Your Office

Microsoft® Office 2016
Volume 1

Amy Kinser

JACOBSON | KINSER | KOSHAREK | MORIARITY

PEARSON

Boston   Columbus   Indianapolis   New York   San Francisco
Amsterdam   Cape Town   Dubai   London   Madrid   Milan   Munich   Paris   Montréal   Toronto
Delhi   Mexico City   São Paulo   Sydney   Hong Kong   Seoul   Singapore   Taipei   Tokyo

Editorial Director: Andrew Gilfillan
Senior Editor: Samantha McAfee Lewis
Team Lead, Project Management: Laura Burgess
Project Manager: Anne Garcia
Program Manager: Emily Biberger
Development Editor: Nancy Lamm
Editorial Assistant: Michael Campbell
Director of Product Marketing: Maggie Waples
Director of Field Marketing: Leigh Ann Sims
Product Marketing Manager: Kaylee Carlson
Field Marketing Managers: Joanna Sabella & Molly Schmidt
Marketing Assistant: Kelli Fisher

Senior Operations Specialist: Maura Zaldivar-Garcia
Senior Art Director: Diane Ernsberger
Manager, Permissions: Karen Sanatar
Interior and Cover Design: Studio Montage
Cover Photo: Courtesy of Shutterstock® Images
Associate Director of Design: Blair Brown
Product Strategy Manager: Eric Hakanson
Vice President, Product Strategy: Jason Fournier
Digital Product Manager: Zachary Alexander
Media Project Manager, Production: John Cassar
Full-Service Project Management: Cenveo Publisher Services
Composition: Cenveo Publisher Services

Credits and acknowledgments borrowed from other sources and reproduced, with permission, in this textbook appear on appropriate page within text.

Pearson Education Ltd., London
Pearson Education Singapore, Pte. Ltd
Pearson Education, Canada, Inc.
Pearson Education–Japan
Pearson Education Australia PTY, Limited

Pearson Education North Asia Ltd., Hong Kong
Pearson Educación de Mexico, S.A. de C.V.
Pearson Education Malaysia, Pte. Ltd.

Library of Congress Cataloging-in-Publication Data available upon request

PEARSON

3 17
ISBN-13: 978-0-13-432080-9
ISBN-10: 0-13-432080-8

I dedicate this series to my Kinser Boyz for their unwavering love, support, and patience; to my parents and sister for their love; to my students for inspiring me; to Sam for believing in me; and to the instructors I hope this series will inspire!

Amy S. Kinser

I dedicate this book to the three most imaginative, exciting, and encouraging pages in my book of life; Paige, Emma, and Jerra!

Kristyn A. Jacobson

For my wife, Amy, and our two boys, Matt and Aidan. I cannot thank them enough for their support, love, and endless inspiration.

J. Eric Kinser

To my husband John, for his love, patience, and encouragement to follow through with my desire to write; to my sons Alex and Justin for their love and support; to my parents, who pushed me to "do" and told me I could; to a special colleague, Ann for her help and support; and to the memory of my best friend Betty who lives on in my heart.

Diane L. Kosharek

I dedicate this book to my beautiful and amazing wife, April. Without her support and understanding, this would not have been possible. Also, to my wonderful son, Patton, whose strength to overcome so many obstacles in his life, inspires me to continue to do my best work.

Brant Moriarity

Amy S. Kinser, Esq., Series Editor

Amy holds a B.A. degree in Chemistry with a Business minor from Indiana University, and a J.D. from the Maurer School of Law, also at Indiana University. After working as an environmental chemist, starting her own technology consulting company, and practicing intellectual property law, she has spent the past 15 years teaching technology at the Kelley School of Business in Bloomington, Indiana. Currently, she serves as the Director of Computer Skills and Senior Lecturer at the Kelley School of Business at Indiana University. She also loves spending time with her two sons, Aidan and J. Matthew, and her husband J. Eric.

Kristyn A. Jacobson

Kristyn holds an M.S. in Education from the University of Wisconsin-La Crosse and a B.S. in Business Education from the University of Wisconsin-Eau Claire. She has been a faculty member and department chair of the Business Technology department at Madison College in Madison, Wisconsin for over 14 years. She also serves as the curriculum coordinator for Microsoft Excel beginning, intermediate, and advanced level courses for the college. As well as teaching, Kristyn provides training to businesses on the Microsoft Office Suite including MS Project, project management, customer service, personal productivity, and time management. Prior to teaching at Madison College, she taught at a business college in Des Moines, Iowa where she helped implement their online learning program while also teaching traditional business courses.

J. Eric Kinser

Eric Kinser received his B.S. degree in Biology from Indiana University and his M.S. in Counseling and Education from the Indiana School of Education. He has worked in the medical field and in higher education as a technology and decision support specialist. He is currently a senior lecturer in the Operations and Decision Technology Department at the Kelley School of Business at Indiana University. When not teaching he enjoys experimenting with new technologies, traveling, and hiking with his family.

Diane L. Kosharek

Diane is a full-time Business Technology faculty member at Madison College in Madison, WI. In addition to her faculty role, she works closely with business and industry specialists, developing and delivering tailored training solutions to employees in areas such as customer service, software applications and business writing skills. Prior to joining Madison College, she worked as a Technology Training Consultant, providing consultation and production assistance to teaching faculty and staff to incorporate appropriate technology in their courses to enhance learning. Diane holds a Bachelor's Degree in Education from the University of Wisconsin-Madison and a Master's Degree in Educational Computing from Cardinal Stritch University.

Brant Moriarity

Brant P. Moriarity earned a B.A. in Religious Studies/Philosophy and a M.S. in Information Systems at Indiana University. He is a Senior Lecturer at the Indiana University's Kelley School of Business where he teaches topics such as data management and analysis, as well as the strategic use of Information Systems in business. He is also the founder of Beats Per Minute Technologies, LLC, bringing the benefits of business analytics to small businesses and non-profit organizations.

POWERPOINT

INTEGRATED PROJECTS

Welcome to the Team Letter 1

The **Your Office** team would like to thank the following reviewers who have invested time and energy to help shape this series from the very beginning, providing us with invaluable feedback through their comments, suggestions, and constructive criticism.

We'd like to thank all of our conscientious reviewers, including those who contributed to our previous editions:

Sven Aelterman
Troy University

Nitin Aggarwal
San Jose State University

Heather Albinger
Waukesha County Technical College

Angel Alexander
Piedmont Technical College

Melody Alexander
Ball State University

Karen Allen
Community College of Rhode Island

Maureen Allen
Elon University

Wilma Andrews
Virginia Commonwealth University

Mazhar Anik
Owens Community College

David Antol
Harford Community College

Kirk Atkinson
Western Kentucky University

Barbara Baker
Indiana Wesleyan University

Kristi Berg
Minot State University

Kavuri Bharath
Old Dominion University

Ann Blackman
Parkland College

Jeanann Boyce
Montgomery College

Lynn Brooks
Tyler Junior College

Cheryl Brown
Delgado Community College West Bank Campus

Bonnie Buchanan
Central Ohio Technical College

Peggy Burrus
Red Rocks Community College

Richard Cacace
Pensacola State College

Margo Chaney
Carroll Community College

Shanan Chappell
College of the Albemarle, North Carolina

Kuan-Chou Chen
Purdue University, Calumet

David Childress
Ashland Community and Technical College

Keh-Wen Chuang
Purdue University North Central

Suzanne Clayton
Drake University

Amy Clubb
Portland Community College

Bruce Collins
Davenport University

Linda Collins
Mesa Community College

Margaret Cooksey
Tallahassee Community College

Charmayne Cullom
University of Northern Colorado

Christy Culver
Marion Technical College

Juliana Cypert
Tarrant County College

Harold Davis
Southeastern Louisiana University

Jeff Davis
Jamestown Community College

Jennifer Day
Sinclair Community College

Anna Degtyareva
Mt. San Antonio College

Beth Deinert
Southeast Community College

Kathleen DeNisco
Erie Community College

Donald Dershem
Mountain View College

Sallie Dodson
Radford University

Joseph F. Domagala
Duquesne University

Bambi Edwards
Craven Community College

Elaine Emanuel
Mt. San Antonio College

Diane Endres
Ancilla College

Nancy Evans
Indiana University, Purdue University, Indianapolis

Christa Fairman
Arizona Western College

Marni Ferner
University of North Carolina, Wilmington

Paula Fisher
Central New Mexico Community College

Linda Fried
University of Colorado, Denver

Diana Friedman
Riverside Community College

Susan Fry
Boise State University

Virginia Fullwood
Texas A&M University, Commerce

Janos Fustos
Metropolitan State College of Denver

John Fyfe
University of Illinois at Chicago

Saiid Ganjalizadeh
The Catholic University of America

Randolph Garvin
Tyler Junior College

Diane Glowacki
Tarrant County College

Jerome Gonnella
Northern Kentucky University

Lorie Goodgine
Tennessee Technology Center in Paris

Connie Grimes
Morehead State University

Debbie Gross
Ohio State University

Babita Gupta
California State University, Monterey Bay

Lewis Hall
Riverside City College

Jane Hammer
Valley City State University

Marie Hartlein
Montgomery County Community
College

Darren Hayes
Pace University

Paul Hayes
Eastern New Mexico University

Mary Hedberg
Johnson County Community College

Lynda Henrie
LDS Business College

Deedee Herrera
Dodge City Community College

Marilyn Hibbert
Salt Lake Community College

Jan Hime
University of Nebraska, Lincoln

Cheryl Hinds
Norfolk State University

Mary Kay Hinkson
Fox Valley Technical College

Margaret Hohly
Cerritos College

Brian Holbert
Spring Hill College

Susan Holland
Southeast Community College

Anita Hollander
University of Tennessee, Knoxville

Emily Holliday
Campbell University

Stacy Hollins
St. Louis Community College Florissant
Valley

Mike Horn
State University of New York, Geneseo

Christie Hovey
Lincoln Land Community College

Margaret Hvatum
St. Louis Community College Meramec

Jean Insinga
Middlesex Community College

Kristyn Jacobson
Madison College

Jon (Sean) Jasperson
Texas A&M University

Glen Jenewein
Kaplan University

Gina Jerry
Santa Monica College

Dana Johnson
North Dakota State University

Mary Johnson
Mt. San Antonio College

Linda Johnsonius
Murray State University

Carla Jones
Middle Tennessee State University

Susan Jones
Utah State University

Nenad Jukic
Loyola University, Chicago

Sali Kaceli
Philadelphia Biblical University

Sue Kanda
Baker College of Auburn Hills

Robert Kansa
Macomb Community College

Susumu Kasai
Salt Lake Community College

Linda Kavanaugh
Robert Morris University

Debby Keen
University of Kentucky

Mike Kelly
Community College of Rhode Island

Melody Kiang
California State University, Long Beach

Lori Kielty
College of Central Florida

Richard Kirk
Pensacola State College

Dawn Konicek
Blackhawk Tech

John Kucharczuk
Centennial College

David Largent
Ball State University

Frank Lee
Fairmont State University

Luis Leon
The University of Tennessee at Chattanooga

Freda Leonard
Delgado Community College

Julie Lewis
Baker College, Allen Park

Suhong Li
Bryant Unversity

Renee Lightner
Florida State College

John Lombardi
South University

Rhonda Lucas
Spring Hill College

Adriana Lumpkin
Midland College

Lynne Lyon
Durham College

Nicole Lytle
California State University, San Bernardino

Donna Madsen
Kirkwood Community College

Susan Maggio
Community College of Baltimore County

Michelle Mallon
Ohio State University

Kim Manning
Tallahassee Community College

Paul Martin
Harrisburg Area Community College

Cheryl Martucci
Diablo Valley College

Sebena Masline
Florida State College of Jacksonville

Sherry Massoni
Harford Community College

Lee McClain
Western Washington University

Sandra McCormack
Monroe Community College

Sue McCrory
Missouri State University

Barbara Miller
University of Notre Dame

Johnette Moody
Arkansas Tech University

Michael O. Moorman
Saint Leo University

Kathleen Morris
University of Alabama

Alysse Morton
Westminster College

Elobaid Muna
University of Maryland Eastern Shore

Jackie Myers
Sinclair Community College

Russell Myers
El Paso Community College

Bernie Negrete
Cerritos College

Melissa Nemeth
Indiana University, Purdue University, Indianapolis

Jennifer Nightingale
Duquesne University

Kathie O'Brien
North Idaho College

Michael Ogawa
University of Hawaii

Janet Olfert
North Dakota State University

Rene Pack
Arizona Western College

Patsy Parker
Southwest Oklahoma State Unversity

Laurie Patterson
University of North Carolina, Wilmington

Alicia Pearlman
Baker College

Diane Perreault
Sierra College and California State University, Sacramento

Theresa Phinney
Texas A&M University

Vickie Pickett
Midland College

Marcia Polanis
Forsyth Technical Community College

Rose Pollard
Southeast Community College

Stephen Pomeroy
Norwich University

Leonard Presby
William Paterson University

Donna Reavis
Delta Career Education

Eris Reddoch
Pensacola State College

James Reddoch
Pensacola State College

Michael Redmond
La Salle University

Terri Rentfro
John A. Logan College

Vicki Robertson
Southwest Tennessee Community College

Jennifer Robinson
Trident Technical College

Dianne Ross
University of Louisiana at Lafayette

Ann Rowlette
Liberty University

Amy Rutledge
Oakland University

Candace Ryder
Colorado State University

Joann Segovia
Winona State University

Eileen Shifflett
James Madison University

Sandeep Shiva
Old Dominion University

Robert Sindt
Johnson County Community College

Cindi Smatt
Texas A&M University

Edward Souza
Hawaii Pacific University

Nora Spencer
Fullerton College

Alicia Stonesifer
La Salle University

Jenny Lee Svelund
University of Utah

Cheryl Sypniewski
Macomb Community College

Arta Szathmary
Bucks County Community College

Nasser Tadayon
Southern Utah University

Asela Thomason
California State University Long Beach

Nicole Thompson
Carteret Community College

Terri Tiedeman
Southeast Community College, Nebraska

Lewis Todd
Belhaven University

Barb Tollinger
Sinclair Community College

Allen Truell
Ball State University

Erhan Uskup
Houston Community College

Lucia Vanderpool
Baptist College of Health Sciences

Michelle Vlaich-Lee
Greenville Technical College

Barry Walker
Monroe Community College

Rosalyn Warren
Enterprise State Community College

Sonia Washington
Prince George's Community College

Eric Weinstein
Suffolk County Community College

Jill Weiss
Florida International University

Lorna Wells
Salt Lake Community College

Rosalie Westerberg
Clover Park Technical College

Clemetee Whaley
Southwest Tennessee Community College

Kenneth Whitten
Florida State College of Jacksonville

MaryLou Wilson
Piedmont Technical College

John Windsor
University of North Texas

Kathy Winters
University of Tennessee, Chattanooga

Nancy Woolridge
Fullerton College

Jensen Zhao
Ball State University

Martha Zimmer
University of Evansville

Molly Zimmer
University of Evansville

Mary Anne Zlotow
College of DuPage

Matthew Zullo
Wake Technical Community College

Additionally, we'd like to thank our MyITLab team for their review and collaboration with our text authors:

LeeAnn Bates
MyITLab content author

Jennifer Hurley
MyITLab content author

Becca Lowe
Media Producer

Ralph Moore
MyITLab content author

Jerri Williams
MyITLab content author

Real World Problem Solving for Business and Beyond

The *Your Office* series provides the foundation for students to learn real world problem solving for use in business and beyond. Students are exposed to hands-on technical content that is woven into realistic business scenarios and focuses on using Microsoft Office as a decision-making tool.

Real world business exposure is a competitive advantage.

The series features a unique running business scenario—the Painted Paradise Resort & Spa—that connects all of the cases together and exposes students to using Microsoft Office to solve problems relating to business areas such as finance and accounting, production and operations, sales and marketing, and more. Look for the icons identifying the business application of each case.

Active learning occurs in context.

Each chapter introduces a realistic business case for students to complete via hands-on steps that are easily identified in blue-shaded boxes. Each blue box teaches a skill and comes complete with video, interactive, and live auto-graded support with automatic feedback.

Coursework that is relevant to students and their future careers.

Real World Advice, Real World Interview Videos, and Real World Success Stories are woven throughout the text and in the student resources. These share how former students use the Microsoft Office concepts they learned in this class and had success in a variety of careers.

Outcomes matter.

Whether it's getting a good grade in this course, learning how to use Excel to be successful in other courses, or learning business skills that will support success in a future job, every student has an outcome in mind. And outcomes matter. That is why we added a Business Unit opener to focus on the outcomes students will achieve by working through the cases and content of each chapter as well as the Capstone at the end of each unit.

No matter what career students may choose to pursue in life, this series will give them the foundation to succeed. And as they learn these valuable problem-solving and decision-making skills while becoming proficient in using Microsoft Office as a tool, they will achieve their intended outcomes, making a positive impact on their lives.

The **Outcomes focus** allows students and instructors to focus on higher-level learning goals and how those can be achieved through particular objectives and skills.

- **Outcomes** are written at the course level and the business unit level.
- **Chapter Objectives list** identifies the learning objectives to be achieved as students work through the chapter. Page numbers are included for easy reference. These are revisited in the Concepts Check at the end of the chapter.
- **MOS Certification Guide** for instructors and students directs anyone interested in prepping for the MOS exam to the specific series resources to find all content required for the test.

Business Application Icons

Customer Service

Finance & Accounting

General Business

Human Resources

Information Technology

Production & Operations

Sales & Marketing

Research & Development

Real World Interview Video

Blue Box Videos

Soft Skills

The **real world focus** reminds students that what they are learning is practical and useful the minute they leave the classroom.

- **Real World Success** features in the chapter opener share anecdotes from real former students, describing how knowledge of Office has helped them be successful in their lives.
- **Real World Advice boxes** offer notes on best practices for general use of important Office skills. The goal is to advise students as a manager might in a future job.
- **Business Application icons** appear with every case in the text and clearly identify which business application students are being exposed to (finance, marketing, operations, etc.).
- **Real World Interview Video icons** appear with the Real World Success story in the business unit. Each interview features a real businessperson discussing how he or she actually uses the skills in the chapter on a day-to-day basis.

Features for active learning help students learn by doing and immerse them in the business world using Microsoft Office.

- **Blue boxes** represent the hands-on portion of the chapter and help students quickly identify what steps they need to take to complete the chapter Prepare Case. This material is easily distinguishable from explanatory text by the blue-shaded background.
- **Starting and ending files** appear before every case in the text. Starting files identify exactly which student data files are needed to complete each case. Ending files are provided to show students the naming conventions they should use when saving their files. Each file icon is color coded by application.
- **Side Note** conveys a brief tip or piece of information aligned visually with a step in the chapter, quickly providing key information to students completing that particular step.
- **Consider This** offers critical thinking questions and topics for discussion, set apart as a boxed feature, allowing students to step back from the project and think about the application of what they are learning and how these concepts might be used in the future.
- **Soft Skills icons** appear with other boxed features and identify specific places where students are being exposed to lessons on soft skills.

Study aids help students review and retain the material so they can recall it at a moment's notice.

- **Quick Reference boxes** summarize generic or alternative instructions on how to accomplish a task. This feature enables students to quickly find important skills.
- **Concept Check** review questions, which appear at the end of the chapter, require students to demonstrate their understanding of the objectives.
- **Visual Summary** offers a review of the objectives learned in the chapter using images from the completed solution file, mapped to the chapter objectives with callouts and page references, so students can easily find the section of text to refer to for a refresher.

- **MyITLab™ icons** identify which cases from the book match those in MyITLab™.
- **Blue Box Video icons** appear with each Active Text box and identify the brief video, demonstrating how students should complete that portion of the Prepare Case.

Extensive cases allow students to progress from a basic understanding of Office through to proficiency.

- **Chapters all conclude with Practice, Problem Solve, and Perform Cases** to allow full mastery at the chapter level. Alternative versions of these cases are available in Instructor Resources.
- **Business Unit Capstones all include More Practice, Problem Solve, and Perform Cases** that require students to synthesize objectives from the two previous chapters to extend their mastery of the content. Alternative versions of these cases are available in Instructor Resources.
- **More Grader Projects** are offered with this edition, including Prepare cases as well as Problem Solve cases at both the chapter and business unit capstone levels.

Instructor Resources

The Instructor's Resource Center, available at www.pearsonhighered.com/irc includes the following:

- AACSB mapping that identifies which cases and exercises in the text prepare for AACSB certification
- Business application mapping, which provides an easy-to-filter way of finding the cases and examples to help highlight whichever business application is of most interest
- Annotated Solution Files with Scorecards, which assist with grading the Prepare, Practice, Problem Solve, and Perform cases
- Data and solution files
- Rubrics for Perform cases in Microsoft Word format, which enable instructors to easily grade open-ended assignments with no definite solution
- PowerPoint presentations with notes for each chapter
- Lesson plans that provide a detailed blueprint to achieve chapter learning objectives and outcomes and best use the unique structure of the business units
- Complete test bank, also available in TestGen format
- Syllabus templates for 8-week, 12-week, and 16-week courses
- Additional Practice, Problem Solve, and Perform cases to provide variety and choice in exercises at both the chapter and business unit levels
- Scripted Lectures, which provide instructors with a lecture outline that mirrors the chapter Prepare case

Student Resources

Student Data Files

Access the student data files needed to complete the cases in this textbook at www.pearsonhighered.com/youroffice.

Available in MyITLab

MyITLab®

- **Blue Box Videos** walk students through the activity in each blue box, illustrating how to perform a task while explaining the business context of the case.
- **Real World Interview Videos** introduce students to real professionals discussing how they use Microsoft Office in their daily work. These videos provide real world relevance to answer the question "Why is this content important to me?" There are videos in each Business Unit.
- **Audio PowerPoints** provide a lecture review of the chapter content and include narration.
- **Grader Projects** provide live-in-the-application training and assessment with immediate feedback and detailed reports for students to practice, learn, and remediate.
- **eText** is available in some MyITLab courses.

MyITLab for Office 2016 is a solution designed by professors for professors that allows easy delivery of Office courses with defensible assessment and outcomes-based training. The new **Your Office 2016** system will seamlessly integrate online assessment, training, and projects with MyITLab for Microsoft Office 2016!

Dear Students,

If you want an edge over the competition, make it personal. Whether you love sports, travel, the stock market, or ballet, your passion is personal to you. Capitalizing on your passion leads to success. You live in a global marketplace, and your competition is global. The honors students in China exceed the total number of students in North America. Skills can help set you apart, but passion will make you stand above. *Your Office* is the tool to harness your passion's true potential.

In prior generations, personalization in a professional setting was discouraged. You had a "work" life and a "home" life. As the Series Editor, I write to you about the vision for *Your Office* from my laptop, on my couch, in the middle of the night when inspiration struck me. My classroom and living room are my office. Life has changed from generations before us.

So, let's get personal. My degrees are not in technology, but chemistry and law. I helped put myself through school by working full time in various jobs, including a successful technology consulting business that continues today. My generation did not grow up with computers, but I did. My father was a network administrator for the military. So, I was learning to program in Basic before anyone had played Nintendo's Duck Hunt or Tetris. Technology has always been one of my passions from a young age. In fact, I now tell my husband: don't buy me jewelry for my birthday, buy me the latest gadget on the market!

In my first law position, I was known as the Office guru to the extent that no one gave me a law assignment for the first two months. Once I submitted the assignment, my supervisor remarked, "Wow, you don't just know how to leverage technology, but you really know the law too." I can tell you novel-sized stories from countless prior students in countless industries who gained an edge from using Office as a tool. Bringing technology to your passion makes you well rounded and a cut above the rest, no matter the industry or position.

I am most passionate about teaching, in particular teaching technology. I come from many generations of teachers, including my mother who is a kindergarten teacher. For over 12 years, I have found my dream job passing on my passion for teaching, technology, law, science, music, and life in general at the Kelley School of Business at Indiana University. I have tried to pass on the key to engaging passion to my students. I have helped them see what differentiates them from all the other bright students vying for the same jobs.

Microsoft Office is a tool. All of your competition will have learned Microsoft Office to some degree or another. Some will have learned it to an advanced level. Knowing Microsoft Office is important, but it is also fundamental. Without it, you will not be considered for a position.

Today, you step into your first of many future roles bringing Microsoft Office to your dream job working for Painted Paradise Resort & Spa. You will delve into the business side of the resort and learn how to use *Your Office* to maximum benefit.

Don't let the context of a business fool you. If you don't think of yourself as a business person, you have no need to worry. Whether you realize it or not, everything is business. If you want to be a nurse, you are entering the health care industry. If you want to be a football player in the NFL, you are entering the business of sports as entertainment. In fact, if you want to be a stay-at-home parent, you are entering the business of a family household where *Your Office* still gives you an advantage. For example, you will be able to prepare a budget in Excel and analyze what you need to do to afford a trip to Disney World!

At Painted Paradise Resort & Spa, you will learn how to make Office yours through four learning levels designed to maximize your understanding. You will Prepare, Practice, and Problem Solve your tasks. Then, you will astound when you Perform your new talents. You will be challenged through Consider This questions and gain insight through Real World Advice.

There is something more. You want success in what you are passionate about in your life. It is personal for you. In this position at Painted Paradise Resort & Spa, you will gain your personal competitive advantage that will stay with you for the rest of your life—*Your Office*.

Sincerely,

Amy Kinser

Series Editor

Painted Paradise

RESORT & SPA

Welcome to the Team!

Welcome to your new office at Painted Paradise Resort & Spa, where we specialize in painting perfect getaways. As the Chief Technology Officer, I am excited to have staff dedicated to the Microsoft Office integration between all the areas of the resort. Our team is passionate about our paradise, and I hope you find this to be your dream position here!

Painted Paradise is a resort and spa in New Mexico catering to business people, romantics, families, and anyone who just needs to get away. Inside our resort are many distinct areas. Many of these areas operate as businesses in their own right but must integrate with the other areas of the resort. The main areas of the resort are as follows.

- The **Hotel** is overseen by our Chief Executive Officer, William Mattingly, and is at the core of our business. The hotel offers a variety of accommodations, ranging from individual rooms to a grand villa suite. Further, the hotel offers packages including spa, golf, and special events.

  Room rates vary according to size, season, demand, and discount. The hotel has discounts for typical groups, such as AARP. The hotel also has a loyalty program where guests can earn free nights based on frequency of visits. Guests may charge anything from the resort to the room.

- **Red Bluff Golf Course** is a private world-class golf course and pro shop. The golf course has services such as golf lessons from the famous golf pro John Schilling and playing packages. Also, the golf course attracts local residents. This requires variety in pricing schemes to accommodate both local and hotel guests. The pro shop sells many retail items online.

  The golf course can also be reserved for special events and tournaments. These special events can be in conjunction with a wedding, conference, meetings, or other events covered by the event planning and catering area of the resort.

- **Turquoise Oasis Spa** is a full-service spa. Spa services include haircuts, pedicures, massages, facials, body wraps, waxing, and various other spa services—typical to exotic. Further, the spa offers private consultation, weight training (in the fitness center), a water bar, meditation areas, and steam rooms. Spa services are offered both in the spa and in the resort guest's room.

  Turquoise Oasis Spa uses top-of-the-line products and some house-brand products. The retail side offers products ranging from candles to age-defying home treatments. These products can also be purchased online. Many of the hotel guests who fall in love with the house-brand soaps, lotions, candles, and other items appreciate being able to buy more at any time.

  The spa offers a multitude of packages including special hotel room packages that include spa treatments. Local residents also use the spa. So, the spa guests are not limited to hotel guests. Thus, the packages also include pricing attractive to the local community.

- **Painted Treasures Gift Shop** has an array of items available for purchase, from toiletries to clothes to presents for loved ones back home including a healthy section of kids' toys for traveling business people. The gift shop sells a small sampling from the spa, golf course pro shop, and local New Mexico culture. The gift shop also has a small section of snacks and drinks. The gift shop has numerous part-time employees including students from the local college.

- The **Event Planning & Catering** area is central to attracting customers to the resort. From weddings to conferences, the resort is a popular destination. The resort has a substantial number of staff dedicated to planning, coordinating, setting up, catering, and maintaining these events. The resort has several facilities that can accommodate large groups. Packages and prices vary by size, room, and other services such as catering. Further, the Event Planning & Catering team works closely with local vendors for floral decorations, photography, and other event or wedding typical needs. However, all catering must go through the resort (no outside catering permitted). Lastly, the resort stocks several choices of decorations, table arrangements, and centerpieces. These range from professional, simple, themed, and luxurious.

- **Indigo5** and the **Silver Moon Lounge**, a world-class restaurant and lounge that is overseen by the well-known Chef Robin Sanchez. The cuisine is balanced and modern. From steaks to pasta to local southwestern meals, Indigo5 attracts local patrons in addition to resort guests. While the catering function is separate from the restaurant—though menu items may be shared—the restaurant does support all room service for the resort. The resort also has smaller food venues onsite such as the Terra Cotta Brew coffee shop in the lobby.

Currently, these areas are using Office to various degrees. In some areas, paper and pencil are still used for most business functions. Others have been lucky enough to have some technology savvy team members start Microsoft Office Solutions.

Using your skills, I am confident that you can help us integrate and use Microsoft Office on a whole new level! I hope you are excited to call Painted Paradise Resort & Spa **Your Office**.

Looking forward to working with you more closely!

Aidan Matthews
Aidan Matthews
Chief Technology Officer

Microsoft Windows 10

Chapter 1 | EXPLORE WINDOWS
AND FILE MANAGEMENT

Prepare Case

Information Technology

Painted Paradise Golf Resort & Spa — Employee Introduction to Microsoft Windows 10

Aidan Matthews, Chief Technology Officer of the Painted Paradise Golf Resort & Spa, has decided to upgrade computers to the brand-new Windows 10 operating system. There are considerable differences between different versions of Windows. Painted Paradise employees have asked for help in making the transition, as some are used to Windows 7 and some are used to Windows 8.1. Windows 10 merges the best features of Windows 7 and Windows 8.1.

You have been asked to plan a workshop to train personnel in all departments to use the new operating system efficiently. Aidan has asked that you start by learning the Windows 10 interface. He wants you to focus on fundamental skills but would also like you to introduce new features that will enhance productivity, such as the enhanced search functionality. Making the transition to Windows 10 will require employees not only to learn the new version of the hotel's software, but also to be comfortable with the operating system on a daily basis. This chapter will focus on demonstrating new features in Windows 10.

StockLite/Shutterstock

Student data file needed for this chapter:

w1001ch01DataFiles.zip

You will save your files as:

w1001ch01Notes_LastFirst.rtf

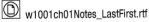
w1001ch01QuadrantsSnip_LastFirst.jpg

w1001ch01StartSnip_LastFirst.jpg

w1001ch01Zipped_LastFirst.zip

3

Exploring the Windows 10 Interface

Microsoft Windows 10 is the latest version of the Windows operating system. The **operating system** is **system software** that controls and coordinates computer hardware operations so that other programs can run efficiently. The operating system acts as an intermediary between **application software** — programs that help the user perform specific tasks, such as word processing — and the computer hardware. The operating system also helps the user perform essential tasks such as displaying information on the computer screen, saving data on a storage device, and sending documents to a printer. The operating system can have multiple programs open at the same time and switch between programs easily, using several different methods. When an operating system is running properly, users are focused on the applications that the system supports rather than on the system itself.

Microsoft releases a new version of Windows every few years to take advantage of improvements to hardware and to add new features. Like previous versions of Windows, Windows 10 uses a **graphical user interface (GUI)**, an interface that uses visual icons, which are small images representing programs, files, websites, or other locations. This type of interface helps the user interact with the hardware and software in a simpler fashion. When Windows 8 was released, it introduced a number of new features that left even experienced users in need of some retraining. Since the release of Windows 95, the center of the Windows experience has been the Start button. Windows 8 moved away from the Start button and toward a touch-screen type of interface, similar to what you may have become accustomed to with smartphones. Windows 10 returns to the Start menu but blends the touch-friendly features from Windows 8 into the operating system.

The goals for this version of Windows were to make the operating system simpler to use, have better search capability, blend the Windows 8 Start screen and Start menu into one, and create a universal operating system for all devices — for example, Windows 10 runs both on a desktop and a mobile phone.

REAL WORLD ADVICE | **Your Phone Is a Computer!**

Windows 10 is universal for all devices — but what does that really mean? If you put Windows 10 on a phone, it will still look different on your phone and on your laptop. Windows 10 uses screen size to determine how things will look. While things look different, the software is the same. This is not something that is important just for developers to know. It means you can take your phone, plug it into a monitor that is not connected to a computer, and your phone *becomes* the computer. You can then interact with the large screen size and do anything that a normal PC can do — assuming that your phone has enough computing power!

The types of functionality that Windows 8 introduced have been included, incorporated, blended, or removed in Windows 10. Illustratively, Windows 8 had both traditional Windows programs and applications. In Windows 8, these two behaved differently. In Windows 10, programs and applications both work the same, which increases the usability.

One of the main goals of Windows 10 is a universal operating system for all devices — including the Xbox gaming system. There are apps that allow your PC or Windows phone to interact with the Xbox. You can even stream your Xbox games to your PC. What would be the purpose of doing this? What are the advantages of doing so? What are the disadvantages or challenges in making an operating system universal for all devices?

Microsoft is offering a free upgrade to Windows 10 for qualified new or existing Windows 7, Windows 8.1, and Windows Phone 8.1 devices that upgrade in the first year. Once a qualified Windows device has been upgraded to Windows 10, Microsoft will continue to keep it up to date for the supported lifetime of the device, keeping it more secure and introducing new features and functionality over time — for no additional charge.

QUICK REFERENCE	Features Removed from Prior Windows Versions

Some of the features of prior versions of Windows have been removed in Windows 10. In some instances, the feature has been replaced by a better counterpart. Other features have not been replaced. Thus, you should evaluate your needs before deciding to upgrade.

- DVD playback — instead uses the new, free Movies & TV app.
- Desktop gadget — will no longer work at all.
- Preinstalled games — such as Solitaire will not be installed. Instead, use the free game apps in the Windows Store.
- Floppy drives — instead use newer media to store files such as a USB drive. Floppy drives that connect via a USB will not work anymore.
- Windows Updates — your system **will** still update. However, some versions — such as Windows Home — will no longer allow you to control and defer updates. Instead, updates will be automatic. The Pro and Enterprise versions of Windows will still allow the user to defer updates.

Start and Shut Down Windows

Windows starts automatically when a computer is switched on unless it has been configured otherwise. The first time a device is started, it will ask questions to get the machine connected to a network and a Microsoft account. That account is then loaded as a user. After that, the **Lock Screen** — the default view when no one is using the computer — will appear. By default, the Lock Screen rotates through different background images, called the Windows 10 Lock Screen Spotlight Collection, and it varies across devices. The Lock Screen also displays the date and time. Also, in the lower right corner, there are battery and wireless level indicators. To get to the **Login Screen**, where a user can enter login credentials, a user needs to just click once or swipe upwards. If user accounts are set up, a list of users appears in the lower left corner. If the desired account is not activated, a user can **click** — press the left mouse button one time — on the desired account.

If the account has a password, the password is needed to proceed. A password can be a typed password, or an account can be configured to be a touch pattern on a picture, a numeric pin, or facial recognition. This prevents other users from accessing the documents or other personal data of other users. A school or business may have a different logon procedure because many people may be sharing a computer.

Windows 8 and later versions start up more quickly than previous versions of the operating system, thanks to a feature called hybrid boot. In previous versions of the operating system, users tended to shut down completely rather than use the sleep and hibernate options. When the computer was idle, it often went into sleep mode to minimize power consumption. Hibernate was similar to sleep. Hibernate was a good option for laptops, allowing users to decrease startup times and use even less battery power than sleep. However, it would often take longer to go into hibernate mode than it would to fully shut down the machine, as the system often had to save large amounts of information to the hard drive before hibernating. Hybrid boot is now the default shut down option for Windows. As its name implies, it provides the best of both worlds with fast startups while not having to wait long for the system to shut down.

Starting and Shutting Down Windows

Windows 10 provides multiple ways to shut down Windows. If the user is not logged in, the button to shut down is in the lower right corner. When the user is logged in, the Start menu has the option to shut down with Power. The Start menu also has options for File Explorer, Settings, All apps, and Most used apps. Also in the Start menu, clicking on the Microsoft login at the top allows the user to sign out or switch accounts. In this exercise, you will explore the process of starting and shutting down Windows.

To Start and Shut Down Windows

a. Switch on your computer, and then wait a few moments.

b. Click **once** or swipe **upwards**. The Login Screen appears.

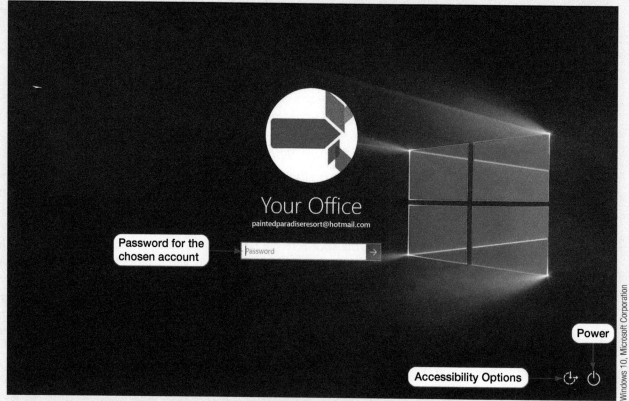

Figure 1   Login Screen

SIDE NOTE
Touch Screens
Remember if you have a touch screen, you can also swipe upwards to move from the Lock Screen to the Login Screen.

c. In the lower right corner on the Login Screen, click **Power** ⏻. Then click **Shut down**.

d. Switch on the computer again, and then wait a few moments. If necessary, follow any sign-in instructions required for the computer you are using. The Windows desktop is displayed.

e. Click **Start** ⊞ and then **Power** ⏻. Click **Restart**.

f. If necessary, follow any sign-in instructions required for the computer you are using. The Windows desktop is displayed.

Explore the Desktop and Start Menu

The default screen for the operating system is the desktop. The desktop includes a **desktop background** — the picture or pattern that is displayed on the desktop; various icons — small images representing programs, files, websites, or other locations; and the **taskbar** — the bar at the bottom of the desktop that contains the Start button ⊞, a Cortana search box, a series of buttons representing pinned apps and all open programs, and the **taskbar notification area** — which displays information about the status of programs running in the background, a clock, the option to safely remove devices such as USB flash drives, and other options that can be customized.

A default configuration of the desktop contains a single icon for the Recycle Bin. The **Recycle Bin** temporarily stores any deleted files from your computer until they are restored or permanently deleted. The default background is an image of the Windows logo.

Somewhere on the screen will be a **mouse pointer** — an arrow that shows the position of the mouse. A mouse or other pointing device is used to interact with objects on the screen, to open programs, or to select commands. Depending on what the user does with the pointer and clicking, Windows reacts differently.

QUICK REFERENCE	Mouse Actions

Pointing — moving the mouse over something such as a desktop icon — highlights it and may bring up a **ScreenTip** — a short on-screen description.

Single-clicking — only selects an icon, folder, or file. Single-clicking a button, such as ⊞, will result in the associated action, such as opening the Start menu. Single-clicking a Tile will open the program or app.

Single-click pause and single-click again — on an icon, folder, or file selects the item and allows you to rename it.

Double-clicking — an icon opens the program, file, or location that is represented by the icon.

Right-clicking — pressing the right mouse button opens a **shortcut menu** — a group or list of commands — containing commands related to the right-clicked item (these menus may also be referred to as contextual menus).

Windows 10 has **gesture recognition** for devices with touch capability. This allows the user to control the computer with finger gestures instead of mouse clicks. Gestures allow you to perform actions such as zooming and switching programs by performing certain movements. Some of the gestures from Windows 8 remain; others no longer exist or perform different tasks. Windows is smart enough to realize when a user uses a gesture instead of a mouse. Thus, when the user accesses some programs and menus with gestures, they may look a little different for touch than when you use a mouse. While not every-thing is different, Windows has been optimized for touch. Windows even has a **tablet mode** — in which every interaction is expected to be touch. The directions in this book assume that a mouse is used.

Desired Action	Gesture	Gesture
Open or select	Tap once on an item — similar to a single mouse click	
Bring up Tile options on the Start menu	Press and hold down on the Tile — similar to a right mouse click	
Open a file	Double-tap — similar to a double mouse click	
Show all open applications in Task View and switch applications	Swipe out from the left and then touch the desired application	
Zoom out/reduce object size	Pinch	
Zoom in/enlarge object size	Stretch — start with two fingers pinched and spread fingers apart	
Show the Action Center with Notifications	Swipe out from the right bezel	
Rotate a picture	Put two fingers on the item and turn in the desired direction — only some items can be rotated	
Show Cortana (if previously enabled)	Swipe upwards from the bottom left	
Show the System Calendar	Swipe upward from the bottom right corner under the system time	

Table 1   What gestures can you use?

Exploring the Desktop and Recycle Bin

Windows offers many ways to personalize and customize the desktop. Some of these can lead to higher efficiency and more productivity. Others are just for fun and might become distracting if overdone. In this exercise, you will explore the elements of the desktop and the Recycle Bin.

To Explore the Desktop and Recycle Bin

a. If your computer is not already running, switch the computer on and log in (if necessary). After you log in, the desktop is displayed.

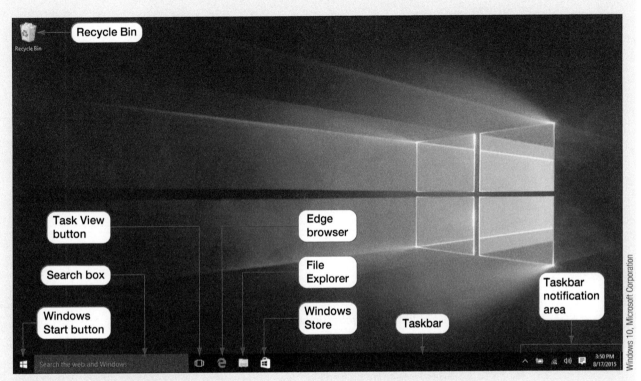

Figure 2   Desktop elements

b. On the desktop, point to the **Recycle Bin**. Notice the ScreenTip — Contains the files and folders that you have deleted.

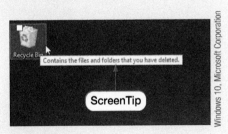

Figure 3   ScreenTip

c. Double-click the **Recycle Bin**.

The Recycle Bin opens up in a window that is not maximized. You can open multiple windows and arrange them however you want. These windows are the reason Windows is named Windows.

In the top-right corner of the Recycle Bin window, notice the Minimize ⬚, Maximize/Restore Down ⬚, and Close ⨯ buttons, which are common to all windows.

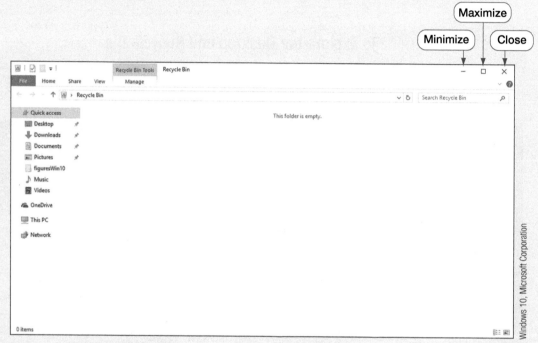

Figure 4　Recycle Bin window elements

d. Click **Close** ⨯.

e. Point to the **Recycle Bin** again, and then right-click.

A shortcut menu is displayed, showing context-sensitive commands or commands that can be performed relating to the Recycle Bin — such as emptying the Recycle Bin. Note that you can also open the Recycle Bin by clicking Open on the shortcut menu.

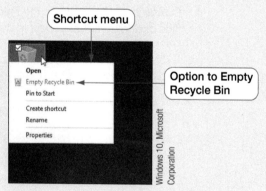

Figure 5　Shortcut menu

f. Point to a **blank area** on the desktop and then right-click. A different shortcut menu appears, listing options that can be performed relating to the desktop.

g. Click a **blank area** of the desktop to close the shortcut menu without making a selection.

REAL WORLD ADVICE | Using the Recycle Bin

Files sent to the Recycle Bin remain on the computer's hard drive — a disk drive inside your computer, also called the local drive — until the Recycle Bin is emptied. As long as a file is in the Recycle Bin, it can be restored to its original location. This is similar to putting a piece of paper in a trashcan. As long as the trashcan has not been emptied, you can still retrieve the piece of paper. Once the Recycle Bin has been emptied, the file is extremely difficult to recover. The Recycle Bin does take up hard drive space. Thus, if space is a concern, emptying the bin will gain hard drive space.

Do not expect files on USB flash drives or other auxiliary storage devices to appear in the Recycle Bin. Only files that are deleted from your hard drive are placed in the Recycle Bin, so be extra careful when deleting files from removable devices.

Navigating the Start Menu

The Start screen and Charms from Windows 8 no longer exist. Instead, the Start menu in Windows 10 is a mixture of the Tiles from Windows 8 and the Start menu from prior versions of Windows. The Start menu can be made full screen and then resembles the look of the Windows 8 Start screen.

The new Windows 10 Start menu has two distinct areas. On the left side, a user can access his or her Microsoft account settings, the File Explorer, Settings, Most Used applications, Power, and All apps. The left side integrates Windows 7 features into the Start menu. On the right side, a user sees default Tiles plus any additional Tiles that have been pinned to the Start menu. The right side integrates Windows 8 features into the Start menu. Depending on the computer, there may be many Tiles or only a few.

On the right side of the menu, the **Tiles** — picture representations of the program or application — on the Start menu represent programs and applications that can be opened. These are similar to shortcut icons found on the desktop or taskbar in previous versions of Windows. Much like icons in previous versions of Windows, they can be customized. A user can change the placement and size of the Tiles and can add, delete, and group Tiles.

Tiles may also be **Live Tiles**, which provide a constant stream of information. For example, the Mail Tile shows recent items in your inbox, updated frequently. Some Internet connections, including some cell phone networks and satellite, do not include unlimited data. In such a case, a user may use the option to turn the Live Tile off.

If desired, a user can also resize the Start menu to full screen. In this exercise, you will navigate and explore the Start menu.

To Expand and Collapse the Start Menu

a. Click **Start** ⊞.

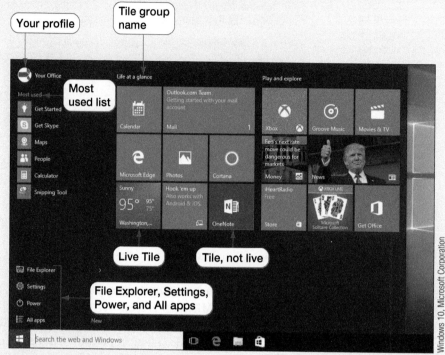

Figure 6   Start menu

Troubleshooting

Does your Start menu have different Tiles or different applications in the Most used list than shown in Figure 6? If you have different applications or programs installed, it *should* look different. Even if this is the first time you have used this device, Microsoft allows users to sync settings and applications across devices. Thus, you may see on the Start menu some applications that you installed on a different device than the one you are on!

---

b. Point to the upper edge of the Start menu until your mouse turns into the **Vertical Resizing** pointer ⬍. Move your mouse-pointer to the right edge of the Start menu until your mouse turns into the **Horizontal Resizing** pointer ⬌.

c. If you prefer, resize the Start menu to your desired size. Depending on how many programs and apps you have pinned to the Start menu, you may also see a scroll bar on the right side.

Opening a Program with the Start Menu

Opening a program from within the Start menu is as easy as clicking on a Tile. In this exercise, you will open and close the News application using the Start menu.

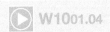
SIDE NOTE
Already Pinned?
If it is pinned to your Start menu, you could also click directly on the News Tile rather than going to All apps.

To Open a Program with the Start Menu

a. If needed, click **Start** ▦.

b. In the lower left corner, click **All apps**.

c. Scroll and find the **News** app. Click **News**.

The News app opens in a new window. In Windows 10, unlike Windows 8, all applications and programs open in a traditional window. The window does not open full screen.

Figure 7   The News app

d. In the upper right corner of the News app window, click **Close** ⨯.

Customize the Start Menu and Taskbar

The Start menu and the taskbar can both be customized. The easiest way to customize in the Start menu itself is by right-clicking and accessing the shortcut menus. Depending on the underlying program or applications, the options that are presented to the user will change. However, all programs and application Tiles have the options to Pin/Unpin to/from Start, Pin/Unpin to/from taskbar, and Resize. If the Tile is a Live Tile, there is also a toggle to Turn live tile on/off. Also, when a user right-clicks under the Most used applications list, one additional option appears: Don't show in this list. Depending on the type of program or application Tile, a few other options may also appear.

QUICK REFERENCE	Tile Customization

When a user right-clicks on a command or Tile in the Start menu, the following can be customized:

1. **Pin to Start** or **Unpin from Start** adds or removes the Tile representing the selected app to or from the Start menu.

2. **Pin to taskbar** or **Unpin from taskbar** adds or removes the shortcut to the app to or from the taskbar.

3. **Resize** provides for one of four Tile size display options on the Start menu: Small, Medium, Wide, and Large.

4. **Turn live tile on** or **Turn live tile off** toggles the use of live data on the Tile display.

5. **Don't show on this list** appears only when a user right-clicks in the Most used applications list — not in All apps. This will make it so that the application never shows up in the Most used list. The application will still appear in All apps.

Pinning Start Menu Tiles and Turning Off Live Tiles

Less frequently used apps can take up space on the Start menu, making it difficult to locate the apps that you use most frequently. To avoid this problem, you can pin additional installed apps to the Start menu or unpin the ones that you do not use as often. In this exercise, you will pin the Sports and WordPad apps to the Start menu. You will also turn off and on the Live Tile for the Sports app.

SIDE NOTE

Using a Touch Screen
Press and hold the app
Tile, and then tap Pin to
Start.

To Pin a Tile and Turn Off Live Tiles in the Start Menu

a. Click **Start** ▦.

b. In the lower left corner, click **All apps**.

c. Find the **Sports** app. Right-click **Sports** and click **Pin to Start**.

The Sports Tile now appears on the right side as a Tile. Notice it is a Live Tile that previews current sports information and news.

> **Troubleshooting**
>
> If the Sports app is not on your list of All apps, go to the Windows Store. In the store, search for and install the free Sports app. If you decide you don't want it, you can always uninstall the app after you are done with your work for this chapter.
>
> If it does not appear as a Live Tile, launch and close the Sports app. If the tile still does not show live information, try restarting your computer.

Figure 8 Pinned to Start

> **Troubleshooting**
>
> If Tile options display Unpin from Start, the Tile feature is already on the Start menu and you can proceed to the next step. If the Tile appears to not be a Live Tile, click off the Start menu and then click the Start menu again.

SIDE NOTE
Live Tiles
Live Tiles will continually access your network. If network connection speed, data usage, or battery life is a concern, turn the Live Tile off.

d. On the right side of the Start menu, right-click the **Sports** live title.

e. Click **Turn live tile off**. Now the Sports app shows the generic Tile rather than live information.

> **Troubleshooting**
>
> If Tile options display Turn live tile on, the Live Tiles feature is already disabled on the Tile and you can proceed to the next step.

f. Right-click the **Sports** title and click **Turn live tile on**. Now, the Sports app shows live sports information again. The Tile is a little small for reading the live information. You will fix that in the next exercise.

> **Troubleshooting**
>
> If a live feed is not shown on the Tile, click the Tile to open the Sports app for the first time, and then press the ⊞ on your keyboard to return to the Start menu. If the live information still does not show, restart the computer.

g. If necessary in the lower left corner, click **All apps**. Scroll and find the **Windows Accessories** group. Programs and applications can be put into groups in the Start menu.

h. Click the **arrow** to expand the group and scroll down to see WordPad. Right-click **WordPad** and select **Pin to Start**.

Notice, WordPad is not a Live Tile. WordPad is a no-frills app for creating and editing files that contain text.

i. If necessary in the lower left corner, click **All apps**, scroll and find the **Windows Accessories** group, and click the **arrow** to expand the group.

j. Right-click **Snipping Tool** and select **Pin to Start**.

> **S** **CONSIDER THIS** | **Pin Everything**
>
> Why do you think that all of the Windows apps are not automatically pinned to the Start menu? How do you decide which apps to pin and which apps to search for when needed? How many apps are too many for the Start menu?

Resizing, Moving, and Grouping Start Menu Tiles

Windows provides options to arrange Tiles on the Start menu to fit each user's unique needs and preferences. Tiles can be displayed using one of four sizes and can display, where applicable, live data on Tiles using any size option other than Small. To move a Tile to a new location, simply drag (click and hold the left mouse button, move the pointer to where you want the item to be placed, and then release the mouse button) the Tile into position. Tiles can be arranged in groups with or without assigned names. Entire groups can be rearranged using the same drag method. In the next exercise, you will resize the WordPad Tile and move the Sports app Tile.

To Resize Tiles and Move Tiles in Start Menu

a. If necessary, click **Start** ⊞.

b. Click and drag the **WordPad** Tile down approximately 1/4 inch below the left side of the Sports Tile. As you drag, notice when you move a Tile, Windows automatically puts it into a new group.

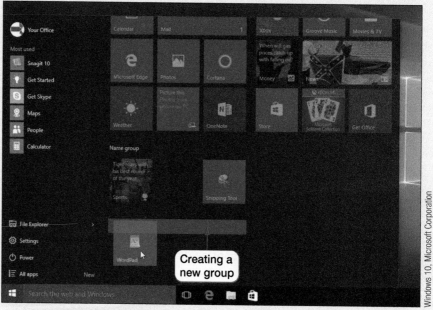

Figure 9   Create a new group

c. Click and drag the **Snipping Tool** Tile down into the same group, to the right of the WordPad Tile.

d. Point to the **blank space** between the Sports and the WordPad Tile. The Name group ▦ button appears to the top right of the group. Click **Name group.**

e. Type Tools and then press ⟨Enter⟩ to name the group.

f. Right-click the **Sports** Tile. Click **Resize** and then **Wide**. Now the live Sports news is easier to read.

QUICK REFERENCE	Tile Size Options

Windows screen Tiles support four size options:

- Small — square format one fourth the size of the Medium size, half as wide and half as tall
- Medium — square Tile four times the size of the Small Tile, half the size of the Wide Tile, and one fourth the size of the Large size
- Wide — rectangular format twice the width of the Medium size
- Large — square format four times the size of the Medium size: twice as wide and twice as tall

Uninstalling a Program Using the Start Menu

When a user right-clicks on some Tiles, additional options will appear in the shortcut menu. These options are available only on supported programs: Uninstall, Run as a different user, Run as administrator, and Open file location. In this exercise, you will view all of the options available in the shortcut menu.

To Uninstall a Program in the Start Menu

a. If necessary, click **Start** ▦.

b. In the Life at a glance group (a default group on installation) right-click the **Weather** app. Notice the options and the absence of the Uninstall option. This app cannot be uninstalled through the Start menu.

c. Right-click the **Sports** Tile. Notice the options, including the Uninstall option.

d. Right-click the **WordPad** Tile. Notice the additional options such as Run as administrator.

QUICK REFERENCE	Additional Start Menu Options

When a user right-clicks an application in the Start menu, the following additional options may appear:

1. **Uninstall** removes the app and associated files from your computer.

2. **Run as a different user** allows the user to run a program under a different account — either local or a Microsoft account.

3. **Run as administrator** allows the user to run a program under an administrator account — either local or a Microsoft account. This is particularly useful when the user is not an administrator.

4. **Open file location** will open the folder in the Start menu folders containing the program shortcut. Changing the shortcuts in this folder will change the user's Start menu.

Pinning a Program to the Taskbar

The taskbar is the long horizontal bar at the bottom of your screen. The taskbar can be customized through the process of pinning and unpinning apps or the customization of the taskbar notification area. For users who routinely interact with the desktop view of Windows or use a number of desktop applications in Windows, pinning apps to the taskbar can make the frequently used programs readily available, saving time returning to the Start menu to open them.

Similar to pinning apps to the Start menu, pinning an app to the taskbar places an icon in a consistent and convenient location for routine access to the most frequently used apps on the computer. Both traditional desktop applications and Windows Store apps can be pinned to the taskbar.

In this exercise, you will pin the WordPad app to the taskbar.

W1001.08

To Pin an App to the Taskbar

a. If necessary, click **Start** ▦.

b. Locate **WordPad**, right-click the **Tile**, and then click **Pin to taskbar**.

> ### Troubleshooting
> If you cannot locate the desired app on the Start menu, use the Search or All apps view of the Start menu to locate the program.

c. Press ▨. This returns you to the desktop but leaves any open windows open.

Verify that the WordPad app is pinned to the taskbar. If you need to take a break before finishing this chapter, now is a good time.

> WordPad icon
> pinned to the taskbar

Figure 10   WordPad pinned to the taskbar

Windows 10, Microsoft Corporation

 CONSIDER THIS | **Why Pin to the Taskbar?**

If all open apps are automatically displayed on the taskbar, what is the benefit of pinning an app to the task-bar? What apps would you benefit from pinning to the taskbar? Which ones might not be worth pinning?

Use Windows 10 Search and Cortana

Microsoft Windows has always included a search tool. Microsoft has greatly enhanced search capabilities in Windows 10 through **Cortana**, a clever personal assistant that previously was found only on the mobile version of Windows.

When Cortana is allowed, she is accessed by a search box.

- When Cortana is first enabled, this search box will say *Hello Name, what can I do for you today?* for a few seconds.
- When a device is first turned on, the search box will say *Name, Hello!* for a few seconds.
- Usually, the search box that says *Ask me anything* is on the taskbar.
- If Cortana is not allowed, the box on the taskbar will say *Search the web and Windows* instead of *Ask me anything*.

When a user clicks in the Search the web and Windows box for the first time, Cortana asks the user to allow Cortana, instructs the user to log into a Microsoft account, and asks a series of questions, including the user's name. If Cortana is not allowed, the Search the web and Windows will only search and cannot do any of the other Cortana actions.

A user can interact with Cortana by typing into the Ask me anything box or by speaking to Cortana by clicking the microphone icon to the right of the Ask me anything — of course, the device must have a microphone for this to work. When using voice, the user starts by saying, "Hey Cortana." At the Windows 10 launch, Cortana is not available in all countries and languages. Further, some Cortana actions are not supported on all devices — a user needs a phone to make a phone call, for instance.

When allowed, Cortana is much more than just a searching tool. If the user logs into a Microsoft account, Cortana can keep track of the user's calendar. Cortana will also suggest news and can even tell the user a joke! Cortana adapts to the user. The more a user uses Cortana, the more she learns and adapts to the user. In the future, Microsoft plans to allow a user to even use Cortana to connect to a Facebook account.

QUICK REFERENCE	How Do You Interact with Cortana?

Cortana can do many different things for you. When talking to Cortana, you start with **Hey Cortana** — for example, you might say, "Hey Cortana, tell me a joke." When typing into the Ask me anything box, you do not need to type her name. You can just type your request — for example, Tell me a joke. When you talk to Cortana, she will talk back. When you type, she will respond on screen. See Table 2 for examples of what Cortana can do for you.

Action*	What the user says or types	Result
Phone	Hey Cortana, call mom.	Cortana finds mom's phone number and places a call.
Messaging	Hey Cortana, text Eric.	Cortana finds Eric's number and asks what the text should say.
Calendar	Hey Cortana, put a meeting at work on my calendar.	Cortana asks questions about the event and then adds it to your calendar.
Reminders	Hey Cortana, when Aidan calls, remind me to thank him.	Cortana asks for any additional details and then sets the reminder. When Aidan calls, the phone will display "Thank him" above where a user accepts the call.
Note	Hey Cortana, take a note.	Cortana will ask what the note should say and then saves it to OneNote.
Alarm	Hey Cortana, set an alarm.	Cortana asks for when and sets the alarm.
Music	Hey Cortana, play Dave Matthews Band.	Cortana starts playing any songs by Dave Matthews Band in your Music app.
Places	Hey Cortana, is there a Starbucks near me?	Cortana displays a list of one or more nearby Starbucks.
Computer Search	Change battery settings	Cortana searches the computer and provides a list of options. Press Enter and she will launch where you change battery settings.
Web Search	Windows Help	Cortana shows a list with a Bing Search first. Press Enter and she will launch the Bing results.

Table 2   What can Cortana do for you?

*Some features only work on particular devices, such as a smart phone.

CONSIDER THIS | **Would Cortana Make You More or Less Efficient?**

Cortana is a personal assistant that was designed to help make your life easier. In what ways could it make your life easier and more efficient? Are there any ways in which Cortana could be distracting or hinder you while you work?

Using Windows Search

When Cortana searches the user's computer, she will find results for programs, applications, computer settings, folders, and not only file names, but also contents of files. The only requirement for searching the contents of a file is that the file be in an indexed folder. **Indexed folders** are locations the Windows search tool has already searched and for which it has produced a keyword list. Common indexed locations include the Documents folder on the hard drive. Removable media, such as USB flash drives and CDs, cannot be indexed.

If Cortana does not find anything on the computer, she will treat the inquiry as a web search and launch the Bing results in the default web browser — in Windows 10, that is a new browser called Edge. In this exercise, you will use Cortana to search for resorts in New Mexico. You know that some of the employees at Painted Paradise will want to monitor what competitors are doing.

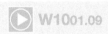

To Search in Windows 10 with Cortana

a. If you took a break, turn on your computer and log into Windows. Also, if necessary, return to the desktop.

b. Click the **Search the web and Windows** box on the taskbar. If your computer displays *Ask me anything* or a greeting with your name in the search box instead of *Search the web and Windows*, Cortana is already enabled. Skip to step e.

> ### Troubleshooting
>
> If you do not have a Microsoft account, you can obtain a free Microsoft account through any browser at https://signup.live.com. You can still search without allowing Cortana. However, the taskbar will say *Search the web and Windows* instead of *Ask me anything*. This chapter is written as if you have Cortana allowed.

c. Click in the **affirmative** such as Next, I Agree, Allow, or I'm in! to enable Cortana. Once you click in the affirmative, Cortana may ask you to sign into a Microsoft account if you did not log into Windows with a Microsoft account. Sign into your Microsoft account if Cortana asks you to.

> ### Troubleshooting
>
> If you clicked in the Search the web and Windows before this exercise and did not allow Cortana, Cortana will not prompt you to allow her to work. To allow her, click in the **Search the web and Windows box** on the taskbar. Then in the upper left side, click Cortana Setting ⚙ and then move the top slider to On. Cortana can give you suggestions, ideas, reminders, alerts, and more.
>
> Note that if you are working on a public computer, an administrator may have not allowed Cortana.

SIDE NOTE

Cortana Suggestions

Pressing Enter after your search will launch the first result. If you want one of Cortana's alternative suggestions, click the one you want.

d. Click **I agree**, type the name you want Cortana to call you, click **Next**, and answer any of the questions that Cortana asks about your personal preferences.

e. In the search box, click **Ask me anything**.

Figure 11 Cortana

f. Type resorts in new mexico.

Notice the first result is to do a Bing Search for what you typed. However, Cortana also makes suggestions for alternative search suggestions, which may vary from the figure below.

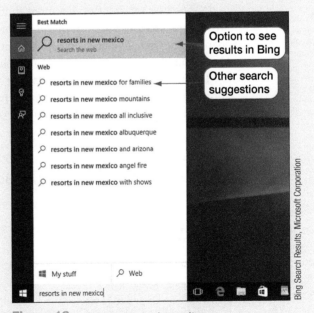

Figure 12 Cortana search results

g. Press Enter. Notice, Cortana launches the Bing search results in the new Windows 10 default browser — Edge.

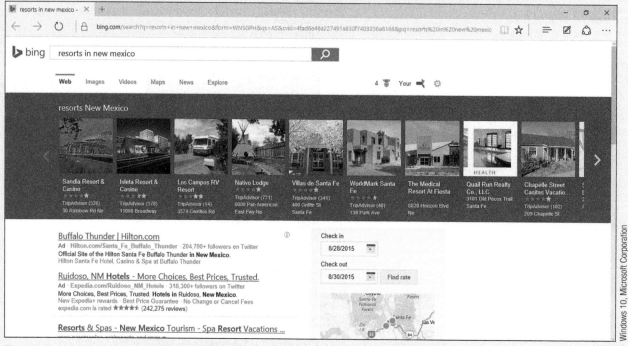

Figure 13 Cortana search results in Edge

h. In the upper right corner of the Edge browser window, click **Close** ⊠

Accessing and Managing the Cortana Notebook and Settings

Cortana's Notebook is where she keeps track of what the user likes and wants Cortana to do. The user can tell Cortana more about his or her interests and even where the user's favorite places are to visit. All of the information in the Notebook helps Cortana learn and adapt to the user. The user can also set hours when Cortana should be quiet by using the Quiet hours in the expanded settings of the Action Center!

In the same area, a user can also set various settings, from turning Cortana off to allowing Cortana to detect information from emails to add to the user's calendar, such as a recently booked flight. In this next exercise, you will add the Business & Tech event category to the notebook and explore the settings.

W1001.10

SIDE NOTE
Informing Cortana
In this exercise, you will only modify one preference for Cortana. The Quick Reference after this exercise explains the ways in which you can inform Cortana and Cortana can inform you.

To Access and Manage the Cortana Notebook and Settings

a. On the taskbar, click **Ask me anything**.

Troubleshooting

Do you not have *Ask me anything* in the taskbar? Then you have not allowed Cortana. If you have not allowed Cortana, you will not be able to do most of this exercise. See the previous exercise for help with allowing Cortana. You can still search without allowing Cortana. However, the taskbar will say *Search the web and Windows* instead of *Ask me anything*.

b. In the upper left corner, click **Cortana menu** ☰. Notice, the Cortana menu expands and labels the icons.

Figure 14   Cortana menu

c. Click **Notebook** ▣. Cortana pulls up About Me, Connected Accounts, Settings, and a list of items in your notebook, which contains information about you that Cortana uses.

d. In the list, click **Events**. Event cards are by default turned off. Click **Off** to turn on events.

e. Click **Add an event category**.

f. Click **Business & tech** and then click **Add**. Then, click **Save**.

g. Click **Notebook** ▣ and then **Settings**.

Scroll through and read the various settings, including Bing SafeSearch settings and Other privacy settings. Modify the settings according to your personal preference.

QUICK REFERENCE	Cortana Menu Options

⌂ **Home** — the default screen where Cortana shows you some suggestions and greets you.

▣ **Notebook** — where you can help Cortana get to know you and your interests including Connected Accounts and Settings.

♀ **Reminders** — where you can have Cortana set reminders for you.

⚐ **Feedback** — where you can provide Microsoft with your opinion on Cortana.

Getting Windows Help

Windows 10 has changed dramatically from Windows 8 and Windows 7. The changes are enough to leave even an experienced user scratching his or her head. Thanks to the taskbar search, finding help could never be easier. In the next exercise, you will search for Windows Help.

 W1001.11

To Use Windows Help and Support

a. If necessary, on the taskbar, click in the **Ask me anything** or **Search the web and Windows** box.

b. Type Windows help.

Notice that search finds several different ways you could get help. One option is for a Microsoft Support web page. However, search also found suggested changes to your search. Your results may vary from Figure 15.

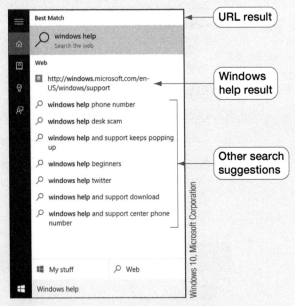

Figure 15 Cortana Windows Help search results

c. Click the option starting with http://windows.microsoft.com. The web browser opens to the support page where you could further look for help or search.

d. In the upper right corner of the Edge browser window, click **Close** ⨉. If you need to take a break before finishing this chapter, now is a good time.

Working with Windows and Desktops

Windows 10 can run applications — apps — or software programs. Traditionally, programs were software designed to run on Windows, such as Microsoft Office. Apps started on mobile devices as lightweight software that perform a specific task, such as playing music or checking your email. The difference between a program and an app is just the way the software is published, designed, installed, and consumed. At their core, they are both programming code. Simply put, an **app** is application software that must be installed from a store — in Windows it is the Windows Store. A **program** is application software that the user will install directly from the download installer or from the company that wrote the program.

In versions of Windows before Windows 10, apps and programs behaved very differently. A major improvement with Windows 10 over prior versions is that apps now open in a traditional window and behave the same, from a user's standpoint, as programs. Generally, apps are designed more for when Windows is used in tablet mode or with a touch screen. Programs usually have more functionality but are designed more for use with a traditional keyboard and mouse. At times, this may be confusing. A user who has both the mail app and Microsoft Outlook installed will have two locations to check his or her email. Windows will come with some preinstalled apps, such as the News app, and some preinstalled programs, such as WordPad and the Snipping Tool.

QUICK REFERENCE	When Do I Need to Use the Windows Store?

While you go straight to the manufacturer for programs, the Windows Store is the source for all apps created for Windows 10. In the store, you can browse through a specific category or collection of apps, such as free apps. You can also search for apps by keywords. Your account area is linked to your Microsoft account. You can manage apps that you have purchased or installed. You can update apps that need updating. If you uninstall an app and later want to reinstall it, you can do so here without paying for the app again. To get to the Windows Store, click on **Ask me anything** or **Search the web and Windows** on the taskbar, type Windows Store, and press Enter. If pinned to the taskbar, you can also click the **Windows Store** on the taskbar.

REAL WORLD ADVICE	When Should I Use an App and When Should I Use the Program?

The good news is that applications — apps — and programs work the same in Windows 10, once installed. Generally, you should use apps, such as the Mail app, when you use tablet mode or your finger. You should use a program, such as Outlook, when you have a keyboard/mouse or when you need additional functionality that is not in the app. However, it really is up to your personal preference! In Windows 10, the only real difference to you, the user, is how they are installed.

The updated apps in Windows 10 are a large improvement from the Windows 8.1 apps. For example, many large cities now have a 3D view that is very useful. Take the time to explore these new apps!

In this section, you will demonstrate how to move, size, and manage both single and multiple windows — both programs and apps — and how to work with multiple desktops.

Open and Manage a Window

A **window** is what displays when you open a program or app. It has standard features across all programs and apps and gives Windows its name. Windows can be moved, resized, minimized to a taskbar button, and maximized to fill the entire screen. Several windows can be open at the same time and can be manipulated in the same way.

Opening, Moving, and Sizing a Window

There are several ways to open windows. You have already opened windows using icons on the desktop, Tiles on the Start menu, and the Search box on the taskbar. All windows have similar components. The bar at the top of a window is the **title bar**. On the right side of the title bar are three control buttons that let you minimize, maximize or restore down, and close a window. If a window is maximized, the center button changes to the Restore Down button. Clicking this button when the window is maximized restores the window to its previous size and location.

The title bar can be used to move a window that is not maximized to another location on the desktop. Many windows also display icons on the left side of the title bar that represent the program that is open. Clicking the icon opens a menu of commonly used commands. To the right of this icon, many Microsoft programs display a Quick Access Toolbar with Save, Undo, and Redo buttons. Clicking the arrow to the right of these buttons displays the Customize Quick Access Toolbar menu that lets the user add other buttons to the Quick Access Toolbar. Windows also display the name of the document or file that is open and the name of the program you are using — except in File Explorer which shows the location. The borders of a window allow you resize the window if the window is not maximized.

All versions of Windows include a text-editing program named WordPad. Though not as powerful as word processing programs (such as Microsoft Word or OpenOffice Writer), WordPad is free and preinstalled. You will use the WordPad program in the following exercise to practice moving and resizing a window. In this exercise, you will create and save notes of new features of Windows 10 that you want to share with other employees at Painted Paradise.

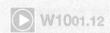 W1001.12

To Open, Move, and Size a Window

a. If you took a break, turn on your computer and log into Windows. Also, if necessary, return to the desktop with no programs or apps open.

b. Click **Start** ▦.

c. Click the **WordPad** Tile.

WordPad opens in a new window. Notice the title bar also displays Document, which is the current file name, and WordPad, the name of the open program. The word "Document" will be replaced by the name of the file once it has been created and saved. WordPad also displays a ribbon, which is common to many Microsoft applications.

> **Troubleshooting**
>
> If the WordPad Tile is not on your Start menu, click All apps, find WordPad in the list, and click.

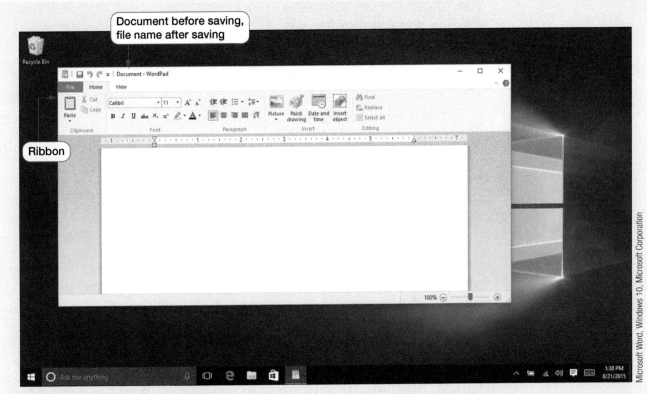

Document before saving,
file name after saving

Ribbon

Figure 16 The WordPad window

SIDE NOTE
Window Won't Resize?
If the Maximize button is dimmed, the window cannot be resized. Dialog boxes — boxes that present information or require a response from the user — may display only a Close button.

d. In the WordPad window, type Notes and press Enter.

e. Type Start menu and press Enter.

f. Type Cortana and press Enter.

g. Type Apps open in a Window.

h. On the File tab, click **Save**. Browse to the location where you are saving your files.

i. Type w1001ch01Notes_LastFirst (using your last and first name), and then click **Save**. Notice that the file name now appears on the title bar.

j. Point to the middle of the title bar. Click and drag **down** a little. This is how you move a window.

k. Point to the lower right corner. Your pointer will change to 🔲. Click and drag **up** and to the **left** a little. This is one way to resize a window.

l. Leave the WordPad window open for the next exercise.

Certain versions of Microsoft Office include the OneNote application. OneNote is designed to allow you to keep track of notes in electronic notebook files. OneNote features options for you to type anywhere on a page, organize related pages into sections, and keep many sections within a notebook. You may have a notebook for your computer class with a section for each chapter of the main textbook. Each section may contain a number of pages related to that section.

OneNote also allows you to paste documents and pictures from the Internet, and it automatically keeps track of the original website address. Users with tablets can use a digitizer pen and handwrite notes as well. Windows handwriting recognition has greatly improved over previous versions.

You can save the files to the Internet as well, so you can open and modify the document from a number of different computers. To access OneNote, you can use the Start menu, Cortana, or Note in the Action Center.

Minimizing, Maximizing, and Restoring a Window

When you minimize a program, the window is removed from the desktop, but the program is still running on the computer. The program button on the taskbar shows that it is still available but not active. When you close a program, the window is removed from the screen, and the program closes and is removed from your computer's memory. When a program is closed, the program button is removed from the taskbar unless it has been pinned there. In this exercise, you will minimize, maximize, and restore the WordPad window.

To Minimize, Maximize, and Restore a Window

a. On the right side of the WordPad title bar, click **Minimize** $\boxed{-}$.

   The window is removed from the screen, but notice that the WordPad icon is still displayed on the taskbar with a light blue line at the bottom indicating that a WordPad window is open.

b. Point to **WordPad** on the taskbar. A thumbnail window is displayed, giving you a chance to preview what the window looks like. Click the **WordPad** thumbnail.

c. On the right side of the WordPad title bar, click **Maximize** $\boxed{\square}$. The WordPad window now fills the entire screen. Note that a maximized window cannot be moved or resized.

d. On the right side of the WordPad title bar, click **Restore Down** $\boxed{\square}$. WordPad returns to the original size.

e. Leave the WordPad window open for the next exercise.

Open and Manage Multiple Windows

The Windows operating system supports multitasking, which is the ability to run more than one program or application at once. Many users take full advantage of this feature. You may be running Edge to log into Facebook while you type a document in Microsoft Word, listen to music in iTunes, and play World of Warcraft. You may not realize that while you are running these programs, other applications such as your antivirus software are also running. The ability to multitask presents great advantages over older operating systems, but it can slow down the computer. A computer should not necessarily run 10 applications at once just because it can. If you find that your computer is running slowly, a quick fix might be to do less multitasking.

Switch Option	Method
Taskbar Task View button	Opens Task View, where you can click the window you want.
Windows + Tab key combination	Press and hold [⊞] and then press [Tab] to launch Task View.
Gesture	Swipe from the left bezel toward the right. Windows opens Task View.
Alt + Tab key combination	Press and hold [Alt] and then press [Tab] repeatedly to cycle through all open windows. When the program you want is highlighted, release the [Alt] button.
Taskbar buttons	On the taskbar, click the button for the program in which you want to work to switch to that program. The program appears in front of the other windows and becomes the active window.

Table 3   Switching between programs

Often, you will want to work with several programs at the same time so that you can move data among them, or you may want to have several windows open in the same program so that you can compare different documents. Learning to manage multiple windows makes it easy to quickly access a window you want to use. You can also arrange open windows in ways that help you work more productively.

Even if multiple programs are open, you can only work in the **active window** — the window in which you can move the mouse pointer, type text, or perform other tasks. This is the window that is on top or in front of any other window. Only one window can be active at a time.

Using Task View

Several methods are available for switching between programs or windows, as shown in Table 3. New to Windows 10, the easiest way to switch between windows is through the use of Task View. In the next exercise, you will explore switching between WordPad and the News app using Task View.

To Use the Task View

a. If you do not see the WordPad window, click **WordPad** on the taskbar.

> **Troubleshooting**
> If WordPad is not on the taskbar, click the Start button, and then locate and click WordPad from the Start menu.

b. Click **Start** ▦.

c. Click the **News** app Tile. The News app launches in a new window. Depending on how much you resized WordPad in the previous exercise, you may not see WordPad or you may see a portion on the window behind the News app.

d. On the taskbar, click **Task View** ▣. Task View launches and displays all open Windows as preview images. If you have other programs open besides News and WordPad, you will see those as well.

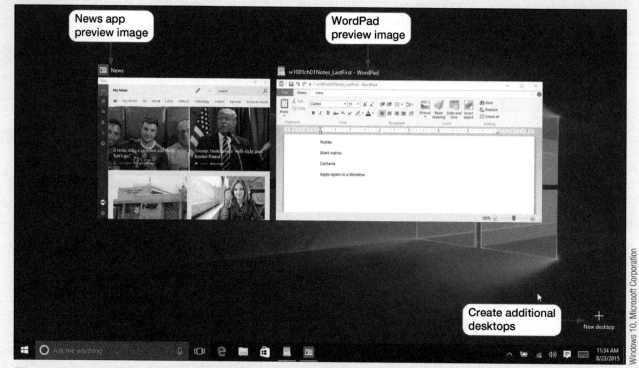

Figure 17 Task View

Windows 10, Microsoft Corporation

e. Click the preview image for **WordPad**. Windows makes WordPad the active window.

f. Press  and Tab at the same time. Task View opens again.

g. Click the preview image for **News**. Windows makes News the active window.

h. On the News app window, click **Close** ×. Leave WordPad open for the next exercise.

SS CONSIDER THIS | **Why Use Key Combinations?**

There are literally hundreds of key combinations. You probably will not want to take the time to memorize all possible key combinations. However, if there is a command you use frequently, it might be worth looking up the key combination on the Internet or in Help. What are some common commands you perform frequently that might be worth finding key combinations for?

Snapping and Shaking Windows

Snap is a quick way to arrange open windows by dragging them to the edges of your screen. Depending on your screen resolution, up to four apps can be docked side by side. When the window snaps to the edge of the screen in the middle, it will take up exactly half of the current screen. When the window snaps to the edge of the screen in the corner, it will take up exactly one fourth of the current screen.

When multiple windows are open, you can minimize all but the active window by using **Shake** — shaking the title bar to minimize all other windows. This method will leave the user with only one window displayed, and it is a good way to clear up a cluttered screen.

In this exercise, you will need to open two programs, practice snapping programs and apps side-by-side and in quadrants, and shake to clean up the view.

To Snap Side by Side, Snap in Quadrants, and Shake Windows

a. If necessary, open WordPad.

b. On the taskbar, click **Ask me anything** or **Search the web and Windows**.

c. Type paint and press Enter. The Paint program opens in a new window and becomes the active window.

d. On the taskbar, click **Ask me anything** or **Search the web and Windows**.

e. Type store and press Enter. The Windows Store opens in a new window and becomes the active window.

f. Point to the middle of the title bar of the **Store window**. Click and drag it to the **middle of the left edge** of the screen. The Store window snaps to the left. On the right, a preview image is shown of all other open windows.

g. Click the **Paint** preview image. Now Paint is snapped to the right.

SIDE NOTE

Screen Resolution

Your screen resolution must be at least 1024 × 768 to have multiple windows and apps on your screen at the same time. To check your resolution, go to Start menu, Settings > System, and then select Advanced display settings.

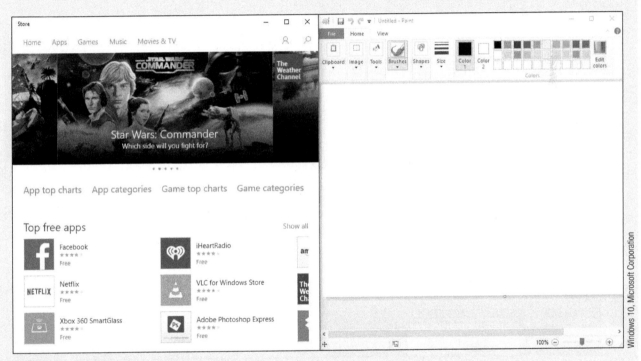

Figure 18 Windows docked side by side

SIDE NOTE

Minimize Everything?

If you want to minimize all windows including the Sports app, you can use the keyboard shortcut of pressing ⊞ and D at the same time.

h. On the taskbar, click **Ask me anything** or **Search the web and Windows**.

i. Type edge and press Enter. The Edge browser opens in a new window and becomes the active window.

j. Point to the middle of the title bar of the **Store** window. Click and drag to the **right**. The Windows store is undocked. With all the open windows, the screen now looks messy.

k. Point to the middle of the title bar of the **Store** window. Click and shake **the window**. All of the windows remain open but are minimized. Only the Windows Store is active.

l. Point to the middle of the title bar of the **Store** window. Click and drag to the **upper left corner**. The Store window is now snapped to the upper left quadrant.

Troubleshooting

If your computer will not snap to quadrants, you may be on a device whose resolution is too low. If this happens, snap the Sports app (left) and Paint (right) side by side again and proceed to the next exercise.

m. On the taskbar, click **WordPad**.

n. Point to the middle of the title bar of **WordPad**. Click and drag to the **upper right corner**. WordPad is now snapped to the upper right quadrant.

o. On the taskbar, click the **Edge** browser.

p. Point to the middle of the title bar of the **Edge** browser. Click and drag to the **lower left corner**. News is now snapped to the lower left quadrant.

q. In the last quadrant, click the **Paint** preview image.

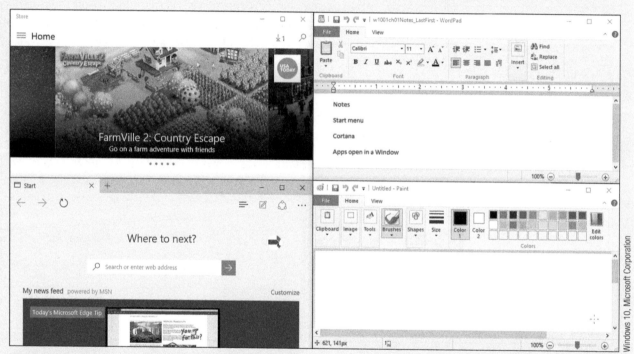

Figure 19   Windows snapped in quadrants

r. Leave your screen with the four windows snapped for the next exercise.

CONSIDER THIS | **Using Apps Side by Side**

What practical benefits exist in viewing apps side by side? What are some apps that you would use side by side to improve efficiency?

Using the Snipping Tool

To have your workshop attendees take before-and-after images of their screen, you will use the Snipping Tool. The Snipping Tool allows you to take a **snip** — a picture of your current screen. For many years, people have been able to take pictures of their screen using the Print Screen key on their keyboard, but that requires pasting the image into a photo editing tool to save it. The Snipping Tool was introduced to personal computers to streamline this process. The Snipping Tool can be used in any area that requires taking snips of what is on a screen. Authors can use it to take pictures of their screens to add to a textbook. People creating manuals for software can take snips to help users understand how to use their product. The tool can be used to show a technical support person what an error on the screen looks like. Any time you need an image of screen contents, you can create one using this program.

One drawback to the Snipping Tool is that it does not allow you to take snips of the Lock Screen, Login Screen, or Start menu. To capture images of these, you will need to press the Print Screen key on your keyboard, open the Paint program, and then paste. You can then save your image. Another drawback is that the Snipping Tool doesn't allow you to capture shortcut menus.

In this exercise, you will use the Snipping Tool to capture a screenshot of the desktop with Windows Store, WordPad, Edge, and Paint open in quadrants. You will also use the Print Screen option to capture a screenshot of the Start menu and save the image using the Paint app.

To Use the Snipping Tool

a. The Windows Store, WordPad, Edge browser, and Paint windows should be snapped in quadrants. If your resolution was insufficient for quadrants, Store and Paint should be snapped side-by-side. If not, repeat the previous exercise before continuing.

b. On the taskbar, click **Ask me anything** or **Search the web and Windows**.

c. Type snipping tool and press Enter. The Snipping Tool opens on top of the other windows.

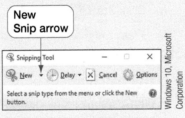

Figure 20   Snipping Tool

d. Click the **New Snip** arrow and then click **Full-screen Snip**. The Snipping Tool opens the image. Notice that the Snipping Tool window does not show in the image. Tools at the top allow you to highlight or write on the image if desired.

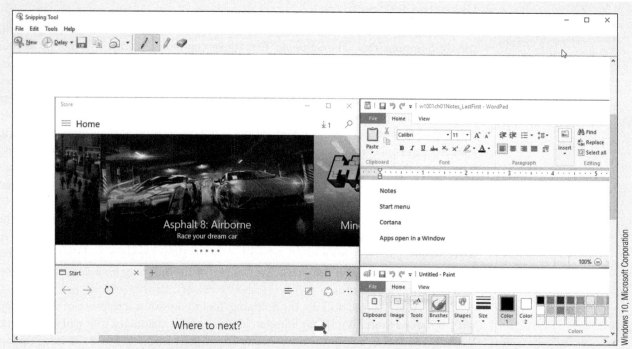

Figure 21 Snipping Tool with image

e. On the menu bar, click **File** and then click **Save As**. Browse to the location where you are saving your files.

f. Click the File name box and then type w1001ch01QuadrantsSnip_LastFirst (using your last and first name).

g. Click the **Save as type** arrow, click **JPEG file (*.JPG)**, and then click **Save**.

h. Click **Close** ☒ in the top-right corner of the Snipping Tool window to close it.

i. Click **Close** ☒ in the top-right corner of the **Windows Store**, **WordPad**, and the **Edge** browser. Leave Paint open.

j. Point to the middle of the title bar for **Paint** and double-click. The Paint window is restored.

k. Click **Start** ⊞.

l. Press the PrtScr key on your keyboard.

> ### Troubleshooting
> What if your keyboard does not have a Print Screen key? Many laptops do not have a Print Screen key. You can search the web for alternative keyboard combinations along with the type of keyboard/device. For example, on a Surface Pro keyboard, the shortcut is pressing the Function N key and the Spacebar Spacebar at the same time.

m. Click the title bar of the **Paint** window to close the Start menu and make Paint the active window.

n. On the Home tab, in the Clipboard group, click **Paste**.

SIDE NOTE
Copying and Pasting
In every Windows program, the keyboard shortcut for copy is `Ctrl` and `C`. The keyboard shortcut for paste is `Ctrl` and `V`.

o.   Click the **File** tab and then click **Save**. Browse to the location where you are saving your files.

p.   Type w1001ch01StartSnip_LastFirst. Click the **Save as type** arrow, click **JPEG (*.JPG)**, and then click **Save**.

q.   Click **Close** `×` in the top-right corner of Paint to close the program. If you need to take a break before finishing this chapter, now is a good time.

QUICK REFERENCE	Snipping Tool Options and Save Types

The Snipping Tool can capture four different types of snips:

*   Free-form Snip — allows for any type of selection of content on the screen in varied shapes and sizes
*   Rectangular Snip — allows for a rectangular selection of content anywhere on the screen, varying in size according to user selection
*   Window Snip — automatically captures the entire window selected, varying in size according to the window size and position
*   Full-screen Snip — automatically captures the entire screen, varying in size according to the screen resolution

The Snipping Tool can save the screen capture in one of the following file types:

*   Portable Network Graphic file (PNG) (*.PNG)
*   GIF file (*.GIF)
*   JPEG file (*.JPG)
*   Single file HTML (MHT) (*.MHT)

Create and Use Multiple Desktops

Earlier in this chapter, you explored the desktop. New to Windows 10, a user can now configure multiple desktops in addition to the multiple windows. **Multiple virtual desktops** allow the user to configure different Start menus and experiences for different purposes — and switch easily between them.

These days, many people have multiple devices for different uses. Who wants to see work email on a Friday night? With a single desktop, the user gets notifications for his or her work email even if the user does not want to see them. Many users, seeing an email from the boss on a Friday night, will feel compelled to react–in essence working on a Friday night and being on call whenever the user is on the device. To avoid these situations, many users have multiple devices so that they will not see the work email until Monday.

Thanks to multiple desktops, a user can get closer to using one device and still keeping that separation. To create multiple desktops, open Task View and then, in the lower right corner, click the New desktop button. Then a user can switch between the two desktops in the Task View. Windows that are open on one desktop will not be open on the other desktop. In settings under System and then Multitasking, a user can specify which windows are shown on the taskbar and appear when using `Alt` + `Tab`.

Using Computer Settings and Protecting the Computer

With Windows 10, Microsoft has streamlined notifications and settings making them more user friendly. Microsoft put considerable effort into grouping settings into new categories, making settings easier to find. Further, a user can find any setting by simply searching for what he or she wants.

Use Windows 10 Notifications and Settings in the Action Center

If a user swipes from the right bezel in Window 10, the Charms from Windows 8 will not appear. Instead, a newly revamped Action Center task pane appears. The **Action Center** is where notifications appear and where a user can quickly get to most settings. You can also click the Action Center button . When you point your mouse to the Action Center button on the taskbar, you will not see the words "Action Center." Instead, the Action Center button on the taskbar will say either *New notifications* or *No new notifications*.

When a user first sees the Action Center task pane by clicking the button or swiping from the right bezel, the words *Action Center* appear at the top. The notifications in the Action Center task pane appear at the top — if you have any. Notifications can perform the action without opening the associated app. For example, you can respond to an instant message without leaving the Action Center task pane. At the bottom of the Action Center task pane, you can expand or collapse to see more or fewer settings.

Seeing and Clearing Notifications, Exploring Settings, and Personalizing the Desktop

Notifications help you keep up with the world. However, notifications can also get backed up and unmanageable when overused. Managing notifications effectively will make you more efficient. In this next exercise, you will look at any notifications you have and find the settings for notification management.

QUICK REFERENCE	Categories of Settings

- **System**   display, notification, apps, power, storage, and other general system settings
- **Devices**   connecting devices, Bluetooth, printers, scanners, pens, and any other settings for devices
- **Network & Internet**   Wi-Fi, airplane mode, data usage, and other connectivity settings
- **Personalization**   desktop backgrounds, colors, Lock Screen, and themes
- **Accounts**   all settings for various accounts and account access on the machine, including Microsoft accounts
- **Time & language**   date, time, region, speech, and language settings
- **Ease of Access**   settings for interacting with the computer, including a magnifier, closed captioning, and a narrator
- **Privacy**   all privacy settings for devices, such as a camera, location, and apps
- **Update & security**   updating, recovery, Windows Defender, backup, and other settings related to keeping the computer secure and updated

W1001.17

To See and Clear Notifications, Explore Settings, and Personalize the Desktop

a. If you took a break, turn on your computer and log into Windows. Also, if necessary, return to the desktop with no open windows.

> **SIDE NOTE**
> **Gestures**
> A right bezel swipe in Windows 10 opens the Action Center.

b. On the taskbar in the lower right corner, point to the **Action Center** . A screen tip will appear indicating either New notifications or No new notifications.

Windows 10, Microsoft Corporation

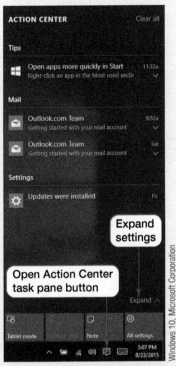

Figure 22 Action Center with collapsed settings

Windows 10, Microsoft Corporation

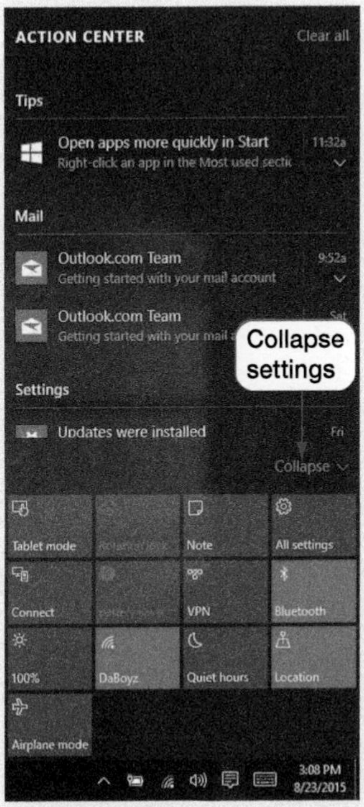

Figure 23 Action Center with expanded settings

c. Click the **Action Center** . The Action Center task pane appears along the right of the screen. If you have any notifications, they will be listed at the top. At the bottom are the Quick Action settings.

> **SIDE NOTE**
> **Clearing a Notification**
> You can also click and drag or swipe from left to the right to clear a notification.

d. If you have a notification, you can click the Notification and take action on the item. If the notification still appears after you are done, you can point to the notification and then click **Close** in the upper right corner of that notification to clear an individual notification.

e. If necessary, click **Expand** to see all settings. The expanded settings may vary depending on your computer settings.

f. If you want to clear all notifications, click **Clear all** in the upper right corner of the screen.

g. Click **All settings** and then click **System**.

h. On the right side, scroll down and click **Advanced display settings**.
Notice your screen resolution setting. The higher the resolution, the smaller the items on the screen will appear. The lower the resolution, the larger the items will appear. The resolution depends on the quality and size of the monitor or screen. For items such as the Microsoft ribbon, the interface will be different at different resolutions. This can be frustrating if your screen does not match the figures in this book. The figures in this book were taken at 1366 × 768.

i. If available and you desire, change your resolution to **1366 × 768** to match the figures in this book.

j. In the upper left corner, to the left of the word Settings, click the **back arrow** ←.

k. On the left side, click **Notifications & actions**. Read through all of the settings you can change for the notifications. In particular, look at how you can modify the quick actions that appear on the collapsed Action Center and icons that appear on the taskbar. You can also turn notifications off for individual apps.

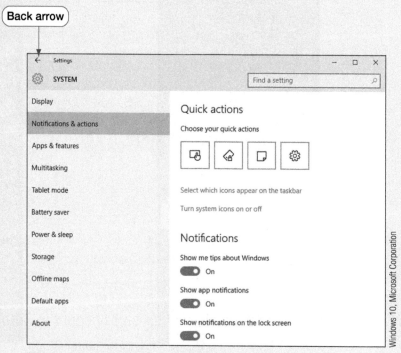

Figure 24 Notifications settings

Windows 10, Microsoft Corporation

SIDE NOTE
Settings
This chapter will take you to some of the settings in Windows but not all of them. You will find that taking the time to look around in the settings is very valuable.

l. In the upper left corner, to the left of the word Settings, click the **back arrow** ←. Then click **Personalization**.

m. Under Choose your picture, click the preview image that has someone running on a **beach**. Your desktop background has now changed to look like a beach scene.

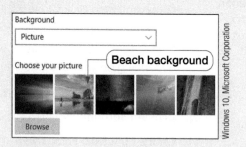

Figure 25 Beach background

Windows 10, Microsoft Corporation

n. Take some time to explore the different settings. Then click **Close** ✕ to exit Settings.

Associating a Microsoft Account in Settings

Microsoft allows you to sign into Windows using a Microsoft account. In this context, the term "Microsoft account" refers to what was previously known as a Windows Live ID. You can create a new Microsoft account for any existing email address or set up a free outlook.com or hotmail.com account to sign in. In other words, Gmail and Yahoo! users can use their regular email accounts as their login. You will be able to choose to log into a local account, which exists only on a single machine, or a Microsoft account.

Signing in using a Microsoft account is an example of cloud computing. Cloud computing allows you to keep files on the Internet rather than on the client computer. The advantage is that even if the client computer fails, files and settings are still safe. A single Microsoft account identifies you as a user on all computers you sign into, the Windows Store, the People app for collaboration with family and friends, and your OneDrive cloud storage space.

You do not have to use a Microsoft account in this version of Windows, but Microsoft has introduced a number of features that make it attractive. Personal settings, photos, and documents can be saved to a Microsoft account rather than to the local machine. Installed apps will follow you to any machine. This will reduce the need for home users to set up a home network, as they can simply log into each machine with their Microsoft account.

Your college or work policy may not allow you to log in this way, but if it does, you will have access to the same files at school and work that you do at home. Using this type of account will reduce the problems associated with forgetting or losing a USB flash drive.

Note this can be undone at any point by going back to Settings, selecting Accounts, and selecting Disconnect on the Your account screen.

In this exercise, you will associate a new or existing Microsoft account with the current user on your PC.

To Associate a Microsoft Account in Settings

a. On the taskbar, click **Action Center** .

b. Click **All settings**.

c. Click **Accounts** and then, if necessary, on the left side click **Your account**.

d. Click **Sign in with a Microsoft Account**.

> **Troubleshooting**
>
> If you have already signed in using a Microsoft account on this PC, the option to Sign in with a Microsoft account will be replaced by the option to Manage my Microsoft account or Sign in with a Local account instead. In that case, you do not need to complete this activity. If your screen says Verify my Microsoft account, click the link and follow the security prompts to verify the account.

e. Follow the directions on the screen. If asked, do not set up a pin at this time.

> **Troubleshooting**
>
> If you don't have a Microsoft account yet, instead click **Create a new account**. Then follow the prompts on the screen to enter your personal information. You will be asked to verify with a text message. If you cannot do that, click *Use a different verification option* or *I can't do this right now* for other options.

f. On the Your account screen, verify that **your Microsoft account email address** is displayed below the account name.
   At this point, any other Windows 10 devices you log into using your email address will have access to the same applications, files, and settings.

g. Click **Close** ☒ to close Settings.

Setting Up a Picture Password or PIN

Windows 10 has a number of security features. In an effort to give the desktop operating system features that users enjoy on mobile devices, Microsoft has introduced multiple login methods — a traditional password, a picture password, a PIN, or Windows Hello. **Windows Hello** is a feature new to Windows 10 that allows the operating system to use the camera to recognize your face rather than typing a password. You must first add a PIN before you can use Windows Hello. A user can also adjust the password policy to require a password after the display is off for a period of time. Many of these setups will be done by using a wizard. **Wizards** are used to guide you through complex tasks.

For some users, a combination of a picture and gestures is more intuitive than remembering a password. The additional methods can provide greater ease of use in logging into the computer. Picture passwords allow you to select a picture and define a series of patterns that need to be "drawn" to unlock the system. With Windows Hello you need only look at your computer and it uses your face like a thumbprint. However, the image recognition software could unlock for someone who looks similar to you. Picture passwords will be more commonly used on mobile devices and home devices; public computer labs will likely not utilize this feature.

Users also have the option in Windows to add an alternative to a password with a personal identification number, or PIN. A PIN is a four-digit numeric pass code. In this exercise, you will create a picture password and a PIN.

Password	Security Rating	Rationale
abc123	Weak	Though it involves letters and numbers, this is a short password.
qwerty	Weak	Though not in the dictionary, this is a common password.
password	Medium	Though it may seem clever to choose a password so simple, this is one of the first passwords hackers guess. It gets a Medium rating for length.
pearsoned	Medium	Password length is good, but if you work for Pearson Education, this would be too obvious.
poptart8675309	Strong	Length of password and combination of letters and numbers make this a stronger password.
efiafaabnatbycc	Strong	Length of password and randomness of letters make this difficult to guess.
Efiafaabnat-bycc@8675309	Very strong	Capital letters, symbols, numbers, and password length make this nearly impossible to guess — if protected correctly.

Table 4 Security of passwords

REAL WORLD ADVICE **Picture Passwords and Dirty Hands!**

A picture password can make logging into a computer much easier. However, imagine what the screen would look like if the user had grease from French fries on his or her hands. That would leave visible marks on the screen, and by holding the device at the right angle, another person could detect the password. The moral here is keep your hands — and your touch screen — clean!

W1001.19

SIDE NOTE
Changing a Picture Password
You can change or remove a picture password from the Sign-in options screen at any time.

SIDE NOTE
Picture Password Gestures
The gestures can be a tap, a straight line, or a circle. Create a set of three gestures that you will remember.

To Set Up a Picture Password or PIN

a. On the taskbar, click **Ask me anything** or **Search the web and Windows**. Then type password and press Enter. The search opens Settings to the place where you can change Sign-in options.

b. Under the Picture password heading, click **Add**.

c. If prompted, type **your password**, and then click **OK**.

d. On the Welcome to picture password screen, click **Choose picture**.

e. Locate a picture of your choosing on the computer, network, or OneDrive account and then click **Open**.

f. On the How's this look? screen, click **Use this picture**.

g. Using the mouse or touch screen, if available, draw **three gestures** on the picture.

h. Re-enter the **gestures** to verify, and click **Finish**.

i. Under the PIN heading, click **Add**.

j. If prompted, type **your password**, and then click **OK**.

k. Type a **four-digit PIN** and press Tab. Re-enter the **same four-digit PIN** and then click **OK**.

l.   Click **Close** ⌧ to return to the desktop.

Once you have set up a PIN and/or a picture password, you can use it to log in from the main screen. You can click Sign-in options to access any of the alternate login methods discussed here. You will demonstrate to your workshop attendees how they can use some of the alternate login methods.

 CONSIDER THIS | **Multiple Sign-in Options for the Same Account**

What benefit is there to configuring multiple sign-in options for the same account? Which of the methods is the most secure? The least secure? The easiest to use? The hardest to use? What are the benefits of using Windows Hello? What if you are a twin?

Managing Windows Updates

Windows checks for updates on a regular basis and automatically installs them. However, you should still know where you can force the device to look for updates — which is particularly useful when a new virus attacks. Otherwise, Windows checks only every couple of hours.

To Manage Windows Updates

a.   Click **Start** ▦ and click **Settings**.

b.   Click **Update & security**. If you wanted to see whether any updates exist, you would click Check for updates.

c.   Click **Advanced options** and make sure, under Choose how updates are installed, that **Automatic (recommended)** is selected. Here, you can also view your update history.

> ### Troubleshooting
> Some versions of Windows 10 will not let you choose anything but Automatic updates. Thus, if you do not see Advanced options, your version of Windows is already set for Automatic updates.

d.   Click **Close** ⌧ to close the Settings window.

Managing Windows Defender

Windows has built-in virus protection called **Windows Defender**. A **virus** is malicious code that intends to harm your computer, use your computer's resources, or collect sensitive information about the user. Usually, virus protection should be turned on all of the time to protect the computer. From time to time, the protection needs to be turned off to complete a task, such as installing a program the user trusts that requires virus protection to be turned off. The user may also want to exclude certain files from being scanned to speed up access to files that he or she trusts. A user who suspects a virus may choose to force an update.

To Use Windows Defender

a. On the taskbar, click **Ask me anything** or **Search the web and Windows** and type windows defender. Click **Windows Defender settings**. Windows Defender settings are launched.

b. Scroll down and click **Use Windows Defender**.

The Windows Defender is launched. From the first screen, you can force a Scan now. You can also see your real-time current scan status. If Windows Defender is currently scanning, it will also show you.

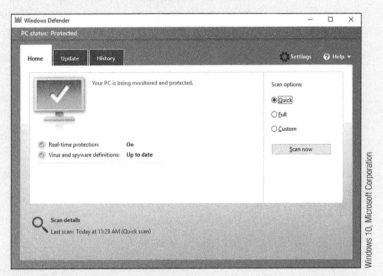

Figure 26   Windows Defender

c. Click the **Update** tab. Here, you can see the last time your virus and spyware definitions were updated. You can force an update as well. However, there is usually no need to do so; Defender will automatically check for these.

d. Click the **History** tab. Here, you can see any issues or items you have excluded from being scanned.

e. Click **Close** ☒ to close Windows Defender. Click **Close** ☒ to close the Settings window.

Access Advanced Computer Settings

Microsoft has done a good job of getting the most important settings into the Settings window, which is launched from either the Start menu or the Action Center. However, there are more settings. A user may need to access advanced settings to troubleshoot a problem or do something more advanced, such as updating a **device driver** — the software that tells the computer how to communicate to a piece of hardware such as a printer. Particularly when a user updates Windows for an older machine, knowing how to get to the more advanced settings is very helpful. Also, when a user searches online to troubleshoot a particular problem, he or she may find advice to use these more advanced settings.

Accessing Advanced Settings and the Control Panel

The most common place to look for additional settings is the Control Panel. The Control Panel has existed in Windows for a long time. It was the main place to access settings for many years. The user interface is not as user friendly as the newer Settings window. Still, not all settings have been moved to the newer user interface.

To Access Advanced Settings and View the Control Panel

a. Click **Start** ▓ and then click **All apps**.

b. Scroll down and click the **arrow** ▼ next to the **Windows System** group. In the Windows System group, click **Control Panel**. The more traditional view of the Control Panel settings opens in a new window.

> **Troubleshooting**
>
> Depending on the settings on your account, you may not be able to access advanced settings. An administrator may have restricted your access, in which case you will not be able to complete this exercise or the next.

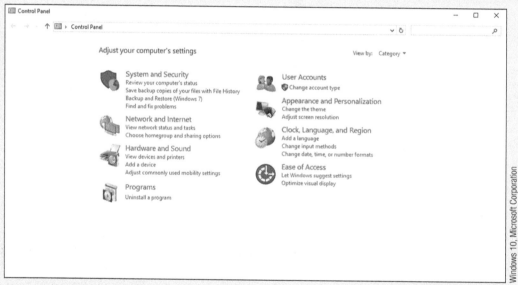

Figure 27   Control Panel

c. Read through the various categories and explore the settings. When done, click **Close** ☒ to close the Control Panel.

Managing Windows Firewall

Windows has a built-in firewall. A **firewall** is software that controls incoming and outgoing network traffic. It helps the computer decide what to trust and what not to trust. The firewall helps to prevent hackers or malicious software from getting into your computer. The firewall settings are accessed through the Control Panel. A user can also get to the Control Panel and all other advanced settings by right-clicking the Start button. In the next exercise, you will locate and explore the settings for the Windows firewall.

To Protect the Computer with Windows Firewall

a. Point to **Start** ⊞ and right-click. A menu with all the advanced settings appears.

Figure 28   All advanced settings

b. Click **Control Panel** and then **System and Security**.

c. Click **Windows Firewall**. Explore and read the firewall settings. When done, click **Close** ⊠. If you need to take a break before finishing this chapter, now is a good time.

Working with Edge and File Explorer

By default, several apps and programs are installed with Windows 10, including a new Internet browser called Edge. Apps and programs routinely create **files** — stored information associated with a particular file type or program. For example, Microsoft Word creates a document file. Various file types have an associated **file extension** — a code after the file name that is preceded by a period and usually consists of three or four letters. Microsoft Word is not one of the default programs in Windows 10. To install a new program, the user gets the installation files straight from the manufacturer — for Word, that is Microsoft. For new apps, the user must find and install from the Windows Store. How you organize the files that you create using these programs and apps is very important — even more important than how you organize them on the Start menu. In this next section, you will learn about Windows Store and the new Edge browser. You will also learn how to use File Explorer to organize your files in folders.

Explore the Edge Browser

Microsoft's old web browser, Internet Explorer, has traditionally been the default browser in Windows. Any **browser** allows users to view web pages. The address bar can be used to enter a **URL (Uniform Resource Locator)**, or website address; to search the web using your default search engine; or to get search suggestions as you type. Internet Explorer is still a program installed in Windows 10. To open it, just search for it on the taskbar in the Ask me anything or Search the web and Windows box. However, Internet Explorer is being phased out.

In the Windows 10 operating system, the default browser is **Edge**. Microsoft went back to the drawing board to create a more streamlined, effective, faster, and more capable browser. Edge also is now the default PDF reader. A **PDF** is a type of file that shows text and images as they would appear in a printed document. Edge will not work in previous versions of Windows.

As with all new programs and apps, Edge is likely to change and have additional functionality over time. This section is written as Edge appeared at the Windows 10 release and this book's publication.

QUICK REFERENCE	Advantages of Edge

Edge is better than Internet Explorer. The list below shows why!

- Edge, Bing, and Cortana are deeply integrated. For example, Cortana will allow you to add an appointment when you select information that appears to be appointment information.
- You can annotate a web page, save it locally or in the cloud, and share it with others. Imagine marking up an article and saving a colleague time by reading only the important parts!
- Edge has increased support for JavaScript extensions — and takes them to a whole new level.
- Edge is **faster** because it is not backward compatible.
- Edge has more uniform format and display of web pages — even across different devices — because of a reinvented engine.
- In Windows 10, Edge is the default PDF reader, but Windows 10 still has all the support for Adobe.

In this section, you will explore the basics of using Edge.

Using the Edge Address Bar for Search

The address bar in Edge is located across the top of the screen. It can be used to directly access a website by URL, to search the web by using the default search engine — by default Bing — or to get suggestions of websites as you type. In this exercise, you will explore using the address bar.

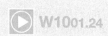

To Search the Web with Edge

a. If you took a break, turn on your computer and log into Windows. Also, if necessary, return to the desktop with no open windows.

b. On the taskbar, click **Ask me anything** or **Search the web and Windows**. Type Edge. If the Edge browser is the first option, press [Enter]. If it is not the first option, click the option for the Edge browser or click Edge <img_1 /> on the taskbar. If needed, click the **Start** tab.

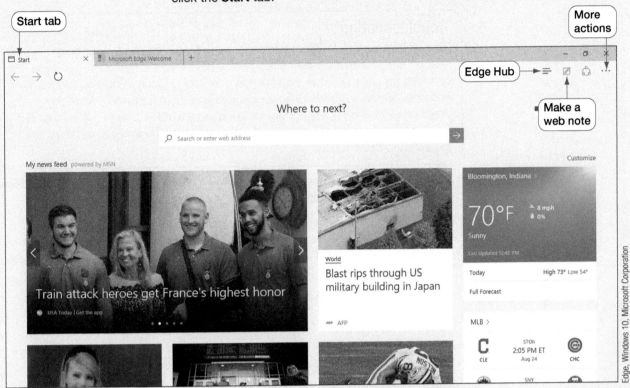

Figure 29 The Edge browser

c. Under the words Where to next? click in the **Search or enter web address** box. If you see a default search engine different than Figure 29, click in the search box for that search engine. Type New Mexico resorts and then press [Enter]. The Bing — or other default search — results appear. Leave these results up for the next exercise.

REAL WORLD ADVICE | **Setting Your Default Search Engine**

In the upper right corner of the browser window, click ..., click Settings, scroll to the bottom, and click View advanced settings. Then scroll down to *Search in the address bar with* and click Bing. Click <Add new> and follow the prompts. While the Bing browser is excellent, everyone has personal preferences. Using the search engine you like best will increase your productivity.

Marking Up the Web

Edge can do something new that other browsers cannot do. You can take a web page and annotate — or make markings. You can do it with a mouse or with your finger or pen if you have a touch device.

W1001.25

To Mark Up a Site and Save to Favorites

a. Your Edge browser should be open with the search results from the previous exercise. Scroll through the results.

Notice, some of the search results are paid advertisements. You know this because right under the title of the result it says *Ads* in small light print, or it will be listed in a group that says *Advertisement*.

Troubleshooting

Your web page looks different! What's happening? Your web page may look different for many reasons. Edge may not be your default browser if you changed the default. Edge may change over time. In fact, Windows, programs, and apps all change and are updated more and more frequently. All of the directions in this book are correct for Windows 10 at the time of publishing. But our world is changing at a more and more rapid pace — and we, as users, are expected to figure it out!

---

b. In the upper right corner, click **Make a Web Note** 📝. Notice a new bar appears across the top with options such as using a pen or a highlighter.

c. In the upper left corner, click **Pen** 🔽.

Your mouse works like a pen, and you can draw on the web page. By default, the pen is blue. If you want a different color, after you click Pen 🔽, click in the lower right corner of Pen 🔽. There, you can pick a different color.

d. Using your mouse, click and drag to draw a **circle** around the first advertisement — you may need to scroll down. If you do not see an advertisement, circle the first search result.

e. Click 💬 **Add a typed note**. Now you can add a typed note. If you have a touchscreen and pen device, you can use the pen to write a handwritten note.

f. Click inside the **circle** you drew near the word **Ads** and type Painted Paradise should consider purchasing an ad with Bing.

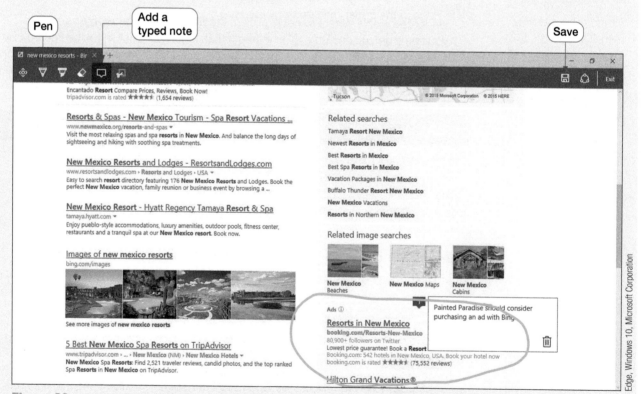

Figure 30   Annotated web page

g. In the upper right corner, click **Save Web Note** 🖫 and then click **Favorites**. Under Name, click in the box and name the file w1001ch01Websearch_LastFirst using your last and first name. Click **Add**.

Edge has now saved your notes under your Favorites. You can also choose to save it to a Reading list. You also could have chosen to Share 🗗. However, you need to use the OneNote or Reading list app to share. Your options may vary.

h. If necessary, in the upper right corner, click **Exit** to leave web marking.

i. In the upper right corner, click **Hub** 📰. This launches a hub containing your Favorites, Reading list, History, and Downloads.

j. Under Favorites, click **w1001ch01Websearch_LastFirst**. If needed, scroll down to see your markup.

Edge shows you the marked-up web page. If you look in the address bar, notice that it does not start with http:// but with file://. This means that the file was saved locally to your machine.

Viewing Browser History and Downloads in the Edge Hub

Most interaction in Edge comes from the Edge Hub. In the **Edge Hub**, you can manage your favorites and reading list. You can manage and open your downloads. And you can view and clear your browsing history.

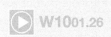

SIDE NOTE

Pinning Your Hub

If you find that you use the Edge Hub frequently, in the upper right corner you can click the pin to keep the hub open and docked to the right.

To View the Browsing History and Recent Downloads in the Edge Hub

a. In Edge in the upper right corner, click **Hub** 📰.

b. Click **History** 🕘.

c. Click **Clear all history**. If you desire, click **Clear**.

The computer has now cleared out prior web pages that you visited. However, the computer will still store where you go from this moment on. You can also click More Actions ⋯ and click New InPrivate window to prevent Edge from storing the history of your browsing. Also under More Actions ⋯ and then Settings, you can click View advanced settings and even enable Cortana in Edge.

Use OneDrive and Work with Folders, Files, and Compression

OneDrive is Microsoft's cloud storage tool associated with your Microsoft account. **Cloud storage** allows you to keep files on the Internet rather than on the client computer. This is beneficial for files that you may need to access from a variety of computers or locations.

In Windows 10, OneDrive is completely integrated. In other words, the user does not need a separate app or program — unless the user is on a Windows 10 phone device or a non-Windows device. To save a file to OneDrive, you need only save it to the OneDrive folder on the computer.

If you are working in a public computer lab, this may or may not be enabled. In that case, you can still access your OneDrive through a web browser. Another benefit to accessing your OneDrive account through a web browser, even when you use your Microsoft account to log into the computer, is the ability to use Office Online, a web-based suite of

Microsoft Office applications including Word Online, Excel Online, PowerPoint Online, and OneNote Online. These apps provide access to the functionality of Microsoft Office even on computers where Microsoft Office has not been installed.

You can also access your files on machines running something other than Windows 10, such as an Android or iPad. Simply visit the store for your device — such as Apple Store or Google Play — and search for the appropriate OneDrive app.

In this section, you will download the files for this book to your OneDrive and learn the basics of the OneDrive app in Windows 10 and Word Online, accessible through your OneDrive account in a web browser.

REAL WORLD ADVICE | **Backing Up Your Files**

The beauty of OneDrive is that your files are automatically backed up in Windows 10. If you are not using a computer lab that restricts this feature, your files are automatically saved locally on your computer and on Microsoft's cloud web storage servers. Thus, if you drop and break your device, all of your files are still there. Further, with the appropriate apps installed, you can access your files from any device, including Apple and Android devices.

Opening OneDrive in the Cloud

To use the OneDrive app to access your personal content, you must already have a Microsoft account and use that account to log into the computer that is running Windows 10. If you do not have a Microsoft account, you can create one at http://onedrive.live.com and then, depending on rights to the computer, add the account as an additional user or add your Microsoft account to your local account, as discussed earlier. In a public computer lab, you may just be asked to log in when you first go to OneDrive online.

In this exercise, you will launch OneDrive in the Edge browser, create a new folder on your OneDrive, and upload the screenshots you saved earlier in the chapter.

REAL WORLD ADVICE | **How Much Can I Store on OneDrive?**

At the time of the writing of this book, everyone gets 15 GB of free space on OneDrive. Videos, images, music, and PDF files tend to take up the most space. If you find that you are using up all your free space, Microsoft has many ways you can increase the amount for free — for example, you can get another 15 GB of space for selecting to automatically upload photos to OneDrive. Search the web for other currently available offers. If that still isn't enough, you can purchase additional space through Microsoft for a yearly fee based on the amount you choose.

To Access OneDrive Files Online with a Browser and Upload a File

a. If the Edge browser is not already open, press the ⊞, type Edge, and click the result for the Edge browser.

b. Click in the **Address bar** at the top, type https://onedrive.live.com, and then press Enter. If Edge brings up a list of Bing search results, click the result for OneDrive.

c. If necessary, click **Sign In** and enter your Microsoft account email address and your password if prompted.

d. If you saved your files from this chapter to OneDrive, then your files may already be in OneDrive. If this is the case, skip to step h. Otherwise, click **Upload**.

e. In the Open dialog box, navigate to **where you saved your files** earlier in this chapter. Click **w1001ch01Notes_LastFirst.rtf**.

f. Hold down the Ctrl key and click **w1001ch01QuadrantsSnip_LastFirst.jpg** and **w1001ch01StartSnip_LastFirst.jpg**.

SIDE NOTE
Click and Drag Instead!
If you restore down the window for the Edge browser, you can also click and drag the files from your desktop or File Explorer into the browser to upload.

Troubleshooting

What if you saved the files from earlier in this chapter to different places? Simply repeat steps e through g for each of the three files.

g. Click **Open**. If necessary, scroll down to see the uploaded files.

Your files are uploaded, and a status window shows when the upload is complete. Your files were not put in any particular folder but in the base folder of your OneDrive — also referred to as the **root**. You may also have noticed that a few folders — such as Documents — may or may not already exist by default.

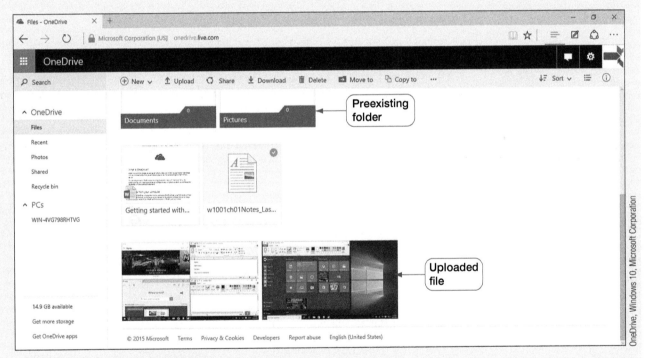

Figure 31 OneDrive after uploading

h. Leave your OneDrive open in the Edge browser for the next exercise.

Using Office Online

Office Online is a web-based suite of Microsoft Office applications, including Word Online, Excel Online, PowerPoint Online, and OneNote Online. These web apps are designed to provide core functionality for viewing, creating, and editing Word documents, Excel workbooks, PowerPoint presentations, and OneNote notebooks directly in the web browser. For full functionality, each web app includes the option to open in the full desktop application if it is installed on the computer.

To Use Office Online and Save to OneDrive

a. OneDrive should already be open in the Edge browser from the previous exercise.

b. At the top of the window under OneDrive, click **New**, select **Folder**, type Office Online - Last First using your last and first name, and then click **Create**.

c. Click **Office Online - Last First**. You are now in the folder you just created.

d. Click **New**, and then select **Word document**. Word Online opens a new blank document.

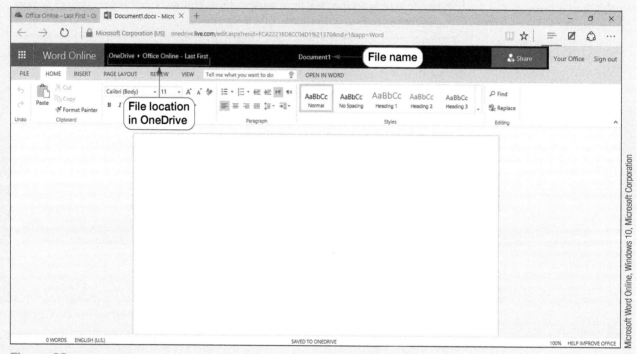

Figure 32   Office Online

e. On the Home tab, in the Styles group, click **Heading 1**, type OneDrive Overview, and then press Enter.

f. Type OneDrive provides online storage for my documents, pictures, and more with the convenience of online versions of Microsoft Word, Excel, PowerPoint, and OneNote.

g. In the title bar to the right of Office Online - Last First, click **Document1**. This selects the word Document1.

h. Type w1001ch01OneDrive_LastFirst using your last and first name, and then press Enter. Your file is now saved by that name to the Office Online - Last First folder in OneDrive.

i. On the title bar, click **Office Online - Last First**. This returns you to the view of your folder and files.

j. Point to the Office Online - Last First document preview, and in the upper right corner, click the **circle**.

k. Unless your instructor specifies otherwise, click **Share**, type your instructor's email address in the To box, and then click **Share**. In the Share screen, click **Close**.

l. In the upper right corner, click **Close** ✕ to close Edge.

Work with Folders and Files in File Explorer

File Explorer — formerly known as Windows Explorer — is a program used to create and manage folders and files. In the previous exercises, you briefly used this program to interact with your OneDrive. File Explorer uses a storage system similar to what you would use in a file cabinet. A file cabinet has drawers to divide files, and each drawer contains folders, which can contain files and more folders. Thus, a **folder** is a container used to store related documents or files.

The same idea applies to the way computers store data. A computer storage device might be a hard drive or a USB flash drive. The storage device may contain a number of folders, subfolders, and files. In this way, a storage device is similar to a file cabinet, which has drawers that contain folders and subfolders, which contain files.

File Explorer ▇ can be accessed in Windows 10 by clicking on the taskbar icon. The interface across the top — known as the **ribbon** — allows users to interact with the operating system using tabs at the top of the screen and is common to most Microsoft programs.

The new File Explorer ribbon has been reorganized into three tabs: Home, Share, and View. Additionally, when you click certain objects, a contextual tab will appear. The **contextual tab** expands the ribbon to display commands specific to the selected item. Within each tab on the ribbon, there are a number of commands. These commands are divided into **ribbon groups**, which are collections of related commands on a ribbon tab.

In addition to the tabs found on the ribbon, users will notice there is a title bar at the top of the window with the usual window options such as minimize. The **File Explorer address bar** is the toolbar immediately below the ribbon. It includes Back and Forward buttons ⬅ ➡, which allow users to browse folders as they would in a web browser. This also displays the current file path and allows users to perform searches for files.

Below this toolbar, Windows displays two panes, or divisions, similar to window panes in a house. The left pane, also called the **navigation pane**, displays locations where users can find files, such as Quick Access, OneDrive, This PC, and Network or more depending on the computer. The right pane, also called the **file list**, opens initially to recent folders and files. Once the user navigates to a folder, the file list will show files and folders. The status bar is located at the bottom of a window. It provides information about the selected window or object.

Modifying the **Quick Access** allows users to browse through locations they have previously marked as important. OneDrive is online cloud storage space associated with a Microsoft account. **This PC** allows the user to view the contents of the computer's storage devices, including the hard drive, CD/DVD drive, and attached USB flash drives. A **USB flash drive** is a small storage device that plugs into a computer's USB port and usually holds large amounts of information. **Network** allows users to browse files stored on network drives rather than on local drives. The Network location is more commonly used in a business environment.

In this section, you will explore folders and file management in File Explorer and OneDrive.

 CONSIDER THIS | **USB or Cloud?**

Today, you have many options for moving your files from computer to computer. USB flash drives are one popular choice. However, cloud technologies such as OneDrive and Dropbox are gaining in popularity. With Windows 10, OneDrive is complete integrated into the build with no app needed for PCs. What are the pros and cons of using a USB versus using cloud technology? What about the security of your files in both choices?

Using the OneDrive and File Explorer

In Windows 10, you interact with OneDrive and all of your files on the computer by using File Explorer. As previously discussed, a separate app or program is not needed in Windows 10. By default, File Explorer is pinned to the taskbar. In this next exercise, you will open and view OneDrive with File Explorer.

 W1001.29

SIDE NOTE

Customizing the Quick Access

You can customize the File Explorer Quick Access by right-clicking and choosing Pin/Unpin to/from. Quick Access.

To View OneDrive from File Explorer

a. On the taskbar, click 📁 **File Explorer**. This opens File Explorer in Quick Access mode.

Notice the areas of File Explorer. On the left pane, known as the navigation pane, you can change between locations under Quick Access, Network, This PC, and OneDrive. Depending on the computer, you may see even more options. On the right pane, you see Frequent folders and Recent files. Once you navigate to a folder, you will see the files on the right side, known as the file list.

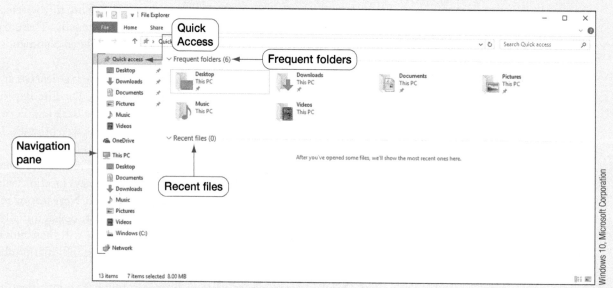

Figure 33 File Explorer in Quick Access mode

b. On the left pane, click **OneDrive**.

You should see the Office Online - Last First folder and the three files you uploaded online.

Troubleshooting

If you do not see an option for OneDrive, you may be in a public computer lab with this function disabled. If so, you will not see the option for OneDrive and will not see the folder and file from the previous exercise. In this case, complete the rest of this chapter using the desktop. Then upload everything to OneDrive via the web browser as demonstrated in the previous exercise.

You may also need to connect OneDrive. If so, follow the prompts to connect OneDrive.

You also may have used a different online account than what is logged into the machine. Alternatively, your computer may not have synced with the cloud yet. The files that you uploaded were relatively small, so it should not take long to sync if you used the same account in both places.

---

c. Click **Close** ☒ to close File Explorer.

Downloading and Extracting Compressed Files for the Your Office Series

Downloading files and saving them to OneDrive has never been easier. Windows 10 uses **syncing** — continually checking for new versions to put your files both on the local computer and the cloud. Depending on the file size, this sync can happen really fast or can take a little longer. If you turn off your device before you finish syncing, the computer will try again the next time the device is turned on. However, if you are in a public computer lab that allows the syncing, you could lose your work if you do not wait until all of the items are synced. In that situation, you can alternatively upload with the web interface, which provides more obvious feedback about when the file has been successfully uploaded.

The files that Aidan has already accumulated are online as a **compressed file** — a file that contains many files grouped together and reduces the file size; the most common file extension of compressed files is .zip, and the files are referred to as "zipped." To use the files, you will need to download them from the Internet location, save them to your local computer, and then extract them for use.

When you download a compressed file from the Internet or if you receive a zipped folder from someone, you will need to extract the files to view them. When you select a zipped folder in the navigation pane, a contextual tab appears on the ribbon. This contextual tab is named Compressed Folder Tools and has a tab named Extract. Users can click Extract all to browse to a location or may select a location from the list in the Extract To area of the tab.

In this exercise, you will download a compressed file from online and then extract the files into your student data files folder on your computer.

 W1001.30

To Download and Extract a Compressed Folder

a. Press ⊞ and type Edge. Press Enter In the address bar, type www.pearsonhighered.com/youroffice and then press Enter. If your computer brings up search results, click the one for Pearson.

> **Troubleshooting**
>
> At the time this chapter was written, not all websites were working in Edge. This is one of the unfortunate effects of using a brand-new browser. If you find yourself in that situation, click More Actions ⋯ and then click Open with Internet Explorer, which has better backward compatibility.

b. Through the web site options, locate and click **Your Office Getting Started with Microsoft Windows 10**, and then follow the links to **download the files** for this book. Click **the link** for the files.

c. At the bottom of the screen, click **Open**.

d. If prompted, choose **File Explorer** to open the file and click **OK**.

In the address bar of File Explorer, notice that Internet Explorer automatically saved the compressed file to the This PC Downloads folder. This is a local folder in Windows 10 where all browsers save downloaded files — unless you tell or configure the browser to do otherwise. You see a folder with the files that are in the compressed file. If you do not see the files inside the compressed file, open File Explorer, navigate to your Downloads folder, and double-click the compressed file. However, you do not want to use or work on the files inside of the compressed file. You want to extract them first.

e. On the Compressed Folder Tools Extract tab, click **Extract all**. The Extract Compressed (Zipped) Folders dialog box opens.

f. Click **Browse**, and then in the left pane, click **OneDrive**. If OneDrive is not available — for example if you are in a public computer lab — navigate to the location where you would like to store your files. You could put them on the desktop and then use the web interface to upload to OneDrive. You could also use a school resource or external medium such as a USB drive.

g. Click **Select Folder** to place the files in that folder.

h. Make sure the **Show extracted files when complete** check box is checked, and then click **Extract**. When the extraction process is complete, a new File Explorer window opens to the root of OneDrive or wherever folder you selected to extract the files. Notice, this zip placed all of the files in a folder named **w1001ch01DataFiles**. Depending on how a zip file is created, it may just extract files without a folder.

i. Double-click the **w1001ch01DataFiles** folder to display the extracted files. If you placed them in OneDrive and OneDrive is set up properly, a green checkmark should appear on the file or folder icon once the file is synced to the cloud.

j. Behind the new window of extracted files, close the **w1001ch01DataFiles.zip** window. Keep the **w1001ch01DataFiles** window open for the next exercise.

QUICK REFERENCE | **Have My Files Synced?**

When you are in File Explorer in the OneDrive folder, a small green checkmark will appear briefly when that file or folder has been successfully synced to the cloud. During active syncing, a small blue sync icon will show. You should wait for the checkmark to appear before you power down or log off the device. If there is a conflict or problem with syncing, a small red X will appear, and you will get a notification. Click the notification or log into the web interface to resolve the issue.

REAL WORLD ADVICE | **Other Methods of Unzipping**

This exercise shows how to use the Windows Compressed Folder tool. Other compression tools, such as WinZip, WinRAR, and 7-Zip, may be installed on your machine. If double-clicking launches one of these programs, you can instead right-click w1001ch01DataFiles.zip and select Open with. From there, select File Explorer.

Navigating and Changing Views in File Explorer

You can view all the drives, folders, and files that are part of your computer's storage system using File Explorer. In the next exercise, you will learn how to move between folders and understand where files are located.

SIDE NOTE

Expanding and Collapsing Folders
You can also expand and collapse folders by double-clicking the folder name in the navigation pane.

To Navigate and Change Views in File Explorer

a. From the previous exercise, the File Explorer window should be open to the w1001ch01DataFiles folder.

b. Click the **View** tab, and in the Layout group, click **Large icons**.

Now the icons for your files for this chapter are larger and easier to read. Because this is the OneDrive location on your computer, these files exist on your local computer but are also synced with the cloud, as was previously discussed.

c. You decide that you prefer the smaller icons. Click the **View** tab and in the Layout group, click **Details**.

d. In the address bar to the right of the w1001ch01DataFiles, click the **empty white space** in the address bar.

This shows you precisely where your files are stored locally on your PC. Usually, this will be C:\Users\username\OneDrive\w1001ch01DataFiles — where username is what you used to sign into the machine. The C:\ represents the drive on which the files stored; the letter C is typical, but it can be other letters. For example, if you navigate in Explorer to a USB drive, it will have another letter — which letter will depend on the computer.

e. Press Esc to get out of the address bar. Then in the address bar, click **OneDrive**.

This brings you back to the root of your OneDrive on your local computer. If you have used the same Microsoft account throughout this chapter, you should see the w1001ch01DataFiles, Office Online - Last First folder and the three files you uploaded online.

f. In the navigation pane, if necessary, point to **This PC** and click the **arrow** ⟩ on the left to expand the folder. The arrow changes to point downwards, and a list of folders and drives is displayed that correspond to the storage locations on the local computer.

g. In the navigation pane, under This PC, click **Windows (C:)**, **OS (C:)**, or some other letter. The file list displays all files and folders on the local computer, including the files that make Windows run.

h. In the navigation pane, under This PC, click **Downloads**. By default, the file list shows all of the files you have downloaded from a browser — assuming you did not specify a different location for saving.

i. Close **File Explorer**.

REAL WORLD ADVICE | **How Does Windows Know That My Word Document Is a Word Document?**

The Windows operating system uses file extensions to determine which programs are used to open a file. The file extension is usually the three or four characters listed after a period in the file name. For example, Document1.**docx** would be associated with Microsoft Word if you have Word installed. If the file extension is changed, the file may no longer open properly. By default, the operating system hides file extensions to prevent accidental renaming. If your installation of Windows shows file extensions, you can click the View tab of File Explorer and uncheck the box labeled File name extensions to hide extensions.

Eight layout options exist for folders in File Explorer in Windows 10:

- Extra large icons
- Large icons
- Medium icons
- Small icons
- List
- Details
- Tiles
- Content

Creating and Naming a New Folder

Aidan has already collected numerous files that all employees need. He has put some of these files in folders but wants help to better organize them. He asks you to use his files as an example when demonstrating how to create folders and organize files.

You suggest creating folders to hold specific types of files, such as documents, pictures, and presentations. It is always a good idea to organize related files. You can use a USB drive, your OneDrive, or your desktop. In this exercise, you will create a folder called Windows Practice to hold the files that will be used for the exercises in this chapter.

W1001.32

To Create and Name Folders

a. On the taskbar, click **File Explorer** .

b. Browse to the location where you plan to store your files. If you are using a USB flash drive, double-click This PC to find it. Figures in this chapter will use OneDrive.

c. Click the **Home** tab, and in the New group, click **New folder**.

d. Type Windows Practice and then press Enter.

e. Double-click the **Windows Practice** folder that you just created. The file list will be empty.

f. Click the **Home** tab, in the New group, click **New folder**, type Resort Documents, and then press Enter.

g. Verify that your Windows Practice folder contains the subfolder. Leave this window open for the next exercise.

REAL WORLD ADVICE | Contact Information

Many places with computer labs, such as libraries, colleges, and schools, have a lost and found that contains dozens of USB flash drives. Often, users do not include any contact information on their device, so the drive will sit in a lost and found, unclaimed. You can use the techniques discussed in this business unit to create a folder named Contact Information and add a small WordPad document containing a cell phone number or an email address. It might save you a headache someday. With all the information users store on USB flash drives, losing information is often more costly than losing hardware.

Managing Existing Folders

As you create more and more files, the original folders that you created may no longer meet your needs. You can move folders to a new location or copy them so that they exist in two or more locations. You can also rename folders if the original name no longer fits, and you can delete folders when they are no longer needed. As you work with folders, you will often find that the name you first assigned to a folder is not relevant anymore. There will also be times when you have a folder that contains files you no longer need. Just as you would shred and discard paper files that are outdated, you will want to delete folders that are no longer needed.

In this exercise, you will help organize the files that you downloaded and extracted to your computer by copying them into your Windows Practice folder.

In the following exercises, you will copy, move, rename, and delete folders.

W1001.33

SIDE NOTE
Sorting Folder Contents
To sort folder contents, click the headings in Details view to sort on that column. Click again to sort in reverse.

To Manage Existing Folders

a. From the previous exercise, you should have your Windows Practice folder open. If necessary, restore the window so that it is not maximized.

b. Click and drag the **title bar of the window** to the middle left side of the screen to snap it to the left.

c. Press ⌃Ctrl and N to open another File Explorer window. Browse to the **w1001ch01DataFiles** folder in the location where you are storing your files, such as OneDrive. Five folders and numerous files are displayed in the file list.

Troubleshooting

If the folder contents do not match the list shown, on the View tab of the ribbon, in the Layout group, click Details, and then in the Show/hide group, if necessary, click to select File name extensions. Also, if you do not have the green checkmark on the file, that is okay. The green checkmark will appear only if you are using OneDrive.

d. Click and drag the **title bar of the w1001ch01DataFiles window** to the middle right side of the screen to snap it to the right. Now you can see both sets of files.

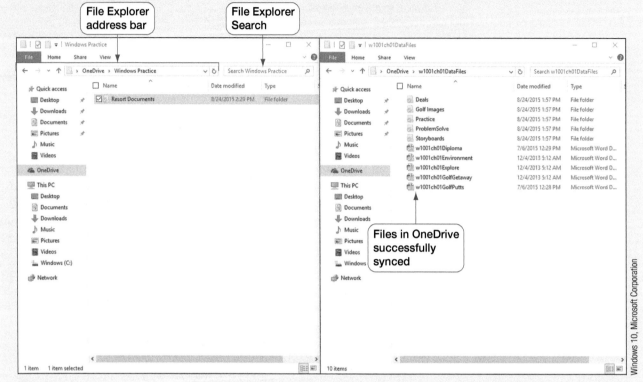

File Explorer address bar

File Explorer Search

Files in OneDrive successfully synced

Windows 10, Microsoft Corporation

Figure 34 Two File Explorer windows snapped

e. In the right window in the file list, click **Deals** once. Then press and hold down the Ctrl key on your keyboard, and then drag the **Deals** folder into the white blank space in the Windows Practice window on the left side. Holding the Ctrl key down forces it to copy instead of moving.

Copying or Moving?
The combination of left-clicking and dragging files from one location to another on the same storage device results in a move. Left-click dragging to a different device results in a copy.

f. When the ScreenTip **Copy to Windows Practice** displays, release the mouse button and then release the Ctrl key. The Deals folder now appears under both the w1001ch01DataFiles folder and the Windows Practice folder.

g. On the left Windows Practice window, double-click **Deals**.

Notice, there are eight images and a subfolder called Flyers in this folder. The subfolder called Flyers used to contain files of deal flyers that used the images. Aidan deleted those files because they were outdated. However, he still wants to keep the images for future documents.

h. In the left window, click the **Flyers** folder. Press the Delete key to delete it. On the address bar, click **Windows Practice** to return to that folder.

SIDE NOTE

Keyboard Shortcuts
You can also select a folder and, to copy, use Ctrl + C to copy and Ctrl + V to paste. To move it, you can use Ctrl + X to cut and Ctrl + V to paste

i. In the left Windows Practice window, right-click **Deals** and select **Rename**.

j. Type Resort Images and press Enter. You have now renamed the folder to a more appropriate name.

k. In the right window, right-click **Golf Images** and drag it on top of the Resort Images folder. When you release the mouse button, you will be given the option to move or copy. Select **Move here**. The Golf Images folder is moved to the Resort Images folder and is no longer visible in the file list in the right window.

60   CHAPTER 1 | Microsoft Windows 10

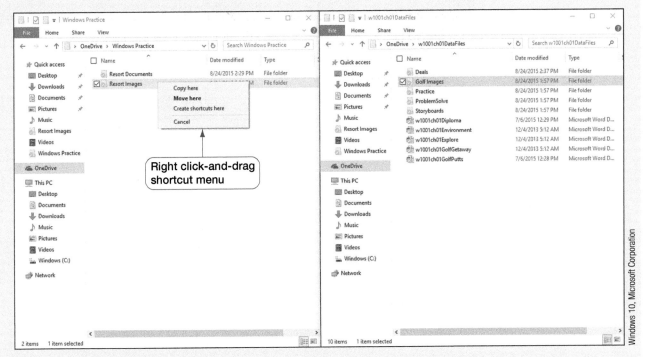

Figure 35 Moving the Golf Images folder

l. In the left Windows Practice window, double-click **Resort Images**. Notice that there are now images files and a subfolder named Golf Images. On the address bar, click **Windows Practice** to return to that folder.

m. Leave both windows open and snapped for the next exercise.

REAL WORLD ADVICE | **How Can Deletions Not Be Permanent?**

Files deleted from your devices may not be permanently deleted even if you empty the Recycle Bin. Data recovery specialists can often recover information from storage devices. This is often done as part of police criminal investigations. If you throw away a hard drive, someone can recover your personal information from it even if you have deleted the information and formatted the drive. You can physically destroy the device, but even that might not be enough. A free program named Darik's Boot and Nuke (DBAN), downloadable at www.dban.org, is a utility that will wipe the contents of your hard drive to conform to U.S. Department of Defense standards.

Managing Existing Files

The procedures that you just practiced with folders can also be applied to files. As you create more documents, you will often find that you did not anticipate how your files would need to be organized. Files can be copied or moved to new locations. They can also be renamed or deleted when no longer needed.

Attribute	Old File Naming Constraints — Still Used by Some Web Systems	Windows 10 File Naming Constraints
Maximum Number of Characters	8	255
Disallowed Characters	Spaces and the following symbols: \ / ? : * " > < | [ ]	The following symbols: \ / : * ? " > < |
Allowable Characters	Letters, numbers, and some symbols	Letters, numbers, spaces, and some symbols

Giving files a meaningful name is essential to efficiently locating your files and sharing files with others. Many years ago, descriptive file names were difficult to create because of naming constraints. Names could be only eight characters long. Spaces were not permitted. Today, file names can be much longer and can include many more characters.

Does that mean you should give your files lengthy names? Not necessarily. A name that is too long can distract from being meaningful as much as one that is too short. Further, some web systems will still remove any characters after the first eight and replace spaces with underscores when the file is uploaded. Thus, the best practice is to make the name just long enough to be meaningful. Meaningful document names can be extremely useful and make finding files easier.

In the following exercise, you will further help Aidan organize his files by moving, copying, renaming, and deleting files.

W1001.34

To Copy, Move, Rename, and Delete Files and Folders

a. From the previous exercise, you should have a File Explorer window snapped to the left open to Windows Practice. You should also have a File Explorer window snapped to the right and open to w1001ch01DataFiles.

b. In the right window, if necessary, scroll to the right and click **Type** in the file list. This sorts all of the files by the type of file. Click the first document **w1001ch01Diploma**.

c. Press and hold the [Shift] key, and then click the fifth document down **w1001ch01GolfPutts**. Release the [Shift] key. All the documents have been selected.

d. Press [Ctrl] and [C] at the same time to copy the selected files to the Clipboard,

e. In the left window, double-click **Resort Documents** and then press [Ctrl] and [V] at the same time to paste the five documents. The documents are copied to the Resort Documents folder and now are in both windows. In the address bar, click **Windows Practice** to return to that folder.

f. Right after you copy the files, you realize that you probably should have moved them instead. You decide to delete them from the original folder. If the files are no longer selected, follow steps b and c again to select the documents in the right window. Make sure the right window is the active window.

SIDE NOTE

To Replace or to Skip?

When you are copying a file to a folder that contains a file that has the same name, click Compare info for both files to see details of both to help you decide whether to replace or skip the file.

g. Press Delete. The files are now deleted from the w1001ch01DataFiles folder in the right window.

h. In the right w1001ch01DataFiles File Explorer window, double-click the **Storyboards** folder. You see one image, w1001ch01ConferenceAttendees, in that folder.

i. Click and drag the **w1001ch01ConferenceAttendees** image from the right window to the Resort Images folder in the left window. When the ScreenTip **Move to Resort Images** displays, release the mouse button.

Troubleshooting

Your ScreenTip says Copy instead of Move! The ScreenTip will depend on where you copy from and where you copy to. If both locations are on the local drive, the default action is move. If you are using a USB drive, as suggested, copy is the default action. If your ScreenTip says Copy when you want Move, you have two options. You can right-click and drag — and then select Move. Alternatively, you can use Ctrl + X to cut and Ctrl + V to paste, creating the same effect as moving.

---

j. In the right window in the address bar, click **w1001ch01DataFiles** to return to that folder. Leave the two windows open for the next exercise.

QUICK REFERENCE	Multiple Methods

There can be literally dozens of ways to accomplish the same task in File Explorer. Of course, whichever way is comfortable for you is fine, but it can be instructive to look at other ways.

- **Home tab**   Many of the commands demonstrated previously can be accessed on the Home tab. Commands such as Move to, Copy to, Delete, and New folder all appear on the Home tab in File Explorer.

- **Right-click**   When you right-click a file or a folder, there are options to rename or delete the selected object.

- **Right-drag**   You are probably used to dragging by holding down the left mouse button. If you drag a file or folder while holding down the right mouse button, Windows will give you the option to Move or Copy when you release the mouse button.

- **Key Combinations**   There are a number of key combinations you can use to replace mouse operations.

- **Rename**   Select a file, and press F2.

- **Select all files**   Hold down the Ctrl key and press A ((Ctrl) + A).

You can also perform a move by cutting files and then pasting them, or you can perform a copy by copying files and then pasting them.

- **Copy**   Hold down the Ctrl key and press C ((Ctrl)+C).

- **Cut**   Hold down the Ctrl key and press X ((Ctrl)+X).

- **Paste**   Hold down the Ctrl key and press V ((Ctrl)+V).

Using the Search Box in File Explorer

Windows 10 includes powerful search tools that make locating files easy. Unlike the Cortana search, the search box in File Explorer is limited by default to the current location in your file structure, making it easier to locate file contents without the distraction of additional results from Cortana — even though Cortana can still find your files.

The search box feature of File Explorer can be used to search for files and content contained within the displayed folder or any subfolders. Using options on the Search Tools Search tab on the ribbon, you can limit searches to specific locations and filter the results by date, time, size, and other properties of the files.

In this exercise, you will use the File Explorer search box to locate all files in the Windows Practice folder and subfolders that contain the word "organic."

To Use the Search Box in File Explorer

a. From the previous exercise, you should have a File Explorer window snapped to the left that is open to Windows Practice. You should also have a File Explorer window snapped to the right that is open to w1001ch01DataFiles.

b. In the upper right corner of the left window, click **Search Windows Practice**.

c. On the Search Tools Search tab, in the Location group, if necessary, click **All subfolders** to highlight the button.

d. Aidan knows that he wrote a report on the environment but cannot remember what he named it. He knows that he talked about organic foods. If necessary, click in the search box again, and then type organic.

The document, w1001ch01Environment should be among the search results.

e. On the right side of the search term, click ⨯ to close the search.

f. On the right File Explorer window, which is open to w1001ch01DataFiles, click **Close** ⨯. Leave the File Explorer Windows Practice open for the next exercise.

Creating Compressed Files

If you have ever had to email multiple files to someone at once, you know that many email programs make it tedious to attach many files simultaneously. Some will also limit the number of attachments, so sending 15 small files would require multiple email messages, and you would risk accidentally missing a file or attaching the same file twice.

In addition, in attaching files to an email message, it is impossible to maintain folder structure. For example, if you wanted to email some files from a subfolder named 2017 and some files from a subfolder named 2018, the recipient would not be able to distinguish which files were in which folder. Windows provides a solution for this. Users can create a zip file containing a number of files and folders.

Files containing graphics, video, or sound are often too large to transfer easily. Windows 10 allows users to compress one or more files into a single zipped folder with a .zip extension. Files that are stored in a zip file take up less storage space and are easier to transfer via email or uploading.

The ability to create zipped files is not new. In previous versions of Windows, this function was often referred to as compressed folders. Many professionals used the term "zipped" instead of "compressed," and Microsoft seems to have made the term "zip" more prominent, perhaps to match the terminology used by many professionals.

You will zip the files in the Windows Practice folder to send to Aidan. The Details pane will display the size of the files before and after compressing.

To Copy Files and Folders to a Compressed Folder

a. If necessary, open File Explorer and navigate to the **Windows Practice** folder.

b. On the Home tab, in the Select group, click **Select all**. The status bar indicates that two items are selected.

c. On the Share tab, in the Send group, click **Zip**. After a few moments, during which time the files are compressed, a new folder with a zipper icon appears in the file list.

d. Type w1001ch01Zipped_LastFirst, using your last and first name, and then press Enter. The file is renamed.

> ### Troubleshooting
>
> When renaming files with file extensions shown, be careful not to edit or delete the extension (e.g., .zip). It is important to keep the correct file extension to ensure that the file can be opened properly later.

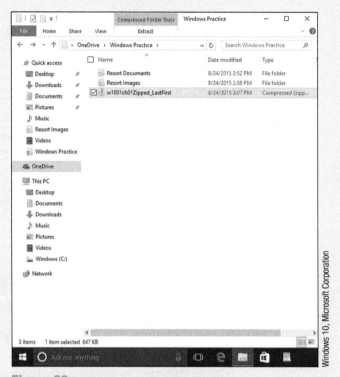

Figure 36   Final Windows Practice folder

e. Click **Maximize** ☐ to maximize the window. On the View tab, in the Panes group, click **Details pane**.

Look at the Details pane. Notice the size of the zipped folder. This should reflect a savings in space. Other files may show a much greater compression rate.

f. In the file list, double-click **w1001ch01Zipped_LastFirst** and then double-click **Resort Documents**. Click each of the files and observe the Compressed size, Size, and Ratio values in the Details pane.

g. Submit your **w1001ch01Zipped_LastFirst.zip** file as directed by your instructor.

Concept Check

1. What are two locations where power options can be located in Windows 10? p. 6

2. What is the desktop and what is the Start menu? p. 7

3. What is the benefit of pinning to the Start menu and taskbar? How are the two different? p. 13, 17

4. How can you search in Windows 10 and what are the benefits of allowing Cortana? p. 18–20

5. What is a window? p. 25

6. How many apps can be displayed while snapped in Windows 10 and what is Task View? p. 29–32

7. What is the purpose of the Action Center, where do you find it, and what is in it? p. 36–38

8. What are the options for signing in to Windows 10? Where do you find the Control Panel? p. 40, 43–44

9. What is the Edge browser and how is it different than older browsers? p. 45–46

10. What are options for saving files both locally and in the cloud? What is the difference between the cloud and the local drive? What is a compressed file? p. 49, 53–56

Key Terms

Action Center 36
Active window 29
Address bar in File Explorer 53
App 25
Application software 4
Browser 45
Click 5
Cloud storage 49
Compressed file 55
Contextual tab 53
Cortana 18
Cortana's Notebook 22
Desktop background 7
Device driver 43
Edge 46
Edge Hub 49
File 45
File Explorer 53
File extension 45
File list in File Explorer 53

Firewall 44
Folder 53
Gesture recognition 7
Graphical user interface (GUI) 4
Indexed folders 20
Live Tile 11
Lock Screen 5
Login Screen 5
Mouse pointer 7
Multiple virtual desktops 35
Navigation pane 53
Network in File Explorer 53
Office Online 51
OneDrive 49
Operating system 4
PDF 46
Program 25
Quick Access 53
Recycle Bin 7
Ribbon 53

Ribbon group 53
Shake 30
Snap 30
Snip 33
Syncing 55
System software 4
Tablet mode 8
Taskbar 7
Taskbar notification area 7
This PC 53
Tile 11
Title bar 26
URL (Uniform Resource Locator) 45
USB flash drive 53
Virus 42
Window 25
Windows Defender 42
Windows Hello 40
Wizard 40

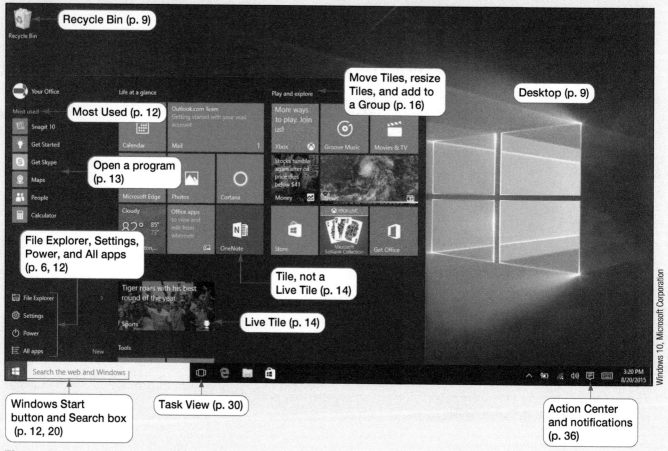

Figure 37   Desktop and Start menu

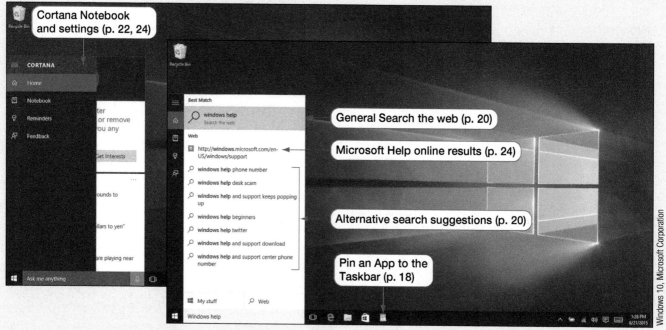

Figure 38   Search and Cortana

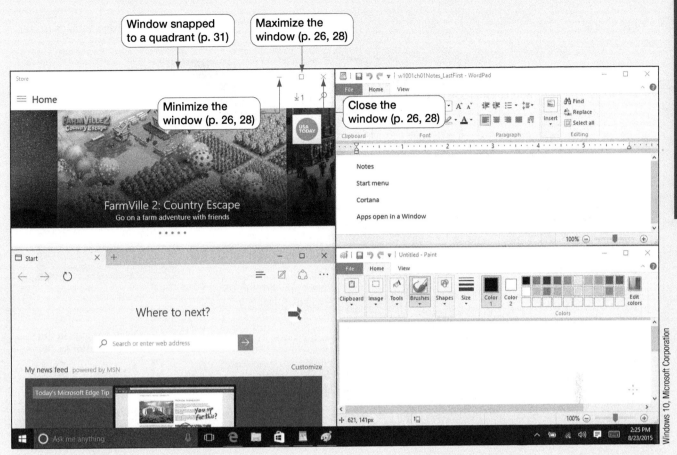

Window snapped to a quadrant (p. 31)

Maximize the window (p. 26, 28)

Minimize the window (p. 26, 28)

Close the window (p. 26, 28)

Windows 10, Microsoft Corporation

Figure 39 Manage multiple windows

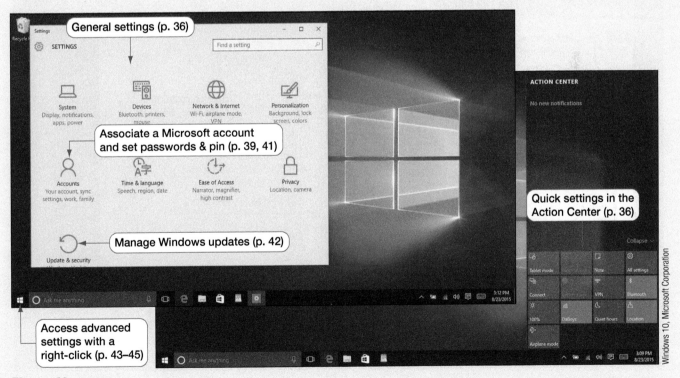

General settings (p. 36)

Associate a Microsoft account and set passwords & pin (p. 39, 41)

Manage Windows updates (p. 42)

Quick settings in the Action Center (p. 36)

Access advanced settings with a right-click (p. 43–45)

Windows 10, Microsoft Corporation

Figure 40 Settings

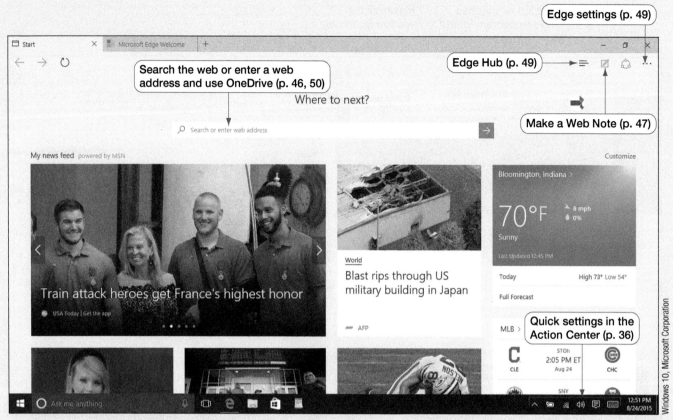

Edge settings (p. 49)

Search the web or enter a web address and use OneDrive (p. 46, 50)

Edge Hub (p. 49)

Make a Web Note (p. 47)

Quick settings in the Action Center (p. 36)

Windows 10, Microsoft Corporation

Figure 41 Edge

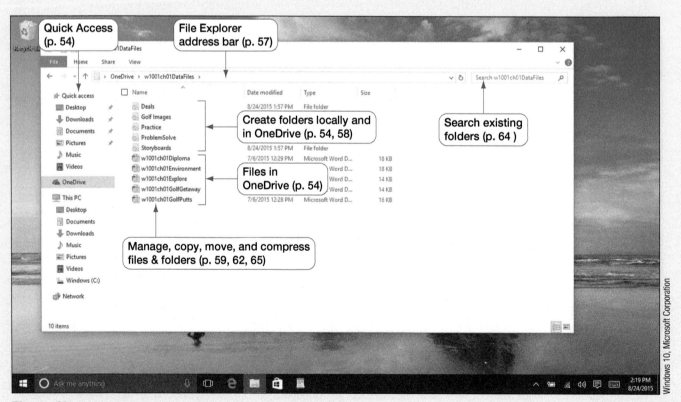

Quick Access (p. 54)

File Explorer address bar (p. 57)

Create folders locally and in OneDrive (p. 54, 58)

Search existing folders (p. 64)

Files in OneDrive (p. 54)

Manage, copy, move, and compress files & folders (p. 59, 62, 65)

Windows 10, Microsoft Corporation

Figure 42 File Explorer and folders

Student data file needed:

 w1001ch01PracticeData.zip unzipped in the chapter from w1001ch01DataFiles.zip

You will save your file as:

w1001ch01Events_LastFirst.zip

Organizing Folders and Files for the Event Planning Department

General Business

Patti Rochelle, the Corporate Event Planner at Painted Paradise Golf Resort & Spa, would like you to continue working with the event planning staff to help them develop strategies for organizing folders and files. Because employees must often fill in for one another, Patti thinks it would be helpful if her staff could develop a common folder hierarchy. She has asked you to show them how to set up folders that will be useful for the various events that take place at the Painted Paradise Resort.

a. If necessary, log in to Windows, and then navigate to the desktop.

b. Open File Explorer, navigate to the location where your student data files are stored, and then click **w1001ch01PracticeData.zip** that you unzipped in the chapter from the w1001ch01DataFiles.zip file in the Practice folder.

c. On the Compressed Folder Tools Extract tab, click **Extract all** and then click **Extract**. All of the files are extracted to a folder called w1001ch01PracticeData, where your student data files are stored. Snap this window open to the w1001ch01PracticeData to the right. If still open, close the window showing the contents of the compressed files.

d. In a new File Explorer window, navigate to the location where you are saving your files, and then create a new subfolder named **w1001ch01Events_LastFirst**, using your last and first name. Double-click **w1001ch01Events_LastFirst** and snap it to the left.

e. Create two subfolders in the **w1001ch01Events_LastFirst** folder named **Conferences** and **Weddings**.

f. In the right window showing the **w1001ch01PracticeData** folder, verify that the files are sorted **alphabetically** from A to Z by name — on the View tab, in the current view group, Sort by.

g. On the left window, double-click **Conferences** to open the Conferences folder. In the right window, click **w1001ch01ConferenceAttendees.jpg**, hold down Shift, and then click **w1001ch01ConferencePueblo.jpg**.

h. Copy the **five selected files** to the **Conferences** subfolder inside the **w1001ch01Events_LastFirst** folder.

i. On the left window in the address bar, click **w1001ch01Events_LastFirst** and then double-click the **Weddings** folder.

j. In the right window, select the six files with the word **Menu** in the file name, and then copy them to the **Weddings** subfolder inside the **w1001ch01Events_LastFirst** folder. Close the right File Explorer window.

k. Maximize the left window showing the Weddings folder. Right-click **w1001ch01MenuStart.pptx**, and then select **Rename**.

l. Type w1001ch01MenuPresentation and then press Enter.

m. Right-click **w1001ch01MenuChefWMF.wmf** and then click **Delete**.

n. Right-click **w1001ch01MenuSalsa.jpg** and then click **Rename**.

o. Type w1001ch01MenuSalsaAppetizer and then press Enter.

p. In the address bar, click **w1001ch01Events_LastFirst** to return to that folder. Click **Conferences**, hold down Shift, and then click **Weddings** to select both folders.

q. Click the **Share** tab and then, in the Send group, click **Zip**. This creates a zip file named Conferences.zip.

r. Right-click **Conferences.zip** and then click **Rename**.

s. Type w1001ch01Events_LastFirst and then press Enter.

t. Close **File Explorer** and then submit your file as directed by your instructor.

Problem Solve 1

Student data file needed:

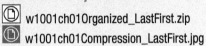 w1001ch01Sonny.zip unzipped in the chapter from w1001ch01DataFiles.zip

You will save your files as:

w1001ch01Organized_LastFirst.zip

w1001ch01Compression_LastFirst.jpg

Uncompressing and Organizing Old Files

General Business

Sonny Fuller, the head concierge for the Painted Paradise Resort & Spa, recently retired. The information technology department for the resort created a zip folder containing the files from the Documents folder on Sonny's computer. You have been asked to sort through his files and organize them.

a. Extract the contents of the **w1001ch01Sonny.zip** file located in the Problem Solve folder into a new folder in the location where you are saving your files, named **w1001ch01Organized_LastFirst**, using your last and first name.

b. Use the search box to locate any files referencing **ElDorado** and then delete them, as they are no longer needed. Verify that the File contents option is selected on the Search Tools Search tab, in the Options group, in the Advanced options menu. Clear the search box contents to redisplay the remaining files.

c. Delete all **JPG** files.

d. Create a new subfolder named **WMFs**.

e. Delete the files named **w1001ch01DealsMassageWMF** and **w1001ch01DealsGolferWMF**, as they are no longer needed.

f. Move the remaining files with **WMF** in the file name into the **WMFs** subfolder.

g. Rename the **w1001ch01Sonny** Word document to **w1001ch01Putts**.

h. Create a new subfolder named **Documents**.

i. Copy all the files that are of a **Microsoft Word Document** type — .docx file extension — into the **Documents** folder.

Critical Thinking

The directions had you copy the files to a folder. Thus, you now have two copies of the Word documents. Is this a good idea from an organizational standpoint? Give at least one example showing why this may be desirable. Give at least one example showing why this may be problematic. Answer as directed by your instructor.

j. Zip the **w1001ch01Organized_LastFirst** folder to create a file named **w1001ch01Organized_LastFirst.zip**, using your last and first name.

k. Open the **w1001ch01Organized_LastFirst.zip** file and evaluate the amount of compression. Of the two subfolders you created in this exercise, open the one that achieved the greatest compression. Snap it to the left side of your screen.

l. Open another window of File Explorer. Navigate to and open **w1001ch01Organized_LastFirst.zip**. Of the two subfolders that you created in this exercise, open the one that achieved the least compression. Snap it to the right side of your screen.

m. Take a screenshot of your screen with both File Explorer windows snapped. Save the snip as **w1001ch01Compression_LastFirst.jpg**, using your last and first name.

n. Close **File Explorer** and then submit your files as directed by your instructor.

Student data file needed:

No data file needed

You will save your files as:

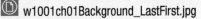

w1001ch01EvalSolution_LastFirst.zip

w1001ch01Evaluation_LastFirst.docx

w1001ch01Background_LastFirst.jpg

Evaluating a Windows Setup

Information
Technology

Locate a computer with Windows 10 installed on it, other than your own. This can be a computer in your school computer lab or a public library, or it can be a friend's or relative's computer. You will objectively evaluate the setup of this computer, examining the login process, desktop, Start menu, and screen saver options.

a. Using this other computer with Windows 10 installed, restart the computer and note the login procedure. Note whether a password is required or the system logs in automatically. Can you log in using a PIN or picture password?

b. Log in to the computer if necessary. Open WordPad. Create a new document and save it as **w1001ch01Evaluation_LastFirst**, using your last and first names. Write **your name** on the first line, your **course and instructor name** on the second, the **date** on the third, and a **description of which machine you evaluated** on the fourth. Create a blank line and then proceed with your evaluation.

c. Summarize the **login options** that you noted in step a. Do you think the **login procedure** for this computer is too restrictive or not restrictive enough?

d. Minimize your document, and notice the **desktop** background. Take a screenshot of the desktop background and save it as a JPEG file named **w1001ch01Background_LastFirst**, using your last and first names.

e. Switch back to **w1001chEvaluation_LastFirst**. In a new paragraph, describe whether you find **the desktop background** appropriate or not.

f. Minimize your document, search for screen saver in the Ask me anything or Search the web and Windows, and display the **screen saver** options. Take note of which screen saver is selected (if any) and how long a delay there is before the screen saver activates.

g. Switch back to **w1001ch01Evaluation_LastFirst**. In a new paragraph, describe whether you think that the **screen saver delay setting** is appropriate or not and which screen saver was selected.

h. Display the **Start menu** and take note of how it is organized.

i. In a new paragraph, describe the positives and negatives about the way the **Start menu** is set up on this computer.

j. In a new paragraph, add any other noteworthy observations about the computer's setup. Add any recommendations you would make to the person who maintains that machine. Save **the document** and exit **WordPad**.

k. Open File Explorer. Create a zip file named **w1001ch01EvalSolution_LastFirst**, using your last and first name, that contains w1001ch01Evaluation_LastFirst.rtf and w1001ch01Background_LastFirst.jpg.

l. Close **File Explorer** and then submit your files as directed by your instructor.

Common Features of Microsoft Office 2016

Chapter 1	UNDERSTANDING THE COMMON FEATURES OF MICROSOFT OFFICE

OBJECTIVES

1. Understand the Office suite and applications   p. 76

2. Start, save, and manipulate Office applications and use the Office ribbon   p. 77

3. Manipulate, correct, and format content using tools such as the Font group and Tell me what you want to do   p. 93

4. Formatting using the ribbon, contextual tools, and other menus   p. 104

5. Use the Help window and ScreenTips   p. 111

6. Printing and sharing files   p. 113

7. Insert Office add-ins   p. 116

Prepare Case

MyITLab® Grader Homework

Sales & Marketing

General Business

Painted Paradise Resort & Spa Employee Training Preparation

The gift shop at the Painted Paradise Resort & Spa has an array of items available for purchase, from toiletries to clothes to souvenirs for loved ones back home. There are numerous part-time employees, including students from the local college. The gift shop frequently holds training luncheons for new employees. Your first assignment will be to prepare three documents for a meeting with your manager, Susan Brock: a starting file for meeting minutes, the agenda for the meeting, and an Excel budget. To complete this task, you need to understand and work with the common features in the Microsoft Office Suite.

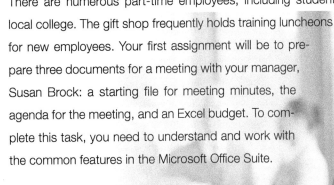

Michaeljung/Shutterstock

Student data files needed for this chapter:

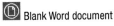 Blank Word document

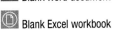 Blank Excel workbook

 cf01ch01Agenda.docx

cf01ch01Logo.jpg

You will save your files as:

 cf01ch01Minutes_LastFirst.docx

 cf01ch01Agenda_LastFirst.docx

 cf01ch01Budget_LastFirst.xlsx

 cf01ch01Budget_LastFirst.pdf

Working with the Office Interface

When you walk into a grocery store, you usually know what you are going to find and that items are likely to be in approximately the same location, regardless of which store you are visiting. The first items you usually see are the fresh fruits and vegetables, while the frozen foods are typically near the end of the store. This similarity among stores creates a comfortable and welcoming experience for the shopper, even if the shopper has never been in that particular store. The brands may be different, but the food types are the same. Canned corn is canned corn.

Microsoft Office was designed to create that same level of familiarity and comfort with its ribbons, features, and functions. Each application has an appearance or user interface that is similar to the appearance or interface of the other applications. The interface for Microsoft Office 2016 has introduced new color schemes, the default being a colorful appearance. The new look is minimalist; even the ribbon is hidden by default — unless a setting from a prior version of Office carries into your Office 2016 installation. In this section, you will learn to navigate and use the Microsoft Office interface.

Microsoft Office Suite and Different Versions

Microsoft Office 2016 is a suite of productivity applications or programs that are available for purchase separately or as a package. The exact applications available depend on the package installed. Office 2016 is available in greater variety and flexibility than ever before.

QUICK REFERENCE	Programs in Office 2016

- **Microsoft Word** is a word-processing program. This application can be used to create, edit, and format **documents** such as letters, memos, reports, brochures, resumes, and flyers.
- **Microsoft Excel** is a **spreadsheet** program — a two-dimensional grid that can be used to model quantitative data and perform accurate and rapid calculations with results ranging from simple budgets to financial and statistical analyses.
- **Microsoft PowerPoint** is a **presentation** program — an oral performance aid that uses slides or a stand-alone presentation such as those at kiosks.
- **Microsoft OneNote** is a planner and note-taking program.
- **Microsoft Outlook** is an e-mail, contact, and information management program.
- **Microsoft Access** is known as a **relational database** — or three-dimensional database software — because it is able to connect data in separate tables, allowing you to make the most efficient storage of your data.
- **Microsoft Publisher** is a desktop publishing program that offers professional tools and templates to help communicate a message easily in a variety of publication types, saving time and money while creating a polished and finished look.
- **Microsoft Skype for Business** — formerly known as Lync — is a unified communication platform.

With Office 2016 and Windows 10, Microsoft has embraced the concept of flexible versions for multiple platforms such as Windows Phone, iPads, Android devices, and even a web browser. Different versions of Office have different levels of functionality, but Microsoft has tried to keep the universal user interface as similar as possible.

Microsoft Office 2016 is available in several different suite packages from home to enterprise. This book is written with Microsoft Office 365 ProPlus — other packages do not contain the database program Access. Furthermore, most schools have special educational pricing and versions. You should consult your instructor or institution for further information.

For non-educational consumers, Office 2016 is available in two main pricing schemes. You can purchase Office 2016 the traditional way from a retailer for a one-time fee. You can then install the software on exactly one computer. Alternatively, Office 2016 can be purchased by subscription for a yearly or monthly fee. This version is called Office 365. It is the same product as Office 2016, but it comes with more frequent updates, the ability to be installed on more than one computer, more OneDrive storage space, free minutes in Skype, and several other additional perks. At the time of this writing, the Office 365 version is competitively priced to be less expensive for most people despite the monthly or yearly fee. For the latest in pricing and options, you can visit http://office.microsoft.com.

REAL WORLD ADVICE — Help, I Have a Mac!

Traditionally, Office has been available in different versions for Windows and Macs with different functionality, such as the absence of the Access program in the Mac versions. Instead of using the Mac version of Office, two other popular options exist for using Office on a Mac: virtualization and dual boot.

Virtualization of Office on a Mac uses software that mimics Windows in order to run Office. In any major search engine, search for "PC virtualization on Mac" and you will find many software options for emulating a PC on a Mac. While many virtualization programs promise to mimic entirely, there can be some — usually minor — differences.

Dual boot is the ability to choose the operating system on startup. **Bootcamp** is the Mac software that allows the user to decide which operating system — Mac operating system or Windows — to run. When the computer is turned on, the user is given the choice of operating system. Thus, the user can run the Windows version of Office under the Windows operating system.

You should consult your instructor about the policy in your course. Policies on the usage of the Mac operating system vary greatly from course to course and from school to school.

Typically, using Office requires you to have a free Microsoft account. If you are working in a computer lab or enterprise version of Windows 10, you may not need to sign into a Microsoft account to run Office or Windows 10. If you are running Office on a personal computer, you will need to have a Microsoft account. You can create the account when you install Windows 10. If you do not have an account, you need to sign up for one at https://signup.live.com and follow the on-screen instructions. Your first name, last name, and profile image for your Microsoft account will appear in various screens of Windows and Microsoft Office.

Start, Save, and Navigate Office Applications

Each Office application has its own specific application Start screen. From the **application Start screen**, you can select a blank document, workbook, presentation, database, or one of many application-specific templates. Files that have already been created can also be opened from this screen. When existing files are double-clicked from a File Explorer window, the Start screen is not needed and does not open.

Opening Microsoft Word and the Start Screen

Once you start working with these applications, you can have more than one application or more than one instance of the same application open at a time. This means that you can open one file in Word in one window and also open another file in Word in a different window. In this exercise, you will start Microsoft Word so you can create a beginning file for meeting minutes.

CF01.01

To Open Microsoft Word and Use the Start Screen

SIDE NOTE
Windows 10
This book is written for Windows 10. If you are using Windows 8, open your charms, click Search, and then type Word. If using Windows 7, search the Start menu for Word.

a. On the taskbar, click into the **Ask me anything** or **Search the web and Windows** box. Type Word. The search results display. Verify the first result is Word 2016, and then press [Enter]. Pressing Enter automatically selects the first search result. Microsoft Word opens to the Word Start screen.

> ## Troubleshooting
>
> If Word 2016 is not the first option, you will need to use your mouse to select Word 2016 from the search results.

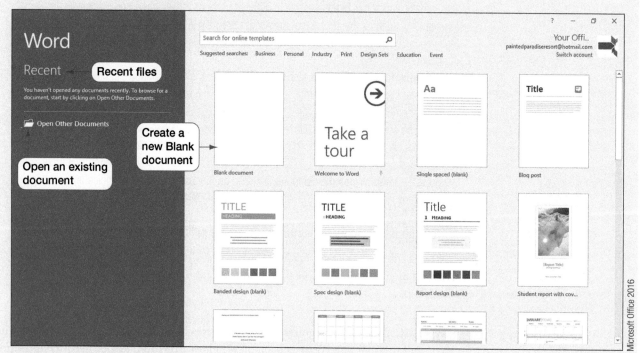

Figure 1   Word Start screen

b. Click **Blank document**. A new Word document opens.

Notice the words Document1 – Word appear on the title bar. This means that the document has not been saved yet. The insertion point is at the beginning of the document.

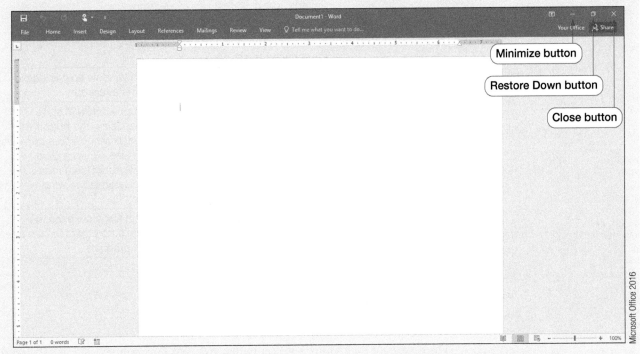

Figure 2 New Word document

Using the Ribbon and Ribbon Display Options

Office has a consistent design and layout that help to make its programs familiar and comfortable to the user. Once you learn to use one Office 2016 program, you can use many of those skills when working with other Office programs. The **ribbon** is the row of tabs across the top of the application. The ribbon display changes according to the screen resolution of your monitor. The figures in this text are set to a screen resolution of 1366 × 768. When open, the ribbons look like Figure 3.

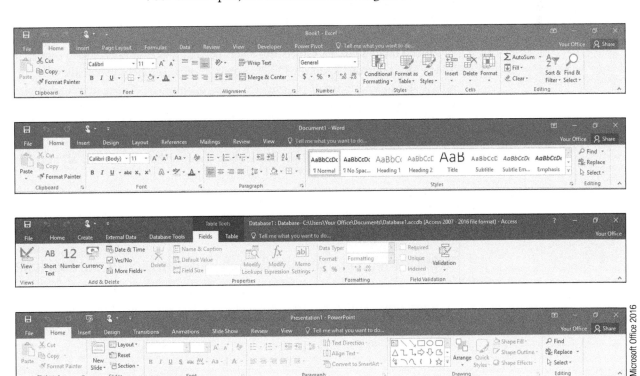

Figure 3 Ribbons of Excel, Word, Access, and PowerPoint

Button	Keyboard Shortcut	Action
Ribbon Display Options ⊞	Ctrl and F1 (toggles between collapsing and showing the ribbon)	Auto-Hide Ribbon, Show Tabs, and Show Tabs and Commands
Minimize −	Alt and Space	Hides a window so it is visible only on the taskbar
Restore Down ⊡ or **Maximize** □	Alt and Space	When the window is at its maximum size, the button will restore the window to a previous, smaller size. When a window is in the Restore Down mode, the button expands the window to its full size.
Close ×	Alt and F4	Closes a file; also, exits the program if no other files are open for that program

Table 1 Top right ribbon buttons

The ribbon for each Office application has two tabs in common: the File tab and the Home tab. The File tab is the first tab on the ribbon and is used for file management needs such as saving and printing. The Home tab is the second tab and contains the commands for the most frequently performed activities, such as copying, cutting, and pasting. The commands on these tabs may differ from program to program. Other tabs are program specific, such as the Formulas tab in Excel, the Design tab in Word and PowerPoint, and the Database Tools tab in Access. The ribbon is further subdivided into **groups** — logical groupings of related commands.

By default, the ribbon is hidden. This allows you more room to work with your document rather than having the ribbon take up screen space with buttons and tools. However, hiding the ribbon makes it harder to perform tasks while learning Office. To open the ribbon, you need to pin it open. All directions and figures in this book will assume that the ribbon is pinned open.

Touch mode switches Office into a version that makes a touch screen easy to use. The Touch Mode button 👆 on the Quick Access Toolbar can help you easily switch between mouse and touch modes. If your device has a touch screen, Office may automatically put your ribbon in touch mode.

One feature common to all of the application ribbons is the four buttons that appear in the top right corner of an application title bar as shown in Table 1.

In this exercise, you will pin the ribbon open so that you can see all of the tabs and commands. You will also add a title to the document.

To Pin the Ribbon Open and Switch Between Mouse and Touch Mode

a. In the top right corner, click **Ribbon Display Options** ⊞ and then click **Show Tabs and Commands**. The ribbon opens with the Home tab selected.

Troubleshooting

Does your ribbon looks different? Your ribbon may seem to have condensed or expanded buttons and groups. The most common causes are different screen resolution, auto-detecting touch mode, or a smaller program window. Since the ribbon changes to accommodate the size of the window or screen, buttons can appear as icons without labels, and a group can be condensed into a button that must be clicked to display the group options. So do not worry! All of the same features are on the ribbon and in the same general area.

All of the figures in this book use a screen resolution of **1366 × 768**. Setting your computer to that resolution, if it is available, will minimize this issue. In Windows 10, you can find the screen resolution by right-clicking the desktop, clicking Display settings, and clicking Advanced display settings.

Touch/Mouse Mode in the Quick Access Toolbar

Title bar name for unsaved documents

Ribbon Display Options

Save button

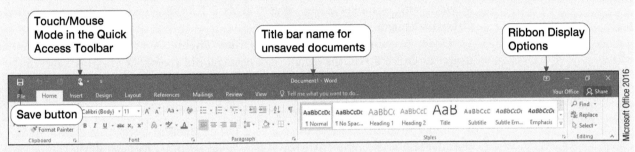

Figure 4   Word with ribbon pinned open

b. In the Quick Access Toolbar in the top left corner, click **Touch/Mouse Mode** 🖑. Then click **Touch**. If your ribbon does not change, you were already in Touch mode — and you most likely have a device with a touch screen.

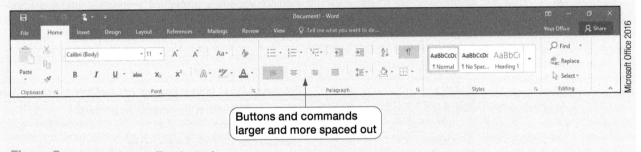

Buttons and commands larger and more spaced out

Figure 5   Word ribbon in Touch mode

c. All the figures in this text were made in mouse mode. In the Quick Access Toolbar in the upper left, click **Touch/Mouse Mode** 🖑. Then click **Mouse** to ensure that you are in mouse mode.

d. With your insertion point still at the beginning of the document, type Meeting Minutes – Budget Meeting.

Using Office Backstage, Your Account, and Document Properties

Office Backstage provides access to the file-level commands, such as saving a file, creating a new file, opening an existing file, printing a file, and closing a file, as well as program options and account settings. Backstage is accessed via the File tab. Office Backstage includes an area called Account. This enables you to log into your Microsoft account or switch accounts. You can also see a list of connected services and add services, such as LinkedIn and Skype. Table 2 lists the areas that you can modify in Office Backstage.

Under Account, you can see what **Office Theme** — or color scheme — you are using. In Office 2016, the default is a new colorful theme. While this looks modern, the best theme for accessibility for people with vision impairments or color blindness is the White theme. For this reason, all of the figures in this book were made with the White theme after this next exercise.

Under Account, you can also see your **Office Background** — an artistic design in the upper right area of the title bar. Again for accessibility reasons, all the figures in this text were made with No Background. In this exercise, you will look at Backstage for your meeting minutes starting document.

Area	Description
Info	Adding properties, protecting, inspecting, and managing a document.
New	Creating a new blank or template-based document.
Open	Opening a file from your computer, recent documents list, or OneDrive account.
Save	Save your file to your computer or OneDrive account.
Save As	Save your file with a new name, as a new file type, or to a different location.
Print	Preview and print your document.
Share	Share your file by invitation, e-mail, online presentation, or blog post.
Export	Change the file type or create a PDF/XPS document.
Close	Close the file without closing the application.
Account	User and product information, including connected services.
Options	Launches the Application Options dialog box with many options, including advanced options.

Table 2 Office Backstage

CF01.03

To Use Backstage to Set Account Settings and View Document Properties

a. Click the **File** tab and then, in the left pane, click **Info**.

Notice the file properties on the right side of the window. Since you have not saved yet, most of the properties are blank. The properties will appear once the file has been saved.

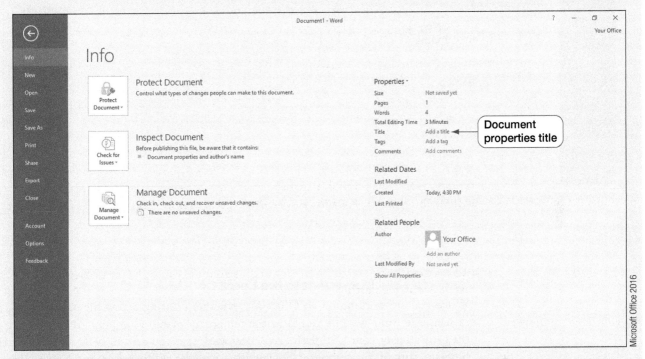

Figure 6 Word Backstage, info page

b. In the properties, click **Add a title**, and then type Budget Meeting Minutes LastFirst, using your last and first name.

c. In the left pane, click **Account**.

If your Microsoft account is already connected, you will see your information and links to access and modify your account. If it is not connected, you will see an option to sign in. In a computer lab, you may see something entirely different, depending on your administrator's setup. If desired and needed, you can sign in to your account now.

Notice that you can also check for updates and see your version of Office. As Microsoft updates in between new versions of Office, your version may change the way the interface works slightly from these instructions. This book is written for version 16.0.6001.1033.

d. If you would like your screen to match the figures in this text, ensure that the **Office Background** is set to **No Background** and the **Office Theme** is set to **White**. Leave Backstage open for the next exercise.

The best theme for accessibility for people with vision impairments or color blindness is the White theme and No Background. For this reason, from this point forward all figures in this book were made with the White theme.

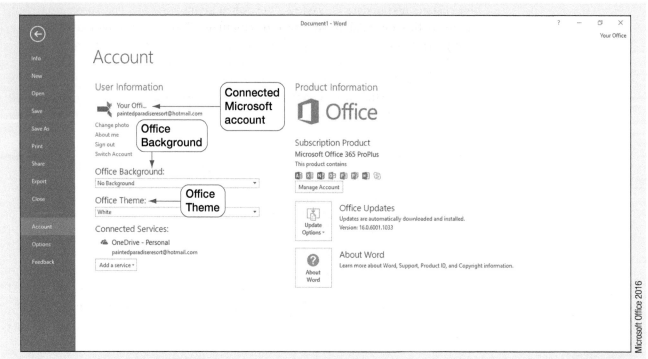

Figure 7 Word Backstage Account name, White theme, and No Background

Saving a New Document to the Local OneDrive That Syncs to the Cloud

While you are working on an Office file, whether creating a new file or modifying an existing file, your work is stored in the temporary memory on your computer, not on the hard drive or your USB flash drive. Any work that you do will be lost if you exit the program, turn off the computer, or experience a power failure or computer crash without you or the program's automatic save function saving your work. To prevent losing your work, you need to save your work and remember to do so frequently — at least every 10 minutes or after adding several changes. That saves you from having to re-create any work you did before the last save.

You can save files to the hard drive, which is located inside the computer; to an external drive, such as a USB flash drive; to a network storage device; or to OneDrive or another cloud storage service. Office has an **AutoRecovery** feature — previously called AutoSave — that will attempt to recover any changes made to a document since your last save if something goes wrong, but this should never be relied upon as a substitute for saving your work manually.

Traditionally, for file storage, files are saved locally on a hard drive or an external storage device such as a USB drive. **A USB drive** is a small, portable storage device — popular for moving files back and forth between a lab, office, and/or home computer. However, USB drives are easily lost, and file versions and backups are usually maintained manually, potentially causing versioning problems.

With Windows 10 and Office 2016, cloud file storage technologies are easier to use than ever. **OneDrive** — Microsoft's cloud storage solution — is fully integrated into File Explorer and Backstage. **Cloud computing** is computing resources, either hardware or software, on remote servers being used by a local computer over the Internet. Apps exist for all of your devices, even Apple and Android devices, that connect to your files on the cloud. Other cloud storage systems also exist, such as Dropbox, Google Drive, and Box.

When you edit a file, your computer or device automatically updates the file in the online storage location. All of the other computers and devices check the online storage for changes and update as needed. Thus, when saving your file, you automatically place a copy online and in all of your synced computers. This creates an online backup if your computer crashes. Additionally, there is no USB drive to lose. File versioning problems are also minimized — in fact, OneDrive by default keeps all versions of your file for you, just in case. Once all applications have been properly set up, you have your files everywhere you want them and shared with exactly who needs them without having multiple copies of files around or e-mailing attachments.

REAL WORLD ADVICE | **Not All Terms of Service Are the Same**

Terms of service for online cloud storage services vary. Some services require you to waive your rights to file content. You really should read the terms of service before signing up for any online service. If you do not, you may not "own" your own files.

Your school's computer lab may or may not be integrated with cloud storage. In this case, you can always log into the cloud storage via a web browser and upload your files. For OneDrive, the URL is http://onedrive.live.com. If you are unsure about your school's computers, ask your instructor.

REAL WORLD ADVICE | **Backing Up to the Cloud**

Best practice still dictates bringing files to important meetings on a physical drive such as a USB drive as backup. Cloud technologies are dependent on an Internet connection. Suppose you show up for a presentation and cannot get to your files because of a poor Internet connection. Your presentation is likely to be a disaster.

The Save As option in Office Backstage gives you direct access to OneDrive, which you can access with your Microsoft account — except Access, which requires you to save locally. With Windows 10, you have a local folder that is directly accessible from the File Explorer and automatically syncs with OneDrive. Thus, you can sync Access files in the local syncing OneDrive folder.

When you save a file, you must provide a name. A file name includes the name you specify and a **file extension** — a few letters that come after the period in the name — assigned by the Office program to indicate the file type. The file extension may or may not be visible, depending on your computer settings. You can check your computer's setting in the File Explorer window under the View tab in the Show/Hide group. The check box for File name extensions should be checked to see file extensions, as shown in Figure 8. Each Office program adds a period and a file extension after the file name to identify the program in which that file was created. Table 3 shows the common default file extensions for Office.

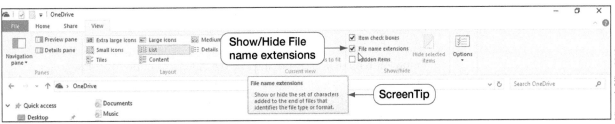

Figure 8 File Explorer extension setting

Application	Extension
Microsoft Word 2016	.docx
Microsoft Excel 2016	.xlsx
Microsoft PowerPoint 2016	.pptx
Microsoft Access 2016	.accdb

Table 3   Office 2016 default file extensions

Name your file with a descriptive name that accurately reflects the content of the document, workbook, presentation, or database, such as "January 2017 Budget" or "012017 Minutes". The descriptive name can include uppercase and lowercase letters, numbers, hyphens, spaces, and some special characters — excluding ? "/ | < > * : — in any combination.

A file exists on your local machine at a **file path** — the physical location of the file starting with a letter that represents the drive and separating folders with a "\". This could be to your hard drive, usually the C:\ drive. Or it could be a USB drive that could be any letter of the alphabet, such as G:\. Assuming your main hard drive is C:\, the OneDrive location on your local computer is C:\Users\username\OneDrive — where username is the username you logged in with. Thus, if you put a file called Meeting.docx in your local OneDrive — and not in a subfolder — the file path combined with the file name would be C:\Users\username\OneDrive\Meeting.docx.

The file path and name combined can include a maximum of 255 characters including the extension. Even though Windows 10 can handle a long file name, some systems cannot. Thus, shorter names can prevent complications in transferring files between different systems.

In this exercise, you will save the meeting minutes document to OneDrive or the location where you are saving your files.

To Save a Workbook to the Local OneDrive Folder That Syncs to the Cloud

a. If necessary, return to Backstage by clicking the **File** tab. Then, on the left pane, click **Save As**.

Notice there is an option for Save and Save As. Save saves a file to the location in which it already exists with the same name. Since this is a new, never saved file, Save and Save As work the same. You will work with an existing file to understand the difference later in this chapter.

b. Click on **This PC**. You may see a folder icon that links to Documents. You will also see recent locations, potentially your OneDrive. If you see OneDrive here, you can click on it. You can also click on Browse to open the Save As dialog box.

c. If you are logged into your Microsoft account, double-click **OneDrive**. If you want to navigate to a subfolder in your OneDrive, do so now.

If you are saving your files to a different location, double-click This PC. In the Save As dialog box, navigate to the location where you are saving your project files.

d. In the Save As dialog box in the File name box, change the name to cf01ch01Minutes_LastFirst, using your last and first name. Click **Save**.

Notice the Save as type menu. This determines the file type and extension. In Word, the default is .docx.

Troubleshooting

You are not connected to OneDrive! If this is your PC, log into your Microsoft account as directed in the previous exercise. If you cannot do that, such as in a computer lab, double-click **This PC** or **Browse** and navigate to a location where you would like to store your files.

You can store the files on the desktop and then upload them at http://onedrive .live.com when you are finished. If you do this, make sure all files are closed before you upload them.

Alternatively, you can save the files to a USB drive or other location of your choosing.

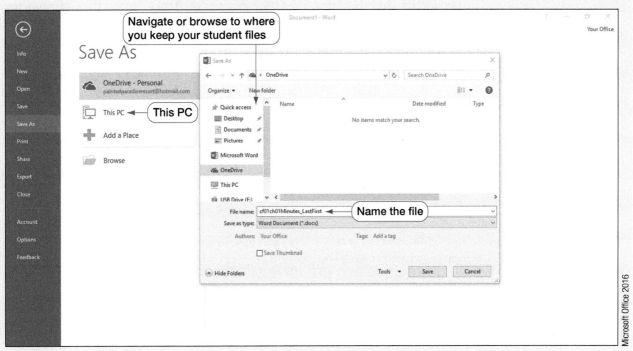

Figure 9 Word Save As

e. Click **Minimize** ‒ . Then on the taskbar, click **File Explorer** .

f. In the left Navigation pane, Click **OneDrive** or otherwise navigate to where you saved your file. In the file list, verify that your file is there.

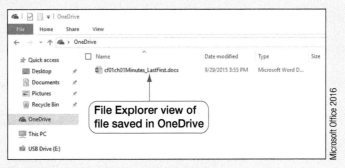

Figure 10 Word file in File Explorer

g. In the top right corner of File Explorer, click **Close** × .

h. On the taskbar, point to the **Word icon** until you see the Live Preview of your file. Click the **Live Preview** to maximize your file again.

Closing a File, Reopening from the Recent Documents List, and Exiting an Application

When you are ready to close a file, you can click the Close command in Office Backstage. If the file you close is the only file that's open for that particular program, the program window remains open with no file in the window. You can also close a file by using the Close button ⊠ in the top right corner of the window to exit the window. If you exit the window, it will close both the file and the program. Exiting programs when you are finished with them helps to save system resources and keeps your Windows desktop and taskbar uncluttered. It also prevents data from being accidentally lost. Importantly, files must be closed before being uploaded to the web, copied to a new location, or attached to an e-mail; otherwise you risk corrupting the file.

Office's **roaming settings** are a group of settings that offer easy remotely synced user-specific data that affect the Office experience. Across logins, these settings remain the same. When signing into Office, the user will experience Office the same way, whether on a desktop, a laptop, or a mobile device.

Roaming settings include Most Recently Used (MRU) list, Documents and Places, MRU Templates, Office Personalization, Custom Dictionary, List of Connected Services, Word Resume Reading Position, OneNote — custom name a notebook view, and in PowerPoint the Last Viewed Slide.

As a part of roaming settings, Office keeps a list of your most recently modified files in the **Most Recently Used list**. As the list grows, older files are removed to make room for more recently modified files. You can pin a frequently used file to always remain at the top of the list. To clear the recent files, right-click any file in the recent files list, and select the option to clear unpinned files. In this exercise, you will close the meeting minutes and reopen it from the most recently used list; then you will close the file and Word.

To Close a File and Exit an Application

a. Verify that you saved your file properly in the previous exercise and know the location to which you saved the file.

b. Click the **File** tab, and then click **Close**. The file closes, but Word remains open.

c. Click the **File** tab, and then click **Open**. On the right, you should see your file in the Most Recently Used list organized by last saved date — labeled Today, Yesterday, Last Week, or Older.

d. Click **cf01ch01Minutes_LastFirst**. Your file opens from the originally saved location.

e. Click **Close** ⊠. Since this was the only open document, the document closes and Word exits.

Opening an Existing File in Microsoft Word and Then Saving as Another Name

You create a new file when you open a blank document, workbook, presentation, or database. If you want to work on a previously created file, you must first open it. When you open a file, it copies the file from the file's storage location to the computer's temporary memory and displays it on the screen. When you save a file, it updates the storage location with the changes. Until then, the file exists only in your computer's memory. If you want to open a second file while one is open, the keyboard shortcut of pressing Ctrl and then pressing O will display the Open tab of Office Backstage. Using the keyboard shortcut of Ctrl + F12 will launch the Open dialog box without taking you to Office Backstage.

Many times, you will open a file that already exists rather than starting a new file. You can open the program and then open the file. You also can double-click a file in File Explorer, and the file will open in the associated program. When you have an existing file open, the Save command saves the file to the current location with the same name. If you want to change the name of a file or save it to a different location, you will need to use the Save As command. This allows you to specify the save options. When you use Save As, it allows you to select any location and give the file a new name.

When you open files that you downloaded from the Internet, accessed from a shared network, or received as an attachment in e-mail, the file usually opens in a read-only format called **Protected View** in Reading Mode. In Protected View, the file contents can be seen and read, but you cannot edit, save, or print the contents until you enable editing. If you see the information bar right under the ribbon and you trust the source of the file, simply click the Enable Editing button on the information bar.

REAL WORLD ADVICE | **Sharing Files Between Office Versions**

Different Office versions are not always compatible with one another. The general rule is that files created in an older version can always be opened in a newer version but not the other way around — an Office 2016 file is not easily opened in earlier versions of Office. Sharing files with Office 2003 users is a concern because different file extensions were used. For example, .doc was used for Word files instead of docx, .xls instead of .xlsx for Excel, and so on.

It is possible to save the Office 2016 files in a previous file format. To save in one of these formats, use the Save As command, and click the 97-2003 file format. If the file is already in the format of a previous version of Office, it will open in Office 2016 and be saved with the same format in which it was created. However, if a file is saved with the extension of a previous version, it may lose anything created with newer features.

If you have not already done so, you need to download the files for this text at http://www.pearsonhighered.com/youroffice. In this exercise, you will open an existing file and save it with another name. Susan Brock has already started an agenda for your meeting with her but has asked you to finish it.

To Open an Existing File

a. On the taskbar, click in **Ask me anything** or **Search the web and Windows** and type Word. Click the **Word 2016** search result. The Word Start screen opens.

b. Click **Open Other Documents** in the left pane, and then click **Browse**. Navigate through the folder structure to the location of your student data files, and then double-click **cf01ch01Agenda**.

The agenda previously started by Susan Brock opens in Word.

c. If necessary, click Enable Editing. If you needed to click Enable Editing, your file opened in Protected View.

d. Click the **File** tab, click **Save As**, and then double-click **This PC**. In the Save As dialog box, navigate to the location where you are saving your project files, and then change the file name to cf01ch01Agenda_LastFirst, using your last and first name. Click **Save** 🖫.

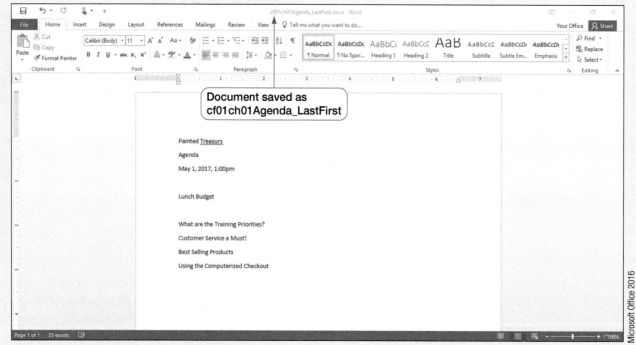

Figure 11 Beginning the Agenda document

Zooming, Scrolling, and Navigating with Keyboard Shortcuts

To get a closer look at the content within the program, you can zoom in. Alternatively, if you would like to see more of the contents, you can zoom out. Keep in mind that the zoom level affects only your view of the document on the screen and does not affect the printed output of the document. It is similar to using a magnifying glass on a page of a book to make the words look bigger — the print on the page is still the same size. Therefore, do not confuse the zoom level with how big the text will print — it affects only your view of the document on the screen.

On the right side of the status bar in the lower right corner is a slide control that permits zooming in Word from 10% to 500%. The minus and plus buttons provide an easy method to change the view size, or you can drag the Zoom Slider. In Excel and PowerPoint, the zoom range is from 10% to 400%. When zoom is used, text is sometimes shifted off the viewing screen. Depending on the program and the zoom level, you might see the vertical or horizontal scroll bars or both scroll bars, which can be used to adjust what is displayed in the window. The scroll bars have arrows that can be clicked to shift the workspace in small increments in a specific direction and a scroll box that can be dragged to move a work space in larger increments. Touch screens allow you to zoom in and out by using pinch and stretch gestures. In addition to zooming and scrolling, you can navigate the file using keyboard shortcuts.

REAL WORLD ADVICE Using Keyboard Shortcuts and KeyTips

Keyboard shortcuts — keyboard equivalents of software commands — are extremely useful, and some are universal to all Windows programs. They allow you to keep your hands on the keyboard instead of reaching for the mouse — increasing efficiency and saving time. Some companies have even take the mouse away from their interns to force them to use keyboard shortcuts. Keyboard shortcuts are also very useful for accessibility and people with vision impairments.

Pressing Alt will toggle the display of **KeyTips** — or keyboard shortcuts — for items on the ribbon and Quick Access Toolbar. After displaying the KeyTips, you can press the corresponding letter or number to request the action from the keyboard.

For multiple-key shortcuts, you hold down the first key listed and press the second key once. Some common keyboard shortcuts are listed below.

Ctrl + C	Copy the selected item
Ctrl + X	Cut the selected item
Ctrl + V	Paste a copied or cut item
Ctrl + A	Select all the items in a document or window
Ctrl + B	Bold selected text
Ctrl + Z	Undo an action
Ctrl + Home	Move to the top of the document
Ctrl + End	Move to the end of the document

In this exercise, you will zoom in and out on the agenda document and navigate it with keyboard shortcuts.

 CF01.07

To Zoom, Scroll, and Navigate with Keyboard Shortcuts

a. The insertion point should be at the beginning of the document right before the word "Painted," and the insertion point should be blinking.

b. On the Word status bar, drag the **Zoom Slider** to the right until it reaches **500%**. The document is enlarged to its largest size. This makes the text appear larger.

c. Press Ctrl + End. This takes you to the end of the document.

> **Troubleshooting**
>
> As discussed in the Windows 10 chapter, if the End key is shared with a function key as on many laptops, you may have had a different result. Ensure that your button is behaving as the End key and not as a function key. This is device specific, and you may need to do a web search to figure it out. If necessary, use the scroll bar instead.

> **d.** On the Word status bar, click **500%**.
>
> Notice that this percentage is the Zoom level button that opens the Zoom dialog box. This dialog box provides options for custom and preset settings.

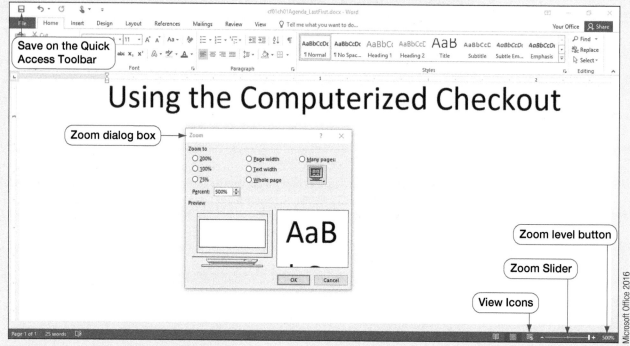

Figure 12 Zoom controls and dialog box

Microsoft Office 2016

> **e.** Click **Page width**, and then click **OK**.
>
> The Word document zooms to its page width. Notice that this zoom level will give you the maximum size without creating a horizontal scroll bar.
>
> **f.** Right-click the **scroll box** in the scroll bar. Then select **Top** to return to the beginning of the document.
>
> Notice that the document scrolled to the top but did not move the insertion point. The keyboard shortcut of Ctrl + Home takes you to the top and moves the insertion point.
>
> **g.** Press Ctrl + Home and notice that the insertion point moves to the top as well.
>
> **h.** **Save** 🖫 the document.

Using the Quick Access Toolbar to Save a Currently Open File

In addition to Office Backstage, Office provides several ways to save a file. To quickly save a file, simply click Save 🖫 on the Quick Access Toolbar or use the keyboard shortcut of pressing Ctrl + S. The **Quick Access Toolbar** is the series of small icons in the top left corner of the title bar that can be customized to display commonly used buttons.

When this method is used, the program simply saves the file to its current location with the same name. Once you save a file the first time, the simple shortcut methods to save any changes to the file work fine to update the existing file — as long as you do not need to change the file name or location with the Save As command. In this exercise, you will save your file to its current location with the same name as previously given.

To Save an Existing File with the Quick Access Toolbar

a. In the top left corner in the Quick Access Toolbar, click **Save** 🖫.

The file is now saved to the same location and with the same name you designated earlier in this chapter. Although you have not made changes since the document was last saved, best practice is to save your files frequently.

Manipulate, Correct, and Format Content in Word

A personal brand is important in business. If a person dresses poorly, colleagues may assume that this person's work is poor as well. In the business world, everything a person does influences the way colleagues and superiors view that person, including the content and formatting of the files he or she produces. Thus, understanding appropriate content and formatting is very important — it is a direct reflection of you as a professional.

 REAL WORLD ADVICE | **It Is Not the Place for Jokes!**

Business documents and files are rarely if ever appropriate for jokes. Consider a job applicant who lists, as the last thing in his or her resume, "Will work for food" — this has actually happened. The job applicant may have wanted to convey that he or she had a good sense of humor. But in reality, the message shows that the job applicant did not understand that humor was inappropriate in this situation or he or she did not take getting the job seriously.

 CONSIDER THIS | **Consider Your Personal Brand**

Have you thought about your personal brand? Are you the creative person? Are you the efficient person? Describe your brand. Give an example of how you were influenced positively or negatively by the way another person presented themselves or their work.

Checking Spelling

Checking spelling is a must — and it is easy in Office. There are no excuses for spelling mistakes. Everyone makes typos, but that is no excuse for poor spelling. Further, you need to understand your audience and purpose before using jargon, acronyms, text abbreviations, or other informal language. Using informal language in a business chat in Skype is appropriate. However, in a business meeting agenda, formal language is expected.

In this exercise, you will correct a spelling mistake.

CF01.09

To Correct Spelling

SIDE NOTE

Spelling Pane

The spelling pane can also be an effective way to check an entire document. Subsequent chapters will cover more on spell check.

a. Notice the second word on the first line is misspelled as "Treasurs" instead of "Treasures." Since it is misspelled, Word put a wavy red line under the word to indicate the mistake. A green wavy line indicates a grammar mistake. A blue wavy line indicates that there could be a mistake but it is not grammar or spelling — such as using "from" instead of "form".

b. Right-click the misspelled word **Treasurs**. Click the first option for **Treasures**.

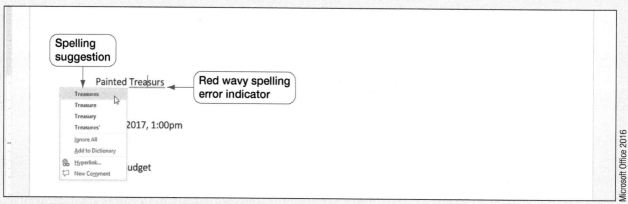

Figure 13   Correcting spelling in a document

c. Save 🖫 the document.

Showing Formatting Symbols, Entering, Copying, and Pasting Text

Many keys, such as Spacebar, Enter, and Tab, insert nonprinting characters in a document. For example, when you press Tab, text is indented and a tab "character" is inserted. Sometimes called formatting marks, nonprinting characters are by default not displayed on the screen. These formatting marks are not shown when the document is printed, even when they are displayed on the screen. When content is entered, these marks can change the way the text is shown, is located, and is formatted. Thus, displaying formatting symbols can help you see everything in your document.

As you add content, you will inevitably find an occasion when copying and pasting the text will save you time. Of course, someone looking at the end product will have no way of knowing what you typed by hand and what you copied and pasted. In many instances, copy and paste not only will save you time but also will increase accuracy — assuming that you do not copy a mistake! In this exercise, you will enter the top three products at the gift store. Along the way, you will copy and paste to enter text as efficiently as possible.

94   CHAPTER 1 | Common Features of Microsoft Office 2016

CHAPTER 1

To Show Formatting Symbols, Enter, Copy, and Paste Text

a. On the Home tab, in the Paragraph group, click **Show/Hide** ¶. The hidden formatting symbols now show. Notice the only hidden symbols in this document are a paragraph mark indicating the end of a paragraph and a dot representing spaces.

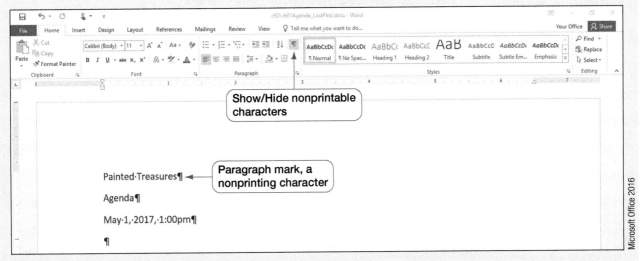

Figure 14 Hidden formatting characters

SIDE NOTE
Mouse Versus Keyboard
If you have trouble using the keyboard to select text, use the mouse instead. In the end, it does not change your document. Knowing both methods is about speed.

b. If necessary, scroll until you see the words **Best Selling Products** and then click after the **s** in Products to place your insertion point at the end of that line. Press Enter.

Pressing Enter creates a hard return that creates a new paragraph. Word will automatically wrap text in a paragraph down to the next line.

c. Type Golf Clubs. The top three products are three different kinds of golf clubs. To save time, you will use copy and paste.

d. Hold down the Shift key, and press the ← **ten** times to select the words Golf Clubs.

You can use Shift and arrow keys to select, rather than the mouse. Depending on the situation, the mouse could be faster or the keyboard could be faster. Therefore, it is useful to know how to use both. Notice when you pressed the arrow for the tenth time, it automatically selected the paragraph mark.

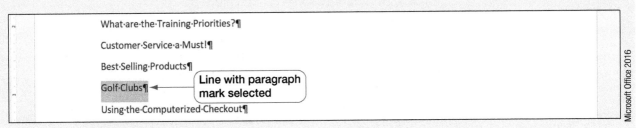

Figure 15 Paragraph mark selected

e. Press Ctrl + C. This copies the text to the Office Clipboard to use anytime you want, even multiple times, until the clipboard is replaced with something else.

f. Click after the **s** in Golf Clubs to place the insertion point at the end of the line. Then press Spacebar and type Junior.

g. Press Enter and then press Ctrl + V. This pastes the contents of the Clipboard onto that line. Then press ← to return to the second line that says "Golf Clubs."

h. Press Spacebar and then type Beginner.

i. Press Enter and then press Ctrl + V. This pastes the contents of the Clipboard onto that line. Then press ← to return to the third line that says "Golf Clubs."

j. Press Spacebar and then type Pro.

k. Press Delete twice to remove the extra hard returns that were copied.

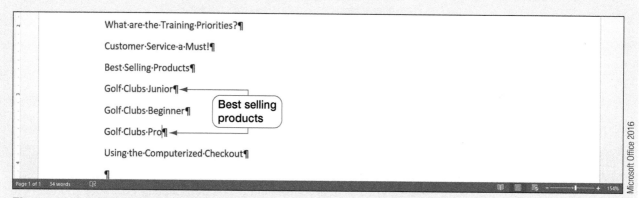

Figure 16 Top products entered

l. Save the document.

Using Undo and Redo

Everyone makes a typo from time to time, and you are going to make mistakes that you need to undo. The easiest way to do that is through the Undo and Redo buttons in the Quick Access Toolbar. In this exercise, you will add some text to your agenda, undo it, and then add better text.

CF01.11

To Use Undo and Redo

a. Press Ctrl + End to place the insertion point at the end of the document.

b. Type Open and Close Steps. After you type that, you realize that the word "Procedures" would be a better word choice than "Steps."

c. In the top left corner in the Quick Access Toolbar, click the **arrow** to the right of Undo Typing ↰.

d. Verify that the list is letting you undo by the letter. If not, see the troubleshooting below. Click the item on the list that says **Typing "S"** that was the first letter to the word Steps.

> ## Troubleshooting
>
> If your version of Office does not undo by the letter, you may see an option for only the phrase Typing "Steps." If you do, click that option. You may also see an option for the whole phrase Typing "Open and Close Steps." If you do, click that option and then, in the next step, you will have to redo the entire line by typing Open and Close Procedures.

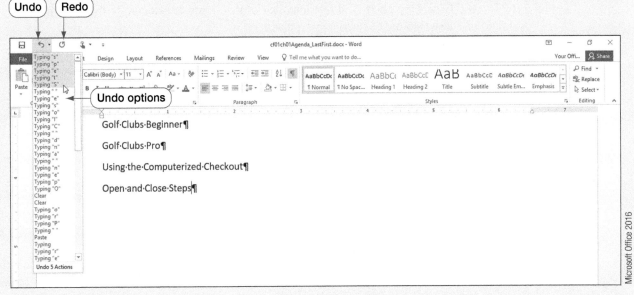

Figure 17 Undo typing steps

e. Type Procedures. The word "Steps" is undone, and you have entered a better word choice. Undo and Redo can be used for almost anything you do, not just typing.

f. **Save** 💾 the document.

Using the Navigation Pane, Finding Text, and Replacing Text

Sometimes, you may not know where certain text is in a document. Or you may need to replace text with something different. You can use Find and Replace on the ribbon rather than manually looking for text and changing it. If you click Find on the Home tab, it opens the Navigation pane on the left side of the window with a search box. **A pane** is a smaller window that often appears to the side of the program window and offers options or helps you to navigate through completing a task or feature. If you click Replace, it opens the Find and Replace **dialog box**, which is a window that provides more options or settings beyond those provided on the Navigation pane. All three of the top-selling products are actually Wilson Golf clubs. In this exercise, you will find the words "Golf Clubs" and replace them with the more precise brand of Wilson Golf Clubs.

REAL WORLD ADVICE	What to "Find" in a Find and Replace?

Be careful what you look for in a find and replace. If you are not careful, you can end up replacing items that should not have been. If this ever happens, remember the Undo command!

SIDE NOTE

Be Careful with Replace All

When using Replace All, be very careful. It is easy to unintentionally change text that should not have been changed.

To Use Find and Replace

a. On the Home tab, in the Editing group, click **Find**. The Navigation pane appears on the left. You could find all of the instances of Golf Clubs from this pane. However, you cannot do a find and replace operation from here. In the top right corner of the Navigation pane, click **Close** ⊠ to close that pane.

b. On the Home tab, in the Editing group, click **Replace**. The Find and Replace dialog box opens.

c. Click in the **Find what** box, and type Golf Clubs.

d. Click in the **Replace with** box, and type Wilson Golf Clubs.

e. Click **Find Next**. The first instance of the words is selected in the document. All three instances need to be replaced.

f. Click **Replace All**. All three instances are updated, and a message box appears. Click **OK**, and click **Close** ⊠ to close the Find and Replace dialog box.

g. Press Ctrl + Home to move the insertion point to the beginning of the document. **Save** 🖫 the document.

Using the Font Group and the Font Dialog Box

One of the most commonly used groups on the ribbon is the Font group. A **font** is the way the letters in words look, including the size, weight, and style. In the Font group, you can change many attributes of the words, including color, size, alignment, type of font, and common emphasis.

Clicking a command will produce an action. For example, the Font group on the Home tab includes buttons for bold and italic. Clicking any of these buttons will produce an intended action. So if you have selected text to which you want to apply bold formatting, simply click the Bold button, and bold formatting is applied to the selected text.

Some buttons are **toggle buttons** — one click turns the feature on and a second click turns the feature off. When a feature is toggled on, the button remains highlighted. Clicking toggles the setting on and off. Bold is an example of a toggle button.

Some buttons have two parts: a button that accesses the most commonly used setting or command and an arrow that opens additional options. A **gallery** is a set of menu options that appears when you click the arrow next to a button. A normal arrow will bring up the options or enable you to scroll through the options. If there is a More arrow ▾, it brings up all of the options.

For example, on the Home tab, in the Font group, the Font Color button 🅰 ▾ includes a gallery of the different colors that are available for fonts. If you click the button, the default is to apply the last color used, which is displayed on the icon. To access the gallery for other color options, click the arrow next to the Font Color button.

Some commands open other menus. These commands expand to a list of options when the arrow next to the list is selected. Whenever you see an arrow next to a button, this is an indicator that more options are available. Then you can click on the option from the list that you want.

Some ribbon groups include a diagonal arrow in the bottom right corner of the group, called a **Dialog Box Launcher** 🗗, which opens a corresponding dialog box. Click the Dialog Box Launcher to open a dialog box. It often provides access to more precise or less frequently used commands along with the commands that are offered on the ribbon; thus, using a dialog box offers the ability to apply many related options at the same time and from one location.

In this exercise, you will change the formatting of the font to be more appropriate.

SIDE NOTE

Text Selection

You can double-click to select a single word or triple-click to select the entire paragraph. You can also use ⇧Shift and arrow keys to select text.

To Use the Font Group and Font Dialog Box

a. If necessary, press ⎡Ctrl⎤ + ⎡Home⎤ to place your insertion point at the beginning of the document.

b. On the Home tab in the Paragraph group, click **Center** ≡. The title is centered across the top.

c. On the first line, click before the **P** in Painted Treasures, and then drag to right after the **s** to select the words "Painted Treasures."

d. On the Home tab, in the Font group, click **Increase Font Size** A˄ three times. The title is now larger.

e. On the Home tab, in the Font group, click the **arrow** next to the Font gallery. Scroll down the list, and click **Verdana**. The font changes.

f. On the Home tab, in the font group, click the **arrow** next to Font color A ˅. Under Standard Colors, select **Dark Red**.

g. On the Home tab, in the font group, click **Bold** B.

h. Click before the **L** in Lunch Budget, and drag to the **t** to select Lunch Budget.

i. On the Home tab, in the Font group, click the **arrow** next to Font Size 11 ˅. Click **14**. The font increases in size to 14 points.

j. On the Home tab, in the Font group, click the **Dialog Box Launcher** ⌐. The Font dialog box opens. Under Font style, click **Italic**.

Figure 18 Font dialog box

k. Click **OK**. The dialog box closes.

l. **Save** ⊟ the document.

Using the Style Gallery and Bullets with Live Preview

Live Preview lets you see the effects of menu selections on your document file or selected item before making a commitment to a particular menu choice. The menu or grid shows samples of the available options. Not all additional options under arrows have Live Preview. Using Live Preview, you can experiment with settings before making a final choice.

Predefined Styles are a type of preset formatting. You will learn more about styles later. However, styles allow for more advanced features, such as a Table of Contents. They can also be customized. So if you later decide that Heading 2 should be in a larger font size, you change the style, and it changes every instance of Heading 2 in your document. Finally, and for the purpose of this chapter, styles help you apply aesthetically pleasing formatting very quickly — and can also be helpful for users with vision color impairments.

When you click on the More arrow ⏷ for styles, you will see the Styles gallery. Point to a text style in the Styles gallery, and the selected text or the paragraph in which the insertion point is located appears with that text style. Moving the pointer from option to option results in quickly seeing what your text will look like before you make a final selection. To finalize a change to the selected option, click the style.

Bullets are symbols that appear before each item to create a list of items. Typically, bullets also have different spacing than a normal paragraph and have the Live Preview option. When you click on the Bullets ☰⏷ arrow, a library menu appears that allows you to pick the symbol you wish to use.

In this exercise, you will add a style to the gift shop agenda using styles and some simple bulleting. In business, agendas usually do not need a lot of formatting. However, a little bit of formatting can actually change what the content conveys to others and provide clarity to your content.

To Use the Styles Gallery and Bullets to Observe Live Preview

a. Click and drag to select the second and third lines starting with **Agenda** and ending with **1:00pm**.

b. On the Home tab, in the Styles group, click **More** ⏷. Point to the option for **Intense Quote**. Notice, the document shows the Live Preview. If you move your mouse over other style options, the document will change accordingly.

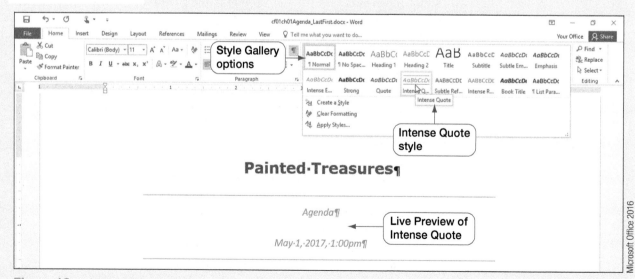

Figure 19 Styles Live Preview

SIDE NOTE

Closing a Gallery

Press [Esc] to close a gallery without making a selection. Alternatively, you can click outside the gallery menu.

c. Click **Intense Quote**. The Intense Quote style is now applied to those two lines.

d. If necessary, scroll down until you see the golf clubs you entered. Click and drag starting with **Wilson Golf Clubs Junior** down to the last of the three types of golf clubs, **Wilson Golf Clubs Pro**.

e. On the Home tab, in the Paragraph group, click **Bullets** [≣ ▾]. The lines now display as a bulleted list. Notice that after the bullet symbol, the formatting symbol for a tab appears, indicating space between the symbol and the words.

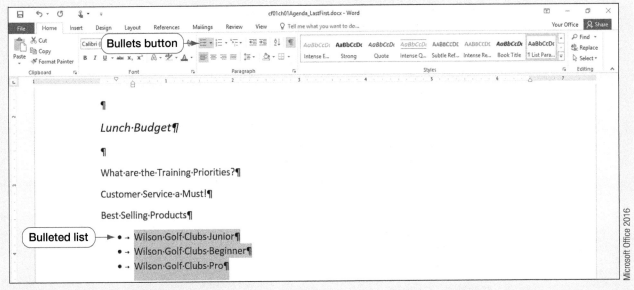

Figure 20 Bulleted list

f. **Save** 🖫 the document.

Inserting a Comment and Footer Using the Tell me what you want to do Box

New in Office 2016, all of the programs have a **Tell me what you want to do** box in the title bar — "Tell me" for short. This tool is particularly useful when you want to do something but do not know where a command is located in the ribbon. This tool will not just take you to help on that item — though it does provide options for that as well. It actually performs the action for you. Although the Tell me feature is not currently connected to Cortana or speech recognition, it is easy to see that as a potential feature upgrade in the future.

Under the Tell me what you want to do search results, you also have an option for a Smart Lookup, which is new to Office 2016. With Smart Lookup, you can open search results and do research without leaving the application. Instead, it brings up the results in the Inights pane.

A comment allows you to leave a note for another person to read and reply. Comments are great for collaboration and can be easily deleted before the document is final. A footer allows you to put text at the bottom of every page. Footers are great for placing the page number, your name, or even the file name. You will learn more about comments and footers in a later chapter and will add basic ones in this exercise. The Tell me feature is great for using and finding features you do not know a lot about.

In this exercise, you will use this tool to add a comment and a footer to the agenda. Susan, the gift shop manager, has asked you to send back to her the updated agenda. You need to add a comment to ask her a question.

To Use Tell Me to Insert a Comment and Footer

a. Place your insertion point at the end of the line Using the Computerized Checkout so that the insertion point is after the **t** and before the **paragraph** mark.

b. In the title bar, click in the **Tell me what you want to do . . .** box and type Add Comment. Notice that command options are listed first. Next, you have the option to open the Help window on the topic you entered. Finally, you can select Smart Lookup, which opens the Insights pane on the right with Bing web search results.

c. Click the first result **Insert Comment**. Tell me adds the comment and places your insertion point in the comment. Type Is there existing documentation to use?

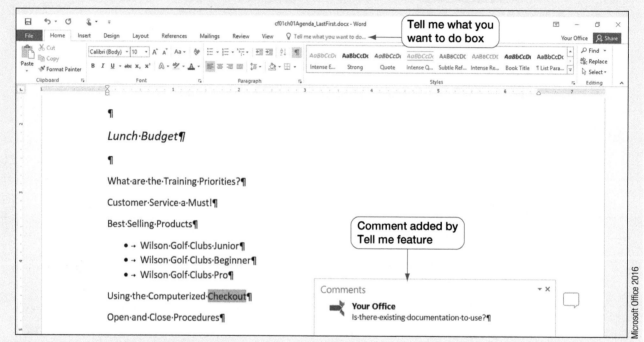

Figure 21   Inserted comment

d. If necessary, scroll to the left and press Ctrl + End to place your insertion point at the end of the document.

e. In the title bar, click in the **Tell me what you want to do . . .** box and type Add a footer, and then click the first result **Add a Footer**. In the submenu, select the second option **Blank (Three Columns)**. Tell me adds the footer and places your insertion point in the footer.

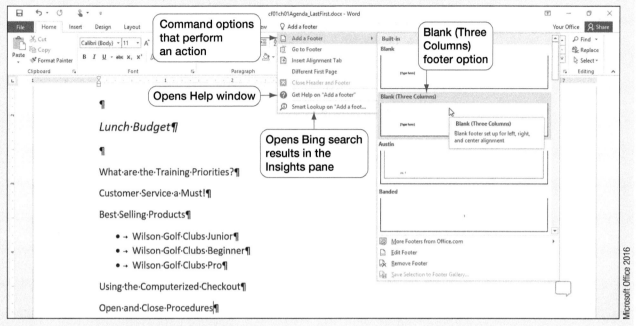

Figure 22 Adding a footer with Tell me

f. On the left side, click **[Type here]** and type First Last, using your first and last name.

g. In the middle, click **[Type here]** and type Course Name, using your class's name.

h. On the right side, click **[Type here]** and type InstructorLast, using your instructor's last name.

i. Press Esc to exit the footer, and then press Ctrl + Home to return to the beginning of the document.

j. **Save** 🖫 the document, and then click **Close** ☒ to close Word. Submit your file as directed by your instructor. If you need to take a break before finishing this chapter, now is a good time.

REAL WORLD ADVICE **Saving Files**

Most programs have an added safeguard or warning dialog box to remind you to save if you attempt to close a file without saving your changes first. Despite that warning, best practice dictates that you save files before closing them or exiting a program. If you select the wrong option on the warning by accident, you will lose work. Remembering to save before you close prevents this kind of accident.

Best practice also dictates saving often. The more often you save, the less work you can lose in the event of an unexpected closing of the application. Pressing Ctrl + S takes only a few seconds. Train yourself now to use this keyboard shortcut regularly and often. If you do, it will become second nature and save you from losing work in the future!

Formatting, Finding Help, and Printing in Office

The accuracy and quality of your content are the most important aspect of your files. However, even the most high-quality, accurate file is much harder to use if it is formatted poorly causing confusion for anyone who looks at it. After accuracy, clarity of your file to others — and even yourself — is extremely important. It is much more than just making a file look "pretty."

For example, imagine a table of numbers. The title says "2016 Sales," and the numbers in the table do not have any dollar signs. What does that mean? Are the numbers the total quantities sold — known as sales volume? However, the word "sales" many times means dollar amounts. Did someone forget the dollar signs and these numbers really show how much was sold in dollars before costs are removed — known as sales revenue? This example highlights how a simple format issue could confuse users and cause poor decision making. Do a search on the web for "Excel mistakes costing companies big money" and you will find numerous examples.

In this section, you will learn how to appropriately format your budget, how to print a copy to take notes on at the meeting, and how to find help.

Format Using Various Office Methods

Generally speaking, too much formatting is just as bad as too little. You need to be aware of accessibility for vision-impaired individuals — discussed in depth later in this text. Styles in Office provide nice options for users who don't have an artistic eye. Remember that less can be more. However, some formatting, if not done, can lead to incorrect conclusions. For example as mentioned earlier, there is a number labeled Sales in Excel. Without a clearer title or currency formatting, how does a user know whether that is sales in dollars or in quantity sold?

Earlier in the chapter, you added a small amount of formatting that helped the clarity of your agenda. Now you are ready to create your budget in Excel.

Creating a New Excel Workbook

An Excel file is referred to as a **workbook**. Each Excel workbook can contain many different worksheets. Each sheet has rows represented by numbers and columns represented by letters of the alphabet. The intersection of any row and column is a **cell**. For example, cell B2 refers to the cell where column B and row 2 intersect. The **active cell** is the currently selected cell. In a new worksheet, the active cell is the first cell of the first row, cell A1.

On a personal computer, you may prefer to use the Windows Start menu to open the program, but in a computer lab or on an unfamiliar computer, the search method may be preferable. In this exercise, you will search for and open Microsoft Excel to create a new workbook to start a budget for the training budget that you will finish in your meeting with Susan Brock, the gift shop manager.

To Create a New Excel Workbook

a. On the taskbar, click **Ask Me Anything** or **Search the web and Windows**. Type **Excel**.

b. Click on **Excel 2016** in the search results. The Excel Start screen is displayed.

c. Click **Blank workbook**. A new Excel spreadsheet opens.

Notice, the words Book1 - Excel appear on the title bar. This means that the workbook has not been saved yet. This opens a blank workbook with one worksheet named Sheet1. The active cell is A1.

d. Press Ctrl + F1 . The ribbon is pinned open so that you can see all of the commands. on the Home tab.

> **Troubleshooting**
>
> You pressed the keyboard shortcut, but nothing happened or something else happened. Are you working on a laptop? If so, then you may need to hold down the `Fn` key as well. The function keys on a laptop are generally assigned to other things, such as volume. You can change these key assignments, but they are specific to the device — you may need to search the web to find out how to change them on yours.
>
> On a Microsoft Surface, you can press `Fn` and `CapsLock` to make the function keys work without pressing the `Fn` keys. If you have a laptop, it is worth the time to figure out how to do this on your machine. Keyboard shortcuts greatly increase your speed and efficiency. Finally, you can always use the Ribbon Display Options button ⊡ instead.

e. Click the **File** tab, click **Save As**, and then double-click **This PC**. In the Save As dialog box, navigate to the location where you are saving your project files, and then change the file name to cf01ch01Budget_LastFirst, using your last and first name. Click **Save** 🔲.

Using Excel to Enter Content, Apply Italics, and Apply a Fill Color

As was discussed earlier in the chapter, Office uses a common interface between all of the applications. This does not mean an identical interface. While some things are the same, how they are applied or how they work may be slightly different. For example, in Excel, if you select the cell, the formatting options apply to the entire cell — not just part of the text inside of a cell. By contrast, in Word, you select precisely the words for which to change the font color. To make only a single word a different color in Excel, you must select the specific text you want inside the cell first. Some formatting must be applied to the entire cell, such as number type — Currency, Text, and Date, among others. When exploring features that are common to the Office applications, you need to experience how a feature can be slightly different or very different in an application-specific way.

In this exercise, you will add content to the budget, apply italic to some cells, and apply different background color to others.

To Use the Italic Button and the Fill Color Button

a. Click cell **A6** to make it the active cell. Then type Budget and press `Enter`. The text is inserted into the cell, and the cell below becomes the active cell.

b. Click cell **A8**. Type Expenses and press `Enter`.

c. In cell A9, type Food and press `Enter`.

d. In cell A10, type Drinks and press `Enter`.

e. Click cell **A8** to make it the active cell. Then, on the Home tab, in the Font group, click **Italic** ⊡. The toggle button applies italic to cell A8, and the button is highlighted.

f. Click cell **B6**. Type 500 and press `Ctrl` + `Enter`. The value is entered in the cell, and the active cell remains B6.

g. With B6 active, on the Home tab, in the Font group, click the **Fill Color arrow** . The color options appear. Point to the colors to find **Green, Accent 6, Lighter 60%**. At the writing of this text, that is the third color down in the far right column. Click **Green, Accent 6, Lighter 60%**.

> ## Troubleshooting
>
> What if that color is not there? Microsoft has taken to updating Office more often than just every new version. Thus, things can change over time — and color placement in the galleries is one of those things. The best way to find the color is to point to the name. If the color you need is not there, pick the standard color — which does not change — of light green.

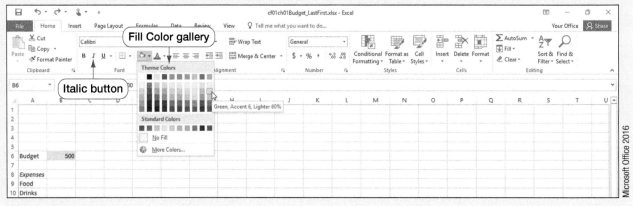

Figure 23 Fill color

h. **Save** the spreadsheet.

Opening an Excel Dialog Box

Excel has dialog boxes, just like Word. The Format Cells dialog box is probably the most used dialog box in Excel, as it allows you to specify many things. Most important, it allows you to specify the type of data in the cell, such as Currency or Text. Since spreadsheets use many calculations, specifying the type of data is very important.

In this exercise, you will use a dialog box to format some of the cells in the budget you are beginning for your manager, Susan Brock.

To Use the Dialog Box Launcher to Format a Number

a. If necessary, click cell **B6** to make it the active cell. Then, on Home tab, in the Number group, click on **Number Format Dialog Box Launcher**. The Format Cells dialog box opens to the Number tab.

b. On the left side, under Category, click **Currency**.

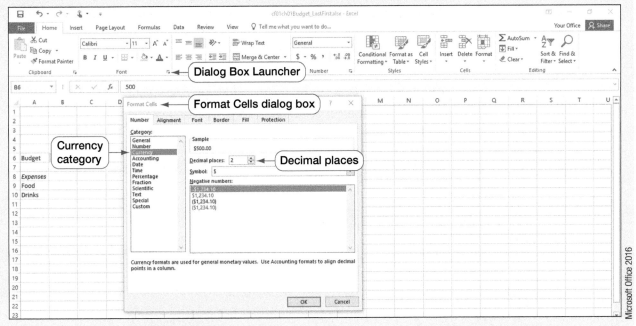

Figure 24 Format Cells dialog box, Number tab

c. Click **OK**. The cell now shows a dollar sign before the number. Notice that the default of two decimals is applied.

d. **Save** 💾 the spreadsheet.

Inserting Images and Using Contextual Tools to Resize

In Word, Excel, PowerPoint, and Publisher, you can insert pictures from a file, a screen shot, or various online sources. The online options include inserting images within the Office Online Pictures collection, via a Bing search, or from your own OneDrive. Be careful when you insert Online Pictures — you must ensure that you have the right to use the image you selected for the purpose you want.

The term "contextual tools" refers to tools that appear only when needed for specific tasks. Some tabs, toolbars, and menus are displayed as you work and appear only if a particular object is selected. Because these tools become available only as you need them, the workspace remains less cluttered.

A **contextual tab** contains commands related to selected objects so that you can manipulate, edit, and format the objects. Examples of objects that can be selected to display contextual tabs include a table, a picture, a shape, or a chart. A contextual tab appears to the right of the standard ribbon tabs. The contextual tab disappears when you click outside the selected object — in the file — to deselect the object. In some instances, contextual tabs can also appear as you switch views.

In this exercise, you will insert a Painted Treasures Gift Shop logo into the budget you are beginning for your manager, Susan Brock. This budget will become a part of Susan's larger budget that she must present to the CEO of Painted Paradise in an internal memo once a year. Logos are an excellent way to brand both internal and external communications.

CF01.19

To Insert an Image and Use the Contextual Tab to Resize

a. Press [Ctrl] + [Home] to make cell A1 — the beginning of this worksheet — the active cell.

b. Click the **Insert** tab. Then, in the Illustrations group, click **Pictures**. Navigate to the location of your student data files, click **cf01ch01Logo.jpg**, and then click **Insert**. The image is inserted, and the Picture Tools Format contextual tab displays. Notice the image is too big and needs to be resized.

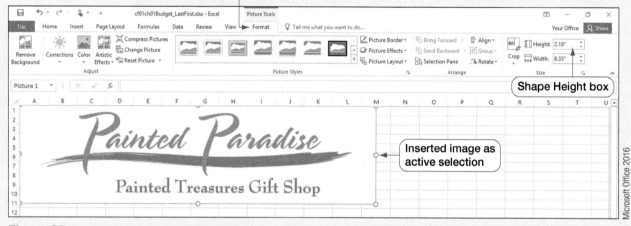

Figure 25 Picture Tools Format contextual tab

c. In Picture Tools, on the Format contextual tab, in the Size group, click in the **Shape Height** box. Then type 1 and press [Enter]. The image now fits the spreadsheet more appropriately.

d. Click cell **A6**. The contextual tab disappears because the image is no longer selected.

e. **Save** 💾 the spreadsheet.

REAL WORLD ADVICE | **What Is Creative Commons and Why Should You Care?**

Office used to provide clip art pictures that were free to use. Office 2016 instead searches web sources for images. By default, it will find images that have Creative Commons licenses. These are images for which the copyright owner has chosen to allow anyone to use the image without commercial compensation. However, it is up to YOU to make sure that image really is free to use. You must read the specific license for that image to be sure your use is acceptable — otherwise, you could be sued for copyright infringement — which is why you should care. When you insert the image, the source URL will be listed on the bottom. Click the link to open the source URL. From there, it may or may not be easier to find the license that is specific to that URL. When in doubt, do not use the file, or contact the owner before using.

Formatting Using the Mini Toolbar

The **Mini toolbar** appears after text has been selected and contains buttons for the most commonly used formatting commands, such as font, font size, font color, center alignment, bold, and italic. The Mini toolbar button commands vary for each Office program. The toolbar disappears if you move the pointer away from the toolbar, press a key, or click the workspace. All the commands on the Mini toolbar are available on the ribbon; however, the Mini toolbar offers quicker access to common commands, since you do not have to move the mouse pointer far away from the selected text for these commands.

In this exercise, you will edit some of the cells in your budget with the Mini toolbar.

To Use the Mini Toolbar to Make a Cell Bold

a. Double-click cell **A6** to place the insertion point in the cell. Double-clicking a cell enables you to enter edit mode for the cell text.

b. Double-click cell **A6** again to select the text. The Mini toolbar appears, coming into view directly above the selected text. If you move the pointer off the cell, the Mini toolbar becomes transparent or disappears entirely. If you don't move it too far away, you can move the pointer back over the Mini toolbar, and it becomes completely visible again. If it doesn't reappear, double-click on the text again.

> ## Troubleshooting
>
> If you are having a problem with the Mini toolbar disappearing, you may have inadvertently moved the mouse pointer to another part of the document. If you need to redisplay the Mini toolbar, right-click the selected text, and the Mini toolbar will appear along with a shortcut menu. Once you have selected an option on the Mini toolbar, the shortcut menu will disappear and the Mini toolbar will remain while in use — or repeat the prior two steps, then make sure the pointer stays over the toolbar.

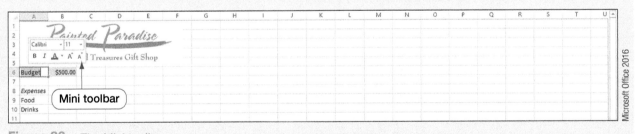

Figure 26   The Mini toolbar

c. In the Mini toolbar, click **Bold** B and press Enter.

d. **Save** 🖫 the spreadsheet.

The Mini toolbar is particularly helpful with the touch interface. When Office recognizes that you are using touch instead of a mouse or digitizer pen, it displays Mini toolbars that are larger and designed to work with fingers more easily. An example of a touch Mini toolbar in Excel Touch mode is shown in Figure 27.

Microsoft Office 2016

Figure 27 The Mini toolbar in Touch mode

Opening Shortcut Menus and Format Painter

A **shortcut menu** is a list of commands related to a selection that appears when you right-click — click the right mouse button. Shortcut menus are also context sensitive and enable you to quickly access commands that are most likely to be needed in the context of the task being performed. This means that you can access popular commands without using the ribbon. Included are commands that perform actions, commands that open dialog boxes, and galleries of options that provide a Live Preview. The Mini toolbar also opens with the shortcut menu when you click the right mouse button. If you click a button on the Mini toolbar, the shortcut menu closes, and the Mini toolbar remains open, allowing you to continue formatting your selection.

The **Format Painter** ☑ allows you to copy a format and apply it to other selections. This allows you to format in one place and quickly apply all of the same formatting elsewhere. If you click the Format Painter button once, Format Painter will turn off after you use it just once. If you double-click the Format Painter, it leaves Format Painter active until you click the Format Painter button again or press [Esc]; leaving Format Painter active allows you to apply the formatting to multiple locations.

In this exercise, you will add some additional information to the budget you are beginning for your manager. You will also edit some of the cells using a shortcut menu and copy the format using Format Painter.

To Use a Shortcut Menu and Format Painter

a. Click cell **B9**. Type 450 and press Enter. Cell B10 should now be the active cell.

b. With cell B10 active, type 50 and press Enter.

c. Right-click cell **B9** to display the shortcut menu.

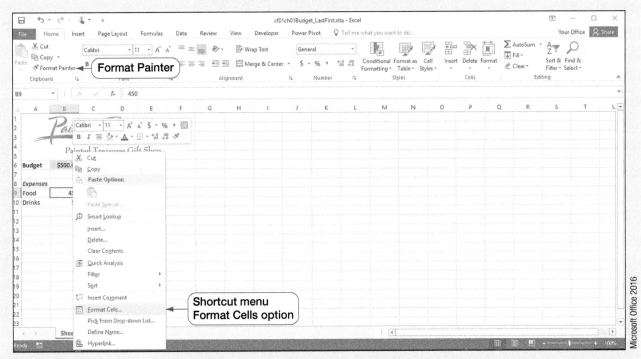

Figure 28   The shortcut menu

> **SIDE NOTE**
>
> **Double-click the Format Painter**
>
> If you double-click the Format Painter, it will stay on until you click the Format Painter again, allowing you to apply the formatting to more than one cell.

d. Click **Format Cells**.

e. In the Format Cells dialog box, under Category, click **Currency** and then click **OK**.

f. With B9 as the active cell, on the Home tab, in the Clipboard group, single-click **Format Painter**. Your insertion point now appears with a paintbrush next to it.

g. Click cell **B10**. Notice that B10 changes to currency format and the Format Painter is turned off.

h. **Save** the spreadsheet.

Find Help, Print, and Share in Office

Office **Help** can give you additional information about a feature or steps for how to perform a new task. Your ability to find and use Help can greatly increase your Office proficiency and save you time from seeking outside assistance. Office has several levels of help, from a searchable search window to more directed help such as ScreenTips.

The Help window provides detailed information on a multitude of topics, as well as access to templates, training videos installed on your computer, and content available on Office.com — the website maintained by Microsoft that provides access to the latest information and additional Help resources. To access the contents at Office.com, you must have access to the Internet from the computer. If there is no Internet access, only the files installed on the computer will be displayed in the Help window. The easiest way to access Help is through pressing F1 — in some of the programs. If available, this will take you directly to an article about what is actively selected.

Pointing to any command on the ribbon will display a **ScreenTip** with screen text to indicate more information. You may have seen these while working earlier in the chapter. They are very useful to learn what the command on the button will do.

Using the Help Window and ScreenTips

In this exercise, you will view a ScreenTip and learn how to insert a footer using Excel Help and then add a footer to the meeting minutes.

To Access Office Help and Insert a Footer

a. With your Excel budget open, press F1. The Excel Help window opens.

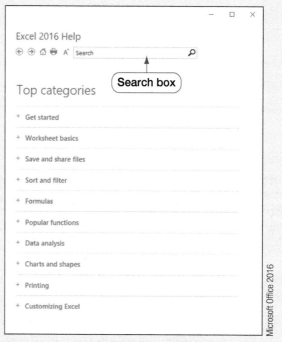

Figure 29   The Excel Help window

b. In the search box, type add a footer and press Enter. Then click the first link, and read about how to add a footer. When you are done, click **Close** ✕ to close the Help window.

c. Click the **Page Layout** tab, and then, in the Page Setup group, point your mouse to **Print Titles**. Notice the ScreenTip with a link for Tell me more. If you clicked on Tell me more, it would take you to the Help window specifically for Print Titles.

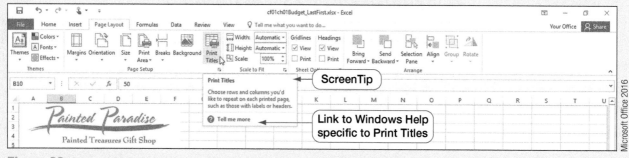

Figure 30   ScreenTip

d. On the **Page Layout** tab, in the Page Setup group, point your mouse to the **Page Setup Dialog Box Launcher** [⌐]. Notice the ScreenTip, this time without the Tell me more option. Click the **Page Setup Dialog Box Launcher** [⌐].

e. Click the **Header/Footer** tab, and then click **Custom Footer** to display the Footer dialog box.

f. Click in the **Left section** and type First Last, using your first and last name.

g. Click in the **Center section** and click **Insert File Name** [🗎].

h. Click in the **Right section** and type InstructorLast, using your instructor's last name.

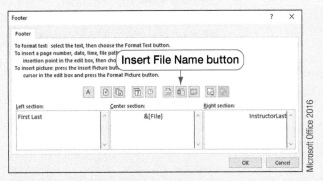

Figure 31   The Footer dialog box

i. Click **OK**, and then click **OK** again. The footer is inserted. In Normal view, you will not see the footer. You will see the footer in the next exercise.

j. **Save** [💾] the spreadsheet.

Accessing the Share Pane

In Office, many ways exist for sharing files. There are times when you will need a paper copy — also known as a hard copy — of an Office document, spreadsheet, or presentation. When a printed version is not needed, a digital copy will save paper and costs. Office provides many ways to share your document. You can use traditional ways of sharing by printing or exporting a PDF. From the Share link in Office, you can invite other people to share the document, and you can specify whether others are allowed to edit the document if the file is saved to OneDrive. From Office Backstage, the document can be e-mailed to others, transformed into an online, browser-not-required presentation, or posted to a blog.

New in Office 2016, you can share your file without leaving your file. In the top right corner, next to your account image, click Share. This will open the Share task pane. From there, you can add a person, choose whether he or she can edit or just view the file, and even give a personal message. In addition, new with Office 2016, you and those you share with can all be editing the document in real time. You will be able to see the changes being made to the document while you are also making changes. To do this, you must have the file saved in your OneDrive and be logged into your Microsoft account.

Changing Views

In each of the Office applications, there are different ways to view the file. For example, in Word, you can view in Read Mode, as a Web Layout, Outline, or Draft. In Excel, it is particularly important to change your view to Page Break Preview before attempting to print a file. This view shows you where the page breaks will happen and, if needed, allows you to modify them. Also, Page Layout view will allow you to view any headers and footers before printing. In this exercise, you will change to Page Break Preview and the Page Layout view to ensure that everything will fit on one page.

CF01.23

SIDE NOTE

Adjusting Page Breaks

From Page Break Preview you can click and drag to adjust page break lines.

To Change Views to Preview How a File Will Print

a. Click the **View** tab, and then, in the Workbook Views group, click **Page Break Preview**. Excel Zooms to 60% and shows each page with blue lines. The budget will fit on one page, and no adjustments are needed.

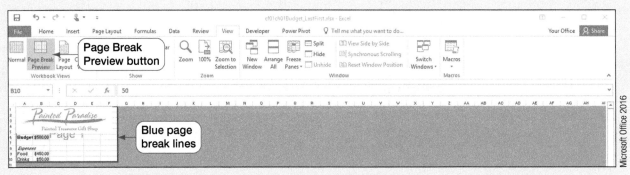

Figure 32 Page Break Preview

b. On the View tab, in the Workbook Views group, click **Page Layout**. Scroll down and verify that the footer you created in a prior exercise looks correct.

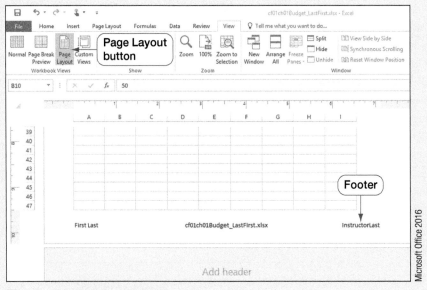

Figure 33 Page Layout view

114   CHAPTER 1 | Common Features of Microsoft Office 2016

c. On the View tab, in the Workbook Views group, click **Normal** to return to the normal Excel view. Press Ctrl + Home to make cell A1 the active cell.

d. **Save** 🖫 the spreadsheet.

Printing a File

Before printing, carefully consider whether a paper copy is necessary. Even in the digital world, paper copies of documents make more sense in many situations. Always review and preview the file and adjust the print settings before sending the document to the printer as you did in the prior exercise. Many options are available to fit various printing needs, such as the number of copies to print, the printing device to use, and the portion of the file to print. The print settings vary slightly from program to program. Printers also have varied capabilities; thus, the same file may look different from one computer to the next, depending on the printer that is connected to it. Doing a simple print preview will help to avoid having to reprint your document, workbook, or presentation, which requires additional paper, ink, and energy resources.

In this exercise, you will print the budget on which notes can be handwritten during the meeting so that you can update the spreadsheet with more detail later.

CF01.24

To Print a File

a. In Excel, click the **File** tab to open Office Backstage.

b. Click **Print**. The Print settings and Print Preview appear. Verify that the Copies box displays **1**.

c. Verify that the correct printer — as directed by your instructor — appears in the Printer box. Choices may vary depending on the computer you are using. If the correct printer is not displayed, click the Printer arrow, and then click to choose the correct or preferred printer from the list of available printers.

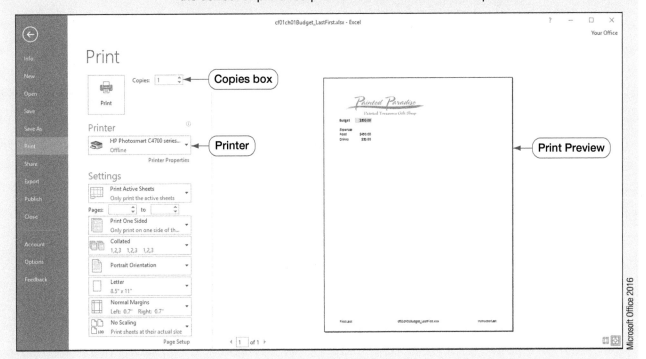

Figure 34   Backstage Print

d. If your instructor asks you to print the document, click **Print**.

Exporting a PDF

When you want to give someone else a document, consider whether an electronic version of the file is better than a printed copy. **A portable document format (PDF)** file is a type of file that ensures that the document will look the same on someone else's computer. For example, different computers may have different fonts installed. A PDF maintains the fonts used in the original document. Even if the computer on which the file is being viewed does not have the same fonts as the computer that was used to create the file, the viewer will see the correct font. PDFs are a common file format used in business to share documents because of the readily available free readers. In Word, you can edit a PDF. Also, in Windows 10, the default PDF reader is now the new Edge browser. You can still install the Adobe reader program and set it as the default if you prefer.

In this exercise, you will export a PDF of the budget file so you can e-mail a copy to your colleagues who are also attending the meeting.

To Create a PDF File

a. If you are not already in Office Backstage, click the **File** tab. Click **Export**, and then click **Create PDF/XPS**.

b. Navigate to the location where your student files are stored. Verify that the file name selected is **cf01ch01Budget_LastFirst.pdf**. Notice settings in the Publish as PDF or XPS dialog box for optimizing for publishing online versus printing. Since your colleague will print this document, the default setting of Standard is appropriate.

c. Click **Publish**. Close the **PDF** file. If the PDF opens in the default reader — in the Windows 10 Edge browser — then close the reader.

d. **Save** 🖫 the spreadsheet and click **Close** ⊠ to close this file and exit Excel. Submit your files as directed by your instructor.

 CONSIDER THIS | **Sending or Sharing Files Electronically**

Sending an electronic file can be easier and cheaper than sending a printed copy to someone. Sharing a file also saves on e-mail quotas. What should you consider when deciding the type of file to send? When you send an application-specific file, such as a Word or Excel file, what happens if the recipient does not have the relevant Office application installed? When you send a PDF, how easy is it for a recipient to edit a document? How does the file type affect the quality of a recipient's printout?

Insert Office Add-ins

To enhance the features of Office, you can install **Add-ins for Office** from Microsoft's Office Store. These Add-ins run in the side pane to provide extra features such as web search, dictionary, and maps. There are different Add-ins for the different Office programs. You must be signed into Office with your Microsoft account to take advantage of them.

QUICK REFERENCE	Installing Add-ins for Office

1. Open up any Office application in which you want to use apps.

2. Go to the Insert tab, and then select My Add-ins arrow. Select See All from the menu.

3. The Office Add-ins window appears, showing all the apps you have installed to your Microsoft account under My Apps. If you see the app you want, select the app, and then click Insert.

4. If you do not see the app you want, click Store link or Office Store button.

5. Search for the Add-in you want, and then follow the steps online to install the Add-in to your account. You may have to sign into your Microsoft account.

6. Once the Add-in has been installed, return to the Office application and repeat steps 2 and 3.

Concept Check

1. What kind of Microsoft program do you need to create a budget? p. 76

2. What are the advantages of using OneDrive instead of a USB flash drive? p. 84

3. What is the difference between Save and Save As? p. 82

4. How do you pin open the ribbon? Explain what can be done in Office Backstage. p. 80–82

5. Explain a way to copy and paste. What advantages are there to knowing keyboard shortcuts? p. 90

6. What is the Tell me what you want to do feature and how is it different from Help? p. 101

7. Describe three different ways of making text bold. p. 109

8. What is a contextual tab? p. 107

9. Describe ways to obtain help in Office 2016. p. 111

10. How could you share a newsletter with all the members of your business fraternity without printing the document? p. 113, 116

11. What are the Add-ins for Office? p. 117

Key Terms

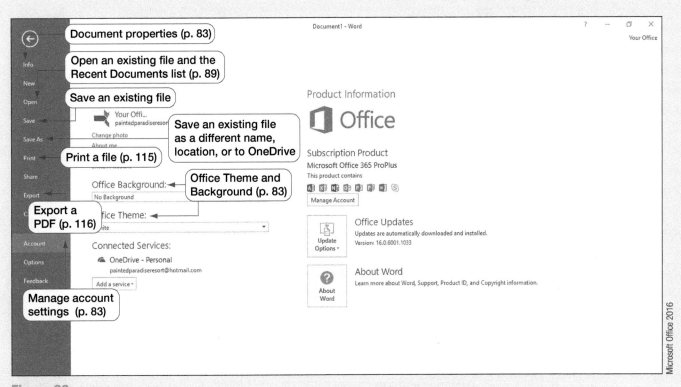

Go to Office backstage (p. 83)

Use the Tell me what you to do box (p. 102)

Change how the ribbon displays

Undo and redo actions (p. 96)

Touch and Mouse Mode (p. 80)

Find and replace (p. 98)

Using the Font group and the Font dialog box launcher (p. 99)

Show formatting symbols (p. 95)

Close a file and exit an application (p. 88)

Use the Style gallery and Live Preview (p. 100)

Check spelling and use buttons (p. 94)

Paragraph symbol (p. 95)

Zoom

Microsoft Office 2016

Figure 35

Document properties (p. 83)

Open an existing file and the Recent Documents list (p. 89)

Save an existing file

Save an existing file as a different name, location, or to OneDrive

Print a file (p. 115)

Office Theme and Background (p. 83)

Export a PDF (p. 116)

Manage account settings (p. 83)

Microsoft Office 2016

Figure 36

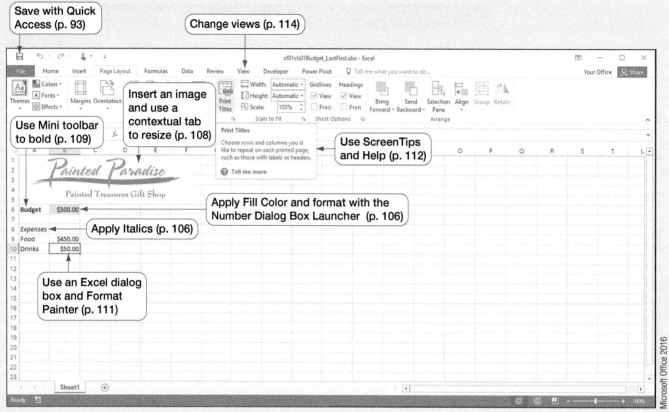

Save with Quick Access (p. 93)

Change views (p. 114)

Insert an image and use a contextual tab to resize (p. 108)

Use Mini toolbar to bold (p. 109)

Use ScreenTips and Help (p. 112)

Apply Fill Color and format with the Number Dialog Box Launcher (p. 106)

Apply Italics (p. 106)

Use an Excel dialog box and Format Painter (p. 111)

Figure 37

Microsoft Office 2016

Practice 1

Student data file needed:
 Blank Word document

You will save your file as:
 cf01ch01TrainingAgenda_LastFirst.docx

Creating an Agenda

Human Resources

Susan Brock, the manager of the gift shop, needs to write an agenda for the upcoming training session she will be holding. You will assist her by creating the agenda.

a. On the taskbar, click Ask Me Anything or Search the web and Windows. Type Word. Click on **Word 2016** in the search results. The Word Start screen is displayed when Word is launched.

b. Click **Blank document**.

c. Click the **File** tab, click **Save As**, and then double-click **This PC**. In the Save As dialog box, navigate to the location where you are saving your project files, and then change the file name to cf01ch01TrainingAgenda_LastFirst, using your last and first name. Click **Save**. If necessary, on the Home tab, in the Paragraph group, click Show/Hide to show nonprinting characters.

d. Press Ctrl + Home to ensure that the insertion point is at the beginning of the document. On the Home tab, in the Font group, click **Bold**.

e. Type Training Agenda, and then press Enter.

f. Click **Bold** to toggle the feature off.

g. Position the insertion point to the left of the word **Training**, press and hold the left mouse button, drag the insertion point across the text to the end of the word **Agenda**, and then release the mouse button. All the text in the line should be highlighted.

h. On the Home tab, in the Font group, click the **Font Size** arrow. Select **20** to make the font size larger.

i. In the Paragraph group, click **Center** ≣. In the Font group, click the **arrow** next to Font Color ⌐A⌐ and select **Blue**.

j. Click the second line, type **today's date**, and then press ⌐Enter⌐ twice.

k. In the Paragraph group, click the **Bullets** arrow. Under the Bullet Library, click the **circle** bullet.

l. Type Welcome trainees 2:00 pm, and then press ⌐Enter⌐.

m. Type Using the Register, and then press ⌐Enter⌐.

n. Type Customer Service Policies, and then press ⌐Enter⌐.

o. Type Wrap-Up, and then press ⌐Enter⌐ twice to turn off bullets.

p. Type Questions?. On the Home tab, in the Styles group, click **Heading 2**.

q. **Save** 🖫 the document.

r. Click the **Insert** tab, and then, in the Header & Footer group, click the **Footer** arrow, and then select the first option **Blank**.

s. On the Header & Footer Tools Design tab, in the Insert group, click **Document Info**, and then click **File Name**.

t. On the Header & Footer Tools Design tab, in the Close group, click **Close Header and Footer** to exit the footer.

u. **Save** 🖫 the document, exit Word, and then submit your file as directed by your instructor.

Problem Solve 1

Homework

Student data files needed:

🗋 cf01ch01Letter.docx

🗋 cf01ch01Cookies.jpg

You will save your file as:

🗋 cf01ch01Letter_LastFirst.docx

Midnight Sweetness Loan Letter

Finance & Accounting

Recently, you opened a business with a few partners called Midnight Sweetness. With the slogan "No more starving late-night studies," the business specializes in delivering freshly baked cookies, brownies, and other sweet treats to local college students. Midnight Sweetness has been a huge success. Currently, you rent a small building that includes major kitchen appliances. Now you and your partners are looking for a bank loan to expand your business. As part of your presentation to the bank, you must write a cover letter highlighting some parts of your business. The letter is written, but now you will add formatting to make it easier to read.

a. Open the cf01ch1Letter document. Save your file as cf01ch01Letter_LastFirst, using your last and first name. Click Enable Editing if necessary. If necessary, show nonprinting characters.

b. Place the insertion point before the **M** in Midnight Sweetness. Insert the cf01ch01Cookies image.

c. Resize the image to be **1"** in height.

d. Format the company name, Midnight Sweetness, to **bold**, **Dark Red** font color, font size **36**, and font of **Georgia**.

e. Find the two spelling errors with a red wavy line, and correct the **mistakes** in the text.

f. Midnight Sweetness has three offerings: Freshly baked cookies, Homemade brownies, and Other sweet treats. Change the three paragraphs listing the offerings to a **bulleted** list using regular bullets.

g. Midnight Sweetness is trying to achieve four things: a larger kitchen, more office space, additional baking equipment, and additional baking supplies. Change the four paragraphs of what the company is trying to achieve to a **numbered** list with **Number alignment: Left** style that uses the number without the parenthesis.

h. Select the second and third lines of the document containing the address. Cut the address to the clipboard.

i. Insert a **blank** footer. Paste the **two address lines** to the footer. Verify that the footer does not have any blank paragraphs — only the two address lines. Verify that there is only one blank paragraph between the company name and the line that reads "Dear Mr. Garth."

j. In the footer, change the font color of both lines of the address to **Dark Red**, and **Center** the text.

k. In the blank line between the company name and "Dear Mr. Garth," type the **current date**.

l. After the letter closing, on the paragraph below "Sincerely," type First Last, using your first and last name. Erase any blank paragraphs below your name.

m. Apply the style **Emphasis** to your name, change the font size to **14**, and change the font color to **Dark Red**. Press Ctrl + Home to place the insertion point at the beginning.

n. Save the document, exit Word, and then submit your file as directed by your instructor.

Critical Thinking

These directions told you how to format the letter. Do you have any suggestions for improvements or anything that might be problematic? Do you think the letter looks professional? Is the content of the language in the letter professional and appropriate? You may suggest changes that you have not learned how to make yet. Answer as directed by your instructor.

Perform 1: Perform in Your Career

Student data files needed:
📄 cf01ch01Herb.xlsx
📄 cf01ch01Herb.docx

You will save your files as:
📄 cf01ch01Herb_LastFirst.xlsx
📄 cf01ch01Herb_LastFirst.docx

Harry's Herbs

General Business

You are interning for a local nursery. One of the employees, Harry, specializes in herbs. Every year, he does an herb sale as a fundraiser for the local homeless shelter. Another intern began to create these files — but is unexpectedly unavailable to finish them. Your supervisor has asked you to help get ready for the event by preparing documents associated with the schedule.

a. Open the Excel file **cf01ch01Herb**. Save your file as cf01ch01Herb_LastFirst, using your last and first name.

b. Change the **font, fill color**, and **font color** of the merged cell A1:D1, and make the font size **16 or larger**. Choose professional colors.

c. Format the merged cell from A2:D2 to be **bold**.

d. Format cells A3:A5 as **italic**.

e. Format cell **A6** so that it matches or complements the coloring you applied to the merged cell A1:D1, and make the font size **larger**.

f. Paint the format from cell A6 to **A13**, **A19**, **A24**, and **A28**.

g. Change the text in cell **D7** to **Details**, and make D7 **bold**. Then copy and paste to put the same label in cells **D14**, **D20**, **D25**, and **D29**.

h. Apply bold to all of the cells with one of these three labels **Master Gardener Advice and Classes**, **Daily** and **Hourly**.

i. Add any other formatting that will make this spreadsheet look more professional or have more clarity. Do not change any more of the content or move cells.

j. Add a custom footer that contains **First Last**, using your first and last name, in the Left section and the **File Name** in the Right section. Do not worry if the file will not print on a single page.

k. **Save** the spreadsheet, exit Excel, and then submit your file as directed by your instructor.

l. Open the Word file **cf01ch01Herb.docx**. Save your file as cf01ch01Herb_LastFirst.docx, using your last and first name.

m. Correct all spelling mistakes.

n. Before the word Schedule in the title, add the word **Tuesday**.

o. Add **am** and **pm** to the times appropriately — Tuesdays overall hours are 10:00 am to 8:00 pm.

p. Change the **font colors**, **background colors**, **font sizes**, and **styles** to make the schedule easier to read and understand. Match the colors you used in cf01ch1Herb_LastFirst.xlsx.

q. Add a custom footer with **First Last**, using your first and last name.

r. **Save** the document, and close Word. Submit your work to your instructor as directed.

Perform 2: Perform in Your Life

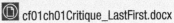

Student data files needed:

 Blank Word document

cf01ch01Vintage.docx

cf01ch01Dinner.xlsx

You will save your file as:

cf01ch01Critique_LastFirst.docx

Improving the Appearance of Files

Your boss at a local vintage clothing store has asked you to review a spreadsheet and a document — made by a prior employee — and make suggestions on what to do to improve the appearance of the document and spreadsheet. Examine the two files cf01ch01Vintage and cf01ch01Dinner. Then do the following.

Human Resources   Finance & Accounting

a. Open a new blank document in Word, and then save the file as cf01ch01Critique_LastFirst, using your last and first name.

b. List five items that you would change in the document and why.

c. List five items that you would change in the spreadsheet and why.

d. Add a footer with First Last, using your first and last name, and the file name.

e. Exit Word, and then submit your file as directed by your instructor.

Additional Chapter Cases are available at www.pearsonhighered.com/youroffice

Additional Cases

Word Business Unit 1

Understanding Business Documents

Word processing is one of the most common tasks in computing. Understanding how to create, edit, and format word-processing documents is an essential business skill. Whether the goal of the document is to create a resume or to communicate with colleagues, Word can greatly enhance the development of a document. This business unit will focus on developing essential skills such as formatting text, using templates to facilitate development, and designing the layout of a document.

Learning Outcome 1

Understand the basics of word-processing software to develop effective, professional business documents.

REAL WORLD SUCCESS

"During my job search, I was having a difficult time getting called in for an interview. I realized that with so many applicants out there, having a resume that stands out is an exceedingly important aspect of getting to the next step. Fortunately, I was able to take advantage of Word's formatting capability to make my resume look much more professional and help me land the interviews I had been striving for."

- Chris, recent graduate

Learning Outcome 2

Use a blank document or template to create, edit, and format letters, memos, flyers, and other business communication.

REAL WORLD SUCCESS

"I work as a systems technician at an IT company. I am in charge of creating the agendas and writing the minutes for our weekly group meetings. Using Word's built-in templates has saved me a considerable amount of time. I download the template, edit the fields, make my changes, and I'm done. I am able to produce a professional-looking document in a very short amount of time."

- Nikil, recent graduate

Microsoft Word 2016

Prepare Case

MyITLab®
Grader
Homework

Customer
Service

Sales &
Marketing

Putts for Paws Golf Tournament Memo

Painted Paradise Resort & Spa sponsors an annual charity golf tournament, with proceeds benefiting a different organization each year. This year, the tournament is spotlighting the Santa Fe Animal Center. The goal is to raise money for the center as well as to facilitate the adoption of as many animals as possible to loving homes. Your assignment is to review and edit a memorandum to the employees of the hotel's event-planning staff. The memo provides a summary of tournament activities and sponsorship opportunities so the staff can answer questions and encourage participation.

Tania Thomson/Shutterstock

Student data files needed for this chapter:

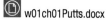 w01ch01Putts.docx

w01ch01PuttsPDF.pdf

You will save your files as:

 w01ch01Putts_LastFirst.docx

w01ch01Putts_LastFirst.pdf

 w01ch01PuttsPDF_LastFirst.pdf

Understanding Business Communication

Communication, both verbal and written, is a regular part of daily life. When you converse with others, you want your listeners to understand your meaning and to become engaged in the topic. It is important that written communication both reflect your objectives and convey your messages exactly as you intend. Excellent communication skills are crucial in the success of a business — so much so that American businesses spend $3.1 billion annually training people to communicate effectively.

Business communication is defined as communication between members of an organization for the purpose of carrying out business activities. Always remember that the way you communicate verbally and in writing is often the first and most lasting impression that others have of you. In fact, communication skills are often the factor that sets you apart from others in a company. The importance of these skills cannot be overstated. Often referred to as a *soft skill*, excellent written and oral communication abilities can identify you as one of the most valued employees in a business.

Communication is not a one-way street. It is not a monologue; it is a dialogue. If your audience does not interpret your message exactly as you intended, the communication has failed. Students often spend an inordinate amount of time developing technical skills in software and business operations, but they give too little credence to the importance of understanding the target audience and communicating on a level at which both the sender and the receiver can understand each other. Regardless of the message topic, always take time to identify and understand your audience. In this section, you will explore the topic of business communication, identifying standard business letter styles, standard memo styles, and effective methods of communication.

Use Word-Processing Software

Word processing is often cited as one of the main reasons to use a computer. People in businesses, schools, and homes use word-processing software daily to create, edit, and print documents. It is used to create reports, letters, memos, newsletters, flyers, business cards, and many other documents. Within documents, you can format text, adjust margins, insert graphics, organize data into tables, create charts, and easily make revisions. Clearly, word-processing software is a versatile tool that can enable you to efficiently create effective documents for written communication.

Although you can select from several word-processing software packages with a wide range of capabilities and cost, Microsoft Word is the leading word-processing program in terms of usage and sales. This textbook provides information on **Microsoft Word 2016**, Microsoft's most current version of its word-processing software.

Opening a File

When you open Microsoft Word 2016, the **Word Start screen** is displayed so that you can easily begin to work with new or existing files. A list of recent documents is displayed in the left pane along with an option to open other documents from OneDrive, your hard drive, or other web locations. The right pane enables you to select a new blank document or choose from a variety of templates.

You are ready to begin work on your memorandum. In this exercise, you will start Word 2016, open the memorandum file, and save it with a new name.

W01.00

To Open a Document

a. On the taskbar, click **Ask Me Anything** or **Search the Web and Windows**. Type Word.

b. Click on **Word 2016** in the search results. The Word Start screen is displayed when Word is launched.

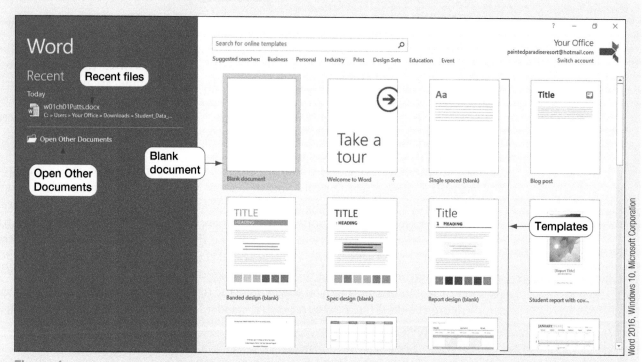

Figure 1   Word Start screen interface

Word 2016, Windows 10, Microsoft Corporation

SIDE NOTE
Windows 10
This book is written for Windows 10. If you are using Windows 8, open your charms, click Search, and then type Word. If you are using Windows 7, search the Start menu for Word.

c. Click **Open Other Documents** in the left pane, and then click **This PC**. Navigate through the folder structure to the location of your student data files, and then double-click **w01ch01Putts**. A memorandum providing information on the upcoming Putts for Paws golf tournament opens.

Read through the memorandum, noting the various elements of a memo, such as the header and body. You will address the grammatical and typographical errors later in this chapter.

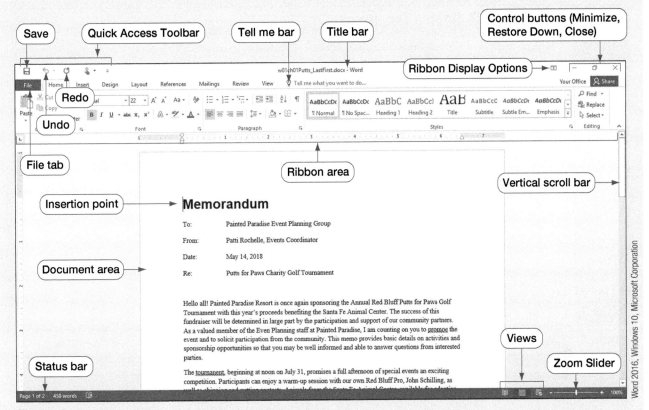

Figure 2 Word interface

SIDE NOTE

Save on the Quick Access Toolbar

Click Save 🖫 on the Quick Access Toolbar to quickly save your file with the same name to the same location.

d. On the File tab, click **Save As**.

The File tab includes both Save and Save As options. As you learned in the Common Features chapter, the Save command behaves the same as the Save As command the first time you save a new file — both commands will ask you to specify a location and name for the file. The next time you save the file, you can simply click the File tab and click Save, saving the file in the same location with the same file name.

e. Click **This PC**. Navigate to the location where you are saving your files.

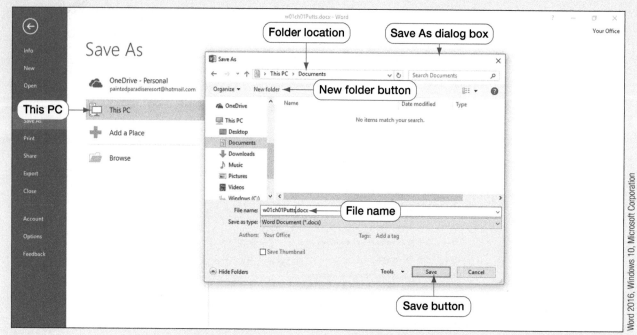

Figure 3   Save As dialog box

f. Click in the **File name** box, and then change the file name to w01ch01Putts_LastFirst, using your last and first name.

g. Click **Save**. If you need to take a break before finishing this chapter, now is a good time.

> **Troubleshooting**
>
> If the Your document will be upgraded to the newest file format message appears, click OK. If you do not want to see this warning again, click the Do not ask me again check box before clicking OK. This occurs the first time you use Save As to save a file that was originally created in a previous version of Word.

REAL WORLD ADVICE   **Minimize Distractions**

Word gives you the ability to open multiple documents at the same time. Each opened document is shown as an overlapped Word icon on the Windows taskbar. Unless you have a specific need to have several documents open, perhaps because you need to copy text from one to another, it is best to keep the number of open documents to a minimum. This will enable you to focus on your current project.

Develop Effective Business Documents

When you talk with others, you get immediate feedback in the form of body language and conversation. Usually, you have an accurate feel for how your message is received, and you are able to elicit responses from your target audience. However, once a word has been spoken, it cannot be retracted. You can give much more forethought to the selection of words to be included in written communication. In the absence of body language, however, it can be difficult for a reader to understand your tone. By carefully considering your objectives and your audience, you can craft a well-worded document that achieves your purpose.

QUICK REFERENCE | Developing Effective Business D

A document containing grammatical errors, misspellings, informal wording, or inaccurate facts might lead others to consider you careless or not credible. Think through the following when creating business documents:

1. Consider your objectives and your audience.

2. Keep your communication concise and clear.

3. Review a document several times for grammar, punctuation, spelling, and proper wording.

4. If possible, have a trusted colleague provide feedback before you send a letter or memo.

5. Humor is difficult to convey in written communication — try to avoid it.

6. Avoid the use of uppercase letters, which can mislead a reader and convey an unintended message.

7. Use active voice rather than passive voice when possible.

8. Never air your frustration or anger in written communication.

S$_S$ REAL WORLD ADVICE | Preparing Business Correspondence

Before writing any document, allow ample time for planning. Ask yourself these questions first: Who is my target audience? Do I understand the audience and what they are looking for in my communication? What is the purpose of my document? How can I build support for my message? What information do I need to include? Answering these questions will enable you to effectively communicate your message.

Work with Business Correspondence

Business documents include many forms of written communication. Some are considered internal communication, while others are external communication. Examples of written internal communication are memos, in-house newsletters, and email. Effective internal communication can create a better work atmosphere and increase productivity, as employees are more likely to understand and support the goals and objectives of the company. Effective external communication through letters, brochures, reports, and newsletters can promote a healthy corporate image and serve to attract and retain customers.

At this point, you should understand the importance of planning a document and understanding your target audience. This section of the chapter focuses on the technical aspects of letters and memos — how to structure a letter and memo and exactly what elements to include.

REAL WORLD ADVICE | Document Formats

Although you may be familiar with generally accepted styles for letters, memos, and even emails, always check with your place of employment when creating business documents. Some businesses require employees to adhere to a specific format. For example, a company might require that the company logo be included in all correspondence or that a specific letterhead be used. Painted Paradise Resort & Spa has a style guide that will be used to format the documents used in this chapter. There may be rules about the use of headings, enclosures, or attachments. Become familiar with the specifics related to your workplace.

Working with Memos and Business Letters

The main difference between a memo and a letter is the target audience. Much less prescriptive than a letter, a memo is intended for internal distribution. The typical audience for a memo is your coworkers and colleagues. A memo generally includes the word "Memo" or "Memorandum" followed by a heading area, the body of the memo, and end notations if necessary (see Figure 4).

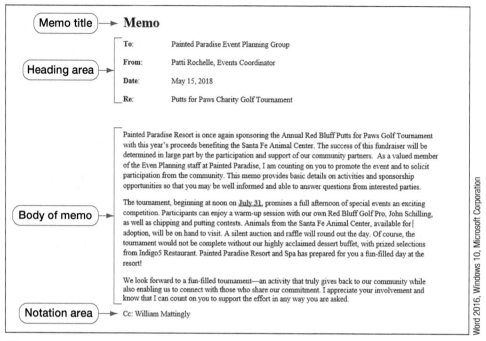

Figure 4   Memo style

Business letters are generally intended for external distribution between two businesses or between a business and one or more clients. For this reason, business letters tend to be more formal and longer than memos. The three accepted letter styles are shown in Table 1 and Figure 5.

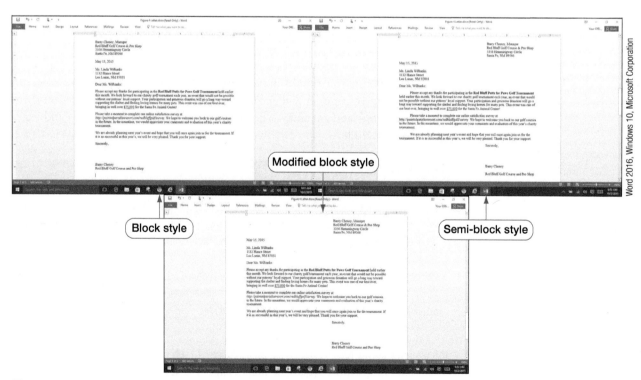

Figure 5   Letter styles

Letter Style	Description
Block	The entire letter is left-aligned and single-spaced except for double spacing between paragraphs
Modified block	The body of the letter is left-aligned and single-spaced except for double spacing between paragraphs; the date and closing are left-aligned slightly to the right of center
Semi-block	Identical to modified block style except that each body paragraph is indented 1/2 inch

Table 1 Letter styles

 CONSIDER THIS | **Be Careful with Written Words**

Experts have suggested that email messages are like postcards in that they can be read by anyone who is involved in their delivery or happens to see them. Letters, memos, and any other form of written communication are not much more private. With that in mind, do you have any suggestions for composing written communication so as to maintain as much privacy as possible?

QUICK REFERENCE | **Business Letter Components**

Some business letter components are required and some are optional, as you will see in the following description. Refer to Figure 6 for a visual summary of letter components.

1. **Heading** — Includes the writer's address and the date of the letter; if you are using letterhead, you may not need to include an address.

2. **Inside address** — Shows the name and address of the recipient of the letter.

3. **Salutation** — Directly addresses the recipient by title and last name; follow the salutation with a colon, as in "Dear Mr. Durham:".

4. **Reference** — or **subject line** — May replace the salutation if you are not sure who will be receiving the letter; may also be used in addition to a salutation.

5. **Body** — The message area.

6. **Complimentary close** — The letter ending, always followed by a comma; usually in the form of "Sincerely yours," although other possibilities include "Respectfully," "Respectfully yours," and "Sincerely."

7. **Signature block** — Most often two to four blank lines after the complimentary close, followed by your typed name and, whenever possible, your position. The blank space is for your written signature.

8. **End notations** — One or more abbreviations or phrases that have important functions. They include initials (capital letters for the writer and lowercase letters beneath for the typist), enclosures (usually abbreviated "Enc" or "Encl" and followed by a very brief summary of the enclosure), and copies (an indication of any other recipients of the letter, such as "Cc: Ms. Jane Clemmons").

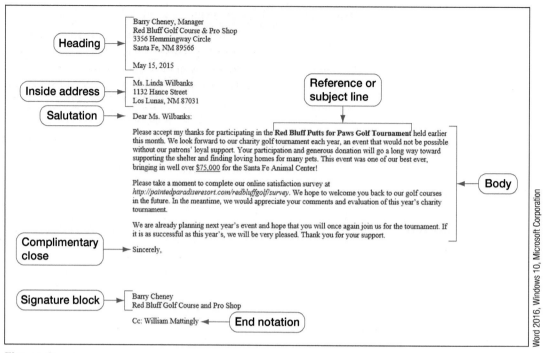

Figure 6 Components of a letter

Editing a Document

Word-processing software such as Word 2016 can facilitate the creation of your business communication. Word enables you to easily revise or update your text to effectively reach your audience. For example, as you look back over a project, you might want to change wording, add emphasis effects — such as italics and boldfacing — or adjust line spacing. This section begins with an overview of the Word interface and then discusses character formatting and paragraph formatting. In addition, you will learn to use Word's proofreading tools to help you find and correct errors.

REAL WORLD ADVICE **Saving Time with KeyTips**

KeyTips enable you to access ribbon commands without ever taking your hands off the keyboard. Press [Alt] on the keyboard to display KeyTips for each Ribbon tab or Quick Access Toolbar command, as shown in Figure 7, and then press a corresponding key to select a ribbon item. Additional key tips will be displayed if necessary. Pressing [Alt] a second time or pressing [Esc] will remove the KeyTips. When you use KeyTips, most ribbon commands can be accessed by pressing only three keys.

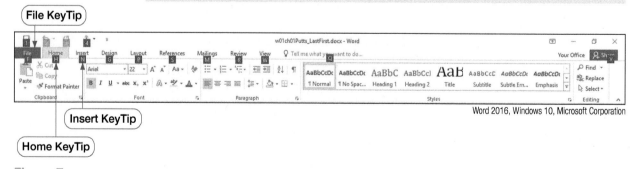

Figure 7 KeyTips

Explore the Word Interface

You were previously introduced to several of elements of the Word interface, such as the Quick Access Toolbar, the ribbon, and the status bar, in the Common Features chapter.

View	Description of View
Print Layout	Shows all margins, headers, footers, graphics, and other features that will be displayed when a document is printed; provides a close approximation to the way a document will look when printed
Web Layout	Shows how a document will appear in a web browser
Outline view	Shows the structure of a document in a hierarchical fashion; expands or collapses details to show only what is necessary
Draft view	Includes the ribbon but does not show margins, headers, footers, columns, tables, or other graphical objects; used to edit and format in a text-only environment
Read Mode	Provides an interactive screen-reading experience; lets you define your column width, page color, and preferred layout; lets you zoom in and out of graphical objects, translate words, and search on Bing; user interface is minimized to avoid reading distractions

Table 2 Document views

With only slight differences, these items serve a similar purpose in each of the Office applications: Access, Excel, PowerPoint, and Word.

The Word interface is unique in comparison to other Office applications because of its large document area in which you can type. As you type, your text automatically wraps from one line to the next. **Word wrap**, the feature that enables you to continue typing without pressing Enter, places a **soft return** at the end of each line. The placement of a soft return automatically changes when you change the length of the line by modifying the margins or simply by adding or deleting words.

When you press Enter, Word inserts a **hard return**. The placement of a hard return does not change when text is reformatted. Only the user can change the placement of a hard return. Hard returns are commonly used at the end of a paragraph or a distinct line, such as a date or salutation (see Figure 8).

Changing the View

Word provides a number of ways to view your document. Each view serves a different purpose, displaying its own features and elements, as shown in Table 2. The default view in Word 2016 is Print Layout. A **default** setting is one that is automatically in place until you specify otherwise.

Word 2016 also uses the Ribbon Display Options ⊞ found on the title bar, to the left of the window control buttons. These options enable you to configure the ribbon interface regardless of the current view. You can auto-hide the ribbon, show ribbon tabs only, or show the full ribbon with both tabs and commands, which is the default.

Showing Nonprinting Characters

Many keys, such as Spacebar, Enter, and Tab, insert **nonprinting characters** in a document. For example, when you press Tab, text is indented and a tab "character" is inserted. Sometimes called **formatting marks**, nonprinting characters are not displayed on the screen by default. These formatting marks are not shown when the document is printed, even when they are displayed on the screen. Figure 8 shows a document with nonprinting characters displayed.

As you continue working with the memorandum, you realize that choosing to show or hide nonprinting characters is ultimately a matter of preference. Many experienced Word users find that displaying nonprinting characters is helpful in trying to fix formatting errors caused by hard returns, tabs, spaces, or page breaks. In this exercise, you will experiment with different views of the memo and work with nonprinting characters.

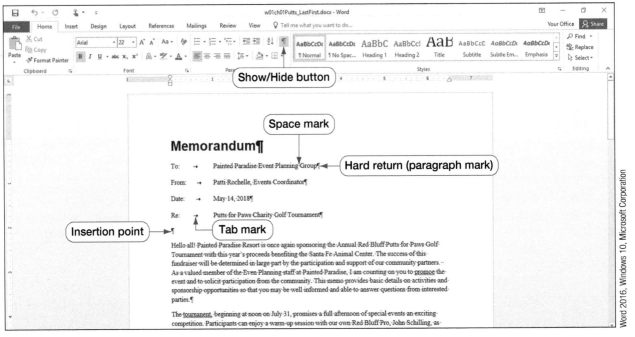

Figure 8　Nonprinting characters displayed

Word 2016, Windows 10, Microsoft Corporation

To Change the View and Show Nonprinting Characters

a. If you took a break, open the **w01ch01Putts** document. Click the **View** tab, and then, in the Views group, click **Read Mode**.

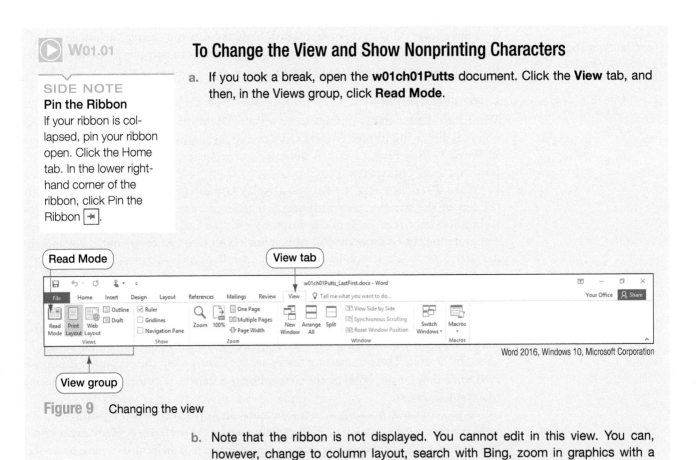

Figure 9　Changing the view

Word 2016, Windows 10, Microsoft Corporation

b. Note that the ribbon is not displayed. You cannot edit in this view. You can, however, change to column layout, search with Bing, zoom in graphics with a double-click, find text, and use your arrow keys to scroll. Press → to move to the next page. Press ← to return to the first page.

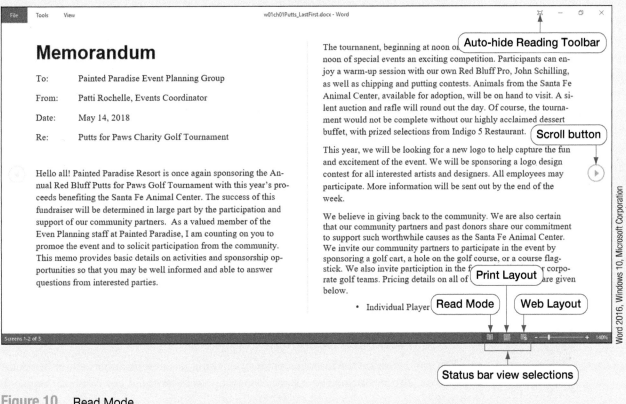

Figure 10 Read Mode

Word 2016, Windows 10, Microsoft Corporation

SIDE NOTE
What Is a Toggle?
A button that switches
between an on and
off state each time it
is clicked is called a
toggle.

c. Click **Print Layout** 🔲 on the status bar to return to Print Layout.
   Print Layout, along with Read Mode and Web Layout, is available on both the View
   tab and the right side of the status bar. The view options on the status bar are
   always available, regardless of which Ribbon tab is selected.

d. Click the **Home** tab, and then, if necessary, in the Paragraph group, click
   Show/Hide ¶ to show nonprinting characters (see Figure 8).

> **Troubleshooting**
> If nonprinting characters are already displayed, the display will be toggled off when
> you click Show/Hide. In that case, click Show/Hide once again to display them.

e. Click to place the insertion point before the paragraph mark ¶ that is displayed
   just beneath the **Re:** paragraph. Press Delete. The paragraph mark is deleted, and
   the text moves up.

f. Click **Save** 💾 on the Quick Access Toolbar to save the document.

Insert and Delete Text

You will often find it necessary to insert or delete text. Recall that an **insertion point** is
the blinking black bar that indicates the position where the next character will be placed
(see Figure 8). By default, text is inserted at the insertion point, within the existing text.
For example, you might notice that you left a word out of a sentence. In that case, click
where you want the new text to be placed and type. Text automatically shifts to make
room for the new entry.

Keys	Resulting Insertion Point	Keys	Resulting Insertion Point
PgUp	Up one page	Home	Beginning of the current line
PgDn	Down one page	End	End of the current line
←	Left one character	Ctrl+Home	Beginning of the document
→	Right one character	Ctrl+End	End of the document
↑	Up one line	Ctrl+→	Left one word
↓	Down one line	Ctrl+←	Right one word

Table 3   To reposition the insertion point

You can delete text in several ways. Press Backspace repeatedly to remove characters to the left of the insertion point. Press Delete to remove text to the right of the insertion point. You can also select text by dragging and then press Delete.

Be careful when deleting text. Deleted text can be retrieved only by retyping it or by clicking Undo on the Quick Access Toolbar — if you are quick enough! The Undo action works only if you invoke it fairly quickly after the unwanted deletion. It will undo the most recent action. Repeatedly clicking Undo will undo each action performed, one by one, in the reverse of the order in which they were performed.

Moving Around a Document

You can reposition the insertion point by clicking in a new location within the document. You can also reposition the insertion point by using keys and key combinations as shown in Table 3.

As you will notice when making your next set of changes to the memorandum, scrolling does not change the position of the insertion point; rather, it changes the section of the document that is currently in view. Even after you scroll to another location in a document, newly typed text will be inserted back at the position of the insertion point. To avoid this common error, always make a habit of noting the position of the insertion point before you begin to type. When text is inserted in the wrong location, click Undo on the Quick Access Toolbar. You will position the insertion point to insert and delete text in the memo.

 W01.02

SIDE NOTE
Deleting Characters
When you want to remove text or nonprinting characters, press Backspace to remove characters to the left of the insertion point, or press Delete to remove characters to the right.

To Move Around a Document and Change the Zoom Level

a. Press Ctrl+End to position the insertion point at the end of the document.

b. Press Ctrl+← to place the insertion point before the exclamation point. Continue pressing Ctrl+← until the insertion point is before the word **effort** on the last line. Type the, and then press the Spacebar once.

c. Press Ctrl+Home to move the insertion point to the beginning of the document. The date is incorrect. It should be "May 15, 2018." Click to place the insertion point after the number **4** in the date. Press Backspace, and then type 5.

d. Click the **View** tab, and then, in the Zoom group, click **Zoom**. Click **200%**, and then click **OK**. Drag the vertical and horizontal scroll bars to view the document. Dragging the scroll bar changes the area of the document that is displayed, but it does not physically reposition the insertion point. Note that the insertion point remains in the same position as where you placed it in step c. You can move the insertion point only by clicking in another location in the document or by using a keyboard shortcut, several of which are described in Table 3.

e. On the status bar, drag the **Zoom Slider** to the left to reduce the size of the document to **100%**.

f. **Save** the document.

Viewing Backstage and Working with Word Options

As you learned in the Common Features chapter, Microsoft Office **Backstage view** is a collection of common actions and settings that apply to the current document. For example, the Print menu enables you to preview the document, set print options, and print. The Options menu enables you to customize Word according to your preference, such as customizing the ribbon, changing the default location where files are saved, or automatically displaying paragraph marks. In this exercise you will examine Backstage view.

QUICK REFERENCE	Backstage View

Backstage view is best defined as a collection of common actions, properties, and settings related to an open file. Following is a brief summary of the commands found in Backstage view:

1. Info — View and set document properties and security permissions, inspect your document for hidden content, and manage versions.
2. New — Open a new blank document or use a template to create a new document.
3. Open — Open an existing document.
4. Save — Save a file.
5. Save As — Save a file with a new name, location, or file type.
6. Print — Print an open document.
7. Share — Send an open document through email, publish it as a blog post, or save to OneDrive for others to view.
8. Export — Save an open document in a different format, including PDF or XPS.
9. Close — Close an open document.
10. Account — Gain access to product information and your Office account.
11. Options — Customize Word preferences.

W01.03

To Use Backstage View

a. Click the **File** tab to open Backstage view.

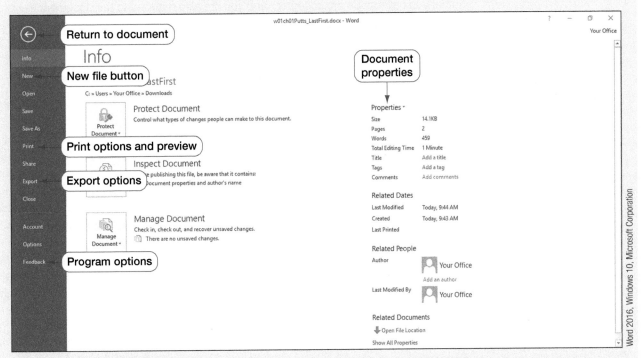

Figure 11 Backstage view

SIDE NOTE

Adding Document Properties

To add additional properties to your document, click Properties, select Advanced Properties, and then click the Summary tab to add document properties.

SIDE NOTE

Exit Backstage View

Alternatively, you can press [Esc] to return to your document from Backstage view.

b. Click **Print** to preview your document.

Selecting the Print option displays the document as it will appear when printed. It also enables you to select print options such as the number of copies to print, change the margins and page orientation, and select a printer. You will explore print settings later in the chapter.

c. Taking a moment to review some of the other Backstage commands. Click **New**, **Share**, and **Export**.

Notice the options available in each of these areas. You will explore Open, Save As, Print, and Options later in this chapter.

d. Click **Options**. The Word Options dialog box opens.

Note the categories on the left side, such as General, Display, and Proofing. Click a category to view related settings that you can confirm or change. Keep in mind that these changes are global, not local. For example, if you change the way Word corrects spelling errors, the change applies to the current document and to all future documents. In effect, you are modifying the Word installation, not just the current Word document. For that reason, you may not be allowed to change these options if you are working in a computer lab.

e. Ensure **General** is selected in the Word Options dialog box. General options enable you to change global settings, such as your user name and initials.

f. Click **Proofing** in the Word Options dialog box.

Word Options in the Proofing group change how spelling and grammatical errors are corrected.

g. Click **Customize Ribbon** in the Word Options dialog box.

You can select or deselect tabs that you want to include on the ribbon, and you can indicate commands to be included in groups. Click the Customize button to create your own keyboard shortcuts.

h. Click **Cancel**.

When you click Cancel, you return all settings to their previous state, even if you have made changes, and you are returned to the document. If you click OK, all changes that you have made are accepted, and you are also returned to the document.

Format Characters

Character formatting is used to change the physical appearance of your text. For example, you may want to make a word bold, underline a sentence, or apply a blue color to an entire paragraph. Many of these formats are available on the Home tab in the Font group. For example, to make a sentence bold, select the sentence, and then click Bold [B]. If you change your mind, select the same sentence, and then click Bold [B] to reverse the effect. Regardless of the change, however, always keep the purpose of the document in mind. While you might have fun experimenting with color and unique fonts in a newsletter, you will need to take a more conservative approach when editing a business document.

Selecting and Deleting Text

You must first select text before applying character formats. Selecting text is easy: Simply position the pointer before the text, press and hold the mouse button, drag to highlight the text, and then release the mouse button. To deselect text, simply click anywhere outside of the selection.

Using this method to select text, however, can present challenges when the area of selection is too small or too large. Imagine trying to select a 200-page document solely by dragging. Although this is possible, it would take some time and patience to drag through 200 pages. Similarly, it can be difficult to select a single word without including the surrounding spaces. Table 4 presents some keyboard shortcuts to selecting blocks of text. In this exercise, you will experiment with some of these shortcuts when making your next set of changes.

To Select	Do This
One word	Double-click the word
One sentence	Press and hold Ctrl while you click in the sentence
One paragraph	Triple-click the paragraph
Entire document	Press Ctrl + A
One line	Position the pointer in the left margin beside the line to select; when the pointer becomes a white arrow, click to select the line
One character to the left of the insertion point	Press Shift + →
One character to the right of the insertion point	Press Shift + ←
One block of text	Click where the selection is to begin, hold down Shift, and then click where the selection is to end
Two nonadjacent blocks of text	Select the first block of text, hold down Ctrl, and then select the second block of text

Table 4   Shortcuts to selection

 W01.04

To Edit a Document

a. The Painted Paradise Resort & Spa Style Guide requires the use of the word "Memo" not "Memorandum". Press Ctrl + Home. Move the pointer into the left margin, just to the left of the word **Memorandum**, to change the pointer to ⚐. Click to select the line of text. When you click in the left margin — the selection area — the entire line to the right of the pointer is selected. Type Memo. The word "Memorandum" will be replaced with "Memo".
Alternatively, you can double-click the word Memorandum to select it.

b. Triple-click in the **third paragraph** of the memo body — the paragraph beginning with **This year** — to select it. Press Delete to delete the paragraph.

Troubleshooting

If only one word is selected, you double-clicked instead of triple-clicked. Click anywhere to deselect the current selection, and then triple-click the paragraph once more.

c. In the first paragraph of the body of the memo, select the first sentence **Hello all!** making sure to include the space after the exclamation point. Scroll to the bottom of the document, press and hold Ctrl, and then select the last sentence, **Hope to see you there!** Do not select the paragraph mark. After both sentences are selected, release Ctrl, and then press Delete to delete both sentences simultaneously.
When you select a word, the space following the word is also selected. If necessary, use Shift + ← or Shift + → to select only the characters you desire.

    d. **Save** ⊟ the document.

Changing Font Type, Size, and Color

An essential feature of word processing is its ability to easily manipulate text — characters, words, sentences, and paragraphs. One such way is through the use of fonts. A **font** is a character design, including qualities such as typeface, size, and spacing. A typeface is a style of printed characters. Typeface, combined with character size and the amount of spacing between characters, makes up a font. You can choose to use the default font — Calibri, 11pt — which is the specified font when you begin a new document in Word 2016, or you can select from a number of additional fonts. With experience, you will develop font preferences and will understand that some font selections are better suited for certain document types than are others.

The Font group on the Home tab shows the current font and font size where the insertion point is located. When you click the Font arrow, a list of fonts is displayed, each font shown as a sample of the actual font. Theme fonts are shown first, followed by recently used fonts. The remaining fonts are listed in alphabetical order. The **Live Preview** feature enables you to preview the change to your selected text. Simply select the text and hover the mouse over any font selection. If you like the change, click the font to select it.

The two main categories of typefaces are serif and sans serif. A **serif font**, such as Times New Roman, has small, thin lines, or hooks, that end the main stroke of each letter. These lines are the serifs. Because a serif font is easy to read in large amounts of text, it is a good choice for printed material, such as reports and lengthy documents. Newspapers and books almost always use serif fonts for body text. Other serif fonts are Bodoni and Century Schoolbook.

The word "sans" means "without" in French. A **sans serif font**, then, is without the ending strokes that are typical of a serif font. The clean, simple lines of a sans serif font work well with titles, logos, and headings. Because the decorative strokes of serif fonts can often appear blurred on a computer screen, web developers prefer sans serif fonts for web page readability. Common sans serif fonts include Arial, Helvetica, Verdana, and Geneva. Figure 12 compares serif and sans serif fonts.

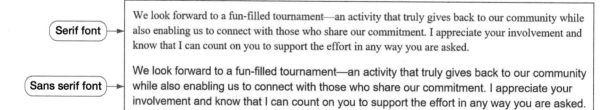

Figure 12   Sans serif and serif fonts   Word 2016, Windows 10, Microsoft Corporation

Another characteristic of a font is its spacing. A font's spacing is either **monospaced** or **proportional**. If you consider how you would print words, you can envision giving more space to some characters than to others. For example, printing the letter "w" typically requires more space than printing the letter "l." Giving more horizontal space to some letters and less to others is an example of proportional spacing. Alternatively, all the characters in a monospaced font, such as Courier New, take up the same amount of horizontal space. Monospaced text, sometimes referred to as fixed-width, is appropriate for tables and financial reports in which text must line up neatly in columns and rows. Figure 13 compares monospaced and proportional fonts.

```
This is an example of a monospaced font. Each character requires the
same amount of space.
```

This is an example of a proportional font. Each character requires only the space that is necessary for display. For example, the *m* requires more space than the letter *i*.

Word 2016, Windows 10, Microsoft Corporation

Figure 13   Monospaced and proportional fonts

Regardless of which font type you select, you can apply additional attributes, including reducing or increasing the font size and changing the color. All of these options are located in the Font group on the Home tab. Font size is measured in points (abbreviated *pt*), each point being equivalent to 1/72 of an inch. A typical font size for the body of a document is 11-pt or 12-pt. Report titles and headings typically use a larger font size. You can also change font color, apply highlighting, and add text effects. Text effects enable you to enhance text by adding a shadow, outline, reflection, or glow. Such effects can be very effective in certain documents as you draw attention to headers or text blocks.

Although you can quickly learn the mechanics of how to select a typeface, or font, you will want to develop skills in preparing business documents — selecting an appropriate font and text style for the project under development. As you progress through this business unit, you will be presented with tips for creating well-designed business documents. In this exercise, you will change the formatting of text in the memo.

REAL WORLD ADVICE | **Selecting an Appropriate Font for Business Correspondence**

If your documents do not conform to typical business standards, your boss will most likely notice. Do not risk your professional image to make a document look a little longer or shorter. A serif font at 11-pt or 12-pt size is a good choice for printed material such as letters, memos, and reports. The accepted standard is Times New Roman 12-pt. Avoid overly ornate or abnormal fonts, such as Comic Sans MS.

Longer documents, such as reports, will often use more than one font. Be consistent with your use of fonts in these cases. For example, use one font style for all headings, one font style for all captions, and one font style for the main body of the document.

Ss CONSIDER THIS | **Going Mobile**

In today's mobile world, correspondence is often displayed on a computer screen or mobile device. Do you think such mobile correspondence would be better received in a sans serif font, such as that used by web designers, or should you stay with a serif font that is more traditionally associated with business correspondence?

To Change Character Formatting

a   Press Ctrl+Home. Double-click the word **Memo** to select it.

b. Click the **Home** tab, in the Font group, click the **Font** arrow, and then select **Times New Roman**.

c. With Memo still selected, click the **Font Size** arrow, and then select **20**. Click anywhere in the document to deselect the text.

The heading is now consistent with the Painted Paradise Resort & Spa Style Guide, the standard for all business documents that are produced within the organization.

Word 2016, Windows 10, Microsoft Corporation

Figure 14   The Font group

d. Select **To** on the second line of the memo. Notice that the colon is not selected. Click **Bold** B on the Mini toolbar. Similarly, select and bold the words **From**, **Date**, and **Re**.

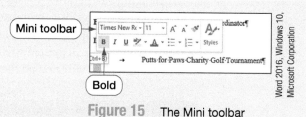

Word 2016, Windows 10, Microsoft Corporation

Figure 15   The Mini toolbar

Troubleshooting

If you do not see the Mini toolbar when the pointer is near the selection, right-click the selected text to reveal the Mini toolbar along with shortcut menu options. Once you click an option on the Mini toolbar, the shortcut menu disappears and the toolbar remains available for the selected text.

e. Select **July 31** in the second paragraph of the body of the memo.

f. On the Home tab, in the Font group, click the **Font Dialog Box Launcher** 🔲. Under Font style, select **Bold**. Click the **Underline style** arrow, and then select the **thick dark line selection** — under the double underline selection. Click the **Font color** arrow, and then, under Standard Colors, select **Dark Red** in the first column. Click **OK**. The date is now bold, dark red, with a thick underline.

Figure 16 Font dialog box

SIDE NOTE

Undo with Ctrl + Z

Alternatively, you can press Ctrl + Z to undo a change.

g. Click **Undo** on the Quick Access Toolbar to undo the bold, underline, and font color change.

When you click Undo once, it enables you to undo the most recent action. If the action that you want to reverse is not the most recent, you can still undo it by clicking Undo repeatedly. Each time you click Undo, an action is reversed, in the order in which you performed the steps. You can also select an action to undo when you click the Undo arrow and select the action.

h. Click **Redo** on the Quick Access Toolbar to reapply the formatting. When you click Redo, the most recent "undone" action is redone.

i. **Save** the document.

QUICK REFERENCE	Four Different Methods to Change Character Formatting

Assume that the text is selected.

1. **Ribbon:** Click a formatting option in the Font group.

2. **Mini Toolbar:** Move the pointer to reveal the Mini toolbar, and then specify formatting.

3. **Keyboard Shortcut:** Press Ctrl + Shift + P to open the Font dialog box, and then specify formatting.

4. **Dialog Box Launcher:** Click the Dialog Box Launcher in the Font group, and then specify formatting.

REAL WORLD ADVICE	Why Use the Font Dialog Box?

Use the Font dialog box when applying several formatting effects at one time, especially if those effects are not common — such as superscript, subscript, or small caps.

Format Paragraphs

The way you define a paragraph and the way Word defines a paragraph are likely very different. While you may have learned to define a paragraph as a group of two or more sentences with a common idea or concept, Word defines a paragraph as identified by a hard return, which is inserted every time you press Enter. By that definition, a blank line with a hard return is a paragraph. A single line, such as the title of a report with a hard return, is also a paragraph. It is important to understand how Word identifies paragraphs, because while some formatting is applied at the character level — such as font size, color, and bold — and affects all selected characters, other formatting is applied at the paragraph level and affects all selected paragraphs. If a paragraph is not selected, however, Word applies the formatting to the paragraph that contains the insertion point. Paragraph formatting options are found in the Paragraph group on the Home tab.

This section will cover paragraph alignment, line spacing, and paragraph spacing. Bullets, lists, indents, and tabs, also defined as paragraph spacing, will be covered later in this business unit.

Adjusting Paragraph Alignment

Alignment determines how the edges of a paragraph align with the left and right margins (see Figure 17). Alignment settings apply to all text within a paragraph. By default, paragraphs in a Word document are **left-aligned**, which means that lines of text begin evenly on the left but include an uneven, or ragged, right edge. Left-aligned text is easy to read; therefore, it is the primary form of alignment of paragraphs in letters, reports, and memos. Text that is **right-aligned** is the reverse: Text is aligned on the right with a ragged left edge. Right-aligned text is often used for short lines such as dates, figure captions, and headers. Text that is **centered** places the middle of each line precisely in the center of the page, between the left and right margins. Report titles and major headings are usually centered. **Justified** (some-times called *fully justified*) is an alignment style that spreads text evenly between the right and left margins so that lines begin on the left margin and end uniformly on the right margin. Such alignment can cause awkward spacing as text is stretched to fit evenly between the margins, as you will see when you try to justify the memorandum. Newspaper articles and textbooks are often formatted in justified alignment. In this exercise, you will change the alignment of paragraphs in the document.

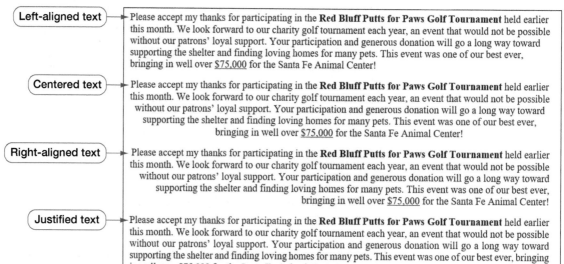

Figure 17 Alignment examples

W01.06

To Adjust Alignment

a. Select **all paragraphs** in the body of the memo, starting with the line beginning with **Painted Paradise Resort is** and ending at the end of the document.

b. On the Home tab, in the Paragraph group, click **Justify** ≡, and then click anywhere in the document to deselect the selection. All paragraphs are evenly aligned on both the left and right margins.

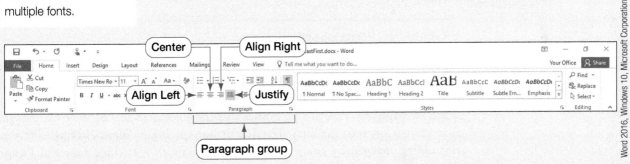

Figure 18 Adjusting alignment

Word 2016, Windows 10, Microsoft Corporation

c. Click **Undo** ↺ on the Quick Access Toolbar to undo paragraph alignment.
    Justify is an alignment that is often used in published documents, such as newspapers and magazines, but it is not suitable for a memo.

d. Press Ctrl + Home, and then, in the Paragraph group, click **Center** ≡.
    As you recall, alignment applies to an entire paragraph — text ending with a hard return. To apply paragraph formatting, simply click within the line of text that identifies the paragraph to be formatted, and then apply your formatting.

e. Click **Center** ≡ again to reverse the change.
    Centering the word Memo is not an attractive change and is not an accepted practice in the design of business documents, so you return alignment to left-align.

f. **Save** 💾 the document.

Working with Paragraph Spacing

Paragraph spacing is defined by the space before and after paragraphs. Generally, there is more space between paragraphs than there is within paragraphs (see Figure 19). The extra spacing between paragraphs makes a document easier to read.

Paragraph spacing is measured in terms of points, with a point equal to 1/72 of an inch. Settings are generally specified in units of six — 0 pt, 6 pt, 12 pt, 18 pt — though you can set the spacing to any value in the Paragraph dialog box. The default paragraph spacing for a new, blank document is 8 pt. Set it to 0 to remove paragraph spacing.

Paragraph spacing can be set to *before* or *after* the paragraph, and making that choice is much like the old adage "Which came first — the chicken or the egg?" Most often, it does not make a difference how you interpret the spacing because either way you are creating space between paragraphs. As a general rule, most spacing is specified *after* a paragraph.

Working with Line Spacing

Just as paragraph spacing is defined by the space between paragraphs, **line spacing** is defined by the space between the lines of a paragraph. Similar to paragraph spacing, line spacing applies to an entire paragraph. A double-spaced paragraph has a line spacing value of 2.0, while a single-spaced paragraph has a line spacing value of 1.0.

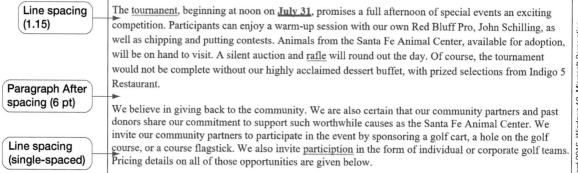

Figure 19 Paragraph and line spacing

Figure 19 shows a document with both paragraph and line spacing. The line spacing for the first paragraph is set to 1.15, while the line spacing for the second paragraph is set to 1.0, or single spacing. Note the difference in white space between the lines. The paragraph after spacing is set to 6 pt. Notice that there is more space between the paragraphs than there is between the lines. The default line spacing in Word 2016 is 1.08, though this can be changed by going to the Home tab and then clicking Line and Paragraph Spacing ‡☰ ▾ in the Paragraph group.

W01.07

SIDE NOTE

Layout Tab

Alternatively, you can change the paragraph spacing from the Layout tab.

To Work with Paragraph and Line Spacing

a. Press Ctrl+Home to move the insertion point to the beginning of the document.

b. Select the four lines in the heading area of the memo beginning with the text **To:** and ending with **Charity Golf Tournament**. In the Paragraph group, click the **Paragraph Dialog Box Launcher** ⬚. The Paragraph dialog box opens, enabling you to adjust both paragraph and line spacing.

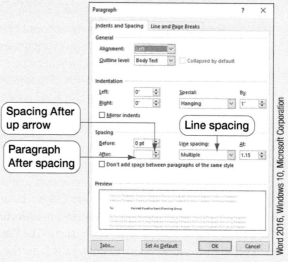

Figure 20 Spacing in Paragraph dialog box

c. In the Paragraph dialog box, under Spacing, click the **After** up arrow two times to increase it to **12 pt**. This will add a little more white space in the heading area. Each time you click the arrow, the spacing value is adjusted by 6, starting with 0. Click **OK**. Instead of clicking the arrow, you can simply click in the Spacing Before or Spacing After box and type a value, such as 12. The value that you type does not have to be a multiple of 6.

d. Click anywhere in the third paragraph of the body memo, beginning with **We believe**. In the Paragraph group, click **Line and Paragraph Spacing** . Notice that the current setting is 1.0. Select **1.15** to change the line spacing to be consistent with the rest of the document.

The extra white space makes the document easier to read.

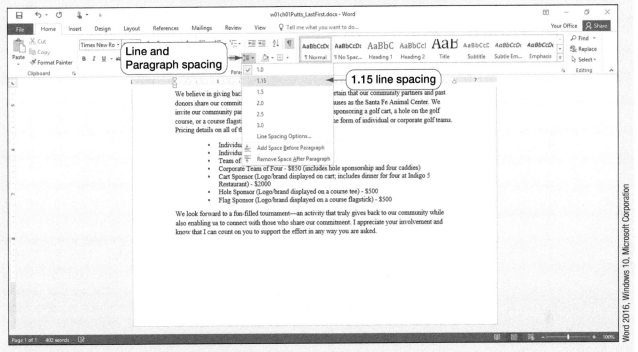

Figure 21 Spacing options in the Paragraph group

e. **Save** 🖫 the document.

REAL WORLD ADVICE **How and When to Choose Line Spacing**

When you use the Paragraph dialog box to select line spacing, you have more choices than simply single spacing and double spacing. You can also select Exactly, At Least, or Multiple. *Exactly* enables you to choose a highly precise line spacing that remains fixed at a specified point size. *At Least* lets you specify a minimum line spacing while allowing Word to adjust the height if necessary to accommodate such items as drop caps, which are oversized letters that sometimes begin paragraphs. The At Least setting is more commonly used in desktop publishing. *Multiple* enables you to set line spacing at an interval other than single, double, or 1.5.

Proofread a Document

Reviewing, or proofreading, a document is an essential step in the process of creating an effective document. As you review a document, you will most likely identify text that is misspelled or incorrectly used. Word enables you to make sweeping changes to a document with very little effort. In this section, you will learn to how to quickly correct spelling mistakes, to use the AutoCorrect feature to correct common typing mistakes as they occur, and to find and replace items within a document.

Checking Spelling and Grammar

By default, Word checks spelling as you type, underlining in red any words that are not found in Word's dictionary. Sometimes the underlined words are not actually misspelled but instead are names or technical terms that Word does not recognize. In that case, you can ignore the flagged text. Grammatical, capitalization, and spacing errors are underlined in green. Word usage errors, such as using "lose" instead of "loose," are underlined in blue. Occasionally, the underlined text is not an error at all but is part of the document formatting or wording that you prefer to leave as is. Often, the "grammatical error" is simply too many spaces between words. Display nonprinting characters to quickly identify and remove any extra spaces. Word's **Spelling & Grammar** tool may not catch every occurrence of a word usage, grammatical, or spelling error, as you will discover in the following exercise. Therefore, always proofread the document yourself.

 CONSIDER THIS | **The Importance of Proofreading**

Should you rely solely on a spelling checker for your proofreading needs? Before answering that question, try typing the following paragraph into a Word document. Which words are flagged? Which are not? Are any even flagged at all?

Eye enjoyed meeting u the other day. After further revue, we feel Ur resume is per fict. Peas call me with any farther questions.

To Check Spelling and Grammar

a. Press [Ctrl]+[Home]. Right-click the wavy red underlined word in the first paragraph of the body of the memo, **promoe**. Select **promote** in the shortcut menu of suggested correct spellings.

When you right-click a flagged spelling mistake, a shortcut menu is displayed. You can then choose to accept a suggestion or to ignore the error. If none of Word's suggested corrections are appropriate, you can edit the document to correct the misspelling or grammatical mistake.

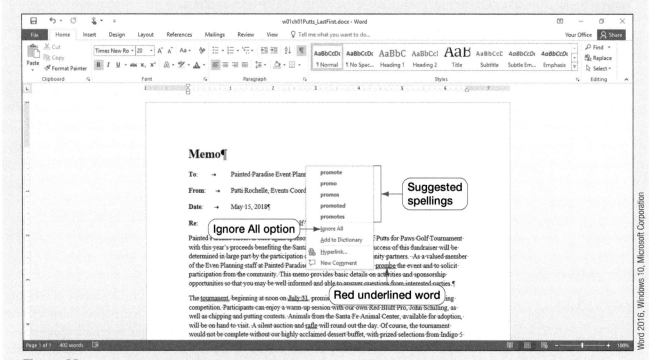

Figure 22 Correcting spelling

Troubleshooting

If you right-click outside the underlined area, the displayed shortcut menu will not include the appropriate selections.

b. Click the **Review** tab, and then, in the Proofing group, click **Spelling & Grammar**. The Spelling pane appears. Position the pointer in the title area of the Spelling pane until it changes to a four-headed arrow ⟐, and then double-click to dock it to the side of the window (make it stationary). If the pane was already docked before you double-clicked, you will see no change.

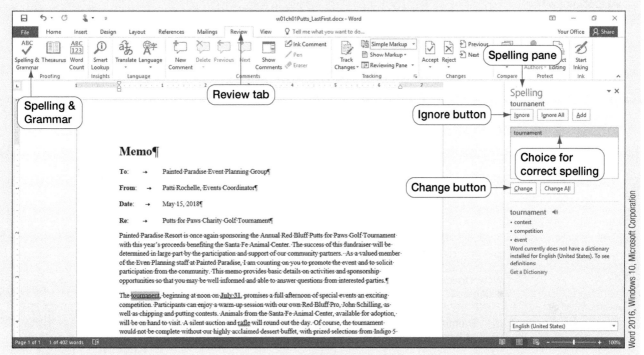

Figure 23 Spelling pane

c. The first misspelled word to be presented will be "tournanent". Select the correct spelling from the list of choices, and then click **Change**. Word will proceed through the entire document, presenting each error for your consideration. Repeat this process for the remaining errors (raffle and participation). Click **OK** when the spelling and grammar check is complete.

d. Drag the vertical scroll bar to view the first two body paragraphs. Locate the word usage error in the first paragraph of the body of the memorandum. The word "Even" should be "Event." The word is not flagged as a spelling error because it is not misspelled. Click after the word **Even**, and then type t.

e. **Save** 🖫 the document.

Using AutoCorrect

Have you ever noticed that when you begin a new line or sentence with a lowercase word, Word automatically changes the first letter to uppercase? **AutoCorrect** is a feature that automatically corrects common typing mistakes as they occur. For example, you might notice that you sometimes type "adn" when you meant to type "and". Similarly, the word "the" is often typed "teh". AutoCorrect automatically fixes these errors. You can also create AutoCorrect entries to correct words that you often misspell.

AutoCorrect can also be customized to expand frequently used abbreviations or to apply special formatting, such as replacing (c) with ©. For example, you will configure AutoCorrect to replace "pp" with "Painted Paradise Resort & Spa".

SIDE NOTE
What will AutoCorrect replace?
Autocorrect will only replace "pp" if the letters are solitary. The "pp" in "happy" would not be replaced.

To Use AutoCorrect

a. Click the **File** tab, click **Options**. The Word Options dialog box opens. Click **Proofing**, and then under the AutoCorrect options section, click **AutoCorrect Options**.

You will often use the phrase "Painted Paradise Resort & Spa" in documents that you prepare for the resort. You will create an AutoCorrect entry to simplify that entry. When you create an AutoCorrect entry, the replacement will apply not only to text that you type in the current document, but also to all Word documents that you create on your computer after you have added the entry.

b. Type pp in the **Replace** box.

c. Type Painted Paradise Resort & Spa in the **With** box.

Troubleshooting

If the words "Painted Paradise Resort & Spa" are displayed in the With box before you type them, another student might have worked with this exercise before you at the same computer. In that case, the AutoCorrect entry has already been created. Verify that the "pp" entry is in the list of AutoCorrect entries. If so, skip to step e.

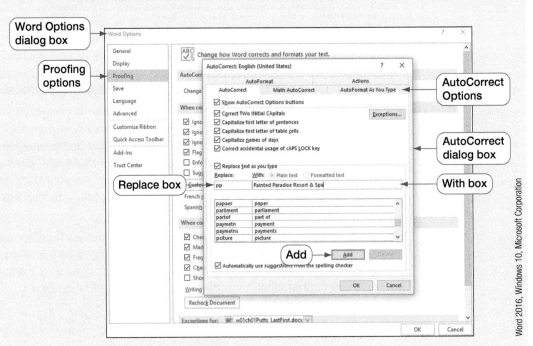

Figure 24 AutoCorrect

d. Click **Add**.

You know that you will often use the word "resort" in the documents that you prepare. However, you tend to type quickly, sometimes reversing the order of letters, resulting in "resrot."

e. Scroll through the list of replacements to see whether the text "resrot" has been added to the list. If you do not see "resrot" in the replacement list, click in the **Replace** box, delete the text pp, and then type resrot. Click in the **With** box, delete any existing text, and then type resort. Click **Add**, click **OK**, and then click **OK** again to close the Word Options dialog box.

f. Click at the end of the second paragraph of the memo body, after the text **Indigo 5 Restaurant**. (Click after the period.) Press [Spacebar]. Type pp has prepared for you a fun-filled day at the resrot! (Type the word "resrot" misspelled as shown.) As you type the letters "pp" and press [Spacebar], the text will adjust to show "Painted Paradise Resort & Spa." As you type "resrot!" the text will automatically adjust to show the word "resort."

g. Because you may be in a computer lab, you should remove the two AutoCorrect entries created in this exercise. Click the **File** tab, click **Options**, click **Proofing**, and then click **AutoCorrect Options**. Scroll through the list of AutoCorrect entries, click **pp**, and then click **Delete**. Scroll through the list, click **resrot**, click **Delete**, click **OK**, and then click **OK** again to close the Word Options dialog box.

h. **Save** 🖫 the document.

Finding and Replacing Text

Finding a particular word or phrase and replacing it with another might not seem to be a huge undertaking if you are working with a very short document. But consider the challenge if the document was much longer — such as a 400-page dissertation. Perhaps you have consistently misspelled a name or are simply searching for a keyword. If the incorrect text appears repeatedly in a lengthy document, you could conceivably save a great deal time by using Word's **Find and Replace** feature.

The **Navigation Pane** provides a set of related features for getting around a document and searching for content. The Navigation Pane is displayed to the left of an open document. To open the Navigation Pane, select Navigation Pane in the Show group on the View tab. The Navigation Pane is also displayed when you click the Home tab and then click Find. Alternatively, you can press [Ctrl]+[F]. If you are looking for a particular word, phrase, graphic, formula, or footnote, the Navigation Pane can help you find the item quickly. In this exercise, you will use Find and Replace to make changes to the memo.

 W01.10

To Find and Replace

a. Press [Ctrl]+[Home] to position the insertion point at the beginning of the document. Click the **Home** tab, and then, in the Editing group, click **Replace**.
Because you often make the mistake of using the word "Indigo 5", with a space before the 5, instead of "Indigo5", you want to find all occurrences of "Indigo 5" and replace them.

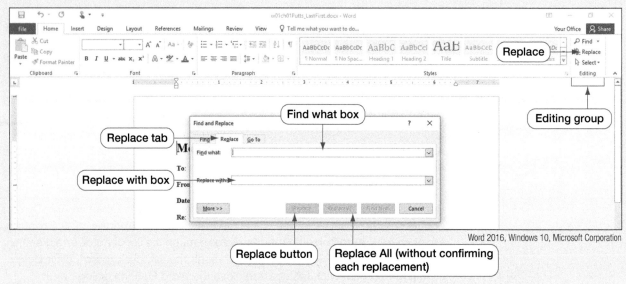

Word 2016, Windows 10, Microsoft Corporation

Figure 25   Replace tab in the Find and Replace dialog box

b. Click in the **Find what** box, delete any text if necessary, and then type Indigo 5 with a space before the 5. Press Tab. In the **Replace with** box, type Indigo5 with no space.

SIDE NOTE
Use Caution with Find and Replace
Replace All does not ask for your confirmation, so it can be a dangerous activity if you have not carefully thought through the possible changes.

c. Click **Replace All** so that you will not be asked to confirm every replacement. Two replacements are made. Click **OK**.

d. Click the **Find** tab.
   The words "caddy" and "caddies" appear in various places throughout the flyer. You will use a **wildcard** to find each occurrence of words that contain "cad"; this should identify each of these words. Because you care only that a search result contains "cad" and you know that what follows those letters is irrelevant to your search, you will use the asterisk (*) wildcard. For example, the word "caddy" includes two additional letters following "cad", while the word "caddies" includes four additional letters. Because wildcard searches are case sensitive (the option to deselect Match Case is unavailable) results will display only words that contain "cad," not "Cad."

Wildcard Symbol	Represents
*	Any number of characters, including none
?	One character
#	One number

Table 5   Find and Replace wildcards

SIDE NOTE
To Go To a Page Number
On the Home tab, in the Editing group, click the Find arrow, and then select Go To. Enter a page number, and then click Next.

e. Click in the **Find what** box, and then remove any existing text if necessary. Type cad* (with no spaces) and then click **More**. Click **Use wildcards**, and then click **Find Next**. The first word containing the text "cad" is displayed.

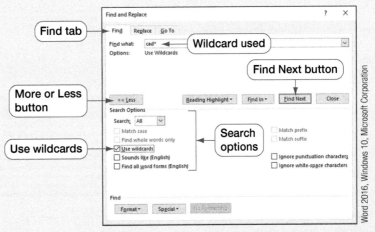

Find tab

Wildcard used

Find Next button

More or Less button

Use wildcards

Search options

Word 2016, Windows 10, Microsoft Corporation

Figure 26 Find tab in the Find and Replace dialog box

> **Troubleshooting**
>
> If the Find and Replace dialog box hides the search result, click the dialog box title bar, and drag the dialog box out of the way.

f. Click **Find Next** to view another word that contains "cad." Continue clicking **Find Next** until the search is complete, click **OK**, and then click **Close** ⊠ to close the Find and Replace dialog box.

SIDE NOTE

Navigation Pane Shortcut

Press Ctrl+F to quickly open the Navigation Pane.

g. On the Home tab, in the Editing group, click **Find**. The Navigation Pane appears to the left of the document. Be sure any text in the **Search** box is highlighted, type tournament, and then press Enter.

All occurrences of the word "tournament" are temporarily highlighted in the flyer. Because the flyer is a one-page document, it is easy to see all the matches. If the document were longer, you could scroll through the pages to view the results.

Tabs in the Navigation Pane provide even quicker access to search results. If a document includes sections with titles formatted in a heading style (Heading 1, Heading 2, etc.), click Headings in the Navigation Pane to see search results organized by section. You can see the resulting pages when you click Pages and all resulting text when you click Results.

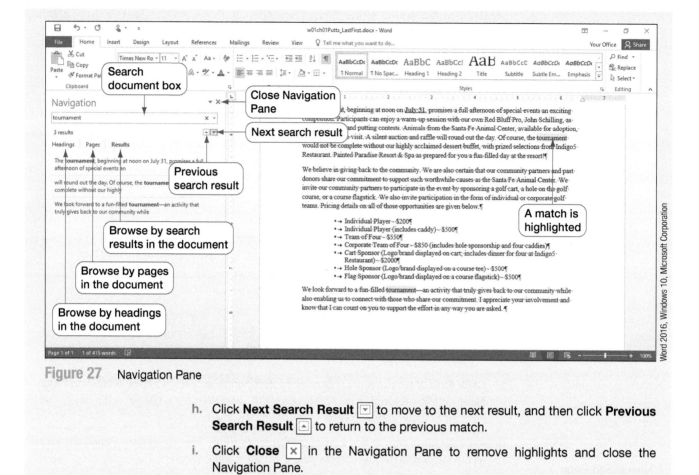

Figure 27 Navigation Pane

h. Click **Next Search Result** ⊡ to move to the next result, and then click **Previous Search Result** ⊡ to return to the previous match.

i. Click **Close** ⊠ in the Navigation Pane to remove highlights and close the Navigation Pane.

j. **Save** 🖫 the document.

Insert a Header and Footer

A **header** or **footer** consists of one or more lines of text or graphics printed in the top or bottom margin of a document. A header appears in the top margin; a footer appears in the bottom margin. Headers and footers are not included in a document by default.

The most commonly used footer is a page number. A page number footer automatically increases in increments so that all pages are properly numbered. When you specify a header or footer, the item appears on all pages unless you specify otherwise. For example, you can indicate that a header or footer is to appear only on odd or even pages. You can choose to set a header or footer on all pages except the first page, which is helpful if the first page is a cover page or the title page of a report. You can also choose to include headers or footers in only one section of a document. You will learn to create sections in Chapter 2.

You can insert a header or footer by simply double-clicking in the top or bottom margin of a document. The insertion point is displayed in the header or footer area, with the rest of the document grayed out. At that point, you can type text, such as your name, and align it using the alignment options on the Home tab. You can also use Tab to position text. A header or footer has three sections: left, center, and right. Press Tab to go from one section to the next. For example, enter your name in the left section, press Tab to move to the center and insert a company name, and then press Tab to move to the right to insert a page number.

You can also insert a header or footer when you click the Insert tab and select Header or Footer in the Header & Footer group. If you like, you can select from a gallery of predesigned header or footer styles. A header or footer style might include colored horizontal lines and preselected and aligned fields such as a page number.

As you work in a header or footer area, the ribbon adjusts to display the Header & Footer Tools Design contextual tab. These tools are displayed only when an item or object — such as a header — is selected. Items on the tab relate directly to the selected object. To return to the document text and exit the header or footer area, double-click in the body of the document, or click Close Header and Footer on the Header & Footer Tools Design tab.

Adding Fields to a Header or Footer

In the case of a header or footer, you can choose to include document information such as a page number, the file name, or the author name. Thus, if the file name, page number, or author ever changes, the new change will be reflected in your document. Word 2016 also utilizes the Document Info button, which will enable you to quickly add some of the more common fields, such as the author, file path, document title, and file name. Although it is not common practice to include a file name or page number within a header or footer of a one-page business memo, you will include it in this exercise so that your instructor can easily identify the memo as belonging to you.

To Insert Headers and Footers

SIDE NOTE

To Open a Header or Footer

Alternatively, you can double-click in the header or footer area.

a. Click the **Insert** tab, and then, in the Header & Footer group, click **Footer**. Select **Edit Footer** to create your own.

The document text appears grayed out, and the insertion point is displayed in the footer area. The ribbon is expanded to include the Header & Footer Tools Design tab. These tools contain commands that are related to the currently selected item, which is a footer.

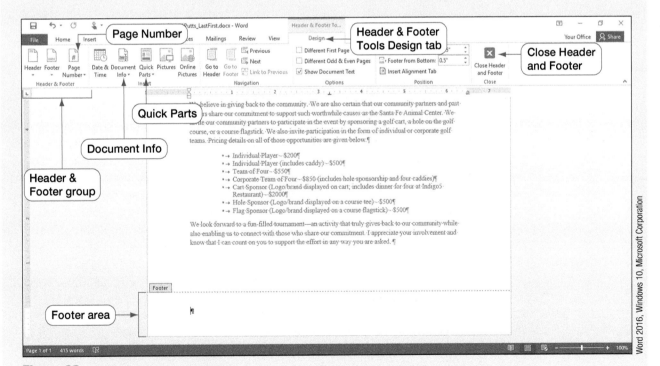

Figure 28 Inserting headers and footers

b. Type Painted Paradise Resort & Spa, and then press Tab.

c. Under Header & Footer Tools, on the Design tab, in the Header & Footer group, click **Page Number**. Point to **Current Position**, select **Plain Number**, press Tab, and then type Internal Communication.

You have included a page number as part of the footer. Choose Current Position so that you can control where the page number field is placed.

d. Select the entire line of the footer. Click the **Home** tab, and then, in the Font group, click the **Font** arrow, and then select **Times New Roman**. While the text is still selected, click the **Font Size** arrow, and then select **10**.

e. Double-click the body of the memo to close the footer and return to the body of the document.

The footer will now appear grayed out to indicate that you are working in the main body of the document.

f. Click the **Insert** tab, and then, in the Header & Footer group, click **Header**. Select **Edit Header** to create your own.

SIDE NOTE

Use Document Info Button to Insert the File Name

Alternatively, on the Header & Footer Tools Design tab, in the Insert group, click Document Info, and then select File Name.

g. Under Header & Footer Tools, on the Design tab, in the Insert group, click **Quick Parts**. Select **Field**. The Field dialog box opens. Scroll down the Field names list, select **FileName**, and then click **OK**. Click the **Home** tab, and then, in the Paragraph group, click **Center** ≡.

You have included the file name as part of the header, making it convenient to identify the source of the document. As was previously mentioned, you will not often include a file name header in a business memo. You are including it here so that your instructor can easily identify the memo as belonging to you.

h. Double-click in the body of the memo to close the header and return to the body of the document.

You can also click Close Header and Footer to return to the document.

i. **Save** 💾 the document.

REAL WORLD ADVICE	Using Headers and Footers

A primary purpose of headers and footers, especially when used in academic and business reports, is to identify pages as belonging to a particular project. If you include your name, the company name, or a project name in a footer, you will be reminded with each page of the document's origin and purpose. Research papers and books might include page and chapter numbers in a header or footer. Use headers and footers where appropriate to add organization and professionalism to a document.

QUICK REFERENCE	To Insert Page Numbers in a Header or Footer

1. Open the header or footer.

2. On the Header & Footer Tools Design tab, click Page Number in the Header & Footer group.

3. Select Current Position.

4. Select Plain Number or any other desired format.

5. Align and format the text in the header or footer as necessary.

Save and Close a Document

You will often need to save and close your work to reopen it at a later time. By default, Word 2016 saves files in a .docx format, which is different from the .doc format used in Word 97 - 2003. Word still enables you to save your file in the previous Word 97 - 2003 format if you prefer or in a variety of other formats. In the following sections, you will also learn how to save your file as a PDF file or directly to the cloud, an Internet storage concept. Regardless of how you save your file, do not forget to save your work often. Saving often will prevent you from losing your work in the event of a system failure, formatting error, or other unexpected disruption.

Saving a Document to OneDrive

When you save a file, you must specify a location. That location might be a flash drive if you are working in a computer lab or perhaps a hard drive on your own computer. Recognizing the mobile lifestyle of most people today, Microsoft built functionality into Word 2016 that enables you to save files directly to the cloud and open them on any computer, even if that computer does not have Word 2016 installed.

Cloud computing allows users to keep files at a location that is connected to the Internet rather than on the user's computer. When you save files to the cloud, you are actually saving the files to a server that is accessible through an Internet storage service, such as a **OneDrive** account. OneDrive is web storage space that Microsoft makes available to you at no cost. When you sign up for OneDrive storage, you are given access to up to 15 GB of space in which you can create folders and upload documents, workbooks, presentations, and other files. In addition, with the release of Office 2010, Microsoft introduced Office Web Apps, a web-based version of Word, PowerPoint, Excel, and OneNote. Office Web Apps has limited functionality, lacking many of the features that you find in a locally installed Office suite, but core editing and formatting commands are still included.

QUICK REFERENCE	Creating a Strong Password

Passwords should be easy to remember but difficult for anyone to guess. Whether you are Internet shopping, managing your email, or creating a OneDrive account, here are some tips that can help you to create a strong password:

1. Include at least 14 characters, including numbers and letters — both uppercase and lowercase.
2. Do not use real words, as software used by ill-intentioned hackers can quickly check every word in the dictionary.
3. Use the first letter of every word in a favorite song, poem, or phrase, combined with numbers that are easily remembered.
4. Do not use personal information, such as your pet's name or a middle name.
5. Use the entire keyboard, including special characters.
6. Do not use the same password for all of your online activity.
7. Do not use your username as the password.

Saving a Document to a PDF File

PDF (Portable Document Format) is a file type that preserves most formatting attributes of a source document, regardless of the software with which it was created. It is a format that can easily be viewed on multiple platforms. The only software that is required to read or print a PDF file is Adobe Reader, which is available as a free download at **www.adobe.com/products/reader/**. For example, if you create a .docx file using Word, Microsoft Word will be required in order to view the file. However, if you create a PDF file, a user can easily view the file using Adobe Reader without having to purchase any additional software. Previous version of Word have been able to save a document as a PDF file; however, Word 2016 has the ability to edit PDF documents, discussed later in this chapter. In this exercise, you will create a PDF file of your memorandum.

REAL WORLD ADVICE | **Why Save a Document as a PDF?**

Saving a document as a PDF file will ensure accessibility by others, regardless of how the file was created or the type of computer the recipient is using.

- A PDF format will preserve the appearance of your document — the font size, the spacing, and the placement of graphics will remain the same, regardless of the software being used to view the document.

- A PDF format is secure, is not easily altered, and cannot be modified without leaving an "electronic footprint" — a trail of modifications.

To Save a Document

a. Click to place the insertion point just before the word **Pro** in the second sentence of the second body paragraph. Type Golf, and then press Spacebar. You have now specifically identified the type of professional by changing "Pro" to "Golf Pro."

Troubleshooting

If you see any unnecessary spaces, click to the right of the unnecessary space and press Bksp to remove it — or click to the left of the space and press Delete to remove it. If a space is needed, click where the space is to be placed, and press Spacebar as necessary to add a space or spaces.

---

b. **Save** ⊟ the document.
Because you made changes to the file, you will save it before creating a PDF file.

c. Click the **File** tab, and then click **Export**. Verify that Create PDF/XPS Document is selected under Export, and then click the **Create PDF/XPS** button. Navigate to the location where you are saving your files.
Note that the Save as type box displays PDF (*.pdf) to indicate that the document will be saved as a PDF file.

d. Because you do not want the PDF file to open after publishing, click to deselect the **Open file after publishing** check box if necessary.

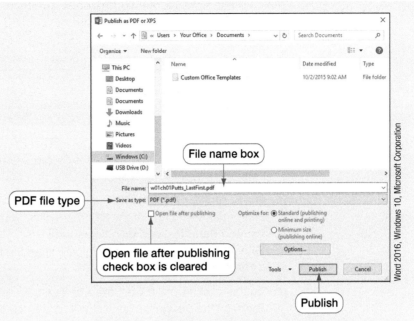

Figure 29 Publish a PDF or XPS dialog box

e. Click **Publish** to save the file as w01ch01Putts_LastFirst.pdf.

Troubleshooting

If a PDF version of the file opens in a reader, you did not deselect the Open file after publishing check box. Simply close the reader and continue with the next step.

---

f. Click **Close** ☒ to close this file and exit Word. If the "Want to save your changes to w01ch01Putts_LastFirst?" message appears, click **Save**.

Editing a PDF File

A PDF file is not easily modified. In the past, the source file and the purchase of a PDF editor were required to edit a PDF file. Word 2016 has a feature called PDF Reflow, which enables you to easily convert PDF files into Word documents. PDF Reflow is not intended to replace PDF-reading software; rather, it allows you to make changes to an existing PDF file. Any PDF file can be modified, though text-based files are preferred. A copy of the PDF file is converted into a Word document, so the original PDF file will remain intact. As you will see in the following exercise, converting a PDF file is not always a seamless process, but with a few simple changes, you will successfully edit the PDF file without having to edit the original source file.

You have been informed that the price of a Flag Sponsor for the Putts for Paws Charity Golf Tournament has been changed from $500 to $600. In this exercise, you will open the PDF version of the document with Word and make the necessary changes.

 W01.13

To Edit a PDF File

a. Start **Word**, click **Open Other Documents** in the left pane, and then click **This PC**. Navigate through the folder structure to the location of your student data files, and then double-click **w01ch01PuttsPDF**.

Make sure to select the PDF file, not the .docx file. Look for the icons in front of the file to help you distinguish between .docx files and PDF files. The PDF file will have the PDF icon in front of its name.

> ### Troubleshooting
>
> If you are not using the Adobe PDF Reader application, the icon for PDF files on your PC will be different from the one shown in Figure 29.

b. Click **Open** to open the file. If the "Word will now convert your PDF" message appears, wait until the pointer appears, and then click **OK**.

c. Press Ctrl+End. After the PDF is converted to a Word document, the footer is now part of the main body of the file. Triple-click the last line of the file, beginning with **Painted Paradise**, and then press Delete.
You remove the line that was originally intended to be the footer. You can now add a corrected footer to the document.

d. Double-click in the **footer area** to insert a new footer. Under Header & Footer Tools, on the Design tab, in the Insert group, click **Document Info**, and then select **File Name**. On the **Home** tab, in the Paragraph group, click **Center** ☰. Press Enter. Type Firstname Lastname, using your first and last name. Double-click in the main body of the memo to close the footer.

e. Scroll to the last bulleted item before the last body paragraph. At the end of the line beginning with **Flag Sponsor**, change the price from $500 to $600.

f. Click the **File** tab, click **Export**, and then click **Create PDF/XPS**. If necessary, click to deselect the **Open file after publishing** check box so that the PDF file does not open. Navigate to the location where you are saving your files, click in the **File name** box, and then change the file name to w01ch01PuttsPDF_LastFirst, using your last and first name. Click **Publish**.

g. Click **Close** ☒ to close this file and exit Word. The Want to save your changes to w01ch01PuttsPDF.pdf? message will appear. Click **Don't Save** because you do not want to create another Word document from the PDF file.

 CONSIDER THIS | **Changing a PDF document**

In the previous exercise, details about the Putts for Paws Charity Golf Tournament were changed. The PDF document was modified, but the original Word document was not. This means that in the original Word document, the price for being a Flag Sponsor remains incorrect. How else could the editing process be handled to address both documents?

Print a Document

Printing and previewing commands are accessed via Backstage view. In earlier versions of Word, it was a bit cumbersome to preview a document before printing because the Print and Preview actions were located in separate areas of the Word command structure. Backstage view brings those actions together, displaying a preview of the document when you click Print. Although you cannot edit a document in print preview, you can take a quick last look before printing.

Exploring Print Settings

Once in Backstage view, you can select several options related to printing a document. By default, new documents in Word are created in portrait orientation, in which the document is taller than it is wide. Documents that are wider than they are tall might be better printed in landscape orientation. You can easily change the page orientation and other print settings in Backstage view. You will experiment with some of these options in the next exercise.

To Preview and Print a Document

a. Start **Word**. Your most recent files will be displayed on the left. Click **w01ch01Putts_LastFirst** from the Recent list. (Recall that your last name and your first name will be shown instead of LastFirst.)
   Make sure to open the w01ch01Putts_LastFirst file and not the w01ch01PuttsPDF_LastFirst file. You can point to the file name to reveal a ScreenTip to verify that the full file name is w01ch01Putts_LastFirst.

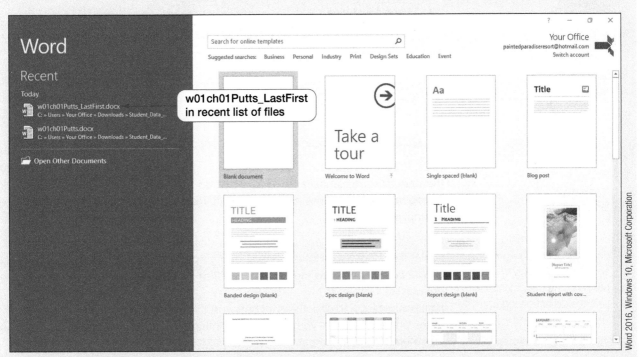

Figure 30   Recent files

b. Click the **File** tab, and then click **Print**.
   Note the preview of the memorandum that is displayed on the right. Options, such as number of copies, orientation, and printer selection, are available under Print.

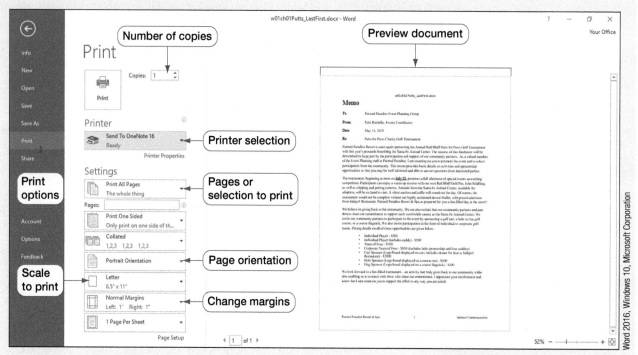

Figure 31 Print settings

c. In the Copies box, increase the number of copies to **2**.

d. Click **Portrait Orientation**, and then select **Landscape Orientation** to change the orientation to landscape. This is not an accepted format for memos. Click **Landscape Orientation**, and then select **Portrait Orientation** to return to the original orientation.

e. Click **Print All Pages**, and note that if the document were a multipage document, you could choose to print only the current page, a custom range of pages, or only a selection of pages in the document. Click **Print All Pages** again to close the options list.

If desired, you could click the Print button at this time to send the document directly to the printer. Because you will not be printing the document in this exercise, you will return to the document.

f. Press Esc to return to the document.

g. Click **Close** to close this file and exit Word. Because you did not make any additional changes to the document, if the "Want to save your changes to w01ch01Putts_LastFirst?" message appears, click **Don't Save**. Submit your files as directed by your instructor.

Concept Check

1. Which version of Microsoft Word is used in this textbook? Word enables you to easily format text in a document. What are some other features available in Word? p. 127

2. When you write business communication, it can be difficult for a reader to understand your tone. Always keep your communication brief and concise. What are some other guidelines to follow in writing business communication? p. 130

3. What is the difference between a memo and a business letter? What is the difference between a block letter, a modified block letter, and a semi-block letter? p. 131

4. Show/Hide is referred to as a toggle. What is a toggle? What purpose does Show/Hide serve? There are five ways to view your document: Print Layout, Web Layout, Outline view, Draft view, and Read Mode. Which view does not display hard returns, and why? p. 137

5. What is the first thing you must do before formatting characters? What are some examples of character formatting? p. 140

6. What is the difference between paragraph spacing and line spacing? What is a specific example of when you would decrease paragraph spacing in a business letter? p. 147

7. What is the difference between the Spelling & Grammar tool and the AutoCorrect feature? p. 150

8. What can you add to a header or footer? What is the difference between typing the page number in a footer and inserting the page number field? p. 156

9. What is a PDF file, and why would you use it? Can you edit a PDF file in Word? p. 159

10. You can select several options related to printing a document in Backstage view. Explain why you might use these options even if you are not planning to send your document to a printer. p. 162

Key Terms

AutoCorrect 151
Backstage view 139
Block 133
Business communication 127
Centered 146
Cloud computing 159
Default 135
Draft view 135
Find and Replace 153
Font 142
Footer 156
Formatting mark 135
Hard return 135
Header 156
Insertion point 137

Justified 146
KeyTips 134
Left-aligned 146
Line spacing 147
Live Preview 142
Microsoft Word 2016 127
Modified block 133
Monospaced font 142
Navigation Pane 153
Nonprinting characters 135
OneDrive 159
Outline view 135
Paragraph spacing 147
PDF (Portable Document Format) 159

Print Layout 135
Proportional font 142
Read Mode 135
Right-aligned 146
Sans serif font 142
Semi-block 133
Serif font 142
Soft return 135
Spelling & Grammar 150
Toggle 137
Web Layout 135
Wildcard 154
Word processing 127
Word Start screen 127
Word wrap 135

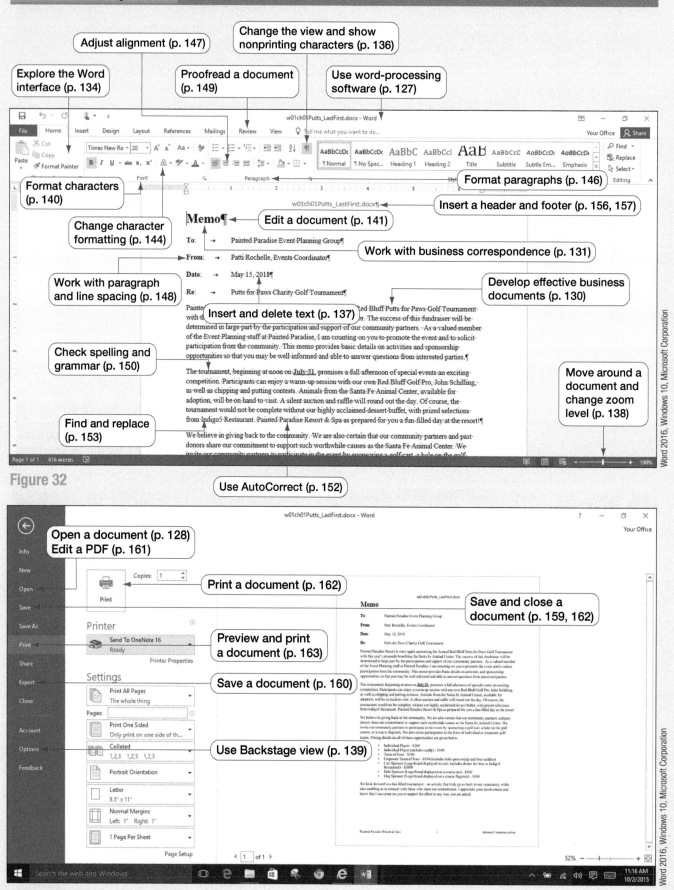

Figure 32

Figure 33

Student data file needed:

 w01ch01Thanks.docx

You will save your files as:

 w01ch01Thanks_LastFirst.docx

 w01ch01Thanks_LastFirst.pdf

Sales &
Marketing

Customer
Service

Thank You Letter

The Putts for Paws Golf Tournament was a tremendous success! Over 80 golfers enjoyed a day on the greens putting for the Santa Fe Animal Center. You plan to send a thank-you letter to each participant. Your first step is to create a standard letter that will be used as a template once you are ready to create the remaining letters. For this exercise, you will use a standard business format to create a single professionally formatted letter that is free of spelling and grammatical mistakes.

a. Start **Word**, click **Open Other Documents**, in the left pane, and then double-click **This PC**. Navigate through the folder structure to the location of your student data files, and then double-click **w01ch01Thanks**. A draft of a thank-you letter is displayed.

b. If necessary, click **Show/Hide** in the Paragraph group to display formatting marks.

c. Click the **File** tab, click **Save As**, and then double-click **This PC**. In the **Save As** dialog box, navigate to the location where you are saving your project files, and then change the file name to w01ch01Thanks_LastFirst, using your last and first name. Click **Save**.

d. Select the text beginning with **Barry Cheney, Manager** and ending with **1132 Hance Street**. On the Home tab, in the Paragraph group, click the **Paragraph Dialog Box Launcher**. In the Paragraph dialog box, under Spacing, click the **After** down arrow twice to set the spacing to **0 pt** and remove the After spacing completely. Click **OK**, and then click anywhere to deselect the text.

e. Select **$75,000** in the first paragraph in the body of the letter. Do not select the space following the dollar amount. With **$75,000** selected, in the Font group, click **Underline**.

The easiest way to select a word without including the following space is to move the insertion point to the beginning of the word and then use Shift+→ to select only the characters you need. The space after "$75,000" should not be underlined. If it is, select the single space and click Underline in the Font group to remove the underline.

f. Press Ctrl+A to select the entire document. In the Font group, click the **Font** arrow, and then select **Times New Roman**. With the text still selected, click the **Font Size** arrow, and then select **11**. Click anywhere to deselect the text.

g. Press Ctrl+Home to place the insertion point at the beginning of the document. Change the date from **May 10, 2018** to May 15, 2018. Locate the word **often** in the second paragraph in the body of the letter. Double-click the word to select it, and then press Del.

h. Click the **Review** tab, and then, in the Proofing group, click **Spelling & Grammar**. Change any misspelled words as they are presented by selecting the correct word and clicking **Change**. If a flagged word is not actually misspelled, as in a correctly spelled last name, street name, or city name, ignore the error by clicking **Ignore**. Click **OK**.

i. Proofread the document to make sure you did not overlook any misspellings or incorrect word usage. Correct any errors.

You will find two word usage errors that Word did not identify in the first and last paragraphs of the memo body.

j. Click the **File** tab, click **Options**, click **Proofing**, and then click **AutoCorrect Options**.

k. Click in the **Replace** box, and then type bc. Click in the **With** box, and then type Barry Cheney. Click **Add**, click **OK**, and then click **OK** again.

   Because you often type the manager's name, Barry Cheney, you create an AutoCorrect entry so that the letters "bc" automatically convert to "Barry Cheney."

l. Press Ctrl+End to place the insertion point at the end of the document. Type bc, and then press Spacebar. The words "Barry Cheney" are displayed. Press Enter, and then type Red Bluff Golf Club & Pro Shop. Do not press Enter.

m. Press ↑ once to position the insertion point in the above line, Barry Cheney. Click the **Home** tab, and then, in the Paragraph group, click the **Paragraph Dialog Box Launcher**. Remove the paragraph **After** spacing by changing the spacing to **0 pt**. Click **OK** to close the Paragraph dialog box.

n. Scroll to the top of the document. Select **Red Bluff Putts for Paws Golf Tournament** in the first paragraph in the body of the letter. On the Home tab, in the Font group, click **Bold**.

o. Select the **URL (web address)** in the second paragraph in the body of the letter, starting with **http** and ending with **survey**. On the Home tab, in the Font group, click **Italic**, to italicize the web address.

p. Select the **first four paragraphs** of the letter, starting with the line **Barry Cheney, Manager**, and ending with the line **Santa Fe, NM 89566**. On the Home tab, in the Paragraph group, click **Align Left**. Click anywhere to deselect the text.

q. Click the **File** tab, and then click **Print** to see a preview of the document. Press Esc to return to the document.

   After viewing the preview, you realize that you forgot to add a header and footer.

r. Click the **Insert** tab. In the Header & Footer group, click **Footer**, and then select **Edit Footer**. You will include your name and the file name in the footer so that your instructor can identify your submission. Type Firstname Lastname, using your first and last name, and then press Enter. Under Header & Footer Tools, on the Design tab, in the Insert group, click **Document Info**, and then select **File Name**.

s. In the Close group, click **Close Header and Footer**.

t. Click the **Insert** tab. In the Header & Footer group, click **Header**, and then select **Edit Header**. Type Painted Paradise Resort & Spa. Select the **text** in the header. Click the **Home** tab, and then, in the Font group, click the **Font Color** arrow. Select **Dark Red**, the first color under Standard Colors. With the text still selected, click the **Font Size** arrow, and then select **14**. In the Paragraph group, click **Center**. In the Close group, click **Close Header and Footer**.

u. Click the **File** tab, and then click **Options**. You will remove the AutoCorrect entry that you created in this exercise. Click **Proofing**, and then click **AutoCorrect Options**. Scroll through the list, select **bc**, click **Delete**, click **OK**, and then click **OK** again.

v. Press Ctrl+Home to place the insertion point at the top of the document. Click the **Home** tab, and, in the Editing group, click **Replace**. Click in the **Find what** box, delete any text if necessary, and then type Club. Press Tab. In the Replace with box, type Course. Click **Replace All**. Two replacements are made. Click **OK**, and then click **Close**.

w. **Save** the document.

x. Click the **File** tab, and then click **Export**. Click **Create PDF/XPS**, navigate to the location where you are saving your files, make sure the **Open file after publishing check box** is **not selected**, and then click **Publish** to create a PDF file with the same name.

y. Click **Close** to exit Word. Click **Save**, if the Want to save your changes to w01ch01Thanks_LastFirst message appears. Submit your files as directed by your instructor.

Customer
Service

Student data file needed:
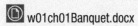 w01ch01Banquet.docx

You will save your files as:
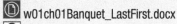 w01ch01Banquet_LastFirst.docx
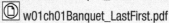 w01ch01Banquet_LastFirst.pdf

Banquet Confirmation Letter

Mr. John Fisher reserved the banquet room at the Indigo5 restaurant for a dinner meeting of local businesses. You will send a confirmation letter to the customer review-ing the details of the agreement. Finish editing the letter, and then save the letter as both a Word document and PDF file.

a. Open the Word file, **w01ch01Banquet**. Save your file as w01ch01Banquet_LastFirst, using your last and first name.

b. If necessary, click **Show/Hide** in the Paragraph group to display formatting marks.

c. Select the first nine paragraphs of the letter, starting with the line that begins **Alberto Dimas, Restaurant Manager** and ending with the line that begins **1234 Pine**. Change the Paragraph After spacing to **0 pt**.

d. Scroll to the end of the document, select the line **Alberto Dimas**, and change the Paragraph After spacing to **0 pt**.

e. Select the entire document. Change the font to **Times New Roman**, and then change the font size to **12**. With the entire document still selected, change the line spacing to **1.15**.

f. Change the alignment of the salutation to **Align Left**.

g. Change November **11** in the first paragraph to November 14.

h. Place the insertion point at the end of the document. Press Enter twice. Type cc: Catering Department. AutoCorrect will automatically convert "cc" to "Cc".

i. Place the insertion point at the top of the document. Correct all the **spelling and grammar** errors. Ignore words that are not misspelled, such as names, streets, and cities.

j. Place the insertion point at the top of the document. Replace all occurrences of **Indigo 5** (with a space before the 5) with Indigo5 (no space before the 5).

k. Insert a footer with the **File Name** field centered.

l. Insert a header with the text Painted Paradise Resort & Spa. Select all the text in the header, and change the font to **Times New Roman**, the font color to **Dark Red**, and the font size to **14**. **Center** the text in the header.

m. Because your customer may request that you send a copy of the letter via email, save the letter as a **PDF** file with the same name.

n. Save the document, exit Word, and then submit your files as directed by your instructor.

Sales &
Marketing

Student data file needed:
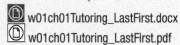 w01ch01Tutoring.docx

You will save your files as:
w01ch01Tutoring_LastFirst.docx
w01ch01Tutoring_LastFirst.pdf

College Tutoring Services

You have just started working at a campus tutoring service. The service offers free tutoring in a wide variety of subjects to all students. This year, the service wants to contact all new and returning students to let them know the hours of operation and the departments that offer tutoring services. A document has already been started that will advertise the service to students on campus. You have been asked to make some formatting changes to the document that can be printed out for students who will be attending events around the university.

a. Open the Word file **w01ch01Tutoring**. Save your file as w01ch01Tutoring_LastFirst.docx, using your last and first name.

b. Display the nonprinting characters.

c. Insert a header containing the text Campus Tutoring Services. Center the text in the header.

d. Select all text in the document, and change the font to **Times New Roman**, **12 point**.

e. In the second paragraph, beginning with **From:**, add a space after the colon, and then type your First and Last name. In the third paragraph, beginning with **Date:**, type September 24, 2018. In the fourth paragraph, beginning with **RE:**, type Campus Tutoring Services.

f. Adjust the line spacing of the document to **1.15**. Select the three paragraphs beginning with **Re:** and ending with **campus tutor!**, and adjust the paragraph After spacing to **12 point**.

g. Format the paragraphs that list the services hours and departmental listings to differentiate them from the rest of the document. Remember to keep the document professional in appearance.

h. Locate the paragraph that begins with **Fall Semester Hours**. Change the color of the font and bold the text to differentiate it from the rest of the document. Apply the same formatting changes to the paragraph beginning with **Departments offering**.

i. Proofread your file, and correct spelling or usage errors. Assume that any names and email addresses listed in the document are correct.

j. Insert a footer containing the services contact information (found in the last paragraph of the document). Make at least two formatting changes to the text in the footer.

k. Save the document, and then save the letter as a PDF so that it can be distributed easily electronically.

l. Exit Word, and then submit your file as directed by your instructor.

Additional
Cases

Additional Chapter Cases are available at www.pearsonhighered.com/youroffice

Microsoft Word 2016

Chapter 2 | CREATE AND EDIT A DOCUMENT

Sales & Marketing

OBJECTIVES

1. Create a new document   p. 172
2. Understand Word styles   p. 178
3. Copy and clear formats   p. 184
4. Add bullets, numbers, and symbols   p. 187
5. Set line and paragraph indents   p. 189
6. Work with templates p. 192
7. Change page setup p. 195
8. Change page background   p. 198
9. Use themes   p. 203

Prepare Case

Red Bluff Golf Course & Pro Shop Caddy School Flyer

Each spring, Painted Paradise Resort & Spa sponsors a caddy school that is open to current and aspiring caddies. The four-day event teaches the basics of caddying and provides an opportunity for participants to caddy for a golf tournament. A prize of a $25 gift certificate from the Red Bluff Bistro, located between the 9th and 18th greens, is giving away on the last day of the caddy school. Your assignment is to create, edit, and format a flyer providing information about the caddy school. You will copy most of the information for the flyer from a memo that the golf course manager sent you. In addition, you will create the $25 gift certificate to the Red Bluff Bistro, using an existing template.

Sebastien Burel/Shutterstock

Student data files needed for this chapter:

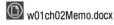 w01ch02Memo.docx

 Blank Word document

You will save your files as:

 w01ch02School_LastFirst.docx

 w01ch02Gift_LastFirst.docx

Creating and Styling a Document

Written communication is the most common form of correspondence used in business, its ultimate goal being to effectively deliver a message. Microsoft Word's extensive formatting capabilities can help you achieve this goal. Because the reader's first impression will be the visual layout of the document, its appearance can have as great an impact as the actual words used. Formatting can emphasize important points, help to organize data, and ultimately make the document easier to read. In this section, you will create, format, and design a document using styles, themes, indents, bullets, and numbering. You will also learn to create a new document based on a template that contains styles and formatting that can be customized.

Create a New Document

Word enables you to start a new project by either using a template or opening a new blank document. Templates, covered later in this chapter, enable you to create a new document based on an existing design and layout. Most often, though, you will start a new blank document to create your own layout and structure. Many refer to this as "starting a document from scratch." There are two ways to start a new document. When Word is launched, choose Blank document from the Word Start screen to display a blank workspace and begin typing. If you are currently in Word, click New in Backstage view, and then click Blank document.

Opening a New Blank Document

You will open a new blank document so that you can start work on the caddy flyer. In this exercise, you will start Word and create a blank document.

W02.00

To Create a New Document

a. Start **Word**. The Word Start screen is displayed. Click **Blank document** in the right pane. A blank Word document opens.

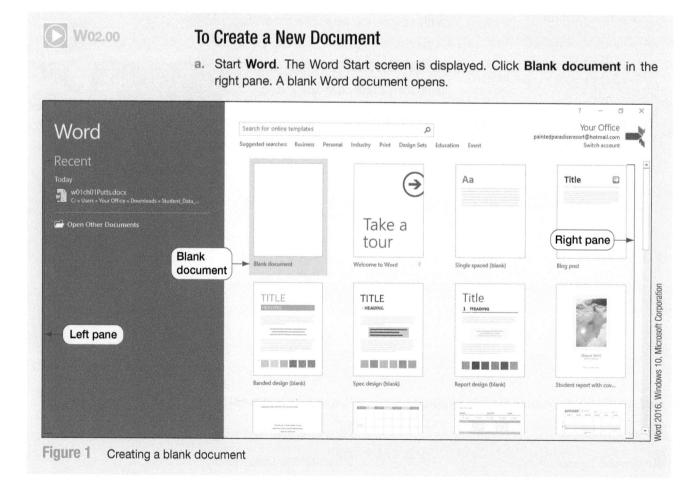

Figure 1   Creating a blank document

b. Click the **File** tab, click **Save As**, and then double-click **This PC**. In the **Save As** dialog box, navigate to where you are saving your project files, and then change the file name to w01ch02School_LastFirst, using your last and first name. Click **Save**.

Adding Text and Displaying the Ruler

When you work with indents and margins, you need to specify placement in terms of inches. For example, for a research paper, you might want to indent a quote 1 inch from both the left and right margins. In addition, measurements are needed when you try to align graphics, tabs, tables, and charts. The use of a **ruler** can simplify those settings by providing a visual guide of the measurements. Word provides both a vertical ruler and a horizontal ruler. In this exercise, you will begin adding text to the flyer. If you do not see the ruler in your flyer, you will turn it on and begin entering the introductory text.

W02.01

SIDE NOTE
Pin the Ribbon
If your ribbon is collapsed, pin your ribbon open. Click the Home tab. In the lower right-hand corner of the ribbon, click Pin the Ribbon ⊣.

To Display the Rulers and Begin Editing

a. If necessary, click the **Home** tab, in the Paragraph group, click **Show/Hide** ¶ to display nonprinting characters.

b. If the horizontal and vertical rulers are not visible at the top and left sides of the window, click the **View** tab, and then, in the Show group, click **Ruler**.

c. Type the following four paragraphs, pressing Enter after each paragraph, including after the last line.
Painted Paradise Resort & Spa
Invites you to participate in a
Caddy School
Sponsored by

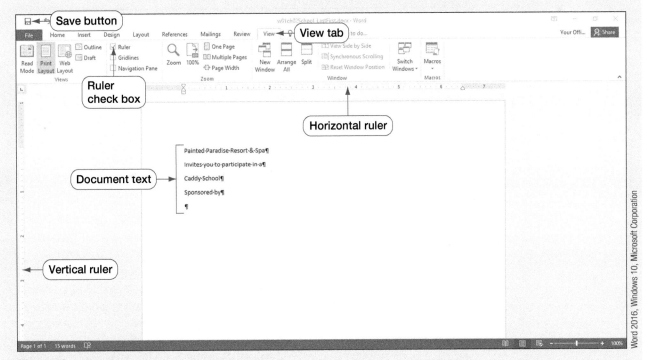

Figure 2 Added text with ruler displayed

d. **Save** 🖫 the document.

Cutting, Copying, and Pasting Text

You will seldom create a document that you do not change later. Often, those changes involve moving or copying text from one location to another. In Office, you are not limited to copying within only one document. You can copy text from a Word document and paste it in an Excel worksheet, a PowerPoint presentation, another Word document, or even another location, such as an e-mail message.

In Windows, the **Clipboard** is an area of memory that is reserved to temporarily hold text that has been cut or copied. When you **copy** text, you place a copy of the selected text on the Clipboard. The original text remains in your document. When you **cut** text, the text is removed from its original location and moved to the Clipboard. You can then **paste** the text from the clipboard into a document. However, the Clipboard can hold only one item at a time. When you cut or copy another selection, the new item overrides the current contents of the Clipboard. For this reason, you usually cut or copy text and then immediately paste it into a new location.

If you need to work with multiple selections, you can open the Office Clipboard by clicking the Dialog Box Launcher in the Clipboard group. With the Clipboard pane open, the **Office Clipboard** can hold up to 24 selections of text or graphics that can be pasted into Office documents. The **Clipboard pane** shows the most recently cut or copied item first. You can select any item in the Clipboard pane and paste it in another location. Keep in mind that the Clipboard pane must be open in order to work with multiple selections.

Table 1 identifies several methods of cutting, copying, and pasting a selection. Regardless of which method you prefer, the first step is to select the text you want to copy or cut. Because the process of cutting, copying, and pasting is universal, you will want to remember shortcuts for those operations — shortcuts that are also applicable to many other applications, including other Office programs. The methods described in Table 1 assume that you intend to paste immediately after cutting or copying.

To Select Text and Then Do This	
Copy	• Click Copy in the Clipboard group on the Home tab OR • Right-click the selection, and click Copy on the shortcut menu OR • Press Ctrl+C
Cut	• Click Cut in the Clipboard group on the Home tab OR • Right-click the selection, and click Cut on the shortcut menu OR • Press Ctrl+X
Paste	• Click Paste in the Clipboard group on the Home tab OR • Right-click in the position where the insertion should occur, and click one of the Paste Options on the shortcut menu OR • Press Ctrl+V

Table 1   Copy, cut, and paste

REAL WORLD ADVICE   Paste Preview

Have you ever pasted a selection only to realize that it did not result in the effect that you intended? Normally, in these instances, the only solution is to press Ctrl+Z or click Undo. Word 2016 provides a **Paste Preview** feature, much like Live Preview, so that you can preview the effect of a change before you accept it. After you copy a selection, move your insertion point to where you intend to paste the text. Click the Paste arrow in the Clipboard group, and point to one of the Paste Options preview buttons to preview the change. Keep Source Formatting retains the formatting from the source, or original document. Merge Formatting maintains most of the formatting from the destination document, which is the document into which a cut or copied item is pasted. It does, however, retain the emphasis formatting options from the source document, such as bold and italics. Keep Text Only discards certain things that were present in the source, such as images and formatting. Click the preview button to accept the change. Other preview options are available depending on the data you are copying, such as Use Destination Styles or Picture.

The golf course manager has sent you a memo with specific information that he would like you to include in the flyer. In this exercise, you will open the memo, copy the necessary information, and paste it into your flyer. You will format the information later in the chapter.

W02.02

To Copy Text from One File into Another

a. Click the **File** tab, click **Open**, and then double-click **This PC.** Navigate to the location of your student files, and then double-click **w01ch02Memo.** You will now have two Word documents open at the same time — the flyer, w01ch02School_LastFirst, and the memo you just opened, w01ch02Memo.

> **Troubleshooting**
>
> If you see only one document, it is probably because one document is hiding behind the other. Click in the title bar of the Word document displayed, and then drag it to the side to reveal the other document. Move and resize both documents as desired.

b. Select the paragraphs beginning with **The Red Bluff Golf Course** and ending at the end of the document.

c. With the text still selected, on the Home tab, in the Clipboard group, click **Copy** 📋.

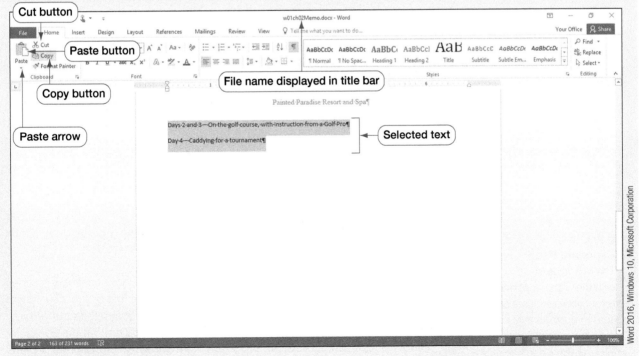

Figure 3 Clipboard group

d. Click the title bar of the **w01ch02memo** document, and then drag it to the middle of the right side of the screen. The window will snap to the right, and any other open windows will appear on the left side of the screen.

e. Click in the preview of the **w01ch02School_LastFirst** document to snap it to the left side of the screen and make it the active document. Press Ctrl+End to move to the end of the document.

f. Click the **Home** tab, and then in the Clipboard group, click **Paste**.
Click the Paste button instead of the Paste arrow. The Paste button is actually a combination of the Paste command and the Paste arrow. When you click the Paste command, the most recently cut or copied item is pasted at the position of the insertion point. When you click the Paste arrow, you can choose a Paste option or use the Paste preview.

g. **Save** the **w01ch02School_LastFirst** document.

h. Click the **w01ws02Memo** document to make it the active document. **Close** the **w01ch02Memo** document. Because you may have accidentally made changes to the memo document, you may be asked to save the changes. If this happens, click **Don't Save**.

> **Troubleshooting**
>
> If you accidentally closed the w01ch02School_LastFirst document, go to Backstage view, and then click Open. Click w01ch02School_LastFirst in the Recent Documents list to open it, and then redo step f.

Dragging and Dropping Text

If you plan to copy or cut and paste text within the same document and if the beginning and ending locations are within a short distance of each other, you can simply drag text to paste a selection. First select the text to copy or cut, and then position the pointer over the selection to display the pointer as a white arrow. Drag the selected text to the new location to move it, or press and hold Ctrl while you drag the selection to copy it. Before you release the mouse button, a small vertical bar will appear, indicating the position where the text will be placed. You are ready to make revisions in the flyer. In this exercise, you will use various copy, cut, and paste techniques to make changes to the flyer.

To Work with the Clipboard

a. Click the **Home** tab, and in the Clipboard group, click the **Dialog Box Launcher**. If necessary, position the pointer in the **title area** of the Clipboard pane until it changes to a four-headed arrow, and then double-click to dock it to the side of the window (making it stationary).
The Clipboard pane is displayed on the left. Although it is not necessary to open the Clipboard pane unless you plan to cut or copy multiple items, you view it here simply to illustrate the concept of the Clipboard. As you continue to cut or copy text, the text will be shown in the Clipboard pane. Until you turn off the computer or otherwise lose power, you can paste any item shown in the Clipboard pane, regardless of its order.

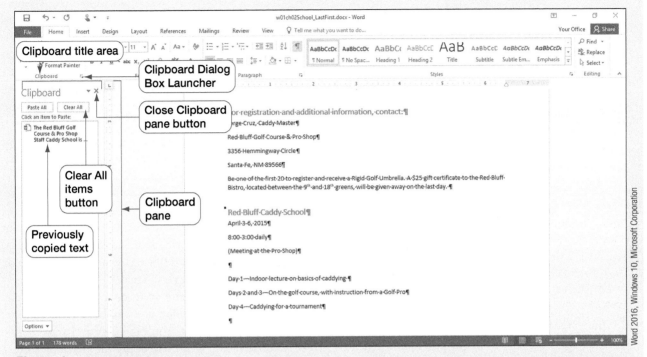

Clipboard title area

Clipboard Dialog Box Launcher

Close Clipboard pane button

Clear All items button

Clipboard pane

Previously copied text

Word 2016, Windows 10, Microsoft Corporation

Figure 4 Clipboard pane

b. In the paragraph under the heading **The Red Bluff Golf Course & Pro Shop Staff**, select the word **basics**. With the pointer, drag the selection to the left until a small vertical line shows just before the word **caddying**, and then release the mouse button.

SIDE NOTE

Alternate Way to Copy

Select the text to be copied, right-click the selection, and then select Copy on the Shortcut menu.

c. Click to place the insertion point just before the "c" in the word **caddying.** Type of, and then press Spacebar.

d. If necessary, scroll down to view the **For registration and additional information, contact** heading. Select the name **Jorge Cruz**. Do not select the comma. On the Home tab, in the Clipboard group, click **Copy**. The selection is displayed as the first item in the Clipboard pane.

e. Scroll to the end of the document, and then select the words **a Golf Pro** in the second to last line of the document. At the top of the Clipboard pane, click **Jorge Cruz** to paste the text. The selected text is replaced by the pasted text.

f. In the Clipboard pane, click **Clear All**.
All items are removed from the Clipboard. If you want to delete only one selection, point to the selection, click the arrow that appears beside the item, and then click Delete.

g. In the top-right of the Clipboard pane, click **Close** ×.

Troubleshooting

If you closed the w01ch02School_LastFirst document instead of the Clipboard pane, then you clicked the window Close button instead of the Close button on the Clipboard pane. In this case, reopen the w01ch02School_LastFirst file.

SIDE NOTE

Alternate Way to Paste

Copy text, right-click in the location where you want the next text to appear, and then click one of the Paste Options on the shortcut menu.

h. **Save** the document.

Understand Word Styles

A **style** is a set of formatting characteristics that you can apply to selected text. Word provides sets of predefined styles in the Quick Styles gallery that can be found in the Style group on the Home tab. In addition to these, Word enables you to create and apply your own styles. Using styles, you can simplify the task of formatting text, and you can be sure that similar elements have the same formatting. When creating a report, for example, you will most likely want all major headings to be formatted identically, with the same font and alignment settings. Simply apply an appropriate style to all headings, and the job is done. Because a style can include any number of formatting options, you can save a great deal of time when you apply a style instead of setting each format option individually, especially if the style includes many complex format settings.

Styles ensure that similar elements have the same formatting, resulting in a cohesive, attractive document. A style can include any number of formatting options. For example, you can create a single style consisting of bold, Times New Roman 12 point font, red font color, and 12 pt paragraph After spacing. This single style can be saved and then applied to any element of your document as often as desired. Simply select your text, and then on the Home tab, click the desired style from the Quick Styles gallery.

Most styles are considered to be either a **character style** or a **paragraph style**. Character styles set the formatting of font, font size, color, and emphasis — underline, bold, or italic — to individual characters or selections. You can apply a character style to any area of selected text. If text is not selected, Word will apply the character format to the current word — the word containing the insertion point. A paragraph style sets alignment, spacing, and indentation formatting. Paragraph styles are applied to entire paragraphs. Therefore, to apply a paragraph style to a single paragraph, simply position the insertion point within the paragraph and select the style. To apply a style to multiple paragraphs, you must first select the paragraphs.

A few styles are neither character nor paragraph styles but are instead linked styles. A linked style behaves as either a character style or a paragraph style, depending on what you select. For example, if you click within a paragraph without selecting any specific text and then select the Heading 1 style, the entire paragraph is formatted with both font and paragraph characteristics, such as color and alignment. However, if you select only one word or a limited amount of text within the paragraph and then apply the Heading 1 style, only the font characteristics are applied. For example, the font color may change, but alignment does not.

Working with Styles

The default style for all new documents is called Normal. Normal style is a paragraph style with specific spacing and formatting characteristics. Although that style might be appropriate for some documents, it will not be the best choice for all documents. You can easily select another style that is more appropriate for either the entire document or selected text or paragraphs. Normal style formats text as 11 pt Calibri font, left-aligned, with 1.08 line spacing, and 8 pt after paragraph spacing. In this exercise, you will use various existing styles from the Styles gallery to format the text in the caddy flyer.

W02.04

SIDE NOTE

Pointing

Recall that "point to" refers to hovering — not clicking — the mouse over text to view a ScreenTip or active Live Preview.

To Apply Styles

a. Press [Ctrl]+[Home] to move to the beginning of the document. Click the **Home** tab, in the Styles group, click **More** ⊡ to display the Styles gallery. In the Styles gallery, point to **Heading 1**. Live Preview shows the effect that the style will have on the selected text.

b. Without clicking, point to another **heading style**, and observe that effect. Click on **Heading 1.** The Heading 1 style is applied to the first paragraph.

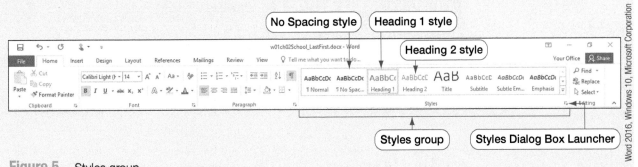

Figure 5 Styles group

c. Click in the third paragraph of the document, **Caddy School**, and then in the Styles gallery, click **Heading 1**.

Notice the extra white spacing that appears above the line when you apply the Heading 1 style. You will fix this later in the chapter.

d. Apply the **Heading 2** style to the second and fourth paragraphs of the document, **Invites you to participate in a** and **Sponsored by**.

e. Press Ctrl+End to move to the end of the document. Select the three paragraphs beginning with **Day 1** and ending with **tournament**. On the Home tab, in the Quick Styles gallery, click **No Spacing**. The lines are now set to single spacing, with no before or after paragraph spacing.

f. **Save** 🖫 the document.

QUICK REFERENCE	Adding the Current Style to the Quick Access Toolbar

To determine the current style, simply click in the text area and look in the Quick Styles gallery. However, the Quick Styles gallery does not always contain a complete list of all styles. In this case, either open the Styles pane or add a Styles list to the Quick Access Toolbar. Do the following to add a Styles list to the Quick Access Toolbar.

1. Click the File tab.

2. Click Options.

3. Click Quick Access Toolbar.

4. Click the Choose commands from arrow, and then select Commands Not in the Ribbon.

5. Scroll through the list, and then click Style.

6. Click Add, and then click OK.

7. You can now click in any paragraph within the document, and the current style will be displayed in the Styles list on the Quick Access Toolbar.

Using the Navigation Pane

Related styles in the Quick Styles gallery (Styles group) are designed to work together. For example, the Heading 2 style is designed to color coordinate with and look subordinate to the Heading 1 style. Additionally, if you use built-in heading styles, Word can automatically generate a table of contents and organize your document into a series of headings. On the basis of the headings applied through Styles, Word lets you quickly move around within your document and move headings from one location of a document to another using the **Navigation Pane**. When you move headings, the heading and all of its content will move to the desired location. In this exercise, you will use the Navigation Pane to move headings within a document.

To Work with the Navigation Pane

SIDE NOTE

Viewing the Navigation Pane

Alternatively, you can view the Navigation Pane by pressing Ctrl+F.

a. Press Ctrl+Home to move to the beginning of the document.

b. Click the **View** tab, and then in the Show group, click the **Navigation Pane** check box. If necessary, double-click the **title area** of the Navigation Pane to dock it to the side of the window.

   A hierarchical outline of your document is displayed. In the Navigation Pane, click any heading to move the insertion point to that location in the document. Notice only heading styles appear in the list.

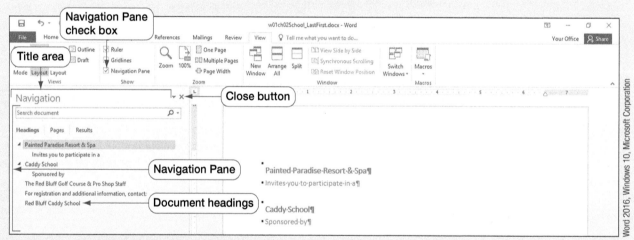

Figure 6   Navigation Pane

c. In the Navigation Pane, click the last heading, **Red Bluff Caddy School**, and drag it up one level so that the line that appears above the section starting with **For registration and additional information, contact**. Notice the heading, along with all of its text, is moved in the document.

   Long heading names may be only partially displayed in the Navigation Pane.

d. In the top right corner of the Navigation Pane, click **Close** . The Navigation Pane closes.

e. Point to the last heading in the document, **For registration and additional information, contact**. A gray triangle will appear to the left of the heading. Click the **triangle** to collapse the section. The text within this section disappears.

f. Point again to the heading **For registration and additional information**, contact:. A white triangle appears to the left of the heading. Click the **triangle** next to the section heading to expand the section and to view the text again.

g. **Save** the document.

Creating a New Style

Normal is the default style when you begin a new document, but it does not single-space text. If you prefer to single-space your documents, you can simply modify the Normal style to single-spacing. Occasionally, however, you cannot find a style that contains any of the formatting options that you need for a selection. In that case, you can create a new style, which will then be available to use throughout the current document. When you no longer need a style, you can delete it. Be careful though — deleting a style will remove its formatting options from any text where the style has been applied. In this exercise, you will create a new style called Lower Paragraph and apply it to the second and fourth lines of the caddy flyer.

REAL WORLD ADVICE | **Base New Styles on Similar Existing Styles**

Because style headings are used to organize your document, it is a good idea to base new headings styles on existing heading styles. For example, if you need a new heading style, first set your text to any of the current heading styles, such as Heading 1 or Heading 2. Make any necessary changes, and then create a new style. Because the new style is now based on a heading style, it will be included in the Navigation Pane and can easily be added to a Table of Contents. Similarly, when you create a new style for the body of your document, base the style on an existing body style. When headings are included in the Navigation Pane, reorganization is very easy.

 W02.06

To Define a New Style and Edit a Document

a. Press `Ctrl`+`Home` to move to the beginning of the document. Select the second paragraph, **Invites you to participate in a**. Click the **Home** tab, and then in the Paragraph group, click **Center** ☰.

SIDE NOTE
To Select a Font Color
Click the Font Color arrow in the Font group to display a palette of colors, and then point to a color to display a ScreenTip identifying its name.

b. With the text still selected, in the Font group, click the **Font Size** arrow `11 ▾`, and then select **14**. Click the **Font Color** arrow `A ▾`, and then under Theme colors, in the fourth column and first row, select **Blue-Gray, Text 2**.

c. In the Styles group, click the **Dialog Box Launcher** `⌐` to open the Styles pane. If necessary, double-click the **title area** of the Styles pane to dock it.

d. In the Styles pane, click **New Style** 🍴, and then in the Create New Style from Formatting dialog box, click in the **Name** box and delete any text. Type Lower Paragraph, and then make sure **Add to the Styles gallery** and **Only in this document** options are selected.

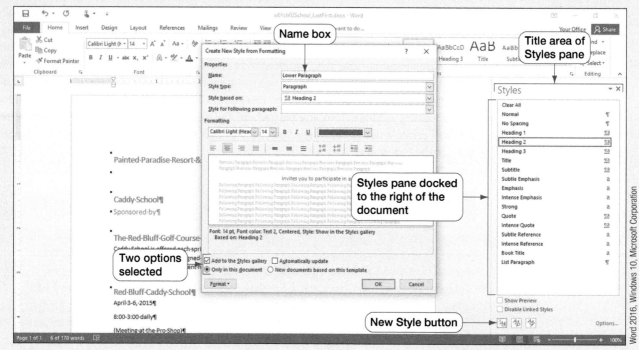

Figure 7 Creating a new style

SIDE NOTE

Selecting a Style

Alternatively, you can select the Lower Paragraph style directly from the Styles gallery, in the Styles group on the Home tab.

e. Click **OK**. Click anywhere in the fourth paragraph, **Sponsored by**, and in the Styles pane, click **Lower Paragraph**.

Because the new style is based on Heading 2 — a heading style — the new style will be included in the Navigation Pane under the Headings tab.

f. **Save** the document.

Modifying a Style

Word enables you to modify current styles. A modified style is saved and then is available to use throughout the current document. You can modify styles even if you have already applied those styles to elements of your document. When you change a style's formatting options, the new options are immediately applied to all text that has been formatted in that style within the current document. That means if your research paper includes ten major headings, all of which have been formatted in a certain style, modifying that style immediately causes all ten headings to reflect the new settings. These changes to the style can be made to only the current document or to all future documents. However, if you change the style for all future documents, the original settings will no longer be available. In this exercise, you will modify the Heading 1 and Normal styles in the caddy flyer.

To Modify a Style

a. If the Styles pane is not already open, on the Home tab, in the Styles group, click the **Dialog Box Launcher** 🗔.

> **Troubleshooting**
>
> If you click the Styles Dialog Box Launcher when the Styles pane is open, the Styles pane will close. Just click the Dialog Box Launcher a second time to reopen the Styles pane.

b. In the Styles pane, point to **Heading 1**, and then note the style description that displays. Because you plan to repeat the Heading 1 style in this document but with different font and alignment settings, you will modify the style.

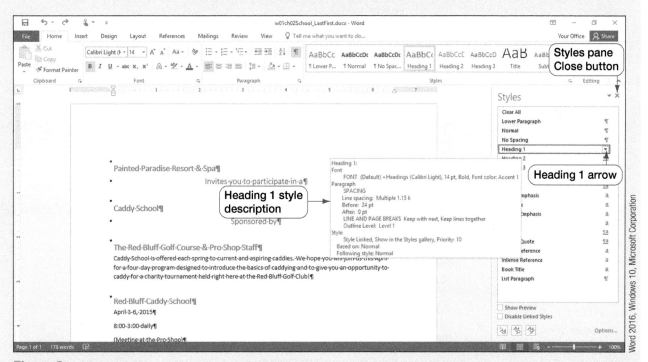

Figure 8 Styles pane

c. Click the **Heading 1** arrow, and then select **Modify**. The Modify Style dialog box opens.

> **Troubleshooting**
>
> If you accidentally clicked Heading 1 instead of the arrow, click Undo, and then repeat step c.

d. Under Formatting, click **Center** 🖹. Click the **Font Size** arrow 11 ▾, and then select **18**.

e. Click the **Font Color** arrow ▾, and then under Theme colors, in the fourth column and first row, select **Blue-Gray, Text 2**.

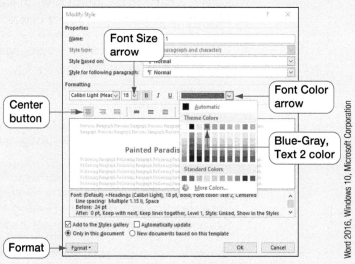

Figure 9 Modify Style dialog box

f. Click the **Format** button, and then select **Paragraph**. Under Spacing, click the **Before** down arrow to display **18 pt**, and then click the **After** up arrow three times to display **18 pt**. Click **OK** to close the Paragraph dialog box, and then click **OK** to close the Modify Style dialog box.
All previous Heading 1 styles in your document have been updated with the new formatting changes.

g. In the Styles pane, point to **Normal**, click the **Normal** arrow, and then select **Modify**. Under Formatting, click **Center** ▤. Click the **Format** button, and then select **Paragraph**. Under Spacing, click the **After** down arrow two times to display **0 pt**. Click **OK** to close the Paragraph dialog box, and then click **OK** to close the Modify Style dialog box.
This centers and adjusts the spacing of the text under the headings.

SIDE NOTE
Increase White Space
Alternatively, increase the paragraph After spacing to add more white space.

h. Scroll to the bottom of the document. Because you notice that white space is needed after the address, click to place the insertion point at the end of the line **Santa Fe, NM 89566**, and then press Enter.

i. In the top right corner of the Styles pane, click **Close** ☒ to close the Styles pane.

j. **Save** ▤ the document.

REAL WORLD ADVICE | **Creating a Shortcut Key for a Style**

If you often apply a particular style, you might find it cumbersome to continually find and click the style on the Styles pane or in the Quick Styles gallery. Instead, you might want to create a shortcut key combination for the style. To do this, modify the style, and then click the Format button. Select Shortcut key, and then in the Press new shortcut key box, press the keys that you want assigned to the style and then click Assign. For example, you can assign Alt + T, B to a style named Text Body.

Copy and Clear Formats

A document's visual appearance can draw attention to the content and encourage readers' interest. Achieving the right combination of format settings is not always an easy task, but once done, you will probably want to recreate the same format elsewhere in the same document. Similar to the principle of cut and paste, the **Format Painter** is a tool that enables you to quickly copy a format from one location to another. For example, perhaps you have formatted a caption to be 10-pt Times New Roman font, in blue font color. Because you want all captions to be formatted identically, simply select the first caption and use Format Painter to copy the formatting to the other captions.

Using Format Painter

In this exercise, you will add a shadow effect to the first heading of the document and then use the Format Painter to copy the format to the next heading.

 W02.08

To Use the Format Painter

a. Press ⌨Ctrl+⌨Home to move to the beginning of the document. Select the first paragraph of text, **Painted Paradise Resort & Spa**. Click the **Home** tab, and in the Font group, click **Text Effects and Typography** [A⌄], and then point to **Shadow**. Under Outer, in the first column and second row, click **Offset Right**.

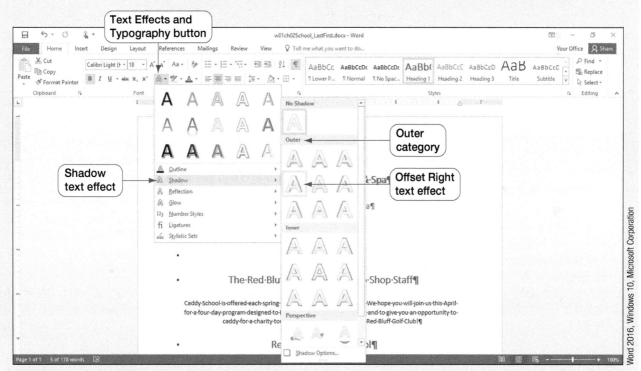

Figure 10   Text effects

b. With the text **Painted Paradise Resort & Spa** still selected, in the Clipboard group, click **Format Painter** [paintbrush icon]. As you move the mouse pointer over the text in the document, note that it resembles a paintbrush [paintbrush icon].

c. Select the third paragraph of the document, **Caddy School**.
The formatting from the first paragraph was applied to the third paragraph.

d. **Save** [save icon] the document.

Using Format Painter on Multiple Selections

As you saw in the previous exercise, clicking Format Painter enables you to copy a format to a single selection. To copy a format to multiple locations, simply double-click Format Painter. This functions like a modified toggle key. The Format Painter is now turned on, and the copied format can be pasted multiple times. Click Format Painter again to turn it off. In this exercise, you will format "Day 1" in the caddy flyer and then use the Format Painter to copy the format to the remaining days.

W02.09

To Use Format Painter on Multiple Selections and to Clear Formatting

a. Verify that **Caddy School** is still selected. Click the **Home** tab, and in the Clipboard group, Double-click **Format Painter** ⟮✷⟯.

b. Select the remaining headings, **The Red Bluff Golf Course & Pro Shop Staff**, **Red Bluff Caddy School**, and **For registration and additional information, contact:**. The formatting from the first two headings is copied to all the headings.

c. With the Format Painter still on, select the three lines in the document starting with line **Day 1 — Indoor lecture on basics of caddying** and ending with line **Day 4 — Caddying for a tournament**. On the Home tab, in the Clipboard group, click **Format Painter** ⟮✷⟯ to turn off the Format Painter.
    You decide that this particular formatting is not attractive for three lines of text.

d. With the text still selected, on the Home tab, in the Font group, click **Clear All Formatting** ⟮✦⟯. All character formatting is removed, and the text is returned to the Normal style. Click anywhere to deselect the text.

Clear All Formatting

Figure 11   Clear formatting

Word 2016, Windows 10, Microsoft Corporation

e. Select only the text **Day 1**, not the entire paragraph. On the Home tab, in the Font group, click **Underline** ⟮U⟯, and then click **Bold** ⟮B⟯.

f. Double-click **Format Painter** ⟮✷⟯, select the text **Days 2 and 3**, and then select **Day 4**. The formatting from the first day is copied to all the days. Click **Format Painter** again to turn the feature off.

g. **Save** ⟮💾⟯ the document.

Add Bullets, Numbers, and Symbols

Lists can make your document easier to read and emphasize major points to your readers. For example, if your document is outlining steps in a process, you could number those steps for better readability. You might even consider developing an itemized or bulleted series of summary points. Word provides three types of lists: Bullets, Numbering, and Multilevel List. A bulleted list uses shapes and symbols. The default **bullet** is a round, filled-in, black circle. A numbered list uses numbers, Roman numerals, or letters; the default numbered list consists of numbers followed by a period. A multilevel list is a hierarchical list consisting of numbers, letters, or symbols. Typically, numbered lists are used to indicate sequence, and bulleted lists are used when the order of the list items is not important.

Lists are simply a series of paragraphs. Recall that the definition of a paragraph is any text that ends with a hard return. To list items in a document, type each item, and then press [Enter]. You can then select the list of items and apply a bullet or number format. You can also apply a list format before you begin to type. To do this, click the Bullets, Numbering, or Multilevel List button to turn on the format, and then begin to enter text for the list. Click the button again to return to normal formatting. Use the Increase Indent and Decrease Indent buttons to quickly create multilevel lists. Press the Increase Indent button on a bulleted line to move the bulleted item to the right, creating a second-level list. The Decrease Indent button will move the item to the left one level.

Inserting and Modifying Bullets

Typically, a bulleted list is prefaced by a circle shape, though Word also provides checks, squares, and other symbols. If you prefer a bullet that is not included in Word's Bullet Library, you can create your own. You can select a symbol for your bullet, or you can modify the format of an existing bullet, such as changing its color or size. In addition, you can include a personal picture as a bullet or select from Microsoft's picture gallery at Office.com.

You want to make the day-by-day schedule stand out in the caddy flyer. In this exercise, you will experiment with numbering and bullets to see which is the most attractive option.

W02.10

SIDE NOTE
Change Numbering
To change numbering in a list, right-click on the number, and select either Set Numbering Value or Continue Numbering.

To Insert Bullets or Numbers

a. Select the three lines starting with the line **Day 1 — Indoor lecture on basics of caddying** and ending with the line **Day 4 — Caddying for a tournament**.

b. Click the **Home** tab, and in the Paragraph group, click **Numbering** [icon]. Because the days already include numbers, you decide Numbering does not look appropriate.

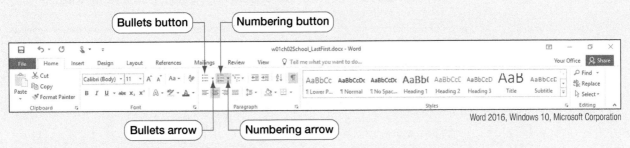

Word 2016, Windows 10, Microsoft Corporation

Figure 12   Applying bullets and numbering

c. On the Quick Access Toolbar, click **Undo** to remove Numbering.

d. With the three lines still selected, click the **Bullets** arrow to view additional bullet styles. Select the **black square shape**.

e. Click the **Bullets** arrow again, and then select **Define New Bullet** to open the Font dialog box.

f. Click **Font** in the Define New Bullet dialog box, click the **Font color** arrow, and then under Theme colors, in the fourth column and first row, select **Blue-Gray, Text 2**. Click **OK** to close the Font dialog box, and then click **OK** again to close the Define New Bullet dialog box. Click anywhere to deselect the text.

g. **Save** the document.

Inserting Symbols

Symbols are characters that do not usually appear on a keyboard, such as © or ™. Word provides a gallery of symbols from which you can select. Some frequently accessed symbols are considered special characters, such as a nonbreaking hyphen or double opening and closing quotes. In this exercise, you will insert the trademark symbol after the word "Rigid" in the caddy flyer.

 W02.11

To Insert Symbols

a. Press Ctrl+End to move to the of end the document, and then in the paragraph beginning with **Be one of the first 20**, click immediately after the word **Rigid** to position the insertion point.

b. Click the **Insert** tab, and then, in the Symbols group, click **Symbol**.
   A few of the most commonly used symbols are shown.

c. Select **More Symbols**. The Symbol dialog box opens and displays more symbols.

d. Click the **Special Characters** tab, and then click **Trademark**. Click **Insert**, and then click **Close**. The Trademark symbol is inserted after the word "Rigid."

Troubleshooting
If you have more than one trademark symbol in your document, you clicked Insert too many times. Simply delete the extra symbols from the document.

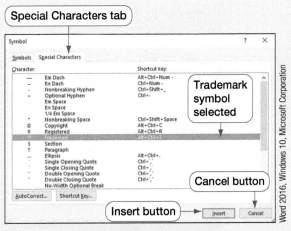

Figure 13 Symbol dialog box

e. **Save** 🔲 the document.

Set Line and Paragraph Indents

As you recall, a semi-block letter style requires the first line of each paragraph to be indented from the left margin. Such an indent is called a **first-line indent**. Typically, the first line of a citation in a bibliography begins at the left margin and all other lines are indented. That indent style is called a **hanging indent**. In writing a research paper, a lengthy quote is often indented an equal distance from left and right margins. Indenting an entire paragraph from the left margin is called a **left indent**. Similarly, indenting from the right margin is a **right indent**. You create indents in a document by using either the Paragraph dialog box or the ruler. Figure 14 provides examples of indents.

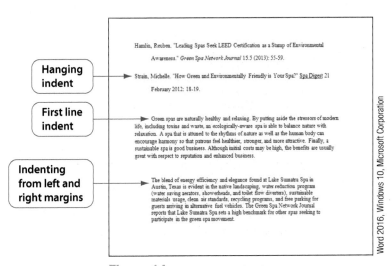

Figure 14 Examples of indents

Paragraph Indentation

Indentation is considered to be a type of paragraph formatting. Therefore, unless you are indenting several paragraphs, you do not need to select a block of text. Simply click within the paragraph to be indented, or select an indent setting before typing a paragraph. Word provides several tools that enable you to specify indents. The Paragraph dialog box, located on the Home tab, and the ruler provide access to all the indents — first-line, hanging, left, and right. The Home tab provides buttons to increase and decrease the left indent by 1/2-inch tab intervals. The Layout tab enables you to quickly modify the left and right indents.

The bulleted schedule needs to be indented in the caddy flyer. In this exercise, you will use the ruler, the Paragraph dialog box, and the Layout tab to experiment with the left indent until you find a setting that looks attractive.

REAL WORLD ADVICE	Is There an Easier Way to Create a First-Line Indent?

The easiest way to set a first-line indent is to press Tab⇥ before you begin to type. By default, that action indents the first line of each paragraph 0.5 inch from the left margin, though you will learn how to change the 0.5 inch default setting in the next business unit. To remove a first-line indent created by a tab, simply position the insertion point in front of the tabbed text and then press Bksp.

W02.12

To Indent Paragraphs

a. Select the three paragraphs starting with line **Day 1 — Indoor lecture on basics of caddying** and ending with line **Day 4 — Caddying for a tournament**. You decide that centering the schedule does not look attractive.

b. Click the **Home** tab, and in the Paragraph group, click **Align Left** ≣, and then click **Increase Indent** ≣ to move the lines to the right.

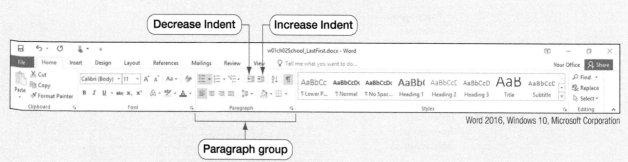

Word 2016, Windows 10, Microsoft Corporation

Figure 15 Indentation on the Home tab

c. With the text still selected, in the Paragraph group, click the **Paragraph Dialog Box Launcher** ⌐. Under Indentation, click the Left up arrow until it displays **1"**. Make sure to change the indent to 1" and not 0.1". Click **OK** to close the Paragraph dialog box.

Because all three paragraphs are selected, each paragraph — or line in this case — is indented by 1 inch.

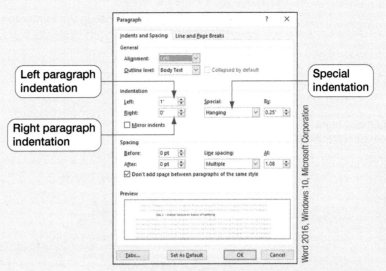

Left paragraph indentation

Right paragraph indentation

Special indentation

Word 2016, Windows 10, Microsoft Corporation

Figure 16 Indentation in the Paragraph dialog box

Troubleshooting

If only one line is indented, you did not have all three lines selected. Select the remaining lines and repeat step b.

d. To adjust the indentation visually, you decide to use the ruler. Point to the **Left Indent** ▢ marker on the ruler.

When you point to the square on the ruler, you will see a ScreenTip indicating that the marker is for the left indent. Just above the Left Indent marker is a small marker that represents a hanging indent. On the top of the side of the ruler is a marker representing a first-line indent. On the right side of the ruler, note the small marker, similar to the hanging indent. It represents a right indent. You can drag any of those markers to set a corresponding indent.

e. Drag the Left **Indent marker** ▢ on the ruler to the **2"** ruler mark to increase the left indent. As you drag, notice the vertical guide that moves with you, giving a visual clue to placement within the document. Keep the text selected.

First Line Indent marker

Hanging Indent marker

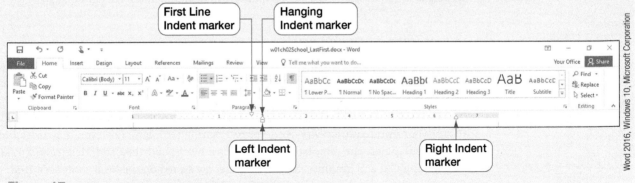

Word 2016, Windows 10, Microsoft Corporation

Left Indent marker

Right Indent marker

Figure 17 Indentation using the ruler

Troubleshooting

If you drag a marker other than the Left Indent marker, your text may not line up cleanly at the 2 inch mark. In that case, click Undo, and then repeat steps c and d.

f. Click the **Layout** tab, and then in the Paragraph group, under Indent, click the **Left** down arrow to decrease the left indent to **1.5"**. Click anywhere in the document to deselect the text.

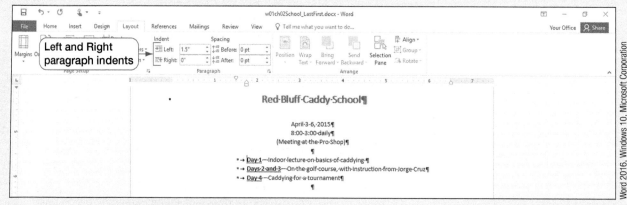

Figure 18   Indentation on the Layout tab

g. **Save** 🖫 the document.

h. Click the **File** tab, and then click **Close**. The document closes, but Word remains open.

Work with Templates

A **template** is a document that is used as a starting point for another document. It has a pre-established format and layout. A template has very little content of its own, perhaps only headings or very generic sample text. For example, a resignation letter template may contain sample text and addresses, structured in a semi-block style that you can modify to suit your own requirements. Another resignation template, however, may use a block style layout. Select the template that suits your needs, and then add, delete, and modify the existing text and graphics. Some templates are stored on the local computer, from the Office installation; others are available from Microsoft's online site, Office.com.

Working with Templates

A template's sample text and headings are sometimes stored in named placeholders. To chan...
text in a placeholder, click in the placeholder to select the text, and then format as necessary. In addition, a placeholder can be moved to a new location in the template, or deleted.

A gift certificate of $25 to the Red Bluff Bistro will be given away on the last day of the Caddy School. In this exercise, you will download a template to create the gift certificate and then fill in the placeholders with the necessary information.

To Work with Templates

a. Click the **File** tab, and then click **New**.
   This is similar to the Word Start screen because you can create a new file from either a blank document or a template.

b. Click in the **Search for online templates** box, type gift certificates, and then press Enter. Point to any **gift certificate** to reveal its full name.

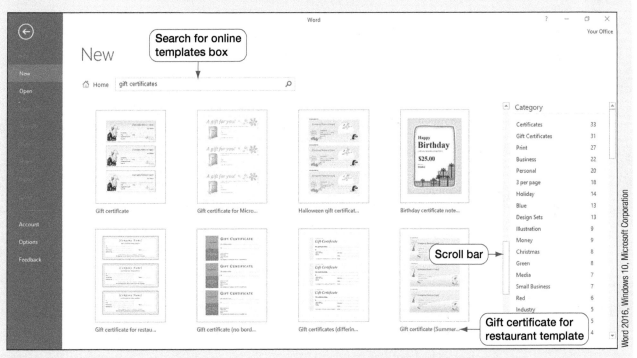

Figure 19 Searching for a template

c. Scroll down, click **Gift certificate for restaurant**, and then click **Create**. Three gift certificates appear in the document.

Troubleshooting

If you have trouble locating the Gift certificate for restaurant template, click in the Search for online templates box again, and type "restaurant gift certificate". Click the thumbnail of the Gift certificate for restaurant template, and then click Create.

---

d. Click **Save** 🖫, double-click **This PC**, and then navigate to where you are saving your project files. Save the file with the file name of w01ch02Gift_LastFirst, using your last and first name. Click **Save**. If you are asked about saving in a new file format, click **OK**.

Because this is the first time you are saving this file, you are required to specify a name and location for the file.

e. In the top certificate, click in the placeholder **Company Name**. The Company placeholder field is displayed, and the text in the placeholder is selected.

Troubleshooting

If the text in the placeholder is not selected, triple-click in the placeholder area to select the text.

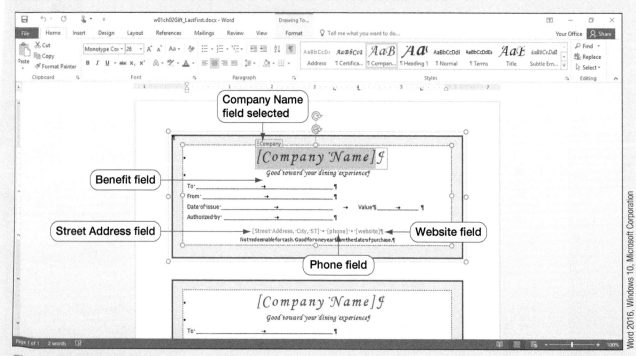

Figure 20 Restaurant template

f. Making sure not to press Enter, type Red Bluff Bistro.

g. Click anywhere in the line **Good toward your dining experience**. The Benefit placeholder field is displayed, and the text is selected.

h. Making sure not to press Enter, type $25 meal at Red Bluff Bistro.

i. Click anywhere in the field **Street Address, City, ST** to select the text. Making sure not to press Enter, type 3356 Hemmingway Cir, Santa Fe, NM.

j. Similarly, change the phone placeholder text to 505-555-1387, and change the website placeholder text to www.paintedparadiseresort.com. Click outside the certificate to deselect the text.

k. Select the text **Value $** and the **underline**, and then press [Delete].
    Because this text is not a placeholder, it is not automatically deleted from the other two certificates.

l. Delete the text **Value $** and the **underline** from the other two certificates.

m. **Save** 🖫 the document. Word automatically fills in the fields for the remaining two gift certificates in the template, though the formatting is not applied.

n. Click the **File** tab, and then click **Close**. If you need to take a break before finishing this chapter, now is a good time.

Formatting a Document

You have explored formatting at the character level and at the paragraph level. Formatting at the document level affects the pages in the document. For example, you may want to change the page margins or add a page border. When working with a lengthy document, knowing how to apply formats that affect an entire document can get a job done quickly and easily. In this section, you will explore page layout settings, learn to adjust margins, change page orientation, modify backgrounds, use borders, and work with themes.

Change Page Setup

The page setup of a document includes settings such as margins, orientation, and alignment. A format can be applied to the entire document or, as you will learn in a later chapter, to individual sections and pages. Selections on the Layout tab enable you to easily complete these tasks.

Changing Page Orientation and Margins

A document presented in **portrait orientation** is taller than it is wide, while **landscape orientation** displays a page wider than it is tall. The default orientation for a document is portrait. Use Backstage view or the Layout tab to change the orientation.

 CONSIDER THIS | **Selection of Page Orientation**

Typically, portrait orientation is most suitable for documents. Can you identify any kinds of documents that would be more attractive or effective in landscape orientation?

The blank space at the top, bottom, left, or right side of a document is called a **margin**. If you do not specify otherwise, all margins are set at 1 inch by default. Inevitably, you will find a need to change margins in some documents. For example, reducing the margins can sometimes make the difference between being able to fit all the text on one page and having one or two extra lines on a second page. Word provides a collection of predefined margin settings from which you can select, or you can easily define custom margins if you need to be more specific.

REAL WORLD ADVICE | **Changing Default Margins**

The default margins are 1 inch on all sides. What if your company requires 2 inch top and bottom margins? Instead of modifying the margins for each document you create, Word enables you to change the default margin setting. If you set your own Custom Margins and then select Set As Default, the new margin settings will be in effect each time you begin a new document, thus saving you time.

You can set the margins and page orientation of a document in the same location.

1. Click the Layout tab.
2. Click Margins in the Page Setup group.
3. Click Custom Margins to display the Page Setup dialog box.
4. Change the Margins settings.
5. Under Orientation select Portrait or Landscape.
6. Click OK.

 W02.14

To Change Page Orientation and Margins in a Document

a. Click the **File** tab, and then click **Open**. In the Recent Documents list, click **w01ch02School_LastFirst**.

b. Click the **Layout** tab. In the Page Setup group, click **Orientation**, and then select **Landscape**. You see the resulting document layout and decide that you prefer Portrait orientation for this document. On the Quick Access Toolbar, click **Undo** 5.

c. In the Page Setup group, click **Margins**, and then select **Custom Margins**.

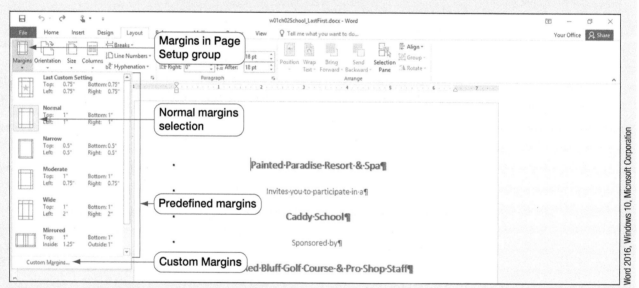

Figure 21 Selecting margins

d. Under Margins, select the text in the **Top** box, type .75, and then press Tab⇆. In the same way, change the **Bottom**, **Left**, and **Right** margins to .75.

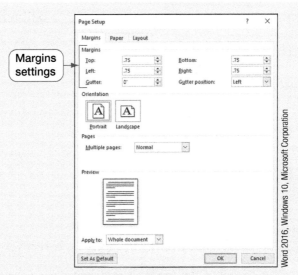

Margins settings

Figure 22 Define custom margins

Word 2016, Windows 10, Microsoft Corporation

e. Click **OK** to close the Page Setup dialog box. All margins on the document have been changed from 1 inch to 0.75 inch.

f. **Save** the document.

Centering a Page Vertically

As you recall, when you click Center in the Paragraph group, text is centered between the left and right margins. Word also provides a way to center the text between the top and bottom margins. This is known as centering a page vertically and is commonly used in creating cover pages and flyers. Word allows you to vertically center either selected text in a document or all pages in a document. In this exercise, you will change the margins and vertically align the text in the caddy flyer. You will also experiment with the orientation of the flyer.

REAL WORLD ADVICE   **A Quick Way to Design a Cover Page**

Although you can develop a cover page by centering a page vertically, you can let Word do the work for you instead. On the Insert tab, in the Pages group, you can select from several installed cover styles or select cover pages from Office.com.

W02.15

SIDE NOTE
Vertically Center Selection
If you want to vertically center only a selection of text, click the Apply to arrow and select Selected text..

To Work with Page Layout Settings

a. Click the **View** tab, and then in the Zoom group, click **One Page**. By reducing the magnification, you are better able to see the results of changes made to the page layout.

b. Click the **Layout** tab, and then in the Page Setup group, click the **Page Setup Dialog Box Launcher** . In the Page Setup dialog box, click the **Layout** tab.

c. Click the **Vertical alignment** arrow, and then select **Center**. The text on the flyer is centered vertically. Click **OK**.

SIDE NOTE
Change the Orientation and Margins
You can set margins and orientation in Backstage view under Print. The changes are then immediately displayed in the print preview.

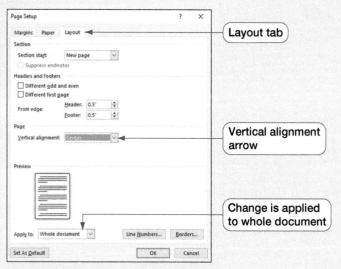

Figure 23 Centering a page vertically

d. **Save** the document.

Change Page Background

The default page background for Word 2016 is white with no border or graphics. Although you never want to go overboard with color or graphics, you might need to enhance a document with color, borders, or even texture. These and other page background settings are located on the Design tab in Word 2016.

In limited cases, a change to a more colorful or textured background might better suit the document's purpose and audience. Keep in mind brightly colored documents can be expensive to print and are generally not necessary or appropriate for business documents. Colored backgrounds can liven up greeting cards, flyers, business cards, or personal stationery, but the background should never overwhelm the text.

REAL WORLD ADVICE | **Printing a Page Background**

Changing the color of a page background is no guarantee that the colored background will print. Always carefully scrutinize readability when using a background color.

Inserting a Watermark

A **watermark** is text or a picture that appears behind document text. A watermark can add interest or identity to a document. For example, documents often include a DRAFT watermark, indicating that they are not in their final form. Figure 24 shows a document with a watermark. If you include a watermark, it will be displayed only in Print Layout or when the document is printed. Word provides built-in text and graphics that you can select as a watermark, or you can create your own. You can lighten a watermark so that it does not interfere with the readability of the document, or you can remove the current watermark. In this exercise, you will change the page background color of the caddy flyer and add a DRAFT watermark.

Memo

To:	Painted Paradise Event Planning Group
From:	Patti Rochelle, Events Coordinator
Date:	May 12, 2015
Re:	Putts for Paws Charity Golf Tournament

Painted Paradise Resort is once again sponsoring the Annual Red Bluff Putts for Paws Golf Tournament with this year's proceeds benefiting the Santa Fe Animal Center. The success of this fundraiser will be determined in large part by the participation and support of our community partners. As a valued member of the Event Planning staff at Painted Paradise, I am counting on you to promote the event and to solicit participation from the community. This memo provides basic details on activities and sponsorship opportunities so that you may be well informed and able to answer questions from interested parties.

The tournament, beginning at noon on July 31, promises a full afternoon of special events an exciting competition. Participants can enjoy a warm-up session with our own Red Bluff Golf, John Schilling, as well as chipping and putting contests. Animals from the Santa Fe Animal Center, available for adoption, will be on hand to visit. A silent auction and raffle will round out the day. Of course, the tournament would not be complete without our highly acclaimed dessert buffet, with prized selections from Indigo5! Restaurant. Painted Paradise Resort and Spa has prepared for you a fun-filled day at the resort!

We believe in giving back to the community. We are also certain that our community partners and past donors share our commitment to support such worthwhile causes as the Santa Fe Animal Center. We invite our community partners to participate in the event by sponsoring a golf cart, a hole on the golf course, or a course flagstick. We also invite participation in the form of individual or corporate golf teams. Pricing details on all of those opportunities are given below.

- Individual Player - $200
- Individual Player (includes caddy) - $500
- Team of Four - $550
- Corporate Team of Four - $850 (includes hole sponsorship and four caddies)
- Cart Sponsor (Logo/brand displayed on cart; includes dinner for four at Indigo5! Restaurant) - $2000
- Hole Sponsor (Logo/brand displayed on a course tee) - $500
- Flag Sponsor (Logo/brand displayed on a course flagstick) - $500

We look forward to a fun-filled tournament—an activity that truly gives back to our community while also enabling us to connect with those who share our commitment. I appreciate your involvement and know that I can count on you to support the effort in any way you are asked

(Watermark)

Figure 24 Including a watermark

To Change a Page Color and Add a Watermark

a. Click the **Design** tab, and in the Page Background group, click **Page Color**, and then point to any color selection in the color palette without clicking.
A Live Preview of the selection is displayed. Explore the effect of several colors. For even more color detail, you can click More Colors. If you prefer a gradient or texture fill, click Fill Effects. Other effects include patterns or even pictures.

b. Under Theme Colors, in the first column and second row, select **White, Background 1, Darker 5%**. A pale gray background is added to the page.

c. In the Page Background group, click **Watermark**.
The gallery provides selections from a predefined list. Because the flyer must be approved before distribution, you will include a DRAFT watermark.

d. Scroll through the predefined watermarks, and then select **DRAFT 1**.

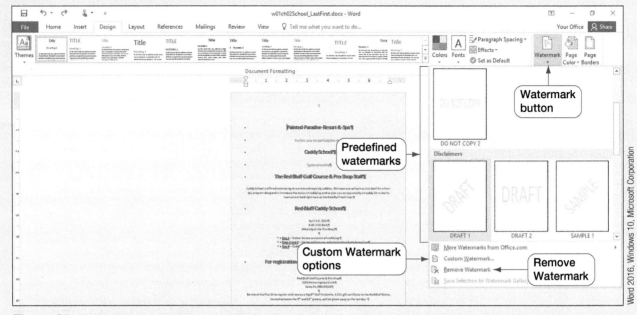

Figure 25 Creating a watermark

e. In the Page Background group, click **Watermark**, and then select **Custom Watermark**. The Printed Watermark dialog box opens. Because the watermark is a little too transparent, click the **Semitransparent** check box to deselect it and make the watermark darker and easier to read. Click **OK** to close the dialog box.

f. **Save** 🖫 the document.

Adding a Page Border

A page border, a line or graphic that surrounds a page, works especially well in flyers and customized stationery. A page border is most appropriate for one-page documents; it is seldom necessary to include one in a multiple-page document. In this exercise, you will add a page border to the Caddy School flyer.

 W02.17

To Add a Page Border

a. Click the **Design** tab, and in the Page Background group, click **Page Borders** to open the Borders and Shading dialog box. Under Setting, click **Shadow**.
    In the Preview pane, in the Borders and Shading dialog box, a preview of the page border appears.

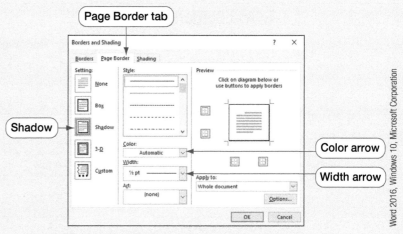

Figure 26 Adding a page border

Word 2016, Windows 10, Microsoft Corporation

b. While you are still on the Page Border tab of the Borders and Shading dialog box, click the **Color** arrow, and then under Theme Colors, in the fourth column and first row, select **Blue-Gray, Text 2**. Click the **Width** arrow, select **1 pt**, and then click **OK** to close the dialog box.
A shadow border is applied to the flyer.

c. Click the **View** tab, and then in the Zoom group, click **100%**.

d. **Save** 💾 the document.

Adding Borders and Shading

The addition of borders and shading can add emphasis to one or more paragraphs or to the entire document. Although the most frequently used borders are bottom, top, left, right, or outside, Word provides a wide range of additional specialty borders. Borders are available in the Paragraph group on the Home tab and in the Page Background group of the Design tab in applying borders to the entire document page. As you apply a border to a paragraph, you can specify line style, color, and weight. In addition, you can apply shading or a background color to a bordered area. When used in conjunction with a border, shading can add definition and draw attention to one or more paragraphs.

Because the use of shading and borders is a type of paragraph formatting, you do not have to select the paragraph. Instead, the selected border or shading is applied only to the paragraph in which the insertion point is positioned. Of course, to apply a border or shading to more than one paragraph, you must select all those paragraphs.

In this exercise, you will add a border to the Red Bluff Caddy School section. After adding the border, you will shade and indent the section from the left and right margins.

REAL WORLD ADVICE | **Highlighting Text Versus Shading**

Paragraph shading adds background color to one or more paragraphs. If you want to add background color to a smaller selection of text rather than to an entire paragraph, you can add highlighting by selecting text and clicking the Text Highlight Color arrow in the Font group on the Home tab.

W02.18

To Add Borders and Shading

a. Select the four lines beginning with **Red Bluff Caddy School** and ending with **(Meeting at the Pro Shop)**.

b. Click the **Home** tab, and then in the Paragraph group, click the **Borders** arrow ⊞ ▾.

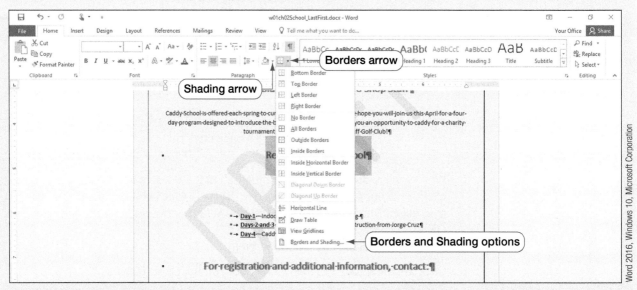

Figure 27   Selecting a border

c. Select **Borders and Shading**. The Borders and Shading dialog box opens, with the Borders tab selected.

d. Under Setting, click **Box**, and then under Style, scroll down the list and select the **double underline** (seventh from top). Because you selected text before applying the border, the Apply to box is set to Paragraph.

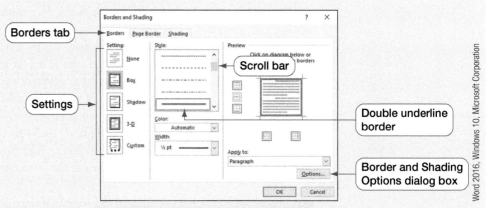

Figure 28   Borders and Shading dialog box

e. Click **Options** to open the Border and Shading Options dialog box, and then click the **Bottom** up arrow three times to display **4 pt**. Click **OK** to close the Border and Shading Options dialog box, and then click **OK** to close the Borders and Shading dialog box. Do not deselect the text.

Because the style of text had no paragraph After spacing, you increased the spacing after the last line of text to 4 pt in the Border and Shading Options dialog box. This increased the white space above the bottom border.

f. With the text still selected, in the Paragraph group, click the **Shading** arrow , and then under Theme colors, in the first column and fourth row, select **White, Background 1, Darker 25%**.

g. With the text still selected, click the **Layout** tab, and then in the Paragraph group, change the **Left** and **Right** values to **1.5"** each, and then click anywhere in the document to deselect the text.

h. **Save** the document.

Use Themes

A **theme** is a set of design elements that enables you to create professional, color-coordinated documents with minimal effort. Color, fonts, and graphics can be combined to provide a unified look for a document and can even coordinate with other Office applications to create "matching" files. For example, a PowerPoint presentation that includes a certain theme can be matched to a Word document using the same color coordination. A company might require a certain theme so that all documents portray a unified or branded look.

CONSIDER THIS | **Global Theme**

Businesses today must think globally. The use of technology simplifies worldwide communication and facilitates global marketing. Communicating in so many diverse cultures can be quite a challenge. When creating a theme or common design to represent your business globally, what considerations are necessary to be effective in a worldwide market?

Working with a Theme

Themes are located in the Document Formatting group of the Design tab. As you point to a theme, you see a Live Preview of the effect of the theme on the document text. Click on the theme to accept the change.

Even a blank document is based on a theme. If you do not specify otherwise, the default theme, which is called Office, is in effect when a new document is created. When you click the Font Color arrow on the Home tab, you will see colors divided into Theme Colors and Standard Colors. The Theme Colors set is a group of colors that work well together for a particular theme. A theme contains four text and background colors, six accent colors, and two hyperlink colors. Similarly, Theme Fonts is a set of fonts that coordinate with the theme. Each theme identifies one font for document headings and another for body text. Because theme colors are designed to complement one another, it is a good idea to select colors from a single theme's color palette to ensure compatibility.

If you like some elements of a theme but want to change others, you can select Theme Colors, Theme Fonts, or Theme Effects in the Document Formatting group of the Design tab. Each group of coordinated colors, fonts, or effects is identified by name. Select an existing group, or if desired, you can customize the individual colors or fonts within a group. In this exercise, you will apply a theme to the flyer.

To Work with a Theme

a. Click the **Design** tab, and then in the **Document Formatting** group, click **Themes**.

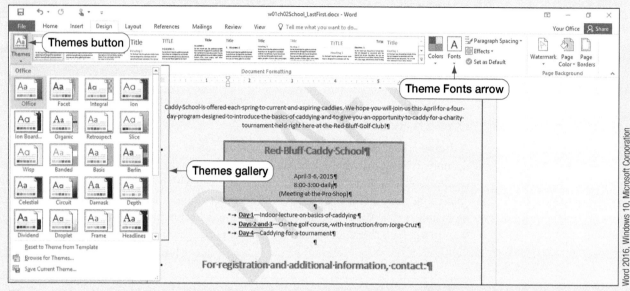

Figure 29   Selecting a theme

b. Click **Integral**.

A new theme has been applied to the entire document. The font, font color, and effects have been changed throughout the flyer. You like the new theme but prefer it to have a different font.

c. On the Design tab, in the Document Formatting group, click **Theme Fonts** ⒶA. Scroll through the font selections, pausing on several to view the effect on the document, and then select **Times New Roman-Arial**.

You have now set Times New Roman as the font for all headings in this theme and Arial as the font for all body text.

d. Click the **Home** tab, and then in the Font group, click the **Font Color** arrow Ⓐ, noting the different theme colors.

Because you have selected a different theme, the font color selections have changed. Notice that in the third column, first row of the theme colors Ice Blue, Background 2 is listed as the color. In the default document theme, Gray-25%, Background 2 is located in the same position under theme colors.

e. **Save** ⒽΗ the document, exit Word, and then submit your files as directed by your instructor.

Concept Check

1. What are some techniques to copy, cut, and paste text in a document? p. 174

2. Why would you use styles? When would you use a Heading 1 style versus a Heading 2 style versus the Normal style? Why would you use the Navigation Pane? When you modify an existing style or create a style, the style is available to use throughout your document. Would you ever want the style to be available in all future documents? p. 178–182

3. Provide an example of when you might want to use the Format Painter. p. 185–186

4. What is the difference between a bulleted list and a numbered list? When should you use a numbered list? p. 187

5. What is the difference between a left indent, a right indent, a hanging indent, and a first-line indent? List three different ways to change a left or right indent. p. 189

6. What is a template? What is the difference between creating a new file from scratch and creating a new file based on a template? What is a business example in which you might use a template? p. 192

7. When would you use landscape versus portrait orientation? What is the difference between center-aligned text and centering your page vertically? What is a margin? p. 195

8. What is a watermark? How are watermarks used in a business environment? p. 198

9. What is the difference between page borders and borders on text? p. 200–201

10. What is the default theme when you create a new document? Why would you use themes? p. 203

Key Terms

Bullet   187
Character style   178
Clipboard   174
Clipboard pane   174
Copy   174
Cut   174
First-line indent   189
Format Painter   185
Hanging indent   189

Landscape orientation   195
Left indent   189
Margin   195
Navigation Pane   179
Office Clipboard   174
Paragraph style   178
Paste   174
Paste Preview   174
Portrait orientation   195

Right indent   189
Ruler   173
Style   178
Symbol   188
Template   192
Theme   203
Watermark   198

Visual Summary

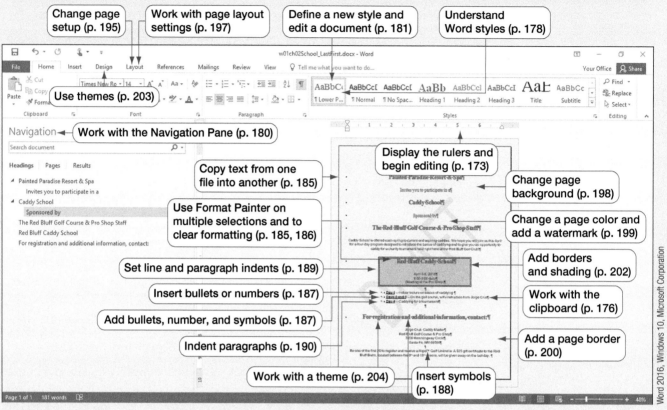

Figure 30

Callouts in Figure 30:
- Change page setup (p. 195)
- Work with page layout settings (p. 197)
- Define a new style and edit a document (p. 181)
- Understand Word styles (p. 178)
- Use themes (p. 203)
- Work with the Navigation Pane (p. 180)
- Copy text from one file into another (p. 185)
- Use Format Painter on multiple selections and to clear formatting (p. 185, 186)
- Set line and paragraph indents (p. 189)
- Insert bullets or numbers (p. 187)
- Add bullets, number, and symbols (p. 187)
- Indent paragraphs (p. 190)
- Work with a theme (p. 204)
- Display the rulers and begin editing (p. 173)
- Change page background (p. 198)
- Change a page color and add a watermark (p. 199)
- Add borders and shading (p. 202)
- Work with the clipboard (p. 176)
- Add a page border (p. 200)
- Insert symbols (p. 188)

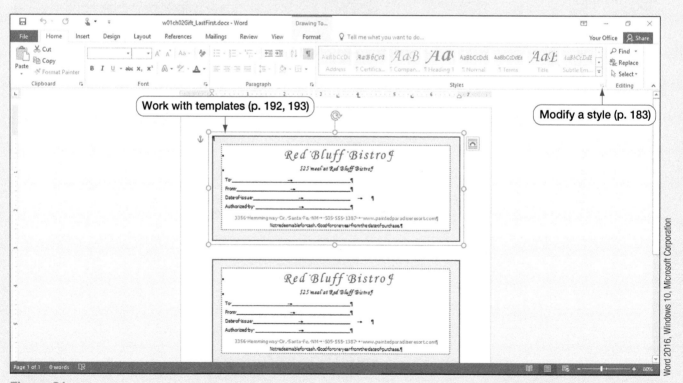

Figure 31

Callouts in Figure 31:
- Work with templates (p. 192, 193)
- Modify a style (p. 183)

Student data file needed:
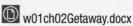 w01ch02Getaway.docx

You will save your file as:
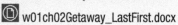 w01ch02Getaway_LastFirst.docx

Production &
Operations

Women's Golf Getaway

Each fall, the Red Bluff Golf Course & Pro Shop hosts a weekend golf getaway for women. The three-day event combines golf lessons, rounds of golf, an evening reception, regional cuisine, and luxury accommodations at the Painted Paradise Resort & Spa. It is open to women of all ages, and participants receive instruction from two of the top golf pros in the country. The Women's Golf Getaway program provides instruction for all skill levels and is one of the most attended annual events of the resort. You will prepare a document, containing the event details, that will be used to advertise the event.

a. Start **Word**, click **Open Other Documents**, and then double-click **This PC.** Navigate to the location of your student files, and then double-click **w01ch02Getaway**.

b. If necessary, on the Home tab, in the Paragraph group, click **Show/Hide**.

c. Click the **File** tab, click **Save As**. Double-click **This PC**, and then navigate to where you are saving your project files. Change the File name to w01ch02Getaway_LastFirst, using your last and first name. Click **Save**.

d. Click anywhere in the paragraph that begins with **We are pleased**. On the Home tab, in the Styles group, click the **Dialog Box Launcher**, and then click **New Style**.

e. You will create a new style for the body of the document.

- In the **Name** box, type Getaway Body.
- Click the **Font** arrow, and then select **Arial**. Click the **Font Size** arrow, and then select **12**.
- Click **Format**, and then select **Paragraph**. Under Indentation, click the **Left** up arrow to display **0.5"**, and then click the **Right** up arrow to display **0.5"**. You have set a 0.5 inch left and right indent.
- Under Spacing, change **Before** and **After** to **18 pt**.
- Click **OK**, and then click **OK** again to close the Create New Style from Formatting dialog box and to apply the style to the paragraph beginning with **We are pleased**.

f. Click in the paragraph beginning with **Join us at the**, and then in the Styles pane, click **Getaway Body**. Similarly, apply the **Getaway Body** style to the paragraph beginning with **We are ready to welcome you**.

g. Press Ctrl+Home, select the text **Women's Golf Getaway** in the first paragraph under the title, and then in the Font group, click **Bold**. Click to place the insertion point at the end of the paragraph, after **October 12-14, 2018.**, and then press Enter.

h. In the Paragraph group, click the **Bullets** arrow, and then under Bullet Library, select the **check mark**. Type the following lines, pressing Enter after each line, including the last line. A checkmark bullet will appear before each line that you type.

Do you love to play golf?

Do you enjoy a resort atmosphere?

Do you feel the need to pamper yourself?

i. Click the **File** tab, and then click **Print**.
Because you see that landscape might not be the best orientation for this document, you change the orientation to portrait.

j. Press Esc to return to the document. Click the **Layout** tab, and then in the Page Setup group, click **Orientation**, and then select **Portrait**.

k. Select the three bulleted lines, and then in the Paragraph group, change **Left** to **2"**.

l. Select the five lines beginning with **Luxury suite accommodations** and ending with **Saturday lunch at Red Bluff Bistro**. In the Styles pane, click **Emphasis**. With the text still selected, click the **Home** tab, and then in the Paragraph group, click **Center**, click the **Font Size** arrow, and then select **12**.

m. Select the five lines beginning with **Patti Rochelle, Event Planning Manager** and ending with **prochelle@paintedparadiseresort.com**. In the Styles pane, click **No Spacing**. With the text still selected, in the Paragraph group, click **Center**. Close the Styles pane.

n. Press [Ctrl]+[Home] to move to the top of the document. Click anywhere in the first line of the document, **Red Bluff Golf Course & Pro Shop**. On the Home tab, in the Clipboard group, double-click **Format Painter**. Scroll to the bottom of the document, select the lines **Reserve your place today!** and **Painting Your Perfect Getaway!**. In the Clipboard group, click **Format Painter** to turn off the Format Painter.

o. You decide that your document needs a little more white space. Click anywhere in the line **Luxury suite accommodations**. Click the **Layout** tab, and then in the Paragraph group, change the paragraph **Before** spacing to **30 pt**. Similarly, for the line **Saturday lunch at Red Bluff Bistro**, change the paragraph **After** spacing to **30 pt**.

p. Click to place the insertion point in front of the **S** in the sentence **Spaces fill up fast**. Press [Bksp] twice to remove the space and the period. Click the **Insert** tab, and then in the Symbols group, click **Symbol**, and then select **More Symbols**. Click the **Special Characters** tab, click **Em Dash**, click **Insert**, and then click **Close**.

q. Click the **Layout** tab, and then in the Page Setup group, click **Margins**, and then select **Narrow**.

r. Click **Margins**, select **Custom Margins**, and then in the Page Setup dialog box, click the **Layout** tab. Click the **Vertical alignment** arrow, select **Center** to center the document vertically, and then click **OK**.

s. Click the **Design** tab, and then in the Page Background group, click **Page Borders** to open the Borders and Shading dialog box. If necessary, select the Page Border tab selected. Click **Box** under Setting, and then click **OK**.

t. In the Document Formatting group, click **Themes**, and then select **Facet**.

u. In the Page Background group, click **Page Color**, and then in the first column and second row, click **White, Background 1, Darker 15%**.

v. Select the five lines beginning with the line **Luxury suite accommodations** and ending with **Saturday lunch at Red Bluff Bistro**. Click the **Home** tab, and then in the Paragraph group, click the **Borders** arrow, and then select **Borders and Shading**. The Borders and Shading dialog box opens with the Borders tab selected.

w. Under Setting, click **Box**, and then click **OK**.

x. Click the **Layout** tab, and then in the Paragraph group, under Indent, change **Left** to **1"**, and then change **Right** to **1"**.

y. Click the **Insert** tab, and then in the Header & Footer group, click **Footer**, and then select **Edit Footer**. In the Insert group, click **Document Info**, and then select **File Name**. Click the **Home** tab, and then click **Center**. Double-click in the body of your document to close the footer.

z. Click the **Design** tab, and then in the Page Background group, click **Watermark**. Scroll down, and then select the **DRAFT 1** watermark.

aa. In the Page Background group, click **Watermark**, and then click **Custom Watermark**. Click the **Semitransparent** checkbox to deselect it, and then press **OK**.

bb. Select the first paragraph of the document. Change the font size to **26**.

cc. **Save** the document, exit Word, and then submit your file as directed by your instructor.

Student data file needed:

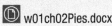 w01ch02Pies.docx

You will save your file as:

w01ch02Pies_LastFirst.docx

Production & Operations

Pie Contract Letter

Indigo5 is sending a contract letter to a local baker outlining the terms of their agreement for pies. The restaurant manager, Alberto Dimas, has drafted a document in Modified Block style. He would like you to edit and format it further.

a. Open the Word document, **w01ch02Pies**. Save the document as w01ch02Pies_LastFirst, using your last and first name.

b. Display the formatting marks and the ruler if they are not already displayed.

c. Select the first four paragraphs, starting with **Alberto Dimas, Manager** and ending with **Santa Fe, NM 87594**. Set a **4"** left indent. Click anywhere to deselect the text.

d. Select the first three lines, starting with **Alberto Dimas, Manager** and ending with **3356 Hemmingway Circle**. Change the Paragraph After spacing to **0 pt**.

e. Select the three lines starting with **Ms. Marcy Niche** and ending with the line **5678 Alamo Drive NW**. Change the paragraph After spacing to **0 pt**.

f. Click anywhere in the line **Lemon Meringue — 4**. Using the Format Painter, paste this format to the other three pie lines: **Apple — 6**, **Pecan — 4**, and **Pumpkin — 6**.

g. Arrange the list of pies in alphabetical order.

h. Select the four lines starting with **Apple — 6** and ending with **Pumpkin — 6**. Insert the default **Bullet** style (round black bullet) to the list of pies. Change the color of the bullets to **Orange, Accent 6, Darker 50%** (Under Theme Colors, column 10, row 6). Set the left indent to **1"**.

i. Add a dollar sign to the price of each pie in the bulleted list.

j. Change the line spacing of the entire document to **Single** (1.0).

k. Open the Styles pane. Click to place the insertion point in one of the bulleted lines. Note the **Book Title** style is selected in the Styles pane. Modify the Book Title style to remove **bold** from the bulleted lines.

l. Click anywhere in the paragraph beginning with **As we discussed on the phone**. Point to the First Line Indent marker on the ruler, and then drag to set the first line indent to **0.5"**. Similarly, for the paragraph beginning with **If sales are satisfactory**, change the first line indent to **0.5"**.

m. Select the last four paragraphs, starting with the line **Sincerely**, and ending with the line **Alberto Dimas, Manager**. Set the left indent to **4"**. The selection will include two blank paragraphs.

n. Change the top and bottom margins of the document to **1.25"**.

o. Remove the current watermark, and then insert the **CONFIDENTIAL 1** watermark.

p. **Save** the document, **exit** Word, and then submit your file as directed by your instructor.

Critical Thinking

What changes would you suggest to the letter completed in this exercise to enhance the professional appearance of the document? What aspects of the document would you change? How could you change the document to make it more apparent that it originated from the Painted Paradise Resort & Spa or the Indigo5 restaurant? You may suggest changes to the document that were not covered in this chapter.

Student data file needed:

 Blank Word document

You will save your file as:

 w01ch02BookSale_LastFirst.docx

Public Library Book Sale

Sales & Marketing

You are coordinating a book sale at your local public library. The goal of the book sale is to raise funds for new initiatives at the library. You need to prepare a letter that will be sent to the members, news media, vendors, and business supporters of the library.

a. Start Word, and then create a new blank document. Save the document as w01ch02BookSale_LastFirst, using your last and first name.

b. If necessary, show the ruler and nonprinting characters.

c. Enter your local public library's name and address in the first three paragraphs of the document. Modify the paragraph spacing on the first two lines of the address to eliminate the extra space after the paragraphs. Set the Left indent to 5[dp] for the first three paragraphs of the document.

d. Enter the date as Month Day, Year (for example, May 1, 2018).

e. Address the letter to:

Ms. Rebekah Holcomb

4143 Sodales Ave.

Santa Fe, NM 89566

f. Add an appropriate salutation and a paragraph of text describing the book sale. Include what types of activities and refreshments will be available along with any other relevant information.

g. Individually list the hours of the book sale and any activities included in the prior paragraph. Apply bullets to each list.

h. Select the paragraph listing the book sale hours, including the paragraph mark. Create a style named LastFirst using your last and first name.

i. Modify the style to make it bold, green (use the standard color), 12 pt and with no additional spacing after the paragraph.

j. Apply the LastFirst style to the paragraph listing the activities for the book sale.

k. Delete all blank lines in the document.

l. Place your first and last name in the signature block. Change the paragraph format so that there is no extra space after your name and 18 points of space before your name.

m. Add a Custom Watermark. Use a Text Watermark with the text Library Book Sale. Set the rest of the watermark options to the default values.

n. Save the document, exit Word, and then submit your file as directed by your instructor.

Additional Chapter Cases are available at www.pearsonhighered.com/youroffice

Additional Cases

Understanding **Word Fundamentals**

This business unit had two outcomes:

Learning Outcome 1

Understand the basics of word-processing software to develop effective, professional business documents.

Learning Outcome 2

Use a blank document or template to create, edit, and format letters, memos, flyers, and other business communication.

In Business Unit 1 Capstone, students will demonstrate competence in these outcomes through a series of business problems at various levels, from guided practice, problem solving an existing document, and performing to create new documents.

More Practice 1

Student data file needed:

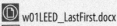 w01LEED.docx

You will save your files as:

w01LEED_LastFirst.docx

w01LEED_LastFirst.pdf

Research/
Development

Sales &
Marketing

Environmental Alliance Sustainable Hotel Information

You have prepared a rough draft of an information sheet for the Santa Fe Environmental Alliance Trade Show, an event that showcases buildings that are Leadership in Energy and Environmental Design (LEED) certified or that otherwise contribute to a more environmentally aware Santa Fe area. Painted Paradise Resort & Spa has recently attained LEED certification, having met a rigorous set of standards for sustainable construction and operation. The information sheet highlights the resort's environmental construction and activities. Before the document is ready for final distribution, you will modify it so that it includes appropriate headings, paragraph and document formatting, and text emphasis. You will save the file as a Word document and a PDF file. In addition, you will ensure that it is error free.

a. Start **Word**, click **Open Other Documents** in the left pane, and then double-click **This PC**. Navigate through the folder structure to the location of your student data files, and then double-click **w01LEED**.

b. If necessary, show nonprinting characters.

c. Click the File tab, click **Save As**, and then double-click **This PC**. In the **Save As** dialog box, navigate to where you are saving your project files, and then change the file name to w01LEED_LastFirst, using your last and first name.

d. Select the first paragraph, **Painted Paradise Resort & Spa**. Click the **Home** tab, in the Styles group, click **More**, and then apply the **Title** style from the Styles gallery. Select the second paragraph, **A Leader in Energy and Environmental Design**, and then apply the **Subtitle** style.

e. Click anywhere in the paragraph beginning with **Santa Fe is on a quest**. In the Styles group, click the **Dialog Box Launcher** to open the Styles pane. In the Styles pane, click **New Style**, and then in the Create New Style from Formatting dialog box, click in the **Name** box and delete any text, and then create a new style called Body Paragraph with the following characteristics:

- **Times New Roman** font with a font size of **11**
- **Justified** alignment

- **Blue, Accent 1, Darker 25%** font color (Under Theme Colors, in the fifth column and the fifth row)
- With the Create New Style from Formatting dialog box still open, click **Format**, and then select **Paragraph**.
- Under Special, select a **First line** indent of **0.5"**.
- Under Spacing, set After to **12 pt**.
- Under Line spacing, select **1.5 lines**.
- Click **OK** to close the Paragraph dialog box, and then click **OK** to close the Create New Style from Formatting dialog box.

f. Select the paragraph beginning with **Painted Paradise Resort & Spa recently became a LEED-certified hotel**. Apply the **Body Paragraph** style.

g. In the Styles pane, point to the **Normal** style, and then click the **arrow**. Select **Modify**, set the font color to **Blue, Accent 1, Darker 25%**, and then click **OK**.

h. Select the paragraph beginning with **Conservation doesn't have to mean deprivation**. With the paragraph selected, complete the following steps.
- In the Font group, click **Bold**.
- In the Paragraph group, click the **Borders** arrow, and then select **Borders and Shading**. Under Setting, click **Box**, and then click **OK**.
- In the Paragraph group, click the **Shading** arrow. Under Theme Colors, in the fifth column and third row, select **Blue, Accent 1, Lighter 60%**.
- In the Paragraph group, click the **Paragraph Dialog Box Launcher**, and then set a **0.5"** left and right indent. Click **OK**.

i. Under the **Guest Room Enhancements** heading, click to place the insertion point immediately after the word **Plus** in the first numbered paragraph. Click the **Insert** tab, and then in the Symbols group, click **Symbol**, and then select the **Trade Mark Sign** symbol (™).

j. Select the four numbered paragraphs, beginning with the paragraph starting with **Carpeting certified**, and ending with **televisions**. Click the **Home** tab, in the Paragraph group, click the **Bullets** arrow, and then click the **right arrowhead**.

k. Select the heading **Green Roof**, and then in the Styles gallery, apply the **Heading 2** style. Using the Styles pane, modify the **Heading 2** style to have a font size of **12**, **Arial** font, **bold** text, and a **6 pt** paragraph After spacing.

l. Apply the **Heading 2** style to all other headings: **Guest Room Enhancements**, **Solar Panels**, **Water Usage and Air Quality**, **Building Material**, **Kitchen**, and **Lighting**. Close the Styles pane.

m. Place the insertion point at the beginning of the paragraph **Building Material**. Type Recycled and press (Spacebar). Place the insertion point at the beginning of the paragraph **Kitchen**. Type Energy-Efficient and press (Spacebar).

n. Click the **View** tab, and then in the Show group, click **Navigation Pane**. Rearrange the headings and their content so they appear in alphabetical order. For example, the first category should be **Energy-Efficient Kitchen**, followed by **Green Roof**, and so on.

o. Close the Navigation Pane. Place the insertion point at the start of the paragraph beginning with **Santa Fe is on a quest**, and then press (Enter) to add one blank paragraph.

p. Click the **Layout** tab, in the Page Setup group, click **Margins**, and then select **Normal**.

q. Press (Ctrl)+(Home) to move the insertion point to the beginning of the document. Bold the words **Painted Paradise Resort & Spa** wherever they appear in the document. To do this using Find and Replace, click the **Home** tab, and then in the Editing group, click **Replace**. In the **Find what** box, type Painted Paradise Resort & Spa, and then in the **Replace with** box type Painted Paradise Resort & Spa. If necessary, click the **More** button to display additional Search Options. Click **Format**, select **Font**, click **Bold**, and then click **OK**. Click **Replace All**. Four replacements should be made. Click **OK**, and then close the dialog box.

r. Press Ctrl + Home . Click the **Review** tab, and then in the Proofing group, click **Spelling & Grammar**. Correct any errors. Note that **Plyboo** is not misspelled.

s. Proofread the document to make sure you did not overlook any misspellings or incorrect word usage. Correct anything that is not correct. You will find one word usage error that Word did not identify in the second sentence under the "Green Roof" heading.

t. Click the **Insert** tab, in the Header & Footer group, click **Footer**, and then select **Edit Footer**. Enter your first name and last name separated by a space. Press Tab twice. On the Header & Footer Tools Design tab, in the Insert group, click **Document Info** and then select **File Name**. Press Spacebar . In the Header & Footer group, click **Page Number**, point to Current Position, and then select **Plain Number**. Double-click anywhere in the document to close the footer.

u. Click the **Design** tab, and then in the Document Formatting group, click **Themes** and then select **Slice**.

v. In the Page Background group, click **Watermark**, scroll down, and then select **DRAFT 1**.

w. **Save** the document.

x. Click the **File** tab, and then click **Export**. Click **Create PDF/XPS**, navigate to the location where you are saving your project files, make sure the **Open file after publishing check box** is not selected, and then click **Publish** to create a PDF file with the same name.

y. Save the document, exit Word, and then submit your files as directed by your instructor.

Problem Solve 1

MyITLab®
Grader
Homework

Student data file needed:

 w01Directions.docx

You will save your files as:

w01Directions_LastFirst.docx

w01Directions_LastFirst.pdf

Directions to Local Attractions

Sales & Marketing

Production & Operations

Guests at the Painted Paradise Resort & Spa often ask the concierge staff for directions to the many attractions within driving distance of the resort. You have been asked to prepare a detailed list of driving directions to the most popular destinations, which the concierge staff can then hand to a guest upon request. You will work with a document begun by another staff member, enhancing the document for visual appeal and making sure that it is error free and easy to read.

a. Open the Word document, **w01Directions**. Save your file as w01Directions_LastFirst, using your last and first name.

b. Show nonprinting characters.

c. Select the first two paragraphs in the document, beginning with **Painted Paradise** and ending with **Directions to Santa Fe**. **Center** and **Bold** the two paragraphs

d. Select the first paragraph, beginning with **Painted Paradise**, and then change the font size to **18**. Select the second paragraph, beginning with **Directions to Santa Fe**, and then change the font size to **16**.

e. Place the insertion point at the beginning of the third paragraph of the document, **Canyon Road**. Create a new style called Attraction. The new style should include **bold** text and **6 pt** spacing after the paragraph. Apply the new style to the remaining two paragraphs of the address information, beginning with **602 Canyon Road** and **ending with Santa Fe, NM 87501**.

f. Apply the **Attraction** style to the three other attraction names and addresses in the document.

g. Move the insertion point to the beginning of the document. Use the spelling checker, correcting words that are misspelled and ignoring those that are not. There are no misspellings in the attraction addresses or in any street names, and "Railyard" should be left as one word.

h. After proofreading the document, you decide to remove the last 0 for the mileages listed as .10 miles, .20 miles, .30 miles, and .40 miles. For example, instead of stating a mileage as .20 miles, you prefer .2 miles. Use **Replace** to replace all occurrences of .10 to .1, and then all occurrences of .20 to .2, and so on.

i. Convert the seven paragraphs of directions to Canyon Road beginning with the paragraph **Make a sharp right turn on S. Guadalupe Street** and ending with the paragraph **Arrive at the Canyon Road Arts Center on the right** to a **numbered list**. With the seven paragraphs still selected, change the line spacing to **1.0** for all the items in the list.

j. Similarly, apply a **numbered list** and **single line spacing** to all other sets of instructions in the document.
   Each set of instructions should begin with the number 1. If this is not the case, simply right-click on the first numbered item of each list, and then select Restart at 1 from the shortcut menu.

k. Locate the **Museum Hill** instructions. Insert a new numbered step between steps 4 and 5 with the text Turn Left on Camino Lejo. Do not press Enter and include the period. Note that the new paragraph will now be numbered with a 5.

l. Select the **Bandelier National Monument** section, beginning with paragraph **Bandelier National Monument** and ending with the paragraph **8. Turn left on**. Cut the text and paste it to the top of the list, above the Canyon Road address and below the paragraph beginning with **Directions**.
   If necessary, insert one paragraph mark above the paragraph **Bandelier National Monument**, one paragraph mark above the paragraph **Canyon Road address**, and one paragraph mark above the paragraph **Museum Hill**.

m. Select the three address paragraphs for the Bandelier National Monument, starting with **Bandelier National Monument** and ending with **Los Alamos, NM 87544**. Apply a **Box** border with a **Tan, Background 2, Darker 10%** shaded fill. With the paragraphs still selected, apply a right indent of **4.2″**.

n. Copy the formatting of the Bandelier address to all other sets of addresses in the document. Remember to toggle the Format Painter on so that you can quickly copy the format to all the other sections.

o. Change the theme to **Ion Boardroom**.

p. Insert a header with the **File Name** field, center-aligned. Close the header.

q. Because you need the concierge staff's approval, insert the **DRAFT 1** watermark.

r. Preview the document from Backstage view. Notice that the landscape orientation is not appropriate. Change the orientation to **Portrait**. Return to the document.

s. Create a PDF, with the same file name, in case any of the guests prefer to have the directions sent to them via e-mail.

t. **Save** the document, exit Word, and then submit your files as directed by your instructor.

Grader

Homework

Student data file needed:

 Blank Word document

 w01Items.docx

You will save your files as:

 w01Menu_LastFirst.docx

 w01Menu_LastFirst.pdf

Indigo5 Special Event Menu

Sales & Marketing   Production & Operations

The Indigo5 restaurant at Painted Paradise Resort & Spa is hosting a special employee appreciation day. They are creating a special menu for the event. This menu will be posted outside the restaurant and e-mailed as a PDF to all employees of the resort and spa. You have been asked to create and design the menu for the event, and then export a copy of the menu as a PDF. The menu items that will be prepared for the event have been sent to you by Indigo5's Chef Robin Sanchez.

a. Start **Word**, in the **Search for online templates** box, type Menu, and press Enter. Create a new document from the **Party Menu (sun and sand design)** template. Save your file as w01Menu_LastFirst, using your last and first name. If prompted to upgrade to the newest file format, click **OK**.

b. Show nonprinting characters.

c. Select the text **Menu** and type Indigo5 Restaurant. Apply the **Title** style to the text.

d. Insert a new paragraph and type Employee Appreciation Event. Change the font size to **24**.

e. Select all text in the document and change the font to **Cambria**.

f. Open the Word document **w01Items**. If necessary, show nonprinting characters. The document contains a list of four menu items that will be offered at the event, each with a short description of the item. Copy the text in the paragraph containing the text **Avocado Salsa**. Do not copy the paragraph symbol. Switch to the **w01Menu_LastFirst** document. Click on the first **Item** placeholder and paste the copied text into the document.

g. Repeat this process for the remaining three menu items, replacing each menu item placeholder with the name from the w01ps2Items document.

h. Switch to the **w01Items** and copy the text in the paragraph beginning with **Mashed avocadoes**. Do not copy the paragraph symbol. Switch to the **w01Menu_LastFirst** document. Click on the first **A brief description of the dish.** placeholder and paste the copied text into the document.

i. Repeat this process for the remaining three descriptions, replacing each menu item description placeholder with the description from the w01Items document.

j. Delete the last **Item** placeholder and **A brief description of the dish.** placeholder.

k. Open the Styles pane. Click the **Normal** arrow and modify the paragraph **After** spacing to **54 pt**.

l. Set the margins to **Normal**.

m. Place the insertion point at the end of the last item description. Insert a new paragraph and type Please join us in celebrating all Painted Paradise Resort & Spa employees on this special day! including the exclamation mark.

n. Select the text from the prior step and change the font size **20** point. Center the text on the page. Change the font color to **Gold, Accent 2**.

o. Save the document. Export the document as a PDF with the same file name.

p. Save the document, exit Word, and then submit your files as directed by your instructor.

What is the advantage of using a template in an organization? How does this impact the branding of the organization? What are the advantages and disadvantages? For example, what happens if an employee makes poor design changes to the template?

Perform 1: Perform in Your Life

Student data file needed:

📄 Blank Word document

You will save your files as:

📄 w01SaleLetter_LastFirst.docx

📄 w01SaleFlyer_LastFirst.docx

Community Garage Sale

Production & Operations

In this project, you will create a letter to be sent to all homeowners in the community who might want to participate in the Annual Community Garage Sale. You will also create a flyer that will help promote the sale. Participants may host garage sales at any time throughout the weekend of May 4 - 6, 2018. The letter will include specific information to be used in the ad for your garage sale. Although the content is up to you, be sure to include at least two body paragraphs informing the Chamber of Commerce in your city of your intent to participate and specific details of information you want included in your ad.

a. Start **Word**, open a new blank document, and then save the document as w01SaleLetter_LastFirst, using your last and first name.

b. Using the Block style, include your address in the heading area. Include the components of a letter found in Chapter 1. Use the current date as the date. Locate the address of the Chamber of Commerce in your local community and use their address as the inside address on the letter.

c. You will write the content of the letter, but keep in mind you are providing a general description of your event. Be sure to include the following information:
   • Your first and last name
   • Your e-mail
   • Your phone number
   • Your address (street address, city, state, ZIP)
   • Description of your sale (dates of participation, times, and location)
   • List of types of items for sale in a standard bulleted list

d. Spell-check, and then proofread the document. Include the file name field as a footer, center-aligned. Save and close the document.

e. Create a one-page flyer, incorporating design elements that will generate enthusiasm and interest in the event. Save the flyer as w01SaleFlyer_LastFirst, using your last and first name.

f. Include specific information about the dates, times, and location of the event and a general list of items for sale.

g. Define appropriate margins for the flyer that differ from the default **Normal** margins.

h. Use at least two but no more than three Word styles in the flyer.

i. Include two different fonts and font sizes in the flyer. Use at least one instance of bold, italic, and underline formatting in the flyer.

j. Include one decorative bulleted list (using a symbol or picture for the bullets) in the flyer.

k. Select an appropriate page border.

l. Include a page color on the flyer. Center the page vertically.

m. Include the file name field as a footer, center-aligned.

n. Spell-check and then proofread the document.

o. Save the document, exit Word, and then submit your files as directed by your instructor.

Perform 2: Perform in Your Career

Student data file needed:

⬛ Blank Word document

You will save your files as:

⬛ w01Picnic_LastFirst.docx

⬛ w01Picnic_LastFirst.pdf

Annual Spring Picnic

Sales & Marketing

As a work-study student in the Student Services Department of your local community college, you have been asked by your supervisor to create a document announcing the Student Senate's Annual Spring Picnic, which is held on campus each spring. Using Word, download a flyer template to use as a starting point in creating your announcement. Insert relevant data and remove any unnecessary fields or information from the template. Save the file as a PDF document that will be e-mailed to various departments and student organizations on campus. The announcement will also be displayed on bulletin boards in the student center and at other visible points around campus. Format the document to create a professional-looking announcement that is easy to read. The document should include all of the necessary details about the spring picnic event, and your design should generate enthusiasm for the event and communicate a fun spring theme.

a. Start **Word**. Choose the Spring Flyer template or search for another appropriate flyer or announcement template design. Save the document as w01Picnic_LastFirst, using your last and first name.

b. Use the template as a guideline to help you get started, and then format the document as needed for the occasion, adding or deleting fields and placeholders as necessary. Include event time, date, and location in your document. Also include details about the types of food and refreshments that will be provided and at least two activities that will be held at the event.

c. Remove any unused or unnecessary items from the template.

d. Include a footer, with your first and last name, center-aligned.

e. Adjust the font, color, size, and style of text, ensuring a coordinating color scheme throughout your design theme. While making your design choices, maintain the readability of the document. Limit your fonts to two.

f. Spell-check and proofread for errors.

g. Create a PDF copy of the announcement to e-mail to your supervisor for approval. Name the PDF file w01Picnic_LastFirst, using your last and first name.

h. Save the documents, exit Word, and then submit your files as directed by your instructor.

Student data file needed:

Blank Word document

You will save your file as:

w01Welcome_TeamName.docx

PTO New Family Welcome Information

Customer
Service

You are the current Parent Teacher Organization president for your child's school. The PTO is creating a welcome packet containing information that is often requested by new families. The packet will include PTO contact information, along with information on each of the upcoming PTO functions. The chairs for each function will edit the document with their specific information. Before you begin, sit down with your team members to discuss the layout, the style, and any special formatting characteristics you plan to use. Remember, only one person can edit the document at any single time, so make sure you plan ahead by determining what each team member will be responsible for contributing and when they will make their updates.

a. Select one team member to set up the document by completing steps b–e.

b. Open your browser, and navigate to either www.onedrive.live.com, www.drive.google.com, or any other instructor-assigned tools. Be sure all members of the team have an account on the chosen system (Microsoft, Google, Dropbox, etc.).

c. Start **Word**, create a new document, and then name it w01Welcome_TeamName, where TeamName is the name assigned to your team by your instructor.

d. Share the file with the other members of your team, making sure that each team member has the appropriate permissions to edit the document.

e. Type in the following text, and then save the file.

Contact Information
PTO Meeting Information
Getting Started Volunteering
Back-to-School Picnic
Father-Daughter Dance
President's Day Walk-a-Thon
Mother-Son Breakfast
Auction
Contributions

f. The team is responsible for adding the appropriate information under each of the headings listed above. Divide the work evenly. At a minimum, include the following information:

Contact Information: Include contact information for the PTO President, PTO Vice President, PTO Treasurer, PTO Secretary, New Family Chair, Volunteer Coordinator, Auction Co-Chair, another Auction Co-Chair, Back-to-School Picnic Chair, Father-Daughter Dance Chair, Walk-a-Thon Chair, and Mother-Son Breakfast Chair.

PTO Meeting Information: Include information on when and where the PTO meeting takes place each month, how long the meeting takes, and any other necessary information.

Getting Started Volunteering: Include easy ways for a parent to volunteer, such as lunch room duty, recess monitor, and library volunteer.

Upcoming PTO Events: Include the following for each of the PTO events (Back-to-School Picnic, Father-Daughter Dance, President's Day Walk-a-Thon, Mother-Son Breakfast, and Auction).

When:

Where:

Information:

Volunteers:

g. List each team member's first and last name under the Contributions heading. Include a summary of each member's planned contributions in this section. Include any additional information required by your instructor.

h. Enter a main heading (not a header) at the top of the document. Apply the Title style to the heading.

i. Format the document appropriately. Create a new style for the subheadings.

j. Use lists appropriately.

k. Insert a footer, include the first and last name of the team members in the footer, and then format the footer appropriately.

l. Apply an appropriate theme. Use color appropriately.

m. Use at least two fonts and two different font sizes. Use bold and italic.

n. Make any necessary additions.

o. Proofread the document.

p. Once the assignment is complete, share the documents with your instructor or turn them in as your instructor directs. Make sure that the instructor has permission to edit the contents of the folder.

Perform 4: How Others Perform

Student data file needed:

 w01Garden.docx

You will save your file as:

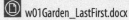 w01Garden_LastFirst.docx

Arbor Day Business Letter

Sales & Marketing

You are the manager of the Smarty Plants Nursery in Lebanon, Texas. With Arbor Day approaching, the nursery is planning a promotion of historical plants and trees. Perfect for school field trips or history lovers, the promotion will include plants that are representative of various eras of American history.

You will finalize a cover letter, originally created by your assistant, informing the Ebersold Botanical Garden of the program. Working from a draft, you will make sure the paragraphs flow well and that the document is formatted using the block style. In addition, you will format paragraphs and develop appropriate styles. Your goal is to produce an attractive, well-formatted document that is informative, readable, and error free.

a. Open the w01Garden, and then save the document as w01Garden_LastFirst, using your last and first name. The letter is from a local plant nursery, introducing a new program that offers seedlings from historical plants.

b. Edit the document so that it is in block style. Study the various parts of the letter (recipient address, date, return address, salutation, etc.), and then make any adjustments you find necessary.

c. Select an attractive font type and size for the document.

d. Create a new style for the paragraphs in the body of the letter, using an appropriate paragraph spacing. Apply the style to all body paragraphs except the numbered items.

e. The paragraphs are not in logical order. Rearrange them so they flow well.

f.   Check the spelling. If you are not certain whether a word is misspelled, look it up online or in a dictionary.

g.   Because the items listed in the numbered list are not sequential items, numbers are not the best choice. Use bullets and indentation of your choice instead.

h.   Make sure the document fits on one page. If it extends to two pages, adjust the margins, spacing, and/or font size to reduce it to one.

i.   Include a footer with the file name field, center-aligned.

j.   Make any other improvements you think necessary.

k.   Save the document, exit Word, and then submit your file as directed by your instructor.

Word Business Unit 2

Impressing with Sophisticated Documents

Tools within Word enable a variety of ways to enhance a text document. Inserting images, SmartArt, or WordArt can visually enhance a document without distracting from its purpose. Setting tabs and breaks in a document or creating a table from text can also enhance the appearance of material in a document. The comments and track changes features are used, collaborating on a Word document is more efficient. Word can also quickly generate references such as a bibliography or a works cited page or use endnotes and footnotes to annotate a document. Finally, Word can work with other Microsoft Office applications as a communication tool by creating merged letters, labels, and envelopes. This business unit will guide you through the use of these tools to leverage Word's collaborative and documenting capabilities.

Learning Outcome 1

Include tables, page, column, and section breaks, and insert objects in Word to create appealing and professional documents.

REAL WORLD SUCCESS

"I teach first grade and use Word daily to create center activities that tie in with the concepts we're learning—worksheets to help them practice our new skills and mini-assessments to check mastery of concepts. I'm able to easily make the activities fun and appealing with Clip Art, WordArt, and SmartArt so they take on more of a game-like look, making the students more willing and excited to complete them."

– Amanda, elementary teacher and recent graduate

Learning Outcome 2

Use tools in Word to develop a bibliography or works cited page, collaborate with track changes and comments; and create mail merge documents for letters, labels, and envelopes.

REAL WORLD SUCCESS

"I am in charge of the quarterly and annual reporting to the Securities and Exchange Commission. From our internal compilation of the report to the final sign-offs by an outside firm, the process takes less than 30 days to complete. This is due mainly to the facilitation of tracked changes in MS Word, allowing the many reviewers to make comments directly on the electronic document. Without using the Track Changes feature, this process could take two to three months. Thank goodness for Microsoft Word. Otherwise, everyone would be asking for extensions from the SEC!"

– PB, alumnus and CFO

Microsoft Word 2016

Chapter 3 | INCLUDE TABLES AND OBJECTS

OBJECTIVES

1. Use WordArt p. 223
2. Create SmartArt p. 231
3. Insert a text box p. 235
4. Insert graphics p. 237
5. Set tabs p. 240
6. Create a table p. 243
7. Work with page breaks p. 253
8. Work with sections p. 254
9. Insert text from another document p. 255

Sales & Marketing

Prepare Case

Turquoise Oasis Spa Services Publication

The Turquoise Oasis Spa has been recognized as one of the leading spas in the nation. It was rated by *Traveler's Choice* magazine as the third best spa in the nation and was recently awarded accreditation by the Day Spa Group, a nationally recognized accrediting association for spas and wellness groups. The Day Spa Group sponsors *Relax*, a quarterly publication that spotlights leading spas. Turquoise Oasis Spa will be featured in the next issue. You are responsible for collecting information and preparing the article. You want to include information on spa benefits and packages, highlighting the spa's unique location, facilities, and treatments. Using Word to create the document, you will include text, graphics, WordArt, and SmartArt. In the process, you will work with tabs, tables, and text from other documents.

Valua Vitaly/Shutterstock

Student data files needed for this chapter:

 w02ch03Relax.docx

 w02ch03SpaCover.docx

 w02ch03Service.jpg

You will save your file as:

 w02ch03Relax_LastFirst.docx

Including Objects in a Document

It is important to create documents that communicate your message effectively. One approach is to use a combination of text and pictures or graphical images. Decorative headings and graphics can add spark, drawing attention to the topic. A shaded box with text can emphasize or restate an item of interest. Charts and tables can add organization to a document, summarizing and diagramming data. All of these "objects" enhance a document if used in the right context. An **object** is an item that you can work with independently of the surrounding text. You can insert an object, resize it, format it, and even delete it without affecting the document text. Word objects include pictures, shapes, WordArt, text boxes, SmartArt, charts, and screenshots. The challenge is to use objects in moderation, always keeping a document's main purpose in mind. In this section, you will learn to insert and modify objects in a Word document.

Use WordArt

WordArt is a Word feature that modifies text to include shadows, outlines, colors, gradients, and 3-D effects. It also shapes text in waves, curves, and angles. You can format existing text as WordArt, or you can insert new WordArt text into a document. You can also drag WordArt to various places within the document.

Opening the Starting File

In this exercise, you will open a rough draft of the spa article. You will display nonprinting characters and then save the file with a new name.

To Open the Starting File

a. Start **Word**, click **Open Other Documents** in the left pane, and then double-click **This PC**. Navigate through the folder structure to the location of your student data files, and then double-click **w02ch03Relax**. If necessary, click **Enable Editing**. A rough draft of the article opens.

b. If necessary, on the HOME tab, in the Paragraph group, click **Show/Hide** ¶ to display nonprinting characters. If the ruler is not displayed, click the **View** tab, in the Show group, click the **Ruler** check box.

c. Click the **File** tab, click **Save As**, and then double-click **This PC**. In the **Save As** dialog box, navigate to the location where you are saving your project files, and then change the file name to w02ch03Relax_LastFirst, using your last and first name. Click **Save**.

Creating and Selecting a WordArt Object

The Insert tab includes an Insert WordArt command that produces a gallery of WordArt styles from which you can choose. When an object is first created, a dashed border will appear around the object. Similarly, a dashed border also appears when you click in the object to select it. A dashed border indicates the text is selected — ready for you to enter text, delete text, or format portions of the text. Click the dashed border to change it to a solid border. A solid border indicates the entire WordArt object is selected and that any changes will now be applied to the entire object. Click outside the selected object to deselect it. When an object is selected, with either a dashed or solid border, the ribbon displays **contextual tabs** — specialized tabs containing commands related to that object. When you deselect the object, the contextual tabs disappear. For example, when you select a WordArt object, Word displays the Drawing Tools contextual tab with the Format tab. Other selected objects, such as charts or SmartArt, cause other contextual tabs to be displayed, with commands related to the specific object.

You are ready to begin work on your article. Scroll through the article. You will notice the article contains a WordArt object at the bottom of the document. In this exercise, you will create a new WordArt object at the top of the article and then modify the object at the bottom of the article.

To Create and Select WordArt

SIDE NOTE
Pin the Ribbon
If your ribbon is collapsed, pin your ribbon open. Click the Home tab. In the lower right corner of the Ribbon, click Pin the Ribbon ⊞.

a. Triple-click in the first line of the document, **Turquoise Oasis Spa**, to select the entire paragraph. Click the **Insert** tab, and then in the Text group, click **Insert WordArt** ⊿ WordArt ▾.

The WordArt gallery presents several styles to choose from. If you position the pointer over a style, a ScreenTip displays the style name.

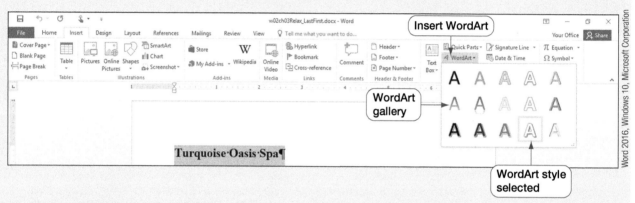

Figure 1 WordArt gallery

SIDE NOTE
Triple-Click
Remember, when you triple-click in a paragraph, you select all of the text, including the ending paragraph mark.

b. In the fourth column and third row, click **Fill - White, Outline — Accent 2, Hard Shadow — Accent 2.** The selected text now appears as a WordArt object. You will fix the spacing of the surrounding text later in the chapter.

c. Click outside of the WordArt object to deselect it and to see the result.

d. Press [Ctrl]+[End] to position the insertion point at the end of the document. Notice the WordArt object at the bottom of the document with the text **A passion for helping people relax**. Click anywhere in the **WordArt** object to select it. A dashed border appears around the WordArt object. Position the pointer on the **dashed border** until it changes to a four-headed arrow, and then click the **dashed border**. The border changes to a solid line, indicating the entire WordArt object is selected.

SIDE NOTE
Solid Border on WordArt
A solid border indicates the entire object is selected. Any format change will now affect all the text within the object.

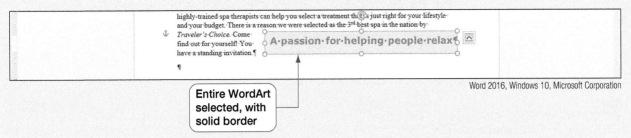

Entire WordArt selected, with solid border

Figure 2   WordArt with solid border

e. Click the **Home** tab. In the Font group, click the **Font Color** arrow , and then, under Theme Colors, in the second column and first row, select **Black, Text 1**.

> **Troubleshooting**
>
> If the formatting was applied to a portion of the text, the "entire" WordArt was not selected. On the Quick Access Toolbar, click Undo. Click the dashed border, changing it to a solid line, and then reapply the change.

f. In the WordArt, double-click the word **relax** to select it, and then in the Font group, click **Underline** . Notice the dashed border when a portion of the WordArt is selected.

g. Click outside of the WordArt object to deselect it and to see the result, and then click **save** on the Quick Access Toolbar.

Formatting a WordArt Object

The Format tab that is shown when a WordArt object is selected includes options for modifying WordArt styles, color, and text. The Shape Styles group enables you to change the fill, outline, effect, and style of the box surrounding the WordArt selection. To enhance the actual text of a WordArt selection, select a different WordArt style, or select a text fill, outline, or effect within the WordArt Styles group. In this exercise, you will use options in the Shape Styles group and the WordArt Styles group to modify the WordArt objects in the spa article.

 W03.02

To Format WordArt

a. Press Ctrl+Home to position the insertion point at the top of the document, and then click in the **Turquoise Oasis Spa** WordArt object to select it.

b. Click the **Format** tab, and in the Shapes Styles group, click **More** , and then place the pointer over any style to reveal the ScreenTip. Live Preview shows the effect of each potential selection.

c. In the second column and the second row, click **Colored Fill - Blue, Accent 1**.

> **Troubleshooting**
>
> If you do not see a Format tab under Drawing Tools, the WordArt is not selected. Click anywhere in the WordArt to select it and to display the Format tab.

d. With the WordArt object still selected, in the Shape Styles group, click **Shape Effects**. Point to **Bevel**, and then under Bevel, in the first column and second row, click **Angle**.

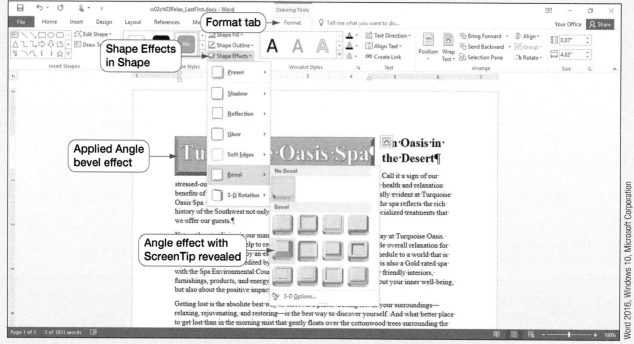

Figure 3 Shape effects

e. In the WordArt Styles group, click **Text Effects** A·, and then point to **Transform**.

A gallery of transform effects is displayed. As you move the pointer over each effect, you see a preview of the effect on the selected WordArt object.

f. Under **Warp**, in the first column and second row, click **Chevron Up**. The text slants upward and then down in a chevron effect.

g. Drag the **orange circle**, located near the top left border of the WordArt object, up slightly to reduce the chevron effect. You can drag the orange circle up or down to reduce or increase the transform effect.

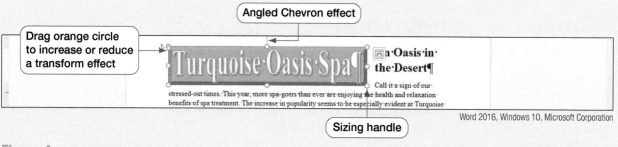

Figure 4 Modifying a text effect

h. Click outside the WordArt object to see the result. **Save** 🖫 the document.

Resizing a WordArt Object

When an object is selected, small circles will appear on the dashed or solid border surrounding the object. These circles are called **sizing handles** and are located in the center and corners of the border surrounding an object. To resize an object, simply drag a sizing handle to increase or decrease the size of the object. If you drag a corner handle, the height and width of the object change size simultaneously. For more precise sizing, adjust the height and width selections in the Size group on the Format tab. You can also resize a WordArt object by changing the font size. Word will resize the object, making it larger or smaller to accommodate the new font size.

The WordArt objects in the article are not sized correctly. In this exercise, you will resize the WordArt object at the top of the document, using the Shape Height and Shape Width boxes on the Format tab, and you will resize the WordArt object at the bottom of the page by adjusting the font. You will also make a format modification to give the WordArt a little more spark.

To Resize WordArt

a. Click in the **Turquoise Oasis Spa** WordArt object once to select it. On the Format tab, in the Size group, click the **Shape Height** 0.29" down arrow once to change the height to **0.8"**. Similarly, change the value in the Shape Width box to **6.5"**.

   You can leave the dashed border on the WordArt for sizing, since resizing an object automatically affects the entire WordArt object.

Shape Height and Shape Width boxes

Word 2016, Windows 10, Microsoft Corporation

Figure 5   Resizing WordArt

b. Click outside of the WordArt object to deselect it. Press Ctrl+End to position the insertion point at the end of the document, and then click in the WordArt object containing the text **A passion for helping people relax** to select it.

c. If necessary, click the **dashed border** of the WordArt to select the entire WordArt and to display a solid border. On the **Home** tab, in the Font group, change the font size to **20**.

> ### Troubleshooting
> If only a portion of the text changes to a 20-pt font size, you did not select the entire WordArt object. Click Undo, and then select the entire WordArt object and reapply the change.

d. With the WordArt object still selected, click the **Format** tab, and then in the Shape Styles group, click **Shape Fill**. Point to **Gradient**, and then under Variations, in the second column and first row, select **Linear Down**. Click outside of the WordArt object to deselect it.

e. **Save** 🔲 the document.

QUICK REFERENCE	Dashed Borders Versus Solid Borders

1. A solid border around an object indicates the entire object is selected. You can apply formats related to the entire object at this time — centering the object, formatting all the text in the object, and so on.

2. A dashed border around an object indicates that the text, or a portion of the text, is selected. You can add text, delete text, or format the selected text.

Repositioning a WordArt Object Using Alignment Guides and Live Layout

To move a WordArt object, select the object, position the pointer on a border of the object to change the pointer to a four-headed arrow, and then drag the object to a new location. When moving an object to the top, middle, or bottom of a document, or to the top of a paragraph, Word automatically displays green **alignment guides** to help you place the object in the exact location. The guides disappear when the object is released or when the guides are not needed anymore.

When dragging an object, the **Live Layout** feature will reflow the text around the object in real time so you can see the result before actually placing the object. The way text wraps around the WordArt is determined by the object's **text wrap** setting. With a WordArt object selected, you can click the Format tab and then click Wrap Text in the Arrange group to determine the current text wrap setting or to change its setting. Text wrap options are shown in the Quick Reference. The Layout Options button 🔲 that appears at the top right of a selected object enables you to quickly and easily select a text wrap setting.

QUICK REFERENCE	Text Wrap Options

The following text wrap options are available on the Format tab or by using the Layout Options button.

Text Wrap Option	Effect
In Line with Text	A graphic or other object that is positioned directly in the text of a document at the insertion point and responds as another character in the paragraph. This is the default setting when a picture is inserted into a document.
Square	Text wraps on all sides of the object, following the border of an invisible square. This is the default setting when existing text is converted into WordArt.
Tight	Text follows the shape but does not overlap it. The text adheres closely to the object's shape but is always an equal distance from the edge.
Through	Text follows the shape, filling any open spaces in the object.
Top and Bottom	Text appears above and below the borders of an object.

Text Wrap Option	Effect
Behind Text	The object appears behind the text. Unless the fill color exactly matches the text color, both the object and the text will be visible.
In Front of Text	The object appears on top of the text, obscuring the text unless there is no shape fill or the fill is set to semitransparent. This is the default setting when a WordArt object is created from scratch. Text will not wrap around the object; rather, it will stay behind the object at all times.

In addition, you can position a WordArt object within a document using the Position button, also on the Format tab in the Arrange group. The Position options enable you to place an object in a preset location within a document with Square text wrapping. You can place an object in the top, middle, or bottom of a document — situated at the top, middle, or right side horizontally. As you explore options in the Position gallery, you can see the effect of each option on a selected object.

The WordArt object at the bottom of the document needs to be repositioned. In this exercise, using the alignment guides and text wrap feature, you will move the WordArt object to a better location.

To Reposition WordArt

a. If necessary, press Ctrl+End to position the insertion point at the end of the document. Click in the WordArt object containing the text **A passion for helping people relax**.

b. Click the **Layout Options** button ⬚ to the right of the object, and then under **With Text Wrapping**, in the first column and second row, click **Top and Bottom**. Click anywhere in the document to view the result. Text will now appear above and below the WordArt object and not to its side.

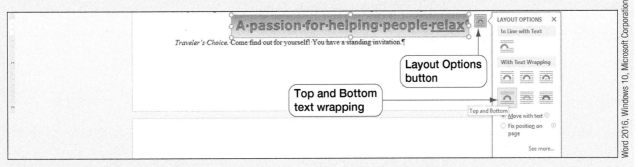

Figure 6 Layout Options button

SIDE NOTE

Center-Align an Object on the Page

Alternatively, on the Format tab, in the Arrange group, click Align Objects, and then select Align Center.

c. Click in the **WordArt** object again. Place the pointer on a **border** of the WordArt object so that the pointer changes to a four-headed arrow ⬚. Drag the **object** just above the text **Join Us at Turquoise Oasis Spa**, minimizing the white space above and below the object. Continue dragging it slowly to the center of the page. When the green vertical alignment guide appears in the middle of the page, release the object. The object will be center-aligned on the page.

You may need to move the WordArt object up and down slightly to find the location with the least amount of white space above and below it.

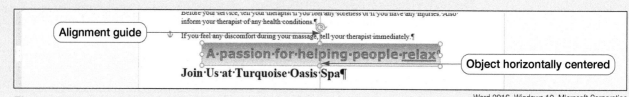

Figure 7   Repositioning WordArt

    d.   Click outside of the WordArt object to deselect it, and then **save** 🖫 the document.

Understanding Anchors

You may have noticed that an image of an anchor appears in the left margin when a WordArt object is selected. When text wrapping is set to something other than In Line with Text, the **anchor** shows which paragraph the object is associated with. Once an object is anchored to a paragraph, it stays with the paragraph. If the paragraph is moved to another location of the document, the object moves with it. When you move the WordArt object, the object anchor will move to the closest paragraph unless the Lock Anchor option is set. You can access the Lock Anchor option when you select More Layout Options from the Wrap Text menu. To associate the object with a different paragraph, drag the anchor.

      To improve readability, one of the WordArt objects in the article needs a little more white space above and below it. In this exercise, you will use your knowledge of anchors to easily increase the white space.

To Anchor a WordArt Object

    a.   Click in the WordArt object containing the text **A passion for helping people relax**. Notice the anchor ⚓ displayed to the left of the paragraph just above the WordArt. Point to the **anchor** so that the pointer changes to a four-headed arrow, and then drag the anchor down so that it is positioned to the left of the paragraph **Join Us at Turquoise Oasis Spa**.

Figure 8   Anchors

    b.   Click before the word **Join** in the line just below the WordArt, and then press Enter to insert a blank line and open some space above the WordArt.
Because the object is anchored to the paragraph, moving the paragraph moves the WordArt.

    c.   Click in the **WordArt** object to view the anchor, and then drag the anchor up so that it is positioned to the left of the paragraph beginning with **If you feel any discomfort**.

    d.   Click before the word **Join** in the line just below the WordArt, and then press Enter to insert a blank line below the WordArt.

    e.   Since the object is now anchored to the previous paragraph, moving this paragraph does not move the WordArt.

    f.   **Save** 🖫 the document.

REAL WORLD ADVICE | **Repeating Text or an Object on Every Page of a Document**

Have you ever wanted to create a customized header or footer that contains more than just page numbers? For example, suppose you needed specific text or an image to repeat on every page of your document. Insert a header or footer, and then insert text or an object (such as an image or text box) into it. The text or object will now appear on every page of the document. Because it is anchored in the header, changing text or spacing in the document will not affect the text or objects such as a text box.

Create SmartArt

SmartArt is a visual representation used to communicate processes, concepts, or ideas that would otherwise require a great deal of text to describe. Using SmartArt, you can create diagrams such as organization charts, process flows, relationship charts, cycle diagrams, and step-by-step processes. Word 2016 includes over 200 SmartArt diagrams in nine categories. Click SmartArt in the Illustrations group of the Insert tab to select from the SmartArt categories, including one that enables you to insert your own pictures within SmartArt shapes. Once a SmartArt object has been created, you can format the entire SmartArt or its individual shapes. You can include your own text in SmartArt shapes, and you can format SmartArt with color, special effects, and font selections. When a SmartArt diagram is selected, the ribbon displays the SmartArt Tools contextual tab with the Design and Format tabs.

Identifying Types of SmartArt

Using SmartArt saves a great deal of time that would otherwise be spent describing a process or even designing a chart yourself. The built-in SmartArt diagrams enable you to quickly portray a situation or process. You can select from nine categories of SmartArt, as described in the following Quick Reference. When you select a SmartArt object, consider the main points in the process or concept and the relationships between the main points. Choose the design that best describes your concept, and then create one shape per main point. In this exercise, you will create a two-shaped cycle SmartArt for the spa article, representing the mind and body in a continuous cycle. You will then add a third shape to represent the spirit in the cycle.

QUICK REFERENCE | **Types of SmartArt**

The nine categories of SmartArt are listed below.

1. List — Nonsequential information
2. Process — Steps in a process or timeline
3. Cycle — A continual process
4. Hierarchy — Top-down relationships or organization chart
5. Relationship — Connections
6. Matrix — How parts relate to a whole
7. Pyramid — Proportional relationships with the smallest part on top or, in an inverted pyramid, on the bottom
8. Picture — Arrangements of pictures in a relationship
9. Office.com — Additional layouts available from Office.com

W03.06

To Create SmartArt and Add Text

SIDE NOTE
ScreenTip
Point to each different SmartArt design to display a ScreenTip containing a name.

a. Scroll to the top of the document. Click to place the insertion point at the end of the third body paragraph, immediately after the text **in a very long while**. Press Enter. Click the **Insert** tab, and then in the Illustrations group, click **SmartArt**. The Choose a SmartArt Graphic dialog box appears. Select **Cycle** from the list of categories to the left, and then select **Nondirectional Cycle** in the fourth column, first row. Click **OK**.

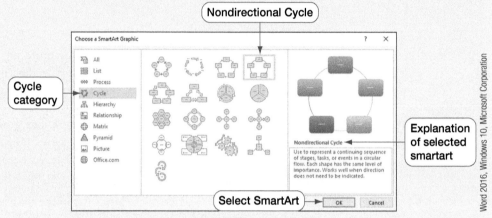

Figure 9   Inserting SmartArt

SIDE NOTE
SmartArt Text Pane
The SmartArt Text pane simplifies the task of typing text in SmartArt shapes. Click or use the arrow keys to move from bullet to bullet.

b. If necessary, scroll to view the SmartArt. If you do not see a SmartArt Text pane, click the **small rectangular box containing a left arrow** in the middle of the left border of the SmartArt object. With the insertion point next to the first bullet, type Mind. Do not press Enter. Click beside the second **bullet**, and then type Body. Alternatively, to enter text in a shape, click in the shape and type.

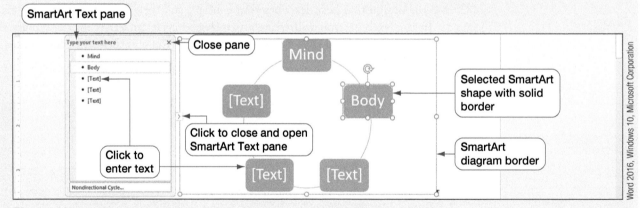

Figure 10   SmartArt text pane

c. **Close** ⊠ the SmartArt Text pane. Click in one of the three remaining **SmartArt** shapes that display "[Text]". If necessary, click the **dashed line** on the shape to change the border to a solid line. With the shape selected, press Delete to delete the shape, and then press Delete two more times to delete the two remaining shapes without text. Click outside the SmartArt graphic to deselect it.

Troubleshooting

If you have more than three remaining shapes without text, you pressed [Enter] when typing the bulleted list of data. Remove any extra shapes as discussed in step c.

d. **Save** 🔲 the document.

Modifying SmartArt

You will often find that you need to add a shape to a SmartArt diagram to better depict a process. Although you can easily specify whether a new shape should appear before or after an object, by default a new shape is added after a selected shape. To select a shape, click inside the shape. While some tasks affect the text within the individual shapes, other tasks affect the entire shape or even the entire SmartArt diagram. Therefore, it is important to pay careful attention in making selections within SmartArt, as shown in the Quick Reference.

You realize that you forgot to insert a SmartArt shape representing spirit. In this exercise, you will add a shape to the SmartArt in the spa article and then resize the entire SmartArt diagram.

QUICK REFERENCE	How to Select SmartArt	
To Select	**Click**	**Resulting Border**
The text within a shape	Text within a shape	Dashed border on shape
A shape	Blank area within a shape, next to its text or the dashed border of a shape	Solid border on shape
The entire SmartArt diagram	The white space outside of a shape but within the SmartArt diagram	One border around entire SmartArt
The entire SmartArt diagram	The outside border of the SmartArt diagram	One border around entire SmartArt

To Modify SmartArt

a. Select the entire **SmartArt** by clicking next to one of the shapes within the SmartArt diagram in the white space area. A box will appear around the entire SmartArt, and none of the individual shapes will have a dashed or solid border.

Troubleshooting

If a dashed or solid border is displayed around any of the individual shapes, the individual shape has been selected as opposed to the entire SmartArt. In that case, click in the white space just outside the shape to select the entire SmartArt.

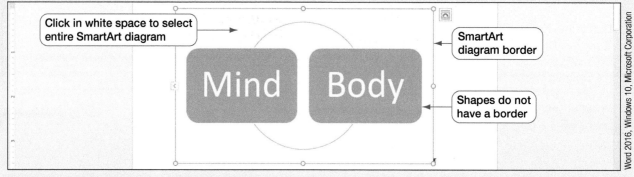

Figure 11   Selecting the entire SmartArt diagram

b. Under SmartArt Tools, on the Design tab, in the Create Graphic group, click **Add Shape**, and then type Spirit. The font size adjusts in the shape to accommodate the new text.

> ### Troubleshooting
>
> If you do not see the Add Shape command, you may have clicked the wrong Design tab. Select the diagram, and then click the Design tab under SmartArt Tools.

c. Because an individual shape is selected, click in the white space just outside the shape to select the entire **SmartArt diagram**. Click the Format tab. In the Size group, click in the **Shape Height** box, and then type 2.5. Press Enter.

> ### Troubleshooting
>
> If only one shape was resized, then the entire SmartArt diagram was not se-lected, but rather an individual shape, indicated by a dashed border around the shape. On the Quick Access Toolbar, click Undo. Click in the white space to the left or right of the individual shape to select the entire SmartArt, and then resize the diagram.

d. If necessary, scroll to view the SmartArt diagram. Click outside the SmartArt diagram to deselect it, and then **save** 🖫 the document.

Formatting SmartArt

The Design tab and Format tab, found on the SmartArt Tools contextual tab, provide many options for formatting SmartArt. After creating a diagram, you might want to explore other styles and color selections. The Design tab — typically used to format the entire SmartArt object — provides a SmartArt Styles gallery and a Layouts gallery, with options for enhancing and modifying a diagram. The Format tab contains many of the commands used to format the individual shapes of a diagram. In this exercise, you will format the layout and style of the SmartArt diagram in the spa article. You will then add a new color style to the diagram.

To Format SmartArt

a. Select the entire **SmartArt diagram**. Under SmartArt Tools, click the **Design** tab, and then in the Layouts group, click **More** ⊡. Point to any **selection** in the Layouts gallery, and view the effect on the selected SmartArt. In the first column and first row, select **Basic Cycle**.

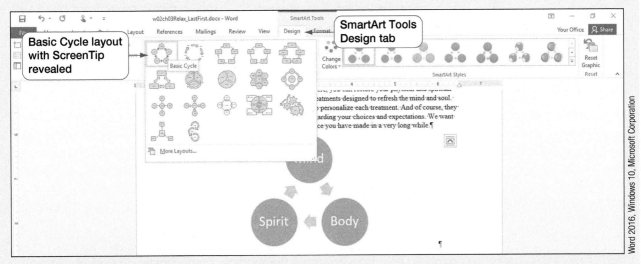

Figure 12 Modifying SmartArt

SIDE NOTE

Color an Individual Shape

To change the color of an individual shape, select the shape, and then on the Format tab, in the Shape Styles group, click Shape Fill.

---

b. With the entire SmartArt still selected, in the SmartArt Styles group, point to any style in the SmartArt Styles gallery to view the effect on the SmartArt diagram. Click **More** to explore other style options, and then under 3-D, in the first column and first row, select **Polished**.

c. With the entire SmartArt still selected, in the SmartArt Styles group, click **Change Colors**. Point to any **selection**, and view the effect on the SmartArt diagram. Under Accent 1, in the third column, click **Gradient Range-Accent 1**.

d. Click the **Home** tab,

e. Click outside the SmartArt diagram to deselect it, and then **save** the document.

Insert a Text Box

A **text box** is an object that gives you control of text placement in a document. It is literally a box of text that you can format just as you would any other drawing object. A text box can be placed anywhere on your page, without regard to the margins. It is often used for information that needs to stand out, such as in a margin or in a diagram. A text box can also help you control the layout of your document, as it limits the text to certain areas. For example, projects such as newsletters, business cards, and greeting cards are easily created by using multiple text boxes to position text in specific areas of a document. Once created, you can shade the text box, add a border to it, rotate it, and add special effects, such as shadows or special fills. When a text box in a document is selected, Word displays the Drawing Tools contextual tab with the Format tab.

Creating a Text Box

Word provides a selection of text boxes that you can insert into your document with predefined sizes, shapes, colors, fonts, and placement. Once inserted into a document, a text box can be easily modified to suit your needs. You can also insert a text box from scratch by using the Draw Text Box option. The pointer will change to a plus sign symbol, and you can click in the document to create a narrow blank text box that you can then format and resize. You can also drag the plus sign pointer — the precision select pointer — and draw a blank text box of any size. In this exercise, you will add a text box at the bottom of the spa article to hold the spa address. You will create a text box, add the address into the text box, and then resize the text box.

To Create and Resize a Text Box

a. Press Ctrl+End to move the insertion point to the end of the document. Click the **Insert** tab. In the Text group, click **Text Box**, and then select **Simple Text Box**. A text box is inserted in your document.

b. Click the **Home** tab, and then in the Styles group, click **No Spacing** to single-space the text.

c. Type Turquoise Oasis Spa, and press Enter. Type Painted Paradise Resort & Spa, and press Enter. Type 3356 Hemmingway Circle, and press Enter. Type Santa Fe, NM 89566, but do not press Enter.

> ### Troubleshooting
> If text appeared in your document and not in the text box, the text box was not selected. Click Undo to remove the text from the document. Click to place the insertion point in the text box, and then redo step c.

d. Point to a **border** of the text box so the pointer appears as a four-headed arrow, and then click the **dashed border**. The border is now solid, and the entire text box is selected. On the Format tab, in the Size group, click the **Shape Height** 0.29" up arrow to increase the height to **1"**.

e. Click outside the text box to deselect it, and then **save** the document.

Modifying a Text Box

Both the Text box and SmartArt graphics use the same Format tab. It includes options for modifying styles, color, and text. Because you want the address to stand out, in this exercise, you will color and shade the text box in the spa article. You will also vertically align and center-align the text within the text box.

To Modify a Text Box

a. Click in the **text box** to select it, and then, if necessary, click the dashed border to select the **entire text box**. On the Format tab, then in the Shape Styles group, click **More**. Point to a **style** to view the effect on the selected text box. In the second column and fifth row, select **Moderate Effect-Blue, Accent 1**.

b. In the Shape Styles group, click **Shape Effects**, and then point to **Shadow**. Under Outer, in the first column and first row, select **Offset Diagonal Bottom Right**. A slight shadow appears to the right and bottom of the shape.

c. In the Text group, click **Align Text**, and then select **Middle**. The text is now centered vertically in the box.

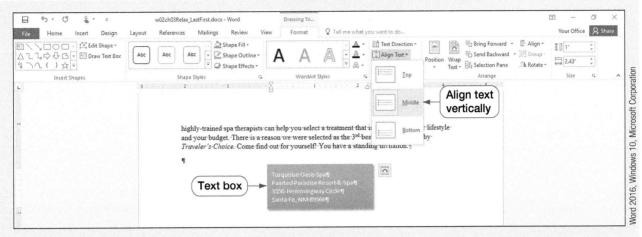

Figure 13 Vertically align text

d. With the entire text box still selected, click the **Home** tab, and then in the Paragraph group, click **Center** to center the text horizontally within the text box.

e. Click outside the text box to deselect it, and then **save** 🖫 the document.

CONSIDER THIS | **SmartArt Without Borders**

You can remove the border and fill of all the SmartArt shapes within a SmartArt diagram. When might you want to do this? How does it compare to creating a series of text boxes?

QUICK REFERENCE	**Align a Text Box Versus Aligning Text Within a Text Box**

1. To align a text box horizontally or vertically on a page, on the Format tab, in the Arrange group, click Align Objects.
2. To align text horizontally within the text box, on the Home tab, in the Paragraph group, click one of the alignment buttons.
3. To align text vertically within the text box, on the Format tab, in the Text group, click Align Text.

Insert Graphics

Newsletters, business cards, and other specialty documents can be enhanced with the addition of graphical illustrations — pictures and clip art. For example, when creating a family newsletter, you might want to include a personal picture saved on a disk drive; or when creating a flyer for a Fourth of July party, you might include an image of a flag from the Internet. You can then crop, recolor, set the text wrap, or format these graphics with outline styles and various artistic effects. To delete a picture or clip art, simply select the graphic and press ⌈Delete⌋. Word 2016 also enables you to insert online videos using a Bing or YouTube search.

Inserting a Picture

A **picture** is a photo or graphical image that is saved on a storage device. You can save your photos on a CD or disk drive and then insert a photo into a document. The photo becomes a graphic object that you can manage just as you do other objects — resizing, formatting, and wrapping text as needed. If you locate a picture or graphic image online that you want to use in a document, you can save the graphic to a CD or disk drive and then insert the image into your document. The Online Pictures command, in the Illustrations group of the Insert tab, enables you to insert pictures from a Bing Image Search or from a OneDrive account. You can even insert a picture from your Facebook or Flickr account. Keep in mind, though, when copying images from the Internet, you must take care to adhere to all copyright laws.

When a picture is inserted into a document, Word displays the Picture Tools contextual tab with the Format tab.

Formatting a Picture

When a picture is inserted in a document, it is surrounded by a solid border that includes sizing handles. To resize the photo, drag a handle. You should always drag a corner handle so the picture is resized proportionally. If you drag a center handle, the picture will be skewed. To ensure that a picture does not get skewed, on the Format tab, click the Layout Dialog Box Launcher in the Size group, and select Lock aspect ratio to maintain the picture's size ratio. To move a picture, point to a border — not a handle — so it appears as a four-headed arrow, and then drag to move the picture to a new location.

When a picture is selected, the Format tab is displayed on the ribbon. The Format tab includes options for changing the picture style, adding a border, adding special effects, cropping the picture, and wrapping text. You can even apply color corrections and add artistic effects.

You have a picture saved on your disk drive that you want to include in the spa article. In this exercise, you will insert the picture, change its text wrap setting, and adjust its color.

To Insert and Format a Picture

a. Press [Ctrl]+[Home], and then click at the beginning of the third body paragraph immediately before **Getting**.

b. Click the **Insert** tab. In the Illustrations group, click **Pictures**, and then navigate to the location of your student data files. Click **w02ch03Service**, and then click **Insert**.
A picture of a spa service is inserted in the document at the position of the insertion point. The picture is selected, as you can tell by the border surrounding it. The border includes sizing handles.

c. On the Format tab, in the Arrange group, click **Wrap Text**, and then select **Square**. Text wraps around the picture on the right, in a square fashion.

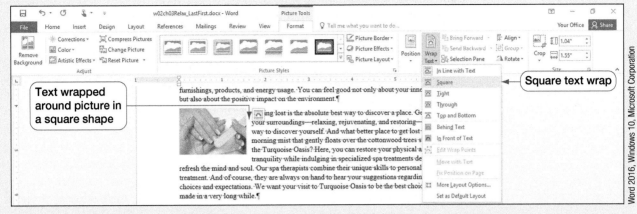

Figure 14 Picture with wrapped text

Word 2016, Windows 10, Microsoft Corporation

SIDE NOTE

Inserting Online Videos from the Insert Tab

In the Media group, click Online Video. Search for a video using Bing or YouTube, or copy its embedded code and paste it into the box provided.

d. In the Size group, click the **Shape Height** [⇳ 0.29" ⇳] down arrow one time to decrease the height to 1 inch.

e. In the Adjust group, click **Color**, and then under Recolor, in the second column and third row, select **Blue, Accent color 1 Light**.

f. Click outside the picture to deselect it, and then **save** 🖫 the document. If you need to take a break before finishing this chapter, now is a good time to take a break.

Working with Tabs and Tables

Recall that most fonts use proportional spacing. For example, the letter "w" will typically use more horizontal space on a line than the letter "i". Thus, typing "wham" followed by a space will not position your insertion point in the same location as typing "lilt" followed by a space. For this reason, it is nearly impossible to align data in columns using spaces.

Tab stops and tables can be used to help align text and to create columns of data. A **tab stop** is a location where the insertion point will stop when you press ⌷Tab⌷. Press ⌷Tab⌷ to move from one tab stop to the next. Word stores paragraph formatting, such as tab stops, in the paragraph marks at the end of a paragraph. Thus, when you press ⌷Enter⌷, the tab stops are copied to the next paragraph. The same tab stops can then be used in sequential paragraphs, enabling you to start or end text in the same location, thus creating columns of aligned data. Perhaps you are preparing a table of contents. You could type the chapter or topic and then leave a set amount of space before typing a page number. By setting a right-aligned tab stop, you can be sure all page numbers line up evenly. Alternatively, you can define a **table** as a grid of columns and rows. A table **cell** is the intersection of a column and a row. Typing text in the table cells will keep your rows of data aligned. You can even select a predesigned table style to draw attention to table text.

Although both methods enable you to align text in columns, each has unique features that make it appropriate for various applications. In this section, you will format documents with tabs, and you will learn to summarize data in tables.

Set Tabs

Recall that a tab stop is a location where the insertion point will stop when you press Tab. If you do not specify tab stops, the default tab stop is set at every 1/2 inch on the ruler. If you press Tab once, the insertion point stops 1/2 inch from the left margin. Press Tab again to stop at 1 inch. Most often, though, you will create your own tab stops, which will temporarily override the default settings. As was mentioned earlier, tab stops are applied to the current paragraph and all subsequent paragraphs that you will type from that point forward until you decide to remove them or reset them. You can remove the tab stops from a paragraph at any time or even reset them to new positions.

You will frequently select from five tab types, as shown in Table 1. Tab stops you create will appear on the horizontal ruler. A **left tab** aligns text on the left, while a **right tab** aligns text on the right. A right tab stop is appropriate for a table of contents or menu, where numbers need to be aligned on the right. A **decimal tab** aligns text on a decimal point, such as a columnar list of student grades, where grades might have varying places to the right of the decimal point. A **center tab** aligns text evenly to the left and right of the tab stop. You can add **leaders** to a tab stop so that a row of dots or dashes is displayed before a tab stop, such as on restaurant menus where a line of dots precedes a menu price. A **bar tab** inserts a vertical bar at the tab stop, creating a line, or separator, between columns of data.

Marker	Tab name	Description
⌞	Left tab	Aligns the left edge of the text under the left tab
⊥	Center tab	Aligns the middle of the of the text under the tab
⌟	Right tab	Aligns the right edge of the text under the right tab
⊥	Decimal tab	Aligns numbers by the decimal point 123.45 1.2345 1234.5
❘	Bar tab	Acts as a divider bar Positions a vertical under the tab stop

Table 1   Tab stops

Using the Ruler to Set Tabs

In most cases, the easiest way to set a tab stop is to use the ruler. The default tab stop is left, but you can easily select another tab type by clicking the **tab selector** to the left of the horizontal ruler. Click the tab selector once to select a center tab stop ⊥. Click again to select a right tab stop ⌟, and then click again to select a decimal tab stop ⊥. After selecting the tab type, simply click the location on the ruler where the tab stop is to be placed. You can move a tab stop by dragging it along the ruler. If you want to delete a tab, drag it off the ruler. Once you create a tab stop, simply press Tab to move the insertion point to that location, and then begin typing.

You decide to align the spa days and hours using tabs. The extra white space will add readability and give it a more professional look. In this exercise, you will create tab stops using the ruler.

To Set Tabs Using the Ruler

a. If you took a break, open the **w02ch03Relax** document. Scroll to the bottom of the second page, and click to place the insertion point before the paragraph mark ¶ that is displayed just beneath the **Spa Hours** heading.

b. If the ruler is not displayed, click the **View** tab, and then in the Show group, click the **Ruler** check box. Point to the tab selector to the left of the ruler to view the ScreenTip. Verify that a Left Tab ⌊ is selected. If a Left Tab is not selected, click the tab selector until a Left Tab is selected. Point to the **1.5"** mark on the horizontal ruler, and then click to set a left tab stop. Click the **4"** mark to set another left tab stop, and then click the **5"** mark to set a third left tab stop.

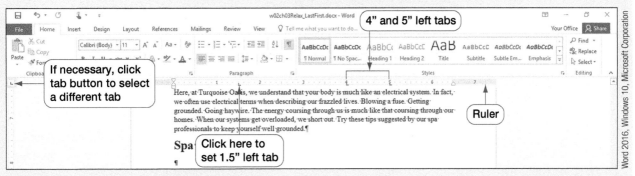

Figure 15 Using the ruler to set tabs

c. You realize that you need to adjust the tabs. On the ruler, click the **5"** tab stop, and then drag it down, off the ruler to remove it. Point to the left tab stop at **1.5"**, and then drag it to the **2"** mark.

You have created a 2 inch left tab stop and a 4 inch left tab stop. You will enter text at the tab stops in the next set of steps.

> ### Troubleshooting
> If you accidentally create extra tabs while trying to move a tab, simply drag the extra tabs off the ruler to remove them.

d. **Save** 🖫 the document.

Using the Tabs Dialog Box

It can be difficult to create exact tab stops using a ruler. For example, if you click to place a left tab stop at the 1" mark, you might instead place it at 1.1" or perhaps at 0.9". The Tabs dialog box enables you to create precise tab stops. If you plan to use tab leaders — dots or dashes that precede a tab stop — you must make that selection in the Tabs dialog box. You can also clear tab stops and set a default tab stop measurement. Click the Tabs button in the Paragraph dialog box to open the Tabs dialog box. In this exercise, you will adjust the tab stops in the spa article using the Tabs dialog box.

W03.13

To Set Tabs Using the Tabs Dialog Box

a. Press Tab, and then type Monday-Friday making sure not to leave a space before or after the dash. Press Tab, and then type 7:00 a.m.-11:00 p.m., making sure not to leave a space before or after the dash. Press Enter.

b. Press Tab, type Saturday, and then press Tab. Without leaving a space before or after the dash, type 7:00 a.m.-Midnight, and then press Enter. Press Tab, and type Sunday. Press Tab, and type Closed. Do not press Enter.

c. You realize the tab stops need to be adjusted again. Select the three lines containing the spa hours, starting with **Monday** and ending with **Closed**. On the Home tab, in the Paragraph group, click the **Paragraph Dialog Box Launcher**. Click **Tabs** at the bottom of the dialog box.

You will replace the 2 inch tab stop with a 1 inch tab stop, and you will specify a dot leader for the space between the days and times. Leaders are attached to the tabs that follow them, so you will adjust the 4 inch tab stop to include a dot leader.

d. Click in the **Tab stop position** box. If necessary, clear any text, type 1, and then click **Set** to create a 1 inch left tab stop.

e. In the list under the Tab stop position box, select **2"**. If you did not set the tab stop precisely at 2", you might not see that exact tab stop. In that case, select the tab stop position closest to 2", and then click **Clear**.

f. In the list under the Tab stop position box, select **4"**. If you did not set the tab stop precisely at 4", you might not see that exact tab stop. In that case, select the tab stop position closest to 4", and then in the Leader area, select option **2** (dot leader).

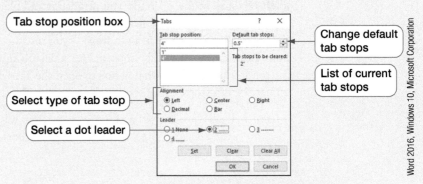

Figure 16   The Tabs Dialog Box

g. Click **OK**. The tabs are adjusted, and the dot leader is displayed.

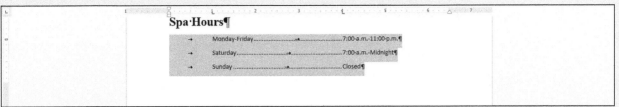

Figure 17 The Tabbed Text

h. **Save** the document.

Create a Table

A table is often used to summarize data, such as sales totals for various divisions of a company or enrollment data for college classes. A table typically includes headings that identify each column or row that contains data. For example, if you are summarizing sales data for company divisions, the headings in row 1 could be "Division" and "Sales." Data for each division would be displayed in the subsequent rows, as shown in Figure 18. If there are four divisions in the company, the table will include five rows: one header row and four rows of data.

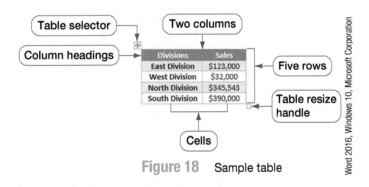

Figure 18 Sample table

When you create a table, you specify the number of columns and rows. Word then creates a blank table with those specifications. New data can be entered into a table cell, and pressing Tab will move from one cell to the next. Often, the number of rows and columns you indicate turns out to be more or less than what is actually necessary. Adding and deleting columns and rows is a simple task, enabling you to easily change a table structure. You can even merge cells to accommodate long entries or table titles. If you want to add a little spark to the table, choose from a gallery of preexisting table designs. You can also add shading and modify borders. You can even remove all the borders from the table. A borderless table may appear to be similar to tabbed data, but the table format enables you to change column widths easily and wrap text within a cell.

The Table Tools contextual tab with the Design tab and Layout tab enable you to change the table layout and design, insert rows and columns, merge cells, sort table data, create sums and averages, change styles, and modify table properties. Before formatting table text, however, you must first select it, as shown in the Quick Reference.

1. Select all text in a cell — Position the pointer just inside the left edge of the cell until the pointer becomes a slanted black arrow and click.

2. Select a row — Position the pointer in the left margin to the left of the row until the pointer becomes a white arrow ⬁, and then click.

3. Select a column — Position the pointer on the top border of the column until the pointer becomes a downward black arrow ⬇, and then click.

4. Select the entire table — Click the table selector ⊞ at the top-left corner of the table. The **table selector** at the top left corner of a table enables you to select the entire table. You can drag the resize handle in the bottom-right corner of the table to resize the table.

Entering Data in a Table

When you insert a table, Word creates an empty grid of columns and rows. You can enter data in a cell by clicking in the cell and typing. To move to another cell, simply click in the cell; you can also press Tab or any of the directional arrows to move to an adjacent cell. Most often, you will press Tab to continue completing the table. As you type in a cell, Word automatically wraps text that reaches the end of the cell, increasing the cell's height — along with all other cells in the row — to accommodate the entry. If you want to add another line within a cell, you can press Enter to add a blank paragraph.

Information on the specialty spa packages needs to be added to the article. In this exercise, you will present the information in a 3 × 4 table. The table will draw attention to the data while maintaining readability.

W03.14

To Create a Table

a. Click to place the insertion point at the end of the **first paragraph** under the heading **Specialty Spa Packages** after the text **fancy!**, and then press Enter. Click the **Insert** tab, and then in the Tables group, click **Table**. A table grid is presented for you to specify the number of columns and rows to include in the table.

b. As you point to the different squares in the grid, a Live Preview of the table is displayed in the document. Click to select a table with three columns and four rows, a **3 × 4** Table (column 3, row 4).

Figure 19 Creating a table

Word 2016, Windows 10, Microsoft Corporation

c. With the insertion point in the **top left cell** of the table, type Spa Package and press Tab to move to the adjacent cell. Type Services, and press Tab. Type Prices, and press Tab to move to the first cell of the second row.
Note that all three columns are of equal width and each row is the same height. If nonprinting characters are shown, you will see an end-of-cell mark in each cell and an end-of-row mark at the right side of each row.

d. With the insertion point in the first cell of the second row, type Body Package (2 hours), and then press Tab. Type Oasis Massage. Because two spa services are included in the Body Package, you will list them all within the same cell. Press Enter. The pointer is positioned on the next line in the same cell. Type Oasis Mani-Pedi. Do not press Enter.

e. Press Tab, type $135, and press Tab.

f. Type the following text in the remaining two rows of the table. Remember to press Tab to move from cell to cell and press Enter when listing the spa services in the second column. Do not press Tab or Enter after typing $325.

Soul Package (3 hours)	Oasis Massage Oasis Mani-Pedi Mini-Facial	$185
Mind Package (4 hours)	Oasis Massage Oasis Facial Oasis Mani-Pedi Paradise Fruit Bar	$325

Troubleshooting

If a new row appears at the bottom of the table, you pressed Tab after typing $325. Click Undo.

g. Click the **table selector** ⊞ to select the entire table. Click the **Home** tab, and then in the Styles group, click **No Spacing**, and then click outside the table to deselect it.

h. Point to the top of the second column — the **Services** column — so the pointer appears as a downward black arrow ↓. When the pointer becomes a downward black arrow, click to select the **column**.

i. Point to the **left of a row**. When the pointer becomes a large white arrow ⇗, click to select the **row**.

j. Point just **inside the left edge of a cell** so the pointer appears as a right-directed black arrow ◼. You can then click to select everything in the cell.

k. Click to place the insertion point in front of the **S** in the text **Spa Package**, and then drag to select multiple cells.

l. Practice selecting columns, rows, and cells. If you accidentally make any changes, click Undo ↺.

m. **Save** 🖫 the document.

QUICK REFERENCE	Selecting Elements in a Table

1. Select all text in a cell — Position the pointer just inside the left edge of the cell until the pointer becomes a right-directed black arrow ◼, and then click.

2. Select a row — Position the pointer in the left margin to the left of the row until the pointer becomes a white arrow ⇗, and then click.

3. Select a column — Position the pointer on the top border of the column until the pointer becomes a downward black arrow ↓, and then click.

4. Select the entire table — Click the table selector ⊞ at the top left corner of the table.

Inserting and Deleting Columns and Rows

You will seldom develop a table that is perfect the first time. Most often, you will need to modify the number of rows or columns after the table is created. As you enter text in the last cell of a table, you can press Tab to insert a new row at the end of the table. That method works well for adding a row at the end of the table, but what if the new row should be inserted between two existing rows? Simply click to position the insertion point in a row or column that is to appear next to the new row or column. Click the Layout tab, and in the Rows & Columns group, select Insert Above, Insert Below, Insert Left, or Insert Right. An alternative is to use one-click row and column insertion. To add a new row, position the pointer just to the left of a table between two existing rows. A control with a plus sign appears outside the table (see Figure 20). Click the plus sign to add a new row above the control. Similarly, to add a new column, point to the top of the table between two existing columns, and then click the plus sign control to add a new column to the left of the control.

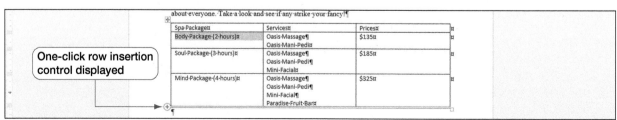

Figure 20 One-click row insertion

Word 2016, Windows 10, Microsoft Corporation

Deleting a column or row is not the same as deleting the contents of a column or row. To delete the contents, simply select the row or column and press Delete. The data in the row or column is deleted, but the empty row or column remains. You can then enter new data in the row (or column). When you delete a row or column, the entire row or column and all its contents are removed. Select the row or column, and click Delete in the Rows & Columns group on the Layout tab. You can then choose to delete cells, columns, rows, or the entire table. You can delete multiple rows and columns by selecting them first.

You realize you forgot to add information on the Balance Package. In this exercise, you will delete the Soul Package row from the table, since the spa no longer offers it, and then add a row containing information on the Balance Package. You will also add to the top of the table a row that you will later format as a heading.

W03.15

SIDE NOTE

Adding a New Row at the Bottom of the Table

Position the insertion point in the last cell of the table, and then press Tab.

To Insert and Delete Rows

a. Click anywhere in the **Soul Package** row. Under Table Tools, click the **Layout** tab. In the Rows & Columns group, click **Delete**, and then select **Delete Rows**. The Soul Package row is removed.

b. Point to the **left of the bottom border**, just outside the table, to display a control with a plus sign ⊕. Click the **plus sign** to add a new row, click in the first cell of the new row, and then type Balance Package. Press Tab, and then type Mind Package plus a one-night hotel stay with full breakfast. Press Tab, and then type $575. Do not press Enter or Tab.

c. Click in any cell in **row 1**. You will insert a top row so you can include a table heading. In the Rows & Columns group, click **Insert Above**. A new row is added at the top of the table.

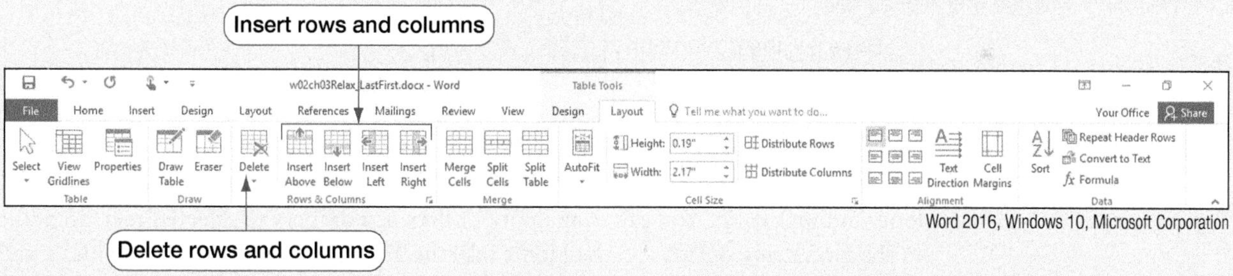

Insert rows and columns

Delete rows and columns

Word 2016, Windows 10, Microsoft Corporation

Figure 21 Insert and delete rows

d. **Save** 🔲 the document.

Merging and Splitting a Row

Cells can be merged or split. Often, as an afterthought, you will decide that several cells should be merged to enable a title to extend across the width of a table. Or perhaps a lengthy cell should be split to enable you to organize information within a cell. In addition to options for splitting and merging cells, the Layout tab includes options for aligning your data once you have split or merged cells. In this exercise, you will add a heading in the top row of the table, merge the cells, and then center the data within the new row.

W03.16

To Merge a Row

a. Click in the **first cell of the first row**, and then type Specialty Spa Packages.

b. Point to the **left of the first row** until a white arrow appears. Click to select the **top row** of the table. On the Layout tab, in the Merge group, click **Merge Cells** to merge all cells in the row into one cell. The first row can now be used as a title row.

c. In the Alignment group, click **Align Center** ▤.

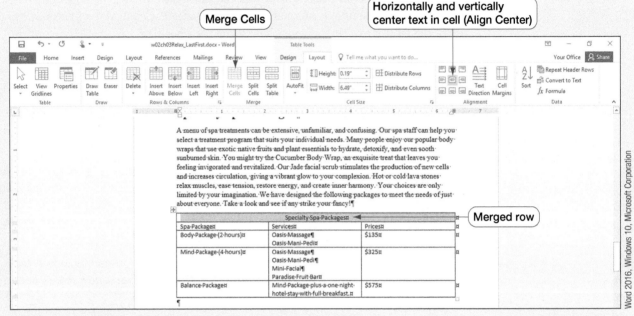

Figure 22 Merged and aligned row

d. **Save** 🖫 the document.

Formatting a Table

Once selected, text in a table can be formatted in a variety of ways. You can identify options in the Font group of the Home tab to format selected text, such as bold, shading, font, and font color. You can even apply bullets or numbers to selected text. In addition to the formatting options on the Home tab, the Table Tools Design tab provides a gallery of table styles with preexisting colors, borders, shading, and other design elements to quickly and easily format your table. You can then choose to add further shading, color, and formatting to the style. Some table styles apply a different color to the first row or to the first column to emphasize the header row or column. Other styles apply alternating color to rows, called banded rows. Still others apply alternating color to columns, called banded columns. Word organizes table styles on the basis of a plain, grid, or list design, as shown in Table 2. Word 2016 also features the Border Painter, which enables you to quickly format borders of the table. In this exercise, you will add some spark to the Specialty Spa Packages table. You will add a table style and then modify the style by adding shading and removing bold.

Table Style Categories	Description
Plain	More black-and-white table design options
Grid	Tables designed to present data in a grid (with column separators)
List	Tables designed to present list-oriented data (with fewer column separators)

Table 2 Word 2016 table styles

To Format a Table

a. Click the **table selector** ⊞ in the top left corner of the table to select the entire table. Under Table Tools, click the **Design** tab, and then in the Table Styles group, click **More**. Scroll down to view all the styles, and then under **List Tables**, in the second column and third row, select **List Table 3 - Accent 1**. The table is formatted to include a shaded blue title area and blue borders.

b. Select the **second row** of the table containing the Spa Packages, Services, and Prices headings. In the Table Styles group, click the **Shading** arrow, and then under Theme Colors, in the fifth column and third row, select **Blue, Accent 2, Lighter 60%**.

c. Click the **table selector** ⊞ to select the entire table. Click the **Home** tab, and then in the Font group, click **Bold** B to remove bold from the table.

d. Click to place the insertion point **below the table**, just in front of the paragraph mark. Press Delete to remove the extra paragraph mark.

e. **Save** 🖫 the document.

REAL WORLD ADVICE | **Aligning Graphics in Your Document**

Have you ever tried to insert multiple graphics side by side in a document? Aligning and spacing multiple graphics evenly can be a challenging task. Create a table with no borders to quickly align your pictures. For example, if you are inserting three pictures in a row, side by side, create a one-row table with three columns. Then remove the borders, and insert each picture into its own cell. It is that simple!

Resizing and Aligning a Table

The Table Tools Layout tab enables you to align text horizontally or vertically within cells, change the text direction within a cell, modify cell margins, and change heights and widths. When Word creates a table, all columns and rows are of equal width and height. As you enter text in a table cell, Word will automatically increase row height to accommodate additional text if necessary. The column width, however, will remain the same. If you want to manually change column width or row height, you can drag a row or column border. For more precise resizing, click Properties in the Table group of the Layout tab, and indicate a measurement for a selected table, column, row, or cell. The alignment buttons on the Home tab, in the Paragraph group, enable you to align a table horizontally on a page. In this exercise, you will resize the table width, center the table horizontally on the page, and then add vertical inside borders.

To Resize and Align a Table

SIDE NOTE
Alternative Way to Resize a Table
Position the pointer on a border of the table until it changes to a double-headed arrow. Drag to resize.

a. Point to the table, and then click the **table selector** ⊞ to select the table. Under Table Tools, click the **Layout** tab, and then in the Table group, click **Properties**. The Table Properties dialog box is displayed. On the Table tab, under **Size**, click the **Preferred width** check box, and then click the arrow as needed to resize the table to **5"**.

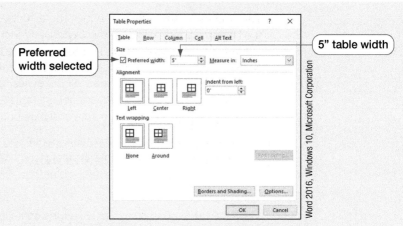

Figure 23 Table properties dialog box

b. Click **OK**. Click the **Home** tab, and then in the Paragraph group, click **Center** ☰ to center the table horizontally on the page.

c. Under Table Tools, click the **Layout** tab, and then in the Alignment group, click **Align Center** ▤ to center the text within each cell of the table. You do not find this change attractive, so on the Quick Access Toolbar, click **Undo** ↺ to undo the alignment change.

d. Under Table Tools, click the **Design** tab. In the Borders group, click **Pen Color**, and then under Theme Colors, in the fifth column and first row, select **Blue, Accent 1**. In the Borders group, click the **Borders** arrow, and then select **Inside Vertical Border**.

e. Click outside the table to deselect it, and then **save** 🖫 the document.

Converting Text into a Table

Word enables you to quickly convert existing text to a table. The key is indicating how the text is separated on each row — or paragraph. If your text is separated by using commas, the first paragraph will be entered into the first row of the table, with text in between each comma placed into individual columns. In this exercise, using existing text, you will create a one-column table based on the five benefits of massages. Since you need only one column per paragraph, you will use the paragraph mark as the separator.

W03.19

SIDE NOTE

Changing the Horizontal Borders
Alternatively, in the Borders group, select the border style, and then click Borders. Select Bottom Border, Top Border, and Inside Horizontal Border.

To Convert Text into a Table

a. In the **Specialty Spa Massages** section, select the five lines starting with the line **Increasing the body's energy flow** and ending with the line **Reducing insomnia, stress, and fatigue**.

b. Click the **Insert** tab. In the Tables group, click **Table**, and then select **Convert Text to Table**.
The Convert Text to Table dialog box appears. Word will automatically place each line — paragraph — of data into a row. Notice "Paragraphs" is selected under the Separate text at section. This will determine how the columns are created. Since there is only one paragraph mark per row in your data, Word will create only one column in the table. You can override this by changing the Number of columns value. You will accept all the defaults.

c. In the Convert Text to Table dialog box, click **OK**. Under Table Tools, click the **Layout** tab. In the Cell Size group, click **AutoFit**, and then select **AutoFit Contents**. Word will automatically determine the best column width for the table data.

d. With the table still selected, under Table Tools, click the **Design** tab, and then in the Borders group, click **Border Styles**, and then under Theme Borders, in the first column and third row, select **Double solid lines, 1/2 pt**. The pointer changes to a brush to indicate that the Border Painter is turned on. Click **each horizontal line** of the table.

> ### Troubleshooting
> If the Border Painter turns off while you are trying to create the border, simply click Borders in the Borders group again to turn it on.

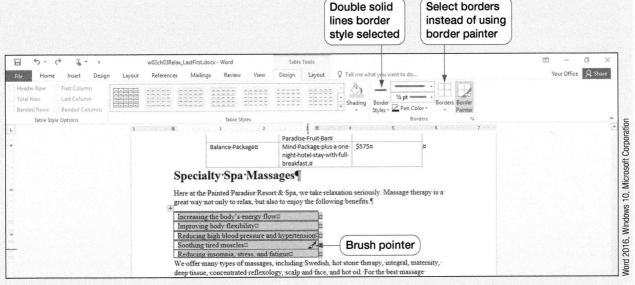

Figure 24   Border painter

e. Press Esc to turn off the border painter. With the table still selected, click the **Home** tab, and then in the Paragraph group, click **Center** ☰.

f. Click outside the table to deselect it, and then **save** 🖫 the document.

Sorting Table Data

You can sort, or rearrange, rows on the basis of the contents of one or more columns. For example, if a table includes divisions of a company in one column and their sales in another column, you can sort the table to place rows in order according to the divisions' sales. If more than one division has the same sales value, you can sort by both sales and division names so that if their sales are identical, the matching records will then be sorted by division names.

You can sort in alphabetic, numeric, or chronological order in either ascending or descending fashion. Alphabetically, the letter "Z" is higher than the letter "A," so a descending alphabetic sort would place records in order from "Z" to "A", while an ascending sort would arrange them from "A" to "Z." In this exercise, you will sort the Specialty Spa Massages table in alphabetic order. You will then sort the Specialty Spa Packages table by price in descending order — with the most expensive package at the top of the list.

To Sort a Table

a. Point to the table, and then click the **table selector** ⊞. Under Table Tools, click the **Layout** tab, and then in the Data group, click **Sort**. The Sort dialog box opens. At the bottom of the dialog box, under **My list has**, verify that **No header row** is selected.

The first column (Column 1) is correctly assumed to be the sort field. If such were not the case, you could click the Sort by arrow and select another column. The field is a Text field, and the sort order is assumed to be Ascending. If any of those assumptions were not correct, you would change them in the dialog box.

b. Click **OK**, and then click outside the table to deselect it. The benefits of massages are rearranged alphabetically.

c. Scroll up to locate the Specialty Spa Packages table, and then select the **last four rows** of the table, starting with **Spa Package** and ending with **$575**. On the Layout tab, in the Data group, click **Sort**.

d. Under **My list has**, click **Header row** to indicate that the selected data contains headers. Notice that Spa Package is assumed to be the sort field. Click the **arrow** next to **Spa Package**, and then select **Prices**. Under **Sort by**, on the right, click **Descending**, and then click **OK**. Click outside the table to deselect it. The Spa Service records are now sorted by price, in descending order.

If your table contains a merged row, do not select it when sorting data within the table; otherwise, you may find yourself selecting the entire table.

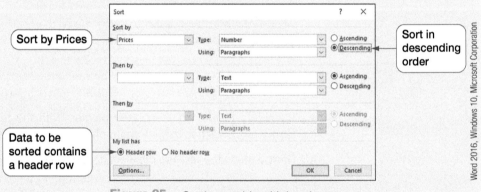

Figure 25   Sorting a table with headers

e. **Save** 💾 the document. If you need to take a break before finishing this chapter, now is a good time to take a break.

 CONSIDER THIS | **Selecting Appropriate Objects**

With the multitude of objects provided by Word, including WordArt, SmartArt, charts, and tables, you should take care to include objects that are appropriate for the documents in which they appear. When would you use one object rather than another? Does it have more to do with the type of document you are working with — school, personal, business — or more with the way you present and format the object?

Managing Pages

When a document includes more than one page of text, there is always a possibility that a page will end awkwardly. A heading may show up at the bottom of a page, with the contents of that section displayed on the next page. Or perhaps only the first line of a paragraph shows at the bottom of a page, with the remainder of the paragraph on the next page. Always be sure to preview a document before printing so you can identify and correct an unattractive page ending. You will now explore ways to manage the end of a page, making sure that each page ends attractively. You will also learn to format text in sections.

Work with Page Breaks

A **page break** is the break where one page ends and another one begins. Word automatically separates pages according to a standard page size, inserting a soft page break when you reach the end of a page. As you add and delete text, Word automatically adjusts the page break. Occasionally, you will want to insert a page break in a different location than where Word locates it. For example, when a heading shows on one page with the remainder of the section on the next page, you might want to force a page break immediately before the heading to keep the heading and its text together. When typing a report that is divided into sections or chapters, you will probably want to insert a page break at the end of each section to ensure that each section or chapter begins on a new page. You can manually insert a page break from either the Insert tab or the Layout tab.

Avoiding Orphan and Widow Lines

Orphans and widows are lines that dangle at the beginning or ending of a page. An **orphan** is the first line of a paragraph when the line is alone at the bottom of a page. The rest of the paragraph appears at the top of the next page. A **widow** is the last line of a paragraph when the line is alone at the top of a page. The first part of the paragraph appears at the end of the previous page. Widows and orphans affect the readability of a document, breaking the flow of text. Because you generally want to avoid widows and orphans, Word automatically sets Widow/Orphan control to prevent their occurrence, ensuring that at least two lines of a paragraph appear together.

Working with the End of a Page

You notice that the spa hours are split apart; some of the hours are listed at the end of page two, and the rest are displayed at the top of page three. In this exercise, you will insert a page break so that all of the spa hours are listed together at the top of page three. You will also verify that Widow/Orphan control is turned on.

 W03.21

SIDE NOTE
Inserting Page Breaks
Alternatively, you can press Ctrl+Enter to insert a page break.

To Work with the End of a Page

a. If you took a break, open the **w02ch03Relax** document. Press Ctrl+Home. Click the **View** tab, and then in the Zoom group, click **Multiple Pages**. Scroll to view all four pages. Note that page three begins awkwardly, with the spa hours split between pages two and three.

b. Click to place the insertion point in front of the heading **Spa Hours**. Click the **Layout** tab. In the Page Setup group, click **Breaks**, and then select **Page**.

c. A page break is inserted. If you are in Print Layout view, with nonprinting characters displayed, you will see the page break. Click the **View** tab, and then in the Zoom group, click **100%**.

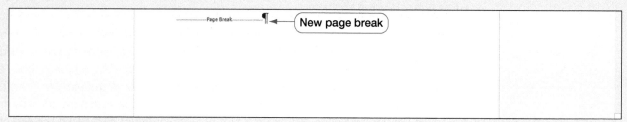

Figure 26 Inserting a page break

Word 2016, Windows 10, Microsoft Corporation

d. Click the **Home** tab. In the Paragraph group, click the **Paragraph Dialog Box Launcher**, and then click the **Line and Page Breaks** tab. Verify the **Widow/Orphan control** check box is selected. If it is not, click to select it. Click **OK**. By default, Word is configured to avoid orphan and widow lines.

e. **Save** 🖫 the document.

Work with Sections

A document can be divided into **sections**, which are areas that can be formatted differently. Each section can have its own orientation, margins, headers, footers, and any other document format. Suppose you have a document that is formatted in the portrait orientation but the last page contains a table that is best suited for landscape orientation. In that case, you simply define a separate section for the table and apply landscape orientation to that section. The rest of the document will remain in portrait orientation.

Inserting a New Section

Options on the Layout tab enable you to assign a section break, which divides a document and begins a new section at that point. When you insert a section break, you will see a dotted line with the words "Section Break" if nonprinting characters are displayed. You can insert a Continuous section break, which starts at the position of the insertion point but does not break the page flow. For example, if you are creating a newsletter, you might want the title of the newsletter to be centered horizontally but all text beneath that point arranged in columns. After centering the title, insert a Continuous section break so the remaining text can be formatted in columns on the same page without affecting the title. A Next Page section break begins a section on a new page.

Day Spa Group requires that all articles include a cover sheet in landscape orientation, with contact information related to the submission. The body of the report should be in portrait orientation. In this exercise, you will insert a Next Page section break after the cover page and change the orientation of the cover page.

▶ W03.22

SIDE NOTE
Deleting a Section Break
Display nonprinting characters, click the section break, and then press Delete .

To Insert a New Section

a. Press Ctrl+Home. Click the **Layout** tab, and then in the Page Setup group, click **Breaks**. Under the Section Breaks category, select **Next Page** (do not select Page).
You have just created a new blank page at the top of your document.

b. Press Ctrl+Home to place the insertion point at the top of the new page. On the Layout tab, in the Page Setup group, click **Orientation**, and then select **Landscape**. The new page is set to landscape orientation. Because the new page is in a different section, the remaining pages in the document are still set to portrait orientation.

c. Click the **Design** tab, and then in the Page Background group, click **Page Borders**. The Borders and Shading dialog box opens with the Page Border tab selected. Under Setting, click **Box**. Click the **Apply to** arrow, select **This section**, and then click **OK**.

d. Click the **View** tab, and then in the Zoom group, click **Multiple Pages**. The first page should be in landscape orientation, and the second page should be in portrait orientation. The border should only be on the first page. You will insert the remaining text into the cover sheet later in the chapter.

e. In the Zoom group, click **100%**.

f. **Save** 🔲 the document.

Insert Text from Another Document

Word makes it possible to insert text from another document without using copy and paste. If you need to insert an entire document into your current document, use the Object command on the Insert tab. If you have text that you often insert into various documents, save the text in a separate file, and then insert the file into your documents. Not only can you save time by reusing text, but you also minimize typing errors.

Creating a Cover Page by Inserting Text from Another Document

Because you must often include a cover page for articles, you have saved the necessary information in a separate document. In this exercise, you will insert the text from the saved document into the cover page.

W03.23

To Insert Text from Another Document

a. Press Ctrl + Home to place the insertion point at the top of the new page.

b. Click the **Insert** tab. In the Text group, click the **Object** arrow 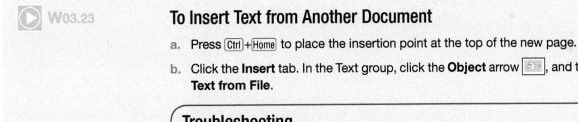, and then select **Text from File**.

> **Troubleshooting**
> If you click Object instead of the arrow beside it, you will see an Object dialog box. Close the dialog box, and redo step b.

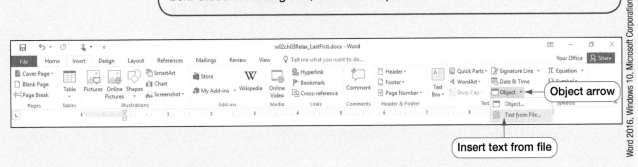

Figure 27   Inserting text from another file

c. Navigate to the location of your student data files, and then double-click **w02ch03SpaCover**.

d. Click the **View** tab, and then in the Zoom group, click **Multiple Pages** to view your article.

e. Click the **Layout** tab, and then in the Page Setup group, click the **Dialog Box Launcher**. In the **Page Setup** dialog box, click the **Layout** tab, click the **Vertical alignment** arrow, select **Center**, and then click **OK**. You have vertically centered text on the cover page.

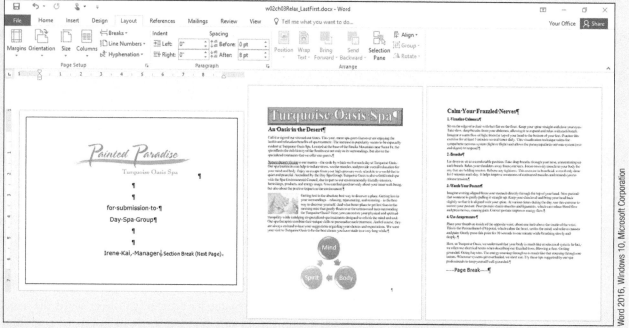

Figure 28   Cover page

f. After reviewing the article, Click the **View** tab, and in the Zoom group, click **100%**.

g. **Save** the document, exit Word, and then submit your file as directed by your instructor.

Concept Check

1. What is the difference between creating WordArt and using Text Effects and Typography in the Font group? p. 223

2. What is a SmartArt graphic, and what is an example of how you could use the Hierarchy layout in a business setting? p. 231

3. What are two ways to create a text box, and what are some examples of when you would use a text box in your document? p. 235

4. What is the difference between Pictures and Online Pictures in the Illustrations group? p. 237

5. Describe how to insert tabs using the ruler and the Tabs dialog box. p. 242

6. Although both tabs and tables enable you to align text in columns, each has unique features that make it appropriate for various applications. What are some examples of when you would use a table versus a tab? p. 243

7. What is a page break? What is the difference between a widow and an orphan? p. 253

8. What are some examples of when you would need to create a new section? p. 254

9. How do you insert all the text from one document into another document without using the copy and paste feature? Why would you use this feature? p. 255

Key Terms

Alignment guides 228
Anchor 230
Bar tab 240
Cell 239
Center tab 240
Contextual tabs 223
Decimal tab 240
Leader 240
Left tab 240

Live Layout 228
Object 223
Orphan 253
Page break 253
Picture 237
Right tab 240
Section 254
Sizing handle 227
SmartArt 231

Tab selector 240
Tab stop 239
Table 239
Table selector 244
Text box 235
Text wrap 228
Widow 253
WordArt 223

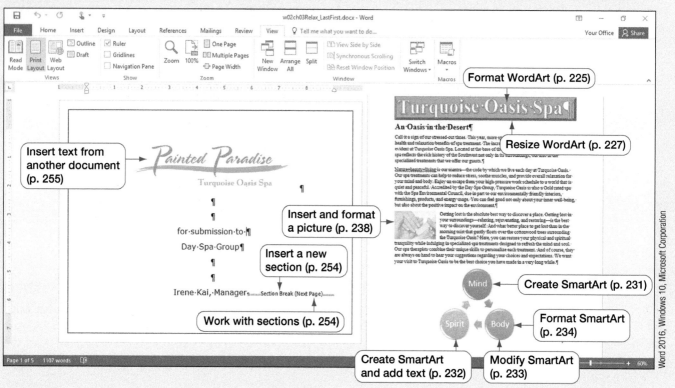

Figure 29

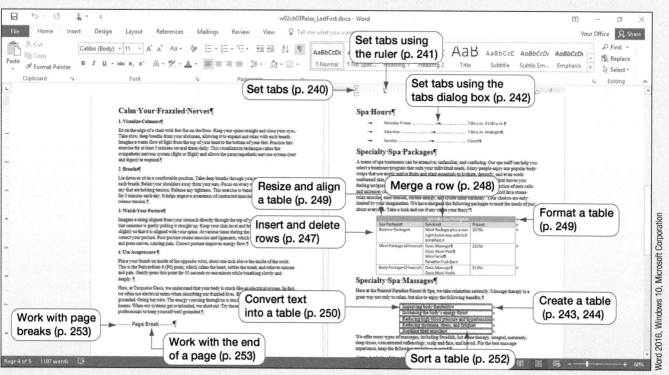

Figure 30

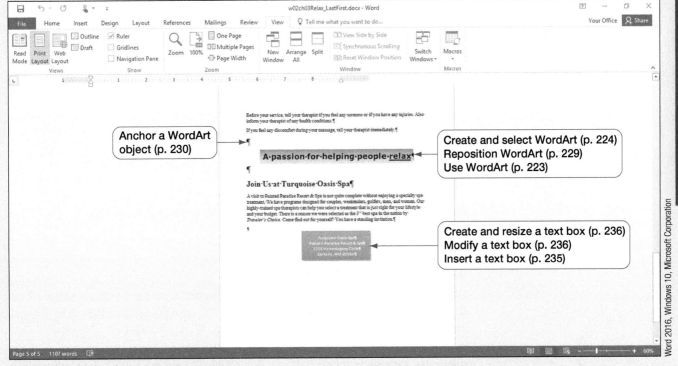

Before your service, tell your therapist if you feel any soreness or if you have any injuries. Also inform your therapist of any health conditions.¶

If you feel any discomfort during your massage, tell your therapist immediately.¶

¶

A·passion·for·helping·people·relax◀

¶

Join·Us·at·Turquoise·Oasis·Spa¶

A visit to Painted Paradise Resort & Spa is not quite complete without enjoying a specialty spa treatment. We have programs designed for couples, weekenders, golfers, men, and women. Our highly-trained spa therapists can help you select a treatment that is just right for your lifestyle and your budget. There is a reason we were selected as the 3ʳᵈ best spa in the nation by *Traveler's Choice*. Come find out for yourself! You have a standing invitation.¶

¶

Turquoise Oasis Spa¶
Painted Paradise Resort & Spa¶
3356 Hemmingway Circle¶
Santa Fe, NM 89566¶

Anchor a WordArt object (p. 230)

Create and select WordArt (p. 224)
Reposition WordArt (p. 229)
Use WordArt (p. 223)

Create and resize a text box (p. 236)
Modify a text box (p. 236)
Insert a text box (p. 235)

Figure 31

Practice 1

Student data files needed:

 w02ch03SpaExcl.docx

w02ch03SpaTable.docx

w02ch03SpaLogo.jpg

You will save your file as:

w02ch03SpaExcl_LastFirst.docx

Spa Exclusives

Sales & Marketing

The website for Turquoise Oasis Spa includes a link that will enable visitors to the site to register for Spa Exclusives, a program that e-mails reminders of spa specials and product sales. Visitors are asked to indicate an interest category — Fitness, Group Events, Spa Boutique, or Spa Treatments — and to provide an e-mail address. Each month, a targeted flyer is sent by e-mail and also made available as a link on the Spa Exclusives Member web page. This month, you are preparing a flyer that highlights items in the spa boutique. The flyer will be prepared as a Word document and sent as an e-mail attachment. It will also be available on the Painted Paradise Resort & Spa website.

a. Start **Word**, click **Open Other Documents**, and then double-click **This PC**. Navigate to the location of your student files, and then double-click **w02ch03SpaExcl**. Click the **File** tab, click **Save As**, double-click **This PC**, and then navigate to where you are saving your files. Change the **File name** to w02ch03SpaExcl_LastFirst, using your last and first name, and then click **Save**.

b. Click the **Insert** tab. In the Illustrations group, click **Pictures**, navigate to the location of your student data files, and then double-click **w02ch03SpaLogo** to insert the logo.

c. Select **Spa Specials for July 2018**. Click the **Insert** tab, and then in the Text group, click **Insert WordArt**. In the second column and third row, select **Fill - Black, Text 1, Outline - Background 1, Hard Shadow - Accent 1**. In the Arrange group, click **Wrap Text**, and then select **Top and Bottom**. In the Arrange group, click **Align**

Objects, and then select **Align Center** to center it horizontally on the page. Click outside of the WordArt to deselect it.

d. Press `Ctrl`+`A` to select the entire document. Change the font to **Verdana** and the font size to **14**. The text in the objects will not change.

e. If the horizontal ruler is not displayed, click the **View** tab, and then in the Show group, click the **Ruler** check box. Press `Ctrl`+`End`, click the **tab selector** at the left of the ruler, and then continue clicking until it displays a **Right Tab** symbol. Click to place a right tab stop at **6"** on the ruler.

f. Type Lavender Bath Salts, and press `Tab`. Type $30, but do not press `Enter`. On the Home tab, in the Paragraph group, click the **Paragraph Dialog Box Launcher**. Click the **Tabs** button, click **2** in the Leader group, and then click **OK**. Press `Enter`, and then enter the following three items, pressing `Tab` between each item and its price. Press `Enter` after each item, including after the last entry of "$8".

Lavender Shower Gel $18
Lavender Lip Balm $3
Signature Lavender Lotion $8

g. Click the **Insert** tab. In the Text group, click **Text Box**, and then select **Simple Text Box**. Click the **Shape Height** down arrow in the Size group until **0.8"** is displayed, and then click the **Shape Width** up arrow until **6"** is displayed.

h. With the text in the text box still selected, click the **tab selector** at the left of the ruler until it displays a Left Tab symbol. Click **2.5"** on the horizontal ruler to set a left tab stop, and then click **4.5"** to set another left tab stop.

i. With the text in the text box still selected, type Painted Paradise Resort & Spa in the box, and then press `Tab`. Type 3356 Hemmingway Circle, and press `Tab`. Type (505)555-0806. Press `Enter`, and then type www.paintedparadiseresort.com.

j. Click the dashed line surrounding the text box to make it solid, indicating the entire text box is selected. Click the **Home** tab. In the Paragraph group, click **Center**, and then change the font size to **12**. In the Paragraph group, click **Line and Paragraph Spacing**, and then select **Remove Space After Paragraph**.

k. Click the **Format** tab, and then in the Shape Styles group, click **Shape Fill**. Under Theme Colors, in the ninth column and third row, select **Aqua, Accent 5, Lighter 60%**. Click **Shape Outline**, point to **Weight**, and then select **1½ pt**. In the Text group, click **Align Text**, and then select **Middle** to align the text vertically.

l. Point to the anchor for the text box, and drag the anchor up so that it is positioned to the left of the text **Signature Lavender Lotion**. This will keep the text box anchored to the last paragraph of the first page.

m. Press `Ctrl`+`End`. Click the **Layout** tab, and then in the Page Setup group, click **Breaks**, and then select **Next Page**. In the Page Setup group, click **Orientation**, and then select **Landscape**.

n. Click the **Insert** tab. In the Text group, click the **Object** arrow, and then select **Text from File**. Navigate to the location of your student data files, and then double-click **w02ch03SpaTable**.

o. Select the six paragraphs beginning with **11-A-231, Body** and ending with **Ultra Healing Lotion, $20.95**. On the Insert tab, in the Tables group, click **Table**, and then select **Convert Text to Table**. The Convert Text to Table dialog box is displayed. Under AutoFit behavior, click **AutoFit to contents**, and then under Separate text at, click **Commas**. Click **OK**.

p. Click anywhere in the **first row** of the table. Under Table Tools, click the **Layout** tab, and then in the Rows & Columns group, click **Insert Above**. Click in the **first cell** of the first row, type Item #, and then press `Tab`. Type the following text, pressing `Tab` after each entry:

Category
Product
Size
Description
Price

q. Point to the **top border** of the first column until the pointer changes to a black downward arrow, and then click to select the **first column**. Under Table Tools, on the Layout tab, in the Cell Size group, click in the **Table Column Width** box, and then change the value displayed to **1.5"**. Press [Enter] to view the result. Similarly, change the column width of the Size column to **0.9"**.

r. Under Table Tools, click the **Design** tab, and then in the Table Styles group, click **More**. Under Grid Tables, click **Grid Table 4 - Accent 5**.

s. Click the **table selector** to select the entire table, and then in the Alignment group, click **Align Center Left** to align the text vertically and to the left in each cell. Select the **first row**, and then in the Alignment group, click **Align Center** to align the text horizontally and vertically in each cell of the first row.

t. Click in any table **cell**, and then in the Data group, click **Sort**. Under My list has, confirm **Header row** is selected. Click the **Sort by** arrow, and then select **Category**. Click the **Then by** arrow, and then select **Product**. Click **OK**.

u. Press [Ctrl]+[End]. Click the **Insert** tab. In the Header & Footer group, click Footer, and then select Edit Footer. In the Insert group, click **Document Info**, and then select **File Name**. **Center** the text in the footer, and then double-click anywhere in the document to close the header and footer.

v. Click the **View** tab, and then in the Zoom group, click **Multiple Pages** to view your document. Save the document, exit Word, and then submit your file as directed by your instructor.

Problem Solve 1

MyITLab®
Grader
Homework

Student data files needed:

 w02ch03Specials.docx

w02ch03IndigoLogo.jpg

You will save your file as:

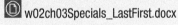 w02ch03Specials_LastFirst.docx

Weekly Dinner Specials

Sales & Marketing

Indigo5 posts a flyer highlighting its dinner specials each day. You will enhance the starting document by adding the dinner specials into a SmartArt diagram. You will then format the SmartArt. You will also add a WordArt object, a picture, tab stops, and a footer to the document.

a. Open the Word document, **w02ch03Specials**. Save the document as w02ch03Specials_LastFirst, using your last and first name.

b. Display the formatting marks and the ruler if they are not already displayed.

c. Insert the **w02ch03IndigoLogo.jpg** picture, located with your student data files, into the document. Center-align the logo horizontally on the page.

d. Select Weekly Dinner Specials, and then, on the Insert tab, click **WordArt**. Click **Gradient Fill – Purple, Accent 4, Outline – Accent 4** (column 3, row 2). Apply **Top and Bottom** text wrap. Center-align the object horizontally on the page.

e. Click **Text Effects** in the WordArt Styles group. Point to Shadow, and then apply the **Perspective Diagonal Upper Right** shadow effect (under Perspective, column 2, row 1).

f. Apply the **Light 1 Outline, Colored Fill – Purple, Accent 4** shape style (column 5, row 3). Click outside of the WordArt object to deselect it.

g. Move the insertion point to the end of the document. Insert a **Vertical Block List** SmartArt object (under the List category).

h. If necessary, open the SmartArt Text pane. With the insertion point next to the first bullet in the SmartArt Text pane, type Sunday. Click beside the second bullet, type Sundried Tomato Lasagna, and then press [Delete] to remove the next bullet.

i. Click beside the third bullet, and type Monday. Click in the next bullet, type Sweet Chili Chicken Breast, and then press [Delete] to remove the next bullet.

j. Similarly, add the Charred New York Strip Steak for Tuesday, and remove the next bullet. Close the SmartArt Text pane.

k. Click the outer border of the SmartArt object to select the entire diagram. Make sure none of the shapes within the SmartArt object are selected. If they are, click the outside border again. Under SmartArt Tools, click the **Design** tab. Click **Add Shape** in the Create Graphic group, and then type Wednesday. Click **Add Bullet** in the Create Graphic group, and then type Peppery Pork Tenderloin. Click the outer border of the SmartArt object to select the entire diagram.

l. Similarly, add three more shapes and three more bullets with the following information, making sure to select the entire SmartArt object before adding a shape:

Thursday	Lamb Rack
Friday	Sesame Crusted Salmon
Saturday	Prime Rib

m. Select the entire SmartArt object . On the Home tab, in the Paragraph group, click **Center** to align the SmartArt horizontally on the page.

n. Under SmartArt Tools, click the **Design** tab. Click Change Colors in the SmartArt Styles group. Scroll down, and under the Accent 4 category, click **Colored Outline – Accent 4** (first selection under Accent 4).

o. Press [Ctrl]+[End]. Press [Enter] twice. Set a **1" left tab** and a **6" right tab with a dot leader**. Press [Tab]. Type Call for Reservations, and then press [Tab]. Type 505-555-5656, and then press [Enter].

p. Insert a footer with the file name field centered. Close the header and footer.

q. Click the **View** tab, and then, in the Zoom group, click **One Page** to view your document. Save the document, exit Word, and then submit your file as directed by your instructor.

Critical Thinking

What would be an effective way to distribute this document? Would it be best posted to a physical location or distributed electronically? Describe specific techniques in detail for distributing information about the annual herb sale.

Perform 1 : Perform in Your Career

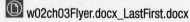

Student data files needed:

📄 w02ch03Flyer.docx

📄 w02ch03Activities.docx

You will save your file as:

📄 w02ch03Flyer.docx_LastFirst.docx

Annual Plant Sale Fundraiser

Sales & Marketing

General Business

You are a volunteer at a local elementary school. The school is hosts a plant sale annually as a fundraiser. You need to prepare a flyer that will be sent to parents, news media, vendors, and various supporters of the school. The flyer will also be posted in stores, churches, the local library, and possibly other locations in the community.

a. Open the Word file, **w02ch03Flyer**. Save your file as w02ch03Flyer_LastFirst, using your last and first name.

b. Use Online Pictures to search Bing for a picture of plants, gardening, schools, or other related images. Insert the picture in the upper left of the document. Size the picture to be approximately 2 inches square.

c. Use WordArt to create a title for the flyer, **Annual Plant Sale**. Format it with a style of your choosing. If necessary, move the WordArt object to ensure that it does not overlap the image inserted in the prior step.

d. At the end of the document, insert the text from the file named **w02ch03Activities**. Ensure that the text is inserted under the image and SmartArt object from the prior steps.

e. Select all the text starting with **Plant Sale Activities** and ending with the paragraph that begins with **Vendor Alley**. Convert it to a table, and separate the text at paragraphs.

f. Merge the cells containing the bulleted items below the **Classes** and **Ongoing Activities** headings.

g. Format the table, using an appropriate table style.

h. Insert a footer with the file name centered.

i. Save the document, exit Word, and then submit your file as directed by your instructor.

Additional
Cases

Additional Chapter Cases are available at www.pearsonhighered.com/youroffice

Microsoft Word 2016

Chapter 4 | SPECIAL DOCUMENT FORMATTING AND MAIL MERGE

Prepare Case

Sales & Marketing

Research & Development

Turquoise Oasis Spa Newsletter

The Turquoise Oasis Spa is considering an incremental program that will phase in environmental improvements. The spa also will start a newsletter, *Solutions*, to help market the new program. As a graduate class requirement, you will edit a research report on this program and help to develop the newsletter. You will use Word to develop the "happenings at the oasis" section, formatting text in columns and including graphics. You will also develop a cover letter to accompany the full-version of the newsletter. You will use Word's mail merge feature to personalize the letter and to produce mailing labels.

Konstantin Sutyagin/Shutterstock

Student data files needed for this chapter:

 w02ch04Addresses.accdb

w02ch04Letter.docx

w02ch04Research.docx

w02ch04ResortStyleGuide.docx

w02ch04Review.docx

w02ch04SpaLogo.jpg

w02ch04SpaNews.docx

w02ch04Wine.jpg

You will save your files as:

w02ch04Addresses_LastFirst.accdb

w02ch04Labels_LastFirst.docx

w02ch04Letter_LastFirst.docx

w02ch04Merged_LastFirst.docx

w02ch04Research_LastFirst.docx

w02ch04Review_LastFirst.docx

w02ch04SpaNews_LastFirst.docx

Creating a Research Report

Most composition classes require that you write a research report. The very words "research report" strike fear into the hearts of many college students. However, researching a topic might not be the most difficult part of the assignment. Instead, ensuring that your report is in the correct format, according to an identified style guide, might be the bigger challenge.

A **style guide**, or style manual, is a set of standards for creating documents. A style manual is not as concerned with the selection of wording as it is with the standardized documentation of citations and general page characteristics such as margins, spacing, headers, footers, and page numbers. A **citation** is a reference to a published or unpublished source. Although it may seem that adherence to a particular style is yet another hurdle to clear in the already challenging chore of writing a research report, it is really very helpful. When you follow set rules for citing works, meaning giving credit to the original author, you are less likely to inadvertently plagiarize. Adherence to a style also gives your instructor the ability to work through a report's ideas and to judge the validity of your work and other students' reports in a consistent manner.

REAL WORLD ADVICE | **What Is Plagiarism?**

When writing any sort of paper, you should be very careful not to plagiarize. **Plagiarism** occurs when you present the ideas, data, or phrasing of another author as if it were your own. In effect, you mislead other people into believing that it is your own original work when in fact you are in effect stealing it from someone else. Regardless of the writing style guide that you use, you must identify the source of information, and you must identify all quoted material by means of quotation marks or indentation on the page. You can be charged with plagiarism for the following activities:

- Copying, paraphrasing, or quoting any person or source without giving proper credit
- Presenting another person's published or unpublished work as your own, with or without permission

---

There is no universally accepted style guide for all writing. Instead, different industries, different academic disciplines, and even different journals within a discipline tend to favor one or another standard style. As you progress through a field of study, you will be required to write papers that adhere to a prescribed style manual. You will find a wealth of information on the various writing style guides, both in print and online.

When assigning a research report, your instructor will identify the preferred writing style. The major writing style guides are MLA, APA, Chicago, and CSE. The report's subject matter is often what determines the style. Some styles are preferred by the social sciences, while others are the choice of humanities or sciences. Each style has unique requirements for the treatment of citation of sources, preparation of a bibliography, and creating a title page. Some elements of a writing style even address such topics as when to spell out numerals. For example, should you write the number "thirty-one" or "31"?

MLA (Modern Language Association) style is often used in the humanities, including English, foreign languages, philosophy, religion, art, architecture, and literature. MLA is generally considered simpler and more concise than other styles. It requires brief parenthetical citations that are keyed to an alphabetic list of works cited at the end of the paper. Available for over 50 years, the style is widely followed internationally, including in North America, Brazil, China, India, and Japan. The association publishes two manuals: *MLA Handbook for Writers of Research Papers* and *MLA Style Manual and Guide to Scholarly Publishing*.

APA (American Psychological Association) is preferred by the social sciences, including business, economics, communication, justice, education, geography, law, political science, and sociology. Originating in 1929, the style was developed to simplify the communication of scientific ideas in a consistent manner. It focuses on the presentation of technical ideas and research and is often the required style for the compilation of literature reviews and experiment reports. The association publishes the *Publication Manual of the American Psychological Association*, which contains the APA's style requirements.

Chicago (University of Chicago) style is concerned primarily with the preparation and editing of papers and books for publication. As such, it is less prescriptive with regard to such items as a title page or an abstract — a summary of the research or paper contents. Since 1906, Chicago has been the recognized standard with regard to American English style, grammar, and punctuation. Offering writers a choice of several different formats, Chicago style requires only that the result is clear and consistent. *The Chicago Manual of Style* provides guidance to writers using Chicago style.

CSE (Council of Science Editors) is the primary style used in the sciences, such as biology, chemistry, computer science, engineering, environmental sciences, geology, math, health sciences, physics, and astronomy. Previously known as CBE (Council of Biology Editors), the association publishes *Scientific Style and Format: The CBE Manual for Authors, Editors, and Publishers*, which provides detailed guidelines for using CSE style.

In this section, you will edit and format a research report.

 CONSIDER THIS | **Plagiarism?**

In 2004, a school board chairman in North Carolina delivered a commencement speech that was identical to one given several years earlier by Donna Shalala when she was U.S. Secretary of Health and Human Services. Although he first claimed to have written the speech himself, he eventually admitted that he had found the speech by searching the Internet for "commencement speeches." He claimed that he thought it was a "generic speech" and therefore he didn't have to attribute it, and he didn't think he was doing any harm. What do you think?

Format a Research Report

Regardless of the writing style in use, a research report typically includes several standard elements. A title page, a copyright page, a dedication, a table of contents, and a list of illustrations and tables are all possibilities for the front matter — the pages preceding the actual report. Different styles require some or all of those parts. The body of the research report is the typed text, including the report, appropriate citations, headers, and footnotes. At the end of the report is reference material, which could include appendices, a bibliography or references, a glossary, and an index. The body of the report is usually double-spaced with the exception of indented block quotes, which are single-spaced. Footnotes should also be single-spaced.

Opening the Starting File

You are working on a research report on the sustainable spa industry. A sustainable establishment includes building features and resources that conserve energy and protect the environment, such as low-flow water fixtures and solar lighting. In this exercise, you will open a rough draft of the report. You will also display nonprinting characters, view the rulers, and save the file with a new name.

SIDE NOTE
Pin the Ribbon
If your ribbon is collapsed, pin your ribbon open. Click the Home tab. In the lower right corner of the ribbon, click Pin the Ribbon 📌.

To Open the Starting File

a. Start **Word**, click **Open Other Documents** in the left pane, and then click **This PC**. Navigate through the folder structure to the location of your student data files, and then open **w02ch04Research**. A rough draft of the research report opens.

b. If necessary, on the Home tab, in the Paragraph group, click **Show/Hide** ¶ to display nonprinting characters.

c. If the horizontal and vertical rulers are not visible at the top and left sides of the document, click the **View** tab, and then in the Show group, click **Ruler**.

d. Click the **File** tab, click **Save As**, and then click **This PC**. In the Save As dialog box, navigate to where you are saving your project files, and then save the file name as w02ch04Research_LastFirst, using your last and first name. Click **Save**.

Pages in a research report are numbered, with a few exceptions. The title page and dedication do not display page numbers, but they are included in the page count. The front matter is numbered with consecutive lowercase Roman numerals: I, II, III, and so on. The remaining pages are numbered with Arabic numerals: 1, 2, 3, and so on. The exact placement of page numbers depends upon the writing style in use.

Both MLA and APA are well-accepted writing styles in college composition classes. With the exception of page numbering rules and heading alignment, the two styles are very similar. Although you will use MLA style for the document in this chapter, a quick review of APA formatting guidelines would enable you to easily format the research report in APA style. An MLA document should be formatted as follows:

- Set top, bottom, right, and left margins to 1 inch.
- Double-space the document.
- Use 12 pt Times New Roman font.
- Indent the first line of each paragraph one-half inch.
- Right-align your name and a page number in the header of all pages except the first.

Working with Spacing and Indentation in a Research Report

You have reviewed the document for adherence to MLA formatting rules and have found some discrepancies. In this exercise, you will double-space the body of your report and remove the paragraph After spacing. You will also set a 0.5 inch first-line indentation.

To Work with Spacing and Indentation in a Research Report

a. Select all body paragraphs, beginning with **Often associated** and ending at the end of the document. On the Home tab, in the Paragraph group, click the **Paragraph Dialog Box Launcher** ⬚.

b. Under Indentation, click the **Special** arrow. Select **First line** to indent the first line of each paragraph 0.5 inch.

c. Under Spacing, click the **After** down arrow to set a **0 pt** paragraph After spacing. Click the **Line spacing** arrow, and then select **Double**. Click **OK**.

d. Click anywhere in the document to deselect the paragraphs. Scroll to the bottom of the first page, and then select the heading **Seeking LEED Certification**.

e. Because the heading should be aligned on the left margin, you will move the first-line indent to the 0" mark. On the ruler, drag the **First Line Indent** marker ▽ to the left to align it with the left margin at the 0" mark. Similarly, adjust the first-line indent ▽ for the heading **Living in Harmony with Nature**, which is located after the second paragraph on page two.

f. **Save** 🖫 the document.

Working with Headers in a Research Report

You continue to review your research report for adherence to MLA formatting rules. In this exercise, you will add a right-aligned header with your last name and the current page number to all pages except the first.

To Work with Headers in a Research Report

a. Press Ctrl+Home. In the first line of the document, change **Firstname** to your first name, and change **Lastname** to your last name.

b. Click the **Insert** tab, in the Header & Footer group, click **Header**, and then select **Edit Header**. Click the **Home** tab, and then in the Paragraph group, click **Align Right** ▤.

   You will insert a right-aligned header including your last name and a page number, as required by MLA style.

c. Type your last name, and then press Spacebar. Under Header & Footer Tools, click the **Design** tab. In the Insert group, click **Quick Parts**, and then select **Field**. In the Field dialog box, scroll through the **Field names** list, and then select **Page**. Under Field Properties, in the Format group, select the first item in the list, **1, 2, 3**. Click **OK**.

d. In the Options group, click the **Different First Page** check box because you do not want the header to be displayed on the first page of the report. **Close** the header.

e. Click the **View** tab, and then in the Zoom group, click **Multiple Pages** to view the report. Scroll through the report, noting that it includes four pages and that the header is displayed on all pages except the first.

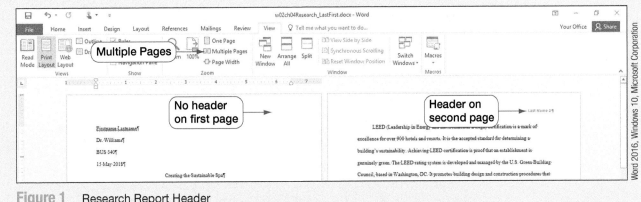

Figure 1 Research Report Header

Word 2016, Windows 10, Microsoft Corporation

f. In the Zoom group, click **100%**. **Save** the document.

Inserting Citations

Referencing, or citing, is the act of giving credit for ideas and information in a research report. If you quote someone, use someone else's words or ideas, or include information taken from another person's work, you must indicate the source of your information. Including a reference to a published or unpublished source is necessary whether you use the exact words of the source or whether you paraphrase it. You must always give credit so that you are not in danger of plagiarism.

An in-text reference is information that you include next to text to give credit to another source. For example, the information can include the author's name and page number in parentheses. This parenthetical reference should be short to minimize interruption of the text itself. It should be placed at the end of a paragraph if the entire paragraph is borrowed or at the end of a sentence if the following sentence is your own work or is identified by another citation. The purpose of an in-text citation is to direct the reader to the correct entry in the list of works cited at the end of your research report or to help locate the source in a library. Rules for including citations vary among the writing styles, but in general you are required to list the author or publication name along with a year, with an optional page number.

You are not required to reference information that is assumed to be general knowledge in the field, nor should you reference text that is your own summary or determination based on your research. The conclusion of a research report most often comprises your thoughts and suggestions, so references are seldom included in a report's conclusion.

 CONSIDER THIS | **What Is General Knowledge?**

You do not need to cite general knowledge, such as the distance from the earth to the moon or the date when the Voting Rights act was signed into law, but you do need to give credit for knowledge from the work of others. Therefore, you should have a clear definition in mind to help you make the distinction. How would you define general knowledge?

Word includes reference tools that enable you to accurately include citations according to one of several writing styles. Enabling Word to format the citations means that you do not have to pay as much attention to learning the minutiae of a particular writing style. Although a style guide is handy, it becomes less necessary when Word assists you in the referencing task. The References tab contains several tools that you will become familiar with when you format a research report.

REAL WORLD ADVICE | **When to Place a Citation**

Although Word simplifies the technical task of citing research, you must still remember to include citations. The task is easier if you place citations in the text as you write the paper. If you wait until the paper is finished, you must backtrack to locate material and position citations. If you have to backtrack, you risk missing a citation and plagiarizing.

Several citations have already been inserted into your research report. In this exercise, you will insert an additional journal and a website citation. You will also edit one of the citations in the document and reuse a previous citation.

 W04.03

SIDE NOTE
Move from Field to Field

Press Tab to move to the next field.

To Insert Citations

a. At the top of the second page, in the first sentence of the first paragraph, place the insertion point after the word **resorts** but before the period. The information in this first sentence came from a journal that you will reference.

b. Click the **References** tab. In the Citations & Bibliography group, click the **Style** arrow, and then if necessary, select **MLA Seventh Edition**. In the Citations & Bibliography group, click **Insert Citation**. Notice the existing citations. Click **Add New Source**. In the Create Source dialog box, click the **Type of Source** arrow, and then select **Journal Article**.

c. Because MLA style requires a volume number and an issue number for a journal, you must show more areas than the ones currently displayed in the dialog box. Click the **Show All Bibliography Fields** check box to expand the areas shown. Insert the information shown below. You may need to scroll down the listing to locate these fields on the list.

Title	The Greening of the Spa Industry
Journal Name	LEED News
Year	2015
Pages	58
Volume	68
Issue	4

Figure 2 Adding a Journal Citation

d. Click **OK** when you have finished entering the data.

The citation (The Greening of the Spa Industry) is inserted at the end of the sentence.

e. Scroll down to the second paragraph on the second page. Before the last sentence of the paragraph, click in the **(Clairday)** citation. A content control is displayed around the citation. Click the **arrow** on the right of the content control, and then select **Edit Citation**. Click in the Pages text box, type 48, and then click the **Author**, **Year**, and **Title** check boxes to suppress the display of those items within the citation.

Because the author's name is mentioned in the sentence, you are revising the parenthetical citation so it includes a page number but no author name.

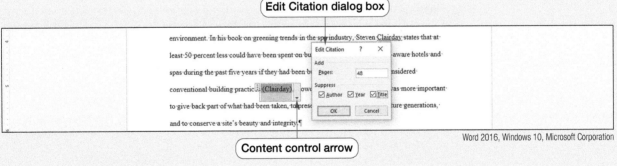

Word 2016, Windows 10, Microsoft Corporation

Figure 3 Editing a Citation

f. Click **OK**. Scroll down to the bottom of the second page. Under the heading **Living in Harmony with Nature**, in the first sentence, click after the word **future** but before the period. On the References tab, in the Citations & Bibliography group, click **Insert Citation**, and then select **Clairday, Steven**.

Because you are reusing a citation to refer to work referenced earlier, you can simply select the citation from the list.

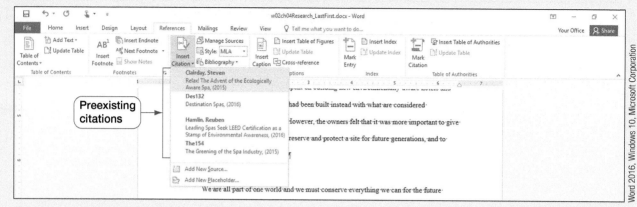

Figure 4 Reusing a Citation

g. Near the bottom of the third page, in the sentence ending with **accountability expected of a green spa**, click after the word **spa** and before the period. In the Citations & Bibliography group, click **Insert Citation**, and then select **Add New Source**. Click the **Type of Source** arrow, scroll down the list, and then select **Web site**. Click the **Show All Bibliography Fields** check box. Type the information below:

Name of Web Page	The Green Spa Industry
Year Accessed	2018
Month Accessed	April
Day Accessed	12
URL	http://www.spanetworknews.com/green

h. Click **OK**, and then **save** the document.

QUICK REFERENCE	Helpful Tips for Placing Citations

1. For regular text citations, always place a citation outside a quotation and before a punctuation mark that ends a sentence.

2. For long quotations that have been set off — indented — from the main text, place a citation after the punctuation mark.

3. If possible, include reference information such as an author's name in the sentence to avoid long parenthetical information.

REAL WORLD ADVICE | Managing Sources

Did you know that Word maintains two lists of sources — a Master List and a Current List? When you create a source in a research report, the citation is added to both lists. The Current List contains cited sources for the current document. The Master List includes sources that are available for use in any document on the local computer. This means that by using the Master List, you can include sources in the current document that were used in a previous document. This keeps you from having to retype the information. Sources from the Current List are included in the document's bibliography. Note that the Master List is retained only on the computer on which the document was created. If you save the document to another computer's storage device, the Master List is not included. However, the Current List is saved with the document, so it accompanies the document even if the document is saved to another location.

Adding Footnotes and Endnotes

Both **footnotes** and **endnotes** are used to direct a reader to a specific source of information referred to in a paper. Footnotes are placed numerically at the bottom of the page where a direct reference is made; endnotes appear in a numerical list at the end of the paper but before the bibliography or works cited page. A footnote is required each time a document is referenced in a paper, possibly yielding several footnotes citing the same source. A general rule of thumb is that if you include footnotes to identify references, you do not need endnotes. Word makes it easy to include footnotes and endnotes, using options on the References tab.

When you include a footnote or an endnote, you place a number or symbol in superscript — slightly elevated from the line — to the right of the source information that you want to reference. The detailed reference is then keyed to the same number or symbol at the end of the page (footnote) or at the end of the document (endnote). If you use footnotes or endnotes, you do not need to include parenthetical information beside the source.

Footnotes and endnotes are not used as often as they once were. Since 1988, the MLA has recommended parenthetical information instead of footnotes. Parenthetical references are directly tied to a works cited list, which serves as a comprehensive list of all references throughout a paper. A works cited page or a bibliography is generally required in university composition classes and is standard practice in the preparation of research reports.

Including parenthetical information does not mean that you cannot use footnotes to provide more detailed descriptions of statements or facts in the paper. A research report can appear cluttered if you overuse footnotes or endnotes, but depending on the writing style used and your instructor's preference, you might be required to include them. For example, you can use a footnote to provide an explanation of statistics. You might also define or illustrate a concept included in the report, providing a personal comment. Using a footnote is a great way to further describe a concept without having to incorporate it into the written paragraph. That way, you do not risk wasting space with overly explanatory text, perhaps losing or diverting the attention of the reader.

If you choose to include footnotes, keep in mind that most writing styles limit a footnote to only one sentence. In a bibliography, however, each entry consists of three sentences. The first sentence gives the author name, the second is the title statement, and the last describes publication information, including publisher and publication date. In this exercise, you will add a footnote to your document and then change the superscript numeral to an asterisk.

To Add and Edit Footnotes

a. Scroll to the second page. In the first paragraph, place the insertion point immediately after the period following **Washington, DC**. You will add a footnote providing additional information on the LEED program.

b. On the References tab, in the Footnotes group, click **Insert Footnote**.
A numeral superscript has been placed where the insertion point was located. A divider is placed at the foot of the current page, and the same superscripted numeral begins the footnote. You will type additional text to make the comment.

c. Type LEED is the primary internationally recognized building certification system for environmental awareness. Include the period.

> **Troubleshooting**
> If the insertion point is displayed at the end of the document instead of the bottom margin of the current page, you clicked Insert Endnote instead of Insert Footnote. Click Undo, and repeat steps b and c.

d. Double-click the superscripted number **1** in the footnote to return to the reference in the document.

> **Troubleshooting**
> If double-clicking the footnote number does not advance you to the footnote in the document, you probably clicked near, but not on, the number. Double-click the footnote number in the footnote area of the report again.

e. Drag to select the superscripted number **1** after the words **Washington, DC**. Because this is the only footnote you will include in the document, you decide to define a symbol instead of a number for the footnote designator. You will use an asterisk.

f. On the References tab, in the Footnotes group, click the **Footnote & Endnote Dialog Box Launcher** ⌁, and then click the **Symbol** button.

g. Confirm that the Font box displays **Symbol**. Scroll up if necessary, and then near the middle of the first row, click the **asterisk (*)**. If you do not see the symbol, click in the **Character code** box, and then type 42.

Figure 5   Selecting a Footnote Symbol

h. Click **OK**, and then click **Insert**. The footnote symbol is changed to an asterisk in both the document reference and the footnote itself.

i. Select the entire **footnote text**. Click the **Home** tab, and then in the Font group, change the font size to **9** and the font to **Times New Roman**.

j. **Save** 🖫 the document.

Develop a Bibliography or Works Cited Page

A **bibliography** is an alphabetic list of all documents or sources used during the research of a paper even if they were not specifically referenced in the paper. A bibliography can help other people understand the basis for your work. They can also use your bibliography as a springboard, perhaps consulting some of the same sources as they continue to study the subject of your research. Although similar to a bibliography, a **works cited** page serves a different purpose. Only the sources that you actually referenced in the paper are included as works cited. The rule is, if you place a parenthetical reference in a paper, there must be a corresponding item in the list of works cited. The major difference is that a bibliography is more inclusive, listing all sources, whether they were referenced or not. A works cited page is considered part of the document, continuing the page numbering, whereas a bibliography is a separate component.

MLA style uses the term "Works Cited" to refer to the works cited page; APA style prefers "References." The terms are synonymous. Each is an alphabetic list of works that you have referenced in the body of a research report. Entries are placed in alphabetic order by last names of authors or editors or by first words of titles.

Options on Word's References tab enable you to easily add citations, footnotes, endnotes, bibliographies, and works cited pages. Word prepares the bibliography or works cited page directly from the parenthetical citations that you included when you used the Insert Citation command. Having selected the writing style (e.g., MLA, APA), Word formats all citations and the works cited page appropriately. You can edit the bibliography page to include additional sources or to modify existing ones if necessary.

Using an Annotated Bibliography

An **annotated bibliography** is a special type of bibliography that compiles references along with a short paragraph summarizing or reviewing the value of the source to the research project. Creating an annotated bibliography gives you a chance to consider several sources, evaluating each to determine its applicability and value to your project. If your instructor requires an annotated bibliography, you should begin preparing the bibliography as you conduct your research, and you should consult relevant writing style rules to ensure adherence to a particular style. For each source, include not only the title and other pertinent publication information, but also a paragraph of 150 words or less that summarizes the article or book as follows:

- Purpose or main focus
- Target audience for the work
- Relevance to the research topic
- Features that are unique or that should be helpful
- Author's credibility and background
- Author's conclusions and observations

Creating a Bibliography or Works Cited Page

Although a writing style manual (e.g., MLA, APA, Chicago) can be helpful as you develop various parts of a research report, you can also rely on Word to correctly format bibliography and works cited pages. The Citations & Bibliography group on the References tab includes a Bibliography option from which you can insert a predesigned bibliography or works cited page. You can also choose to insert a bibliography page with no heading or title so you can manage it more independently. Regardless of which approach you take, you should always confirm the resulting page meets all requirements of the particular style you are following. Just as you would proofread a document instead of relying solely on Word's spelling checker, you should consult a writing style manual to make sure your bibliography or works cited page is correct.

When Word creates a bibliography or works cited page, it places all citations in a **field**, which is a unit that is recognized as a single entity. The name of the field does not change, but its contents can. The Citations field is a unit that can be updated if you add more references to the document. In fact, when you click any text on a bibliography or works cited page, a content control tab, titled Update Citations and Bibliography, appears at the top of the selected list of citations. If you have included additional citations in the body of the research report, clicking the content control tab automatically updates the bibliography. You can also change bibliography entries into static text, which removes the field designation and enables you to treat the text as normal, editing and deleting references as needed. In this exercise, you will create a Works Cited page in your research report.

To Create a Works Cited Page

a. Press Ctrl+End.

SIDE NOTE

Insert a Page Break
Alternatively, press
Ctrl+Enter to insert a page break.

b. Because a bibliography or list of works cited must begin on a new page, you will insert a manual page break so text will begin on the following page.

c. Click the **Layout** tab. In the Page Setup group, click **Breaks**, and then select **Page**.

d. Click the **References** tab. In the Citations & Bibliography group, click **Bibliography**, and then select **Works Cited**. The sources that you inserted as you created the research report will be placed alphabetically under the title Works Cited.

SIDE NOTE

Insert a Bibliography
Click Bibliography, and then select Bibliography, which includes all citations but without a page title.

e. Scroll up to view the Works Cited page, which has five entries. The Works Cited title is left-aligned above the entries. Click any **entry** to select the Works Cited field. Note that all entries are shaded, indicating they are considered a single unit. You will also see the Update Citations and Bibliography content control tab, which you will use later in the chapter to update the works cited page.

Update Citations and Bibliography content control

Citations and Bibliography field

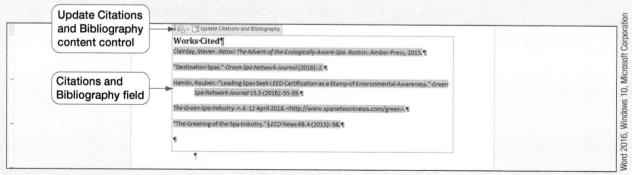

Figure 6 Works Cited Page

f. **Save** the document.

Editing a Bibliography or Works Cited Page

The only distinction that Word makes between a bibliography and a works cited page is the title. All sources that you have created in the paper are included in the bibliography or list of works cited. However, a bibliography differs from a works cited page in that a bibliography includes all resources, even those that are not cited in the paper. Therefore, the bibliography included with your research report might not be complete after Word creates it. In that case, you will need to edit the page to include other resources that helped you develop the paper. You can add and edit sources using the Manage Sources button on the References tab. You can also modify a source directly from the parenthetical information in your document.

In reviewing your research report, you determine that one of the citations should be updated and corrected. In this exercise, you will edit the citation source, thus updating the works cited to include the new information. You will then format the Works Cited page according to MLA style.

W04.06

SIDE NOTE
Edit a Source
Alternatively, on the References tab, click Manage Sources. Select the source from the Current List, and click Edit.

To Edit an Existing Source and to Update Works Cited

a. Scroll to the second page, and locate the **(48)** reference in the second paragraph. Click in the **(48)** citation. A content control appears around the citation. Click the Citation Options arrow on the right, and then select **Edit Source**.

b. Click the **Show All Bibliography Fields** check box. Click in the **Year** box, and then change the year to **2018**. Scroll down, click in the **Edition** box, and then type 2nd ed. including the period. Click **OK**. If you are asked to update the master source list and the current document, click **Yes**. MLA style requires an edition for a book if it is a second edition or later.

c. Press Ctrl+End. Scroll up slightly, and note that the Clairday reference still includes 2015 as the year. Click any reference in the **Works Cited page** to display the content control, and then click **Update Citations and Bibliography**. The works cited list is updated with the new edition and year in the Clairday reference.

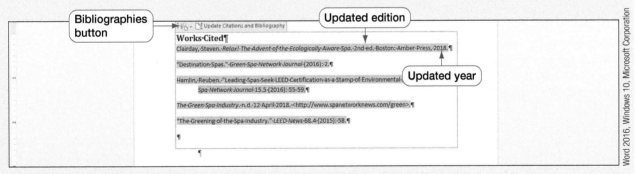

Figure 7 To Update Works Cited

d. Click the **Bibliographies** button on the left side of the content control tab, and then select **Convert bibliography to static text**.

The bibliography or works cited page that Word includes is not exactly as required by MLA style. Because you must edit the page slightly to accommodate MLA style, you convert the field to regular, or static, text. After you convert the page, it can no longer be updated automatically if citations are changed, so convert to static text only after all updates are complete.

e. Select all text on the Works Cited page, including the Works Cited title. Click the **Home** tab, and change the font size to **12** and the font to **Times New Roman**. With the text still selected, change the paragraph **After** spacing to **0 pt** and the Line spacing to **Double**. Center the title **Works Cited**. If necessary, click outside the Works Cited area to deselect the text. The Works Cited page is now formatted according to MLA style.

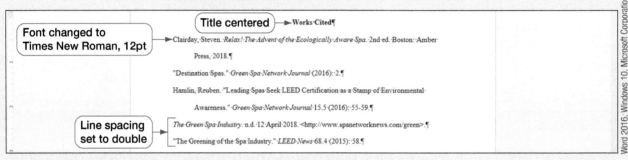

Figure 8 Works Cited in MLA Format

f. **Save** 💾 the document. Click the **File** tab, and then click Close to close the w02ch04Research_LastFirst file. The Word application remains open.

g. If you need to take a break before finishing this chapter, now is a good time.

Reviewing a Document

Word enables multiple people to collaborate on a project with the Tracking and Comment tools on the Review tab. A **comment** is a note or annotated text that may be added to a document. Comments might be added as a means of reviewing a document. You can also add comments to your own document to remind yourself, for example, to verify an address or research a topic in more depth. The **Track Changes** tool enables you to keep track of all additions, and deletions, and formatting changes in a document. Typically, the original author will turn on the Track Changes feature and then send the document for review to one or more people. The reviewers will make their changes and return the document to the original author. The changes are tracked with revision marks. For example, deletions are typically marked with strikeout lines, and additions are indicated with underlines, though the marks can vary depending on how you set up your preferences. The original author can then choose to accept or reject those changes. In this section, you will track changes, accept and reject changes, and work with comments.

Work with Comments

Comments can be displayed in the Reviewing pane or in the margin of the document. The comment will contain your user name and the time the comment was created. You can set how your name will appear in a comment by setting the User name in the General section of the Word Options dialog box. When the document contains comments from multiple users, Word will automatically color code the comments, one color per user. For new documents created in Word 2016, the comments will display the user's picture if the user signs in with a Microsoft account. In addition, Word enables you to easily contact the reviewers via an e-mail, IM, or chat link. In Word 2016, a user can also reply directly to a comment so an entire discussion is saved as one unit. Comments can also be marked as done. This will shrink the comment and gray it out. This gets the comment out of the way but keeps the information accessible if needed.

Reviewing Comments

You asked your boss to review your research report, providing suggestions wherever possible. In this exercise, you will open the document he returned to you and review the comments. You will reply to a comment and mark the comment as done.

To Reply to Comments

a. If you took a break, start **Word**. Click the **File** tab, and then click **This PC**. Navigate through the folder structure to the location of your student data files. Double-click **w02ch04Review** to open the document your boss returned to you.

b. Click the **File** tab, click **Save As**, and then click **This PC**. In the **Save As** dialog box, navigate to where you are saving your project files, and then change the file name to w02ch04Review_LastFirst, using your last and first name.

c. Click the **Review** tab. In the Tracking group, click the **Display for Review** arrow [Simple Markup ▾], and then, if necessary, select **All Markup**.

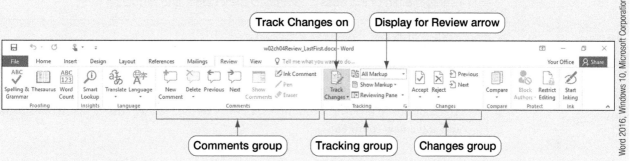

Figure 9 Review Tab

d. Press Ctrl+Home. On the **Review** tab, in the Comments group, click **Next** to view the first comment, starting with **I think they changed their name**.

Troubleshooting

If you are not viewing the comment, you might have clicked Next in the Changes group instead of the Comments group. Click Next in the Comments group.

---

e. If necessary, scroll to the right of the document. Click the **Reply** button 🔁 in the comment to reply to the comment. Type Verify name. including the period.

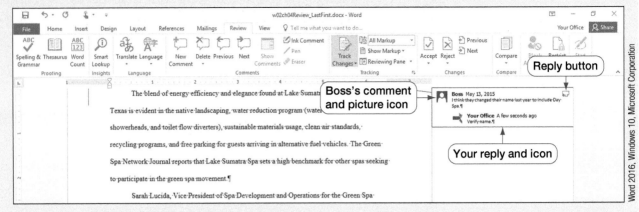

Figure 10 Reply to a Comment

    f. Point to the left of the boss's comment, in the picture icon , and then right-click. Select **Mark Comment Done** from the shortcut menu. The entire comment will be grayed out, and the text will shrink down, but the comment remains in the document for future access.

> **Troubleshooting**
> If just your comment is grayed out, you pointed to the left of your reply instead of to the left of the boss's comment. Click Undo, and redo step f.

    g. **Save** 🖫 the document.

Deleting and Adding Comments

You continue to review the comments. In this exercise, you will delete the second comment and add a new comment.

W04.08

SIDE NOTE
Delete All Comments
On the Review tab, in the Comments group, click the Delete arrow, and then select Delete All Comments in Document.

To Delete and Add Comments

    a. Press Ctrl+End. On the Review tab, in the Comments group, click **Previous** to view the comment at the end of the document, **Great job!** In the Comments group, click **Delete**. If you clicked the Delete arrow instead of the Delete button, simply select Delete.

Figure 11 Delete a Comment

b. Scroll to the middle of page three. At the beginning of the second paragraph, select the word **Sarah.** In the Comments group, click **New Comment**, and then type Verify spelling. including the period.

c. **Save** 🖫 the document.

QUICK REFERENCE | **Printing Comments**

1. On the Review tab, click Show Markup.
2. Select Comments.
3. In Backstage view, click Print, and then click Print All Pages.
4. Select Print Markup.

Track Changes

Click the Track Changes button on the Review tab to track all changes from that point on. Click the Track Changes button again to turn the feature off. When the feature is turned off, changes made to the document will not be monitored, though previous changes made while the feature was on will still be documented until they have been rejected or accepted. Word 2016 enables you to Lock Tracking to ensure that all changes made to a document will be monitored. A password is required to lock and unlock tracking. Once it is turned on, changes cannot be accepted or rejected, though comments can still be deleted.

REAL WORLD ADVICE | **Track Changes Indicator on the Status Bar**

Right-click the status bar, and then select Track Changes from the shortcut menu. A Track Changes indicator will appear on the status bar set to ON or OFF depending on whether or not the Track Changes feature is active. This is an easy way to determine whether your changes are being tracked. You can even click the indicator for a quick and easy way to turn the feature on and off without having to click the Review tab.

Viewing a Changed Document

Word provides four ways to view tracked changes and comments. By default, in **All Markup** view, comments and formatting changes appear to the right of the document, while addition and deletion marks appear directly in the document. The Track Changes Options dialog box enables you to modify how you view these changes. **Simple Markup** provides a less cluttered view of the document, using red vertical lines to indicate changes and balloons to indicate comments. Simply click the vertical red lines to view the changes in All Markup view; click again to hide the changes and return back to Simple Markup view. Similarly, click a balloon to view a single comment, and then click again to hide the comment. The Original view enables you to view the original document without any of the changes. The No Markup view enables you to view the final document if you were to accept all the suggested changes. The changes are still there but are hidden from view. The next time the document is opened, the changes will be displayed. Keep in mind, the only way to permanently remove the tracked changes from a document is to accept or reject them. You can accept or reject one change at a time or all at one time. In this exercise, you will review the changes made to the document. The first thing you will do is to turn off the Track Changes feature so further changes are not tracked. You will then experiment with the different tracking views.

To Turn Off Track Changes and to Change Tracking Views

a. Press [Ctrl]+[Home]. As you review the document, you realize that you entered the wrong course number. In the third line of the document, place the insertion point immediately after **BUS 340**, and then type 1.

b. You realize the Track Changes feature is still on. On the Quick Access Toolbar, click **Undo** 🔄. On the Review tab, in the Tracking group, click **Track Changes** to turn the feature off. Type 1, and notice that the text is now added without tracking.

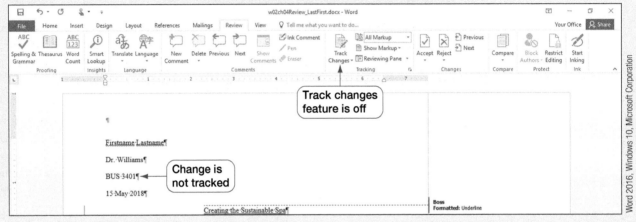

Figure 12   Tracking Group

c. In the Tracking group, click the **Display for Review** arrow [Simple Markup ▾], and then select **Simple Markup**. Notice the changes to the document. Tracked changes are indicated with red vertical lines in the left margin. Scroll down to view the comments at the end of the document. Comments are indicated by balloons in the right margin.

> **Troubleshooting**
> If the comments are still visible, ensure that on the Review tab, in the Comments group, the Show Comments button is not selected.

Figure 13   Simple Markup

SIDE NOTE
View Comments in Simple Markup View
Simply click the balloon to view the comment, and then click anywhere in the document to hide the comment.

d. Press Ctrl+Home. Click the **first red vertical line** in the left margin. The view changes to All Markup, and the red vertical line changes to a gray color.
   You can click the gray vertical line to return to Simple Markup view. Because you prefer to view all the changes at one time, you will remain in All Markup view.

e. **Save** 🖫 the document.

Accepting and Rejecting Changes

You will now incorporate the changes your boss made into the document. Because the Track Changes feature was turned on when he made the changes, you can accept or reject the changes as you see necessary. In this exercise, you will reject the first change, accept the second change, and then automatically accept the remaining changes.

 W04.10

To Accept and Reject Changes

a. Press Ctrl+Home. On the Review tab, in the Changes group, click **Next Change** 📄 to view the first change. Because MLA style does not support underlined titles, in the Changes group, click **Reject and Move to Next** 🗙.

> **Troubleshooting**
> If you click the Reject arrow, select Reject and Move to Next.

b. The change was rejected, and the next change is highlighted. Because MLA does not support extra spacing before the body of the document, you will accept this change to remove the spacing. In the Changes group, click **Accept**. Make sure to click the Accept button, not the Accept arrow.

c. Because you plan to accept the remaining changes, in the Changes group, click the **Accept** arrow, and then select **Accept All Changes**. The comments remain, but the changes have now been applied to the document.

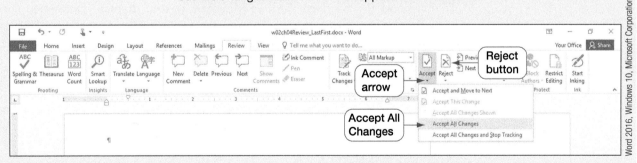

Figure 14 Accept All Changes

d. **Save** 🖫 the document. Click the **File** tab, and then click **Close** to close the w02ch04Review_LastFirst file. The Word application remains open.

e. If you need to take a break before finishing this chapter, now is a good time.

Creating a Newsletter

A **newsletter** is a regular publication that is distributed in print, through e-mail, or as a link on a web page. A newsletter is designed to provide information of interest to a defined group of people. Its main purpose is to convey information in a form that is easy to read, using design techniques that consolidate points so they are quickly understood. Catchy graphics and color add an element of entertainment and hold the reader's interest.

Newsletters can be designed for internal distribution to employees of a company or for external communication to customers, clients, or patrons. Information included in a company newsletter could just as easily be included in a memo, but the newsletter's columnar format, the vibrancy of the text, and eye-catching graphics are effective ways to grab a reader's attention. Clubs, churches, societies, and professional associations use newsletters to provide information of interest to their members. An organization might include news and upcoming events as well as contact information for general member inquiries. Often used as a marketing strategy, a regularly scheduled newsletter can be an effective way to draw attention to a company or a cause and to create enthusiasm among clients. In this section, you will create and format the newsletter for the Turquoise Oasis Spa.

REAL WORLD ADVICE | **When Should You Use an E-Zine?**

An e-zine is an electronic magazine or newsletter, delivered via e-mail or available online. You can duplicate the content from the electronic version to use in a printed newsletter, and you can encourage visits to your website by printing a link at the bottom of all pages of the printed newsletter. An electronic newsletter or e-zine can reach customers outside your immediate geographic area, give you greater exposure, and may even open new business channels. The ideas and strategies for printed and online newsletters are the same. The only difference is that printed material is more expensive to generate and to distribute. PDF is often used as the format for distribution of electronic newsletters because most computers have the ability to display PDF documents, and the recipient is not able to manipulate the contents without PDF-editing software.

Work with Columns

Many newsletters are designed with text in **columns**, narrow vertical sections of text. A column draws the eye downward, enabling you to scan through information fairly quickly. Because the column widths are narrower, the lines of text are shorter. This can give the impression that minimal reading is required, making the document more inviting to read. A section break is a common element in a Word newsletter, enabling you to format a newsletter heading or an ending line differently so the format does not affect other text that may be presented in columns. An entire document can be formatted in columns, or, with the use of section breaks, column formatting can be limited to specific sections. You can define up to three columns in each section or page.

Formatting in Columns

The Columns command on the Layout tab enables you to format an entire document in columns or to limit columns to one or more specific sections. Word evenly spaces columns with equal width by default, but you can specify column width in inches if you need to customize more specifically. You can even specify the width of the spacing between the columns. Word also enables you to display a line between the columns. In this exercise, you will open the rough draft of the newsletter excerpt. You will then format the body of the newsletter using a three-column layout, keeping the title and the picture in the original one-column layout.

To Format a Newsletter in Columns

a. If you took a break, start **Word**. Click the **File** tab, and then double-click **This PC**. Navigate to the location of your student data files, and then double-click **w02ch04SpaNews**. A rough draft of the newsletter excerpt opens.

b. Click the **File** tab, click **Save As**, and then click **This PC**. In the **Save as** dialog box, navigate to the location where you are saving your project files, and then change the file name to w02ch04SpaNews_LastFirst, using your last and first name. Click **Save**.

c. Place the insertion point immediately before the heading **Children at the Oasis**. Click the **Layout** tab. In the Page Setup group, click **Columns**, and then select **Three**.

   The entire document is formatted in a three-column layout. Because you prefer to keep the title and picture in a one-column layout, you will undo the format and use the Columns dialog box to specify where to begin the column.

d. On the Quick Access Toolbar, click **Undo** ↰. If necessary, place the insertion point immediately before **Children at the Oasis**. In the Page Setup group, click **Columns**, and then select **More Columns** to open the Columns dialog box.

e. Under Presets, click **Three**. A preview shows three columns of equal width. Click the **Apply to** arrow, and then select **This point forward**.

> **SIDE NOTE**
> **Apply Columns to Selected Text**
> Select text to be arranged in columns, click Columns, and then simply select One, Two, Three, Left, or Right.

Three columns

Columns dialog box →

Preview →

This point forward

Figure 15 Columns Dialog Box

Word 2016, Windows 10, Microsoft Corporation

f. Click **OK**. Click the **View** tab, and then in the Zoom group, click **One Page**.

   The inserted continuous section break is now visible, and all text after the section break is formatted in three evenly spaced columns. However, the columns are not balanced, as they end unevenly. You will address that problem later in this chapter.

g. In the Zoom group, click **100%** to return the view to normal size. **Save** 🖫 the document.

Inserting a Drop Cap

A **drop cap** is a design element in which the first letter of a paragraph is shown as a large graphic representation of the letter. You often see drop caps in magazines and books. They tend to draw the eye to the beginning of an article, providing interest and eye appeal. A drop cap can be placed in the margin next to the paragraph or with text wrapped around the character. In this exercise, you will set a drop cap for the first letter of the first body paragraph.

To Insert a Drop Cap

a. In the first body paragraph, place the insertion point immediately before the text **Join us for mom-and-child**.

b. Click the **Insert** tab. In the Text group, click **Add a Drop Cap** ⬚, and then select **Dropped**.

   If you need more precision, you can click Drop Cap Options. However, most often, the orientation of the drop cap is appropriate without any additional settings. The letter "J" appears in large print at the left of the paragraph, with text wrapped around it.

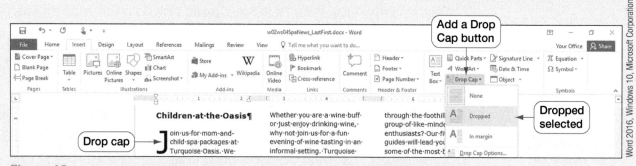

Figure 16 Inserting a Drop Cap

c. Click anywhere in the document to deselect the drop cap. **Save** ⬚ the document.

Balancing Columns

Columns seldom end evenly. Although columns rarely contain identical amounts of text, you will definitely want to avoid having column headings begin awkwardly at the end of a column, or having a small amount of text in a column. In this exercise, you will insert a column break to manually align the columns in a more even fashion.

To Insert a Column Break　　　　　　　　　　　**Use File:** w02ch04SpaNews

a. Scroll down and place the insertion point immediately before **An Evening of Wine Tasting**.

   The first column ends unattractively, with a heading and none of its text. You will insert a column break before the wine heading to move it to the next column.

b. Click the **Layout** tab. In the Page Setup group, click **Breaks**, and then select **Column**. The heading is moved to the top of the second column.

c. **Save** ⬚ the document.

Using Pictures in a Columnar Layout

Newsletters, business cards, and other specialty documents can be enhanced with the addition of pictures. After inserting a graphic, you can crop, recolor, set the text wrap, or format these graphics with outline styles and various artistic effects. In addition, Word enables you to place graphics in between two columns. Insert the picture, set the text wrap and other effects, and then drag the picture into the white space. The part of the picture that overlaps with the text in the column will maintain its text wrap setting. In this exercise, you will insert a graphic between the first two columns to enhance the body of the newsletter.

W04.14

To Insert a Picture in a Columnar Layout

a. Under **An Evening of Wine Tasting**, place the insertion point immediately before **Whether you are a wine buff**.

b. You want to insert a picture of a wine glass to enhance the body of the newsletter. Click the **Insert** tab, and then in the Illustrations group, click **Pictures**. Navigate to the location of your student data files, and then double-click **w02ch04Wine**.

c. On the **Format** tab, in the Arrange group, click **Wrap Text**, and then select **Square**.

d. Drag to position the **picture** as shown. Use the alignment guide to line up the picture with the right edge of the first column.

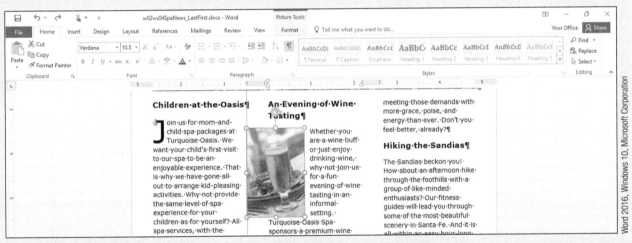

Figure 17   Positioning a Picture

e. Click anywhere in the document to deselect the picture. **Save** 🔲 the document.

Use a Style Guide to Format a Newsletter

As you recall, a style guide is a set of standards for the writing and design of written or edited materials. Organizations and companies use their own style guides to ensure that documents conform to corporate image and policy. Style guides help to maintain uniformity and consistency to all publications written for internal or external use. Style guides vary from organization to organization and can range from a couple of pages to hundreds of pages. Many style guides include rules on the use of punctuation, grammar, capitalization, and abbreviations; placement of logos; and font types, colors, and sizes. A style guide can even include information for conducting research.

The Painted Paradise Resort & Spa has recently produced a style guide that includes a section on how to format a business letter: 11-pt or 12-pt Times New Roman font, 1 inch margins, Plain Number page numbers, resort logo centered in the header, and watermarks when appropriate. All new written communication is expected to follow the Painted Paradise Resort & Spa style guide, which is available in your student data files. Following is an excerpt from the style guide, which includes guidelines that are applicable to the creation of any newsletter. Refer to the style guide for a complete list of guidelines.

- Communicate clearly, consistently, and truthfully.
- Check the newsletter for spelling and grammatical errors before distributing it.
- Provide your contact information.
- Keep the format simple.
- Avoid the use of such words as "we," "us," or "I." Instead, use "you" or "your."
- Provide a simple way to navigate the newsletter, especially if it spans more than one page. A front page sidebar is a great place for navigational aids, as is a short table of contents.
- Select a short, to-the-point newsletter title. The title should be uncluttered and does not need to include the word "newsletter" or start with the word "The." Consider using words ending in "ing" whenever possible or words with news appeal, such as "alert," "connection," "digest," and "happenings."
- Use colors and graphics to enhance the newsletter and to increase the user's interest. Incorporate the company's logo in some area of the newsletter. Use the company's colors wherever possible.

Inserting a Company Logo in a Header

The Painted Paradise Resort & Spa has recently developed a style guide, which states that logos should be incorporated in all publications. In this exercise, to conform to the logo rules in the style guide, you will insert the company logo in the header of the document.

To Insert a Graphic in a Header

a. Click the **Insert** tab. In the Header & Footer group, click **Header**, and then select **Edit Header**.

b. Under Header & Footer Tools, on the Design tab, in the Insert group, click **Pictures**. Navigate to the location of your student data files, and then double-click **w02ch04SpaLogo** to insert the graphic in the header. On the **Format** tab, in the Size group, click in the **Shape Height** box, type 1", and then press Enter.

c. Click the **Home** tab, and then in the Paragraph group, click **Center** ☰.

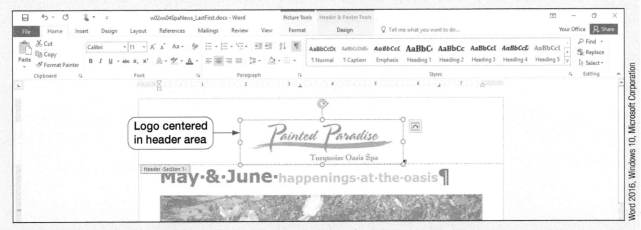

Figure 18   Logo in the Header

    d. Double-click anywhere in the body of the newsletter to close the header.
       The logo is now placed in the document as mandated by the Painted Paradise Resort & Spa style guide.

    e. **Save** the document.

REAL WORLD ADVICE | **Image Copyrights**

Images can also be inserted by using the Online Pictures feature on the Insert tab. This feature inserts images from a Bing Search, OneDrive, Facebook, or Flickr. However, the images that are located by searching these sources may be copyrighted, meaning that you cannot insert them into a document without permission of the copyright owner and possibly payment of a fee. The Bing Image Search option will initially return images in the public domain and images with Creative Commons licenses. Images in the public domain are not subject to copyright and are free to use. The Creative Commons are available for use with few or no restrictions, depending on the preferences of the copyright owner. Details about the Creative Commons can be found at: http://creativecommons.org. It is your responsibility to verify the ownership and usage restrictions that apply to any image you want to use in your work. Even an image in the Creative Commons can have restrictions — particularly for restrictions on commercial use. If you violate a copyright, the copyright owner can sue you!

Formatting a Newsletter

Word provides millions of color choices, each color represented by an **RGB** color — a color system in which red, green, and blue are combined in various proportions in order to produce other colors. In most cases, each red, green, and blue value is represented by a number range of 0 to 255. Use these three values to match a color. For example, to match the turquoise blue in the newsletter, select the turquoise text and then click the Font Color arrow. Choose More Colors, and then in the Colors dialog box that opens, look at its values, listed on the Custom tab. Use those values to recreate the color at any time.

You are ready to add the finishing touches to the newsletter. In this exercise, you will modify the title of the newsletter by changing the font and applying a bottom border. You will then use the company colors, which are listed in the Painted Paradise Resort & Spa style guide, to precisely match the color of the border to the logo colors. Finally, you will apply a picture style to the wineglass graphic and add a footer containing the company website address.

To Format a Newsletter

a. Place the insertion point anywhere in the title of the newsletter, **May & June happenings at the oasis**. On the Home tab, in the Paragraph group, click the **Borders** arrow ⊞ ▾, and then select **Borders and Shading**.

b. In the Borders and Shading dialog box, click the **Color** arrow, and then select **More Colors**. The Colors dialog box opens. Click the **Custom** tab, click in the **Green** box, delete the current value, and then type 167. Press Tab, and then type 157.

You have matched the border color to the turquoise blue color according to the RGB value listed in the Painted Paradise Resort & Spa style guide.

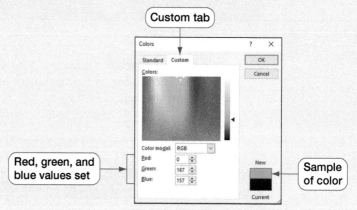

Figure 19 Colors Dialog Box

c. Click **OK** to close the Colors dialog box. In the Borders and Shading dialog box, click the **Width** arrow, and then select **1½ pt**. Under Preview, click **Bottom Border** ⊞ ▾. The border will be applied to the under the title paragraph.

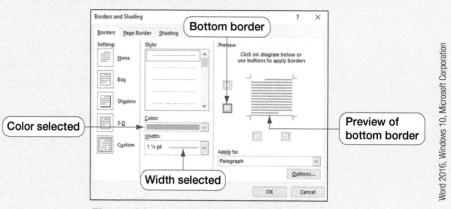

Figure 20 Creating a Bottom Border

SIDE NOTE

Format a Hyperlink in a Document

Press Enter or Spacebar after a URL to convert it to a hyperlink.

Alternatively, select the text to link, click the Insert tab, and click Hyperlink. Type the URL in the Address box.

d. Click **OK**. Select the words **happenings at the oasis** in the title of the newsletter. Set the font to **Lucida Handwriting**.

e. Click to select the **wineglass** graphic. Click the **Format** tab, and then in the Picture Styles **more** arrow, click **Soft Edge Rectangle**. Click anywhere in the document to deselect the picture.

f. Click the **Insert** tab. In the Header & Footer group, click **Footer**, and then select **Edit Footer**. Type http://www.paintedparadiseresort.com. Center the text in the footer, and then close the footer.

g. Click the **View** tab, and then in the Zoom group, click **One Page** to view the newsletter.

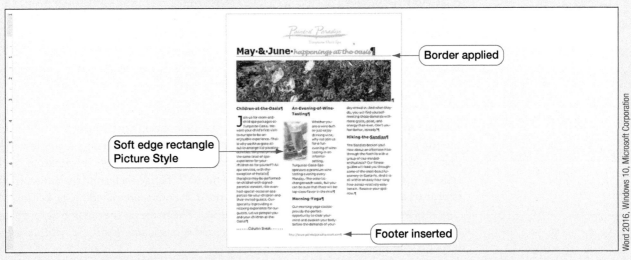

Figure 21 Final Newsletter

h. In the Zoom group, click **100%**. **Save** the document. Click the **File** tab, and then click **Close** to close w02ch04SpaNews_LastFirst. The Word application remains open.

i. If you need to take a break before finishing this chapter, now is a good time.

S_S CONSIDER THIS | Columns Versus Boxes

You checked Office.com for a relevant newsletter template that you could modify. To your surprise, when you open the newsletter template that you selected, the newsletter columns are organized in boxes instead of Word columns. Why do you think the template's designer chose to use boxes instead of formatting in columns? Can you identify any advantages or disadvantages to using boxes as columns?

Creating a Mail Merge Document

The term "mail merge" is a little misleading. The term suggests that the process focuses only on preparing documents for mailing, and although that is a primary application, it is not the only reason to use the feature. Actually, **mail merge** simplifies the task of preparing documents that contain identical formatting, layout, and text but in which only certain portions of each document vary. Perhaps you are preparing a document announcing a new product line that you plan to distribute to your client base. To personalize the announcement, you want to include the client's name and company in the body. The bulk of the announcement is text that will not vary, but the client name and company name should be inserted as if they were part of the original document. You will include a field for each piece of variable data in the document and then simply merge, or copy, data into those fields from a master list of clients and companies.

Obviously, mail merge is the ideal vehicle for generating mailing labels, envelopes, address lists, and personalized letters and handouts. In addition to generating mailings, mail merge can be helpful in the preparation of multiple e-mails and electronic faxes. To prosper, a company needs to maintain a well-informed client base in which each customer is made to feel a part of the company's success.

You will work with two files during a mail merge process: the main document and the data source. In the example given above, the announcement of the new product line is the **main document**. It consists primarily of text that will not change regardless of how many times it is duplicated. The **data source** contains the variable information, such as specific client and company names. Those items will change each time the announcement is printed or otherwise duplicated. Items in the data source are called fields, because their contents will vary. A field is much like a mailbox. The name on the outside never changes, but the contents change often. For example, the client name field is a holding area for actual client names.

The main document contains not only text that does not change, but also **merge fields**, which are references to the fields in the data source. When the two documents are merged, Word replaces each merge field with data from the data source. Ultimately, the two documents are merged into a third document that is a combination of the main document and the data source. However, if you are merging to the printer, fax, or e-mail, you will not actually save a copy of the third document. In this section, you will create and complete a mail merge.

Use Mail Merge

Mail merge is a step-by-step process, achieved by using the Mailings tab in Word. You indicate the type of mail merge — letters, labels, envelopes, e-mails, or directory — that the starting document, which is called the main document, will use and the location of the data source. You can then edit the data source and choose which fields to include in the document.

If you are creating mailing labels or envelopes, you will not have a main document. Instead, you will simply begin with a blank document. Similarly, you do not have to begin with a data source. Instead, you can create a field list during the mail merge process. Of course, it is much more common to use a data source of fields that you can call on for use in more than one merged document. Your Outlook Contacts can also serve as a data source.

Before completing the mail merge, you can preview the document and make changes if necessary. Although the most common option is to merge to a document, you can also merge to an e-mail. Simply indicate where the text should be sent, enter a subject line, and select a format option. The document will automatically be sent to all e-mail recipients that you indicated earlier in your data source.

Creating a Mail Merge Document

You will be sending each of your spa clients a letter informing them of the regular newsletter mailings that Turquoise Oasis Spa is beginning. You will also include the first newsletter in your mailing. You will use two documents for the mail merge process: the main document and the data source. In this exercise, the main document is the letter that you will send to the spa clients on your mailing list. The data source is an Access database containing your client address list. You will copy the data source to where you are saving your project files. You will then open the form letter in Word and review it to become familiar with its content. You will format the date to be updated automatically each time the letter is opened.

To Review the Main Document

a. If you took a break, start **Word**. Open **File Explorer**. Navigate to the location of your student data files. Right-click **w02ch04Addresses**, and then select **Copy** from the shortcut menu. Navigate to the location where you are saving your project files, right-click the folder or disk drive, and then select **Paste**. Locate the file that you pasted, right-click it, and then select **Rename** from the shortcut menu. Type w02ch04Addresses_LastFirst, using your last and first name, and then press Enter. **Close** File Explorer.

b. In Word, click the **File** tab, and then click **This PC**. Navigate through the folder structure to the location of your student data files, and then double-click **w02ch04Letter**. A form letter opens that you will be mailing to your client base.

c. Click the **File** tab, click **Save As**, and then click **This PC**. In the **Save As** dialog box, navigate to the location where you are saving your project files, and then change the file name to w02ch04Letter_LastFirst, using your last and first name.

d. You will personalize this letter for each of your clients. During the mail merge process, you will replace the bracketed information with data from your client address list, which is your data source.

e. Place the insertion point immediately before the **left bracket** before **[Current Date]**, and then press Delete **14 times** to remove the left bracket, the text, and the right bracket. Do not remove the final paragraph mark.
You will insert the current date, in the format "August 6, 2018." When you insert the date, you can specify that it be updated automatically, which means that each time the document is opened, the date will change to reflect the current date.

> **Troubleshooting**
> If you mistakenly remove the final paragraph mark beside the date, click Undo and repeat step d.

f. Click the **Insert** tab, and then in the Text group, click **Insert Date and Time**. The Date and Time dialog box opens.

g. Click the **third selection** from the top, indicating the current date is to be displayed in the format of Month Day, Year, such as August 6, 2018. If necessary, click the **Update automatically** check box to select it, and then click **OK**.

h. Click in the **current date** in the letter to display the content control, which is indicated by the shaded area and the Update tab. This indicates that the date is a field that will update automatically.

i. Click outside the content control to deselect it. **Save** the document.

SIDE NOTE
Should You Always Set the Date to Update Automatically?
Do not set the date to update automatically if the date needs to reflect the date of the document creation.

Beginning a Mail Merge

Options on the Mailings tab enable you to create a merged document, edit the data source, and create envelopes and labels. Perhaps the simplest way to begin the process is to work with the Mail Merge wizard. A wizard leads you through a process step by step. Simply respond to the prompts to produce a desired result. In this exercise, you will start the Mail Merge Wizard and then select the document to use to start the mail merge. You will use a form letter that you will personalize later for each client.

W04.18

SIDE NOTE
Dock the Mail Merge Pane
Double-click the title area in the Mail Merge pane to dock the pane in place.

To Begin a Mail Merge

a. Click the **Mailings** tab. In the Start Mail Merge group, click **Start Mail Merge**, and then select **Step-by-Step Mail Merge Wizard**. The Mail Merge pane opens, enabling you to complete the mail merge process one step at a time.

From the Start Mail Merge menu, you can work with letters, e-mail messages, envelopes, labels, or directories.

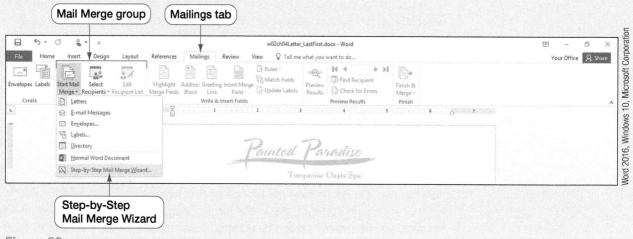

Figure 22 Start the Step-by-Step Mail Merge Wizard

b. In the Mail Merge pane, in the Select document type area, confirm that **Letters** is selected.

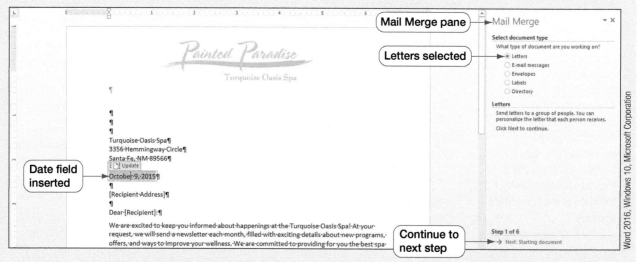

Figure 23 Selecting the Document Type

c. In the Mail Merge pane, click **Next: Starting document**. In the Select starting document area, confirm that **Use the current document** is selected.

The document that you choose here is the main document. Although the main document is often the currently open document, as is the case here, you could alternatively indicate that a template is to be used or that you prefer to use a previously saved document.

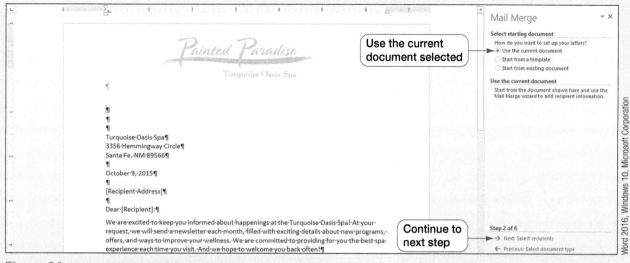

Figure 24 Selecting a Starting Document

Selecting a Data Source

A data source is a list of fields that contains variable data. For example, a list of mailing addresses, including names, street addresses, cities, and states, can supply data for a client mailing. A Word table containing such data can serve as a data source, as can an Excel worksheet, an Access database, and an Outlook contacts list. If you keep the data source current, you can reuse it countless times in the preparation of documents that require such variable data. Keep in mind that when you merge a document with a data source, formatting is not incorporated. For example, if text is bolded in a data source, the text will not carry the bold format into the merged document. Instead, you must format in the merged document as well.

In this exercise, you will select the data source containing your names and addresses and will then sort the data. You will also modify one of the addresses in the data source.

To Select a Data Source

a. In the Mail Merge pane, click **Next: Select recipients**. In the Select recipients area, confirm that **Use an existing list** is selected.

In most cases, you will be working with a predefined list — a Word table, Excel worksheet, or Access database. However, if you have not yet created a data source, you can select Type a new list to create a list of data. In this case, the data source is an Access database that was created earlier to include client mailing addresses.

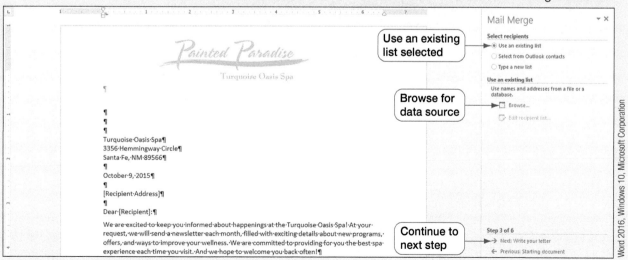

Figure 25 Selecting a Data Source

b. In the Use an existing list area, click **Browse**.
Earlier, you copied the Access database that will be used as your data source to the location where you save your Word projects. It is always a good idea to include the main document and the data source in the same storage location so the main document will always have the data source at hand.

c. Navigate to the location where you save your Word projects, and then double-click **w02ch04Addresses_LastFirst**. The Mail Merge Recipients dialog box opens. Note that all of the records in the data table are checked, indicating that each of them will be included in a letter. You can deselect any record that you do not wish to include. In this case, you will include them all.

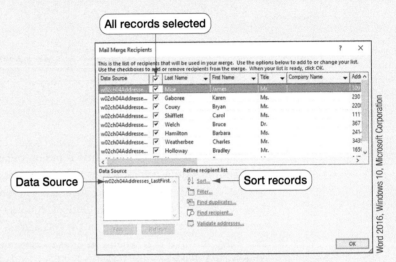

Figure 26   Mail Merge Recipients Dialog Box

d. The last names are sorted in the correct order. Click **Sort**.
The Filter and Sort dialog box includes several selections related to sorting, filtering, and editing the recipient list. You will sort the list by last name.

e. Click the **Sort by arrow**, and then select **Last Name**. Click **OK**.
The default sort order is ascending. Although you will sort by only one field, note that you could also refine the sort to include secondary fields in the event of duplicates in the primary sort field. For example, you could sort by Last Name and then by First Name.

f. In the Mail Merge Recipients dialog box, in the Data Source box, select the **w02ch04Addresses_LastFirst** file name, and then click **Edit**.
You can edit records, changing data and adding new contacts. You can also remove records. Dana Nye's address has changed.

g. In the Edit Data Source dialog box, click the address **347 Maple Drive**, delete the current address, and then type 3213 Main Street. Select the name **Dana**, and then change it to your first name. Select the name **Nye**, and then change it to your last name. Click **OK**, and then click **Yes** when asked whether to update the recipient list. Click **OK** to close the Mail Merge Recipients dialog box.

h. In the Mail Merge pane, click **Next: Write your letter**.

Completing the Letter

To complete the letter, you will identify specific data to be inserted from the data source into the main document. Since the mail merge process is commonly used for preparing mailings, Word is designed to simplify the use of mailing addresses. Although you could work with the recipient name, street address, city, state, and zip as separate fields, Word incorporates them all into a single unit called an Address block, with the fields automatically positioned in a correct mailing format. In this exercise, you will add the Address Block to your form letter.

 W04.20

To Insert an Address Block

a. Place the insertion point immediately in front of the left bracket before **[Recipient Address]**, and then press Delete **19 times** to remove the brackets and text, leaving the paragraph mark.

You should see three paragraph marks between the date and the salutation. The insertion point should be displayed before the second paragraph mark.

b. In the Mail Merge pane, in the Write your letter area, click **Address block**. The Insert Address Block dialog box opens. Confirm that **Insert recipient's name in this format** is checked.

c. From the address formats shown, select the second item in the list, **Joshua Randall Jr.** This will format the address block to include only the first and last name of recipients.

d. Confirm that **Insert postal address** is selected so the entire address including street address, city, state, and zip will be included in the address block.

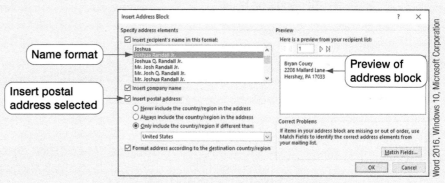

Figure 27 Selecting an Address Block

e. Click **OK**. A merge field, **<<AddressBlock>>**, is inserted in the letter. The field begins and ends with double characters that appear to be left- and right-facing arrows.

f. Click in the **AddressBlock** field in the letter, and note that the entire field is shaded, indicating that it is now considered a unit.

g. Click outside the AddressBlock field to deselect it.

Inserting a Salutation Line

A salutation is included in a typical business letter. Although the format can vary slightly, it typically includes a title and a last name followed by a colon. You can include any fields from the data source in any order, providing for appropriate spacing between each field. In this exercise, to finish the personalization of the letter, you will include a salutation to include the client's title and last name, followed by a colon.

To Design a Salutation

a. Place the insertion point immediately in front of the left bracket before **[Recipient]**. Press Delete **11 times** to remove both brackets and the word **Recipient**. Do NOT delete the colon or the space before it.

b. With the insertion point in front of the colon, in the Mail Merge pane, click **More items**. The **Title** is already selected. Click **Insert**, and then click **Close**. The Title field is inserted into the document. Press Spacebar so a space is placed between the title and the last name. Click **More items** again, click **Last Name**, and then click **Insert**.

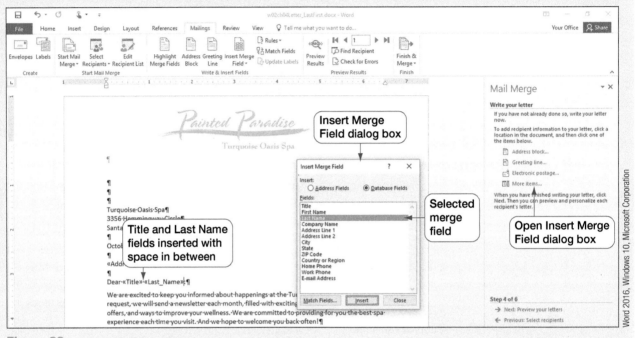

Figure 28 Selecting Merge Fields

c. Click **Close** to close the Insert Merge Field dialog box. The salutation line, with two merge fields, is displayed. In the Mail Merge pane, click **Next: Preview your letters**.

Previewing Letters

Before completing the merge, you will want to preview the finished result. The Preview step of the mail merge process presents a document with the actual data from the data source in place of the merge fields. This will display a letter with an address and a salutation instead of the placeholders that were visible earlier. Before the merge is complete, the preview enables you to check for formatting errors. In this exercise, you will preview the letters and then make a change to the font.

To Preview a Merged Document

a. In the Mail Merge pane, to the right of **Recipient: 1**, click the **Next Recipient** button ⟩⟩ to view another letter. Click the **Next Recipient** button ⟩⟩ again. You can page forward or backward among letters, although all the letters are identical except for the address and salutation.

b. Press Ctrl+A to select the entire document.
Before completing the merge, you can edit the letter if necessary. Because the Painted Paradise Resort & Spa style guide requires business letters to use the Times New Roman font, you will change the font for the entire letter.

c. Click the **Home** tab, and then in the Font group, change the font to **Times New Roman**. In the Mail Merge page, click the **Next Recipient** button ⟩⟩ to view another letter. You can page forward or backward among letters to confirm that the font change has been applied.

d. In the Mail Merge pane, click **Next: Complete the merge**.

Completing a Mail Merge

The last step of the Mail Merge Wizard completes the merge, resulting in a document with one page for each recipient. In this case, because you are sending letters to nine recipients, the merged document will include nine pages. The resulting document is separate from the main document and the data source, and therefore must be saved as a separate file. In this exercise, you will save the individual letters to the location where you are saving your files.

To Complete the Merge

a. In the Mail Merge pane, in the Merge area, click **Edit individual letters**. The Merge to New Document dialog box opens.
The Merge to New Document dialog box enables you to specify whether to merge all letters or a subset into a new document. In this case, you will merge all letters, so the default option All is correct as selected. Alternatively, clicking Print in the Mail Merge pane instead of Edit individual letters will print the letters directly to the computers default printer.

b. Click **OK**. Scroll through the letters, noting that each letter is in its own page section, as is indicated by the Next Page section break dividing each letter from the next.
Each address and salutation is unique to the recipient, but the bodies of all the letters are identical. Any changes at this time will be applied only to the individual letter in which they are made. For example, if you need to fix a spelling mistake in the body of the letter, you will need to fix it in each letter individually.

c. The file name, shown in the title bar, begins with Letters, indicating that this is a new document. Click the **File** tab, click **Save As**, and then click **This PC**. In the **Save As** dialog box, navigate to the location where you are saving your project files, and save the merged letters as w02ch04Merged_LastFirst, using your last and first name.

d. Click the **File** tab, and then click **Close** to close w02ch04Merged_LastFirst. You have closed the new file containing all the merged letters. The original main document, w02ch04Letter_LastFirst, remains open, as is indicated on the title bar. The original w02ch04Letter_LastFirst file requires the data source in order for you to view the merged letters or make changes to the mail merge. Use this file to update and regenerate the merged letters if necessary.

e. **Save** 🔲 the original main document, **w02ch04Letter_LastFirst**. Click the **File** tab, and then click **Close** to close the w02ch04Letter_LastFirst document. Word remains open.

REAL WORLD ADVICE | **Using an Excel Worksheet as a Data Source**

An Excel worksheet, which is a grid of columns and rows, is a logical choice in creating a table of mailing addresses to use as a data source for a mail merge. When you are creating the Excel worksheet, do not leave a blank row between the column headings and the mailing records. Also, give column headings recognizable titles, such as First Name and Last Name, so that Word can connect the fields with its mail merge blocks. Be sure to include separate columns for different elements of an address, such as Street Address, City, State, and Zip Code. When working through the Mail Merge Wizard, you will select an existing list for the data source and navigate to the Excel workbook. Open the workbook, and then select the worksheet that contains the data source. At that point, you can edit, filter, and sort records in the Excel data source just as you would with other data sources, such as an Access or Word table.

Create Mailing Labels and Envelopes

To create mailing labels and address envelopes, you use the same method that you use to create merged letters. In this case, you want to create one mailing label for each record in the data source. Using Word's Mail Merge feature, you simply select labels, specify the label type and size, and then select or create the data source. Insert the fields, and then adjust the font and positioning of the data to suit the needs of your project. The mail merge process creates a layout of the label sheet. You then load the label sheets into the printer and print.

When you create envelopes, the entire envelope is fed through the printer, so the address is printed directly on the envelope. To address envelopes, begin with a new blank document. Using Word's Mail Merge wizard, step through the process of creating an envelope. This process creates a layout of the addressed envelopes in your document, which you then print directly on the envelopes. During this process, you select the envelope type and the data source. You then arrange the data source fields and format the layout if necessary. Although mailing labels are probably easier to manage than envelopes, there may be occasions when an envelope is more suitable.

Selecting Labels

When creating labels, you begin with a blank Word document. Use Mail Merge to design and format a sheet of labels in your document. Then the label sheets can be loaded into the printer, and the labels can be printed. The Mail Merge feature enables you to select from numerous label types, including mailing, folder, and even name tag labels. Although the most common type of label used is a mailing label, it is by no means the only choice. Labels are listed by manufacturer, such as Microsoft, 3M, and Avery. Avery is such a standard that you will often find other label types providing an Avery equivalent number so you can use the label in a Word mail merge process. In this exercise, you will use the same data source to create labels that was used to create the merged letters. You will print the labels on Avery 5160 Easy Peel Address labels.

To Select Labels

a. Click the **File** tab, click **New**, and then click **Blank document**. Click the **Mailings** tab. In the Start Mail Merge group, click **Start Mail Merge**, and then select **Step-by-Step Mail Merge Wizard**.

b. In the Mail Merge pane, in the Select document type area, select **Labels**. Click **Next: Starting document**. In the Select starting document area, confirm that **Change document layout** is selected, and then in the Change document layout area, click **Label options**. You must indicate the label type for Word to correctly design the label sheet.

c. Click the Label vendors arrow, and then scroll if necessary to select **Avery US Letter**. Scroll through the list of product numbers to locate and select **5160 Easy Peel Address Labels**.

> **Troubleshooting**
> If you are having trouble locating the 5160 Easy Peel Address Labels in the list of product numbers, click an item the Product number box and type 5160. This will take you to all products beginning with 5160.

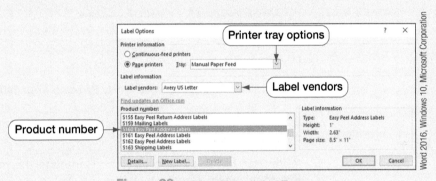

Figure 29 Selecting a Label Type

d. Click **OK**. The document now reflects the layout of the label type 5160 Easy Peel Address Labels. In the Mail Merge pane, click **Next: Select recipients**.

Selecting Recipients and Arranging Labels

As you learned in the previous section, you need to select recipients from a data source. You can then filter the data, sort it, delete records, edit records, and insert records. Word will then insert fields from the data source into your document in a mailing label format, duplicating the fields for each label so each label contains a different recipient. In this exercise, you will select the recipients, arrange the labels, and then complete the merge.

To Select Recipients and Arrange Labels

a. In the Mail Merge pane, in the Select recipients area, confirm that **Use an existing list** is selected, and then click **Browse**. Navigate to the location where you are saving your project files, and double-click **w02ch04Addresses_LastFirst** to select the data source.

b. Click **Sort**, click the **Sort by** arrow, and then select **Last Name**. Click **OK**. The mailing labels will be printed alphabetically by last name. Click **OK**.

c. In the Mail Merge pane, click **Next: Arrange your labels**. Confirm that the insertion point is located in the top left label. Click **Address block** in the Arrange your labels area, select the second option, **Joshua Randall Jr.**, and then click **OK**. An Address Block is inserted into the first label.

d. In the Mail Merge pane, in the Replicate labels area, click **Update all labels** to add an Address Block field in each label.

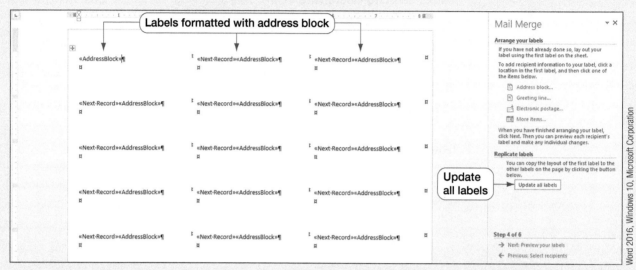

Figure 30   Arranging Mailing Labels

e. In the Mail Merge pane, click **Next: Preview your labels**. Labels with four lines will not fit properly on the labels. Press Ctrl+A to select all mailing labels. Click the **Home** tab, and then in the Styles group, click **No Spacing** so all text fits more neatly within each label space.

f. In the Mail Merge pane, click **Next: Complete the merge**, and then click **Edit individual labels**. Confirm that All is selected, and click **OK**.
   The completed mailing label document is displayed. After loading a sheet of mailing labels in the printer, you can print the mailing labels. Note that the merged mailing labels are actually a document that you can save, if you like, and then print at a later time.

g. The file name, shown in the title bar, begins with **Labels**, indicating that this is a new document. Click the **File** tab, click **Save As**, and the click **This PC**. In the **Save As** dialog box, navigate to the location where you are saving your project files, and save the merged labels, calling the document w02ch04Labels_LastFirst, using your last and first name. Click the **File** tab, and then click **Close** to close w02ch04Labels_LastFirst.

h. You will now close the original labels document without saving the changes. Click the **File** tab, and then click **Close** to close the original labels document. Click **Don't Save** when asked to save the changes. Exit **Word**. Submit your files as directed by your instructor.

CONSIDER THIS | **Mailing Labels or Envelopes?**

Word allows you to create addresses on envelopes as well as mailing labels. Is there a preference for one over the other? Do you feel any differently when you receive a letter that is addressed on an envelope without a mailing label?

Concept Check

1. List six specific guidelines to follow in using MLA style. p. 267

2. What is the difference between a bibliography and a works cited page? p. 275

3. What is a comment? Where do comments appear in your document? p. 278–279

4. What is the difference between the All Markup and Simple Markup views? p. 281

5. How would you create a document in which the title is positioned across the top of the document but the text under the columns is formatted in a three-column layout? p. 284

6. What is a style guide? Why would a company use one? p. 287–288

7. What is mail merge? What is an example of why you would use mail merge in a business? p. 291

8. What is the difference between creating labels and creating envelopes in mail merge? p. 300

Key Terms

Visual Summary

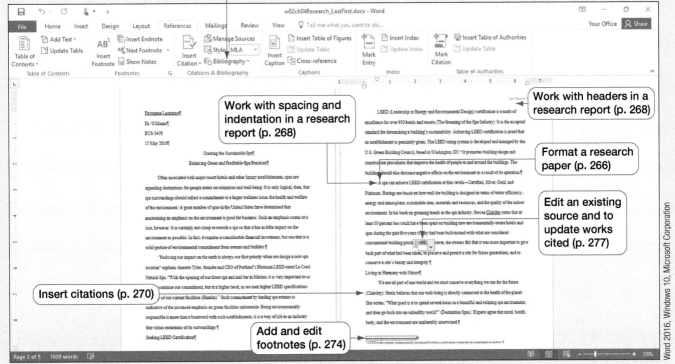

Create a works cited page (p. 276)
Develop a bibliography or works cited page (p. 275)

Work with spacing and indentation in a research report (p. 268)

Work with headers in a research report (p. 268)

Format a research paper (p. 266)

Edit an existing source and to update works cited (p. 277)

Insert citations (p. 270)

Add and edit footnotes (p. 274)

Word 2016, Windows 10, Microsoft Corporation

Figure 31

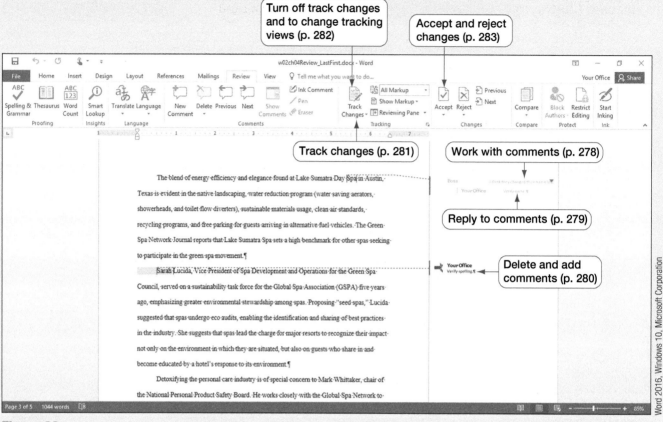

Turn off track changes and to change tracking views (p. 282)

Accept and reject changes (p. 283)

Track changes (p. 281)

Work with comments (p. 278)

Reply to comments (p. 279)

Delete and add comments (p. 280)

Figure 32

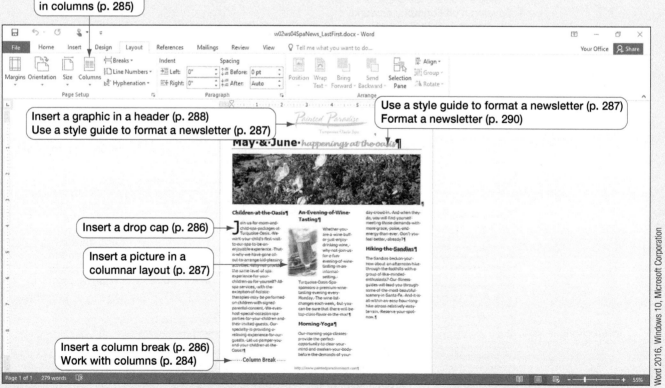

Format a newsletter in columns (p. 285)

Insert a graphic in a header (p. 288)
Use a style guide to format a newsletter (p. 287)

Use a style guide to format a newsletter (p. 287)
Format a newsletter (p. 290)

Insert a drop cap (p. 286)

Insert a picture in a columnar layout (p. 287)

Insert a column break (p. 286)
Work with columns (p. 284)

Figure 33

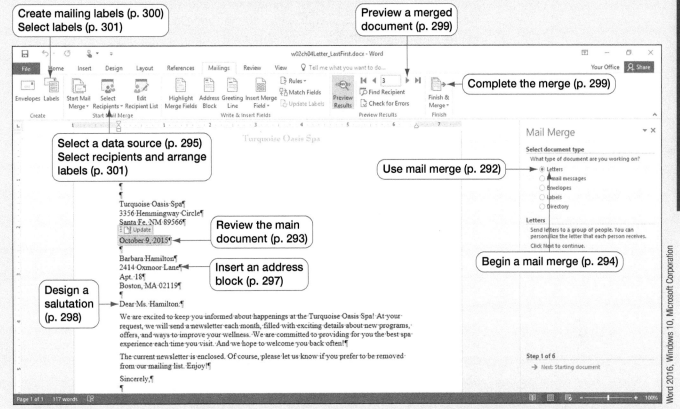

Create mailing labels (p. 300)
Select labels (p. 301)

Preview a merged document (p. 299)

Complete the merge (p. 299)

Select a data source (p. 295)
Select recipients and arrange labels (p. 301)

Use mail merge (p. 292)

Review the main document (p. 293)

Begin a mail merge (p. 294)

Insert an address block (p. 297)

Design a salutation (p. 298)

Word 2016, Windows 10, Microsoft Corporation

Figure 34

Practice 1

Student data files needed:

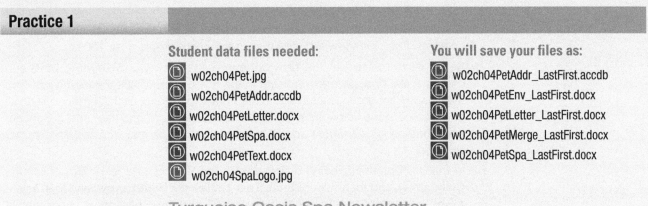

w02ch04Pet.jpg

w02ch04PetAddr.accdb

w02ch04PetLetter.docx

w02ch04PetSpa.docx

w02ch04PetText.docx

w02ch04SpaLogo.jpg

You will save your files as:

w02ch04PetAddr_LastFirst.accdb

w02ch04PetEnv_LastFirst.docx

w02ch04PetLetter_LastFirst.docx

w02ch04PetMerge_LastFirst.docx

w02ch04PetSpa_LastFirst.docx

Sales & Marketing

Production & Operations

Turquoise Oasis Spa Newsletter

The Turquoise Oasis Spa has expanded to include a center for pets — Turquoise Oasis Pet Pals. Guests of the Painted Paradise Resort & Spa often place their pets in the resort's pet lodge, and the spa is capitalizing on that group by offering pet spa services. Pets can enjoy massages, baths, grooming, and pedicures. In addition, Turquoise Oasis Pet Pals offers a full line of pet clothing and grooming accessories in the on-site boutique. Occasional seminars with pet professionals and veterinarians are hosted in the pet lounge, which also provides play space. The new pet center is spotlighted in the summer edition of **Solutions**, the Turquoise Oasis Spa's quarterly newsletter. You will develop the first page of the newsletter in this exercise. Your boss also requested that addressed envelopes, rather than mailing labels, be used to mail out the newsletter. You will prepare the envelopes.

a. Open File Explorer. Navigate to the location of your student data files, and then right-click **w02ch04PetAddr**. Select **Copy**. Navigate to the location where you are saving your project files, right-click the folder (or disk drive), and then select **Paste**. Locate the file that you pasted, right-click it, and then select **Rename**. Type w02ch04PetAddr_LastFirst, using your last and first name, and then press Enter.

b. Start **Word**, click **Open Other Documents**, and then double-click **This PC**. Navigate to the location of your student data files. Double-click **w02ch04PetSpa** to open the rough draft of the newsletter page.

c. Click the **File** tab, and then click **Save As**. Save the document as w02ch04PetSpa_LastFirst, using your last and first name. If necessary, on the Home tab, in the Paragraph group, click **Show/Hide**.

d. Press [Ctrl]+[End]. Click the **Layout** tab. In the Page Setup group, click **Columns**, and then select **More Columns**. The Columns dialog box displays. Under Presets, click **Left** to create two columns, with the left column slightly smaller than the right column. Click the **Apply to** arrow, and then select **This point forward**. Click **OK**. Note that the horizontal ruler displays two uneven columns, with more space in the column on the right.

e. In the Paragraph group, change the paragraph **After** spacing to 0 pt.

f. Click the **Home** tab, change the font size to **18**, and then change the **Font Color** to **Black, Text 1**.

g. Type SUMMER 2018, and then press [Enter]. Type TURQUOISE OASIS SPA, and then press [Enter] twice.

h. Click the **Insert** tab. In the Text group, click the **Object** arrow, and then select **Text from File**. Navigate to the location of your student data files, and double-click **w02ch04PetText**. The text is inserted in the document. Press [Delete] to remove the extra paragraph mark at the end of the document.

i. Scroll to the bottom of the document, and then click to place the insertion point immediately in front of the paragraph **Experience Turquoise Pet Pals**. Click the **View** tab, and then in the Zoom group, click **One Page**. With the entire page displayed, column changes that you make are more evident.

j. Click the **Layout** tab. In the Page Setup group, click **Breaks**, and then select **Column** to insert a column break so the entire article appears to the right of the contents. Click the **View** tab, and then in the Zoom group, click **100%**.

k. Select all of the text in the **first column**, beginning with **SUMMER 2018** and ending at the **final paragraph mark** in the first column. Click the **Home** tab, and then in the Font group, click **Bold**. In the Paragraph group, click **Center** so text will be centered in the first column. Click the **Borders** arrow, and then select **Borders and Shading**. The Borders and Shading dialog box opens, with the Borders tab selected.

l. In the Borders and Shading dialog box, in the Setting area, click **Box**. Click the **Color** arrow, and then select **Black, Text 1**. Click the **Width** arrow, and then select **1½ pt**. In the Borders and Shading dialog box, click the **Shading** tab, click the **Fill** arrow, and then select **Aqua, Accent 5, Lighter 40%**. Click **OK**.

m. Center and bold the text **Experience Turquoise Pet Pals** at the top of the second column. Click before the word **Share** in the second paragraph of the second column. Click the **Insert** tab, and then in the Illustrations group, click **Pictures**. Navigate to the location of your student data files, and then double-click **w02ch04Pet**. In the Size group, click in the **Shape Height** box, and then type 1. In the Arrange group, click **Wrap Text**, and then select **Square**.

n. Insert a **footer** with the **File Name** field centered. Close the footer. Save and close the document. Keep Word open.

o. Click the **File** tab, click **Open**, and then double-click. **This PC**, and then navigate to the location of your student data files. Double-click **w02ch04PetLetter**. The letter will serve as the main document for a mail merge. It is a cover letter that will accompany the newsletter, inviting spa clients to an open house for Turquoise Oasis Pet Pals. Click the **File** tab, and then save the document as w02ch04PetLetter_LastFirst to the location where you are saving your files, using your last and first name.

p. Place the insertion point immediately before [Current Date], and then press Delete 14 times to delete both brackets and the text but leaving the paragraph mark. The insertion point should be positioned before the second blank paragraph between the inside address and the **[Recipient]** line. Click the **Insert** tab. In the Text group, click **Insert Date and Time**, and then select the third date format, showing month, day, and year, similar to **April 3, 2018**. Click **Update automatically** if necessary, and then click **OK**.

q. Click the **Mailings** tab. In the Start Mail Merge group, click **Start Mail Merge**, and then select **Step-by-Step Mail Merge Wizard**. Confirm that **Letters** is selected as the document type, and then click **Next: Starting document**.

r. Confirm that **Use the current document** is selected, and then click **Next: Select recipients**.

s. Confirm that **Use an existing list** is selected, and then click **Browse**. Navigate to the location where you are saving your project files, and double-click **w02 ch04PetAddr_LastFirst**. Click **Sort**. Click the **Sort by** arrow, select **Last Name**, and then click **OK**.

t. In the Data Source box, click **w02ch04PetAddr_LastFirst.accdb**, and then click **Edit**.

u. In the First Name column, click **Barbara**, delete the name, and then type your first name. Replace the Last Name, **Alim**, with your last name. Click **OK**, click **Yes** when asked whether to update the recipient list, and then click **OK**.

v. Click **Next: Write your letter**. Click before the first bracket on the **[Recipient]** line, and then remove the entire line of text, with the exception of the final paragraph mark. In the Mail Merge pane, click **Address block**. Under Specify address elements, click **Joshua Randall Jr.**, and then click **OK**.

w. Place the insertion point immediately after the **r** in **Dear** but before the colon. With the insertion point positioned before the colon, press Spacebar. In the Mail Merge pane, click **More items**. Select **Title**, click **Insert**, and then click **Close**. Press Spacebar, and then click **More items**. Select **Last Name**, click **Insert**, and then click **Close**. Click **Next: Preview your letters**.

x. You remember that the new Painted Paradise Resort & Spa style guide requires the logo to be placed in the header of all business letters. Click the **Insert** tab. In the Header & Footer group, click **Header**, and then select **Edit Header**. Under Header & Footer Tools, on the **Design** tab, in the Insert group, click **Pictures**. Navigate to the location of your student data files, and then double-click **w02ch04SpaLogo** to insert the graphic in the header.

y. In the Size group, change the **Shape Height** of the logo to **1"**. Click the **Home** tab, and then in the Paragraph group, click **Center**. Double-click the **body** of the letter to close the header.

z. Click **Next: Complete the merge**, click **Edit individual letters**, and then click **OK**. Note that the resulting merged document includes nine pages, with one letter on each page. Also note that the letters are arranged alphabetically by last name.

aa. Click the **File** tab, and then save the merged document as w02ch04PetMerge_LastFirst, using your last and first name. Save and close all open documents, but do not exit Word.

ab. Click the **File** tab, and then click **New**. Click **Blank document**, and then start the **Step-by-Step Mail Merge Wizard**.

ac. Click **Envelopes** in the Select document type area, click **Next: Starting document**, and then click **Envelope options**.

ad. The Envelope Options dialog box appears. You can select an envelope type, and you can indicate a font size and type. Options on the Printing Options tab enable you to identify printing methods.

ae. The default envelope size is Size 10. Leave the size as is, or click the **Envelope size** arrow to select **Size 10** if it is not displayed. Click **OK**.

af. Click **Next: Select recipients**. In the Select recipients area, confirm that **Use an existing list** is selected, and then click **Browse**. Navigate to the location where you are saving your project files, and then double-click **w02ch04PetAddr_LastFirst**. The data source is displayed, with all records selected. You will print an envelope for all recipients. Click **OK**.

ag. Click **Next: Arrange your envelope**. Click before the paragraph mark in the delivery address area in the lower middle of the **envelope**, and then in the Mail Merge pane, click **Address block**. The Insert Address Block dialog box appears. Click **Joshua Randall Jr.** to select a recipient name format, and then click **OK**.

ah. Click **Next: Preview your envelopes**. Click the left or right arrow in the **Preview your envelopes** area to view the envelopes.

ai. Click before the first paragraph mark in the top left corner of the envelope. You will type a return address. Type Turquoise Oasis Spa, and then press Enter. Type 3356 Hemmingway Circle, and then press Enter. Finally, type Santa Fe, NM 89566.

aj. Click **Next: Complete the merge**, click **Edit individual envelopes**, and then click **OK**.

ak. The file name, shown in the title bar, begins with **Envelopes**, indicating that this is a new document. Click the **File** tab, and then save the merged envelopes as w02ch04PetEnv_LastFirst, using your last and first name. Close w02ch04PetEnv_LastFirst.

al. Close the original envelopes document without saving it, exit Word, and then submit your files as directed by your instructor.

Problem Solve 1

Homework

Student data files needed:

 w02ch04Benefit.docx

w02ch04BenAddr.xlsx

You will save your files as:

w02ch04BenAddr_LastFirst.xlsx

w02ch04Benefit_LastFirst.docx

w02ch04BenLabels_LastFirst.docx

w02ch04BenMerge_LastFirst.docx

Benefit Merge Letter

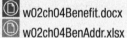

Sales & Marketing

The Painted Paradise Resort & Spa Event Planning committee is holding its annual Stomp Out Cancer sports-themed fundraiser, benefitting the local Santa Fe cancer center. The benefit will be held at the Indigo5 restaurant. You created a letter to mail to clients who have previously signed up for information on the fundraiser. Your assistant has reviewed the letter for errors. Now you will open the reviewed document and accept or reject the changes as you deem necessary. You will then finish formatting the letter and use Word's mail merge feature to personalize each letter.

a. Open File Explorer. Navigate to the location of your student data files, and then right-click **w02ch04BenAddr**. Select **Copy**. Navigate to the location where you are saving your project files, right-click the folder (or disk drive), and then select **Paste**. Locate the file that you pasted, right-click it, and then select Rename. Type w02ch04BenAddr_LastFirst, using your last and first name, and then press J

b. Open the Word file, **w02ch04Benefit**. Save your file as w02ch04Benefit_LastFirst, using your last and first name. If necessary, click **Show/Hide** to display nonprinting characters.

c. Turn the **Track Changes** feature off. Click the **Display for Review** arrow, and select **All Markup**.

d. **Reject** the $10 to $15 ticket price change because you have confirmed that the ticket price will be $10 for advance purchase. **Accept** all other changes.

e. Delete the comment at the beginning of the document.

f. Select the eight lines containing the bulleted items. Apply a **two-column** layout to the **selected text**. If necessary, insert a Column Break to ensure that four items appear in each column.

g. Select the entire document, and change the font to **Times New Roman**.

h. Place the insertion point at the end of the sentence listing the hours of the benefit. Insert a footnote. Type Children's menus available upon request. including the period.

i. Delete the text [Current Date]. Do not delete the paragraph mark at the end of line. Insert the current date field, using the format Month Day, Year, as in October 10, 2018. Make sure the date is set to **Update Automatically**.

j. Start the **Step-by-Step Mail Merge Wizard**. Confirm that **Letters** is selected as the document type. Proceed to the next mail merge step.

k. Confirm that **Use the current document** is selected as the starting document. Proceed to the next mail merge step.

l. Confirm that **Use an existing** list is selected in selecting recipients. Browse and select **w02ch04BenAddr_LastFirst** as the data source. Because this is an Excel spreadsheet, confirm that Sheet1$ is selected and that **First row of data contains column headers** is selected. Click **OK**. Sort the records alphabetically by Last Name.

m. Select **w02ch04BenAddr_LastFirst.xlsx** in the Data Source box, and then click **Edit**. Change Pedro Bohls to **your First and Last name**. Click **OK**, and then click **Yes** to update the recipient list. Proceed to the next mail merge step.

n. Click before the first bracket on the [Recipient] line, and then remove the entire line of text except the final paragraph mark. Insert an **Address block**, using the **Joshua Randall Jr.** format.

o. Place the insertion point immediately after the "r" in "Dear:" but before the colon. With the insertion point positioned before the colon, press the spacebar. Insert the **Title** and **Last Name** fields, separated by a space. Proceed to the next mail merge step to preview the letters.

p. When you preview the letters, you notice you forgot to add a footer. Insert a footer with the **File Name** field centered.

q. Proceed to the next mail merge step to complete the merge. Edit the individual letters, selecting all the records. Save the merged document as **w02ch04BenMerge_LastFirst**, and then close the w02ch04BenMerge_LastFirst.docx document.

r. Before printing and mailing or sending your document electronically to its target audience, it is important to know how many items have been created. List two methods of checking the number of recipients without creating individual documents. Why is this important to know? Have you ever received a mailing that was not intended for you? If so, how did that change your perception of the company?

s. Save and close the **w02ch04Benefit_LastFirst** file. Keep Word open.

t. Open a new blank document. Start the **Step-by-Step Mail Merge Wizard**. Create a **Labels** mail merge document. Use the **Avery US Letter** label vendor and the **5162 Easy Peel Address Labels** product number. Use **w02ch04BenAddr_LastFirst** as the data source. Make sure **Sheet1$** is selected and that **First row of data contains column headers** is selected. You do not need to sort or edit the data source.

u. Press Ctrl+Home. Insert an **Address block** using the **Joshua Randall Jr.** format and then **Update** all labels. Preview the labels, and confirm that your name appears on one of the labels. Apply the **No Spacing** style to all the labels. Complete the merge, and then **Edit individual labels**. Make sure eleven labels are included. Save the labels sheet as w02ch04BenLabels_LastFirst, and then close the document.

v. Close the remaining open document without saving, exit Word, and then submit your files as directed by your instructor.

Perform 1: Perform in Your Career

Student data file needed:

w02ch04Newsletter.docx

You will save your files as:

w02ch04Newsletter_LastFirst.docx

w02ch04Newsletter_LastFirst.pdf

Student Organization Newsletter

Sales & Marketing

A student organization at your college is sponsoring a beginning-of-the-year social event for new and returning students. The event will feature local restaurants, career events services, and games for students to engage in. You have been given a listing of events and have been asked to make a newsletter that can be distributed to advertise for the event.

a. Start **Word**. Open the file w02ch04Newsletter. Save your file as w02ch04Newsletter_LastFirst.

b. Select all the text starting with the paragraph **Food** and ending with the paragraph that begins with **Get involved**. Convert the text into a two- or three-column format depending on the space requirements of the remaining steps.

c. Use Online Pictures and Bing Image Search to find pictures of students meeting together, pizza or other food items, or other related images.

d. Apply a Picture Style to each image you insert into the document.

e. Size the pictures to fit within the text and columns you have arranged. Insert the pictures beside the activity illustrated, some on one side and some on the other.

f. Use WordArt to create a title for the flyer, using the text **Beginning of the Year Social**. Apply at least two types of formatting to the WordArt. Size it so that it fills most of the page width.

g. Insert a Simple Text Box listing the date of the event as Friday, September 14, 2018 and the hours of the event as 5pm-11pm. Include the location of the event in the Student Union Building.

h. Apply an appropriate Page Color to the document.

i. Insert a Footer into the document with the file name centered in the footer.

j. Save the file. Create a PDF file with the same name, exit Word, and then submit your files as directed by your instructor.

Additional Cases

Additional Chapter Cases are available at www.pearsonhighered.com/youroffice

Word Business Unit **2** CAPSTONE

Understanding Word Fundamentals

This business unit had two outcomes:

Learning Outcome 1

Include tables, page, column, and section breaks; and insert objects in Word to create appealing and professional documents.

Learning Outcome 2

Use tools in Word to develop a bibliography or works cited page; collaborate with track changes and comments; and create mail merge documents for letters, labels, and envelopes.

In Business Unit 2 Capstone, students will demonstrate competence in these outcomes through a series of business problems at various levels including guided practice, problem solving an existing document, and performing to create new documents.

More Practice 1

Student data files needed:

 w02FieldDay.docx

 w02Text.docx

w02VictoryLogo.jpg

You will save your file as:

 w02FieldDay_LastFirst.docx

College Field Day

Sales & Marketing

Victory Community College was very successful with its sports camp and has decided to hold a field day when students can compete in various events. Your assignment is to prepare a one-page flyer with details about each competitive event. You will use a two-column layout with graphics and WordArt. Because this a first draft, you will include a watermark and comments before sending it to your supervisor for approval.

a. Start **Word**, click **Open Other Documents**, and then double-click **This PC**. Navigate to the location of your student data files, open **w02FieldDay**, and then save the document as w02FieldDay_LastFirst where you are saving your project files, using your last name and first name. If necessary, click **Show/Hide** to display nonprinting characters. If necessary, click the **View** tab, and then in the Show group, click **Ruler** to display the horizontal and vertical rulers.

b. Select the text **Field Day**. Click the **Insert** tab, and then in the Text group, click **Insert WordArt**. In the second column and first row, select **Fill - Blue, Accent 1, Shadow**.

c. Click the **Format** tab, and then in the Arrange group, click **Wrap Text**. Select **Top and Bottom**.

d. On the Format tab, in the WordArt Styles group, click **Text Effects**. Point to Shadow, and then under Perspective, in the first column and in the first row, select **Perspective Diagonal Upper Left**. In the Size group, change the Shape Width to **6.7"**.

e. Click the **Insert** tab, and in the Header & Footer group, click **Header**, and then click **Edit Header**. On the **Design** tab, in the Insert group, click **Pictures**. Insert the picture **w02VictoryLogo** from your student data files. In the Size group, change the Shape Height to **1.2"**. In the Picture Styles group, click **More**, and then apply the **Drop Shadow Rectangle** picture style. Click the **Home** tab, and in the Paragraph group, click **Center**. Double-click anywhere in the document to close the Header.

f. Place the insertion point immediately after **First Annual** in the first paragraph after the WordArt. On the **Home** tab, in the Paragraph group, click the **Paragraph Dialog Box Launcher**, and then click **Tabs**. In the **Tab stop position** box, type **6.5**. Select a **Right tab** with a **dot** leader. Click **Set**, and then click **OK**.

g. Place the insertion point immediately before **Attention All Students and Faculty**. Click the **Layout** tab, and then in the Page Setup group, click **Columns**, and then select **More Columns**. Under Presets, click **Two**, click the **Apply to** arrow, and then select **This point forward**. Click **OK**. A continuous section break has been added to the document. All text below the break will be formatted into a single column. Note that the horizontal ruler displays two columns.

h. Select **Attention All Students and Faculty**. Click the **Home** tab, and in the Styles group, click the Styles Dialog Box Launcher to open the Styles pane, and then click the **New Style** button. Name the style Topic Heading, change the font to **14**, **Bold**, **Orange**, **Accent 2**, and then click **OK**. **Close** the Styles pane.

i. Apply the Topic Heading style to the text **Tug of War**, **Sack Race**, **Balloon Toss**, and **Tire Roll**.

j. Insert a **blank line** above Tug of War. With the insertion point on the blank line, click the **Insert** tab. In the Text group, click the **Object** arrow, and then select **Text from File**. Navigate to the location of your student data files, double-click **w02Text** to insert the text into the document, and then press Delete to remove the extra paragraph mark at the end of the document.

k. Select the three paragraphs beginning with the line **Stop by the Athletic Complex office** and ending with the line **E-mail** jmusark@victory.edu. Click on the **Home** tab. In the Paragraph group, click **Bullets**, and then click **Decrease Indent**.

l. Place the insertion point in front of the **Tug of War** topic heading, and press Enter. On the blank line, type Schedule of Events, and then press Enter. If necessary, apply the **Topic Heading** style to the text.

m. Click the **Insert** tab. In the Tables group, click **Table**, and then insert a table with **two columns and six rows** (2 × 6 table).

n. Click the **table selector** to select the entire table. Click the **HOME** tab, and then in the Paragraph group, click **Center**. With the table still selected, in the Styles group, click **Normal**. Complete the table as follows, pressing Tab after each entry except the last.

9:00 a.m.	Tug of War
10:00 a.m.	Sack Race
11:00 a.m.	Balloon Toss
12:00 p.m.	Lunch
1:00 p.m.	Tire Roll
2:00 p.m.	Awards

o. Click in the **first row** of the table. Click the **Table Tools Layout** tab, and in the Rows & Columns group, click **Insert Above**, and then type All events will be held on the South lawn. Do not include the period.

p. Select the **first row** of the table. On the Table Tools Layout tab, in the Merge group, click **Merge Cells**. In the Alignment group, click **Align Center**. In the Cell Size group, click **AutoFit**, and then select **AutoFit Contents**.

q. Click the **Table Tools Design** tab, and then in the Table Styles group, click **More**. Scroll down, and under List Tables, click the **List Table 2 - Accent 2** style.

r. Place the insertion point in front of the text **Tug of War**. Click the **Layout** tab. In the Page Setup group, click **Breaks**, and then select **Column**.

s. Select the word **Lunch** in the table. Click the **Review** tab. In the Comments group, click **New Comment**, and then type Is this enough time for lunch?, including the question mark.

t. Click the **Design** tab. In the Page Background group, click **Watermark**, and then under Disclaimers, select the **DRAFT 2** watermark.

u. Preview the document to view the final result.

v. Save the document, exit Word, and then submit your file as directed by your instructor.

Problem Solve 1

MyITLab®
Grader
Homework

Student data files needed:

 w02Chef.jpg

 w02Cook.docx

w02CookAddr.accdb

 w02IndigoLogo.jpg

You will save your files as:

 w02Cook_LastFirst.docx

 w02CookLabels_LastFirst.docx

 w02CookAddr_LastFirst.accdb

Indigo5 Cooking School

Sales &
Marketing

The Indigo5 Cooking School is offered every Tuesday afternoon in the Indigo5 kitchen. The cooking school is popular with resort guests as well as local residents[em]so much so that reservations must be made far in advance. Cooking school students don aprons and learn to prepare everything from informal luncheons to elegant dinners. Recipes from the cooking school are included on the Indigo5 website as well as in the in-house cookbook sold at the resort's Painted Treasures Gift Shop. To promote the cooking school and to encourage advance reservations, you will prepare a mailing to past guests and a select number of local residents. You will format and update the one-page flyer. You will then create mailing labels to send the flyer out.

a. Open **File Explorer**. Navigate to the location of your student data files. Copy the file **w02CookAddr** to the location where you are saving your project files, and rename it as w02CookAddr_LastFirst.

b. Open the Word document, **w02Cook**. Save your file as w02Cook_LastFirst using your last and first name. If necessary, show nonprinting characters and display the horizontal and vertical rulers.

c. If necessary, turn the Track Changes feature off. If necessary, switch to the **All Markup** view. **Accept all** changes. **Delete** the comment.

d. Insert the Indigo5 logo from your student data files, **w02IndigoLogo**, in the header. Change the height of the logo to **0.8"**. Change the color of the logo to **Grayscale**, and then **center** the logo in the header. Close the header.

e. Change the font size for the entire document to **12 pt** and the line spacing to **1.15**.

f. Select the four paragraphs beginning with **Don your apron** and ending with http://www.paintedparadiseresort.com. Convert the text to a table. In the Convert Text to Table dialog box, select **AutoFit to contents**, and then accept the other default settings. Apply **Align Center** to the text within the table, and then **center** the table horizontally on the page.

g. Remove the inside borders of the table. Apply the **Tan, Background 2, Darker 10%** shading to the table.

h. Select the first paragraph of text in the document, **Indigo5 Cooking School**, and then insert a **Fill-Black, Text 1, Shadow** WordArt object. Apply a **Top and Bottom** text wrap to the WordArt.

i. Apply a **Tan, Background 2, Darker 50%** Text Fill to the WordArt.

j. Apply the **Deflate** (under Warp, column 2, row 6) Transform text effect. Apply **Align Center** to the WordArt on the page.

k. Select the two paragraphs beginning with **Bring a bit** and ending with **Santa Fe Pasta Salad**. Center, bold, and then change the font size to **14**.

l. Apply a **36 pt** paragraph **Before** spacing to the paragraph beginning with **Bring a bit**.

m. Select the recipe ingredients and instructions, beginning with **1 pound uncooked tri-color pasta** and ending with **Season with salt and white pepper**. Do not select the ending paragraph mark. Apply a **two-column** format to the selected text.

n. Place the insertion point immediately in front of the text **Cook the pasta al dente**. Insert the **w02Chef** picture from your student data files. Change text wrapping to **Square**. Change the picture height to **2"**. Apply the **Snip Diagonal Corner, White** picture style to the chef picture. Apply **Align Center** to the picture.

o. Place the insertion point in front of the paragraph beginning with **Cook the pasta al dente**. Insert a column break.

p. Press Ctrl+End. Insert a **Simple Text Box**. Change the width of the text box to **5"** and the height to **0.5"**. Type Indigo5 looks forward to welcoming you to our kitchen!, including the exclamation mark. Center the text vertically and horizontally within the text box. Change the font size to **14 pt**. Apply a **Tan, Background 2, Darker 10%** Shape Fill.

q. Insert a footer. Clear any current tabs, and then insert a **6"** right tab stop. Type Indigo5 Cooking School, press Tab, and then insert the **File Name** field. Close the footer.

r. Preview the page as it will appear when printed. Save and close the document, but keep Word open.

s. Open a new **blank document**. Start the **Step-by-Step Mail Merge Wizard**. Select **Labels as the** document type, and then proceed to the next step of the mail merge. Click on **Label options**, and then select the **Avery US Letter** vendor and the **5160 Easy Peel Address Labels** product number. Proceed to the next step of the mail merge.

t. Browse to the location where you are saving your project files, and then open the **w02CookAddr_LastFirst** file as the data source. Edit the data source, and change the **Dana Nye** entry, using your first and last name. Sort the labels in ascending order by last name. Proceed to the next step of the mail merge.

u. Press Ctrl+Home. Insert an Address block using the **Joshua Randall Jr.** format, and then **Update all labels**. Preview the labels, and confirm that your name appears as one of the labels. Apply the **No Spacing** style to all the labels. Complete the merge, and edit all the individual labels. Save the document with all the labels as w02CookLabels_LastFirst, and then close the document.

v. Close the remaining open document without saving.

w. Exit Word, and then submit your files as directed by your instructor.

Student data files needed:

 w02Travel.docx

 w02SpaLogo.jpg

 w02ExpenseTable.docx

w02TravelAddr.xlsx

You will save your files as:

 w02Travel_LastFirst.docx

 w02TravelMerged_LastFirst.docx

w02TravelAddr_LastFirst.xlsx

Travel Expenses

Accounting

Painted Paradise Resort & Spa has sent spa managers Irene Kai and Meda Rodate along with various spa employees to several conferences over the past year. You have been asked to help create a document that can be merged from a list of conference attendees and used in the future to better track travel and expenses. Two documents have been provided to begin the process of building a formal travel expense tracking system for the resort.

a. Open **File Explorer**. Navigate to the location of your student data files. Copy the file **w02TravelAddr** to the location where you are saving your project files, and rename it as w02TravelAddr_LastFirst.

b. Open the Word document, **w02Travel**. Save your file as w02Travel_LastFirst, using your last and first name. If necessary, show nonprinting characters and display the horizontal and vertical rulers.

c. Insert a **header**. With the insertion point in the header, insert the **w02SpaLogo** graphic from your student data files. Change the height to **1"**, and then center the **logo** in the header. Close the header.

d. Place the insertion point at the end of the document. Insert the text from the **w02ExpenseTable** document.

e. Select the six paragraphs of text beginning with **Expense Type** and ending with **Totals**. Convert the **text** to a **table**, and separate the text by **tabs**.

f. Insert a new row above the first row, and merge the cells. Type Enter Conference Information Below, and then align the text to the center of the cell.

g. In the last row of the table, merge the **first two cells**. Align the text to the center right of the cell.

h. Format the table using the **List Table 3-Accent 3** style (fourth column, third row under List Tables).

i. Change the font of the entire document to **Times New Roman**. Change the font size to **12 pt**.

j. Insert a **footer** into the document. Place the **file name** in the footer, and **center** the text in the footer.

k. Use the **Step-by-Step Mail Merge Wizard** to begin a mail merge process for **letters**. Use the **current document** for the merge.

l. For this document, **use an existing list** for the recipients. **Browse** and navigate to where you are saving your project files, and then select **w02TravelAddr_LastFirst** as the data source. Select **Sheet1$** as the table. Select **w02TravelAddr_LastFirst** in the Data Source box, and then click **Edit**. In the last record in the table, replace **Kelly** with your first name, and replace **Masters** with your last name. Choose to update, and save changes to the recipient list.

m. Replace the text **Please enter your name here** in the document with the first name, last name, and e-mail fields. Keep a space between the first name and last name fields. Place the e-mail address field on the line below the first name and last name fields.

n. Place the insertion point after the colon in the paragraph beginning with **Conference Information**, and press Enter. Insert the **Conference Name** field, and press Enter. Insert the **Street Address** field, and press Enter.

o. Insert the **City**, **State**, and **Zip Code** fields. Insert a comma and a space character between the City field and the State field. Insert a space between the State field and the Zip Code field. Save the document.

p. Preview the letters, and then complete the **merge**. Select **Edit individual letters**. Save the document as w02TravelMerged_LastFirst, using your first and last name, and then close the document.

q. Save and close any remaining documents, exit Word, and submit your files as directed by your instructor.

Critical Thinking

When being reimbursed for travel, an employee is often asked for receipts in addition to a list of expenses. List three ways in which an employee can include electronic documentation along with the document created in this Problem Solve. What if the original receipt was lost[em]what other forms of proof could an employee offer? Provide at least three examples. Why would a company want copies of the receipts in addition to a listing of expenses?

Perform 1: Perform in Your Life

Student data file needed:

📄 Blank Word document

You will save your files as:

📄 w02Resume_LastFirst.docx

📄 w02Cover_LastFirst.docx

📄 w02Companies_LastFirst.accdb

📄 w02CoverMerge_LastFirst.docx

📄 w02CoverEnv_LastFirst.docx

Resume, Cover Letter, and Envelopes

Human Resources

As you prepare to seek employment, you are aware of the importance of an attractive resume and cover letter. Websites such as www.monster.com provide resume and cover letter tips, and Microsoft provides templates for both resumes and cover letters. Using a resume template, you will prepare your resume. You will also prepare a cover letter, providing potential employers with information on your employment goals. You will then create a data source, with addresses of employers, so you can personalize the cover letter. Finally you will create envelopes to mail your packet.

a. Start **Word**. Search the online templates for a **resume** template. Download an appropriate resume template, and then save the resume as w02Resume_LastFirst.

b. Modify the resume document to include information specific to your educational and professional preparation. Enhance the resume in any way you like, keeping in mind the need to present a concise, professional document. Follow any additional directions given by your instructor. Save and close the document, but keep the Word application open.

c. You will now create a cover letter. You can create a new blank document to start your cover letter from scratch, or you can search the online templates for an appropriate cover letter. You may even choose to search monster.com for ideas, which you can then incorporate into a new blank document. Save the document as w02Cover_LastFirst.

d. Insert a date field to be automatically updated in the cover letter. Personalize the cover letter to include information specific to your job search. Because the letter will be the basis for a mail merge document, include placeholders for the address block and the salutation. Save the document.

e. Begin a mail merge, using the Step-by-Step Mail Merge Wizard to create letters.
- The merge is to produce letters, using the current document.
- You will create the data source. In Step 3 of the Mail Merge Wizard, under the Select recipients area, select **Type a new list**. Then click **Create**. Type at least eight complete address records, using fictitious addresses if you like. Click **New Entry** to start a new address. Click **OK** when the list is complete, navigate to where you are saving your files, and then save the data as w02Companies_LastFirst.
- Sort the recipients alphabetically by last name.
- Include an AddressBlock and an appropriate salutation so each letter is individualized.
- Preview your letters. Adjust the spacing in the address block and salutation area, if necessary.
- Complete the merge, and then edit the individual letters. Save the file containing all the letters as w02CoverMerge_LastFirst. Close the file. Save and close the **w02Cover_LastFirst** file. Keep Word open.

f. Use the Step-by-Step Mail Merge Wizard to create envelopes for the employers to whom you are sending the cover letter.
- Use a Size 10 envelope size.
- Use the **w02Companies_LastFirst** file as the data source. Sort the recipients alphabetically by last name.
- If necessary, show nonprinting characters to help you properly place the address block. Type your address in the return address area, and then enter an appropriate address block in the delivery address area.
- Preview the envelopes, and then adjust the spacing and font as necessary.
- Complete the merge, and then edit the individual letters. Save the document containing all the envelopes as w02CoverEnv_LastFirst. Close the file, and then close any remaining files without saving. Exit Word.

g. Submit your files as directed by your instructor.

Perform 2: Perform in Your Career

 Student data file needed:
    w02NSIDAddr.accdb

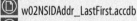 **You will save your files as:**
    w02NSIDAddr_LastFirst.accdb
    w02NSID_LastFirst.docx
    w02NSIDMerge_LastFirst.docx

NSID Scholarships

Sales & Marketing

You are employed as the marketing director for the National Society of Interior Designers (NSID). Your job responsibilities include preparing marketing and educational material to promote the society and to encourage new membership. NSID has partnered with the Interior Design Educators Group to provide scholarship opportunities for interior design students. You will prepare a letter to be sent to high school guidance counselors outlining the various scholarship programs provided by NSID. You will then create a mail merge document, combining addresses from a data source with the letter.

a. Copy **w02NSIDAddr** from the student data files to the location where you are saving your files, renaming it w02NSIDAddr_LastFirst, using your last and first name. Start **Word**, and then begin a new document. Save the document as w02NSID_LastFirst.

b. The font should be 11-pt Times New Roman. In block letter style, type your address as shown below, replacing Firstname and Lastname with your first and last name.

Firstname Lastname, Marketing Coordinator
National Society of Interior Designers
134 Greenfield Street
Fort Worth, TX 76102

c. Insert a date field so that the date will be updated automatically. The format is Month Day, Year (for example, September 2, 2018).

d. Leave space for a mailing address that will be inserted in the mail merge process. The salutation should include the word **Dear:**, with space left for a recipient's name to be placed during the mail merge process.

e. Compose a letter to guidance counselors encouraging them to inform students of the exciting opportunities in the interior design field. Include in the letter that interior design is more than the knowledge of color, fabrics, and design. An interior designer must also be proficient with budgets, computers, and communication. Remind the counselors that the field of interior design has expanded over the years to include even more specialties, such as eco-friendly and antique architectural designs. Inform them of the scholarships that are available through the partnership of NSID with the Interior Design Educators Group. List the scholarships in the form of a table, as shown below. You should note in your letter that additional information about specific requirements for each scholarship is available through the NSID website, www.NSIDDesign.com/careers, or by calling (555) 555-0088.

Scholarship	Sponsor	Award
NDFA Scholarship	National Design and Furnishings Association	$1,500/semester
Metropolis Design	In Sync Design Professionals	$1,500/semester plus all books
Student Design Award Competitions	National Society of Interior Designers	$2,000/semester

f. Apply an attractive design style to the scholarship table, or create your own, using shading and bordering. Insert a row above the first row, merge the cells, and enter the text Interior Design Scholarships. Center all the text in the table.

g. Resize columns if necessary to provide the best readability and use of space. Center the table horizontally on the page.

h. Design a SmartArt diagram (perhaps a process chart) in the letter to graphically indicate the progression to a career in interior design. Include the following steps, in sequence, in the SmartArt diagram.

Practice your skills at home
Seek an industry mentor
Explore scholarships
Network and market yourself

i. End the letter with a closing paragraph and a complimentary close. Adjust the size of the table and SmartArt so the letter fits on one page. If necessary, change the design layout of the SmartArt or edit the text in the letter. Save the document.

j. Begin the Step-by-Step Mail Merge Wizard to create a Letters mail merge, using the current document. You will merge the letter with an existing data source called **w02NSIDAddr_LastFirst**, which you copied and renamed in step a. Edit the data source, and then change one of the entries to include your first and last name. Sort the data alphabetically by last name.

k. Insert an AddressBlock. Insert the appropriate fields in the salutation. Preview the letters, and then complete the merge by editing the individual letters. Save the file containing all the letters as w02NSIDMerge_LastFirst. Close the document, save **w02NSID_LastFirst**, and then exit Word. Submit your files as directed by your instructor.

Perform 3: Perform in Your Team

Student data file needed:

 Blank document

You will save your file as:

 w02Welcome_GroupName.docx

Freshman Ambassador Program

Sales & Marketing

You are an honors student at Southeast University who has been selected to participate in the ambassador program to welcome incoming freshmen to campus. You have been assigned to work with a group of fellow ambassadors whose task it is to create an informational sheet welcoming incoming freshmen and addressing many of their questions or concerns. Arrange to meet with your group to assign specific tasks to each member, who will then be responsible for gathering and writing an informational section (or more) to include in the document. Once a rough draft has been typed, format and design the document with a page layout that is not only readable and informative, but also visually appealing to promote enthusiasm for the start of the new school year. Think about incorporating the school colors in your design.

a. Divide the document sections to be written and the word-processing responsibilities evenly among the group members. Suggested section topics may include the following.
- Welcome and orientation to campus
- Advising and peer mentoring
- Registration
- Academic policies and procedures
- Library and tutoring services
- Financial aid and scholarship opportunities
- Residential life and campus activities
- Parking and dining services
- Health and wellness center
- Information technology and social media
- Community resources and activities

Research your topic(s), and write a rough draft of your section(s) before continuing with the word-processing portion of the project.

b. Select one group member to set up the document by completing steps c through e.

c. Open your browser, and navigate to www.onedrive.live.com, www.drive.google.com, or any other instructor-assigned location. Be sure all members of the group have an account on the chosen Microsoft, Google, or other system.

d. Start **Word**, and create a new blank document. Save the document as w02Welcome_GroupName, where GroupName is the name assigned to your group by your instructor.

e. Share the w02Welcome_GroupName file with the other members of your group, and make sure that each group member has the appropriate permissions to edit the document.

f. Each group member will then type the rough draft sections within the file.

g. As a group, select a design theme for the entire document. Adjust theme colors and fonts as desired, possibly using your school colors.

h. Change margins and line/paragraph spacing for the document, keeping related information together.

i. Consider enlarging the font size to indicate the importance of the title and section headings. Maintain consistency throughout the document.

j. Use the visual tools in Word, such as Styles, Illustrations, WordArt, and Page Colors and Borders, to create a visually appealing document. Again, think school colors.

k. Consider using tables to organize text information in rows and columns or using SmartArt graphics to indicate a process.

l. Insert a cover page with the document title, group member names, and current date.

m. If the document is more than one page long, insert page numbers in a decorative footer.

n. Correct any spelling or grammatical errors. Make any other improvements you think necessary.

o. Save the document, exit Word, and submit your files as directed by your instructor.

p. Make sure that the instructor has permission to edit the file with comments.

Perform 4: How Others Perform

Student data file needed:

 w02Music.docx

You will save your file as:

 w02Music_LastFirst.docx

Music Program

Sales & Marketing

As a parent volunteer for the Band & Instrument Department of River City College, you have been asked by the Music Director to edit and finalize the program for this upcoming fall's Music Showcase held at the local River Bluffs Theatre. A document has been started already, but several issues with how it has been constructed make it difficult to read. Make changes to the document to organize the program details attractively to highlight the musical arrangements chosen by the student performers as well as the variety of musical instruments on which these selections will be played. Format the document to create a professional-looking program that is easy to read for all ages of community members in attendance.

a. Open the Word document, **w02MusicData**. Save your file as w02MusicData_LastFirst, using your last and first name.

b. The currently selected page color is very dark and could make the text difficult for some people to read. Apply a page color that conveys a fall theme but improves the legibility of the document. Adjust the color and width of the border as you like.

c. The current font in the document is difficult to read and not appropriate for this event. Change the font to Times New Roman for the document.

d. Center-align the top four lines of the program (the title and subtitles).

e. Near the beginning of the document, the words **Music Showcase** have been converted into WordArt. Change the layout options such that the text wraps around the top and bottom of the WordArt object.

f. To better illustrate each artist and musical selection, set a right dot leader tab for the musical selections above and below **Intermission**. Ensure the performers are aligned at the left margin and the musical selections are aligned at the right tab set at the right margin of your document.

g. Adjust the line spacing of the document, keeping related information together while placing extra spacing between musical selections. Your document should be balanced and fit on one page. Adjust margins as you see fit.

h. The text **Intermission** should be differentiated from the listing of musical performers and musical selections. Center-align and add font style or WordArt to the **Intermission**. Consider using all caps and adding spacing above and below this line.

i. Include at least one additional fall or music-related image. Format, size, and position as you choose.

j. Spell-check the document, assuming all names of performers and musical selections are spelled correctly.

k. Make any other improvements you think necessary.

l. Save the document, exit Word, and submit your file as directed by your instructor.

Excel Business Unit 1

Understanding the Fundamentals

Data is vital to businesses to help them determine their profits or their losses, their place in a competitive market, and/or their ability to branch into new markets. Businesses use Excel to structure and process data to create information to help in decision making purposes. To use Excel effectively, you need to plan, structure, and format workbooks appropriately. This business unit will introduce you to the fundamentals of creating and working with an Excel workbook.

Learning Outcome 1:

Use Excel to enter text, number, date, and time data to create efficient and effective worksheets.

REAL WORLD SUCCESS

"My family has operated the same farm for four generations. When I graduated from college, I decided to become the first woman to run the family farm. I now track all of our production inputs and outputs using Excel. The high-quality information I produce with Excel has made our farm more efficient and more profitable. Farming is a business, and a successful business requires intelligence in handling information as much as, or more than, it requires intelligence in any other critical business activity."

- Leah, recent graduate

Learning Outcome 2:

Use Excel to effectively communicate information through the use of functions and worksheet formatting.

REAL WORLD SUCCESS

"I worked in an insurance agency while I was in college. Part of my job was to administer marketing strategies. Every month, we received data from our parent company that identified prospective clients. I used Excel to calculate a ranking so I could contact prospects with the highest potential value first. Agency performance was significantly improved as a result, and I received a regional award for efficiency improvement."

- Mike, alumnus and insurance agent

Microsoft Excel 2016

OBJECTIVES

1. Understand spreadsheet terminology and components p. 325

2. Navigate worksheets and workbooks p. 327

3. Document your work p. 331

4. Enter and edit data p. 334

5. Work with cells and cell ranges p. 337

6. Adjust columns and rows p. 345

7. Manipulate worksheets and workbooks p. 350

8. Preview, print, and export workbooks p. 358

Prepare Case

Finance & Accounting

Red Bluff Golf Course & Pro Shop Golf Cart Purchase Analysis

The Red Bluff Golf Course & Pro Shop makes golf carts available to its members for a fee. Recently, the resort has been running out of carts. The time has come for the club to add more golf carts to its fleet. Club manager Barry Cheney, wants to use Microsoft Excel to analyze the purchase of golf carts by model, price, and financing parameters.

Laura Gangi Pond / Shutterstock

Student data file needed for this chapter:

 e01ch01GolfCarts.xlsx

You will save your files as:

e01ch01GolfCarts_LastFirst.xlsx

e01ch01GolfCarts_LastFirst.pdf

e01ch01Mowers_LastFirst.xlsx

Getting Started with Excel

Data plays an integral part in supporting business. Without data, businesses cannot determine their effectiveness in the market, let alone their profit or loss performance. In addition, as businesses grow and change, the types of data collected by a particular business are among the few things that remain relatively static over time. Jobs change, products change, and businesses grow, shrink, or evolve into different lines of business — even into different organizations — on the basis of customer and market demands. However, the types of data that businesses gather and analyze are relatively constant. Much of the same information is required about customers, vendors, products, services, materials, transactions, and so on regardless of the type of business or its stage of growth. Data tracking typically expands as new data is made available and deemed necessary for business purposes or as new technologies easily capture data that was prohibitive to track in the past. Many things may change, but the type of information remains the same.

Data requires processing — categorizing, summarizing, counting, averaging, statistical analysis, and formatting for effective communication — to reveal information that the data itself cannot tell you. With an application such as Excel, it is possible to structure data and to process it in a manner that creates information for decision-making purposes.

Understand Spreadsheet Terminology and Components

Excel is a spreadsheet program that can be used to manage, analyze, and share information. With the help of Excel, you can reveal underlying trends, calculate values, make predictions, make recommendations, and display or share information with large or small amounts of data.

To learn the efficient and effective utilization of Excel, you must know the terminology and components of a spreadsheet. If you are unsure where something is located or how Excel is functioning, you can use the Excel Help feature. You can access Excel Help by pressing the F1 key or by typing your question into the *Tell me what you want to do ...* or *Search the web or Windows ...* section on the ribbon.

What Is a Spreadsheet?

Excel is a spreadsheet application. **A spreadsheet** is a collection of data that is organized in a row and column format. The intersection of each row and column is called a **cell**. **A row** is a horizontal set of cells that encompasses all the columns in a worksheet. A **column** is a vertical set of cells that encompasses all the rows in a worksheet. Each cell can contain text, numbers, formulas, and/or functions. A **formula** is an equation that produces a result and may contain numbers, operators, text, and/or functions. **A function** is a built-in program that performs a task such as calculating a sum or average. Both formulas and functions must always start with the equal sign (=). In Excel, each instance of a spreadsheet is referred to as a **worksheet**, which is a grid of columns and rows in which data is entered.

From balancing an accounting ledger to creating a financial report, many business documents use Excel spreadsheets. Excel spreadsheets are designed to support analyzing business data, representing data through charts, and modeling real world situations.

Spreadsheets are also commonly used to perform **what-if analysis**. In what-if analysis, you change values in spreadsheet cells to investigate the effects on calculated values of interest. What-if analysis allows you to examine the outcome of the changes to values in a worksheet.

Spreadsheets are used for much more than what-if analysis, however. A spreadsheet can be used as a basic collection of data in which each row is a record and each column is a field in the record. **A record** is all of the categories of data that pertain to one person, place, thing, event, or idea and are formatted as a row in a worksheet. A **field** is an item of information in a worksheet column that is associated with something of interest.

Spreadsheets can be built to act as a simple accounting system. Businesses often use spreadsheets to analyze complex financial statements and information. Excel can calculate statistical values such as mean, variance, and standard deviation. Excel can even be used for advanced statistical models such as forecasting and regression analysis. Spreadsheet applications "excel" at calculations of almost any kind.

What Is a Workbook?

Excel files are known as workbooks. A **workbook** is a file that contains one or more worksheets. In Microsoft Excel 2016, workbooks have a file extension of .xlsx. By default, a new, blank workbook contains one worksheet, identified by a tab at the bottom of the Excel window titled Sheet1. As additional worksheets are added, each is given a default name. For example, two new worksheets would be given the names Sheet2 and Sheet3. The **active worksheet** is the worksheet that is visible in the Excel application window and is denoted by a white tab — unless a tab color has been applied — with bold letters and a thick bottom border. Worksheets that are not active are denoted by gray tabs — unless tab colors have been applied — with normal letters. The number of worksheets that can be contained in a workbook is determined by the amount of available memory.

Once a workbook has been created, any changes to it will need to be saved. Save can accomplish this task; however, Save As is useful for saving a copy of a file with a new name. Save As is also useful for creating a backup of a file or for creating a copy of a workbook when you want to use that workbook as the starting point for another workbook.

In this exercise, to get started on the golf cart analysis, you will open a workbook that club manager Barry Cheney has prepared for you and then will save the workbook with a new name.

 E01.00

SIDE NOTE
Windows 10
This book is written for Windows 10. If you are using Windows 8, open your charms, click Search, and then type Excel. If using Windows 7, search the Start menu for Excel.

SIDE NOTE
Pin the Ribbon
If your ribbon is collapsed, pin your ribbon open. Click the Home tab. In the lower right-hand corner of the ribbon, click Pin the Ribbon ⊞.

To Start Excel and Open, Save, and Rename a Workbook

a. On the taskbar, click **Ask Me Anything** or **Search the web and Windows**. Type Excel.

b. If necessary, click on **Excel 2016** in the search results.

c. As explained in the Common Features chapter, the Excel Start screen is displayed when Excel is launched. Click **Open Other Workbooks** in the left pane, and then double-click **This PC**. Navigate through the folder structure to the location of your student data files, and then double-click **e01ch01GolfCarts**. If a Security Warning message displays, click the **Enable Editing** button.

A workbook providing data to analyze the purchase of golf carts by model, price, and financing opens.

d. Click the **File** tab, click **Save As**, and then double-click **This PC**. In the Save As dialog box, navigate to the location where you are saving your project files, and then change the file name to e01ch01GolfCarts_LastFirst, using your last and first name. Click **Save**.

S **CONSIDER THIS** | **Excel Can Store a Vast Amount of Data**

There are 1,048,576 rows × 16,384 columns = 17,179,869,184 cells in an Excel 2016 worksheet. With so much capacity, it can be tempting to use Excel as a database. What other Office application would be better for storing vast amounts of data?

REAL WORLD ADVICE | **AutoRecover and Quick Save — Outsmart Murphy!**

Computers are not perfect. While life's imperfections often make things interesting, they are also an opportunity for Murphy's Law: Anything that can go wrong, will go wrong. However, never fear — AutoRecover and Quick Save are here!

Excel automatically saves your work every 10 minutes, but you can change that interval. Click the File tab, click Options, and then click Save. In the Excel Options dialog box, change the value in the Save AutoRecover information every box. The saved copies of your work are called AutoRecover files. If your computer shuts down unexpectedly, Office will recognize that the file you were working on was not closed properly and will give you the option of opening the most recent AutoRecover file.

The Ctrl+S shortcut quickly saves your file to the same location as the last save. Whenever you make a significant change to your file, save it immediately using the quick save keyboard shortcut.

QUICK REFERENCE | **Back Up Your Workbook!**

It is a good idea to back up your workbook when you are about to make significant changes to it, when those changes have been made, and/or when you have finished working for the moment.

To make a backup of your workbook, do the following.

1. Click the File tab, click Save As, and then click Browse.

2. In the Save As dialog box, navigate to the location where you are saving your files. In the File name box, type the name of your file, such as YourFile_yyyy-mm-dd, where yyyy-mm-dd is today's date. Click Save.

If possible, best practice is to store backup files on an entirely different drive, such as a USB drive, or to a cloud service such as OneDrive.

Save As not only saves a copy of your file, but also changes the file Excel has open. YourFile_yyyy-mm-dd will be the open file, and the title bar at the top of the Excel application window will display the new file name. Click Close and open your original file before continuing your work.

Navigate Worksheets and Workbooks

Workbooks often contain more than a single worksheet. Sometimes the worksheets are related to each other, such as monthly sales data. Other times, worksheets may be separate from the rest of the data and used only to document the workbook's worksheet(s). To effectively develop and use workbooks and worksheets, you must be able to navigate within worksheets and between worksheets in a workbook.

Navigating Between Worksheets

Workbooks may contain more than one worksheet. The worksheet tabs are located on the bottom left side of the Excel window. Each tab represents a single worksheet in the workbook.

The active worksheet — the worksheet that is visible — is readily identifiable because the background color of its worksheet tab is white and it has a thick bottom border. To make a different worksheet active, click its worksheet tab. When you open a workbook that you have not worked with before, it is a best practice to spend some time familiarizing yourself with its worksheets.

You may have noticed that the golf carts workbook you have opened contains four worksheets. In this exercise, you will navigate among worksheets to familiarize yourself with their contents.

 E01.01

To Change the Active Worksheet

a. Click on the **GolfCartPurchases** worksheet tab to make it the active worksheet. This worksheet is the start of a purchase analysis for replacement of the Red Bluff Golf Course fleet of golf carts.

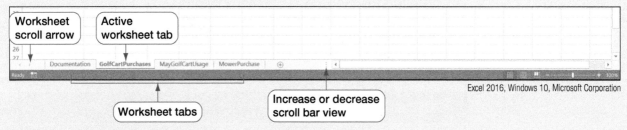

Excel 2016, Windows 10, Microsoft Corporation

Figure 1   Change the active worksheet

b. Click the **MayGolfCartUsage** worksheet tab. This worksheet is an analysis of golf cart usage for the month of May that Barry Cheney developed to assess whether the number of carts in the current fleet is optimal.

c. Click the **MowerPurchase** worksheet tab. This worksheet is an analysis of the five different types of mowers available for purchase.

d. Click the **Documentation** worksheet tab. You may need to scroll left using the worksheet scroll arrows to see the Documentation worksheet tab. This worksheet is used to document the contents of the workbook. Documentation is an important component of a well-structured workbook.

e. **Save** 🖫 the workbook.

> ## Troubleshooting
> All the figures in this text were taken at a monitor resolution of 1366 × 768. Higher or lower resolution will affect the way Excel displays ribbon options.

Once Excel is open, it is important to recognize the components of the worksheet window so that you can effectively use a workbook and navigate within a worksheet. As Figure 2 shows, the worksheet window has many components.

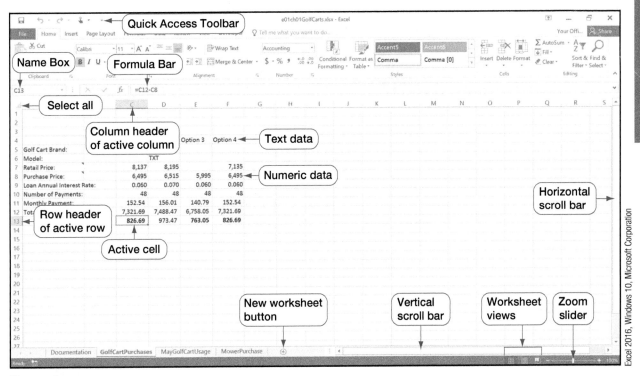

Figure 2   The worksheet window

Navigating Within Worksheets

Whether a worksheet is small or extremely large, navigation from one cell to another is necessary to enter or edit numbers, formulas, functions, or text. Navigation requires an understanding of how Excel handles rows, columns, and cells.

Each row is identified by a number in ascending sequence from top to bottom. Each column is identified by a letter in ascending sequence from left to right. Each cell has a default name called a **cell reference**. A cell reference refers to a particular cell or range of cells within a formula or function instead of a value. The cell reference is a combination of its column letter and row number. For example, the intersection of column A and row 1 has a cell reference of A1, and the intersection of column D and row 20 is cell D20.

Navigating in a small worksheet is simple: Point to the cell, and click to make it the active cell. The **active cell** is the recipient of an action, such as a click, calculation, or paste. When a cell becomes the active cell, the border around it changes to a thick, green line. Any data you enter via the keyboard is placed into the active cell. Worksheet navigation is simply defined as moving the location of the active cell.

When a part of a worksheet is out of view, it may be because the worksheet is too large to be displayed completely in the visible application window. In this case, use the vertical and horizontal scroll bars to shift other parts of the document into view. The vertical scroll bar is on the right side of the application window, and the horizontal scroll bar is at the bottom right of the application window. It is important to note that scrolling does not move the active cell; it only changes your view in the worksheet.

A **keyboard shortcut** is a keyboard equivalent for a software command that allows you to keep your hands on the keyboard instead of reaching for the mouse to make ribbon selections. Keyboard shortcuts allow rapid navigation in a worksheet without having to use the mouse. It is considered best practice to learn and use keyboard shortcuts whenever possible.

There are several keyboard shortcuts that may be used to navigate a worksheet and move the active cell.

Keyboard Shortcuts	Moves the Active Cell
Enter	Down one row
Shift + Enter	Up one row
→ ← ↓ ↑	One cell in the direction of the arrow key
Home	To column A of the current row
Ctrl + Home	To column A, row 1 (cell A1)
Ctrl + End	To the last cell, highest number row and far-right column, that contains information
End + → End + ← End + ↓ End + ↑	To the last cell containing data in the arrow direction before an empty cell if the first cell in the direction of the arrow beyond the active cell contains data To the next cell in the arrow direction that contains information if the first cell in the direction of the arrow beyond the active cell is empty
PgUp PgDn	Up one screen, down one screen
Alt + PgUp	Left one screen
Alt + PgDn	Right one screen
Ctrl + PgUp Ctrl + PgDn	One worksheet left One worksheet right
Tab Shift + Tab	One column right One column left

For large worksheets, Go To allows rapid navigation. Although the worksheet you are currently working with is not large, knowledge of how to use the Go To dialog box to navigate directly to any cell in the worksheet by specifying a cell reference is a skill that you may find useful. In this exercise, you will learn to navigate within a worksheet.

E01.02

To Navigate Within a Worksheet

a. Click the **GolfCartPurchases** worksheet tab, and then press Ctrl + Home to make **A1** the active cell. Press the ↓ six times, and then press → four times. The active cell should be **E7**. Type 6495, and then press Ctrl + Enter to keep cell E7 active.

b. Press ← once, and then press ↑ two times. The active cell should be **D5**. Type EZ-GO, and then press Enter.
   Notice that the active cell is now **D6**. Pressing Enter moved the active cell down one row.

c. On the Home tab, in the Editing group, click **Find & Select**, and then click **Go To**. The Go To dialog box appears. Click in the **Reference** box, and type D13.

Excel 2016, Windows 10, Microsoft Corporation

Figure 3 Go To dialog box

d. Click **OK**. The active cell is now D13. On the Home tab, in the Font group, click **Bold** B.

e. Press Home. This takes you to column A of the row with the active cell. The active cell should be **A13**. Type Total Interest Cost:, and then press Enter.

f. Press Ctrl + Home to return the active cell to A1.

> **Troubleshooting**
>
> The active cell is repositioned by using the mouse pointer or keyboard. Even experienced users often scroll through a worksheet and press an arrow key only to find themselves returned to the active cell where they began scrolling.

g. **Save** the workbook.

Touch Devices

If you have a device such as a tablet PC with a touch screen, you can control Excel 2016 using your finger. The commands on the ribbon and in shortcut menus are the same, but Excel recognizes when you have touched the screen and enables **touch mode**. In touch mode, the ribbon and shortcut menus are enlarged to make selecting commands with your fingertip easier. Figure 4 shows the Excel interface in touch mode.

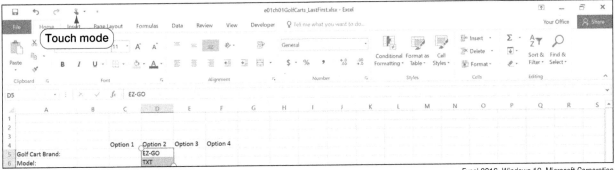

Excel 2016, Windows 10, Microsoft Corporation

Figure 4 Touch mode in Excel 2016

Document Your Work

Workbooks may be used by people who did not develop them. Even if a workbook will never be used by anyone other than its builder, best practice dictates that you document a workbook and its worksheets.

Documentation is vital to ensure that a workbook remains usable. A well-documented workbook is much easier to use and maintain, particularly for a user who did not develop the workbook. You may use a workbook on a regular basis, you may even have developed it, but over time you may forget how the workbook operates.

Documentation takes several forms, such as descriptive file and worksheet names, worksheet titles, column and/or row titles, cell labels, cell comments, or a dedicated documentation worksheet. Many people do not take the time to document adequately because they do not think that it is time spent productively. Some do not think it is necessary because they do not think anyone else will ever use the workbook. However, for a workbook to be useful, it must be accurate, easily understood, flexible, efficient, and documented. While accuracy is most important, an undocumented workbook can later create inaccurate data. Where documentation is concerned, less is not more — more is more.

While documentation worksheets generally include documentation for an entire workbook, comments can be created specifically to add documentation to a worksheet and address individual fields, calculations, and so on and are included as content in an individual cell.

Using Comments to Document a Workbook

A cell **comment** is a text box, similar to a sticky note, that is attached to a cell in a worksheet in which you can enter notes or give instructions. In this exercise, you will insert comments into a worksheet to document a workbook.

To Document a Workbook Using Comments

a. On the **GolfCartPurchases** worksheet, notice the red triangles in the upper right corners of cells A7 and A8. The triangle indicates the existence of a comment. Point to cell A7. The comment that appears defines Retail Price.

b. Click cell **A9**. Click the **Review** tab.

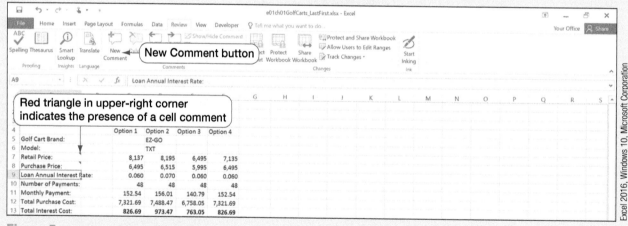

Figure 5   Insert a cell comment

c. In the Comments group, click **New Comment** to create a comment.

d. In the comment box, select the text **user name** — not the colon — that is automatically inserted into the comment. Press Del to delete the text.

e. With the insertion point to the left of the colon, type Annual Interest Rate, and then press the → twice, and then type Annual rate of interest in decimal or percentage format.

			Option 2	Option 3	Option 4
4					
5	Golf Cart Bra	Comment box	EZ-GO		
6	Model:		TXT		
7	Retail Price:	8,137	8,195	6,495	7,135
8	Purchase Price:	6,495	6,515	5,995	6,495
9	Loan Annual Interest Ra	Annual Interest Rate: Annual rate of interest in	0.070	0.060	0.060
10	Number of Payments:	decimal or percentage	48	48	48
11	Monthly Payment:	format.	156.01	140.79	152.54
12	Total Purchase Cost:		7,488.47	6,758.05	7,321.69
13	Total Interest Cost:	826.69	973.47	763.05	826.69

Figure 6 Documenting a worksheet using a comment

SIDE NOTE
Cell Comments
To close a comment, you can also click any other cell within the worksheet.

f. Press Esc twice to close the comment. Cell A9 now has a red triangle in the top right corner to indicate the presence of a comment.

g. **Save** 🖫 the workbook.

Using a Worksheet for Documentation

A well-structured worksheet is self-documenting in that there are descriptive titles, column headings, and cell labels. However, a separate documentation worksheet includes information that is not generally specified in a worksheet, such as authorship, modification dates, modification history, or specific information that should be noted. Documentation worksheets go beyond the file properties that are automatically stored by Excel when a workbook is saved. For example, a documentation sheet could include the indication of cell comments or an explanation of calculations being performed, which could assist the user of the workbook.

In this exercise, you will update the documentation worksheet to include your name as well as the addition of the cell comment you added previously.

E01.04

To Document a Workbook Using a Documentation Worksheet

a. Click the **Documentation** worksheet tab. You may have to scroll left in the worksheet tabs. Click cell **A8**, and then type the **current date** in mm/dd/yyyy format.

b. Press Tab. In cell **B8**, type your name in Firstname Lastname format. Press Tab. In cell **C8**, type Added comment to a key heading on the GolfCartPurchases worksheet, and then press Enter.

c. **Save** 🖫 the workbook.

REAL WORLD ADVICE	Failing to Plan Is Planning to Fail

Winston Churchill said, "He who fails to plan, plans to fail." The first step in building a worksheet should be planning. There are several questions that you should consider before you begin entering information.

- What is the objective of the worksheet? Is it to solve a problem? Is it to analyze data and recommend a course of action? Is it to summarize data and present usable information? Is it to store information for use by another application?
- Do you have all of the data necessary to build this worksheet?

- What information does your worksheet need to generate?
- How should the information in your worksheet be presented? Who is the audience? What form will best present the worksheet information?

Plan your work before you begin. The time spent planning will be saved several times over, and the end result will be of higher quality.

Enter and Edit Data

In building and maintaining worksheets, the ability to enter, edit, and format data is fundamental. As data is entered via the keyboard, the data appears simultaneously in the active cell and in the formula bar. Figure 7 shows the result when a cell is double-clicked to place the insertion point into cell contents. If you click in the formula bar, the insertion point is displayed in the formula bar.

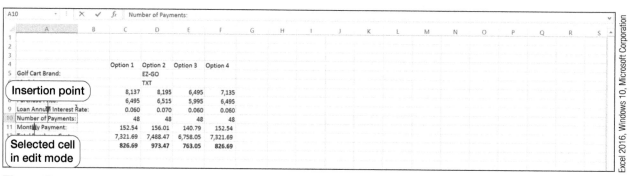

Figure 7   Editing data in a cell

Using Text, Number, Date, and Time Data in Cells

Cell entries can consist of text data or numerical data. **Text data** consists of any combination of printable characters, including letters, numbers, and special characters available on any standard keyboard. By default, text data is left-aligned in a cell

Numeric data consists of numbers (0–9) in any form not combined with letters and special characters such as the period (decimal) and/or hyphen (to indicate negative values). Technically, special characters such as the dollar sign ($) or comma (,) are not considered numeric. They are displayed only for contextual and readability purposes and are not stored as part of a numeric cell value. By default, numeric data is right-aligned in a cell.

In Excel, date data and time data are special forms of numeric data. **Date data** is data recognized by Excel as a date. Data formatted as a date takes the form of a serial number, with the number 1 representing January 1, 1900. **Time data** is data recognized by Excel as representing time. Time data is represented as a decimal value where .1 is 144 minutes, .01 is 14.4 minutes, and so on. Information entered in a recognized date and/or time format will be converted automatically to an Excel date and/or time value. If Excel recognizes a value as a date/time, it will right-align the entry. If you enter a date or time that is not recognized, Excel treats the information as text and left-aligns it in the cell.

Table 1 includes examples of valid dates and times that can be entered into Excel and how they will be displayed by default.

Enter	Excel Displays	Enter	
December 21, 2018	21-Dec-18	1:00 p	
21 Dec 2018	21-Dec-18	1 a	
Dec 21, 2018	21-Dec-18	13:00	13:00

Table 1   Date and time entries and how Excel displays dates

The GolfCartPurchases worksheet not only contains text, numbers, and date information, it also contains formulas and functions. Although you will not learn about formulas and functions until the next chapter, it is important to note that they appear throughout the Golf Carts workbook. A formula performs a mathematical calculation (or calculations) using data in the worksheet to calculate new values, as in cell D12 of the GolfCartPurchases worksheet. A function is a built-in program that performs operations against data and returns a value, as in cell D11 of the GolfCartPurchases worksheet.

After reviewing the GolfCartPurchases worksheet, you think that the worksheet is missing an appropriate title to help with understanding its contents. In this exercise, you will add worksheet titles and edit existing information.

 E01.05

SIDE NOTE
Keyboard Shortcut for Undo
Ctrl+Z is a fast and efficient method of performing an Undo ↺.

SIDE NOTE
Use Undo History
If you need to undo a change but have made other changes since making that change, click the Undo arrow ↺ to see the change history.

To Enter Information into a Worksheet

a. Click the **GolfCartPurchases** worksheet tab, click cell **A2**, type Red Bluff Golf Course & Pro Shop, and then press Enter. Notice the active cell is cell A3.

b. In cell **A3**, type Golf Cart Purchase Analysis, and then press Enter. Notice that Excel displays the text as left-aligned.

c. In cell **A4**, type 6/6/2018, and then press Enter. Notice that Excel displays the date as 6/6/2018 and is right-aligned.

d. In cell **G4**, type Option 5, and then press Enter. Notice that the text in cell G4 is left-aligned.

e. Notice the value in cell D11 of 156.01. Click cell **D9**, type 0.06, and then press Enter.

    Notice that the monthly payment in cell D11 changes to 153.00. The values in cells D11, D12, and D13 are automatically recalculated because those cells contain formulas.

f. Click on cell **D11**, and then view the function in the Formula Bar. Also click on cells **D12** and **D13** to view the formulas of those cells in the Formula Bar.

> **Troubleshooting**
> If the monthly payment is larger than it should be, you may have entered 0.6. That is actually 60% for calculation purposes. You must enter the percentage 6% or enter 0.06, the decimal equivalent of 6%.

g. **Save** 🖫 the workbook.

Wrapping Text and Line Breaks

By default, Excel places all information in a single line in a cell. Text that is too long to fit in a cell is displayed over adjoining cells to the right unless those cells also contain information. If adjoining cells contain information, lengthy text from cells to the left is not fully displayed.

...tion can be avoided by changing the alignment of a cell to wrap words or ...rd returns into text to force wrapping at a particular location. In this exer- ...l wrap text in a cell.

...ap Text in a Cell

Click the **Documentation** worksheet tab, and then click cell **C8**. Notice how the contents of cell C8 appear to be displayed over cell D8.

b. Click the **Home** tab and in the Alignment group, click **Wrap Text**. The vertical size of row 8 is increased to display all content within the boundaries of cell C8.

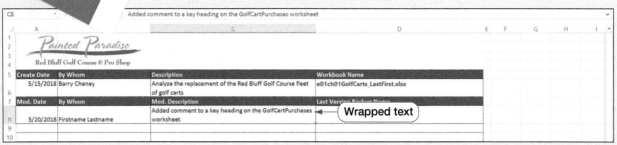

Figure 8 Wrap text in a cell

Excel 2016, Windows 10, Microsoft Corporation

c. Click the **GolfCartPurchases** worksheet tab.

d. Click cell **A3**, and then click in the **Formula Bar** immediately to the right of the word **Cart**. Press Delete to remove the space between Cart and Purchase, and then press Alt+Enter to insert a line break, often referred to as a hard return.

e. Press Ctrl+Enter to complete the entry. Notice how only the words before the hard return are visible on the formula bar.

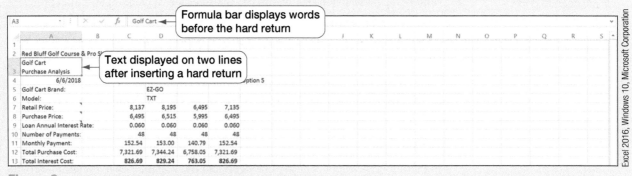

Figure 9 Insert a hard return to control text wrap location

f. **Save** the workbook.

Work with Cells and Cell Ranges

Part of what makes a worksheet an efficient tool is the ability to perform actions that affect many cells at once. Knowing how to work with cells and cell ranges is an important part of maximizing your efficiency. **Cell range** refers to the cells in the worksheet that have been selected. A cell range can reference a single cell, several contiguous cells, or noncontiguous cells. A **contiguous cell range** consists of multiple selected cells, all directly adjacent to one another — for example, A1:A10. When you read a range such as A1:A10, the colon stands for "through." A **noncontiguous cell range** consists of multiple selected cells with at least one cell not directly adjacent to other cells.

Cutting, Copying, and Pasting

Copy and paste copies everything in a cell, including formatting. Cut and paste moves everything in a cell, including formatting. However, through Paste Options and Paste Special, you can control exactly what is placed into the destination cells. When you copy or cut data in Excel, the data is placed in the Clipboard. The **Clipboard** is a temporary storage location where information that was cut or copied is stored until you paste, move, or clear the information. A **destination cell** is the location cell to be modified by a move or paste operation.

In this exercise, you will make changes to the GolfCartPurchases worksheet by using the cut, copy, and paste in Excel.

 E01.07

SIDE NOTE
Keyboard Shortcuts
The keyboard shortcut for **Cut** is Ctrl+X; the shortcut for **Copy** is Ctrl+C; and the shortcut for **Paste** is Ctrl+V.

To Cut, Copy, and Paste Cells

a. On the GolfCartPurchases worksheet, click cell **D5**. On the Home tab, in the Clipboard group, notice that the Paste option is unavailable — it is light gray in color.

> **Troubleshooting**
>
> If the Paste option is not grayed out on your screen, you could have another application open in which you have been copying information and therefore information remains on the Office Clipboard. To clear the Clipboard, click the Clipboard arrow, and select Clear All from the Clipboard pane, and then close the Clipboard pane.

b. In the Clipboard group, click **Cut**. The solid border around cell D5 changes to a moving dashed border.

c. Click cell **C5**.

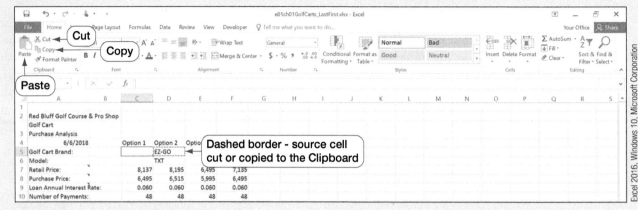

Figure 10 Cut, copy, and paste

d. In the Clipboard group, click **Paste**.

e. Click cell **D6**, and then, in the Clipboard group, click **Copy**. The solid border around cell D6 changes to a moving dashed border. Click cell **C6**, and then, in the Clipboard group, click **Paste**.

f. Press Esc to clear the Clipboard and remove the dashed border from around cell D6. Notice that once the Clipboard has been cleared by pressing Esc, Paste becomes unavailable again.

g. **Save** the workbook.

Selecting Cell Ranges

By using the mouse, multiple cells can be selected simultaneously. Selected cells can be contiguous to each other, or they can be noncontiguous. Once multiple cells have been selected, they can be affected by actions such as clear, delete, copy, paste, formatting, and many others while offering the convenience of performing the desired task only once for the selected cells. In this exercise, you will select, copy, and paste to contiguous and noncontiguous selections.

 E01.08

SIDE NOTE

Shift can be used in combination with other navigation keys and/or the mouse to select a contiguous range of cells.

To Select, Copy, and Paste to Contiguous and Noncontiguous Selections

a. On the GolfCartPurchases worksheet, click cell **C5**. Press Shift+↓. The active cell border expands to include **C5:C6**.

b. Press Ctrl+C to copy the selected cells to the Clipboard. Click cell **E5**, and then press Ctrl+V to paste the Clipboard contents to the selected cell.

<table>
<tr><td rowspan="2">SIDE NOTE
Ctrl can be used in combination with other navigation keys and/or the mouse to select non-contiguous cell ranges.</td><td>c. Click cell D5, press and hold Ctrl, click cell F5, and then release Ctrl.</td></tr>
<tr><td>d. Press Shift + →.</td></tr>
</table>

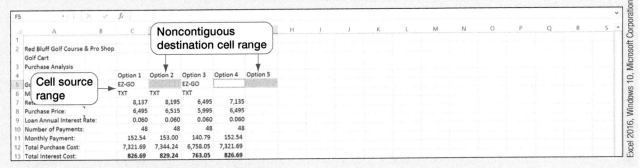

Figure 11   Selecting a noncontiguous cell range

e. Press Ctrl + V, and then press Esc to clear the Clipboard.

> ## Troubleshooting
> If nothing pasted when you pressed Ctrl + V, it could be that you lost the copy command by pressing another cell or command. Retry by selecting C5:C6, pressing Ctrl + C, and then repeating step c.

f. **Save** 🖫 the workbook.

QUICK REFERENCE	Selecting Cell Ranges

There are several ways to select a contiguous range of cells.

- Expand the active cell by dragging the mouse.
- Select the first cell in the range, press Shift, and click the last cell in the desired range.

A contiguous range of rows or columns can be selected in the following ways.

- Click a row or column header. Drag the mouse pointer across the headers to select contiguous rows or columns.
- Click a row or column header, press Shift, and then click the header of the last row or column you wish to select.

Once a cell or contiguous range of cells has been selected, you can add noncontiguous cells and ranges by pressing Ctrl and using any of the above methods for selecting ranges that do not involve Shift.

Dragging and Dropping

As worksheets are designed, built, and modified, it is often necessary to move information from one cell or range of cells to another. One of the most efficient ways to do this is called "drag and drop." In this exercise, you will drag and drop cells to reorganize a worksheet.

 E01.09

SIDE NOTE

Drag and Drop

A ghost range, also referred to as a destination range, and a destination range ScreenTip are displayed as a pointer is moved to show exactly where the moved cells will be placed.

To Drag and Drop Cells

a. On the GolfCartPurchases worksheet, click and drag to select the cell range **A2:A4**.

b. Point to the **border** of the selected range. The mouse pointer changes to a move pointer.

c. Click and hold the left mouse button, and then drag the selected cells up one row to cell range **A1:A3**.

d. Drop the dragged cells by releasing the mouse button.

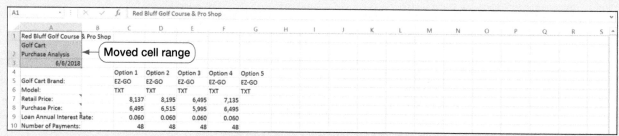

Figure 12   Moved cell range

Excel 2016, Windows 10, Microsoft Corporation

e. Select the range **F7:F13**. Move the mouse pointer until it is over the **border** of the selected range in column F. The mouse pointer changes to a move pointer. Press and hold Ctrl. The move pointer changes to a copy pointer. Drag the selected range until the ghost range is directly to the right of column F, over range **G7:G13**. Release the mouse button, and then release Ctrl.

f. Cell range F7:F13 has been copied to cell range G7:G13.

g. **Save** the workbook.

QUICK REFERENCE	Moving Cells

Moving cells may cause formulas to break. After moving a cell or range of cells, always double-click any formulas to ensure that they still reference the appropriate cells.

Modifying Cell Information

Copying and pasting content from one range of cells to another range or ranges is a highly efficient way to reuse parts of a worksheet. The range you just copied into column G contains information that is calculated by using formulas in the cell range G11:G13.

However, once you have duplicated a cell or cell range, it is usually necessary to change some content.

If only part of the content is to change, a cell can be placed into edit mode. In edit mode, the active cell will contain an insertion point. Double-click the cell to enter edit mode, and use arrow keys or click to position the insertion point at the desired location. Cells can also be edited by using the Formula Bar.

If all the cell content is to be replaced, click the cell once to make it the active cell, and then begin entering the new content. All cell content will be replaced when you begin typing to enter the new content for the selected cell.

In this exercise, you want to correct the GolfCartPurchases worksheet to reflect the correct golf cart brands and prices.

E01.10

SIDE NOTE

Alternate Method
Press the F2 key to place a cell in edit mode.

To Modify Worksheet Contents by Changing Copied Information

a. On the GolfCartPurchases worksheet, click cell **D6**, type RXV, and then press →. Notice that the entire contents of the cell are replaced with the new text.

b. Double-click cell **E6**, press Home to go to the left margin of the cell, type Freedom, and then press Spacebar once so the formula bar displays **Freedom TXT**. Press Tab.

c. In cell **F6**, type Freedom RXV, and then press Tab.

d. In cell **G6**, type The Drive, and then press Enter.

e. Click cell **G7**, type 6995, and then press Enter. In cell **G8**, type 6350, and then press Ctrl+Enter.

   Notice that when you changed the value in cell G8, the Monthly Payment, Total Purchase Cost, and Total Interest Cost were recalculated because these cells contain formulas.

f. Click cell **G5**, type Yamaha, and then press Enter.

g. Select the range C6:G6. On the Home tab in the Alignment group, click Wrap Text, and then press Ctrl+Home.

A1   ▾ : × ✓ _fx_   Red Bluff Golf Course & Pro Shop

	A	B	C	D	E	F	G	H	I	J	K	L	M	N	O	P	Q	R	S
1	Red Bluff Golf Course & Pro Shop																		
2	Golf Cart Purchase Analysis																		
3	6/6/2018																		
4			Option 1	Option 2	Option 3	Option 4	Option 5												
5	Golf Cart Brand:		EZ-GO	EZ-GO	EZ-GO	EZ-GO	Yamaha												
6	Model:		TXT	RXV	Freedom TXT	Freedom RXV	The Drive												
7	Retail Price:		8,137	8,195	6,495	7,135	6,995												
8	Purchase Price:		6,495	6,515	5,995	6,495	6,350												
9	Loan Annual Interest Rate:		0.060	0.060	0.060	0.060	0.060												
10	Number of Payments:		48	48	48	48	48												
11	Monthly Payment:		152.54	153.00	140.79	152.54	149.13												
12	Total Purchase Cost:		7,321.69	7,344.24	6,758.05	7,321.69	7,158.24												
13	Total Interest Cost:		826.69	829.24	763.05	826.69	808.24												

Excel 2016, Windows 10, Microsoft Corporation

Figure 13   Modified worksheet

h. **Save** the workbook.

Inserting and Deleting Cells, Clearing Cells, and Cell Ranges

It is sometimes necessary to insert or delete cells to make a worksheet easier to read or to improve its appearance. Inserting or deleting cells is not the same as inserting or deleting entire rows or column. If you insert a cell in a worksheet where data already exists, Excel will adjust the current data by shifting cells down or to the right. If you delete a cell in a worksheet where data already exists, Excel will shift cells up or to the left.

Worksheet data can either be cleared or deleted; there is a difference. Clearing contents from a cell does not change the location of other cells in the worksheet. Deleting a cell shifts surrounding cells in a direction determined from a prompt. When you are editing a string of characters in a cell, pressing Delete works exactly as you would expect. When you are not in edit mode, pressing Delete clears content but does not delete the cell or cells.

You want to change the appearance of the golf cart purchase analysis worksheet. In this exercise, you will insert and delete cells.

 E01.11

To Insert, Delete, or Clear Cells and Cell Ranges in a Worksheet

a. On the GolfCartPurchases worksheet, click cell **B5**. On the Home tab, in the Cells group, click **Delete** ⊠. Notice that the brand headings in row 5 moved to the left one cell.

> ### Troubleshooting
>
> If nothing happened, you may have pressed the Delete button on the keyboard. Click the Delete ⊠ button in the Cells group. If you click the Delete arrow, you can then click Delete Cells in the list.

b. Click cell **B4**. Click the **Delete** arrow, and then click **Delete Cells**.

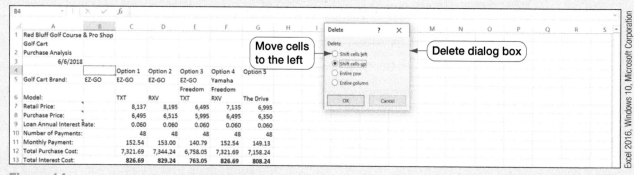

Figure 14 Delete dialog box for deleting cells

c. From the Delete dialog box, click **Shift cells left**, and then click **OK**.

d. Select the range **B6:B13**. Right-click the selection, and then select **Delete** from the shortcut menu. Verify **Shift cells left** is selected, and then click **OK**. The remaining cell values in rows 6:13 moved left one cell.

e. Click cell **B5**, and then, in the Cells group, click **Insert** ⊞.

   Notice how the contents of column B shifted down a row and no longer align appropriately with the labels in column A. You will undo this change.

f. Click **Undo** ↰ from the Quick Access Toolbar to undo the last action.

g. Click in Cell **B6**, press (Delete), and then press (Ctrl)+(Enter). Notice how the content of cell B6 is cleared but the cell is not deleted. Click **Undo** ↰.

h. **Save** ⊟ the workbook.

Merging and Centering Versus Centering Across

The titles in the golf cart analysis worksheet are in cells A1:A3. Although they contain the correct information to communicate the purpose of the golf cart analysis worksheet, that information might be better presented with some formatting improvements.

Titles that identify the general purpose of a worksheet are often at the top and centered above worksheet content. Clicking the Center button ☰ from the Alignment group of the Home tab will center contents only within the active cell. However, the **Merge & Center** feature ☷ ▾ combines selected cells into a single cell and then centers the text within that single cell. Merge & Center can be applied to horizontal or vertical cell ranges. Content in the left and/or top cell of the selected range is centered; all other data in the selected range is lost.

If more than one row of cells need to be centered, another option is to use the Center Across Selection command. Center Across Selection removes the borders between cells such that a selected range looks like a single cell, but the original cells remain, the borders between them are hidden, and the content is centered across the cells. Center Across Selection can be applied only horizontally. Additionally, Center Across Selection will never replace the data in the other cells.

In this exercise, you will center the headings in rows 1:3 to improve the appearance of the golf cart purchase analysis worksheet.

 E01.12

To Merge & Center Headings

a. On the GolfCartPurchases worksheet, press `Ctrl`+`Home` to return to cell **A1**. Left-click and drag until range **A1:F1** is selected. On the Home tab, in the Alignment group, click **Merge & Center** ☷ ▾.

   Notice how the content of cell A1 appears to span across the six columns even though the content still remains in cell A1.

b. Select the range **A2:F3**. In the Alignment group, click **Merge & Center** ☷ ▾.

   Notice the warning message. If you Merge & Center data in more than one cell at a time, only the data in the upper left cell of the selected range will be kept; the rest will be lost.

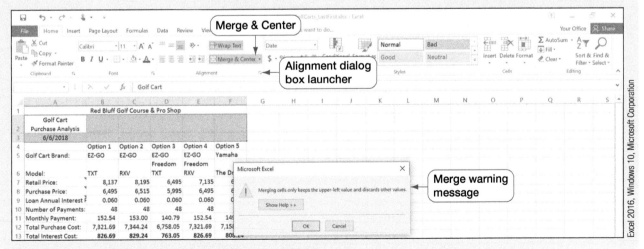

Figure 15 Merge and center a range containing multiple values

c. Click **Cancel**. You do not want to lose the data in cell A3.

> **Troubleshooting**
>
> If you clicked OK instead of Cancel, press Ctrl + Z to undo the last change and go back to step b.

d. With range A2:F3 still selected, on the Home tab, in the Alignment group, click the **Alignment** Dialog Box Launcher ⬏. This opens the Format Cells dialog box.

e. With the **Alignment** tab selected, click the **Horizontal** arrow, and then click **Center Across Selection**.

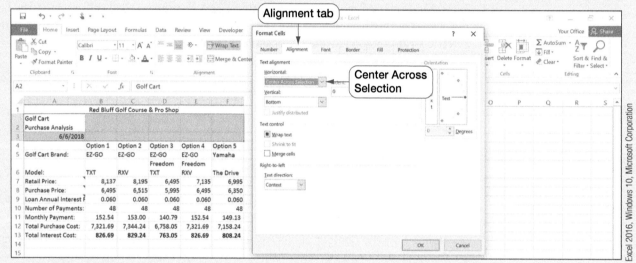

Figure 16 Center Across Selection

f. Click **OK**. Cell A2 content is centered across cell range A2:F2, and cell A3 content is centered across cell range A3:F3.

g. **Save** ⊟ the workbook.

SS CONSIDER THIS | **Merge & Center and Cell Range Selection**

Try this: Try to select cell range A1:D17. Try to select cell range A1:B9. Now select cell range A2:F17.

Merge & Center 🔲▾ creates a single cell that can cause problems if you want to select a range of cells that includes only part of the merged cell range. Center Across Selection does not cause this problem.

Some Excel users think that Merge & Center should never be used. Do you agree?

Adjust Columns and Rows

Any worksheet created has default column widths and row heights. As you build, refine, and modify a worksheet, it is often necessary to add and/or delete columns and rows or to change column widths and/or row heights for formatting and content purposes. Fortunately, Excel makes these activities easy to accomplish.

Selecting Contiguous and Noncontiguous Columns and Rows

To manipulate columns and rows, you must first indicate which of each you wish to affect by your actions. As with cells and cell ranges, you can select entire columns, entire rows, multiple columns, and multiple rows. You can select noncontiguous columns and rows, and you can even select multiple columns and multiple rows at the same time.

QUICK REFERENCE	Selecting Columns and Rows

- To select a column or row click the header — the letter or number, respectively — in the header.
- To select a range of contiguous columns or rows, point to and click the header at the start of the range you want to select. Hold down the mouse button, and then drag to select additional columns or rows, or click the header of the column or row at one end of the range you want to select, press and hold Shift, and then click the header of the column or row at the other end of the range.
- To select noncontiguous columns or rows, click the header of the first column or row you want to select. Press and hold [Ctrl], and then click the headers of any additional columns and/or rows you want to select.
- To select all cells in a worksheet, point to the Select All ☐ button, and when the pointer changes to ⊕, click the left mouse button. Click any cell to cancel the selection.

Inserting and Deleting Columns or Rows

It is sometimes necessary to insert or remove rows or columns in a worksheet. The user may need to add or delete data, or perhaps it is necessary to refine the white space in a worksheet to improve its readability. **White space** refers to blank areas of a worksheet that do not contain data or documentation — regardless of the actual color. The blank space gives a document visual structure and creates a sense of order in the mind of the worksheet user.

A selected range is defined as a contiguous set of cells, columns, or rows that are all part of a single contiguous selection. However, how you select cells, columns, and rows determines whether they are a single contiguous range or are considered separate individual selections.

If you click column C, press and hold Shift, and click column E, you have created a contiguous selection of columns C:E. All three columns are highlighted as a group. But if you click column C, press and hold [Ctrl], click column D, and then click column E, you have just selected three individual columns — three individual selections. In this situation, Excel treats columns C, D, and E as noncontiguous columns — there is a white border highlighted between the columns. Whether columns or rows are contiguous or noncontiguous has an effect on how actions such as Insert are applied to a worksheet.

You want to make the golf cart analysis worksheet easier to read and to use by refining the white space. There is also a need to add some white space to the golf cart purchases worksheet because the columns and rows of information for the different golf carts are too close together. One way to add white space is to insert blank columns or blank rows to not only separate the data but also add visual interest to the worksheet. In this exercise, you will insert and delete sheet columns and rows to adjust the white space in a worksheet.

To Insert or Delete Columns and Rows

a. On the GolfCartPurchases worksheet, click cell **A4**. On the Home tab, in the Cells group, click the **Insert** arrow.

b. Click **Insert Sheet Rows**. Excel inserts a row above the active cell location and moves all cells in row 4 and below down.

c. Right-click the header for **row 8**.

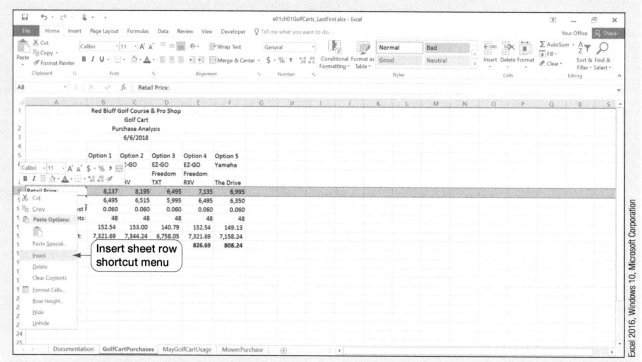

Figure 17   Inserting a sheet row by row header

d. Select **Insert** on the shortcut menu. Excel inserts a row above row 8 and moves all cells in row 8 and below down one row.

e. Select the range **A11:A12**. In the Cells group, click the **Insert** arrow, and then click **Insert Sheet Rows**. Excel inserts a row for each row in the selected range.

> ### Troubleshooting
> If you clicked the Insert button from the Cells group instead of the Insert arrow, Excel will default to inserting extra cells only, instead of a row. Press Ctrl+Z to undo the last change, and then repeat step e.

SIDE NOTE

Alternate Method

To delete a sheet row, you can also right-click a row header, and select **Delete** from the shortcut menu.

f. Select the **row headers** for rows **15:16**, and in the Cells group, click **Insert**.

Inserting two rows above and below rows 13 and 14 appears to be too much. Often, you cannot tell until you try, but the worksheet might look better if a couple of the rows of white space were removed.

g. Click the header for **row 11**, press Ctrl, and then click header for **row 15**. In the Cells group, select **Delete**.

SIDE NOTE

Alternate Method

To add or delete a column, right-click the column header, and select **Insert** or **Delete** from the shortcut menu.

h. Click the header for column C to select column C, and then, in the Cells group, select **Insert** ▦. A new column is added to the **left** of the selected column.

i. Click the header for **column E**, press and hold Ctrl, and then select **column F** and **column G** by clicking on each column header individually. Notice the white line between the columns. This is not a selected range of columns; it is three individually selected columns.

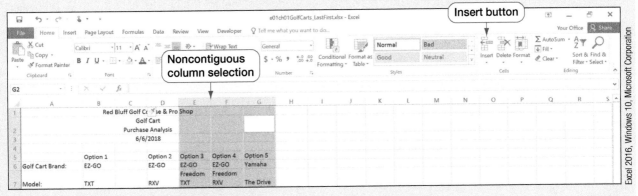

Figure 18   Selecting noncontiguous columns

SIDE NOTE

Selecting Several Rows or Columns Using Shift

Click the header of the first row or column, press Shift, and then click the last row or column.

j. In the Cells group, click **Insert** ▦.

A column has been inserted to the left of each selected column because columns E, F, and G were selected as noncontiguous individual columns. Had you selected columns E:G as a single contiguous selection, three columns would have been inserted to the left of column E.

> **Troubleshooting**
>
> If you now have three blank columns to the left of column H, you selected columns E:G as a contiguous selection. Press Ctrl+Z to Undo, and repeat steps b and c.

Notice also that the merged and centered cells in rows 1:3 expanded to include the inserted columns. This ensures that the content in rows 1:3 remains centered over the columns that were in the original merged range.

k. **Save** 🖫 the workbook.

Adjusting Column Width and Row Height

You have inserted columns and rows to add additional white space, but there is still a need to refine the amount of white space in the worksheet. At this point, there is too much — the information is spread too far apart.

Column width and row height often need to be adjusted for a couple of reasons. One reason is to reduce the amount of white space a blank column or row represents in a worksheet; the other is to allow the content of cells in a row or column to be displayed properly. Column width is defined in characters. The default width is 8.43 characters. The maximum width of a column is 255 characters. Row height is defined in points. A point is approximately 1/72 of an inch (0.035 cm). The default row height in Excel is 15 points, or approximately 1/6 of an inch (0.4 cm). A row can be up to 409 points in height (about 5.4 inches).

In this exercise, you will manually adjust column width and row height to improve the appearance of a worksheet.

 E01.14

SIDE NOTE
Alternate Method
To adjust column width, you can also right-click the selected columns, select Column Width from the pop-up menu, enter the desired column width, and click OK.

To Manually Adjust Column Width and Row Height

a. On the GolfCartPurchases worksheet, select the header for column **C**, press and hold Ctrl, and then select columns **E**, **G**, and **I**.

b. In the Cells group, click **Format** 🔲. In the Cell Size list, click **Column Width**, and then, in the Column Width dialog box, type 2.

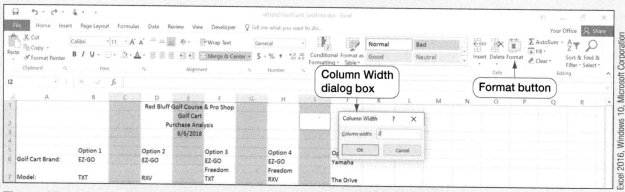

Figure 19   Column Width dialog box

SIDE NOTE
Alternate Method
To adjust row height, you can also right-click the selected rows, select Row Height from the pop-up menu, enter the desired row height, and click OK.

c. Click **OK**. By changing the column width, there is less white space between the columns.

d. Click the **row 4** header, press and hold Ctrl, and then select headers for rows **11** and **14**.

e. In the Cells group, click **Format** 🔲, and then, in the Cell Size list, click **Row Height**. In the Row Height dialog box, type 7, and then click **OK**.

f. **Save** 🔲 the workbook.

Changing Column Widths Using AutoFit

By using the AutoFit feature, column width and row height can be adjusted automatically on the basis of the width and height of selected content. AutoFit adjusts the width of columns and the height of rows to allow selected content to fit. Care is required in adjusting column widths so that data in unselected cells is not truncated or improperly displayed.

In this exercise, you will use AutoFit to adjust column width to adjust the appearance of a worksheet.

SIDE NOTE

AutoFit Row Height

AutoFit Row Height works in exactly the same manner as AutoFit Column Width.

To Use AutoFit to Adjust Column Width

a. On the GolfCartPurchases worksheet, click cell **A7**, press and hold Ctrl, and then select cells **B7**, **D7**, **F7**, **H7**, and **J7**.

b. On the Home tab, and then, in the Cells group, click **Format**, and in the Cell Size list, click **AutoFit Column Width**.

Since AutoFit sizes columns to the selected content, which in this case was individual cells, columns B and D are too narrow to display most of their numeric information, so now the information is displayed as a series of number signs (#). Notice also that column A is too narrow to display the content of most of the cells in range A6:A17, so content is truncated on the right.

c. Select column **A** by clicking the column A header, press and hold Ctrl, and then select columns **B**, **D**, **F**, **H**, and **J**.

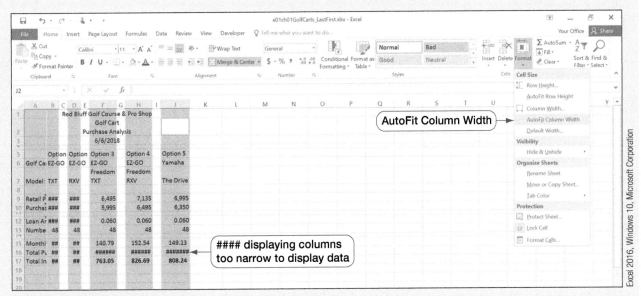

Figure 20   AutoFit Column Width results for selected cells

SIDE NOTE

Alternate Method

If you see number (#) signs in columns, point to the line between two column headers, and when the mouse pointer changes to ✛, double click.

d. In the Cells group, click **Format**. In the Cell Size list, click **AutoFit Column Width**.

Since columns were selected instead of individual cells, the columns are automatically adjusted to the widest content in the column, resulting in no number signs.

Column width can also be set manually. Column A could be a little wider than was set by AutoFit Column Width.

e. Click cell **A1** to deselect the columns. Point to the border between column A and column B. The pointer should change to ✛. Click and hold the left mouse button. Drag the mouse to the right until column A has a width of **26.00** (293 pixels). Notice the column width ScreenTip. NOTE: The number of pixels corresponding to a width of 26.00 may vary based on your monitor's screen resolution.

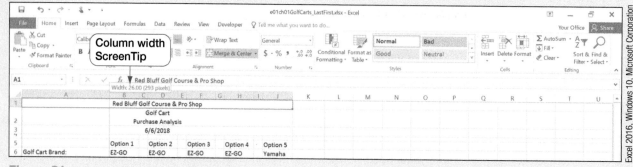

Figure 21   Manually adjust column width

f. Release the left mouse button, and then **Save** 🖫 the workbook.

g. If you need to take a break before finishing this chapter, now is a good time.

REAL WORLD ADVICE   **Quick Ways to Adjust Column Width and Row Height**

You can quickly adjust column width and row height using any of the following methods.
1. Point to the line between two column headers. The mouse pointer will change to ⟷.
2. Click and hold the left mouse button, and move the mouse left or right to adjust the width of the column to the left of the pointer, or double-click to use the AutoFit feature.

The same procedure can be used to adjust row height.
1. Point to the line between two row headers; the pointer will change to ↕.
2. Click and hold the left mouse button, and then move the mouse up or down to adjust the height of the row above the pointer, or double-click to use the AutoFit feature.

If multiple columns or rows are selected, adjusting the width or height for one selected column or row adjusts the width or height for all.

Working With and Printing Workbooks and Worksheets

Worksheets must often be printed for discussion at meetings, for distribution in venues where paper is the most effective medium, or to send digitally in a printed file format. Excel has a lot of built-in functionality that makes printed worksheets easy to read and understand. Further, as workbooks grow to include multiple worksheets and evolve to require maintenance, it is necessary to be able to create new worksheets, copy worksheets, delete worksheets, and reorder worksheets.

Manipulate Worksheets and Workbooks

Worksheets can be added to a workbook, deleted from a workbook, moved or copied within a workbook, or moved or copied to other workbooks. Sheet names are displayed on each sheet's tab at the bottom of the application window, just above the status bar (see Figure 22). The white worksheet tab identifies the active worksheet. Gray worksheet tabs identify inactive worksheets.

When a workbook contains a large number of worksheets or when the worksheets have very long names, some worksheet tabs may not be visible in the application window.

To bring tabs that are not visible into view, use the worksheet tab scrolling buttons to the left of the worksheet tabs.

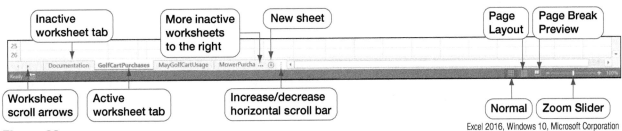

Figure 22   Worksheet tabs and controls

Creating a New Workbook

When you first open Excel, you can click Blank workbook to create a new, blank workbook. However, sometimes you may wish to create a blank workbook when Excel is already open. This can be accomplished on the File tab in Backstage view.

Barry Cheney used the golf cart analysis as an example to create an analysis of lawn mowers he is considering for purchase. The MowerPurchase worksheet is located in the Golf Carts workbook. Barry wants to present the mower analysis at an upcoming staff meeting. Therefore, he asked you to create a separate workbook for the mower analysis. In this exercise, you will create a new workbook and move or copy the appropriate worksheets to the new workbook.

  E01.16

To Create a Blank Workbook

a. If you took a break, open the **e01ch01GolfCarts** workbook. Click the **File** tab to access Backstage view, and then click **New**.

b. Available templates will appear in the right pane. Click **Blank workbook**. You will leave Backstage view and see the new blank workbook. You now have two files open in Excel.

c. Click the **File** tab, click **Save**, and under Save As, click **Browse**. In the Save As dialog box, navigate to the location where you are saving your files. In the File name box, type e01ch01Mowers_LastFirst using your last and first name.

d. Click **Save**. You have now created a new, blank workbook.

Moving and Copying Worksheets Between Workbooks

Well-developed worksheets are often used as the starting point for new worksheets. Excel makes it easy to copy worksheets from one workbook to another.

Barry has asked you to create a separate workbook for the mower analysis. In this exercise, to save yourself some time, you have decided to copy the MowerPurchase and Documentation worksheets from the GolfCarts workbook to the new Mowers workbook instead of recreating them.

To Move or Copy a Worksheet to Another Workbook

a. Press Ctrl+Tab to make **e01ch01GolfCarts_LastFirst** the active workbook.

> **Troubleshooting**
>
> If Ctrl+Tab did not make e01ch01GolfCarts_LastFirst the active workbook, there are two possible explanations. One is that you have more than two workbooks open. If that is the case, you need to press Ctrl+Tab more than once to cycle through open workbooks until e01ch01GolfCarts_LastFirst is active. The other possibility is that you closed e01ch01GolfCarts_LastFirst. In this case, you will need to open the file, at which time it will be the active workbook.

b. Right-click the **MowerPurchase** worksheet tab, and then select **Move or Copy** in the shortcut menu.

c. In the Move or Copy dialog box, click the **To book** arrow, and then click **e01ch01Mowers_LastFirst**. Leave Sheet1 selected in the **Before sheet** section.

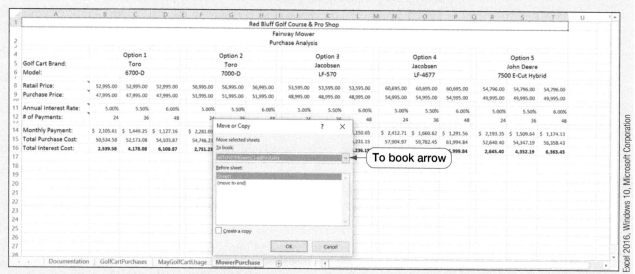

Figure 23   Move or Copy dialog box

d. Click **OK**. The MowerPurchase worksheet is moved to the e01ch01Mowers_LastFirst workbook, which is now the active workbook.

e. Press Ctrl+Tab to make **e01ch01GolfCarts_LastFirst** the active workbook.

f. If necessary, scroll to the left to view the Documentation worksheet. Right-click the **Documentation** worksheet tab, and then select **Move or Copy** in the shortcut menu. In the Move or Copy dialog box, click the **To book** arrow, and then click **e01ch01Mowers_LastFirst**. In the **Before sheet** box, click **Sheet1**, and click the **Create a copy** check box.

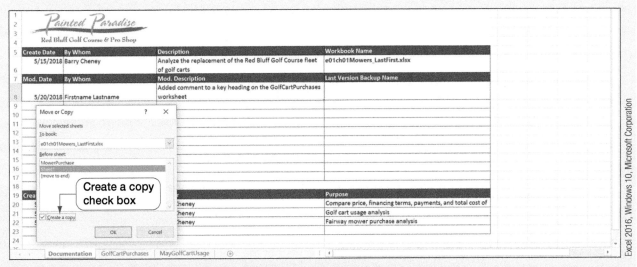

Figure 24 Copy a worksheet to another workbook

g. Click **OK**. The Documentation worksheet is copied to the e01ch01Mowers_LastFirst workbook, which is now the active workbook.

h. In the Documentation worksheet of the **e01ch01Mowers_LastFirst** workbook, select cell range **A20:D21**. Press and hold Ctrl, select cell **C8**, and then press Delete.

i. Right-click the header for row **22**, and select **Cut**. Right-click the header for row **20**, and then click **Paste**. The documentation that had been in line 22 should now be in line 20.

j. Double-click cell **C6**. Position the insertion point after **carts**, delete **fleet of golf carts**, type fairway mowers, and then press Enter. Click **Save** 💾.

k. Press Ctrl+Tab to make **e01ch01GolfCarts_LastFirst** the active workbook. In the **Documentation** worksheet, select cell range **A22:D22**, and press Delete.

l. **Save** 💾 the workbook.

Deleting, Inserting, Renaming, and Coloring Worksheet Tabs

Unused worksheets are a form of clutter in a workbook and add unnecessary size to the stored workbook file, so it is best practice to delete any unused sheets in a workbook. Do so with caution, however, because deleting a worksheet removes it from a workbook. This action cannot be undone. Inserted worksheets are by default given a name such as "Sheet2" in which the number is one larger than the last number used for a worksheet name. An inserted worksheet is automatically the active worksheet. To insert a worksheet, move to the right of the list of worksheet tabs, and click New sheet ⊕. In Excel 2016, new worksheets are always inserted to the right of the active worksheet.

The default worksheet names are not particularly descriptive and do nothing to help document the contents or purpose of a worksheet. Worksheets can be renamed in two ways: by double-clicking the worksheet tab and typing a descriptive name or by right-clicking the worksheet tab and then clicking Rename on the shortcut menu. Worksheet names can be up to 31 characters long. Worksheet tabs can also be colored to add interest or for visual separation of the worksheets.

Now that you have created a separate workbook for the mower purchase analysis, Barry wants you to prepare a worksheet in the golf cart purchase analysis to extend the golf cart usage analysis to the month of June. He has asked you to create a new worksheet and to use the May usage analysis as a starting point. You just need to create the worksheet and get it ready for Barry to enter the data later. First, you should remove any unnecessary worksheets from the mower analysis workbook.

In this exercise, you will delete, insert, rename, and color worksheets.

SIDE NOTE
Be Careful — There Is No Undo!
Most workbook and worksheet manipulation, such as deleting a worksheet, cannot be undone.

To Delete, Insert, Rename, and Color Worksheet Tabs

a. Press Ctrl+Tab to make **e01ch01Mowers_LastFirst** the active workbook, and then right-click the **Sheet1** worksheet tab.

b. Select **Delete** in the shortcut menu. Click **Save** 🖫.

c. Now prepare a new golf cart usage analysis worksheet for June. Press Ctrl+Tab to make **e01ch01GolfCarts_LastFirst** the active workbook.

d. Click the **MayGolfCartUsage** worksheet tab.

e. Click **New sheet** ⊕ to the right of the worksheet tabs. A new Sheet1 worksheet is inserted to the right of the MayGolfCartUsage worksheet.

f. Double-click the **Sheet1** worksheet tab, type JuneGolfCartUsage, and then press Enter.

g. Right-click the **JuneGolfCartUsage** worksheet tab, and point to **Tab Color**.

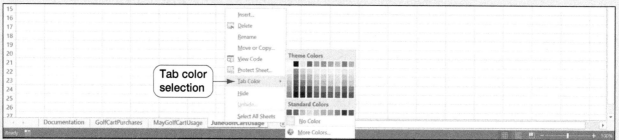

Figure 25 Worksheet tab color

Excel 2016, Windows 10, Microsoft Corporation

h. Select **Blue, Accent 1** in the top row, fifth column.

i. Right-click the **MayGolfCartUsage** worksheet tab, point to **Tab Color**, and then select **Orange, Accent 2** in the top row, sixth column.

j. **Save** 🖫 the workbook.

Using Series (AutoFill)

The AutoFill feature is a powerful way to minimize the effort required to enter certain types of data. **AutoFill** copies information from one cell or a series in contiguous cells into contiguous cells in the direction in which the fill handle is dragged. AutoFill is a smart copy that will try to guess how you want values or formulas changed as you copy. Sometimes, AutoFill will save significant time by changing the contents correctly. Other times, AutoFill changes the contents in a way you did not intend. When that happens, Auto Fill Options 🖳 makes options available that may be helpful.

The fill handle is a small green square in the bottom right corner of the active cell border. To engage the AutoFill feature, drag the fill handle in the direction in which you wish to expand the active cell. When you point to and drag the fill handle, the mouse pointer is a thin black plus sign [+].

To make the JuneGolfCartUsage worksheet ready for data entry, in this exercise you will copy and then clear some of the May data. You will also generate date information for June.

To Quickly Generate Data Using AutoFill

E01.19

a. On the MayGolfCartUsage worksheet, press Ctrl+Home to make cell A1 the active cell, and then press Ctrl+A to select the entire worksheet.

b. Press Ctrl+C to copy the contents of the MayGolfCartUsage worksheet.

c. Click the **JuneGolfCartUsage** worksheet tab, press Ctrl+Home to ensure that cell A1 is the active cell, and then press Ctrl+V to paste the contents from the May worksheet.

d. Click cell **A11**. If necessary, scroll down until you can see cell A41. Press and hold Shift, and then click cell **A41**. Cell range A11:A41 should be selected. Press Delete.

e. June contains one less day than May. Therefore, you need to delete one row of the daily data. Right-click the header for **row 12**, and then select **Delete** in the shortcut menu.

f. Double-click cell **H3**, delete the word **May**, and then type June.

g. Click cell **A11**. Type 06/01/2018, and then press Ctrl+Enter.

h. Click and hold the fill handle, drag the fill handle down until the border around the cell range expands to include cells **A11:A40**, and then release the left mouse button.

Notice that the date is incremented by one day in each cell from top to bottom. Also notice the Auto Fill Options ☐ button.

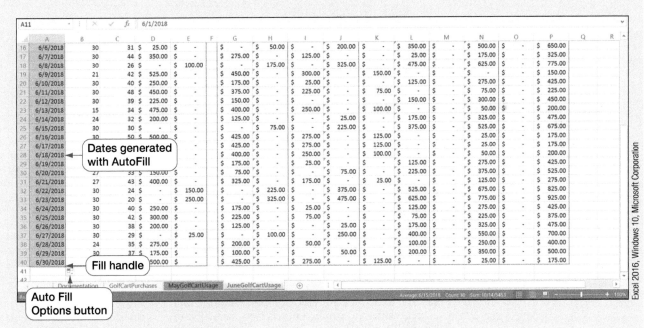

Figure 26 Generate data using AutoFill

i. Click the **Auto Fill Options** ☐ button.

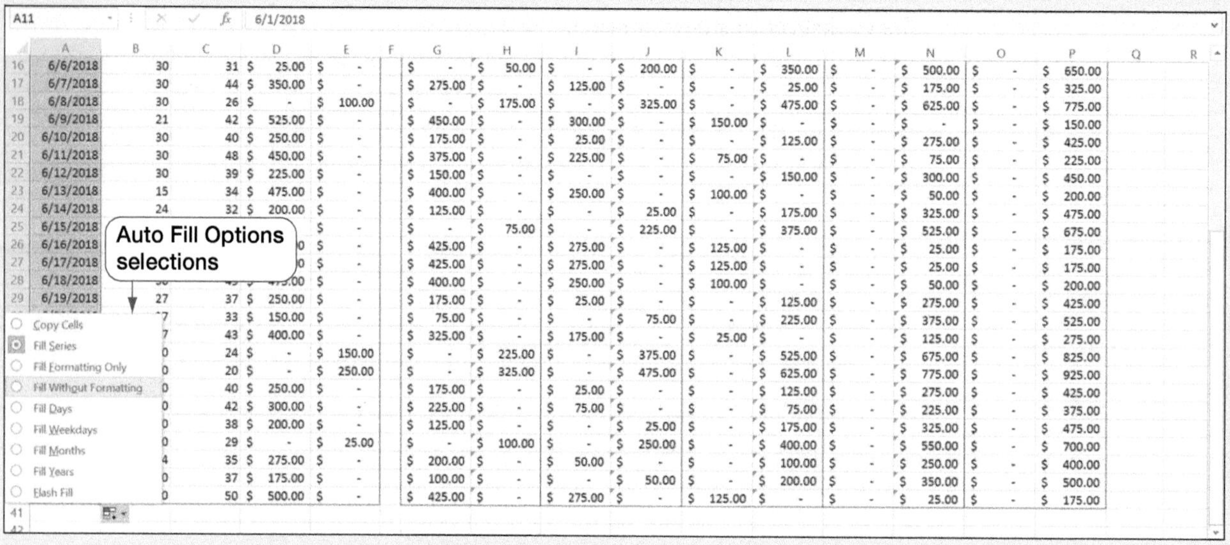

	A	B	C	D	E	F	G	H	I	J	K	L	M	N	O	P
16	6/6/2018	30	31	$ 25.00	$ -		$ -	$ 50.00	$ -	$ 200.00	$ -	$ 350.00	$ -	$ 500.00	$ -	$ 650.00
17	6/7/2018	30	44	$ 350.00	$ -		$ 275.00	$ -	$ 125.00	$ -	$ -	$ 25.00	$ -	$ 175.00	$ -	$ 325.00
18	6/8/2018	30	26	$ -	$ 100.00		$ -	$ 175.00	$ -	$ 325.00	$ -	$ 475.00	$ -	$ 625.00	$ -	$ 775.00
19	6/9/2018	21	42	$ 525.00	$ -		$ 450.00	$ -	$ 300.00	$ -	$ 150.00	$ -		$ -	$ -	$ 150.00
20	6/10/2018	30	40	$ 250.00	$ -		$ 175.00	$ -	$ 25.00	$ -	$ -	$ 125.00	$ -	$ 275.00	$ -	$ 425.00
21	6/11/2018	30	48	$ 450.00	$ -		$ 375.00	$ -	$ 225.00	$ -	$ 75.00	$ -	$ -	$ 75.00	$ -	$ 225.00
22	6/12/2018	30	39	$ 225.00	$ -		$ 150.00	$ -	$ -	$ -	$ -	$ 150.00	$ -	$ 300.00	$ -	$ 450.00
23	6/13/2018	15	34	$ 475.00	$ -		$ 400.00	$ -	$ 250.00	$ -	$ 100.00	$ -	$ -	$ 50.00	$ -	$ 200.00
24	6/14/2018	24	32	$ 200.00	$ -		$ 125.00	$ -	$ -	$ 25.00	$ -	$ 175.00	$ -	$ 325.00	$ -	$ 475.00
25	6/15/2018				$ -		$ -	$ 75.00	$ -	$ 225.00	$ -	$ 375.00	$ -	$ 525.00	$ -	$ 675.00
26	6/16/2018						$ 425.00	$ -	$ 275.00	$ -	$ 125.00	$ -	$ -	$ 25.00	$ -	$ 175.00
27	6/17/2018						$ 425.00	$ -	$ 275.00	$ -	$ 125.00	$ -	$ -	$ 25.00	$ -	$ 175.00
28	6/18/2018						$ 400.00	$ -	$ 250.00	$ -	$ 100.00	$ -	$ -	$ 50.00	$ -	$ 200.00
29	6/19/2018	27	37	$ 250.00			$ 175.00	$ -	$ 25.00	$ -	$ -	$ 125.00	$ -	$ 275.00	$ -	$ 425.00

Auto Fill Options selections

Fill options menu: Copy Cells / Fill Series / Fill Formatting Only / Fill Without Formatting / Fill Days / Fill Weekdays / Fill Months / Fill Years / Flash Fill

Figure 27 AutoFill Options menu

Excel 2016, Windows 10, Microsoft Corporation

j. Click **Fill Without Formatting** so the border of cell A40 does not disappear. Press Home to deselect the AutoFill range.

k. If necessary, scroll to the left, and then click the **Documentation** worksheet tab. Click cell **A22**, and then press Ctrl+; to insert today's date. Press Tab, type JuneGolfCartUsage, and then press Tab. Type your name in Firstname Lastname format, press Tab, and then type G.

Since you entered text, Excel examines other contiguous cells that contain content in the same column and uses the AutoComplete feature, which completes the entry with other cell contents that begin with "G".

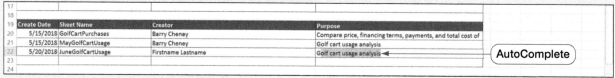

	Create Date	Sheet Name	Creator	Purpose
19				
20	5/15/2018	GolfCartPurchases	Barry Cheney	Compare price, financing terms, payments, and total cost of
21	5/15/2018	MayGolfCartUsage	Barry Cheney	Golf cart usage analysis
22	5/20/2018	JuneGolfCartUsage	Firstname Lastname	Golf cart usage analysis ◄ AutoComplete

Figure 28 AutoComplete

Excel 2016, Windows 10, Microsoft Corporation

Troubleshooting

If you didn't see the AutoComplete feature after typing a G, the AutoComplete feature may be disabled. To enable the AutoComplete feature, click the File tab, select Options, Advanced, and then check Enable AutoComplete for cell values.

l. Press Enter to accept the AutoComplete suggestion.

m. **Save** 🖫 the workbook.

Moving or Copying a Worksheet

The order of worksheets in a workbook can be changed by reordering the worksheet tabs. To move a worksheet, make the worksheet you wish to move the active worksheet by clicking on its tab. Click and hold the worksheet tab, drag the worksheet tab to its new location, and drop it by releasing the mouse button. As a worksheet is dragged, a small black triangle will appear between worksheet tabs. This indicates the location where the worksheet will be inserted if the mouse button is released.

If a new worksheet needs to be created that will be similar to another worksheet in the workbook, the worksheet can be copied to save time. To copy a worksheet within a

Excel 2016, Windows 10, Microsoft Corporation

workbook, after clicking on the worksheet tab, press and hold Ctrl, and drag a copy of the worksheet to a new location.

In the golf carts workbook, the Documentation worksheet is the first worksheet tab on the far left. Painted Paradise Resort & Spa standards require the Documentation worksheet to be the far-right worksheet in a workbook. In this exercise, you will move and copy worksheets.

E01.20

To Move and Copy a Worksheet

a. In the e01ch01GolfCarts_LastFirst workbook, click and hold the **Documentation** worksheet tab. The mouse pointer will change to the move worksheet pointer. Drag the mouse to the right until ▾ appears to the right of the JuneGolfCartUsage worksheet tab.

19	Create Date	Sheet Name	Creator	Purpose
20	5/15/2018	GolfCartPurchases	Barry Cheney	Compare price, financing terms, payments, and total cost of
21	5/15/2018	MayGolfCartUsage	Barry Cheney	Golf cart usage analysis
22	5/20/2018	JuneGolfCartUsage	Firstname Lastname	Golf cart usage analysis
23				
24				

Move worksheet triangle

Documentation GolfCartPurchases MayGolfCartUsage JuneGolfCartUsage

Figure 29 Move a worksheet

Excel 2016, Windows 10, Microsoft Corporation

SIDE NOTE

Copying a Worksheet
Worksheets can also be copied by right-clicking the worksheet tab and selecting **Create a copy** from the Move or Copy dialog box.

b. Release the mouse button. The Documentation sheet is now the last worksheet tab on the right.

Barry has decided that he wants the most recent golf cart usage analysis to be first (leftmost) in the sequence of worksheets. You need to move the JuneGolfCartUsage worksheet tab to the left of the MayGolfCartUsage worksheet tab.

c. Click and hold the **JuneGolfCartUsage** worksheet tab, drag to the left of MayGolfCartUsage, and then release the mouse button. The worksheets are now in the following order from left to right: GolfCartPurchases, JuneGolfCartUsage, MayGolfCartUsage, and Documentation.

Barry also wants you to create a JulyGolfCartUsage worksheet. He has decided that three months of usage data will help him better determine the number of carts to purchase. Rather than creating a new worksheet and then copying a range of cells from another worksheet, this time you will copy the MayGolfCartUsage worksheet in its entirety to a new worksheet.

d. Click and hold the **MayGolfCartUsage** worksheet tab, and then press and hold Ctrl. The mouse pointer will change from 🔩 to the Copy Worksheet pointer 🔩. Move the mouse to the left until ▾ appears to the left of the JuneGolfCartUsage worksheet tab. Release the mouse button.

e. A copy of the MayGolfCartUsage worksheet has been created, called "MayGolfCartUsage (2)". Double-click the **MayGolfCartUsage (2)** worksheet tab, type JulyGolfCartUsage, and then press Enter.

f. Right-click the **JulyGolfCartUsage** worksheet tab, point to **Tab Color**, and then select **Gold, Accent 4**, in the top row, eighth column.

g. Double-click cell **H3**, delete the word **May**, and then type July.

h. Click cell **A11**. Type 07/01/2018, and then press Ctrl+Enter.

i. Double-click the **fill handle** to fill the dates in the range A11:A41 Scroll, if necessary, to see row 41. Click the AutoFill Options ⊞, and then select **Fill Without Formatting**.

j. Press Ctrl+Home to deselect the Auto Fill range.

k. Click the **Documentation** worksheet tab, click cell **A23**, and then press Ctrl+; to insert today's date. Press Tab, type JulyGolfCartUsage, and then press Tab. Type your name in Firstname Lastname format, press Tab, and then type G and press Enter to use Auto Complete to fill in the remainder of the text.

l. Click the **JulyGolfCartUsage** worksheet tab.

SIDE NOTE

Navigating Between Worksheets

Press Ctrl+PgUp to go to the prior worksheet. Press Ctrl+PgDn to go to the next worksheet.

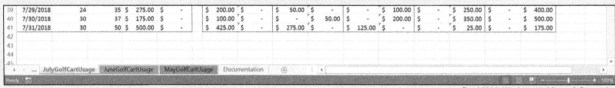

39	7/29/2018	24	35	$ 275.00	$ -		$ 200.00	$ -		$ 50.00	$ -		$ -		$ 100.00	$ -		$ 250.00	$ -		$ 400.00
40	7/30/2018	30	37	$ 175.00	$ -		$ 100.00	$ -		$ -	$ 50.00		$ -		$ 200.00	$ -		$ 350.00	$ -		$ 500.00
41	7/31/2018	30	50	$ 500.00	$ -		$ 425.00	$ -		$ 275.00	$ -		$ 125.00		$ -		$ -		$ 25.00	$ -		$ 175.00

JulyGolfCartUsage JuneGolfCartUsage MayGolfCartUsage Documentation

Figure 30   Worksheet tabs moved and copied

Excel 2016, Windows 10, Microsoft Corporation

m. **Save** 🖫 the workbook.

Preview, Print, and Export Workbooks

Excel has a great deal of flexibility built into its printing functionality. To appropriately present your work in printed form, it is important that you understand how to take advantage of Excel's previewing, printing, and exporting features.

Using Worksheet Views

In the bottom right corner of the application window are three icons that control the worksheet view. **Normal view** ▦ is what you use most of the time when building and editing a worksheet. Only the cells in the worksheet are visible; print-specific features such as margins, headers, footers, and page breaks are not displayed.

Page Layout view ▦ shows page margins, print headers and footers, and page breaks. It presents you with a reasonable preview of how a worksheet will print on paper.

Page Break Preview ▦ does not show page margins, headers, or footers, but it allows you to manually adjust the location of page breaks. This is particularly helpful when you would like to force a page break after a set of summary values and/or between data categories and force part of a worksheet to print on a new page.

Excel places a default page break wherever it is necessary to split content between pages. If the size of content changes, the location of a default break can change. A hard page break remains in its defined location until you move it. Changes in content size have no effect on the location of a hard page break. In this exercise, you will switch among worksheet views and adjust page breaks.

To Switch Among Worksheet Views and Adjust Page Breaks

a. Select the **e01ch01Mowers_LastFirst** workbook, and click the **MowerPurchase** worksheet tab.

b. Click the **File** tab, and then click **Print**.

Notice that the worksheet does not print on a single page; nor does information break across pages correctly.

c. Press ⌈Esc⌋ to leave Backstage view, and then click **Page Break Preview** 🔲 on the status bar.

Only the part of the worksheet that will print is displayed. A dashed blue border indicates where printing will break from one page to another.

d. Use the Zoom Slider ⌈━━━━━┃━━━⌋ to decrease the zoom level to make the pages as large as possible without having any data not be visible in the application window.

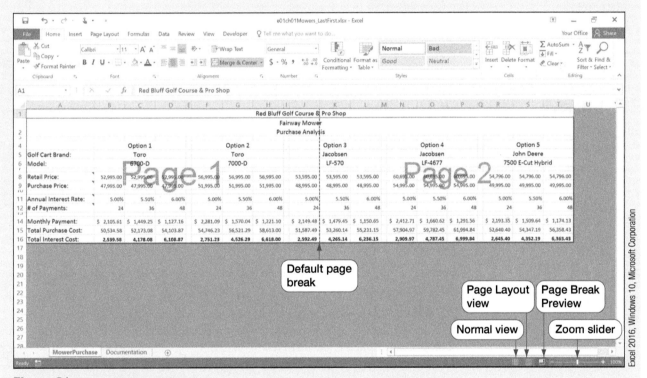

Figure 31   Page Break Preview

Now move the default page break, since it divides Option 3 between two pages.

e. Move the mouse pointer over the **vertical dashed line** between columns **J** and **K** to display the Vertical Page Break pointer ↔. Click and drag the page break between columns **I** and **J**.

Notice that the page break changes to a solid blue line. By moving the page break, you changed it from a default break to a hard page break. Now you need to insert a new page break so that Option 5 will print on a separate page.

f. On the ribbon, click the **Page Layout** tab — not Page Layout on the status bar.

g. Click cell **R2**. In the Page Setup group, click **Breaks**, and then select **Insert Page Break**.

Two page breaks are inserted: a horizontal page break above the active cell and a vertical page break to the left of the active cell. You want only the vertical page break between columns Q and R.

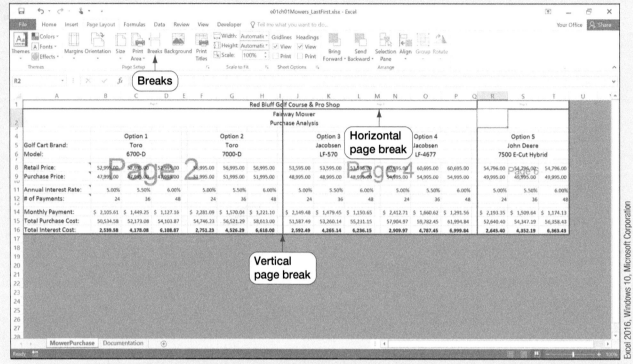

Figure 32 Horizontal and vertical page breaks in Page Break Preview

h. Point to the **horizontal page break**, and the mouse pointer will change to ↕. Drag the horizontal page break off the bottom or top of the print area to remove it. There should now be a page break after column I and a page break after column Q.

Notice that the titles in rows 1:2 are split between two pages. You need to remove them from the print area.

i. Point to the **top border**, and the mouse pointer will change to the Horizontal Page Break pointer ↕. Click and hold the left mouse button, and then move the top border down until it is between rows 2 and 3.

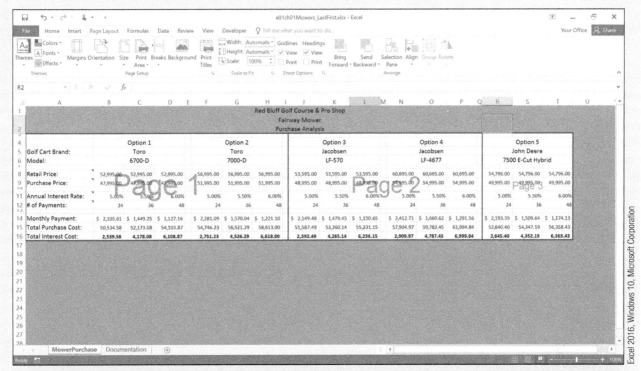

Figure 33 Page Break Preview

j. Click **Page Layout** 🗔 on the status bar, and then press Ctrl+Home. Page Layout view displays the worksheet with print margins. A thin border shows which part(s) of the worksheet will be printed on a page and also shows the location of the header.

k. Click **Normal** ▦ on the status bar. The thin lines between rows 2 and 3, between rows 16 and 17, between columns I and J, and between columns Q and R show the print area and the locations of page breaks.

l. **Save** 🗄 the workbook.

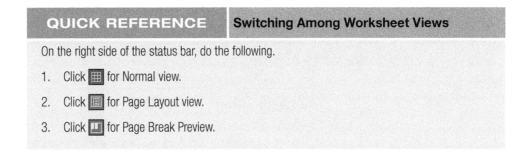

QUICK REFERENCE	Switching Among Worksheet Views

On the right side of the status bar, do the following.

1. Click ▦ for Normal view.

2. Click 🗔 for Page Layout view.

3. Click ▥ for Page Break Preview.

Using Print Preview and Printer Selection

Print Preview is the backstage view of how a document, workbook, presentation, table, or other object will appear when printed. You can use the scroll bar on the right or the page navigation arrows on the bottom to view additional pages if your worksheet requires more than one page to print.

More than one print device can be made available to a computer. Always pay attention to the printer name before printing, and be sure to select the device you want to use. The default printer is selected automatically and is usually acceptable. When a different printer is required, click the Printer Status arrow to see a list of available devices.

Printing a worksheet is as simple as clicking the Print button on the Print tab in Backstage view. If you want to print more than one copy, change the number in the Copies box to the right of the Print button. The copy count can be increased or decreased by clicking the arrows or by clicking in the Copies box and entering the number of copies from the keyboard. In this exercise, you will print preview your workbook to prepare it for distribution.

To Print Preview

a. On the MowerPurchase worksheet, click the **File** tab, and then click **Print**. If your computer has access to a printer, the Printer box displays the default printer. Click the Printer Status arrow to determine what print devices are available on your network. The right pane displays a preview of what will print.

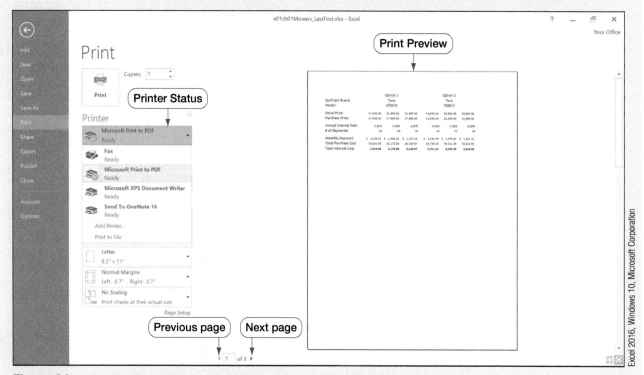

Figure 34 Print Preview and the Printer list

> ### Troubleshooting
> The list of devices displayed in the Printer list is determined by your installation, so the list of available printers will not match those shown in Figure 34.

b. Click the **Next Page** button ▶ to view page 2, and then click the **Next Page** button ▶ to view page 3.

Notice that pages 2 and 3 do not have any row headings. None of the pages have a page title. There is more to be done before this worksheet is ready for printing.

c. Press Esc to leave Backstage view.

d. **Save** 🖫 the workbook.

Using Print Titles

When a worksheet is too large to print on a single page, it is often difficult to keep track of what information is being viewed from one page to another. Headers, such as those in column A of the golf cart analysis, are printed only on the first page.

Print titles can be included on each printed page so every column and/or row is labeled and easily identified from one page to another. Since you set page breaks between cart categories, you should print at least one column on each page that identifies cell contents in each row. In this exercise, you will specify print titles to prepare the worksheet to print.

To Specify Print Titles

a. On the MowerPurchase worksheet, click the **Page Layout** tab, and then, in the Page Setup group, click **Print Titles**. The Page Setup dialog box will appear.

b. On the Sheet tab of the Page Setup dialog box, under Print titles, in the **Columns to repeat at left** box, type A:A as shown in Figure 35.

   The Print Titles feature requires the specification of a range, even when only a single column will be printed — thus the need to enter column A as A:A.

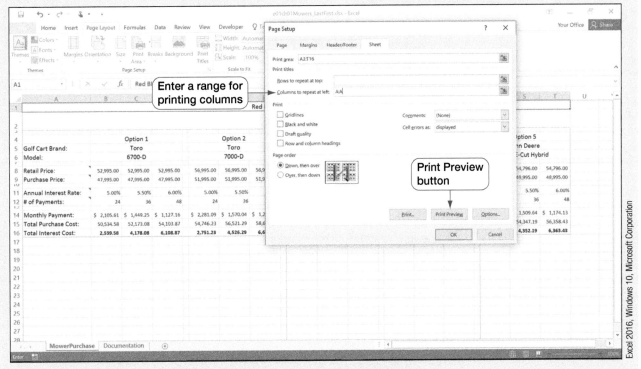

Figure 35   Sheet tab in the Page Setup dialog box for creating print titles

SIDE NOTE
Alternate Method
You can also press the Excel Back button ⊙ to exit Backstage view.

c. Click **Print Preview**. In the Print Preview pane, click ▶ to view page 2, and then click ▶ again to view page 3.

d. Notice that pages 2 and 3 now have row headings. Press Esc to exit Backstage view.

e. **Save** ⊟ the workbook.

Adding Headers and Footers

There are often items of information that should be included on a printed document that are not necessary in a worksheet. These items might include the following.

- Print date
- Print time
- Company name
- Page number
- Total number of pages
- File name and location

Headers place information at the top of each printed page. Footers place information at the bottom of each printed page. Headers and footers are divided into three sections: left, center, and right. Information can be placed in any combination of the sections. You may include information in either the header or the footer or both, as deemed necessary. In this exercise, you will add a header and a footer to prepare the worksheet to print.

To Add a Header and a Footer

a. On the **MowerPurchase** worksheet tab, press Ctrl+Home to make A1 the active cell.

b. Click **Page Layout** 🔲 on the status bar. If necessary, use the **Zoom Slider** ─────┃─────+ to adjust zoom to 100%.

c. Click **Add header** in the top margin of Page Layout view. The Design tab for Header & Footer Tools will appear on the ribbon. If necessary, click the **Header & Footer Tools Design** tab.

d. Click the left section of the header, and then, in the Header & Footer Elements group, click **Current Date**.

e. Click the center section of the header, type Red Bluff Golf Course && Pro Shop, press Enter, type Mower Purchase Analysis, and then press Tab. The ampersand (&) performs a special function in headers and footers. It indicates the start of a field name. To display "&" in the print header, it must be entered twice.

f. In the right section of the header, in the Header & Footer Elements group, click **Page Number**, press Spacebar to add a space, type of, and press Spacebar to add a space.

g. In the Header & Footer Elements group, click **Number of Pages**.

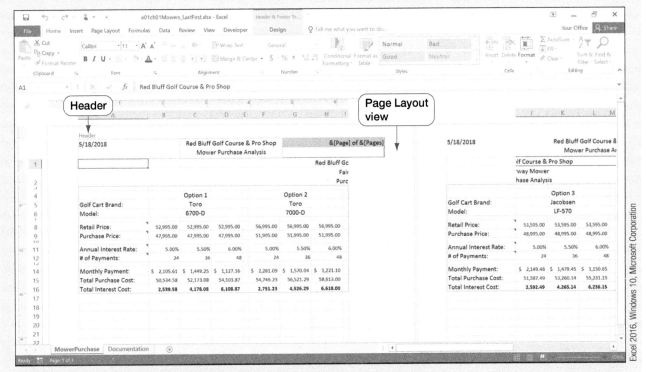

Figure 36 Page Layout view with header information added

h. In the Navigation group, click **Go to Footer**.

i. Click the left section of the footer, and then, in the Header & Footer Elements group, click **File Name**. Select any cell in the worksheet, press Ctrl+Home, and then, on the status bar, click **Normal** 🔲.

j. Click the **File** tab, and then click **Print**. In the Print Preview pane, scroll through the pages to see that the header and footer are added to every page.

k. If your computer is attached to a printer, the Printer Status control displays the default printer. If you want to print to a different printer, click the Printer Status arrow next to the printer name, and then select the desired printer from the list. If requested by your instructor, click **Print**. If you are not instructed to print, press Esc.

l. **Save** 🔲 and **Close** ✖ the e01ch01Mowers_LastFirst workbook, and then submit your file as directed by your instructor.

Changing Page Margins and Scaling

Page margins are the white space at the edges of the printed page. Normal margins for Excel are 0.7 inch on the left and right sides of the page, 0.75 inch on the top and bottom of the page, and 0.3 inch for the header and footer if included.

Margins can be changed to suit conventions or standards for an organization, to better locate information on the page, or to avoid a page break at the last column or line of a worksheet.

It is not uncommon for worksheets to be too large to print on a single page or to be so small that they appear lost in the top left corner of the page. Scaling changes the size of the print font to allow more of a worksheet to be printed on a page or for a worksheet to be printed larger and use more page space. A printed worksheet that has been scaled to fit a sheet of paper generally looks more professional and is easier to read and understand than a worksheet that is printed on two pages that uses only a small part of the second page.

Barry Cheney wants you to prepare the golf cart analysis workbook for printing. Before you print, you want to preview the pages and make and adjustments in page margins or scaling to be sure the worksheets print on single pages. In this exercise, you will change the scaling and page margins of three worksheets.

To Change Page Margins and Scaling

a. On the **e01ch01GolfCarts_LastFirst** workbook, click the **MayGolfCartUsage** worksheet tab. Click the **File** tab, and then click **Print**. Notice that the worksheet would not fit on one page if it were to be printed.

b. Under Settings, click the Scaling arrow — the last setting. Select **Fit All Columns on One Page**.

c. Click the **Margins** arrow, just above the Scaling setting, and then, in the Margins list, select **Narrow**. Press Esc.

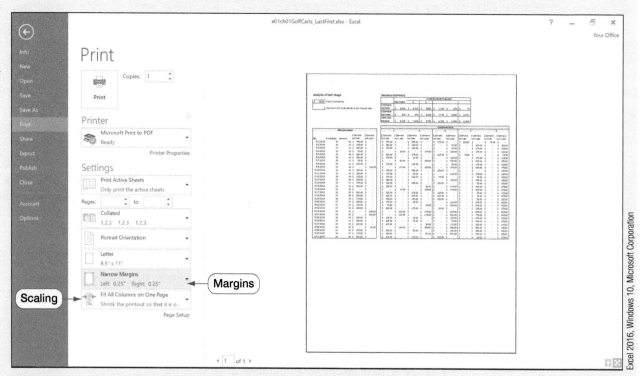

Figure 37 Print Preview with scaling control and narrow margins

d. Repeat steps b through c for the **JuneGolfCartUsage** and **JulyGolfCartUsage** worksheet tabs.

e. **Save** the workbook.

Changing Page Orientation and Print Range

Worksheets can be oriented to print on paper in one of two ways: portrait or landscape. **Landscape orientation** indicates that the page is wider than it is tall. Landscape orientation is generally used when a worksheet has too many columns to print well on a single page in portrait orientation. **Portrait orientation** indicates that the page is taller than it is wide. Scaling the worksheet to fit all columns on a single page can work in portrait orientation, but if scaling makes the data too small to be readable, landscape orientation is an option.

Print range defines what part of a workbook will be printed. The default is Print Active Sheets. This is often adequate, but you can also choose to print only a selected range of cells or to print the entire workbook.

Barry Cheney does not like the last printout you produced of the Documentation worksheet; the print is too small. He suggests changing the page orientation to landscape. In this exercise, you will change the page orientation of a worksheet.

To Change Page Orientation and Print Range

a. Click the **Documentation** worksheet tab. Click the **File** tab and then click **Print**.

b. Click the **Orientation** arrow — fourth from the bottom under Settings — and then select **Landscape Orientation**.

c. Click the Print Range arrow — the first setting under Settings — and then select **Print Entire Workbook**. Notice that five pages will print.

d. Scroll through the pages to preview how the workbook would print. Click **Print** if requested by your instructor, or press Esc.

e. **Save** 🖫 the workbook.

Exporting a Workbook to PDF

Portable Document Format (PDF), which was developed by Adobe Systems in 1993, is a file type that preserves most formatting attributes of a source document regardless of the software in which the document was created. PDF preserves exactly the original "look and feel" of a document but allows the document to be viewed in many different applications. Exporting to PDF is a great way to document your worksheets. One way to distribute a worksheet or workbook in a manner that allows it to be read by anyone with a free PDF reader application is to export the worksheet or entire workbook to PDF.

Now that you have the e01ch01GolfCarts_LastFirst workbook prepared for distribution, Barry wants a PDF version. In this exercise, you will export the workbook to PDF.

To Export a Workbook to PDF

a. With the **e01ch01GolfCarts_LastFirst** workbook open, click the **File** tab, and then click **Export**.

b. In the right pane, under Create a PDF/XPS Document, click **Create PDF/XPS**.

c. In the Publish as PDF or XPS dialog box, click **Options**. In the Options dialog box, under Publish what, click **Entire workbook**.

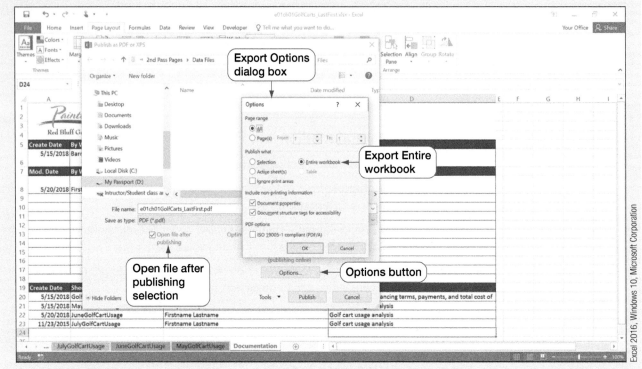

Figure 38 Export Options dialog box

d. Click **OK**. In the Publish as PDF or XPS dialog box, be sure **Open file after publishing** is checked.

e. Navigate to where you are saving your Excel files, verify the file name listed in the File name box to be e01ch01GolfCarts_LastFirst using your last and first name, and then click **Publish**.

f. Once the PDF file has been created, it may be opened in Reader, the built-in Windows 10 PDF document viewer.

Troubleshooting

Your PDF file may not open in Reader if a different PDF reader, such as Adobe Reader, is installed as the default PDF file reader. If the PDF file displays in a different reader, close the reader and skip step g.

g. Right-click anywhere on the screen. A menu bar will appear at the bottom of the screen. Click **More**.

h. Click **Close** to close the PDF file.

i. **Save** 🖫 the workbook, exit Excel, and then submit your files as directed by your instructor.

Concept Check

1. Explain the following terms for a reader who is not familiar with Excel.

   - Worksheet p. 325
   - Workbook p. 326
   - Cell p. 325
   - Row p. 325
   - Column p. 325
   - Spreadsheet p. 325

2. How do you quickly navigate to the last row in a worksheet that contains data? What happens when you press End in Excel? How do you move from one worksheet to another in Excel? What purpose does the Go To dialog box serve? How do you access the Go To dialog box? p. 330

3. Why is documentation important? Why do many people not properly document their workbooks? What are the possible costs associated with inadequate documentation? p. 333

4. What happens if you select a cell that contains important data, type "Your Office", and then press Enter? How does the outcome change if you first double-click a cell that contains important data, type "Your Office", and then press Enter? p. 340–341

5. How do you select noncontiguous cells? Is the ability to select noncontiguous cells important to the effective use of Excel? If yes, why? If no, why make use of noncontiguous cell selection? p. 345

6. Describe two ways in which columns and rows can be inserted and deleted. p. 345

7. How do you reorder worksheets in a workbook? p. 351

8. Explain the purpose of print titles, page headers, and page footers and describe when you would use them. What are page orientation and scaling, and how can they be used in tandem to allow you to efficiently print a professional-looking worksheet? p. 363

Key Terms

Active cell 329
Active worksheet 326
AutoFill 354
Cell 325
Cell range 337
Cell reference 329
Clipboard 337
Column 325
Comment 332
Contiguous cell range 337
Date data 334
Destination cell 337

Field 325
Formula 325
Function 325
Keyboard shortcut 329
Landscape orientation 366
Merge & Center 343
Noncontiguous cell range 337
Normal view 358
Numeric data 334
Page Break Preview 358
Page Layout view 358
Portable Document
    Format (PDF) 367

Portrait orientation 366
Print Preview 361
Record 325
Row 325
Spreadsheet 325
Text data 334
Time data 334
Touch mode 331
What-if analysis 325
White space 345
Workbook 326
Worksheet 325

Export a workbook to PDF (p. 367)

Understand spreadsheet terminology and components (p. 325)

Use AutoFit to adjust column width (p. 349)

Manipulate columns and rows (p. 345)

Manipulate cells and cell ranges (p. 337)

Wrap text in a cell (p. 336)

Enter and edit data (p. 334)

Manually adjust column width and row height (p. 348)

Merge & Center headings (p. 343)

Navigate within a worksheet (p. 330)

Select, copy and paste to contiguous and noncontiguous selections (p. 338)

Delete columns and rows (p. 345)

Modify worksheet contents by changing copied information (p. 341)

Insert and delete cells and cell ranges in a worksheet (p. 342)

Cut, copy, and paste cells (p. 337)

Document a workbook using comments (p. 331, 332)

Enter information into a worksheet (p. 335)

Navigate within worksheets and workbooks (p. 327)

Quickly generate data using AutoFIll (p. 355)

Delete, insert, rename, and color a worksheet (p. 354)

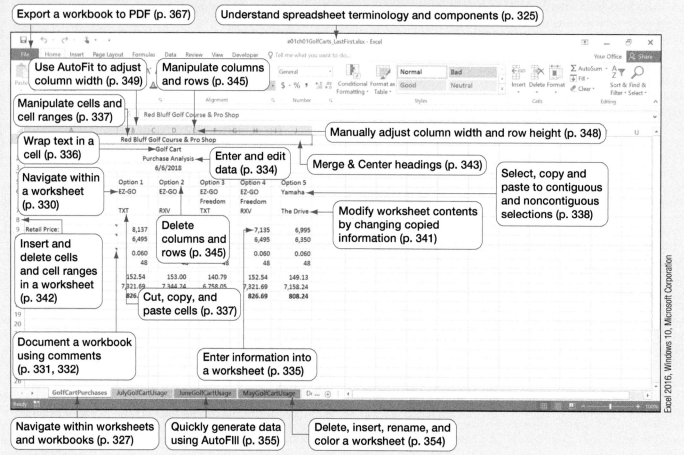

Figure 39

Create a workbook (p. 351)

Print preview (p. 362)

Preview, export, and print worksheets (p. 358)

Change page orientation and print range (p. 367)

Change page margins (p. 366)

Change page scaling (p. 366)

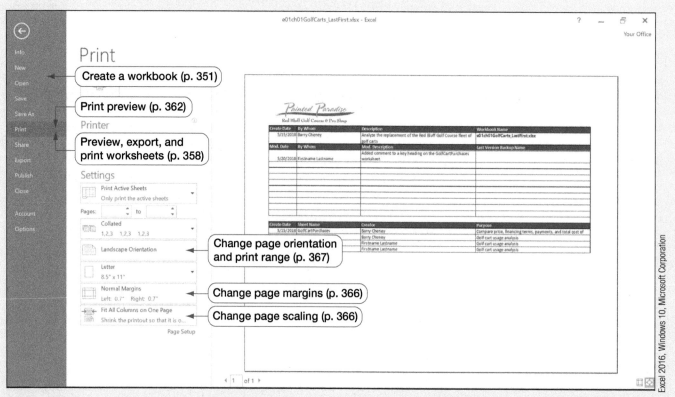

Figure 40

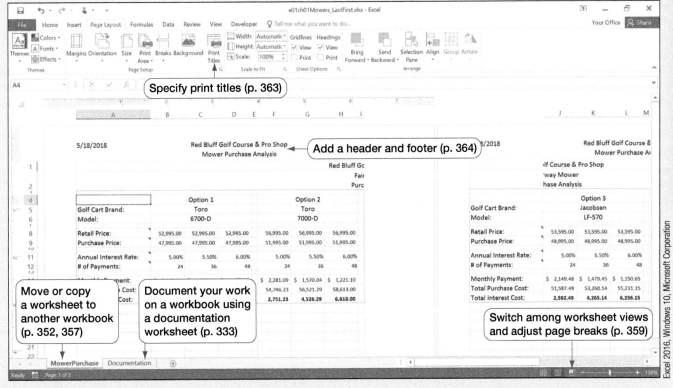

Specify print titles (p. 363)

Add a header and footer (p. 364)

Move or copy a worksheet to another workbook (p. 352, 357)

Document your work on a workbook using a documentation worksheet (p. 333)

Switch among worksheet views and adjust page breaks (p. 359)

Excel 2016, Windows 10, Microsoft Corporation

Figure 41

Practice 1

Student data file needed:	You will save your files as:
e01ch01WeddingPlan.xlsx	e01ch01WeddingPlan_LastFirst.xlsx
	e01ch01WeddingPlan_LastFirst.pdf

Red Bluff Resort Wedding Planning Worksheet

Sales & Marketing

Weddings are becoming an important part of the Painted Paradise Resort & Spa's business, so Patti Rochelle started a worksheet to improve the wedding-planning process for her staff. Last year, the resort hosted three weddings per week, on average, and it has done as many as six in a weekend. The worksheet Patti wants you to finish will allow for changes in pricing to be immediately reflected in the planning process.

You have been given a workbook that includes product/service categories, prices, and an initial worksheet structure to help standardize the process and pricing of weddings. You will build a worksheet that calculates the price of a wedding and doubles as a checklist to use as weddings are set up, to ensure that subcontractors, such as DJs, are reserved in a timely fashion and that all contracted services are delivered.

a. Start Excel, click **Open Other Workbooks** in the left pane, and then double-click **This PC**. Navigate through the folder structure to the location of your student data files, and then double-click **e01ch01WeddingPlan**. If a Security Warning message displays, click the **Enable Editing** button.

b. Click the **File** tab, click **Save As**, and then double-click **This PC**. In the Save As dialog box, navigate to the location where you are saving your project files, and then change the file name to e01ch01WeddingPlan_LastFirst, using your last and first name. Click **Save**.

c. Double-click the active **Sheet3** worksheet tab, type WeddingPlanner, and then press Enter. Double-click the **Sheet1** worksheet tab, and then type Documentation as the new name for the worksheet. Press Enter, click cell **B20**, and then type WeddingPlanner. Press Ctrl+Home.

d. Right-click the **Sheet2** worksheet tab, and then select Delete.

e. Click the **WeddingPlanner** worksheet tab if necessary. Type the information into the indicated cells as follows.

Data Item	Cell	Value
Wedding Date	B2	6/18/2018
Start Time	D2	4 p
End Time	D3	5 p
Reception Start Time	G2	6 p
Reception End Time	G3	12 a
Total Hours	B5	8
Reception Hours	D5	6
Estimated Guests	B7	300
Piano Player (Hours)	C28	1
String Quartet (Hours)	C29	2
DJ (Hours)	C32	4

f. Click cell **E2**. Point to the border of the active cell, and when the mouse pointer changes, click and hold the left mouse button, drag cell E2 to cell **G7**, and then release the mouse button.

g. Select cell range **F2:G3**, press Ctrl+X, click cell **H7**, and then press Ctrl+V. Select cell range **C2:D3**, press Ctrl+X, click cell **H4**, and then press Ctrl+V.

h. Select cell range **A2:B2**, press Ctrl+X, and then click cell **G3** to make it the active cell. Press Ctrl+V, and then select columns **G:I**. On the Home tab, in the Cells group, click the Format arrow, and then click **AutoFit Column Width**.

i. Select columns **B:C**, and in the Cells group, click **Format**, and then click **Column Width**. Type 17 in the Column Width box, and then click **OK**.

j. Click the header for column **E**, and then right-click and select **Delete** from the shortcut menu to delete the column. Right-click column E, select Column Width, type 2 in the Column Width box, and then click **OK**.

k. Press Ctrl+Home. Select **A1:H1** and in the Alignment group, click **Merge & Center**.

l. Right-click the header for Row 1, select Row Height, type 20 in the Row Height box, and then click **OK**.

m. Select cell range **B9:C9**, press Ctrl, and then select cell range **B34:C34**. In the Alignment group, click **Merge & Center**.

n. Click cell **A27**, and then, in the Cells group, click the **Insert** arrow, and then click **Insert Sheet Rows**.

o. Click **Page Layout** view on the status bar, scroll to the bottom of the worksheet, and click in the left section of the Add footer. If necessary, under Header & Footer Tools, click the **Design** tab. In the Header & Footer Elements group, click **File Name**, and then click a cell in the worksheet. Press Ctrl+Home, and then click **Normal** on the status bar.

p. Click the **Documentation** worksheet tab. Repeat step m to insert the file name in the footer.

q. Click cell **A8**, and then type **today's date** in mm/dd/yyyy format. Click cell **B8**, and type your name in Firstname Lastname format. Click cell **C8**, type Completed Ms. Rochelle's initial work; reorganized worksheet to function better as a checklist, and then press Ctrl+Enter. On the Home tab, in the Alignment group, click **Wrap Text** to wrap the text in cell C8.

r. Click and hold the **Documentation** worksheet tab, and then move the Documentation worksheet to the right of the WeddingPlanner worksheet to make it the last sheet.

s. Click the **WeddingPlanner** worksheet tab, click the **File** tab, and then click **Print**. Click the Scaling arrow, and then select **Fit All Columns on One Page**. Exit Backstage view.

t. Click the **Documentation** worksheet tab. Click the **File** tab, and then click **Print**. Click the **Orientation** arrow, and then select **Landscape Orientation**. Click the Scaling arrow, and then select **Fit All Columns on One Page**.

u. Click **Export**, and then click **Create PDF/XPS**. Click **Options**. In the Options dialog box, under Publish what, click **Entire workbook**, and then click **OK**. Navigate to the folder where you are saving your files. In the File name box, type e01ch01WeddingPlan_LastFirst using your last and first name. Verify **Open file after publishing** is checked, and then click **Publish**. View the pages, and then close the PDF.

v. Save the workbook, exit Excel, and then submit your files as directed by your instructor.

Problem Solve 1

MyITLab®
Grader
Homework

Sales & Marketing

Finance & Accounting

Student data file needed:

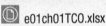 e01ch01TCO.xlsx

You will save your file as:

 e01ch01TCO_LastFirst.xlsx

Automobile Total Cost of Ownership

Most people own, or will at some time own, an automobile. Few actually take the time to calculate what owning an automobile actually costs — called total cost of ownership. This is an important calculation for both individuals and businesses. You will complete the development of an automobile total cost of ownership worksheet for your supervisor, Jan Bossy, CFO at Kallio Auto Sales.

a. Open the Excel file, **e01ch01TCO**. Save your file as e01ch01TCO_LastFirst, using your last and first name.

b. Rename **Sheet1** Documentation. Rename **Sheet2** AutoTCO.

c. Delete **Sheet3**.

d. On the AutoTCO worksheet, type the Value information into the indicated cells as follows.

Data Item	Cell	Value
Miles Driven / Year	E4	15000
Fuel Cost / Gallon	E5	3.00
MPG	E6	26

e. Merge and center the worksheet heading across cell range **A1:F1**.

f. Select cell range **C16:C22**, and then copy the selected range to the Clipboard. Select cell range **D16:F16**, and paste the Clipboard contents into the selected range.

g. Select cell range **B15:C15**. Use AutoFill to expand the selected range to **B15:F15**.

h. Insert a row above row 15.

i. In cell **B15**, type 5-year Total Cost of Ownership Analysis, and then select cell range **B15:F15**. Apply **Center Across Selection**.

j. Add the file name in the left footer of the AutoTCO and Documentation worksheets.

k. Click cell **A8**, and then enter **today's date** in mm/dd/yyyy format. Click cell **B8**, and then type your name in Firstname Lastname format. Click cell **C8**, and then type Completed Ms. Bossy's automobile total cost of ownership worksheet. Apply **Wrap Text** to cell **C8**. Click cell **B20**, type AutoTCO.

l. On the **AutoTCO** worksheet tab, apply **AutoFit Column Width** to column A. Change the column width of columns **B:F** to **12**.

m. Move the AutoTCO worksheet to the left of the Documentation worksheet.

n. For printing the AutoTCO worksheet, set its orientation to **Landscape Orientation**. For the Documentation worksheet, set its orientation to Landscape Orientation, and then set the scaling to **Fit All Columns to One Page**. Set the Print Range to **Print Entire Workbook**, and then print the workbook as directed by your instructor.

o. Save the workbook, exit Excel, and then submit your file as directed by your instructor.

Perform 1: Perform in Your Career

Student data file needed:

 e01ch01IncProp.xlsx

You will save your file as:

 e01ch01IncProp_LastFirst.xlsx

Property Investment Analysis

Finance & Accounting

You were recently hired by O'Miller Property Investment for an internship. A determining factor in Kelsie O'Miller's decision to give you this opportunity was based on your ability to work with Microsoft Excel. Ms. O'Miller just started a workbook that she wants to use to compare properties under consideration for acquisition.

She has asked you to finish the worksheet by formatting and expanding the worksheet to allow the side-by-side comparison of six properties.

a. Open the Excel file, **e01ch01IncProp**. Save your file as e01ch01IncProp_LastFirst, using your last and first name.

b. Rename the **Sheet3** worksheet PropertyAnalysis, and then rename the **Sheet1** worksheet Documentation. Delete the **Sheet2** worksheet.

c. On the PropertyAnalysis worksheet tab, set the width of column A so that no portion of any row heading is hidden, and then delete column **B**.

d. Insert new rows into the worksheet above Loan APR, Income, Interest Paid Year 1, and Net Carrying Costs.

e. Copy all of the information for a loan, and paste two more loan columns to the right of column F. Use the AutoFit feature to adjust the column width of the new loan columns if necessary.

f. Use AutoFill to number the loans in row 4.

g. Type the following information into the indicated columns.

Data Item	G	H
Purchase Price	450000	499000
Down Payment	50000	60000
Loan APR	0.06	0.055
Income	95000	105000
Property Taxes	6500	7250
Repairs	12000	10000
Insurance	5000	5500
Advertising	600	650

h. Center the worksheet titles — the top two lines — across all columns that contain headings and data. Adjust row height where necessary so that the titles are entirely visible.

i. Insert a column between the columns that contain loan information. For any column to the left of a column that contains loan data, set the column width to **3**.

j. Move the values for Depreciation Years and Income Tax Rate one column to the right to C29:C30.

k. Add a comment to cell **C30** stating Income tax rate may increase.

l. In the **Documentation** worksheet, insert today's date into cell **A8**. Type your name in Firstname Lastname format into cell **B8**, and then type into cell **C8** an appropriate description of your activities in this workbook. Change any other necessary information in the Documentation worksheet.

m. Add the file name to the left page footer on both worksheets.

n. Move a worksheet so that the worksheets are in the following order from left to right: PropertyAnalysis, Documentation.

o. For printing the PropertyAnalysis worksheet, set its orientation to **Landscape**. For printing the Documentation worksheet, set its orientation to **Landscape Orientation**, and then set scaling to **Fit All Columns on One Page**. Set Print Range to **Print Entire Workbook**. Press Esc.

p. Save the workbook, exit Excel, and then submit your file as directed by your instructor.

Additional Chapter Cases are available at www.pearsonhighered.com/youroffice

Additional
Cases

Microsoft Excel 2016

Chapter 2 | FORMATS, FUNCTIONS, AND FORMULAS

Finance and Accounting

OBJECTIVES

1. Format cells, cell ranges, and worksheets p. 377

2. Create information with functions p. 396

3. Calculate totals in a table p. 401

4. Create information with formulas p. 404

5. Use conditional formatting to assist in decision making p. 408

6. Hide information in a worksheet p. 413

7. Document functions and formulas p. 414

Prepare Case

Red Bluff Golf Course & Pro Shop Sales Analysis

The Red Bluff Golf Course & Pro Shop sells products ranging from golf clubs and accessories to clothing displaying the club logo. In addition, the Pro Shop collects fees for rounds of golf and services such as lessons from golf pro John Schilling.

Manager Aleeta Herriott needs to track Pro Shop sales by category on a day-by-day basis. Sales, at least to some extent, are a reflection of traffic in the Pro Shop and can be used to help determine staffing requirements on different days of the week. In addition, summary sales data can be compared to inventory investments to determine whether the product mix is optimal, given the demands of the clientele.

Each item or service at the time of sale is recorded in the Pro Shop point-of-sale (POS) system. At the end of each day, the POS system produces a cash register report with categorized sales for the day. This is the data source of each day's sales for the worksheet. Aleeta has created an initial layout for a sales analysis workbook, but she needs you to finish it.

Bikeriderlondon/Shutterstock

Student data files needed for this chapter:

 e01ch02WeekSales.xlsx

 e01ch02red_bluff.jpg

You will save your files as:

 e01ch02WeekSales_LastFirst.xlsx

 e01ch02WSFormulas_LastFirst.pdf

Worksheet Formatting

To be of value, information must be communicated effectively. Effective communication of information generally requires the information is formatted in a manner that aids in proper interpretation and understanding.

Some of the most revolutionary ideas in history were initially recorded on a handy scrap of paper, a yellow legal pad, a tape recorder — even a paper napkin. Communication of those ideas generally required that they be presented in a different medium and that they be formatted in a manner that aided other people's understanding. The content may not have changed, but the format of the presentation is important. People are more receptive to well-formatted information because it is easier to understand and to absorb. While accuracy of information is of the utmost importance, of what use is accurate data that is misunderstood? In this section, you will manipulate a worksheet by formatting numbers, aligning and rotating text, changing cell fill color and borders, using built-in cell and table styles, and applying workbook themes.

Format Cells, Cell Ranges, and Worksheets

There are several ways to present information. If different technologies, mediums, and audiences are considered, a list of more than 50 ways to present information would be easy to produce. The list could include varied communication methods such as books, speeches, websites, tweets, RSS feeds, and bumper stickers. However, an analysis of such a list would reveal generic communication methodologies.

- Oral
- Written narrative
- Tabular
- Graphical

Excel is an application specifically designed to present information in tabular and graphical formats. **Tabular format** is the presentation of text and numbers in tables — essentially organized in labeled columns and numbered rows. **Graphical format** is the presentation of information in charts, graphs, and pictures. Excel facilitates the graphical presentation of information via charts and graphs based on the tabular information in worksheets.

 E02.00

To Get Started

a. Start **Excel**, click **Open Other Workbooks** in the left pane, and then double-click **This PC**. Navigate through the folder structure to the location of your student data files, and then double-click **e01ch02WeekSales**. If a Security Warning message displays, click the **Enable Editing** button.

b. Click the **File** tab, click **Save As**, and then double-click **This PC**. In the Save As dialog box, navigate to the location where you are saving your project files, and then change the file name to e01ch02WeekSales_LastFirst, using your last and first name. Click **Save**.

Number Formatting

Through number formatting, context can be given to numbers, reducing the need for text labeling, such as for date and/or time values. Most of the world's currencies can be represented in Excel through number formatting. Financial numbers, scientific numbers, percentages, dates, times, and so on all have special formatting requirements and can be properly displayed in a worksheet. The ability to manipulate and properly display many different types of numeric information is a feature that makes Excel an incredibly powerful and ubiquitously popular application.

Numbers can be formatted in many ways in Excel. The most common formats are shown in Table 1.

Format Name	Ribbon	Number Format List	Keyboard Shortcut	Example
Accounting	$ ·	(icon)		$ (1,234.00)
Comma*	,		Ctrl + Shift + !	(1,234.00)
Currency		(icon)		-1,234.00
			Ctrl + Shift + $	($1,234.00)
General		ABC 123	Ctrl + Shift + ~	-1234
Number		General ▾		-1234.00
Percentage	%	%	Ctrl + Shift + %	-7.00%
Short Date		(icon)		6/28/2018
			Ctrl + Shift + #	28-Jun-18
Time		(icon)		6:00:00 PM
			Ctrl + Shift + @	6:00 PM

*Comma format is Accounting format without a currency symbol.

Table 1   Common number formats

Your manager, Aleeta Herriott, has asked you to format the WeeklySales worksheet so the data is easier to understand. You think using simple Excel formatting such as the Accounting Number Format, Currency Format, Comma Style, Percent Style, and Decimals will make the worksheet more readable. In this exercise, you will format numbers on the WeeklySales worksheet.

To Format Numbers

a. On the WeeklySales worksheet tab, select cell range **B6:H6**. Click the **Home** tab, and then, in the Number group, click **Accounting Number Format** [$ ·]. The top row of numbers is often formatted with a currency symbol to indicate that subsequent values are currency as well.

> **Troubleshooting**
> If any of the cells you just formatted display a series of number signs (#), select the cell(s), and in the Cells group, click Format [icon], and then, under Cell Size, click AutoFit Column Width.

b. Select cell range **B7:H8**, and then, in the Number group, click **Comma Style** [,].

c. Select cell range **C29:C30**, press and hold Ctrl, click cell **C33**, and then select **C36:C38**. In the Number group, click **Percent Style** [%], and then in the Number group, click **Increase Decimal** [←.0 .00] once.

d. Click cell **C31**, press Ctrl, and then click **C34**. In the Number group, click the **Number Format** arrow General ▾, and then select **More Number Formats**. The Format Cells dialog box is displayed. Under Category, select **Currency**.

e. Double-click the Decimal places box, and type 0.

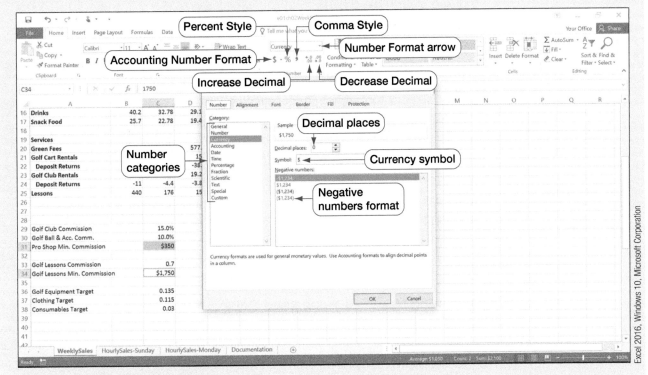

Figure 1 Number Format options

SIDE NOTE

Comma Style

The Comma Style is simply the Accounting Number Format without a monetary symbol.

f. Click **OK**, and then **Save** 🖫 the workbook.

Accounting Number Format Versus Currency Number Format

The Accounting and Currency number formats are both intended for monetary values.

The Accounting format has the following characteristics.

- Negative numbers are enclosed in parentheses.
- The currency symbol is aligned to the left side of the cell.
- Zero values are displayed as a long dash (—) aligned at the decimal position.
- The decimal place is aligned.

The Currency format has the following characteristics.

- Negative numbers can be identified with a dash (–), parentheses, or displayed in red. The red color option can be combined with parentheses as well.
- The currency symbol is placed directly left of the value.
- Zero values are displayed as 0 with zeroes in each decimal place.

It is important to understand the differences so you can make intelligent formatting decisions. For appearance purposes, best practice is to try to use only the currency OR only the accounting format in the same table or with numbers that are next to one another.

Displaying Negative Values and Color

Negative numbers often require more than parentheses or a hyphen to call attention to the fact that a value is less than zero. The phrase "in the red" is often used to describe financial values that are less than zero, so, not surprisingly, Excel makes it very easy to display negative numbers in a red font color.

To draw attention to negative numbers, in this exercise you will format the worksheet to display negative numbers in red.

E02.02

Alternate Method

To launch the Format Cells dialog box, you can also right-click the number(s) you wish to format and select Format Cells from the menu.

To Display Negative Numbers in Red

a. On the WeeklySales worksheet, select cell range **B20:H22**. On the Home tab, in the Number group, click the **Number Format** arrow [General ▾], and then select **More Number Formats**.

b. Under Category, select **Number**. If necessary, type a 2 in the Decimal places box. Select **Use 1000 Separator (,)**. Under Negative numbers, select the **red negative number format (1,234.10)**, and then click **OK**. You will change the format of rows 23:25 in a later exercise.

> ### Troubleshooting
> If the negative numbers in B22:H22 are not displayed in red, you didn't select the correct negative number format. Press Ctrl + Z, and repeat steps a and b.

c. **Save** 🖫 the workbook.

Formatting Date and Time

Excel stores a date and time as a number in which the digits to the left of the decimal place are the number of complete days since January 1, 1900, inclusive. The right side of the decimal place is the decimal portion of the current day, which represents the current time. This date system allows Excel to use dates in calculations. For example, if you add 7 to today's date, the result is the date one week in the future.

While this is useful for computer systems and applications such as Excel, people have not been taught to interpret time in this manner, so unformatted date and time values — those displayed in General format — mean little or nothing to us. Date and time formatting allows Excel date and time values to be displayed in a fashion that allows human interpretation. A heading that identifies a column as date values gives context to the information, but in the case of date information, without proper formatting, it is for the most part unusable by the reader.

In this exercise, you will format cells with date and time formats.

 E02.03

To Format a Cell or Cell Range as a Date or Time

a. On the WeeklySales worksheet, click cell **B4**; this is an unformatted date in Excel.

b. On the Home tab, and in the Number group, click the **Number Format** arrow [General ⌄], and then select **Short Date**. Click and hold down the left mouse button on the **fill handle,** drag the fill handle right until the border around the active cell expands to include cells **B4:H4**, and then release the left mouse button. The date in cell B4 has been incremented by one day in each of the cells in C4:H4.

c. Notice the series of number (#) signs in F4:H4. Select columns **F:H**. In the Cells group, click **Format** 🗔, and then select **AutoFit Column Width**. Next you want to format numbers to appropriately reflect time.

d. Click the **HourlySales-Sunday** worksheet tab. Select cell range **A6:A7**. In the Number group, click the **Number Format** arrow [General ⌄].

   Notice the Time format includes hours, minutes, and seconds. You have no need to display seconds, so you need to use the Format Cells dialog box to access additional time formats.

e. Select **More Number Formats**. Under Category, select **Time**. In the Type box, select **1:30 PM**.

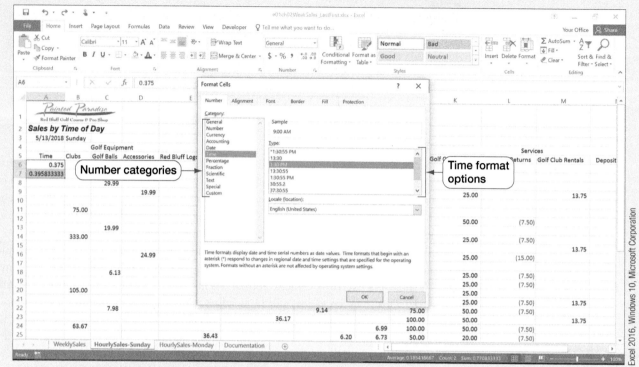

Figure 2   Format Cells dialog box

f. Click **OK**. With A6:A7 still selected, click and hold the **fill handle**, and then drag the **fill handle** down to encompass cells **A6:A28**.

The series in cell range A6:A7 has been expanded through cell A28. Note each cell is incremented by 30 minutes from the cell above. The 30-minute increment was determined by the time difference between cells A6 and A7. That is why you selected two cells before using AutoFill in cell range A6:A28.

g. **Save** ⊟ the workbook.

CONSIDER THIS | **Excel stores time values as decimal portions of one day as follows.**

- 1 = 1 day = 1,440 minutes
- .1 = 144 minutes = 2:24 AM
- .01 = 14.4 minutes = 12:14:24 AM

For this system to work in conjunction with date values, 0 and 1 are displayed as equivalent time values: 12:00:00 AM. However, in reality, once a time value increases to 1, the date is incremented by 1 day and time reverts to 0. Would you be able to adapt if your digital watch or cell phone showed time the way Excel stores it? Would there be any advantages if time were actually displayed and handled in this format? What about date values?

Aligning Cell Content

Cell alignment allows cell content to be left-aligned, centered, and right-aligned horizontally, as well as top-aligned, middle-aligned, and bottom-aligned vertically. Certain cell formats are aligned left or right by **default** — automatically in place unless you specify otherwise. Number formats are right-aligned, including date and time formats. Text formatting aligns cell contents to the left by default. For the most part, horizontal alignment changes will be made to alphabetic content such as titles, headings, and labels.

To improve the appearance of the data labels, in this exercise you will align text on the WeeklySales worksheet.

E02.04

To Align Text

a. Click the **WeeklySales** worksheet tab, select cell range **A5:A25.**

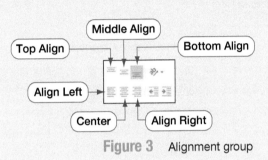

Figure 3 Alignment group

b. In the Alignment group, click **Align Right** .

c. Click cell **A5**, press and hold Ctrl, and then select cells **A10**, **A15**, and **A19**. In the Alignment group, click **Align Left** , and then, in the Alignment group, click **Increase Indent** .

d. Select cell range **I4:J4**, and then click **Align Right** . The content in J4 is truncated (cut off), so the width of column J needs to be increased.

e. Point to the border between the headers for columns J and K. The mouse pointer will change to . Double-click to apply AutoFit to the width of column J.

f. Select cell range **B4:J4.**

g. In the Alignment group, click **Bottom Align** .

In the next exercise, you will rotate the dates in cell range B4:H4. Applying Bottom Align ensures the contents of cell range B4:J4 will align at the bottom of the cell once the dates have been rotated.

h. **Save** the workbook.

Setting Content Orientation

Sometimes it is helpful to display information at an angle or even vertically rather than in the standard horizontal left to right. This is particularly true for tabular information. When you are formatting charts and graphs, rotating textual content can be very helpful in presenting information in a space-efficient yet readable manner.

You think the dates on the WeeklySales worksheet appear too close to one another. In this exercise, you will rotate text on the WeeklySales worksheet.

To Rotate Text

a. On the WeeklySales worksheet, select cell range **B4:J4**.

b. In the Alignment group, click **Orientation** [≫▼].

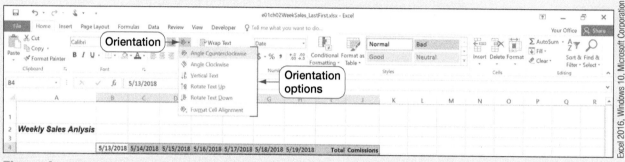

Figure 4   Orientation list

c. Select **Angle Counterclockwise**.

d. In the Alignment group, click **Center** [≡], and then, in the Font group, click **Bold** [B].

e. **Save** [💾] the workbook.

Changing Fill Color

Fill color refers to the background color of a cell. It can be used to categorize information, to band rows or columns as a means of assisting the reader to follow information across or down a worksheet, or to highlight values.

It is generally best practice to use muted or pastel fill colors. Bright colors are difficult to view for long periods of time and often make reading difficult. Bright background colors should be used sparingly to highlight a value that requires attention, such as a value outside normal operating parameters.

In this exercise, to make some of the worksheet data labels stand out, you will fill cells and cell ranges with background color.

 E02.06

To Change Cell Background Color

a. On the WeeklySales worksheet, select the cell range **B4:J4**. Press [Ctrl], and then select cell range **A5:A25**. In the Font group, click the **Fill Color** arrow [🖌▼] to display the color palette. Under Theme Colors, point to any color in the palette, and a ScreenTip will appear identifying the color name.

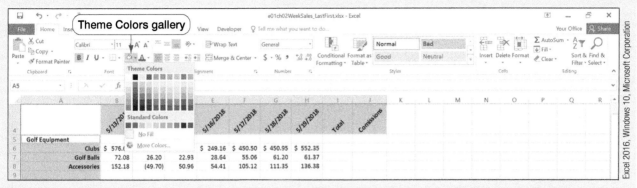

Figure 5 Theme colors

b. Select **Gold, Accent 4, Lighter 40%** (eighth column, fourth row).

c. Click cell **A4**. Click **Fill Color**. Notice that the fill color applied in step b is now applied to A4.

d. Click cell **A9**, press Ctrl, and then select cells **A14** and **A18**. In the Font group, click the **Fill Color** arrow, and then select **No Fill**.

e. **Save** the workbook.

Adding Cell Borders

In the previous exercise, you changed the background color in a range of cells. When the background color is changed for a range of contiguous cells, cell borders are no longer visible. If it would be preferable to have visible cell borders, cell borders can be formatted to make them visible.

In this exercise, on the WeeklySales worksheet, you want to have the worksheet total rows identified, so you have decided to format the cells using borders.

E02.07

To Format Cell Borders

a. On the WeeklySales worksheet, select cell range **B4:J4**, press Ctrl, and then select cell range **A5:A25**.

b. In the Font group, click the **Borders** arrow.

> **Troubleshooting**
> The Borders button may look different in your Excel application window than it does when referenced in this text; this is because the Borders button in the Font group of the Home tab displays the last border setting applied.

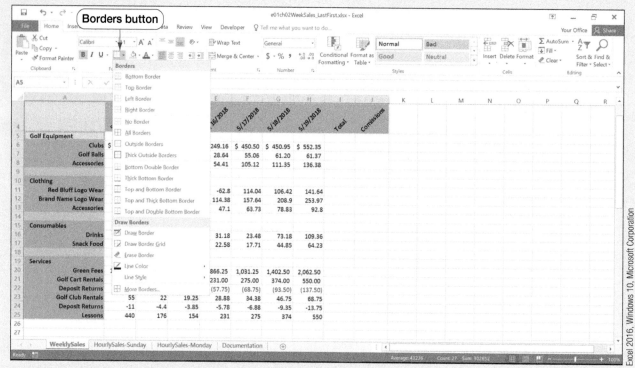

Figure 6 Borders list

c. In the Borders list, select **All Borders**.

d. Click cell **A5**, press Ctrl, and then select cells **A10**, **A15**, and **A19**. In the Font group, click the **Borders** arrow, and then, in the Borders list, select **Thick Bottom Border**.

e. Click cell **J9**, click the **Borders** arrow, and then select **Top and Double Bottom Border**.

f. Select cell range **B9:I9**, press Ctrl, and then select cell ranges **B14:I14**, **B18:I18**, and **B26:I26**. Click the **Borders** arrow, and then select **Top and Bottom Border**.

g. Select cell range **B27:I27**, click the **Borders** arrow, and then select **Bottom Double Border**.

h. **Save** worksheet.

REAL WORLD ADVICE | Formatting — Less Is More

Too much formatting results in a worksheet that is difficult to look at, is difficult to read, and conveys a sense that the designer lacked a plan. Here are some formatting guidelines.

- Format for a reason, not just for appearances.
- Use at most three fonts in a worksheet. Use each font for a purpose, such as to differentiate titles.
- Use color only to assist in readability, categorization, or identification purposes. For example, use organization colors for titles, use bright colors to highlight small details, and use background colors for categorization.
- Background colors should be pale, pastel colors. Bright background colors are tiring for the reader and can become painful to look at after a while.
- Special characters such as the dollar sign ($) should be applied only as necessary. A dollar sign in the first value of a column of numbers is often sufficient to identify its values as monetary. Then format subtotals and totals with a dollar sign to differentiate them.

Copying Formats

Formatting a cell can consist of several steps involving fonts, colors, sizes, borders, alignment, and so on. You gain a significant efficiency advantage by reusing your work. Once a cell has been formatted properly, you can apply the formatting properties to other cells. Copying formats from one cell to another saves a great deal of time.

Format Painter is a tool that enables you to copy the format of objects, such as text or pictures, to other objects. To use the Format Painter, simply select the cell that is the source of the format you want to copy, click the Format Painter in the Clipboard group on the Home tab, and then select the cell or range of cells you want to "paint" with the source cell's formatting. To paint a format to more than one nonadjacent cell, you can double-click Format Painter and then select nonadjacent cells. Once you have finished applying the format to nonadjacent cells, press Esc or click the Format Painter again to turn off the feature.

In this exercise, to save time formatting the WeeklySales worksheet, you will use the Format Painter to copy formats.

E02.08

SIDE NOTE
How to Use the Format Painter Multiple Times
Double-click the Format Painter, and it will remain active until you click it again or press Esc.

To Use the Format Painter to Copy Formats

a. On the WeeklySales worksheet, click cell **B22**, and then, in the Clipboard group, click **Format Painter** . The mouse pointer will change to . Select cell range **B23:H25**.

b. Click cell **B6**, double-click **Format Painter** , and then select cell range **B11:H11**. Select cell range **B16:H16**, select cell range **B20:H20**, and then click **Format Painter** to toggle it off.

c. Click **Format** , and then select **AutoFit Column Width**.

d. **Save** the workbook.

Using Paste Options/Paste Special

When a cell is copied to the Clipboard, there is much more than a simple value ready to be pasted to another location. Formats, formulas, and values are all copied and can be selectively pasted to other locations in a workbook.

Different paste options are shown in Table 2. Although there are a large number of paste options, most worksheet activities require only a few of these options. Paste 📋, Paste Formatting 🖌️, and Paste Values 📋 will accomplish most of what you will need to do. The various paste options are additive, in that you can first paste a value to a copied cell and then paste the format from the copied cell, after which you could paste the formula from the copied cell.

Button	Function	Pastes
📋	Paste	All content from the Clipboard to a cell
🖌️	Formatting	Only the formatting from the Clipboard to a cell
📋	Values	Only the value from the Clipboard to a cell
📋	Formulas	Only the formula from the Clipboard to a cell
📋	Paste Link	A link (e.g., =A25) to the source cell from the Clipboard to a cell
📋	Transpose	A range of cells to a new range of cells with columns and rows switched

Table 2 Paste options

In this exercise, you will use the Paste Options to copy formats in the WeeklySales worksheet.

 E02.09

To Use Paste Options to Copy Formats

a. On the WeeklySales worksheet, click cell **B7**. In the Clipboard group, click **Copy** 🗒️ to copy cell B7 to the Clipboard. Select cell range **B12:H13**, press Ctrl, and then select cell range **B17:H17**.

b. Right-click the selected range. The shortcut menu is displayed, which includes options that are determined by the context of the object that is the focus of the right-click.

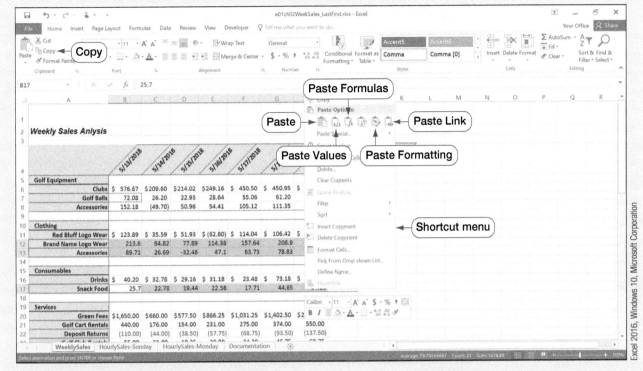

Figure 7 Paste Options menu

c. Point to each button on the Paste Options menu, and notice what happens in the selected cell range.

d. On the Paste Options menu, click **Formatting** 📋, and then press ⎋Esc to clear the Clipboard.

e. **Save** 🖫 the workbook.

Checking the Spelling of a Worksheet

Not only should worksheets be professionally formatted, they should also contain correct spelling. Even professionally formatted worksheets can be confusing if they contain misspelled words or phrases. Unlike other Microsoft applications such as Word, Outlook, or PowerPoint, by default Microsoft Excel does not automatically check for misspelled text. Also, Excel does not have a grammar checker, as Word, Outlook, and PowerPoint do.

If a single cell is selected, Excel begins checking the spelling from the active cell. Excel checks spelling only on the active worksheet, not the entire workbook, but it will spell check the entire worksheet, including any comments, page headers, footers, and graphics. If you have a range of cells selected, Excel will check spelling only on the range of cells, not the entire workbook. There are several ways to check the spelling of a worksheet. On the Review tab, in the Proofing group, select the Spelling button. For easy reference, the Spelling ✓ command can be added to the Quick Access Toolbar.

In this exercise, you will check the spelling on the WeeklySales worksheet.

 E02.10

To Check Spelling

a. On the WeeklySales worksheet, press Ctrl + Home to make A1 the active cell.

b. Click the **Review** tab, and then in the Proofing group, click **Spelling**.

c. The first spelling error was found, and the Spelling dialog box is displayed.

SIDE NOTE

AutoCorrect

You can use the Excel AutoCorrect feature to correct typos or add words to the dictionary. Select File, Options, Proofing, AutoCorrect Options.

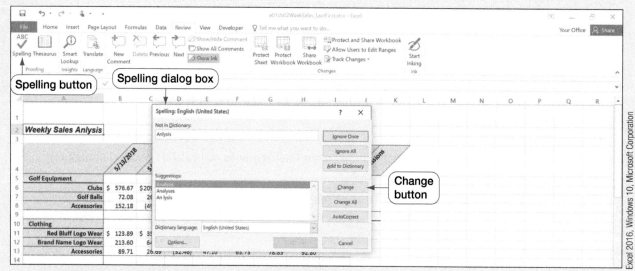

Figure 8   Spelling dialog box

SIDE NOTE

Quick Access Spelling

To add the Spelling button to the Quick Access Toolbar, click the Customize Quick Access Toolbar arrow, and select Spelling.

d. Verify **Analysis** is selected in the Suggestions box, and then click **Change**.

e. A second spelling error was found. Verify **Commissions** is selected in the Suggestions box, and then click **Change**. There were only two spelling errors on this worksheet; therefore, the spell check is finished.

f. Click **OK**, and then **Save** the workbook.

SIDE NOTE

Alternate Method

You can also press the F7 key to begin to spell check a worksheet.

Inserting a Picture

Painted Paradise Resort & Spa has logos for each of its core businesses. All documents must include the appropriate logo whenever possible. Excel allows images, such as logos, to be inserted into a worksheet. Images are not contained in a cell, as data is, but can be sized to fit cell borders by using the Snap to Grid feature.

In this exercise, you will insert an image into a worksheet.

 E02.11

To Insert an Image into a Worksheet

a. On the WeeklySales worksheet, click cell **A1**.

b. Click the **Insert** tab, and then, in the Illustrations group, click **Pictures**. In the Insert Picture dialog box, navigate to the location where your student data files are stored, click the **e01ch02red_bluff** file, and then click **Insert**.

c. Click the **Picture Tools Format** tab, and then, in the Arrange group, click **Align** [icon]. If Snap to Grid is not selected — it does not have a border around it as shown around View Gridlines — then select **Snap to Grid**.

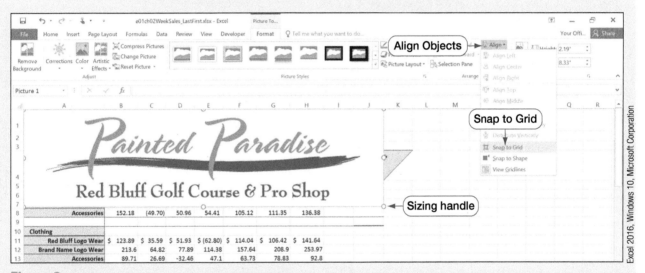

Figure 9   Insert a picture and toggle on Snap to Grid

d. Click and hold the right horizontal sizing handle, and then drag the edge of the **logo** to the left until it snaps to the border between columns **B** and **C**. Click and hold the bottom vertical sizing handle, and then drag the bottom edge of the logo up until it snaps to the border between rows **1** and **2**. Click cell **B6** to deselect the picture.

e. **Save** [icon] the workbook.

Using Built-In Cell Styles

Built-in cell styles are predefined and named combinations of cell and content formatting properties that can be applied to a cell or range of cells to define several formatting properties at once. A built-in cell style can set the font, font size and color, number format, background color, borders, and alignment with just a few clicks of the mouse. Built-in cell styles allow for rapid and accurate changes to the appearance of a workbook with very little effort.

To change the appearance of the HourlySales-Sunday worksheet, in this exercise you will apply built-in cell styles on the HourlySales-Sunday worksheet.

 E02.12

To Apply Built-In Cell Styles

a. Click the **HourlySales-Sunday** worksheet tab, and if necessary click the **Home** tab.

b. Click cell **B4**, press ⌃Ctrl, and then select cell **H4**.

c. In the Styles group, click **Cell Styles** 📋. The Cell Styles gallery appears.

> ### Troubleshooting
> If you do not see the Cell Styles button 📋, it may be that your screen has a different resolution and the Cell Styles button has been expanded.

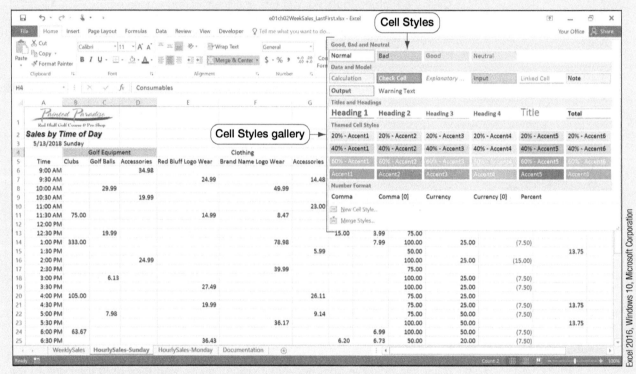

Figure 10 Cell Styles gallery

d. Under Themed Cell Styles, click **20% - Accent1**.

e. Click cell **E4**, press ⌃Ctrl, and then select cell **J4**. In the Styles group, click **Cell Styles**, and then select **40% - Accent1**.

f. Select cell range **A3:B3**, press ⌃Ctrl, select cell range **B4:O5,** and then select **A5:A33**.

g. Click **Cell Styles**, and then, under Titles and Headings, select **Heading 4**. Click cell **B6**.

Notice in cell range B4:O4, the Accent1 cell background colors have not changed.

h. Select cell range **B29:O29**, and in the Styles group, click **Cell Styles**, and then, under Titles and Headings, select **Total**.

i. Press ⌃Ctrl+Home, and then **Save** 💾 the workbook.

Applying Table Styles

Data can be formatted as an Excel table. A **table** is a powerful tabular data-formatting tool that facilitates data sorting, filtering, and calculations. Once a collection of data has been defined as a table by the application of a table style, it has special table properties not available to data that is simply entered into rows and columns of cells.

A **table style** is a predefined set of formatting properties that determine the appearance of a table. One of the useful features of a table style is the ability to "band" rows and columns. **Banding** is alternating the background color of rows and/or columns to assist in visually tracking information. Banding can be accomplished manually by changing the background color of a range of cells — a row, for example — and then pasting the formatting into every other row. Manually banding a table is a tedious process at best. By applying a table style to a selected range of rows and columns, banding is accomplished in a couple of clicks. Most important, table banding is dynamic. If a row or column is inserted into — or deleted from — the worksheet, the banding is automatically updated. If banding is done manually, insertions and deletions require the banding to be manually updated as well.

Tables also allow for calculations in a total row such as summations, averages, or counts for each column in the table. These calculations are possible without table formatting; however, a table simplifies them.

In this exercise, you will apply a table style to cell ranges.

E02.13

SIDE NOTE

Column Names in a Table

Each table column must have a unique header. Excel will append a number to any columns with duplicate names to make them unique.

To Apply a Table Style to a Cell Range

a. Click the **HourlySales-Monday** worksheet tab.

b. Click the cell range **A5:O28**. Click the **Home** tab, and then, in the Styles group, click **Format as Table**. The Table Styles gallery appears.

c. Under Medium table styles, select **Table Style Medium 2** — second column. The Format As Table dialog box appears.

d. Since row 5 contains column headings, be sure **My table has headers** is checked.

Excel 2016, Windows 10, Microsoft Corporation

Figure 11 Format As Table dialog box

e. Click **OK**. The range is formatted as a table, and the Table Tools Design contextual tab appears.

Notice the rows of table data are in descending order by time. The arrow next to each column heading in the table in row 5 allows you to sort or filter the entire table by the information in each column.

f. In cell **A5**, click the Filter arrow.

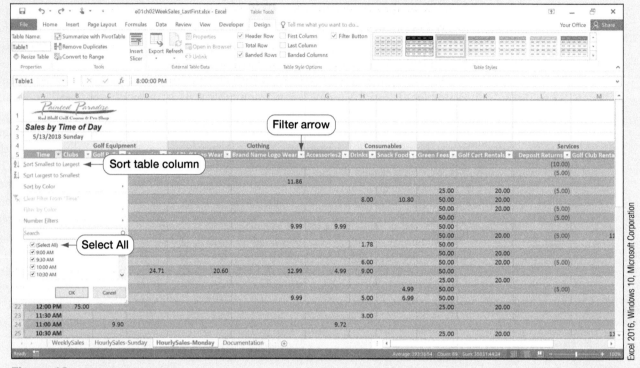

Figure 12 Filter menu

g. On the displayed list, click **Sort Smallest to Largest**. Notice the sort indicator ↓↑ on the Time column filter arrow.

> **Troubleshooting**
>
> Is the Table Tools Design tab not available when you want to select it? Check to make sure the active cell is somewhere in the table you formatted. A worksheet can contain many tables. Excel makes the Table Tools Design tab available only when the active cell is part of a formatted table.

SIDE NOTE

Alternate Method

To convert a table into a normal range of cells, you can right-click any cell in the table, point to Table on the shortcut menu, and then select Convert to Range.

h. Click cell **B10**. Scroll down until row 5 disappears at the top of the window.

Notice what happens to the column headers. If the active cell is inside a table, when you scroll table column headings off the visible application window, table column headings replace worksheet column headings. Also notice the sort arrow on the Time column filter arrow.

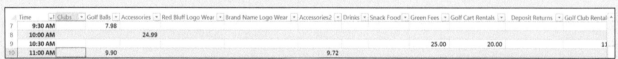

Figure 13 Column headers become table column names

Excel 2016, Windows 10, Microsoft Corporation

i. Click the **HourlySales-Sunday** worksheet tab. Select cell range **A5:O28**. In the Styles group, click **Format as Table**. Under Medium table styles, select **Table Style Medium 9**. The Format As Table dialog box appears. Be sure **My table has headers** is checked, and then click **OK**.

You do not want the table functionality on the HourlySales-Sunday worksheet, so you will convert the table out of table format.

j. Click the **Design** tab, and then, in the Tools group, click **Convert to Range**. In the alert box that appears, click **Yes**.

Convert to Range removes all table functionality but leaves in place the headers and cell formatting of the selected table design. This is a great way to quickly format a range with a theme and row banding, but if you do not want the data filtering and other table features, you can keep the visual formatting.

k. Click cell **B6**, and then **Save** 🔲 the workbook.

Changing Themes

A **theme** is a collection of fonts, styles, colors, and effects associated with a theme name that enables you to create professional, color-coordinated documents quickly. The default theme — the theme that is automatically applied unless you specify otherwise — is the Office theme. Changing the assigned theme is a way to very quickly change the appearance of the worksheets in your workbook. When a different workbook theme is applied, the built-in cell styles in the Styles group on the Home tab change to reflect the new workbook theme. Applying a workbook theme ensures a consistent, well-designed look throughout your workbook.

In this exercise, to ensure all the worksheets in the Week Sales workbook have the same formatting features, you will apply a theme to the workbook.

 E02.14

To Change the Theme

a. On the HourlySales-Sunday worksheet, click the **Page Layout** tab, and then, in the Themes group, click **Themes**. The Themes gallery is displayed.

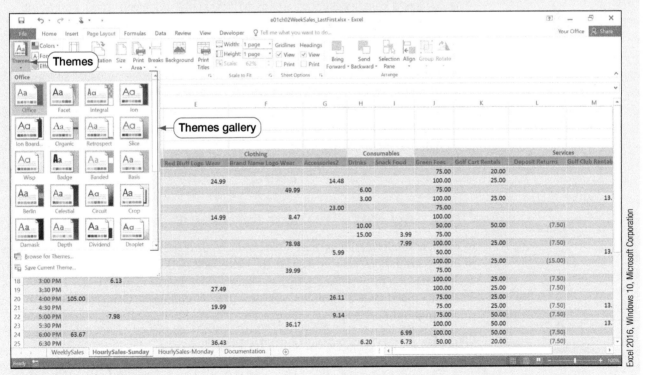

Figure 14 Themes gallery

b. Scroll down, and then select the **Parallax** built-in theme.

Note any cell that was assigned a cell style now reflects the corresponding cell style in the Parallax theme. For example, click the Home tab, and see that the default font has changed to Corbel.

c. Click the **HourlySales-Monday** worksheet tab. Note the Parallax theme has been applied to this worksheet as well as the HourlySales-Sunday worksheet.

d. Click the **Page Layout** tab. In the Themes group, click **Themes**, and then select the **Metropolitan** theme.

The table styles applied to these worksheets reveal the extent to which a change in theme can change the appearance of a worksheet. Note also that themes affect the entire workbook. A theme cannot be selectively applied to individual worksheets in a workbook.

e. Click the **WeeklySales** worksheet tab, and then click the **Home** tab.

Notice the background colors that were set by using cell formatting are also affected by the new workbook theme. Also notice for any cell in which a font was not explicitly set, the font has changed to Calibri Light.

f. **Save** 🖫 the workbook.

g. If you need to take a break before finishing this chapter, now is a good time.

REAL WORLD ADVICE	Formatting Does Not Change the Data Value, but Formatting Can Make Information More Valuable

Formatting affects how information is displayed and understood. It does not change the value stored in a cell. Special formatting characters such as the dollar sign ($) and comma (,) are not stored with values, but they make financial values easier to read and to understand. Formatting helps to turn data into information.

The next time you are adding formatting to a worksheet, ask yourself, "Does this formatting make my worksheet easier to understand?" or "Does this formatting add value in other ways?" such as confirming your organizational identity or its look and feel. If the answer to both questions is "No," maybe you should reconsider.

Remember formatting does not change a data value, but it certainly can add information value. If formatting does not add value, it is likely unnecessary and may detract from the overall value of your worksheet. Consider your formatting decisions carefully.

Creating Information for Decision Making

In Excel, new information is most often produced through the use of functions or formulas to make calculations against data in the workbook. Often, the objective is to improve decision making by providing additional information. In this section, you will manipulate data using functions and formulas, and you will add information using conditional formatting to highlight or categorize information on the basis of problem-specific parameters.

Create Information with Functions

Functions are one of Excel's most powerful features. A **function** is a built-in program that performs operations on data. Function syntax takes the following form:

function name (argument 1, …, argument n)

where "function name" is the name of the function and arguments inside the parentheses are the values the function requires. Different functions require different arguments. **Arguments** are variables or values the function requires in order to calculate a solution. Arguments can be entered as letters, numbers, cell references, cell ranges, or other functions. Some functions do not require any arguments at all. There are more than 400 functions built into Excel that can be categorized as financial, statistical, mathematical, date and time, text, and several others. Collectively, these are referred to — not surprisingly — as **built-in functions**.

Part of what makes functions so useful is the use of cell references as arguments. **Cell references** refer to a particular cell or range of cells within a formula or function instead of a value. Cell references enable you to use information from a particular cell or cell range in a function. Recall that a cell reference is the combination of a cell's column and row addresses. When a function that includes a cell reference as an argument is copied, the cell reference is changed to reflect the copied location relative to the original location. For example, suppose a function in cell B26 calculates the sum of cells B1:B25; if you copy the function from cell B26 to cell C26, the function in cell C26 will automatically be changed to sum C1:C25 — the copied function will be relatively adjusted one column to the right.

Using the SUM, COUNT, AVERAGE, MIN, and MAX Functions

Of the more than 400 functions built into Excel, commonly used functions such as SUM, COUNT, AVERAGE, MIN, and MAX are readily available via the AutoSum $\boxed{\Sigma \text{ AutoSum } \cdot}$ button in the Function Library group on the Formulas tab or in the Editing group on the Home tab. There are two ways to use AutoSum functions. You select either the **destination cell(s)**, the cell(s) that received the result of an operation such as Paste or an AutoSum function, or the **source cell(s)**, the cell(s) that contain the data supplied to the function.

When you invoke AutoSum with the destination cell(s) selected, Excel inspects your worksheet and automatically includes a range adjacent to the active cell. Adjacent cells above the active cell are used by default. If there are no adjacent cells above, then adjacent cells to the left are used for the range. Excel does not inspect cell ranges to the right or below the active cell.

If a column of source cells is selected, if the cell at the bottom of the selected range does not contain data, the bottom cell is treated as the destination cell. If a row of source cells is selected, if the far-right cell in the selected range does not contain data, the far-right cell is treated as the destination cell. If the bottom or far-right cell contains data, the next open cell is used as the destination cell. Table 3 contains examples of the different ways in which data can be included in a function.

Type of Data	Function
Numbers	=SUM(1,3,5,7,11,13)
Cell range	=AVERAGE(B3:B25)
List of noncontiguous cells	=COUNT(B3,B9,C5,D14)
Column or columns	=SUM(J:J) or =AVERAGE(J:L)
Row or rows	=MIN(9:9) or =MAX(9:11)
Combination	=MIN(B3,B9:B15,C12/100,D:E)

Table 3   Function variations

Using the SUM Function by Selecting Destination Cells

The **SUM function** is a commonly used function that adds all numeric information in a specified range, list of numbers, list of cells, or any combination. In this exercise, you will generate new information in the Weekly Sales worksheet by selecting destination cells and inserting the SUM function.

To Use the SUM Function by Selecting Destination Cells

a. If you took a break, open the **e01ch02WeekSales** workbook, and, if necessary, navigate to the **WeeklySales** worksheet tab.

b. Click cell **B9**. On the Home tab, in the Editing group, click **AutoSum** ∑ AutoSum ▾. Excel inspects the cells above B9 and suggests that you want to sum range B6:B8 by surrounding it with a dashed, moving border.

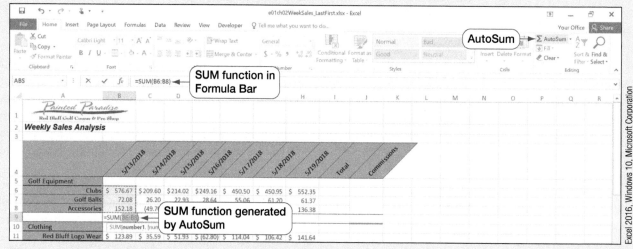

Figure 15 AutoSum range

c. Since the suggested range is correct, press Ctrl + Enter. Notice the Accounting Number Format is automatically applied to cell B9. Drag the fill handle to copy the formula to **C9:H9**.

SIDE NOTE

Double-Click AutoSum

If you are sure Excel will predict the correct range, double-click the AutoSum.

---

d. Select cell range **B14:H14**, press and hold Ctrl, and then select cell ranges **B18:H18**, **B26: H26, I6:I9, I11:I14, I16:I18**, and **I20:I26**. Click **AutoSum** ∑ AutoSum ▾.

e. In the Cells group, click **Format** , and then select **AutoFit Column Width**.

AutoSum will operate on noncontiguous cell ranges as well, but it must be handled a little differently. To calculate the total sales for each day, you must sum the category totals.

SIDE NOTE

SUM Shortcut

SUM can be quickly invoked by pressing Alt + =.

---

f. Click cell **B27**, and then click **AutoSum** ∑ AutoSum ▾. AutoSum recognizes that cell B26 contains a SUM function and selects only B26 as the predicted range. Press and hold Ctrl; select cells **B18, B14**, and **B9**; and then click **AutoSum** ∑ AutoSum ▾ again.

g. Drag the fill handle to copy the formula to **B27:I27**. If any of the cells display a series of number signs (#), in the Cells group, click **Format** , and then select **AutoFit Column Width**.

h. Press Ctrl + Home, and then **Save** the workbook.

Using the SUM Function by Selecting Source Cells

Inserting a function using AutoSum after selecting source cells works particularly well when the source range does not contain contiguous data, as in the HourlySales - Sunday worksheet. In the next exercise, you will generate new information in the HourlySales - Sunday worksheet by selecting source cells and inserting a SUM function using the AutoSum button.

 E02.16

To Use the SUM Function by Selecting Source Cells

a. Click the **HourlySales-Sunday** worksheet tab.

b. Select cell range **B29:B6**. If you start your selection with the cell where you wish to insert the SUM function, then when the function is inserted, you will see it in the formula bar.

SIDE NOTE
Error Warning Symbol
If you see a green triangle in the upper right corner of a cell, point to the triangle to get a warning symbol ⚠; Excel believes there may be an error in your formula.

c. Click the **AutoSum** button ∑ AutoSum ▾ to insert a SUM function.

Since the bottom cell in the selected range did not contain data, the SUM function is placed into cell B29.

d. Select cell range **B6:P29**. You have included a row of empty cells below your destination range and a column of empty cells to the right of your destination range. In this case, you are actually selecting both the source and destination cells. Click the **AutoSum** button ∑ AutoSum ▾. You may have to scroll to the right to see column P.

Click cell **B6** to deselect the selected range, and then **Save** 🖫 the workbook.

Using COUNT and AVERAGE

The **COUNT function** returns the number of cells in a cell range that contain numbers. It can be used to generate information such as the number of sales in a period by counting invoice numbers, the number of people in a group by counting Social Security numbers, and so on.

The **AVERAGE function** returns the average (mean) from a specified range of cells. The sum of all numeric values in the range is calculated and then divided by the count of numbers in the range. Essentially the AVERAGE function is SUM/COUNT. COUNT and AVERAGE can be inserted in any manner by which the SUM function can be inserted.

In this exercise, you will calculate averages and counts for the HourlySales - Sunday worksheet and take advantage of the AutoSum feature that places results in the first open cell following a selected destination range.

To Use the COUNT and AVERAGE Functions

a. On the HourlySales-Sunday worksheet, select cell range **B6:O28**. In the Editing group, click the **AutoSum** arrow Σ AutoSum ▾.

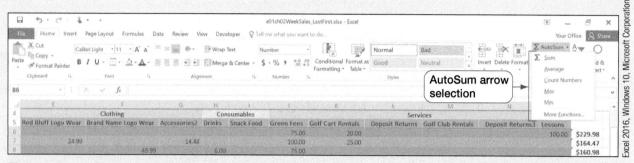

Figure 16   AutoSum arrow selection

b. Select **Average**.

Notice Excel expanded the selected range to include row 29 but inserted the AVERAGE functions into row 30, the first available empty cells below the selected destination range. Click cell O30. Also notice the AVERAGE function in cell O30 does not include row 29; it includes the rows specified in the originally selected range.

c. Select cell range **B6:O28**, click the **AutoSum** arrow Σ AutoSum ▾, and then select **Count Numbers**.

Once again, AutoSum expanded the selected range to include row 29, but this time it inserted the COUNT functions into row 31, the first available empty cells below the selected destination range.

d. **Save** 🖫 the workbook.

Using MIN and MAX

An average gives you an incomplete picture. If your instructor states that the average score on the exam is 75%, you do not have any information about the actual score distribution. Everyone in the class may have gotten a C with a low of 71% and a high of 79%. Conversely, no one may have gotten a C; it may be that half the class got an A and half got an F. Both situations could result in a 75% average but with very different distributions. You should never rely on the average without looking at additional statistics that help to complete the picture. While many statistics exist to do this, the minimum value and the maximum value provide at least a little more insight into the distribution of data by defining the extremes. The **MIN function** and **MAX function** examine all numeric values in a specified range and return the minimum value and the maximum value, respectively.

In this exercise, you will use the MIN and MAX functions to find the smallest and largest values in a range of cells.

To Use the MIN and MAX Functions

a. On the HourlySales-Sunday worksheet, select cell range **B6:O28**, click the **AutoSum** arrow Σ AutoSum ▾, and then select **Max**.

The MAX functions were inserted into row 32, the first available empty row below the selected destination range.

b. Rather than selecting cell range **B6:O28** over again, press Shift + ↑ to remove row 29 from the selected range. Cell range B6:O28 should now be selected. Click the **AutoSum** arrow ∑ AutoSum ▾ , and then select **Min**.

The MIN functions were inserted into row 33, the first available empty row below the selected destination range. The functions inserted into the HourlySales - Sunday worksheet can be used to calculate the same values in the HourlySales - Monday worksheet. They simply need to be copied between worksheets.

c. Click the header for **row 29**, press and hold Shift, and then click the header for **row 33**. In the Clipboard group, click **Copy** 📋.

d. Click the **HourlySales-Monday** worksheet tab, click cell **A29**, and then, in the Clipboard group, click **Paste** 📋.

The functions in rows 29:33 in the HourlySales-Sunday worksheet have been copied to the same locations in the HourlySales-Monday worksheet.

e. **Save** 💾 the workbook.

Calculate Totals in a Table

Not only can an Excel table be used to format worksheet data, a table can be applied to a range of cells that is to be managed separately from other data in the same worksheet. When a range is formatted as a table, the range is structured such that every column is assigned a name, either by the user or automatically by Excel. When a range of data is formatted as a table, you will see filter buttons on each column name, the data formatted with a table style, a sizing handle in the lower right corner of the table, and the Table Tools Design tab on the ribbon. Data in a table can be easily sorted and/or filtered by the values in each column. When you filter data, you choose which data is visible and which is not. Visible data is included in table calculations, and hidden data is not.

Using Tables and the Total Row

An Excel table can include a total row that allows you to calculate a number of different statistics for each column in the table. The HourlySales-Monday worksheet has been formatted as a table. In the next exercise, you will add a total row and use the total row to sum each column in the table.

To generate a statistic such as the sum, average, or standard deviation in a total row, you click the filter arrow and select from the menu. A table total row uses the SUBTOTAL function to generate values. The **SUBTOTAL function** is a function that will run calculations only on the data that is in the subset when a filter is applied. Therefore, when the SUBTOTAL function is used in a table, Excel calculates results based on only data that is visible in a table. When you filter table data, the SUBTOTAL values will automatically be recalculated. The SUBTOTAL function can return any of 11 different values, including all of the AutoSum functions, product, standard deviation, and variance.

An extensive discussion of structured references is outside the scope of this text, but since a table is a data structure defined by its column titles, you can perform calculations by referencing the column titles — the structure identifiers — in the table. In this exercise, you will use Sum in a table's total row, and you will filter table results.

To Use Sum in a Table Total Row and Filter the Results

a. On the HourlySales-Monday worksheet, click cell **B28** to place the active cell inside the table range. The Table Tools Design tab is displayed. Click the **Design** tab, and then, in the Table Style Options group, click the **Total Row** check box.

This adds a special total row that works with the table format to total each column as you specify. Notice the formulas you copied into this worksheet in the previous exercise have been moved down one row.

b. Click cell **B29**, and then click the **Function List** arrow ⬜ next to cell B29.

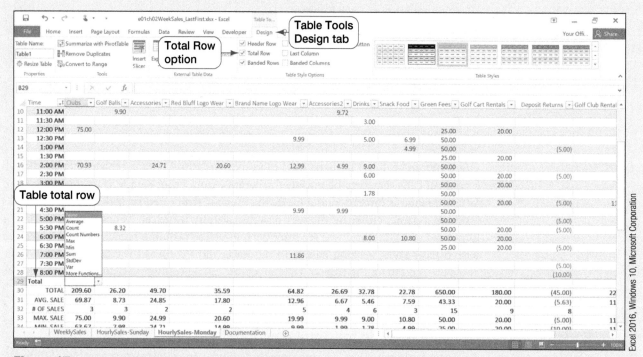

Figure 17   Calculating the sum in a table total row

c. Select **Sum**.

Excel does not need to predict the summed range for a table. It automatically sums all the visible rows in the table column. Notice the formula bar. Even though you selected Sum from the Table Totals menu, Excel uses a SUBTOTAL function in a table total row.

d. Drag the fill handle to copy cell B29 to cell range **C29:O29**. Select AutoFit Column Width if necessary. Notice how rows 28:29 have the same values.

e. In cell **A5**, click the **filter arrow** ⬜. Since this is the Time column, you can filter the table data by selecting — or deselecting — values in the time column. Click **(Select All)** to deselect all time values in the table. Then click **9:00**, **9:30**, **10:00**, **10:30**, **11:00** and **11:30**. This will filter the table to display only sales in the morning hours.

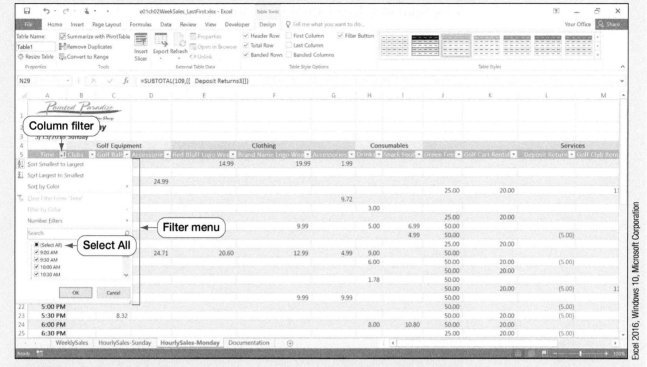

Figure 18 Table filter menu

f. Click **OK**, and then click cell **B29**.

Figure 19 Filtered table total row

Notice in Figure 19 that the Total values in row 29 no longer equal the TOTAL values in row 30. The SUBTOTAL function that calculated the sums in row 29 included only the visible data. You filtered the table to exclude all hours of 12:00 PM or later. Notice rows 12:28 are hidden — rows 12:28 are not included in the SUBTOTAL calculations in row 29.

In Figure 19, notice the formula bar displays the function in cell B29, that is, =SUBTOTAL(109,[Clubs]). This formula uses a structured reference that is unique to tables in Excel. It is the equivalent of =SUBTOTAL(109,B6:B28), but it uses the column name in the table to identify the range against which the function is to act. The number "109" indicates that the SUBTOTAL function is to calculate a sum. The Quick Reference lists the values for different SUBTOTAL statistics.

g. **Save** ⊟ the workbook.

SIDE NOTE
What Is the SUBTOTAL Function?
To learn more about the SUBTOTAL function (or other functions), press F1, type SUBTOTAL (or the name of another function) into the Search box, and press Enter.

The first argument listed in the SUBTOTAL function identifies the statistic to be calculated. Functions 1 through 11 return values that include all values in the specified range. Functions 101 through 111 return values that include only the visible values in the specified range.

Function # All values	Function # Visible values	Statistic
1	101	AVERAGE
2	102	COUNT
3	103	COUNTA
4	104	MAX
5	105	MIN
6	106	PRODUCT
7	107	STDEV
8	108	STDEVP
9	109	SUM
10	110	VAR
11	111	VARP

One quirk associated with the SUBTOTAL function is that when it is used to calculate statistics against a table, the function number visibility is irrelevant. For example, if you specify function number 9 and then filter the table data such that only part of the table data is visible, only visible data will be included in the calculation. Value visibility is a factor in SUBTOTAL function calculations only for data not included in a table.

Create Information with Formulas

A **formula** allows you to perform basic mathematical calculations using information in the active worksheet and other worksheets to calculate new values; formulas can contain cell references, constants, functions, and mathematical operators. Formulas in Excel have a very specific syntax. In Excel, formulas always begin with an equal sign (=). Formulas can contain references to specific cells that contain information; a **constant**, which is a number that never changes, such as the value for π (pi); **mathematical operators** such as +, −, *, /, and ^; and functions. Cells that contain formulas can be treated like any other worksheet cell. They can be referenced, edited, formatted, copied, and pasted.

If a formula contains a cell reference, the cell reference in the formula changes when the formula is copied and then pasted into a new location. The new cell reference reflects a new location relative to the old location. This is called a relative cell reference. For example, as shown in Figure 20, when the formula in the left column is copied one column to the right and two rows down, the cell references in the formula change to reflect the destination cell relative to the original cell. Consequently, columns A and J are changed to B and K, respectively — one column right, and rows 3 and 12 are changed to 5 and 14, two rows down. Note that the column and row numbers of the cells that contain the formulas are not shown in Figure 20. The active cell address does not matter in relative addressing. All that matters is the relative shift in columns and rows from source to destination and the cell references in the formula.

Excel 2016, Windows 10, Microsoft Corporation

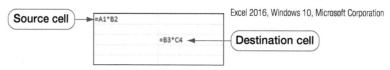

Figure 20   Relative referencing when copying from a source cell to a destination cell

Relative cell references allow you to reuse formulas in a well-designed worksheet. You can enter a formula once and use it many times without having to reenter it in each location and change the cell references. Simply copy the formula and paste it to a new location.

Further, relative references adjust formulas to ensure correctness when the structure of the worksheet changes. If a column is inserted to the left of a cell referenced in a formula or a row is inserted above a cell referenced in a formula, the cells referenced by the formula will be adjusted to ensure the formula still references the same relative locations.

Using Operators

Excel formulas are constructed by using basic mathematical operators very similar to those used in everyday mathematics and exactly the same as those used in most programming languages. Table 4 contains the mathematical operators recognized in Excel.

Operation	Operator	Example	Formula Entered in Current Cell
Addition	+	=B4+B5	Assign the sum of B4 and B5 to the current cell.
Subtraction	-	=B5-B4	Assign the difference of B4 and B5 to the current cell.
Multiplication	*	=B5*3.14	Assign B5 multiplied by 3.14 to the current cell.
Division	/	=B5/B4	Assign the result of dividing B5 by B4 to the current cell.
Exponentiation	^	=B4^2	Assign the square of B4 to the current cell.

Table 4 Mathematical operators in Excel

Applying Order of Operations

The **order of operations** is the order in which Excel processes calculations in a formula that contains more than one operator. Mathematical operations execute in a specific order, which can be remembered by using the mnemonic PEMDAS.

1. (P) Parentheses
2. (E) Exponentiation
3. (M) Multiplication
4. (D) Division
5. (A) Addition
6. (S) Subtraction

Excel scans a formula from left to right while performing calculations using the above order of operation rules. Thus, you can control which part of a calculation is performed first by enclosing parts of a formula in parentheses. Portions of a formula enclosed in parentheses are evaluated first, following the previously listed order. Table 5 contains some examples of the effect of order of operations on formula results.

Formula	Result	Formula	Result
=4-2*5^2	-46	=(5+5)*4/2-3*6	2
=(4-2)*5^2	50	=(5+5)*4/(2-3)*6	-240
=5+5*4/2-3*6	-3	=(5+5)*4/(2-3*6)	-2.5

Table 5 Order of operations

Golf pro John Schilling is paid a commission on golf lessons. He earns 70% of all lesson fees received by the Pro Shop. Pro Shop manager Aleeta Herriott is in charge of all golf club sales. She receives a 15% commission on all sales of clubs and a 10% commission on golf balls and accessories. In this exercise, you will calculate commissions using formulas.

To Calculate Commissions Using Formulas

a. Click the **WeeklySales** worksheet tab, and then click cell **J25**. In this cell, you will calculate the commissions John Schilling earned on golf lessons. The total revenue from golf lessons for the week is in cell I25, and the commission paid for golf lessons is in cell C33.

b. Type =, click **I25**. Excel puts the cell reference of I25 into the formula.

c. Type *, click **C33**. Excel puts the cell reference of C33 into the formula.

SIDE NOTE

Alternate Method

To enter the formula in J25, type =I25*C33, and then press Enter.

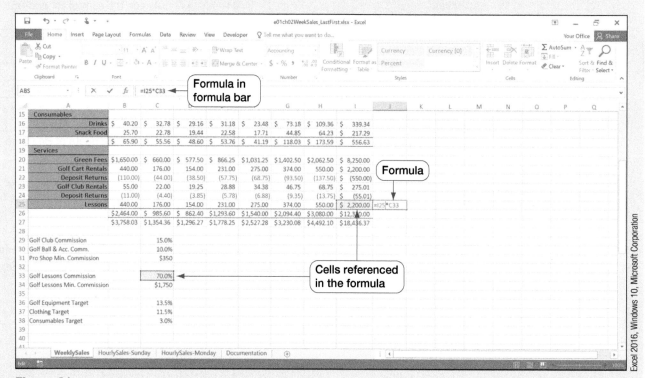

Figure 21 Entering a formula in a cell

d. Press Enter. The active cell is now J26, and the formula in cell J25 multiplies I25 and C33. AutoFit the column width as necessary.

Next, you need to calculate the commissions that Aleeta Herriott earned selling golf clubs in the Pro Shop by multiplying the total golf club sales for the weekly by the commission percentage on golf club sales.

e. Click cell **J6**. Type =, click cell **I6**, type *, click cell **C29,** and then press Enter.

SIDE NOTE

Alternate Method

To enter the formula in J7, type =(I7+I8)*C30, and then press Enter.

Next, you need to calculate the commission earned on Pro Shop accessories by multiplying the sum of golf ball and accessory sales for the week by the appropriate commission.

f. Click cell **J7**. This cell has been merged. Type =(, click **I7**. Type +, click **I8**. Type)*, click **C30**, and then press Enter.

You added the parentheses to ensure cells I7 and I8 are added before they are multiplied by cell C30. Next you need to sum Aleeta Herriott's commissions.

SIDE NOTE
Alternate Method
In cell J9, type =SUM(J6:J7), and then press Enter.

g. Click cell **J9**, and then double-click the **AutoSum** button Σ AutoSum ⏷.

After adding the formula in cell J9, you notice the error message in the upper left corner in cell I9. Excel believes there may be an error in the formula in cell I9 because the formulas in cell I9 and J9 differ. Because both formulas are correct, you want to remove the error message.

h. In cell **I9,** click the **Error** ◆ arrow.

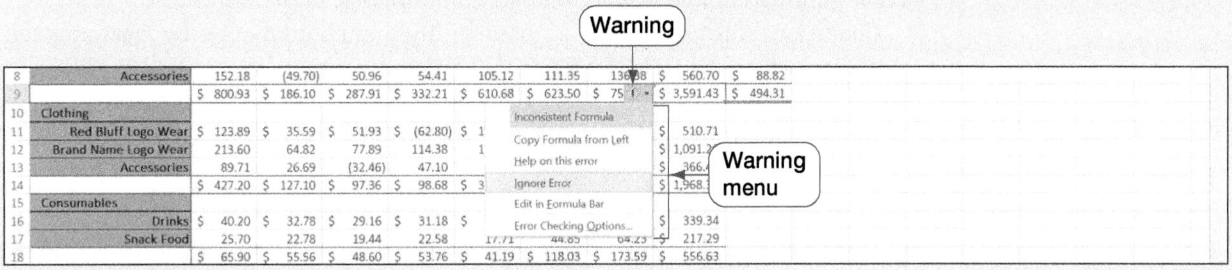

Figure 22   Error Message menu

Excel 2016, Windows 10, Microsoft Corporation

i. Select **Ignore Error**, and then **Save** 🖫 the workbook.

Troubleshooting

Excel allows you to copy formulas from one location to another and adjusts cell references to ensure calculation accuracy. This is not necessarily true when a formula is moved from one location to another, however. If you move a formula by dragging it from one location to another, cell references do not change. Be sure you double-check a formula after you move it to ensure it is still producing a correct result.

REAL WORLD ADVICE   **An Alternative to Typing Cell References**

An alternative — and more accurate — method of typing cell references into a formula is to type only the operators and then select the cells from the worksheet. The steps to enter the daily sales total in the Weekly Sales worksheet would be as follows.

1. Select cell B27.

2. Type =.

3. Click cell B9, and then type +.

4. Click cell B14, and then type +.

5. Click cell B18, and then type +.

6. Click cell B26, and then press Enter.

This method of building formulas is much less error prone than typing cell references.

Use Conditional Formatting to Assist in Decision Making

As was discussed previously, one of the primary purposes of information analysis in Excel worksheets is to assist in decision making. People are often influenced by the format in which information is presented. Worksheets can be very large — thousands of rows and dozens of columns of information. The number of calculated items can be daunting to analyze, digest, and interpret. To the extent to which Excel can be used to assist the decision maker in understanding information, decision-making speed and quality should improve.

Conditional formatting can aid the decision maker by changing the way information is displayed based on rules specific to the problem the worksheet is designed to address.

Highlighting Values in a Range with Conditional Formatting

Conditional formatting allows the specification of rules that apply formatting to a cell as determined by the rule outcome. It is a way to dynamically change the visual presentation of information in a manner that adds information to the worksheet.

Conditional formatting can be used to highlight information by changing cell fill color, font color, font style, font size, border, and number format and by adding visual cues such as scales and icons. In the next exercise, you will apply conditional formatting to highlight the sales figures in each category that are above average for each day's sales.

To Highlight High and Low Category Sales and to Display Negative Accounting Number Formatted Cells in Red

a. On the WeeklySales worksheet, select cell range **B9:H9**. Click the **Home** tab, and in the Styles group, click **Conditional Formatting**. Point to **Top/Bottom Rules**, and then select **Top 10 Items**. In the Top 10 Items dialog box, in the **Format cells that rank in the TOP** box, double-click **10**, and then type 1.

b. Click the **with** arrow, select **Green Fill with Dark Green Text**.

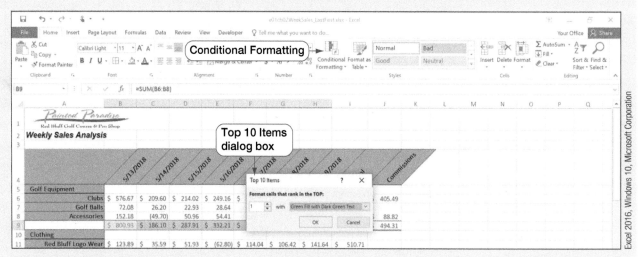

Figure 23 Top 10 Items dialog box

c. Click **OK**. With cell range B9:H9 still selected, in the Styles group, click **Conditional Formatting**, point to Top/Bottom Rules, and then select **Bottom 10 Items**. In the Bottom 10 Items dialog box, in the **Format cells that rank in the BOTTOM** box, double-click **10**, and then type 1. Click **OK** to accept the Light Red Fill with Dark Red Text.

Now you can copy the formatting you just added to B9:H9 to the other category totals and to the overall totals in the WeeklySales worksheet.

d. With cell range **B9:H9** still selected, in the Clipboard group, double-click **Format Painter** . Select cell ranges **B14:H14, B18:H18,** and **B26:H26.** Click **Format Painter** to turn off the Format Painter.

Recall that Accounting Number Format does not include the option to display negative numbers in red — notice cell C8. This can be accomplished with conditional formatting.

SIDE NOTE
Want Negative Numbers in Blue?
In the with box, click Custom Format, click Color, and choose a different color for negative numbers.

e. Select cell range **B6:I27.** In the Styles group, click **Conditional Formatting** , point to **Highlight Cells Rules,** and then click **Less Than.** In the **Format cells that are LESS THAN** box, type 0. Click the **with** box arrow, and then select **Red Text.** Click **OK.**

f. **Save** the workbook.

Applying Conditional Formatting to Assess Benchmarks Using Icon Sets

Conditional formatting can also be used to highlight whether or not a value satisfies particular criteria such as a benchmark. The staff in the Pro Shop is guaranteed a minimum commission amount — stored in cells C31 and C34. The resort management prefers that a staff member's commissions exceed the minimum. You can use conditional formatting to clearly identify whether or not Aleeta Herriott's commissions in the Pro Shop and John Schilling's commissions for lessons exceed the contractual minimum.

In this exercise, you will use conditional formatting with icon sets to highlight above-minimum commissions.

 E02.22

To Use Conditional Formatting with Icon Sets to Highlight Above-Minimum Commissions

a. On the WeeklySales worksheet, click cell **J9.** In the Styles group, click **Conditional Formatting** , point to **Icon Sets,** and then select **More Rules.** In the New Formatting Rule dialog box, under Select a Rule Type, make sure **Format all cells based on their values** is selected.

b. Under Edit the Rule Description, click the **Icon Style** arrow, and then select the first item in the list, **3 Arrows (Colored)** — you will have to scroll up.

c. Under Icon, next to the yellow arrow icon, click the arrow, and then select the red down arrow for the middle Icon box; the Icon Style box will change to Custom. In the bottom Icon box, next to the red arrow icon, click the arrow, select **No Cell Icon,** and then select **Number** in both **Type** boxes.

d. Double-click in the top **Value** box, and then press Delete. Click the **Collapse** button , select cell **C31** — the minimum commission for the Pro Shop manager — and then click the **Expand** button .

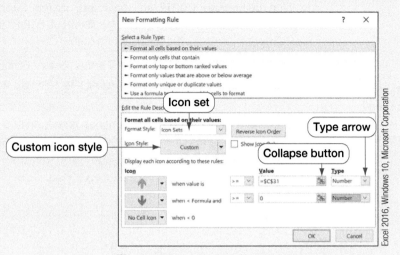

Figure 24   Conditional Formatting icon sets

e. Click **OK**. Now you can use the conditional format you just created for the golf lessons commission in cell J25.

f. With cell **J9** selected, click **Format Painter** , and then click cell **J25** to paste formatting, including conditional formatting.

g. With **J25** still selected, in the Styles group, click **Conditional Formatting** , and then select **Manage Rules**. The Conditional Formatting Rules Manager dialog box is displayed.

h. In the Conditional Formatting Rules Manager dialog box, click **Edit Rule**. In the Edit Formatting Rule dialog box, under Display each icon according to these rules, double-click the top **Value** box.

i. Click the **Collapse** button in the top Value box. Click cell **C34** — the minimum commission for the RBGC golf pro — and then click the **Expand** button .

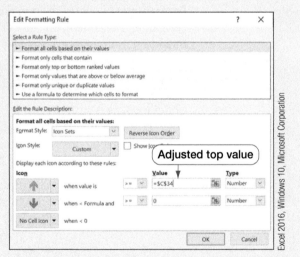

Figure 25   Conditional Formatting modifying an icon set

j. Click **OK**, and then click **OK**. AutoFit the column width of column J.

k. **Save** the workbook.

Using Conditional Formatting to Assess Benchmarks Using Font Formatting

In the previous exercise, you used arrow icons to indicate whether or not Aleeta Herriott and John Schilling had met commission minimums. Any of the conditional formatting features can be used to visually highlight benchmark satisfaction. Aleeta has used historical sales data to identify a proportion of weekly sales that is a minimum goal (benchmark) for each product category.

In this exercise, you will format weekly sales totals to be displayed in a bold and green font if they meet or exceed benchmarks.

E02.23

To Highlight Sales That Meet or Exceed Benchmarks

a. On the WeeklySales worksheet, click cell **I9**. In the Styles group, click **Conditional Formatting** . Point to **Highlight Cells Rules**, and then select **More Rules**. In the New Formatting Rule dialog box, under Select a Rule Type, select **Use a formula to determine which cells to format**.

b. In the **Format values where this formula is true box**, type =I9/I27>=C36 (golf equipment percentage of total sales compared to the golf equipment target percentage of sales).

In using a formula to determine which cells to format, the conditional format always starts with an equal sign, which is followed by a conditional test. If that condition is TRUE then the formatting is applied. If the condition is FALSE, then it will not apply the formatting.

Figure 26 Conditional Formatting using a formula

c. Click **Format**. In the Format Cells dialog box, on the Font tab, in the Font style box, select **Bold**, and then click the **Color** arrow. Under Standard Colors, select **Green**.

d. Click **OK** twice. If necessary, AutoFit Column Width on cell I9.

e. Click cell **I14**. In the Styles group, click **Conditional Formatting** . Point to **Highlight Cells Rules**, and then select **More Rules**. In the New Formatting Rule dialog box, under Select a Rule Type, select **Use a formula to determine which cells to format**. Type =I14/I27>=C37. Click **Format**. On the Font tab, in the Font style box, click **Bold**, and then click the **Color** arrow. Under Standard Colors, select **Green**. Click **OK** two times.

f. Click cell **I18**. In the Styles group, click **Conditional Formatting** . Point to **Highlight Cells Rules**, and then select **More Rules**. In the New Formatting Rule dialog box, under Select a Rule Type, select **Use a formula to determine which cells to format**. Type =I18/I27>=C38. Click **Format**. On the Font tab, in the Font style box, click **Bold**, and then click the **Color** arrow. Under Standard Colors, select **Green**. Click **OK** two times.

g. **Save** the workbook.

Removing Conditional Formatting

Once conditional formatting has been applied to a cell or range of cells, it may be necessary to remove the conditional formatting without affecting other cell formatting or cell contents. Conditional formatting can be removed from a selected cell or cell range, and it can be removed from the entire sheet, depending on which option is chosen.

When you applied the conditional formatting to cell range B6:I27 to display negative numbers in red regardless of the number format, several cells that did not contain data were also conditionally formatted. Although applying conditional formatting to a large range of cells all at once is efficient, applying it to cells that do not contain data in the current design may cause unforeseen problems as the worksheet is modified in the future. You need to remove the conditional formatting in the empty cells.

S S CONSIDER THIS | **How Might You Use Conditional Formatting?**

Can you think of ways you could use conditional formatting in worksheets to aid in making personal decisions? Could you use conditional formatting as an aid in tracking your stock portfolio? Monthly budget and expenses? Checking account?

In this exercise, you will remove the conditional formatting in the empty cells.

E02.24

SIDE NOTE
Alternate Method
To remove conditional formatting, click Conditional Formatting, select Manage Rules, click Delete Rule.

To Remove Conditional Formatting from a Range of Cells

a. On the WeeklySales worksheet, select cell range **B10:I10**, press Ctrl, and then select cell ranges **B15:I15** and **B19:I19**.

b. In the Styles group, click **Conditional Formatting** , and then select **Manage Rules**. Notice the Cell Value < 0 rule that was applied to the selected ranges even though the ranges do not contain any data. Click **Close**.

c. In the Styles group, click Conditional Formatting, and then point to **Clear Rules**. Select **Clear Rules from Selected Cells**.

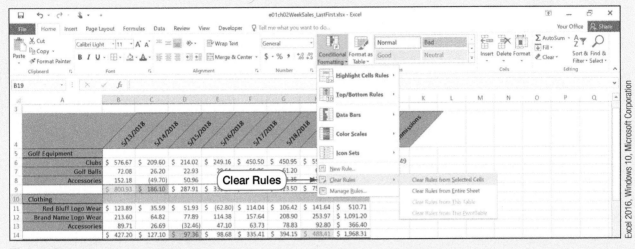

Figure 27 Remove Conditional Formatting

d. Save 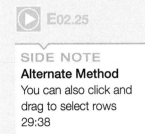 the workbook.

Hide Information in a Worksheet

A worksheet can contain information that may not be necessary, or even desirable, to display. For example, detailed information used to calculate totals might be hidden until such time that the person using the worksheet would like to see it.

Hiding information in a worksheet is relatively simple. Entire worksheet rows and columns can be hidden. Simply select the rows and/or columns to be hidden by clicking on the row or column heading. Point to the selected row or column heading(s), right-click, and then select Hide on the displayed shortcut menu.

Gridlines are very helpful in visualizing and navigating a workbook during development, but some users feel gridlines clutter a worksheet. Gridlines can be "hidden" simply by unchecking the Gridlines box in the Show group on the View tab.

Hiding Worksheet Rows

In the WeeklySales worksheet, rows 29:38 contain parameters that are used to calculate commissions, to identify minimum commission levels, and to specify sales percentage benchmarks for golf equipment, clothing, and consumables. Once the WeeklySales worksheet has been fully developed, there is little need to have this data visible. In fact, having this kind of data visible can be problematic in that a user could inadvertently or intentionally change the data and cause the worksheet to display incorrect information.

In this exercise, you will hide rows 29:38 from view in the WeeklySales worksheet.

E02.25

SIDE NOTE
Alternate Method
You can also click and drag to select rows 29:38

To Hide Rows in a Worksheet

a. On the WeeklySales worksheet, click the heading for row **29** in the WeeklySales worksheet, press and hold Shift, and then click the heading for row **38**.

b. Right-click anywhere in the selected rows.

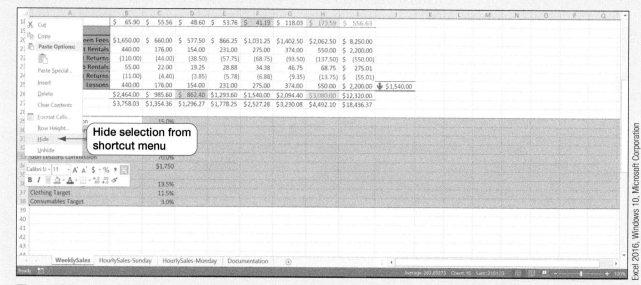

Figure 28 Shortcut menu

c. Select **Hide** on the shortcut menu, and then press `Ctrl` + `Home`.

d. **Save** 🖫 the workbook.

Hiding Worksheet Gridlines

Gridlines assist in identifying cells in manipulating a worksheet. Once a worksheet is complete, some people think gridlines detract from a worksheet's professional appearance. In this exercise, you will turn off, or hide, gridlines in the WeeklySales worksheet.

 E02.26

To Hide Gridlines in a Worksheet

a. On the WeeklySales worksheet, click the **View** tab, and then, in the Show group, click to deselect the Gridlines check box and turn the gridlines off.

Notice the worksheet now has a white background. To many users, this is much more visually appealing than a worksheet in which gridlines are visible.

b. **Save** 🖫 the workbook.

Document Functions and Formulas

An important part of building a good worksheet is documentation. Aleeta Herriott included the standard documentation worksheet in the Week Sales workbook and updated it to reflect what she had accomplished before assigning completion of the workbook to you.

Showing Functions and Formulas

What is displayed in a cell that contains a function or a formula is the calculated result. The function or formula that generated the displayed value is visible only one cell at a time by selecting a cell and then looking at the formula bar. When the Show Formulas feature is turned on, the calculated results are hidden and functions and formulas are shown in the cells instead, whenever applicable.

Show Formulas is very helpful in understanding how a worksheet is structured. It is an essential aid in correcting errors or updating the function of a worksheet. A worksheet that has Show Formulas turned on can be printed and/or exported for documentation purposes.

In this exercise, you will view worksheet formulas and export a formulas worksheet to a PDF.

To View Worksheet Formulas and Export to PDF

a. On the WeeklySales worksheet, click the **Formulas** tab, and then, in the Formula Auditing group, select **Show Formulas** 📝.

Cells now display formulas rather than values. Notice that Show Formulas also displays cell data without formatting.

b. Use the **Zoom Slider** ⎯⎯⎯⎯⎯⎯⎯⎯ on the status bar to move the zoom level so you can view the entire worksheet on the monitor.

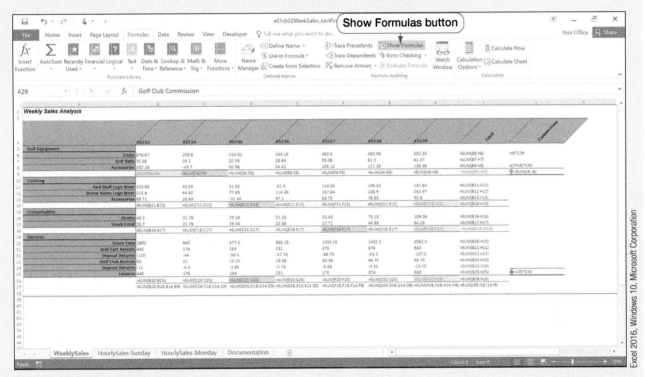

Figure 29 Show formulas

c. Click the **Page Layout** tab, and then, in the Scale to Fit group, click the **Width** arrow, and then select **1 page**. This will scale your worksheet to print in the width of a single page.

d. In the Scale to Fit group, click the **Height** arrow, and then select **1 page**. This will scale your document to print in the height of a single page.

e. In the Page Setup group, click **Orientation**, and then select **Landscape**.

f. Click the **File** tab to enter Backstage view, and then click **Export**. Under Create a PDF/XPS Document, click **Create PDF/XPS**. In the Publish as PDF or XPS dialog box, double-click the File name box, and then type e01ch02WeeklySalesFormulas_LastFirst, using your last and first name. Make sure **Open file after publishing** is checked. Click **Publish**.

g. The WeeklySales worksheet with Show Formulas turned on is displayed as a PDF document in Reader. Close Reader.

h. Click the **Formulas** tab, and then click **Show Formulas** 🔣 to toggle off Show Formulas and return to the default Normal view.

i. Use the Zoom Slider ⊟━━━━━┃━━━━━⊞ on the status bar to set the zoom to 100%.

j. **Save** 🖫 the workbook.

REAL WORLD ADVICE | **Print Formula View for Documentation**

You need to document your workbooks. As the worksheets you develop become more complex — using more functions and formulas — the need for documentation increases. Once your worksheet is complete, one vital documentation step is to print the formulas of your worksheet. If anything ever goes wrong with your worksheet in the future, the formulas printout may be the fastest way to fix it. Remember that an environmentally-friendly documentation option can be to print to Portable Document Format (PDF). A PDF preserves exactly the original "look and feel" of a document but allows its viewing in many different applications.

Updating Existing Documentation

You have made some significant and very important improvements to the Week Sales workbook. You must document the updates that require identification or explanation. In this exercise, you will update the existing documentation worksheet.

To Update Existing Documentation

a. Click the **Documentation** worksheet tab, and then complete the following.

- Click cell **A8**, type today's date in mm/dd/yyyy format, and then press Enter.

- Click cell **B8**, type your name in Firstname Lastname format, and then press Enter.

- Click cell **C8**, type Green background for high sales, and then press Enter.

- In cell **C9**, type Red background for low sales, and then press Enter.

b. Add the file name to the left page footer on all sheets.

c. Click the **WeeklySales** worksheet tab. Click the **File** tab, and then click **Print**. Under Settings, click the **Print Active Sheets** arrow, and then click **Print Entire Workbook**. If requested by your instructor, click **Print**.

d. **Save** 🖫 the workbook, exit Excel, and then submit your files as directed by your instructor.

REAL WORLD ADVICE | **The Power and Risk of "Machine Decision Making"**

Never forget that tools such as Excel are decision-making aids, not decision makers. Certainly, there are highly structured situations, such as a product mix problem, that can be programmed into a worksheet in Excel such that the result is the decision. Excel is also used for the analysis of information in less highly structured problems. In addition, not all factors in a decision can typically be quantified and programmed into a worksheet.

Computers make calculations; people make decisions.

Concept Check

1. Why should you format data in Excel? How might you format data for a person who is color-blind? p. 377–381

2. What are the different functions made available via the AutoSum button? What does each function calculate? p. 397

3. What are the advantages of calculating totals in a table total row? p. 401

4. What character precedes all formulas and functions in Excel? What purpose do parentheses serve in Excel formulas? p. 404–405

5. What is conditional formatting? How can conditional formatting assist in decision making? p. 408

6. List two reasons why it may be necessary to hide rows or columns of information in a worksheet. p. 413

7. Why might you choose to print the formulas of a worksheet? Why is the PDF file format good for saving documentation? p. 416

Key Terms

Argument 397
AVERAGE function 399
Banding 393
Built-in cell style 391
Built-in function 397
Cell alignment 383
Cell reference 397
Conditional formatting 408
Constant 404
COUNT function 399

Default 383
Destination cell 397
Fill color 384
Format Painter 387
Formula 404
Function 396
Graphical format 377
Mathematical operator 404
MAX function 400
MIN function 400

Order of operations 405
Source cell(s) 397
SUBTOTAL function 401
SUM function 398
Table 393
Table style 393
Tabular format 377
Theme 395

Visual Summary

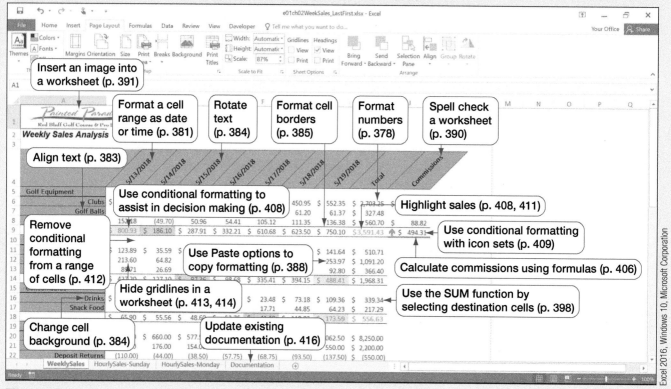

Insert an image into a worksheet (p. 391)

Format a cell range as date or time (p. 381)

Rotate text (p. 384)

Format cell borders (p. 385)

Format numbers (p. 378)

Spell check a worksheet (p. 390)

Align text (p. 383)

Use conditional formatting to assist in decision making (p. 408)

Highlight sales (p. 408, 411)

Remove conditional formatting from a range of cells (p. 412)

Use conditional formatting with icon sets (p. 409)

Use Paste options to copy formatting (p. 388)

Calculate commissions using formulas (p. 406)

Hide gridlines in a worksheet (p. 413, 414)

Use the SUM function by selecting destination cells (p. 398)

Change cell background (p. 384)

Update existing documentation (p. 416)

Figure 30

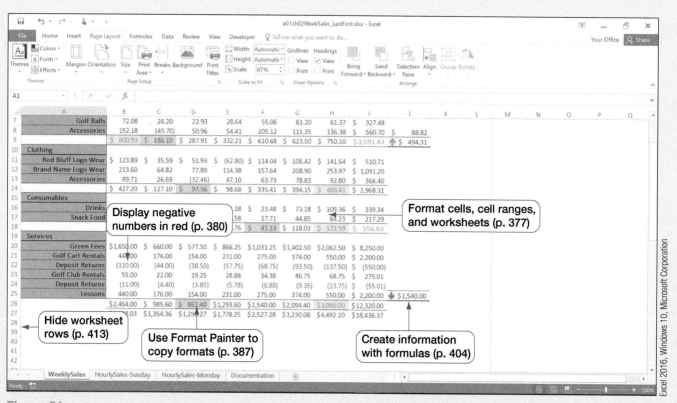

Display negative numbers in red (p. 380)

Format cells, cell ranges, and worksheets (p. 377)

Hide worksheet rows (p. 413)

Use Format Painter to copy formats (p. 387)

Create information with formulas (p. 404)

Figure 31

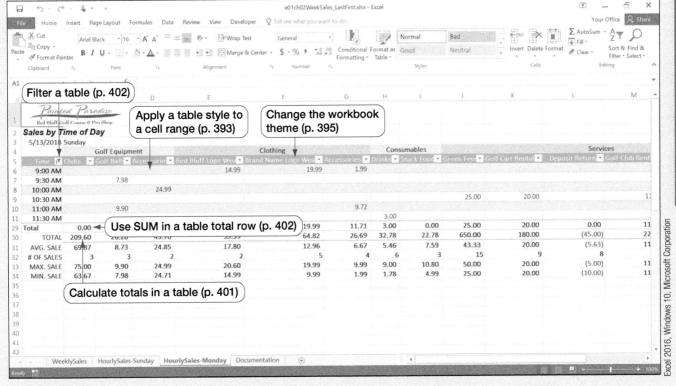

Figure 32

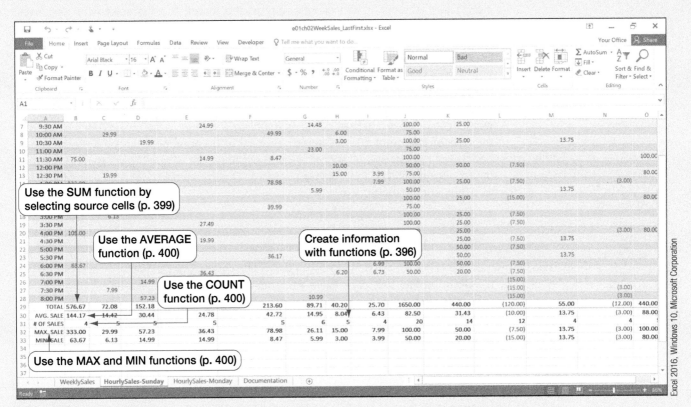

Figure 33

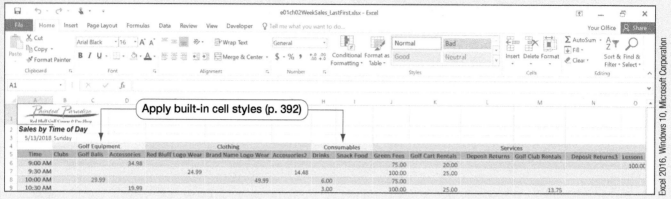

Figure 34

Apply built-in cell styles (p. 392)

Practice 1

Student data files needed:

 e01ch02SpaSchedule.xlsx

e01ch02turquoise_oasis.jpg

You will save your files as:

e01ch02SpaSchedule_LastFirst.xlsx

e01ch02SpaSchedule_LastFirst.pdf

Spa Schedule

Production & Operations

Irene Kai, another manager at the Turquoise Oasis Spa, has exported sales data from a database program into an Excel spreadsheet to facilitate the analysis of services received by a client during a visit to the spa. This spreadsheet is in the initial development stages, but the intention is to keep track of the treatments performed on an individual client during the client's stay at the resort, the therapist who performed each service, and the treatments that seem most popular. This will allow the staff to review spa usage in a visually appealing layout, notice trends in treatment choices, and improve the scheduling of therapist. In the future, it might lead to the mailing of special promotions to regular or repeat customers, a reevaluation of pricing, or the addition or deletion of treatments on the basis of popularity.

Irene has imported the data and created a workbook that will consist of three worksheets. One worksheet contains the clients' names, a list of the dates of service, the type of treatment ad-ministered, the cost of the treatment, and the therapist who performed that service. A second worksheet has a list of spa therapists and the days of the week and times that each is available. The third worksheet contains information to document the workbook.

a. Open Excel, click **Open Other Documents** in the left pane, and then double-click **This PC**. Navigate through the folder structure to the location of your student data files, and then double-click **e01ch02SpaSchedule**. If a Security Warning message displays, click the **Enable Editing** button.

b. Click the **File** tab, click **Save As**, and then double-click **This PC**. In the Save As dialog box, navigate to the location where you are saving your project files, and then change the file name to e01ch02SpaSchedule_LastFirst, using your last and first name. Click **Save**.

c. Click the **ScheduleByDate** worksheet tab. Click the **Page Layout** tab, and then, in the Themes group, click **Themes**, and then select **Droplet** from the gallery.

d. Click cell **A1**. Click the **Home** tab, and then, in the Cells group, click **Format**, and then click **Row Height**. Type 60 in the Row height box, and then click **OK**.

e. Click cell **E1**. Click the **Insert** tab, and then, in the Illustrations group, click **Pictures**. Navigate to the location where your student data files are stored, click **e01ch02turquoise_oasis.jpg**, and then click **Insert**. Click the **Picture Tools Format** tab, and then, in the Arrange group, click **Align**. If necessary, select **Snap**

to Grid. Click the right horizontal sizing handle, and snap the right edge of the logo to the border between columns **F** and **G**. Click the bottom vertical sizing handle, and snap the bottom edge of the logo to the border between rows **1** and **2**.

f. Select the cell range **A2:J2**. Click the **Home** tab, and then, in the Alignment group, click **Merge & Center**. In the Styles group, click **Cell Styles**, and then click **Heading 4** in the gallery.

g. Select cell range **A4:J4**, click **Cell Styles**, and then click **Heading 3** in the gallery.

h. Click cell **A2**, and then, in the Clipboard group, click **Copy**. Select cell range **A26:A30**, right-click cell **A26**, and then, in the Paste Options shortcut menu, select **Formatting**. In the Alignment group, click **Align Left**.

i. Click cell **A6**. In the Clipboard group, click **Format Painter**, and then select cell range **A7:A23**.

j. Select cell range **I6:I23**. In the Number group, click the **Number Format** arrow, and then select **Currency**. In the Number group, click **Decrease Decimal** two times.

k. Select cell range **C6:C23**. Click the **Number Format** arrow, and then select **More Number Formats**. In the Type box, select **1:30 PM**, and then click **OK**.

l. Click cell **J10**. Click **AutoSum**, select the cell range **I6:I9**, and then press Enter. Click cell **J13**. Click **AutoSum**, select the cell range **I11:I12**, and then press Enter. Click cell **J18**. Click **AutoSum**, select cell range **I14:I17**, and then press Enter. Click cell **J21**. Click **AutoSum**, select cell range **I19:I20**, and then press Enter. Click cell **J24**. Click **AutoSum**, select cell range **I22:I23**, and then press Enter.

m. Click cell **C28**, type =MAX(J6:J24), and then press Ctrl+Enter. Click cell **J24**, click the **Format Painter**, and then click cell **C28**.

n. Select cell range **A4:J24**. In the Styles group, click **Format as Table**, and then select **Table Style Medium 3** from the gallery. In the Format as Table dialog box, click to select **My table has headers**, and then click **OK**. On the Design tab, in the Table Style Options group, click **Total Row**. On the **Home** tab, click cell **J10**, click **Format Painter**, and then click cell **J25**.

o. In the Editing group, click **Sort & Filter**, and then click **Filter** to turn off column filters.

p. Select cell **J10**, press and hold Ctrl, and then select cells **J13**, **J18**, **J21**, and **J24**. In the Styles group, click **Conditional Formatting**, point to Highlight Cells Rules, and then select **Greater Than**. Type =C$31 in the Format cells that are GREATER THAN box. Click the **with** arrow, and then select **Custom Format**. In the Format Cells dialog box, on the Font tab, in the Font style box, select **Bold**. Click the Color arrow, and select **Green, Accent2** from the palette. Click **OK**, and then click **OK** again.

q. Click the **TherapistSchedule** worksheet tab. Select cell **C8**, type Monday, and then press Ctrl+Enter. Click and hold the fill handle, and then expand the active cell to encompass cell range **C8:C14**. Press Ctrl+C. Click cell **C16**, press and hold Ctrl, and then click cell **C24**. Press Ctrl+V.

r. Select cell range **A6:D6**. In the Styles group, click **Cell Styles**, and then select **40% - Accent5** from the gallery. In the Font group, click **Bold**.

s. Select cell range **A8:A14**. Press Ctrl, and then select cell ranges **B8:B14**, **A16:A22**, **B16:B22**, **A24:A30**, and **B24:B30**. In the Alignment group, click **Merge & Center**. In the Alignment group, click **Orientation**, and then select **Vertical Text**. In the Alignment group, click **Middle Align**. In the Font group, click **Bold**. Select columns A:B. In the Cells group, click **Format**, and select **AutoFit Column Width**.

t. Right-click the header for row **5**, and then click **Delete**.

u. Click the **Documentation** worksheet tab. Click cell **A8**, insert today's date, and then press Tab. Type your name in cell B8 in the Firstname Lastname format. Click cell **C8**, and then type Calculated daily totals. Press Enter. Type Determined maximum day's sales. Press [Enter]. Type Formatted daily sales totals that met target as green and bold. Press [Enter]. Press [Ctrl]+[Home].

v. Click the **ScheduleByDate** worksheet tab. On the **Page Layout** tab, in the Page Setup group, click **Orientation**, and then select **Landscape**. In the Scale to Fit group, click the **Width** arrow, and then select **1 page**.

w. Spell check the entire workbook. Insert the **file name** on the left page footer on all worksheets.

x. On the **File** tab, click **Export**, and then, under Create a PDF/XPS Document, click **Create PDF/XPS**. Be sure **Open file after publishing** is not checked. Click **Options**. In the Options dialog box, under Publish what, click **Entire workbook**, and then click **OK**. Navigate to the folder where you are saving your files. In the File name box, type e01ch02SpaSchedule_LastFirst using your last and first name, and then click **Publish**.

y. Save 💾 the workbook, exit Excel, and then submit your files as directed by your instructor.

Problem Solve 1

MyITLab®
Grader
Homework

Student data file needed:

 e01ch02Portfolio.xlsx

You will save your file as:

e01ch02Portfolio_LastFirst.xlsx

Stock Portfolio Monthly Dividend Income

Finance &
Accounting

One method that people use to provide income during their retirement years is investing in dividend-paying stocks. The dividends allow investors to make withdrawals from their retirement account without having to reduce their invested principal. Michael Malley, president and chief investment officer of your new employer, Excellent Wealth Management, has developed a worksheet to show how a portfolio of stocks can create an additional income stream for his clients. You are asked to determine how much income the current portfolio is generating in order to assist with future investment decisions in the form of adding to current investments or diversifying and adding other dividend-paying investments.

a. Open the Excel file, **e01ch02Portfolio**. Save your file as e01ch02Portfolio_LastFirst, using your last and first name.

b. **Center** and **bold** cell range **B2:F3**.

c. Merge & Center cell range **A1:N1**. Apply the **Title** cell style, and then **Bold** the range.

d. Select cell range **N12:N16** and **N20:N24**, and then calculate row totals using the **SUM** function.

e. Calculate the average of Total Dividends Received in cell **G8**.

f. Apply cell style **Heading 3** to cells **G7**, **B10**, and **B18**.

g. Apply the **Currency** format to cell ranges **B4:F4**, **B6:F6**, **B8:G8**, **B12:N16**, and **B20:N25**.

h. In cell **B7**, calculate the yield of Prime Steel — the annual dividends per share divided by the price per share. Copy the formula to cell range **C7:F7**. Format the yield figures as Percent Style with two decimal places.

i. Hide rows **10:17**.

j. Format cell range **A19:N24** as a table with headers. Apply **Table Style Light 11**. Sort by **STOCK** from **A-Z**, and then turn off Filters.

k. Add the Total Row to the table, and calculate the total of columns B:N.

l. Apply a top border to cell range **A25:N25**.

m. Apply cell style **40% - Accent3** to cell ranges **A20:A25**, **B25:N25**, and **N20:N24**.

n. Apply Conditional Formatting to cell range **B20:M24**. Display **the Top 10 Items** as **Green Fill with Dark Green Text**.

o. Turn off **gridlines** in the Dividend Portfolio worksheet.

p. In the **Documentation** worksheet, enter today's date in mm/dd/yyyy format into cells **A8** and **A20**. In cell B8, type your name in the Firstname Lastname format. In cell **C8**, type Completed Mr. Malley's monthly dividend income worksheet. Make cell **A1** the active cell.

q. Spell check the entire workbook. Insert the file name on the left page footer on all worksheets.

r. For the **DividendPortfolio** and **Documentation** worksheets, set the Orientation to **Landscape**, and then set the **Width** to **1 page**. Change Print Settings to **Print Entire Workbook**. Print your workbook as directed by your instructor.

s. Save the workbook, exit Excel, and then submit your file as directed by your instructor.

Critical Thinking   The FIVE stock yields the highest dividends. What decision regarding the FIVE stock can be drawn from this result? The PULSE stock yields the lowest dividends. Should this stock be sold based off of this data? Why or why not?

Perform 1: Perform in Your Life

Tracking Stock Price Movements

Finance & Accounting

Excel can be used to track changes in stock prices over time. Not only can you record the actual prices, but by using formulas and some formatting, you can easily calculate the percentage changes in price and pick out the winners and losers in your portfolio.

After you have demonstrated your Excel skills for Mr. Malley, he would like you to work with some real data for a client (your instructor). The client may decide to modify the specifications given below. Because customer service is of the utmost importance to Excellent Wealth Management, be sure to follow any client requests very carefully.

a. Open the Excel file, **e01ch02PriceChanges**. Save your file as e01ch02PriceChanges_LastFirst, using your last and first name.

Use a website that provides access to historic stock price data for steps b through d. Options include, but are not limited to, finance.yahoo.com and google.com/finance.

b. Select five companies that are publicly traded. Enter the company name in each cell, starting with B3:F3. Format the titles to look professional. In the cells immediately below each company name, enter the ticker symbol — the abbreviation that the company's stock uses.

c. Enter the eight most recent dates that denote the first trading day of a quarter, starting in cell A5:A12. For example, the first trading day of 1Q2016 was 1/2/2016. The first trading day of 2Q was 4/1/2016. Format the dates entered as Long Date. Adjust the widths of columns A:F to fit the data you entered.

d. Look up the historic closing prices for each stock for the dates entered in step c, and then enter these values into the corresponding cells.

e. Under the first company's historic closing price data, calculate the minimum price that was observed. Copy the formula to the cells under each of the other companies' historic price data.

f.　Under the minimum price that was calculated, determine the maximum closing price that was observed. Copy the formula to the appropriate cell for each of the other companies.

g.　For each company, calculate the Current Gross Margin as the closing price for the most recent quarter minus the closing price of the first quarter.

h.　Format the historic price data, the minimum and maximum closing prices, and the current gross margin with an appropriate format.

i.　Select the range that contains the historic closing prices for the first company. Apply conditional formatting to the range using the Gradient Fill Green Data Bar.

j.　Right-align row headings (A5:A12), and center the company names and tickers for each range. Merge & Center the heading Price Performance across columns B:F. Merge & Center Excellent Wealth Management across all of the columns used in the worksheet, and then apply the Title cell style and bold. Make sure all of the data is visible in each of the cells.

k.　Apply an appropriate heading cell style to all row and column headings, and then apply an appropriate cell style to the ticker symbols.

l.　Apply an appropriate workbook theme, and then adjust the widths of columns A:F if necessary.

m.　Copy the worksheet to a new worksheet named Auditing. Move the Auditing worksheet to the right of the Stocks worksheet. Show the formulas in this worksheet, and then adjust the column widths of columns A:F to fit the displayed content.

n.　Update the Documentation worksheet to reflect the changes that have been made to the workbook. Spell check the entire workbook. Insert the file name on the left page footer on all worksheets.

o.　Click the Stocks worksheet tab, and then adjust print settings to ensure a usable printed worksheet and to print all worksheets in the workbook. Adjust the Auditing worksheet to print on one page.

p.　Save the workbook, exit Excel, and then submit your file as directed by your instructor.

Additional Cases

Additional Chapter Cases are available at www.pearsonhighered.com/youroffice

Understanding the Fundamentals

This business unit had two outcomes:

Learning Outcome 1:

Use Excel to enter text, number, date, and time data to create efficient and effective worksheets.

Learning Outcome 2:

Use Excel to effectively communicate information through the use of functions and worksheet formatting.

In the Business Unit 1 Capstone, students will demonstrate competency in these outcomes through a series of business problems at various levels from guided practice to problem solving an existing spreadsheet to performing to create new spreadsheets.

More Practice 1

Student data files needed:

 e01BeverageSales.xlsx

 e01Indigo5.jpg

You will save your files as:

 e01BeverageSales_LastFirst.xlsx

e01BeverageSales_LastFirst.pdf

 Product & Operations

 Accounting & Finance

Beverage Sales and Inventory Analysis

The Painted Paradise Resort & Spa offers a wide assortment of beverages through the Indigo5 restaurant and bar. The resort must track the inventory levels of these beverages as well as the sales and costs associated with each item. Restaurant manager Alberto Dimas has asked you to analyze the inventory and sales data found in the worksheet. There are four categories of beverages: beer, wine, soda, and water. You also have three inventory figures: Starting, Delivered, and Ending. You will work with a beverage sales workbook to generate an analysis of beverage sales in which you identify units sold of each beverage, cost of goods sold, revenue, profit, profit margin, and appropriate totals and averages.

a. Open **Excel**, click **Open Other Documents** in the left pane, and then double-click **This PC**. Navigate through the folder structure to the location of your student data files, and then double-click **e01BeverageSales**. If a Security Warning message displays, click the **Enable Editing** button.

b. Click the **File** tab, click **Save As**, and then double-click **This PC**. In the Save As dialog box, navigate to the location where you are saving your project files, and then change the file name to e01BeverageSales_LastFirst, using your last and first name. Click **Save**.

c. On the **BeverageSales** worksheet tab, select cell range **C2:K2**, and then click **Merge & Center** for the selected range. Apply the **Title** cell style to the selected range.

d. Select cell range **C3:K3**, and then click **Merge & Center** for the selected range. Apply the **Heading 4** cell style to the selected range.

e. Insert a hard return at the specified locations in the following cells. Be sure to remove any spaces between the words, and then press Alt + Enter to insert the hard return.

- Between **Starting** and **Inventory** in C6

- Between **Inventory** and **Delivered** in D6

- Between **Ending** and **Inventory** in E6

f. Make the following calculations.

- Click cell **F7**. Calculate Units Sold by adding Starting Inventory to Inventory Delivered and then subtracting Ending Inventory. Type =, click cell **C7**, type +, click cell **D7**, type -, and then click cell **E7**. Press Ctrl + Enter, and then copy the formula in cell F7 to cell ranges **F8:F12**, **F15:F18**, **F21:F25**, and **F28:F29**. If any cells contain a series of number signs (#), select the column. On the **Home** tab, in the Cells group, click **Format**, and then click **AutoFit Column Width**.

- Click cell **H7**. Calculate Cost of Goods Sold as Units Sold multiplied by Cost Per Unit. Type =, click cell **F7**, type *, and then click cell **G7**. Press Ctrl + Enter, and then copy the formula in cell H7 to cell ranges **H8:H12**, **H15:H18**, **H21:H25**, and **H28:H29**. If any cells contain a series of number signs (#), select the column, and then apply **AutoFit Column Width**.

- Click cell **J7**. Calculate Revenue as Units Sold multiplied by Sale Price Per Unit. Type =, click cell **F7**, type *, and then click cell **I7**. Press Ctrl + Enter, and then copy the formula in cell J7 to cell ranges **J8:J12**, **J15:J18**, **J21:J25**, and **J28:J29**. If any cells contain a series of number signs (#), select the column, and then apply **AutoFit Column Width**.

- Click cell **K7**. Calculate Profit Margin as (Revenue - Cost of Goods Sold)/Revenue. Type =(, click cell **J7**, type -, click cell **H7**, type)/, and then click cell **J7**. Press Ctrl + Enter, and then copy the formula in cell K7 to cell ranges **K8:K12**, **K15:K18**, **K21:K25**, and **K28:K29**.

g. Select cell ranges **C13:F13**, **C19:F19**, **C26:F26**, and **C30:F30** and cells **H13**, **J13**, **H19**, **J19**, **H26**, **J26**, **H30**, and **J30**. Click **AutoSum**. If any cells contain a series of number signs (#), select the cells, and then apply **AutoFit Column Width**.

h. Click cell **C31**. Calculate the total number of items in Starting Inventory for all categories combined by using the SUM() function. Type =SUM(C13,C19,C26,C30), and then copy cell C31 to cell range **D31:F31** as well as cells **H31** and **J31**. If any cells contain a series of number signs (#), select the cells, and then apply **AutoFit Column Width**.

i. Make the following formatting changes.

- Format the row height of row 6 to 30.

- Select cell range **A6:K29**, and then apply **AutoFit Column Width**.

- Select cell range **C6:K6** along with cells **B13**, **B19**, **B26**, **B30**, and **B31**. Apply **Align Right**.

- Select cell ranges **C13:K13**, **C19:K19**, **C26:K26**, and **C30:K30**. Add a **Top and Bottom Border** to the selected cell ranges.

- Select cell range **C31:K31**, and then add a **Bottom Double Border** to the selected range.

j. Select cell range **C7:F31**. Format the selected range as **Number** with a comma separator and **zero** decimal places. Select cell range **G7:J31**, and then format the selected range as **Number** with a comma separator and **two** decimal places.

k. Copy cell **K12**, and then from **Paste Options**, paste **Formulas** into cells **K13**, **K19**, **K26**, **K30**, and **K31**. Select cell range **K7:K31**. Format the selected range as **Percentage** with two decimal places. If any cells contain a series of number signs (#), select the cells, and then apply **AutoFit Column Width**.

l. Select cells **H13**, **J13**, **H19**, **J19**, **H26**, **J26**, **H30**, **J30**, **H31**, and **J31**. Format the selected cells as **Currency**. If any cells contain a series of number signs (#), select the cells, and then apply **AutoFit Column Width**.

m. Select cell range **F7:F12**. Use **conditional formatting** to highlight the beer with the highest number of units sold for the week as **Green Fill with Dark Green Text**. Use **Top 10 Items** in Top/Bottom Rules, and then change the number of ranked items to 1.

n. Copy cell **F12**. Select cell range **J7:J12**. Right-click the selected cell range, and then under **Paste Options**, click **Paste Formatting**. Continue pasting conditional formatting as follows:

- Select cell range **F15:F18**, right-click the selection, and then click **Paste Formatting**.

- Select cell range **J15:J18**, right-click the selection, and then click **Paste Formatting**.

- Select cell range **F21:F25**, right-click the selection, and then click **Paste Formatting**.

- Select cell range **J21:J25**, right-click the selection and then click **Paste Formatting**.

- Select cell range **F28:F29**, right-click the selection and then click **Paste Formatting**.

- Select cell range **J28:J29**, right-click the selection and then click **Paste Formatting**.

o. Select cell range **J7:J12**, press Ctrl, and then select cell ranges **J15:J18**, **J21:J25**, and **J28:J29**. Click **Increase Decimal** two times.

p. Select cell range **A6:K6**, press Ctrl, and then click cells **A14**, **A20**, and **A27**. Click **Cell Styles** and then, in the Themed Cell Styles group, apply **Accent6** to the selected cells. With the cells still selected, press Ctrl, and then select cell ranges **B13:K13**, **B19:K19**, **B26:K26**, and **B30:K31**. Click **Bold**.

q. Delete row **4**.

r. Press Ctrl + Home. Click the **Insert** tab, and then in the Illustrations group, click **Pictures**. Navigate to the location of your student data files, and then click **e01mpIndigo5**. Click **Insert**. Under **Picture Tools**, on the **Format** tab, in the Arrange group, click **Align**, and then click **Snap to Grid**. Drag the square resizing handle on the right side of the logo left until the right border is between columns **B** and **C**. Drag the square resizing handle on the bottom of the logo and up until the bottom border is between rows **4** and **5**.

s. Click the **Page Layout** tab, in the Themes group, click **Themes**, and then click **Organic** to change the workbook theme. Click the **Home** tab, and then in the Cells group, click the **Format** button and select **AutoFit Column Width** to columns A:K. Click the **Page Layout** tab, and in the Page Setup group, click the **Orientation** arrow. Select **Landscape**. In the Scale to Fit group, change the Width to **1 page**, and then press Ctrl + Home.

t. Click the **Documentation** worksheet tab, click cell **A8**. Press Ctrl+; (semicolon), press Ctrl + Enter, and then press Tab. In cell **B8**, type your name in the Firstname Lastname format, and then press Tab. In cell **C8**, type Formatted BeverageSales worksheet, and then press Enter. Press Ctrl + Home.

u. Click the **Insert** tab, in the Text group, click Header & Footer. In the Navigation group, click **Go to Footer**, and then insert the **file name** in the left footer of all worksheets.

v. Check the spelling on both worksheets.

w. Click the **BeverageSales** worksheet tab.

x. Click the **File** tab, click **Export**, and then under Create a PDF/XPS Document, click **Create PDF/XPS**. Be sure Open file after publishing is not checked. Click **Options**. In the Options dialog box, under Publish what, click **Entire workbook**, and then click **OK**. Navigate to the folder where you are saving your files. In the File name box, verify e01mpBeverageSales_LastFirst is the file name, and then click **Publish**.

y. Save the workbook, exit Excel, and then submit your files as directed by your instructor.

Problem Solve 1

Student data file needed:

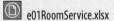 e01RoomService.xlsx

You will save your file as:

 e01RoomService_LastFirst.xlsx

Accounting & Finance

Room Service Analysis

The Painted Paradise Resort & Spa offers an extensive array of food and drinks available for delivery to guests' rooms. For the convenience of in-room delivery, guests pay a premium price for the service. Recently, the resort has asked representatives from both the hotel and the restaurant to start tracking the charges by room type and day of the week. From this information, management hopes to determine which types of guests are ordering room service.

a. Open the Excel file, **e01RoomService**. Save your file as e01RoomService_LastFirst, using your last and first name.

b. Click the **RoomServiceAnalysis** worksheet tab, and then apply the formatting as follows:

- Select cell range **A2:H2**, and then apply Merge & Center.

- Select cell **A2**, and then apply the **Heading 2** cell style.

- Select cell range **B7:H23**, and then apply the **Comma Style** (,) number style.

- Select cell range **B22:H22**, and then set the number of decimals to **0**.

- Format cell ranges **A4:A23** and **B6:H6** as cell style **Heading 4** and **Align Right**. Select cell ranges **A7:A23** and **B6:H6**, and then set the Fill Color to **Green, Accent 6, Lighter 60%**. Click cell **A6**, and then click **Fill Color** to apply the color Green, Accent 6, Lighter 60%.

- Insert a hard return between **Villa** and **Suite** in cell **G6** (remember to remove the space between the two words).

- Set the width of column **A** using **AutoFit Column Width**. Set the width of columns **B:H** to **12**.

c. Increase the height of row 1 to **55**.

d. Select the **picture** in cell A1. Set the picture alignment to **Snap to Grid**. Position the graphic with the right edge between columns **F** and **G** and the left edge between columns **C** and **D**.

e. Calculate the following using **AutoSum** with source cells selected. Use cell range **B7:G13** as the source range for the remainder of this step.

- Add a total in row **14**.

- Average the values in row **15**.

- Calculate the minimum value in row **16**.

- Calculate the maximum value in row **17**.

f. Calculate the total for each row of data in column H in cell ranges **H7:H14** and **H19:H20**, and cell **H22**. Make sure the number of decimal places in cell H22 is set to 0.

g. Calculate the average individual sales per day for One Double rooms in cell **B23**. Divide the total sales for the week by the number of rooms divided by the number of days in a week (7). Copy the formula to cell range **C23:H23**.

h. Apply the Data Bar conditional formatting to cell range **H7:H13**. Select the **Orange Data Bar** under the Gradient Fill.

i. Apply the Total cell style to cell range **B14:H14**, and then apply Accounting Number Format to cell ranges **B14:H17**, **B19:H20**, and **B23:H23**.

j. Turn off the worksheet **gridlines**. Apply the **Headlines** theme.

k. Insert the file name into the left section of the page footer for both worksheets in the workbook.

l. For both worksheets, set page orientation to **Landscape** orientation, and set scaling to **Fit All Columns on One Page**.

m. Check the spelling of both worksheets.

n. In the **Documentation** worksheet, type today's date in cells **A8**. In cell **B8**, type your name in Firstname Lastname format. In **C8**, type Completed the RoomServiceAnalysis worksheet.

o. Save the workbook, exit Excel, and then submit your file as directed by your instructor.

Critical Thinking
After reviewing the completed RoomServiceAnalysis worksheet, which types of guests are ordering room service the most. Identify the top 2 types. Which types of guests are ordering room service the least? Identify the bottom 2 types. What decisions could management make about room service from analysis worksheet?

Problem Solve 2

Grader
Homework

Student data file needed:

 e01AutoBody.xlsx

You will save your files as:

e01AutoBody_LastFirst.xlsx

e01AutoBody_LastFirst.pdf

Auto Shop Sales Analysis

Accounting & Finance

You are the office manager for Jim's Auto Shop. A new body shop just opened a few blocks away, and your boss, Jim Love, is concerned that sales have declined. He has started a workbook of services offered at the auto shop and included the last six month's sales. He has asked that you complete the workbook by creating formulas to calculate the total sales of each service. Jim also wants you to determine the largest-selling service at the auto shop and to call attention to these services by formatting them appropriately. From this completed workbook, Jim will determine whether he should continue to offer all services or focus on fewer services to stay competitive.

a. Open the Excel file, **e01AutoBody**. Save your file as e01AutoBody_LastFirst, using your last and first name.

b. Rename Sheet1 Sales. Rename Sheet2 Documentation.

c. On the **Sales** worksheet, set the horizontal alignment for A1:H1 and then A2:H2 to **Center Across Selection**.

d. Increase the height of row **1** to 30. Hide row **3**.

e. Click cell **H4**, and type Total. Click in cell **A15**, and type Total.

f. Select cell **B4**. Use AutoFill to fill through **G4**. Apply the Angle Counterclockwise orientation to cell range **B4:H4**.

g. In cell range **B15:G15**, use a function to calculate the monthly totals.

h. In cell range **H5:H15**, use a function to calculate the total of each service offered.

i. Select cell range **A4:H4**, and then apply the **Heading 3** style to the cell range. Select cell **A1**, and then apply the **Title** style. Select cell **A2**, and then apply **Heading 4** style.

j. Select cell ranges **B5:H5** and **B15:H15**, and then apply the **Accounting Number Format**.

k. Select cell range **B6:H14**, and then apply the **Comma** style format.

l. Select cell range **B15:H15**, and then apply the **Total** style.

m. Select cell range **B5:H15**, and then decrease the decimals to zero decimal places.

n. In cells **A17**, **A18**, and **A19**, enter the labels Average, Largest, and Smallest, respectively. **Right-align** cell range A17:A19.

o. In **B17**, use a function to determine the average sales for January

p. In **B18**, use a function to determine the largest sale for January.

q. In **B19**, use a function to determine the smallest sale for January.

r. Copy the formulas in cell range B17:B19 to cell range **C17:G19**. If necessary, decrease the decimals to zero decimal places.

s. Select cell range **H5:H14**. Apply the **Gradient Fill Light Blue Data Bar** to the range of cells.

t. Select cell range **B5:G14**, and apply a conditional format to highlight any sales less than $1,000 with **Light Red Fill**.

u. Hide the **Gridlines** of the **Sales** worksheet.

v. Click the **Documentation** worksheet. In cell **A8**, type today's date. In cell **B8**, type your name in the Firstname Lastname format. In cell **C8**, type Calculated totals for the services and products for the past six months. **Wrap the text** of cell **C8**. Type Sales in cell **B20**.

w. Enter the file name in the left footer of both worksheets. Check the spelling of both worksheets.

x. Change the scaling of the **Sales** worksheet to **Fit all Columns on One Page**. Change both worksheets to **Landscape** orientation.

y. Show the formulas of the Sales worksheet, and then export the worksheet to **PDF**. Do not open the file after publishing. Save the PDF as e01AutoBody_LastFirst using your last and first name. Remove the formulas view from the Sales worksheet.

z. Save the workbook, exit Excel, and then submit your files as directed by your instructor.

Perform 1: Perform in Your Life

Student data file needed:
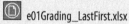 e01Grading.xlsx

You will save your file as:
e01Grading_LastFirst.xlsx

Grade Analysis

Information Technology

Most students are concerned about grades and want to have some means of easily tracking grades, analyzing their performance, and calculating their current grade (as much as is possible) in every class. You will create a grade analysis workbook to assist you with tracking, calculating, and analyzing your performance in your classes.

a. Open the Excel file, **e01Grading**. Save your file as e01Grading_LastFirst, using your last and first name. Rename Sheet1 with a name appropriate for this exercise.

b. A grading scale of 90-80-70-60 was entered into the worksheet. If necessary, adjust the grading scale as desired. Classes and class assignments have been entered into the workbook. Adjust to your classes and class assignments as desired.

c. Include the following calculations,

• Using a function, calculate the total possible points for each class.

• Using a function, calculate your total score for each class.

• Using a formula, calculate the percentage earned on each assignment for each class.

• Using a formula, calculate the total percentage earned in each class.

d. In cell E46, using a formula, calculate the average total percent earned in all classes.

e. In cell E47, using a formula, calculate the lowest total percent earn in all classes.

f. You are striving for an A in each course. Apply conditional formatting to the total percentage earned in each course based on the grading scale. For example, when 90% or greater is earned, a format is applied. When less than 90% is earned, a different format is applied.

g. Format the worksheet appropriately. Rename and color the worksheet tab containing your grade data.

h. Include a completed and well-structured Documentation worksheet.

i. Insert the file name in the left footer of all worksheets. Check the spelling of both worksheets.

j. Modify any page settings to ensure that each of your worksheets will print on a single page. Specify portrait or landscape orientation as is appropriate to maximize readability.

k. Save the workbook, exit Excel, and then submit your file as directed by your instructor.

Perform 2: Perform in Your Career

Student data file needed:

 Blank Excel workbook

You will save your file as:

e01TimeTrack_LastFirst.xlsx

Personal Time Tracking

Accounting & Finance

Human Resources

You have started working as a computer programmer with BetaWerks Software Corporation. The company requires you to track the time that you spend doing different things during the day each week. This helps the company to determine how many of your hours are billable to customers. You have several different projects to work on as well as a few training sessions throughout the week. The company pays for one 15-minute coffee break and a one-hour lunch each day. Any additional time is considered personal time.

a. Start Excel, and then open a blank workbook. Save your file as e01TimeTrack_LastFirst, using your last and first name. Rename Sheet1 with a name appropriate to this exercise.

b. Create a worksheet to track your time for the company this week. The following requirements must be met.

- The worksheet should identify the first day of the workweek with a title such as Week of mm/dd/yyyy.

- Your time must be broken down by project/client and weekdays.

- Time not billable to a project should be classified as Unbillable.

- Unbillable time should be broken into at least two categories: Breaks and Work.

c. Set up your worksheet so you can easily calculate the amount of time you spent working on each account, in meetings, in training, and on breaks according to the following information.

- Monday, you spent two hours in a meeting with your development team. You will bill this to the BetaWerks Software company as unbillable hours. After the meeting, you took a 20-minute coffee break. After your break, you spent two hours and 15 minutes working on your project for Garske Advising. After a one-hour lunch, you attended a two-hour training and development meeting. Before heading home for the day, you spent two hours working on the ISBC Distributing project.

- Tuesday morning, you spent four hours on the Klemisch Kompany project. To help break up the morning, you took a 20-minute coffee break at 10:00. You had time for only a 30-minute lunch because you had to get back to the office for a team-building activity. The activity lasted 40 minutes. To finish the day, you spent four hours working on the Garske Advising assignment.

- Wednesday morning, you spent two hours each on the Garske Advising and Klemisch Kompany projects. Lunch was a quick 30 minutes because you had a conference call with Mr. Atkinson from ISBC at 1 p.m. The conference call took one hour, and then you spent an additional three hours working on the ISBC project.

- Thursday, the day started with a 30-minute update with your supervisor. Following the meeting, you were able to spend two hours on the ISBC project. After a 15-minute coffee break, you started on a new project for K&M Worldwide for 90 minutes. You took a 45-minute lunch break and then spent two and a half hours on the Klemisch Kompany project and two hours on your work for L&H United.

- Friday started with a two-hour training and development session about a new software package that BetaWerks is starting to implement, followed by a 15-minute coffee break. After your coffee break, you were able to squeeze in two more hours for L&H United before taking a one-hour lunch. After lunch, you put in four hours on the Klemisch Kompany project before finally going home for the week.

d. BetaWerks bills your time spent on each account according to the following rates.

Klemisch Kompany	$275
Garske Advising	$250
ISBC Distributing	$225
K&M Worldwide	$175
L&H United	$200

e. Your salary is $100,000/year with benefits. Given two weeks of vacation, you cost BetaWerks $2,000 in salary and benefits per week.

f. Include in your worksheet a calculation of your profit/loss to BetaWerks for the week.

g. Be sure to document your worksheet using a separate Documentation worksheet, comments, and instructions.

h. Modify any page settings to ensure that each of your worksheets will print on a single page. Specify portrait or landscape orientation as is appropriate to maximize readability.

i. Insert the file name in the left footer of all worksheets.

j. Save the workbook, exit Excel, and then submit your file as directed by your instructor.

Perform 3: Perform in Your Team

Student data file needed:

 Blank Excel workbook

You will save your file as:

 e01CheckRegister_TeamName.xlsx

Check Register

Finance & Accounting

You volunteer time with a local nonprofit, the Mayville Community Theatre. Because of your business background, the board of directors has asked you to serve as the new treasurer and to track all the monetary transactions for the group.

a. Select one team member to set up the document by completing steps b through e. Then continue with step d.

b. Open your browser, and then navigate to either https://www.onedrive.live.com, https://www.drive.google.com, or any other instructor-assigned location. Be sure all members of the team have an account on the chosen system, such as a Microsoft or Google account.

c. Create a new workbook, and then save it as e01CheckRegister_TeamName. Replace Name with the number assigned to your team by your instructor.

d. Rename Sheet1 as CheckRegister-TeamName. Replace Name with the number of your team.

e. Share the worksheet with the other members of your team. Make sure that each team member has the appropriate permission to edit the document.

f. Hold a team meeting, and make a plan. Lay out on paper the worksheet you are going to build, discuss the requirements of each of the remaining steps, and then divide the remaining steps (steps g through n) among team members. Note that the steps should be completed in order, so as each team member completes his or her steps, he or she should notify the entire team, not just the team member responsible for the next step.

g. Create the Check Register worksheet to track receipts and expenditures that should be assigned to one of the following categories: **Costumes**, **Marketing**, **Operating and Maintenance**, **Scripts and Royalties**, and **Set Construction**. Also track the following for each receipt or expenditure: the date, amount of payment, check/reference number, recipient, and item description.

h. Enter the following receipts and expenditures under the appropriate category.

Date	Item	Paid To	Check or Ref. #	Amount
11/1/2018	Starting Balance	N/A		$1793.08
11/2/2018	Royalties for "The Cubicle"	Office Publishing Company	9520	–$300.00
11/2/2018	Scripts for "The Cubicle"	Office Publishing Company	9521	–$200.00
11/5/2018	Building Maintenance — Ticket Office	Fix It Palace	9522	–$187.92
11/8/2018	Patron Donation	N/A	53339	$1,000.00
11/12/2018	Costumes for "The Cubicle"	Jane's Fabrics	9523	–$300.00
11/21/2018	Building Materials for set construction of "The Cubicle"	Fix It Palace	9524	–$430.00
11/30/2018	TV and Radio ads for "The Cubicle"	AdSpace	9525	–$229.18
11/30/2018	General Theater Operating Expenses — November	The Electric Co-op, City Water Works	9526	–$149.98
12/15/2018	Ticket Revenue from "The Cubicle"	N/A	59431	$1,115.50
12/31/2018	General Theater Operating Expenses — December	The Electric Co-op, City Water Works	9527	–$195.13

i. Money is deposited periodically into the checking account. Include a column to track deposits.

j. Finally, include a column to track the running balance. This should be updated any time money is deposited into or withdrawn from the account.

k. If the running account balance drops below $1,000, there should be a conditional formatting alert for any balance figure below the threshold.

l. Document the check register using a separate Documentation worksheet and comments where helpful.

m. Modify any page settings to ensure that each of your worksheets will print on a single page. Specify portrait or landscape orientation as is appropriate to maximize readability.

n. Insert the file name in the left footer on all worksheets in the workbook. Include a list of the names of the students in your team in the right section of the footer.

o. Save the workbook, exit Excel, and then submit your file as directed by your instructor.

Perform 4: How Others Perform

Student data file needed:

e01ProjectBilling.xlsx

You will save your file as:

e01ProjectBilling_LastFirst.xlsx

Project Management Billing

Finance & Accounting

John Smith works with you at the Excellent Consulting Company. Each week, consultants are required to track how much time they spend on each project. A worksheet is used to track the date, start time, end time, project code, description of work performed, and number of billable hours completed. At the bottom of the worksheet, the hours spent on each project are summarized so clients can be billed. In your role as an internal auditor, you have been asked to double-check a tracking sheet each week. By random selection, you need to check Mr. Smith's tracking worksheet this week. Make sure his numbers are accurate, and ensure that his worksheet is set up to minimize errors. His worksheet is also in need of formatting for appearance and clarity.

a. Open the Excel file, **e01ProjectBilling**. Save your file as e01ProjectBilling_LastFirst, using your last and first name.

b. Check all calculated figures for accuracy. If you subtract Start Time from End Time and multiply the difference by 24, the result is the number of hours between the two times.

c. Calculate the totals for the items in column J.

d. Examine client totals, and then correct any problems with formulas.

e. Apply formatting, such as cell styles, bold, and a theme, to improve the appearance of the worksheet.

f. Apply any data formatting that will make the data easier to interpret.

g. Add workbook documentation as directed by your instructor.

h. Insert the file name in the left footer on all worksheets in the workbook.

i. Modify any page settings to ensure that each of the worksheets will print on a single page. Specify portrait or landscape orientation as is appropriate to maximize readability.

j. Save the workbook, exit Excel, and then submit your file as directed by your instructor.

Excel Business Unit **2**

Conducting **Business Analysis**

Businesses often have to manage large amounts of data on a daily basis. This can be a difficult feat for any business employee. However, Excel can help you organize large amounts of data, making that data easier to manage, update, and analyze. You can also use Excel to report or present information to internal and external customers, company stakeholders, or your supervisor. This business unit will introduce you to the importance of using Excel for business analysis.

Learning Outcome 1

Use Excel to create formulas and functions to perform calculations, analyze data, solve problems, and help in making wise business decisions.

REAL WORLD SUCCESS

"The skills I have learned through Excel have become incredibly valuable in my everyday life. I recently worked at a private golf course and was asked to create an inventory workbook to track beverage cart sales. This would allow the golf course to forecast demand and predict the amount of starting inventory we needed to maintain. In addition, we needed to use functions that would be user-friendly for the beverage cart employees. At the end of the day, the beverage cart employees would count to see how many items from the set amount of inventory were missing, input the numbers into the Excel workbook. Then Excel would compute the amount of sales the beverage cart employee would need to turn in. The remaining amount would equal the tips the employee had earned. The use of Excel functions helped the golf course to track not only its inventory but also its profits."

- Miri, alumnus

Learning Outcome 2

Use Excel to create a variety of detailed charts appropriate to the data that will visually represent and analyze the data.

REAL WORLD SUCCESS

"In my internship, I used a combo chart to analyze inventory trends over time, presenting inventory buildup or shrinkage on one axis and production levels on another. I was able to use this visual representation to better understand supply chain coordination throughout a quarter, providing my superiors with data to improve our operating efficiency. By combining these charts with charts presenting demand variance, our company was able to pinpoint sources of inventory buildup and higher operating costs."

- Steven, alumnus

Microsoft Excel 2016

Chapter 3	CELL REFERENCES, NAMED RANGES, AND FUNCTIONS

Prepare Case

Sales & Marketing

Finance and Accounting

Painted Paradise Resort & Spa Wedding Planning

Clint Keller and Addison Ryan have just booked a wedding at Painted Paradise Resort & Spa. When requested by a happy couple, the Turquoise Oasis Spa coordinates a variety of events including spa visits, golf massages, and gift baskets made up of various spa products. Given the frequency of wedding events at the Turquoise Oasis Spa, Meda Rodate has asked for your assistance in modifying an Excel workbook that can be used and reused to plan these events in the future.

Goran Bogicevic/Shutterstock

Student data file needed for this chapter:

 e02ch03Wedding.xlsx

You will save your file as:

 e02ch03Wedding_LastFirst.xlsx

Referencing Cells and Named Ranges

The value of Excel expands as you move from using the spreadsheet for displaying data to analyzing data in order to make informed decisions. As the complexity of a spreadsheet increases, techniques that promote effective and efficient development of the spreadsheet become of utmost importance. Integrating cell references within formulas and working with functions are common methods used in developing effective spreadsheets. These skills will become the foundation for more advanced skills.

A **cell reference** refers to a particular cell or range of cells within a formula or function instead of a value. A cell reference contains two parts: a column reference, which is the alphabetic portion that comes first, and a row reference, which is the numeric portion that comes last. For example, cell reference B4 refers to the intersection of column B and row 4. When a formula is created, you can simply use values, such as =5*5. However, writing a formula without cell references is limiting. Formulas with cell references are substantially more powerful. For example, the formula =B4*C4, where cells B4 and C4 contain values to be used in the calculation, allows the formula to reference a cell (or cell range) rather than a value (or values). This means that when data changes in an individual cell, any formulas that reference the cell are automatically recalculated.

A **named range** is a group of cells that have been given a name. The name can then be used within a formula or function. In this section, you will use cell referencing and named ranges to build a worksheet model for planning events at the Turquoise Oasis Spa.

Understand the Types of Cell References

There are three types of cell referencing: relative, absolute, and mixed. A **relative cell reference** is a cell reference that changes automatically when the formula or function is copied to another location. The change in the cell reference will reflect the number of rows and/or columns from which the cell was copied relative to its original location. Relative cell references are the default in Excel. An **absolute cell reference** is the exact address of a cell when both the column and the row need to remain constant regardless of the position of the cell when the formula is copied to other cells. When an absolute cell reference is used, a cell reference does not change if a formula or function is copied to another location. An absolute cell reference is specified by placing a dollar sign ($) in front of both the column letter(s) and the row number(s). For example, to make B4 an absolute reference, you would specify $B$4. A **mixed cell reference** is a combination of relative and absolute cell references. In a mixed cell reference, the column or row portion of the reference is absolute, and the corresponding row or column is relative. For example, $B4 is a mixed reference in which the column is absolute and the row is relative. B$4 is a mixed reference in which the column is relative and the row is absolute. In essence, the dollar sign ($) sign locks down the letter or number it precedes so the letter or number will not change when copied.

QUICK REFERENCE	Types of Cell Referencing

Below are examples of the types of cell referencing for cell A5.

1. Relative cell referencing: =A5+B5
2. Absolute cell referencing: =$A$5+B5
3. Mixed cell referencing: =$A5+B5
4. Mixed cell referencing: =A$5+B5

Cell referencing is a useful feature when formulas need to be copied across ranges in a spreadsheet. When you create a spreadsheet and develop a formula that will not be copied elsewhere, absolute cell referencing and mixed cell referencing are not necessary.

However, data arranged in a table may require a formula to perform calculations on each row, or record. Excel allows this process to be completed quickly and easily by using cell referencing. The formula can be constructed once and then quickly copied across a range of cells.

REAL WORLD ADVICE | **Creating Dynamic Workbooks**

The use of cell references in formulas helps to make spreadsheets in Excel extremely powerful. By using a cell reference to refer to a value in a formula, you can make your spreadsheet flexible. In other words, using cell references makes your spreadsheet easier to use and more efficient. If something about your business changes and requires an update to a value in your spreadsheet, you need only make the update in one place.

Opening the Starting File

Meda Rodate would like for the Turquoise Oasis Spa to become more efficient in planning for wedding events. She has asked for your help in designing an Excel workbook to accomplish this goal. You will begin in this exercise by opening the wedding planning workbook and organizing the number and pricing of spa gift baskets by creating common Excel functions using various types of cell referencing.

E03.00

SIDE NOTE
Pin the Ribbon
If your ribbon is collapsed, pin your ribbon open. Click the Home tab. In the lower right corner of the ribbon, click Pin the Ribbon.

To Open the Wedding Workbook

a. Start **Excel**, click **Open Other Workbooks** in the left pane, and then double-click **This PC**. Navigate through the folder structure to the location of your student data files, and then double-click **e02ch03Wedding**. If a Security Warning message displays, click the **Enable Editing** button.

b. Click the **File** tab, click **Save As**, and then double-click **This PC**. In the Save As dialog box, navigate to the location where you are saving your project files. Change the file name to **e02ch03Wedding_LastFirst**, using your last and first name. Click **Save**.

c. Click the **Insert** tab, and then, in the Text group, click **Header & Footer**.

> **Troubleshooting**
> If you do not see the Text group, look for the Text button and click the Text arrow, which will open the Text group and show the various commands.

---

d. On the Header & Footer Tools Design tab, in the Navigation group, click **Go to Footer**. Click the **left section of the footer**, and then, in the Header & Footer Elements group, click **File Name**.

e. Click any cell on the spreadsheet to move out of the footer, and press Ctrl+Home to return to cell A1.

f. Click the **View** tab, and in the Workbook Views group, click **Normal**, and then click the **Home** tab. Click **Save**.

Using Relative Cell Referencing

Relative cell referencing (as shown in Figure 1) is the default reference type in constructing formulas in Excel. Remember that relative cell referencing changes the cell references in a formula if it is copied or otherwise moved to another location. This includes the use of copy and paste or the AutoFill feature to copy a formula to another location. If a formula is copied to the right or left, the column references will change in the formula. If a formula is copied up or down, the row references will change in the formula.

Relative cell referencing is useful in situations in which the same calculation is needed in multiple cells but the location of the data needed for the calculation changes relative to the position of the calculation cell. The GiftBaskets worksheet of the Wedding workbook contains a list of individual items that are included in the different types of gift baskets offered at the Turquoise Oasis Spa. The worksheet contains the prices for individual items in the baskets, the number of each item in the basket, and the prices of each basket.

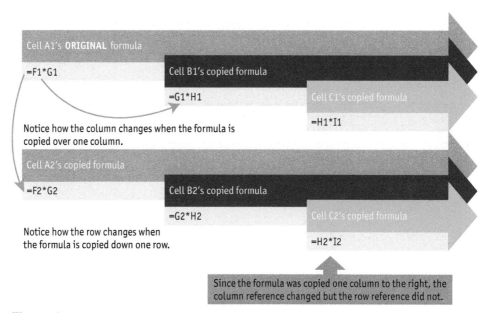

Figure 1 Understanding cell referencing

The Turquoise Oasis Spa allows wedding parties to specify up to three different kinds of custom gift baskets. Each gift basket can contain up to four different items in each basket. The workbook has been set up such that cells with a blue fill need to be changed from one event to another. In this exercise, you will use relative cell referencing to display the total number of items in each type of gift basket.

E03.01

SIDE NOTE
You can also use AutoFill with a formula in a vertical range by selecting the range, pressing Ctrl, and typing D.

SIDE NOTE

Viewing Formulas
You can view your formulas by pressing Ctrl+~.

To Use Relative Cell Referencing

a. Click the **GiftBaskets** worksheet if necessary, and then click cell **F9**.

b. On the Home tab, in the Editing group, click **AutoSum** , and then press Ctrl+Enter.

c. Click the **AutoFill handle** + on the bottom right corner of cell **F9**, and then drag down to copy the formula to cell **F11**.

Notice that the formula in cell F11 refers to cells B11:E11. Since the formula was copied down, the row reference changed from 9 to 10 and finally to 11.

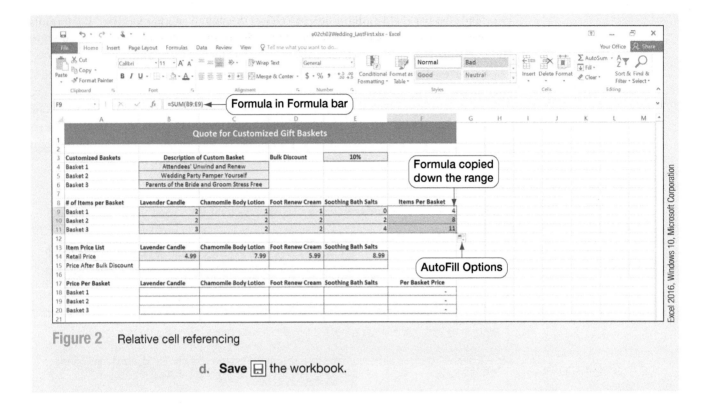

Figure 2　Relative cell referencing

d. **Save** 💾 the workbook.

Using Absolute Cell Referencing

Absolute cell referencing (as shown in Figure 3) is useful when a formula needs to be copied and the reference to one or more cells within the formula must not change as the formula is copied. Thus, the column and row address of a referenced cell remains constant regardless of the position of the cell when the formula is copied to other cells.

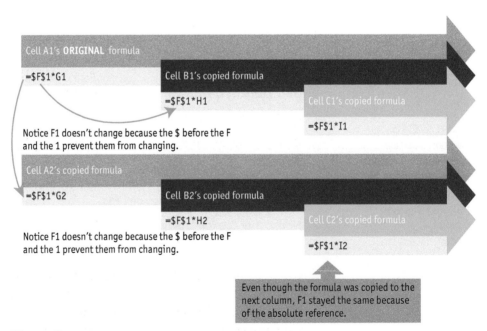

Figure 3　Understanding absolute cell referencing

Meda has decided to offer a bulk percentage discount on all gift baskets purchased for this event because of the large number being ordered. In this exercise, you will modify the formulas in cells B15:E15 of the GiftBaskets worksheet using absolute cell referencing to include this discount.

 E03.02

To Use Absolute Cell Referencing

a. On the **GiftBaskets** worksheet, click cell **B15**.

b. Type =B14-(B14*$E$3), and then click **Enter** ✓ to the left of the Insert Function button ƒₓ.

c. Click the **AutoFill handle** + on cell **B15**, and then drag to the right to copy the formula to cell **E15**.

Notice that the formula in cell E15 refers to cell E3. The dollar signs in front of the column letter and row number force Excel to keep the same cell reference as the formula is copied.

Also, notice that the dollar sign before row 3 is not required, since the formula was not copied to a different row. However, no matter where this formula is copied to on the worksheet, the calculation should always use cell E3. Thus, common practice is to put a dollar signs before the column and row, making the cell reference absolute.

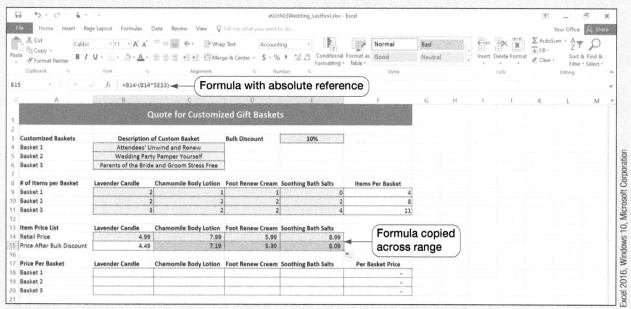

Figure 4 Absolute cell referencing

d. **Save** 🖫 the workbook.

Using Mixed Cell Referencing

Mixed cell references can be very useful in the development of spreadsheets. Mixed cell references refer to referencing a cell within the formula where part of the cell address is preceded by a dollar sign to lock — either the column letter or the row value — as absolute reference. This will leave the other part of the cell as relatively referenced when the formula is copied to new cells. Figure 5 shows a representation of how mixed cell referencing works.

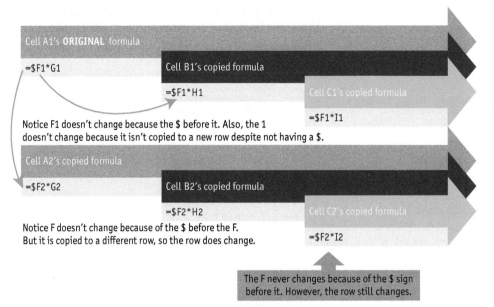

Cell A1's **ORIGINAL** formula

=$F1*G1

Cell B1's copied formula

=$F1*H1

Cell C1's copied formula

=$F1*I1

Notice F1 doesn't change because the $ before it. Also, the 1 doesn't change because it isn't copied to a new row despite not having a $.

Cell A2's copied formula

=$F2*G2

Cell B2's copied formula

=$F2*H2

Cell C2's copied formula

=$F2*I2

Notice F doesn't change because of the $ before the F. But it is copied to a different row, so the row does change.

The F never changes because of the $ sign before it. However, the row still changes.

Figure 5   Understanding mixed cell referencing

REAL WORLD ADVICE   **Layout of a Spreadsheet Model**

Think of a spreadsheet model as an interactive report. Some of the data is static and may not change often, if ever. Some of the data, as in the wedding planning workbook, will need to change with each use of the spreadsheet. It can be helpful to color code cells so anyone using the spreadsheet can easily see which cells require a change and which should be left alone. For example, in the Wedding workbook, cells with a blue fill are cells that need to be updated from one event to another.

If you need to verify that the formula has the correct relative and absolute referencing after it has been copied or moved into other cells within the spreadsheet, a quick and easy verification method is to examine one of the cells in edit mode. Best practice dictates following these steps.

1. Double-click a cell containing the formula to enter edit mode.
2. In edit mode, notice that the color-coded borders around cells match the cell address references in the formula. Using the color-coding as a guide, verify that the cells are referenced correctly.
3. If the referencing is incorrect, notice which cells are not referenced correctly.
4. Edit the cell references, and then, if necessary, recopy the corrected formula.
5. Always recheck the formula again to see whether your correction worked when it was copied into other cells or cell ranges.

To exit out of edit mode, press Esc to return to the original formula. Another way of entering edit mode is to press the A key.

Repeat this process as needed. Instead of typing the dollar signs within your cell references, F4 can be used to change the type of cell referencing. If the insertion point is placed within a cell reference in your formula, press F4 one time, and Excel will insert dollar signs in front of both the row reference and the column reference. If you press F4 again, Excel places a dollar sign in front of the row number only. If you press F4 a third time, Excel places a dollar sign in front of the column reference and removes the dollar sign from the row reference. Pressing F4 a fourth time returns the cell to a relative reference.

QUICK REFERENCE — Using F4

F4 can be used to change the type of cell referencing.

1. Press F4 one time to place a dollar sign in front of both the column and row values (absolute reference).
2. Press F4 a second time to place a dollar sign in front of the row value only (mixed reference).
3. Press F4 a third time to place a dollar sign in front of the column value only (mixed reference).
4. Press F4 a fourth time to remove all dollar sign characters (relative reference).

Meda has asked you to update the range B18:E20 to include formulas that calculate the price of individual items included in each basket type. In this exercise, you will do so, using mixed cell referencing.

E03.03

SIDE NOTE
Alternate Method
You can click the Enter button ✓ to the left of the Insert Function button ƒx on the Formula Bar for the same result as Ctrl+Enter.

To Use Mixed Cell Referencing

a. On the **GiftBaskets** worksheet, click cell **B18**.

b. Type =B9*B$15, and then press Ctrl+Enter.

c. Click the **AutoFill handle** + on cell **B18**, and then drag down to copy the formula to cell **B20**.

   Notice that the formula in cell B20 still refers to cell B15. The dollar sign in front of the row heading forces Excel to use row 15 as the referenced row no matter where the formula is copied to. However, the column will change as the formula is copied to the left or right in the worksheet.

d. With range **B18:B20** still selected, click the **AutoFill handle** + on cell **B20**, and then drag to the right to copy the formulas to the range **E18:E20**. Notice that as the formulas are copied, column B changes, while the row reference to row 15 remains unchanged as the formula is copied to the range.

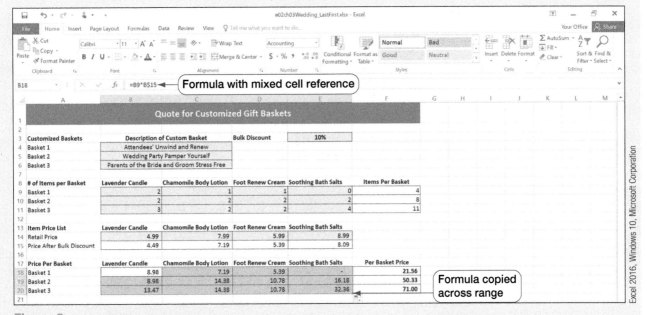

Figure 6 Mixed cell referencing

e. Click cell **E14**, type 11.99, and then press Enter.

Notice that the values in cells E19:E20 have been updated. For reference, E20 previously displayed 32.36; now it displays 43.16.

f. **Save** 💾 the workbook.

 CONSIDER THIS | **Cell Referencing**

In cell B18 of the GiftBaskets worksheet, the formula uses mixed cell referencing by referring to cell B$15. Would there have been a different result if absolute referencing ($B$15) had been used? Would there have been a different result if relative referencing (B15) had been used? Why would these options be incorrect?

REAL WORLD ADVICE | **Building for Scalability**

When you develop a spreadsheet, you should consider the potential for the model to expand. A good spreadsheet model allows the user to add more data as needed. Instead of assuming that current conditions will never change, your spreadsheet should be built to accommodate growth. While developing the model, you may consider using hypothetical data so you can see how the model will look when it has real data.

QUICK REFERENCE | **Understanding Referencing Based on Copy Destination**

Cell references in a formula can change when copied. To understand where to put a dollar sign, you must understand how the cell references will change when copied. Excel determines what to change by the original location and the copy destination. Remember that the dollar sign locks down the letter (column) or number (row) it precedes so it will not change.

Original Location	Copy Destination	Column Becomes	Row Becomes	Considerations
A1	Formula will not be copied.	N/A	N/A	Cell referencing is irrelevant.
A1	A5	The column reference will not change.	The row reference will change by 4 rows.	Adding a dollar sign before the column is irrelevant. Add a dollar sign before the row if the row should not change.
A1	C1	The column reference will change by 2 columns.	The row reference will not change.	Add a dollar sign before the column if the column should not change. Adding a dollar sign before the row is irrelevant.

(Continued)

QUICK REFERENCE	Understanding Referencing Based on Copy Destination (Continued)			
Original Location	**Copy Destination**	**Column Becomes**	**Row Becomes**	**Considerations**
A1	C5	The column reference will change by 2 columns.	The row reference will change by 4 rows.	Since both the column and row references will change, add a dollar sign before any references that should not change.

Create Named Ranges

Once you are comfortable working with formulas and cells, there is a natural progression to using named ranges and functions. As has been mentioned, a named range is a group of cells that have been given a name that can then be used within a formula or function. Named ranges are an extension of cell references and provide a quick alternative for commonly used cell references or ranges.

Spreadsheet formulas that use cell references, such as =C5*C6, may be easy to interpret when they are simple. However, as the size and complexity of the workbook increase, so do the difficulty and time needed to incorporate cell references in formulas. This is especially the case with workbooks that use multiple worksheets. The use of named ranges enables a developer to quickly develop formulas that make sense. It also increases the readability of formulas to other individuals who are using the same workbook. For example, the formula =SUM(BasketSubtotals) is much easier to interpret than =SUM(C23:C25). Also, named ranges create absolute referencing when used in a formula. You can quickly understand the formula if it is written with assigned names you designate.

Creating Named Ranges Using the Name Box

Named ranges are easy to create as you develop a spreadsheet. A named range can be either a single cell or a group of cells. Most named ranges are groups of cells used within multiple formulas. A simple way to name a range is to select the range and use the Name Box to create the name. This allows for a custom name to be given to the range. In naming ranges, a descriptive name should be used for the range being named. Named ranges do have some restrictions on the types of characters that can be used. Named ranges cannot start with a number and cannot contain spaces, and the name cannot resemble a cell reference.

QUICK REFERENCE	Conventions for Naming Ranges

Below is a list of conditions that must be meet when creating named ranges.

1. Names for ranges must start with a letter, an underscore (_), or a backslash (\ ).
2. Create names that provide specific meaning to the range being named.
3. Spaces cannot be used in creating a named range. Instead, use an underscore or a hyphen character, or capitalize the first letter of each word (e.g., HairStyles).
4. Do not use combinations of letters and numbers that resemble cell references.

In this exercise, you will create a named range using the Name box. This named range can then be used in future calculations as an absolute cell reference.

E03.04

To Create a Named Range Using the Name Box

a. On the **GiftBaskets** worksheet, select the range **C23:C25**.

b. Click in the **Name Box** to select the existing text. Type BasketSubtotals, and then press Enter to create a new named range. Notice that when the range C23:C25 is selected, the text BasketSubtotals is displayed in the Name box.

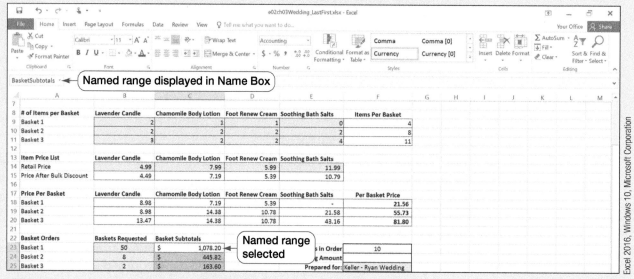

Figure 7   Name range applied to C23:C25

SIDE NOTE

Selecting a Range
Click the Name Box arrow to display a list of all named ranges in a workbook. Click any named range in the Name Box to select that range in a worksheet.

Troubleshooting

If you click outside of the Name Box before pressing Enter, the named range will not be created.

c. **Save** 🖫 the workbook.

Modifying Named Ranges

If a named range has been created incorrectly, it can be redefined by selecting the correct data and naming the range again. Alternatively, the Name Manager can be used to modify an existing range or to view a list of already defined ranges. The **Name Manager** can be used to create, edit, delete, or troubleshoot named ranges in a workbook.

Currently, the range BasketsRequested includes only gift basket options 2 and 3. In this exercise, you will modify the named range that was previously created in the workbook to include all basket options.

E03.05

To Modify a Named Range

a. On the **GiftBaskets** worksheet, click the Name box arrow, and then click **BasketsRequested**.

Notice that the range selected is B24:B26. This is the incorrect range. The correct range is B23:B25.

b. Click the **Formulas** tab, and then, in the Defined Names group, click **Name Manager**.

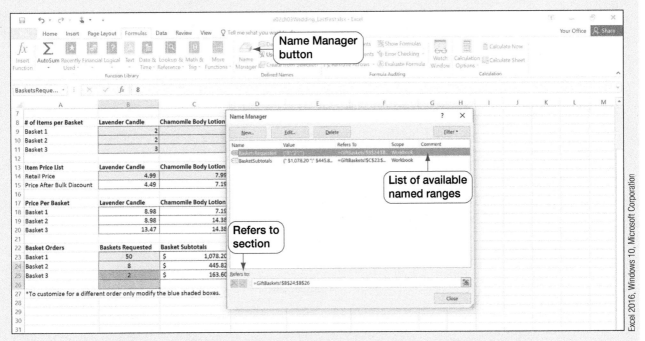

Figure 8 Name Manager dialog box

c. From the displayed list of names, click **BasketsRequested**, and then, in the Refers to section in the box, select the text **GiftBaskets!$B$24:$B$26**.

d. Type **$B$23:$B$25**, click **Close**, and then click **Yes** to accept the changes to the named range.

e. Click the Name box arrow, and then click **BasketsRequested**. Notice that the correct range, B23:B25, is now selected.

f. **Save** 🖫 the workbook.

Using Named Ranges

Using named ranges in place of cell references is a simple process. Instead of typing in the cells that you want to use in a formula, you can type the range name you have created. Excel will begin to recognize the name you are typing and offer to automatically complete the name for you. Another method of using named ranges is to use the Paste Name feature in Excel. While typing a formula, you can press F3 to view a list of named ranges in the workbook and then insert it into the formula you are constructing. A third way of using named ranges is the Use in Formula button in the Defined Names group of the Formulas tab. When typing a formula, click the Use in Formula arrow and select an available range name.

1. Type the range name when entering a formula.

2. While typing a formula, press [F3] to view and select a range name.

3. While typing a formula, click the Formulas tab, and then, in the Defined Names group, click Use in Formula to view and select a range name.

Meda has requested that the worksheet display the total amount that the wedding party is to be billed for the gift baskets being made. In this exercise, you will use a named range to create a calculation to display the total price of the requested gift baskets in the worksheet.

 E03.06

To Use Named Ranges in a Formula

a. Click the **GiftBaskets** worksheet if necessary, and then click cell **F24**.

b. Type =SUM(B, and then notice that a list of functions and named ranges beginning with the letter "B" appear in a list.

    The named ranges appear with a 🔲 next to the name of the range. The functions have (fx) to the left of the function name.

c. Type ask. Notice the two range names that appear in the list.

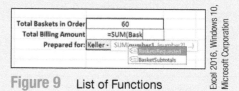

Figure 9 List of Functions

d. Press [↓], and then press [Tab] to select the BasketSubtotals named range. Press [Ctrl]+[Enter] to complete the formula.

e. **Save** 🔲 the workbook.

Creating Named Ranges from Selections

At times, your worksheet's data will be organized in such a way that the names for your ranges exist in a cell in the form of a heading for each row or each column in the data set. Rather than selecting each row or column separately, which is a time-consuming process, you can use the Create from Selection method.

The Create from Selection method produces multiple named ranges from the headings in rows, columns, or both from the data set. The key element is to realize that the names for the ranges need to exist in a cell adjacent to the data range. Most commonly, these names are row or column headers that make for very convenient names for each row or column of data.

Meda has asked you to create named ranges for the item subtotals for each type of gift basket. In this exercise, you will create the named ranges. You will then apply them to the formulas in cells F18:F20.

E03.07

To Create Named Ranges and Apply the Names to Formulas

a. On the **GiftBaskets** worksheet, select the range **A18:E20**.

b. On the **Formulas** tab, in the Defined Names group, click **Create from Selection**. The Create Names from Selection dialog box opens.

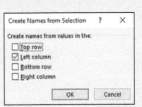

Figure 10   Create Names from Selection dialog box

Excel 2016, Windows 10, Microsoft Corporation

SIDE NOTE

Alternate Method

After you have selected the range of data you wish to name, the keyboard shortcut Ctrl+Shift+F3 will create a single named range or multiple named ranges from the selection.

c. Confirm that the **Left column** check box is selected, and then click **OK**.

d. Select the range **B18:E18**.

Notice that the Name box displays the name Basket_1. In creating the named range, Excel replaced all space characters in the name with underscore characters. Ranges B19:E19 and B20:E20 will appear similarly.

e. Select the range **F18:F20**, and then, in the Defined Names group, click the **Define Name** arrow, and then click **Apply Names**. Notice that Excel has detected three potential named ranges that can be substituted into the formulas in the selected range.

Apply Names dialog box → ← **Names detected in selected cells**

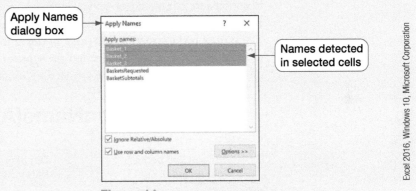

Figure 11   Apply Names dialog box

Excel 2016, Windows 10, Microsoft Corporation

f. Click **OK**. Notice in the Formula Bar that the formula in cell F18 now reads =SUM(Basket_1).

g. **Save** 🖫 the workbook. If you need to take a break before finishing this chapter, now is a good time.

Understanding Functions

A **function** is a built-in formula that performs operations against data based on a set of inputs. Excel uses functions to calculate output on the basis of the input provided. Functions can be fairly simple, such as using the SUM function that totals the contents of the cells in a range. Functions can also be more complex. For example, calculating a monthly loan payment is accomplished by providing various arguments: the loan amount, number of payments, and interest rate. An **argument** is a variable or value the function requires to calculate a solution. As long as you have the correct inputs, Excel will perform the calculation for the function. Some functions do not require arguments. In this section, you will use common business functions to continue building the worksheet to be used for planning events at the Turquoise Oasis Spa.

Create and Structure Functions

Functions are composed of several elements and need to be structured in a particular order. In discussing functions, you need to be aware of the syntax of an Excel function. The **syntax** is the structure and order of the function and the arguments needed for Excel to run a function. If you understand the syntax of a function, you can easily learn how to use new functions quickly. The syntax for a function is represented in Figure 12.

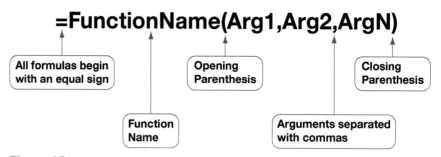

Figure 12   Syntax of a function

The FunctionName is any function that is in the Excel library. Examples are SUM, COUNT, and TODAY. With all functions, a pair of parentheses () are required after the FunctionName that may contain arguments associated with the function. Functions such as SUM() have one or more arguments that are required. If the required argument or arguments are not supplied, an error will occur. Some functions, such as TODAY(), do not have any arguments. These functions do not need any inputs to be able to generate output. The TODAY() function uses the clock on the computer to return the current date. Even though no arguments are needed, the () parentheses are always included, which helps Excel understand that a function is being used.

Arguments can be either required or optional. The required arguments always come before any optional arguments. Arguments are separated by commas. Optional arguments are identified by square brackets [] around the argument name. You never type the square brackets into the actual construction of the function; they are used only to inform you that the argument is optional.

For example, the syntax for the SUM function is

=SUM(number1, [number2], . . .)

The first argument is required; the SUM function must have a number, cell, or range to begin the calculation. The second argument — a second cell or range — is optional. Notice that the second argument uses square brackets to identify that it is optional. The periods after the second argument indicate that one or more arguments can be added as needed. The SUM function can hold up to 255 arguments.

Arguments, like variables in a math equation, need to be appropriate values that are suitable for the function. With Excel, the acceptable values can take six common forms, including other functions, as shown in Table 1.

Form of Input	Example	Explanation
Numeric value	5	Type the value
Cell reference	C5	Type the cell or range of cells
Named range	SALES	Type the name of the range
Text string	"Bonus"	Type the text with quotation marks so Excel will recognize it as a text string rather than a named range
Function	SUM(C5:C19)	Type a function using the correct syntax of the function name, pair of parentheses, and any arguments
Formula	(C5+D5)/100	Type the formula using correct mathematical formula structure

Table 1   Function argument formats

Functions are typically categorized for easy access. The primary categories are shown in Table 2. Functions can be found on the Formulas tab under these categorical names. They can also be searched to find the usage and syntax of functions that are unfamiliar.

Category	Description
Compatibility	A set of functions that are compatible with older versions of Excel
Cube	Working with data and filtering, similar to pivot tables
Date & Time	Working with serial date and time values
Engineering	Working with engineering formulas and calculations
Financial	Working with common financial formulas
Information	Providing data about cell content within a worksheet
Logical	Evaluating expressions or conditions as being either true or false
Lookup & Reference	Working with indexing and retrieving information from data sets
Math & Trig	Working with mathematics
Text	Working with text strings
Statistical	Working with common statistical calculations
Web	Working with URL, XML, and web services connections

Table 2   Function categories

Use and Understand Math and Statistical Functions

At the most fundamental level, spreadsheets are used to perform calculations. These calculations may result in loan payments, GPA calculations, profit margins, or even age calculations. Excel has a large array of functions available for simple and complex mathematical functions. There are functions available to sum, count, perform algebra or trigonometry, and create a wide range of statistical calculations.

Using Math and Trig Functions

The math and trigonometry functions are useful for various numerical manipulations. For example, there are several functions that round data in a cell or calculation. The **ABS function** returns the absolute value of the number analyzed by the function. A cell or calculation resulting in the number −4 would be returned as 4 by the ABS function. The **INT function** rounds down any decimal values associated with a number to the nearest whole integer. The **ROUND function** is important when you want to round a number to a specific number of digits. The ROUND function can round values to the left or right of the decimal in a number. For example, using the ROUND function, you could change the number 115.89 to 116 by rounding to the ones place. You could also display 120 by rounding to the integer value to the tens place. While ROUND will round to the nearest digit, ROUNDDOWN and ROUNDUP can be used to force the rounding in a particular direction.

When a function is used to round data, the result of that function is used in future calculations. This is different from formatting a cell to a specific number of decimal places, as formatting does not change the underlying data.

Commonly used math functions are shown in Table 3.

Function	Usage
ABS(number)	Returns the absolute value of a number
INT(number)	Rounds a number down to the nearest integer
RAND( )	Returns a random number from 0 to less than 1
RANDBETWEEN(bottom,top)	Returns a random integer between the numbers you specify
ROUND(number,num_digits)	Rounds a number to a specified number of digits
ROUNDDOWN(number,num_digits)	Rounds a number down to a specified number of digits
ROUNDUP(number,num_digits)	Rounds a number up to a specified number of digits

Table 3 Commonly used math functions

There are two common methods for creating functions: by using the Function Arguments dialog box and by typing the function in the cell. The **Function Arguments** dialog box provides additional information and previews results of the function being constructed. When you are first developing the skills for using functions in Excel, the Function Arguments dialog box can be very valuable. As you gain more experience with functions, you will depend less on the Function Arguments dialog box, particularly when nesting multiple functions together.

Meda has received some historical data on wedding events that she would like to have summarized. In planning new events, referring to this historical data will be helpful. The data contains four items of interest.

1. The number of days spent by wedding parties at the Painted Paradise Resort & Spa. Previously, the value was calculated by using decimal values based on check-in and checkout times. Meda would like this data to be in integers, or whole numbers of days. Since wedding parties receive a late checkout time, these values would need to be rounded down to the nearest whole number.

2. The price of merchandise that was returned after the wedding took place — the price in the column represents the money refunded to customers for the merchandise. The system used at the spa erroneously allowed employees to enter some of this data as either negative or positive values. In the new system, this data must be displayed as positive values.

3. Data displaying the amount spent in total by each wedding party at the Turquoise Oasis Spa. The average of this column has been calculated in the WeddingSummary worksheet cell C2. Currently, the average is formatted to display too many decimal places. However, the actual value of the cell has many more than two decimals. Meda plans to use this average in subsequent calculations. Formatting the cell to two decimals will not change the value of the cell. Thus, the value needs to be rounded to two decimals.

4. Data indicating whether the bridal party from the wedding is a member of the spa. The system used by the spa indicates a 1 for spa members and a null value for nonmembers. When this data was imported into Excel, the result for nonmembers was the text "Null".

In this exercise, you will summarize these data items, using the INT and ABS functions.

E03.08

SIDE NOTE

Alternate Method

Instead of typing B9 in the Function Arguments dialog box, you can click cell B9. The cell reference will be supplied automatically.

To Use the INT and ABS Functions

a. If you took a break, open the **e02ch04Wedding** workbook, click the **WeddingSummary** worksheet, and then click cell **C9.**

b. To the left of the formula bar, click **Insert Function** f_x. Click the **Or select a category** arrow, and then select **Math & Trig.**

c. In the Select a function box, scroll down, click **INT**, and then click **OK.**

d. Type **B9**, and notice that to the right of the dialog box, you see the value currently in cell B9. Under the current value, you will see a preview of the result of the INT function.

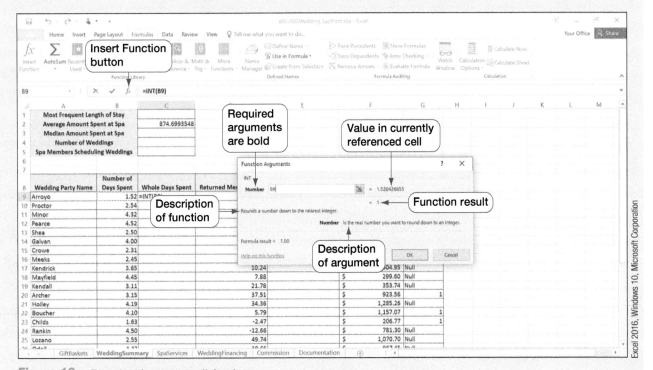

Figure 13 Function Arguments dialog box

e. Click **OK**, and then double-click the AutoFill handle $\boxed{+}$ to copy cell **C9** down to **C39**.

Notice that the values in column B have now been rounded down to the nearest whole number. Illustratively, the value of cell C24 is 4.00 even though the value in cell B24 is 4.50. Since all of the values are now whole days without a decimal value, the format for C9:C39 should have decimals decreased to zero decimals.

f. With the range **C9:C39** selected, click the **Home** tab, and then, in the Number group, click **Decrease Decimal** $\boxed{.00 \atop \rightarrow .0}$ twice.

SIDE NOTE

Function Help

Click the Help on this function link in the lower left of the Function Arguments dialog box to open Excel Help for the function being used.

g. Click cell **E9**, and then click **Insert Function** $\boxed{f_x}$. If necessary, click the **Or select a category** arrow, and then verify that **Math & Trig** is selected.

h. In the Select a function box, click **ABS**, and then click **OK**.

i. In the Function Arguments dialog box, in the Number box, type D9, and then click **OK**. Double-click the AutoFill handle $\boxed{+}$ to copy cell **E9** down to **E39**. All values in column E now appear as positive numbers.

j. **Save** $\boxed{\Box}$ the workbook.

S$_S$ CONSIDER THIS | **Exploring Functions**

Use the Insert Function button in the formula bar to find a function with which you are not familiar. Read the description for the function in the Insert Function dialog box. Use Microsoft Help or the Internet to learn more about the function, and share your findings with another person. Did you have any trouble understanding the function? Is the Insert Function button a useful tool for exploring new functions?

Inserting a Function Using Forumlas

Formula AutoComplete can help you construct formulas without using the Function Arguments dialog box. This is accomplished by typing the equal sign and typing the function name directly into the cell. Excel will still provide guidance if you use this method. Additionally, as needed, you can always enter the Function Arguments dialog box to get more assistance.

When you initially type in the beginning of a function name, the Formula AutoComplete listing of functions will be shown, from which you can select the appropriate function. Formula AutoComplete will provide a list of functions and named ranges that match the text after the equal sign. The list will automatically reflect changes as you type in more letters. Excel will even display a short description of the function when the function name is highlighted. As the function names appear, you can use $\boxed{\uparrow}$, $\boxed{\downarrow}$, $\boxed{\rightarrow}$, $\boxed{\leftarrow}$, or mouse to move through the listing. To select a function, press $\boxed{\text{Tab}}$ or double-click the selected function.

Once the function is selected, the arguments will be listed in a movable tag, called a ScreenTip, to provide guidance in completing the function. The argument you are currently editing will be displayed in bold. If you have entered some of the arguments, you can click the argument in the ScreenTip, and Excel will relocate the insertion point to that argument. In this exercise, you will insert the ROUND function, using Formula AutoComplete.

To Insert a Function Using Formula AutoComplete

a. On the **WeddingSummary** worksheet, double-click cell **C2** to begin editing the function.

b. Click after the **equal sign** to place the insertion point before the AVERAGE function. Type ROUND(to begin the new function.

Notice how the Formula AutoComplete suggested possible functions while you typed "round". Also, notice that the number argument is shown in bold to indicate that this is the argument being edited.

Figure 14 Screen Tip showing ROUND function

c. Click after the **ending parenthesis** for the AVERAGE function, type , — a comma — and then notice in the ScreenTip that the num_digits argument of the ROUND function is in bold.

d. Type 2) to complete the num_digits argument. This will round the result of the AVERAGE function to two decimal places. Press Ctrl + Enter.

Notice that the value in cell C2 is now $874.70, rounded to two decimal places. It is important to know that if you had formatted cell C2 to display only two decimal places, the cell would also show $874.70 on the screen. However, formatting does not change the value. So even though the cell would show $874.70, the cell value used in subsequent mathematical calculations would still be $874.6993548. If you increase the number of decimals for cell C2 after using the ROUND function, you will see that the cell value is changed to $874.700000.

e. **Save** 🖫 the workbook.

REAL WORLD ADVICE **Rounding Versus Formatting**

Formatting text as currency will only give the appearance of true rounding. Any calculations using a cell formatted as currency but containing extra decimal places will include all decimal places in the calculation. Using the ROUND function will eliminate extra decimal places. Thus, future calculations will use the value displayed as a result of the ROUND function.

Using Statistical Functions

Similar to mathematical functions, statistical functions, as shown in Table 4, handle common statistical calculations such as averages, minimums, and maximums. Statistical functions are extremely useful for business analysis, as they aggregate and compare data. Common descriptive statistics are used to describe the data. The average, median, and mode are common descriptive statistics that help describe the nature of a data set. They help understand and predict future data.

Statistical Functions	Usage
AVERAGE(number1,[number2],...)	Returns the average from a set of numbers
COUNT(value1,[value2],...)	Counts the number of cells in a range that contain numbers
COUNTA(value1,[value2],...)	Counts the number of cells in a range that are not empty
COUNTBLANK(range)	Counts the number of empty cells in a range
MEDIAN(number1,[number2],...)	Returns the number in the middle of a set of numbers
MAX(number1,[number2],...)	Returns the largest number from a set of numbers
MIN(number1,[number2],...)	Returns the smallest number from a set of numbers
MODE.SNGL(number1,[number2],...)	Returns the value that occurs most often within a set

Table 4   Commonly used statistical functions

The **MEDIAN function** is used to measure the central tendency or the location of the middle of a set of data. For example, in the number set 1 to 3, 2 would be the middle of the data or the median.

Another measure commonly used to locate data in a range is mode. There are two methods for calculating the mode — the value that occurs most often — of a range of data in Excel 2016. The **MODE.SNGL** function returns the most frequently occurring value in a range of data. If more than one number occurs multiple times in a range of data, the **MODE.MULT** function can be used to return a vertical array, or list, of the most frequently occurring values in a range of data.

The **MODE function**, like MODE.SNGL, returns the most frequently occurring value in a range of data. It is important to note that in Excel 2010, this function was replaced by MODE.SNGL and MODE.MULT. The MODE function is still available in Excel 2010, 2013, and 2016 to provide backwards compatibility with earlier versions of Excel. Because of this, the function will appear in the Formula AutoComplete menu with a warning icon ⚠ next to it.

The **COUNTA function** is a useful function for counting the number of cells within a range that contain any type of data. Using COUNTA is a great method to count the number of records in a data set that may include numbers and letters. This is different from the COUNT function.

The **COUNT function** returns the number of cells in a range of cells that contain numeric data.

On the WeddingSummary worksheet, column G contains a list indicating whether or not the bridal party were members of the spa. When the data was imported into Excel, the system used by the spa marked members with the number one. Nonmembers were marked with the text "Null". Meda has asked you to find the most frequently occurring number of days stayed by a wedding party, the median amount spent by wedding parties at the spa, the number of weddings held at the spa, as well the number of members who have scheduled weddings. In this exercise, you will find this data using statistical functions.

E03.10

SIDE NOTE
Creating Formulas
When creating formulas, to avoid typing mistakes, you can use your mouse to click and drag a cell or a range of cells.

To Use Statistical Functions

a. On the **WeddingSummary** worksheet, click cell **C1**.

b. Type =MODE.SNGL(C9:C39), and then click Enter ✓.

Cell C1 now displays 4, the most frequently occurring number of days stayed by a wedding party.

c. Click cell **C3**, type =MEDIAN(F9:F39), and then press Enter.

Cell C3 now displays the median amount spent by wedding parties at the spa, $899.77, representing the middle value as compared to the data for the average amount spent at the spa.

d. Click cell **C4**, type =COUNTA(A9:A39), and then press Enter.

The COUNTA function counts all of the cells that contain values in the range A9:A39 to display the 31 wedding parties represented in the data.

e. Click cell **C5**, type =COUNT(G9:G39), and then press Ctrl+Enter.

The COUNT function counts the numbers occurring in the range G9:G39 to display 16 spa members scheduled weddings.

f. **Save** 💾 the workbook.

1	Most Frequent Length of Stay	=MODE.SNGL(C9:C39)
2	Average Amount Spent at Spa	=ROUND(AVERAGE(F9:F39),2)
3	Median Amount Spent at Spa	=MEDIAN(F9:F39)
4	Number of Weddings	=COUNTA(A9:A39)
5	Spa Members Scheduling Weddings	=COUNT(G9:G39)

Figure 15 Statistical functions in formula view   Excel 2016, Windows 10, Microsoft Corporation

Use and Understand Date and Time Functions

Date and time functions are useful for entering the current day and time into a worksheet as well as for calculating the intervals between dates. This category of functions is based on a serial date system in which each day is represented sequentially from a starting point. In Microsoft applications, that standard is 1/1/1900, which has a serial number of 1. Thus, dates before January 1, 1900, will not be recognized by the system. Interestingly, when Apple initially made its starting point, it began in 1904. Excel settings can be changed to use the Apple starting point, but it is generally accepted practice to keep the default setting of 1/1/1900 as the starting point. Using two different starting points for dates in Excel spreadsheets can cause significant problems. Common date and time functions are shown in Table 5.

Function	Usage
DATE(year,month,day)	Returns the number that represents the date in Microsoft Excel date-time code
DATEDIF(date1,date2,interval)	Returns the time unit specified between two dates, including the two dates (inclusive)
DAY(serial_number)	Returns the day of the month, a number from 1 to 31
MONTH(serial_number)	Returns the month, a number from 1 to 12
NETWORKDAYS(start_date,end_date,[holidays])	Returns the number of whole workdays between two dates, inclusive; does not count weekends and can skip holidays that are listed
TODAY( )	Returns the computer system date
WEEKDAY(serial_number, [return_type])	Returns a number from 1 to 7 representing the day of the week. Can be set to return 0–6 or 1–7
WEEKNUM(serial_number, [return_type])	Returns the week number in the year, which week of the year the date occurs
YEAR(serial_number)	Returns the year of a date, an integer in the range 1900–9999

Table 5   Common date functions

CONSIDER THIS | **Dates in Microsoft Applications**

Do you suppose the same Microsoft employees developed Access, Excel, Word, and PowerPoint? Is it possible that even within a company, there may have been differences in the starting date? Does Access use the same 1/1/1900 for its date starting point? See if you can find out.

Using Date and Time Functions

Since Excel tracks time by the number of days that have occurred since 1/1/1900, time is represented by the decimal portion of this number. The decimal is based on the number of minutes in a day (24*60=1440). Thus, a 0.1 decimal is equal to 144 minutes. A full date and time value — such as 5/14/2018 8:35 AM — would appear as 43234.35763. There are 43234 days between 1/1/1900 and 5/14/2018. The time of 8:35 AM is represented by the .35763 portion of the number.

The TODAY and NOW functions are two common functions for inserting the current date into a spreadsheet. There is a difference between these functions. The key difference is that the **TODAY function** simply inserts the current date into a cell, while the **NOW function** inserts the current date and time into a cell. If you think about it, the TODAY function works only with integer representation of days, while the NOW function uses decimals to include the time in addition to the day. Both functions can be formatted to show just the date, and you can work with time calculations that mix the two functions. Common time functions are listed in Table 6.

Function	Usage
HOUR(serial_number)	Returns the hour in a time value, from 0 to 23
MINUTE(serial_number)	Returns the minute in a time value, from 0 to 59
SECOND(serial_number)	Returns the number of seconds in a time value, from 0 to 59
NOW( )	Returns the computer system date and time

Table 6   Common time functions

Be careful when using NOW versus TODAY, especially when doing date calculations. Both functions use a serial number, counting from 1/1/1900. But the NOW function also includes decimals for the time of day, while TODAY works with integer serial numbers. At noon on 5/1/2018, the NOW function has the value of 43221.5, while the TODAY function has a value of 43221.0. If you are using these date functions inside another function, this could change the result if you are comparing a date the user provided. The TODAY function should be used if a user will be inserting the date into Excel by hand so the hand-typed value will be compared or used in a calculation with the function, eliminating the decimal issue.

DATEDIF function is a useful date function because it enables you to calculate the time between two dates. The function can return the time unit as days, months, or years. However, while all the other functions are listed and can be found in Excel, neither Help nor the Function Library offers any information about the DATEDIF function. You will not find any information on the DATEDIF function unless you search the Microsoft site. Since no information exists on it within Excel, this is one function that you must hand type and do the research to understand the syntax. Nonetheless, DATEDIF is one of the more useful date functions.

The syntax of the function is

=DATEDIF(date1, date2,interval)

The first argument is the starting date in time — the older date — and the second argument is the ending date in time — the newer, more recent date. It may be helpful to remember that time lines are usually depicted as moving from left to right, just as they would be listed in the DATEDIF function. The third argument is the interval that should be used, such as the number of months or days between the two dates. The interval is expressed as a text value and therefore must be surrounded by quotes for correct syntax. The viable interval options are shown in Table 7.

Interval	Description
"D"	Returns the number of complete days between the dates
"M"	Returns the number of complete months between the dates
"Y"	Returns the number of complete years between the dates
"MD"	Returns the difference between days in two dates, ignoring months and years
"YM"	Returns the difference between months in two dates, ignoring days and years
"YD"	Returns the difference between days in two dates, ignoring years

Table 7   Unit value options for DATEDIF

The options "D", "M", and "Y" are commonly used to calculate differences between dates. For example, using "Y" for the Interval argument is common practice for calculating an age. The options "YM", "YD", and "MD" are not as commonly used because they ignore certain aspects of the date structure. For example, using "YM" for the Interval argument with the dates 7/1/2017 and 9/12/2018 will result in a value of 2. This is because the "YM" unit value ignores the years in the two dates and calculates only the number of whole months between July (7) and September (9). Using "M" in the Interval argument will result in the value 14, the more commonly expected result.

Meda has asked for your help in completing an analysis of customers in the Keller-Ryan wedding party who have requested spa services. She would like the current date to appear in cell B1 of the spreadsheet and the current age of customers to appear in column C. In this exercise, you will use common date functions to complete the analysis.

 E03.11

To Use Date and Time Functions

a. Click the **SpaServices** worksheet tab, and then click cell **B1**.

b. Type =TODAY(), and then press Ctrl+Enter.

   Notice that cell B1 now displays the current date. Each time the worksheet is opened or when a cell is edited, the current date will be updated and displayed in cell B1. Since the time of day is not relevant here, the TODAY function is preferred over the NOW function.

c. Click cell **C5**, type =DATEDIF(B5,$B$1,"Y"), and then press Ctrl+Enter.

SIDE NOTE
Alternate Method
You could also use the TODAY function in the formula in place of the absolute reference to B1. For example, the formula could be =DATEDIF(B5,TODAY(),"Y").

   In this formula, B5 is the start date, $B$1 is the end date, and the "Y" stands for years. Using an absolute reference to cell **B1** will allow you to copy the formula down a range. Since the interval is set to year, the result is that the age of the guest is always current in this calculation.

Troubleshooting

No ScreenTip will appear when you type the DATEDIF function. If the DATEDIF function returns a #NUM! error, the most likely problem is mixing up the order of the two dates within the function. The first date should be the earliest date, and the second date should be the most recent one. The other common error is actually typing in a date as the argument. Typing 12/3/2018 will be interpreted as division instead of a date. The value must be either in serial date format or typed inside of quotation marks.

d. Double-click the **AutoFill handle** + to copy cell **C5** down to **C22**. The current ages of all guests are now displayed in column C.

e. **Save** 🔲 the workbook.

 CONSIDER THIS | **Calculating Days**

Do you really need to use the DATEDIF function to calculate the difference between days — the "D" unit? In what other way could you calculate the difference? What would that formula look like?

Use and Understand Text Functions

Excel is frequently used to bring data together from multiple different locations and/or systems, including text data. Many times, the data is inconsistent from one source to another. For example, one workbook could list names as First Name Last Name — Olivia Stone — and the next may list names as Last Name, First Name — Stone, Olivia. In situations like this, knowing how to alter text data is extremely valuable and can save a lot of time.

There are many reasons why text data in a cell may need to be altered. Names in a cell may need to be separated or combined. Several pieces of data may be stored in a single cell but need to be separated into many columns of data for easier analysis. Excel contains a wide array of functions and features that allow for the manipulation of text data. Some newer features when Excel are optimized for touch screen devices. This makes it easier to manipulate data when using Excel on a mobile device such as a tablet computer.

Text functions are functions that manage, manipulate, and format text data. They can be used to change the appearance of data, such as displaying text in all lowercase letters. Text functions can also be used to cleanse text. **Cleansing text** involves removing unwanted characters, rearranging data in a cell, or correcting erroneous data.

Using Text Functions

Data stored as text is commonly referred to as a string. Text functions can change the way data is viewed, cut a string of text into multiple pieces, or combine multiple pieces of text together into one string of text. While most text functions can be used individually, they become increasingly powerful when nested together to transform text. Common text functions are defined in Table 8.

Function	Usage
CONCATENATE(text1,text2,...)	Joins textl, text2,...,textn together into a single string value.
FIND(find_text,within_text,[start_num])	Finds find_text in within_text. The search begins at start_ num (start_num defaults to 1) and is case sensitive. The starting position of find_text is returned. If the find_text is not present, an error will be returned.
LEFT(text,[num_chars])	Returns a string num_chars long from the left side of text. Num_chars defaults to 1.
LEN(text)	Returns a number that represents the number of characters.
MID(text,start_num,num_chars)	Returns a string extracted from text beginning in position start_num that is num_chars long.
RIGHT(text,[num_chars])	Returns a string num_chars long from the right side of text. Num_chars defaults to 1.
TRIM(text)	Returns text with any leading, trailing, or extra spaces between words removed.
UPPER(text)	Returns text with all characters in uppercase.
PROPER(text)	Returns text with only the first letter in uppercase. All other letters will return in lowercase.
SEARCH(find_text,within_text,[start_num])	Finds find_text in within_text. The search begins at start_ num (start_num defaults to 1) and is case insensitive. The starting position of find_text is returned. If the find_text is not present, an error will be returned.
TEXT(value,format_text)	Returns a number value as a string with the format specified in format_text.

Table 8   Common text functions

The **LEFT function** returns the characters in a text string based on the number of characters you specify, starting with the far-left character in the string. The number of characters the LEFT function will return is defined in the num_chars argument. This number can be simply typed in, or it can be more dynamically calculated by using other functions. The **FIND function** searches for a specified string of text in a larger string of text and returns the position number where the specified text begins. By using the FIND function in the num_chars argument of the LEFT function, a dynamic formula can be constructed to separate a portion of text from one cell into another.

Meda has asked that you rearrange some of the data on the SpaServices worksheet. Column A contains a list of guests' first and last names. To provide better customer service, Meda would like the first names of the guests in a separate column that can be used later. The names in column A are arranged in a consistent format. The text in the cell begins with the guest's first name followed by a single space character. After the space character is the guest's last name. Given this format, the space character can be used by text functions to separate the first name from the last name. In this exercise, you will use the FIND and LEFT functions to display only the first name of the guests in column D.

To Nest the FIND and LEFT Functions

a. On the **SpaServices** worksheet, click cell **D5**.

b. Type =LEFT(A5, to begin the text function. The LEFT function will begin at the left side of cell A5 and return all characters from position 1 until the number specified by the num_chars argument.

c. Type FIND(" ",A5)), and then press Ctrl+Enter to complete the function. Be sure to enter a space between the quotation marks.

Notice that the name Olivia appears in cell D5. To separate the first name, you take advantage of the text pattern of the space. To separate text, you must identify the text pattern. To use text functions, the pattern must be consistent in some way. Here, the FIND function looks for the space character that separates the first and last names. For cell A5, the FIND function returns a 7 because the name Olivia contains six characters and the space after the name is the seventh character. Since you will not want to include the space character, the TRIM function can be used to remove it.

d. Double-click cell **D5** to begin editing the function. Click after the **equal sign** to place the insertion point before the LEFT function. Type TRIM(to begin the TRIM function.

e. Click after the last **closing** parenthesis. Type), and then press Ctrl+Enter to complete the TRIM function. The number of characters displayed in cell D5 is now 6, as the trailing space character has been removed.

f. Double-click the AutoFill handle + to copy cell **D5** down to **D22**. The first names of all guests are now displayed in column D.

Figure 16 Result of nesting the LEFT and FIND functions

g. **Save** 🖫 the workbook.

Using Flash Fill

The Flash Fill feature in Excel 2016 makes data cleansing easier and faster than using traditional text functions. **Flash Fill** recognizes patterns in data as you type and automatically fills in values for text and numeric data. Flash Fill involves less typing than text functions, and this makes it easier to use on mobile or touch screen devices.

To work correctly, Flash Fill must be completed in a column adjacent to the data being manipulated. There are two ways to use Flash Fill. Providing two suggested values will initiate the automatic Flash Fill to a suggestion for cleansing your data. This suggestion will be previewed along the column adjacent to the data. Pressing Enter will accept the suggestion and populate the column of cells. Flash Fill can also be initiated on the Data tab. This is useful for cleansing data in cells that are not directly adjacent to the data or for numeric data. Flash Fill will not automatically suggest values for numeric data.

The SpaServices worksheet includes a list of the city and state of origin for each guest who will be attending the wedding. Separating these values into individual columns will be helpful for future tasks such as counting the number of guests from each state. In this exercise, you will use the Flash Fill feature to separate the guests' city and state of origin into individual columns.

 E03.13

To Use Flash Fill

a. On the **SpaServices** worksheet, click cell **G5**.

b. Type Bernalilo, and then press Enter to move to cell **G6**.

c. Type F, and notice that the Flash Fill suggestion appears down the column of data. Press Enter to accept the suggestion.

Notice that column G now contains only the city names from the list of cities and states in column F.

d. Click cell **H5**, type NM, and then press Ctrl+Enter.

Since the State column is not next to the column with the city and state text, typing a suggested value for Flash Fill will not work. Using the Flash Fill button from the Data tab will accomplish the task of isolating the state from column F.

e. Click the **Data** tab, and then, in the Data Tools group, click **Flash Fill**.

Notice that column H now contains only the state abbreviations from the list of cities and states in column F.

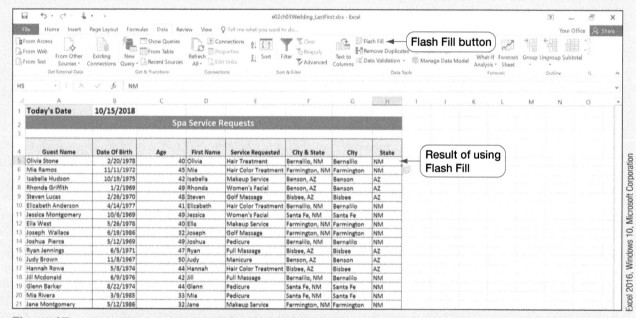

Figure 17 City names and state abbreviations separated with Flash Fill

f. **Save** 🖫 the workbook.

Use Financial and Lookup Functions

Excel has many functions available to help businesses make decisions. These decisions may include calculating payments on a loan or returning data from a table based upon a specific value in a worksheet. The ability to combine these processes in more complex tasks is even more powerful. For example, a lookup function can retrieve an interest rate from a table of data to be used in a subsequent loan calculation. As with other functions, lookup and reference functions can be very effective when combined with financial functions.

Using Lookup and Reference Functions

Lookup and reference functions look up matching values in a table of data. Lookup and reference functions can be used for simple matches or complex retrieval tasks. This can be as simple as retrieving a value from a vertical or horizontal list or as complex as finding the value of a cell within a table of data at a given row and column intersection. Common lookup and reference functions can be found in Table 9.

Function	Usage
HLOOKUP(lookup_value,table_array, row_index_num,[range_lookup])	Finds lookup_value in the top row of table_array and returns a value from row_index_num
INDEX(array,row_num,[column_num])	Returns a value from array by indexes specified as row_num and column_num
MATCH(lookup_value,lookup_array, [match_type])	Finds lookup_value in lookup_array
VLOOKUP(lookup_value,table_array, col_index_num,[range_lookup])	Finds lookup_value in the first column of table_array and returns a value from col_index_num

Table 9   Common lookup and reference functions

The **VLOOKUP function** matches a provided value in a table of data and returns a value from a subsequent column — similar to looking up a phone number in a phone book. The "V" signifies that the function matches the provided value vertically in the first column of the table of data. The syntax of a VLOOKUP is

=VLOOKUP(lookup_value, table_array, col_index_num, [range_lookup])

The lookup_value argument can be any text, any number, or a reference to a cell that contains data. The table_array argument is a range in a spreadsheet. The range can be a single column of cells or multiple columns of cells. The VLOOKUP function will match the lookup_value in the first column of the supplied table_array. The col_index_num is the column number of the corresponding value that will be returned. The optional range_lookup argument allows the VLOOKUP to perform an approximate or exact match.

The range_lookup argument is TRUE for an approximate match. An approximate match allows the VLOOKUP to return the first value less than the range_lookup in the first column of the table_array. For example, looking up the value 50 on a range containing 45 and 55 would return 45. To get an exact match, the range_lookup argument should be set to FALSE. An exact match will force the VLOOKUP to find the same value supplied in the lookup_value in the first column of the table_array. If the value cannot be found, the function will return an error.

The Turquoise Oasis Spa has recently partnered with a local bank to offer financing to customers who are booking large, costly events. Booking spa services is usually one of the last things guests will do. Thus, some guests will book fewer services than they desire because of budget concerns. The spa is hoping that offering a financing package and discounts for large events will increase revenue.

As part of the workbook you are building for the spa, Meda has asked that you finish the WeddingFinancing worksheet that she started. This worksheet contains cells to enter information about guest weddings being planned. The worksheet already has cells prepared for entering the cost of the event, the down payment supplied by the guest, the annual interest rate, and the term of the loan in years.

You have been asked to complete this worksheet so that when a wedding is scheduled, the guest will have an understanding of the basic elements of the financing plan. In this exercise, you will use a lookup function to return the discount that the spa will provide based on the total cost of the wedding event being planned.

To Use the VLOOKUP function

a. Click the **WeddingFinancing** worksheet tab, and then click cell **B7**.

b. Click **Insert Function** f_x. In the Search for a function box: type VLOOKUP, click **Go**, and then click **OK**. The Function Arguments dialog box is now open.

c. In the Lookup_value, type B3 as the lookup value to match on the list of discounts, and then press `Tab`.

d. In the Table_array, type E4:F8, and then press `Tab`.

e. In the Col_index_num, type 2, and then press `Tab`.

f. In the Range_lookup, type TRUE.

The VLOOKUP matches the value in B3 on the range E4:E8. When a match is found, the corresponding row value from column F will be returned. By placing TRUE as the range_lookup argument, the VLOOKUP will perform an approximate match; true is the default setting for this function. This means that an event costing $37,000 will return a 5.0% discount.

SIDE NOTE

Lookup Table Array

Notice the values in the table array (E4:F8) are listed in ascending order; otherwise, the correct value may not be returned.

SIDE NOTE

Table Array Text

Uppercase text and lowercase text are equivalent in lookup table arrays.

Troubleshooting

If the VLOOKUP function returns a #N/A error, check to make sure the range_lookup argument is TRUE. Using FALSE for the argument will force the VLOOKUP into an exact match. Since $37,000 is not listed in E4:E8, an error will be returned.

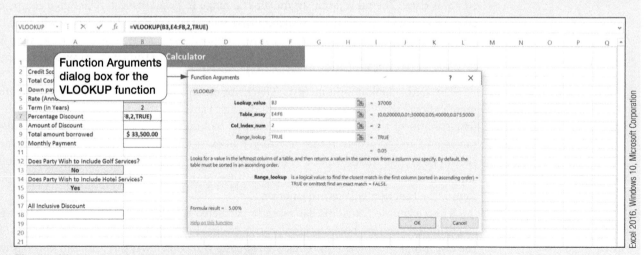

Figure 18 Function Arguments dialog box for the VLOOKUP function

g. Click **OK** to complete the VLOOKUP function and get a result of 5.00%.

h. Click cell **B8**, type =B3*B7, and then press Enter. This will apply the 5.00% discount to the $37,000 event cost, resulting in a discount of $1,850.00.

i. **Save** 🖫 the workbook.

| REAL WORLD ADVICE | Approximate and Exact Matches |

If the range_lookup argument is left blank, it will default to TRUE for an approximate match. If the range_lookup should be FALSE but is mistakenly left blank, an incorrect result will be returned.

Using Financial Functions

Having a foundational knowledge of financial terms is an important element of succeeding in both your personal life and your professional life. Some common financial terms that you will see and hear or possibly use in an Excel spreadsheet are shown in Table 10.

Financial Term	Definition
APR	The annual percentage rate; an interest rate expressed in an annual equivalent
Compound interest	The interest charged on both the principal and the interest that accumulates on a loan
Interest payment	The amount of a payment that goes toward paying the interest accrued
NPV	The net present value of future investments
Period	The time period of payments, such as making payments monthly
Principal payment	The amount of a payment that goes toward reducing the principal amount
Principal value	The original amount borrowed or loaned
PV	Present value — the original value of the loan
Rate (and APR)	The interest rate per period of a loan or an investment
Simple interest	The interest charged on the principal amount of a loan only
Term	The total time of a loan, typically expressed in years or months

Table 10 Financial terminology

Financial functions are a set of predefined functions that can be used for common financial calculations, such as interest rates, payments, and analyzing loans. Some common financial functions are listed in Table 11.

PMT(rate,nper,pv,[fv],[type])	Calculates periodic payment for a loan based on a constant interest rate and constant payment amounts
IPMT(rate,per, nper,pv,[fv],[type])	Calculates periodic interest payment for a loan based on a constant interest rate and constant payment amounts
PPMT(rate,per,nper,pv,[fv],[type])	Calculates periodic principal payment for a loan based on a constant interest rate and constant payment amounts
NPV(rate,value1,[value2]...)	Calculates the net present value based on a discount interest rate, a series of future payments, and future income

Table 11   Common financial functions

A common and useful financial function is the PMT function. The **PMT function** determines the periodic payment for a loan based upon constant payments and interest rate. The PMT function by default returns a negative value. The function is really calculating an outflow of cash, a payment to be made. Within the financial and accounting industry, an outflow of cash is considered a negative value. In other words, this function assumes that you are actually making a payment — taking money out of your pocket to give to someone else, or a negative value to you. Since some people may be confused by seeing the value as negative, the value can be made positive by simply inserting a negative sign before the function or placing the absolute value function — ABS() — around the PMT function.

The syntax of the PMT function is

=PMT(rate,nper,pv,[fv],[type])

The first argument is the rate, which is the periodic interest rate. It is important to remember that the interest rate must be for each period. Most loans are discussed in terms of annual percentage rate (APR), while the period would be a shorter time period such as quarterly or monthly. The APR would need to be divided by 12 to get an equivalent monthly interest rate.

The second argument is nper, which is the number of periods or total number of payments that will be made for the loan. Again, many loans are discussed in years, while the payments would be monthly. Therefore, you will often need to determine the total number of periodic payments with a calculation.

The third required argument is PV, which is the present value of an investment or loan — the amount borrowed that needs to be paid back. The last two arguments are optional. The FV argument is the future value attained after the last payment is made. If this argument is left blank, the PMT function assumes FV to be zero. The type argument indicates when a payment is due. If it is left blank, the PMT function assumes that payments are due at the end of a period; if the type argument is supplied, payments are assumed to be due at the beginning of a period.

In this exercise, you will calculate the monthly payment for the customer for the event being planned, using the PMT function.

To Use the PMT Function

a. On the **WeddingFinancing** worksheet, click cell **B10**.

b. Type =-PMT(to begin the PMT function.

   As was mentioned previously, the PMT function is calculated by default as a negative value. The negative sign before the PMT function will display the final result as a positive number.

Unit Conversions

Be careful when converting the arguments of the PMT function. Monthly payments are converted by using 12; quarterly payments are converted by using 4.

c. Type B5/12, to complete the rate argument. Because the interest rate in cell B5 is annual, you need to divide by 12 to get the interest rate per payment — in this case, monthly.

d. Type B6*12, to complete the number of periods argument. Because the term of the loan is in years, you will need to multiply the term by 12 to get the total number of payments — in this case, months — in the loan.

e. Type B9), and then press ⌃Ctrl+⏎Enter to supply the present value of the loan and complete the PMT function.

f. The original loan amount was $37,000. Cell B9 takes the original amount in B3, subtracts the down payment supplied in cell B4, and subtracts the amount of the discount in cell B8.

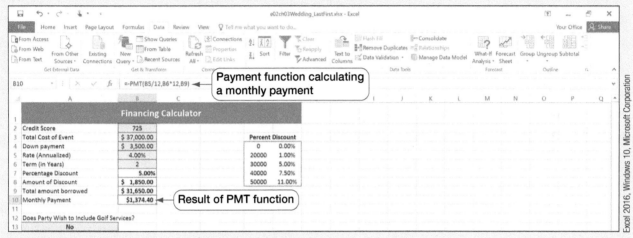

Figure 19 PMT function used to calculate a monthly payment

g. **Save** 🖫 the workbook.

Use Logical Functions and Troubleshoot Functions

In constructing a spreadsheet, the need will often arise to evaluate criteria in a range of cells and make a decision based on those criteria. Excel contains functions that can evaluate a wide range of criteria and return customized results. For example, a comparison of two cells to see whether their values are the same may result in a cell displaying TRUE, a customized text response, or even performing another calculation. As the formulas become more complicated, errors may occur in the spreadsheet. Understanding some basic spreadsheet troubleshooting techniques can help you to easily correct these errors.

Using Logical Functions

Logical functions return a result based upon evaluating whether a logical test is true or false. For example, the statement "The sky is blue" is a declaration that can be evaluated as true. If the statement was "Is the sky blue?" the response would be a yes/no instead of true/false. So all logical functions are structured around the concept of declaring a position or statement that Excel will evaluate and return as True or False.

The best way to think of a declaration is to think of using comparison symbols such as the =, >, <, or >= symbols as shown in Table 12. When you set up a statement of X > Y, Excel can evaluate that comparison as true or false.

Comparison Operator Symbol	Example	Declarative Clause
<	A < B	A is less than B
>	A > B	A is greater than B
=	A = B	A is equal to B
<=	A <= B	A is less than or equal to B
>=	A >= B	A is greater than or equal to B
<>	A <> B	A does not equal B

Table 12   Comparison operators

The IF function is the most commonly used logical function. The **IF function** will return one of two values depending upon whether the supplied logical test being evaluated is true or false. The syntax of the IF function is

=IF(logical_test,[value_if_true],[value_if_false])

The first argument is the logical_test, the statement you want to evaluate as TRUE or FALSE. Excel will then evaluate it as either true or false. The second argument is the result you want to display in the cell if the expression is evaluated as true. The third argument is the result you want to display in the cell if the expression is evaluated as false.

Notice that only the logical_test argument is required. The last two arguments are optional. If you leave them out, Excel will automatically return TRUE or FALSE as the result of the function. However, it is much more common and expected that you will supply something for all three arguments. If you consider the context, logical statement, and results of the IF function, the structure begins to fall into place.

It is possible to create intricate logical statements using the AND and OR functions. These functions allow you to evaluate multiple logical statements within a single IF function. The **AND function** is a logical function that returns TRUE if all logical tests supplied are true; otherwise, it returns FALSE. The **OR function** is a logical function that returns TRUE if any one logical test supplied is true; otherwise, it returns FALSE. The components can incorporate values, cells, named ranges, and even other functions. Common logical functions and their usage are listed in Table 13.

Logical Functions	Usage
IF(logical_test,[value_if_true],[value_if_false])	Returns one of two values depending upon whether the logical statement is evaluated as being true or false
IFERROR(value,value_if_error)	Returns a specified value if a function or formula returns an error; otherwise, it returns the value of the function or formula
AND(logical1,logical2,...)	Returns true if logical1, logical2,...logical255 all return true
OR(logical1,logical2,...)	Returns true if any one of logical1, logical2,...logical255 return true

Table 13   Common logical functions

 CONSIDER THIS | **Variations in Constructing Formulas**

In Excel, a formula can be written in many ways. Some are more efficient than others. At a minimum, every IF statement can be written in two ways. Why? Provide an example for each way.

To encourage couples getting married to use the resort for all of their wedding services, the Painted Paradise Resort & Spa is offering an all-inclusive discount of $500.00. The availability of the discount to the guests must be evaluated in two steps. First, the discount can be offered only if the guest's credit score is at least 650. Second, the wedding party must use both the golf course and the hotel as part of the event.

In this exercise, you will use common logical functions to evaluate whether a wedding party is eligible for the all-inclusive discount. If the wedding party is eligible, they will receive a $500 discount. If they are not eligible, the cell should display a zero.

 E03.16

To Use the IF and the AND functions

a. On the **WeddingFinancing** worksheet, click cell **C10**.

b. Click the **Formulas** tab, and in the Function Library group, click **Logical**, and then click **IF** to begin the IF function and enter the Logical_test argument.

The credit score of the guest is located in cell B2. The IF function will need to test for a value in this cell of greater than or equal to 650.

c. With the insertion point in the Logical_test, type B2>=650 for the logical_test argument. Press Tab to enter the value_if_true argument.

The IF function should return the text "Sufficient Credit Score" if the value in B2 is 650 or greater. If the value is less than 650, the text "Insufficient Credit Score" should be returned.

d. Type Sufficient Credit Score, and then press Tab to enter the Value_if_false argument.

e. Type Insufficient Credit Score.

SIDE NOTE

Using Text in Formulas

Note in the Functions Arguments dialog box how Excel supplied quotation marks around the Value_if_true text. If you type this formula in a cell, you must add the quotation marks.

Figure 20 Function Arguments dialog box

f. Click **OK** to complete the IF function. Use the AutoFit feature on column C. Notice that since the value in B2 is 725, the text "Sufficient Credit Score" is returned by the IF function.

g. Click cell **A18**, and then type =IF(to begin the IF function.

Since the discount requires both golf services and hotel services to be used by the wedding party, the AND function will be used in the logical test of the IF function to evaluate this criterion.

h. Type AND(A13="Yes",A15="Yes"), to insert the AND function into the IF function and complete the logical_test argument.

The AND function will now return TRUE if cells A13 and A15 both contain the text "Yes". Otherwise, it will return FALSE to the IF function.

i.   Type 500, to complete the Value_if_true argument.

   If the AND function returns TRUE, the number 500 will be displayed in cell A18. This will give a $500 discount to the wedding party.

j.   Type 0) to complete the Value_if_false argument and complete the IF function. Press [Ctrl] and [Enter].

   If the AND function returns FALSE, the number 0 will be displayed in cell A18, and no discount will be given. Notice that no discount is currently given, as cell A13 displays No.

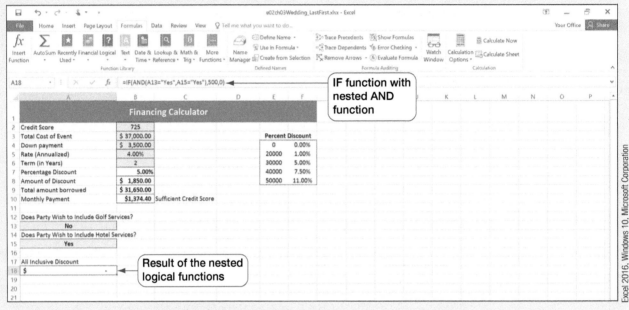

Figure 21   IF function with nested AND function

k.   Click cell **A13**, type Yes, and then press [Ctrl]+[Enter]. Cell A18 now displays the discount value of $500.00, as both cells A13 and A15 display Yes.

l.   **Save** [icon] the workbook.

IF functions can range from simple tests of a statement to complex, nested formulas. Table 14 shows four examples of IF functions with varying levels of complexity.

Context: Display the word "Good" if the exam score in J10 is greater than or equal to the target goal of 80 which is in cell B2. If it is worse than 80, display the word "Bad".

Example: =IF(J10>=$B$2,"Good","Bad")

Interpretation: If the value in cell J10 is greater than or equal to the value in B2, the text "Good" is displayed. Otherwise, the text "Bad" is displayed.

Context: Display the status of an employee meeting his or her goal of getting a number of transactions where transactions are listed in the range of A2:A30 and the target number of transactions are in cell C3.

Example: =IF(COUNT(A2:A30)>=C3,"Met Goal"," ")

Interpretation: If the count of transactions that are listed in range A2:A30 is greater than or equal to the value in C3 (the target goal for the employee), the employee met his or her goal and the text "Met Goal" should be displayed. Otherwise, the goal was not met, and no value should be displayed. This can be accomplished by supplying two quotation marks with no characters typed between them.

Context: For tracking any projects that have not been completed, check the text in H20, and if it does not say "Complete", assume that the project is not complete and calculate how many months are left when A3 has today's date and A4 has the targeted completion date.

Example: =IF(H20<>"Complete", DATEDIF(A3,A4,"M"),0)

Interpretation: If H20 does not say "Complete" to represent a completed project, calculate the number of months left based on dates in cells A3 and A4. Otherwise, show a zero.

Context: Determine salary by checking whether the employee generated less revenue than his or her goal listed in B2. If so, the employee simply gets the base pay. If the employee does meet his or her goal or generates more revenue than the goal, the employee gets a bonus, which is a percent of sales added to the base pay. Since this may result in a value that has more than two decimals, the result needs to be rounded to two decimals.

Example: =ROUND(IF(SUM(Sales)<B2,Base,Base+BonusPercent*(SUM(Sales))),2)

Interpretation: The ROUND() function will round the result to two decimals. Inside the ROUND function, the SUM(Sales) functions will sum the range named Sales to give the total sales. The IF statement then indicates that IF the total Sales is less than the value in B2 (the sales goal), provide the value that is in the range called Base (Base pay). Otherwise, the total Sales must be greater than or equal to B2, and the pay would be calculated as the Base (Base pay) plus the value in the named range BonusPercent times the total Sales.

Table 14 Examples of IF functions

 CONSIDER THIS | **What IF There Are Three Options?**

An IF statement can handle just two results: true and false. Are most real world situations that simple? How could you use an IF statement if there are more than two results? It is possible!

Troubleshooting Functions

Logical functions dramatically increase the value of a spreadsheet. However, on the path to learning how to use functions, and even as an experienced spreadsheet user, you will still make typing errors during the development of functions. Excel does an excellent job of incorporating clues to help you determine where you have gone astray with a function.

When you make a mistake with a function that prevents Excel from returning a viable result, Excel will provide an error message. While these may seem cryptic initially, they can be interpreted. Typically, an error message will be prefaced with a number symbol (#).

Examples are #VALUE!, #N/A, #NAME?, or #REF!. Over time, you will learn to recognize common issues that would cause these error messages.

There are numerous ways to troubleshoot erroneous functions in Excel. When you encounter an error, you can quickly check the cell references and arguments of the function by double-clicking the cell to edit the function. This is beneficial because while a function is being edited, Excel will outline any cells or ranges included in the function and display the ScreenTip for the function. You can also press the F2 key to place a cell in edit mode. Auditing options are available in the Formula Auditing group of the Formulas tab as well.

On the Commission worksheet, Meda has set up a quick analysis that rewards the employee who schedules the event with a commission on the total cost of the event. The commission earned is then added to the base event pay for the employee. The base event pay is contingent upon the employee level. After setting up the worksheet, Meda noticed an error in one of the cells. Additionally, the table located in the Commission worksheet states that managers have a base event pay of $1,250. However, the value shown for the manager in the worksheet is only $750. In this exercise, you will troubleshoot the problem.

To Troubleshoot a Function

a. Click the **Commission** worksheet tab, and then click cell **B4**.

Notice the #N/A error being returned by the VLOOKUP function in the cell. Recall that this error commonly occurs because a value cannot be found on a list.

b. Click the **Error Message** button next to cell **B4**. Notice the error message states that a value is not available.

c. Click cell **B4** again, and then press F2 to edit the formula.

Notice the outlines around the cells that are part of the VLOOKUP function. From this view, you can verify that cell B3 is correctly referenced as the lookup value. Cells E4:F8 are correctly referenced as the table array. The column index number will return a value from column F if a value is found in column E.

Notice that the range_lookup argument is set to FALSE. This means that the lookup is performing an exact match. Since $17,000 does not occur in the range E4:E8, the VLOOKUP will return a #N/A error.

d. Place the insertion point at the end of the **range_lookup** argument, and then delete the text **FALSE**. Type TRUE, and then press Ctrl+Enter to fix the formula. Notice that the value 5.00% now appears in cell B4.

e. Double-click cell **B8** to edit the formula.

Notice that the range_lookup argument is set to TRUE. This means that the lookup is performing an approximate match and is returning the incorrect base event pay rate.

f. Place the insertion point at the end of the **range_lookup** argument, and then **delete** the text **TRUE**. Type FALSE, and then press Ctrl+Enter to fix the formula. Notice that the value $1,250 now appears in cell B8.

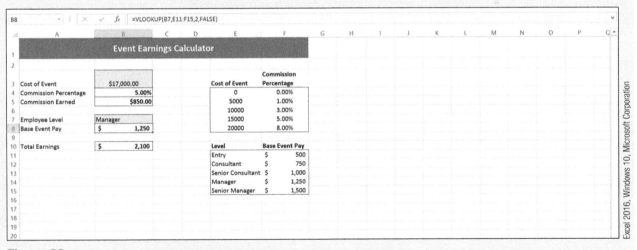

Figure 22   Worksheet with IF functions corrected

g. Complete the Documentation worksheet according to your instructor's directions.

h. Insert the file name in the left footer of all worksheets.

i. **Save** 🖫 the workbook, exit Excel, and then submit your file as directed by your instructor.

As you develop a spreadsheet, follow these guidelines for creating formulas and functions.

1. Use parentheses for grouping operations in calculations in order to get the correct order. However, do not overuse parentheses, as this quickly adds to the complexity of the formula. For example, use =SUM(Sales) instead of =(SUM(Sales)).

2. When inserting numbers into a function, use formatting such as 10000. Do not enter 10,000, with a comma. In Excel, the comma is a formatting element and is used to separate arguments. Best practice for functions and formulas dictates entering the 10000 value in a cell and then using the cell address in the formula.

3. Insert currency as 4.34 instead of $4.34 to avoid confusion with relative and absolute cell referencing. Then format the cell that will contain the result as Accounting or Currency. Best practice for functions and formulas dictates entering the 4.34 value in a cell and then using the cell address in the formula.

4. Enter percentages as decimals, such as .04. Then format the number as a percentage.

5. Logical conditions have three parts: two components to compare and the comparison sign. Do not type >5 when there is no value to evaluate as being greater than 5.

6. Use the negative sign, as in -333, to indicate negative numbers in formulas, rather than (333).

7. Always put quotation marks around text unless it is a named range. Numeric values do not require quotation marks unless the number will be used in a textual context and not for a mathematical calculation. An example of numbers in a textual context would be a zip code or telephone number.

8. Avoid unneeded spaces in formulas. Excel will allow a function such as =SUM(A2:A10). Best practice dictates typing the function as =SUM(A2:A10) with no extra spaces.

Concept Check

1. Explain the three different types of cell referencing. p. 437

2. Why are named ranges useful? What limitations are there in creating the names for ranges? p. 445

3. Why is the syntax of an Excel function important? How can you distinguish between required and optional portions of a function? p. 450–451

4. In the mathematical and statistical functions, what are the differences between the ROUND function and the INT function? Give a business example of when you would use each. p. 452

5. What is the difference between the TODAY() function and the NOW() function? Why is this difference important? p. 458–459

6. What are common uses for text functions? Why is the Flash Fill feature useful on mobile devices? p. 461–463

7. Explain the difference between the TRUE and FALSE arguments for the range_lookup argument of a VLOOKUP function. Give a business example of how you would use a VLOOKUP with a PMT function. p. 465–468

8. Give a business example in which an IF function would be useful. How would using the AND or OR functions in the logical_test argument change the way the IF function works? p. 469–473

Key Terms

ABS function 452
Absolute cell reference 437
AND function 470
Argument 450
Cell reference 437
Cleansing text 461
COUNT function 456
COUNTA function 456
Date and time functions 457
DATEDIF function 459
Financial functions 467
FIND function 462

Flash Fill 463
Function 450
Function arguments 452
IF function 470
INT function 452
LEFT function 461
Logical functions 469
Lookup and reference functions 465
MEDIAN function 456
Mixed cell reference 437
MODE function 456
MODE.MULT function 456

MODE.SNGL function 456
Name Manager 446
Named range 437
NOW function 458
OR function 470
PMT function 468
Relative cell reference 437
ROUND function 452
Syntax 450
Text function 461
TODAY function 458
VLOOKUP function 465

Visual Summary

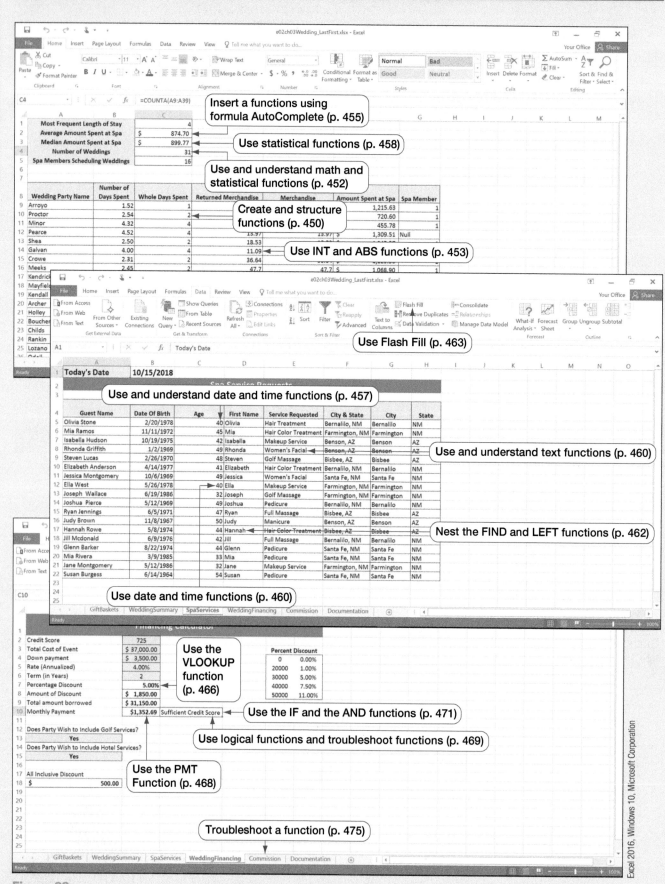

Figure 23

Excel 2016, Windows 10, Microsoft Corporation

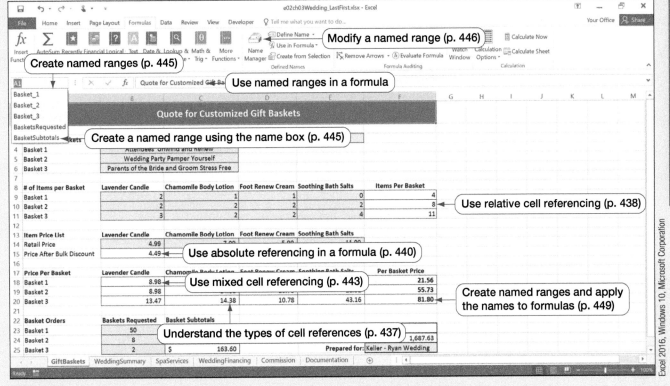

Figure 24

Practice 1

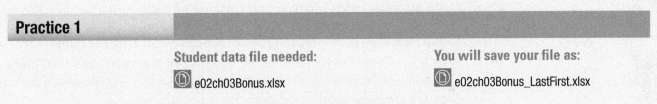

Student data file needed:

📄 e02ch03Bonus.xlsx

You will save your file as:

📄 e02ch03Bonus_LastFirst.xlsx

Massage Therapist Bonus Workbook

Human
Resources

Finance and
Accounting

Meda Rodate has been constructing a workbook that will enable her to analyze the goals for massage therapists and calculate their pay. The massage therapists have a base pay and earn commission on massages along with a bonus. Meda has asked that you make some modifications to the workbook that she began to facilitate her analysis.

a. Start **Excel**, click **Open Other Workbooks** in the left pane, and then double-click **This PC**. Navigate through the folder structure to the location of your student data files, and then double-click **e02ch03Bonus**. If a Security Warning message displays, click the **Enable Editing** button.

b. Click the **File** tab, click **Save As**, and then double-click **This PC**. In the Save As dialog box, navigate to the location where you are saving your project files, and then change the file name to e02ch03Bonus_LastFirst, using your last and first name. Click **Save**.

c. Click the **Bonus** worksheet tab, and then click cell **J17**. Click in the Name box, type Bonus, and then press Enter.

d. Click the **Formulas** tab, and then, in the Defined Names group, click **Name Manager**. Click **Christy** in the list of named ranges in the workbook.

e. In the **Refers to** box, delete the existing range, and then type =Bonus!$B$12:$K$12. Click the Enter button, and then click **Close**.

f. Click cell **B4**, type =B3, and then press F4 twice to create the mixed cell reference B$3. Type *A4, and then press F4 three times to create the mixed cell reference $A4. Press Ctrl+Enter.

g. Click the **AutoFill** handle, and then drag down to copy the formula to cell **B8**. With the range B4:B8 still selected, click the **AutoFill** handle, and then drag to the right to copy the formulas to the range **B4:K8**.

h. Click cell **F19**, type =SUM(Christy), and then press Enter. Repeat this process for cells **F20:F22**, replacing the named range in the SUM function with the name of the **therapist** in cells **A20:A22** respectively.

i. Click cell **D25**, type =C19*C25, and then press Ctrl+Enter. Double-click the **AutoFill** handle to copy the formula to cell **D28**.

A bonus is earned if the therapist attains two goals: first, the generated actual revenue for a therapist is greater than the goal for that therapist and, second, the actual number of massages completed for a therapist was greater than or equal to the goal of that therapist. If the goal is met, cells D19:D22 and G19:G22 should display a 1; otherwise, they should display a 0.

j. Click cell **D19**, type =IF(C19>=B19,1,0), and then press Ctrl+Enter. Double-click the **AutoFill** handle to copy the formula to cell **D22**.

k. Click cell **G19**, type =IF(F19>=E19,1,0), and then press Ctrl+Enter. Double-click the **AutoFill** handle to copy the formula to cell **G22**.

If both goals are met, cells E25:E28 should display the bonus amount in cell J17; otherwise, they should display 0.

l. Click cell **E25**, type =IF(AND(D19=1,G19=1),Bonus,0), and then press Ctrl+Enter. Double-click the **AutoFill** handle, and then drag down to copy the formula to cell **E28**.

m. Click cell **F25**, type =B25+D25+E25, and then press Ctrl+Enter. Click the **AutoFill** handle, and then drag down to copy the formula to cell **F28**.

n. On the **Insert** tab, in the Text group, click **Header & Footer**. On the Header & Footer Tools Design tab, in the Navigation group, click **Go to Footer**. Click in the left footer section, and then, in the Header & Footer Elements group, click **File Name**.

o. Click any **cell** on the spreadsheet to move out of the footer, and then press Ctrl+Home. On the **View** tab, in the Workbook Views group, click **Normal**.

p. Click the **Documentation** worksheet. Click cell **A8**, and then type in today's date. Click cell **B8**, and then type your name in the Firstname Lastname format. Complete the remainder of the Documentation worksheet according to your instructor's directions.

q. Save the workbook, exit Excel, and then submit your file as directed by your instructor.

Problem Solve 1

MyITLab®
Grader

Homework

Productions and
Operations

Finance and
Accounting

Student data file needed:

e02ch03Renovations.xlsx

You will save your file as:

e02ch03Renovations _LastFirst.xlsx

Painted Paradise Resort & Spa Scenario

Lesa Martin, a member of the support/coordination staff for the conference center at Painted Paradise Resort & Spa, has created a worksheet to keep track of the renovations being made to the three rooms that are used for conferences and the two technology centers that are used for computer-based presentations and interactive sessions. The technology centers are equipped with workstations, are networked, and have Internet accessibility. This spreadsheet is simple and designed only for Lesa and her associates to keep a handle on the renovation progress and estimate the increase in capacity and revenue that might occur as a result of the renovations.

a. Open the Excel file, **e02ch03Renovations**. Save your file as e02ch03Renovations_LastFirst, using your last and first name.

b. On the **Renovations** worksheet in cell **G6**, enter a formula using an absolute reference to determine the new capacity that the Musica Room will hold based on the capacity in cell F6 and the percentage in cell B13.

c. Copy this formula to the range **G7:G10**.

d. Assign the name range IncreaseInRevenue to cell **B14**.

e. In cell **I6**, enter a formula to determine the increase in revenue for the Musica Room based on the revenue figure in cell H6 and the percentage in cell B14. Use the named range in cell B14 when entering this formula.

f. Copy this formula to the range **I7:I10**.

g. In cell **D6**, enter the appropriate date function to determine the length in days of the expected renovation for the Musica Room.

h. Copy this function to the range **D7:D10**.

i. In cell **B15**, enter the function to calculate the median length of renovations in days. Give the cell the name range MedianDays.

j. In cell **J6**, enter a logical function to display the word **Under** in the cell if the renovations are going to take fewer than or equal to the median number of days calculated in cell B15; otherwise, have the word **Over** display. Use the named range for B15 when entering this formula.

k. Copy this function to the range **J7:J10**.

l. In cell **B21**, enter a function that will calculate the monthly payment for the loan amount in cell B18, based on the Annualized Rate in B19, and the number of years in the Term in cell B20. Display the monthly payment as a positive value.

m. Assign the named range **RoomClassification** to A24:B27.

n. In cell **K6**, using a lookup function, create a formula to determine the projected room classification based on the projected quarterly revenue after renovations in cell I6. Use the name range RoomClassification when entering this formula.

o. Copy this formula to the range **K7:K10**.

p. Add the **File Name** in the left footer of the Renovations sheet. Return to Normal view if necessary.

q. On the **Documentation** worksheet in cell **A8**, type today's date. In cell **B8**, type your name in the Firstname Lastname format. Complete the remainder of the Documentation worksheet according to your instructor's directions.

r. Save the workbook, exit Excel, and then submit your file as directed by your instructor.

Critical Thinking

The Renovations workbook contains named ranges. What are the benefits of using named ranges in formulas?

Not all workbooks benefit from naming cells or ranges of cells. Can you explain a scenario in which it would not be wise to use names or named ranges?

Perform 1: Perform in Your Life

Student data file needed:

 e02ch03RealEstate.xlsx

You will save your file as:

e02ch03RealEstate_LastFirst.xlsx

Finance and Accounting

Real Estate Workbook

You are interning at Schalow Real Estate firm. Your supervisor has asked you to cleanse the data in a spreadsheet so that she can analyze it and look for trends. She asks that you create new columns as directed. Format all currency spreadsheet values using the Currency Number Format, and display two decimal places. Fill all formula and functions through the appropriate rows.

a. Open the Excel file, **e02ch03RealEstate**. Save your file as e02ch03RealEstate_LastFirst, using your last and first name.

b. On the Sold worksheet, create a column named Price/SqFt in column N, and then create a formula to calculate the price per square foot based on of the square footage and the price sold.

c. Create a column named Down PMT, and then create a formula that will calculate a down payment of 20% of the sold price.

d. Create a column named Days on MKT, and then create a formula to calculate the number of days each property was on the market.

e. Create a column named Monthly Payment. Create a formula to calculate the monthly mortgage payment for each property. With a mixed reference, use the interest rate found in cell V2. With a mixed reference, use the term in cell W2. Deduct the down payment from the sold price to calculate the amount financed. Edit the function to display positive numbers.

f. Create a column named Monthly Taxes. Each development has a different tax rate. Use a lookup function to look up the **Development ID** from the Sold worksheet, and determine that development's **Tax Rate** from the Development worksheet. Then, to determine the actual tax, multiply the tax rate by the sold price, and divide the tax by 12. This will determine the amount to save each month to pay the taxes at the end of the year (Month Tax).

   To reference a lookup table on a different worksheet, click on the worksheet tab that contains the lookup table, select the range, type a comma (,), and then click the original worksheet tab.

g. Create a column named Monthly Insurance. The cost to insure homes is different in different neighborhoods. Use a lookup function to look up the **Development ID** and determine that development's Insurance Rates from the Development worksheet. Then multiply the insurance rate by the sold price, and divide by 12 to determine the monthly payment.

h. Create a column named Total Payment. Add the monthly tax and insurance to the monthly payment to determine how much the homeowner needs to live in the newly purchased home.

i. Ensure that your columns are sufficiently wide to display their content fully. Wrap the text in the header rows on each worksheet as necessary. Format the workbook professionally.

j. On the **Documentation** worksheet in cell **A8**, type today's date. In cell **B8**, type your name in the Firstname Lastname format. Complete the remainder of the Documentation worksheet according to your instructor's directions.

k. Add the file name to the left footer on all sheets.

l. Save the workbook, exit Excel, and then submit your file as directed by your instructor.

Additional Cases

Additional Chapter Cases are available at www.pearsonhighered.com/youroffice

Microsoft Excel 2016

Chapter 4 | EFFECTIVE CHARTS

Prepare Case

Sales & Marketing

Turquoise Oasis Spa Sales Reports

The Turquoise Oasis Spa managers, Irene Kai and Meda Rodate, are pleased with your work and would like to see you continue to improve the spa spreadsheets. They want to use charts to learn more about the spa. Meda has given you a spreadsheet with some data and would like you to develop some charts. Visualizing the data with charts will provide knowledge about the spa for decision-making purposes.

Sea Wave/Fotolia

Student data files needed for this chapter:

 e02ch04SpaSales.xlsx

 e02ch04TurquoiseOasis.jpg

You will save your file as:

 e02ch04SpaSales_LastFirst.xlsx

Designing a Chart

With Excel, you can organize data so it has context and meaning. **Data visualization** is the graphical presentation of data with a focus on qualitative understanding. It is central to finding trends and supporting business decisions. Modern data visualization can involve beautiful and elegant charts that include movement and convey information in real time. Charts are at the heart of data visualization. Charts enlighten you as you compare and contrast data and examine how it changes over time. Learning how to work with charts means not only knowing how to create them but also realizing that each type of chart can discover or emphasize different knowledge.

While it may seem simple to create a pie chart or a bar chart, there are many considerations in creating charts. Like a picture, a chart can be worth a thousand words. However, different people may interpret a chart differently if it is not well developed. A well-developed chart should provide context for the information without overshadowing key points. Finally, it is easy to confuse people with the choice and layout of a chart. A chart should use accurate and complete data. The objective should be to provide a focused, clear message. In today's data-rich world, many interpretations or messages can be extracted from the data. Businesses have three primary objectives in charting: data analysis, hypothesis testing, and persuasion.

In data analysis, the Excel chart is used to manipulate the data to try to evaluate and prioritize all the interpretations or messages. There may be a need to create multiple charts, using a variety of data sources, layouts, and designs as data is interpreted.

Ideas or hypotheses may be made about the data. Charts can visually support or refute hypotheses. For example, maybe you have the impression that a certain salesperson performs better than the other salespeople. You could support or refute your hypothesis by charting their sales data.

If you have a position you want the data to support visually, you could consider using an Excel chart to help persuade your audience of your position. You will need to select a specific and appropriate chart layout, use the necessary data, and design a chart that conveys your message clearly and unambiguously. Further, you have an ethical obligation to represent the data accurately. Misrepresenting data can result in lawsuits or termination of employment.

Regardless of the objective, even a small set of data allows you to create a variety of charts, each offering a different understanding of the data. In this chapter, you will start with understanding the concepts for creating a chart in Excel and understanding which type of chart will depict the information in the best and most efficient manner.

Explore Chart Types, Layouts, and Styles

When you decide to represent data visually, you need to make some initial decisions about the basic design of the chart. These initial decisions include the location of the chart, the type of chart, the general layout and style, and what data you will be using. These elements can be set initially and modified later. Best practice dictates that you first consider and develop the basic design of the chart.

Regardless of the location or type of chart, the process of creating a chart starts with the organization of the data on the spreadsheet. The typical structure is to have labels across the top of the data, along the left side of the data, or both. While the labels do not have to be directly next to the data, this position helps in selecting data and making your chart. The data may have been brought in from an external data source, such as Access. The data may need to be filtered, calculated, or reorganized before a chart is created. Keep in mind that not all data is organized in a way that allows for the creation of charts.

When you are ready to create a chart, select the cells that contain both the label headings and the data. People rarely create a perfect chart the first time. You might start a chart, work with it for a while, and then realize that a different chart type would better convey the information. Fortunately, Excel provides ample flexibility in designing charts. Thus, if you change your mind, you can modify the chart or simply start over.

Opening the Starting File

In this exercise, you will review a pie chart that displays the use of portable massage tables by different therapists at the Turquoise Oasis Spa.

SIDE NOTE
Pin the Ribbon
If your ribbon is collapsed, pin your ribbon open. Click the Home tab. In the lower right corner of the ribbon, click Pin the Ribbon ⊡.

SIDE NOTE
Screen Size
Not all screen sizes are the same. If you cannot see all of a tab's groups, you may need to click a arrow to make a button visible.

To Open the SpaSales Workbook

a. Start **Excel**, click **Open Other Workbooks** in the left pane, and then click **This PC**. Navigate through the folder structure to the location of your student data files, and then click **e02ch04SpaSales**. The workbook containing sales data for the Turquoise Oasis Spa opens.

b. If necessary, click Enable Editing. Click the **File** tab, and then click **Save As,** and then click **This PC**. In the Save As dialog box, navigate to the location where you are saving your project files, and then change the file name to e02ch04SpaSales_LastFirst using your last and first name. Click **Save**.

c. On the **TableUse** worksheet, click the **Insert** tab, and in the Text group, click **Header & Footer**.

d. On the **Header & Footer Tools Design** tab, in the Navigation group, click **Go to Footer**. If necessary, click the left section of the footer, and then, in the Header & Footer Elements group, click **File Name**.

e. Click any **cell** on the worksheet to move out of the footer, press [Ctrl]+[Home], and then, on the status bar, click **Normal** ▦.

f. Click **Save** 🖫.

Modifying an Existing Chart

A chart is an object in Excel. Clicking on the chart will allow you to modify aspects of the chart or even change the type of chart. When you click an existing chart, you are activating the chart area. The border of the chart will be highlighted, while the middle of the sides and the corners of the chart will have selection handles, which can be used to resize the chart. The chart border can also be used to move the entire chart to a new location within the spreadsheet. When a chart is selected, the Chart Tools contextual tab will appear on the ribbon. To the right of the chart, the Chart Formatting Control will appear as three buttons that provide quick access to common functions such as chart elements, chart layout, and filtering of chart data.

When a chart is selected by clicking on the chart, the data used in creating the chart will be highlighted in the worksheet, offering a visual clue of the associated data. In the TableUse worksheet, you will see a pie chart describing the use of massage tables by individual therapists at the spa. When the chart is selected, a purple border surrounds the data that represents the legend labels. The range with a blue border is the data that represents the data series for the pie slices. **A data series** is a group of related data values to be charted. **A data point** is an individual data value in a data series. A chart may contain multiple data series or a single data series.

REAL WORLD ADVICE	First Impressions

First impressions are important with charts. You want the audience to receive the correct message during the initial moments. An audience that is distracted by the look and feel of the chart may stop looking for the message in the chart or extend the chaotic personality of the chart to the presenter. Thus, the chart can become a reflection on you and your company.

To quickly identify the value of the data series, Meda Rodate has asked you to modify the existing pie chart on the TableUse worksheet by adding data labels, which you will do in this exercise. Since you will be modifying a pie chart, Meda prefers the addition of percentage labels over the value labels for each data series. She has also asked you to change the chart style to improve its appearance. In this exercise, you will modify an existing chart.

To Modify an Existing Chart

a. On the **TableUse** worksheet, notice the pie chart located to the right of the data on this worksheet.

b. Click the **chart border** of the chart to select the chart and display the Chart Tools contextual tabs.

c. To the right of the chart, click **Chart Elements** ⊞, and then click to select **Data Labels**. This will display the number of times each therapist used a portable massage table in the corresponding slice of the pie chart.

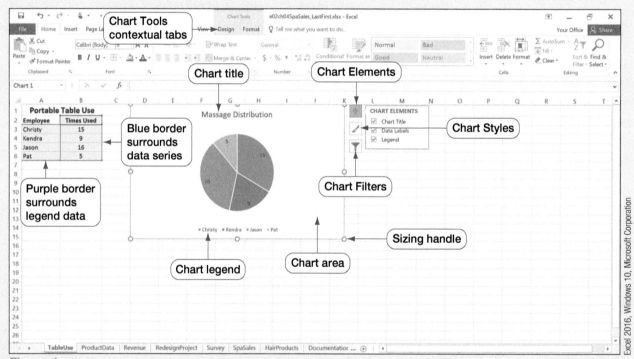

Figure 1 Selected pie chart

d. Click the **Data Labels** arrow, and then select **More Options**. This will open the Format Data Labels task pane.

e. Under Label Options, click to select **Percentage**, and then click to deselect **Value**. On the Format Data Labels task pane on the right side of the screen, click close ✕.

f. Click the **chart border** of the pie chart, click **Chart Styles** 🖌, and then scroll down and point to **Style 3**. Notice that the chart changes to display a live preview of the style.

g. Click **Style 3**, and then click **Chart Styles** 🖌 to close the control. The chart now displays the percentage of portable table use for each massage therapist at the spa.

h. **Save** 🖫 the workbook.

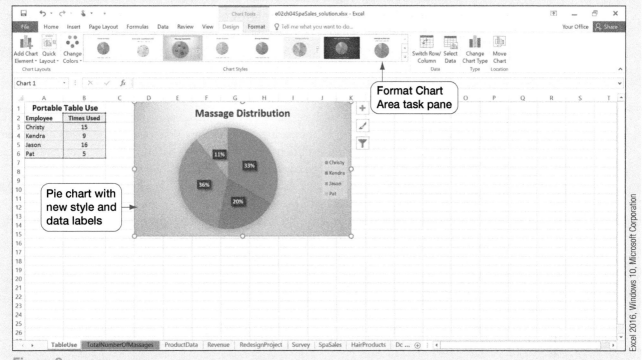

Figure 2 Modified chart

 CONSIDER THIS | **Misleading Charts**

Charts are supposed to frame information. However, charts in newspapers, online articles, and magazines sometimes lead the viewer to an incorrect assumption or conclusion. Look for a chart that is misleading. Discuss the context and possible incorrect conclusions that could be drawn from the chart, and consider the ethical aspect for the creator of the chart.

QUICK REFERENCE | **Working with Chart Objects**

It is possible to navigate through a chart using some of these guidelines.

- Click the chart border to activate the Chart Tools contextual tabs.
- Click chart objects to select individual chart components.
- Click outside a chart object or press [Esc] to deselect an object.
- On the Chart Tools contextual tabs, on the Format tab, in the Current Selection group, use the Chart Elements box to select specific chart objects.
- Use border corner handles to resize selected objects.
- Click a chart object and drag to move the chart object.

Explore the Position of Charts

When designing a chart, consider the chart location, as this might affect the flexibility of moving and resizing your chart components. There are two general locations for a chart: either within an existing worksheet as an embedded chart or on a separate worksheet, referred to as a chart sheet. An **embedded chart** exists as an object on the same worksheet with the data. A **chart sheet** is a special worksheet that is dedicated to displaying chart objects. Excel 2016 has several features that allow you to quickly analyze data. Two of these are the Quick Analysis tool and the Recommended Charts feature. The **Quick Analysis** tool is a contextual tool that appears when you select data in a worksheet and offers single-click access to formatting, charts, formulas, PivotTables, and sparklines. The Recommended Charts feature is located on the Insert tab on the ribbon. The **Recommended Charts** feature quickly analyzes a selection in a worksheet and recommends chart types that best fit your data. The Recommend Charts option also appears in the Quick Analysis tool under the Chart heading.

Creating Charts in an Existing Worksheet

Placing a chart within a worksheet can be very helpful, allowing you to display the chart beside the associated data source. In comparing charts side by side, placing the charts on the same worksheet can also be handy. Additionally, placing a chart within the worksheet may offer easy access to chart components when copying and pasting components into other applications.

To aid in the analysis of the data, Irene Kai would like the data on the ProductData worksheet to be organized and presented in an effective graphical manner. Specifically, she would like to compare the total number of massages given over an eight-week period of time. In this exercise you will create a chart in an existing worksheet.

E04.02

SIDE NOTE
Axis Labels
When creating a chart, be sure to select the appropriate data labels as well as the data. Failure to do so may produce an incomplete and confusing chart.

To Create a Chart in an Existing Worksheet

a. Click the **ProductData** worksheet tab, and then select the range **A2:B12** as the data to use for creating a chart. Notice that once the data is selected, the Quick Analysis tool is displayed below and to the right of cell B12.

b. Click **Quick Analysis** 📊, and then click **Charts**.

c. Point to the **Clustered Column** chart suggestion. Notice that a Live Preview of the chart is displayed.

Troubleshooting

If Live Preview is not displaying, it may be that your taskbar is in triple height. Try changing your taskbar to double or single height.

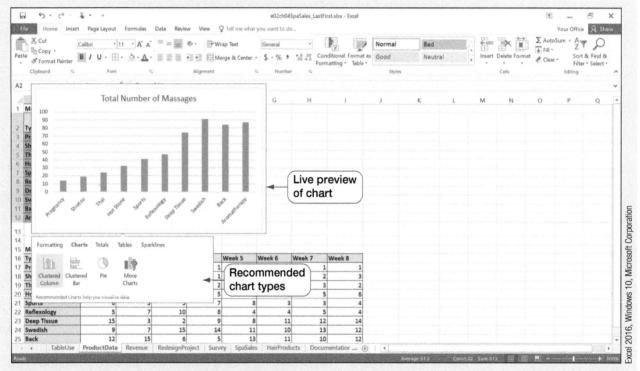

Figure 3 Quick Analysis tool with a suggested chart

E04.03

d. Click **Clustered Column** to insert the chart into the worksheet.
Notice that the chart appears on the currently active worksheet and shows colored borders surrounding the associated data linked to the chart. This chart displays the total number provided of each type of massage offered by the spa.

e. Click the **chart border.** When the pointer appears as a four-way arrow , drag the border to move the chart to the right of the data so the top left chart corner is in cell **D2**.

f. **Save** 🖫 the workbook.

SIDE NOTE
Resizing a chart
You can resize a chart by clicking and dragging a sizing handle. Be careful not to click the corners or middle areas of the chart border if you want only to move a chart.

Modifying a Chart's Position Properties

When a chart is created in Excel, it is placed by default on a worksheet as an embedded chart. The default property settings resize the chart shape if any of the underlying rows or columns are changed or adjusted. Therefore, if the width of a column that lies behind the chart is increased, the chart width will increase accordingly. It is possible to change this setting, locking the size and position of the chart so it does not resize or move when columns or rows are resized, inserted, or deleted.

Meda is concerned that if additional data is added to the ProductData worksheet, the data may require the underlying columns to be widened or new columns to be inserted. If the default settings on the chart are not adjusted, the chart could become distorted when changes are made to the worksheet. In this exercise, you will modify the chart's position properties.

To Modify the Chart Position on a Worksheet

a. On the **ProductData** worksheet, right-click the **chart border** of the clustered column chart, and then select **Format Chart Area**. This will open the Format Chart Area task pane.

b. In the Format Chart Area task pane, click **Size & Properties** 🔲, and then click the **Properties** arrow to expand the **Properties** group.

c. Click **Move but don't size with cells.**

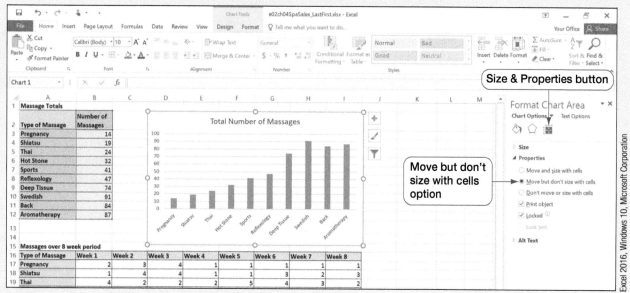

Figure 4 Format Chart Area task pane

d. On the Format Chart Area task pane, click **Close** ☒. **Save** 🖫 the workbook.

The chart size will not be resized if the width or height of the columns or rows underneath are changed or adjusted, but the chart will move along with the cells beneath the chart. From here, you can easily move the chart by dragging the border, or you can resize the chart by clicking and dragging the sizing handles.

Placing Charts on a Chart Sheet

A chart sheet is a worksheet that contains only a chart object. The familiar cell grid is replaced with the actual chart. Having the chart on a separate chart sheet can make it easier to isolate and print on a page. Chart sheets are also useful when you want to create a set of charts and easily navigate between them by worksheet names rather than by looking for them on various worksheets. Because of the nature of chart sheets, the data associated with the chart will be on a different worksheet.

Irene has mentioned that she would like to use this chart in future presentations and would like to be able to easily isolate and print the chart. To facilitate this, in this exercise, you will move the chart to a chart sheet.

 E04.04

SIDE NOTE

Alternate Method
To move a chart to a chart sheet, you can also right-click the chart and select Move Chart from the shortcut menu.

SIDE NOTE

Cutting and Pasting a Chart
You can move a chart to another sheet by cutting and pasting the chart. This does not create a chart sheet; rather, it creates an embedded chart on a new sheet.

To Move a Chart to a Chart Sheet

a. On the **ProductData** worksheet, select the **clustered column chart**.

b. On the **Chart Tools Design** tab, in the **Location** group, click **Move Chart**. The Move Chart dialog box is displayed.

c. In the Move Chart dialog box, click the **New sheet** option. In the New sheet box, clear the **existing name**, and then type TotalNumberOfMassages. Click **OK**.

Notice that you now have a new chart sheet tab in your workbook. By default, the new sheet is placed to the left of the current sheet. This chart sheet is exclusively for the chart and will not have the normal worksheet appearance.

d. Applying a color to the worksheet tab will allow the chart sheet to be easily distinguished from the rest of the worksheets in the workbook. Right-click the **TotalNumberOfMassages** worksheet tab. Point to **Tab Color**, and then click **Blue, Accent 1** in the first row, fifth column as the tab color.

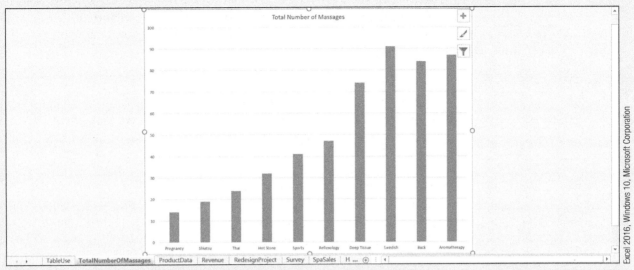

Total Number of Massages

| ‹ › | TableUse | **TotalNumberOfMassages** | ProductData | Revenue | RedesignProject | Survey | SpaSales | H ... ⊕ | ‹ |

Figure 5   Total number of massages bar chart sheet

e. **Save** 💾 the workbook.

Understand Different Chart Types

In creating a chart, it is important to choose the correct type of chart to use. Each chart type conveys information in a particular way. The chart type sets the tone for the basic format of the data and what kind of data is included. Thus, it helps if you become familiar with the types of charts that are commonly used for business decision making and for presentations. Always consider which type is appropriate for the message you are trying to convey.

Creating Pie Charts

Pie charts are commonly used for depicting the relationships of the parts to the whole, such as comparing staff performance within a department or comparing the number of transactions of each product category within a time period.

For a pie chart, you need two data series: the labels and a set of corresponding values. This is similar to the data selection made in the TableUse sheet to indicate the percentage of times each person used the portable massage table. Note that the data can be described as a percentage of the whole, as in the chart.

The questions you have will influence what textual data you will include in any chart. If you are exploring a usage fee for each time a table is used, then having the percentage would indicate which therapist is contributing the most fees, and the actual numbers may not be a crucial element. When you create a chart, examine it to see whether it answers your questions.

In this exercise, you will create a simple pie chart that shows the proportion of total revenue each of four different massage types earned for the spa in the month of June.

 E04.05

To Create a Pie Chart

a. Click the **Revenue** worksheet tab, and then select the range **A1:E2**.

b. Click **Quick Analysis** 📈, click **Charts**, and then click **Pie**.

c. Click the **chart border**, and then drag to move the chart to the top left corner of cell **G4**. This will place the chart to the right of the data set.

d. Point to the **bottom right corner** of the chart until the pointer changes to ⬂, and then drag to the chart so the bottom right corner is over cell **M17**. The chart displays the proportion of revenue generated by each massage type.

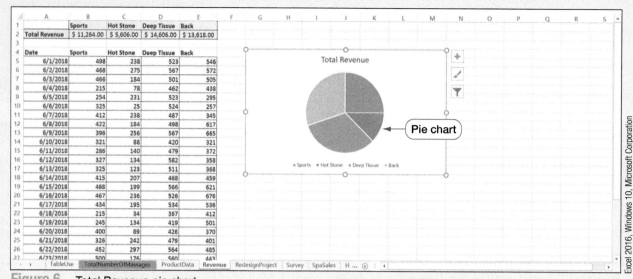

▲	A	B	C	D	E
1		Sports	Hot Stone	Deep Tissue	Back
2	**Total Revenue**	$ 11,264.00	$ 5,606.00	$ 14,606.00	$ 13,618.00
3					
4	**Date**	**Sports**	**Hot Stone**	**Deep Tissue**	**Back**
5	6/1/2018	498	238	523	546
6	6/2/2018	468	275	567	572
7	6/3/2018	466	184	501	505
8	6/4/2018	215	78	462	438
9	6/5/2018	254	231	523	295
10	6/6/2018	325	25	524	257
11	6/7/2018	412	238	487	345
12	6/8/2018	422	184	498	617
13	6/9/2018	396	256	567	665
14	6/10/2018	321	88	420	321
15	6/11/2018	286	140	479	372
16	6/12/2018	327	134	582	358
17	6/13/2018	325	123	511	368
18	6/14/2018	415	207	468	459
19	6/15/2018	468	199	566	621
20	6/16/2018	467	236	526	676
21	6/17/2018	434	195	534	536
22	6/18/2018	215	34	367	412
23	6/19/2018	245	134	419	501
24	6/20/2018	400	89	426	370
25	6/21/2018	326	242	479	401
26	6/22/2018	452	297	564	485
27	6/23/2018	500	176	560	443

Total Revenue — Sports, Hot Stone, Deep Tissue, Back

Pie chart

Figure 6 Total Revenue pie chart

e. **Save** 💾 the workbook.

Even though all the data is used to show every massage type, you do not have to use all the data. If the goal is to examine the data and extract a portion of the information, such as the fact that several massage types have low or high average ratings, it may be better to show only a few massage types rather than including too much information. Showing a subset of massage types may help to emphasize particular ratings.

In determining how to proceed once the data has been initially examined, start developing hypotheses and questions. For example, it may be that hot stone massages are too new and need to be marketed more, as they currently represent a small portion of revenues. Develop questions, and then use the data to determine the validity of the questions and make strategic decisions.

Creating Line Charts

Line charts help to convey change in data over a period of time. They are great for exploring how data in a business, such as sales or production, changes over time. Line charts help people to interpret why the data is changing and to make decisions about how to proceed. For example, in examining a heart rate on an electrocardiogram, a doctor is looking at data over time to see what has been happening. The doctor wants to determine if there are issues, and then make decisions about whether the patient should go home, be given medications, or have surgery.

To create a line chart, you need to have at least one set of labels and at least one set of corresponding data. It is possible to have multiple data series, each series representing a line on the chart. You have been provided with data that lists revenue generated by four different types of massages. The data is organized by day throughout the month of June.

In this exercise, you will create a line chart displaying daily revenue by massage type in June. Irene would like each day to appear as a point on the line that is created and each massage type to be a separate line on the chart.

To Create a Line Chart

a. On the **Revenue** worksheet tab, click cell **A4**, press [Ctrl], and then press [A] to select the entire data set, including the labels.

b. Click **Quick Analysis** 📊, click **Charts**, and then click **Line**. The chart displays the revenue generated by each type of massage through the month of June.

c. Click the **Chart Tools Format** tab. In the Current Selection group, click the **Chart Elements** arrow, and then click **Chart Title** to select the chart title. Type Revenue by Massage Type for June, and then press Enter.

d. Click the **chart border**, and then drag to move the chart to place the top left corner in cell **G20**. This will place the chart to the right of the data set.

e. Point to the **bottom right corner** of the chart until the pointer changes to ⌖, and then drag to resize the chart so the bottom right corner is over cell **M34**.

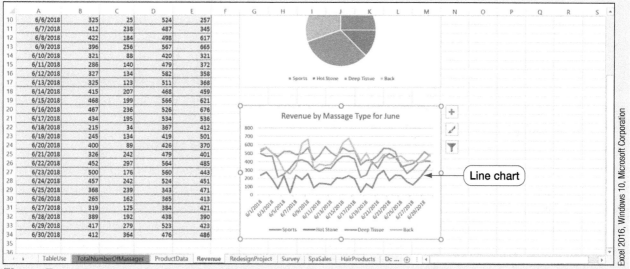

Figure 7   Revenue by Massage Type for June line chart

> ## Troubleshooting
>
> If you end up with a chart that looks dramatically different from what you would expect, check the colored borders around the linked data set. It is very common to select all the data in a table when the intention was to select just part of the data. If too much data was selected, you can delete the selected chart by pressing Delete and then try recreating the chart with the appropriate data. Alternatively, you could select the corner of a colored link data border and drag the border to adjust the set of data. The blue border data is displayed in the chart. When that border is adjusted, the associated label data is automatically adjusted accordingly. The chart is also automatically adjusted so changes can be immediately seen.

f. **Save** 🖫 the workbook.

Creating Column Charts

Column charts are useful for comparing data sets that are categorized, such as departments, product categories, or survey results. Column charts are also useful for showing categories over time where each column represents a unit of time. Column charts are good for comparisons either individually, in groups, or stacked. Column chart data can easily allow for grouping of data so comparisons of the groups can occur.

On the TotalNumberOfMassages chart sheet, it is easy to interpret that pregnancy massages represent a small portion of the total massages provided. By contrast, Swedish, aromatherapy, back, and deep tissue massages represent a large portion of the data.

Creating Bar Charts

Bar charts are useful for working with categorical data. Bar charts are similar to column charts except the bars are horizontal representations of the data rather than vertical. Like column charts, bar charts can depict a single piece of data, can be grouped data series, and can be stacked.

Stacked bar charts can be useful when you want to see how the individual parts add up to create the entire length of each bar. A stacked bar chart can display changes over time for products or services. Stacked charts should be considered when the sum of the data values is as important as the individual items.

In this exercise, you will create a stacked bar chart that will assist Meda and Irene to visualize the status of a project to redesign the massage therapy rooms.

E04.07

SIDE NOTE

Selecting Nonadjacent Columns
To select nonadjacent columns when creating a chart, you must first select the first column of data, then press and hold the Ctrl key, and then select the second column of data.

To Create a Stacked Bar Chart

a. Click the **RedesignProject** worksheet tab.

b. Select the range **A3:A8**, press and hold down the Ctrl key, and then select the range **C3:D8**.

c. Click the **Insert** tab, and in the Chart group, click **Recommended Charts**.

d. Click **Stacked Bar**, the second selection on the Recommended Charts tab of the Insert Chart dialog box. Click **OK**.

e. Position the chart so the top left corner is over cell **A10**.

f. Click the **chart title**, type Project Redesign Status, and then press Enter.

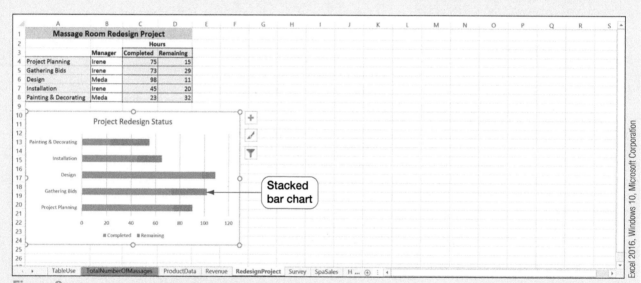

Figure 8 Project Redesign stacked bar chart

g. **Save** the workbook.

The stacked bar chart helps Irene and Meda to determine the status of the redesign phases The chart shows which phases are nearly complete and which phases still need more time to complete. They can use the information to determine whether they need to assign more resources to a phase, such as painting and decorating, to be sure it gets completed in the desired time.

Creating Scatter Charts

A **Scatter chart**, also called XY (Scatter), is a particular type of chart that conveys the relationship between two numeric variables. This type of chart is very common as a statistical tool depicting the correlation between the two variables. The standard format is to have the x-axis (horizontal) data in the left column and the y-axis (vertical) data in the right column(s).

Irene and Meda have data from a survey showing the requested temperature of the room used for massages and the age of the customer. This data may reveal important information about what temperature is typically requested by customers in different age groups. In this exercise, you will create a scatter chart of the requested temperatures of rooms and ages of customers.

To Create a Scatter Chart

a. Click the **Survey** worksheet tab, and then select the range **A2:B53**. This will include the data and labels for Age and Temp.

b. Click **Quick Analysis** 📋, click **Charts**, and then click **Scatter**.

c. Click the **chart border**, and then drag to move it to the right of the data so the top left corner is over cell **E2**.

   The default scale of the chart does not bring out any trends in the data. Adjusting the scaling of the y-axis will help to display any trends. You will adjust the scale of the y-axis later in this chapter.

d. Click the **Chart Title**, type Relationship Between Age and Temperature, and then press Enter. This chart shows the relationship between increasing age and temperatures requested for massages.

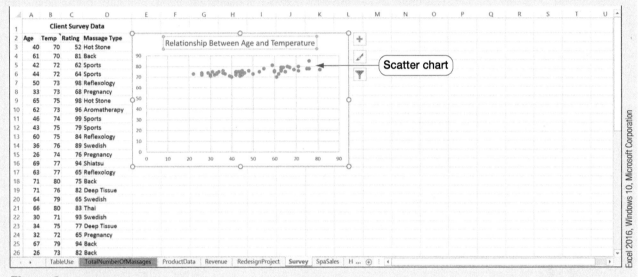

Figure 9 Scatter chart of temperature

e. **Save** 💾 the workbook.

Creating Area Charts

An **area chart** is a variation of a stacked line chart that emphasizes the magnitude of change over time and visually depicts a trend. The area chart stacks a set of data series and colors each area that is created. This type of chart provides a nice visual presentation because each colored layer changes, by growing or shrinking as it moves across time periods. With an area chart, the horizontal x-axis is typically a time sequence. The area chart could also use categories instead of time on the horizontal x-axis, where each layer again is showing the individual contribution to the area; thus, it is a quantitative chart that shows growth or change in totals.

Irene has asked you to create a chart to further understand the differences in the types of massages given over the past eight weeks at the spa. She is particularly interested in Pregnancy, Shiatsu, and Thai massages. In this exercise, you will create an area chart for this purpose.

To Create an Area Chart

a. Click the **ProductData** worksheet tab, and then select the range **A16:I19**.

b. Click **Quick Analysis** 📊, click **Charts**, and then click **Stacked Area.** Notice that there are two chart choices for stacked charts. You will select the second for Stacked Area.

c. Click the **Chart Title**, type Massage Types Over 8 Week Period, and then press Enter.

d. Click the **chart border**, and then drag to move the chart so the top left corner is over cell **D2**.

e. With the chart border still selected, point to the lower right sizing handle, and then drag to resize the chart so the lower right corner of the chart is over **I14**.

This chart shows the total number of massages offered for each of the past eight weeks with emphasis placed on three different massage types.

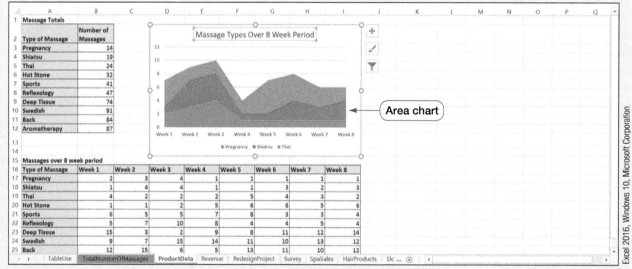

Figure 10   Area chart of three types of massages over past eight weeks

f. **Save** 💾 the workbook.

Creating Combination Charts

A **combination chart** displays two different types of data by using multiple chart types in a single chart object. Combination charts can enhance the understanding of data when the scale of data being charted varies greatly. For example, consider monitoring the number of items sold in the spa to customers over a 12-month span of time. To fully comprehend the data, it would be helpful to explore both the number of items sold and the profit from items sold. However, a single item may cost hundreds of dollars. This makes creating a chart to compare these two pieces of data difficult. In prior versions of Excel, creating a combination chart was a difficult and time-consuming process. In Excel 2016, combination charts are a standard chart type.

Meda has asked you to analyze the quantities of spa products sold from the prior year's sales and compare the result to the profits over the same time span. Currently, only data from January to November is available. In this exercise, you will create a chart to which the December data can be added when it becomes available.

To Create a Combination Chart

a. Click the **SpaSales** worksheet tab, and then select the range **A2:C13**.

b. Click **Quick Analysis** 📊, click **Charts**, and then click **More Charts**.

c. In the Insert Chart dialog box, click the **All Charts** tab. From the list of charts, click **Combo**.

Before you insert the chart, you will have an opportunity to customize how the data will look. The default chart shows the month on the x-axis while using a line chart for profit (in red) and a clustered column chart for quantity sold (in blue).

d. At the bottom of the dialog box, to the right of **Profit**, click to select the **Secondary Axis** check box. This scales the line chart for profit on a separate axis from quantity, allowing the trend over time between the two to be compared. Click **OK**.

e. Click the **Chart Title**, type Quantity Sold and Profit, and then press Enter.

f. Click the **chart border**, and then drag to move the chart so the top left corner is over cell **E1**.

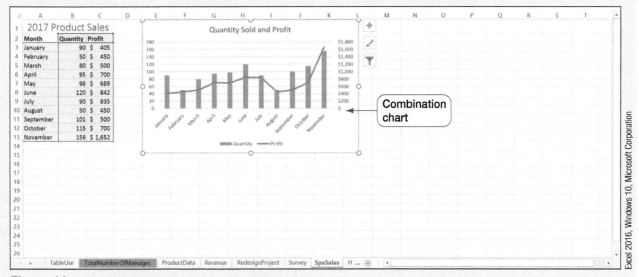

Figure 11 Combination chart of quantity sold and profit

g. **Save** 💾 the workbook.

This chart compares the number of spa products sold and the profit from products sold in the same chart. Notice that in January, the profit for items sold is lower than might be expected from the quantity sold.

h. If you need to take a break before finishing this chapter, now is a good time.

QUICK REFERENCE	Chart Selection Guidelines

- **Pie**   Used for comparing the relationship of parts to a whole
- **Line**   Shows changes within a data series; often used with time on the x-axis
- **Column**   Compares data vertically; can incorporate a time element and groups
- **Bar**   Compares data horizontally; stacked bar can show progress or growth
- **Scatter**   Used for correlations, exploring the relationship between two variables
- **Area**   Used to highlight areas showing growth over time or for categories; a variation of a line chart
- **Combination Chart**   Used to display two different types of data in a single chart

Exploring Chart Layouts

As you have seen, a chart can help to answer questions and may even generate more questions. This can help in moving toward the understanding of information, which can also lead to better decision making. Creating these initial charts to explore data is quick and efficient and informs the user.

When a chart is presented to other people, the context of the chart is of utmost importance. Without context, your audience must try to guess the context. You need to provide meaning. Providing context means providing textual guidance to the audience. The audience will see the chart, but you need to inform them more about the data. Thus, labels are another crucial element needed to provide context in charts. The labels include the chart title and axes titles, legend, and data labels. All these elements should work cohesively to complete a picture of what the chart is trying to convey to the audience. In this section, you will change the appearance of charts by altering their layout and color patterns. You will also modify chart titles and the titles of the chart axes.

Change Chart Data and Styles for Presentations

While the default chart settings are pleasant visually, you can still improve the look and feel of the chart. The chart layouts are available under the Chart Tools contextual tabs, on the Design tab, in the Chart Layouts group. Excel provides many options for arranging the components on a chart. This includes placement of the titles and legend as well as the display of information such as the data point values.

Chart styles are a variation of chart layouts. Where chart layouts focus on location of components, styles focus more on the color coordination and effects of the components. Chart styles are located on the Chart Tools Design tab, in the Chart Styles group. For easier access, Excel 2016 displays the Chart Style icon to the right side of any chart when it is selected. The choices mix color options with shadows and 3-D effects to create a variety of styles. You can also start with a style and then adapt it to suit your needs.

Worksheet data is the underlying data for the chart and labels. Therefore, if data or labels change on the worksheet, the chart will also change because charts are connected to data in the worksheet. There can be many reasons for needing to modify data. For example, there might be a data entry error that needs to be corrected, or an employee might have changed her last name.

Not only can you modify a chart by modifying the worksheet data it was created from, you can also modify how the chart is displaying the data. For example, if the data needs to be swapped between the data points and the axis data, you can use the Data group to switch rows and columns or select new data for a chart.

Changing the Data and Appearance of a Chart

Because charts in Excel are connected to data on the worksheet, changes to the data are automatically reflected in the chart. This is extremely useful if you have a model that is using some calculations that are then used in a chart. You can do what-if analysis by changing data in a worksheet; the corresponding changes will appear on the chart.

Charts may need to be modified when the amount of data being charted needs to be changed. For example, a chart might have too much information included, making it difficult to get a clear picture. Conversely, a chart may need to be modified as new data becomes available. If the new data is adjacent to the existing data, it is a simple process to expand the existing data series. This is achieved by resizing the borders around the data series after activating the chart.

Irene has just provided you with the December data for quantity and profit for the spa. She has also mentioned that there is an error in the quantity in January sales. In this exercise, you will add the December data to the SpaSales worksheet, adjust the combination chart accordingly, and correct the January data. You will also modify the appearance of the chart.

To Modify the Layout and Data in an Existing Chart

a. If you took a break, open the **e02ch04SpaSales** workbook and, if needed, navigate to the **SpaSales** worksheet. Click cell **A14**.

b. Type December, and then press Tab⇆. Type 165, and then press Tab⇆. Type 1701, and then press Ctrl+Enter.

c. Click the **chart area** portion of the chart. Click the **sizing handle** on the lower edge between cells **A13** and **B13**, and then drag the sizing handle down one row so the range **A2:C14** is now being charted. The chart will now include the quantity sold and profits for the month of December.

d. On the **Chart Tools Design** tab, in the Type group, click **Change Chart Type**.

e. Near the bottom of the Change Chart Type dialog box, next to the **Profit** series, click the **Chart Type** arrow. Select **Area**, and then click **OK**.

f. To the right of the chart, click **Chart Styles** 🖊, scroll down, and then click **Style 6**. Click **Chart Styles** 🖊 to close the style gallery.

g. On the **Chart Tools Design** tab, in the Chart Layouts group, click **Quick Layout**. In the displayed gallery, click **Layout 9**.

Notice that the new layout added labels for the x-axis and y-axis on the chart. These axis titles will be revised at a later point.

h. On the worksheet, click cell **B3**, enter 125, and then press Tab⇆. In cell **C3**, type 650, and then press Enter. Notice that the combination chart reflects the new values.

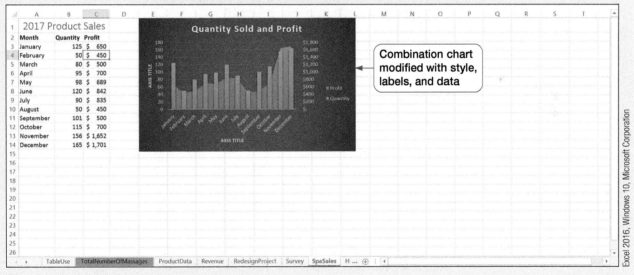

Combination chart modified with style, labels, and data

Excel 2016, Windows 10, Microsoft Corporation

Figure 12 Modified combination chart

i. **Save** 💾 the workbook.

Inserting Objects

If you work for a company, it can be useful to insert the company logo into any chart that is used outside the company. After all, marketing occurs everywhere. It may also be useful to use images to help convey the tone of the presentation. This can be accomplished by inserting an image into the chart.

Irene mentioned that she would be using the chart sheet in the workbook in a variety of presentations and would like it to contain the Turquoise Oasis Spa logo. In this exercise, you will modify the appearance of the chart by inserting the logo and a shape object containing the title of the chart.

E04.12

To Insert Objects into a Chart

a. Click the **TotalNumberOfMassages** worksheet tab.

b. Click the **Insert** tab, and then, in the Illustrations group, click **Pictures**. In the left pane of the Insert Picture dialog box, navigate to the location where you store your student data files, and then click **e02ch04TurquoiseOasis**. Click **Insert**.

c. On the **Picture Tools Format** tab, in the Size group, click the **Shape Height** box. Clear any existing text, type 0.9, and then press Enter.

d. Click in the **Chart Area**. Click the **Chart Tools Design** tab, and in the Chart Layouts group, click **Quick Layout**. In the gallery that appears, click **Layout 4**. Notice that the new layout added labels for the x-axis on the chart.

e. Click any of the columns in the chart. On the **Chart Tools Format** tab, in the Shape Styles group, click the **More** arrow, and then click **Subtle Effect - Orange, Accent 2** in the fourth row, third column.

f. Click the **Insert** tab, and then, in the Illustrations group, click **Shapes**. In the displayed gallery, in the Rectangles group, click **Rounded Rectangle** — the second option. Click below the Turquoise Oasis Spa logo to place the rectangle.

g. Type Number of Massage Services by Type. On the **Drawing Tools Format** tab, in the Size group, click the Shape Height box, type 0.8, and then press Enter. In the Shape Width box, type 2.2, and then press Enter.

h. In the Shape Styles group, click the **More** arrow, and then select **Subtle Effect - Orange, Accent 2** in the fourth row, third column.

i. Select the text in the rectangle. Click the **Home** tab, and in the Font group, click the **Font Size** arrow, and then select **16**.

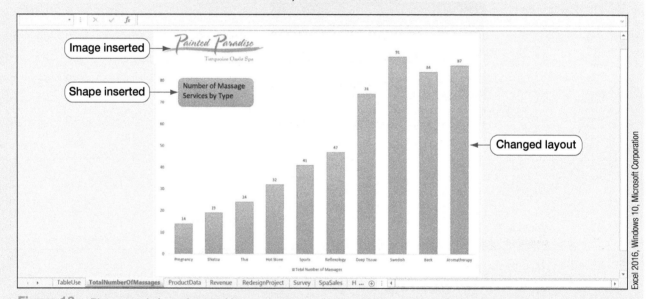

Figure 13 Picture and shape inserted into a chart

j. **Save** the workbook.

Exploring Titles for the Chart and Axes

Chart and axes titles are added easily under the Chart Tools Format tab or with the Chart Elements button that appears on the right side of charts in Excel 2016. Chart titles can be added within the chart, or they can reference cells on the spreadsheet for easy updating.

In this exercise, you will alter the title of the stacked bar chart on the RedesignProject worksheet to match the text in cell A1. You will also clarify the horizontal and vertical axis labels on the combination chart in the SpaSales worksheet.

To Modify Chart Titles and Axis Labels

a. Click the **RedesignProject** worksheet tab, and then click the **chart border** of the stacked bar chart.

b. Click the **chart title** at the top of the chart, and then click the Formula Bar. Type =, and then click cell **A1**.

c. Press Enter.

Notice that the title of the chart now matches the contents of cell A1. If the text in cell A1 is changed, the chart title will be updated automatically.

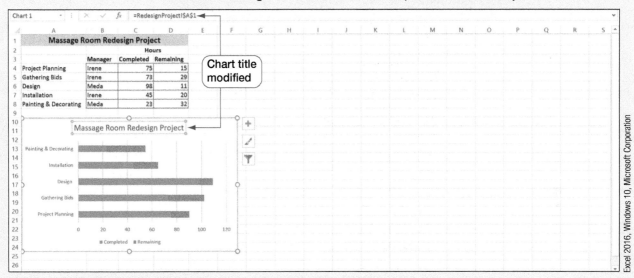

Figure 14 Chart with modified title

d. Click the **SpaSales** worksheet tab, and then click the **chart border** of the combination chart. Click the **Horizontal (Category) Axis Title** box, and then press Del.

e. Click the **Vertical (Value) Axis Title**, type Quantity, and then press Enter.

f. On the **Chart Tools Design** tab, in the Chart Layouts group, click **Add Chart Element**.

g. Point to **Axis Titles**, and then select **Secondary Vertical**. Type Profit, and then press Enter.

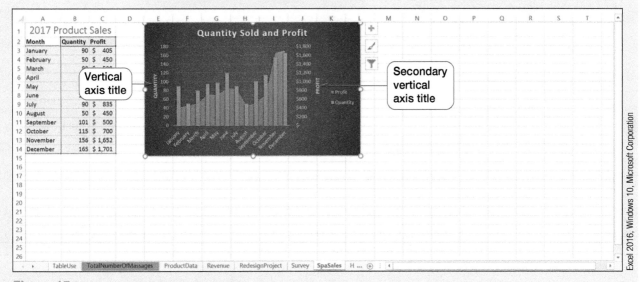

Figure 15 Chart with modified axis labels

h. **Save** the workbook.

Working with the Legend and Labeling the Data

The **legend** is an index within a chart that provides information about the data. With some charts, the legend is added automatically. With other charts, such as pie charts, it is possible to incorporate the same information on or beside each pie slice as labels.

When the parts are labeled on the chart, the legend is not needed and can be removed. Labels can also be added alongside the data on the chart. This is quite informative, as it moves the information from a legend to the data. The data labels can be added, moved, or removed on the Chart Elements button that appears to the right of a selected chart or on the Chart Tools Design tab.

In this exercise, you will modify the revenue charts to make them more visually appealing.

To Work with Legends and Data Labels

a. Click the **Revenue** worksheet tab, and then click the **chart border** of the **line** chart.

b. To the right of the chart, click **Chart Elements** ⊞, point to Legend, click the **Legend** arrow, and then click **Right**. This moves the legend to the right side of the chart. Click **Chart Elements** ⊞ again to close it.

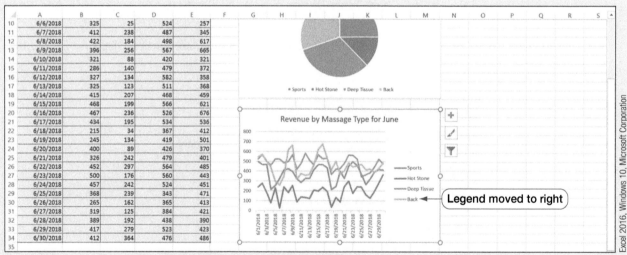

Figure 16 Line chart with legend moved

c. Scroll up if necessary, and click the **chart border** of the **pie** chart. To the right of the chart, click **Chart Elements** ⊞, and then click the **Data Labels** check box. Click the arrow next to Data Labels, and then select **Data Callout**.

d. Click **Legend** to clear the check box. This will remove the legend from the pie chart.

e. Click **Chart Elements** ⊞ again to close the gallery.

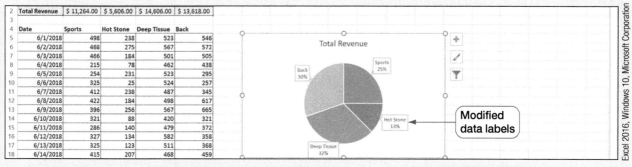

2	Total Revenue	$ 11,264.00	$ 5,606.00	$ 14,606.00	$ 13,618.00
3					
4	Date	Sports	Hot Stone	Deep Tissue	Back
5	6/1/2018	498	238	523	546
6	6/2/2018	468	275	567	572
7	6/3/2018	466	184	501	505
8	6/4/2018	215	78	462	438
9	6/5/2018	254	231	523	295
10	6/6/2018	325	25	524	257
11	6/7/2018	412	238	487	345
12	6/8/2018	422	184	498	617
13	6/9/2018	396	256	567	665
14	6/10/2018	321	88	420	321
15	6/11/2018	286	140	479	372
16	6/12/2018	327	134	582	358
17	6/13/2018	325	123	511	368
18	6/14/2018	415	207	468	459

Modified data labels

Figure 17 Pie chart with modified legend and data labels

f. **Save** 💾 the workbook.

> ### Troubleshooting
>
> Adding and removing chart elements may alter the position of other elements of your chart. You may need to reposition existing or new elements in the chart to clarify the meaning of the chart.

Modifying Axes

The horizontal x-axis and vertical y-axis scales are automatically created through a mathematical algorithm within Excel. However, sometimes the scale needs to be modified, as you have already seen. For example, when the scale of numbers is large, a significant gap can exist from 0 to the first data point. In this case, you can modify the scale to start at a more appropriate number instead of 0, which is the default minimum value for Excel. When you need to compare two or more charts, the scales must be consistent. Any time you put charts side by side, you also need to make sure your x-axis and y-axis scales are the same. Otherwise, your audience may not notice the difference and may make incorrect assumptions or decisions. The axis data may also be too crowded, making it difficult to read. In this situation, you would be able to modify the layout of the scale by adjusting the alignment of the data. The data on the axis can be vertical, horizontal, or even placed at an angle.

The Format Axis task pane is used to manually set the axis options for consistency between a set of charts. Under the Axis Options, the default Excel scale minimum and maximum values are set automatically on the basis of the data. This setting can be changed to allow for customized minimum and maximum values to be applied to the chart. If the source data for the chart is changed, the scale will remain fixed and will not automatically be updated; therefore, any fixed values may also need to be reevaluated as source data changes. In this exercise, you will change the minimum value of a chart.

⏺ E04.15

SIDE NOTE

Deleting Chart Elements

A chart element can be easily removed by selecting the element and pressing ⌫.

To Modify a Chart Axis

a. Click the **RedesignProject** worksheet tab, and then click the **chart border** of the stacked bar chart.

b. Double-click **Horizontal (Value) Axis** for corresponding hours completed and hours remaining. This will open the Format Axis task pane to the Axis Options group. In the Format Axis task pane, if necessary click the Axis Options arrow to expand the **Axis Options** group, and then click in the box for **Minimum**.

c. In the Minimum box, delete the **existing value**, type 20, and then press ⏎.

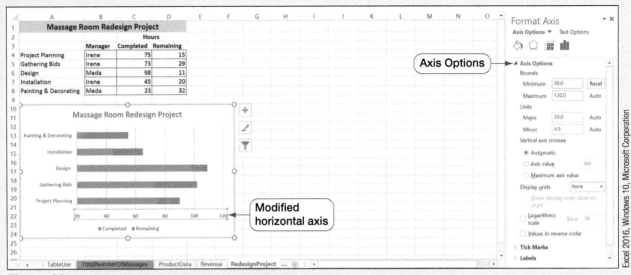

Figure 18 Stacked bar chart with modified chart axis

d. Click the **Survey** worksheet tab, and then select the scatter chart. Double-click the **Vertical (Value) Axis** corresponding to the temperature requested. In the **Axis Options** group, under Bounds, click in the box for **Minimum**.

e. Select the existing number, type 65, and then press (Enter). Notice that the resulting scatter plot has a slight upward trend as the age of the customer increases. This knowledge may lead to decisions that help provide better customer service. You will learn more about modifying axes later in this chapter.

f. On the Format Axis task pane, click Close ☒.

> **Troubleshooting**
>
> If the value you type in any of the Axis Options boxes does not work for your chart, click the Reset button to the right of the box to change the value back to the chart default.

g. **Save** 🖫 the workbook.

Analyzing with Trendlines

A common analysis tool to use within a chart is the trendline. A **trendline** is a line that uses current data to show a trend or general direction of the data. However, data can have a variety of patterns. For scatter plots that explore how two variables interact, a linear trend may be seen. If data fluctuates or varies a great deal, it may be more desirable to use a moving average trendline. Instead of creating a straight line based on all the current data, the moving average trendline uses the average of small subsets of data to set short trend segments over time. The moving average trendline will curve and adjust as the data moves up or down.

The trend or pattern of the data may suggest or predict what will happen in the future. For linear trends, the predicted data can be charted by using a linear trendline added to a scatter chart and the current trend of the data.

Adding a trendline for the scatter chart on the Survey worksheet data may help to confirm the hypothesis that older customers desire a warmer room than younger customers. This may lead the staff to adjust the room temperature before a customer arrives. The staff could predict the desired temperature based on the age of the customer. This could help to improve customer satisfaction. The spa may also want to consider other demographics or characteristics of the customers that allow for providing a customized and personalized service that will build customer loyalty and repeat business. It is easier to retain existing customers than find new ones.

The scatter chart on the Survey worksheet shows that as the age of the customer increases, so does the temperature of the room they request. In this exercise, you will add a trendline to this chart to further illustrate this relationship.

 E04.16

To Insert a Trendline

a. On the **Survey** worksheet, click the **chart border** of the scatter chart.

b. To the right of the chart, click **Chart Elements** ⊕, and then click to select **Trendline**.

c. Click the **Trendline** arrow, and then click **More Options**. In the Format Trendline task pane, click **Fill & Line** ◇.

d. Click the **Dash type** arrow, and then click **Solid** (the first option).

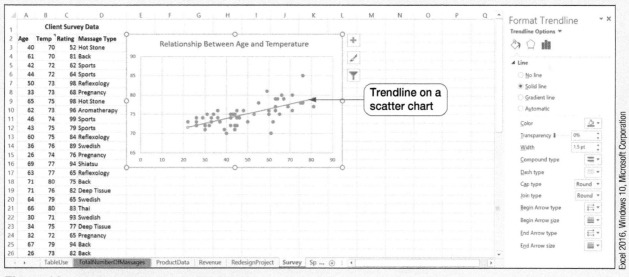

Figure 19 Scatter chart with trendline added

e. In the Format Trendline task pane, click Close ☒.

f. **Save** 🖫 the workbook.

Changing Gridlines

Gridlines are the lines that go across charts to help gauge the size of the bars, columns, or data lines. In Excel, the default is to display the major gridlines (the gridlines at the designated label values) and not to display the minor gridlines (the gridlines between the label values). If the chart is a line or column chart, Excel puts in the horizontal major gridlines; if it is a bar chart, Excel puts in vertical major gridlines. The default is a good starting point, but personal preferences can dictate which lines to display. The Format Major Gridlines task pane allows for the customization of gridlines in a chart.

In this exercise, you will customize the gridlines in your revenue chart.

To Modify Gridlines on a Chart

a. Click the **Revenue** worksheet tab, and then click the **chart border** of the line chart.

b. To the right of the chart, click **Chart Elements** ⊞, point to over Gridlines, click the **Gridlines** arrow, and then select **Primary Major Vertical**.

c. Click **Chart Elements** ⊞ again to close the gallery.

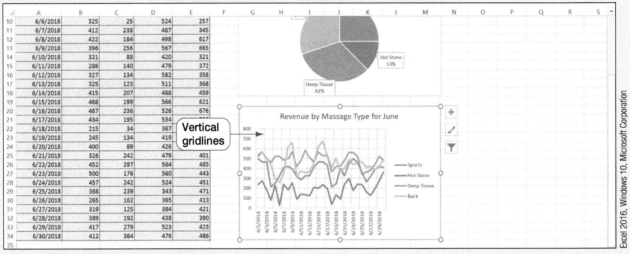

Figure 20 Line chart with modified gridlines

d. **Save** ⊟ the workbook.

QUICK REFERENCE	Chart Trendlines

The following types of trendlines are available within Excel.

- **Linear**   Adds or sets a linear trendline for the selected chart series
- **Exponential**   Adds or sets an exponential trendline for the selected chart series
- **Linear Forecast**   Adds or sets a linear trendline with a two-period forecast for the selected chart series
- **Two-Period Moving Average**   Adds or sets a two-period moving average trendline for the selected chart series

---

REAL WORLD ADVICE	The Timing of Trends

Trends show patterns over time. In analyzing hourly sales at a restaurant, it becomes important to look at more than one day's worth of hourly sales to obtain a better understanding of the trend. Charting multiple days reveals any trends and consistent patterns. For example, maybe the chart shows that on Friday and Saturday, hourly sales are consistently higher than sales on other days of the week. This would suggest a need for scheduling more people to work on Fridays and Saturdays. If only one day had been charted or even just one week, the overall weekly trends may have been missed or interpreted incorrectly.

Edit and Format Charts to Add Emphasis

In formatting a chart, it is important to have a plan in mind as to the overall layout and look and feel. With a well-thought-out plan, it will be easy to apply the desired adjustments to the components with regard to position, color, and emphasis. Typically, you can either create a unique layout or modify one of Excel's many layouts. Either way, being able to make formatting changes is easy and a very useful and powerful way to convey information. In this section, you will explore various ways to format a chart.

Adding Color to Chart Objects

Working some color into charts can be helpful from a marketing perspective. Excel offers options that allow changing the fill color as well as the border color. Chart colors can be added to match a company's color scheme or to highlight certain important aspects of the data. Remember, however, that while it is possible to add value to charts with color, it is also possible to overdo it.

Irene has mentioned to you that she will be using the pie chart on the Revenue worksheet in a presentation. In this exercise, you will enhance the visual appeal of the chart before her presentation.

To Change the Coloring of a Chart

a. On the **Revenue** worksheet, click the **chart border** of the pie chart.

b. On the **Chart Tools Design** tab, in the Chart Styles group, click **Change Colors**, and then, in the gallery that appears, click **Color 4** (the fourth option).

c. On the **Chart Tools Format** tab, in the Shape Styles group, click **Shape Fill**, and then click **Gold, Accent 4, Lighter 60%**.

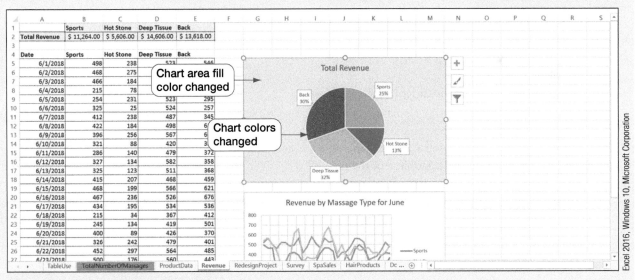

Figure 21 Pie chart with color added

d. **Save** the workbook.

Working with Text

Whether the text is in a shape, title, legend, or axis scale, you can change the formatting of text and the backgrounds of the text objects in charts. The text can be formatted as WordArt, and shapes can be modified to common Shape Styles.

Irene has decided that the pie chart you modified with a new color scheme now has a title that is too difficult to read. In this exercise, you will increase the font size and apply bold to the font in the chart title box to address this problem.

To Format Text Within a Chart

a. On the **Revenue** worksheet, if necessary click the **chart border** of the pie chart.

b. Click the **Chart Title**, click the **Home** tab, and then, in the Font group, click **Bold** **B**. In the Font group, click the **Font Size** 11 arrow, and then select **16**.

c. With the title still selected, click the **Chart Tools Format** tab, and in the WordArt Styles group, click the Quick Styles More arrow to expand the WordArt gallery. Select **Pattern Fill – White, Text 2, Dark Upward Diagonal, Shadow** in the first column, fourth row.

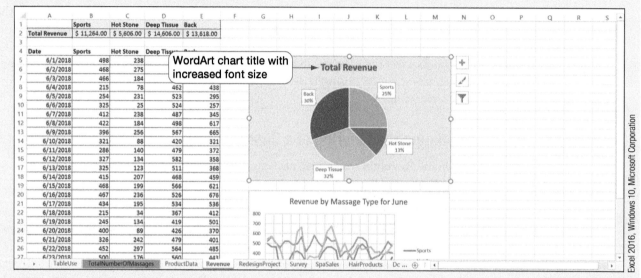

Figure 22 Pie chart with formatted title

d. **Save** the workbook.

Exploding Pie Charts

The traditional pie chart is a pie with all the slices together. Preset options offer a pie chart with a slice pulled slightly away from the main pie, or you can manually move a slice outward, creating an exploded pie chart. This technique allows for highlighting a particular piece of the pie.

As part of her presentation, Irene wants to emphasize the hot stone massage type because it represents the least amount of revenue in the data series. In this exercise, you will create visual emphasis by exploding the slice of the pie chart representing the revenue percentage of hot stone massages.

To Create an Exploding Pie Chart

a. On the **Revenue** worksheet, if necessary click the **chart border** of the pie chart.

b. Click the **pie**. Notice that the entire pie is selected.

c. Click the **Hot Stone** slice of the pie. Notice that only the Hot Stone slice is now selected.

d. Drag the Hot Stone data **slice** slightly to the **right**. The Hot Stone slice is now exploded to show emphasis.

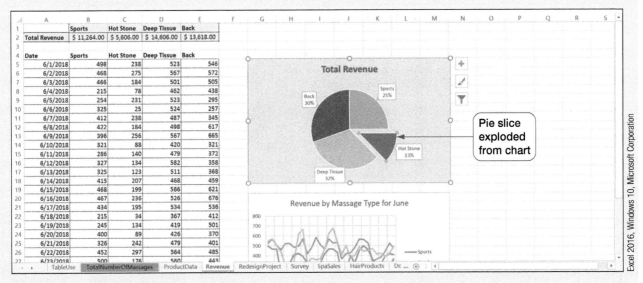

	Sports	Hot Stone	Deep Tissue	Back
Total Revenue	$ 11,264.00	$ 5,606.00	$ 14,606.00	$ 13,618.00
Date	**Sports**	**Hot Stone**	**Deep Tissue**	**Back**
6/1/2018	498	238	523	546
6/2/2018	468	275	567	572
6/3/2018	466	184	501	505
6/4/2018	215	78	462	438
6/5/2018	254	231	523	295
6/6/2018	325	25	524	257
6/7/2018	412	238	487	345
6/8/2018	422	184	498	617
6/9/2018	396	256	567	665
6/10/2018	321	88	420	321
6/11/2018	286	140	479	372
6/12/2018	327	134	582	358
6/13/2018	325	123	511	368
6/14/2018	415	207	468	459
6/15/2018	468	199	566	621
6/16/2018	467	236	526	676
6/17/2018	434	195	534	536
6/18/2018	215	34	367	412
6/19/2018	245	134	419	501
6/20/2018	400	89	426	370
6/21/2018	326	242	479	401
6/22/2018	452	297	564	485
6/23/2018	500	176	560	443

Pie slice exploded from chart

Figure 23 Exploded pie chart

e. **Save** the workbook.

Changing 3-D Charts and Rotation of Charts

The 3-D effect and rotation of a chart are effects that should be used conservatively. They can be done well, or they can be overused, resulting in a chart that goes overboard and distracts from the intended message. You can choose the 3-D effect when starting to develop a chart, or you can apply the effect after creating the chart. Additionally, options are available to rotate the 3-D effect, giving the chart a crisp, distinctive look. The 3-D format can be applied to a variety of objects. The 3-D Rotation setting is intended for the chart area only.

In this exercise, you will use the 3-D effect and rotation to enhance the pie chart showing the total revenue by massage type.

E04.21

To Change the Chart Type to 3-D

a. On the **Revenue** worksheet, if necessary, click the **chart border** of the pie chart.

b. Click the **Chart Tools Design** tab, and then, in the Type group, click **Change Chart Type**.

c. In the Change Chart Type dialog box, if necessary, click the **All Charts** tab. In the left pane, click **Pie**, click **3-D Pie**, and then click **OK**.

d. Double-click the **chart area** to open the Format Chart Area task pane. Click **Effects**, and then click the **3-D Rotation** arrow to expand the 3-D Rotation group.

e. Click in the box for **Y Rotation**, delete the existing value, and then type 50. Click in the box for **Perspective**, delete the existing value, and then type 30.

f. Click the **3-D Format** arrow to expand the 3-D Format group. Click the **Top bevel** arrow, and then click **Cool Slant** in the first row, fourth column. In the Format Chart Area task pane, click Close.

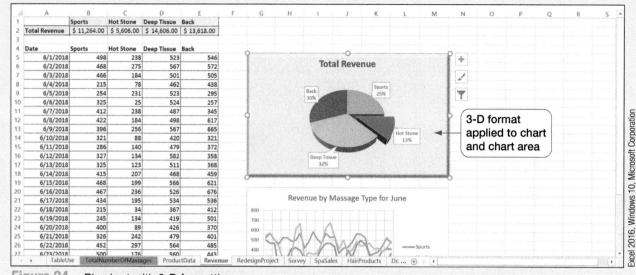

Figure 24 Pie chart with 3-D formatting

g. **Save** 🖫 the workbook.

h. If you need to take a break before finishing this chapter, now is a good time.

QUICK REFERENCE	Formatting Options for Chart Objects

Below are format options for charts and their descriptions.

- **Number**   Format data as currency, date, time, and so on.
- **Fill**   Fill the background of a component with a color, picture, or pattern.
- **Border Color**   Set the color of the border for a component.
- **Border Styles**   Set the thickness and type of border for a component.
- **Shadow**   Add shadowing effect to a component.
- **Glow and Soft Edges**   Add glow and edge effects to a component.
- **3-D Format**   Add 3-D effects to a component.
- **Alignment**   Align text direction for a component, such as left, top, vertical, or horizontal.

Using Charts Effectively

The effectiveness of a chart depends on the chart type, the layout, and the formatting of the data. Charts should provide clarity and expand the viewer's understanding of the data. Charts used in a presentation should support the ideas you want to convey. The charts should highlight key components about an issue or topic being addressed in the presentation. In this section, you will use sparklines and data bars to emphasize data. You will also recognize and correct confusing charts.

Use Sparklines and Data Bars to Emphasize Data

The same data can be viewed through various perspectives, emphasizing different parts of information. Charts typically do three things.

- Support or refute assertions
- Clarify information
- Help the audience understand trends

Sparklines and data bars are tools in Excel that can accomplish these three goals.

Emphasizing Data

As with any set of data, you can reasonably expect to find multiple ideas that could be emphasized in a chart. Typically, in a business setting, one to three key issues might be chosen for discussion. The idea is to eliminate any extraneous data from the chart that does not pertain to the issues being emphasized. Common methods can be employed to emphasize the idea in the chart. When using a single chart, highlight a particular data set within the chart to help focus attention to a key point. Depending on the chart type, the emphasis may be depicted differently, as shown in Table 1.

Single Chart Types	Common Emphasis Methods
Pie chart	Explode a pie slice
Bar/column	Use an emphasizing color on the bar/column
Line	Use line color, weight, and marker size
Scatter	Add a trendline

Table 1 Emphasis methods for single chart types

Exploring Sparklines

Sparklines are small charts that are embedded into the cells in a worksheet, usually beside the data, to facilitate quick analysis of trends. A sparkline can be used within a worksheet to give an immediate visual trend analysis, and it adjusts as the source data changes. The sparkline can graphically depict the data over time through either a line chart or a bar chart that accumulates the data. Sparklines can also depict data points in the series as a win/loss chart. The default setting is for values above 0 to be a win while values below 0 are a loss. This value can be modified under the Format tab by using the Sparkline Axis button.

Irene and Meda would like to better examine sales of hair products at the spa. They have collected some data for you to analyze from the last eight weeks. In this exercise you will add sparklines adjacent to the data to emphasize the trend in products over time.

E04.22

SIDE NOTE
Alternate Method
Sparklines can also be inserted to the right of data by using the Quick Analysis tool.

To Insert Sparklines

a. If you took a break, open the **e02ch04SpaSales** workbook, and then click the **HairProducts** worksheet tab. Select the range **A3:A7**.

b. Click the **Insert** tab, and in the Sparklines group, click **Line**. In the Create Sparklines dialog box, in the **Data Range** box, type C3:N7 and then click **OK**.

c. On the **Sparkline Tools Design** tab, in the Style group, click the **More** arrow, and then select **Sparkline Style Accent 2, Darker 50%** (first row, second column).

The sparklines show the changes in hair products sold over the 12 months represented by the data. Notice that sales of the For Men products were steady until Month 7, when they spiked, then came back down in month 9, and then spiked again in Month 11. This is very easy to visualize with sparklines next to the data.

d. Click cell **A1** to deselect the sparklines.

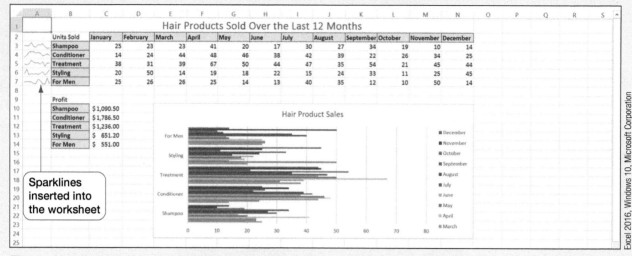

The spreadsheet shows data under the title "Hair Products Sold Over the Last 12 Months":

Units Sold	January	February	March	April	May	June	July	August	September	October	November	December
Shampoo	25	23	23	41	20	17	30	27	34	19	10	14
Conditioner	14	24	44	48	46	38	42	39	22	26	34	25
Treatment	38	31	39	67	50	44	47	35	54	21	45	44
Styling	20	50	14	19	18	22	15	24	33	11	25	45
For Men	25	26	26	25	14	13	40	35	12	10	50	14

Profit	
Shampoo	$1,090.50
Conditioner	$1,786.50
Treatment	$1,236.00
Styling	$ 651.20
For Men	$ 551.00

Sparklines inserted into the worksheet

Figure 25   Sparklines applied to hair products data

e. **Save** 🖫 the workbook.

QUICK REFERENCE	Working with Sparklines

Using the following process will help in the development of sparklines.

- Select any cell within the added sparklines to display the Sparkline Tools contextual tabs.
- Ungroup sparklines using the Ungroup button on the Sparkline Tools Design tab.
- Group sparklines again using the Group button on the Design tab.
- Change colors and styles using the options available in the Style group.
- Choose to show high or low points using the options in the Show group.

Inserting Data Bars

Data bars are graphic components that are overlaid onto data in worksheet cells. The graphic component is added to a cell and interprets a set of data in a range in which the bar and, if necessary, the bar color are adjusted to help a spreadsheet user gain a quick understanding of the data. Data bars can be applied as a one-color solid fill or as a gradient fill from left to right as the numerical value gets bigger. Data bars are components of the Conditional Formatting feature. This technique can be employed with scores, ratings, or other data for which the user would want to do a visual inspection to see a relative scale on the data.

Irene and Meda have requested one more enhancement to the hair products analysis you have already begun. They would like a small visual cue added to a list of profits by hair product type. In this exercise, you will add data bars to the profits of all hair products sold at the spa over the past 12 months to emphasize which products were profitable and which were not profitable.

E04.23

To Insert Data Bars

a. On the **HairProducts** worksheet, select the range **C10:C14**.

b. Click the **Home** tab, and in the Styles group, click **Conditional Formatting**, and then point to **Data Bars**. Under Gradient Fill, click **Green Data Bar** (row one, second option). The inserted data bars clearly show that Conditioner is the highest-grossing product, while For Men is the lowest-grossing product.

c. Click cell **A1** to deselect the data bars.

SIDE NOTE
Alternate Method
Data bars can also be inserted from the Quick Analysis tool. The default color is blue if you are using this method.

Figure 26 Data bars added to profit data

d. **Save** 🖫 the workbook.

Recognize and Correct Confusing Charts

The process of working with and creating visually appealing charts with clear messages involves recognizing when you have a confusing chart. It is possible to have too much information or ambiguous information. This could include missing labels or legends, or there might be textual information on a chart that is not clear. Additionally, a common error is to use the incorrect chart type in analyzing data.

Correcting a Confusing Chart

Irene has pointed out that on the HairProducts sheet, a clustered bar chart was created that is difficult to interpret. The chart is based on the same data from which you created sparklines. Irene would like to be able to use the chart to compare different lines of product. The chart that was created shows the number of units sold as the bars, each product having a different bar for each month in the data. In this exercise, you will correct the chart so that it provides a meaningful representation of the data.

 E04.24

To Correct a Confusing Chart

SIDE NOTE

Suggested Charts
Depending on your data, Excel may suggest a chart with the x-axis and y-axis already switched, saving you a step.

a. On the **HairProducts** worksheet, click the **chart border** of the clustered bar chart.

   Notice that this chart is showing time as a bar chart. Earlier in this chapter, you learned that a line chart is better for trends over time.

b. Click the **Chart Tools Design** tab, and in the Type group, click **Change Chart Type**. In the Change Chart Type dialog box, on the **All Charts** tab, click **Line**, and then click **OK**.

c. In the Data group, click **Switch Row/Column**. Since the data being charted is time sensitive, the time element should be shown on the x-axis.

d. Double-click the **Horizontal (Category) Axis** to open the Format Axis task pane. Click **Text Options**, and then click **Textbox** [⊞].

e. Click in the **Custom angle** box, delete the existing value, and then type -45 and press Enter. On the Format Axis task pane, click Close [×].

f. Click the **Chart Title**, and then type =, click cell **B1**, and then press Enter.

Too many items on a chart can make a chart confusing, as with this line chart. Filtering a chart can improve the chart's readability.

g. Click the **Chart Border** of the line chart. To the right of the chart, click **Chart Filters** [▼], and then, under Series, click **Select All** to deselect all of the product options. Click the check boxes for **Shampoo** and **Conditioner**.

Troubleshooting

If the Chart Elements, Chart Styles, and Chart Filter buttons do not automatically appear to the right of the selected chart, use the horizontal scroll bar to create more space to the right of the selected chart. The buttons will appear only if there is enough space beside the chart.

h. Click **Apply** at the bottom of the Chart Filters gallery, and then click **Chart Filters** [▼] again to close the gallery. Notice that the lines for these two products do not show similar trends, as might be expected.

Troubleshooting

If you cannot see the Apply button on your screen, you may need to close the dialog, move the worksheet up, and try the steps again.

Figure 27   Corrected line chart

Troubleshooting

If you click the chart to see the source data associated with the chart and see only some of the data selected with a blue border, you might have clicked a chart component by mistake instead of the full chart area. To get the data set associated with the entire chart, under Chart Tools, click the Format tab. In the Current Selection group, change the Chart Element to Chart Area. Data associated with the selected component will be highlighted with a colored border.

i. **Save** [💾] the workbook.

Preparing to Print a Chart

Printing charts uses essentially the same process as printing a worksheet. When printing a chart sheet, select the chart sheet, go through the normal printing process, and adjust print options as you would for a worksheet. The chart will be a full-page display. If the chart is on a regular worksheet, it will be printed if you choose to print everything on the worksheet. In this case, the chart will be the size you developed on the worksheet. This is convenient when you want to print some tables or other data along with the chart. Finally, if you want to print just the chart on the worksheet, select the chart first, then choose the Print Selected Chart print option to print only the current chart.

Another useful technique in exploring data through charts is the ability to create static copies of the chart that can be used to compare with later versions. You can, in essence, take a picture of a chart that will not retain the underlying data. In this manner, subsequent versions of the chart can be made into images for comparisons. The process of creating a picture of the chart is to select the chart, copy it, then use the Paste Special option and paste it as a picture. When you paste as a picture, there are multiple picture format options, such as a PNG, JPEG, or GIF files.

In this exercise, you will print the HairProducts chart.

QUICK REFERENCE	Common Charting Issues

These are common issues you should try to avoid in the development of charts.

1. Not enough context; users do not understand the chart.

   - Add titles to the horizontal and vertical axes.
   - Add a chart title that conveys context of time and scope.
   - Add data labels to show percentages or values of chart elements.

2. Too much information is on the chart.

   - Use a subset of the data rather than all the data.
   - Summarize the data so it is consolidated.

3. Incorrect chart type is used.

   - Choose a more appropriate type of chart, such as a line chart for trends.

4. Chart has issues with readability.

   - Check the color scheme to ensure that the text is readable.
   - Check font characteristics such as font type or font size.
   - Move data labels, and remove excess information.
   - Resize the overall chart to provide more area to work.
   - Check the color scheme and formatting so it is professional and does not hide chart information or text.
   - Information or labeling is misleading.
   - Check the scaling to ensure that it is appropriate and labeled with the correct units.
   - Consider the following wording: Does "Sales" mean the number of transactions or the total revenue?

E04.25

To Print a Chart

a. On the **HairProducts** worksheet, click the **chart border** of the line chart.

b. Click the **File** tab, and then click **Print**. Notice that under Settings, the option for Print Selected Chart is selected by default. Also notice that only the chart is displayed in the preview pane. This is because you had the chart selected, not a cell within the worksheet.

c. Click the **Portrait Orientation** arrow, and select **Landscape Orientation**.

d. Verify that the correct printer — as directed by your instructor — appears in the Printer box. Choices may vary depending on the computer you are using. If the correct printer is not displayed, click the Printer arrow, and then click to choose the correct or preferred printer from the list of available printers. If your instructor asks you to print the document, click the **Print** button.

e. Complete the **Documentation** worksheet as directed by your instructor.

f. Insert the file name in the left footer on all worksheets in the workbook.

g. **Save** 🖫 the workbook, exit Excel, and then submit your file as directed by your instructor.

Concept Check

1. What are some important items to consider in choosing the design and layout of a chart? p. 484

2. What are the two possible locations for a chart in Excel? Why would you choose one over the other? p. 487

3. Compare the purpose of a column chart and a pie chart. Give an example of a scenario in which you would use the two different types of charts. When would you create a combination chart to display worksheet data? p. 491–493

4. Why is it important to add elements and styles to charts such as titles, legends, and labels? p. 498

5. List two possible ways to add emphasis to an existing chart. p. 511

6. How are sparklines and data bars different from other chart objects in Excel? What are they commonly used for? p. 511–512

7. What are common mistakes that can be made in designing charts? Why is it important to correct these mistakes in existing charts? p. 513–514

Key Terms

Area chart   495
Bar chart   493
Chart sheet   487
Column chart   493
Combination chart   496
Data bar   512
Data point   485

Data series   485
Data visualization   484
Embedded chart   487
Gridlines   504
Legend   502
Line chart   492
Pie chart   491

Quick Analysis   487
Recommended Charts   488
Scatter chart   494
Sparkline   511
Trendline   505

Visual Summary

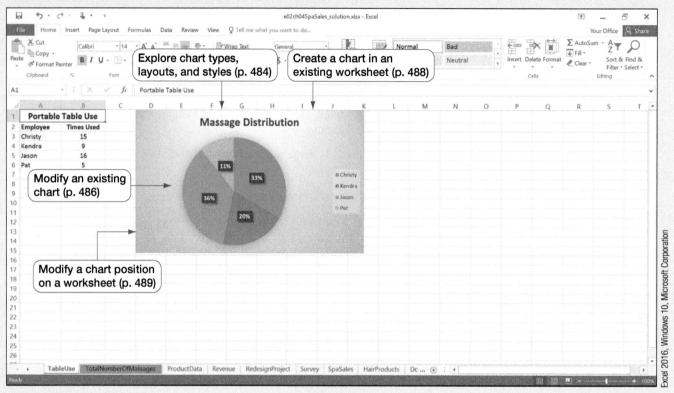

Explore chart types, layouts, and styles (p. 484)

Create a chart in an existing worksheet (p. 488)

Modify an existing chart (p. 486)

Modify a chart position on a worksheet (p. 489)

Figure 28

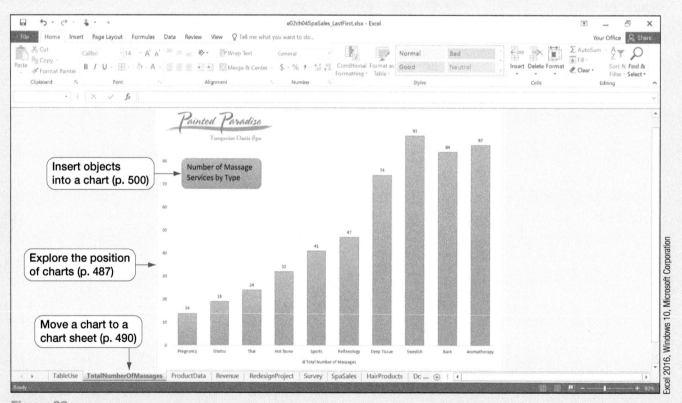

Insert objects into a chart (p. 500)

Explore the position of charts (p. 487)

Move a chart to a chart sheet (p. 490)

Figure 29

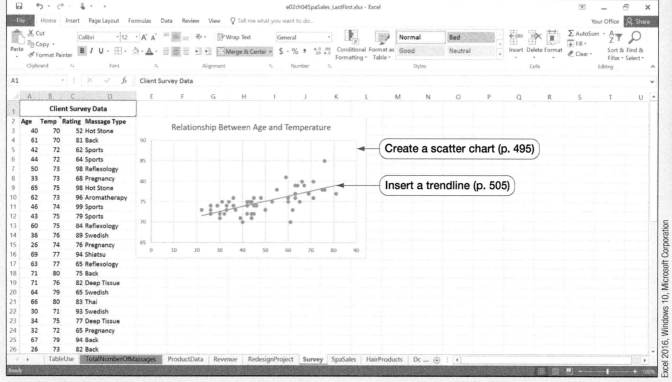

Figure 30

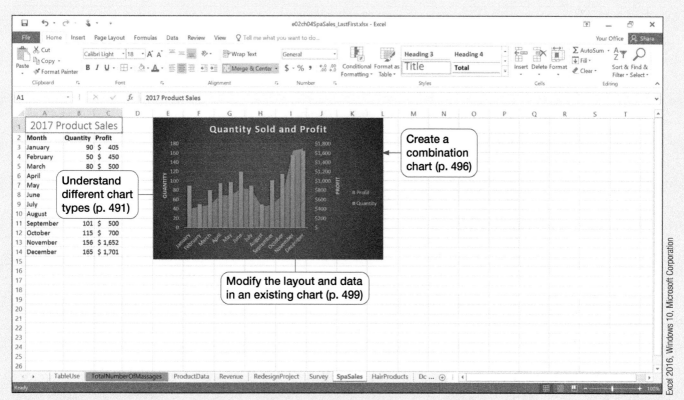

Figure 31

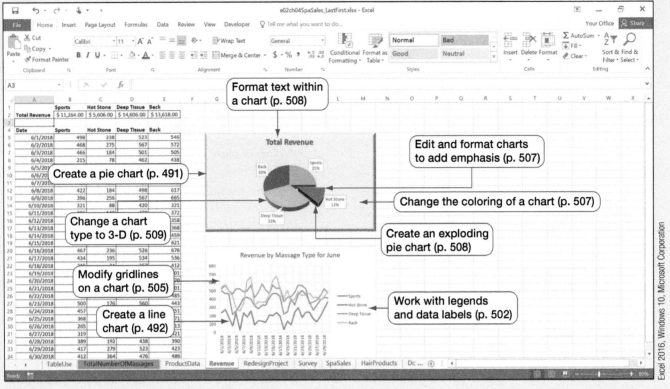

Figure 32

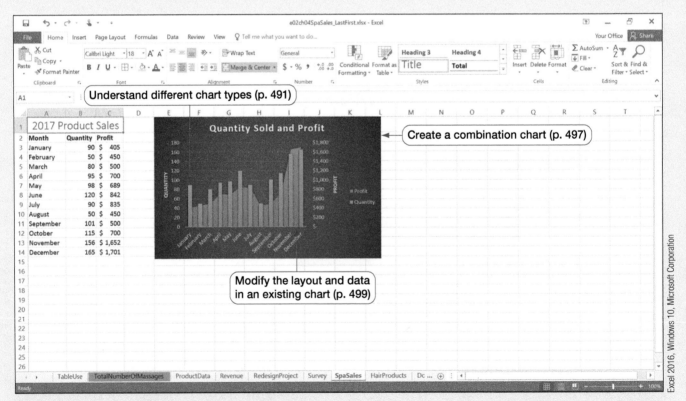

Figure 33

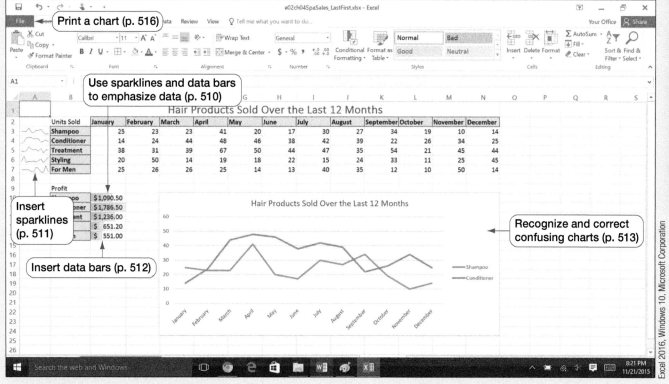

Figure 34

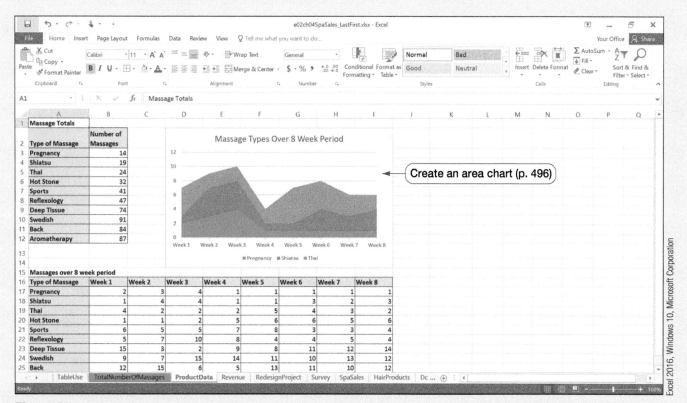

Figure 35

Student data file needed:

 e02ch04Summary.xlsx

You will save your file as:

 e02ch04Summary_LastFirst.xlsx

Product Sales Report

Sales &
Marketing

Irene Kai and Meda Rodate have pulled together data pertaining to sales made by the spa's massage therapists. In addition to massages, the therapists should promote skin care, health care, and other products. With the monthly data, the managers want a few charts developed that will enable them to look at trends, compare sales, and provide feedback to the therapists. You are to help them create the charts.

a. Start **Excel**, click **Open Other Workbooks** in the left pane, and then double-click **This PC**. Navigate through the folder structure to the location of your student data files, and then click **e02ch04Summary**.

b. If necessary, click Enable Editing. Click the **File** tab, then click **Save As**, and then double-click **This PC**. In the Save As dialog box, navigate to the location where you are saving your project files, and change the file name to e02ch04Summary_LastFirst, using your last and first name. Click **Save**.

c. On the **Projections** worksheet tab select the range **A4:B12**. Click **Quick Analysis**, click **Charts**, and then click **Clustered Column**. Click the **chart border**, and position the chart so the top left corner is over cell **D4**. Adjust the size of the chart so the bottom right corner is over cell **J17**.

d. Click the **Chart Title**, and then click in the **formula bar**. Type =, click cell **A1**, and then press [Enter].

   To the right of the chart, click **Chart Styles**, and then click **Style 6** from the list. Click **Chart Styles** again to close the gallery.

e. Double-click the **Vertical (Value) Axis** to open the Format Axis task pane. In the Axis Options, click in the **Minimum** box, clear the existing text, and then type 100. Close the Format Axis task pane.

f. Click the **Transactions** worksheet tab. Select the range **B4:J4**, press and hold [Ctrl], and then select the range **B9:J9**. On the **Insert** tab, in the Charts group, click the **Insert Pie or Doughnut Chart** arrow. Click **Pie**, the first option under 2-D Pie. Click the **chart border** of the chart, and position the chart so the top left corner is over cell **C11**.

g. Click the **Chart Title**, type Total Transactions by Therapist, and then press [Enter].

h. To the right of the chart, click **Chart Elements**. Click the **Data Labels** arrow, and then click **More Options**. In the Format Data Labels task pane, under Label Options, under Label Contains, Click to select **Percentage**. Click **Value** to deselect that label. Under Label Position, select **Outside End**. Close the Format Data Labels task pane.

i. To the right of the chart, click **Chart Elements**. Click the **Legend** arrow, and then click **Right**. Click **Chart Elements** again to close the gallery.

j. Click the **Pie** chart, being careful not to click the label text. Click once again on the **orange pie slice** that has the associated label 6%. Drag the slice slightly **to the right** so it is exploded from the rest of the pie.

k. Click the **Revenue** worksheet tab, and then select the range **B9:J9**. Click the **Insert** tab, and then, in the Sparklines group, click **Line** to add sparklines to the worksheet. In the Data Range box, type B5:J8, and then click **OK**. Click any **cell** outside of the sparklines to deselect the sparklines.

l. On the **Insert** tab, in the Text group, click **Header & Footer**. On the **Header & Footer Tools Design** tab, in the Navigation group, click **Go to Footer**. Click in the **left footer section**, and then, in the Header & Footer Elements group, click **File Name**.

m. Click any **cell** on the worksheet to move out of the footer, and then press ⎡Ctrl⎤+⎡Home⎤. On the status bar, click **Normal**.

n. Click the **Documentation** worksheet tab. Click cell **A8**, and then type in today's date. Click cell **B6**, and then type your name in the Firstname Lastname format. Complete the remainder of the **Documentation** worksheet according to your instructor's directions.

o. **Save** the workbook, close Excel, and then submit your file as directed by your instructor.

Problem Solve 1

Homework

Sales & Marketing

Finance & Accounting

Student data file needed:

 e02ch04Advertising.xlsx

You will save your file as:

e02ch04Advertising_LastFirst.xlsx

Advertising

The marketing manager of the Painted Paradise Golf Resort & Spa, Timothy Smith, has created a spreadsheet of the first six months (first two quarters) of advertising expenses for the various amenities of the resort. He is planning to display the data at the next Board of Directors meeting and wants to create a few charts to make the figures easier to view and the presentation more visually appealing.

a. Open the Excel file, **e02ch04Advertising**. Save your file as e02ch04Advertising_LastFirst, using your last and first name.

b. On the **AdvertisingCosts** worksheet, create a **Line** chart of the data for the total spent on advertising each month from January through June. The primary Horizontal (Category) Axis should be the months of the year, and the Vertical (value) Axis should be the total spent on advertising each month.

c. Change the line chart title to Total Advertising Expenses per Month. Change the Vertical Axis minimum to **$26,000**, and change the chart style to **Style 10**.

d. Move the line chart to a **chart sheet**, and rename the sheet AdvertisingPerMonth. If necessary, move the chart sheet to the **right** of the AdvertisingCosts sheet.

e. Click the **AdvertisingCosts** worksheet tab. Create a **3-D Pie chart** of the amenities and their six-month totals in the range **A16:B22**. Reposition the chart so the left corner of the chart is in cell **C14**.

f. On the 3-D pie chart, insert the title Semi-Annual Advertising Costs. Apply **Style 8** to the chart.

g. Add **Data Callout** as data labels to the 3-D pie chart. Include the **category name** and **percentage** in the data labels.

h. On the 3-D pie chart, slightly explode the segment of the chart that was allocated the **smallest amount** of advertising funds.

i. Double-click the chart area. Select **Effects** in the Format Chart Area task pane, click to expand **3-D Rotation**, and adjust the 3-D rotation to the following:

 a. X rotation of **20**

 b. Y Rotation of **40**

 c. Perspective of **10**

j. On the 3-D pie chart, expand **3-D Format** in the Format Chart Area task pane. Change the Top bevel to **Relaxed Inset** in the second column, first row. Close the Format Chart Area task pane. Resize the chart so the lower-right corner is in H28.

k. In cells **H5:H11**, add **Column sparklines** that chart the advertising expense by amenity type over the months January to June. Apply the style **Sparkline Style Accent 5, Darker 50%**.

l. Update the Documentation worksheet according to your instructor's directions.

m. Insert the file name in the left footer on all worksheets in the workbook.

n. **Save** the workbook, close Excel, and then submit your file as directed by your instructor.

Perform 1: Perform in Your Career

Student data file needed:
e02ch04Homes.xlsx

You will save your file as:
e02ch04Homes_LastFirst.xlsx

Real Estate

Research/
Development

You are interning at Schalow Real Estate Company. Your supervisor needs to know why some houses sell quickly and others take more time. She asks you to create charts from data to help her analyze and look for trends.

a. Open the Excel file **e02ch04Homes**. Save your file as e02ch04Homes_LastFirst, using your last and first name.

b. On the **SoldProperties** worksheet, create a line chart showing the number of days on the market over time. Plot the days on the market on the y-axis and the sold date on the x-axis.

c. Add a **linear trendline** to your chart. Change the trend line Dash type to **Solid**.

d. Format the chart using an appropriate style, and position it below the data in the approximate range **A40:F54**.

e. Create a line chart that shows how the price per square foot of the sold properties has changed over time.

f. Add a **linear trendline** to your chart. Change the trend line Dash type to **Solid**.

g. Format the chart using a style of your choice, and position it below the data in the approximate range **H40:N54**.

h. On the **Summary** worksheet, the first group of data in A2:D11 describes homes sold in all developments. Use that data to create three charts using a style of your choice, and show the following on the three different charts.

  • The Average Number of Days on Market by Development

  • The Average Percent of List Price by Development

  • The Average of Sold Price by Development

i. Create a **new worksheet** in your workbook. Name the new worksheet Charts.

j. Move the three charts showing averages by development to the **Charts** worksheet. Position them in the approximate ranges **A1:I15**, **A17:I31**, and **A33:I47**.

k. On the **Summary** worksheet, type your last name in cell **A38**.

l. Create a chart that shows the average number of days it took a home to sell by salesperson.

m. Format this chart using **Style 8**. Position the chart on the **Charts** worksheet in the range **K1:R15**.

n. Complete the **Documentation** worksheet according to your instructor's directions. Insert the file name in the left footer on all worksheets in the workbook.

o. **Save** the workbook, close Excel, and submit your file as directed by your instructor.

Additional
Cases

Additional Chapter Cases are available at www.pearsonhighered.com/youroffice

Conducting **Business Analysis**

This business unit had two outcomes:

Learning Outcome 1

Use Excel to create formulas and functions to perform calculations, analyze data, solve problems, and help in making wise business decisions.

Learning Outcome 2

Use Excel to create a variety of detailed charts appropriate to the data that will visually represent and analyze the data.

In Business Unit 2 Capstone, students will demonstrate competence in these outcomes through a series of business problems at various levels from guided practice to problem solving an existing spreadsheet and creating new spreadsheets.

More Practice 1

Student data file needed:
 e02Sales.xlsx

You will save your file as:
e02Sales_LastFirst.xlsx

Restaurant Marketing Analysis

Sales & Marketing

Finance & Accounting

The accounting system at the Indigo5 Restaurant tracks data on a daily basis that can be used for analysis to gauge its performance and determine any needed changes. The restaurant is considering entering into a long-term agreement with a poultry company and getting a new refrigeration unit to store the chicken. If Indigo5 enters the agreement, the poultry company agrees to give Indigo5 a substantial discount for a specified period of time. Management would like to stimulate sales for the lowest-revenue-producing chicken item and any chicken items that do not meet a sale performance threshold. To accomplish this, some of the savings will be passed on to the guests by having these chicken items put on special at a lower price.

a. Open **Excel**, click **Open Other Documents** in the left pane, and then double-click **This PC**. Navigate through the folder structure to the location of your student data files, and then double-click **e02Sales**. If a Security Warning message displays, click the **Enable Editing** button.

b. Click the **File** tab, click **Save As**, and then double-click **This PC**. In the Save As dialog box, navigate to the location where you are saving your project files, and then change the file name to **e02Sales_LastFirst**, using your last and first name. Click **Save**.

c. Click the **Indigo5ChickenSales** worksheet, and then click cell **D2**. Enter the formula =TODAY(), and then press Enter.

   Notice the data on the worksheet. The range A13:E18 contains four months of actual sales quantities for each menu item. The range A22:E27 contains the sales projections that Indigo5 made for the same four months before the start of each month.

d. Click cell **B4**, enter the formula =SUM(B22:E22), and then press Ctrl+Enter. In cell B4, double-click the AutoFill handle to automatically fill cell range B4:B9. The range now returns the total quantity projection over the four months for each item.

e. Format range **B4:B9** with comma style, zero decimal places.

f. Click cell **C4**, enter the formula =SUM(B13:E13), and then press Ctrl+Enter. In cell C4, double-click the AutoFill handle to automatically fill cell range C4:C9. The range now returns the total quantity of actual sales over the four months for each item.

g. Format range **C4:C9** with comma style, zero decimal places.

h. Click cell **D4**, enter the formula =AVERAGE(B13:E13), and then press Ctrl+Enter. In cell D4, double-click the AutoFill handle to automatically fill cell range D4:D9. The range now returns the average monthly quantity for actual sales over the four months for each item.

i. Format range **D4:D9** with comma style, two decimal places.

j. Now you need to determine the price for each item to use in revenue calculations. Notice that a list of menu prices is in cells A30:B44. Select the range **A30:B44**. Click the **Name Box**, type Prices, and then press Enter. The price listing is now named Prices to use in later calculations.

k. Now you want to assign the price of each item by looking up the item and exactly matching the item name in the Prices list. Click cell **E4**, enter the formula =VLOOKUP(A4,Prices,2,FALSE), and then press Ctrl+Enter. Be sure to use the range name Prices in the formula. In cell **E4**, double-click the **AutoFill** handle to automatically fill the cell range **E4:E9**.

l. To determine the total revenue for each item, click cell **F4**, enter the formula =E4*C4, and then press Ctrl+Enter. In cell **F4**, double-click the AutoFill handle to automatically fill cell range **F4:F9**.

m. Now you need to determine whether the item fell short of the sales projection or exceeded it. Click cell **G4**, enter the formula =ROUND(C4/B4,2), and then press Ctrl+Enter. In cell **G4**, double-click the **AutoFill** handle to automatically fill cell range **G4:G9**. The range now returns a projection percentage. An item that fell short of the sales projection will be under 100%. An item that exceeded the sales projection will be over 100%.

n. Now you need to determine what item has the highest revenue. Click cell **H4**, enter the formula =IF(F4=MAX($F$4:$F$9),"Best Item",""), and then press Ctrl+Enter. In cell **H4**, double-click the **AutoFill** handle to automatically fill cell range **H4:H9**. The range now returns a blank for all items except the one with the highest sales revenue, which returns Best Item.

o. Next you need to determine which items to put on sale to stimulate sales. An item should be put on sale if its % of Projection is less than the Sale Threshold in cell L4 or if its sales revenue is the lowest. Click cell **I4**, enter the formula =IF(OR(G4<$L$4,F4=MIN($F$4:$F$9)),"Put on Sale",""), and then press Ctrl+Enter. In cell **I4**, double-click the **AutoFill** handle to automatically fill cell range **I4:I9**.

The range now returns Put on Sale for two items: the item with the lowest sales revenue and the item with a % of Projection less than 95%. All other items return a blank.

p. You also need to know how many days the sale will last based on dates given by the poultry company. Click cell **L7**, enter the formula =DATEDIF(L5,L6,"D"), and then press Ctrl+Enter.

q. Select the range **B13:E18**. Click the **Insert** tab, and then, in the Sparklines group, click **Line**. Select the location range **F13:F18**, and then click **OK**. Click the **Sparkline Tools Design** tab, and then, in the Show group, click the **Markers** check box.

r. To represent the data, you want to create a chart comparing the percentage of all sales each item represents. Select the range **A3:A9**. Press and hold Ctrl, and then select the range **F3:F9**.

- Click the **Insert** tab, and then, in the Charts group, click the Insert Pie or Doughnut Chart button. Select the first option for a Pie Chart.
- Click the chart border, and then drag to move the chart so the top left corner is over the top left corner of cell G10. Click on the right resizing handle, and then drag the right chart border to the border between columns L and M. Click the bottom resizing handle, and then move the bottom of the chart to the border between rows **22** and **23**.
- On the **Chart Tools Design** tab, in the Chart Styles group, select **Style 3**.
- Click the chart title, **Total Revenue**. Click a second time on **Total Revenue** to place your insertion point in the title. Erase "Total Revenue", and then type Chicken Sales

Revenue by Menu Item. Decrease the font size of the title text to **14**. Click cell **D1** to deselect the chart.

s. You need to look at loan options for the new refrigeration unit by looking at a quarterly payment as it varies for different numbers of payments — or terms in years — and the annual interest rate. Click the **PoultryLoan** worksheet tab. Indigo5 would like to make quarterly payments (four payments per year). Click cell **C12**, enter the formula =-PMT($B12/4,C$11*4,$C$6), and then press Ctrl+Enter. In cell **C12**, double-click the **AutoFill** handle to automatically fill cell range **C12:C14**. With C12:C14 selected, drag the **AutoFill** handle to column **E** to fill the range **C12:E14**.

Notice that the mixed cell addressing of the dollar sign before the B will make the B stay the same and not change when copied, and the same holds true for the dollar sign before the 11. Notice that when copied, the formula will always contain $C$6, since it has an absolute reference of a dollar sign before both the column and the row.

t. Indigo5 would like to use the option that keeps the payment under $2,000, has the shortest term, and has the lowest interest rate. Click cell **D12**, and then click the **Bold** button to indicate that option as the best.

u. Click the **Indigo5ChickenSales** worksheet tab. Click the **Page Layout** tab, and then, in the Page Setup group, click the **Page Setup Dialog Box Launcher**. Click the **Header/Footer** tab. Click **Custom Footer**, then click the **Insert File Name** button to place the file name in the left section of the footer. Click **OK** twice. Repeat this step for the **PoultryLoan** worksheet.

v. Click the **Documentation** worksheet. Click cell **A8**, and then type in today's date. Click cell **B8**, and then type your name in Firstname Lastname format. Complete the remainder of the **Documentation** worksheet according to your instructor's directions.

w. **Save** the workbook, close Excel, and then submit your file as directed by your instructor.

Problem Solve 1

MyITLab®
Grader
Homework

Student data file needed:

e02B-Trendz.xlsx

You will save your file as:

e02B-Trendz_LastFirst.xlsx

Sales Data Analysis

Finance & Accounting

You are the executive assistant to the director of sales at B-Trendz, Inc., a trendy retail store that has locations in only ten states. The company is considering branching into the online retail market. Your supervisor, Kayla Zimmerman, wants to review last year's sales data and make predictions about this year's sales data before making any decisions on whether or not to begin selling online and, if so, which products may sell well online. You have been asked to determine the best-selling women's and men's clothing line by ranking them on a scale from A to E. Only products that have a ranking of A or B will be considered for online sales. To branch into the online market in the future, next year's total sales must be at least $3,000,000. Finally, if B-Trendz, Inc. begins selling products online, you will need help setting up and maintaining the online store. Several companies have given you their information, and you need to determine which company would best fit the needs for the B-Trendz online website.

a. Open the Excel file, **e02B-Trendz**. Save your file as e02B-Trendz_LastFirst, using your last and first name.

b. The Retail sheet contains 2017 quarterly sales data. You need to complete several calculations on this sheet.

- Calculate the quarterly sales totals for the women's and men's clothing lines.
- Calculate the yearly sales totals for the women's and men's clothing lines.
- In **B36:F36**, calculate the grand totals of women's and men's clothing sales.
- In **B37:E37**, calculate the percentage of sales from women's clothing. Display zero decimal places.

- In **B38:E38**, calculate the percentage of sales from men's clothing. Display zero decimal places.

c. You have been asked to determine whether the grand total yearly sales goals were met. The 2017 yearly sales goals were met if the yearly sales were $25,000,000 or more.
- In cell **G36**, using a logical function, determine whether the yearly sales goals were met. Set the formula to return a value of **Yes** if the goal was met or a value of **No** if the goal was not met.

d. You want to create quick visuals of the quarterly sales of each product line, so you decide to use Sparklines to view the sales at a glance. In **G5:G16**, insert **Line** sparklines based on the data in B5:E16. Add High Point markers. Also add **Line** sparklines for the Men's clothing data in **G21:G32**. Add High Point markers.

e. To determine which clothing lines may sell well online, you decide to rank them on a scale from A to E. First, you want to give the ranking table a range name.
- Select **M4:N8**, and give the range the name Rank.
- In cell **H5**, using a Vlookup function, determine the product line ranking of each product based on the Yearly Sales. Use the range name assigned to the lookup table.
- Copy the formula through **H16**.
- In cell **H21**, using a Vlookup function, determine the product line ranking of each product based on the Yearly Sales. Use the range name assigned to the lookup table.
- Copy the formula through **H32**.

f. You have been told that each product line will be considered for online sales only if the product line has a ranking of A or B. You need to determine which product lines will be considered for online sales.
- In cell **I5**, using a logical function, determine whether the product will be an online product. The product will be an online product if it has a ranking of A or B. Set the formula to return a value of **Yes** if the rank was met and a value of **No** if the rank was not met.
- Copy the formula through **I16**.
- Repeat the same formula for the men's clothing lines starting in cell **I21**, and copy the formula through **I32**.

g. You want to visually compare the women's sales and the men's sales of the product lines. Create two charts.
- Create a 3-D clustered column chart that represents the women's clothing sales based on each product line and the product line's yearly sales. Enter a chart title of Women's Clothing Sales.
- Move the chart so the top left corner of the chart is in cell **K10** and the bottom right corner of the chart is in cell **Q22**.
- Apply **Style 3** to the chart.
- Create a second 3-D clustered column chart that represents the men's clothing sales based on each product line and the product line's yearly sales. Enter a chart title of Men's Clothing Sales.
- Move the chart so the top left corner of the chart is in cell **K23** and the bottom right corner of the chart is in cell **Q38**.
- Apply **Style 3** to the chart.
- Adjust the vertical axis Bounds and Units of the men's clothing chart to match the vertical axis of the women's clothing chart.

h. You want to compare sales percentages of women's and men's clothing and have this chart as a separate chart sheet for ease of printing.
- Create a clustered column chart to compare the sales percentages of women's and men's clothing sales for all four quarters.

- Move the chart to a new chart sheet, and name the new worksheet SalesComparison. Position the SalesComparison worksheet to the right the Retail worksheet.
- Apply **Style 4** to the chart.
- Enter the chart title Sales Comparison. Change the chart title format using WordArt, **Pattern Fill - Blue, Accent 1, Light Downward Diagonal, Outline - Accent 1**. Increase the font of the chart title to **40**.
- Insert a rounded rectangle shape in the top left corner of the chart. Enter the text Women's products consistently outsold men's products.
- Change the size of the rounded rectangle shape to .6" high and 2.25" wide.

i. B-Trendz management believes that with the growing popularity of its clothing products, the company can reach the overall yearly goal of $30,000,000 in sales (the sales goal of 2017 was $25,000,000). You have been asked to determine the approximate increase in sales of each product that would be needed to reach this goal. Assume the same percentage increase for all the products.

- Select the **Predictions** worksheet tab. In cell **B5**, multiply the percent increase in sales in B1 by the 2017 sales for women's Quarter 1 Activeware (B5 of the Retail worksheet). (Hint: To use data from another worksheet in this formula, click the worksheet tab, click the cell you want to multiply by the percentage in cell B1 and then press Enter.) Don't forget that you want at least the amount from the Retail worksheet plus the predicted increase.
- Copy this formula to the range **B5:E16**.
- Total the women's clothing sales as well as the women's quarterly sales.
- Repeat all the above steps for the men's clothing sales.
- In **B36:F36**, total the quarterly and yearly sales for both women's and men's clothing.
- In cell **G36**, using a logical function, you will determine whether the sales goal is met. The sales goal is met if the yearly sales total is greater than or equal to $30,000,000. Set the formula to return a value of **Yes** if goal was met and a value of **No** if goal was not met.
- Using trial and error in cell **B1**, determine the approximate percentage increase that is needed for all products to meet the total sales goal of $30,000,000 in cell G36. Use only whole number percentages.

j. To launch online sales, B-Trendz will need to hire a website development company to set up and maintain the website. To do so, B-Trendz will need to take out a loan to cover the cost of the development and maintenance of the website. You have solicited and received bids from three different companies. For each bid, you need to determine the monthly payment, total loan payment, and total interest.

- Select the **Online** worksheet. In cell **B11**, calculate the monthly payment for the loan given the loan amount, term, and interest for the Online Solutions company. The result should be a positive value.
- In cell **B12**, calculate the total payments over the life of the loan.
- In **B13**, calculate how much total interest will be paid over the life of the loan.
- Copy the range B11:B13 to **D11:D13**.
- You need to recommend which company B-Trendz should use to create and maintain the online website. The best option is based on the company maintaining the website for at least two years and a monthly payment of $2,100 or less. Use a logical function in cell **B15:D15** to return the company name from row 2 if the website will be maintained for at least two years and the monthly payment is $2,100 or less. If the value is false, the cell should remain blank.

k. Complete the **Documentation** worksheet according to your instructor's directions. Insert the **file name** in the left footer section on all worksheets in the workbook.

l. **Save** the workbook, exit Excel, and then submit your file as directed by your instructor.

When calculating the payment for the three potential loans, you were asked to have the function return a positive value. Why is it important to return a positive value of a loan payment? Identify at least two ways to make a payment function return a positive value.

Critical Thinking

Student data file needed:

 e02Advertise.xlsx

You will save your file as:

e02Advertise_LastFirst.xlsx

Advertising Review

Sales & Marketing

The Painted Paradise Resort & Spa has been investing in advertising using different media. When guests check in, the employee asks them how they heard about Painted Paradise Resort & Spa. Based on the customer's response, the employee then notes in the system either magazine, radio, television, Internet, word of mouth, or other. Since almost every guest is asked, the number surveyed represents a significant portion of the actual guests. The past year's data is located on the GuestData worksheet. Every time a guest answers the question by mentioning an advertising source, it is considered a guest result. Ideally, the resort wants to purchase advertising at a low cost but then see as many guest results from that advertising as possible.

Every year, upper management sets the advertising budget before the beginning of the fiscal year, July 1. For the coming year, upper management has given you a larger television budget because of a new video marketing campaign. Also, the advertising contracts get negotiated every year, because the media vendors require a one-year commitment. The contracts are negotiated after the budget has been set. You will develop charts for an upcoming presentation that will discuss a marketing strategy, potential changes to the budget given the new media prices, anticipated monthly guest results, and the prospect of hiring a marketing consulting company with a high retainer that would require a loan.

a. Open the Excel file, **e02Advertise**. Save your file as e02Advertise_LastFirst, using your last and first name.

b. On the **GuestData** worksheet, in cells **A6:J17**, the data indicates the number of guests responding that they heard of the resort from the listed method — Guest Results. Add the following.

  • In cell **H2**, add a COUNTA function to determine the number of months listed in cells A6:A17.

  • In cell **J2**, add a DATEDIF function to calculate the survey duration in years using the 2017 Fiscal Start date and 2018 Fiscal Start date.

  • In cells **B6:B17**, use Flash Fill to return the three-character code for the month — JUL for July.

  • Select cells **L6:M17**, and then name the range **Season**.

  • In cells **C6:C17**, add a VLOOKUP that will exactly match the month in column **B** to return the correct season — Low, Mid, or High — based on the named range **Season**.

  • In cells **D19:J19**, calculate the averages for each column with a rounded value — not just formatted — to zero decimal places.

  • For later use, create the following named ranges.

Cell	Name
D19	AvgMagazine
E19	AvgRadio
F19	AvgTelevision
G19	AvgInternet

c. On the **AdvertisingPlan** worksheet, an analysis of past Guest Results and the new budget have been started. First, you need to finish out the past year analysis. Add the following:

  • In cell **F2**, enter a function that will return the current date.

  • Set the following cells to these formulas.

Cell	Name
D6	=AvgMagazine
D7	=AvgRadio
D8	=AvgTelevision
D9	=AvgInternet

* Note that these are monthly averages. Thus, all calculations on this worksheet are estimates based on the monthly average.

- In cells **E6:E9**, calculate the Amount Spent — a monthly figure — by multiplying the Cost Per Ad and the Ads Placed.
- In cells **F6:F10**, calculate the Cost per Guest Result by dividing the Amount Spent by the Past Guest Results.
- In cells **C10:E10**, calculate the appropriate totals for each column.

d. On the **AdvertisingPlan** worksheet, you need to finish out the new budget year analysis. Add the following.
- In cells **I6:I9**, calculate the Number of Ads that can be purchased based on the New Budget and the New Cost Per Ad in columns **G** and **H.** (Hint: A partial ad cannot be purchased. Further, $300 would not be enough to purchase one radio ad, since the new cost per ad is $325, so you need to create a formula that will round the number down to the nearest integer.)
- In cells **J6:J9**, calculate the Amount to Spend — this is a monthly figure — by multiplying the New Cost Per Ad and the Ads to Place.
- In cells **G10** and **I10:J10**, calculate the appropriate totals for each column. If necessary, change the format for cell I10 to general.
- In cell **H11**, calculate the amount of the budget remaining by subtracting the Amount to Spend total from the New Budget total. Note that the totals are in row 10. A negative number indicates that the new plan is over budget. A positive number indicates that the new plan is under budget and has excess spendable funds.
- In cells **K6:K9**, add a formula that will return **Increase?** if the Ads to Place is equal to zero or if the New Cost Per Ad is less than or equal to the Budget +/- in cell **H11**. Any others should return **Decrease?**. This column now indicates the media types for which the resort may want to consider an increase or decrease in the Ads to Place, along with any necessary budget adjustment.
- In cells **L6:L9**, calculate the Anticipated Guest Results by dividing the Amount to Spend by the Cost per Guest Result — column F. The resulting value — not the just the format — should be rounded to zero decimals.
- In cell **L10**, calculate the appropriate total for Anticipated Guest Results.
- In cell **L11**, calculate the number of anticipated guest results compared to the past by subtracting the Past Guest Results total from the Anticipated Guest Results total. Note that the totals are in row 10. A negative number indicates an anticipated decrease in Guest Results. A positive number indicates an anticipated increase in Guest Results.

e. Starting on the **AdvertisingPlan** worksheet, you need to make two charts for your presentation. Create the following two charts.
- Based on the data in cells **A5:A9**, **D5:D9**, and **L5:L9**, add a **3-D Clustered Column** chart to compare the past guest results to the anticipated guest results based on the new monthly advertising.
- Under chart styles, set the chart to **Style 6**. Then change the title to read PAST VS. ANTICIPATED MONTHLY GUEST RESULTS.
- Move and resize the chart so the top left corner is in cell **A11** and the bottom right corner is in cell **F22**. Set the chart title to **12** pt font size.

- Based on the data in cells **A5:A9**, **D5:D9**, and **E5:E9**, add a **Clustered Column - Line on Secondary Axis Combo Chart**. Move this chart to its own worksheet — chart sheet — named GuestResultsBySpending.

- Under chart styles, set the chart to **Style 6**. Then change the title to read Past Advertising Amount Spent Compared to # of Guest Results Experienced.

- Set the chart title to **18** pt font size, set all axis data labels to **12** pt font size, and set all legend text to **12** pt font size.

f. On the **MarketingConsultants** worksheet, a monthly loan payment analysis has been started. The resort is considering hiring marketing consultants. However, they require a large up-front retainer fee. The resort would need to take out a loan to cover the cost. The resort needs an analysis of the loan payment by varying interest rate and down payment amount. Add the following.

- In cells **D10:H13**, add a **PMT** function to calculate the monthly payment. Enter one formula that can be entered in cell **D10** and filled to the remaining cells. (Hint: Think carefully about where dollar signs are needed for mixed and absolute cell addressing. Also, the down payment can be subtracted from the Retainer — or Principal — Amount in the third argument of the PMT function. Adjust the formula so the result is positive.)

g. Complete the **Documentation** worksheet according to your instructor's directions. Insert the **file name** in the left footer section on all worksheets in the workbook.

h. **Save** the workbook, exit Excel, and then submit your file as directed by your instructor.

Perform 1: Perform in Your Life

Student data file needed:

 e02Ideal.xlsx

You will save your file as:

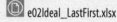 e02Ideal_LastFirst.xlsx

Your Ideal Career Start

Human Resources

Even if this is your first semester, you have probably already begun to think about the type of job or career you want. Further, when you are spending long hours studying, it can be fun to imagine the new car you might buy at your ideal career start after graduation. For this project, pretend — if you need to — that you are graduating this semester. In this project, you need to find currently available jobs and establish criteria to help you pick your most desired position. Then you will find the ideal new car to purchase, but your new position's salary must allow you to afford the monthly payment.

a. Open the Excel file, **e02Ideal**. Save your file as e02Ideal_LastFirst, using your last and first name. Keep the workbook professional, but feel free to optionally add elements such as a picture of your ideal career start or new car.

b. Go to the Internet, and find five or more jobs that interest you. You can select data from multiple websites or just one website (from the same website will be easiest). Search for jobs that you may apply for after graduation. Copy and paste that data into the **JobData worksheet**. Feel free to add columns, move columns, or rename columns to fit your data and style needs.

c. On the **JobData** worksheet, accomplish the following.

- In cell **A1**, add an appropriate title for your career goals.

- In cell **B3**, indicate the website you used to find the job posting (e.g., Monster.com or CareerBuilder.com).

- In cell **B4**, indicate the date you gathered the information.

- In the center header of your worksheet, insert your full name.
- Starting in row 7, complete the columns of data listed on Table 1 below by copying from the Internet and separating — or cleansing — the data using Excel's Flash Fill feature and/or text functions as necessary. You can gather more data than is listed below if it is relevant to picking the ideal job for you. At a minimum, you must have the following.

Data (no extra characters in or around the data)	Description
Company Name	Full name as you would address a letter to the company.
Job Title	Full job title, which needs to be descriptive of the position. For example, "Entry Level" is not a sufficient title. "Application Support Analyst — Entry Level" is a sufficient title.
State	State in which the position is located. State should be in a column by itself, not in combination with the city or address.
Salary	Try not to mix pay types. For example, if you are looking for a salaried position, choose all salaried positions.

Table 1   Required minimum job position data

- Add headers, comments, and/or notes to make clear to your instructor what Excel steps you took to get to the final job data. Leave all formulas you create in the worksheet — show your work, don't delete it. If Flash Fill was used, indicate the range. Keep your work organized.
- Format the JobData worksheet as needed.

d. On the **JobAnalysis** worksheet, copy data from the JobData sheet that you intend to use to help you determine which position(s) to apply for. Add the following elements to this worksheet.

- In cell A1, enter an appropriate worksheet title, and then copy data from the JobData sheet beginning in row 3.
- In Column D, use an IF statement in combination with any other Excel formulas or functions to indicate whether a job is in a state you find desirable. You should indicate a minimum of two states as desirable.
- In cell A16:A18, fill in salary data to establish pay range categories for Below Expected, Expected, and Above Expected based on your personal job expectations.
- Give the salary table data an appropriate range name.
- In column F, use this table in a VLOOKUP to determine the category for each of the positions you are evaluating using the salary table range name.
- In column G, determine whether you will apply for the job. You will apply for the job if the salary has a category of Expected or Above Expected.
- Add any other additional formulas and functions to help you determine the most desirable position.
- The worksheet must ultimately indicate one final Most Desired job position.
- Format the JobAnalysis worksheet as needed.

e. On the **MyNewCar** worksheet, add the following elements.

- In B2:B7, enter data for the ideal car you wish to purchase. In B13:B15, enter three current interest rates for the type of car you wish to purchase. In C12:E12, enter possible terms of the loan in years for the type of car you wish to purchase.
- In cells C13:E15, calculate the monthly payment for your ideal car using the three different interest rates and three different terms of loans.

- In cell B17, input the monthly gross salary by referencing the salary from your most desired job on the JobAnalysis worksheet.
- You need to be able to afford the car you pick. The amount you will be able to afford will vary greatly depending on individual circumstances, such as marital status, credit card debt, and homeowner status. For the purposes of this project, the car you pick cannot have a monthly payment greater than **10%** of your gross salary for your Most Desired job. In C22:E24, determine the percentage of your monthly salary the loan payment would represent.
- Use a conditional format to indicate feasible loan options. If none of the loan options are under 10%, you will have to do one or a combination of the following: pick a new car, increase your down payment, extend your term, or find a lower interest rate.
- Format the MyNewCar worksheet as needed.

f. Build at least one meaningful chart on either the JobAnalysis or MyNewCar worksheet. Include at least a one-sentence explanation near the chart explaining the chart's significance.

g. Complete the **Documentation** worksheet according to your instructor's directions. Insert the **file name** in the left footer on all worksheets in the workbook.

h. **Save** the workbook, exit Excel, and then submit your file as directed by your instructor.

Perform 2: Perform in Your Career

Student data file needed:	You will save your file as:
e02Investment.xlsx	e02Investment_LastFirst.xlsx

Investment Portfolios

Finance & Accounting

You have started working as an investment intern for a financial company that helps clients invest in the stock market. Your manager, Roger Hedding, gives you a spreadsheet detailing some periodic investments in Nobel Energy, Inc. (NBL) made by one of the clients. The client would like a report and charts on the NBL investment and the stock's performance. Your manager has asked you to finish this report.

a. Open the Excel file, **e02Investment**. Save your file as e02Investment_LastFirst, using your last and first name.

b. On the **NBLInvestment** worksheet, add the following calculation.
- In column **F**, starting in row 21, your manager has already entered a formula to calculate total value. Update the formula to return a value of only **two decimals**. (Hint: The cell value needs to change, which is different from merely formatting to two decimals.)
- In column **G**, starting in the second row — cell **G22** — enter a formula to sum up the quarterly investments as of the date in column A to provide a cumulative total. For example, cell G22 should return the sum of the Quarterly investments on 1/2/2016 and 4/1/2016. Next, cell G23 should return the sum of the Quarterly investments on 1/2/2016, 4/1/2016, and 7/1/2016. Thus, column G returns a running total of investments so the last cell — G33 — reflects the total of all investments from 1/2/2016 thru 1/3/2019.
- In column **H**, calculate the Total Growth. The total growth is the Total Value minus the Total Investment. (A result of a negative value means that the investment shrank instead of growing.)
- In column **I**, calculate the Total Growth %. The Total Growth% is the Total Growth divided by the Total Investment.
- In cell **J21**, type 0. In cell **J22**, calculate the Quarterly Growth. The Quarterly Growth is the Total Growth minus the Total Growth from the previous quarter.

- In column **K**, calculate the Quarterly Growth %: The Quarterly Growth % is the Quarterly Growth divided by the Total Investment.
- In column **L**, using a lookup function, calculate the Quarterly Rank based on the lookup table in M1:N7. Assign the range name Rank to the lookup table, and use the range name in the formula.
- In column **M**, using a logical function, determine the Portfolio Status Recommendation. The Portfolio Status is "Good" if the Quarterly Rank is A or B. Otherwise, the Portfolio Status will return a value of "Diversify".

c. Create a **combo chart** for Total Portfolio Performance that displays the Total Value, Total Investment, and Total Growth over time. (Hint: You will need to show a secondary axis for Total Growth.) Apply a chart style. Position the chart above the data in row 20.

d. Create a **combo chart** for Quarterly Performance that displays the Quarterly Growth and the Quarterly Growth % over time. (Hint: You will need to show a secondary axis for Quarterly Total Growth %.) Apply a chart style. Position the chart above the data. You may need to change the Label Position to Low.

e. Complete the **Documentation** worksheet according to your instructor's directions. Insert the **file name** in the left footer on all worksheets in the workbook.

f. **Save** the workbook, exit Excel, and then submit your file as directed by your instructor.

Perform 3: Perform in Your Team

Student data file needed:

 e02Paintball.xlsx

You will save your file as:

e02Paintball_TeamName.xlsx

Paintball Facility Expansion

Productions & Operations

You work for Splat Attack Paintball Range, a popular outdoor paintball facility near a metropolitan area. The range is open Wednesdays through Sundays from the first of April until the end of October every year. With the popularity of the sport of paintball rising and the facility's inability to accommodate the number of paintball party bookings being requested, Splat Attack is considering an expansion of its paintball range. You have been assigned to a team to help with the analysis for an expansion of the range area and overall capacity. Your manager, Amy Trilling, needs help looking at past sales, sales trends, and loan options. Located in the upper Midwest of the United States, Splat Attack has typical Midwest weather. Therefore, part of the facility's marketing strategy is to offer discounted season passes in the colder months if the temperature is 60 degrees or below. Following is a description of the data Amy has provided to you.

Date	Description
Month	The first day of the month for the data in that row.
Passes Sold	The number of paid players and season pass holders who entered the paintball range that month. Attendance does not reflect the time spent on the range. If a player leaves the range and returns, the player is counted only once.
Ticket Sales	All ticket sales that month, including single-day and season passes. If a player buys a season pass in April, the sale is accounted for only in April, yet the player can play throughout the remaining months of that season.
Other Sales	All other revenue besides ticket sales. This is primarily equipment rental and paintballs.
Avg High Temp (Degrees)	The average high temperature for the park that particular month.

a. Select one team member to set up the document by completing steps b through d.

b. Open your browser, and navigate to **https://www.onedrive.live.com, https://www.drive.google.com**, or any other instructor-assigned location. Be sure all members of the team have an account on the chosen system, such as a Microsoft or Google account.

c. Open the Excel file, **e02Paintball**. Save your file as e02Paintball_TeamName, replacing TeamName with the name assigned to your team by your instructor.

d. Share the spreadsheet with the other members of your team. Make sure each team member has the appropriate permission to edit the document.

e. Hold a team meeting to discuss the requirements of the remaining steps. As a team, make an action plan to assign individual and team work and set deadlines for each step.

f. The **Sales** worksheet includes data about past revenue — earned income before any costs. The data on the Sales worksheet could be analyzed in several ways. Add the following to the worksheet.

   - As a team, determine possible range names that can be used in creating formulas for the Sales worksheet.
   - In cell **E4**, add a field labeled Total Sales. In column E, calculate the total sales for each month using range names if appropriate.
   - In cell **F4**, add a field labeled Average Sales per Pass Sold. In column F, calculate the average sales per pass sold for each month.
   - In cell **G4**, add a field labeled % of Total Sales. In column G, using a mixed or absolute reference, calculate each month's percent of the total sales.
   - In cell **J4**, add a field labeled Discount Passes?. In column J, determine whether Splat Attack will offer discount passes based on the facility's marketing strategy.
   - In cell **A12**, add a field labeled Totals. In the cell range **B12:E12**, use a function to calculate the totals.
   - In cell **A13**, add a field labeled Averages. In the cell range **B13:E13**, use a function or formula to calculate the averages.
   - Add any other calculations your team feels are relevant for analyzing Splat Attack's past revenue.
   - As a team, format the worksheet in a professional manner. Adjust column width and row height as appropriate. Apply cell format as necessary for data interpretation.
   - Each team member should independently create and format one or two charts about the data on this worksheet.
   - With a focus on displaying sales peaks and trends, the team should meet to decide which three to five charts to include in the final file.

g. On the **Loan** worksheet, you will find the basic information about two loan options to finance Splat Attack's range expansion. Make the following updates to the loan worksheet.

   - In cells **B8** and **C8**, calculate the Monthly Payment amount for the two loan options for the range expansion. Splat Attack is considering only terms of three or five years.
   - In cells **B12** and **C12**, calculate the Total Loan Payments for the two loan options.
   - In cell **B13**, identify which loan is preferred for Splat Attack's expansion project. The loan is preferred if the total loan payment is the lower of the two.
   - Add any other calculations your team feels are relevant to determining the best loan for Splat Attack.
   - As a team, format the worksheet in a professional manner, applying appropriate theme and cell styles. Adjust column width and row height as appropriate. Apply cell formatting as necessary for data interpretation.

h. Fill out the **TeamComments** worksheet as directed by your instructor.

i. Complete the Documentation worksheet according to your instructor's directions. At the minimum, include enough detail to identify which parts of the worksheets or workbook each team member completed.

j. Insert the **file name** in the left footer on all worksheets in the workbook. In a custom header section, include the names of the students in your team, spreading the names evenly across each of the three header sections: left section, center section, and right section.

k. **Save** the workbook, exit Excel, and then submit your file as directed by your instructor.

Perform 4: How Others Perform

Student data file needed:
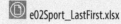 e02Sport.xlsx

You will save your file as:
e02Sport_LastFirst.xlsx

Sports Facility Operations

Productions & Operations

You have recently been hired as an account representative in the business office of Sports Plus, a fitness facility. Your supervisor, Tim Kerr, has requested that you finish an already-started Excel workbook file that identifies the expenses of the sports facility and projects by quarter for the current year. Beyond performing calculations for total expenses by expense category and per quarter, you are expected to create and format a series of professional-looking charts that will assist in the interpretation of the workbook data. The spreadsheet data and visual charts will not only be included in an annual report but also be presented to the board of directors of the company.

You have also been asked to look at the sales of the specific exercise classes for the year and determine which courses should continue to be offered at the facility the following year and which courses should no longer be offered. Finally, you have been asked to predict what percentage increase in the cost of classes would be needed to reach the total sales goal of $40,000.

a. Open the Excel file, **e02Sport**. Save your file as e02Sport_LastFirst, using your last and first name.

b. Rename Sheet1 Expenses. Complete the worksheet by making the following changes.

   • In cell D6, adjust the existing formula by taking **Last Year's Avg Qtr** and multiplying it by the **Target Factor for Increases** for **Qtr 1**. Use mixed referencing when correcting this formula. Copy the formula though **G14**.

   • Check to be sure the SUM function and cell range are correct in cell H6, in which you are calculating the **Total** for **Rent** for the current year only (**Qtr 1 - Qtr 4**). Fill the formula down through Column **H14**.

   • Correct the SUM function in cell **D16**, and then fill the corrected function across through column G.

   • For cell range **D19:D22**, use functions to perform calculations for Qtr1 through Qtr4. Fill the formulas in **D19:D21** across through column G.

   • Apply formatting to improve the appearance of the worksheet as necessary. Apply any data formatting that will make the data easier to interpret.

   • Create a chart to display each expense category and expense amounts for each quarter. Reposition the chart below the worksheet data beginning in A24. Resize the chart so the bottom left corner is in cell D38. Format the chart, and add a descriptive title that represents the information displayed in the chart.

   • Create a chart to display the expense categories and total expenses for the current year. Add percentages as data labels. Reposition the chart below the worksheet data beginning in row 24. Resize the chart so the bottom left corner of the chart is in cell H38. Format the chart, and add a descriptive chart title.

- In I6:I14, insert column Sparklines of the data for Qtr1:Qtr4.
- Modify the page settings to ensure your worksheet will print on a single page. Specify page orientation as is appropriate to maximize readability.

c. Select **Sheet2**, and rename the sheet SalesData. The SalesData worksheet contains sales information for exercise classes offered at the facility. You will finish this worksheet by completing the following.

- In column D, create a formula to calculate the sales total for adult classes and youth classes.
- Calculate the totals of yearly sessions sold and sales total for both adult and youth classes.
- Calculate the total sales of the exercise classes for the fitness facility.
- To determine exercise class ranking for both the adult and youth classes, you will use the lookup table in I2:J7. Give the lookup table the range name Rank, and use the range name when creating the formula.
- Only classes with a ranking of Silver, Gold, or Platinum will be continued the following year. Create a formula to help your supervisor determine whether the courses should continue to be offered for both the adult and youth classes.

d. Select **Sheet3**, and rename the sheet SalesGoal. On the SalesGoal worksheet, you have been asked to predict how much to raise the cost of classes to reach the total sales goal of **$40,000**. You will increase all classes by the same percentage. Finish the SalesGoal sheet by completing the following.

- Referencing the 2016 data from the SalesData sheet, determine the percentage of increase needed in the 2017 cost per class session. The increase is determined by multiplying the 2016 Cost per Class by the Sales Increase Percentage Recommendation. (Hint: Be sure to add 1 to the percentage found in cell D22 to get an accurate increase for the 2017 classes.)
- Since the results on the SalesData worksheet indicated that the low-selling courses should be discontinued, change the yearly sessions sold for Racquetball in cell B15 to 0. You may need to re-determine the percentage increase of cost per class session after deleting the row.
- Through trial and error, determine the recommended percentage of increase in the cost per class session in cell D22 to reach the 2017 sales goal of at least $40,000.

e. Complete the **Documentation** worksheet according to your instructor's directions. Insert the **file name** in the left footer section on all worksheets in the workbook.

f. **Save** the workbook, exit Excel, and then submit your file as directed by your instructor.

Access Business Unit 1

Understanding and Using a Relational Database

Today's businesses rely heavily on having access to accurate, reliable, and consistent data to make decisions. Database management systems (DBMS) such as Microsoft Access provide organizations with the ability to develop relational databases for collecting, storing, and accessing valuable data via tables, queries, forms, and reports.

Learning Outcome 1

Understand the purpose for main database objects in Access: tables, queries, forms, and reports.

Real World Success

"I used Access to create ad hoc reports for managers. My ability to quickly provide data has made me their 'go to' person."

– Art, alumnus, materials analyst

Learning Outcome 2

Based on the needs of an organization, understand and create various types of relationships using different types of keys: primary, foreign, and composite.

Real World Success

"Reports on open issues were very important to my project manager. I set up a database with a main table of open issues. I used foreign keys to link it to employee tables and to a table of priorities. That way, I could generate a report that included the details of any open issues, including who reported it and the priority level of the issue."

– Joseph P., IT intern

Microsoft Access 2016

Chapter 1 | THE FOUR MAIN DATABASE OBJECTS

Prepare Case

Production & Operations

Red Bluff Golf Course Putts for Paws Charity Tournament

The Red Bluff Golf Course & Pro Shop is sponsoring a charity tournament, Putts for Paws, to raise money for the Santa Fe Animal Center. An intern created a database to help run the tournament but did not finish it before leaving. You have been asked to finish the database to track the participants who enter the tournament, the orders they have placed, and the items they have purchased.

Kati Molin / Shutterstock

Student data files needed for this chapter:

 a01ch01Putts.accdb

 a01ch01Participant.accdb

You will save your file as:

 a01ch01Putts_LastFirst.accdb

Understanding the Basics of Databases and Tables

Businesses keep records about everything they do. If a business sells products, it keeps records about its products. It keeps records of its customers, the products it sells to each customer, and each sale. It keeps records about its employees, the hours they work, and their benefits. These records are collected and used for decision making, for sales and marketing, and for reporting purposes. A **database** is a collection of these records. The purpose of a database is to store, manage, and provide access to these business records.

In the past, many databases were paper based. Paper records were stored in files in file cabinets. Each file would be labeled and put in a drawer in a file cabinet. Elaborate filing schemes were developed so that any record could be located quickly. This was highly labor intensive and prone to error. Today, while most businesses use automated databases to store their records, you still see the occasional paper-based system. For example, a realtor's office may still use paper files for client records.

Data can be defined as facts about people, events, things, or ideas. Data is an important asset to any organization as it allows companies to make better business decisions after the data is converted into useful information. **Information** is data that has been manipulated and processed to make it meaningful. For example, if you see the number 2,000 out of context, it has no meaning. If you are told that 2,000 represents the amount of an order in dollars, that piece of data becomes meaningful information. Businesses can use meaningful information to gain a competitive advantage, such as by providing discounts to customers who order more expensive items. An automated database management system, such as Microsoft Access 2016, makes that possible.

Databases are used for two major purposes: for operational processing and for analytical purposes. In operational or transaction-based databases, each sale or transaction that a business makes is tracked. The information is used to keep the business running. Analytical databases are used for extracting data for decision making. The data in these databases is summarized and classified to make information available to the decision makers in the business.

Automated databases provide many advantages over paper databases. The information in the databases is much easier to find in automated form. The information can be manipulated and processed more rapidly. Automated databases can be used to enforce accuracy and other quality standards. In today's fast-paced world, a business needs to manipulate information quickly and accurately to make decisions. Without today's automated databases, a business cannot compete. In this section, you will learn what Access is and learn about the four main object types in an Access database.

Understand the Purpose of Access

Access is a relational **database management system (DBMS)** program created by Microsoft. It is a tool to organize, store, and manipulate data and to select and report on data. Access stores data in tables. Similar data is stored in the same table. For example, if one is storing data about participants in an event, he or she would include all the participants' names, addresses, and telephone numbers in one table.

The power of a database management system comes from the ability to link tables together. A separate table of purchases for the tournament can be linked with the participant table. This allows users to easily combine the two tables; for example, the tournament manager would be able to print out the participants with a record of their tournament purchases.

Understanding the Four Main Objects in a Database

Access has four main database **objects**: tables, queries, forms, and reports. A **table** is the database object that stores data organized in an arrangement of columns and rows. A **query** object retrieves specific data from other database objects and then displays only the data that you specify. Queries allow you to ask questions about the data in your tables. You can use a **form** object to enter new records into a table, edit or delete existing records in a table, or display existing records. The **report** object summarizes the fields and records from a table or query in an easy-to-read format suitable for printing.

Access objects have several views. Each **view** gives you a different perspective on the objects and different capabilities. For example, **Datasheet view** of a table shows the data contents within a table. Figure 1 shows Datasheet view of a participant table. **Design view** shows how fields are defined. Depending on the object, other views may exist. Figure 1 shows a toggle button you can use to switch between Datasheet view and Design view. Figure 2 shows how a participant table would appear in Design view. In Datasheet view, you see the actual participants and their related information. In Design view, you see how the information is defined and structured. Figure 1 shows the charity event participant table. Each row contains corresponding pieces of data about the participant listed in that row. Each row in Access is called a **record**. A record is all of the data pertaining to one person, place, thing, or event. There are 17 participant records in the table. The second participant is John Trujillo.

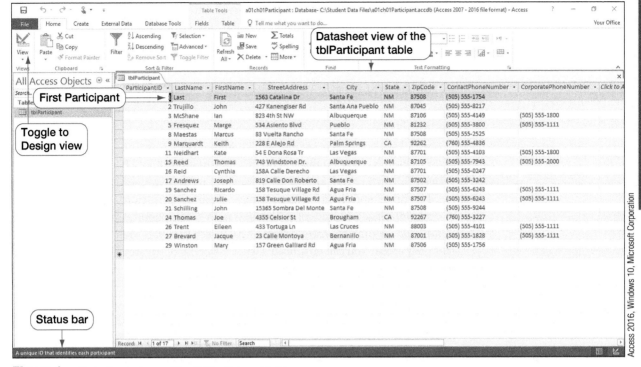

Figure 1 Datasheet view of the tblParticipant table

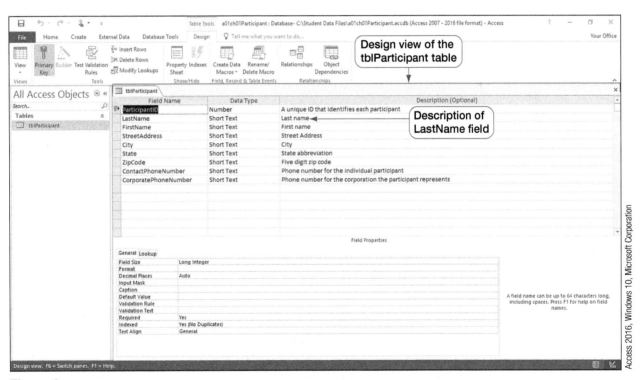

Figure 2 Design view of the tblParticipant table

Each column in Access is called a **field**, often referred to as an attribute. A field or attribute is a specific piece of information that is stored in every record. LastName is a field that shows the participant's last name. As you go across the table rows, you will see fields that represent the participant's first name and address.

Creating a New Database and Templates

When you create a new database, you can design it yourself, starting with an empty database. If you take this approach, you develop the tables, fields, and the relationships — or links — between the tables. This requires you to decide what information you want to keep in your database, how this information should be grouped into tables, what relationships you need, and what queries and reports you need.

The other option in creating a new database is to start with a prebuilt template. A **template** is a structure of a database with tables, fields, forms, queries, and reports. Templates are professionally designed databases that you can either use as is or adapt to suit your needs. You can download a wide variety of templates from Microsoft's Office.com website. Microsoft provides sample database templates for managing assets, contacts, issues, projects, and tasks.

Templates are created by Microsoft employees or other users. You can also download sample databases in which to experiment. The difference between a template and a sample database is that a sample database includes sample data, whereas a template is empty except for the structure and definitions.

Opening the Starting File

For the tournament, the intern created a new database and defined tables specifically for Putts for Paws. You will work with the database that has already been created. In this exercise, you will launch Access and open the database to get started.

A01.00

SIDE NOTE
Windows 10
This book is written for Windows 10. If you are using Windows 8, open your charms, click Search, and then type Access. If using Windows 7, search the Start menu for Access.

To Open the Starting File

a. On the taskbar, click **Ask Me Anything** or **Search the web and Windows**. Type Access.

b. Click on **Access 2016** in the search results.

c. The Access Start screen is displayed when Access is launched. Click **Open Other Files** in the left pane, and then double-click **This PC**. Navigate through the folder structure to the location of your student data files, and then double-click **a01ch01Putts**.

d. A database opens that will be used to track certain aspects of the Putts for Paws charity event. Observe the various database objects that have already been created by the intern.

e. Click the **File** tab, save the file as an **Access Database**, and then click **Save As**. Navigate to the location where you are saving your project files, and then change the file name to a01ch01Putts_LastFirst, using your last and first name. Click **Save**. If necessary, enable the content.

Maneuver in the Navigation Pane

When a database is opened, Access displays the **Navigation Pane** on the left side as shown in Figure 3. This pane allows you to view the objects in the database. The standard view in the Navigation Pane shows all objects in the database organized by object type. You can see that the database has three tables: tblItem, tblOrder, and tblOrderLine. There is one query, one form, and one report.

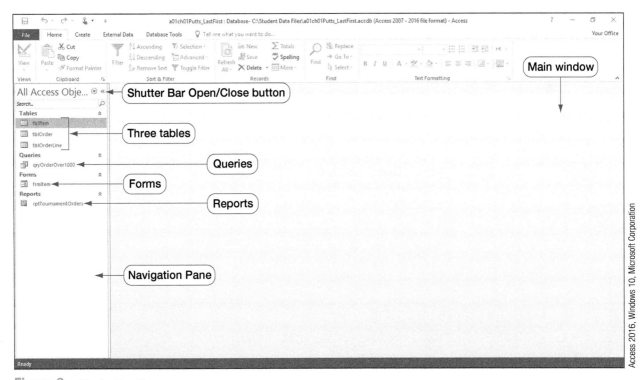

Figure 3   Navigation Pane

Opening and Closing the Shutter Bar

You can work in Access with the Navigation Pane open or closed. In this exercise, you will use the Shutter Bar Open/Close button at the top of the pane to open and close the pane.

A01.01

To Open and Close the Shutter Bar

a. Click the **Shutter Bar Close** button ⟨«⟩ to close the Navigation Pane. Access closes the pane, allowing for a larger workspace in the database, but it leaves the Navigation Pane on the side of the window for when you need it.

b. Click the **Shutter Bar Open** button ⟨»⟩ to open the pane again.

SIDE NOTE

Pin the Ribbon

If your ribbon is collapsed, pin your ribbon open. Click the Home tab. In the lower right-hand corner of the ribbon, click Pin the Ribbon ⟨ ⟩.

Customize the Navigation Pane

While the default view of the Navigation Pane shows all objects such as tables, queries, forms, and reports, organized by object type, you have several choices of views. In this exercise, you will explore the various views.

 A01.02

To Customize the Navigation Pane

a. Click the **Navigation Pane arrow** ⟨ ⟩ to display the Navigation Pane view options. The default view is displayed, which is Object Type and All Access Objects.

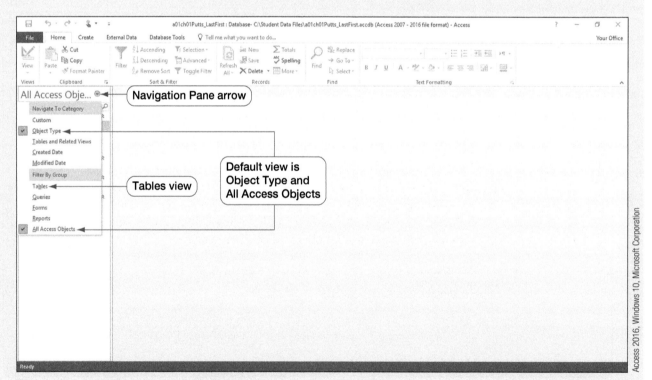

Figure 4 Navigation Pane options: default view

b. Click **Tables**.

Only the three tables are displayed in the Navigation Pane. When you have many objects in a database, it helps to restrict objects that are shown in the Navigation Pane.

c. Click the **Navigation Pane arrow** again, and then click **Tables and Related Views**.

The objects are organized by tables. Any query, report, or form related to a table is listed with that table.

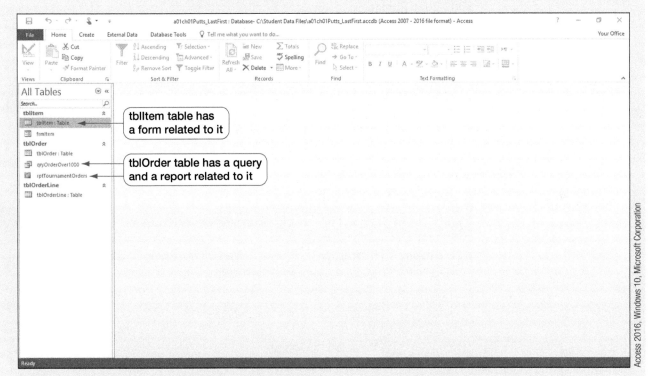

Figure 5 Tables and Related Views in Navigation Pane

Using the Search Box

Currently, there are only a few objects in your database. However, as you work with a database, more objects may be added as you develop reports and queries. As a result, to help you find objects, Access provides a Search box. In this exercise, you will use the search box to locate specific objects within the database.

To Use the Search Box

a. Click in the **Search** box at the top of the Navigation Pane, and then type Order. Access searches for and displays all objects with the word Order in their name.

b. Click the **Clear Search String** button to see all objects again.

c. Click the **Navigation Pane arrow**, click **Object Type**, click the **Navigation Pane** arrow again, and then select **All Access Objects**. This returns you to the default view, which is what will be used throughout this text.

Understanding File Extensions in Access

A **file extension** is the suffix on all file names that helps Windows determine what information is in a file and what program should open the file. However, Windows automatically hides these extensions, so they often go unnoticed. The file name in Figure 6 shows the file name and location followed by its extension ".accdb". Access 2016 uses the same file extension that was used in Access 2007, Access 2010, and Access 2013. This ".accdb" extension indicates that databases created in the four versions are compatible with one another. The file name at the top of the window in Figure 6 also shows that the file version is Access 2007-2016. Be careful not to confuse the DBMS with the database. The DBMS software you are using is Access 2016, but the database is in Access 2007-2016 format.

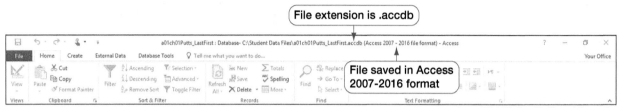

Figure 6   Title bar showing file extension and version

Access 2016, Windows 10, Microsoft Corporation

QUICK REFERENCE	Access File Extensions		
Extension	**Description**	**Version of Access**	**Compatibility**
accdb	Access database files	2007–2016	Cannot be opened in Access 2002–2003
accde	Access database files that are in "execute only" mode; Visual Basic for Applications (VBA) source code is hidden	2007–2016	Cannot be opened in Access 2002–2003
accdt	Access database templates	2007–2016	Cannot be opened in Access 2002–2003
mdb	Access 2002–2003 database files	2002–2003	Can be opened in Access 2007–2016. Access 2007–2016 can save files in this format
mde	Access database files that are in "execute only" mode; Visual Basic for Applications (VBA) source code is hidden	2002–2003	Can be opened in Access 2007–2016. Access 2007–2016 can save files in this format

Understand the Purpose of Tables

Tables store data organized in an arrangement of columns and rows. For illustration, think about the charity event, Putts for Paws. There are many ways participants and companies can participate in the event and help the charity. For example, a participant can play in the event, a company can pay for a foursome to play in the event, or the company can sponsor various items such as a cart, hole, or flag. Painted Paradise needs to keep a record of the available options and what corporations or participants have purchased, as shown in Table 1.

Item ID	Item Description	Quantity Available	Amount To Be Charged	Notes
G1	Golfer — one	100	$200.00	
TEAM	Golfers — team of four	10	$550.00	
CTEAM	Golfers — corporate team of four	10	$850.00	Includes hole sponsorship
CART	Cart sponsor	40	$2,000.00	Logo or brand displayed on cart
HOLE	Hole sponsor	18	$500.00	Logo or brand displayed on hole
FLAG	Flag sponsor	18	$500.00	Logo or brand displayed on flagstick

Table 1 Data in the tblItem table

As was mentioned previously, the power of a **relational database** comes in when you link tables. A relational database is a database in which data is stored in tables with relationships between the tables. The tblItem table shown in Table 1 contains information about items that a participant or corporation can buy to support the charity, including the items available, a description, the quantity available to be sold, the amount that will be charged for the item, and notes about the item. However, you cannot see who has ordered these items. That additional information becomes available when you use relationships to look at other tables.

Importing a Table

Recently, a colleague compiled a list of participants in the charity event in an Access table in another database. In this exercise, you will begin your work for Putts for Paws by importing this participant table from the Participant database into your database. **Importing** is the process of copying data from another file, such as a Word file or Excel workbook, into a separate file, such as an Access database.

A01.04

To Import a Table

a. Click the **External Data** tab, and then, in the Import & Link group, click **Access**. The Get External Data - Access Database dialog box is displayed.

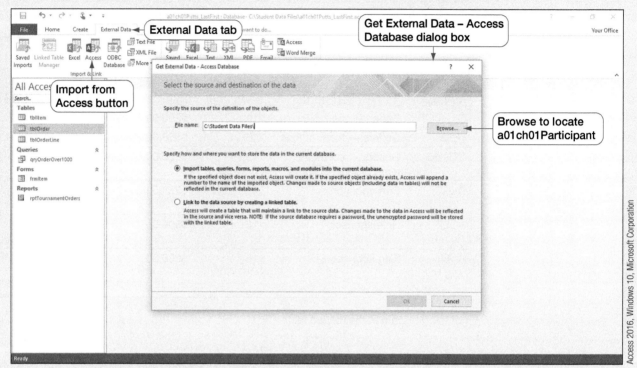

Figure 7 Get External Data - Access Database dialog box

b. Click **Browse**, navigate through the folder structure to the location of your student data files, double-click **a01ch01Participant**, and then click **OK**. Access opens the Import Objects dialog box.

Troubleshooting

If you do not see the Import Objects dialog box, you may have chosen Access from the Export group on the ribbon rather than from the Import & Link group.

---

c. If necessary, click the **Tables** tab. Click **tblParticipant**, and then click **OK**. Access displays the message "All objects were imported successfully."

d. Click **Close** at the bottom of the dialog box.

e. Double-click **tblParticipant** in the Navigation Pane.
   Access opens the table. You may not see exactly the same number of columns and rows in your table, because how much of the table is visible depends on how large your Access window is. You can change the size of the Access window by using your mouse to resize it or by clicking the Maximize button ☐ to maximize the Access window.

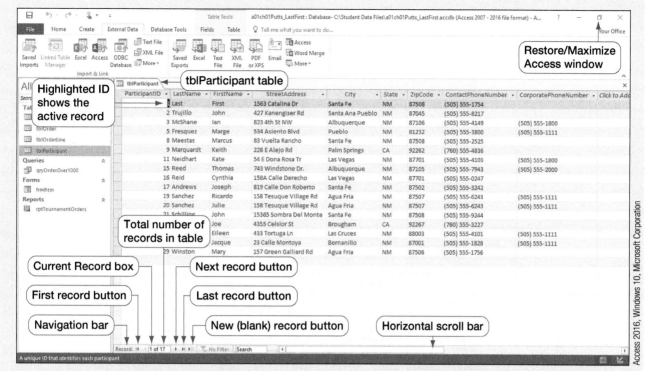

Figure 8 Imported tblParticipant table

REAL WORLD ADVICE | **What Should You Name Your Tables?**

If other people use the database and cannot find the right table, how useful is your database? Therefore, you want to use names that are easy to understand. While Access allows you to give any name you want to a table, the name "tblParticipant" follows a standard naming convention:

- Use a name that starts with "tbl". That allows you to distinguish tables from queries at a glance.

- Follow with a name that is descriptive. You want it to be easy to remember what is in the table.

- Make the name short enough that it is easy to see in the Navigation Pane.

- You can use spaces in table names (e.g., tbl Participant), but avid Access users avoid them because using spaces in table names makes advanced tasks more difficult.

- You can use special characters in names. Some people use underscores where a space would otherwise be, such as tbl_Participant.

Navigating Through a Table

Carefully examine the tblParticipant table. Each row of data contains information about the participant listed in the LastName field. There are 17 participant records in the table, the second record being John Trujillo. In this exercise, you will change the name in the record for the first participant to your name.

To Navigate Through a Table

a. If necessary, click the **First record** button ⏮.

b. Press Tab to move to the LastName field.

c. Replace **Last** in the first record of the LastName field with your last name.
   As you edit the record, notice the pencil icon 🖉 in the record selector. This indicates that you are in edit mode. The changes will not be saved until you exit the record. While in edit mode, you can press Esc to undo any changes.

d. Press Tab to move to the next field, and then replace **First** in the FirstName field with your first name. Press Enter.

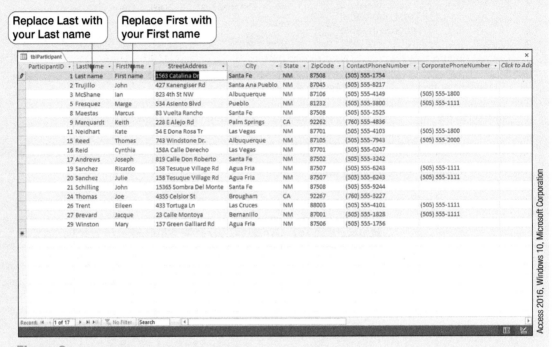

Figure 9   Record edited with your name

Navigating Through a Table with the Navigation Bar

At the bottom of the table, Access provides a **Navigation bar** that allows you to move through the table. You can move record by record, or skip to the end, or if you know a specific record number, you can jump to that record. The highlighted ID shows the active record. When you open the table, the first record is active. In this exercise, you will navigate through the table using the Navigation bar.

To Navigate Through a Table with the Navigation Bar

a. Click the **Next record** button ▶ to move to the second record. The Current Record box changes to show 2 of 17. Access highlights the street address of participant John Trujillo.

b. Click the **Next record** button ▶ again to move to the third participant. The Current Record box changes to show 3 of 17.

c. Click the **First record** button ◀ to return to the first participant.

d. Click the **New (blank) record button** ▶* to go to the first blank row. Alternatively, you could click in the ParticipantID field of the first blank row.

The first blank row at the end of the table is the **append row**. This row allows you to enter new records to the table. Notice that Access displays an asterisk in the **record selector** box — the small box at the left of the record — to indicate that it is the append row. When you type data here, you create a new participant record. Whenever you add a participant, make sure you are in the append row so you are not changing the information for an existing participant. You will add a participant to this empty row.

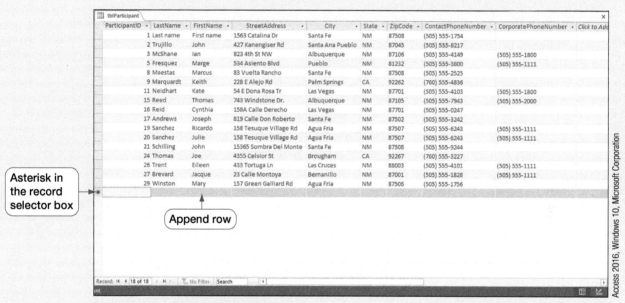

Asterisk in the record selector box

Append row

Figure 10 Append a new record

e. Make sure that the append row (blank row) is selected and that the record selector box contains an asterisk. In the ParticipantID field, type 30. Press Tab to move to the next field, and then, in the LastName field, type Fox.

Alternatively, you can press Enter after typing text in a field to move to the next field. Also, notice that when you start typing, the record indicator changed from an asterisk to a pencil 🖉. The pencil means that you are in edit mode. The record after Fox now becomes the new append row.

f. Press Enter, and then, in the FirstName column, type Jeff.

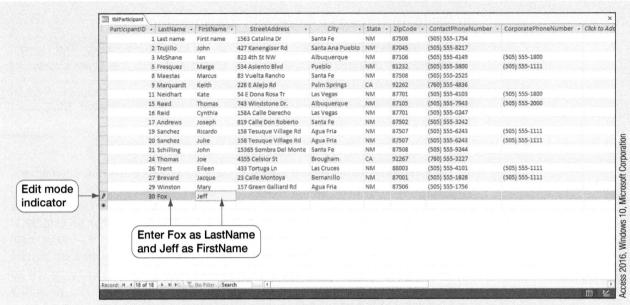

Edit mode indicator

Enter Fox as LastName and Jeff as FirstName

Figure 11 Enter participant Jeff Fox into the append row

SIDE NOTE

Format Symbols in the Phone Field

Notice that as you typed the ContactPhoneNumber into the field the formatting symbols were there to guide you. This is known as an Input Mask and is covered in a later chapter.

g. Continue entering the data for Jeff Fox, using the following information.

StreetAddress	1509 Las Cruces Drive
City	Las Cruces
State	NM
ZipCode	88003
ContactPhoneNumber	5055558786
CorporatePhoneNumber	(leave blank)

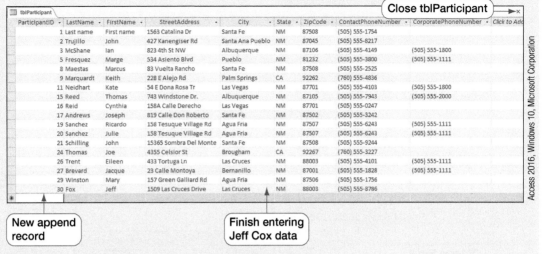

New append record

Finish entering Jeff Cox data

Figure 12 Finish entering the record for Jeff Fox

h. Click **Close** ☒ to close the tblParticipant table. Keep Access and the database open.

Notice that Access did not ask you whether you want to save the table. Access is not like Word or the other Office applications in which you must choose an option to save the file. Access automatically saves the data you enter as you type it.

Understanding Differences Between Access and Excel

An Access table looks similar to an Excel worksheet. Both have numbered rows of data and columns with labels. In addition, both applications allow you to manage data, perform calculations, and report on the data. The major difference between them is that Access allows multiple tables with relationships between the tables, thus the term "relational database." For example, if you are keeping track of participants and the items they order, you create a table of participants and another table of orders. Excel 2016 has some of these features, so it now blurs the distinction between spreadsheets and relational databases.

When you look at Access, you notice that several tables are used for an order. Why use multiple tables for a single order? Figure 13 shows how an order would look in Access and in Excel. The Excel version has to repeat the participant's information on multiple lines. This leads to the following problems.

- **Data redundancy** — With repetition, you create redundant information. John Trujillo bought a cart and a team, so in Excel, you have two rows. You would have to repeat the address information on both records. It is not efficient to enter the address information twice.

- **Errors** — Redundant information leads to errors. If the address needs to be changed, you have to look for all records with that information to make sure it is fixed everywhere.

- **Loss of data** — Suppose that John Trujillo orders just one item. If you deleted the ordered item, it would mean deleting all the information about him as well as the order.

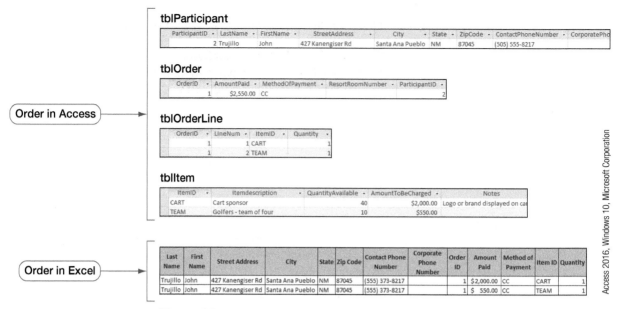

Order in Access

tblParticipant

ParticipantID	LastName	FirstName	StreetAddress	City	State	ZipCode	ContactPhoneNumber	CorporatePho
2	Trujillo	John	427 Kanengiser Rd	Santa Ana Pueblo	NM	87045	(505) 555-8217	

tblOrder

OrderID	AmountPaid	MethodOfPayment	ResortRoomNumber	ParticipantID
1	$2,550.00	CC		2

tblOrderLine

OrderID	LineNum	ItemID	Quantity
1	1	CART	1
1	2	TEAM	1

tblItem

ItemID	Itemdescription	QuantityAvailable	AmountToBeCharged	Notes
CART	Cart sponsor	40	$2,000.00	Logo or brand displayed on car
TEAM	Golfers - team of four	10	$550.00	

Order in Excel

Last Name	First Name	Street Address	City	State	Zip Code	Contact Phone Number	Corporate Phone Number	Order ID	Amount Paid	Method of Payment	Item ID	Quantity
Trujillo	John	427 Kanengiser Rd	Santa Ana Pueblo	NM	87045	(555) 373-8217		1	$2,000.00	CC	CART	1
Trujillo	John	427 Kanengiser Rd	Santa Ana Pueblo	NM	87045	(555) 373-8217		1	$ 550.00	CC	TEAM	1

Figure 13 John Trujillos's order in Access and in Excel

Because Access and Excel have so many common functionalities, many people use the tool that they are more confident using. If you prefer to use both, however, you can easily switch by exporting your data from Access to Excel or from Excel into Access. You can also use one tool for most uses and import your data into the other when you need to.

REAL WORLD ADVICE	**When Do You Use Access Instead of Excel?**

Generally, Access is designed to store data, and Excel is designed to analyze data and model situations. Fortunately, you can easily store data in Access and export a query to Excel for analysis.

Use Access for the following:

- You need to store data in multiple tables.
- You have a very large amount of data, perhaps thousands of records.
- You have large amounts of nonnumeric data.
- You want to run many different queries and reports from your data.

Use Excel for the following:

- Your data fits well into one table.
- You primarily want to do calculations, summaries, or comparisons of your data.

Manually Navigate a Database

Before exploring a database using Access queries, it will prove useful to explore the database manually. This will provide an understanding of what Access can do. Additionally, before developing queries and reports, one should examine the tables and fields so that he or she understands the database.

Using a Manual Query to Explore a Database

Patti Rochelle, the events coordinator at Painted Paradise, wants to send follow-up letters to the participants who have booked a corporate team for the Putts for Paws charity event. She asks you which participants have booked a team. In this exercise, you will first need to discover how a team is indicated in the database. Teams are items that participants can order, so you will start in the tblItem table.

To Use a Manual Query to Discover a Database

a. In the Navigation Pane, double-click **tblItem**.

Access opens tblItem in Datasheet view. Explore the data, and you will notice that a corporate team is indicated as CTEAM.

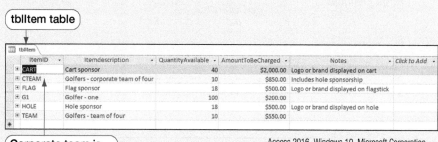

Figure 14 tblItem table

b. Close ✕ the tblItem table.

Next you need to determine which orders include CTEAM. Orders are composed of data from tblOrderLine and tblOrder.

c. Double-click **tblOrderLine** to open the table.

Scan for orders that include CTEAM. There are two: OrderID 4 and OrderID 11.

d. Close ✕ the tblOrderLine table.

e. Double-click **tblOrder** to open the table, and then find OrderID 4 and 11.

You need to find which participants placed these orders. Access uses common fields to relate tables. tblParticipant and tblOrder have ParticipantID in common. You find that the ParticipantID for OrderID 4 is 5 and the ParticipantID for OrderID 11 is 19.

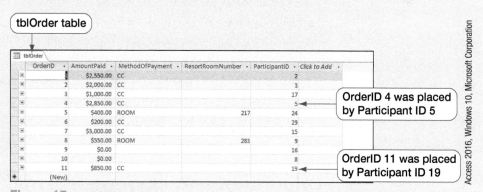

Figure 15 tblOrder table

f. Close ✕ the tblOrder table.

g. Double-click **tblParticipant** to open the table.

Scan for the participants that match the two ParticipantIDs you identified earlier, 5 and 19. You find that OrderID 4 was placed by ParticipantID 5, Marge Fresquez. OrderID 11 was placed by ParticipantID 19, Ricardo Sanchez.

tblParticipant table

ParticipantID 5 is Marge Fresquez

ParticipantID 19 is Ricardo Sanchez

ParticipantID	LastName	FirstName	StreetAddress	City	State	ZipCode	ContactPhoneNumber	CorporatePhoneNumber	Click to Add
1	Last name	First name	1563 Catalina Dr	Santa Fe	NM	87508	(505) 555-1754		
2	Trujillo	John	427 Kanengiser Rd	Santa Ana Pueblo	NM	87045	(505) 555-8217		
3	McShane	Ian	823 4th St NW	Albuquerque	NM	87106	(505) 555-4149	(505) 555-1800	
5	Fresquez	Marge	534 Asiento Blvd	Pueblo	NM	81232	(505) 555-3800	(505) 555-1111	
8	Maestas	Marcus	83 Vuelta Rancho	Santa Fe	NM	87508	(505) 555-2525		
9	Marquardt	Keith	228 E Alejo Rd	Palm Springs	CA	92262	(760) 555-4836		
11	Neidhart	Kate	54 E Dona Rosa Tr	Las Vegas	NM	87701	(505) 555-4103	(505) 555-1800	
15	Reed	Thomas	743 Windstone Dr.	Albuquerque	NM	87105	(505) 555-7943	(505) 555-2000	
16	Reid	Cynthia	158A Calle Derecho	Las Vegas	NM	87701	(505) 555-0247		
17	Andrews	Joseph	819 Calle Don Roberto	Santa Fe	NM	87502	(505) 555-3242		
19	Sanchez	Ricardo	158 Tesuque Village Rd	Agua Fria	NM	87507	(505) 555-6243	(505) 555-1111	
20	Sanchez	Julie	158 Tesuque Village Rd	Agua Fria	NM	87507	(505) 555-6243	(505) 555-1111	
21	Schilling	John	15365 Sombra Del Monte	Santa Fe	NM	87508	(505) 555-9244		
24	Thomas	Joe	4355 Celsior St	Brougham	CA	92267	(760) 555-3227		
26	Trent	Eileen	433 Tortuga Ln	Las Cruces	NM	88003	(505) 555-4101	(505) 555-1111	
27	Brevard	Jacque	23 Calle Montoya	Bernanillo	NM	87001	(505) 555-1828	(505) 555-1111	
29	Winston	Mary	157 Green Galliard Rd	Agua Fria	NM	87506	(505) 555-1756		
30	Fox	Jeff	1509 Las Cruces Drive	Las Cruces	NM	88003	(505) 555-8786		

Access 2016, Windows 10, Microsoft Corporation

Figure 16 tblParticipant table

h. **Close** ☒ the tblParticipant table. If you need to take a break before finishing this chapter, now is a good time to take a break.

You now can tell Patti which participants have booked corporate teams and the addresses to which the follow-up letters should be sent. However, it may seem like that was a lot of work to find out who booked the corporate teams. Access queries make this task easier. It is important to know what data is in your database. While Access will do the hard part of matching tables on common fields and finding the results, you still need to tell it what fields you want and where the fields are located.

REAL WORLD ADVICE | **Closing Tables**

While Access allows you to leave several tables open at the same time, it is a good idea to get into the habit of closing a table when you are done with it.

- First, there are many Access functions that use a table that cannot be completed while the table is open. If you close the table, you no longer risk running into this problem.

- Second, closing tables makes it less likely that you will accidentally change the wrong table.

- Third, each open table requires more memory for Access. With larger tables, Access could be slowed down by having multiple tables open.

Understanding Queries, Forms, and Reports

You have explored tables, the first of the four main object types in Access. As was mentioned previously, the other three object types are queries, forms, and reports. Each object provides a different way to work with data stored in tables. A query is used to ask questions about your data. A form is primarily used to enter data into your database or display data in your database. Reports are used to provide professional-looking displays of your tables that are suitable for printing. In this section, you will work with queries, forms, and reports within your database.

Understand the Purpose of Queries

A query is a way to ask questions about the data. For example, with the Putts for Paws Charity database, queries can be used to get answers to questions like the one asked in the manual query exercise or other questions, such as "What has John Trujillo ordered?", "What orders are over $1,000?", and "Which charity participants are from Santa Fe?" More complex queries can also be created, such as calculating a score given a player's strokes and handicap.

One of the strengths of Access is the ability to ask such questions and get answers quickly. In the previous exercise, you traced who ordered corporate teams. That was difficult because you had to keep track of fields such as ParticipantID in one table and then look them up in another table. If you use queries, Access can match common fields in the tables and trace the order for you.

You will look at two different views of queries in this chapter.

- Datasheet view shows the results of your query.
- Design view shows how the query is constructed. It shows the tables, fields, and selection criterion for the query.

Using the Query Wizard

Access provides wizards to help you with tasks. A **wizard** is a step-by-step guide that walks you through tasks by asking you questions to help you decide what you want to do. Once you have some experience, you can also do the task yourself without a guide.

You would like to know which participants are from Santa Fe, New Mexico. In this exercise, you will use the Query Wizard to create the query getting all participants, and then you will modify the query design to select those from Santa Fe.

REAL WORLD ADVICE | **Using Wizards in Access**

Wizards can sometimes save you time. Access wizards are shortcuts to building objects such as queries, reports, and forms. They select fields, format the data, and perform calculations. After the wizard does the initial formatting, you can always modify the resulting query, report, or form to get exactly what you want.

However, anything that can be done with a wizard could also be done without a wizard. A wizard may limit your choices. On the other hand, starting in Design view requires you to make choices without guidance. Whether you start with a wizard or with Design view is usually personal choice. As you become more comfortable with Access, pick the method you prefer. The results will be the same.

A01.08

To Use the Query Wizard

a. If you took a break, open the **a01ch01Putts** database. Click the **Create** tab, and then, in the Queries group, click **Query Wizard**.

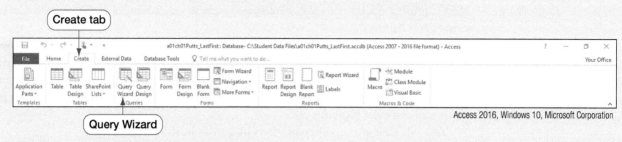

Create tab

Query Wizard

Access 2016, Windows 10, Microsoft Corporation

Figure 17 Create tab on the ribbon

Access displays the New Query dialog box and asks you what kind of query you want to create.

> ## Troubleshooting
>
> If this is the first time that you have used an Access wizard, Access will need to set up the wizards. You will get the message "Setting up wizard" and will need to wait while the wizards are installed.

b. If necessary, click **Simple Query Wizard**, and then click **OK**.

Access asks you which fields you want to include in the query. You have choices of tables or queries as the source for your fields. Your database has four tables to select as a source. You will choose only one table. You could choose fields from multiple tables, but that is not necessary in this query.

c. Click the **Tables/Queries** arrow to see available field sources, and then select **Table: tblParticipant** as the source of your fields.

The dialog box has two lists. The box on the left shows you all available fields from the selected table or query. The box on the right shows you all the fields that you have selected for this query. You use the buttons between the two lists to move fields from one box to the other. By selecting a field and clicking the One Field button ▶ , you move that field from the Available Fields box to the Selected Fields box. Clicking the All Fields button ▶▶ moves all fields.

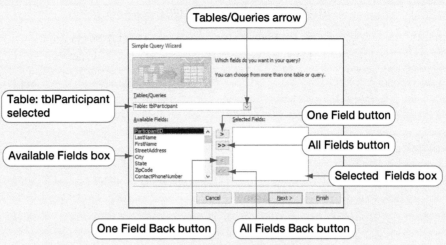

Figure 18 Select tblParticipant

SIDE NOTE

Selecting Fields

Alternatively, you can double-click the field name to move it from the Available Fields box to the Selected Fields box.

d. Under Available Fields, click **LastName**, and then click the **One Field** button $\boxed{>}$. Access moves the LastName field to the Selected Fields box.

e. If necessary, click **FirstName**, and then click the **One Field** button $\boxed{>}$.

f. Click **City**, and then click the **One Field** button $\boxed{>}$.
   Your field list in the Selected Fields box should display fields in the following order: LastName, FirstName, and City.

Troubleshooting

If you accidentally add the wrong field to the Selected Fields box, select the field and use the One Field Back button $\boxed{<}$ to place it back in the Available Fields box.

If you select the fields in the wrong order, Access does not have a way to reorder the fields. It is best to place them all back in the Available Fields box using the All Fields Back button $\boxed{<<}$ and then select them again in the correct order.

---

g. Click **Next** to continue to the next page of the wizard. In the **What title do you want for your query?** box, type qryParticipantSantaFe.

h. Click **Finish**.
   Access shows you the results of your query. Once you have created this query, the query name is displayed under All Access objects in the Navigation Pane.

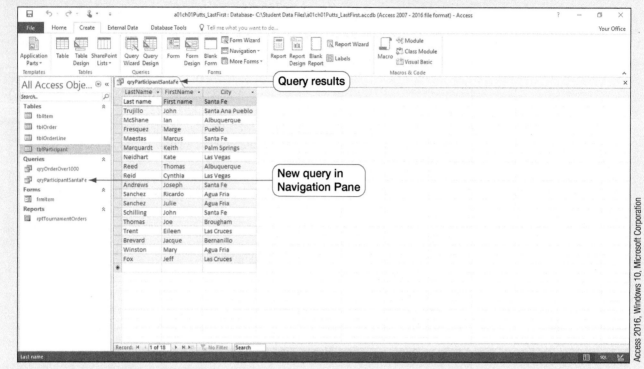

Figure 19   Results of query

i.   **Close** ☒ the query.

Switching to the Design View of a Query

The Query Wizard uses a question-and-answer dialog box to create a query. The other method of creating a query is to use Design view. Design view goes behind the scenes of the data and shows you the detailed structure of an Access object. In this exercise, you will switch to Design view of a query.

A01.09

To Switch to Design View to Modify a Query

a. Right-click **qryParticipantSantaFe** in the Navigation Pane.

b. Select **Design View** from the shortcut menu.

Access opens the Design view of your query. The Design tab is open on the ribbon. The left side of the screen shows the Navigation Pane. The top half of the screen shows the **query workspace**, which is the source for data in the query. In this case, the source is the table tblParticipant. The bottom half is called the **query design grid**. It shows which fields are selected in this query: LastName, FirstName, and City.

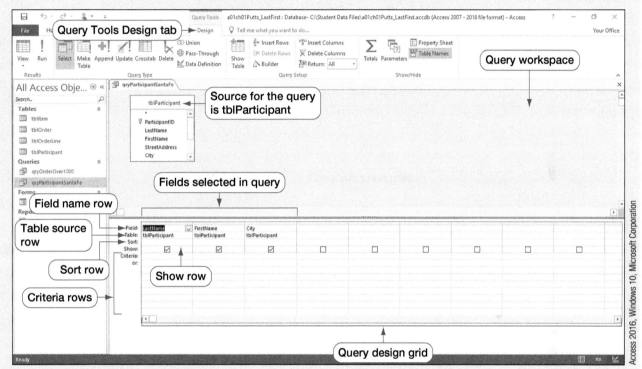

Figure 20 Design view of qryParticipantSantaFe

Specifying Selection Criteria

Each row in the design grid shows information about the field. The top row is Field name. The next row shows the table or source for this field. The Sort row allows you to specify the order of records shown in your query results by setting one or more sort fields. The Show row is a check box that specifies whether the field is shown in the table of query results. The Criteria rows allow you to select certain records by setting conditions for the field contents. In this exercise, you are going to change the query to see which participants are from Santa Fe. You will do that by adding a selection criterion.

A01.10

To Specify Selection Criteria

a. In the Query Design Grid, click the **Criteria** cell in the City column.

b. Type Santa Fe, and then press Enter.

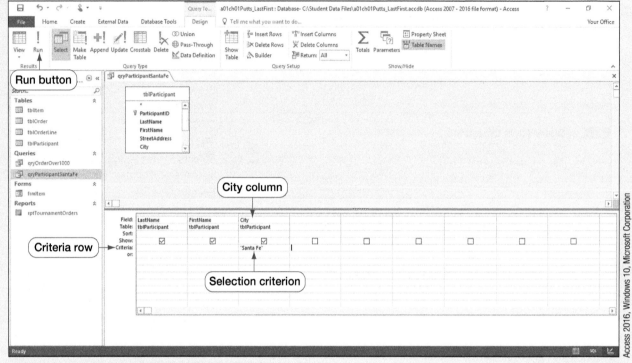

Figure 21 Selection criterion added to City field

SIDE NOTE

Query Criteria
Because "City" is a text field, the criterion is treated as text, and Access adds quotation marks. You can also type the quotation marks.

c. On the Design tab, in the Results group, click **Run**.

Access returns the query results as shown in Figure 22. When you run a query, you should check the results to make sure they make sense. You wanted the participants with a city of Santa Fe, and the participants shown are only from Santa Fe.

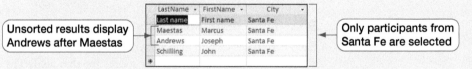

Figure 22 Query results showing participants from Santa Fe

Troubleshooting

If your query results are not what you expect (compare to Figure 22), you made an error in entering your selection criterion. Click the View button on the Home tab to switch back to Design view. Compare your criterion with Figure 21. Make sure that you spelled "Santa Fe" correctly and that it is in the City column.

When you typed Santa Fe as the criterion, you asked Access to select the participants who had a city equal to "Santa Fe". The equals sign is implied, though you can enter it if you wish. Other operators that can be entered in the selection criteria are as follows.

Operator	Meaning	Description
=	Equal to	Selects the records in which the field value is equal to the value provided. If no operator is used, equal to is assumed.
<	Less than	Selects the records in which the field value is less than the value provided.
>	Greater than	Selects the records in which the field value is greater than the value provided.
< =	Less than or equal to	Selects the records in which the field value is less than or equal to the value provided.
> =	Greater than or equal to	Selects the records in which the field value is greater than or equal to the value provided.
< >	Not equal	Selects the records in which the field value is not equal to the value provided.
Between	Between	Selects the records in which the field values listed are within the two values. For example, between 1 and 7 is true for any value between 1 and 7; this includes the value of 1 and the value of 7.

Sorting Query Results

When Access runs a query, it puts the results in a default order based on how the table is defined. As Figure 22 illustrates, having the participants sorted by ID does not make much sense. If no sorting sequence is specified, Access will sort the results of the query by the primary key. In addition, if the query result shows many records, it will be difficult to find a specific record with the default sorting. Usually, you will want to change the sort order so that the order of the results makes sense. In this exercise, you will sort the participants in alphabetical order.

A01.11

To Sort Query Results

a. On the Home tab, in the Views group, click the **View** arrow, and then select **Design View**.

b. Click the **Sort cell** in the LastName column, click the **Selection** arrow ⌄, and then select **Ascending**.

c. Click the **Sort cell** in the FirstName column, click the **Selection** arrow ⌄, and then select **Ascending**.

   Although sorting in Datasheet view is possible, it is best practice always to sort a query in Design view. This allows for sorting by multiple rows with ease, and the sorting sequence becomes part of the underlying query code, which means it can be exported into other applications.

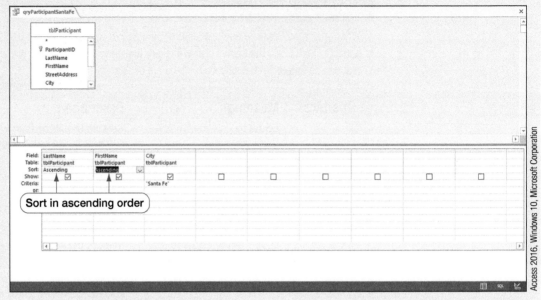

Figure 23 Sorting results of a query

d. On the Design tab, in the Results group, click **Run**.

Access puts the participants in alphabetical order by last name. If there were two participants with the same last name, they would be sorted alphabetically by first name.

Printing Query Results

If you want to print your query results, you can do this on the File tab. Printing tables is done the same way. In this exercise, you will print the results of the qryParticipantSantaFe query.

 A01.12

To Print Query Results

a. Click the **File** tab to display Backstage view.

b. Click **Print**, and then click **Print Preview** to see what the results would look like if printed.

c. If your instructor asks you to print your results, on the Print Preview tab, click **Print**. In the Print dialog box, select the correct printer, and then click **OK**.

d. On the Print Preview tab, click **Close Print Preview**.

e. Click **Save** 🔲.

f. **Close** ☒ the qryParticipantSantaFe query.

> ### Troubleshooting
> If you accidentally closed Access instead of just the query, open Access the same way you did at the beginning of the chapter. In the Recent databases, click the name a01ch01Putts_LastFirst to open the database again.

REAL WORLD ADVICE | Do You Need to Print?

Before you decide to print the results of a query, you may want to consider whether you really need a printed version. If you want to share the results with someone else, often you can share them via e-mail. Access provides an export-to-PDF feature for a query or table that allows you to save the results in PDF format. Right-click the object in the Navigation Pane, point to Export, and then select PDF or XPS. You can then publish your object as a PDF file, which you can e-mail to someone. Alternatively, you can use the External Data tab to export to a PDF format

Understand the Purpose of Forms

A form provides another interface to a table or query beyond the table in Datasheet view. In corporate databases, end users of a database computer system often use forms to enter and change data. You can also use forms to limit the amount of data you see from a table. In a personal database, you can create forms for entering data if you wish.

Forms have three views.

- **Form view** shows the data in the form. This is the view you use to enter or change data. You cannot change the form design in this view.

- **Layout view** shows the form and the data. Some of the form design, such as field lengths and fonts, can be changed in this view. The data cannot be changed.

- Design view shows the form design but not the data. Any aspect of the form design can be changed. The data cannot be changed.

REAL WORLD ADVICE | Layout View Versus Design View

Both Layout view and Design view allow you to change the design of forms. Which view is best for changing design? Part of this is personal preference, but some features can be changed only in Design view. Following are some considerations.

- Layout view shows both the form and the data. When you are changing column widths or field lengths, it is often easier if you see both. You can adjust the sizes while seeing the data and make sure you pick a size that is appropriate.

- Many features can be changed only in Design view. How do you remember which ones? If you prefer Layout view, try it in that view first, and switch to Design view whenever you have trouble changing something.

Creating a Form

There are different types of forms that can be created. The default form shows one record at a time and has each field clearly labeled. In this exercise, you will create a form to make it easier to enter new participants and edit the records of existing participants.

To Create a Form

a. Click **tblParticipant** in the Navigation Pane. Click the **Create** tab, and then, in the Forms group, click **Form**.

b. Click **Save** 🖫 to save the form. In the Save As dialog box, type frmParticipant, and then click **OK**.

   Access creates a form. Notice that the form displays the same Navigation bar that you had in the table. That is because a form is a data entry or display tool for the table. You can use it to navigate through your table. The form is created in Layout view, which allows you make minor changes to the design. You cannot enter data when the form is in Layout view.

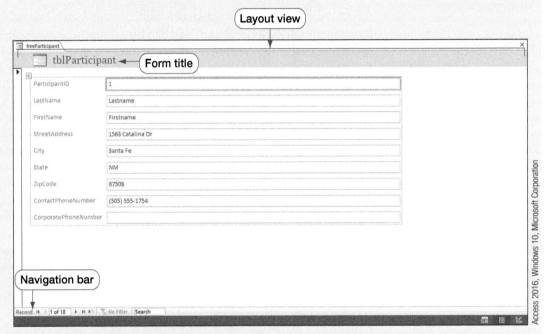

Figure 24 frmParticipant form in Layout View

c. Click the **title** of the form, and then click again to select the **text**. Replace the current title with Participant Form, and then press Enter.

d. **Save** the form.

Entering Data Using a Form

Jackie Silva has asked to register for the tournament. When you are adding a new record, it is very important that you navigate to the append row so you enter the information into a blank record instead of overriding an existing record. In this exercise, you will use your newly created form to add a new record to the participant table.

A01.14

To Enter Data Using a Form

a. On the Design tab, in the Views group, click the **View** arrow, and then click **Form View**. This view allows you to use the form to enter data into the table. Form view opens to existing records, so you must be careful that you do not override any existing data.

b. Click the **New (blank) record button** 🔘 on the Navigation bar. If you see a participant's name in the form, try again. This will be record 19 of 19 in the Navigation bar.

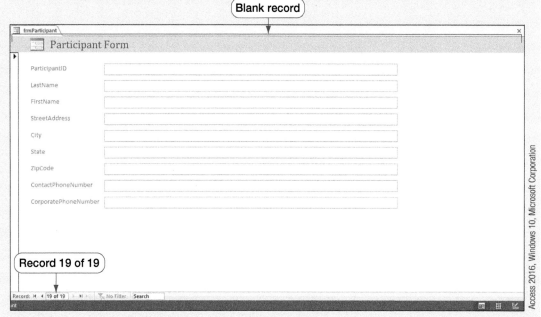

Figure 25 Blank append record

c. Type the following information into the form. Press Enter or Tab to move to each field.

ParticipantID	31
LastName	Silva
FirstName	Jackie
StreetAddress	1509 Main Street
City	Santa Ana Pueblo
State	NM
ZipCode	87044
ContactPhoneNumber	5055553355
CorporatePhoneNumber	(leave blank)

d. **Close** ☒ the form. The participant data you entered in the form is saved to the table.

e.   On the Navigation Pane, under Tables, double-click **tblParticipant**.

f.   Click the **Last Record button** ⏭ on the Navigation bar. Verify that Jackie Silva has been added to your table.

g.   **Close** ⊠ the table.

S S CONSIDER THIS | **Adding Data Directly into a Table Versus Adding Data into a Form**

You have added two participants to your table. Earlier, you added a row to the table and added Jeff Fox. Now you have added Jackie Silva via a form. Which was easier for you? Why would most companies use forms to enter data?

Understand the Purpose of Reports

A report provides an easy-to-read format suitable for printing. A sample report is shown in Figure 26. You can easily provide column totals as needed. When printing data for management presentations, you usually use a report rather than a query. The source of the data for a report can be a table or a query.

Reports have four views.

- **Report view** shows how the report would look in a continuous page layout.
- **Print Preview** shows how the report would look on the printed page. This view allows you to change the page layout.
- Layout view shows the report and the data. Some parts of the report design, such as field lengths and fonts, can be changed in this view.
- Design view shows the report design but not the data. Any aspect of the report design can be changed.

rptParticipantsByCity			
Tournament Participants By City			
City	LastName	FirstName	ContactPhoneNumber
Agua Fria			
	Sanchez	Julie	(505) 555-6243
	Sanchez	Ricardo	(505) 555-6243
	Winston	Mary	(505) 555-1756
Albuquerque			
	McShane	Ian	(505) 555-4149
	Reed	Thomas	(505) 555-7943
Bernanillo			
	Brevard	Jacque	(505) 555-1828
Brougham			
	Thomas	Joe	(760) 555-3227
Las Cruces			
	Fox	Jeff	(505) 555-8786
	Trent	Eileen	(505) 555-4101
Las Vegas			
	Neidhart	Kate	(505) 555-4103
	Reid	Cynthia	(505) 555-0247
Palm Springs			
	Marquardt	Keith	(760) 555-4836
Pueblo			
	Fresquez	Marge	(505) 555-3800

Figure 26   An Access report

Creating a Report Using a Wizard

The report feature in Access allows you to easily design reports that can serve management purposes and look professional. The Report Wizard starts similarly to the Query Wizard in selecting fields for the report. After that, the wizard asks questions about report formatting that were not part of the Query Wizard.

In this exercise, you will create a report listing the participants entered in the tournament with their contact phone numbers. You will group all participants in a city into a single group, alphabetized in ascending order by their names.

 A01.15

To Create a Report Using a Wizard

a. Click the **Create** tab, and then, in the Reports group, click **Report Wizard**. Click the **Tables/Queries** arrow, and then click **Table: tblParticipant**.

SIDE NOTE
Adding Fields
Alternatively, you can double-click each field name that you want to add to the query.

b. Using the One Field button [**>**], move these fields to the Selected Fields box: **LastName**, **FirstName**, **City**, and **ContactPhoneNumber**.

c. Click **Next**. The wizard asks whether you want to add grouping levels.

d. Click **City**, and then click the **One Field button** [**>**] to group by city. When you make this selection, the box on the right of the dialog box shows a preview of what the report grouping will look like.

Figure 27   Add grouping levels

e. Click **Next**.
The wizard asks what sort order you want. You always want to put your report in some order that makes it easy to read and understand. Otherwise, a report with a lot of information is difficult to understand. In this report, you will list participants alphabetically.

f. In the 1 box, click the **Selection arrow** [⌄], and then select **LastName**. If necessary, make sure that the sort order is **Ascending**, meaning in alphabetical order from A to Z.

g. In the 2 box, click the **Selection arrow** [⌄], and then select **FirstName**.

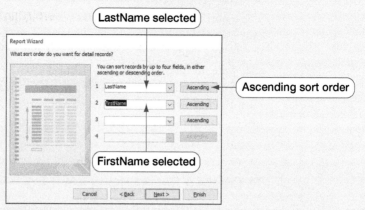

Figure 28   Add sorting

SIDE NOTE
Previewing Reports
Print Preview is the only view that allows you to see page headers and footers and is therefore the best place to check how your report will look when printed or converted to a PDF.

h. Click **Next**. Make sure the default **Stepped** layout and **Portrait** orientation are selected.

i. Click **Next**. In the **What title do you want for your report?** box, type rptParticipantsByCity.

j. Click **Finish**.
   Access displays the report in Print Preview. You notice that the ContactPhoneNumber heading is not fully shown. You can fix that easily in Layout view.

Figure 29   Report in Print Preview

k. Right-click anywhere on the report, and then click **Layout View** from the shortcut menu. Click the heading of the **ContactPhoneNumber** column.

Troubleshooting

If either the Field List Pane or the Property Sheet shows on the right side of the field, click ⊠ to close it.

---

l. Point to the **left border** of the selected heading (ContactPhoneNumber) until the Horizontal Resize pointer is displayed ↔.

m. Drag to the left until you can see the entire column heading.

n. Double-click the **title** of the report, and then change the report title to Tournament Participants By City. Your report should look like Figure 26.

o. **Save** ⊟ the report.
   Notice that the City data is a line above the data in the other columns. That is because the participants are grouped by city. Within a city, participants are sorted alphabetically.

CONSIDER THIS | **Grouping Versus Sorting**

Grouping arranges records together by the value of a single field. Sorting puts the records within a group in a specific order based on field values. When would you choose to sort your records, and when would you group before sorting?

Printing a Report

Reports can be printed in the same way as queries, using the File tab. You can also take advantage of Print Preview to print a report. In this exercise, you will switch from Layout View to Print Preview to see how the report will be printed.

A01.16

To Print a Report

a. Click **Print Preview** on the Status Bar to change to Print Preview. Alternatively, you could change to Print Preview using the View button on the ribbon, as you have done before. If necessary, widen the Report Title so that the entire title is visible.

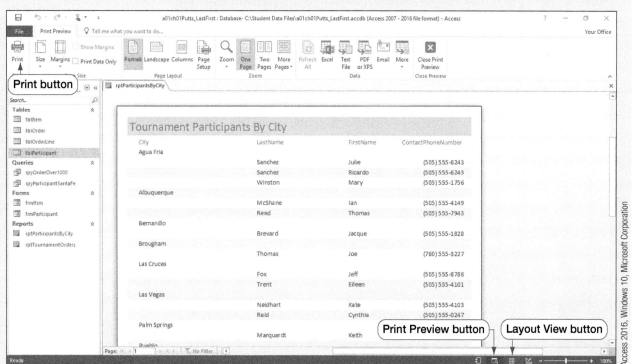

Figure 30 Switch views using the status bar

b. If your instructor directs you to print the report, in the Print group, click **Print**, and then click **OK**.

c. In the Close Preview group, click **Close Print Preview**, and then **close** ☒ the report.

REAL WORLD ADVICE | **When Do You Use a Report Versus a Query?**

Both reports and queries can be used to view data. A report provides a more formal presentation of data and is designed for printing. A query has more selection capabilities, but the formatting is not as attractive. You can combine the two capabilities by first creating the query object and then creating a report using the query as your source.

Back Up a Database

A **backup database** is an extra copy of your database that you can use to protect yourself from the accidental loss of data. You can return to the backup copy if you accidentally delete the real database. The backup copy may not be as current, but it may save you from having to recreate the whole database. If you store the backup on another storage medium, it can also help in cases of hardware failure such as a hard drive crash.

Backing Up a Database

In Access, you make backups by using the Back Up Database command, which is available on **Backstage view** under Save As. If you make multiple backup copies, you will want to give them different names. The backup feature appends the current date to the suggested file name. That allows you to easily distinguish between various versions of the backups, and you can be sure that you are getting the most recent one.

If you ever need a backup, simply return to the most recent copy that you have, and start working with that file. In this exercise, you will back up the a01ch01Putts database.

 A01.17

To Back Up a Database

a. Click the **File** tab, and then click **Save As**. Make sure that **Save Database As** is selected under File Types. Access displays Save Database As options in the right pane.

b. Under **Advanced**, click **Back Up Database**, and then click the **Save As** button. The Save As dialog box appears with a suggested file name that has the current date appended.

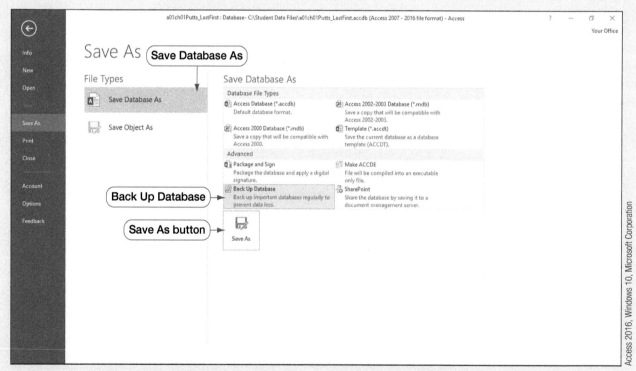

Figure 31 Making a backup copy of a database

c. Navigate to the drive and folder where you want to store your backup, and then click **Save**.

Compact and Repair a Database

As you work on an Access database, the size of the database file increases. When you delete a record or object or if you make changes to an object, Access does not reuse the original space. Access provides a compacting feature that makes more efficient use of disk space. **Compacting** rearranges objects to use disk space more efficiently, thus releasing the now unused space to be used again. If you do not compact your database, its size can get very large quickly. The compact option also looks for damaged data and tries to repair it.

Compacting Your Database

You have two options for compacting.

1. You can perform a single Compact and Repair Database action at any time.

2. You can select Compact on Close.

If you select Compact on Close, Access automatically compacts your database anytime you close it. Both options are available on Backstage view. In this exercise, you will compact and repair the a01ch01Putts database.

To Compact Your Database

a. Click the **File** tab.

b. Click **Compact & Repair Database**.

Access compacts your database, fixes it if necessary, and returns you to the Home tab. On a small database such as Putts for Paws, this action is very fast. On a larger database with many changes made, there may be a noticeable delay.

c. Click the **File** tab, and then click **Options**.

d. Click **Current Database** in the left pane, and then, under Application Options, click the **Compact on Close** check box.

By default, Compact on Close is turned off. Many professionals like to turn on Compact on Close so they do not need to remember to compact the database themselves.

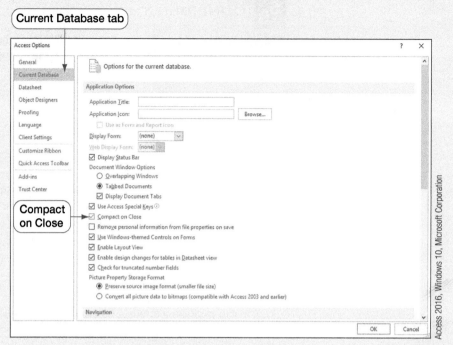

Figure 32 Select Compact on Close

e. Click **OK** to turn this option on. Access warns you that the option will not take effect until you close and reopen the database.

f. Click **OK** again.

g. Exit Access, and then submit your file as directed by your instructor.

Concept Check

1. What is Access? When would you use Access instead of Excel? p. 541, 555

2. What is the Navigation Pane? Where do you find it? p. 545

3. What is a record? What is a field? How are they represented in Access? p. 542, 543

4. How do you manually navigate a database? p. 556

5. How is a query used? What is the difference between Datasheet view and Design view of a query? p. 559

6. How is a form used? p. 567

7. How is a report used? What is Report Layout view? p. 570

8. What is a database backup, and how is it used? p. 574

9. What does it mean to compact and repair your database? What is the difference between a single compact and a compact on close? p. 575

Key Terms

Append row 553
Backstage view 574
Backup database 574
Compacting 575
Data 541
Database 541
Database management system
   (DBMS) 541
Datasheet view 542
Design view 542
Field 544

File extension 548
Form 542
Form view 567
Importing 549
Information 541
Layout view 567
Navigation bar 552
Navigation Pane 545
Object 542
Print Preview 570
Query 542

Query design grid 563
Query workspace 563
Record 542
Record selector 553
Relational database 549
Report 542
Report view 570
Table 542
Template 544
View 542
Wizard 559

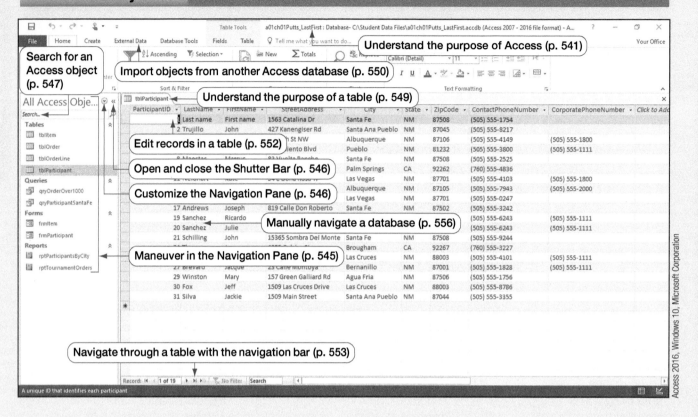

Figure 33

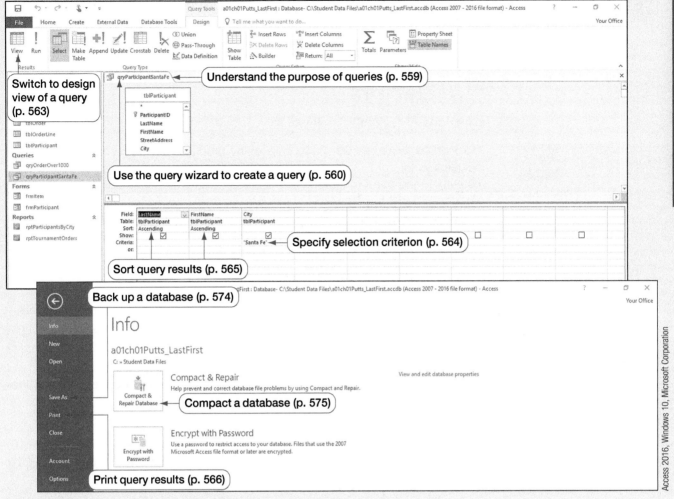

Switch to design view of a query (p. 563)

Understand the purpose of queries (p. 559)

Use the query wizard to create a query (p. 560)

Specify selection criterion (p. 564)

Sort query results (p. 565)

Back up a database (p. 574)

Compact a database (p. 575)

Print query results (p. 566)

Figure 34

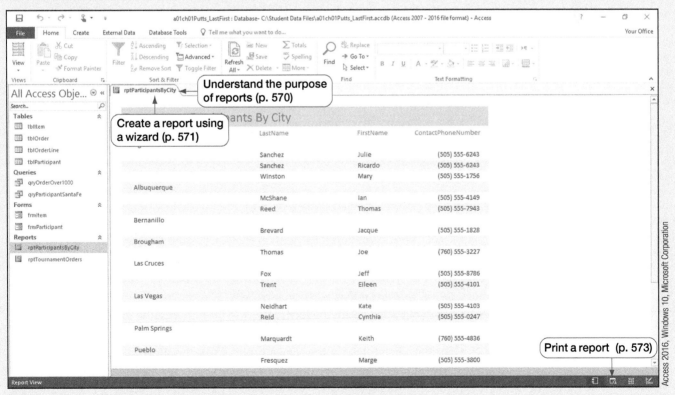

Understand the purpose of reports (p. 570)

Create a report using a wizard (p. 571)

Print a report (p. 573)

Figure 35

Practice 1

Student data files needed:

a01ch01Giftshop.accdb

a01ch01Products.accdb

You will save your file as:

a01ch01Giftshop_LastFirst.accdb

Painted Treasures Gift Shop

Production & Operations

The Painted Treasures Gift Shop sells many products for the resort patrons. These include jewelry from local artists, Painted Paradise linens, products from the resort's restaurant, and spa products. You will create a database that stores the gift shop's products. You will import a table of products from another Access database and create a query to select particular products. You will also create a form to enter new products and an inventory report.

a. Open the Access file, **a01ch01Giftshop**. Save your file as **a01ch01Giftshop_LastFirst**, using your last and first name. If necessary, enable the content.

b. Click the **External Data** tab, and then, in the Import & Link group, click **Access**.

c. In the Get External Data - Access Database dialog box, click **Browse**, navigate through the folder structure to the location of your student data files, double-click **a01ch01Products**, and then click **OK**.

d. In the Import Objects dialog box, select **tblProduct** on the Tables tab, and then click **OK**.

e. Click **Close**.

f. Create a query to find the clothing products.

- Click the **Create** tab, and then, in the Queries group, click **Query Wizard**. Be sure **Simple Query Wizard** is selected, and then click **OK**.

- Click the **Tables/Queries** arrow, and then click **Table: tblProduct** as the source of your fields.

- In this order, select the **ProductID**, **Category**, **ProductDescription**, **Color**, **Size**, and **Price** fields, and move them to the Selected Fields box. Click **Next**, make sure that **Detail (shows every field of every record)** is selected, and then click **Next**.

- Under **What title do you want for your query?**, type qryClothingTypes_iLast using your first initial and last name.

- Click **Finish**. Click the **Home** tab, and in the Results group, click the **View** arrow, and then click **Design View**.

- In the Category Criteria cell, type Clothing, and in the ProductDescription Sort cell, select **Ascending**, and then, in the Results group, click **Run**.

- Save and close the query.

g. Create a form to enter new products.

- Click **tblProduct** in the Navigation Pane. Click the **Create** tab, and then, in the Forms group, click **Form**.

- Click **Save**, and then, in the Save As dialog box, type **frmProduct_iLast** using your first initial and last name. Click **OK**.

- In Layout view, select the **form title**, and then change the text to **Products Form by iLast** using your first initial and last name. Save the form.

- On the Design tab, in the Views group, click the **View** button arrow, and then select **Form View**. Click **New (blank) record**, and then enter the following product in the blank append record.

ProductID	42
ProductDescription	Polo Shirt
Category	Clothing
QuantityInStock	35
Price	30.00
Size	L
Color	Blue

- Close the form.

h. Create an inventory report.

- Click the **Create** tab, and then, in the Reports group, click **Report Wizard**.
- Click the **Tables/Queries** arrow, and then click **Table: tblProduct**.
- Select the fields in the following order: **Category**, **ProductDescription**, **Color**, **Size**, and **QuantityInStock**, and then click **Next**.
- Under **Do you want to add any grouping levels?**, double-click **Category** and **ProductDescription**, and then click **Next**.
- In the 1 box, click the **arrow**, and then select **Color**. In the 2 box, click the **arrow**, select **Size**, and then click **Next**.
- Make sure the layout is set to **Stepped**, change the Orientation to **Landscape**, and then click **Next**.
- Type rptInventory_iLast, using your first initial and last name, as the title for your report, and then click **Finish**.
- Click **Close Print Preview.** On the Design tab, in the Views group, click the **View** arrow, and then click **Layout View**. Change the report title to Inventory Report by iLast using your first initial and last name.

i. Save the database, exit Access, and then submit your file as directed by your instructor.

Problem Solve 1

MyITLab®
Grader
Homework

Student data files needed:

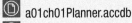 a01ch01Planner.accdb

a01ch01PlanItems.accdb

You will save your file as:

 a01ch01Planner_LastFirst.accdb

Rakes Event Management

Production & Operations

Beth Rakes runs an event-planning service. She is moving toward using Access to manage her business more effectively. In one database, she tracks clients, events, and menus that each client has booked. In another database, she has many decorations reserved for events. She has hired you to consolidate the databases and make some additional changes, which will improve the database's functionality.

a. Open the Access file, **a01ch01Planner**. Save your file as a01ch01Planner_LastFirst using your last and first name. If necessary, enable the content.

b. Import the **tblEventItems** table from the **a01ch01PlanItems** Access database, located with your student data files.

c. Import the **tblDecorations** table from the **a01ch01PlanItems** Access database, located with your student data files.

d. Open **tblClients**. In record **8**, change client **Colorado Rojas'** street address to 725 Second Avenue.

e. Create a form to enter decorations into the **tblDecorations** table, naming the form **frmDecorations**. Change the title of the form to Decorations.

f. Enter the following products as new records. Notice that you do not have to enter the DecorID or the Extended Price because Access automatically fills them in.

DecorID	DecorItem	Color	Category	Quantity	Price	Extended Price
Access automatically fills	Balloons	Red	Miscellaneous	12	1.99	Automatically calculated
Access automatically fills	Balloons	White	Miscellaneous	12	1.99	Automatically calculated

g. **Save** and **close** the form.

h. Create a query for Beth to use to retrieve information on all the different balloon decorations available for events. Use the Query Wizard to create a query listing **DecorID**, **DecorItem**, **Color**, **Quantity**, and **Price** from tblDecorations. Save your query as qryBalloonDecorations.

i. Switch to Design view, and type Balloons in the Criteria row for the DecorItem field. Run the query to observe the results. Save and close the query.

j. Create a query that will return the various types of buffet meals offered for events. Using the Query Wizard, create a query that selects **MenuType**, **CostPerPerson**, and **ServiceType** from tblMenuChoice. Save your query as qryBuffetMeals.

k. Switch to Design view, and type Buffet in the Criteria row for the ServiceType field. Sort the results by **CostPerPerson** in ascending order. Run the query to observe the results. Save and close the query.

l. Create a report showing **EventDate**, **EventName**, **StartTime**, **EndTime**, **Location**, and **TotalAttendees** from tblEvents. Do not add any grouping levels. Sort by **EventDate** and then **EventName** in ascending order. Change to **Landscape** orientation. Name your report rptEvents. In Layout view, change the report title to read Event Report.

m. Save the database, exit Access, and then submit your file as directed by your instructor.

Student data file needed:
 a01ch01Market.accdb

You will save your file as:
a01ch01Market_LastFirst.accdb

Farmer's Market

Production & Operations

You are the owner of a small herb business that cultivates various herbs to sell at the local farmer's market. All of the data from the sale of the herbs are stored in an Access database. You will create a form, a query, and a report to be able to make decisions from the data stored in the database.

a. Open the Access file, **a01ch01Market.accdb**. Save your file as a01ch01Market_LastFirst using your last and first name.

b. Create a form based on **tblHerb**, and name the form frmHerb_iLast using your first initial and last name. Note that since the tblHerb table has a relationship to another table, the form you create includes a subform that shows data related to orders in which the particular herb was sold.

c. Add a new record using **frmHerb_iLast**. Use the following information.

Field Name	Data
HerbID	130
HerbName	Sweet Basil
PotSize	8
Cost	6
Price	18
Light	Full Sun
Height	14"
Spacing	18"
Type	Annual
Uses	Makes Pesto
Other	Pinch flowers to keep the leaves from turning bitter.

d. Create a query based on the **tblHerb** table. Include the fields for **HerbID**, **HerbName**, **PotSize**, **Cost,** and **Price**. Name the query qryHerb_iLast using your first initial and last name. Select only the herbs that come in **8**-inch pots. Sort the results by the **Cost** field in ascending order.

e. Save and close the query.

f. Create a report based on **tblHerb**. Include the fields for **HerbID**, **HerbName**, **PotSize**, **Cost**, and **Price**.

g. Group the report by **PotSize**, and sort it in alphabetical order by **HerbName**. Save the report. Name the report rptHerb_iLast using your first initial and last name.

h. Save the database, exit Access, and then submit your file as directed by your instructor.

Additional Cases

Additional Chapter Cases are available at www.pearsonhighered.com/youroffice

Microsoft Access 2016

Production & Operations

OBJECTIVES

1. Understand database design   p. 585

2. Import data from other sources   p. 588

3. Enter data manually   p. 594

4. Create a table in Design view   p. 598

5. Understand masks and formatting   p. 602

6. Understand and designate keys   p. 606

7. Understand basic principles of normalization   p. 611

8. Understand relationships between tables   p. 613

9. Create a one-to-many relationship   p. 615

10. Create a many-to-many relationship   p. 618

11. Understand referential integrity   p. 623

Prepare Case

Red Bluff Golf Course Putts for Paws Charity Tournament Database

The Red Bluff Golf Course & Pro Shop is sponsoring a charity tournament, Putts for Paws, to raise money for the local pet shelter. You are modifying a database for the tournament that tracks money being raised from the event. The scope of this database is limited to tracking monies. Thus, in this instance, you are not tracking whether a participant is a golfer, volunteer, or other role. Anyone can donate money in the form of hole sponsorship or another donation item. You will want to track monies derived from corporate sponsorship. You will bring in data for the event from various sources, including Excel worksheets and text files.

Rayjunk/Shutterstock

Student data files needed for this chapter:

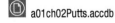 a01ch02Putts.accdb

 a01ch02PuttsGolf.xlsx

a01ch02PuttsCont.xlsx

 a01ch02PuttsVol.xlsx

 a01ch02PuttsDon.txt

You will save your file as:

a01ch02Putts_LastFirst.accdb

Inserting Data into a Database

To manage the golf tournament, the participants, the corporations that participate, the tee times, and the items each participant purchases have to be tracked. Each of these sets of data will be entered into a separate table in the database. In this chapter, you will load tables from already existing databases and from Excel worksheets in addition to creating two new tables.

Understand Database Design

Database design can be thought of as a three-step process:

1. Identify the entities — they become the tables.
2. Identify the attributes — they become the fields.
3. Specify the relationships between the tables.

An **entity** is a person, place, item, or event for which data is to be tracked. For the Putts for Paws tournament database, data on participants, including golfers, donors, and corporate representatives, need to be tracked. The participant data will be stored in a participant table. A single participant is an instance of the participant entity and will become a record in the participant table.

An **attribute** is information about an entity. For example, for each participant, the person's name and address would be considered attributes that will need to be tracked. Each of the attributes will become a field in the table.

A **relationship** is an association between tables based on common fields. The power of Access is easily seen when relationships are created between tables. For example, a relationship can be created between the participant table and the table that contains the orders that participants place.

Later in the chapter, you will look more closely at designing a database. While you explore the database tables and data, think about these general principles or steps to follow.

1. Brainstorm a list of all the types of data you will need.
2. Rearrange data items into groups that represent a single entity. These groups will become your tables.
3. If one item can have several attributes, such as a credit card number, expiration date, name on the card, and security code, then put it into one group that will later become a table of its own. In this example, it would be a group named "credit card".
4. Break each attribute into the smallest attributes; they will become the fields. Give each attribute a descriptive name. For example, split addresses into street, city, state, and ZIP Code.
5. Do not include totals, but do include all of the data needed so the calculation can be done in a query. For example, include the price of an item and the quantity ordered so the total cost can be calculated.
6. Remove any redundant data that exists in multiple groupings. For example, do not put customer names in both the customer grouping and the sales grouping.
7. Ensure that common fields connect the groupings. For example, make sure that there is a common field between the customer grouping and the sales grouping so they can be connected. Later in this chapter, you will learn more about common fields.

Table 1 contains the attributes being tracked for the participant entity in the Putts for Paws tournament database. Next to each attribute is the data type, description, and field size for that attribute. These will be discussed later in the chapter.

Field Name	Data Type	Description	Field Size
ParticipantID	Number	A unique ID that identifies each participant	Long Integer
LastName	Short Text	Last name	25
FirstName	Short Text	First name	20
StreetAddress	Short Text	Street address	35
City	Short Text	City	25
State	Short Text	State abbreviation	2
ZipCode	Short Text	Five-digit ZIP Code	5
ContactPhoneNumber	Short Text	Phone number for the individual participant	14
CorporatePhoneNumber	Short Text	Phone number for the corporation the participant represents	14

Table 1   Fields for tblParticipant

REAL WORLD ADVICE   **Break Compound Fields into Their Parts**

You might wonder why the name and address fields are divided into multiple fields. Would it not be easier to have a single field for Name and a single field for Address? It might be easier for data entry, but it is much more difficult for reporting.

- Break names into first name and last name fields. That means you can sort on people alphabetically by last name and, if two people have the same last name, by first name.

- Break addresses into fields such as StreetAddress, City, State, and ZipCode. This allows reporting by state, city, or other fields.

- For other fields, consider whether you might want to report on smaller parts of the field. For example, for PhoneNumber in some applications, you might want to report on AreaCode. However, that would be rare, so you usually use just one field.

Opening the Starting File

For the golf tournament, you will need to keep track of participants, the corporations that participate, and the items each participant purchases. There are several files that tournament organizers have been keeping about the tournament. In this exercise, you will open the main database file.

 A02.00

To Open the Starting File

a. Start **Access**, click **Open Other Files** in the left pane, and then double-click **This PC**. Navigate through the folder structure to the location of your student data files, and then double-click **a01ch02Putts**. A database opens, displaying tables related to the Putts for Paws tournament.

b. Click the **File** tab, save the file as an Access database, and then click **Save As**. Navigate to the location where you are saving your project files, and then change the file name to a01ch02Putts_LastFirst using your last and first name. Click **Save**. If necessary, enable the content.

Viewing the Design View of a Table

Tables have two views: Datasheet view and Design view. Datasheet view shows the values of the data within the table. Design view shows the structure of the table with the fields and their definitions. In this exercise, you will open a table and switch to Design view to examine the table structure and field properties.

A02.01

SIDE NOTE

Pin the Ribbon

If your ribbon is collapsed, pin your ribbon open. Click the Home tab. In the lower right-hand corner of the ribbon, click Pin the Ribbon ⊣.

To View the Design View of a Table

a. In the Navigation Pane, double-click **tblParticipant** to open it.
   When you open the tblParticipant table, it opens in Datasheet view. In Datasheet view, you can see the information about the participants.

b. On the Home tab, in the Views group, click the **View** arrow, and then select **Design View**. When you switch to Design view, you see the structure of the fields and the field properties.

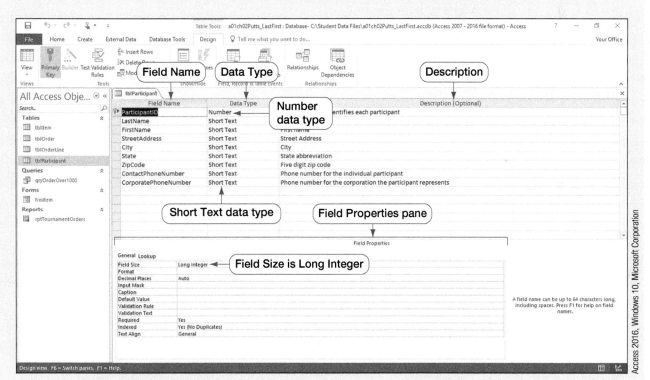

Figure 1 Design view of tblParticipant

The upper pane of Design view has three columns: Field Name, Data Type, and Description. The Field Name is the column label in Datasheet view. **Data types** define the kind of data that can be entered into a field, such as numbers, text, or dates. The data type tells Access how to store and display the field. Number and Short Text are the two most common data types. In this table, you can see that one field is stored as a **Number data type**. That means the data can contain only numeric characters. The **Short Text data type** allows any text and numeric characters to be stored. StreetAddress is the Short

Text data type, so a street address in this database can contain numbers, letters, and special characters. The third column, Description, helps the user to discern the meaning of the field.

The Field Properties pane in Design view gives more information on how the data is stored, entered, and processed. If the ParticipantID field is selected, you can see that its Field Size is Long Integer.

Import Data from Other Sources

The Red Bluff Golf Course & Pro Shop has had different employees collecting data in different ways. Luckily, the applications in the Microsoft Office suite work together. This allows you to import and export — transfer data — easily between Excel and Access. You will import the files from Excel, Access, and Notepad. After importing the data, you will be able to further analyze and refine the table structure for the database. Even though other employees have kept track of the roles that each participant plays, remember that the scope of this database does not include tracking the participants' roles in the event. You are tracking only corporate involvement.

Copying and Pasting Data from Excel

Only a few golfers were entered into the tblParticipant table. Some others were put in an Excel worksheet. In this exercise, you will copy and paste them from Excel into your Access table.

 A02.02

To Copy and Paste Data from Excel

a. Click the **Home** tab, and in the Views group, click the **View** arrow, and then select **Datasheet View**.

b. Open the Excel file **a01ch02PuttsGolf**.

c. In Excel, drag to select **cells A1** through **I9**. On the Home tab, in the Clipboard group, click **Copy** to copy these cells.

d. On the Windows taskbar, click **Access**, and make sure the tblParticipant table is opened to Datasheet view.

e. Click the **record selector** at the beginning of the append row.

f. On the Home tab, in the Clipboard group, click **Paste** to paste the records into Access. In the warning dialog box, click **Yes** to paste the records into the table.

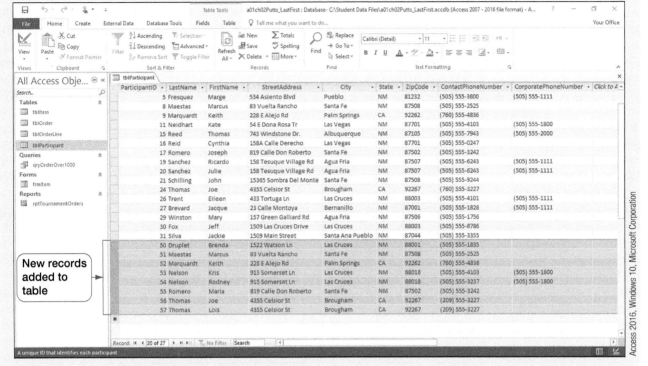

Figure 2 New records added to the tblParticipant table

Troubleshooting

If you accidentally click in a single cell of the append row and try to paste there, you get the error message "The text is too long to be edited." It appears that you are trying to paste all the data into one cell, and Access will not let you continue. If this happens, click OK, indicating that you do not want to put all the text into the one cell.

After that, it may be difficult to exit that row and click in the record selector column. It appears you are trying to paste an invalid row, and Access will not let you continue. You will get an error message saying, "Index or primary key cannot contain a Null value." When you click OK and try to recover, the message will reappear. If this happens, press Esc, indicating that you do not want to keep that record.

g. On the Windows taskbar, click **Excel**, and then **close** ☒ Excel.

h. If necessary, on the Windows taskbar, click Access and then **Close** ☒ tblParticipant.

REAL WORLD ADVICE   **Copying and Pasting from Excel into Access**

If you want to copy and paste from Excel into Access, the columns must be exactly the same in the two applications. There cannot be missing columns or columns in different orders. You cannot paste fields that are nonnumeric into numeric fields. If you have any doubt about the data being compatible, use the Import feature to append the data to the table.

Use Copy and Paste in these situations.

- You started in Access and exported the data to Excel, made additions, and now want to import the data into Access. That way, you know the columns are the same.

- You are copying and pasting the contents of a single field from Excel into Access, such as a street address.

Importing a Worksheet

Access allows you to import an entire worksheet or a smaller portion of a worksheet into a table. This is quite useful, as Excel is so frequently used in organizations. Excel column headings are often imported as field names.

The golf club has been keeping corporate contacts for the event in an Excel worksheet. In this exercise, you will import this Excel worksheet into your tblParticipant table.

 A02.03

To Import a Worksheet

a. Open the Excel file, **a01ch02PuttsCont**.

Notice that the contacts data looks like the tblParticipant table in many ways. However, the corporate phone number immediately follows the participant's name rather than being at the end of the record, as it is in the Access table. An import from Excel into an existing Access table is ideal for this type of import because as long as the columns have the same name, Access will match up the columns, skipping any missing column. You cannot copy and paste the way you did earlier because the columns are not arranged in the same order.

CorporatePhoneNumber immediately follows FirstName

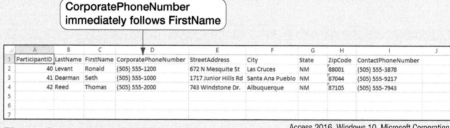

	A	B	C	D	E	F	G	H	I	J
1	ParticipantID	LastName	FirstName	CorporatePhoneNumber	StreetAddress	City	State	ZipCode	ContactPhoneNumber	
2	40	Levant	Ronald	(505) 555-1200	672 N Mesquite St	Las Cruces	NM	88001	(505) 555-3878	
3	41	Dearman	Seth	(505) 555-1000	1717 Junior Hills Rd	Santa Ana Pueblo	NM	87044	(505) 555-9217	
4	42	Reed	Thomas	(505) 555-2000	743 Windstone Dr.	Albuquerque	NM	87105	(505) 555-7943	
5										
6										
7										

Figure 3   Contact data in Excel

Access 2016, Windows 10, Microsoft Corporation

b. **Close** ☒ Excel.

c. In Access, click the **External Data** tab, and then, in the Import & Link group, click **Excel**.

The Get External Data - Excel Spreadsheet dialog box appears.

d. Click **Browse**, navigate through the folder structure to the location of your student data files, and then double-click **a01ch02PuttsCont**.

e. Select **Append a copy of the records to the table**, click the **arrow**, select **tblParticipant**, and then click **OK**.

The Import Spreadsheet Wizard opens, which displays worksheets and named ranges in the Excel workbook.

f. Make sure **Show Worksheets** is selected and the **Corporate contacts** worksheet is highlighted, and then click **Next**.

Access displays the next page of the wizard. This shows that Access found the column headings in Excel and matched them to the field names in Access.

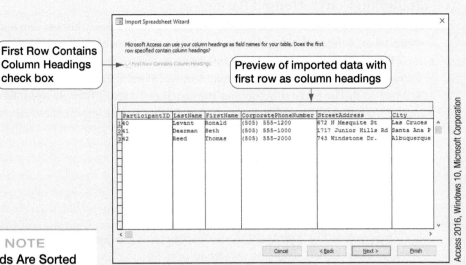

First Row Contains Column Headings check box

Preview of imported data with first row as column headings

Figure 4 Worksheet to be imported

g. Click **Next**, click **Finish**, and then click **Close**.

h. In the Navigation Pane, double-click **tblParticipant** to open the table.

   Your table has the three corporate contacts added. The contacts were imported, and because the field names in Access matched the Excel column headings, the fields were rearranged to match the Access table order.

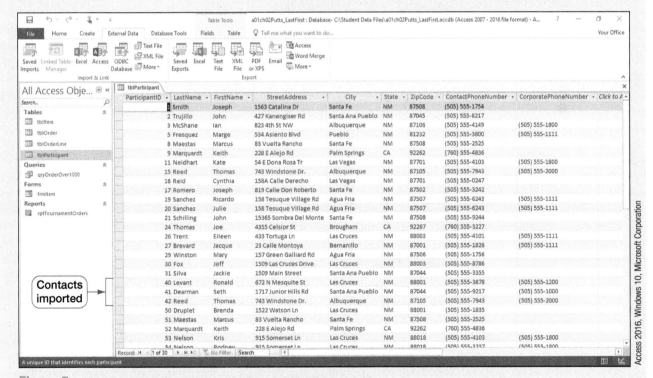

Contacts imported

Figure 5 Corporate contacts imported into the tblParticipant table

i. **Close** ☒ tblParticipant.

Importing from a Named Range

Access allows you to import a smaller portion of a worksheet, known as a named range, into a table. A **named range** is a group of cells that have been given a name.

The golf club has been keeping information about the volunteers for the event in an Excel worksheet. This worksheet contains other information about volunteering that you will not need. The range that contains the contact information for the volunteers has been named VolunteerNamesAddress. In this exercise, you will import those records into the Putts database.

To Import from a Named Range

a. Open the Excel file, **a01ch02PuttsVol**.

   Notice that the Volunteers worksheet contains the volunteer information, in the Volunteers named range, as well as other data.

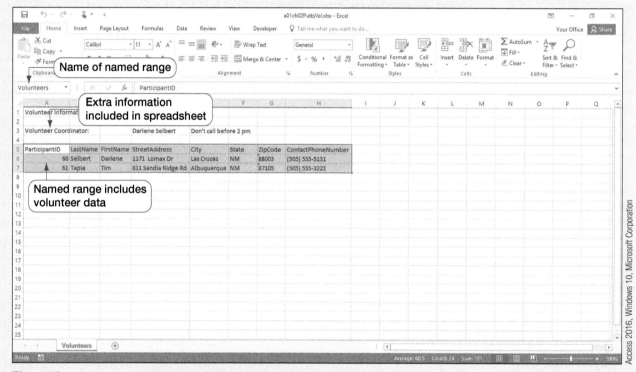

Figure 6   Volunteer worksheet with extra information

b. **Close** ☒ Excel.

c. In Access, on the External Data tab, in the Import & Link group, click **Excel**.
   The Get External Data - Excel Spreadsheet dialog box appears.

d. Click **Browse**, navigate through the folder structure to the location of your student data files, and then double-click **a01ch02PuttsVol**.

e. Select **Append a copy of the records to the table**, click the **arrow**, and then select **tblParticipant**.

f. Click **OK**, and then click **Show Named Ranges**.
   One named range, VolunteerNamesAddress, is displayed and highlighted in the list box.

g. Click **Next**. Access tells you that it found your column headings in Excel and matched them to the field names in Access. Click **Next**.

h. Click **Finish**, and then click **Close**.

i. In the Navigation Pane, double-click **tblParticipant** to open the table. Your table has the two volunteers added for a total of 32 volunteers.

j. **Close** ⨯ the tblParticipant table.

Importing from a Text File

Access enables you to import data from text and Word files. Typically, these files would have data organized in tables. In Word, these tables will have actual rows and columns. In text files, the tables are implied by the separation of the columns. This separation is done by delimiter characters. **A delimiter** is a character such as a tab or comma that separates the fields. The rows in the text tables will be imported as records into your Access table.

The golf course has been keeping information about the donors for the event in a text file. In this exercise, you will import those records into the Putts database.

To Import from a Text File

a. Open the text file **a01ch02PuttsDon**.
    Notice that there are three donors in this file. The fields are separated by unseen tabs.

> ### Troubleshooting
> Your columns may not line up the way Figure 7 shows them lining up. This happens because Notepad does not save font formatting. Notepad does save tabs, so you do not need to worry about any display differences.

Three donors in text file →

Figure 7   Donor text file in Notepad

Access 2016, Windows 10, Microsoft Corporation

b. **Close** ⨯ Notepad.

c. In Access, on the External Data tab, in the Import & Link group, click **Text File**.
    The Get External Data - Text File dialog box appears.

d. Click **Browse**, navigate through the folder structure to the location of your student data files, and then double-click **a01ch02PuttsDon**.

e. Click **Append a copy of the records to the table**, click the **arrow** to select **tblParticipant**, and then click **OK**.

f. Click **Next**, make sure that the **Tab** delimiter is selected, and then click to select the **First Row Contains Field Names** check box.

Tab delimiter selected

First Row Contains Field Names check box selected

Figure 8 Tab delimiter Delimited with First Row Contains Field Names

g. Click **Next**, and then click **Finish**.

h. Click **Close**. Double-click **tblParticipant** to open the table, and verify that the records for Luis Ortiz, Alice Ramirez, and Lisa Victor were imported.

REAL WORLD ADVICE | **Importing an Excel Worksheet into a New Table**

In all the previous examples of importing, you imported into an already existing table. You can also import into a new table. Access creates a table using the column headings for field names. Access defines fields with default definitions. After performing the import, open the table in Design view and adjust fields and properties as necessary. Some things that you should consider in these adjustments are the following.

- What field did Access assign as the primary key for the table? Access defaults to creating a new field called ID for the primary key. Later in the chapter, you will learn what field might work better as a primary key.

- The default length for all short text fields is 255 characters. Adjust the field size properties to sizes that are appropriate for your fields. Check all field definitions for errors.

- Are the field names descriptive? The column headings from Excel might not be appropriate as field names in Access.

Enter Data Manually

If the data does not already exist in another form, you can type the data directly into Access. There are two methods: entering data directly into the table or entering the data in a form.

Entering Data Using Datasheet View

When you open a table in Datasheet view, you can type data directly into the table. In this exercise, you will add a new participant to the tournament by creating a new record in the tblParticipant table.

To Enter Data Using Datasheet View

a. In the tblParticipant table, click in the **ParticipantID** column of the append row, and then type 62.

   As you type the "62", a pencil icon appears in the record selector on the left. The pencil icon means that this record is actively being modified.

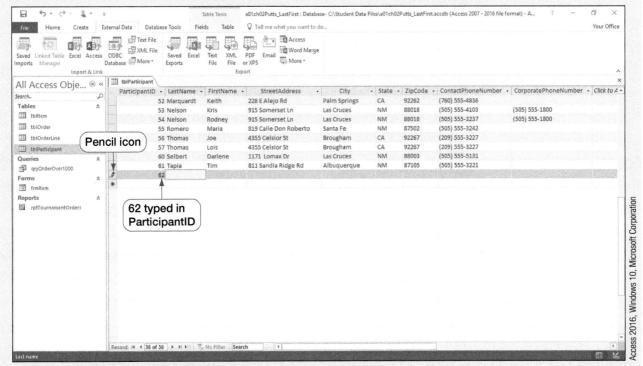

Figure 9 Type 62 in ParticipantID

b. Press Tab to continue filling in the record using the following data.

LastName	FirstName	Street Address	City	State	ZipCode	ContactPhone Number
Gupta	Sanjay	3544 Cornice Blvd	Las Cruces	NM	88001	5055557789

c. Press Tab to go to the next field, and press Tab again to go to the next record. The pencil icon disappears. Unlike Word and Excel, Access immediately saves the data change.

Access immediately saves the changes you make to data. There is very limited undo/redo functionality in Access. If the Undo button ⟲ is dimmed, you cannot undo the change you made.

- Typically, you can undo a single typing change even if you have gone on to the next record. However, if you made several changes to different records, you cannot undo more than the changes to the last record.

- If you have made changes to several fields in a single record, you can click Undo to undo each of them.

- You can also press [Esc] to stop editing a record and revert to the record data as it appeared before you started changing the record.

- If you make an error, you can press [Esc] to get out of the error.

Because of the limited undo features in Access, do not count on being able to undo your changes. You will often find that you cannot. For example, when you delete a record or records, you cannot undo the deletion.

Design changes are not saved until you save the object you changed. Thus, you can undo design changes until you save.

Deleting Data from a Table

You can delete records from a table. These are permanent deletions and cannot be undone. In this exercise, you will delete the record for golfer Kate Neidhart, who needs to withdraw from the tournament.

▶ A02.07

To Delete Data from a Table

a. In the tblParticipant table, click the **record selector** for record 7, Kate Neidhart, ParticipantID 11, to select the row.

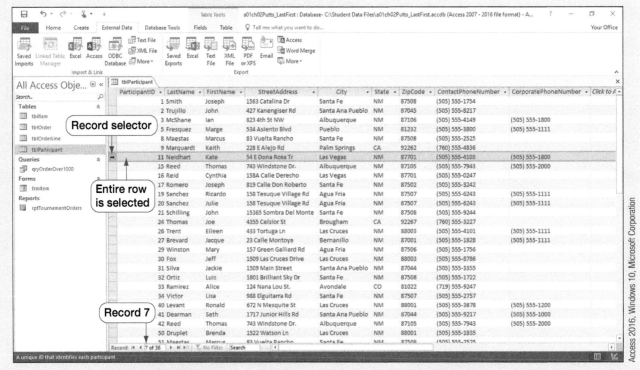

Figure 10 Delete Kate Neidhart's record

b. Right-click the **row**, and then select **Delete Record**.

Because you cannot undo a delete, Access asks whether you are sure you want to delete this record.

c. Click **Yes**. The record is deleted.

> ### Troubleshooting
>
> If you do not get the Access confirmation message asking whether you are sure you want the deletion to occur, the confirmation message setting may be turned off. If you would like to turn it back on, on the File tab, click Options, and then click Client Settings. Scroll down to find the Confirm section under Editing, click the Document deletions check box, and click OK.

Deleting a Field from a Table

You can also delete individual fields from a table. These are also permanent deletions and cannot be undone. The design of the database will be changed to track individual participants separate from corporations. Later in this chapter, you will create a table for the corporations involved with the tournament and include the CorporatePhoneNumber field there. In this exercise, you will delete the CorporatePhoneNumber field from the tblParticipant table. You can delete a field in either Design view or Datasheet view. In Datasheet view, you can see the contents of the field that you are deleting, which gives you an extra check on whether you really want to delete the field.

 A02.08

To Delete a Field from a Table

a. In the tblParticipant table, scroll to the right to find the **CorporatePhoneNumber** column. Point to the **column heading** until it changes to a black down arrow, and then click so the entire column is highlighted. Make sure that you selected **CorporatePhoneNumber** and not **ContactPhoneNumber**.

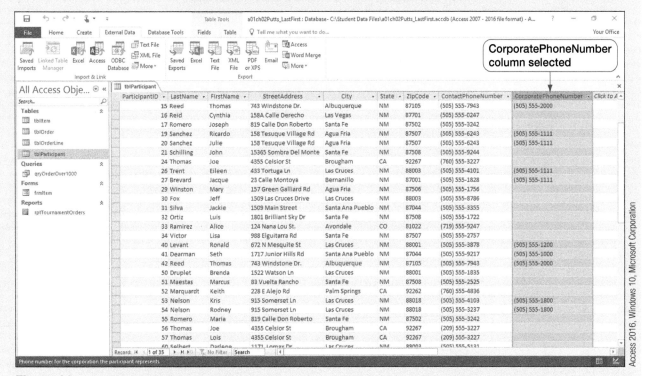

Figure 11 Select the CorporatePhoneNumber column

b. Click the **Home** tab, and then in the Records group, click **Delete**.

Because you cannot undo a deletion, Access asks, "Do you want to permanently delete the selected field(s) and all the data in the field(s)? To permanently delete the field(s), click Yes." Because you are in Datasheet view, you can glance at it and make sure this is the data you want to delete.

c. Click **Yes**. The column is deleted.

d. **Close** ☒ tblParticipant.

> **Troubleshooting**
>
> If, when you clicked in the column heading, you accidentally double-clicked and then clicked Delete, Access blanked out the field name rather than deleting the column. This put you in edit mode, ready to rename the field. Press Esc to cancel edit mode and try again.

e. If you need to take a break before finishing this chapter, now is a good time.

Understanding Tables and Keys

The database needs to be further examined and evaluated with regard to how the tables have been set up. Tables represent entities — or people, places, things, or events that you want to track. Each row represents a single person, place, or other entity. To identify that entity, a primary key field is typically used. A **primary key** field is a field that uniquely identifies the record; it can be any data type, but it should be a field that will not change. For example, a person's name is not a good primary key for two reasons. First, it is not unique — several people may have the same name. Second, a person's name could change. If you define a primary key for a table, the field cannot be blank.

In this section, you will create a table from scratch, minimize file size, facilitate quick data entry, minimize errors, and encourage data consistency as shown in Table 2.

Goal	Example
Minimize file size	If a field is an integer that is always less than 32,767, use Integer rather than Long Integer to define the field.
Facilitate quick data entry, including removing redundant data	Store a state abbreviation rather than the state name spelled out.
Minimize errors	Use the Date/Time data type for dates and not a Text data type. Access will then accept only valid dates and not a date such as 2/31/2018, which is invalid.
Encourage data consistency	Use a Yes/No check box rather than having the word Yes or No typed into a text field, where misspellings could occur.

Table 2 Table design goals

Create a Table in Design View

You want to keep track of corporations that are involved with the tournament. You do not have a source that you can import, so you will need to design and create the table. You will use Design view to enter fields, data types, and descriptions.

Defining Data Types

Data types define the kind of data that can be entered into a field, such as numbers, text, or dates. The data type tells Access how to store and display the field.

QUICK REFERENCE	Data Types	
Data Type	**Description**	**Examples**
Short Text	Used to store textual or character information. Any character or number can be entered into this type of field. You should store any data that will never be used in calculations, such as a Social Security number, as text, not a number. There is an upper limit of 255 characters that can be stored in a Short Text field.	Names, addresses
Long Text	Used to capture large amounts of text. Can store up to 1 gigabyte of characters, of which you can display 65,535 characters in a control on a form or report. This is a good data type to use if you need more than 255 characters in one field.	Comments
Number	Used for numeric data.	Quantity
Date/Time	Used to store a date and/or time.	Start time
Currency	A numeric value that is used for units of currency. It follows the regional settings preset in Windows to determine what the default currency should be. In the United States, the data is displayed with a dollar sign and two decimal places.	Salary
AutoNumber	Used for keys. Access generates the value by automatically incrementing the value for each new record to produce unique keys. For example, it would set the value as 1 for the first record, 2 for the next, and 3 for the third.	ProductID
Yes/No	A checked box in which an empty box is no and a checked box is yes.	EntryPaid
OLE Object	Use to attach an OLE object, such as a Microsoft Office Excel worksheet, to a record. An OLE object means that when you open the object, you open it in its original application, such as Excel. This allows cross-application editing.	SalarySpreadsheet
Hyperlink	Text or combinations of text and numbers stored as text and used as a hyperlink address.	CompanyWebsite
Attachment	Images, worksheet files, documents, charts, and other types of supported files that are attached to the records in your database, similar to attaching files to e-mail messages.	EmployeePhoto
Calculated	A field calculated from other fields in the table. A calculated field may not be edited, as it performs a calculation on other data that is entered.	GrossPay, which is calculated on the basis of HoursWorked and HourlySalary
Lookup Wizard	Lists either values retrieved from a table or query or a set of values that you specified when you created the field.	ProductType, which gives a list of valid types

Determining Field Size

Field size indicates the maximum length of a data field. Whenever you use a Short Text data type, you should determine the maximum number of text characters that can exist in the data to be stored. That number would then be the field size. For example, a state abbreviation can be only two characters long, so the size for this field should be 2. If you allow more than two characters, you are likely to get a mix of abbreviations and spelled-out state names. Limiting the size will limit errors in the data. There is an upper limit of 255 characters for a Short Text field. If you need more than 255 characters, use a Long Text data type.

For numeric fields, the type defines the maximum length or range of values. You should use the number size that best suits your needs. For example, if a value in a field is always going to be a whole number and is never going to be above 32,768, then Integer is the best field size. If the number is currency, you should use the Currency data type instead of Number.

QUICK REFERENCE | **Number Field Sizes**

Field Size	Description
Byte	For integers that range from 0 to 255. These numbers can be stored in a single byte.
Integer	For integers that range from −32,768 to +32,767. Must be whole numbers. Integers cannot have decimal places.
Long Integer	For integers that range from −2,147,483,648 to +2,147,483,647. Long Integers cannot have decimal places. (AutoNumber is a long integer.)
Single	For large numbers with up to seven significant digits. Can contain decimal places. Numbers can be negative or positive. For numeric floating point values that range from -3.4×10^{38} to $+3.4 \times 10^{38}$.
Double	For very large numbers with up to 15 significant digits. Can contain decimal places. Numbers can be negative or positive. For numeric floating point values that range from -1.797×10^{308} to $+1.797 \times 10^{308}$.
Decimal	For numeric values that contain decimal places. Numbers can be negative or positive. For numeric values that range from $-9.999\ldots \times 10^{27}$ to $+9.999\ldots \times 10^{27}$.

Creating a Table in Design View

In this exercise, you will create a new table to track data on the corporations participating in the tournament. You will name the table tblCorporate, add the necessary fields, define data types, add descriptions, and specify field sizes.

A02.09

To Create a Table in Design View

SIDE NOTE

Select Data Type
Alternatively, you can type the first letter of the data type, and it will appear, such as "N" for Number.

SIDE NOTE

Switch Panes
You can press the F6 key to quickly switch to the Field Properties pane.

a. If you took a break, open the **a01ch02Putts** database.

b. Click the **Create** tab, and then, in the Tables group, click **Table Design**.

 Access opens a blank table in Design view. You will enter each field in the appropriate row.

c. Type **CompanyName** for the Field Name, and then press Tab to move to the Data Type column.

 Notice that Short Text is the default data type, so you do not need to make a selection to keep Short Text for this field. For other data types, click the arrow and select the data type.

d. Press Tab to move to the Description column, and then type Name of the company.

e. In the Field Properties pane, type 50 in the Field Size box.

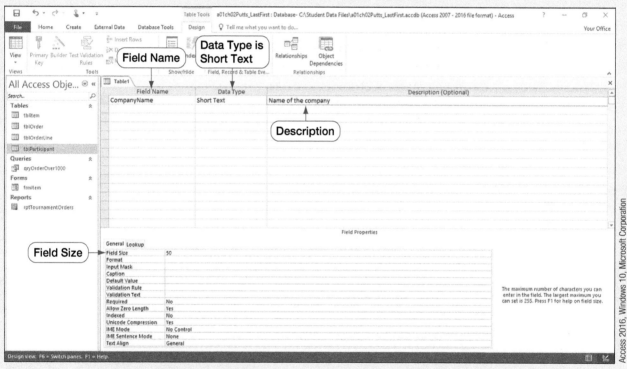

Figure 12   First field in the tblCorporate table

f. Continue defining the table with the following information.

Field Name	Data Type	Description	Field Size
StreetAddress	Short Text	Company's street address	40
City	Short Text	Company's city	40
State	Short Text	State abbreviation	2
ZipCode	Short Text	ZIP Code either 5 or 9 character format	10
PhoneNumber	Short Text	Phone number with area code	14

g. **Save** 💾 the table, name it tblCorporate, and then click **OK**. In the warning message that asks whether you want to create a primary key, click **No**. You will define a key later.

h. **Close** ⊠ tblCorporate.

Changing a Data Type

In Design view, you can change the size of a field. If you decide that a field length needs to be longer, you can change the field without concern. If you make a field length shorter and there was data that needed the longer length, you may truncate those values. For that reason, Access will always warn you that data may be lost if you change the length to a smaller size.

In this exercise, you will change the data type of the Notes field in tblItem so that full, lengthy comments can be added for items.

 A02.10

To Change a Data Type

a. Right-click **tblItem** in the Navigation Pane, and then select **Design View** to open the table in Design view. Notice that Notes is defined with a Data Type of Short Text.

b. Click the **Data Type** column for Notes, click the **arrow** ⌄, and then select **Long Text**. Note that there is no longer a Field Size field. Long Text does not show the maximum field length.

c. **Save** 💾 and **close** ⊠ the table.

Understand Masks and Formatting

One of the values of using a DBMS is that it can make sure that information is entered, stored, and displayed consistently. Masks and formatting are two of the methods that assist in that process.

Defining Input Masks

Access provides a way to consistently enter data, called input masks. For example, phone numbers can be typed (555) 555-5555, 555-5555, or 555-555-5555. An **input mask** defines a consistent template and provides the punctuation, so it does not have to be typed manually. Access also has a wizard that creates automatic masks for Social Security numbers, ZIP Codes, passwords, extensions, dates, and times. You can also create your own custom masks. Input masks can affect how data is stored. In this exercise, you will create an input mask for the PhoneNumber field in tblCorporate.

To Define an Input Mask

a. Right-click **tblCorporate** in the Navigation Pane, and then select **Design View** to open the table in Design view.

b. Click the **PhoneNumber** Field Name to select the PhoneNumber field. In the Field Properties pane, click in the **Input Mask** box.

c. Click the **Build** button ☐ to start the Input Mask Wizard. If necessary, select **Phone Number**.

d. Click **Next** to start the phone number Input Mask Wizard.

Access suggests the format !(999) 000–0000. This means that the area code is optional and will be enclosed in parentheses. The rest of the phone number is required and will have a dash between the two parts. The exclamation mark specifies that characters should be typed from left to right.

e. Click **Next** to accept the format.

f. Access asks whether you want to store the symbols with the data. Select **With the symbols in the mask, like this**.

To save space, Access recommends that an input mask be saved without the symbols. However, the mask characters in this instance will not utilize much space. Keeping the symbols will add clarity for users looking at the data.

g. Click **Next**, and then click **Finish**.

SIDE NOTE

Semicolons in Input Mask

The semicolons indicate that there are three sections of the mask. The dash in the last section shows the placeholder.

Figure 13 Finished input mask

h. **Save** ☐ the table design. On the Design tab, in the Views group, click the **View** arrow, and then select **Datasheet View**.

i. Notice that the columns are not wide enough for the entire heading text to show. Move your mouse pointer to the border between **CompanyName** and **StreetAddress** until it becomes the Horizontal resize pointer ┼, and then double-click the **border** to widen the column.

j. Double-click the **border** after the **StreetAddress** and **PhoneNumber** headings to widen the columns.

k. In the append row, type Tesuque Mirage Market in the CompanyName field. Press Tab to move to StreetAddress.

l. Continue entering the records as follows.

StreetAddress	City	State	ZipCode	PhoneNumber
8 Tesuque Mirage Rd	Santa Fe	NM	87506	5055551111

Notice the input mask in the PhoneNumber makes it easier to type in phone numbers.

m. Double-click the borders in between all fields so that all data are visible. **Close** ☒ tblCorporate, and then, in the Microsoft Access dialog box, click **Yes** to save the layout.

Formatting a Field

In a table design, you can define a Format field property that customizes how data is displayed and printed in tables, queries, reports, and forms. The **Format** property tells Access how data is to be displayed. It does not affect the way the data is stored. For example, you can specify that currency fields are displayed in dollars, such as $1,234.56, in American databases or in euros, such as €1.234,56, in European databases. Formats are available for Date/Time, Number, Currency, and Yes/No data types. You can also define your own custom formats for Short Text and Long Text fields.

QUICK REFERENCE	Format Field Property	
Data Type	**Format**	**Example**
Date/Time	General Date	11/9/2015 10:10:10 PM
	Long Date	Monday, November 9, 2015
	Medium Date	9-Nov-15
	Short Date	11/9/2015
	Long Time	10:10:10 PM
	Medium Time	10:10 PM
	Short Time	22:10
Number and Currency	General Number	Display the number as entered
	Currency	Follows the regional settings preset in Windows. In the United States, $1,234.56. In much of Europe, €1.234,56.
	Euro	Uses the euro symbol regardless of the Windows setting.
	Fixed	Displays at least one digit after the decimal point. In the Decimal Places property, you choose how many fixed digits to show after the decimal point.
	Standard	Use the regional settings preset in Windows for the thousands divider. In the United States, 1,234; in much of Europe, 1.234.
	Percent	Multiply the value by 100 and follow with %.
	Scientific	Use standard scientific notation, for example, 4.5E + 13.
Yes/No	Yes/No	Yes or No display options.
	True/False	True or False display options.
	On/Off	On or Off display options.

A02.12

To Format a Field

a. In the Navigation Pane, right-click **tblOrder**, and then select **Design View**.

b. In the first **blank row**, in the Field Name column, type OrderDate. Select a Data Type of **Date/Time**, and then enter a Description of Date order was placed.

c. Click in the **Input Mask** box.

d. Click **Build** … to start the Input Mask Wizard. When prompted to save, click **Yes**. Select **Short Date**, and then click **Next**.

Access suggests the format 99/99/0000. This means that the month and day are optional and that a four-character year is required. The backslashes are used to separate the month, day, and year.

e. Click **Next** to accept the format, and then click **Finish**.

f. Click in the **Format** property, click the **Format** arrow, and then select **Medium Date**.

Notice that the Property Update Options button 📝 appears. Clicking it would display an option to change the format of OrderDate wherever else it appears. Because it does not appear anywhere else yet, you do not need to click the button.

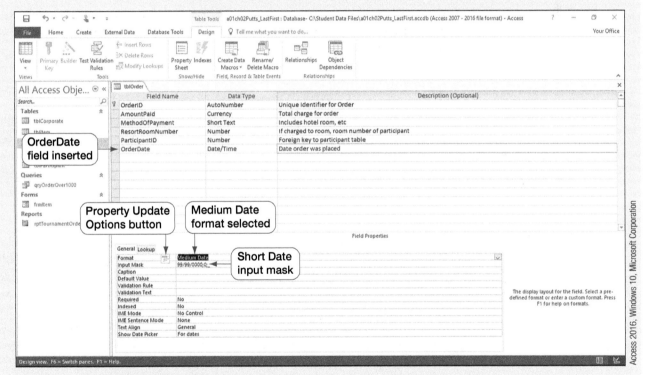

Figure 14   Input mask and formatting

g. **Save** 🖫 the table design, and then, in the Views group, click the **View** button to switch to Datasheet view.

The orders were placed on May 4, 2018, but no date was entered.

h. For the first order, in the OrderDate field, type 05042018. Press the down arrow ⬇ to move to the next record.

Notice that the input mask provides the placeholders and the backslashes, and the display changes to **04-May-18**, the medium date format.

To save time and to avoid making errors, after typing the date and before moving to the next record, select 05042018, press Ctrl+C to copy, and then press Ctrl+V to paste the order date into the other orders.

> ## Troubleshooting
>
> When clicking inside the OrderDate field, be sure to click in the left side of the field to avoid starting in the middle of the input mask.

i. For the second order, type 05042018, and then press the down arrow ⬇ to move to the next record. Again, the display changes to medium date format.

j. Continue typing 05042018 for all the orders.

   Input masks are generally useful for increasing the efficiency and ensuring consistency of data entry. Formatting is useful for changing the way data appears to the end users. As you can see from the above example, having a Short Date input mask makes entering dates easier, and applying a Medium Date format makes viewing the dates easier.

k. **Close** ⊠ the table.

 CONSIDER THIS | **Database Design Principles**

Some principles for database design are shown in Table 2. How do field sizes, formatting, and input masks facilitate these principles? When would you use a format? When would you use an input mask?

Understand and Designate Keys

Each table should have a field that uniquely identifies each of the records in the table. This field is called the primary key. If you know the primary key, you know exactly what record you want. Another type of key is a **foreign key**. A foreign key is a value in a table that is the primary key of another table. The primary and foreign keys form the common field between tables that allows the relationship between two tables to be formed.

Understanding Primary Keys

Each row of a table represents a single instance of an entity. The primary key field is the field that uniquely identifies that instance. Remember that a primary key field should be a field that has values that will not change. When you define a primary key for a table, the field cannot be blank. A common way of defining a primary key is to use a field specifically designed to identify the entity. This is sometimes an arbitrary **numeric key** that is assigned to represent an individual item, such as CustomerID or ProductID. A numeric key is often assigned an AutoNumber data type that Access will fill as the data is entered. Instead of using a numeric key, you can use an already existing field that uniquely identifies the person or item, such as the person's employee ID.

REAL WORLD ADVICE | **Do You Need a Primary Key?**

While Access does not require a primary key for every table, you almost always want to give the table a primary key. What are the advantages of having a primary key?

- It helps to organize your data. Each record is uniquely identified.
- Primary keys speed up access to your data. Primary keys provide an index to a record. In a large table, that makes it much faster to find a record.
- Primary keys are used to form relationships between tables.

Understanding Foreign Keys

A foreign key is a field in a table that stores a value that is the primary key in another table. It is called foreign because it does not identify a record in this table; it identifies a record in another — foreign — table. For example, you have two tables, tblParticipant and tblOrder, in your database. You want to know which participants have placed certain orders. The primary key for your Participant table is ParticipantID. You can add a field called ParticipantID to the Order table that indicates which participant placed the order. ParticipantID is the foreign key in the tblOrder table; it identifies the participant in the tblParticipant table. Figure 15 illustrates this relationship. Foreign keys do not need to be unique in the table. Participants can place several orders.

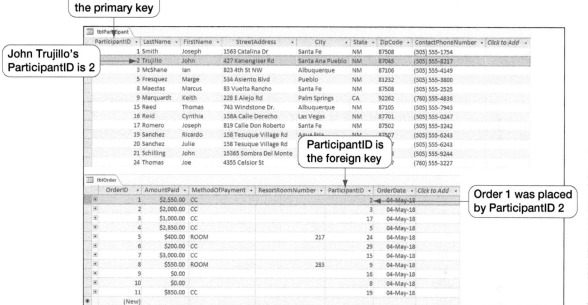

Figure 15   Relationship between the tblParticipant and tblOrder tables

Identifying a Composite Key

Sometimes, two fields are needed to uniquely identify a record. In that case, both fields are used to create the key and are called a **composite key**. For example, a university might identify a class by subject area and course number. The university could have classes Math 101, Math 102, and MIS 101. It takes both subject and course number to identify a single course.

A typical use of a composite key is on an order form. Figure 16 shows a paper form that the golf tournament organizers used before they used Access. To uniquely identify the items that have been ordered, a composite key can be made that combines the order number with the line number of the order form. In this exercise, you will identify a composite key used in the Putts for Paws tournament database.

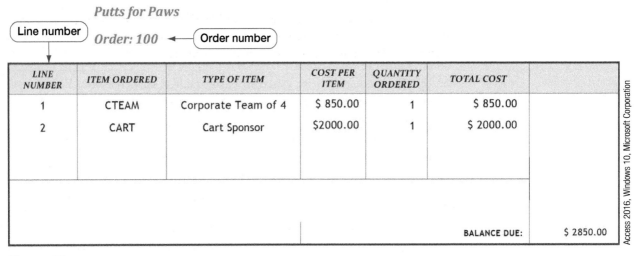

Figure 16   Composite key on paper order form

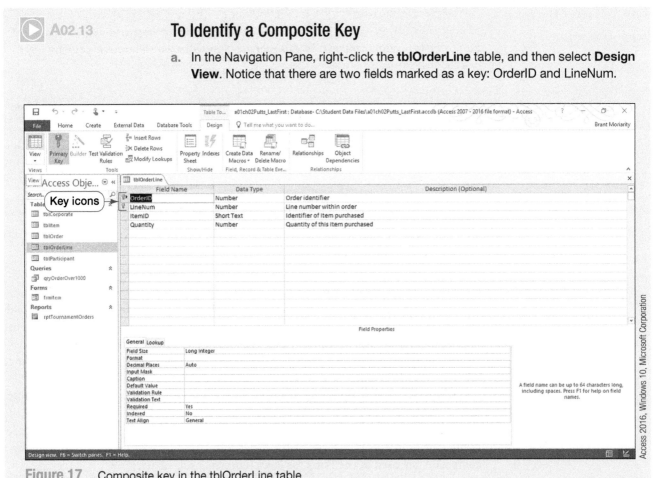

Figure 17   Composite key in the tblOrderLine table

To Identify a Composite Key

a. In the Navigation Pane, right-click the **tblOrderLine** table, and then select **Design View**. Notice that there are two fields marked as a key: OrderID and LineNum.

b. **Close** ☒ the tblOrderLine table.

Defining a Primary Key

Sometimes your data will have a unique identifier that is a natural part of your data. When that is true, you can use the field as a **natural primary key**. If you already identify orders by order number, that would make a good primary key.

The important point is that the natural primary key is a value that will not change. You might start by thinking that telephone number is a natural way to identify a customer. But people change their telephone numbers. When the natural key might change, it is better to use an arbitrary unique number to identify the customer. When natural keys do exist, they are favored over numeric keys.

CONSIDER THIS | **Social Security Number as a Primary Key**

While a Social Security number seems like the perfect primary key, it is seldom used. What privacy concerns might arise in using Social Security numbers? Are there other issues that might arise with using Social Security numbers?

You can use the data type AutoNumber for the primary key. In that case, Access will automatically assign a unique value for every record. You can also define a key as numeric and fill the key values yourself. In this exercise, you will create a numeric primary key for the tblCorporate table.

 A02.14

To Define a Primary Key

a. In the Navigation Pane, right-click **tblCorporate**, and then select **Design View**.

b. On the Design tab, in the Tools group, click **Insert Rows**. Because CompanyName was the active field, a blank row is added above CompanyName.

c. Type CorporateID in the Field Name column.

d. Select **AutoNumber** as the Data Type. The field size is set to Long Integer.

e. Type Unique corporate identifier in the Description column.

f. With the CorporateID row still selected, on the Design tab, in the Tools group, click **Primary Key** to make CorporateID the primary key. A key icon is displayed in the record selector bar.

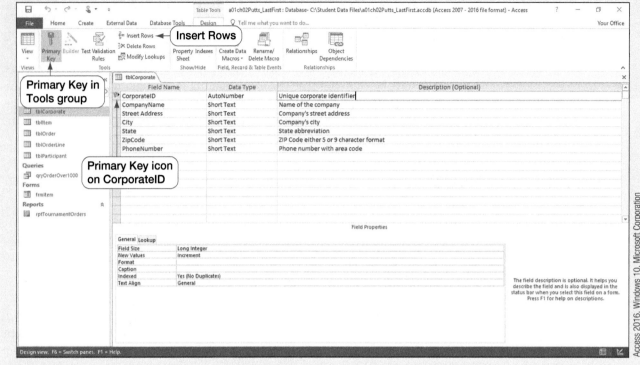

Figure 18 Defining a primary key

g. **Save** [disk icon] your table design. On the Design tab, in the Views group, click **View** to switch to Datasheet view. Notice that Access has populated the CorporateID field with an automatic number of 1. When new records are added the CorporateID field will automatically increment the value by 1.

h. **Close** [X] the tblCorporate table. If you need to take a break before finishing this chapter, now is a good time.

REAL WORLD ADVICE | **Read Error Messages**

The error message "Index or primary key cannot contain a Null value" is one example of an error message that Access displays when you make changes to an Access database that would break the rules you set up in your table design. You should read the error message carefully to understand what it is telling you.

If you get the error message "Index or primary key cannot contain a Null value," that means that one of your records has no entry in the primary key field. Enter the primary key. Often, the issue is that you accidentally entered data in the append record. If you do not want that record to be created, press [Esc] to cancel the addition of the record.

Understanding Relational Databases

One of the benefits of using Access is the ability to add relationships to the tables. This allows you to work with two or more tables in the same query, report, or form. For the tournament database, when you relate tables together, you can ask such questions as "Which golfers are playing for the Tesuque Mirage Market?", "Did the market agree to purchase any other items?", and "Have they paid for those items yet?"

Relationships in a relational database are created by joining the tables together. A **join** is created by establishing a relationship between two tables based on a common field in the two tables, as shown in Figure 19. The tblParticipant table has a field named ParticipantID. The tblOrder table also has a field named ParticipantID. When you create the relationship, Access will match the ParticipantID fields between the two tables to find which participants placed an order. Looking at the table, you can mentally join the two tables to see that John Trujillo has placed an order for $2,550. In this section, you will create relationships between tables, create a report, and check to make sure the relationships you are creating between the tables make sense.

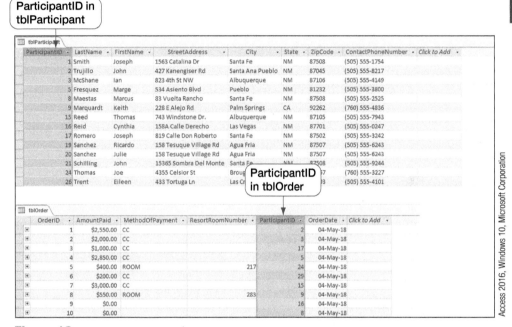

Figure 19   Tables joined between primary and foreign keys

Understand Basic Principles of Normalization

When you work with tables in Access, you want each table to represent a single entity and have data about only that entity. For example, you want tblParticipant to have data about participants and nothing else. You do not want to have data about the corporation they represent or the order they placed. This is why you deleted the CorporatePhoneNumber field earlier in the chapter.

Representing Entities and Attributes

Recall that an entity is a person, place, or item that you want to keep data about. The data you keep about an entity are called attributes. An entity is generally stored in a single table in a relational database. The attributes form the fields or columns of the table. **Normalization** is the process of minimizing the duplication of information in a relational database through effective database design. If you know the primary key of an entity in a normalized database, each of the attributes will have just one value. When you normalize a database, you will have multiple smaller tables, each representing a different thing. There will be no redundant data in the tables. A complete discussion of normalization is beyond the scope of this chapter, but the following sections will give you an idea of why tables should be normalized.

Table 3 shows a nonnormalized view of tblParticipant. Suppose John Trujillo places two orders: Order 1 for $2,550 and Order 2 for $500. You can easily fill in his name and address. However, when you get to the order fields, you cannot fill in the attributes with just one value. You want to enter Order 1 for Order ID and Order 2 for Order ID. You want to enter $2,550 for AmountPaid and $500 for AmountPaid. But you have only one field for each.

Participant ID	Last Name	First Name	Street Address	Other Address Fields	Order ID	Amount Paid
2	Trujillo	John	427 Kanengiser Rd		??????	????

Table 3 Nonnormalized tblParticipant table

For each record's ParticipantID, you do not have a single value for OrderID and AmountPaid because each participant may make several orders. You could have a column for OrderID1 and OrderID2. But how many columns would you make? What if this was for a grocery store where one transaction might contain dozens of items? Any time you do not know how many columns to repeat, the table is not normalized and you need another table. Thus, this table does not fit the principles of normalization. It has two entities in the table: participants and orders.

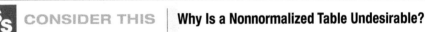 **CONSIDER THIS** | **Why Is a Nonnormalized Table Undesirable?**

If you have a table like that shown in Table 3, you could simply enter a record for each item. If you had five items, you would enter five records in the table. What kind of redundancy does that create? If you used this method, would there be a primary key?

Minimizing Redundancy

Table 4 shows a nonnormalized view of the tblOrder table. In this case, when you know the OrderID, you are able to know the amount paid, the method of payment, and the name and address of the customer who purchased the order.

OrderID	Amount Paid	Method of Payment	Last Name	First Name	Address
1	$2,550.00	CC	Trujillo	John	427 Kanengiser Rd
12	$500.00	CC	Trujillo	John	427 Kanengiser Rd

Table 4 Nonnormalized tblOrder table

However, the table has redundant data. **Redundancy** occurs when data is repeated several times in a database. All of the data about John Trujillo is repeated for each order he makes. That means that the data will need to be entered multiple times. Beyond that, if the data changes, it has to be changed in multiple places. If his address or phone number changes, it will need to be changed in all his order records. Forgetting to change it in one place will lead to inconsistent data and confusion. Again, this table is not normalized because it contains data about two different entities: participant and orders.

In a normalized database, redundancy is minimized. The foreign keys are redundant, but no other data about the entity is repeated.

Understand Relationships Between Tables

To normalize the database, you need to have two tables: one for participants and one for orders. How then do you form a relationship between them? A table represents an entity — or the nouns — in the database. The relationship represents the verb that connects the two nouns. In the example, the two nouns are "participant" and "order." Is there a relationship between these two nouns? Yes. You can say that a participant places an order.

Once you have determined that there is a relationship between the entities, you need to describe the relationship. You do that by asking yourself two questions starting with each entity in the relationship.

- Question 1, starting with the Participant entity: If you have one participant, what is the maximum number of orders that one participant can place? The only two answers to consider are one or many. In this case, the participant can place many orders.

- Question 2, starting with the Order entity: If you have one order, what is the maximum number of participants that can place that order? Again, the only answers to consider are one or many. An order is placed by just one participant.

The type of relationship in which one question is answered "one" and the other is answered "many" is called a one-to-many relationship. **A one-to-many-relationship** is a relationship between two tables in which one record in the first table corresponds to many records in the second table. One-to-many is called the cardinality of the relationship. **Cardinality** indicates the number of instances of one entity that relates to one instance of another entity.

Viewing the Relationships Window

Access stores relationship information in the Relationships window as shown in Figure 20.

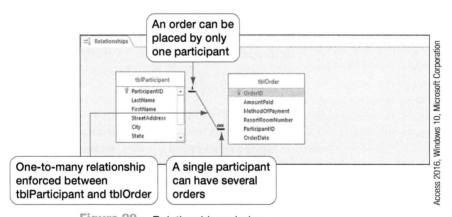

Figure 20 Relationships window

The Relationships window shows tables and the relationships between those tables. Notice the join line between tblParticipant and tblOrder. There is an infinity symbol on the line next to tblOrder. The infinity symbol indicates that a single participant can have several orders. There is a "1" on the line next to tblParticipant. The "1" indicates that an order can be placed by just one participant. Access indicates that a one-to-many relationship is being enforced by displaying a "1" on the one side of the join line and an infinity symbol on the many side.

In this exercise, you will view the Relationships window in the database.

To View the Relationships Window

a. If you took a break, open the **a01ch02Putts** database.

b. Click the **Database Tools** tab, and then, in the Relationships group, click **Relationships**.
   The Relationships window opens. The window shows tables and the relationships between those tables.

Determining Relationship Types

The relationship between tblParticipant and tblOrder is a one-to-many relationship. There are other types of relationships. Consider the relationship between tblOrder and tblItem: An item can be on an order. What is the cardinality? You need to ask yourself the two questions to determine the cardinality.

- Question 1, starting with the Order entity: If you have one order, what is the maximum number of items that can be part of that order? You care about only two answers: one or many. In this case, the order can contain many items. For example, a golfer could buy an entry into the tournament and a T-shirt.

- Question 2, starting with the Item entity: If you have one item, what is the maximum number of orders that that item can be part of? Again, the only answers to consider are one or many. Obviously, you want more than one person to be able to order an entry to the tournament. Therefore, you say that an item can be on many orders.

With both answers being many, this is a many-to-many relationship. A **many-to-many relationship** is a relationship between tables in which one record in one table has many matching records in a second table and one record in the related table has many matching records in the first table. Because these two tables in the charity database do not have a common field, in Access this kind of many-to-many relationship must have an additional table in between these two. This intermediate table is referred to by several synonymous terms: "intersection," "junction," or "link table." You will look at this later in the chapter.

A one-to-one relationship occurs when each question is answered with a maximum of one. A **one-to-one relationship** is a relationship between tables in which a record in one table has only one matching record in the second table. In a small business, a department might be managed by no more than one manager, and each manager manages no more than one department. That relationship in that business is a one-to-one relationship.

There are three types of relationships: one-to-many, many-to-many, and one-to-one. The relationship type is based on the rules of the business. In the charity golf tournament, the relationship between the order and the item is many-to-many, but in another business, it might not be. For example, consider a business that sells custom-made jewelry in which each item is one of a kind. In this case, an item can appear on just one order. Thus, the relationship between order and item in that business would be one-to-many.

When you have a one-to-one relationship, you could combine the two tables into a single table. A single table is simpler than two tables with a one-to-one relationship between them.

- You could keep the two tables separate when the two tables are obviously two different things, such as manager and department. You might want to keep private information about the manager in the manager table. Additionally, this would be easier to change if business rules were to change and multiple managers might manage the same department.

- You should combine the two tables when there are just a few attributes on one of the tables. For example, suppose you wanted to keep only the manager's name in the manager table with no other information about the manager. Then you might consider the manager's name to be an attribute of the department.

Create a One-to-Many Relationship

Consider the relationship between tblParticipant and tblOrder. This is a one-to-many relationship. To form a relationship between two tables, you need the tables to have a field in common. The easiest way to accomplish this is to put the primary key from the table on the one side in the table on the many side. In this case, you would use the ParticipantID from the one side table and add it as a field to tblOrder. The field that you add to the many side is called a foreign key because it is a key to another, or foreign, table. ParticipantID is already a field on the many side table, so you can use it to form the relationship.

| QUICK REFERENCE | Creating a One-to-Many Relationship in Access |

Creating a one-to-many relationship in Access takes three steps.

1. Make sure the two tables have a field in common. Use the primary key from the one side, and add it as a foreign key in the many side table.

2. Form the relationship in the Relationships window. This is done by connecting the primary key of the one side table to the foreign key in the many side table.

3. Populate the foreign key by adding data to the foreign key in the many side table.

Forming a Relationship

Because tblParticipant and tblOrder already have a field in common, you can form the relationship. In this exercise, you will connect the primary key of the one side table to the foreign key in the many side table.

To Form a Relationship

a. On the Database Tools tab, in the Relationships group, click **Show Table**, click **tblParticipant**, and then click **Add**.

b. Click **Close** to close the Show Table dialog box, and then drag the **tblParticipant** table to appear below tblOrder in the Relationships window.

c. Use your pointer to resize **tblParticipant** by dragging the corner of the field list so all fields show. Drag **tblOrder** to the right.

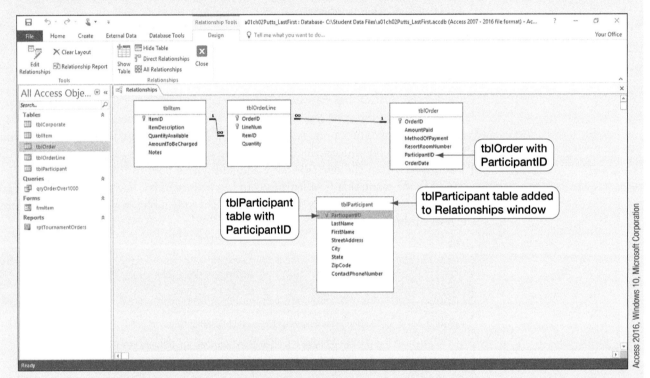

Figure 21   Add tblParticipant table to the Relationships window

d. Drag the primary key, **ParticipantID**, from tblParticipant to **ParticipantID** in tblOrder. Alternatively, you could drag from ParticipantID in tblOrder to ParticipantID in tblParticipant.

e. The Edit Relationships dialog box is displayed. Check that the fields shown in the box are both ParticipantID.

> **Troubleshooting**
>
> If you do not see two fields named ParticipantID in the Edit Relationships dialog box, click Cancel and retry step d.

Notice that Access calls the relationship a one-to-many relationship. This is because the relationship is between a primary key and a foreign key.

f. Click **Enforce Referential Integrity** to select it, and then click **Create**. Later in the chapter, you will look further at what referential integrity accomplishes.

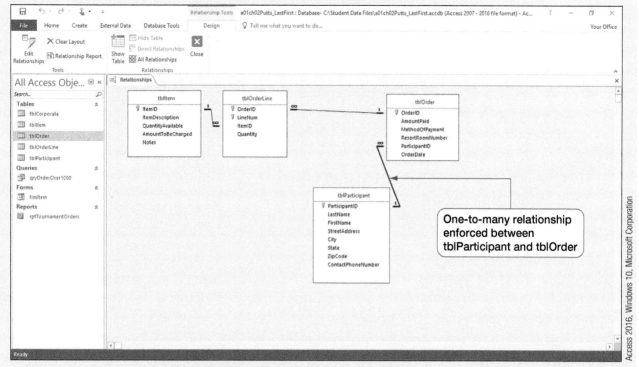

Figure 22 Relationship between tblParticipant and tblOrder

g. On the Relationship Tools Design tab, in the Relationships group, click **Close**. Click **Yes** to save the changes made to the layout.

> ### Troubleshooting
>
> If you get the error message "The database engine could not lock table 'tblParticipant' because it is already in use by another person or process," this means that the tblParticipant table is still open. Close the table, and try again to form the relationship. You should get in the habit of closing tables when you are done with them.
>
> If you get the error message "Relationship must be on the same number of fields with the same data type," this means that the data types for the primary key and the foreign key are different. For example, they must be both Numeric and Long Integer or both Text. Make sure that you are creating the relationship between the correct fields. If you are, check the table designs, and fix the field with the wrong data type.
>
> If you add a relationship that you do not want, right-click the join line, and click Delete. If you want to edit a relationship, right-click the join line, and click Edit Relationship.

Type of Relationship	Alternate Notations	Meaning
One-to-many	1:N or 1:M 1-to-N	A relationship between two tables in which one record in the first table corresponds to many records in the second table but each record in the second table corresponds to just one record in the first table.
Many-to-many	M:N M-to-N	A relationship between two tables in which one record in the first table corresponds to many records in the second table and each record in the second table corresponds to many records in the first table.
One-to-one	1:1 1-to-1	A relationship between two tables in which a record in one table has only one matching record in the second table and each record in the second table corresponds to just one record in the first table.

Create a Many-to-Many Relationship

Unless you are connecting a common field such as a foreign key to the same foreign key in a different table, Access cannot form a many-to-many relationship with a single relationship. Instead, you need to make two one-to-many relationships to represent the many-to-many relationship. As was stated before, tblOrder and tblItem have a many-to-many relationship. An order can have many items on it. Each item can be on many orders. To form this relationship, a new table, tblOrderLine, needs to be added. Both tblOrder and tblItem are related to the new table. The third table is called a junction table. **A junction table** breaks down the many-to-many relationship into two one-to-many relationships.

Look at the relationship between tblOrder and tblOrderLine in Figure 23. It is a one-to-many relationship with orders having many order lines but each order line on just one order. There is also a relationship between tblOrderLine and tblItem. It also is a one-to-many relationship with each order line having just one item but an item being able to be on many order lines, as shown in Figure 23.

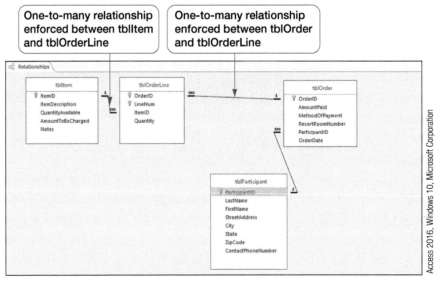

Figure 23 Relationship between tblOrder and tblItem with tblOrderLine

As shown in Figure 24, OrderID 4 has two order lines: one with an item of a corporate team and one with a cart. By traveling from left to right across the three tables, you see that OrderID 4 has many items on it. OrderID 6 has one line: an entry to the tournament. By traveling from right to left across the three tables, you see that an entry to the tournament can be on many orders. Hence, the junction table tblOrderLine forms a many-to-many relationship between tblOrder and tblItem.

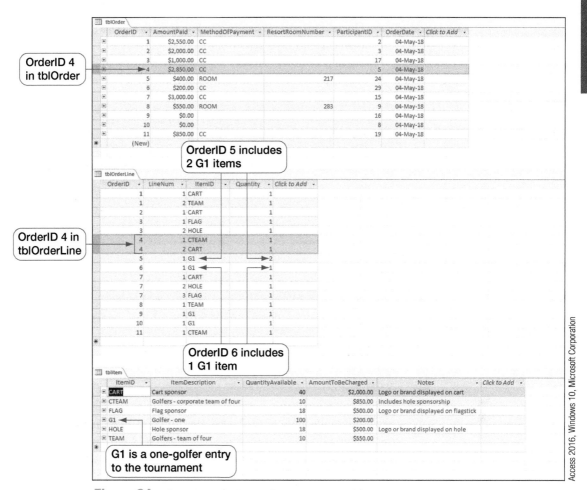

Figure 24 Data in tblOrder, tblOrderLine, and tblItem

tblOrderLine has foreign keys to tblOrder and tblItem. This allows the relationships to be formed. Notice that the relationship between tblOrder and tblOrderLine is formed with OrderID in tblOrder joined to OrderID in tblOrderLine. Similarly, the relationship between tblItem and tblOrderLine is formed from ItemID in tblItem to ItemID in tblOrderLine.

The junction table, tblOrderLine, has one field beyond the key fields: Quantity. This indicates the quantity of each item on the order. As shown in Figure 24, OrderID 5 included two entries to the tournament.

Forming a New Many-to-Many Relationship

Consider the relationship between tblCorporate and tblParticipant. There is a relationship: A participant can represent a corporation. A participant can be a golfer for a corporation, the corporate representative, or a donor. What is the cardinality? You need to ask yourself the two questions to determine the cardinality.

- Question 1, starting with the Corporate entity: If you have one corporation, what is the maximum number of participants that can represent that corporation? You care about only two answers: one or many. In this case, the corporation could be represented by many participants. A corporate team might have four golfer participants.

- Question 2, starting with the Participant entity: If you have one participant, what is the maximum number of roles that participant can represent for the corporation? Again, the only answers to consider are one or many. A participant could be a golfer representing the corporation and also be a corporate representative.

QUICK REFERENCE	Creating a Many-to-Many Relationship in Access

Creating a many-to-many relationship in Access takes four steps.

1. Create a junction table. Create a primary key that will be a unique field for the junction table, and add two foreign keys, one to each of the many-to-many tables. Alternatively, you can create a composite key made up of the two foreign keys.

2. Determine whether there are any fields that you want to add to the junction table beyond the keys.

3. Form two relationships in the Relationships window. This is done by connecting the primary key of one of the original tables to the appropriate foreign key of the junction table. Repeat for the second of the original tables. The junction table is on the many side of both relationships.

4. Populate the junction table.

Creating a Junction Table

Because the relationship between tblCorporate and tblParticipant is many-to-many, you need a junction table. Recall that the junction table breaks down the many-to-many relationship into two one-to-many relationships. In this exercise, you will create the junction table that will represent the role that the participant has for the corporation. The primary key for the junction table will be ParticipantRoleID, an AutoNumber field. You will have two foreign keys: the CorporateID field and the ParticipantID field. You will also add a field named Role that describes the role of the participant. Because the table represents roles, you will call the table tblParticipantRole.

 A02.17

To Create a Junction Table

a. Click the **Create** tab, and then, in the Tables group, click **Table Design**.
   Access opens a blank table in Design view. You will enter each field in the appropriate row.

b. In the Field Name column, type ParticipantRoleID. Press Tab to move to the Data Type column, click the **arrow**, and then select the **AutoNumber** data type.
   Alternatively, you can type the A and "AutoNumber" will appear.

c. Notice that Field Size in the Field Properties pane defaults to Long Integer. Press Tab to move to the Description column, and then type Primary key for tblParticipantRole.

d. On the Design tab, in the Tools group, click **Primary Key** to make the ParticipantRoleID field the primary key.

e. Press Tab to move to the next field. Continue filling in the table with the following information, being sure to enter the field size in the Field Properties pane.

Field Name	Data Type	Description	Field Size
CorporateID	Number	Foreign key to tblCorporate	Long Integer
ParticipantID	Number	Foreign key to tblParticipant	Long Integer
Role	Short Text	Role that participant fills for the corporation	40

f. **Close** ☒ the table, and then, in the Microsoft Access dialog box click **Yes**. Name the table tblParticipantRole, and then click **OK**.

Forming Two Relationships to a Junction Table

The many-to-many relationship will turn into two one-to-many relationships between each of the original tables and the junction table. The rule is that the junction table is on the many side of the two relationships. But you can ask yourself the two questions to determine the cardinality.

- Question 1, starting with the Corporate entity: If you have one corporation, what is the maximum number of participant roles that can represent that corporation? You care about only two answers: one or many. In this case, the corporation could be represented by many participant roles. A corporation could have golfers and corporate contacts.

- Question 2, starting with the ParticipantRole entity: If you have one ParticipantRole, what is the maximum number of corporations that the participant can represent? Again, the only answers to consider are one or many. A ParticipantRole is for a single participant.

Thus, tblCorporate to tblParticipantRole is a one-to-many relationship with Corporate on the one side. You can ask the same questions about the relationship between tblParticipant and tblParticipantRole.

In this exercise, you will create the two one-to-many relationships to the tblParticipantRole table.

 A02.18

To Form Two Relationships to a Junction Table

a. Click the **Database Tools** tab, and then, in the Relationships group, click **Relationships**.

b. On the Design tab, in the Relationships group, click **Show Table**. Select **tblCorporate**, click **Add**, select **tblParticipantRole**, and then click **Add**.

c. **Close** the Show Table dialog box, and then drag the **tables** in the Relationships window so there is some space between the tables to form the relationships.

d. Drag the primary key **ParticipantID** from tblParticipant to **ParticipantID** in tblParticipantRole. Alternatively, you could drag from ParticipantID in tblParticipantRole to ParticipantID in tblParticipant.

e. Access displays the Edit Relationships dialog box. Click **Enforce Referential Integrity** to select it, and then click **Create**.

f. Drag the primary key **CorporateID** from tblCorporate to **CorporateID** in tblParticipantRole.

g. Access displays the Edit Relationships dialog box. Click **Enforce Referential Integrity** to select it, and then click **Create**.

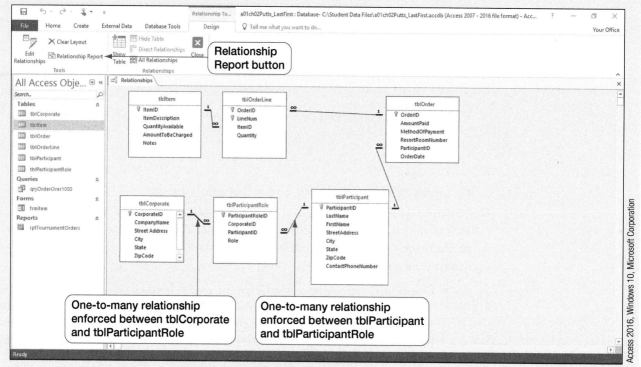

Figure 25   Junction table with two one-to-many relationships

h. On the Design tab, in the Tools group, click **Relationship Report** to create a report for your relationships. **Save** 🖫 the report, accepting the report name **Relationships for a01ch02Putts_LastFirst**, and then click **OK**.

i. If your instructor asks you to print your report, on the Print Preview tab, in the Print group, click **Print** to print the report.

j. In the Close Preview group, click **Close Print Preview**, and then **close** ☒ the Relationships report.

k. **Close** ☒ the Relationships window.

Populating the Junction Table

In this exercise, you will populate the junction table with data to complete the many-to-many relationship.

To Populate the Junction Table

a. Double-click **tblParticipantRole** to open the table in Datasheet view.

b. Click in the **CorporateID** field in the **append row**. Enter a CorporateID of 1, a ParticipantID of 5, and a Role of Corporate Contact. Access automatically numbers ParticipantRoleID as 1.

c. Because the last field is not totally visible, place your pointer in the **border** on the right of the **Role** column heading. When your pointer is a double-headed arrow $+$, double-click the **border** to resize the column. Repeat for each field.

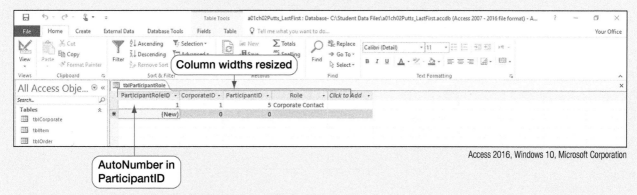

AutoNumber in ParticipantID

Figure 26 tblParticipantRole columns resized

d. Enter the following data in new records as follows.

CorporateID	ParticipantID	Role
1	1	Golfer
1	26	Golfer

e. **Close** $\times$ the table, and then, in the Microsoft Access dialog box, click **Yes** to save the changes to the table layout.

Defining One-to-One Relationships

One-to-one relationships in Access are formed very similarly to one-to-many relationships. You can put a foreign key in either table and establish the relationship by dragging with the primary key in one table joined to the foreign key. You can also make both tables have the same primary key.

Understand Referential Integrity

Referential integrity is a database concept that ensures that relationships between tables remain consistent. When one table has a foreign key to another table, the concept of referential integrity states that you may not add a record to the table that contains the foreign key unless there is a corresponding record in the linked table. Recall that when you created the relationship between tblParticipant and tblOrder, you told Access to enforce referential integrity.

Selecting Cascade Update

When you ask Access to enforce referential integrity, you can also select whether you want Access to automatically cascade update related fields or cascade delete related records. These options allow some deletions and updates that would usually be prevented by referential integrity. However, Access makes these changes and replicates or cascades the changes through all related tables so referential integrity is preserved.

If you select Cascade Update Related Fields when you define a relationship, then when the primary key of a record in the one side table changes, Access automatically changes the foreign keys in all related records. For example, if you change the ItemID in the tblItem table, Access automatically changes the ItemID on all order lines that include that item. Access makes these changes without displaying an error message.

If the primary key in the one side table was defined as AutoNumber, selecting Cascade Update Related Fields has no effect, because you cannot change the value in an AutoNumber field.

Selecting Cascade Delete

If you select Cascade Delete Related Records when you define a relationship, any time you delete records from the one side table, the related records in the many side table are also deleted. For example, if you delete a tblParticipant record, all the orders made by that participant are automatically deleted from the tblOrder table. Before you make the deletion, Access warns you that related records may also be deleted.

 CONSIDER THIS | **Should You Cascade Delete Related Records?**

Consider a customer who has made many orders. If the customer asks to be removed from your database, do you want to remove his or her past orders? How do you think the company's accountants would feel?

Testing Referential Integrity

Enforcing referential integrity ensures that the following rules will be applied when you define the fields in Design view.

- The value in the field on the one side of the relationship is unique in the table. You must use either the primary key of the one side in the relationship or a field that you have set as unique in the table.

- You cannot add a foreign key value on the many side that does not have a matching primary key value on the one side.

- The matching fields on both sides of the relationship are defined with the same data types. For example, if the primary key is numeric and Long Integer, the foreign key must be numeric and Long Integer too. (For purposes of relationships, an AutoNumber primary key is considered Long Integer.)

If these rules are violated, when you try to form the relationship, you will get the following error message: "Relationship must be on the same number of fields with the same data type."

 CONSIDER THIS | **Why Enforce Referential Integrity?**

You can decline to enforce referential integrity on a relationship. What are the pros and cons of enforcing referential integrity? What are the pros and cons of not enforcing referential integrity?

You also cannot change the primary key value in the one side table if that record has related records.

QUICK REFERENCE	Referential Integrity

Access enforces the following rules on defining a relationship with referential integrity.

1. The primary key field values on the one side of the relationship must be unique in the table.
2. The foreign key values on the many side of the relationship must exist as the primary key field for a record on the one side of the relationship.
3. The matching fields on both sides of the relationship are defined with the same data types.

(Continued)

CHAPTER 2

The following rules are applied to data changes when referential integrity is enforced.

1. You cannot enter a value in the foreign key field on the many side table that is not a primary key on the one side table. However, you can leave the foreign key unfilled, indicating that this record is not in the relationship. However, it is not good practice to do this.

2. You cannot delete a record from the one side table if matching records exist in a many side table, unless Cascade Delete has been selected for the relationship, in which case all the matching records on the many side are deleted.

3. You cannot change a primary key value in the one side table if that record has related records in the many side unless Cascade Update has been selected for the relationship, in which case all the matching records on the many side have their foreign key updated.

In this exercise, you will test referential integrity being enforced between the tblParticipant and tblOrder tables by attempting to enter a new order and assign it to a ParticipantID that does not exist and by attempting to delete a participant that has records in the tblOrder table.

To Test Referential Integrity

a. Right-click **tblParticipant**, and then select **Design View**. Notice that ParticipantID is defined as Number and Long Integer.

b. **Close** ☒ tblParticipant, right-click **tblOrder**, select **Design View**, and then click the **ParticipantID** field. Notice that ParticipantID is also defined as Number and Long Integer in the tblOrder table.

c. Click the **Home** tab, and then, in the Views group, click the **View** button to switch to Datasheet View for tblOrder.

d. In the ParticipantID for the last record in the table, type 70, and then press Enter twice.

Access responds with the error message "You cannot add or change a record because a related record is required in table tblParticipant." That is, you cannot add an order to participant 70 because there is no participant 70.

e. Click **OK**, and then change the ParticipantID for the last order to 1. Press Enter twice. ParticipantID 1 is a valid participant, so you can make that change.

f. **Close** ☒ the tblOrder table.

If you enforce referential integrity, you also cannot delete a record from the one side table if matching records exist in the many side table. If you want to delete the record, you must delete the matching records or use Cascade Delete.

g. In the Navigation Pane, double-click **tblParticipant** to open it in Datasheet view.

h. Click the **record selector** of the second row, John Trujillo.

i. On the Home tab, in the Records group, click **Delete**.

Access responds with the error message "The record cannot be deleted or changed because table 'tblOrder' includes related records." That means John Trujillo has placed an order.

j. Click **OK**.

k. **Close** ☒ the tblParticipant table.

Creating a Report Using Two Related Tables

The reason you create a relationship is to join two tables for queries, reports, and forms. In this exercise, you will create a simple report showing participants and their orders by using two related tables.

To Create a Report Using Two Related Tables

a. Click the **Create** tab, and then, in the Reports group, click **Report Wizard**.

b. In the Report Wizard dialog box, click the **Tables/Queries** arrow, and then select **Table: tblParticipant**. Select the **LastName** field, and then click **One Field** >. Select the **FirstName** field, and then click **One Field** >.

c. Click the **Tables/Queries** arrow, and then select **Table: tblOrder**. Select the **OrderID** field, and then click **One Field** >. Select the **AmountPaid** field, and then click **One Field** >.

> **Troubleshooting**
>
> If you clicked Next instead of selecting the tblOrder fields, you can go back a step in the wizard by clicking Back.

d. Click **Next**.

   You can see a preview of how your report will look if you group the report by participants, using the data in tblParticipant. Access uses the one side of a one-to-many relationship as the default for the grouping. This is the grouping you want.

e. Click **Next**. The wizard asks whether you want more grouping levels; however, you do not want any other grouping levels.

f. Click **Next**.

g. Use the arrow to select **OrderID**. Ascending sort order is already selected. Click **Next**.

   The wizard asks you to choose a layout and orientation for your report. You will accept the default Stepped layout and Portrait orientation.

h. Click **Next**.

i. Title your report rptParticipantOrders. Click **Finish**.

   Access connects the participants and orders in a report.

j. Right-click anywhere on the report, and then select **Layout View** from the shortcut menu.

> **Troubleshooting**
>
> If the Field List shows on the right side of the Access window, close it so you can see the entire report layout.

k. Double-click the **title** of the report. Change the report title to Participants and Orders, and press Enter. **Save** your report.

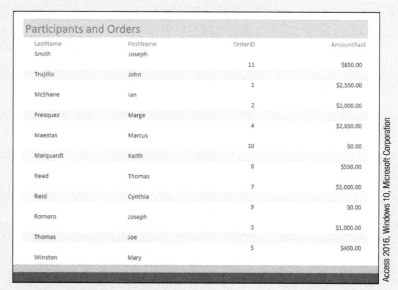

Figure 27   Completed report

l.   If your instructor directs you to print the report, right-click anywhere on the report, switch to **Print Preview**, click **Print** in the Print group, and then click **OK**.

m. **Close** ☒ the report.

n.   Exit Access and then submit your file as directed by your instructor.

Concept Check

1. What is an entity? What is an attribute? What is a relationship? p. 585

2. If you have data in an Excel worksheet, what methods could you use to move the data in Excel to Access? How would you decide between the methods? p. 588, 590, 592, 594

3. Why is it important to type a new record in the blank (append) row rather than on top of another record? p. 594

4. What data types would you use for the following fields: price, phone number, street address, ZIP Code, and notes about product usage? p. 599

5. What is an input mask used for? What is a format used for? Which can affect the way in which data is stored? p. 602, 604

6. What is the purpose of a primary key? p. 598

7. Why is redundancy of data undesirable? p. 612

8. What does it mean to say that there is a relationship between two tables? p. 613

9. How do you create a one-to-many relationship in Access? p. 615

10. How do you create a many-to-many relationship in Access? p. 618–623

11. What does it mean for a relationship to have referential integrity enforced? p. 623

Key Terms

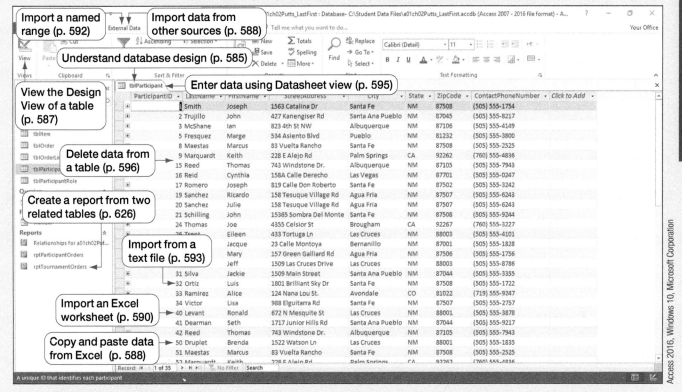

Figure 28

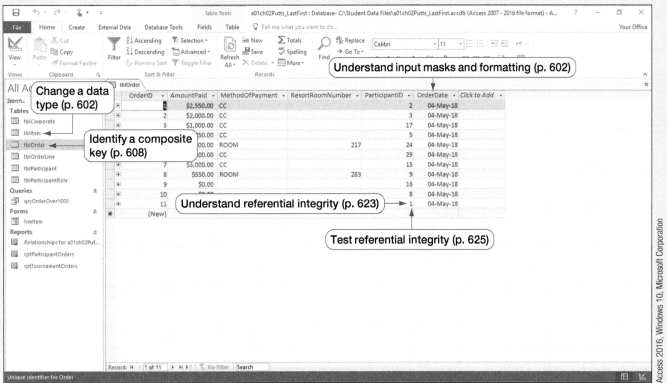

Figure 29

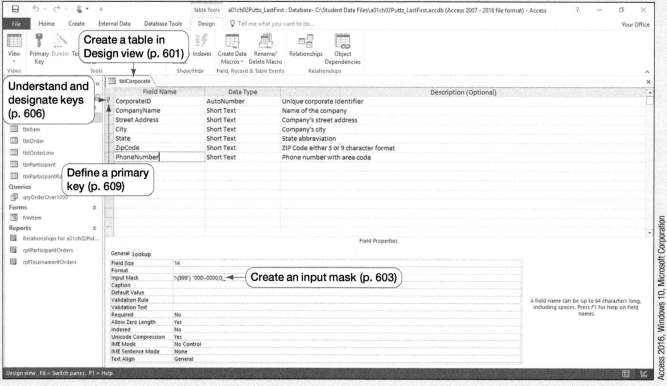

Figure 30

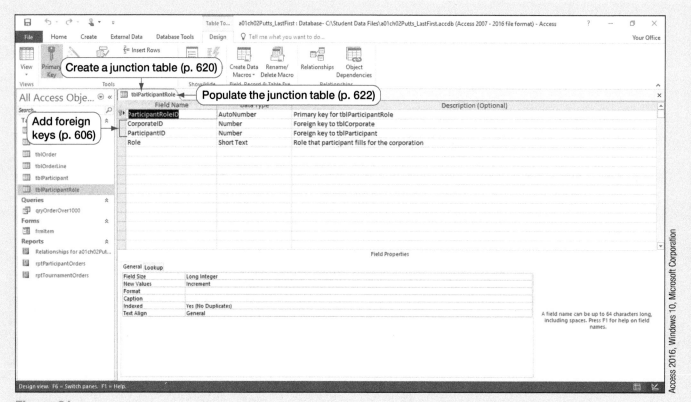

Figure 31

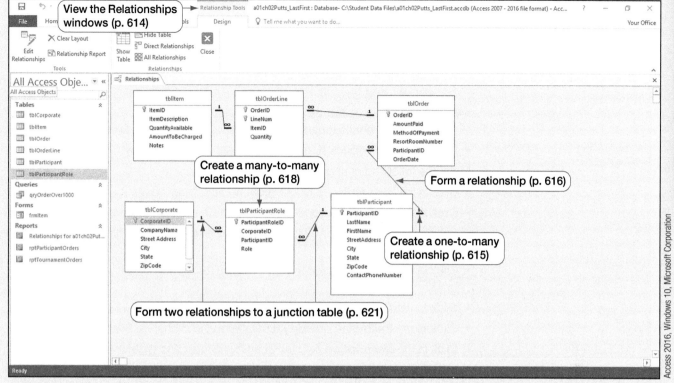

Figure 32

Practice 1

Student data files needed:

Sales & Marketing

a01ch02Giftshop.accdb

a01ch02Products.xlsx

a01ch02Customers.xlsx

You will save your file as:

a01ch02Giftshop_LastFirst.accdb

Painted Treasures Gift Shop

The Painted Treasures Gift Shop sells many products for the resort patrons, including jewelry, clothing, and spa products. You will create a database of customers and their purchases. The three tables that you need are customers, purchases, and products. What are the relationships between these three tables? You will need to create a new table that will serve as a junction table between the two tables, as is necessary to accommodate a many-to-many relationship.

a. Open the Access file, **a01ch02Giftshop**. Save your file as a01ch02Giftshop_LastFirst using your last and first name. If necessary, enable the content.

b. Import data from Excel into the database by completing the following steps.

- Click the **External Data** tab, and then, in the Import & Link group, click **Excel**.

- Click **Browse.** Navigate through the folder structure to the location of your student data files, and then double-click **a01ch02Products**. Make sure **Import the source data into a new table in the current database** is selected, and then click **OK**.

- In the Import Spreadsheet Wizard, note that **tblProduct** is selected, and then click **Next**.
- Be sure that the **First Row Contains Column Headings** check box is selected, click **Next**, and then click **Next** again.
- Select **Choose my own primary key**, make sure **ProductID** is selected as the primary key, and then click **Next**.
- In the **Import to Table** box, change the table name to tblProduct_iLast using your first initial and last name. Click **Finish**, and then click **Close**.
- Right-click **tblProduct_iLast**, and then select **Design View**.

c. Make the following changes to the fields in tblProducts_iLast.

- Click in the **Description** field for ProductID, and type Unique identifier for product.
- Click in the **Field Size** property for ProductID, and select **Long Integer**.
- Click in the **Description** field for ProductDescription, and type Description of product.
- Click in the **Field Size** property for ProductDescription, and change the field size to 40.
- Click in the **Description** field for Category, and type Product category.
- Click in the **Field Size** property for Category, and change the field size to 15.
- Click in the **Description** field for QuantityInStock, and type Quantity of products in stock.
- Click in the **Field Size** property for QuantityInStock, and select **Integer**.
- Click in the **Data Type** field for Price, and select **Currency**.
- Click in the **Description** field for Price, and type Price to charge customer.
- Click the **Description** field for Size, and type Size of product.
- Click in the **Field Size** property for Size, and set the size to 10.
- Click the **Description** field for Color, and type Color of product.
- Click in the **Field Size** property for Color, and set the size to 15.

d. Save the table. Access tells you that some data might be lost because you are making fields shorter in length. Accept this by clicking **Yes**, and then close the table.

e. Create a table in Design view by completing the following steps.

- Click the **Create** tab, and then click **Table Design**. Access opens a blank table in Design view.
- Fill in the fields and change field sizes as noted.

Field Name	Data Type	Description	Field Size
CustomerID	AutoNumber	A unique ID that identifies each customer	Long Integer
LastName	Short Text	The customer's last name	25
FirstName	Short Text	The customer's first name	20
StreetAddress	Short Text	Street address	40
City	Short Text	City address	25
State	Short Text	State abbreviation	2
ZipCode	Short Text	Five-digit ZIP Code	5
ResortHotelRoom	Short Text	Leave blank if not guest	6

- Highlight the **CustomerID** row by clicking the record selector to the left of the field, and then, on the Design tab, in the Tools group, click **Primary Key** to make CustomerID the primary key.
- Save your table design, naming it tblCustomer_iLast using your first initial and last name, and then close the table.

f. Import data into the table by completing the following steps.

- Click the **External Data** tab, and then, in the Import & Link group, click **Excel**.
- Click **Browse**. Navigate through the folder structure to the location of your student data files, and then double-click **a01ch02Customers**.
- Click **Append a copy of the records to the table** if necessary, click the arrow to select **tblCustomer_iLast**, and then click **OK**.
- Click **Next** twice, and then, in the Import Spreadsheet Wizard dialog box, in the Import to Table box, accept the name **tblCustomer_iLast**. Click **Finish**, and then click **Close**. Double-click **tblCustomer_iLast** to open it in Datasheet view.
- In the first record in the table, change the **LastName** and **FirstName** fields to your **last name** and **first name**. Close the table.

g. Create relationships between your tables by completing the following steps.

- Click the **Database Tools** tab, and then, in the Relationships group, click **Relationships**, and then click **Show Table** if necessary.
- Add all four tables in the order **tblCustomer_iLast**, **tblPurchase**, **tblPurchase-Line**, and **tblProduct_iLast** to the Relationships window, and then close the Show Table dialog box.
- Drag the primary key **CustomerID** from tblCustomer_iLast to **CustomerID** in tblPurchase.
- Click **Enforce Referential Integrity**, and then click **Create**.
- Drag the primary key **PurchaseID** from tblPurchase to **PurchaseID** in tblPurchaseLine. Click **Enforce Referential Integrity**, and then click **Create**.
- Drag the primary key **ProductID** from tblProduct_iLast to **ProductID** in tblPurchaseLine. Click **Enforce Referential Integrity**, and then click **Create**.
- Click **Relationship Report**, and then save the report, accepting the name **Relationships for a01ch02Giftshop_LastFirst**. If your instructor directs you to print your results, print the report.
- Close the report, and then close the Relationships window.

h. Create a report of the customers, purchases, and products by completing the following steps.

- Click the **Create** tab, and then, in the Reports group, click **Report Wizard**.
- In the Report Wizard dialog box, click the **Tables/Queries** arrow, and then select **Table: tblCustomer_iLast**. Select the **LastName** and **FirstName** fields.
- Click the **Tables/Queries** arrow, click **Table: tblPurchase**, and then select **PurchaseDate**.
- Click the **Tables/Queries** arrow, click **Table: tblPurchaseLine**, and then select **Quantity**.
- Click the **Tables/Queries** arrow, click **Table: tblProduct_iLast**, select **ProductDescription**, and then click **Next**.
- Accept grouping by **tblCustomer_iLast** and then by **PurchaseDate** by clicking **Next**.
- You do not want any other grouping levels, so click **Next**.

- Click the **arrow** to sort your report by ascending **ProductDescription**, and then click **Next**.
- Change the Orientation to **Landscape**, and then click **Next**.
- Title your report **rptCustomerPurchases_iLast** using your first initial and last name, and then click **Finish**.
- Switch to Layout view.
- Change the title of your report to **Customers and Purchases by iLast** using your first initial and last name.

i. Save the report, exit Access, and then submit your file as directed by your instructor.

Problem Solve 1

Student data files needed:

a01ch02Planner.accdb

a01ch02PlannerDec.txt

You will save your file as:

a01ch02Planner_LastFirst.accdb

Morris Event Management

Production & Operations

Sue Morris has a small event-planning business. She recently decided to transfer her company's data to a database. Although she has started on the database, she is too busy to finish it, so she has hired you to complete the implementation.

a. Open the Access file, **a01ch02Planner**. Save your file as a01ch02Planner_LastFirst using your last and first name. If necessary, enable the content.

b. Sue wants to ensure that certain data is entered correctly. Open **tblClients** in Design view.
- For **Phone**, add an input mask so that fields appear as **(555) 555-5555** with a placeholder of "_", and save with symbols in the mask.
- Change the field size of **State** to 2.
- Change the field size of **ZipCode** to 5.

c. Import the decorations data stored in **a01ch02PlannerDec.txt** into a new table.
- The data is delimited and separated with commas.
- Choose your own primary key of **Field1**.
- Name the table tblDecorations.
- Do not save the import steps.

d. In Design view for **tblDecorations**, make the following changes to the fields.

Current Field Name	New Field Name	Data Type	Description	Field Size
Field1	DecorationID	Number	A unique identifier for the decoration	Long Integer
Field2	Decoration	Short Text	Decoration label	20
Field3	Color	Short Text	Decoration color	10
Field4	Category	Short Text	Type of decoration	20

e. Sue wants to be able to record the decorations that are being reserved for each event. This creates a many-to-many relationship between events and decorations. Create a junction table in Design view.

- Add the following fields (in this order).

Field Name	Data Type	Description	Field Size
EventID	Number	The primary key from tblEvents	Long Integer
DecorationID	Number	The primary key from tblDecorations	Long Integer
NumberReserved	Number	The number of decorations reserved	Long Integer

- Create a composite key using **EventID** and **DecorationID**.
- Save the new table as tblEventDecoration.

f. Open the **Relationships** window, create a one-to-many relationship between **ClientID** in tblClients and **ClientID** in tblEvents. Enforce referential integrity.

g. Create a many-to-many relationship between **tblEvents** and **tblDecorations** using the new junction table.

- Add the **tblEventDecoration** table to the Relationships window.
- Create a one-to-many relationship between **EventID** in tblEvents and **EventID** in tblEventDecoration. Enforce referential integrity.
- Create a one-to-many relationship between **DecorationID** in tblDecorations and **DecorationID** in tblEventDecoration. Enforce referential integrity.
- Create a relationships report accepting the name **Relationships for a01ch02Planner_LastFirst**.
- If your instructor directs you to print the relationships, print your relationship report.

h. Sue has one order to put into **tblEventDecoration**. Type the following new records in the table.

EventID	DecorationID	NumberReserved
3	7	4
3	9	40
3	17	4

i. Use the Report Wizard to create a report showing decorations needed for each event.

- Use the **LastName** and **FirstName** fields from tblClients.
- Use the **EventDate** field from tblEvents.
- Use the **Decoration** and **Color** fields from tblDecorations.
- Use **NumberReserved** from tblEventDecoration.
- View by **tblClients**, and accept the default grouping.
- Sort by **Decoration** in ascending order.
- Change Orientation to **Landscape**.
- Name the report rptEventDecorations, and then modify the report title to be Event Decorations.
- Fix the report columns as necessary so the report fits on one page. If your instructor directs you to print your results, print your report.

j. Save the report, exit Access, and then submit your file as directed by your instructor.

Critical Thinking

Name one other entity that would be useful for Morris Event Management to track in the database and provide an explanation as to why it would be useful.

Student data files needed:

 a01ch02RealEstate.accdb

 a01ch02Development.xlsx

You will save your file as:

 a01ch02RealEstate_LastFirst.accdb

Real Estate Listings Database

Sales & Marketing

You are interning for a local real estate firm. You have been asked to work with a database of your firm's real estate listings. There is data describing each development in the area and listing its amenities in an Excel workbook. Your boss asks that you incorporate the Excel data into the database and report some findings.

a. Open the Access file, **a01ch02RealEstate**. Save your file as a01ch02RealEstate_LastFirst using your last and first name.

b. Open **tblAgent**. Change the first and last name fields for record 1 to your first and your last name.

c. Add a new field named Phone. Create an input mask so that the numbers appear as (336) 555-1234. Store the data without the symbols. Set the field size to 12. Enter ten-digit phone numbers for all the agents.

d. Import the data contained in the Excel file **a01ch02Development** into the database as a table named tblDevelopment_iLast using your first initial and last name. Set **DevelopmentID** as the primary key.

e. Open tblDevelopment_iLast in Design view. Change the field size of DevelopmentID to 15. Change the field size of DevelopmentName to 40. Define the Pool, Playground, BikeTrail, and DogPark fields as **Yes/No** fields. Define HOADues as **Currency**.

f. Create a one-to-many relationship between the **DevelopmentID** field in tblDevelopment_iLast and tblListing. Enforce referential integrity.

g. Create a Relationship Report showing the relationships in the database. Name this report rptRelationships_iLast using your first initial and last name.

h. Use the Report Wizard to create a report showing the sales for each agent.
   - From tblAgent, select the **LastName** and **FirstName** fields.
   - From tblListing, select the **SoldDate** and **SoldPrice** fields.
   - From tblDevelopment_iLast select the **DevelopmentName** field.
   - View the data in the report by tblAgent, and sort in ascending order by SoldDate.
   - Keep the default Stepped layout and Portrait orientation.
   - Name this report rptAgentSales_iLast using your first initial and last name.

i. Edit the report title to read Agent Sales Report.

j. Save the report, exit Access, and then submit your file as directed by your instructor.

Additional Cases

Additional Chapter Cases are available at www.pearsonhighered.com/youroffice

Understanding and Using a Relational Database

This business unit had two outcomes:

Learning Outcome 1:

Understand the purpose for main database objects in Access: tables, queries, forms, and reports.

Learning Outcome 2:

Based on the needs of an organization, understand and create various types of relationships using different types of keys: primary, foreign, and composite.

In Business Unit 1 Capstone, students will demonstrate competence in these outcomes through a series of business problems at various levels from guided practice, problem solving an existing database, and performing to create new databases.

More Practice 1

Student data files needed:

- a01Recipe.accdb
- a01RecipePrep.xlsx
- a01RecipeIng.xlsx
- a01RecipeJunc.csv

You will save your file as:

- a01Recipe_LastFirst.accdb

Indigo5 Restaurant

Production & Operations

Robin Sanchez, the chef of the Painted Paradise Resort's restaurant, Indigo5, wants to keep track of recipes and the ingredients they include in an Access database. This will allow her to plan menus and run reports and queries on the ingredients that are needed. Ingredients have already been stored in Excel worksheets and can be imported from Excel into Access. The dish preparation instructions can be copied from Excel and pasted into Access. Other data will need to be entered. Complete the following tasks.

a. Open the Access file **a01Recipe**. Save your file as a01Recipe_LastFirst using your last and first name. If necessary, enable the content.

b. Create a new table in **Design** view. This table will store specific recipe items.

- Add the following fields, data types, and descriptions. Change field sizes as noted.

Field Name	Data Type	Description	Field Size
RecipeID	Short Text	The recipe ID assigned to each menu item (primary key)	6
RecipeName	Short Text	The recipe name	30
FoodCategory	Short Text	The food category	15
TimeToPrepare	Number	Preparation time in minutes	Integer
Servings	Number	The number of servings this recipe makes	Integer
Instructions	Long Text	Cooking instructions	

- Designate **RecipeID** as the primary key. Save the new table as tblRecipes_iLast using your first initial and last name, and then close the table.

c. Create a form to enter recipes. Select **tblRecipes_iLast**, click the **Create** tab, and then, in the Forms group, click **Form**. Save the form as frmRecipes_iLast using your first initial and last name.

- Enter the following data into frmRecipes_iLast in Form view.

RecipeID	RecipeName	FoodCategory	TimeToPrepare	Servings
REC001	Chicken Soup	Soup	45	8
REC002	Black Beans	Beans	90	6

d. Open the Excel file, **a01RecipePrep**. For each recipe, copy the **Cooking Instructions** from the Excel worksheet, and paste these instructions into the Access field **Instructions**. Close the form, and then close Excel.

e. Import the Excel file **a01RecipeIng**, appending it to **tblIngredients**. Use the **Ingredients** worksheet. There are headers in the first row of this worksheet. Do not save the import steps.

f. Create a new table in **Design** view. This table will serve as the junction table between the tblIngredients and tblRecipes_iLast tables.

- Add the following fields, data types, and descriptions in this order. Change field sizes as noted.

Field Name	Data Type	Description	Field Size
RecipeIngredientID	AutoNumber	The recipe ingredient ID automatically assigned to each recipe ingredient (primary key)	Long Integer
RecipeID	Short Text	The recipe ID from tblRecipes (foreign key)	6
IngredientID	Number	The ingredient ID from tblIngredients (foreign key)	Long Integer
Quantity	Number	The quantity of the ingredient required in the recipe	Double

- Assign **RecipeIngredientID** as the primary key.
- Save the new table as tblRecipeIngredients_iLast using your first initial and last name.
- Close the table.

g. Open the **Relationships** window, and add all three tables to the window.

- Create a one-to-many relationship between **RecipeID** in tblRecipes_iLast and **RecipeID** in tblRecipeIngredients_iLast. Enforce referential integrity. Do not cascade update or cascade delete.

- Create a one-to-many relationship between **IngredientID** in tblIngredients and **IngredientID** in tblRecipeIngredients_iLast. Enforce referential integrity. Do not cascade update or cascade delete.

- Create a relationship report accepting the default name.

- Save the relationships, and then close the Relationships window.

h. The Recipe Ingredients junction data were stored in a comma-separated values file, also known as a csv file. This is a comma-delimited format that can be read by Excel. Access treats a csv file as a text file. Import **a01RecipeJunc** as **Text**, appending it to **tblRecipeIngredients_iLast**. Select **Delimited**, **Comma**, and **First Row Contains Field Names**. Do not save the import steps.

i.   Use the Simple Query Wizard and the data in tblRecipes_iLast, tblRecipeIngredients_iLast, and tblIngredients to create a query that displays the ingredients for each dish. The query results should list **RecipeName**, **Quantity**, **Ingredient**, and **Units**. This will be a **Detail** query. Run your query. Adjust the width of the query columns as necessary. Save your query as qryRecipeIngredients_iLast using your first initial and last name.

j.   Create a report with the source **qryRecipeIngredients_iLast** using the Report Wizard. Select all fields, group by **RecipeName**, and then sort by **Ingredient**. Accept all other defaults. Name your report rptRecipeIngredients_iLast using your first initial and last name.

k.   Modify the report title to be Recipe Ingredients Report by iLast using your first initial and last name. Adjust the report columns as necessary.

l.   Save the report, exit Access, and then submit your file as directed by your instructor.

Problem Solve 1

MyITLab®
Grader
Homework

Production & Operations

Student data file needed:

 a01HotelEvent.accdb

You will save your file as:

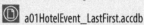 a01HotelEvent_LastFirst.accdb

Group Reservations Database

Patti Rochelle, corporate event planner, wants to be able to track group reservations with the conference rooms that are booked for the event. This will involve tracking conference rooms, groups, and events.

A group can book several events. Each event is booked by just one group. Each event could require multiple conference rooms. Conference rooms can be booked for several events (on different days). You will need a junction table for this relationship. Complete the following tasks.

a.   Open the Access file **a01HotelEvent**. Save your file as a01HotelEvent_LastFirst using your last and first name. If necessary, enable the content.

b.   Create a new table in Design view. This table will store conference rooms.

   • Add the following fields (in the following order). Where necessary, decide upon data types.

Field Name	Data Type	Description	Field Size
ConfRoomID	AutoNumber	A unique identifier for the conference room	Long Integer
RoomName	Pick an appropriate data type.	The name of the conference room	40
Capacity	Pick an appropriate data type.	The capacity of the conference room	Integer

   • Assign **ConfRoomID** as the primary key.

   • Save the new table as **tblConfRooms**.

c.   In this order, enter the following rooms into the table.

RoomName	Capacity
Musica	500
Eldorado	100
Pueblo	25

d. Create a new table in Design view. This table will store groups.

- Add the following fields, data types, and descriptions (in the following order). Where necessary, decide upon data types.

Field Name	Data Type	Description	Field Size
GroupID	AutoNumber	A unique identifier for the group (primary key)	Long Integer
GroupName	Pick an appropriate data type.	Group name	40
ContactFirstName	Pick an appropriate data type.	Contact person first name	30
ContactLastName	Pick an appropriate data type.	Contact person last name	40
ContactPhone	Pick an appropriate data type.	Contact phone number	14

- Define an input mask for contact phone number. Use a mask that will show phone numbers as **(555) 555-5555** with a placeholder of "_", and save with the symbols in the mask.

- Assign **GroupID** as the primary key. Save the new table as tblGroup.

e. Create a new table in Design view. This table will store events.

- Add the following fields, data types, and descriptions (in the following order). Where necessary, decide upon data types.

Field Name	Data Type	Description	Field Size
EventID	AutoNumber	A unique identifier for the event (primary key)	Long Integer
EventName	Pick an appropriate data type.	The name of the event	40
EventStart	Pick an appropriate data type.	Starting date for the event	Short Date
EventLength	Pick an appropriate data type.	Length of the event (in days)	Integer
GroupID	Number	The Group ID from tblGroup (foreign key)	Long Integer

- Make sure that you have assigned EventID as a primary key. Save the new table as tblEvent.

f. Create a new table in Design view. This table will serve as the junction table between tblConfRooms and tblEvent.

- Add the following fields, data types, and descriptions (in the following order). Where necessary, decide upon the field names and data types.

Field Name	Data Type	Description	Field Size
ReservationID	AutoNumber	A unique identifier for the conference reservation (primary key)	Long Integer
EventID	Number	The Event ID from tblEvent (foreign key)	Long Integer
ConfRoomID	Number	The Conference Room ID from tblConfRooms (foreign key)	Long Integer
ReservationDate	Pick an appropriate data type.	Reservation date	Short Date
DaysReserved	Number	Number of days reserved	Integer

- Make sure that you have assigned ReservationID as a primary key. Save the new table as tblConfRes.

g. Open the **Relationships** window.

- Create a one-to-many relationship between the correct field in tblGroup and the correct field in tblEvent. Enforce referential integrity. Do not cascade update or cascade delete.

- Create a one-to-many relationship between the correct field in tblEvent and the correct field in tblConfRes. Enforce referential integrity. Do not cascade update or cascade delete.

- Create a one-to-many relationship between the correct field in tblConfRooms and tblConfRes. Enforce referential integrity. Do not cascade update or cascade delete.

- Create a relationship report, keeping the default name.

h. Enter the following data into the appropriate tables (in the following order). You may need to determine keys along the way.

Group:	Benson & Diaz Law Group
	Contact: Mary Williams (505) 555-1207
Benson & Diaz's Event:	Company Retreat
	Start Date: 2/17/2018
	Length of Event: 2 days
Benson & Diaz's Reservation of the Pueblo Room:	
	Date: 2/17/2018
	Number of Days: 2 days

Group:	Dental Association of Nova Scotia
	Contact: Firstname Lastname (replacing Firstname Lastname with your own name) (902) 555–8765
Dental Association's Event:	Annual Meeting
	Start Date: 2/17/2018
	Length of Event: 5 days
Dental Association's Reservation of the Eldorado Room:	
	Date: 2/17/2018
	Number of Days: 2 days
Dental Association's Reservation of the Pueblo Room:	
	Date: 2/20/2018
	Number of Days: 2 days

Group:	Orchard Growers of the United States
	Contact: Will Goodwin (212) 555-7889
Orchard Growers' Event:	Annual Meeting
	Start Date: 2/17/2018
	Length of Event: 2 days
Orchard Growers' Reservation of the Musica Room:	
	Date: 2/17/2018
	Number of Days: 5 days

i. Create a query using **RoomName** from tblConfRooms and **ReservationDate** and **DaysReserved** from tblConfRes. Save your query as qryEldoradoRoom. Modify the query to select the room named **Eldorado**, sort by **ReservationDate**, and then run the query. Adjust the width of the query columns as necessary. If your instructor directs you to print your results, print your query.

j. Use data from four tables to create a query about the Dental Association of Nova Scotia. The query results should list **GroupName**, **EventName**, **EventStart**, **EventLength**, **RoomName**, **ReservationDate**, and **DaysReserved**. Save your query as qryDentalAssociation. Modify the query to select the group named **Dental Association of Nova Scotia**, sort by **ReservationDate**, and then run the query. Adjust the width of the columns as necessary. If your instructor directs you to print your results, print your query.

k. Create a report from **qryDentalAssociation**. Select all fields. Accept the default view by tblGroup. Sort by **RoomName** and **ReservationDate**. Select **Landscape orientation**. Name your report rptDentalAssociationBooking. Adjust the width of the report columns as necessary. Modify the report title to be Dental Association Booking. If your instructor directs you to print your results, print your report.

l. Save the report, exit Access, and then submit your file as directed by your instructor.

Critical Thinking

In this project, you were asked to pick an appropriate data type for several of the fields. Explain how you determined which data types were most appropriate. Do you think there was more than one appropriate data type for any of the fields? Explain your thinking for one of the choices you made.

Problem Solve 2

MyITLab®
Grader
Homework

Student data files needed:

 a01HotelRoom.accdb

a01HotelType.txt

a01HotelItems.xlsx

You will save your file as:

a01HotelRoom_LastFirst.accdb

Room Inventory Database

Production & Operations

For each room at the hotel, the resort wants to track room types and all inventory items such as furniture, artwork, and appliances. You will build an Access database to do this tracking. The database will have four new tables: tblRoomType, tblRoom, tblItem, and a junction table between tblRoom and tblItem, named tblRoomItem.

a. Open the Access file, **a01HotelRoom**. Save your file as a01HotelRoom_LastFirst using your last and first name. If necessary, enable the content.

b. Create a new table in Design view. This table will store the room types.
   • Add the following fields (in the following order).

Field Name	Data Type	Description	Field Size
RoomType	Short Text	The name of the room type	20
RoomAmenities	Long Text	The amenities that this type of room has	

   • Do not assign a primary key yet.
   • Save the new table as tblRoomType.

c. The data for this table has been stored in a text file delimited with tabs, **a01HotelType**. Import the data, and append it to **tblRoomType**.

- Add a new field to be the primary key. The field should be the first field in the table and should have the following characteristics.

Field Name	Data Type	Description	Field Size
RoomTypeID	AutoNumber	A unique identifier for the room type	Long Integer

d. Create a new table in Design view. This table will store individual rooms.

- Add the following fields, data types, fields sizes, and descriptions (in the following order).

Field Name	Data Type	Description	Field Size
RoomNumber	Short Text	A unique identifier for the room	30
ResortFloor	Number	Floor that the room is on	Integer
SquareFeet	Number	Square feet of this room	Long Integer
RoomTypeID	Number	Foreign key to tblRoomType	Long Integer

- Assign a primary key using the most appropriate field.
- Name the table tblRoom.

e. Enter the following data into the tblRoom table.

RoomNumber	ResortFloor	SquareFeet	RoomTypeID
101	1	500	1
102	1	520	1
106	1	600	2
206	2	600	2
112	1	700	3
120	1	1000	4
231	2	1400	5

f. The resort has been tracking inventory items in Excel. Import the spreadsheet **a01HotelItems** into a new table named tblItem. The first row contains column headings. Do not assign a primary key yet.

g. Make the following design changes to **tblItem**, adding descriptions for all fields.

Action	Field Name	Data Type	Description	Field Size
Add as primary key.	ItemID	AutoNumber	A unique identifier for inventory items	Long Integer
Modify field.	ItemName		Name of item	20
Modify field.	ItemDescription		Description of item	40
Modify field.	Color		Color of item	20
Modify field.	ItemCount		Number of items in hotel	Long Integer
Remove field.	Which rooms			

h. Create a new table in Design view. This table will serve as the junction table between tblRoom and tblItem.

- Add the following fields, data types, field sizes, and descriptions (in the following order).

Field Name	Data Type	Description	Field Size
RoomItemID	AutoNumber	A unique identifier for the room item (primary key)	Long Integer
RoomNumber	Short Text	The room number from tblRoom (foreign key)	30
ItemID	Number	The item ID from tblItem (foreign key)	Long Integer
InventoryCount	Number	Number of items of this type in this room	Long Integer

- Make sure that you have assigned RoomItemID as a primary key. Save the new table as tblRoomItem.

i. Create the following relationships using existing fields and enforcing referential integrity. Do not cascade update or cascade delete.

- Each room is of a single room type. There are many rooms of each type.
- A room may have many items in it. Each type of inventory item may be in many rooms. You will need to use the junction table tblRoomItem to create this relationship.
- Create a relationship report accepting the default report name. If your instructor directs you to print your results, print your report.

j. Enter the following data into **tblRoomItem**.

RoomItemID	RoomNumber	ItemID	InventoryCount
Let Access autonumber as 1.	101	1	1
Let Access autonumber as 2.	102	1	1
Let Access autonumber as 3.	120	1	1
Let Access autonumber as 4.	120	3	1
Let Access autonumber as 5.	120	4	1
Let Access autonumber as 6.	120	8	4
Let Access autonumber as 7.	120	9	3
Let Access autonumber as 8.	101	8	2
Let Access autonumber as 9.	102	8	2
Let Access autonumber as 10.	101	3	1

k. Create a report showing **RoomType** and **RoomAmenities** from **tblRoomType** and **ResortFloor** and **RoomNumber** from **tblRoom**. View by **tblRoomType**, and add a grouping by **ResortFloor**. Sort by **RoomNumber**. Select **Landscape** orientation. Name your report rptRoomType. Change the title of your report to Rooms Listed by Room Type. Adjust the column widths as needed so that all four columns are displayed on each page. If your instructor directs you to print your results, print your report.

l. Create a query listing **RoomNumber** from **tblRoom**, **InventoryCount** from **tblRoomItem**, and **ItemName** from **tblItem**. Save your query as qryTelephone. Modify the query to select the items named **Telephone**, sort by **RoomNumber**, and then run the query. Fix column widths. If your instructor directs you to print your results, print your query.

m. Create a query listing **RoomNumber** and **ResortFloor** from **tblRoom**, **InventoryCount** from **tblRoomItem**, and **ItemName** from **tblItem**. Save your query as qryRoom120Contents. Modify the query to select the room numbered **120**, sort by **ItemName**, and then run the query. Fix column widths. If your instructor directs you to print your results, print your query.

n. Save the query, exit Access, and then submit your file as directed by your instructor.

Perform 1: Perform in Your Life

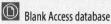

Personal Contact Database

Research & Development

You have decided to keep better track of the contact information of your family, friends, and acquaintances. You will begin with a blank database file, building tables, forms, queries, and reports for typical ways you would use contact information in your personal life. You will track data to include names, mailing addresses, e-mail addresses, cell phone numbers, and birthdates.

a. Start **Access**, and then create a new blank database. Save the database as a01Contacts_LastFirst using your last and first name.

b. When saving any objects in this project, add _iLast using your first initial and last name, to the end of the name.

c. Design a table to store contact information for your family, friends, and acquaintances. Use the following fields: LastName, FirstName, Street, City, State, ZIP, Cell#, Email, and BirthMonth.

   • Insert an AutoNumber field as the first field with the name, ContactID.

   • Add an Input Mask to Cell# with symbols for phone numbers as appropriate.

   • Add an Input Mask with symbols for **ZIP**.

   • For all other fields, determine and enter appropriate data types, descriptions, and field sizes.

   • Save your table as tblContacts_iLast.

d. Enter a minimum of ten records in **tblContacts_iLast**. Widen fields as appropriate to ensure that all information is visible.

e. Using **tblContacts_iLast**, design a columnar form with all fields, and name the form frmContacts_iLast.

f. Using **tblContacts_iLast** and the Report Wizard, design a tabular report named rptPhoneBook_iLast that displays the fields **LastName**, **FirstName**, and **Cell#**. Sort in ascending order by **LastName**. Display report in portrait orientation. Modify the title to be Last Name's Phone Book using your last name. Adjust column widths as appropriate to ensure that all information is visible.

g. Create another report that would be useful, using the Report Wizard. Apply any appropriate groupings and sorting. Adjust column widths as appropriate to ensure that all information is visible. Give the report an appropriate title, and save the report with an appropriate name.

h. Create a query that would be useful. Use a specific criterion to select only a subset of your contacts, and be sure to apply appropriate sorting. Save the query with an appropriate name.

i. Using **tblContacts_iLast**, create a query named qryCity_iLast to find out which contacts reside in a city of your choice. Show the fields **LastName**, **FirstName**, and **City**. Modify the query design to show only the contacts who reside in the city of your choice. Sort in ascending order by **FirstName** or **LastName**. Run the query.

j. Save the query, exit Access, and then submit your file as directed by your instructor.

Student data file needed:

 Blank Access database

You will save your file as:

a01HorseStable_LastFirst.accdb

Bluff Creek Stables Inventory Database

Production & Operations

You live in the Midwest and work as a stable hand for Bluff Creek Stables, a regionally well-known horse barn. This stable provides guided trail rides, horse-drawn wagon and sleigh rides, horse camps, and horseback riding lessons for people of all ages. The stable manager has asked you to complete an inventory database of the horses, farrier care (equine hoof care), and saddle time.

a. Start **Access**, and then create a new blank database. Save the database as a01HorseStable_LastFirst using your last and first name.

b. When saving any objects in this project, add _iLast, using your first initial and last name, to the end of the name.

c. Design a table to store an inventory of the stable's horses. Use the following fields: **HorseID**, **HorseName**, **Breed**, **TrailHorse**, **LessonHorse**, and **GuideHorse**.
   - Assign **HorseID** to be the primary key with the AutoNumber data type.
   - For all fields, enter appropriate data types and descriptions, and apply field sizes. Save your table as tblHorses_iLast.
   - Enter the following data into the table, in this order.

HorseID	HorseName	Breed	TrailHorse	LessonHorse	GuideHorse
1	Pecos	Draft Cross	Yes	Yes	No
2	Joey	Thoroughbred	Yes	No	Yes
3	Tahnee	Paint	Yes	No	Yes
4	Buck	QuarterHorse	Yes	Yes	No
5	Moose	Draft Cross	Yes	Yes	Yes
6	Chip	Paint	Yes	Yes	No
7	Doc	QuarterHorse	Yes	Yes	Yes
8	Buzzard	Draft Cross	Yes	No	No
9	Patches	Warmblood	No	Yes	Yes
10	Champ	Warmblood	No	Yes	No

d. Design a table to store farrier data. Use the following fields: HorseID and DateTrimmed.
   - For all fields, enter appropriate data types and descriptions, and apply field sizes.
   - Save your table as tblFarrier_iLast.

e. Enter the following data into tblFarrier_iLast, in this order.

HorseID	DateTrimmed
1	9/29/2018
2	7/26/2018
3	9/29/2018
4	9/27/2018
5	9/27/2018
6	7/21/2018
7	9/27/2018
8	9/27/2018
9	9/29/2018
10	7/26/2018

f. Design a table to store saddle time. Use the following fields: HorseID, 2016Hours, 2017Hours, and 2018Hours.
- Assign **HorseID** to be the primary key.
- For all fields, enter appropriate data types and descriptions, and apply field sizes.
- Save your table as tblSaddleTime_iLast.

g. Enter the following data into **tblSaddleTime_iLast**, in this order.

HorseID	2016Hours	2017Hours	2018Hours
1	154	115	138
2	37	56	42
3	76	64	106
4	45	55	98
5	90	83	75
6	50	30	30
7	102	80	115
8	45	58	75
9	50	52	120
10	85	67	15

h. Open the Relationships window. Create a one-to-many relationship between HorseID in tblHorses_iLast and HorseID in tblFarrier_iLast. Enforce referential integrity. Do not cascade update or cascade delete.

i. Create a one-to-one relationship between HorseID in tblHorses_iLast and HorseID in tblSaddleTime_iLast. Enforce referential integrity. Do not cascade update or cascade delete.

j. Create a relationship report named rptRelationships_iLast.

k. Create a form based on tblHorses_iLast named frmHorses_iLast.

l. Create a report showing the most current information for each horse. Display the fields **HorseID**, **HorseName**, **Breed**, **DateTrimmed**, and **2018Hours**. Group by **Breed**, and sort in ascending order by **HorseID**. Display report in landscape orientation. Save the report as rptCurrentInfo_iLast.

m. Create a query to find out which horses are both guide and lesson horses. Show the **HorseID**, **HorseName**, **GuideHorse**, and **LessonHorse** fields. Save the query as qryGuideLessonHorses_iLast.

n. Create a query to find out which horses logged more than 100 hours of saddle time in 2018. Show the **HorseID**, **HorseName**, and **2018Hours** fields. Save the query as qry100+Hours_iLast.

o. Exit Access, and then submit your file as directed by your instructor.

Perform 3: Perform in Your Team

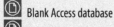

Student data files needed:

Blank Access database

Blank Word document

You will save your files as:

a01Music_TeamName.accdb

a01MusicPlan_TeamName.docx

Production & Operations

Independent Music Label

The owner of an independent music label needs to keep track of the label's groups, the musicians in the groups, and the groups' music, both albums and songs. You have been asked to create a database for the label.

The label owner would like to be able to get a list of groups with all musicians, get a list of groups with albums, select an album and see all songs in the album, and select a group and see their albums with all songs in the album. You will need to design tables, fields, relationships, queries, and reports for the label.

Because databases can be opened and edited by only one person at a time, it is a good idea to plan ahead by designing your tables in advance. You will use a Word document to plan your database and to plan which team member will complete each task.

a. Select one team member to set up the Word document and Access database by completing steps b through e.

b. Open your browser and navigate to either https://www.onedrive.com, https://www.drive.google.com, or any other instructor assigned location. Be sure all members of the team have an account on the chosen system. Create a new folder, and name it **a01MusicFolder_TeamName**. Replace TeamName with the name assigned to your team by your instructor.

c. Start **Access**, and then create a new blank database. Save the database as **a01Music_TeamName**. Replace TeamName with the name assigned to your team by your instructor.

d. Upload the **a01Music_TeamName** database to the **a01MusicFolder_TeamName** folder, and then share the folder with the other members of your team. Verify that the other team members have permission to edit the contents of the shared folder and that they are required to log in to access it.

e. Create a new Word document in the assignment folder and then name it **a01MusicPlan_TeamName**. Replace TeamName with the name assigned to your team by your instructor.

f. In the Word document, each team member must list his or her first and last name as well as a summary of his or her planned contributions. As work is completed on the database, this document should be updated with the specifics of each team member's contributions.

g. Use the Word document to list the fields you need in each table, the primary keys for each table, and the foreign keys.

h. In Access, your team members will need to complete the following steps.
   - Design your tables.
   - Enter data for three music groups into your tables.

Groups	Group Members	Albums	Songs
Clean Green, an Enviro-Punk band	Jon Smith (vocalist and guitar) Lee Smith (percussion and keyboard)	Clean Green	Esperando Verde Precious Drops Recycle Mania Don't Tread on Me
		Be Kind to Animals	It's Our Planet Too Animal Rag Where Will We Live?
Spanish Moss, a Spanish Jazz band	Hector Caurendo (guitar) Pasquale Rodriguez (percussion) Perry Trent (vocalist) Meredith Selmer (bass)	Latin Latitude	Attitude Latitude Flying South Latin Guitarra Cancion Cancion
Your band	Your team members (and their instruments)	You decide	You decide

- Create your relationships. Create a relationship report.
- Create a report showing all groups with all musicians.
- Create a report showing all groups, each group's type, and each group's albums.
- Create a query to select an album from your band and see all songs in the album.
- Create a query to select your band and see all your albums with all songs in the albums.

i. Save the database and the document, exit Access and Word, and then submit your files as directed by your instructor.

Perform 4: How Others Perform

Student data file needed:

 a01Textbook.accdb

You will save your file as:

 a01Textbook_LastFirst.docx

College Bookstore

Production & Operations

A colleague has created a database for your college bookstore. He is having problems creating the relationships in the database and has come to you for your help. What problems do you see in his database design? He has three tables in his database: one for sections of courses, one for instructors, and one for textbooks, as shown in Figures 1, 2, and 3.

a. Open the Access file, **a01Textbook**. Save your file as a01Textbook_LastFirst using your last and first name. You do not need to make changes to this database, but you will want to look at the database in more detail than is shown in the figures.

b. Create a Word document named a01Textbook_LastFirst using your last and first name, where you will answer the remaining questions.

c. Are there any errors in the way fields are defined or named in the tables? In your a01Textbook_LastFirst Word document, list these errors by table.

d. Are there any errors in the way tables are named or defined? In your a01Textbook_LastFirst Word document, list these errors by table.

e. How would you want to define the relationships?
- An instructor can teach many sections; a section is taught by just one instructor.
- A section can have many textbooks; a textbook can be used in many sections.

f. Save the database and the document, exit Access and Word, and then submit your files as directed by your instructor.

Figure 1 Table design for courseSection

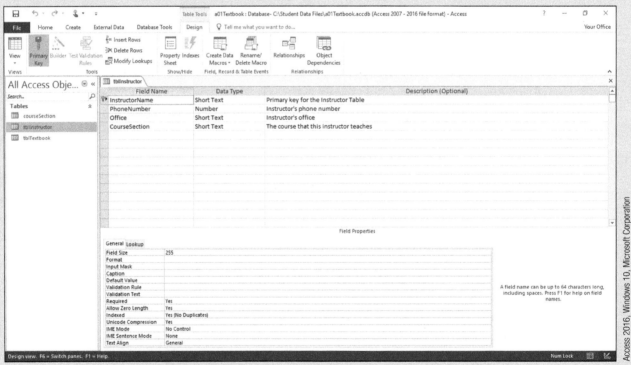

Figure 2 Table design for tblInstructor

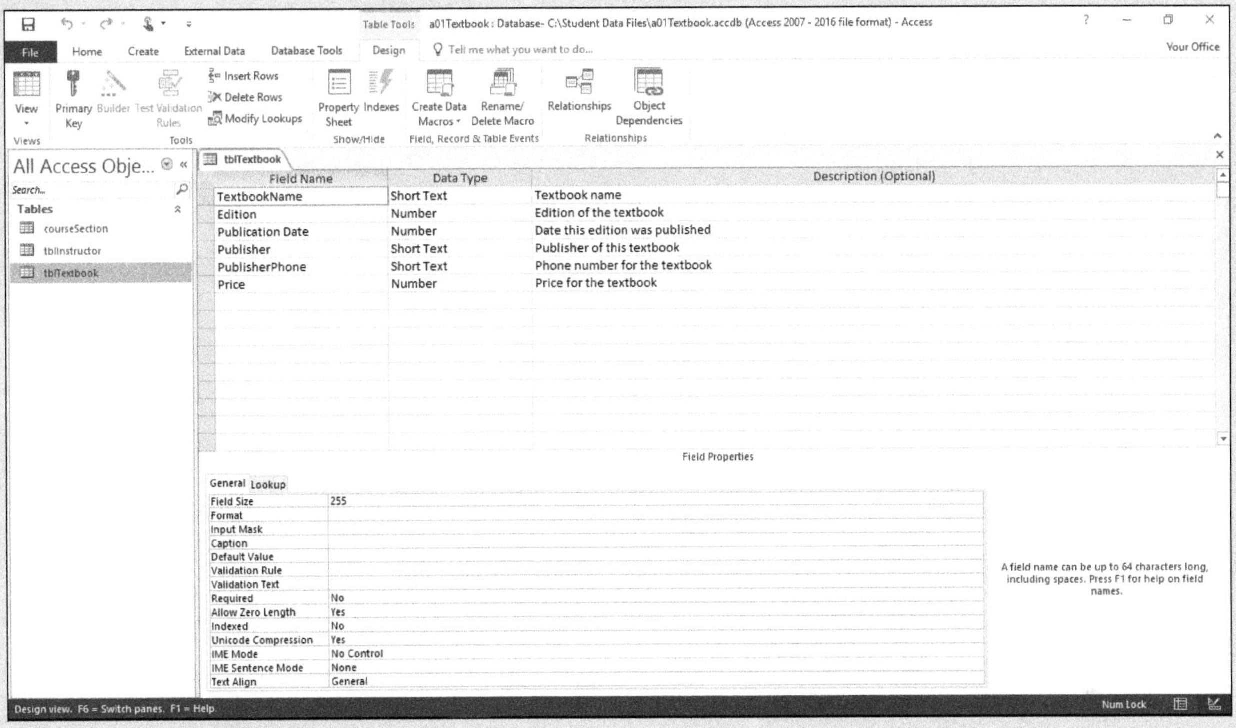

Figure 3 Table design for tblTextbook

Access Business Unit **2**

Accessing, Maintaining, and Presenting Information

Databases are an essential part of operating a business. The ability to navigate and search for data as well as present data is a crucial business function of a database. While simply searching a database table for a specific record is helpful, searching data across multiple tables using sophisticated criteria can reveal important business information. Using forms in Access allows the database user to navigate and enter new information into a database simply and quickly. Queries allow for searching single or multiple tables using complex criteria to return data or reveal new insights from the database. Reports provide a method of presenting data from tables or queries for viewing, printing, or exporting to formats such as PDF documents.

Learning Outcome 1:

Find data in a database by searching tables and designing queries that sort, aggregate, and calculate complex search results.

Real World Success

"My company sells luxury appliances. Sometimes we run out of products and don't have time to wait for the supplier. In the past, I'd have to get on the phone and call all our other locations in the region to see if they had extra that they could spare. Now I run a query, and in less than a minute, I know which location has it and how fast they can ship it. The queries are so popular that I've shared them with all of the managers."

- David, alumnus and procurement specialist

Learning Outcome 2:

Navigate and update information in a database using forms and present information in a database by creating customized reports.

Real World Success

"After I started using Access for entering my data and running reports, my supervisor asked whether I could set up a database for my coworker to use for her job. She didn't know Access, so I created forms for her data entry. She just enters today's data and runs her daily reports."

- Elaine, marketing analyst and alumnus

Microsoft Access 2016

Chapter 3 | QUERIES AND DATA ACCESS

OBJECTIVES

1. Find and replace records in the datasheet   p. 655

2. Modify datasheet appearance   p. 660

3. Run query wizards   p. 661

4. Create queries in Design view   p. 664

5. Sort table and query results   p. 671

6. Define selection criteria for queries   p. 673

7. Create aggregate functions   p. 688

8. Create calculated fields   p. 695

Prepare Case

Turquoise Oasis Spa Data Management

The Turquoise Oasis Spa has been popular with resort clients. The owners have spent several months putting spa data into an Access database so they can better manage the data. You have been asked to help show the staff how best to use the database to find information about products, services, and customers. For training purposes, not all the spa records have been added yet. Once the staff has been trained, the remaining records will be entered into the database.

Subbotina Anna/Fotolia

Student data file needed for this chapter:

 a02ch03Spa.accdb

You will save your file as:

 a02ch03Spa_LastFirst.accdb

Working with Datasheets

Datasheets are used to view all records in a table at one time. Each record is viewed as a row in the table. Records can be entered, edited, and deleted directly in a datasheet. When a table becomes so large that all the records and fields are no longer visible in the datasheet window without scrolling, the Find command can be used to quickly find specific values in a record. In this section, you will find records in a datasheet and modify the appearance of a datasheet.

Find and Replace Records in the Datasheet

The Navigation bar allows you to move to the top and bottom of a table or scroll to a specific record; however, this can be inefficient if your table is large. To manage larger tables, Access provides ways for you to quickly locate information within the datasheet. Once that information has been found, it can then be easily replaced with another value by using the **Replace command**.

If you do not know the exact value you are looking for because you do not know how it is spelled or how someone entered it, you can use a **wildcard character**. A wildcard character is used as a placeholder for an unknown part of a value or to match a certain pattern in a value. For example, if you know that the value you are looking for contains the word "market", you can use a wildcard character at the beginning and end such as *market*.

Opening the Starting File

The owners of the spa have spent several months entering spa data into an Access database so they can better manage the data. You have been asked to help show the staff how best to use the database to find information about products, services, and customers. For training purposes, not all the spa records have been added yet. In this exercise you will open the database and save it with a new file name.

To Open the a02ch03Spa Database

a. Start **Access**, click **Open Other Files** in the left pane, and then double-click **This PC**. Navigate through the folder structure to the location of your student data files, and then double-click **a02ch03Spa**. A database opens displaying tables and queries related to the spa.

b. On the File tab, click **Save As**, save the file as an **Access Database**, and click **Save As**. Navigate to the location where you are saving your project files and then change the file name to a02ch03Spa_LastFirst using your last and first name. Click **Save**. If necessary, enable the content.

Finding Records in a Table

In Datasheet view, you can use the **Find command** to quickly locate specific records using all or part of a field value. In this exercise, a staff member found a book left by one of the guests. A first name was printed on the inside of the book cover. The staff member remembers helping a man named Guy who said he was from North Carolina, but the staff member is not certain of his last name. In this exercise, you will show the staff how to use the Find command to quickly navigate through the table to search for this guest.

To Find Records in the Datasheet

a. In the Navigation Pane, double-click **tblCustomer** to open the table.

b. Add a record at the end of the table with your first name, last name, address, city, state, phone, and e-mail address. Press Tab until the record selector is on the next row and your record has been added to the table.

c. On the Navigation bar, click **First Record** |◄| to go to the first record in the table. On the Home tab, in the Find group, click **Find** to open the Find and Replace dialog box.

d. Replace the text in the Find What box with Guy. Click the **Look In** arrow, and then select **Current document**.

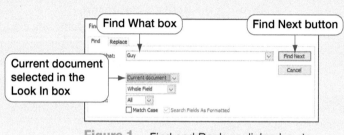

Figure 1 Find and Replace dialog box to find all records for "Guy"

e. Click **Find Next**. Access highlights the first record found for Guy Bowers from Derby, North Carolina (NC). This is a possibility, but there might be a second Guy.

f. Click **Find Next** again to check for more records with Guy. Guy Blake from Suffolk, Wisconsin, is found.

g. Click **Find Next** again to check for more records with Guy. When Access is done searching and cannot find any more matches, you will see the message "Microsoft Access finished searching the records. The search item was not found."

h. Click **OK**, and then click **Cancel** to close the Find and Replace dialog box.

> ### Troubleshooting
>
> If you did not get the results shown above, go back and carefully check the settings in the Find and Replace dialog box. Make sure Match Case is not checked. When Match Case is checked, the search will be case sensitive. Also check to make sure the Look In box shows Current document. If the Look In box shows Current field, Access will look only in the field selected.

Finding and Replacing Records in a Datasheet

Not only can you find records using the Find command, but you can also replace records once you have found them with the Replace command. In a large table, it is helpful to locate a record using the Find command and then replace the data using the Replace command.

The spa receptionist has received an e-mail from Erica Rocha about her upcoming marriage, which will result in a new last name. The receptionist wants to go through the database and find any records related to Erica and change her last name to her married name, Muer. In this exercise, you will show the receptionist how to find Erica in the database and replace her last name of Rocha with Muer.

A03.02

To Find and Replace Records

a. Click the **Home** tab, and in the Find group, click **Find** to open the Find and Replace dialog box.

b. In the Find and Replace dialog box, click the **Replace** tab. In the Find What box, type Rocha, and then, in the Replace With box, type Muer.

c. Verify that Look in: Current document is selected. Leave all other options as they are.

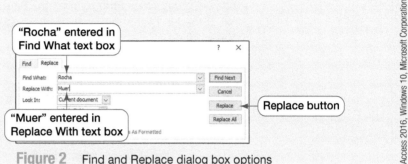

Figure 2   Find and Replace dialog box options

Access 2016, Windows 10, Microsoft Corporation

d. Click **Find Next**. Notice that the first record found has the last name Rocha, but the first name is Emily. Click **Find Next** again. Notice that this is the record for Erica Rocha. Click **Replace**. Click **OK** when you get the message that Microsoft Access has finished searching the records. The Last Name should now be Muer instead of Rocha. Click **Cancel** to close the Find and Replace dialog box.

e. **Close** ⊠ the table.

Using a Wildcard Character

A wildcard character, as shown in Table 1, is used as a placeholder for an unknown part of a value or to match a certain pattern in a value. A wildcard character can replace a single character or multiple characters, which can be both text and numbers.

Wildcard Character	Example
*	Used to match any number of characters; to search for a word that starts with "ar", you would enter ar*.
#	Used to match any single numeric character; to search for a three-digit number that starts with "75", you would enter 75#.
?	Used to match any single character; to search for a three-letter word that starts with "t" and ends with "p", you would enter t?p.
[ ]	Used to match any single character within the brackets; to search for a word that starts with "e", contains any of the letters "a" or "r", and ends with "r", you would enter e[ar]r and get "ear" or "err" as a result.
!	Used to match any single character NOT within the brackets; to search for a word that starts with "e", contains any letter other than "a" or "r", and ends with "r," you would enter e[!ar]r to get anything except "err" or "ear".
-	Used to match any range of characters in ascending order: "a" to "z"; to search for a word beginning with "a" and ending in "e" with any letter between "b" and "t" in between, you would enter a[b-t]e.

Table 1   Wildcard characters

The staff is looking for products with the word "butter" in the name so they can put together a weekly promotion for all these products. In this exercise, you will show them how to use a wildcard character to find the products.

To Use a Wildcard Character to Find a Record

a. In the Navigation Pane, double-click **tblProduct** to open the table.

b. In the first record, click the **ProductDescription** field. Click the **Home** tab, and in the Find group, click **Find** to open the Find and Replace dialog box. Replace the text in the Find What box with *butter*. Click the **Look In** arrow, and then click **Current field**.

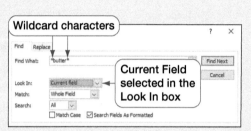

Figure 3   Find records with "butter" in the ProductDescription field

c. Click **Find Next**. The first record found is for ProductID P018 Cocoa Body Butter. Click **Find Next** again to find the record for ProductID P021 Lemon Body Butter.

d. Click **Find Next** again until Access has finished searching the records. When Access is done searching and cannot find any more matches, you will see the message "Microsoft Access finished searching the records. The search item was not found." Click **OK**, and then click **Cancel** to close the Find and Replace dialog box.

Troubleshooting
If Access highlights a record in the table and you cannot see it, drag the Find and Replace dialog box to another area of the screen.

---

e. **Close** ⊠ the table.

Applying a Filter to a Datasheet

A **filter** is a condition you apply temporarily to a table or query. All records that do not match the filter criteria are hidden until the filter is removed or until the table is closed and reopened. A filter is a simple technique to quickly reduce a large amount of data to a much smaller subset of data. You can choose to save a table with the filter applied so when you open the table later, the filter is still available.

You can filter a datasheet by selecting a value in a record and telling Access to filter records that contain some variation of the record you choose, or you can create a custom filter to select all or part of a field value.

When you **filter by selection**, you select a value in a record, and Access filters the records that contain only the values that match what you have selected. A customer came into the spa and stated that she was from Minnesota and had previously been a spa customer but was just browsing today. She left her glasses on the counter, and the staff wants to return them to her. In this exercise, you will help the staff members find all customers from Minnesota to see whether they recognize the customer's name.

A03.04

SIDE NOTE

How to Clear Filters

To delete filters from the table, click Advanced in the Sort & Filter group, and select Clear All Filters.

To Select Specific Records Using a Selection Filter

a. Double-click **tblCustomer** to open the table, locate the first record with an address in the state of Minnesota (MN), and then click the **State** field for that record. Click the **Home** tab, in the Sort & Filter group, click **Selection**, and then click the **Equals "MN"** option.

Access displays three records in which all states are MN for Minnesota.

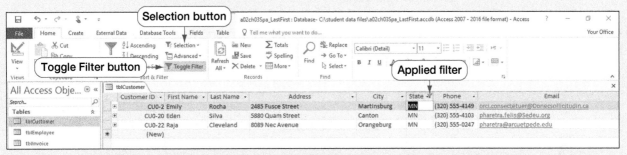

Figure 4   Filtered table for all records containing a state of MN

Access 2016, Windows 10, Microsoft Corporation

b. Click **Save** 🖫. This saves the table with the filter.

The filter is temporary unless you choose to save it with the table or query. If you do save it, the next time you open the table or query, you only have to click Toggle Filter to see the records from the state of Minnesota.

c. **Close** ✕ the table.

d. Double-click **tblCustomer** to open the table. On the Home tab, in the Sort & Filter group, click **Toggle Filter** to see the filtered records.

The Toggle Filter button in the Sort & Filter group allows you to go back and forth between viewing the filtered records and all the records in the table. To remove the filter, click Toggle Filter in the Sort & Filter group. To show the filter again, click Toggle Filter in the Sort & Filter group.

e. **Close** ✕ the table.

 CONSIDER THIS | **Finding Records**

You have now found records using Find and Replace and using a selection filter. What are the advantages of each method? When would you use each?

Using a Text Filter

Text filters allow you to create a custom filter to match all or part of the text in a field that you specify. The staff wants to create a mailing of sample products but cannot send the products to customers with a post office box. In this exercise, you will help the staff find all customers who have "P.O. Box" as part of their address.

A03.05

To Select Specific Records Using a Text Filter

a. Double-click **tblCustomer** to open the table. Select the entire **Address** column by clicking the column name. In the column heading, click the **filter** arrow, point to **Text Filters**, and then click **Begins With**.

b. In the Custom Filter dialog box, type P, and then click **OK**.

Access retrieves the nine records in which the addresses contain a P.O. box number. Notice that Toggle Filter in the Sort & Filter group is selected and the Filtered indicator in the Navigation bar is highlighted. You can toggle between the filtered table and the whole table by clicking on either Toggle Filter or the Filtered indicator. The filter indicator in the column heading indicates whether a filter is currently applied.

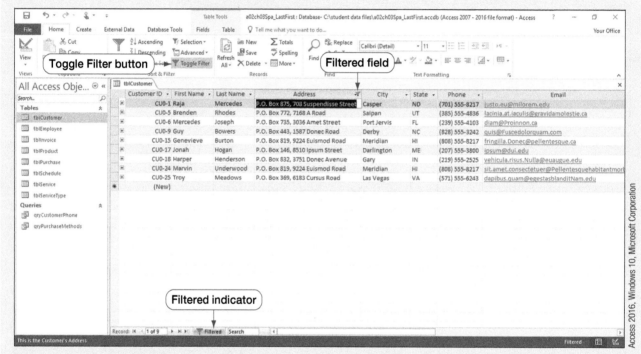

Figure 5 Results of the filter

c. Click **Save** 🖫 to save the table with the new filter applied. **Close** ☒ the table.

Modify Datasheet Appearance

You can change the appearance of your datasheet by changing the font type, font size, column widths, and background colors to make it more readable. **AutoFit** is a feature that can change the column width of the data to match the widest data entered in that field. AutoFit allows you to see all the data in a particular field.

Changing the Look of a Datasheet

The manager is upset because the font is too small and she cannot see all the field headings in the invoice table. In this exercise, you will show her how to make the text larger and the columns wider.

To Change Font Size, Column Width, and Alternating Row Colors

a. Double-click **tblInvoice** to open the table.

b. Click the **Home** tab. In the Text Formatting group, click the **Font Size** arrow 11, and then click **14**.

c. Point to the **right border** of the first field name until the pointer turns into a double-sided arrow, and double-click. The AutoFit feature resizes the column to best fit the data. Repeat this action for all the columns.

d. In the Text Formatting group, click the **Alternate Row Color** arrow, and then under Theme Colors, select **Green, Accent 6, Lighter 40%**. This is the tenth column and the fourth row under Theme Colors. The rows will still be alternating colors, but they will be changed to green.

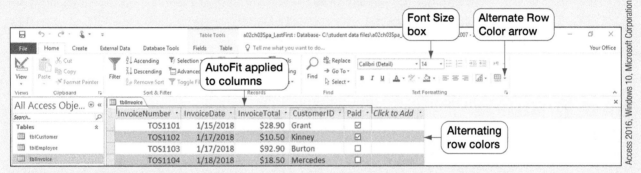

Figure 6   Modified table

e. **Close** the table, and then when prompted to save the changes, click **Yes**. If you need to take a break before finishing this chapter, now is a good time.

Querying the Database

While the Find and Filter features can help you to find data quickly, a query can be created for data that you may need to find again in the future. If you recall, the Simple Query Wizard is used to display fields from one or more tables or queries with the option to choose a detailed or summary query. The Simple Query Wizard does not provide the opportunity to select data criteria. Queries can also be created in Query Design view, which not only allows you to choose the tables and fields to include in the query, but also allows you to select criteria for the field values, create calculated fields, and select sorting options.

In this section, you will create and define selection criteria for queries and create aggregate functions and calculated fields as well as sort query results.

Run Query Wizards

In addition to the Simple Query Wizard, three other query wizards are available to make quick, step-by-step queries.

1. **Crosstab** — Used when you want to describe one field in terms of two or more fields in the table. Example: summarizing information or calculating statistics on the fields in the table.

2. **Find Duplicates** — Used when you want to find records with the same specific value. Example: duplicate e-mail addresses in a customer database.

3. **Find Unmatched** — Used when you want to find the rows in one table that do not have a match in the other table. Example: identifying customers who currently have no open orders.

The Find Duplicates Query Wizard and the Find Unmatched Query Wizard, allow you to find duplicate records or identify orphans by selecting criteria as part of the wizard steps. An **orphan** is a foreign key in one table that does not have a matching value in the primary key field of a related table.

Creating a Find Duplicates Query

The **Find Duplicates Query Wizard** finds duplicate records in a table or a query. You select the fields that you think may include duplicate information, and the wizard creates the query to find records matching your criteria.

The spa receptionist sends out mailings and reminders to spa customers throughout the year. She wants to prevent multiple mailings to the same address to help reduce costs. In this exercise, you will show her how she can use a Find Duplicates query to check for duplicate addresses.

To Find Duplicate Customer Information

a. If you took a break, open the **a02ch03Spa_LastFirst** database. Click the **Create** tab, and then in the Queries group, click **Query Wizard**. Access displays the New Query dialog box and lists the different queries you can select.

b. Select **Find Duplicates Query Wizard**, and then click **OK**.

c. Select **Table: tblCustomer** as the table to search for duplicate field values, and then click **Next**.

> ### Troubleshooting
> If you get a Security Notice, click Open.

d. Under Available fields, click **CustAddress**, and then click the **One Field** button ` > `. Access moves the CustAddress field to the Duplicate-value fields list. This is the field you think may have duplicate data.

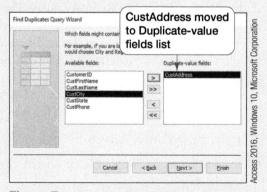

Figure 7 Select the field that may have duplicate data

e. Click **Next**. Click the **All Fields** button ` >> ` to move all available fields to the Duplicate-value fields list to display all the fields in the query results. Click **Next**.

f. Under "What do you want to name your query?", type qryDuplicateCustomers, and then click **Finish**. The result of the query should have two records with the same address.

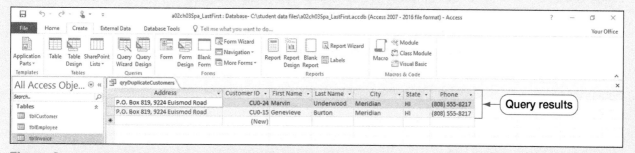

Figure 8   Results from the Find Duplicates query   Access 2016, Windows 10, Microsoft Corporation

g. **Close** ⊠ the query.

Creating a Find Unmatched Query

The **Find Unmatched Query Wizard** is designed to find records in a table or query that have no related records in a second table or query. This can be very helpful if you want to contact inactive customers or mail a notice to past clients who are still listed in the database. The wizard uses the primary key from the first table and matches it with the foreign key in the second table to determine whether there are unmatched records. If a one-to-many relationship exists between the two tables, the wizard will join the two correct fields automatically.

The wizard will try to match the primary key field and the foreign key field if there is a one-to-many relationship between the two tables. If there is not a one-to-many relationship, you can select the fields to be matched manually.

In this exercise, spa management would like to identify customers who have used the spa's services in the past but do not have a current appointment. This means that a record for the customer would be listed in the customer table but not in the schedule table, as shown in Figure 9.

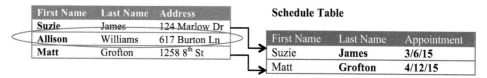

Figure 9   Tables in a Find Unmatched query

Notice that Allison Williams is a past customer, so she is listed in the customer table, but she does not have an appointment scheduled in the schedule table. Her record would be found in a Find Unmatched query comparing the customer and schedule tables. In this exercise, you will show the staff how to find unmatched records.

 A03.08

To Find Unmatched Records

a. Click the **Create** tab, and then in the Queries group, click **Query Wizard**.

b. Select **Find Unmatched Query Wizard**, and then click **OK**.

SIDE NOTE

Manually Select Fields to Match

If your tables are not in a one-to-many relationship, select the fields manually, and use the `<=>` button to move them to the Matching fields box.

c. Select **Table: tblCustomer**, and then click **Next**. This is the table you think has past customers with no upcoming appointments.

d. Select **Table: tblSchedule**, and then click **Next**. This is the table that has customers with upcoming appointments you want to compare to the main tblCustomer table.

e. Under Fields in 'tblCustomer', verify that **CustomerID** is selected, and then under Fields in 'tblSchedule', verify that **Customer** is selected. This is the common field that the wizard will use to compare the tables.

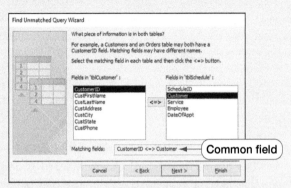

Figure 10 Compare the two tables using their common field

f. Click **Next**, click the **All Fields** button `>>` to add all the fields to the Selected fields list, and then click **Next**.

g. Under "What would you like to name your query?", type qryCustomersWithoutAppointments, and then click **Finish**. You should see the names, addresses, and e-mail addresses of three customers who do not currently have appointments at the spa, including yourself. **Close** `X` the query.

Create Queries in Design View

The query wizards work by prompting you to answer a series of questions about the tables and fields to display and then creating the query based on your responses. Alternatively, you can use Design view to manually create queries. The query window in Design view allows you to specify the data you want to see by building a **query by example**. A query by example provides a sample of the data you want to see in the results. Access takes that sample of data and finds records in the tables you specify that match the example. In the query window, you can include specific fields, define criteria, sort records, and perform calculations. When you use the query window, you have more control and more options available to manage the details of the query design than with the Simple Query Wizard.

When you open Design view, by default the Show Table dialog box opens with a list of available tables and queries to add. You can select a table name and click Add, or you can double-click the table name. Either way, the table will be added to the query window. If the Show Table dialog box is closed, you can drag a table or query from the Navigation Pane to the query window to add it to the query.

The next step in building your query is to add the fields you want to include from the various tables selected to the query design grid. There are a number of ways to add fields to the query design grid.

QUICK REFERENCE	Methods to Add Fields to a Query Design Grid

Action	Description
Drag	Once you click the field name, drag it to any empty column in the query design grid.
Double-click field name	Double-click the field name to add it to the first empty column in the query design grid.
Select from list	Click in the first row of any empty column, click the selection arrow, and select the field name from the list.
Double-click title bar	Double-click the title bar for the table with the fields you want to add, and all the fields will be selected. Drag the fields to the first empty column.
Click, Shift, click	Click a field name, press and hold down the Shift key, and then click another name to select a range of field names. Drag the selected fields to the query design grid.

If you add a field to the wrong column in the query design grid, you can delete the column and add it to the correct column, or you can drag it to another position in the grid.

All fields that have values you want included in a query — either for the criteria or to show in the results — must be added to the query design grid. For example, you may want to find all customers from New Mexico but not necessarily show the state field in the query results. You can use the Show check box to indicate which fields to show in the results and which fields not to show.

REAL WORLD ADVICE	Increasing Privacy Concerns

There are many instances in which the person running the query does not have the right to see confidential information in the database. An example of this is Social Security numbers. Although companies are doing away with this practice, many existing databases still use a customer's Social Security number as a unique identifier. You can include a Social Security number in query criteria, but uncheck the Show box so the actual value does not show in the query results.

Creating a Single-Table Query

A single-table query is a query that is based on only one table in your database. The manager of the spa needs your help to print out a price list for all the products. She wants to see the product description, size, and price for each product, and she wants to see all the records. In this exercise, you will show her how to add only the fields she wants to the query.

A03.09

To Create a Single-Table Query

a. Click the **Create** tab, and then in the Queries group, click **Query Design** to open the query window with the Show Table dialog box.

b. In the Show Table dialog box, select **tblProduct**, and then click **Add**. Click **Close** to close the Show Table dialog box.

> ### Troubleshooting
> If you cannot see the query design grid at the bottom of the query design window, use the pointer ⊞ to drag the top border of the grid up.

SIDE NOTE
Seeing All Fields in a Table
Alternatively, you can scroll down to see all the fields.

SIDE NOTE
Adding fields to the Query Design Grid
Alternatively, you can click the Field arrow in a column of the query design grid and select a table field.

c. Move the pointer to the lower border of **tblProduct** until it becomes a double-sided arrow ⇕. Click and drag down to see all the fields.

d. Double-click **ProductDescription** to add it to the first column of the query design grid. You can also add fields by dragging a field from the table to a column in the query design grid.

e. Click and drag the **Price** field from tblProduct to the **second column** of the query design grid. Repeat the process for the **Size** field.

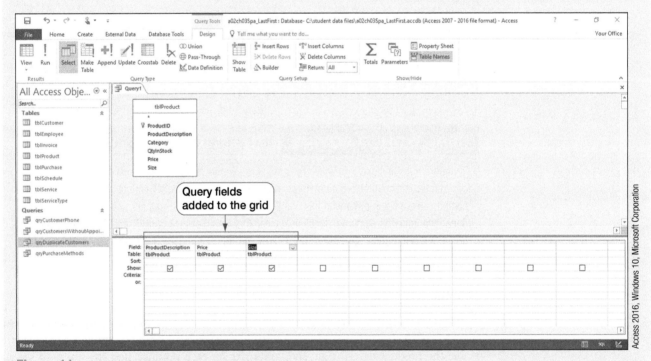

Figure 11   Fields from tblProduct added to the query design grid

f. On the Design tab, in the Results group, click **Run** to run the query. You should have 25 records showing the ProductDescription, Price, and Size (ounces) fields.

g. In the Views group, click the **View** arrow, and then click **Design View**. To move the Size field to the left of the ProductDescription field, point to the **top border** of the **Size** field until the pointer turns into a black arrow ⬇. Click the **ProductDescription** field while the black arrow is displayed, then drag the **Size field** to the left of the **ProductDescription** field.

h. In the Results group, click **Run** to run the query again. The query will still have 25 records, but the field order will be Size (ounces), ProductDescription, and Price.

i. Click **Save** 🖫. In the Save As dialog box, type qryProductPriceList, and then click **OK. Close** ☒ the query.

QUICK REFERENCE	Opening or Switching Views

Access gives you several methods to open objects in different views or to switch views.

1. To open an object in default view, double-click it in the Navigation Pane.

2. To open an object in Design View, right-click it in the Navigation Pane, and select Design View.

3. To switch views for an already open object, on the Home tab, in the Views group, click the View arrow, and then select your preferred view.

4. To switch views for an already open object, right-click the object tab, and then select the preferred view.

5. To switch views for an already open object, the right side of the status bar has small icons for each available view. Hover your mouse pointer over the icon to see the ScreenTip. Click the icon to switch to the preferred view.

REAL WORLD ADVICE	The Importance of Knowing Your Data

Many times, databases are shared by many users. Different people may enter data differently causing errors or inconsistency. Inconsistent data entry can affect the validity of query results. If a value is misspelled or is abbreviated when it should be spelled out, a query may not find the record when it searches using criteria. You must know what your data looks like when you create queries. A quick scan of the records or using Find with a wildcard for certain values may help you find misspellings or other data entry errors before you run your query.

Having some idea of what the query results should look like will also help make sure your query has found the right record set. For example, if you query all customers from New Mexico and think there should be about a dozen but your query shows 75, you should check your table records and your query criteria to see why there might be such a big discrepancy from what you expected.

Viewing Table Relationships

A multiple-table query retrieves information from more than one table or query. For Access to perform this type of query, it uses relationships between the tables, or the common field that exists in both tables to "connect" the tables.

If two tables do not have a common field, Access will join the two tables by combining the records, regardless of whether they have a matching field. This is called the **multiplier effect**. For example, if one table has 10,000 records, another table also has 10,000 records, and these two tables do not have a common field, all records in the first table will be matched with all records in the second table for a total of 100,000,000 records! Depending on the computer's processing power and memory, Access could take a long time to run the query or may even become nonresponsive.

You can view how your tables are related in the Relationships window. **Join lines** are the lines connecting the tables that represent relationships. The field to which the line is pointing in each table represents the common field between the tables. It is helpful to understand how tables are related before you try to create a multiple table query. In this exercise, you will view table relationships to determine how the tables are related.

To View Table Relationships

a. Click the **Database Tools** tab, and in the Relationships group, click **Relationships**. Click the **Shutter Bar Open/Close** button 《 to hide the Navigation Pane and display the whole Relationships window. Take a moment to study the table relationships.

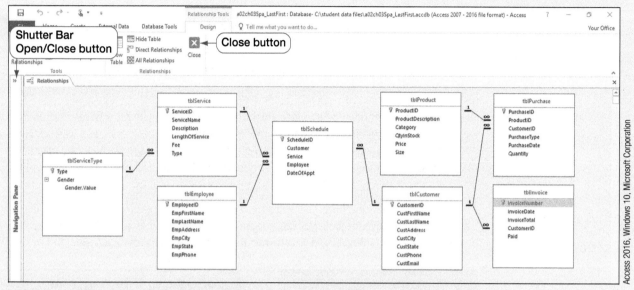

Figure 12   Spa Database table relationships

b. On the Design tab, in the Relationships group, click **Close** to close the Relationships window. Click the **Shutter Bar Open/Close** button 》 to show the Navigation Pane again.

REAL WORLD ADVICE   **Which Tables to Choose?**

You should select only the tables you need when creating a query in the query window. Access treats all the tables selected as part of the query when it executes the query, which means that unnecessary tables added to the query may cause performance problems or incorrect results. Best practice is to do the following.

- Understand the table structure and relationships before you construct your query — refer to the Relationships window often.

- Choose only the tables from which you need data.

- If no data from a table is needed, do not add the table. The exception to this rule is if a table is required to link the many-to-many relationship together. In other words, no table will be left unconnected, and tables can be added to create that connection.

Creating a Query from Multiple Tables

All tables added to a query should be connected by relationships and have a common field. The staff would like to see all services scheduled for each employee. tblEmployee includes the employee names, and tblSchedule lists the services scheduled for each employee. In this exercise, you will create a query that includes records from two tables into one query.

A03.11

SIDE NOTE
Adding Tables from the Navigation Pane
Remember that in addition to selecting the tables from the Show Table dialog box, you can drag tables from the Navigation Pane.

SIDE NOTE
Add Only Necessary Tables
Adding a table to a query without adding fields changes the query results, and the results may not make sense.

To Create a Query from Multiple Tables

a. Click the **Create** tab, and then in the Queries group, click **Query Design**. Click **tblEmployee**, and then click **Add**. Click **Close** to close the Show Table dialog box.

b. Double-click **EmpFirstName** and **EmpLastName** in that order to add the fields to the query design grid.

c. In the Results group, click **Run**. Notice there are 14 employee records.

d. Switch to **Design** view. From the Navigation Pane, drag **tblSchedule** to the query window. In the Results group, click **Run** to run the query again.
Scroll through the table and notice there are 53 records in the query results now and employees names are repeated. Employee names have been matched up with each scheduled service, of which there are 53, but you cannot see any information about the services because no fields from that table have been added. The relationship between the two tables dictates that each employee be listed for each service he or she has scheduled. The relationship also prevents employees without a scheduled appointment from appearing in the results. For example, Mariah Paul does not appear here because she has no appointments scheduled.

e. Switch to **Design** view. In the tblSchedule table, in the following order, double-click **Service**, **DateOfAppt**, and **Customer** to add the fields to the query design grid.

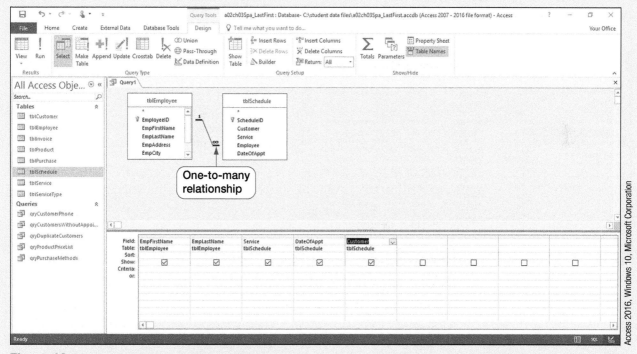

Figure 13 Query window for multiple-table query

f. In the Results group, click **Run** to run the query. Use the **AutoFit** feature on the columns to best fit the data.
Notice there are 53 records again for each service scheduled, but now the details for those services are included in the query because you added the fields to the query design grid.

g. Click **Save** [icon], and under Query Name, type qryEmployeeSchedule, and then click **OK**. **Close** [X] the query.

Removing a Table from a Query to Fix an Undesirable Multiplier Effect

When two tables without a common field are used in a query, you will see the multiplier effect. Recall that the multiplier effect occurs when each record in the first table is matched to each record in the second table.

Someone in the spa wanted to find the phone number for each customer but created a multiple table query using two tables without a common field. One table has 25 records and the other has 26, so the multiplier effect caused the query result to have 650 records! In this exercise, you will run the employee's query and then fix it by removing the second table from the query.

To Remove a Table from a Query

a. In the Navigation pane, double-click **qryCustomerPhone** to run the query. Notice there are 650 records because every customer name is matched with every product. Since there are 25 products, each of the 26 customers is matched with every product for 25 times 26 = 650 records.

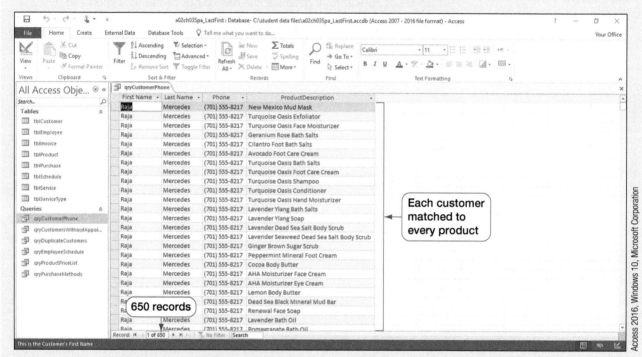

Figure 14   Query with multiplier effect

b. Switch to **Design** view. Notice there is no relationship between tblProduct and tblCustomer, which caused the multiplier effect. You will remove tblProduct from the query.

c. Right-click **tblProduct** in the query window, and then select **Remove Table**. The table is removed from the query window, and the ProductDescription is removed from the query design grid.

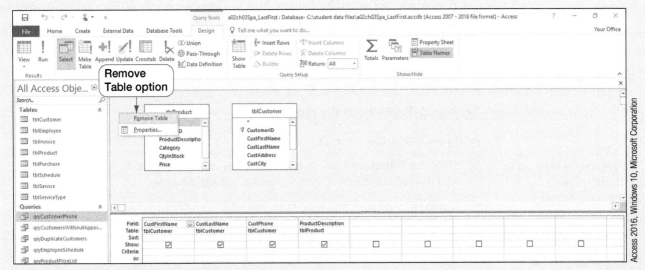

Figure 15 Remove table from query

d. In the Results group, click **Run** to run the query. Notice there are now only 26 records.

e. Click the **File** tab, click **Save As**, and then click **Save Object As**. Click **Save As**, and under Save 'qryCustomerPhone' to, type qryCustomerPhoneFixed, and then click **OK. Close** ☒ the query.

Sort Tables and Query Results

Sorting is the process of rearranging records in a specific order. By default, records in a table or query are sorted by the primary key field. You can change the sort order of a table in a query, which will not affect how the data is stored, only how it will appear in the query results.

Sorting by One Field

To sort records, you have to select a **sort field**, or a field used to determine the order of the records. The sort field can be a Short Text, Long Text, Number, Date/Time, Currency, AutoNumber, Yes/No, or Lookup Wizard field as shown in Table 2. A field may be sorted in either ascending (A to Z) order or descending (Z to A) order.

Type of Data	Sorting Options
Short and Long Text	Ascending (A to Z); descending (Z to A)
Numbers (including Currency and AutoNumber)	Ascending (lowest to highest); descending (highest to lowest)
Date/Time	Ascending (oldest to newest); descending (newest to oldest)
Yes/No	Ascending (yes, then no values); descending (no, then yes values)

Table 2 Methods for sorting data

If you have numbers that are stored as text — phone numbers, Social Security numbers, ZIP Codes — then the characters 1 to 9 come before A to Z in the appropriate order sorted as alphanumeric text.

A table may be sorted by a single field in Datasheet view. When a table is sorted by using a single field, a sort arrow will appear in the field name so you can see that it is sorted. In this exercise, you will show the spa manager how to sort the tblProduct table by category.

A03.13

SIDE NOTE
Alternative Method to Sorting Fields
Alternatively, you can select the field to be sorted and click Ascending or Descending on the Home tab in the Sort & Filter group.

To Sort a Table by a Single Field

a. In the Navigation pane, double-click **tblProduct** to open the table.

b. Click the **Category** column heading arrow, and then click **Sort A to Z**. This will sort the records by the Category field in ascending order.

c. **Close** ☒ the table, and then click **Yes** when prompted to save the changes.

Sorting by More Than One Field

You can also sort by multiple fields in Access. The first field you choose to sort by is called the **primary sort field**. The second and subsequent fields are called **secondary sort fields**.

In Datasheet view, you can sort multiple fields by selecting all the fields at one time and using the Sort & Filter group sorts, but there are some restrictions. First, the fields in Datasheet view must be next to each other, and the sort is executed from left to right; that is, the far-left field is the primary sort field, the next field is a secondary sort field, and so on. Second, you can sort only in ascending or descending order for all fields; you cannot have one field sorted in ascending order and another in descending order. These two restrictions do not exist if sorting is set in Design view. Thus, it is more efficient to create a query and sort by multiple fields using Design view.

Using Design view to sort records allows you to sequence the fields from left to right in an order that makes sense for your desired sort results and allows you to combine ascending and descending sorts. You can also sort in an order different from left to right by adding a field multiple times and clearing the Show check box. In this exercise, you will show the staff how to sort the tblSchedule table by Employee, then Date, and then Service by creating a query from the table and setting up the sort options.

A03.14

SIDE NOTE
How Many Fields Is Too Many?
You may choose up to ten fields to sort by in Design view.

To Sort a Query by More than One Field

a. Click the **Create** tab, and then in the Queries group, click **Query Design**. Double-click **tblEmployee** and **tblSchedule** to add the tables to the query. Click **Close** to close the Show Table dialog box.

b. Double-click **EmpLastName**, **EmpFirstName**, and **EmpPhone** from **tblEmployee** to add those fields to the query design grid. Double-click **DateOfAppt**, **Service**, and **Customer** from tblSchedule to add those fields to the query design grid.

c. Click the **Sort** row for EmpLastName, click the **selection** arrow, and then click **Ascending**. Click **Ascending** for the EmpFirstName, DateOfAppt, and Service fields.

Notice that unlike sorting in Datasheet view, your sorting fields do not need to be next to each other to be sorted in a query.

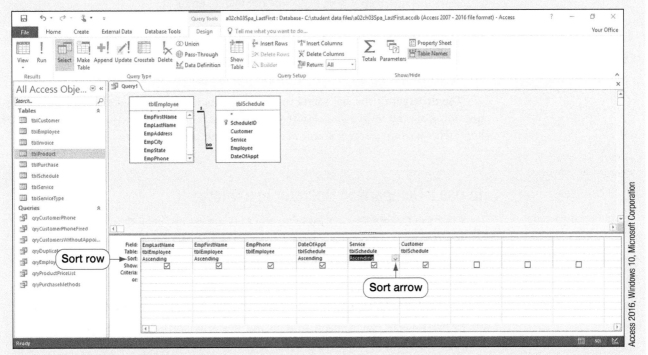

Figure 16 Sort options selected

d. In the Results group, click **Run** to run the query. Use the **AutoFit** feature on the columns to best fit the data.

Notice there are 53 records and the table is sorted by Employee, then Date, then Service.

e. Click **Save** 🖫 , name the query qryEmployeeAppointments, and then click **OK**. **Close** ☒ the query.

Define Selection Criteria for Queries

Databases, including Access, provide a robust set of selection criteria that you can use to make your queries well focused. You can use the different kinds of operators described below to choose criteria for one or more fields in one or more tables.

Using a Comparison Operator

Comparison operators compare the values in a table or another query to the criteria value you set up in a query. The different comparison operators, descriptions, and examples are shown in Table 3. Comparison operators are generally used with numbers and dates to find a range or a specific value. Equal to and not equal to can also be used with text to find exact matches to criteria. For example, to find all states that are not NY, you could enter < >"NY" for the state criterion.

In query criteria, text is identified by quotation marks around it and dates with # in front of and at the end of the date. For example, 1/1/18 would appear as #1/1/18#. Access adds the necessary quotation marks and pound signs, but it is a good idea to double-check.

Operator	Description
=	Equal to
< =	Less than or equal to
<	Less than
>	Greater than
> =	Greater than or equal to
< >	Not equal to

Table 3   Comparison operators

The manager of the spa wants to see all products $10 and under so she can plan an upcoming special on the spa's lower-priced products. In this exercise, you will show her how to use a comparison operator in a query to find those products.

To Use a Comparison Operator in a Query

a. Click the **Create** tab, and then in the Queries group, click **Query Design**. Click **tblProduct**, and then click **Add**. Click **Close** to close the Show Table dialog box.

b. In the following order, double-click **ProductID**, **ProductDescription**, **Size**, **Category**, **QtyInStock**, and **Price** to add the fields to the query design grid.

c. Click in the **Criteria** row for the Price field, and then type <=10.

d. In the Results group, click **Run** to run the query. The results should show six records, all with prices $10 or less.

e. Click **Save** 🖫, under Query Name type qryLowPriceProducts, and then click **OK**.

Hiding Fields That Are Used in a Query

For a field to be used in a query, it must be added to the query grid. If you just want to use the field to define criteria but do not want to see the results of that field in the query, it cannot be removed from the query grid, but it can be hidden from the results.

The manager is happy with the results of the low-price products query you created above, but she would like to post a list of the products without the prices so she can advertise the list as all $10 and under. In this exercise, you show her how that is possible by using the Show check box in the query design grid.

To Use a Field Value in a Query but Not Show the Field in the Results

a. With the **qryLowPriceProducts** query open, switch to **Design** view.

b. In the Price field, click the **Show** check box to clear the check mark.

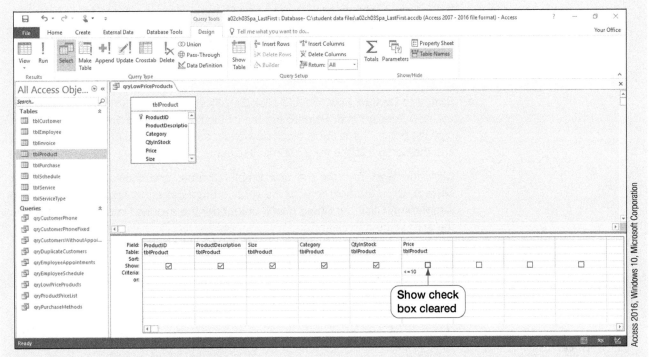

Figure 17   Clearing the Show check box

Access 2016, Windows 10, Microsoft Corporation

c. In the Results group, click **Run** to run the query. The results should show the same six records you found in the previous query but without the price field showing.

d. Click the **File** tab, click **Save As**, and then click **Save Object As**. Click **Save As**, and in Save 'qryLowPriceProducts' to:, type qryTenAndUnder, and then click **OK**. **Close** ☒ the query.

Sorting on a Field That You Do Not Show

The manager liked the employee schedule query you created, but she would like it to show the employee's first name first in the query results. If you put first name first in the grid and then last name, Access will sort by first name first. In this exercise, you will show her how to add a field multiple times to the query design grid to sort fields one way but display them another way.

  A03.17

To Sort a Query by Multiple Fields in a Different Sort Order

a. Click the **Create** tab, and then in the Queries group, click **Query Design**. Double-click **tblEmployee** and **tblSchedule** to add the tables to the query. Click **Close** to close the Show Table dialog box.

b. Double-click **EmpFirstName** and **EmpLastName** from tblEmployee to add those fields to the query design grid. Double-click **DateOfAppt**, **Service**, and **Customer** from tblSchedule to add those fields to the query design grid.

c. Click the **Sort** row for EmpFirstName, click the **selection** arrow, and then click **Ascending**. Click **Ascending** for the EmpLastName, DateOfAppt, and Service fields.

d. In the Results group, click **Run** to run the query. Use the **AutoFit** feature on the columns to best fit the data.

Notice that the results are sorted by first name and not last name; for example, Alex Weaver is shown before Amanda Johnson. You will need to add another first name field to fix the sort order.

e. Switch to **Design** view. Double-click **EmpFirstName** in tblEmployee to add it to the query design grid. Point to the top of the of the second **EmpFirstName** field until the pointer turns into a black downward arrow. Click the **EmpFirstName** field and then drag it to the right of EmpLastName.

f. Click the **Sort** row for the first EmpFirstName, and then change it to **(not sorted)**. Click the **Sort** row for the second EmpFirstName, and then change it to **Ascending**. Click the **Show** check box under the second EmpFirstName field in the third column to clear it.

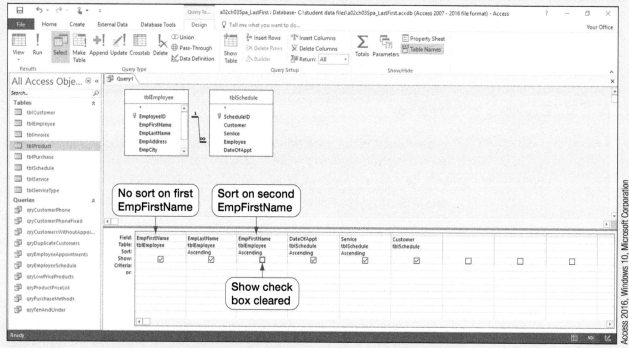

Figure 18 Sort options selected and second EmpFirstName Show check box cleared

g. In the Results group, click **Run** to run the query. The results should show 53 records sorted by employee last name, first name, date, and service. Notice that the main sort is by last name but Alex Weaver comes before Joseph Weaver.

h. Click **Save** 🖫, name the query qryEmployeeSort, and then click **OK**. **Close** ☒ the query.

Using Is Null Criteria

You practiced entering a criterion value to get all records that meet the criterion. You can also select any records that have no value in a field using the Is Null criterion. Null is the absence of any value and is different from blank or zero.

One of the spa workers has created a purchase record without specifying that the order was placed in person. In this exercise, you will show the manager how to locate a record that is missing a value. You will also show her how to change the value in the query and have it changed in the table.

To Use Is Null Criteria

a. Click the **Create** tab, and then in the Queries group, click **Query Design**. Double-click **tblPurchase**, and **tblCustomer** to add the tables to the query window. Click **Close** to close the Show Table dialog box.

b. In the following order, double-click **PurchaseType** and **PurchaseDate** from tblPurchase, and **CustFirstName** and **CustLastName** from tblCustomer to add them to the query design grid.

c. Click in the **Criteria** row for the PurchaseType field, and then type Is Null.

d. In the Results group, click **Run** to run the query. The results show one record: the purchase by Omar Hinton on 1/18/2018. That is the record that the employee forgot to change to In Person.

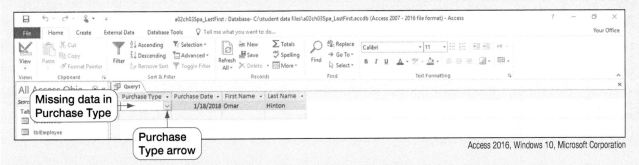

Access 2016, Windows 10, Microsoft Corporation

Figure 19 Change null value in query results

e. Click the arrow under **Purchase Type**, and then change the value to **In Person**. This changes the result in the underlying tblPurchase to be In Person.

f. Click **Save** 🔲, and under Query Name, type qryNullPurchaseType, and then click **OK**. **Close** ✕ the query.

g. Double-click **tblPurchase** to open the table. Notice that Hinton's purchase (PurchaseID = 25) is now indicated as being In Person. **Close** ✕ the table.

h. Double-click **qryNullPurchaseType** to run it. Notice that no records are found, since Hinton's record was corrected. **Close** ✕ the query.

Using Criteria Row with Multiple Criteria

When you create a query, you can specify criteria for one field or for multiple fields. When selecting criteria for multiple fields, you must show how the query selects the records. When criteria are placed on the same Criteria row, Access logically interprets the criteria as related by an and — all criteria are true. For example, the query may need to return orders placed Online and from customers in New Mexico. The query must contain the criterion in which the PurchaseType is Online and the criterion in which the customer State is New Mexico. This task can be easily completed by using the Criteria row in the query design grid. The Criteria row of the query design grid directs Access to look for the first criterion AND the second criterion and so on for each value typed into the same Criteria row in the query. All criteria on the same line are interpreted by Access as an AND logically. In this exercise, you want to help the manager narrow down a sales strategy. She is trying to determine which customers have placed phone orders for products over $10.

A03.19

To Use the Criteria Row

a. Click the **Create** tab, and then in the Queries group, click **Query Design**. Double-click **tblProduct, tblPurchase,** and **tblCustomer** to add the tables to the query window. Click **Close** to close the Show Table dialog box.

b. In the following order, double-click **PurchaseType** from tblPurchase, **ProductDescription** and **Price** from tblProduct, and **CustFirstName** and **CustLastName** from tblCustomer to add them to the query design grid.

c. Click in the **Criteria** row for the PurchaseType field, type Phone, and then for the Price field, type >10.

d. Click in the **Sort** row for the **ProductDescription** field, and then select **Ascending**.

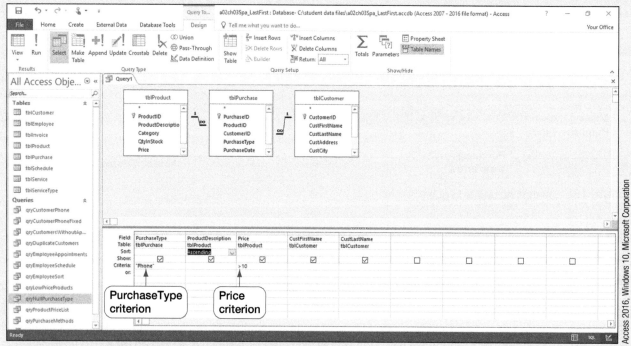

Figure 20 Criteria added for PurchaseType and Price fields

e. In the Results group, click **Run** to run the query. The results show five records with Phone as the purchase type and a price greater than $10. The results are sorted by ProductDescription.

f. Click **Save** 🖫, and under Query Name type qryPhoneAndTen, and then click **OK**. **Close** ✕ the query.

Using the Or Criteria Row

When specifying two or more different criteria for the same field or different sets of criteria in a query, the or row below the Criteria row can be used. For example, if you wanted to know how many customers live in New Mexico or Nevada, you could enter the criterion for the State field on two different lines for the same field in the query design grid — assuming no other criteria for different fields. The query would then run and return records in which the State field equals New Mexico OR where the state field equals Nevada. In this exercise, you will help the manager find all customers who make purchases either by phone or online.

To Use the Or Criteria Row

a. Click the **Create** tab, and then in the Queries group, click **Query Design**. Double-click **tblProduct**, **tblPurchase**, and **tblCustomer** to add the tables to the query. Click **Close** to close the Show Table dialog box.

b. Double-click **PurchaseType** from tblPurchase, double-click **ProductDescription** from tblProduct, and then double-click **CustFirstName** and **CustLastName** from tblCustomer in that order to add them to the query design grid.

c. Click in the **Criteria** row for the PurchaseType field, type Phone. In the **or criteria** row just below the Criteria row in the PurchaseType field, type Online.

d. Click in the **Sort** row, and then select **Ascending** for the PurchaseType and ProductDescription fields.

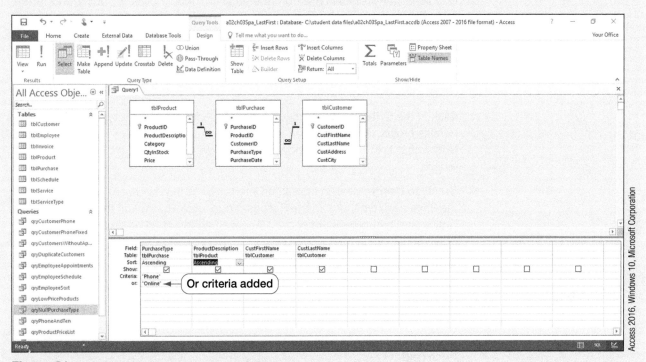

Figure 21   Or Criteria row used for PurchaseType

e. In the Results group, click **Run** to run the query. The results should show 12 records, all with Phone or Online as the purchase type sorted by purchase type and product description.

f. Click **Save** 🖫, name the query qryPhoneOrOnline, and then click **OK**. **Close** ☒ the query.

Using Both the Criteria Row and the Or Criteria Rows in a Query

More complex queries can be created by combining the use of the Criteria row and the or criteria rows. Each row of criteria in the query design grid is returned as a set of records by the query. In other words, records that meet the values on the first Criteria row are returned by the query as one set of records. Records that meet the values on the or criteria row are also returned by the query, as are records on each successive or criteria row in the query design grid. The result is a query containing records that meet the first set of criteria or the second set of criteria and so on. Each line represents a separate set of connected criteria that is logically compared by an OR.

The manager wants you to find all phone purchase types for products over $20 as well as all online purchase types for products over $15. Phone and greater than $20 are one criterion, while Online and greater than $15 are a separate criterion. By specifying each criterion on a separate or criteria row, the query will combine the records meeting each set of criteria. In this exercise, you will create a query that combines two different sets of criteria using the or criteria row.

To Use the Criteria and Or Criteria Rows in a Query

a. Click the **Create** tab, and then in the Queries group, click **Query Design**, and then double-click **tblProduct**, **tblPurchase**, and **tblCustomer** to add the tables to the query. Click **Close** to close the Show Table dialog box.

b. Double-click **PurchaseType** from tblPurchase, double-click **ProductDescription** and **Price** from tblProduct, and then double-click **CustFirstName** and **CustLastName** from tblCustomer in that order to add them to the query design grid.

c. Click in the **Sort** row, and then select **Ascending** for the **PurchaseType** and **Price** fields.

d. Click in the **Criteria** row for the PurchaseType field, and then type Phone. In the Results group, click **Run** to run the query.
Notice that five orders are shown. Access has found all records that are Phone orders.

e. Switch to **Design** view. In the same Criteria row as the PurchaseType of Phone, for the Price field, type >20. In the Results group, click **Run** to run the query.
Notice that two orders are shown. Access has found all records that are phone orders and have prices of over $20.

f. Switch to **Design** view. In the **or criteria** row below the Criteria row, type Online for the PurchaseType field. In the Results group, click **Run** to run the query.
Notice that nine orders are shown. Access has found all records that are phone orders with prices of over $20 or are online orders.

g. Switch to **Design** view. In the same **or criteria** row as Online, type >15 for the **Price** field.

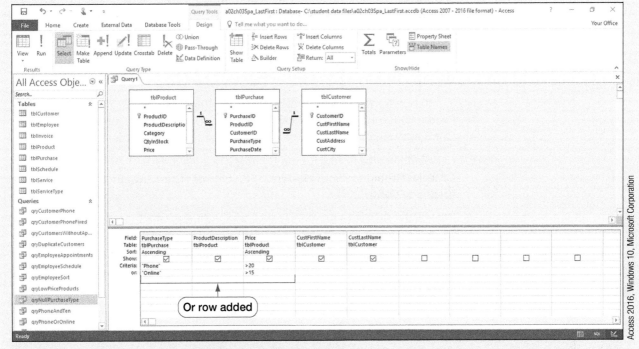

Figure 22 Two criteria rows added for PurchaseType and Price

h. In the Results group, click **Run** to run the query.
Notice that six orders are shown. Access has found all records that are phone orders with prices over $20 or are online orders with prices over $15.

i. Click **Save** 🖫, name the query qryPhoneAndOnline, and then click **OK**. **Close** ☒ the query.

Using AND and OR Logical Operators

When a query is created, it may be necessary to meet multiple criteria for a single field. This can be easily accomplished in the query design grid with the use of logical operators. **Logical operators** are operators that allow you to combine two or more criteria for the same field. Examples of logical operators are shown in Table 4. For example, if you want a record selected when two or more criteria are met for a field, you would use the AND logical operator typed into the Criteria row of the field. Alternatively, if you want a record selected if only one of the criteria is met, you would use the OR logical operator.

Operator	Description
AND	Returns records that meet both criteria
OR	Returns records that meet one or more criteria
NOT	Returns records that do not meet the criteria

Table 4 Logical operators

The manager of the spa wants you to find all phone and online purchase types for products over $10. If you put the purchase type criteria on two rows and the price of >10 in one row, your results will show all records with phone purchase types over $10 or Online purchase types of any amount. Access will treat "Phone" and >10 as AND criteria and then move to the next row, which it will consider an OR criterion. In this exercise, you will create a query using the OR logical operator to find all phone and online purchases over $10.

To Use the OR Logical Operator

a. Click the **Create** tab, and then in the Queries group, click **Query Design**. Double-click **tblProduct**, **tblPurchase**, and **tblCustomer** to add the tables to the query. Click **Close** to close the Show Table dialog box.

b. In the following order, double-click **PurchaseType** from tblPurchase, **ProductDescription** and **Price** from tblProduct, and **CustFirstName** and **CustLastName** from tblCustomer to add them to the query design grid.

c. Click in the **Criteria** row for the PurchaseType field, type Phone, and then in the **Criteria** row for the Price field, type >10. In the **or criteria** row for the PurchaseType field, type Online.

d. Click in the **Sort** row, and then select **Ascending** for the PurchaseType and Price fields.

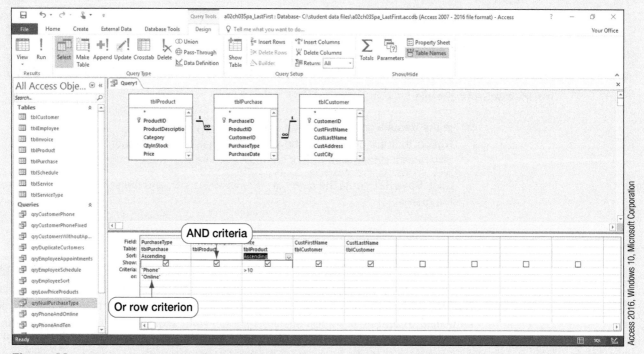

Figure 23   Criteria added to the query design grid

SIDE NOTE

Access Puts in Quotes

You can leave the quotation marks around "Phone" or remove them. Access will add them for Short Text fields.

e. In the Results group, click **Run** to run the query.
   Notice the results are all Phone purchase types with prices over $10 or all Online purchase types, regardless of the price. The manager wants to see Phone or Online purchase types over $10, so this is not correct.

f. Switch to **Design** view. In the **or criteria** row for the PurchaseType field, delete "Online." Click in the **Criteria** row for the PurchaseType field, and then change the criteria to Phone or Online.

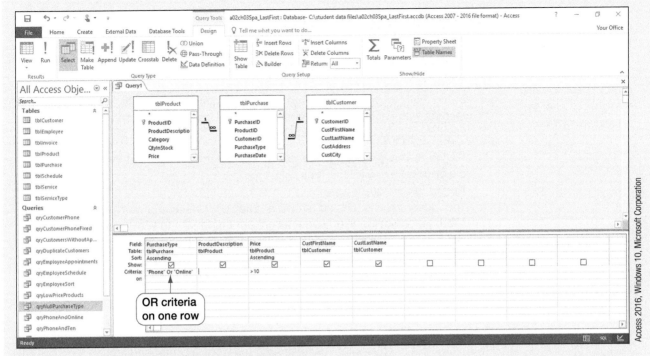

Figure 24   Or criteria added to the query design grid

g. In the Results group, click **Run** to run the query again. The results should now show the 10 Phone or Online purchase types that are over $10.

h. Click **Save** 🖫, and under Query Name, type qryPhoneOrOnlineOverTen, and then click **OK. Close** ☒ the query.

Combining Operators and Multiple Criteria

The more criteria you add to your query, the more difficult it will be to see whether you have the correct results. With multiple criteria, it is good practice to add one criterion, run the query to make sure you are getting the correct results, and then continue adding criteria one at a time.

The spa manager would like to see all of her high-end services listed by price and then service type, and she would like to break down the criteria as follows: Hands & Feet or Body Massage services $50 or more, Facial or Microdermabrasion services over $55, Beauty or Waxing services over $45, and all Botanical Hair & Scalp Therapy services. In this exercise, you will show her how to do this by combining operators and multiple criteria.

To Combine Operators and Multiple Criteria

a. Click the **Create** tab, and then in the Queries group, click **Query Design**, and double-click **tblService** to add the table to the query window. Click **Close** to close the Show Table dialog box.

b. In the following order, double-click **Fee**, **Type**, and **ServiceName** to add the fields to the query design grid.

SIDE NOTE

Wider Columns

You can widen the columns in the query design grid by double-clicking the right border of the column selector bar.

c. Click in the **Criteria** row for the Fee field, type >55, and then in the Criteria row for the Type field, type Facial or Microdermabrasion.

d. Click in the **Sort** row, and then select **Ascending** for the Fee, Type, and ServiceName fields.

e. In the Results group, click **Run** to run the query. The results should show six records with Facial or Microdermabrasion for the Type field, and all values in the Fee field should be greater than $55.

f. Switch to **Design** view. In the **or criteria** row for the Fee field, type >=50, and in the **or criteria** row for the Type field, type "Hands & Feet" or Body Massage. Click **Run** to run the query again.

The query results should show a total of 19 records with types Facial or Microdermabrasion that have fees greater than $55 and with types Hands & Feet or Body Massage that have fees greater than or equal to $50.

Troubleshooting

If you get only 16 records in the results, you did not put the quotation marks around "Hands & Feet". Access will add those quotation marks for you. In this case, Access evaluates the ampersand character (&) as separating two values, so it will put the quotation marks around the word "Hands" and around the word "Feet" so it will look like "Hands" & "Feet". This is different from having the quotations around the whole phrase, which is what you want it to look like. In this case, you should put the quotation marks around the phrase in order for it to appear as "Hands & Feet".

---

g. Switch to **Design** view. Click in the first **blank row** under the or criteria row for the Fee field, type >45, and then for the Type field, type Beauty or Waxing. In the Results group, click **Run** to run the query again.

The results should show a total of 23 records with types Facial or Microdermabrasion that have fees greater than $55, with types Hands & Feet or Body Massage that have fees greater than or equal to $50, and with types Beauty or Waxing that have fees greater than $45.

h. Switch to **Design** view. Click in the **next blank row** under the **or criteria** row for the Type field, and then type "Botanical Hair & Scalp Therapy".

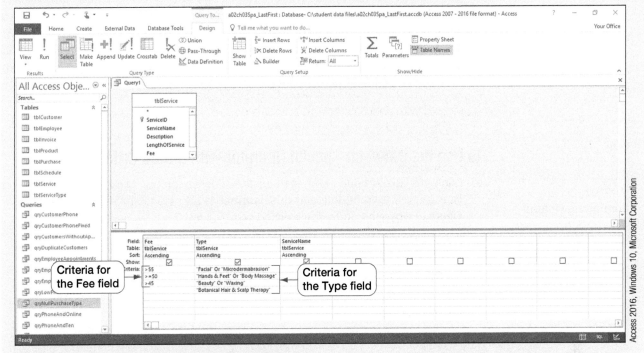

Figure 25 All criteria added to the query design grid

i. In the Results group, click **Run** to run the query again.

The results should show a total of 25 records with types Facial or Microdermabrasion that have fees greater than $55, with types Hands & Feet or Body Massage that have fees greater than or equal to $50, with types Beauty or Waxing that have fees greater than $45, and with all Botanical Hair & Scalp Therapy types.

Troubleshooting

If you still see 23 records, check to see whether you put the quotation marks around "Botanical Hair & Scalp Therapy" and whether you spelled the type correctly.

---

j. Click **Save** 🖫, name the query qryHighEndServices, and then click **OK**. **Close** ☒ the query.

Using Special Operators and Date Criteria

Special operators, as shown in Table 5, are used to compare text values using wildcards (LIKE) to determine whether values are between a range of values (BETWEEN) or in a set of values (IN).

Operator	Description
LIKE	Matches text values by using wildcards. These are the same wildcards that are shown in Table 1.
BETWEEN	Determines whether a number or date is within a range.
IN	Determines whether a value is found within a set of values.

Table 5 Special operators

The manager of the spa would like you to find all services scheduled for February 2018, along with the customer who is scheduled for each of those services. The Between special operator will return results that include and fall between the criteria you enter. As you may recall, in working with dates as criteria, a # in front of each date and another at the end of each date are required to identify the numbers as dates and not a string of text. In this exercise, you will use the Between special operator.

 A03.24

SIDE NOTE
Formatting Criteria
Access will add pound signs (#) around dates and quotation marks around text. However, if the criteria are ambiguous, you should put these symbols in.

To Use the Between Special Operator with a Date Criterion

a. Click the **Create** tab, and then in the Queries group, click **Query Design**. Double-click **tblSchedule** and **tblCustomer** to add the tables to the query. Click **Close** to close the Show Table dialog box.

b. Double-click **DateOfAppt**, **Service**, and **Employee**, from tblSchedule, and then double-click **CustFirstName** and **CustLastName** from tblCustomer in that order to add them to the query design grid.

c. Click in the **Sort** row, and then select **Ascending** for the DateOfAppt, Service, and Employee fields.

d. Click in the **Criteria** row for the DateOfAppt field, and then type Between 2/1/18 and 2/29/18.

e. In the Results group, click **Run** to run the query. Use the **AutoFit** feature on the columns to best fit the data.
Notice that the results do not show services in February. They show services in January. Access is misinterpreting your query criterion.

f. Switch to **Design** view to check the criteria. Move your pointer to the **border** between DateOfAppt and Service until it becomes ⟨⊶⟩. Double-click to see the full criteria.
Notice that since there is no leap day in 2018, Access interpreted the 2/29 as February of 2029 (2/1/2029) and the /18 as a division. This is not what you wanted. This example shows why it is so important to check your results to see whether they make sense.

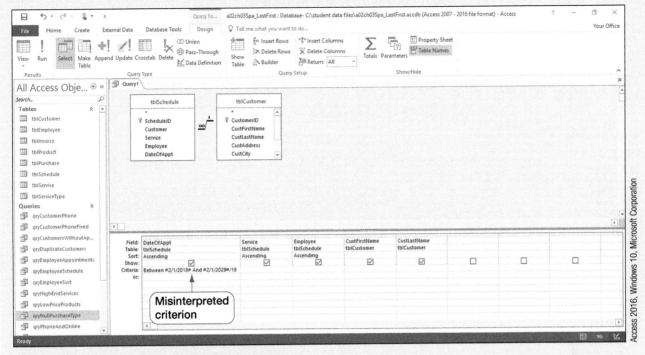

Figure 26 Misinterpreted criterion for DateOfAppt

g. Change the criterion to Between 2/1/18 and 2/28/18. In the Results group, click **Run** to run the query.
   This time, the results are as expected and show 47 appointments in February.

h. Click **Save** 🖫, and under Query Name, type qryFebruaryServices, and then click **OK**. **Close** ☒ the query.

Combining Special Operators and Logical Operators

Special operators can be combined with logical operators. As your criteria get more complex, you need to carefully check how Access interprets your criteria and your results.

The manager of the spa would like you to find all services scheduled for months other than February 2018, along with the customer who is scheduled for each of those services. In this exercise, you will use the LIKE special operator and combine it with the NOT logical operator. This query is very similar to the one you just created, so you will open that query and modify it.

To Combine Logical and Special Operators

a. In the Navigation pane, right-click **qryFebruaryServices**, and then select **Copy**. Right-click anywhere in the **Navigation Pane**, and then select **Paste**. In the Query Name box, type qryNotFebruaryServices. Click OK.

b. Double-click **qryNotFebruaryServices** to open it.

c. Switch to **Design** view. Click in the **Criteria** row for the DateOfAppt field, and then replace the current criteria with Like 2/*/2018. Remember that the asterisk (*) is a wildcard that will select all dates that have a month of 2 and a year of 2018.

d. In the Results group, click **Run** to run the query. Notice that the results show 47 February service appointments.

e. Switch to **Design** view. Type Not before the current criterion so it reads **Not Like "2/*/2015"**.

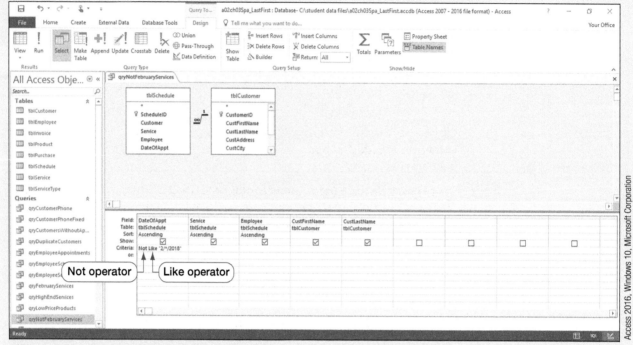

Figure 27   Combined Not and Like operators

f. In the Results group, click **Run** to run the query. Notice that the results now show the six service appointments not in February.

g. **Save** 🖫, and **close** ⊠ your query.

Create Aggregate Functions

Aggregate functions perform arithmetic operations, such as calculating averages and totals, on records displayed in a table or query. An aggregate function can be used in Datasheet view by adding a total row to a table, or it can be used in a query on records that meet certain criteria.

QUICK REFERENCE	Commonly Used Aggregate Functions
There are a number of different aggregate functions that can be used depending on the type of calculation you want to perform.	

1. **Sum** — Calculates the total value for selected records
2. **Average** — Calculates the average value for selected records
3. **Count** — Displays the number of records retrieved
4. **Minimum** — Displays the smallest value from the selected records
5. **Maximum** — Displays the largest value from the selected records

Adding a Total Row

If you need to see a quick snapshot of statistics for a table or query, you can use the total row. The **total row** is a special row that appears at the end of a datasheet that enables you to show aggregate functions for one or more fields. In this exercise, you will help the manager quickly find a total for all unpaid invoices listed in the invoices table and a count of the number of invoices in the table. The invoice table has a Yes/No field, so you will show her how to define criteria for Yes/No.

To Add a Total Row to a Query

a. In the Navigation pane, double-click **tblInvoice** to open it. Notice that the Paid field is a check box. Switch to **Design** view, and for the Paid field, click the **Data Type** box, and see that the Format is Yes/No. **Close** ⊠ the table.

b. Click the **Create** tab, and then in the Queries group, click **Query Design**. Double-click **tblInvoice** and **tblCustomer** to add the tables to the query. Click **Close** to close the Show Table dialog box.

c. Double-click **InvoiceDate**, **InvoiceTotal**, and **Paid** from tblInvoice, and then double-click **CustFirstName** and **CustLastName** from tblCustomer in that order to add them to the query design grid.

d. Click in the **Sort** row, and then select **Ascending** for InvoiceDate.

e. Click in the **Criteria** row for the Paid field, and then type No.

f. In the Results group, click **Run** to run the query. The six unpaid invoices are shown.

g. In the Records group, click **Totals** so that the Total row shows.

h. Click in the **Total row** under the InvoiceTotal field, click the **arrow**, and then select **Sum**. Click in the **Total** row under the First Name field, click the **arrow**, and then select **Count**.

SIDE NOTE

Removing Totals
To remove the total row, on the Home tab, click Totals.

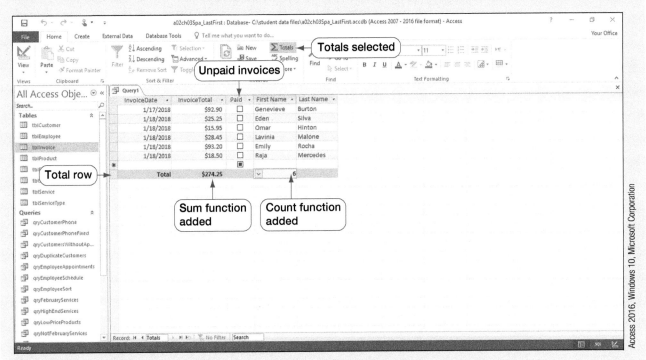

Figure 28 Sum and Count of Unpaid Invoices added to the Total row

i. Click **Save** 🖫, and under Query Name, type qryUnpaidInvoices, and then click **OK**. **Close** ⊠ the query.

Using Aggregate Functions in a Query

Aggregate functions can be used in queries to perform calculations on selected fields and records. One advantage to using aggregate functions in queries, rather than just a total row, is that you can group criteria and then calculate the aggregate functions for a group of records. By default, the query design grid does not have a place to enter aggregate functions, so the column total row must be added from the Query Tools Design tab. Each column or field can calculate only one aggregate function. So to calculate the sum and average on the same field, the field must be added to the grid multiple times.

You have been asked to provide a statistical summary of the spa's product prices. The manager would like to see how many products are offered, the average product price, and the minimum and maximum product prices. In this exercise, you will use aggregate functions to provide this information.

To Use Aggregate Functions in a Query

a. Click the **Create** tab, and then in the Queries group, click **Query Design**. Double-click **tblProduct** to add the table to the query. Click **Close** to close the Show Table dialog box.

b. Double-click **Price** four times to add the field four times to the query design grid.

> **Troubleshooting**
>
> If you clicked the Price field too many times, click the top of the extra Price fields in the query design grid, and press Delete to remove them.

c. In the Show/Hide group, click **Totals** to add a total row to the query design grid.

d. In the first Price column, click in the **Total** row, click the **arrow**, and then select **Count**. In the second Price column, click in the **Total** row, click the **arrow**, and then select **Avg**. Repeat for the next two Price columns, selecting **Min** for the third column and **Max** for the last column.

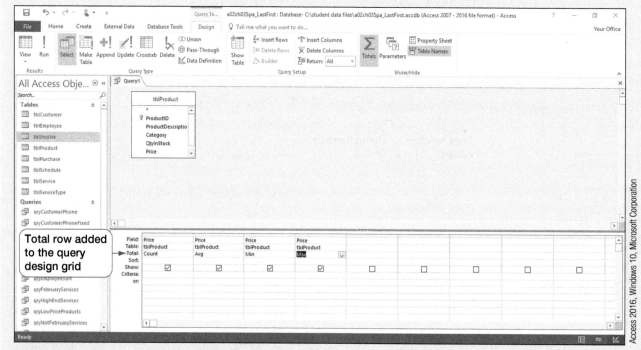

Figure 29 Aggregate functions selected for each column

e. In the Results group, click **Run** to run the query. Because this is an aggregate query and you are calculating one statistic per column, there will be only one record in the results.

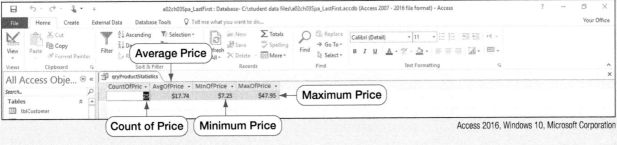

Figure 30 Aggregate query results

f. Click **Save** 🖫, and under Query name, type qryProductStatistics, and then click **OK**.

Changing Field Names

Field names in aggregate queries are a composite of the selected aggregate function and the table field name. For example, the Count function for Price is named CountOfPrice as shown in Figure 30. This name can be misleading, as the aggregate function actually shows the number of products that have a price. The other functions are more descriptively named but still could have more useful names.

The field names assigned in an aggregate query can easily be changed either before or after the query is run. However, you must keep the original field name in the query design grid so Access knows what field to perform the calculation on. In this exercise, you will change the names of the fields in the aggregate query you just created.

To Change the Field Names in an Aggregate Query

a. With qryProductStatistics open, switch to **Design** view.

b. Click in the **Field** row of the first column, and then press Home to move the insertion point to the beginning of the field name. Type Number of Products:. Do not delete the field name Price. The colon identifies the title as separate from the field name. Repeat for the other three fields, and type Average Price:, Minimum Price:, and Maximum Price:. If necessary, use **AutoFit** to resize the columns to see the complete column names.

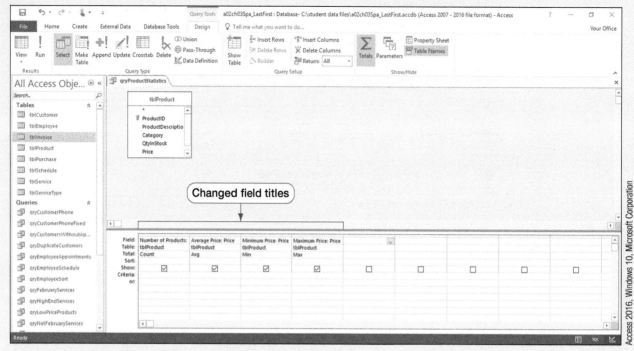

Figure 31 Field titles changed

c. In the Results group, click **Run** to run the query. Use **AutoFit** to resize the columns to see the complete column names.

d. Click **Save** and then **Close** the query.

Creating Calculations for Groups of Records

Not only can you find statistical information for selected records using aggregate functions in a query or for all records using the total row, you can also calculate statistics for groups of records. Creating a group to calculate statistics works the same way as an aggregate query but must include the field to group by. The additional field will not have a statistic selected for the total row, but instead, it will have the default Group By entered in the total row.

In this exercise, you will help the spa manager find the same product price statistics you calculated above but this time grouped by product category.

 A03.29

To Create a Group Calculation

a. In the Navigation pane, right-click **qryProductStatistics**, and then select **Copy**. Right-click anywhere in the **Navigation Pane**, and then select **Paste**. In the Query Name box, type qryProductStatisticsByCategory. Click OK.

b. In the Navigation pane, double-click **qryProductStatisticsByCategory** to open it. Switch to **Design** view.

c. Double-click **Category** to add it to the query design grid. Point to the **top border** of the Category field until the pointer turns into a black downward arrow. Click and drag the **Category** field to the left of the Number of Products: Price column. Notice that the Category Total row displays Group By, so the statistics will be grouped by each category type.

d. In the Results group, click **Run** to run the query. Use **AutoFit** on the columns to best fit the data.

Notice that there are five total rows, one for each category of product.

Figure 32 Query results with calculations

e. Click **Save** 🖫, and **Close** ✕ the query.

Troubleshooting an Aggregate Query

Caution should be used in using aggregate functions. Forgetting to add a function in the total row can cause a large number of records to be retrieved from the database or can result in a combination of records that do not make any sense. You must carefully select which field should have the Group By operator in the total row; many times, only one field will use Group By. Combining search criteria and aggregate functions in a single query can make the query complex. It also makes troubleshooting more difficult if the query does not work. When in doubt, set all your criteria in one query, and then use the aggregate functions in another query based on the query with the criteria. This way, you can first verify that your criteria worked and then concentrate on the aggregate function results.

The manager tried to create an aggregate query to calculate the total number of items and average number of items purchased by different methods: phone, online, and in person. The results made no sense, and she has asked you to help her figure out why. In this exercise, you will troubleshoot the query to determine the problem and correct it.

To Troubleshoot an Aggregate Query

a. Double-click **qryPurchaseMethods** to open the query. Notice the results in the second and third columns are exactly the same when the intent was to have one column contain a total and the other column contain an average.

b. Switch to **Design** view. Look at the second column, **Quantity**, and notice the Total row shows the Group By operator instead of a function. Change this to **Sum**.

c. Rename the second and third column field titles to **Total Quantity** and **Average Quantity**, remembering to put a colon between the name and the Quantity field name.

d. In the Results group, click **Run** to run the query. Use **AutoFit** on the columns to best fit the data.

e. Click the **File** tab, click **Save As**, click **Save Object As**, and then click **Save As**. Under Save 'qryPurchaseMethods' to:, type qryPurchaseMethodsFixed, and then click **OK**.

Formatting a Calculated Field

An aggregate query may give you the correct results, but the formatting may not be what you expected. The fields used in a query that come from a table use the formatting defined in the table design. However, calculated query fields must be formatted in the query design grid using the Field properties sheet. The **Property Sheet** contains a list of properties for fields in which you can make precise changes to each property associated with the field.

The manager does not want to see decimal places for the Average Quantity column. In this exercise, you will show her how to change the formatting of that field.

To Change the Formatting of a Calculated Field

a. With **qryPurchaseMethodsFixed** open, switch to **Design** view.

b. Click the **Average Quantity: Quantity** column. On the Design tab, in the Show/Hide group, click **Property Sheet**.

c. In the Property Sheet pane, on the General tab, click the **Format** box, click the **arrow**, and then select **Fixed**. Click the **Decimal Places** box, and then type 0.

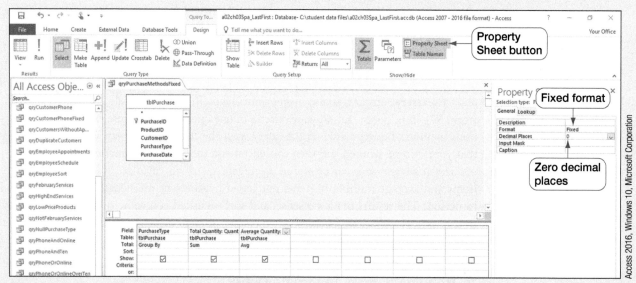

Figure 33 Property sheet open with changes

d. **Close** ☒ the Property Sheet pane, and then **run** the query again. The results should be formatted with no decimal places.

e. **Save** ☐ and **close** ☒ the query.

Create Calculated Fields

In addition to statistical calculations using aggregate functions, you can perform an arithmetic calculation within a query to create a new field. The result of the calculated field is displayed each time you run the query. However, this new field is not part of any other table.

A calculated field can be added to a query using the fields in the query or even fields in another table or query in the database. The calculation can use a combination of numbers and field values, allowing you flexibility in how you perform the calculation. For example, you can multiply a product price stored in the table by a sales tax rate that you enter into the calculation.

Building a Calculated Field Using Expression Builder

The **Expression Builder** is a tool in Access that can help you build calculated fields correctly. Expression Builder provides a list of expression elements, operators, and built-in functions. Its capabilities range from simple to complex.

In this exercise, you will help the spa manager create a query to show what the value of her inventory is, using the Quantity in Stock and Price fields for each product.

A03.32

SIDE NOTE
Expression Box
When you use multiple tables in Expression Builder, the table name is put in front of the field name with an exclamation mark.

To Add a Calculated Field Using Expression Builder

a. Click the **Create** tab, and then in the Queries group, click **Query Design**, and then double-click **tblProduct** to add the table to the query. Click **Close** to close the Show Table dialog box.

b. Double-click **ProductDescription**, **Category**, **QtyInStock**, and **Price** to add the fields to the query design grid.

c. Click in the **Sort** row, and then select **Ascending** for the ProductDescription field.

d. Click **Save** 🖫, and under Query Name, type qryProductInventory, and then click **OK**.

e. Click in the **Field** row in the fifth column, and in the Query Setup group, click **Builder**. The Expression Builder dialog box opens, which is where you will build your formula for the calculation.

f. Under Expression Categories, double-click **QtyInStock** to add the field to the expression box, type * for multiplication, and then under Expression Categories, double-click **Price**. Move the insertion point to the beginning of the expression, and then type Total Inventory:.

Troubleshooting

When you click Expression Builder to create a calculated field and you do not see your field names listed in the Expression Categories box in the middle of the dialog box, it may be that the query has not been saved yet. If the query has not been saved, the field names will not appear, and you will have to type them in the Expression Builder manually instead of clicking them to select them. It is good practice to save your query first and then open the Expression Builder to create a calculated field.

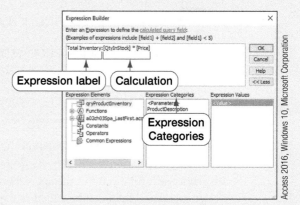

Figure 34 Expression Builder

g. Click **OK** to save the expression and add it to the query design grid.
The field name will show Total Inventory: [QtyInStock]*[Price] and will multiply the quantity by the price.

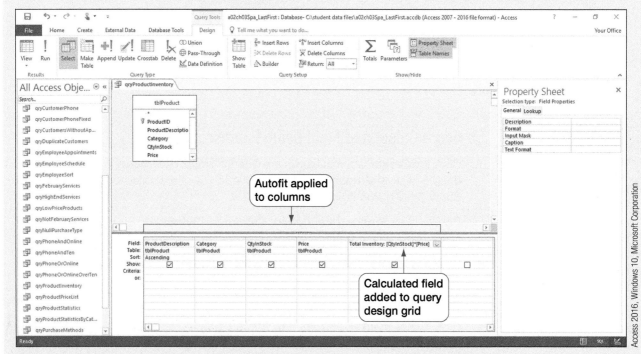

Figure 35 Design grid with calculated expression added

h. In the Results group, click **Run** to run the query. Use **AutoFit** on the Total Inventory column to best fit the data. The results should show 25 records with a new column titled Total Inventory that multiplies the QtyInStock and the Price fields.

i. **Close** ☒ the query, and then click **Yes** when prompted to save changes. **Close** Access.

Concept Check

1. What is a wildcard character? How would you use it to find a record? p. 655

2. Does modifying the datasheet appearance change the data in your database? p. 660

3. What is the difference between the Find Duplicates Query Wizard and the Find Unmatched Query Wizard? p. 661–662

4. What is the multiplier effect, and how can you prevent it from happening? p. 667

5. If you sort on two different fields in a query, which sort is done first? p. 672

6. What is the difference between using AND and OR as logical operators in a query? p. 681

7. What is an aggregate query? Why would you add the same field multiple times to an aggregate query? p. 689–690

8. How does a calculated field differ from an aggregate function? p. 694

Key Terms

Aggregate function   688
AutoFit   660
Comparison operator   673
Crosstab query   661
Expression Builder   695
Filter   658
Filter by selection   658
Find command   655
Find Duplicates Query Wizard   661

Find Unmatched Query Wizard   662
Join lines   667
Logical operator   681
Multiplier effect   667
Orphan   662
Primary sort field   672
Property sheet   694
Query by example   664
Replace command   655

Secondary sort field   672
Sort field   671
Sorting   671
Special operator   685
Text filter   659
Total row   688
Wildcard character   655

Visual Summary

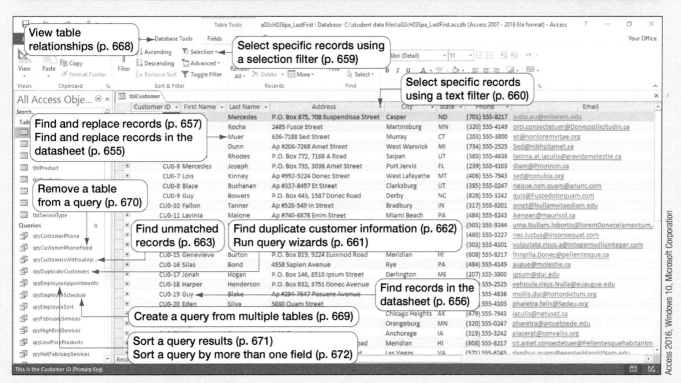

Figure 36

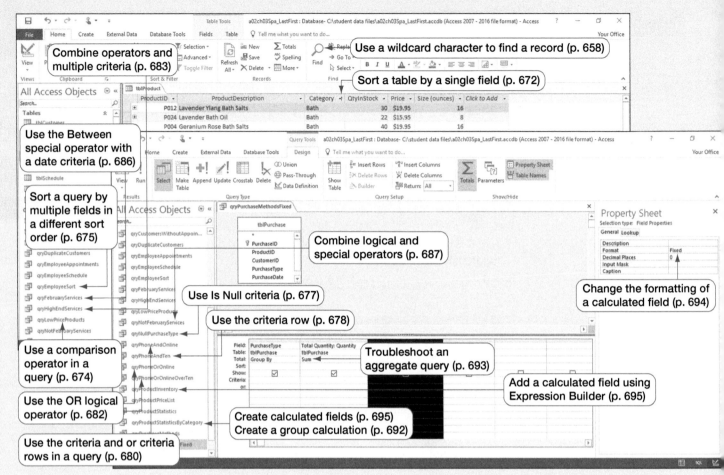

Figure 37

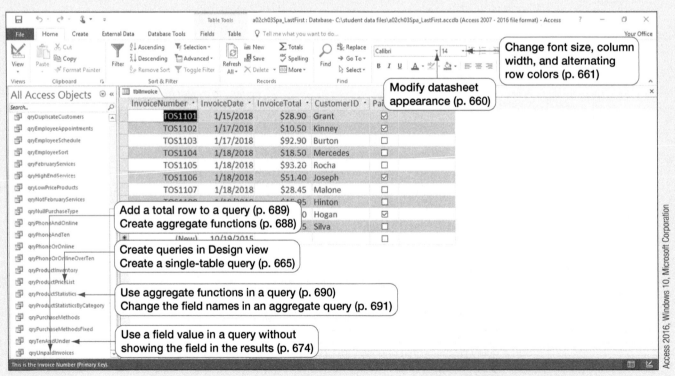

Figure 38

Student data file needed:

 a02ch03Spa2.accdb

You will save your file as:

 a02ch03Spa2_LastFirst.accdb

Turquoise Oasis Spa

Sales & Marketing

The resort is considering hosting a large convention and is trying to sign a multiple-year contract with an out-of-town group. The spa is being asked to provide information about the services, products, and packages it offers. All the information can be found in the database, but it needs to come together in a coherent fashion. You have been asked to answer a number of questions about the spa and provide information to help answer those questions. You will also look for discrepancies or mistakes in the data and correct them as necessary.

a. Start **Access**, click **Open Other Files** in the left pane, and then double-click **This PC**. Navigate through the folder structure to the location of your student data files, and then double-click **a02ch03Spa2**. A database opens displaying tables related to the spa.

b. Click the **File** tab, click **Save As**, save the file as an **Access Database**, and click **Save As**. Navigate to the location where you are saving your project files, and then change the file name to a02ch03Spa2_LastFirst using your last and first name. Click **Save**. If necessary, enable the content.

c. Double-click **tblCustomer** to open the table. Add a new record with your first name and last name, your address, your city, your state, your phone number, and your e-mail address.

d. Use the **Find** command to find spa customers who come from as far away as Alaska.

   • Click in the **State** column for the first record. On the Home tab, in the Find group, click **Find**. Type AK in the Find What box, and then click **Find Next** until Access finishes searching the table. Click **OK**, and then click **Cancel** to close the dialog box. Notice that the Alaska address selected is really a city in Hawaii.

e. Use the Replace command to replace **AK** with HI in the table.

   • On the Home tab, in the Find group, click **Find**. Click the **Replace** tab, and type AK in the Find What box. Type HI in the Replace With box, and then click **Find Next**. When Customer ID CU0-21 is selected, click **Replace**. Click **Find Next** to check for any more similar errors. Click **OK**, and then click **Cancel** to close the dialog box.

f. Click the **arrow** on the State field column, point to **Text Filters**, select **Begins With**, type H in the State begins with box, and then click **OK**. Verify that three records are selected. Save and close the table.

g. Create a query to find which products are purchased by more than one customer.

   • Click the **Create** tab, and then in the Queries group, click **Query Wizard**. Click **Find Duplicates Query Wizard**, and then click **OK**.

   • Click **Table: tblPurchase**, and then click **Next**. Double-click **ProductID**, and then click **Next**. Click the **All Fields** button to add all the fields to the Additional query fields box, and then click **Next**. Under "What do you want to name your query?", type qryDuplicateProducts_iLast using your first initial and last name, and then click **Finish**. Close the query.

h. Create a query to find out which employees currently do not have any customer appointments at the spa.

   • On the **Create** tab, in the Queries group, click **Query Wizard**. Click **Find Unmatched Query Wizard**, and then click **OK**.

- Click **Table: tblEmployee**, and then click **Next**. Select **Table: tblSchedule**, and then click **Next**. Verify that Matching fields shows **EmployeeID <=> Employee**, and then click **Next**. Click the **All Fields** button to add all the fields to the Selected fields column, and then click **Next**.

- Name the query qryEmployeesWithoutAppointments_iLast using your first initial and last name, and then click **Finish**.

- In the Results group, switch to **Design** view. Click the **Sort** row for the EmpLastName field, click the **sort** arrow, and then click **Ascending** to sort the query in ascending order by Last Name. On the Design tab, in the Results group, click **Run** to run the query. Close the query, and then click **Yes** when prompted to save the changes.

i. Create a query to list any customers who are not from New Mexico who have purchased bath products.

- Click the **Create** tab, and then in the Queries group, click **Query Design**. Double-click **tblCustomer**, **tblPurchase**, and **tblProduct** to add the tables to the query window. Click **Close** to close the Show Table dialog box.

- In the following order, from tblCustomer, double-click **CustLastName**, **CustFirstName**, **CustState**; from tblPurchase, double-click **PurchaseDate**; from tblProduct, double-click **ProductDescription**; and from tblPurchase, double-click **Quantity** to add the fields to the query design grid. Click the **Sort** row for the CustLastName and CustFirstName fields, and then select **Ascending**.

- In the **Criteria** row for CustState, type Not NM. In the same **Criteria** row for ProductDescription, type *Bath*.

- Note that the Not in the CustState criteria will be converted to <> by Access and the word Like will be added to the criteria *Bath*.

- On the Design tab, in the Results group, click **Run** to run the query.

- Click **Save**, name the query qryBathProductsNotNM_iLast using your first initial and last name, and then close the query.

j. Create a query to list the spa's services by Type, Name, LengthOfService, and Fee.

- Click the **Create** tab, in the Queries group, click **Query Design**. Double-click **tblService** and **tblServiceType** to add the tables to the query window. Click **Close** to close the Show Table dialog box.

- In the following order, from tblServiceType, double-click **Type**, and from tblService, double-click **ServiceName**, **LengthOfService**, and **Fee** to add the fields to the query design grid. Click the **Sort** row for the Type field, select **Ascending**, and then for the Fee field, select **Descending**. On the Design tab, in the Results group, click **Run** to run the query.

- Use **AutoFit** on all columns to better view the data. Click **Save**, name the query qryServicesAndFees_iLast using your first initial and last name, and then close the query.

k. Create a query to find how much each customer spent on his or her product purchase, including 8% sales tax, but only if the purchase was a quantity greater than 1.

- Click the **Create** tab, and then in the Queries group, click **Query Design**. Add **tblProduct**, **tblPurchase**, and **tblCustomer** to the query window. Click **Close** to close the Show Table dialog box. From tblProduct, double-click **ProductDescription** and **Price**; from tblPurchase, double-click **Quantity**; and from tblCustomer, double-click **CustFirstName** and **CustLastName** in that order to add the fields to the query design grid.

- Click in the **Criteria** row for Quantity, and then type >1. Click **Save**, name the query qryTotalPurchase_iLast using your first initial and last name, and then click **OK**.

- In the sixth column, click in the **Field** row, and then on the Design tab, in the Query Set-up group, click **Builder**. In the Expression Categories column, double-click **Price** to add it to the expression, type *, double-click **Quantity** to add it to the expression, type *, and then type 1.08. Click at the beginning of the expression, type Total Purchase with tax:, and then click **OK**.

- Click the **Sort** row for the Quantity field, click the **arrow**, and then click **Ascending**. In the Results group, click **Run** to run the query.

- Switch to **Design** view. Click the **Total Purchase with tax** field, on the Design tab, in the Show/Hide group, click **Property Sheet**. On the Property Sheet's General tab, click the **Format** arrow, and then select **Currency**. Click the Decimal Places arrow, and then select **2**. Close the Property Sheet, and then on the Design tab, in the Results group, click **Run** to run the query. The Total Purchase with tax field should be formatted with currency and two decimal places.

- Use **AutoFit** on all the columns.

- Close the query, and then click **Yes** when prompted to save the changes.

l. Create an aggregate query to find the average, minimum, and maximum fee for each type of service the spa offers.

- Click the **Create** tab, and then in the Queries group, click **Query Design**. Add **tblService** to the query window. Click **Close** to close the Show Table dialog box. Double-click **Type** one time, and then double-click **Fee** three times in that order to add the fields to the query design grid. In the Show/Hide group, click **Totals** to add the Total row to the query design grid.

- Click in the **Total** row, for the first Fee column, click the **arrow**, and then click **Avg**. For the second Fee column, select **Min**; and for the third Fee column, select **Max**. Click in the **Sort** row in the Type field, click the **arrow**, and then select **Ascending**. In the Results group, click **Run** to run the query.

- Switch to **Design** view. Change the names of the three Fee columns to Average Fee, Minimum Fee, and Maximum Fee in that order, remembering to put a colon before the Fee field name. In the **Results** group, click **Run** to run the query.

- Use **AutoFit** on all the columns.

- Click **Save**, name the query qryFeeStatistics_iLast using your first initial and last name, and then click **OK**. Close the query.

m. Close Access, and submit your file as directed by your instructor.

Problem Solve 1

MyITLab®
Grader
Homework

Student data file needed:

a02ch03Planner.accdb

You will save your file as:

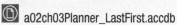
a02ch03Planner_LastFirst.accdb

Rakes Event Management

Production & Operations

Beth Rakes runs an event-planning service. She has a database with clients, events, menus, and decorations. She has hired you to add queries to make the database more useful. You have been given a small database with representative data.

a. Open the Access database **a02ch03Planner**. Save your file as a02ch03Planner_LastFirst using your last and first name. If necessary, enable the content.

b. Open **tblClients**, and change the first and last name in the last record to be your actual name. Create a filter to show only the clients who have a State of **MN**. Save and close the table.

c. Modify tblEvents so the font size is **14**. Adjust the column widths appropriately. Change to an Alternate Row Color of **Gold, Accent 4, Lighter 80%**. Save and close the table.
Create a Find Duplicates query that will show all events on the same date. Show all the fields in the query results. Name the query qryDupDates. Close the query.

d. Create a Find Unmatched query that will return the **last name**, **first name**, **city**, **state**, and **phone** of anyone who is listed as a client in **tblClients** but does not have an event booked. Sort the query in ascending order by last name and then by first name. Name the query qryClientNoEvent. Save and close the query.

> **Critical Thinking**

Of the records returned in this query, which state or states occur most frequently as having clients that do not have booked events?

e. Create a query that will return the client's **last name**, **first name**, **event name**, **event date**, and **rate**. Sort the query in ascending order first by LastName then by FirstName. Name the query qryRates. Add a total row to show total rate. Save and close the query.

f. Create a query that returns all the events with 100 attendees or more. Include event date, event name, location, total attendees, and rate. Sort them by rate (highest to lowest), but do not show the rate in the result. Name the query qryLargeEvents. Save and close the query.

g. Create a query to calculate menu costs. Include from **tblEvents** the **EventDate**, **EventName**, and **TotalAttendees**, and include from **tblMenuChoice** the **MenuType** and the **CostPerPerson**. You will also need to include the **tblMenuItems** table to avoid the multiplier effect. Name the query qryMenuCosts. Calculate MenuCost as TotalAttendees * CostPerPerson. If necessary, format the new field as currency, and sort the results by EventDate (ascending).
Adjust the column widths as necessary. Save and close the query.

h. Create a query that returns the **count**, **sum**, **average**, **minimum**, and **maximum** of all the event rates. Name the fields Event Count, Total Rates, Average Rate, Minimum Rate, and Maximum Rate in that order. Adjust the column widths as necessary. Name the query qryEventRateStats. Save and close the query.

i. Create a query that includes the client **LastName** and **FirstName**, the **EventName**, **EventDate** and **TotalAttendees** for any event in April 2018 that has 200 or more attendees. Sort in ascending order by client LastName and then by FirstName. Name the query qryAprilBigEvents. Save and close the query.

j. Close the database, exit Access, and then submit your file as directed by your instructor.

Perform 1: Perform in Your Career

Student data file needed:	You will save your file as:
🗃 a02ch03HomeSale.accdb	🗃 a02ch03HomeSale_LastFirst.accdb

Real Estate Database

Production & Operations

You are interning at a real estate firm. You supervisor was delighted with your Access skills. She asks you to deliver subsets of data from the database so that she can analyze the data and look for trends.

a. Open the Access database, **a02ch03HomeSale**. Save your file as a02ch03HomeSale_LastFirst using your last and first name. If necessary, enable the content.

b. Open the Relationships window to familiarize yourself with the tables, fields, and relationships in the database. Close the Relationships window.

c. Open **tblAgent**, and add your first and last names where indicated. Close the table.

d. Open **tblDevelopment**, and add your name to the **DevelopmentName** field for the sixth record. Close the table.

e. Create a query that displays the **DevelopmentName**, **Address**, **City**, **State**, and **PostalCode**. Add the listing agent's **ID** and **first** and **last** names. Finally, add the **ListPrice** and **SoldPrice**.

f. Limit your query to only the sold properties, and sort it by development name in ascending order. (Hint: Properties that have been sold will have a sold price; all others will be null.) Save the query as qrySoldProperties_iLast.

g. Make the following modifications to the qrySoldProperties_iLast query.

- Calculate the percent of list price for which each property was sold. For example, a property that listed for $100,000 and sold for $98,000 received 98.0% of its listed price, 98,000/100,000. Format the calculation results as a percent with one decimal place. Name the new field PercentList.

- Add a total row to the Datasheet View of the query. Use it to calculate the average percent of list price and the total of the list price and sold prices. If necessary, resize the columns to view the data.

h. Create a new query based on **qrySoldProperties_iLast**. In the Show Table dialog box, use the Queries tab to view a list of queries in the database. Add the **DevelopmentName**, the **ListPrice**, the **SoldPrice**, and the **PercentList** fields. Aggregate by the development name; sum the price fields; and average the PercentList field. Format the PercentList field as **Percent** with **1** decimal place. Save the query as qrySalesByDevelopment_iLast.

i. Create a new query based on qrySoldProperties. Add the agent's first and last names, the ListPrice, the SoldPrice, and the PercentList fields.

j. Group the data by the agent's last name, sum the ListPrice, and SoldPrice, and average the PercentList field. Sort the data in ascending order by the last name.

k. Calculate the listing agent's commission. Multiply the SoldPrice by 3%. In the total row for the expression, select **Sum**. Name the field Commission and format the field as **Currency**. Save the query as qryCommission_iLast.

l. Create a new query. Add the agent's first and last names, the ListingDate, SoldDate, SquareFeet, and SoldPrice fields. Save the query as qrySaleAnalysis_iLast.

m. Limit the query to sales made in 2017 of properties with more than 2000 square feet.

n. Calculate the number of days each property was on the market by finding the difference between the SoldDate and the ListingDate.

o. Run the query. In Datasheet view, calculate the average number of days the 2017 sold homes were on the market.

p. Close the database, exit Access, and then submit your files as directed by your instructor.

Additional Cases

Additional Chapter Cases are available at www.pearsonhighered.com/youroffice

Microsoft Access 2016

Chapter 4 | USING FORMS AND REPORTS IN ACCESS

Production & Operations

OBJECTIVES

1. Navigate and edit records in datasheets   p. 705

2. Navigate forms and subforms   p. 712

3. Update table records using forms   p. 712

4. Create a form using the Form Wizard   p. 715

5. Modify a form's design p. 721

6. Create a report using the Report Wizard p. 726

7. Customize a report p. 734

8. Save a report as a PDF file   p. 740

Prepare Case

Turquoise Oasis Spa's New Database

The Turquoise Oasis Spa has a database with customer, employee, product, and service information for easier scheduling and access. An intern created the database, and the manager and staff members are struggling to use it to its fullest capacity. You have recently been hired to work in the office of the spa, and you have knowledge of Access, so the manager has asked for your help in maintaining the records and creating forms and reports to help better use the data in the database.

Zadorozhnyi Viktor / Shutterstock

Student data files needed for this chapter:

 a02ch04Spa.accdb

a02ch04Spa.jpg

a02ch04Spa.thmx

You will save your files as:

 a02ch04Spa_LastFirst.accdb

 a02ch04SpaEmployeeSchedule_LastFirst.pdf

Creating Customized Forms

Recall that forms are the objects in Access that are used to enter, edit, or view records in a table. Data can be entered, edited, or viewed directly in the table or in a form. Each option offers advantages and disadvantages.

In Datasheet view, data may be updated directly in the table where it is stored. Datasheet view shows all the fields and records at one time, which provides all the information you need to update your data, unlike in a form or query, where some of the fields or records may not be in view. In this section you will navigate datasheets and forms. Then you will edit data in a table and in a form.

Navigate and Edit Records in Datasheets

As you may recall, you can navigate from record to record or from field to field in a table using the Navigation bar or, in Navigation mode, by using Tab, Enter, Home, End, ↑, ↓, ←, and →. **Navigation mode** allows you to move from record to record and from field to field using keystrokes. To update data in a table, you must be in Edit mode. **Edit mode** allows you to edit, or change, the contents of a field. To switch between Navigation mode and Edit mode, press F2.

If you can see the blinking insertion point in a field, you are in Edit mode. When the text of a field is selected and highlighted, you are in Navigation mode.

QUICK REFERENCE	Keystrokes Used in Navigation Mode and Edit Mode	
Keystroke	**Navigation Mode**	**Edit Mode**
→ and ←	Move from field to field	Move from character to character
↑ and ↓	Move from record to record	Switch to Navigation mode and move from record to record
Home	Moves to the first field in the record	Moves to the first character in the field
End	Moves to the last field in the record	Moves to the last character in the field
Tab and Enter	Move one field at a time	Switch to Navigation mode and move from field to field
Ctrl + Home	Moves to the first field of the first record	Moves to the first character in the field, same as Home
Ctrl + End	Moves to the last field of the last record	Moves to the last character in the field, same as End

Opening the Starting File

The spa collects data about customers, employees, products, and services and uses the data for scheduling. In this exercise, you will open the spa database to get started.

To Open the a02ch04Spa Database

a. Start **Access**, click **Open Other Files** in the left pane, and then double-click **This PC**. Navigate through the folder structure to the location of your student data files, and then double-click **a02ch04Spa**. A database opens displaying tables, forms, and a report related to the spa.

b. Click the **File** tab, click **Save As**, and save the file as an **Access Database**, and click **Save As**. Navigate to the location where you are saving your project files, and then change the file name to a02ch04Spa_LastFirst using your last and first name. Click **Save**. If necessary, enable the content.

Editing a Table in Datasheet View

Datasheet view shows all the records and fields at one time, which is one advantage to using it to update your records. Another advantage is the ability to see all the records in the table, which gives you a perspective on the data you are entering. The spa staff has received a note from a customer who has changed his phone number. In this exercise, you will show the staff how to change that customer's record in the Customer table.

To Edit a Record in a Table in Datasheet View

a. In the Navigation Pane, double-click **tblCustomer** to open the table.

b. Locate the customer with the Customer ID **CU0-12** and the last name **Hinton**.

c. Click in the **CustomerID** field, and then press Tab. You are now in Navigation mode, and the First Name field should be highlighted.

SIDE NOTE

Pin the Ribbon

If your ribbon is collapsed, pin your ribbon open. Click the Home tab. In the lower right-hand corner of the ribbon, click Pin the Ribbon ⊣.

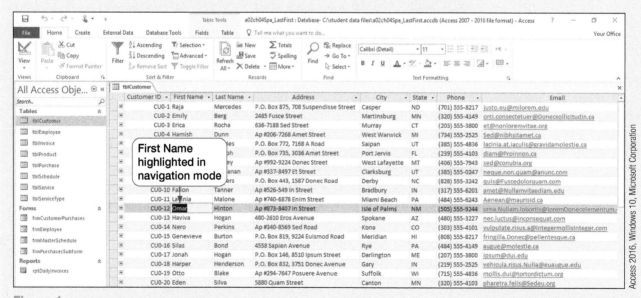

Figure 1 Table in Navigation mode

d. Continue pressing Tab until the **Phone** field is highlighted. Press F2 to switch from Navigation mode to Edit mode. Notice the insertion point is at the beginning of the Phone field and the first character is highlighted. Type 5055552923 to enter the new phone number. Because the field is already formatted as a phone number, it is not necessary to enter parentheses or dashes.

e. Press Tab to switch to Navigation mode and move to the next field.

f. **Close** X the table.

 CONSIDER THIS | **Why Put a Prefix Before a Primary Key?**

CustomerID, the primary key for tblCustomer, is defined as AutoNumber but is formatted to have the prefix "CU0-" (0 is a zero) before the number field. Similarly, EmployeeID, the key for tblEmployee, is formatted to have "EMP00" as a prefix before the number field. What is the advantage of putting a prefix before the primary key to a table? Are there disadvantages? Why were these two prefixes chosen?

Navigate Forms and Subforms

A form is an object in Access that you can use to enter, edit, or view records in a table. A simple form allows you to see records one at a time rather than as a group in Datasheet view.

REAL WORLD ADVICE | **Data Overload!**

You may be asked to create a database for someone else who is not familiar with how a database works or even how the computer works. Your role is to make that person's job as easy as possible so he or she can get work done with as few errors as possible.

Looking at a database table with hundreds or thousands of records in Datasheet view can be very intimidating to some people. Trying to keep track of the record or field you are in can be more difficult as the table grows larger and larger. Often, seeing one record at a time in a form can eliminate data entry errors and allow the user to focus on the information for that particular record.

You navigate records in a form the same way you navigate a table: using buttons on the Navigation bar to move from record to record.

QUICK REFERENCE		Navigation Buttons on the Navigation Bar
Button	**Description**	**What it does**
⏮	First record	Moves to the first record in the table
⏭	Last record	Moves to the last record in the table
◀	Previous record	Moves to the record just before the current record
▶	Next record	Moves to the record just after the current record
▶⁕	New (blank) record	Moves to a new row to enter a new record

When you create a form from two tables that have a one-to-many relationship, the first table you select becomes the **main form**, and the second table you select becomes the **subform**. A form with a subform allows you to see one record at a time from the main form and multiple records in Datasheet view from the other related table. Because you see only one record at a time or one record and a datasheet, navigation tools become important when you are working with forms, as you cannot see all the records at one time.

Navigating a Main Form

Within each record, you can use a combination of Tab, Home, Enter, and End, as well as ↓, ↑, ←, and →, to move from field to field as shown in the Quick Reference Box.

QUICK REFERENCE	Navigating Forms

Navigating a main form

Keystroke	What it does
Tab	Moves from field to field within a record; at the last field in a record, moves you to the first field in the next record
Home	Moves to the first field of the current record
Ctrl + Home	Moves to the first field of the first record of the table
End	Moves to the last field of the current record
Ctrl + End	Moves to the last field of the last record of the table
↓, ↑, ←, →	Move up or down a field of the current record

Navigating a form with a subform

Keystroke	What it does
Tab	Moves from field to field within a main record; at the last field in a record, moves to the first field in the subform; at the last record in the subform, moves to the first field in the next record of the main form
Home	From the main form, moves to the first field of the current record; from the subform, moves to the first field of the current record in the subform
Ctrl + Home	From the main form, moves to the first field of the first record; from the subform, moves to the first field of the first record in the subform
End	From the main form, moves to the last field of the current record in the subform; from the subform, moves to the last field of the current record in the subform
Ctrl + End	From the main form, moves to the last field of the last record of the subform; from the subform, moves to the last field of the last record of the subform
↓, ↑, ←, →	Move up or down a field in the current record in either the form or the subform

In this exercise, you will show the spa staff how to navigate the form frmEmployee, which is a list of all employees, one record at a time.

To Navigate a Single-Table Form

a. In the Navigation Pane, double-click **frmEmployee** to open the form.

b. Click **Last record** [▶|] to go to the last record of the table.

c. Click **First record** [|◀] to return to the first record in the table.

d. Click **Next record** [▶] to go to the next record in the table.

e. Click **Previous record** [◀] to go back to the previous record in the table.

f. **Close** [✕] the form.

Navigating a Form with a Subform

When you are navigating forms with a subform, the Navigation bar buttons at the bottom of the main window are used to navigate the records in the main form, and a second Navigation bar at the bottom of the subform datasheet is used to navigate the records in the subform. The same navigation keystrokes are used; however, they work a little differently when a subform is included.

In this exercise, you will show the spa staff members how to navigate the form frmCustomerPurchases, which shows one customer at a time with all the customer's recent product purchases.

To Navigate a Form with a Subform

a. On the Navigation Pane, double-click **frmCustomerPurchases** to open the form.
   Notice that the form has two parts. At the top is the main form that shows information about the customer. It contains records from the tblCustomer table. The lower part is the subform that shows all the purchases made by the customer. It contains records from the tblPurchase table. There are also two navigation bars: one for the main form and one for the subform.

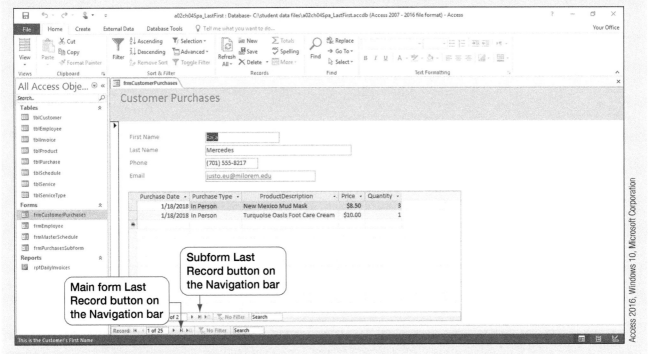

Figure 2 Form with a subform in Datasheet view

b. Click **Last record** ▶| on the subform Navigation bar to highlight the last record in the subform.

c. Click **Last record** ▶| on the main form Navigation bar to go to the last record in the table.

d. Click **Previous record** ◀ on the main form repeatedly to go to record 20 with the customer name Eden Silva.

e. Click **Next record** ▶ in the subform to go to the next record in the subform.

f. **Close** ✕ the form.

Navigating a Split Form

A **split form** is a form created from one table, but it has a Form view and a Datasheet view in the same window. You can view one record at a time at the top of the window and see the whole table in Datasheet view at the bottom of the window. This kind of form is helpful when you want to work with one record at a time and still see the big picture in the main table. In a split form, there are buttons on the Navigation bar to move only from record to record, and each record shown at the top is the record highlighted in the datasheet at the same time. You cannot highlight a different record in the form part and the datasheet part at the same time.

In this exercise, you will show the spa staff how to navigate the form frmMasterSchedule, which shows the schedule as a form and a datasheet in the same window.

To Navigate a Split Form

a. In the Navigation Pane, double-click **frmMasterSchedule** to open the form.

b. Click **Last record** ▶| on the Navigation bar to highlight the last record in both the form and the datasheet.
The customer that appears for the last record has a Schedule ID of S053 and the Customer is Raja.

c. Click the **record selector** in the datasheet with **Schedule ID S046**. The record will be highlighted in the datasheet and also be shown at the top in Form view.

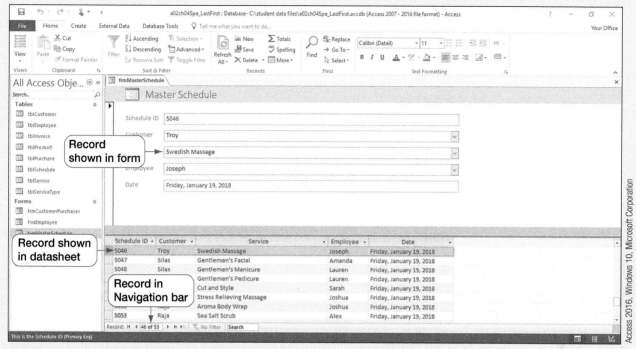

Figure 3 Navigating a split form

d. **Close** ⊠ the form.

REAL WORLD ADVICE   **Using Tabs**

People have become accustomed to using tabs in browsers, and they tend to have many tabs open at one time. In fact, it makes work more efficient because they do not have to keep opening and closing those windows. Unfortunately, Access does not work the same way. Every time you open an object in Access, it opens in a new tab. However, those tabs do not work the same way as tabs in your browser. While websites can be updated when they are open in a browser tab on your desktop, related Access objects cannot be updated when they are open. For example, design changes cannot be made to a table if a related form is open. It is therefore a good idea to close an object when you are done working with it and then reopen it again later when you need it.

Using the Find Command in a Form

Finding data in a form is similar to finding data in a datasheet — you use the Find command. Because you see only one record at a time with a form, using Find can be a quick way to find a record with a specific value in a field and prevents you from having to scroll through all the records in the table one at a time in Form view.

When you are looking for a specific value in a field, you are looking for an exact match. A staff member has asked you to search the employee table to find any employees who may live in Las Vegas so they can try to set up a carpool. In this exercise, you will show the staff member how to use a form to look for that information.

A04.05

To Use the Find Command in a Form

a. In the Navigation Pane, double-click **frmEmployee** to open the form. Press `Tab` to move to the **City** field in the first record.

b. Click the Home tab, and in the Find group, click **Find** to open the Find and Replace dialog box.

c. In the **Find What** box, type Las Vegas. Verify that the Look In text box is Current field, and then click **Find Next**.
Move the Find and Replace dialog box to see all the fields for the current record. The first record with Las Vegas as a value in the City field will be shown.

> ### Troubleshooting
> If you get the message that the search item was not found, make sure you spelled "Las Vegas" correctly.

Figure 4   Find and Replace dialog box

d. Continue to click **Find Next** until Access gives you the message "Microsoft Access finished searching the records. The search item was not found." Click **OK**, and then click **Cancel** to close the Find and Replace dialog box.

Update Table Records Using Forms

Just as you can update data in a datasheet, you can also update data in a form. Remember that a form is just another way to view the data in the table, so when you see a record, you are seeing the record that is actually stored in the table. Nothing is stored in the form.

To make changes to data in a form, you must view the form in Form view. You can also add a record to a table in Form view. Using the Navigation bar, you can go directly to a new record.

QUICK REFERENCE	Updating Tables

Data can be edited in tables, queries, or forms. There are advantages and disadvantages to each method. The table below will help you decide the most appropriate place to edit data.

Method	Advantages	Disadvantages	Typical Situation to Use
Tables	All the records and fields are visible in the datasheet.	The number of records and/or fields in the datasheet can be overwhelming.	A user familiar with Access needs to add a record quickly to a smaller table.
Queries	There may be fewer records and/or fields in the datasheet, making the data more manageable. A form can be based on a query rather than a table.	Not being able to see all the records and/or fields, you may inadvertently change related data in the fields you can see. Not all queries are editable, such as aggregate queries.	A user familiar with Access needs to see and modify appointments booked for a particular day.
Forms	Being able to view one record at a time can make the data seem more manageable.	Not all fields may be included in a form. If fields are missing, some data may mistakenly be left out of a record. Provides a view of only one record at a time.	A user unfamiliar with Access needs to add data to a large table with many records.

Adding Records

When you add a record to a form, you are actually adding the record to the table in which it will be stored. The form will open in Form view, which is the view that allows you to edit the data. As in a datasheet, new records are added at the end of the table, which means that you must go to a blank record to enter new data. In this exercise, you will use the frmEmployee form to add your name to the list of employees in the tblEmployee table.

A04.06

To Add a New Record in a Form

a. On the Navigation bar, click **New (blank) record** .

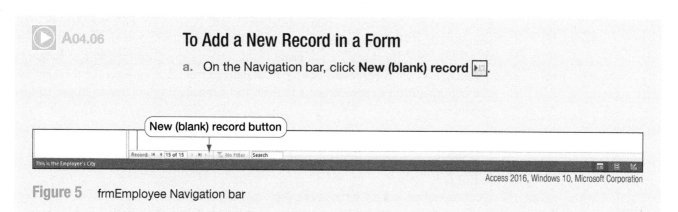

Figure 5   frmEmployee Navigation bar

Access 2016, Windows 10, Microsoft Corporation

b. Type your first name, last name, address, city, state, and phone number in the new record. **Close** ⊠ the form.

c. In the Navigation Pane, double-click **tblEmployee** to open the table, and then click **Last record** ⊮ to see that your record was added. **Close** ⊠ the table.

Editing Records

When you edit a record in a form, you are actually editing the record in the table in which it is stored. Changes to data are saved automatically but can be undone while the table or form is open by using the Undo button or by pressing [Esc] just after the change is made while still in Edit mode.

You have been asked to update the tblEmployee table with recent changes. Mary Murphy has recently changed her phone number, but it has not yet been changed in the table. In this exercise, you will show the staff how to find her record using a form and update her phone number.

To Edit Records Using a Form

a. In the Navigation Pane, double-click **frmEmployee** to open the form. Press [Tab] to move to the **Last Name** field. Click the Home tab, in the Find group, click **Find**, and then in the Find What box, type Murphy. Click **Find Next**.

b. When the record for Mary Murphy is displayed, click **Cancel** to close the Find and Replace dialog box, and then press [Tab] to move to the **Phone** field. Change Mary's phone number to 5055551289.

c. **Close** ⊠ the form.

Deleting Records

Records can be deleted from a single table without additional steps if the table is not part of a relationship. If the table is part of a relationship, referential integrity has been enforced, and the cascade delete option has not been chosen, a record cannot be deleted if there are related records in another table until those records have also been deleted. For example, if you want to delete a customer from tblCustomer and that customer has appointments in tblSchedule, then the appointments for the customer have to be deleted from the tblSchedule before the customer can be deleted from the tblCustomer. This prevents leaving a customer scheduled in one table without the corresponding customer information in another table.

The spa manager would like you to remove Peter Klein from tblEmployee because he has taken a new job and is leaving the spa. You explain to her that if Peter has any appointments scheduled in tblSchedule, those will have to be removed first. She tells you that rather than removing those records, she would like to give those appointments to Alex instead. By changing the name to Alex, those appointments will no longer be linked to Peter, and Peter will be able to be deleted from tblEmployee. In this exercise, you will give Peter's appointments to Alex and remove Peter's record from the table of employees.

> **S₅ CONSIDER THIS** | **Delete with Caution**
>
> Deleting records in a table is permanent. Once you confirm a deletion, you cannot use the Undo button. This is very different from programs such as Excel or Word. Can you think of ways in which you could safeguard your data from accidental deletion?

To Delete a Record with a Form

a. In the Navigation Pane, double-click **frmEmployee** to open the form. In the Find group, click **Find**, and then in the Find What box, type Peter. Click **Find Next**, and then click **Cancel** to close the Find and Replace dialog box.

b. Click the Home tab, and in the Records group, click the **Delete** arrow, and then click **Delete Record**. Access displays a message saying, "The record cannot be deleted or changed because table 'tblSchedule' included related records." Click **OK**.

> ### Troubleshooting
> If Access blanks out the First Name field, you chose Delete rather than Delete Record. Press Esc to undo the deletion, and then choose Delete Record.

c. In the Navigation Pane, double-click **tblSchedule** to open the table. Press Tab to move to the Employee field for the first record. Click the arrow next to **Peter**, and then click **Alex**.

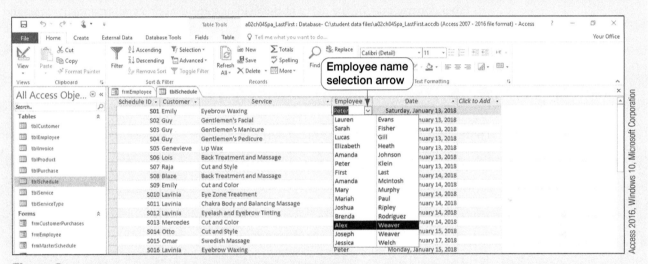

Figure 6   Replacing employee name using the selection arrow

d. On the Home tab, in the Find group, click **Find**, and then in the **Find What** box, type Peter. Click **Find Next**. Click the **arrow** next to the name, and then click **Alex**. Click **Find Next**, and then repeat for the remaining record that has **Peter** listed as the Employee. Click **Cancel** to close the Find and Replace box.

e. **Close** ☒ the table. On the frmEmployee form, make sure the record showing is for **Peter**. On the Home tab, in the Records group, click the **Delete** arrow, and then select **Delete Record**. Click **Yes** to confirm the deletion.

f. **Close** ☒ the form.

Create a Form Using the Form Wizard

Recall that the Query Wizard walks you through the steps to create a query, asking you questions and using your answers to build a query that you can then make changes to if necessary. The Form Wizard works in a similar fashion, walking you through step by step to create a form from one or more tables in your database.

Unlike creating a simple form using the Form button on the Create tab, when you create a form using the wizard, it opens automatically in Form view, ready for you to enter or edit your records. To make changes to the form, you have to switch to either Layout view or Design view.

Creating a Form

Form view is only for viewing and changing data, so to make any changes to the form, you need to switch to either Layout view or Design view. Layout view allows you to make changes to the form while viewing the data at the same time. The effects of your changes can be viewed right away. Design view is a more advanced view that allows you to change the properties or structure of the form. Data is not shown while you are in Design view.

Both Layout view and Design view work with controls, as shown in Figure 7. A **control** is a part of a form or report that you use to enter, edit, or display data. There are three major kinds of controls: bound, unbound, and calculated. A **bound control** is a control whose data source is a field in the table, such as the customer name. An **unbound control** is a control that does not have a source of data, such as the title of the form. A **calculated control** is a control whose data source is a calculated expression that you create. Every field from the table is made up of two controls: a label and a text box. A **label control** may be the name of the field or some other text you manually enter and is an unbound control. A **text box control** represents the actual value of a field and is a bound control. When you add a text box to a form, the label is automatically added as well. However, a label can be added independently from a text box.

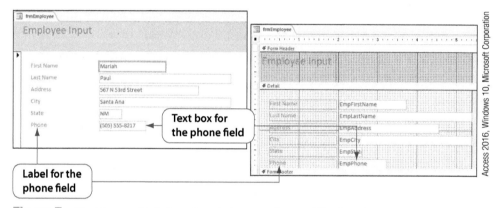

Figure 7   Text box and label controls in Layout view and Design view

The manager of the spa wants the staff to be able to enter and update customer information easily. She thinks it would be much easier to enter data in a form rather than in Datasheet view. In this exercise, you will help her set up the form.

To Create a Single-Table Form

a. Click the **Create** tab, and then in the Forms group, click **Form Wizard**. The Form Wizard dialog box opens.

b. Click the **Tables/Queries** arrow, and select **Table: tblCustomer**. Click the **All Fields** button `>>` to add all the available fields to the Selected Fields box, and then click **Next**.

c. Verify that **Columnar** is selected as the form layout, and then click **Next**.

d. Under "What title do you want for your form?", type frmCustomerInput. Verify that the Open the form to view or enter information option is selected, and then click **Finish**.

The form opens in Form view, so you can immediately start adding or editing records. The form name is also displayed in the Navigation Pane under forms.

e. On the Home tab, click the **View** arrow and select **Design view**. Notice the Form Footer at the bottom of the form window. On the Design tab, in the Controls group, click **Label** Aa. Point to the Form Footer area, and then when your pointer changes to $^{+}_{A}$, drag your pointer to draw a label control about 2.5 inches wide in the top left corner of the Form Footer section. In the new label, type Created by initial Lastname using your first initial and last name.

Troubleshooting

If the Field List pane opens, close it.

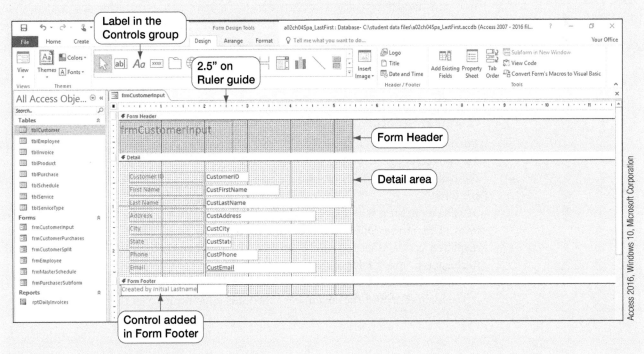

Figure 8 Form in Design view

f. Switch to **Form** view. Verify that your label has been entered in the bottom left corner of the form.

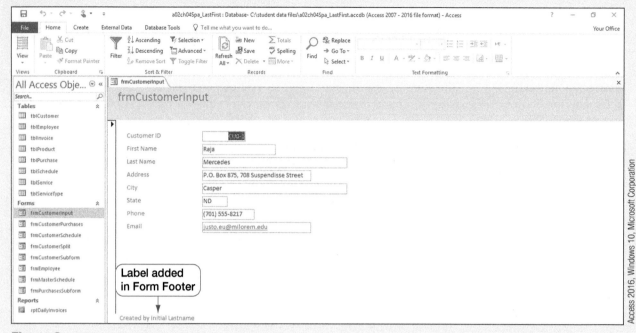

Figure 9 Form with footer added

g. **Close** ⊠ the form, and then click **Yes** to save the changes.

Creating Subforms (Multiple-Table Forms)

There may be times when you want to create a form using two tables. Before you can use two tables in a form, you must make sure there is a one-to-many relationship between the tables. Access will automatically use the common field between the tables to create the form.

The main form will display the first table one record at a time, just like a single-table form. This is the "one" record in the one-to-many relationship. The subform will be displayed as a datasheet below the main form record. This will display the "many" records in the one-to-many relationship.

In this exercise, you will help the staff create another form that shows each customer in the main form and the customer's scheduled appointments in the subform.

 To Create a Subform

a. Click the **Create** tab, and then in the Forms group, click **Form Wizard**. The Form Wizard dialog box opens.

b. Click the **Tables/Queries** arrow, and then select **Table: tblCustomer**. Click the **All Fields** button >> to add all the available fields to the Selected Fields list.

c. Click the **Tables/Queries** arrow, and then select **Table: tblSchedule**. Click the **All Fields** button >> to add all the available fields to the Selected Fields list, and then click **Next**.

d. Verify that by **tblCustomer** is selected and that **Form with subform(s)** is selected, and then click **Next**.

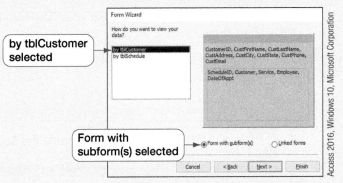

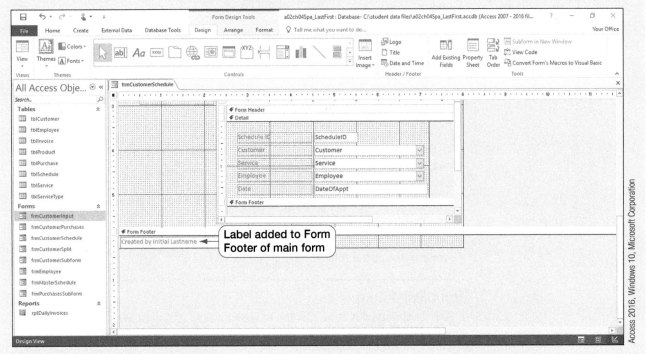

Figure 10 Form options are selected

e. Verify that Datasheet is selected as the subform layout, and then click **Next**.

f. Under What titles do you want for your forms? in the Form field, type frmCustomerSchedule. In the Subform field, type frmCustomerSubform. Verify that the Open the form to view or enter information option is selected, and then click **Finish**.

The form opens in Form view so you can immediately start adding or editing records. The form and subform names are shown in the Navigation Pane.

g. Switch to **Design** view. Scroll to the bottom of the form to see the Form Footer at the base of the main form. On the Design tab, in the Controls group, click **Label** [Aa]. When your pointer changes to [+A], drag your pointer to draw a label control about 2.5 inches wide in the top left corner of the Form Footer section. In the new label, type Created by initial Lastname using your initial and last name.

> ### Troubleshooting
> If the Field List pane shows and blocks parts of the form you need to see, close the Field List pane.

Figure 11 Add footer to main form

h. Switch to **Form** view. Verify that your label has been entered in the bottom left corner of the form.

i. **Close** ☒ the form, and then click **Yes** to save the changes.

 CONSIDER THIS | **Include the Subform?**

When two tables are in a one-to-many relationship and you use the Form button to create a form for the table on the one side of the relationship, the wizard automatically adds a subform for the table on the many side. If you create the form using Form Wizard, you can choose whether to include the subform. When would you want to include the subform? When would you not want to include the subform?

Creating a Split Form

A split form is created from one table and displays each record individually at the top of the window and then again as part of the whole table datasheet in the bottom of the window. This type of form gives you the advantage of seeing each record and the whole table in one place.

The manager would like to see each customer's record individually along with all the records from the customer table. In this exercise, you will show her how to create a split form from the customer table.

 A04.11

To Create a Split Form

a. In the Navigation Pane, click **tblCustomer** one time to select the table, but do not open it.

b. Click the **Create** tab, and then in the Forms group, click **More Forms**, and then select **Split Form**.
A window will open with the split form for the customer table. Notice that the top of the form shows a record individually and the bottom of the form shows the whole table as a datasheet.

c. Switch to **Design** view. Notice that Design view shows only the top of the split form.

d. On the Design tab, in the Controls group, click **Label** Aa, point to the Form Footer area, and then when your pointer changes to ⁺A, drag your pointer to draw a label control about 2.5 inches wide in the top left corner of the Form Footer section. In the new label, type Created by initial Lastname using your first initial and last name.

e. Switch to **Form** view. Verify that your label has been entered in the bottom left corner of the upper form.

Troubleshooting

If your label does not show, switch to Design view, and then switch back to Form view.

---

f. Click **Save** 🖫, and under **Form Name**, type frmCustomerSplit, and then click **OK**. **Close** ☒ the form.

Modify a Form's Design

While creating a form using the wizard is quick and efficient, there may be times when you will want to change how the form looks or add things to the form after you have created it. Formatting, such as colors and fonts, can easily be changed. Controls can be added to a form to include additional fields or labels with text. Pictures and other objects can also be added to a form to make the form more visually appealing.

Often, forms are customized to match company or group color themes or other forms and reports already created by a user. Customizing forms can make them more personal and sometimes easier to use.

Colors, font types, and font sizes are just a few of the formatting changes you can make to an existing form.

Changing the Form Theme

By default, Access uses the Office theme when you create a form using the Form Wizard. Even though there is not a step in the wizard to select a different theme, you can change it once the form has been created. A **theme** is a built-in combination of colors and fonts. By default, a theme will be applied to all objects in a database: forms, reports, tables, and queries. However, you can choose to apply a theme to only the object you are working with or to all matching objects. You can also select a theme to be the default theme instead of Office.

Because the form is displayed in Form view, once it has been created, the first step is to switch to Layout view to make changes to the form itself. Changing the theme will change not only the colors of the form but also the font type and size and any border colors or object colors added to the form. Once a theme has been applied to the form, the colors and fonts can be changed independently of the theme, so you can combine the colors of one theme and a font of another.

The manager of the spa would like to make the customer input form look more like the colors in the spa. The resort has a set of themes that the manager wants to apply to the selected form. In this exercise, you will show her how to change the theme and the fonts for the form. The theme will be applied to all objects in the database. The font change will be applied to this form only.

To Change the Theme of a Form

a. In the Navigation Pane, double-click **frmCustomerInput** to open the form. Switch to **Layout** view.

b. Click the Design tab, and in the Themes group, click **Themes** to open the Themes gallery. Click **Browse for Themes**, navigate to where you stored your data files, click **a02ch04Spa**, and then click **Open**. This applies the spa theme to all objects.

c. On the Design tab, in the Themes group, click **Fonts**. Scroll down, and click the Font theme **Corbel**.

d. Double-click the **form title**, select the existing **text**, which by default is the name of the form, and then type Customer Input. Press Enter.

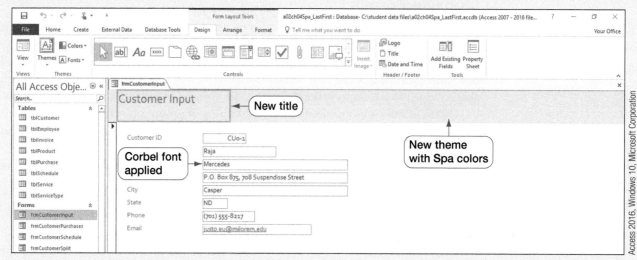

Figure 12 Form with theme, font, and title changed

e. **Save** 🖫 and **Close** ✕ the form.

Resizing and Changing Controls

Controls can be resized to make the form more user friendly. When you create a form using the wizard, the order in which you choose the fields in the wizard step is the order in which the fields are added to the form. Once the form has been created, you may decide the fields should be in a different order. When you click a control in Layout view, an orange border appears around the control. When you select a subform control, an orange border appears around the control, and a layout selector appears in the top-left corner. The **Layout Selector** allows you to move the whole table at one time. Once the control has been selected, you can move it or resize it. You can also change its appearance by adding borders or fill color.

In this exercise, you will work with the spa staff to rearrange the controls on the Customer Schedule form to make data entry easier.

To Resize and Change Controls on a Form

a. In the Navigation Pane, double-click **frmCustomerSchedule** to open it. Notice that the spa theme was applied to this form.

b. Switch to **Layout** view. Click the **Last Name** text box control, and an orange border appears around the control. Point to the **right border** of the control, and then drag it to the left so it lines up with the right border of the First Name text box above.

c. Click the **Address** text box control, and then drag the **right border** to the right until it lines up with the right border of the City text box below.

d. Double-click the **form title**, select the existing **text**, which by default is the name of the form, and then type Customer Schedule. Press Enter.

e. Click the **frmCustomer** subform label, and then press Delete to delete it from the form.

f. Use the AutoFit feature on each column of the subform to best fit the data. Use the scroll bar on the Navigation bar of the subform to scroll to the right to see all the fields. Drag the **left border** of the subform to the left so that all fields are visible without scrolling.

g. In the main form, click the **Customer ID** label control, press and hold Shift, and then click the **Customer ID** text box control to select both controls.

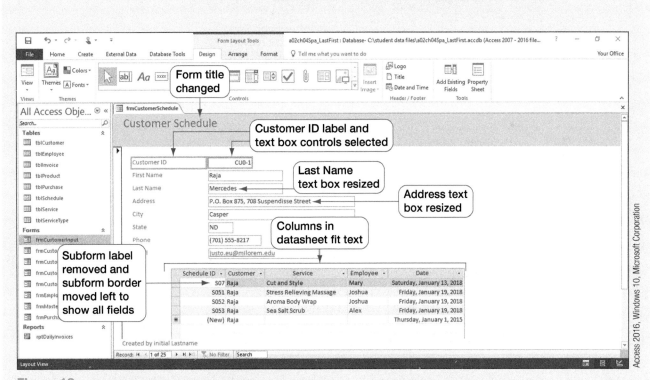

Figure 13 Select both label and name control to delete

h. Press Delete to delete both controls from the form.

i. Click the **Phone** label, hold down Shift, and then click the **Phone** text box, the **Email** label, and the **Email** text box controls.

j. Point to any of the **selected controls**. When the pointer changes to ⬚, drag all four controls up and to the right until they are right next to the First Name and Last Name controls.

> ## Troubleshooting
> If, the fields do not line up when you release the pointer, repeat step j, and then adjust the placement.

SIDE NOTE

Limited Visibility

If you cannot see the whole subform, use the scroll arrow on the right side of the window to scroll down the form.

k. Click the **subform** datasheet to select it. Click the **Layout Selector** ⊞, and then drag it up and to the left so it is just under the State control.

l. Click the **title** of the form to select it. Click the **Home** tab, and in the Text Formatting group, click **Bold** B, click the **Font size** arrow [11 ▾], and then select **28**.

m. Click the **First Name** text box control, hold down Shift, and then click the **Last Name** text box control. On the Home tab, in the Text Formatting group, Click **Bold** B.

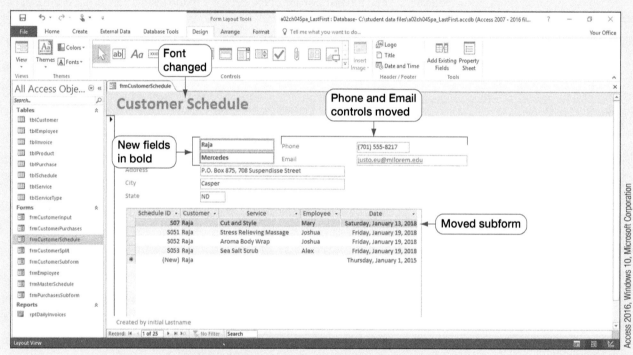

Figure 14 Formatted form and subform

n. **Save** 🖫 the form.

Adding a Picture to the Form

Pictures can be added to forms to make them more appealing. When a picture is added to a form, the same picture will appear for every record in the table. A different picture cannot be added for each record. A picture can be inserted in the header, the footer, or the Detail area of the form where the record values are shown. In this exercise, you will insert the spa's logo in the Detail area of the form to make it more personal for the spa.

A04.14

To Add a Picture on the Form

a. With the frmCustomerSchedule open, in Layout view, click in the **Detail area** of the form to select it. If a text box or label is selected, the Insert Image button will not be available to use.

b. Click the **Design** tab, in the Controls group, click **Insert Image**, and then click **Browse**.

c. In the Insert Picture dialog box, navigate to where your student files are located, click **a02ch04Spa**, and then click **OK**. With the image control pointer 🔲, click in the **form detail** to insert the picture. Drag the corner until the picture is small enough to fit under Email and above the subform.

d. Click the **Layout Selector** ⊞ and move the picture under the **Email** text box. Move your pointer to the **bottom right corner** of the picture until it becomes a diagonal resize pointer 🔲 and drag to make the picture smaller until the picture fits between the Email text box and the subform.

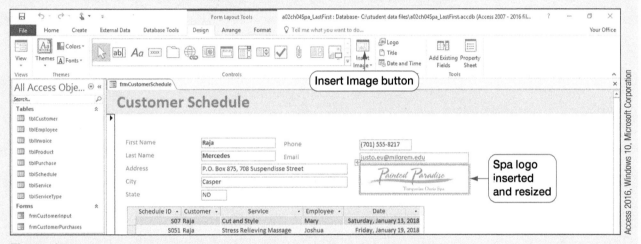

Figure 15 Logo inserted in form

e. **Close** ☒ the form, and then click **Yes** to save the changes.

Printing a Record from a Form

Not only can you see one record at a time using a form, but you can also print one record at a time. Printing a form can be useful if you need only one record's information or if you want to use a form for other people to manually fill in the information.

The spa manager would like you to print a record for a particular customer from the customer form. In this exercise, you will show her how to preview the form first, select one record, and then send it to the printer.

To Preview and Print a Record from a Form

a. In the Navigation Pane, double-click **frmCustomerInput** to open it, and then switch to **Layout** view.

b. Click the **Address** text box control, and then drag the **right border** to the right until it is lined up with the Last Name and City text box controls.

c. Click the **File** tab, click **Print**, and then click **Print Preview**. Notice all the records will print in Form view.

d. Click **Last Page** 🔘 on the Navigation bar to go to the last record. Notice in the Navigation bar that the number of pages for the printed report will be seven.

e. On the Print Preview tab, in the Close Preview group, click **Close Print Preview**.

f. Using the Navigation bar, advance through the customer records to find the record for **Jonah Hogan**.

g. Click the **File** tab, click **Print**, and then click **Print**. In the Print dialog box, in the Print Range section, click **Selected Record(s)**. Click **OK** to print the record if requested by your instructor. Otherwise, click **Cancel**.

When you view all the records in Print Preview, you cannot choose Selected Record(s) in the Print dialog box. To choose Selected Record(s), you must have one record showing in Form view when you click Print.

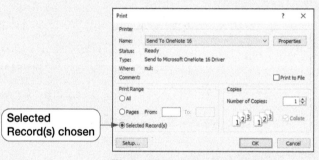

Selected Record(s) chosen

Figure 16 Print one record as a form

h. **Close** ☒ the form, and then click **Yes** to save the changes. If you need to take a break before finishing this chapter, now is a good time.

Creating Customized Reports

While a report and a form may look similar, a form is a method for data entry, and a report is a read-only view of the data that can be formatted for easy printing. A report can be created from either a table or a query. Reports may be based on multiple tables in a one-to-many relationship using a common field to match the records. The "one" record from the first table in the relationship will be shown first — similar to a main form — while the "many" records from the second table will be displayed as detailed records in the **subreport** — similar to a subform. In this section, you will create a report using the Report Wizard and then make changes to the report in Design and Layout views.

Create a Report Using the Report Wizard

The Report Wizard will walk you step by step through the process of building your report. You will choose the table or query to base the report on, and you will choose the fields to include in the report. You will have the option to group the data in your report.

A **group** is a collection of records along with introductory and summary information about the records. Grouping allows you to separate related records for the purpose of creating a visual summary of the data. Groups can be created with data from individual tables or from multiple tables.

For example, a report grouped by the primary table containing customer records would show all the selected fields for a customer and then would list that customer's individual appointments from the secondary table below the customer's record.

Within a report, you can also sort using up to four fields in either ascending or descending order. Once a report has been created using the wizard, it will open in Print Preview. Print Preview provides a view of the report representing how it will look when it is actually printed and provides you with printing options such as orientation, margins, and size. The current date and page numbers are added, and you can navigate the report in this view using the Navigation bar. To make any changes to the report, you can switch to Layout view.

Creating a Single-Table Report

A report can be created by using one table, multiple tables, or a query. A single-table report is a report created from one table. Any or all of the fields can be selected. The spa manager would like to have a report to help the staff with scheduling. In this exercise, you will create a report that will consist of a list of employee names and phone numbers so the staff can contact each other if necessary.

 A04.16

To Create a Single-Table Report Using Report Wizard

a. If you took a break, open the **a02ch04Spa_LastFirst** database. Click the **Create** tab, and then in the Reports group, click **Report Wizard**.

b. Click the **Tables/Queries** arrow, and then select **tblEmployee**.

c. Double-click **EmpFirstName**, **EmpLastName**, and **EmpPhone** from the Available Fields list. Click **Next**.

d. You will not add any grouping levels to this report, so click **Next**.

e. Click the **1 Sort** arrow, select **EmpLastName**, click the **2 Sort** arrow, select **EmpFirstName**, and then click **Next**.

f. Verify that **Tabular** layout and **Portrait** orientation are selected, as well as **Adjust the field width so all fields fit on a page**. Click **Next**.

g. Under What title do you want for your report?, type rptEmployeeList. Click **Modify the report's design**, and then click **Finish**.

h. If necessary, **close** ☒ the Field List pane. On the Report Design Tools Design tab, in the Controls group, click **Label** ⟨Aa⟩, point to the **Report Footer** area, and then when your pointer changes to ⁺A, drag your pointer to draw a label control about 2.5 inches wide in the top left corner of the Report Footer section. In the new label, type Created by initial Lastname using your first initial and last name.

> ### Troubleshooting
> If the Label control is not visible, in the Controls group, click the More button to display the gallery, and then click Label.

i. Switch to **Report** view. Verify that your label is fully shown in the bottom left corner of the report.

SIDE NOTE
Field Order
The order in which you add the fields in the Report Wizard is the order in which the fields will appear on the report.

j. Switch to **Layout** view. Double-click the **form title**, select the existing text, type Employee List and then press Enter.

In Layout view, you should also check that all the report column headers and data show fully. On this report they do, so no further changes are necessary.

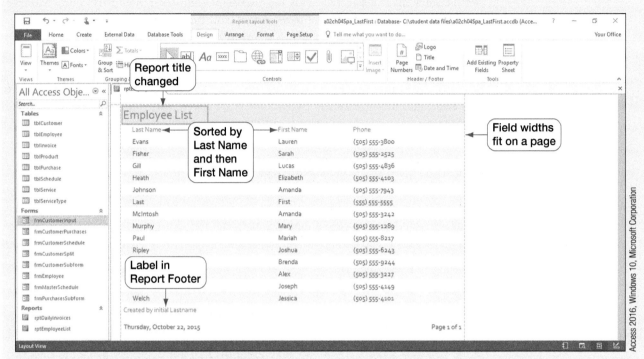

Figure 17 Completed Employee List report

k. **Close** ☒ the report, and then click **Yes** to save the changes.

Creating a Multiple-Table Report

Similar to other objects created by using more than one table or query, a multiple-table report must use tables that have a common field. The first table chosen for the report becomes the primary table, and the next and subsequent tables chosen become the secondary tables.

An employee has a one-to-many relationship with scheduled appointments. Each employee may have more than one appointment, and each appointment is with just one employee. Therefore, tblEmployee will be the primary table, and tblSchedule will be a secondary table.

The manager would like a report that will show all employees' names and their upcoming appointments. This way, the staff members can help coordinate their services for a guest who may be seeing more than one staff member in a day. In this exercise, you will create a multiple-table report that the staff can use for this purpose.

To Create a Multiple-Table Report Using the Report Wizard

a. Click the **Create** tab, and then in the Reports group, click **Report Wizard**.

b. Click the **Tables/Queries** arrow, and then select **Table: tblEmployee**. Double-click **EmpFirstName** and **EmpLastName** in the Available Fields list.

c. Click the **Tables/Queries** arrow, and then select **Table: tblSchedule**. Double-click **Service**, **DateOfAppt**, and **Customer** from the Available Fields list, and then click **Next**.

d. Verify that by tblEmployee is highlighted to view the data by Employee, and then click **Next**.
Notice that Access defaults to viewing the data by primary table, tblEmployee.

e. Double-click **DateOfAppt** to group by the date. Click **Grouping Options**, click the **Grouping intervals** arrow, select **Normal**, and then click **OK**.
Access defaults to grouping dates by Month. Normal groups by date value.

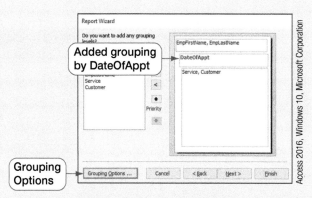

Figure 18   Report Wizard grouping step

f. Click **Next**. Click the **1 Sort** arrow, select **Customer**, and then click **Next**.

g. Verify that Stepped is selected under Layout, and then under Orientation, click **Landscape**. Verify that Adjust the field width so all fields fit on a page is checked. Click **Next**.

h. Under What title do you want for your report?, type rptEmployeeSchedule, and then click **Finish**. The report will open in Print Preview.

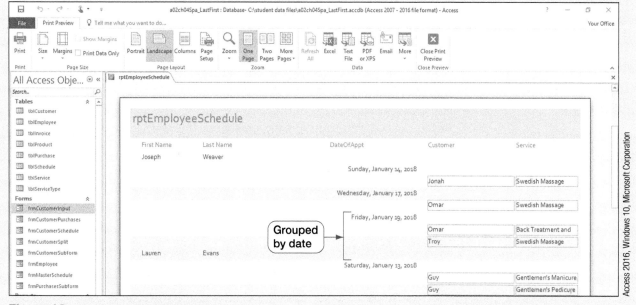

Figure 19   Report in Print Preview

Notice that the appointments are grouped by date. Your date column may not be wide enough to see the dates, but you will fix that in Layout view. Additionally, notice that in Print Preview view, at the bottom of each page of the report is today's date and the page number.

i. Click **Close Print Preview**.

Exploring Report Views

Recall that reports have four different views. Each type of view has its own features.

QUICK REFERENCE	Different View Options for a Report
View Name	**What the View Is Used For**
Print Preview	Shows what the printed report will look like
Layout view	Allows you to modify the report while seeing the data
Report view	Allows you to filter data or copy parts of the report to the Clipboard
Design view	Allows you to change more details of the report design or add other controls that are available only in Design view

When the Report Wizard has finished creating the report, it shows you the report in Print Preview, which is the view that shows you exactly what the report will look like when it is printed. Print Preview adds the current date and page numbers in the page footer at the bottom of each page.

Layout view allows you to change basic design features of the report while the report is displaying data so the changes you make are immediately visible. You can resize controls, add conditional formatting, and change or add titles and other objects to the report in Layout view.

Report view provides an interactive view of your report. In Report view, you can filter records or you can copy data to the clipboard. No page breaks are shown in Report view, so the number of pages at the bottom will show Page 1 of 1.

Design view offers more options for adding and editing controls on a report, as well as options not available in any of the other views.

In this exercise, you will show the spa staff members what a report looks like in the different views and how to switch from one view to another. You will also show them how to make changes in the Layout and Design views.

To Explore Report Views

a. With the rptEmployeeSchedule open, switch to **Layout** view.

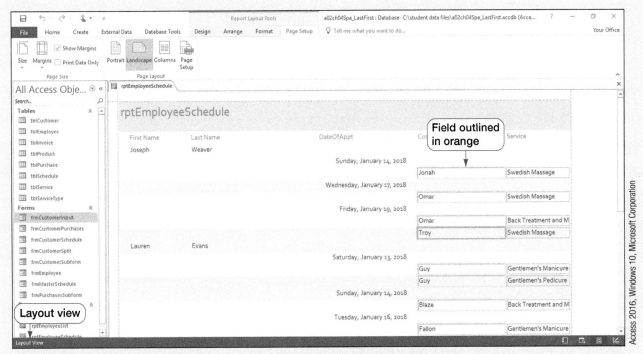

Figure 20 Report in Layout view

Notice the orange border around the first Customer field. Customer is the active field. You can make changes, such as making a column wider, in Layout view.

b. If your dates are not visible, click the **DateOfAppt** column header, press and hold Shift, and then click the **DateOfAppt** text box. Use your pointer to drag the left border of the column to the left so the date is fully shown.

c. Scroll to the **bottom right** of the report.
Notice there is the date and page number in the page footer, but the page number shows page 1 of 1. The actual number of pages will not be calculated until you switch to Print Preview.

d. On the Design tab, switch to **Design** view. Data in Design view is not visible, only the controls in each section of the report are.

e. On the Design tab, in the Controls group, click **Label** Aa, point to the Report Footer area, and then when your pointer changes to ⁺A, drag your pointer to draw a label control about 2.5 inches wide in the top left corner of the Report Footer section. In the new label, type Created by initial Lastname using your first initial and last name.

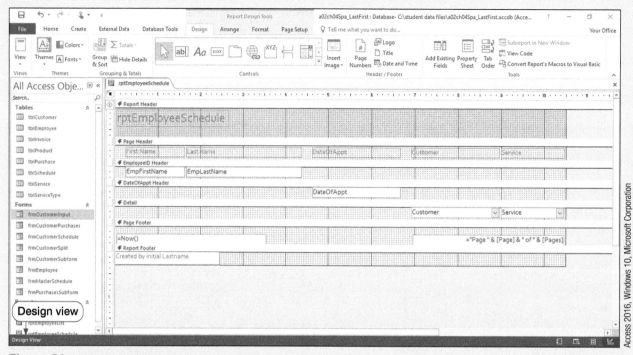

Figure 21   Report in Design view

f. Switch to **Report** view.

g. Scroll to the **bottom** of the report.
   Verify that your label has been entered in the bottom left corner of the report. In Report view, there are no page breaks, so the number of pages at the bottom will show Page 1 of 1.

h. **Save** 🖫 and **close** ✕ your report.

Creating Totals Using the Report Wizard

When you report on numeric data, Access has the ability to calculate sums, averages, minimums, and maximums of the numeric data. The **grand total** calculates the total for all records. **Subtotals** calculate totals for smaller groups of records. In this exercise, you will use the wizard to request these totals. Later, you will add totals to an already created report.

The spa manager asks you to create a report showing the invoices collected each day. In this exercise, you will show her how to provide a daily total as well as a grand total using the Report Wizard.

To Create Report Totals Using the Report Wizard

a. Click the **Create** tab, and then in the Reports group, click **Report Wizard**.

b. Click the **Tables/Queries** arrow, and then select **Table: tblInvoice**. Double-click **InvoiceDate** and **InvoiceTotal** in the Available Fields list. Click **Next**.

c. Double-click **InvoiceDate** to group by the date. Click **Grouping Options…**, click the **Grouping intervals** arrow, and select **Day**. Click **OK**, and then click **Next**.

d. Click the **1 Sort** arrow, and then select **InvoiceDate**.

e. Click **Summary Options…**, and then click the **Sum** check box.

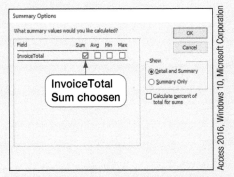

Figure 22   Report Summary Options

f. Click **OK**, and then click **Next**. Verify that Stepped and Portrait are selected, and then click **Next**.

g. Under What title do you want for your report?, type rptInvoiceTotals, and then click **Finish**. The report will open in Print Preview. If necessary, scroll down to see the grand total.

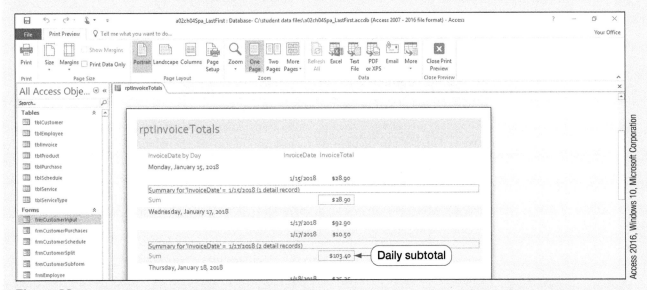

Figure 23   Report with daily subtotals and a grand total

Notice that there is a sum for each day and a grand total of all invoices for all days.

h. **Close Print Preview** and Switch to **Design** view. There is a new footer for InvoiceDate where the sum for each day is shown. There is also a Report Footer where the GrandTotal is shown.

i. On the Design tab, in the Controls group, select **Label** $\boxed{Aa}$, move your pointer to the **Report Footer** just below the existing Grand Total label, and then when your pointer changes to $\boxed{^+_A}$, drag your pointer to draw a label control about 2.5 inches wide in the Report Footer section. In the new label, type Created by initial Lastname using your first initial and last name.

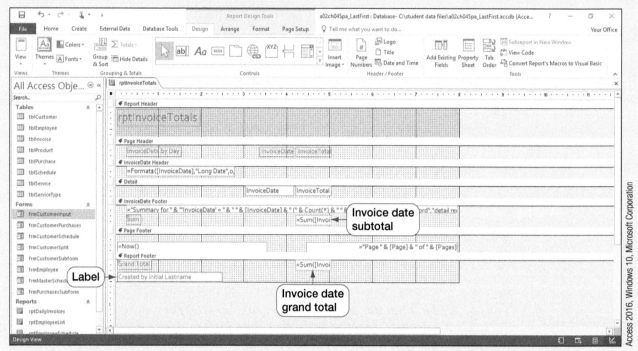

Figure 24 Design view of totals

j. Switch to **Print Preview** to check your label. **Save** $\boxed{\square}$ and **close** $\boxed{\times}$ your report.

Customize a Report

Reports created by the wizard can be easily customized after they have been created and saved. Themes can be applied to just the report or the whole database to change the colors, fonts, or both. Controls, bound and unbound, can be added or modified on the report to make room for more information or to rearrange the information already there.

To break a report into smaller sections, subtotals or groups may be added. Additional sorting options may also be applied or modified. Conditional formatting may also be applied to highlight fields that meet certain criteria.

Moving, Resizing, and Formatting Report Controls

Controls, as defined in the section on forms, are also used in reports. A control can be a text box or another object that has been added to the form either by the wizard or manually in Layout or Design view. Controls can be moved or resized to make the report more readable. In this exercise, you will change the rptEmployeeSchedule schedule report to make it look more like what the manager expected. You will move the date, service, and customer name fields below the employee name, change the heading, and change the formatting to match the resort theme.

To Move, Resize, and Format a Report Control

a. In the Navigation Pane, right-click **rptEmployeeSchedule**, and then click **Layout View**.

b. Click the **DateOfAppt** text box control to select it, and then drag the field to the left so it is just slightly indented under the employee first name.

c. Click the **First Name** label control — the column header. Press and hold ⇧Shift, click the **Last Name** and the **DateofAppt** label controls, and then press Delete.

d. Click the Customer label control, press and hold ⇧Shift, and then click the **Customer** text box, the **Service** label, and the **Service** text box controls. Point to and click any field to drag all the controls to the left, just next to the date field.

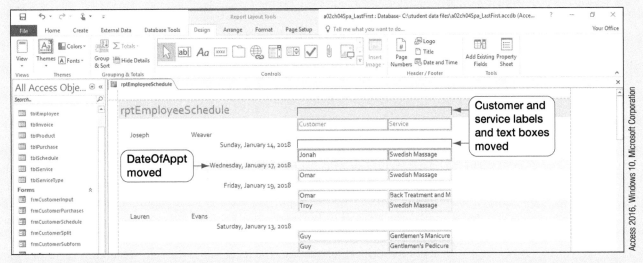

Figure 25 Fields moved

> ### Troubleshooting
> If you drag the controls too far to the left, reselect them and then drag them back to the right.

e. Click the **Service** text box control. Drag the **right border** of the box to the right to fit all the service description. Scroll down to check Chakra Body and Balancing Massage to make sure the description is fully shown. If it is not, drag the border to make the field wider.

f. Click the **Service** text box control, press and hold ⇧Shift, and then click the **Customer** text box control. Click the **Format** tab, in the Control Formatting group, click **Shape Outline**, and then select **Transparent**.

g. Click the employee's **First Name** text box control, press and hold ⇧Shift, and then click the **Last Name** text box control. On the Format tab, in the Control Formatting group, click **Shape Fill**, and then select **Dark Teal Accent 2 Lighter 80%** in the second row of the sixth column under Theme colors. In the Font group, click **Bold** B.

h. Double-click the **title**, select the **text**, type Employee Schedule, and then press Enter.

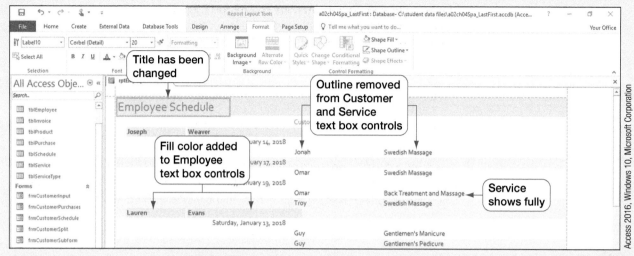

Figure 26 Formatted report in Layout view

i. **Close** ☒ the report, and then click **Yes** to save the changes.

Enhancing a Report with Conditional Formatting

In the previous section, you changed the colors and fonts of fields. You can also arrange for the fonts and colors of fields to change only when certain conditions are met in the field. This is called **conditional formatting**. If a field value meets the conditions you specify, the formatting will be applied. This is a useful tool to automatically highlight sales numbers on a report if they meet a certain threshold or to highlight students' grades when they exceed a certain limit.

To apply conditional formatting, you must select the field value in the field to which you want the formatting applied. You can select a different font color and font effects for the formatting.

The spa manager would like a list of services currently scheduled that cost over $100. The customers who buy these services usually get some special treatment, such as complimentary coffee and tea, and the staff would like to be able to easily see which customers are to get special treatment. In this exercise, you will create a report and apply conditional formatting to all services currently scheduled that cost over $100.

To Apply Conditional Formatting to a Report Field

a. Click the **Create** tab, and then in the Reports group, click **Report Wizard**.

b. Click the **Tables/Queries** arrow, and then select **Table: tblSchedule**. Double-click **DateOfAppt**, **Customer**, and **Service** in the Available Fields list. Click the **Tables/Queries** arrow, and then select **Table: tblService**. In the Available Fields list, double-click **Fee**, and then click **Next**.

c. Verify that by tblSchedule is highlighted, and then click **Next**. You will not add any grouping to this report, click **Next**.

d. Click the **1 Sort** arrow, click **DateofAppt**, and then click **Next**. Verify that Tabular is selected under Layout and Portrait is selected under Orientation. Verify that Adjust the field width so all fields fit on a page is checked. Click **Next**.

e. Under What title do you want for your report?, type rptHighFees, and then click **Finish**. The report will open in Print Preview. **Close Print Preview**, and switch to **Layout** view. If necessary, close the Field List pane.

f. Double-click the title, select the text, type High Service Customers, and then press Enter.

g. Click in the **Fee** text box control, and then, click the **Format** tab, and in the Control Formatting group, click **Conditional Formatting**.

h. In the Conditional Formatting Rules Manager dialog box, click **New Rule**. Verify that Check values in the current record or use an expression is highlighted. Find the three condition text boxes. The first should display Field Value Is. Click in the second condition box, and then select **greater than**. In the third condition text box, type 100.

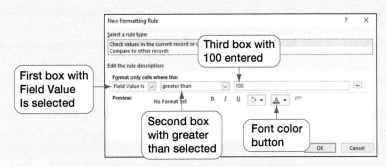

Figure 27   New Formatting Rule dialog box

Access 2016, Windows 10, Microsoft Corporation

i. Below the condition text boxes, click **Bold** B , click the **Font color** arrow, and then click **Dark Red**. Click **OK**, verify that your rule states Value >100, and then click **OK**.
All values greater than $100 in the Fee field will now be highlighted in dark red and bold.

j. Click the **Design** tab, and switch to **Design** view. Click the **Design** tab, in the Controls group, select **Label** Aa , move your pointer to the **Report Footer**, and then when your pointer changes to ⁺A , drag your pointer to draw a label control about 2.5 inches wide in the top left corner of the Report Footer section. In the new label, type Created by initial Lastname using your first initial and last name.

k. Switch to **Report** view. Verify that your label has been entered in the bottom left corner of the report.

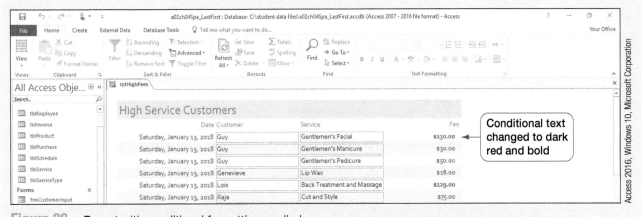

Access 2016, Windows 10, Microsoft Corporation

Figure 28   Report with conditional formatting applied

l. **Close** ✕ the report, and then click **Yes** to save the changes.

1. Click the Format tab in Layout view.
2. Click the field that has the conditional formatting applied.
3. In the Control Formatting group, click Conditional Formatting.
4. Click the rule you wish to delete, and then click Delete Rule.

Applying Grouping and Sorting

The Report Wizard gives you the opportunity to sort and group records. Sometimes reviewing the report reveals an alternative way to group and sort the data. You can change the sorting and grouping options from either Layout view or Design view. Groups are added to a section of the report called the **group header**. Calculations performed on a group in a report are added to a section called the **group footer**. A report may have one or more Group Headers, Group Footers, both, or neither.

In Layout view, you will use the Group, Sort, and Total pane to select the sort fields and grouping fields for a report. This is done after the report has been created by the Report Wizard.

The spa manager would like a report that shows appointment dates and services scheduled for those dates. In this exercise, you will show her how to create the report, and then you will make some changes to it until she likes how the information is presented.

To Add Group and Sort Fields to a New Report

a. Click the **Create** tab, and then in the Reports group, click **Report Wizard**.

b. Click the **Tables/Queries** arrow, and then select **Table: tblSchedule**. Double-click **DateOfAppt**, **Service**, **Customer**, and **Employee** from the Available Fields list. Click **Next**.

c. Click the **One Field Back** button <span> < </span> to remove the Service grouping level. Click **DateOfAppt**, and then click the **One Field** button <span> > </span> to add the date as a grouping level. Click **Grouping Options...**, click the **Grouping intervals** arrow, and then click **Normal**. Click **OK**, and then click **Next**.

d. Click the **1 Sort** arrow, select **Service**, and then click **Next**.

e. Verify that Stepped layout and Portrait orientation are selected. Verify that Adjust the field width so all fields fit on a page is selected. Click **Next**.

f. Under What title do you want for your report? type rptAppointments, and then click **Finish**.

g. Switch to **Design** view. On the Design tab, in the Controls group, select **Label** Aa, move your pointer to the **Report Footer**, and then when your pointer changes to ⁺A, drag your pointer to draw a label control about 2.5 inches wide in the top left corner of the Report Footer section. In the new label, type Created by initial Lastname using your first initial and last name.

h. Switch to **Layout** view. Verify that your label has been entered in the bottom left corner of the report.

i. Click the **DateOfAppt** text box control, click the **Format** tab, in the Font group, click **Align Text Left** ≡. Drag the right border of the DateOfAppt text box to line up with the left border of the Service text box. All the date values should be visible.

j. Click the **Service** text box control, and then drag the left border to the left to make the control wider so all the text can be displayed. Scroll down to the appointments scheduled on January 18, and then confirm that the **Microdermabrasion Treatment (6 sessions)** is showing.

k. Double-click the **title**, select the **text**, and then type Daily Appointments. Press Enter.

l. Click the **Design** tab, in the Grouping & Totals group, click **Group & Sort**, and then notice the Group, Sort, and Total pane that opens at the bottom of the report.

m. Click the line that displays **Sort by Service**, and then click **Delete** ⊠ on the far right of the line. This will delete the sort that was added in the Report Wizard.

n. Click **Add a group** in the Group, Sort, and Total pane, and then select **Employee**.

o. Click the **Employee** text box control, and then drag it to the left until it is under the date. Click the **Employee** label control, press and hold Shift, click the **DateOfAppt** label control, and then press Delete.

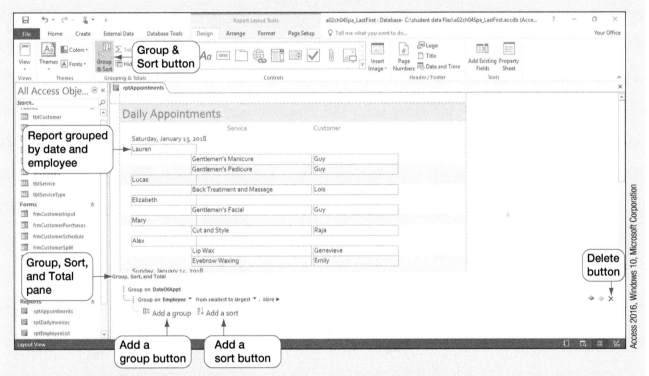

Figure 29 New grouping added to report

p. **Close** ⊠ the Group, Sort, and Total pane, being careful that you are clicking Close and not the Delete button. **Close** ⊠ the report, and then click **Yes** to save the changes.

Adding Subtotals

Earlier, you added subtotals when you created the report using the wizard. However, sometimes seeing the report makes you realize that subtotals would be useful. You can add them in Layout view, using the Group, Sort, and Total pane when you are selecting or modifying groups and sorts for the reports.

In this exercise, you will show the spa manager how to add subtotals to a report that shows all invoices grouped by date.

A04.23

To Add Subtotals to a Report

a. In the Navigation Pane, right-click **rptDailyInvoices**, and then select **Copy**. Right-click in the **Navigation Pane**, and then select **Paste**. In the Paste As dialog box, in the Report Name: box, type rptDailyInvoiceTotals. Click **OK**.

b. In the Navigation Pane, double-click **rptDailyInvoiceTotals** to open the report. Notice the report shows all invoices by day but has no totals.

c. Switch to **Design** view. On the Design tab, in the Controls group, click **Label** Aa. Move your pointer to the **Report Footer**, and then when your pointer changes to ⁺ₐ, drag your pointer to draw a label control about 2.5 inches wide in the top left corner of the Report Footer section. In the new label control, type Created by initial Lastname using your first initial and last name.

d. Switch to **Layout** view. Verify that your label has been entered in the bottom left corner of the report.

e. Click the **Invoice Total** label control, press and hold Shift, click the **Invoice Total** text box control, and then drag the **left border** to the right so the field is narrower but the column heading still shows.

f. Click the **InvoiceTotal** text box control. Click the **Design** tab, and in the Grouping & Totals group, click **Totals**, and then click **Sum**.
Subtotals for each InvoiceDate group will show under the InvoiceTotal details. A grand total will show at the bottom of the report.

g. Right-click one of the subtotal controls, and then click **Set Caption**. A label control will be added next to each subtotal amount that says "InvoiceTotal Total". Double-click the **label** control, select the text, and then type Invoice Subtotal. Press Enter. Repeat the same steps to set a caption for the grand total control, and then change the text to Invoice Total.

h. Double-click the **title**, select the text, and then type **Invoice Amounts**. Press Enter.

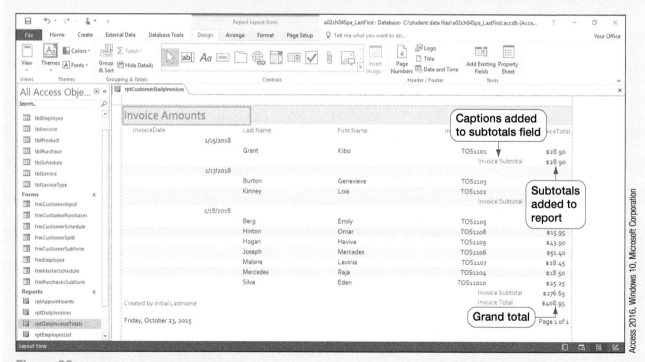

Figure 30   Report with subtotals added

i. **Close** ☒ the report, and then click **Yes** to save the changes.

Save a Report as a PDF File

Reports are formatted printable documents of your data, so the final result of a report will usually be a printout. Alternatively, the report may be shared with other people electronically. When you send a report to someone electronically, they have to have the same program in which the report was created in order to open the report. To avoid this problem, you can save a report as a PDF file, which can be read by Adobe Reader, a free program that can be downloaded from the Internet, or by Word 2016 or several other programs on a computer or mobile device.

To print a report, you use the Print dialog box to select your printing options. Before you print, it is always a good idea to view the report in Print Preview to make sure it looks the way you want. Viewing the report in Layout view and Report view does not show you page breaks and other features of the report as it will look when actually printed. In Print Preview, you have many options to make design changes to your report before you send it to the printer. You can change the margins and orientation, and you can select how many pages, if not all, you want to print.

Creating a PDF File

If you need to distribute the report electronically, you also have the option to save the report as an Adobe PDF file. An **Adobe PDF file** is usually smaller than the original document, is easy to send through e-mail, and preserves the original document look and feel so you know exactly what it will look like when the recipient opens it. The correct terminology for saving a report as a PDF file format is to "publish" the report. When you are saving the report as a PDF, you will see the option to Publish, not to Save or Print.

In this exercise, you will show the staff how to print and publish a PDF file of the employee schedule so it can easily be e-mailed to the staff each week.

 A04.24

To Save a Report as a PDF File

a. In the Navigation Pane, double-click **rptEmployeeSchedule** to open the report. On the Home tab, click the **View** button, and switch to **Print Preview**. Navigate through the pages to make sure the records fit on the pages correctly.

b. On the Print Preview tab, in the Print group, click **Print**.

c. If your instructor instructs you to print, under Print Range, verify All is selected, and then click **OK**. Otherwise, click **Cancel**.

d. On the Print Preview tab, in the Data group, click **PDF or XPS**.

e. In the Publish as PDF or XPS dialog box, navigate to the location where you are saving your files, and then in the File name box, type a02ch04SpaEmployeeSchedule_LastFirst using your last and first name. Click **Publish**. The PDF file automatically opens. **Close** 🖫 the file and the application in which it opened.

f. **Close** the Export - PDF window. **Close** 🖫 the report, and then exit Access.

1. What is the difference between Navigation and Edit modes? How can you tell you are in each mode? p. 705

2. When you add, change, or delete a record in a form, how does it affect the underlying table? Why? p. 712–713

3. What are controls? What is a bound control? What is an unbound control? p. 716

4. What is the difference between a label control and a text box control? Which is bound, and which is unbound? p. 716

5. What is a theme? What is the difference between applying a theme to an entire database and to a single object? p. 720

6. What view will you see when the Report Wizard is done creating a report? What is the difference between Report view, Layout view, Design view, and Print Preview when you are creating a report? Which view will show you the most accurate picture of what your printed report will look like? In which views do you see the data? p. 730

7. What is conditional formatting, and when would you use it? p. 736

8. What is a PDF file, and why would you want to save your report as a PDF? p. 741

Key Terms

Adobe PDF file 741	Group 727	Split form 710
Bound control 716	Group footer 738	Subform 708
Calculated control 716	Group header 738	Subreport 726
Conditional formatting 736	Label control 716	Subtotals 732
Control 716	Layout Selector 722	Text box control 716
Edit mode 705	Main form 708	Theme 721
Grand total 732	Navigation mode 705	Unbound control 716

Visual Summary

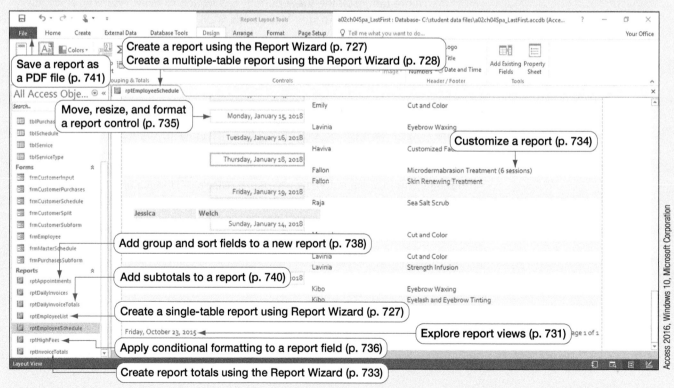

Figure 31

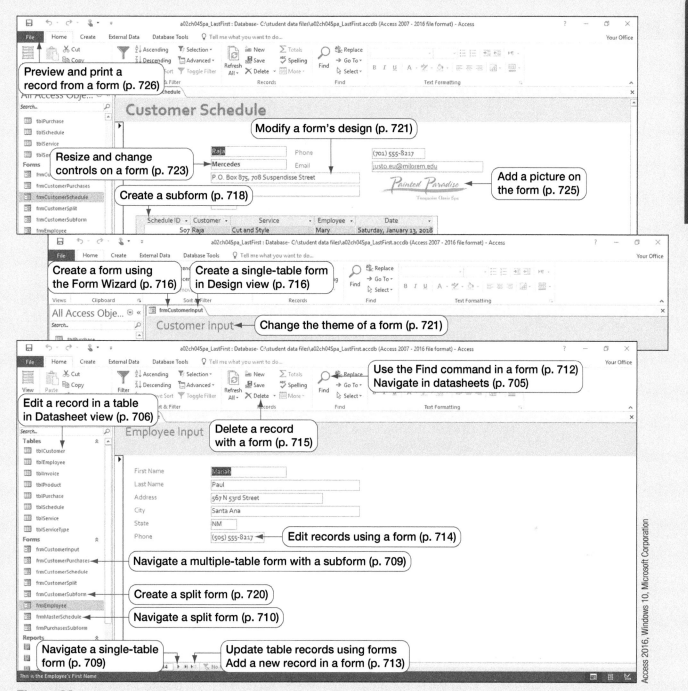

Figure 32

Student data files needed:

 a02ch04Spa2.accdb

 a02ch04Spa.thmx

You will save your file as:

 a02ch04Spa2_LastFirst.accdb

Turquoise Oasis Spa

Human
Resources

The spa has just redecorated the staff lounge and has added bulletin boards and even a computer for the staff members to check their appointments and sign in and out. The manager would like to create reports to post on the bulletin boards with schedule and service information and would also like to make the database as easy to use as possible. You will help to create some of the reports as well as forms to make the database easy for data entry and maintenance.

a. Start **Access**, and then open **a02ch04Spa2**.

b. Click the **File** tab, click **Save As**. Verify Save Database As and Access Database are selected. Click **Save As**. In the Save As dialog box, navigate to where you are saving your files, and then type a02ch04Spa2_LastFirst using your last and first name. Click **Save**. If necessary, in the Security Warning, click **Enable Content**.

c. Create a form that will allow employees to edit their personal information as well as their upcoming appointments.

- Click the **Create** tab, and then in the Forms group, click **Form Wizard**.

- In the Form Wizard dialog box, click the **Tables/Queries** arrow, and then select **Table: tblEmployee**. Click the **All Fields** button to add all the fields to the Selected Fields list.

- Click the **Tables/Queries** arrow, and then select **Table: tblSchedule**. Double-click **Customer**, **Service**, **Employee**, and **DateOfAppt** to add the fields to the Selected Fields list. Click **Next**.

- Verify that the data will be viewed by tblEmployee, and then click **Next**.

- Verify that Datasheet is selected as the layout for the subform, and then click **Next**.

- Name the form frmEmployeeSchedule_iLast using your first initial and last name, name the subform frmSubform_iLast, and then click **Finish**.

- On the main form Navigation bar, click **New (blank) record**, and then add your first name, last name, address, city, state, and phone number. On the Navigation bar, click **First record** to return to the first record in the table, and then click in the **Last Name** field.

- On the Home tab, in the Records group, click the **Delete** arrow, and then click **Delete Record**. Click **Yes** when prompted to delete the record.

- Switch to **Layout** view. Double-click the **title**, select the **text**, and then type Employee Schedule.

- Click the **Last Name** text box control, and then drag the **right border** of the text box to line up with the right border of the First Name text box.

- Click the **subform label**, and then press Delete to delete the control. Click the **Subform**, and then using the layout selector, drag it to the left so it is right below the Phone label. Use AutoFit on all the columns to best fit the data.

- Click the **Employee** field heading in the subform datasheet, and then press Delete to delete the field. Click the **Date** heading in the subform datasheet, and then drag it to the left of the Customer field.

- On the Design tab, in the Themes group, click the **Themes** arrow, click **Browse for Themes**, browse to where you stored data files, click **a02ch04Spa**, and then click **Open**.

- Switch to Design view and, if prompted to save changes, click **Yes**. Click the **Design** tab, and in the Controls group, select **Label**, move your pointer to the **Form Footer**, and then draw a label control about 2.5 inches wide in the top left corner of the Form Footer section. In the new label control, type Created by initial Lastname using your first initial and last name.

- **Close** the form, and then click **Yes** when prompted to save the changes.

d. Create a report to show a list of customers and their purchases.

- Click the **Create** tab, and then in the Reports group, click **Report Wizard**. In the Report Wizard dialog box, click the **Tables/Queries** arrow, and then select **Table: tblCustomer**. Double-click **CustFirstName**, **CustLastName**, **CustState**, and **CustPhone** to add the fields to the Selected Fields list.

- Click the **Tables/Queries** arrow, and then select **Table: tblProduct**. Double-click **ProductDescription** to add the field to the Selected Fields list.

- Click the **Tables/Queries** arrow, and then select **Table: tblPurchase**. Double-click **PurchaseType**, **PurchaseDate**, and **Quantity** to add the fields to the Selected Fields list. Click **Next**.

- Verify that the data will be viewed by tblCustomer, and then click **Next**.

- Double-click **ProductDescription** to add it as a grouping level, and then click **Next**.

- Click the **1 Sort** arrow, click **PurchaseDate**, and then click **Next**. Select a **Stepped** layout and **Portrait** orientation, and then click **Next**.

- Name the report rptCustomerPurchases_iLast using your first initial and last name, and then click **Finish**.

e. Customize the report's appearance.

- Switch to **Layout** view.

- Click the **PurchaseDate** text box control, and then drag the **left border** to the left until the date is visible. Move the **Date** text box control to the left until it lines up under the First Name field.

- Click the **ProductDescription** text box control, and then drag the **right border** to the right until the whole field is visible.

- Click the **ProductDescription** label control, press and hold [Shift], click the **PurchaseDate** label control, click the **PurchaseType** label control, and then press [Delete] to delete the controls.

- Click the **Phone** text box control, and then drag the **right border** so the whole field is visible.

- Double-click the **title**, select the **text**, and then type Customer Purchases.

- **Save** the report.

f. Add totals and subtotals.

- Click the Design tab, and in the Grouping & Totals group, click **Group & Sort** to open the Group, Sort, and Total pane. Click **Group on ProductDescription**, and then click **Delete** to delete the group.

- In the Group, Sort, and Total pane, click **Add a group**, and then select **PurchaseType**. Click the **PurchaseType** text box control — on the far right of report — and then drag it just below the customer's first name and just above the date.

- In the Group, Sort, and Total pane, click **Add a sort**, and then select **ProductDescription**. **Close** the Group, Sort, and Total pane.

- Click the **PurchaseType** text box. Click the **Format** tab, and in the Control Formatting group, click **Conditional Formatting**, and then click **New Rule**. In the second box, select **equal to**, and then in the third text box, type Online. Click the **Font color** arrow, and then under Standard Colors in the first row, select **Purple**. Click **OK** twice.

- With the PurchaseType text box control selected, click the **Design** tab. In the Grouping & Totals group, click **Totals**, and then select **Count Records**. Click the **PurchaseType** text box control, press and hold [Shift], and then click the **subtotal** text box control. Click the **Format** tab, and in the Control Formatting group, click **Shape Outline**, and then select **Transparent**.

- Right-click the **Subtotal** text box control for Record Count, and then select **Set Caption**. Replace the text in the caption box with Orders.

- Scroll to the bottom of the report. Click the **Grand Total** text box control, and then move it under the product description. Right-click the **Grand Total** text box control, and then click **Set Caption**. Replace the text in the caption box with Total Orders.

- Switch to **Design** view. Click the **Design** tab, in the Controls group, select **Label**, move your pointer to the **Report Footer**, and then when your pointer changes, drag your pointer to draw a label control about 2.5 inches wide on the left side of the Report Footer. In the new label control, type Created by initial Lastname using your first initial and last name.

g. **Close** the report, and then click **Yes** when prompted to save the changes.

h. Close your database, exit Access, and submit your files as directed by your instructor.

MyITLab®
Grader
Homework

Student data file needed:

 a02ch04Baseball.accdb

You will save your files as:

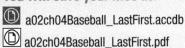 a02ch04Baseball_LastFirst.accdb

a02ch04Baseball_LastFirst.pdf

Baseball Academy

Production & Operations

Matt Davis is a retired baseball player who runs the Baseball Academy, an indoor baseball facility for middle school, high school, and college players. He offers lessons as well as practice times for individuals and teams. Because of his growing clientele and increased record-keeping needs, Matt wants all his records in a database. Although he has already set up a database, he now needs to take the database to the next level of performance by improving his ability to get specific data out of the database. He has hired you to create the forms and reports he needs.

a. Open the Access database, **a02ch04Baseball**. Save the file as a02ch04Baseball_LastFirst using your last and first name. If necessary, enable the content.

b. Create a **split form** to show all the member information from **tblMember**.

- Save the form as frmMemberInput.

- Change the title of the form to be **Member Input**.

- Apply the theme **Organic** to all objects in the database. (Hint: The themes are listed alphabetically.)

- Add Created by initial Lastname to the Form Footer.

- Use the form to add your information to the members table.

- Save and close the form.

c. Use the Form Wizard to create a form that will display in the main form the member's **LastName**, **FirstName**, **Phone**, and **ScheduledDate** and **Fee** in the subform. Keep all other default options. Name the form frmMemberLessons, and name the subform frmSubformLessons.

- Move the right borders of the Member fields so they are all the same width as FirstName.
- Remove the subform label. Move the subform to line up with the Phone label.
- AutoFit the columns in the subform so all the lesson information fits. Resize the subform to fit the columns.
- Change the title of the form to Member Lessons.
- Add Created by initial Lastname to the main form footer. Save and close the form.

d. Use the Report Wizard to create a schedule of lessons for an employee. Include employee **LastName**, **FirstName**, **ScheduledDate**, and member **LastName** and **FirstName**. Accept the default view, add a grouping by **ScheduledDate** with **Normal** grouping intervals, sort by member **LastName** and **FirstName**, use a format of **Stepped** and **Landscape**, and save the report as rptEmployeeSchedule.

- Change the column headers for the member's name to be Member Last Name and Member First Name respectively.
- **Bold** the employee **LastName** and **FirstName** text boxes.
- Left align the ScheduledDate text box.
- Add Created by initial Lastname to the report footer.
- Change the title of the report to Employee Schedule. Save and close the report.

Critical Thinking

How would this report need to be changed to display the schedule by date instead of by employee? List any changes to the report that would need to be made without removing any existing fields from the report. Be sure to discuss both technical changes to the report and design changes. What business needs would be met with the schedule organized by employee? What business needs would be met with the schedule organized by date?

e. Use the Report Wizard to create a report to summarize lessons taught by each employee. Include employee **LastName**, **FirstName**, **ScheduledDate**, **Fee**, and member **FirstName** and **LastName**. Accept the view, add a grouping by **ScheduledDate** with **Normal** grouping intervals, sort by member **LastName** and **FirstName**, add Summary Options to **Average** the **Fee** field, use a format of **Stepped** and **Landscape**, and save the report as rptEmployeeLessons.

- Fix the Fee column width so that all fees and averages show fully.
- Move the **Avg caption** for each date to the right to line up with member's first name. Repeat for the **Avg caption** for employee. Change the captions to read Daily Average and Employee Average.
- Change the column headers for the member's name to be Member Last Name and Member First Name respectively.
- In Layout view, click on the field that starts **Summary for 'ScheduledDate'** and delete it.
- In Layout view, click on the field that starts **Summary for 'EmployeeID'** and delete it.
- Left-align the ScheduledDate text box, and resize the control to fit under the ScheduledDate label.
- Select the **First Name** text label and text box controls, and move them to the left so that they are slightly indented under the report title.

- Move the text box controls and labels for the **ScheduledDate**, **Member Last Name**, **Member First Name**, **Fee**, **Daily Average**, and **Employee Average** to the left to minimize the extra space in the report.
- Apply conditional formatting to make any Employee Average greater than **175** display in bold and red.
- Add Created by initial Lastname to the report footer.
- Change the title of the report to Employee Lessons.
- Print the report as a PDF. Save the file as a02ch04Baseball_LastFirst.pdf using your last and first name.
- Save and close the report.

f. Close your database, exit Access, and submit your files as directed by your instructor.

Perform 1: Perform in Your Career

Student data files needed:

▣ a02ch04Rentals.accdb

▣ a02ch04Room.jpg

You will save your file as:

▣ a02ch04Rentals_LastFirst.accdb

Student Housing Rentals

Production & Operations

You are working for a company that specializes in renting apartments and houses to students at your university. The manager is familiar with your Access skills and has asked you to create a series of forms and reports to improve her ability to add and analyze information in the database.

a. Open the Access database, **a02ch04Rentals**. Save the file as a02ch04Rentals_LastFirst using your last and first name. If necessary, enable the content.

b. Open the Relationships window to familiarize yourself with the tables, fields, and relationships in the database. Open **tblEmployees**, and add your name as a new record in the table.

c. Create a columnar form based on **tblProperties**. Use all the fields in the form, and name the form frmProperties_iLast using your first initial and last name.

d. Change the theme of frmProperties_iLast to **Slice**. Make the Slice Theme the default for the database.

e. Change the font color of all labels in the detail area of the form to **Light Turquoise, Background 2** (first row, third column) under Theme Colors.

f. Insert the house picture **a02ch04Room** on the right side of the form. Adjust the image size to fit between the PropertyID field and the PostalCode field. Change the title in the form to Properties. Add Created by initial Lastname, using your first initial and last name, to the form footer.

g. Create a form with a subform from **tblEmployees**. Use **tblProperties** for the subform data. Name the form frmAgents_iLast, and name the subform frmAgentSubform_iLast, using your first initial and last name.

h. Change the title in the form Header to Our Agents.

i. Remove the **frmAgentsSubform** label. Align the left border of the subform to the Phone label. Use AutoFit to adjust the column width of the subform fields. Adjust the right border of the subform so that the PostalCode field can been seen without scrolling to the right. Add Created by initial Lastname, using your first initial and last name, to the form footer.

j. Create a report from **qryNotRented** showing the **City**, **Property Name**, **Address**, **Pool**, **Playground**, **BikeTrail**, **DogPark**, and **MonthlyRental** fields. Name the report rptNotRented_iLast.

k. Change the title of the report to Available Rentals By City. Group the data by the City.

l. Change the text of the MonthlyRental label to Rent.

m. Display the Count of the Property Name field by City for all cities displayed in the report.

n. Change the caption for the property count by city to Available and the caption for all properties in the report to Total Available.

o. Create a conditional format that adds an Aqua Blue fill color (first row, ninth column) to Available values greater than 1.

p. Modify the spaces between column labels and move or resize the columns to fit the report to a single page width. Ensure that no values are cut off. Add Created by initial Lastname, using your first initial and last name, to the report footer.

q. Close your database, exit Access, and submit your file as directed by your instructor.

Additional Cases

Additional Chapter Cases are available at www.pearsonhighered.com/youroffice

Accessing, Maintaining, and Presenting Information

This business unit had two outcomes:

Learning Outcome 1:

Find data in a database by searching tables and designing queries that sort, aggregate, and calculate complex search results.

Learning Outcome 2:

Navigate and update information in a database using forms and present information in a database by creating customized reports.

In Business Unit 2 Capstone, students will demonstrate competence in these outcomes through a series of business problems at various levels from guided practice, problem solving an existing database, and performing to create new databases.

More Practice 1

Student data files needed:

- a02Recipes.accdb
- a02Indigo5.jpg

You will save your files as:

- a02Recipes_LastFirst.accdb
- a02Recipes_LastFirst.pdf

Indigo5 Restaurant

Production & Operations

Robin Sanchez, the chef of the Painted Paradise Resort's restaurant, Indigo5, has started a database to keep track of the recipes and ingredients that the restaurant includes. Right now, no forms, queries, or reports have been created for this database, so the information available is very limited. You will help to create some queries as well as forms for data entry and reports for the daily management of the food preparation.

a. Start **Access**, click **Open Other Files** in the left pane, and then double-click **This PC**. Navigate through the folder structure to the location of your student data files, and then double-click **a02Recipes**. A database opens displaying tables related to the spa.

b. Click the **File** tab, save the file as an **Access Database**, and click **Save As**. Navigate to the location where you are saving your project files and then change the file name to a02Recipes_LastFirst using your last and first name. Click **Save**. If necessary, in the Security Warning, click **Enable Content**.

c. Click the **Create** tab, and then in the Forms group, click **Form Wizard**. Add all of the fields from **Table: tblRecipes**. From **Table: tblRecipeIngredients**, add **IngredientID**, **Quantity**, and **Measurement**. View the form **by tblRecipes**, and then show the subform as a **Datasheet**. Save the form as frmRecipe_iLast, using your first initial and last name, and save the subform as frmRecipeSubform_ilLast using your first initial and last name. Switch to **Design** view. On the Design tab, in the Controls group, click **Label**, and then add a label about 2.5 inches wide in the top left corner of the form footer that says Created by initial Lastname using your first initial and last name.

d. Switch to **Layout** view. Click the **Design** tab, and in the Themes group, click **Themes**. Click the **Ion Boardroom** theme to apply it to all objects in the database.

e. Click the **Design** tab, and in the Themes group, click Fonts, and then click **Office** to apply it to all objects.

f. Double-click the title of the form, and change it to Recipe Details. Click the **Format** tab, and in the Font group, change the title font size to **28**, and then apply **Bold**.

g. Delete the subform label, and then move the subform to the left under the Instructions label. AutoFit the subform fields **Quantity** and **Measurement** to size them appropriately. Move the **right** border of the subform to the left to fit the subform columns.

h. Click in the form body. On the Design tab, in the Controls group, click **Insert Image**. Click **Browse**, navigate to your student data files, and then locate **a02Indigo5**. Insert the image to the right of the Recipe information. Resize the image as necessary to fit above the Instructions text box.

i. Switch to **Form** view. Click the **Recipe Name** text box. Click the **Home** tab, and in the Find group, click **Find**, and then in the Find What box, type Pasta Napolitana, and then click **Find Next**. Click **Cancel**. Change the Quantity for the IngredientID Honey to 1.

j. Click the **New (blank) record** button on the main form Navigation bar, and then enter the following data. Use the field arrows for the Food Category ID and Subcategory fields.

Recipe Name	Food Category ID	Subcategory	Prep Time (minutes)	Servings	Instructions
Avocado Salsa	Appetizer	Vegetarian	10	6	Peel and mash avocados. Add cayenne pepper, salt, chopped onion, and chopped tomato. Add lime juice and mix well. Refrigerate for at least 4 hours.

Enter the following data into the subform:

IngredientID	Quantity	Measurement
Avocado	2	whole
Tomato	1	cup
Cayenne pepper	.5	teaspoon
Salt	.5	teaspoon
Onions	1	cup
Lime juice	3	tablespoons

Save and close the form.

k. Create a query to show recipes that use the ingredients cumin or paprika. Click the **Create** tab, and in the Queries group, click **Query Design**, and then add **tblRecipes**, **tblRecipeIngredients**, and **tblIngredients**. Include **RecipeName**, **Ingredient**, and **Quantity** in the results. In the **Ingredient Criteria**, type cumin or paprika. Sort in **Ascending** order by Quantity. Run the query, and then use AutoFit on the query columns. Save your query as qryCuminOrPaprika_iLast, using your first initial and last name. Close the query.

l. Create a query to show all ingredients not used in any recipe. Click the **Create** tab, and then in the Queries group, click Query Wizard, click **Find Unmatched Query Wizard**, and then click **OK**. Click **Table: tblIngredients**, and then click **Next**. Click **tblRecipeIngredients**, and then click **Next**. IngredientID will be the common field between the tables. Click **Next**, and then include all the available fields. Click **Next**. Save the query as qryUnusedIngredients_iLast, using your first initial and last name. Click **Finish**. Switch to **Design** view, and sort IngredientID in **Ascending** order. Save and close the query.

m. Create a query to show all recipes that take less than 30 minutes to prepare and are listed with the category of soup or pizza. Click the **Create** tab, and in the Queries group, click **Query Design**, and then add **tblRecipes** and **tblFoodCategories**. Include **RecipeName**, **TimeToPrepare**, and **FoodCategory** in the results. Add the criterion <30 to the TimeToPrepare field to find all recipes that take less than 30 minutes to prepare. Add the criterion soup or pizza to the FoodCategory field. Sort TimeToPrepare in **Ascending** order. **Run** the query. Use AutoFit on each column. Save the query as qryTimeAndCategory_iLast, using your first initial and last name, and then close the query.

n. Create a query to show all recipes that include tomatoes or garlic in their ingredients. Click the **Create** tab, and in the Queries group, click **Query Design**, and then add **tblRecipes**, **tblRecipeIngredients**, and **tblIngredients**. Include **RecipeName**, **Ingredient**, **Quantity**, **Measurement**, and **RecipeID** from tblRecipeIngredients in the results, in that order. Add the criterion tomato or garlic to the Ingredient field. Sort RecipeID in **Ascending** order. **Run** the query. Use AutoFit on each column. Save the query as qryRecipeIngredients_iLast, using your first initial and last name, and then close the query.

o. Create a report that lists all recipes, their instructions, and a list of ingredients. Click the **Create** tab, and in the Reports group, click **Report Wizard**, and then from Table: tblRecipes, add the fields **RecipeName**, **Instructions**, **TimeToPrepare**, and **Servings**. From Query: qryRecipeIngredients_iLast, add the fields **Ingredient**, **Quantity**, and **Measurement** in that order. View your report **by tblRecipes**. Group by **RecipeName**. Sort in **Ascending** order by Ingredient. Accept all other default settings, and then name the report rptRecipes_iLast using your first initial and last name.

- Switch to **Layout** view, and then move the **Ingredient**, **Quantity**, and **Measurement** text boxes to the left under the Instructions field. Delete the **Ingredient**, **Quantity**, and **Measurement** labels. Move the **Servings text box** and **label** to the right. Make the **Prep Time (minutes)** and **Servings** labels wider so the text is visible. Double-click the report **title**, and then change it to Recipes.

- Click the **RecipeName** text box. Click the **Format** tab, and in the Font group, click **Bold**. Move the right border for the **RecipeName** text box to make it wide enough to fit all the text for every record. Scroll down to **Gambas al Ajillo (Shrimp with Garlic)** to make sure the field is wide enough.

- Click the **Quantity** text box, and then move the **left** border to the right to make the field narrower. Click the **Ingredient** text box, and then move the right border to the right to make the field completely visible. Scroll down to see **Garlic** make sure the field is wide enough.

- Click the **Prep Time** text box, and then in the Control Formatting group, click **Conditional Formatting**. Click **New Rule**, select **greater than** in the second box, and then type 15 in the third box. Click **Bold**, change the font color to **Red**, and then click **OK**. Click **OK** again.

- Switch to **Design** view. Click the **Design** tab, and in the Controls group, click **Label**, and then add a label saying Created by initial Lastname, using your first initial and last name, to the Report Footer.

- Save the report, switch to **Report** view to check your report, and then close the report.

- Right-click **rptRecipes_iLast**. Select **Export**, and then select **PDF or XPS**. Navigate to the folder where you are saving your files, and type a02Recipes_LastFirst using your last and first name. In the Open file after publishing box, **clear** the check box, click **Publish**, and then click **Close**.

p. Create a report that lists all ingredients and which recipes they are used in. Click the **Create** tab, and in the Reports group, click **Report Wizard**, and then from **Table:**

tblRecipeIngredients, add the fields **IngredientID**, **Quantity**, and **Measurement**. From **Table: tblRecipes**, add **RecipeName**. Click **Next**, check to make sure you view your data **by tblRecipeIngredients**, click **Next**, and then double-click **RecipeName** to add grouping. Accept all other default options, and then name your report rptIngredientCount_iLast using your first initial and last name.

- Switch to **Design** view. On the Design tab, in the Controls group, click **Label**, and then add a label saying Created by initial Lastname, using your first initial and last name, to the Report Footer.

- Switch to **Layout** view. Click the **Design** tab, and in the Grouping & Totals group, click **Group & Sort**, and then delete the grouping by RecipeName. Click **Add a group**, and then group by **IngredientID**. Move the **IngredientID** text box to the left margin, under the RecipeName label. Click the **Format** tab, and in the Font group, click **Align Left**. Delete the **RecipeName**, **IngredientID**, **Quantity**, and **Measurement** labels.

- Change the title to Ingredient List. Click the **IngredientID** text box, click **Shape Outline**, and then click **Transparent**. Click **Shape Fill**, and then under Theme Colors, click **Dark Purple, Text 2, Lighter 60%**.

- Click the **Quantity** text box. Click the **Design** tab, and in the Grouping & Totals group, click **Totals**, and then click **Sum** to add subtotals. Right-click the **subtotal** text box, select **Set Caption**, and then change the text to Total. Click the **subtotal** text box, and then click the **Format** tab.

- In the Font group, click **Align Right** to change the alignment. Scroll down to the bottom of the report to find the grand total text box (value 84.5), click the text box, and then press **Delete**. Make the **RecipeName** text box wide enough to fit all the text for every record, and scroll to find **Gambas al Ajillo (Shrimp with Garlic)** to check the width.

- Close the Group, Sort, and Total pane. Close the report, and then save your changes.

q. Close the database, exit Access, and then submit your file as directed by your instructor.

Problem Solve 1

MyITLab® Grader
Homework

Student data files needed:

 a02Hotel.accdb

 a02Paradise.jpg

 a02PaintedParadise.thmx

You will save your file as:

 a02Hotel_LastFirst.accdb

Hotel Reservations

Production & Operations

Painted Paradise Resort & Spa has started a database to keep track of its hotel reservations with guest information, reservation information, and additional room charge information. Because no reports, forms, or queries have been built yet, the hotel staff finds that the database is not easy to use. You will create reports, forms, and queries to help the staff better manage the data in the database. Complete the following tasks.

a. Open the Access file, **a02Hotel**. Save your file as a02Hotel_LastFirst using your last and first name. If necessary, enable the content.

b. Open **tblGuests**, and add a new record with your Last Name, First Name, Address, City, State, ZipCode, and Phone. Close the table.

c. Use the Form Wizard to create a form that will allow the staff to enter Room Charges for each guest during their stay. Include the **GuestLastName**, **GuestFirstName**, **City**, **State**, **ChargeCategory**, and **ChargeAmount**. View the data by **tblGuests**. The subform should be in **Datasheet** layout. Accept all other default options, name the form frmGuestRoomCharges, and name the subform frmGuestSubform.

- Add Created by initial Lastname, using your first initial and last name, to the form footer.
- Delete the subform label. Move the **subform** to the left to line up with State. Resize the subform to fit the columns.
- Apply the theme **a02PaintedParadise** to all objects in your database.
- Insert the image **a02Paradise** to the right of the guest fields, resizing as necessary.
- Resize the **First Name** text field to line up with Last Name.
- Change the **title** to Guest Room Charges, and change the font size of the title to **28** and **bold**. Save and close the form.

d. Create a query to find the number of times (count) a room type has been reserved and the average room rate for the room type. Use **RoomType** and **RoomRate** from tblReservations to perform the aggregate query. Sort the query in **Ascending** order by average **RoomRate**.

- Change the field names to Number of Reservations and Average Room Rate.
- AutoFit the **column widths**.
- Add a total line to the query datasheet results. Show the Total Number of Reservations overall.
- Change the alternating row colors to **Rose, Background 2, Darker 10%**.
- Save the query as qryRoomStatistics.

e. Create a query to find guests who have reservations but do not have any room charges. Include all available fields in the results. Sort the query in ascending order by **CheckInDate**. Save the query as qryGuestsWithoutRoomCharges.

f. Create a query to find guests with multiple room charges. Include **GuestID**, **RoomChargeID**, **ReservationID**, **ChargeCategory**, and **ChargeAmount** from tblRoomCharges. Sort the query in ascending order by **ReservationID**. AutoFit the columns. Save the query as qryMultipleRoomCharges.

Critical Thinking

Consider another version of this query. How could this query be altered to display the total number of room charges and the total amount of these charges for each guest with multiple room charges? Which guest has the most room charges? Which guest has spent the highest total amount on room charges?

g. Create a query to find all guests who have reservations in **2018** and who are staying **two or more nights**. Include **GuestFirstName** and **GuestLastName** from tblGuests, and include **CheckInDate**, **NightsStay**, and **NumberOfGuests** from tblReservations. Sort in ascending order by **CheckInDate**. Save the query as qry2018And2.

h. Create a query to find all guests who have reservations in **2017** with **more than three guests** or all guests who are staying **three or more nights** regardless of their check-in date. Include **GuestFirstName** and **GuestLastName** from tblGuests, and include **CheckInDate**, **NightsStay**, and **NumberOfGuests** from tblReservations. Sort in ascending order by **GuestLastName**. Save the query as qryGuestRelations.

i. Create a query to find all guests who are checking in sometime in **April 2018** and who are staying **between two and four nights**. Include **GuestFirstName** and **GuestLastName** from tblGuests, and include **CheckInDate**, and **NightsStay** from tblReservations. Sort in ascending order by **CheckInDate**, but do not show CheckInDate. Save the query as qryAprilReservations.

j. Use the Report Wizard to create a report for all guests with their reservation information. Include **GuestFirstName**, **GuestLastName**, **CheckInDate**, **NightsStay**, **NumberOfGuests**, **RoomType**, and **RoomRate**. View the data by **tblReservation**. Group the report by **CheckInDate** with normal date grouping options. Sort in ascending order by **GuestLastName** and then by **GuestFirstName**. Add an average of **NightsStay**. Change to **Landscape** orientation, accept all other default options, and name the report rptGuestReservations.

- Change the report title to Guest Reservations.
- Add Created by initial Lastname, using your first initial and last name, to the report footer.
- Delete the line that begins **Summary for 'CheckInDate'**.
- Move or resize all necessary fields so all the text is visible.
- Move the caption **Avg** to line up with FirstName. Change the caption to **Average Nights Stay**.
- Change the border of the RoomType text box control to **Transparent**.
- Add conditional formatting so that any **NightsStay** that is more than two nights displays in **Dark Red** and **Bold**. Close the form.

k. Close the database, exit Access, and then submit your file as directed by your instructor.

Problem Solve 2

MyITLab®
Grader
Homework

Production & Operations

Student data files needed:

 a02Hotel2.accdb

 a02Paradise2.jpg

You will save your files as:

 a02Hotel_LastFirst.accdb

 a02Room_LastFirst.pdf

Additional Hotel Reservations

The hotel has asked you to further customize their database. The hotel manager is interested in learning more about how often guests stay and how much they spend on reservations. She is also interested in extracting data from the database about the room types in the hotel. You will create reports, forms, and queries to help the staff better manage the data in the database.

a. Open the Access file, **a02Hotel**. Save your file as a02Hotel_LastFirst using your last and first name. If necessary, enable the content.

b. Open **tblGuests**, and add a new record with your Last Name, First Name, Address, City, State, ZipCode, and Phone. Close the table.

c. Create a query to see which guests had reservations between November 1, 2017, and January 31, 2018, that included either a crib or handicapped accommodations. Show **GuestLastName** and **GuestFirstName** from tblGuests, and show **CheckInDate**, **Crib**, and **Handicapped** from tblReservations. Sort by **CheckInDate**. Name the query qryCribReservations.

d. Create a query to calculate the total room charges per guest. Use the **GuestID** from tblGuests and the **ChargeAmount** from tblRoomCharges. Rename the total field **RoomCharges**. Sort in **Descending** order by **RoomCharges**. AutoFit the **RoomCharges** field. Save the query as qryTotalRoomCharges.

e. Create a query to calculate the total amount due for each guest, including room rate and room charges. Include **GuestLastName** and **GuestFirstName** from tblGuests, include **NightsStay** and **RoomRate** from tblReservations, and include **RoomCharges** from qryTotalRoomCharges. Save the query as qryTotalDue.

- Add a new calculated field to the query to calculate each guest's total amount due based on the room rate, the number of nights they stayed, and room charges. Name the new field **TotalDue**. Sort the query by **GuestLastName** and then by **GuestFirstName** in **Ascending** order. Save the changes, and close the query.

f. Use the Report Wizard to create a report showing the **TotalDue** for each guest. Include all the fields from qryTotalDue. Do not add a grouping level. Sort by TotalDue in **Descending** order. Accept all other default options, and name the report rptTotalDue.
   - Add Created by initial Lastname, using your first initial and last name, to the report footer. Change the title to Guest Total Charges. Add conditional formatting in **Dark Red** and **Bold** for all NightsStay between three and five nights. Adjust all the label sizes to see the headings. Save and close the report.

g. Use the Report Wizard to create a report with data from **tblRoomtypes** and **tblReservations** with the **RoomDescription**, **RoomRate**, **DiscountType**, **NightsStay**, and **CheckInDate**. View the data by **tblRoomTypes**, do not add any other grouping, and sort by CheckInDate in **Ascending** order. Accept all other default options, and name the report rptRoomTypes.
   - Add Created by initial Lastname, using your first initial and last name, to the report footer. Change the title to Room Types. Remove the outline around the **DiscountType** text box.
   - Calculate the number of reservations for each RoomRate. Add a caption, and type Number of reservations. Resize the calculated field so the caption is visible. Add the fill color **Blue, Accent 1, Lighter 60%** to the caption.
   - Calculate the average nights' stay for each **RoomDescription**. Add a caption, and type Average Nights Stay. Add the fill color **Blue, Accent 1, Lighter 60%** to the caption.
   - Remove the sort on **CheckInDate**. Add a new sort by **RoomDescription**, and move it above the **Group on RoomID**. Resize the width of all the labels so all text is visible. Save and close the report.

h. Publish the report as a PDF file. Save the file as a02Room_LastFirst using your last and first name.

i. Use the Form Wizard to create a form to enter room charges along with the charge details. Include **RoomChargeID**, **GuestID**, **ChargeCategory**, **ChargeAmount**, and **Purchase**. View the form by **tblRoomCharges**, and view the subform in a tabular layout. Accept all other default options, name the form frmRoomCharges, and name the subform frmRoomSubform.
   - Add Created by initial Lastname, using your first initial and last name, to the form footer. Change the title to Room Charges. Insert the image **a02Paradise2** to the right of the main form detail, with the top border of the image lined up with the top border of the GuestID text box and the bottom border of the image lined up with the bottom border of the Amount text box.
   - Delete the **frmRoom** label, and move the subform to the left so it aligns with the Amount label.
   - Save and close the form.

j. Close the database, exit Access, and then submit your file as directed by your instructor.

Student data file needed:

Blank Access database

You will save your file as:

a02Schedule_LastFirst.accdb

Class Schedule

Information
Technology

One way to stay organized during the semester is to keep track of your schedule. You will create a database of all your classes and grades. The database should track the class information, your personal schedule, and the location of the class. To be able to use this for more than one semester, you will keep each of the data in separate tables.

Once the tables have been created, you will set up forms to make data entry easier, run queries to get more information, and create reports to help you manage your schedule. For each report, query, or form, make the object attractive and meaningful.

a. Start **Access**, and then click the **Blank desktop database**. Save the database as a02Schedule_LastFirst using your last and first name.

b. To keep track of class information, design a table that includes fields for at least the class number, class description, credits offered, and professor's name. Assign an appropriate primary key, and then save the table as tblClasses.

c. Add the class information for your classes from last semester, or use fictitious classes if necessary. Add at least six classes to the table. AutoFit the columns so all text is visible.

d. To keep track of your class locations, design a table that includes fields for the building number, building name, and campus the building is located on. Assign an appropriate primary key, and then save the table as tblBuilding.

e. Add the location of the classes you entered in step c. Include at least three different locations. Use AutoFit on the columns so all text is visible.

f. To keep track of your schedule, design a table that includes fields for the class number, semester, meeting days, meeting time, location, midterm grade (as a number), and final grade (as a number). Use AutoFit on the columns so all text is visible. Assign an appropriate primary key, and then save the table as tblSchedule.

g. Enter last semester's schedule, or a fictitious one, that includes at least six classes in at least three different locations. The classes and locations should be the ones entered in tblClasses and tblBuildings.

h. Create relationships as appropriate for tblSchedule, tblClasses, and tblBuilding.

i. You would like to be able to enter all your class and schedule information at one time. Create one form that will allow you to enter all the information. Save the form as frmSchedule_iLast, using your first initial and last name.

j. Use the form to enter a new record for this semester. You should enter all the information except grades. Add a new theme to the form, change the title to something more meaningful than the form name, and add Created by initial Lastname, using your first initial and last name, to the form footer. Save and close the form.

k. You would like to see each class individually as well as all the class records at once. Create a form that will show you this view of the data. Change the form title to something meaningful. Save the form as frmClasses_iLast, using your first initial and last name.

l. You want to find out what your average midterm grade and average final grade were each semester. Even though grades are entered for only one semester, create a query to perform this calculation.

- Rename the fields to something more meaningful, and then format the fields to show only two decimal places. Sort the query by Semester in **Descending** order. Save the query as qryAverageGrades_iLast, using your first initial and last name.

m. You want a schedule of last semester's classes only. Create a query that will show you last semester's classes, the instructor for each class, and where and when each class occurred. Save the query as qrySchedule_iLast, using your first initial and last name.

n. Create a report that will show you last semester's schedule organized by each day. Sort it in order of class time.
- Make sure all the fields print on one page of the report and that all the fields are visible. Add Created by initial Lastname, using your first initial and last name, to the report footer. Save the report as rptSchedule_iLast using your initial and last name.

o. You want to know how to schedule your weekends. Create a query to see whether you have classes after 9 A.M. on Friday. When entering your criteria for this query, use the time as formatted in the tblSchedule table. Save the query as qryFridayClasses_iLast using your initial and last name.

p. You also want to know the average of your midterm and final grades for your classes. Create a query to calculate the average grade in each class. Sort the query by an appropriate field. Save the query as qryGrades_iLast using your initial and last name.

q. You want to print a report to show your parents your grades by class for the semester, including the average grade. Create a report that shows the class number, description, credits, midterm grade, final grade, and average grade for each class. Sort by an appropriate field. Resize all labels so all the text is visible. Change the title to something more appropriate. Save the report as rptGrades_iLast using your initial and last name.
- Add Created by initial Lastname, using your initial and last name, to the report footer. Use Conditional Formatting to display all average grades over 90 in red and bold. Save and close the report.

r. Close the database, exit Access, and then submit your file as directed by your instructor.

Perform 2: Perform in Your Career

Student data file needed:
 a02Fitness.accdb

You will save your file as:
 a02Fitness_LastFirst.accdb

Fitness Center

Production & Operations

A new fitness center has opened and is developing a database for keeping track of members. So far the fitness center has two tables, for Membership information and Member information, and another table with Roster Information. No queries, forms, or reports have been created, so the center has asked you to help answer some questions with queries, make data entry easier with forms, and print some reports for reference. For each report, query, or form, make the object attractive and meaningful.

a. Start **Access**, and open the student data file **a02Fitness**. Save the database as a02Fitness_LastFirst using your last and first name.

b. Open each table, and then familiarize yourself with the fields. Open the **Relationships** window, and then note how the tables are related.

c. The staff wants to be able to enter all new member and roster information in the database at one time. Create a form that will allow them to enter the member records and the related membership records for a new member. Give the form a meaningful name. Add Created by initial Lastname, using your initial and last name, to the form footer. Save the form as frmMemberInput_iLast using your initial and last name.

d. Using frmMemberInput, enter yourself as a member. Use your actual name and address; all other information can be fictitious. Join the club today, and have your membership end a year from now.

e. The staff wants to know how old each member is (in whole numbers) as of the date the person joined the club. This will help the staff to plan age-appropriate activities. Create a query to calculate the age of each member as of the date the person joined the club. (Hint: When you subtract one date from the other, you get a total number of days, not years.) Sort the query by an appropriate field. Save the query as qryMemberAge_iLast using your initial and last name.

f. The manager wants to know which membership types are creating the most revenue and which types are the most popular. Create a query to calculate the total number of each membership type and the total fees collected for each membership type. Format the query so the manager will understand exactly what each field represents. Save the query as qryMembershipStatistics_iLast using your initial and last name.

g. The manager would like to know whether any membership types have not been applied for. Find any membership types that are not assigned to a current member. Include all fields from tblMemberships in the query. Save the query as qryMembershipTypesUnused_iLast using your initial and last name.

h. The staff likes to celebrate birthdays at the club. Assume that the current year is 2017. Everyone born in 1977 will turn 40 this year, and the staff would like a list of all those members along with their actual birthdays so the staff can quickly see who is celebrating a birthday each day. Sort the query by an appropriate field. Save the query as qry1977Birthdays_iLast using your initial and last name.

i. The staff likes to see each member's data as an individual record while still being able to view the whole table of data. Create a form that will allow the staff to view the data this way. Add Created by initial Lastname, using your initial and last name, to the form footer. Give the form a meaningful name. Save the form as frmMemberRecords_iLast using your initial and last name.

j. The staff needs a master list of members with their membership information. Create a report that will show member names, date joined, expiration date, and membership type so the staff knows who is a current member and what kind of membership each person has. Save the report as rptExpirationDates_iLast using your initial and last name.
   • Add Created by initial Lastname, using your first initial and last name, to the report footer. Change the report title to something meaningful.
   • Modify rptExpirationDates_iLast so the records are grouped by the month of the expiration date. Conditionally format the expiration date field with bold and colored font so it stands out from the other fields.

k. The staff needs a list of members with the facilities their membership type gives them access to. Create a report so the staff can quickly locate a member's name and determine which facilities the member is allowed to access. Save the report as rptFacilities_iLast using your initial and last name.
   • Add Created by initial Lastname, using your initial and last name, to the report footer.
   • Change the report theme, change the report title to something other than the name of the report, and save the report.

l. Close the database, exit Access, and then submit your file as directed by your instructor.

Student data file needed:

 a02Cars.accdb

You will save your file as:

 a02Cars_TeamName.accdb

River Bluff Car Dealership

Production & Operations

You work as an office manager for River Bluff Car Dealership, a prosperous car dealership near a metropolitan area on the banks of a river. The car dealership operates from two locations: a main location downtown and a second location on the edge of the city on the sunny side of a river bluff. You work as the office manager at the second location, while another office manager works for the main downtown location. Your supervisor has asked you to work with the other office manager to build a database of the existing used and new vehicles in stock at both locations. This database will make it easier for the sales personnel to suggest vehicles for purchase by customers at either location. Within an existing database file, a table and form of vehicles for each location have already been created with vehicle data entered, including makes, models, year, transmission category, selling price, interior/exterior features, color, and mileage. Your supervisor has asked you to work closely with the other office manager to complete a set of queries and reports for an upcoming meeting for River Bluff's sales staff.

a. Select one office manager to set up the document by completing steps b through d.

b. Open your browser, and navigate to https://www.onedrive.live.com, https://www.drive. google.com or any other instructor-assigned location. Be sure both members of the office manager team have an account on the chosen system, such as a Microsoft or Google account.

c. Open **a02Cars**, and then save the database as a02Cars_TeamName, replacing TeamName with the name assigned to your team by your instructor.

d. Share the database with the other office manager on your team. Make sure each member has the appropriate permission to edit the document.

e. Hold an office manager team meeting to discuss the requirements of the remaining steps. Make an action plan to assign individual and team work, as well as deadlines for each step.

f. Create a query qryBluffside5%DiscountSale_TeamName, using your team name, that calculates the Sales Discount amount and Total Sales Price after discount for each make and model of vehicle in stock at the Bluffside location.
   - Show the fields **Make**, **Model**, and **Price**.
   - Add a new calculated field SaleDiscount that multiplies the **Price** by 5%.
   - Add another new calculated field TotalSalesPrice that subtracts the **SaleDiscount** from the **Price**.
   - Format both calculated fields to display in Currency format in Datasheet view.
   - Run the query results.
   - Add a Total row, and use the SUM aggregate function to find the totals for **Price**, **SaleDiscount**, and **TotalSalesPrice**.
   - Adjust the column width of each field as necessary to display all information.
   - Close and save the query.

g. Create a query qryDowntown6CylinderVehicles_TeamName, using your team name, that finds vehicles in the downtown location that operate on six cylinders.
   - Show the fields **Make**, **Model**, and **Price**.
   - Use the **Cylinder** field for a criterion, but do not show it in the query results.
   - Sort in ascending order by **Make**, then **Model**, then **Price**.
   - Run the query results.

- Adjust the column widths of each field as necessary to display all information.
- Close and save the query.

h. Create a query qryBluffsideUsedCarsunder$15,000_TeamName, using your team name, that finds used vehicles under $15,000 at the Bluffside location only.

- Show the fields **Make**, **Model**, **Used/New**, **Color**, and **Price**.
- Use the appropriate criterion to display used vehicles under $15,000.
- Sort in ascending order by **Price**.
- Run the query results.
- Adjust the column widths of each field as necessary to display all information.
- Close and save the query.

i. Create a query qryDowntownUsedCarsover50,000Miles_TeamName, using your team name, that finds used vehicles with mileage over 50,000 at the downtown location only.

- Show the fields **Make**, **Model**, **Price**, and **Mileage**.
- Use the appropriate criterion to display used vehicles with over 50,000 miles.
- Sort in ascending order by **Mileage**.
- Run the query results.
- Adjust the column widths of each field as necessary to display all information.
- Close and save the query.

j. Create a query qryDowntownPrices_TeamName, using your team name, that finds the overall average, minimum, and maximum prices of vehicles at the downtown location only.

- Use the **Price** field to find the Average Price, Minimum Price, and Maximum Price.
- Run the query results.
- Adjust the column widths of each field as necessary to display all information.
- Close and save the query.

k. Using the Report Wizard, create a report rptBluffside5%DiscountSale_TeamName, using your team name, based on the **qryBluffside5%DiscountSales** query.

- Show all fields **Make**, **Model**, **Price**, **SaleDiscount**, and **TotalSalePrice**.
- Group by **Make**, then by **Model**, then by **TotalSalesPrice**.
- Select an appropriate layout for the report.
- Use the report title Bluffside 5% Discount Sale.
- Adjust the column widths to display on one page in portrait orientation. This will ensure there are no blank pages in the report.
- Close and save the report.

l. Using the Report Wizard, create a report rptDowntownVehicleInventory_TeamName, using your team name, based on the **tblDowntownVehicleInventory** table.

- Show the fields **Make**, **Model**, **Year**, **Price**, and **Used/New**.
- Group by **Used/New**, then by **Year**.
- Sort by **Price**.
- Select an appropriate layout for the report.
- Use the report title Downtown Inventory.
- Adjust the column widths to display on one page in portrait orientation. This will ensure there are no blank pages in the report.
- Adjust alignment of field names as necessary to improve readability and format.
- Close and save the report.

m. Close the database, exit Access, and then submit your file as directed by your instructor.

Student data file needed:

 a02SummerCamp.accdb

You will save your file as:

 a02Answers_LastFirst.docx

Summer Camp

Production & Operations

You live in the Midwest and volunteer as kitchen help for Kidz Kamp in June, July, and August of each year. At the start of this summer, the head chef had another volunteer complete a database of meal recipes and main ingredients. Specifically, she requested a set of queries and reports that would provide her with information to plan meals for the week-long summer camps. As you began using the database, you noticed that the queries and reports appeared to be either missing data or presenting incorrect results. Answer the following questions about each of the objects as completely as possible.

a. Start **Access**, and then open **a02SummerCamp**.

b. Create a Word document a02Answers_LastFirst, using your last and first name, where you will answer the questions.

c. Open the form **frmRecipes**. This form was created by using the table **tblRecipes**. The form was supposed to display the fields Recipe Card Number, Recipe Name, Total Prep Time, and Total Cook Time and show one recipe (record) at a time in the window. Why is the form showing the first recipe in the top half of the form and then all recipes at the bottom of the form? How was this form created? How should the form have been created to display only a single recipe at a time?

d. The query qryBreakfast was created to find all breakfast food records in which the food category is "Vegetable". Why are records with meal categories other than breakfast listed? Switch to **Design** view, and explain how you would correct the query.

e. The query qryEarlyJune was created to find all recipes that were last used in the first two weeks of June (from June 1 until June 14). Why is the query returning all results from June? Switch to **Design** view, and explain how you would correct the query.

f. The report rptMainIngredients was created from the table tblIngredients. The chef has requested that the report be modified to be grouped by Food Category in alphabetical order. How could this be accomplished? How would the appearance of the report need to be altered to reflect this change?

g. Close the database, exit Access, and then submit your file as directed by your instructor.

PowerPoint Business Unit 1

Understanding the Art of Presentation

Good communication and presentation skills are essential to becoming successful in business. PowerPoint is one of the most commonly used presentation tools in the world, yet it is often misused by students and professionals alike. Understanding how to use the tools available in PowerPoint to engage the audience and invoke an emotional response is critical to a good presentation. This business unit will provide you with the instruction and guidance you need to create powerful presentations that are tailored to your target audience.

Learning Outcome 1:

Understand the purpose of PowerPoint and how to utilize the available tools to create effective and engaging presentations that are tailored to your audience.

REAL WORLD SUCCESS

"I had a summer internship for a consulting company in Chicago. I had the opportunity to proofread a set of presentation slides that my supervisor was going to use for a meeting with potential clients. I noticed that much of the presentation contained wording geared toward employees instead of potential clients. She really appreciated my feedback and made some changes so that it was more appropriate for the intended audience. She got the clients, and I got a full-time job offer!"

- Tanya, recent graduate

Learning Outcome 2:

Arrange and format text in a presentation to ensure optimal readability and comprehension by your audience and to leverage graphics and images to enhance your presentations.

REAL WORLD SUCCESS

"I remember how cluttered, confusing, and boring the vendor's presentation was. Then the presenter said, 'I think I'm putting Clark to sleep here.' It was embarrassing, but I was on the client team and unimpressed. His company did not win our business that day, and I learned a valuable lesson about the importance of a good presentation. The text and graphics have to come alive, and that's usually up to the presenter."

- Clark, client executive

Microsoft PowerPoint 2016

Chapter 1 | PRESENTATION FUNDAMENTALS

Sales & Marketing

Prepare Case

The Red Bluff Golf Course & Pro Shop Putts for Paws Golf Tournament Presentation

The Red Bluff Golf Course & Pro Shop hosts a tournament each year to benefit the Santa Fe Animal Center. Golf pro John Schilling speaks at community meetings, such as the Community Club and Women's Business Council, to gather sponsors and golfers. He has asked you to assist him with the Putts for Paws tournament this year. Your first assignment is to review and update the PowerPoint presentation he uses during his speeches. This presentation has a persuasive purpose, but it also provides basic information such as the time, date, and cost of the tournament; sponsorship opportunities; and special events.

Zorandim75/Fotolia

OBJECTIVES

1. Plan your presentation with a purpose for an intended outcome p. 765

2. Define the purpose, scope, and audience of a presentation p. 766

3. Plan the presentation content p. 770

4. Work with PowerPoint windows and views p. 772

5. Navigate in Slide Show view and Outline View p. 778

6. Add, reuse, and rearrange slides and change slide layouts p. 782

7. Understand the purpose and benefits of using themes p. 787

8. Edit and move slide content p. 793

9. Utilize proofing and research tools p. 795

10. Save a presentation p. 798

11. Preview and print a presentation p. 799

12. Utilize PowerPoint templates to create presentations p. 802

Student data files needed for this chapter:

 p01ch01LogoRB.png

 p01ch01Sponsor.pptx

p01ch01RedBluff.potx

p01ch01ContactInfo.pptx

p01ch01GolfCourse.pptx

p01ch01RedBluffBG.jpg

p01ch01SponsorStory.docx

You will save your files as:

 p01ch01Sponsor_LastFirst.pptx

 p01ch01SponsorPDF_LastFirst.pdf

p01ch01GolfCourse_LastFirst.pptx

p01ch01SponsorShow_LastFirst.ppsx

Understanding the Purpose of PowerPoint

Microsoft Office PowerPoint 2016 is a software application that enables users to create professional-quality presentations with ease. It is a visual and emotive aid used by a presenter to accompany an oral presentation. Adding visual components to a presentation adds impact and helps to engage the audience and make the presentation memorable. Unfortunately, many people use PowerPoint when they have nothing to say, imagining that the slide show will do all the work for them. Visual aids such as marks on a whiteboard, a test tube full of bubbling liquid, or an electronic slide show support the speaker, but they cannot stand on their own; the presenter must have a message that is compelling enough to command the attention of others.

Presentations are typically displayed on large screens for audiences; however, there are many creative ways to use PowerPoint. Kiosks, for example, which are common in public locations such as malls, banks, hotels, zoos, or museums, and can display self-running PowerPoint presentations that provide information or display advertisements. PowerPoint is a versatile tool that can help to vividly communicate a message. In this chapter, you will explore PowerPoint and get a sense of how it can be used to enhance a presentation.

Plan Your Presentation with a Purpose for an Intended Outcome

PowerPoint presentations can help someone communicate with an audience. Slides add interest and variety to the presentation. Because of the visual nature of the slides, the audience is able to grasp more information. Well-built presentations organize thoughts, stimulate interest, clarify and substantiate a message, reinforce what is said, and often motivate the audience to take some form of action.

REAL WORLD ADVICE   **Defining a Target Audience**

A **target audience** is defined by the general characteristics of the group of people to whom you are planning to present. Asking yourself a few starting questions can help you to identify the audience.

- Why were you invited to speak?
- Why is the topic important to your audience?
- What does the audience know about the topic? How will the audience use the information?
- How large is the audience?
- What is the physical layout of the space in which you will be presenting?
- How long are you expected to speak?

Informing an Audience

Generally, the purpose of presentations will fall into one of three major categories. The first category is informational, and the purpose is to provide facts and figures. A fiscal report in business is an example of an informational presentation. The slides in a financial report may show business income and expense, perhaps employing charts and tables. Another example of an informational presentation is a museum kiosk that provides information about artists, their methods, and the history of the artwork. Yet another example is a class lecture, in which objectives, concepts, examples, and questions for discussion are organized. When information is being presented to an audience, the presenter needs to know what the audience already knows about the topic and how the presenter can support the audience's needs.

Persuading an Audience

The second purpose of a presentation is to persuade. While this type of presentation may contain elements such as facts and figures, the main objective will be to appeal to members of the audience to persuade them to agree with the message. Sales and political presentations are examples of persuasive presentations. Whenever someone is trying to generate support for an idea, fund a proposal, or get people to change their beliefs about something, that person is making a persuasive presentation. For this type of presentation, the presenter needs to know the audience's expectations and biases for or against the topic and how the presenter can relate to the audience on a personal level. The presenter needs to address what the audience is resisting with regard to the position, address what the risks are, and how the audience will be rewarded for taking such risks.

Preparing an Audience

The third purpose of a presentation is to prepare. In this case, the presenter may be preparing an audience for bad times, such as layoffs, or preparing them for good times by cross-training them to do a different type of job. The presenter will include important information and help them to understand the circumstances they will encounter. In order to prepare an audience, their expectations must be known as well as what they already know about the topic.

 CONSIDER THIS | **Are There Mixed Purposes?**

Can a presentation have a mixture of purposes? If you begin with the purpose of persuading an audience, is it possible also to inform them? What role do your personal biases play in the purpose? Can an informational presentation really be devoid of persuasion? If you are preparing an audience for a change, are you also informing and persuading the audience?

Telling a Story

Universally, people listening to a presentation want to know "What is in it for me?" Presentations should focus on answering this question while addressing what the audience members need to know. PowerPoint expert Cliff Atkinson, author of *Beyond Bullet Points*, says, "Your audience doesn't care as much about your company history as they do about whether you can help them solve the specific problems they face. Write a script for your presentation that makes the audience the protagonist, or the main character, who faces a problem that you will help to solve."

Good presenters are often great storytellers. A good story creates a sense of tension that is somehow resolved. Chip and Dan Heath, authors of the bestseller *Made to Stick: Why Some Ideas Die and Others Survive*, encourage presenters to generate unexpected "sticky" ideas: to "break patterns, create mystery, build unique stories, and find knowledge gaps." Give the audience members something unexpected. Make them think. Stir up controversy. Challenge their beliefs. Darrell Zahorsky, former About.com Guide, says to use these techniques as a method to "wake them up." Do not do what everybody else does. A good presenter's job is to stand out.

Define the Purpose, Scope, and Audience of a Presentation

Every presentation begins with planning. According to David A. Peoples, author of *Presentations Plus*, "Ninety-five percent of how well your presentation is going to go is determined before you even start." A good presenter will allow approximately four hours of planning time for each hour of presentation time. You should start by defining the purpose of the presentation. The purpose should be specific, and you should be able to list the objectives of the presentation, using action words. You should determine the outcome you expect from the audience. Clear thinking about what the objectives are, the type of content that will be included, and the composition of the audience will be of great assistance in creating a slide show that truly serves its intended purpose.

Asking the following questions can help a presenter determine his or her objectives:

- What is the purpose? To persuade? To inform? To prepare?
- Why is the topic important?
- Why should the audience be interested?
- What is in it for the audience?
- What is the audience expected to do after the presentation?

Using paper sticky notes to brainstorm the possible main ideas for a presentation has proven useful to many professional presenters. In the early stages, these ideas should not be edited; it is helpful just to spend time generating them. Once you reach a point at which no more ideas come to mind, you should begin eliminating some of the ideas. The goal is to focus the presentation on two to five main ideas. These ideas should be translated into action verb objectives, such as "update our computer systems" or "increase workflow by 15%." The objectives will determine the content of the presentation, determine the scope or level of detail, and enable an effective presentation to be delivered.

With the objectives clearly stated, you should continue to add sticky notes to develop the subtopics of the presentation. These subtopics will likely become the titles on the slides and will make the content of the presentation meaningful because they directly relate to the objectives. You should consider the order of the subtopics and try to provide organization so that you can lead the audience through the presentation and achieve the purpose you have defined. A good presenter must understand and be clear about what needs to be communicated to the audience. If you are unsure of your message, the audience will be too.

Opening PowerPoint

In this exercise, you will open the file for the Red Bluff Putts for Paws Golf Tournament, look at the beginning of a presentation, and review the objectives for the presentation.

To Open a Presentation

a. On the taskbar, click **Ask Me Anything** or **Search the web and Windows**. Type PowerPoint.

b. Click on **PowerPoint 2016** in the search results.

c. The PowerPoint Start screen is displayed when PowerPoint is launched. Click **Open Other Presentations** in the left pane, and then double-click **This PC**. Navigate through the folder structure to the location of your student data files, and then double-click **p01ch01Sponsor**.

d. A simple presentation containing slides with information about the upcoming Putts for Paws Golf Tournament benefit opens. Look through the slides in this presentation, noting the simplicity of the content. You will make improvements to this presentation later in this chapter.

e. Click the **File** tab, click **Save As**, and then double-click **This PC**. In the **Save As** dialog box, navigate to the location where you are saving your project files, and then change the file name to p01ch01Sponsor_LastFirst using your last and first name. Click **Save**.

Pecha Kucha, pronounced "*pe-cha-k'cha*" (Japanese for "chit-chat"), is a unique format for presentations, first used in Tokyo, Japan, in 2003 by a Western architecture firm. This type of presentation automatically displays 20 slides for 20 seconds each, during which the presenter speaks. Although this trend in presentations began with architects, it has spread worldwide, and organized PechaKucha Nights (a trademarked name) now cover topics such as travels, artwork, business, and research. Practicing a Pecha Kucha presentation can help you become a better presenter by learning to be more concise and clear in a short period of time. To give effective short presentations such as Pecha Kucha, you must start early while planning. Think about how Pecha Kucha relates to various online videos you have seen and how it relates to presentation planning.

Considering the Target Audience and Their Needs

Determining the characteristics of the expected audience enables a presenter to produce a presentation that is worthwhile to the audience and achieves the objectives of both presenter and audience. Many characteristics can help to shape a presentation. Consider these questions:

- Why will the audience be there to listen to the presentation?
- What attitudes does the audience have about the topic being presented?
- What does the audience already know about the topic?
- What are the constraints? Are they political? Financial? Knowledge based?
- How will audience use the information being presented?
- What are the demographics of the audience? Number of people? Location of the presentation?
- What technical equipment is available? Will there be a microphone? Computer? Projector?
- What is the size of the audience? Will it be small and intimate or large and formal?

Clearly, there are many things to consider, but knowing the audience will enable you to streamline your presentation, customize the materials, and feel more comfortable as you deliver the presentation.

As you consider the audience's needs, you should answer the following questions.

- What do they want to hear?
- What do they need to know?
- What are the potential benefits to the audience?
- What questions might they have?

Another consideration is to determine what the audience members are doing before and after the presentation. Are they listening to another speaker? Are they about to go home or return to their desks? Have they had lunch? Good presenters try to put themselves inside the metaphorical shoes of the audience. Understanding the audience members' frame of mind can enable you to better prepare to meet their needs.

 CONSIDER THIS | **How Many Audiences Do You Really Have?**

Will your presentation have only one target audience or multiple audiences? Should you plan your presentation around all the different potential audiences or just your main target audience?

Understanding Commonality with the Audience

Understanding the relationship the presenter has with the audience and the relationships the audience members have with each other helps to set the tone for the presentation. You might have to make a presentation to your superiors at work, in which case you will want to make suggestions related to the topic so management can make an informed decision. Another audience might be made up of peers or team members. You may want to engage these audience members by having them share their experiences or expertise. Use "we" language, such as "We can improve our customer service by responding to calls within 1 minute." A special interest group will expect the presenter to focus on the group's concerns as they relate to the topic.

Anticipating Audience Expectations

Audiences anticipate that the presenter has expertise in the topic area. This may mean that you will have to conduct some research so that you have a complete understanding of the subject matter. This additional study can add significant time to the preparation for the presentation. The audience will ask questions. Anticipating their questions and adding these to the planning of the presentation helps the audience to understand the topic more clearly.

An audience that is interested in the topic is concerned with what additional information they can glean from the presentation. For this kind of presentation, you should focus on teaching them about the topic. Another audience may not be quite as interested and may need to be involved in some way with the presentation. Group work or discussions are often the key in this situation. Still another audience will be uninterested in the presentation but forced to attend. Faced with this group, you should strive to include them, too, maybe even directly, but if common ground has not yet been established, this may backfire. A good presenter should stay true to the purpose and objectives of the presentation.

Understanding the Audience's Interaction with the Presentation

The expectation of most audiences is that the topic will be presented with few surprises, cover points A through D, and end on time. Planning for interaction should extend well beyond the standard question-and-answer period. You should consider creatively developing activities that draw the audience into the presentation, using a variety of visual aids, including PowerPoint slide shows, to explain concepts and bringing in an object that everyone can hold, if that is appropriate. Keep in mind that people remember much more when visual aids are used in the presentation.

In planning for the organization of the presentation, you should begin by telling the audience what is going to be discussed. Often, presentations outline the objectives or major topic areas first. Then you should follow through and talk about each item you said would be discussed, in the same order. Finally, you should review what was discussed as a summary of the presentation. Presentations should finish strong with a call to action or an appeal that supports the purpose of the presentation.

REAL WORLD ADVICE | **Everyone Needs a Roadmap**

A good presentation can help to organize the thinking of the audience by providing a roadmap of the presentation. Setting the tone early will draw the audience into listening during the presentation instead of simply reading the text on the slides. The roadmap should be part of the beginning of the presentation, and then a short recap at the end will remind the audience of the important parts in the presentation.

Plan the Presentation Content

Once you have a script, you can begin to visualize the ideas. Developed by the Walt Disney Studio during the 1930s, storyboards are often used in business today to plan ad campaigns, websites, and interactive user interfaces. **Storyboards** are conceptual drawings of a story, much like a comic book. Using a storyboard can enable you to plan and visualize how everything comes together in a scene or sequence of shots, to use the film industry analogy. Being an artist is not a prerequisite to using storyboards to plan presentations. Quick drawings suffice and can remind you of elements you want to include. The best presentations are visual and not all text on the screen. Storyboarding also takes your concentration away from typing on the keyboard and back to the visuals the audience will see. Remember that PowerPoint presentations are not presentation notes but rather visual aids.

Using a Storyboard

Typically, storyboards are composed of three panels situated from left to right — content, layout or action, and audio/visual elements — but this is not a rule. Storyboards should include information about the script, props or visual aids, backgrounds, and transitions. In this exercise, you will review a storyboard for the Red Bluff Putts for Paws Golf Tournament and review the objectives in this presentation.

To Review a Storyboard

a. Start **Word**, click **Open Other Documents** in the left pane, and then double-click **This PC**. Navigate through the folder structure to the location of your student data files, and then double-click **p01ch01SponsorStory**. A sample storyboard opens.

b. Scroll through the document, making note of the content, layout, and visual elements planned for each slide. Notice the progression from opening material about logistics to the golfer incentives, corporate incentives, and contact information.

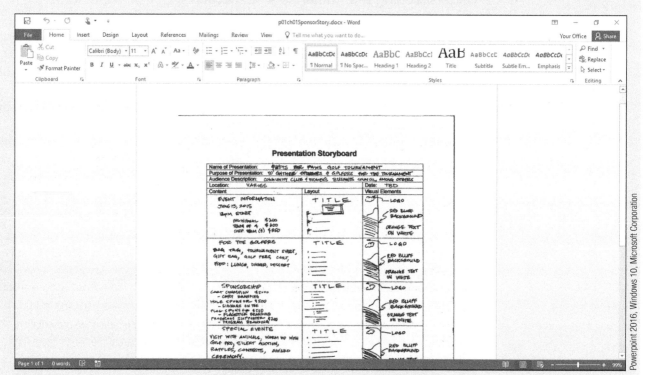

Figure 1 Sponsors storyboard

c. **Close** × Word.

When building a storyboard, you should keep in mind that you will be the focus of the audience. The presentation text and graphics will assist the audience in seeing what is being communicated. People cannot listen and read at the same time. Thus, any text should be minimal and thoroughly edited to include only the main points or key terms. Complete sentences, with the exception of quotations, should be avoided as slide content. When you use complete sentences, you must allow silence during the presentation to give the audience time to read before listening to you. Think like a headline writer, distilling the content down to the essence of the topic. As a presenter, you will want the audience to read and understand your slide in less than ten seconds. People also like numbers in presentation content, such as "Four Hot Tips" or "Three Steps to Success." This helps to organize content in a way that the audience can easily recall.

It has been said that "a picture is worth a thousand words," and in fact, media elements such as photographs, video, audio, charts, and graphics should be the bulk of the presentation. Media can be used to summarize, demonstrate, inject humor, clarify, and reinforce what has been said. As often as possible, use pictures or other visual elements to replace words.

Using Anecdotes and Quotations

Anecdotes and quotations that support the message and can be used either as an opening statement or a closing statement. They can give the presentation credibility. They can convey a startling fact or statistic. Anecdotes, such as stories in the news or personal experiences, can help you connect to the audience by explaining a situation. Quotations that relate to the subject can also add humor to the presentation. If a quote is used in a presentation, it is customary to attribute the quotation to the person who originally said it.

Encouraging Audience Participation

One of the reasons why people enjoy giving presentations is to make a connection with the members of the audience. Encouraging audience participation is an important part of the planning. This is one place in which the evaluation of the audience comes into play. In a large group environment, you will use different strategies than in a conference room meeting. Remarkably, games are very engaging, and audience members become very active when a simple prize is offered, if appropriate. Asking questions of the audience helps to keep them on their toes and gives feedback. However, you should always try to avoid putting someone on the spot or making someone feel uncomfortable. Small group discussions are effective if the presentation is educational in nature or when debate or argument is necessary to make a decision. As with everything else involved with presenting, planning is the key in successful audience participation.

Including Quantitative and Statistical Content

When presenting data, you should resist the urge to put all of the numbers on the screen. If it is necessary for the audience to have all of the numbers, it is better to provide handouts. If you are going to be presenting data, it is best to critically review the numerical data and pull out the important numbers, such as the totals, for the slide.

Converting the numbers into a chart can often enhance a slide show. Visualizing data with charts will allow the audience to better understand the numbers, and audience members are more likely to remember the meaning of the data. A rich visualization will add interest and color to the presentation and can often make a point more clearly than words.

As you create graphs for your presentation, make sure they convey the information in a way the audience can comprehend. Critically view the graphs, and determine whether the point you wish to make is evident. As you select the type of chart, consider these characteristics.

- **Pie chart** — Parts make up a whole; usually contains percentages
- **Bar** or **column chart** — Compares items in rank or changes over a period of time
- **Line chart** — Changes over time, frequency, or relationship between items

Using Appropriate Media

Good media choices — including graphics, audio, and video — stimulate interest, help to clarify important points, and reinforce what has been said. Poor media choices confuse the audience and distract them from purpose of the presentation.

Cliff Atkinson says, "When you overload your audience, you shut down the dialogue that is an important part of decision making." Pointing to research by educational psychologists, he says, "When you remove interesting but irrelevant words and pictures from a screen, you can increase the audience's ability to remember the information by 189% and the ability to apply the information by 109%."

In selecting media, consider the length of the presentation and the technology that will be available in the presentation room.

- Does the media element completely support the objectives?
- Is the media element clear enough for the audience to see and understand?
- Will there be a good Internet connection for loading a web page or a YouTube video?
- Do you want to devote three to eight minutes to a video?

You should be ready to engage the audience regardless of the technology that is available. If the technology does not work as expected, you should be able to adapt appropriately.

Respecting Copyrights

In selecting content for a presentation, it is important to respect copyrights. Copyrights include the rights to reproduce, distribute, create derivative works from, perform, and display intellectual property. Many people believe that everything on the Internet is copyright free, but it is not. Works that are created by individuals, such as photographs, poems and other writing, music, and video, are copyrighted to the individual automatically as soon as they are in a fixed format. Individuals have the right to post their work on the Internet, sell the work to another party, or display the work in any way they see fit.

Copyright law and the Digital Millennium Copyright Act of 1998 address many aspects of how media elements are protected. Best practice is to seek permission before using copyrighted elements in your PowerPoint slide shows. Using the Internet, it is easy to research and request permission to use these elements. Often, permission to use the elements is granted without cost or restriction, and sometimes you can make a direct connection with the person who created the item. In some cases, the copyright holder will request a citation or attribution recognizing his or contribution.

REAL WORLD ADVICE | **Citing Sources**

Depending on the presentation's purpose and audience, you should consider citing the sources you used in creating your presentation. Your instructor or supervisor may prefer a specific citation format, such as APA (American Psychological Association), MLA (Modern Language Association), or the Chicago Manual of Style. You can learn more about the formats on the websites for each.

- APA — www.apa.org
- MLA — www.mla.org
- Chicago Manual of Style — www.chicagomanualofstyle.org

Work with PowerPoint Windows and Views

PowerPoint allows the presentation to be viewed from various perspectives. **Normal view**, shown in Figure 2, is the default view of PowerPoint and displays the left pane and the Slide pane work area. **Outline View** is a view that presents left pane content on the slide in a text hierarchy that allows the presentation creator to focus on the content. In the early stages of presentation development, the focus should be on the quality and brevity of content in the presentation.

PowerPoint also has several panes for editing the presentation. On the left side, the **left pane** allows you to select a slide. In the middle, the **Slide pane** is a large work area, in Normal view, that allows for the editing of text, images, and other objects on the slide. On the bottom, the **Notes pane** allows the addition of speaker notes that the audience will not see.

As the tournament manager working with John Schilling, the golf pro at the Red Bluff Golf Course & Pro Shop, you will modify a persuasive presentation previously created for the Red Bluff Golf Course & Pro Shop Putts for Paws Golf Tournament. John plans to give this presentation to civic groups in the community with the purpose of soliciting financial sponsorship for the tournament, a benefit for the Santa Fe Animal Center. Also, the presentation will encourage golfers to register for the event.

Exploring PowerPoint and Adding Notes

The golf pro has asked you to make some updates to the slides. In this exercise, you will explore the various elements of PowerPoint, review the slide show from the previous year, and add some notes to the presentation.

 P01.02

To Explore PowerPoint and Add Notes

a. Using the file **p01ch01Sponsor_LastFirst**, notice that PowerPoint is divided into three main areas: the Slide pane, the left pane, and the Notes pane. The ribbon is across the top of the window. The status bar is across the bottom.

b. Click through each **slide** in the left pane. Notice the progression from introductory material to the incentives to a call to action.

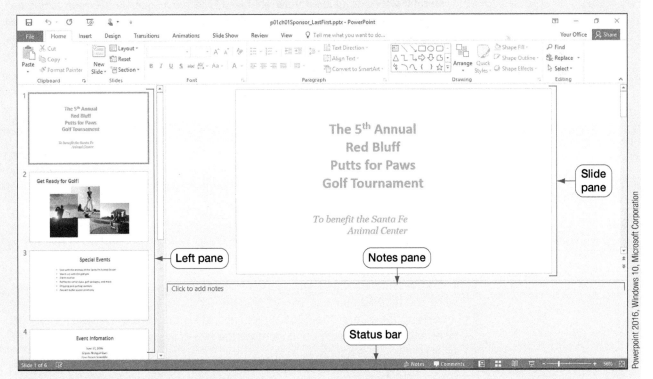

Figure 2 PowerPoint default, Normal View

c. Click the **View** tab, and then, in the Presentation Views group, click **Outline View**. Notice how the left pane changes. Outline View enables you to concentrate only on the text content of the slide presentation.

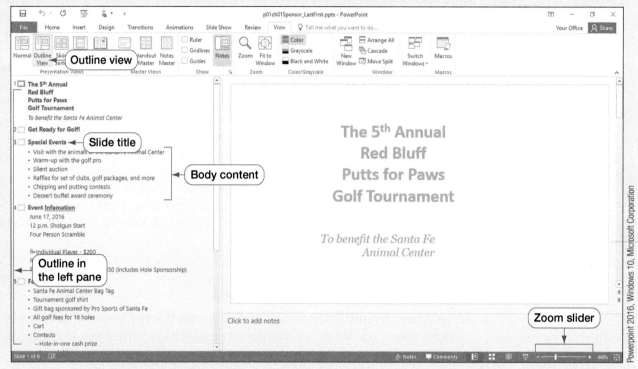

Figure 3   PowerPoint, Outline View

Normal view and Outline View enable you to move quickly between slides by clicking on the slide in the left pane that you want to view. Use the scroll bar on the right side of the Slide pane to move up or down through the slides.

d. In the Presentation Views group, click **Normal**, and then click the thumbnail for **Slide 2**. The left pane displays thumbnail views of the slides in the presentation. The selected slide is displayed in the Slide pane.

e. Point to each of the areas on the status bar located at the bottom-right of the window, and then click the **Slide Sorter** button. Notice that the number of the selected slide and the total number of slides are on the left side of the status bar. On the right side of the status bar are buttons for changing the view and look of the PowerPoint window.

f. Drag the **Zoom Slider** to the right to increase the magnification of the slides to **150%**. Click the **Zoom Out** button on the Zoom Slider until the slide is at **30%** magnification. Click the **Fit slide to current window** button in the status bar to maximize the view of all slides.

g. In the Presentation Views group, click **Normal**. Drag the **divider** between the left pane and the Slide pane to the left until the scroll bar in the left pane disappears, increasing the size of the Slide pane. Next, drag the **divider** between the Slide pane and the Notes pane up to increase the size of the Notes pane until the Zoom level on the status bar reads **33%**.

h. With Slide 2 selected in the Slide pane, click the **Notes** pane, and then type Introduction Name and job title. Press ⏎Enter⏎ to move to the next line, and then type Purpose - Introduce you to the opportunities for sponsorship of the Putts for Paws Golf Tournament and to advocate for the needs of the animals and those who care for them at the Santa Fe Animal Center.

The Notes pane contains the speaker's notes for each slide in the presentation. These notes are not seen by the audience when the presentation is displayed. As the presenter, you can print the notes with the slides or use them in the Presenter view when two displays exist.

j. **Save** 🖫 the presentation.

Displaying the Presentation in Various Views

PowerPoint can display slides in a variety of views. Each view has a purpose, and the available tools change as you switch between views. Normal view is used to edit the slides. **Slide Sorter view** provides options for rearranging slides and reviewing slide transitions. In Slide Sorter view, you see thumbnails of each of the slides. **Reading view** displays the slides one at a time, offering tools such as the title bar Minimize, Maximize/Restore, and Close buttons and navigation buttons for moving between slides. **Slide Show view** is used to display the presentation to an audience. The views are accessed by using the View tab or the view buttons on the status bar. In this exercise, you will explore these various views.

To Zoom and Display a Presentation in Various Views

a. Click the **Slide Sorter** button ⊞ on the status bar.

Slide 2 is highlighted with an orange border because it was the slide selected in the previous view. Thumbnails of all six slides in the presentation are displayed.

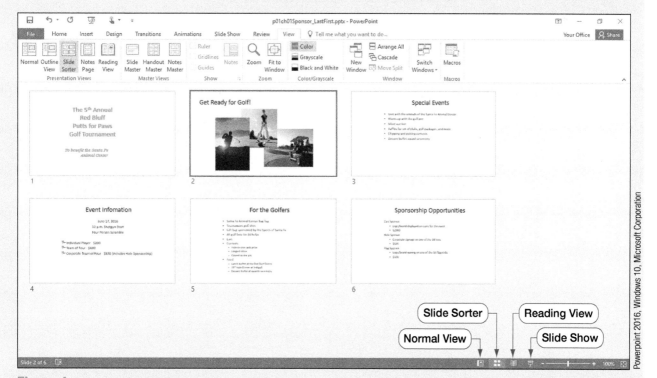

Figure 4 PowerPoint view buttons

b. On the View tab, in the Zoom group, click **Zoom**, and select **50%**.

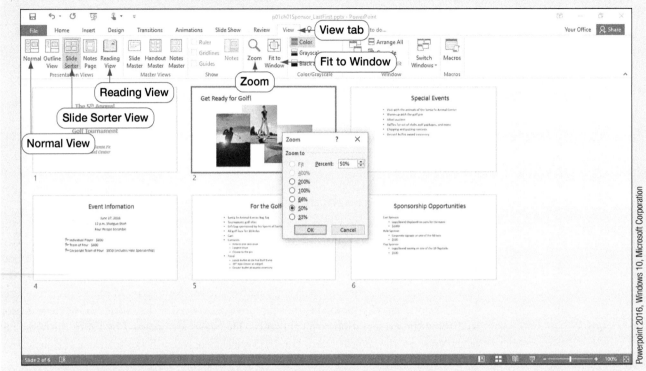

Figure 5   PowerPoint, Slide Sorter view

c. Click **OK**. The thumbnails become smaller, which is useful for displaying more slides in a large slide show.

d. In the Zoom group, click **Fit to Window**. This causes the slides to be displayed as large as possible in this Slide Sorter view.

SIDE NOTE
Reading View
Reading View on the View tab displays the first slide, but Reading View on the status bar displays the active slide.

e. Click **Slide 5**, and then click **Reading View** 📖 on the status bar. Slide 5 is displayed in a view designed for reading on the screen.

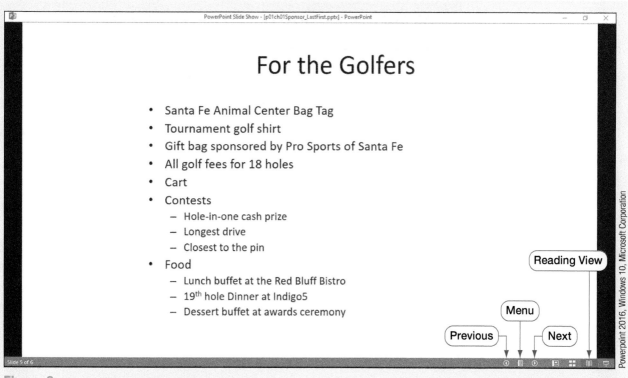

For the Golfers

- Santa Fe Animal Center Bag Tag
- Tournament golf shirt
- Gift bag sponsored by Pro Sports of Santa Fe
- All golf fees for 18 holes
- Cart
- Contests
  - Hole-in-one cash prize
  - Longest drive
  - Closest to the pin
- Food
  - Lunch buffet at the Red Bluff Bistro
  - 19th hole Dinner at Indigo5
  - Dessert buffet at awards ceremony

Reading View

Menu

Previous

Next

Slide 5 of 6

Powerpoint 2016, Windows 10, Microsoft Corporation

Figure 6 PowerPoint, Reading View

SIDE NOTE

Using the Menu
The Reading View menu enables you to navigate through the slides, preview, print, copy, exit, and end a show.

f. Click the **Next** ▶ button on the status bar to view Slide 6. The Next and Previous buttons on the status bar make it easy to navigate through the slide show in this view.

g. Click **Menu** 📄 on the status bar, and then click **Edit Slides**. You return to Slide Sorter view.

h. Click **Slide 2**, and then click **Slide Show** 🖵 on the status bar. Slide 2 fills the primary screen. If a different slide was selected, that slide would have been displayed. If you have two displays, you will also see the Presenter View. The Presenter View is not displayed to the audience. Keep the slide show open as you move to the next section.

Get Ready for Golf!

Primary Slide Show display

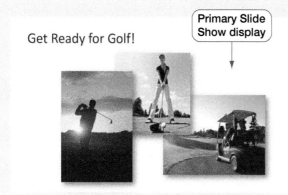

Presenter View when two displays are present

Slide 2 notes typed in Note pane

Powerpoint 2016, Windows 10, Microsoft Corporation

Figure 7 PowerPoint, Slide Show displays

Navigate in Slide Show View and Outline View

Most often, when giving a presentation, you will display the slide show in Slide Show view, advancing each slide after you have spoken about the contents of the slide. PowerPoint offers many methods for advancing the slides and returning to previous slides. Some people prefer to use the mouse to move between the slides; others like to use the keyboard. Windows 10 enables you to gesture on touch devices to navigate a presentation. A presenter remote control can also free you from having to stand close to the computer while giving the presentation.

Navigating the Presentation in Various Views

In this exercise, you will practice various methods of navigating through a slide show.

 P01.04

To Display and Navigate Through a Slide Show

a. If necessary, click **Slide 2**, and then click **Slide Show** 🖵 on the status bar. Click once to advance to the next slide in the presentation. Right-click, and then click **See All Slides**. This view enables you to select a specific slide to display. Click the **Back** button in the top-left corner of the screen.

b. Right-click, and then click **Previous**. Using the mouse, you can advance through the slides, return to previously viewed slides, or select specific slides to display.

Special Events

- Visit with the animals of the Santa Fe Animal Center
- Warm-up with the golf pro
- Silent auction
- Raffles for set of clubs, golf packages, and more
- Chipping and putting contests
- Dessert buffet award ceremony

Slide in Slide Show View →

Shortcut menu →

Powerpoint 2016, Windows 10, Microsoft Corporation

Figure 8 PowerPoint, Slide Show view

c. Press Spacebar to display Slide 3, Special Events, again. Many people like to use the spacebar to advance through their presentations because it is a large key that is easy to find in a darkened room.

d. Use your favorite method to advance to the end of the presentation. When you advance the slides beyond the last slide, a black screen alerts you that you have reached the end of the slide show. While the black screen is showing, any of the methods for moving to the next slide will return you to the view and slide you were at before you started the Slide Show.

e. Use any previous methods described to advance past the black screen, and then, on the View tab, in the Presentation Views group, click **Normal**.

f. **Save** 🖫 the presentation.

> ## Troubleshooting
> To exit a presentation while it is displayed in Slide Show view, press Esc. This returns you to the previous view.

There are many options for navigating through the slide show.

1. To advance to the next slide, either type an N or press `Enter`, `PgDn`, `→`, `↓`, or `Spacebar`. On a touch-enabled surface, start from the right side of the screen and swipe left.

2. To return to a previous slide, either type a P or press `PgUp`, `←`, `↑`, or `Bksp`. On a touch-enabled surface, start from the left side of the screen and swipe right.

3. To view all slides, either type a G or zoom all the way out. To view a specific slide, press the number of the slide, and then press `Enter`.

4. To zoom in, either type a + (plus sign) or stretch or double-tap on a touch-enabled surface.

5. To zoom out, either type a - (minus sign) or pinch or double-tap on a touch-enabled surface.

6. To display a blank black screen, type a B or a . (period). To return to the display, type a B or a . again.

7. To display a blank screen, type a W or a , (comma). To return to the display, type a W or a , again.

8. Using the mouse, click the transparent icons in the lower-left corner of the slide in the Slide Show view.

9. To end the slide show, press `Esc`.

Promoting, Demoting, and Moving Text in Outline View

Outline View displays the titles and bullet points of the slides in the presentation. It is easy to add, modify, and delete text in this view. You can also move the slides by dragging them to new positions in Outline View. Promoting outline text moves it up a level, and demoting outline text moves it down a level.

Some of the slides might appear to be blank in Outline View when in fact they are not blank. Outline text is drawn from the title and content placeholders. Placeholders are objects in PowerPoint that hold different types of content for the presentation. Slides that do not contain text in these placeholders will appear to be blank in Outline View. To make modifications to these slides, you use Normal view.

In this exercise, you will update the golf tournament presentation in Outline View.

To Use Outline View

a. Click **Slide 6**. On the View tab, in the Presentation Views group, click **Outline View**. If necessary, drag the **border** between the outline in the left pane and the Slide pane to increase the amount of text you can see in the outline.

   Minimizing the size of the slide in the Slide pane enables you to focus more on the outline content.

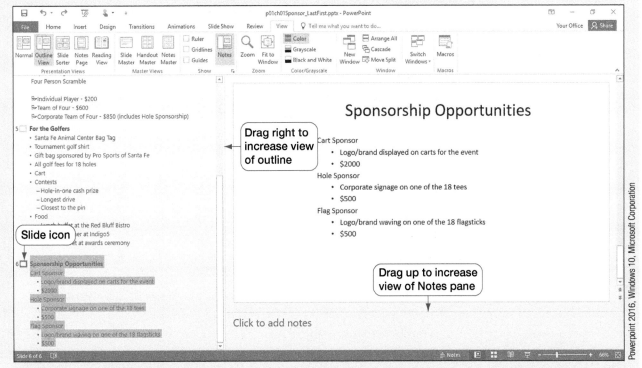

Figure 9 Using Outline View

b. On Slide 6 in the outline on the left pane, position the insertion point at the very end of the bulleted text right after **$500**, and then press Enter. Type the following, pressing Enter after each line:

Program Sponsor
Logo/brand on program materials
$200

c. Place the insertion point anywhere in the text **Program Sponsor**, click the **Home** tab, and then, in the Paragraph group, click **Decrease List Level** 🔲.
    The text has been promoted in the outline. You will change the bullet and font size later.

d. On Slide 5 in the outline on the left pane, click and drag to select the text for the sixth bullet beginning with the word **Contests** and ending with the word **pin**. On the Home tab, in the Clipboard group, click **Cut** 🔲 to remove the text and copy it to the Clipboard.

e. On Slide 3, click to place your insertion point to the left of the word **Chipping** in the fifth bullet, and then, in the Clipboard group, click **Paste**.

f. Select the four bullet points in the outline on the left pane, beginning with the text **Hole-in-one** and ending with **putting contests**, and then, in the Paragraph group, click **Increase List Level** 🔲.
    The text has been demoted in the outline. The pasting process left inconsistent formatting; you will change the bullets and font size later.

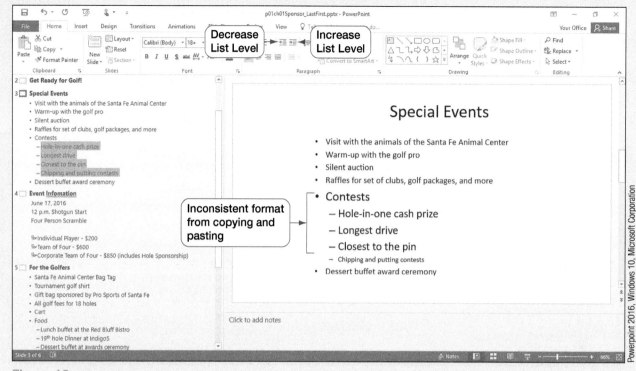

Figure 10 Demoting text

g. **Save** 🔲 the presentation. If you need to take a break before finishing this chapter, now is a good time.

REAL WORLD ADVICE | **Amount of Text on a Slide**

Audience members typically cannot read and listen well at the same time. Text on the screen should be as minimal as possible without sacrificing the message. Some presenters use the 6 × 6 rule to help guide the amount of text. This rule limits the number of words in a line to six and limits the number of lines on a slide to six. Your presentation will be at its best when you minimize text.

Understanding Effective Communication

A good presentation is one that is developed with an eye toward what the audience will see as well as what they will hear. Effective communicators are good storytellers. They have a keen sense about designing imagery to generate interest and about using emotion to create tension.

Add, Reuse, and Rearrange Slides and Change Slide Layouts

PowerPoint includes tools that make it easy to add, modify, and delete content on the slides. It goes further by providing tools that enable you to manipulate the slides. New slides can be added at any point in the presentation and can even be reused from other presentations. The layout of the slides can be changed to present the content better. Unwanted slides can be deleted. In addition, moving slides from one position in the presentation to another is as simple as a drag-and-drop operation.

Adding New Slides

New slides can be easily added to a presentation at any time, using the New Slide button in the Slides group on the Home tab. The current slide show is missing a slide at the beginning that informs the audience of what the presentation will cover. In this exercise, you will add a new slide to the presentation that will outline the topics that are to be covered.

To Add New Slides

a. If you took a break, open the **p01ch01Sponsor** presentation and click the **View** tab.

b. In the Presentation Views group, click **Normal**. Drag the **divider** between the Slide pane and the Notes pane down to decrease the size of the Notes pane until the Zoom level on the status bar reads **60%**.

c. Click **Slide 1**. Click the **Home** tab, and in the Slides group, click the **New Slide** arrow. Several different slide layouts appear.

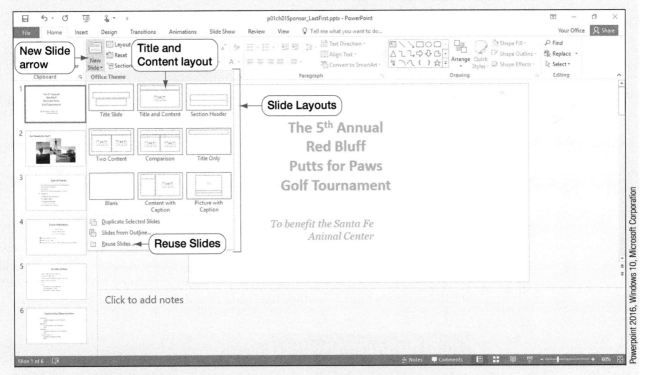

Figure 11   Adding a new slide

d. Click the **Title and Content** slide layout. A new slide is inserted after Slide 1.

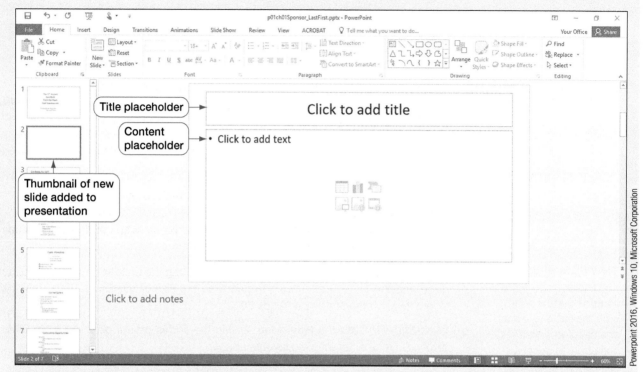

Figure 12   Title and Content slide layout

e. On Slide 2, click the **title placeholder**, and type Overview as the slide title.

f. Click the **content placeholder**, and type the following, pressing Enter after each line:
   Introduction
   Event Information
   Special Events
   Participation Benefits
   Sponsorship Opportunities

g. **Save** ⊟ the presentation

Reusing Slides

Besides adding new slides, you can import slides from other slide shows into the current slide show. You can reuse the slides that you currently have available on your computer or use Slide Libraries that are stored on a server. People with access to the server can share the slides in Slide Libraries, which is an efficient and accurate way to build content.

REAL WORLD ADVICE	Planning the Number of Slides

Plan to display a new slide every two to three minutes. In a 20- to 30-minute presentation, this is a total of ten slides. Be minimalist. The fewer slides, the better. Slides are aides, not a replacement for the presenter or speaker notes. This guideline keeps you on track with timing your presentation as you plan for and deliver your speech. Make sure you prepare for your presentation rather than relying on slides to guide you. How did you feel the last time a presenter read slides to you in lieu of discussion? How did you feel the last time a presenter flipped through slides quicker than you could read, let alone listen?

In this exercise, you will add a slide containing contact information for the tournament. You will reuse a slide from an older presentation to save time.

P01.07

To Reuse Slides

a. Click **Slide 7**.

When new slides are added to a presentation, they are inserted after the selected slide. Since you want the contact information to be at the end of the presentation, you will select the final slide first.

b. On the Home tab, in the Slides group, click the **New Slide** arrow.

c. Click **Reuse Slides**. The Reuse Slides pane opens on the right side of the window.

d. Click **Browse**, and then click **Browse File**. Navigate through the folder structure to the location of your student data files, and then double-click **p01ch01ContactInfo**.

Slide thumbnails from the selected presentation are displayed in the Reuse Slides pane. The title of each slide is listed beside the thumbnail.

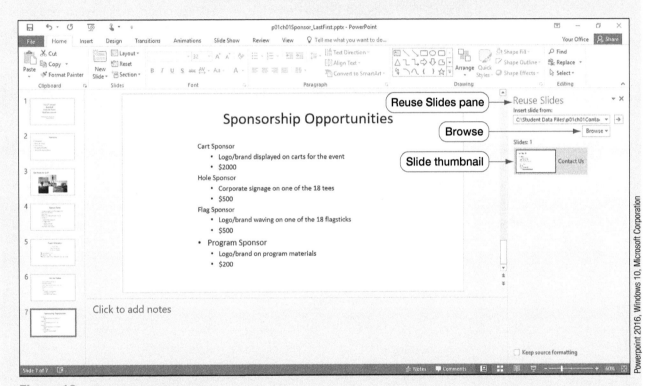

Figure 13 Reuse Slides Pane

e. In the Reuse Slides pane, click the **Contact Us** thumbnail.

The slide is inserted into the current presentation as Slide 8.

f. On the Reuse Slides pane, click **close** ☒. **Save** 🖫 the presentation.

Changing the Slide Layout

Changing the layout of a slide can improve its readability. Similar information should be grouped together. For example, on the Contact Us slide, two sets of contact information are displayed, but by changing the layout, the audience members can better understand which person to contact for their specific needs. The **slide layouts** are provided as part of the theme applied to the presentation.

You can change the layout of the slide either before or after you add information. Placeholders indicate the types of information you can place on the slide. Content slides have placeholders not only for text, but also for graphic elements such as pictures, tables, charts, and media clips. The size of a placeholder can be adjusted by dragging the **sizing handles**. Sizing handles are small boxes or circles in the center and corners of the border surrounding an object that can be used to resize the object.

In this exercise, you will change the layout of the Contact Us slide to one that will improve the readability of the information.

To Change the Slide Layout

a. With Slide 8 selected, on the Home tab, in the Slides group, click **Layout**, and then select **Two Content**. This layout gives you two columns, but all the information is in the first column.

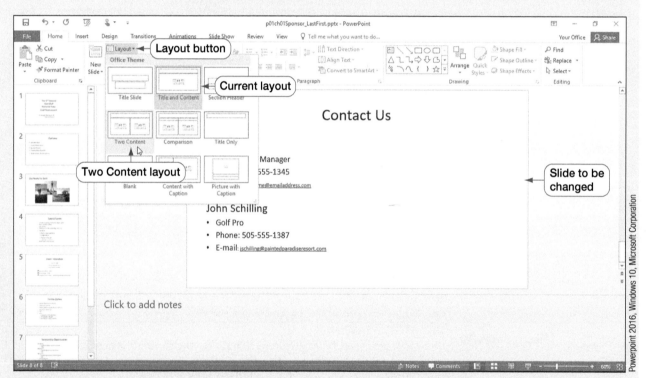

Figure 14   Selecting a slide layout

b. Select **John Schilling's** information, and then drag it to the text box in the right column.

c. Select the **bulleted text** under John's name, and then, in the Font group, decrease the font size to **24**.

d. After the bullet text **E-mail:**, select **John's e-mail address**, and then, in the Font group, decrease the font size to **16**.

e. In the left content placeholder, replace the text **Your Name** using your first and last name, and change the **e-mail address** to your e-mail address.

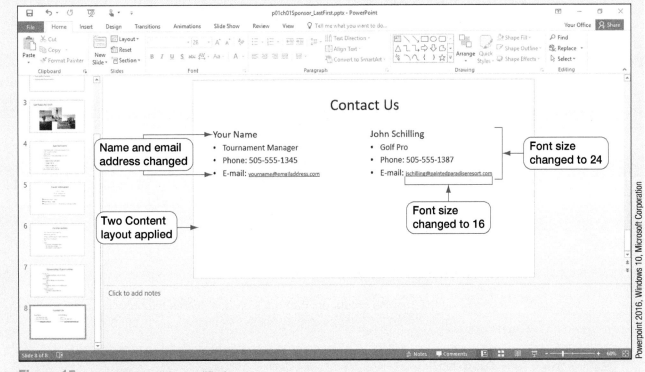

Figure 15 Contact Us slide modified

  f. **Save** the presentation.

Rearranging Slides

Even after the best planning, you may realize that the organization of the presentation would benefit from moving some slides. In PowerPoint there are two ways to do this. You can use the left pane, or you can use Slide Sorter view to drag slides to new positions.

In this exercise, you will improve the flow of the Putts for Paws presentation by moving the Special Events slide into position after the Event Information slide.

P01.09

To Rearrange Slides

  a. Click **Slide 4** on the left pane, and then drag **Slide 4** downward between Slide 5 and Slide 6. The Event Information slide will move up to the Slide 4 position. Release the mouse button.

    You should now have the title slide, Overview, Get Ready for Golf, Event Information, Special Events, For the Golfers, Sponsorship Opportunities, and Contact Us slides shown in this order in the left pane.

  b. **Save** the presentation.

Understand the Purpose and Benefits of Using Themes

PowerPoint enables you to concentrate on the message you are trying to convey to the audience and build the presentation around that message. **Design themes** add visual interest to the message. Background, color, and font selections are included as part of the design themes and can easily be applied to a slide show. In some cases, you may want to build your own theme. Many businesses have a standard corporate theme that makes their presentations recognizable and professional. Themes can be used in the various Microsoft applications, so a theme can be applied to a Word document or Excel workbook that matches the theme of a presentation. Themes can be applied at any time during the development of the presentation, but they will override other formatting changes, so it is best to apply them at the beginning.

Themes should be considered starting places for the design of the presentation. Various aspects of a theme will often need to be changed. Colors, font selections, theme effects, and more can be modified to fit your particular needs. As you apply design themes to a presentation, you should consider the purpose, audience, and message.

Applying a Design Theme

Design themes are available on the Design tab in PowerPoint. In this exercise, you will briefly look at the design themes that are available and select an appropriate theme for the Red Bluff Golf Course. It will provide consistency and add to the visual appeal of the presentation.

P01.10

To Apply a Design Theme

a. Click the **Design** tab.

b. In the Themes group, point to the individual theme thumbnails, pausing momentarily to let Live Preview display the theme on the slide in the Slide pane.

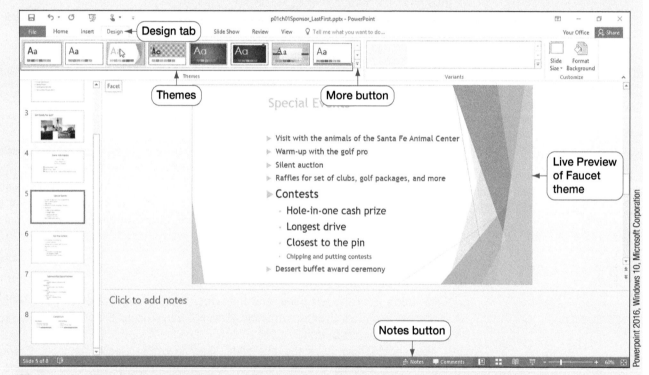

Figure 16   Using design themes

c. In the Themes group, click More ⤓, and then preview additional themes.

d. Select the **Wisp** theme.
    The theme is applied to all slides in the presentation, and on the Design tab, the Variants group populates with available variations. Do not change the variant default.

e. On the status bar, click **Notes** to toggle off the Notes pane and provide more space for the slide. Click through each of the **slides** in the left pane to review the changes made by applying the theme.

f. **Save** ⊟ the presentation.

Modifying Theme Fonts

In selecting fonts to use throughout a presentation, consistency is crucial. Changing fonts throughout can distract the audience, and a wrong font choice, such as Comic Sans, can ruin your credibility. It is acceptable to have multiple fonts throughout the presentation as long as they are used consistently. For example, use one font for all of your slide titles, one for any headings used throughout, and perhaps another for the main body text.

In this exercise, you will modify the heading and body fonts in the applied Wisp theme to match the font standards for all documents produced by the Red Bluff Golf Course & Pro Shop. You will also modify some text added earlier to ensure consistency.

To Modify Theme Fonts

a. Click **Slide 1** in the left pane, if necessary, to display it in the Slide pane.

b. Click the **View** tab, and in the Master Views group, click **Slide Master**. A Slide Master tab appears on the ribbon. Scroll up in the left pane so the first slide — the Master Slide — appears, but keep the Title Slide Layout selected.

c. In the Background group, click the **Fonts** button, and then point to a few **fonts** on the list to view the preview of the title slide. As you view each font group, notice the change to the fonts on the title slide.

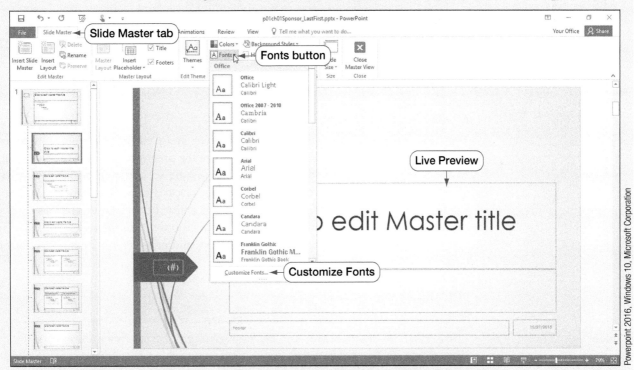

Figure 17 Modifying theme fonts

SIDE NOTE

Searching for Fonts
Rather than scrolling through a long list of fonts, if you already know which font you want to select, try typing the name in the box.

d. Click **Customize Fonts** at the bottom of the Fonts gallery.

e. Click the **Heading font** arrow, and then scroll to and click **Times New Roman**.

f. Click the **Body font** arrow, and then scroll to and click **Calibri**.

g. Select the **text** in the Name box, and then type Red Bluff LastFirst using your last and first name.

Powerpoint 2016, Windows 10, Microsoft Corporation

Figure 18 Creating new theme fonts

h. Click **Save**, and then, in the Close group, click **Close Master View**.

i. Click **Slide 7**, and then select the text **Program Sponsor**. On the Home tab, then in the Font group, in the Font Size box, type 19, and then press Enter. In the Paragraph group, click Bullets :≡ ▾ to deselect it. The bullet has been removed.

j. Click **Slide 5**, and then select the fifth bullet text **Contests**. On the Home tab, in the Font group, in the Font Size box, type 22, and then press Enter. In the Font group, click **Font Color** arrow A ▾, and then select **Black, Text 1, Lighter 25%**.

k. On Slide 5, select the three lines of text beginning with **Hole-in-one** and ending with **Closest to the pin**. On the Home tab, in the Font group, in the Font Size box, type 18, and then press Enter. In the Font group, click **Font Color** to apply the same color previously selected: **Black, Text 1, Lighter 25%**.

l. **Save** 🖫 the presentation.

Modifying Theme Colors

There are many aspects to consider in using color in a presentation. Color can be used to emphasize important elements and to organize the message. Colors are also associated with emotions or qualities, different colors suggesting various things in different parts of the world. For instance, in American culture, black is associated with death, but in Chinese culture, the color associated with death is white. Business presentations are often clean and crisp, while presentations to children are often colorful and whimsical. You should carefully consider the audience, objectives, and message in making selections for color in the presentation.

REAL WORLD ADVICE **Color Associations**

When using color in presentations, consider the psychology of common color associations. In mainstream American culture, people may associate feelings of danger or excitement with red colors. Blue can invoke calm and tranquility, and yellow can invoke cheer or optimism.

As you select the colors for the presentation, it is best to choose the background color first and then place high-contrast colors on top of it. Be careful that the colors do not clash. For instance, a combination of a medium blue background and red text almost vibrates because the colors clash. Select a maximum of four colors to use in a presentation, and keep the colors consistent throughout the presentation. Use the brightest colors as accents in areas needing the most attention. Focus on design, not decoration.

In this exercise, you will change the color of the title and subtitle text to coordinate with the color scheme of the theme.

To Modify Theme Colors

a. Click **Slide 1** on the left pane. Select the title text **The 5th Annual Red Bluff Putts for Paws Golf Tournament**.

You will change the color of the font only on this one slide, so you select just the text you want to change.

b. On the Home tab, in the Font group, click the **Font Color** arrow ⬛ ▾, and then click **More Colors** in the gallery.

c   In the Colors dialog box, if necessary, click the **Custom** tab, and then modify the color numbers at the bottom of the dialog box as follows:

- Red: 190
- Green: 30
- Blue: 45

The color created is a color that matches the Painted Paradise Resort & Spa logo.

d. Click **OK**, and then click outside of the text placeholder. The color of the title text has changed to red.

e. Select the subtitle text, **To benefit the Santa Fe Animal Center**, click the **Font Color** arrow ⬛ ▾, and then click **Red** in the Recent Colors section of the gallery.

f. **Save** 🖫 the presentation.

SIDE NOTE

Custom Colors

For precise image-matching colors, the eyedropper tool under Font Color can sample the image for the color. Image-editing software can also provide RGB number values.

Inserting Slide Footers

Slide footers can be created to further customize a presentation. Slide footers are displayed at the bottom of the slide and can include the slide number, date, company name, and other information. The slide number can also be displayed in the footer section of each slide. This will allow the audience to more easily refer to specific slide numbers if they have questions about content.

The footer in this presentation needs to have slide numbers and the tournament name, Putts for Paws Golf Tournament. In this exercise, you will modify the presentation by placing footers on all slides except the title slide.

To Insert Slide Footers

a. Click the **Insert** tab, and then, in the Text group, click **Header & Footer**.

The Header and Footer dialog box opens. There are two tabs in this dialog box: Slide and Notes and Handouts. You will focus on the Slide tab.

b. In the Include on slide section, click the **Slide number** check box, and then click the **Footer** check box. In the Footer box, type Putts for Paws Golf Tournament. This footer text will appear in the bottom left portion of the slide.

c. Click the **Don't show on title slide** check box.

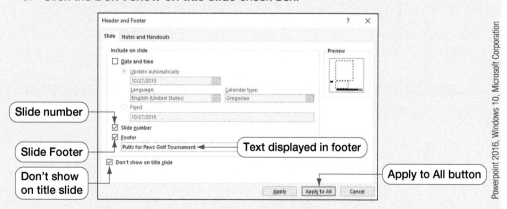

Figure 19 Applying slide footers

d. Click **Apply to All** at the bottom of the dialog box. The footer is applied to all but the title slide. The title slide will contain the name of the golf club, and a footer would detract from the overall design of the title slide.

e. **Save** 🖫 the presentation.

While design themes often include their own slide background colors, patterns, or images, other images can be applied to the background of a slide to give the presentation a more customized look and feel. It is important to remember, when selecting an image, that the text on top of the background must still be easy to read.

Modifying the Slide Background

In this exercise, you will modify the background of several slides by applying an appropriate picture to the background.

 P01.14

To Modify a Slide Background

a. Click **Slide 2**, hold down the Shift key, and then click **Slide 8** to select all but the first slide.

b. Click the **Design** tab, and then, in the Customize group, click **Format Background**. The Format Background pane will open on the right.

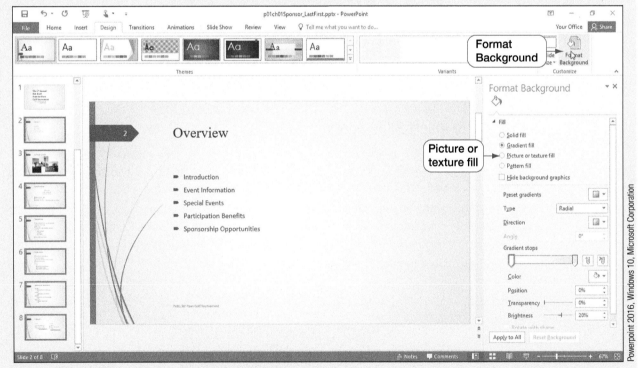

Figure 20 Applying a picture background to slides

c. Click **Picture or texture fill** in the Format Background pane, and then, under Insert picture from, click the **File...** button. Navigate through the folder structure to the location of your student data files, and then double-click **p01ch01RedBluffBG.**

    The image adjusts to fill the background of the selected slides, but because it is a narrow image, it was stretched across the screen. Offsetting it from the right will keep the entire image on the left of the slide and will prevent the image from hindering the readability of the text.

d. Move the **Transparency** slider to **20%**, and set the **Offset right** box to **80%**. Ensure that the remaining offsets are set to **0%**.

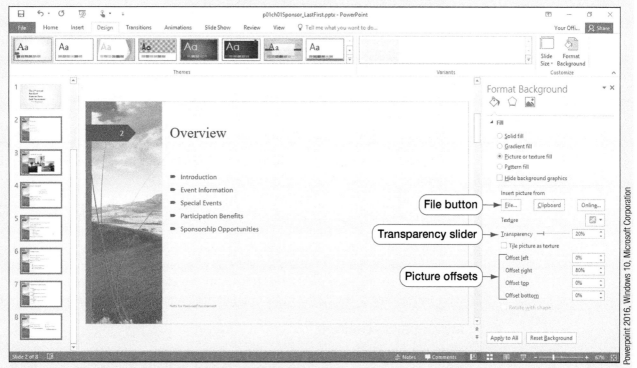

Figure 21   Background image settings applied

e. Click **Slide 1** so the slides are no longer selected together, and then **Close** ☒ the Format Background pane.

f. **Save** 🖫 the presentation.

Edit and Move Slide Content

Presentations can be quickly updated and modified, recycled, and personalized for the current audience. For instance, a sales presentation may have the basic information about the company's products, but for each customer visited, you may wish to update the slide show to include the customer name and date. You may also want to move the slides around so the most relevant products are at the beginning of the presentation.

Editing Slide Content

In this exercise, you will modify the Putts for Paws Golf Tournament presentation by updating some of the text to reflect this year's event.

To Edit Slide Content

a. On Slide 1, select the text **5**, and then type 6, indicating how many years the tournament has been running.

b. Click **Slide 4**. Select the **date**, and then type June 16, 2018.

c. **Save** ⊟ the presentation.

Various design principles apply to slides and serve as useful guidelines as adjustments are made to the presentation. Keep it short and simple. In most cases, the presentation will benefit from simplicity, which allows you to focus attention on the topic. The audience should be able to read and understand the slide in less than ten seconds. This means that the audience members can quickly read the displayed slide and turn their attention back to the presenter.

Aim to design slides with a path the eye can follow naturally. Keep in mind that people who read English are used to beginning at the top left of the page and reading to the lower right. While it may be interesting to place the titles of the slides in the bottom right corner, it may also be very confusing to the audience without some additional clues such as font size, emphasis, or color changes.

Strive to make some important element on each slide dominant while achieving a sense of balance with the remaining elements on the slide. The dominant element can be the title, a quotation, or a graphic. Look at the slides in the presentation, and think about the purpose of each slide. The dominant element should reflect the purpose of the slide.

White space, which is not always white, is space on the slide without text or graphics. It serves as a resting place for the eye. It helps to provide organization to the slides. White space can be used to divide the slides in interesting ways to keep the audience involved.

Moving Slide Content

Slide placeholders, the containers for text and graphic elements, can be moved and resized to improve the use of the white space on your slides. You can also manipulate the placeholders to suggest a relationship between items on the slide. Placeholder adjustments can help to move the eye around the slide.

In this exercise, you will insert the Red Bluff Golf Club & Pro Shop logo into the presentation and move it to an appropriate location on the slide.

To Move Slide Content

a. Click **Slide 8**, then click the **Insert** tab, and then, in the Images group, click **Pictures**. Navigate through the folder structure to the location of your student data files, and then double-click **p01ch01LogoRB**.

b. On the Picture Tools Format tab, in the Size group, click in the **Shape Width** ⊞ box and type 4.5, and then press Enter.

c. Drag the **picture** into the lower right corner of the slide. You can make small adjustments using the arrow keys if necessary.

Figure 22　Moving slide content

    d. **Save** the presentation.

Utilize Proofing and Research Tools

PowerPoint provides access to other tools that can help you as you prepare presentations. The **Smart Lookup** tool provides access to a variety of reference books, dictionaries, research websites, and business and financial sites. The **Thesaurus tool** is a research tool that enables you to select synonyms for words in the presentation. The **Spelling tool** is used to check the spelling of the presentation, offer suggestions for misspelled words, provide audible pronunciations of words, and suggest synonyms. These tools are accessible in the Insights group and Proofing group on the Review tab.

Using the Insights Pane

The Insights pane is powered by Bing, Microsoft's search engine, and can be used to define words and much more. This pane allows you to check facts and develop your ideas for the presentation. The Insights pane includes Wiki articles, and top related searches from the web for any topic.

    You can either access the Insights pane by selecting text in your presentation and on the Review tab, in the Insights group, click Smart Lookup, or by typing your query in the Tell Me box on the ribbon and then click Smart Lookup In this exercise, you will use the Insights pane to research some techniques to persuade the audience members to become sponsors.

> P01.17

To Use the Insights Pane

    a. On the ribbon, click inside the Tell Me box, and type persuade people to donate money. Click **Smart Lookup on "persuade** ....

        A large number of results are returned that relate to the search terms.

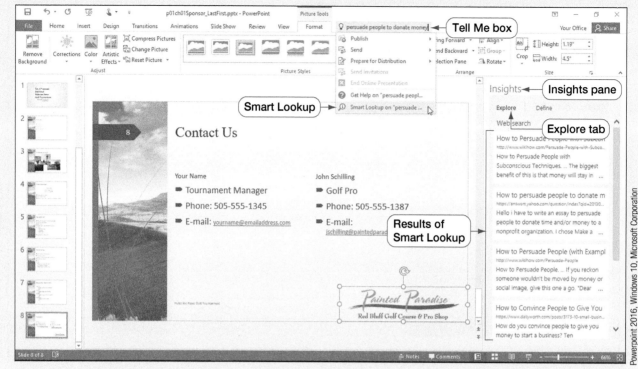

Figure 23 Using the Research pane

b. The Insights pane opens on the right with the Explore tab active. Click the **link** for one of the sites listed in the results. Review the information, and then close the browser window.

c. **Close** ☒ the Insights pane. **Save** ☐ the presentation.

Using the Thesaurus Pane

Slide 7 in the presentation uses the word "sponsor" four times. In this exercise, you will use the thesaurus tool to find other words that have a similar meaning.

To Use the Thesaurus Pane

a. Click **Slide 7** on the left pane, and select the word **Sponsor** in the Cart Sponsor heading. Click the **Review** tab, and in the **Proofing** group, click **Thesaurus**. The Thesaurus Pane opens to the right.

b. Point to **Champion** in the Thesaurus listing, click the **arrow** that appears to the right of the word "Champion," and then click **Insert**. The word **Champion** is applied to the biggest sponsorship opportunity.

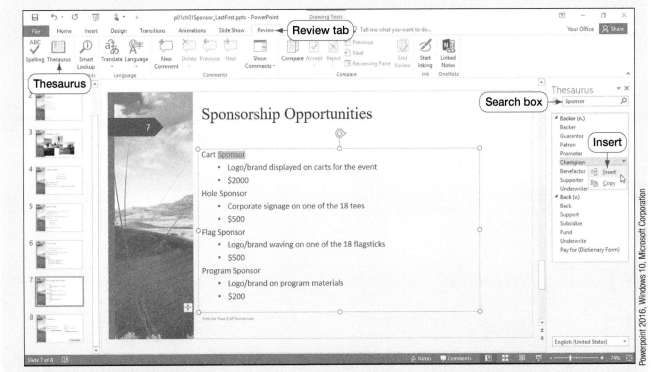

Figure 24 Using the Thesaurus Pane

c. **Close** ☒ the Thesaurus pane. **Save** 🖫 the presentation.

Using the Spelling Pane

An interactive spelling checker is built into PowerPoint that will automatically add a squiggly red line under any misspelled words. However, it flags some words that are actually spelled correctly, so make sure you know the correct spelling. When you are finishing a presentation, it is a good idea to use the spelling checker to check the entire document. In this exercise, you will use the spelling pane to ensure that there are no spelling mistakes in the presentation.

To Use the Spelling Pane

a. On the Review tab, in the Proofing group, click **Spelling**. The Spelling Pane opens to the right. The Spelling pane will take you to each word in the presentation that was flagged as being misspelled and will offer suggestions, if possible, for corrections.

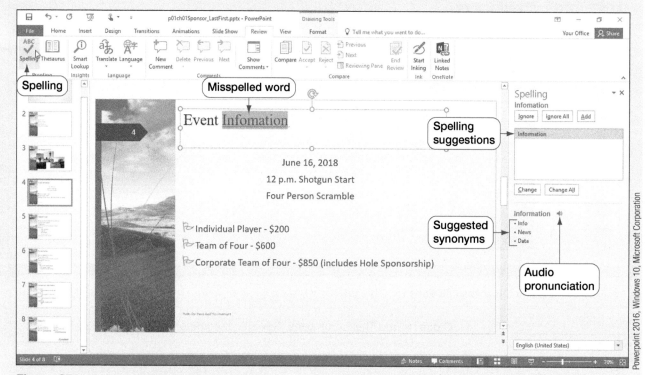

Figure 25   Using the Spelling Pane

b. The slide title for Slide 4 has a typographical error. In the Spelling Pane, click **Change** to correct the typo.

c. Once the spelling check has been completed, click **OK** in the spell check complete message box.

d. **Save** 🖫 the presentation. If you need to take a break before finishing this chapter, now is a good time.

Saving and Printing a Presentation

PowerPoint has many options for saving a presentation to fit different needs. The most common option for saving a presentation is the PowerPoint Presentation format. This format can be opened only with PowerPoint 2007 or later. Because not everyone has the most recent version of the software, some alternative options include saving the presentation so it is compatible with a previous PowerPoint version, saving it in an OpenDocument format, and saving it in a Portable Document Format (PDF).

Save a Presentation

Sometimes it is appropriate to save the file so it opens directly in Slide Show view. **PowerPoint Show** is convenient because you do not have to open the software and then click the Slide Show button. It looks more professional to start the presentation without fumbling with additional clicks. This method also works well if you want to keep other people from editing the slide content, because once all slides have been displayed, the application closes automatically.

Another option is to save the file for distribution on a website via **PDF** (Portable Document Format). When a file is saved as a PDF file, it does not open in PowerPoint but rather in a PDF reader application. This means that PowerPoint cannot be used to update a PDF file. It is important always to save the file in PowerPoint Presentation format too so that the latest version is available in an editable format.

Saving Your Presentation in Different Formats

In this exercise, you will save the Putts for Paws presentation as a PowerPoint Show and as a PDF. Each version will be named differently so you can observe the differences between them.

 P01.20

To Save Your Presentation in Different Formats

a. If you took a break, open the **p01ch01Sponsor** presentation.

b. Click the **File** tab, click **Save As**, and then double-click **This PC**. In the Save As dialog box, navigate to the location where you are saving your project files, and then change the file name to p01ch01SponsorShow_Lastfirst using your last and first name. In the Save as type box, select **PowerPoint Show**, and then click **Save**.

   The file is saved in PowerPoint Show format, and the Normal PowerPoint view is displayed.

c. Click the **File** tab, click **Save As**, and then double-click **This PC**. In the Save As dialog box, navigate to the location where you are saving your project files, and then change the file name to p01ch01SponsorPDF_Lastfirst using your last and first name. In the Save as type box, select **PDF**, and then click **Save**.

   The file is published in PDF format. Close the **PDF**, and return to PowerPoint.

d. Close your **PowerPoint Show**, but keep PowerPoint open. Open the folder where you store your PowerPoint projects. You should now see the several different files saved as a result of this exercise, and you can explore opening the various file types.

Preview and Print a Presentation

Many audiences will request a copy of the presentation for future reference. Many speakers make the PDF version available on a website as an eco-friendly option, but more important, it is a universal format that anyone can read with a free reader. Other speakers will make hard copies of the most important slides in the presentation to distribute after the presentation. For other audiences, handouts with thumbnail versions of the slides are appropriate. The presentation can also be printed in outline format so the audience has the text from the presentation but not the slide graphics, tables, or pictures. The presentation can also be printed by using the Notes Pages option, which prints the slides and the notes in the Notes pane so you can have a copy to use as speaker notes. The decision to print or not depends on the audience and the purpose of the presentation.

 CONSIDER THIS | **When Should You Pass Out Handouts?**

If you have handouts, should you pass them out before you begin the presentation or at the end? Describe a situation in which it would be good to hand them out before the presentation. Is there any reason why it may be distracting for the audience to have printed handouts during a presentation? List some reasons for waiting until the end of the presentation to distribute handouts.

Best practices for printing is to print as few sheets as possible to conserve resources. It is important to use the preview function of PowerPoint to review the potential printout before printing the slide show. Keep in mind that it is more economical to print in black and white than in color or gray scale, especially if you are planning to use a copier to make additional copies.

Printing Slides

Printing each slide individually is time consuming and not generally necessary. At times, one or two slides may contain information that is important. In this exercise, you will print Slides 4 through 8 from the presentation.

To Print Slides

a. Click the **File** tab, and then click **p01ch01Sponsor_LastFirst**, to open the recent presentation.

b. Click the **File** tab, and then click **Print**.

c. Select the **printer name** as directed by your instructor.

d. Click the **Print All Slides** arrow, and then select **Custom Range**.

e. Type 4-8 in the **Slides** box. Be sure to include the dash.

f. Click **Color**, and then click **Pure Black and White**.

g. If your instructor directs you to submit a printed copy, click **Print** after reviewing the Preview pane.

h. Click the **Back** button to return to the presentation in Normal view.

i. **Save** ⊟ the presentation.

Printing Handouts

As you print handouts for your audience, you have many style choices to make. You can print one to nine slides per page, sequencing them either horizontally or vertically. You can choose to frame the slides, scale them to fit the paper, and select high-quality printing.

In this exercise, you will print a copy of your entire presentation to use in a discussion you will have with the golf pro, John Schilling. He will give the presentation at various times during the next month and should review the slides. You will preview a few options before printing the final document.

To Print Handouts

a. Click the **File** tab, and then click **Print**. Click **Custom Range**, and then click **Print All Slides**.

b. Under **Settings**, click **Full Page Slides**, and then click **6 Slides Horizontal** in the Handouts section. The slides are displayed on a single sheet of paper, with Slide 2 next to Slide 1, and so on down the page.

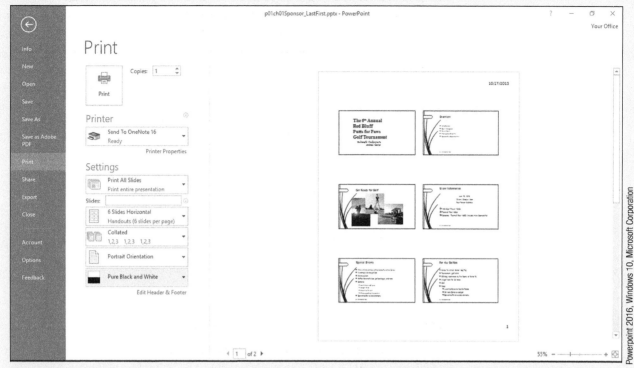

Figure 26 Printing handouts

c. If your instructor directs you to submit a copy of the document, click **Print**.

d. Click the **Back** button to return to Normal view.

e. **Save** ⊟ the presentation.

Printing an Outline

For some audiences, an outline of the presentation is sufficient. The outline displays the headings and body text on the slides but not the graphics. In this exercise, you will print an outline to use as a reminder sheet when you talk to potential sponsors and players.

To Print an Outline

a. Click the **File** tab, and then click **Print**.

b. Click the **Print Layout** arrow, and then click **Outline**.
  The content of the slides is displayed on two pages. You decide that you do not need to have the title slide information or the Contact Us slide, so you will set a range for the Slide numbers 2 to 7.

c. Type 2-7 in the Slides box, and then click the **Next Page** ▶ button, if necessary, to view the outline. Review the document preview.

d. Click **Print** if your instructor directs you to submit a copy of the document.

e. On the File tab, click **Close**, to close the presentation, but leave the PowerPoint application open for the next section.

A PowerPoint **template** is a file with predefined layouts, theme colors and fonts, and possibly sample content that enables the quick production of professional, consistent slide shows. Many people use templates to guide them in creating presentations. For example, templates are available for project status reports, training, quiz shows, and photo albums, to name a few. Templates can be selected as you begin a new PowerPoint presentation or can be applied to one that is already completed or in progress. Many businesses and organizations develop their own custom PowerPoint templates so that every presentation made on behalf of the company has a similar branding. PowerPoint templates can also be downloaded free from Office.com. You can also find free templates by completing an Internet search for "free PowerPoint templates."

Applying a Template to a Presentation

In this exercise, you will take a simple presentation that provides potential new members to the Red Bluff Golf Club & Pro Shop with an overview of what it has to offer and apply a new template that was recently developed by the resort's marketing department.

To Apply a Template to a Presentation

a. Click the **File** tab, and then click the **New** tab. On this tab, you can start a new presentation from blank slides with or without a theme or template applied. You can also search for and use an Office template.

b. Click **Open,** and then double-click **This PC**. Navigate through the folder structure to the location of your student data files, and then double-click **p01ch01GolfCourse**.
   A presentation opens containing ten slides about the Red Bluff Golf Course & Pro Shop.

c. Click each of the **slides** in the left pane, and pay attention to the lack of personalization and branding.

d. Click the **Design** tab, and in the Themes group, click **More** [⌄], and then click **Browse for Themes**. The Choose Theme or Themed Document dialog box opens.

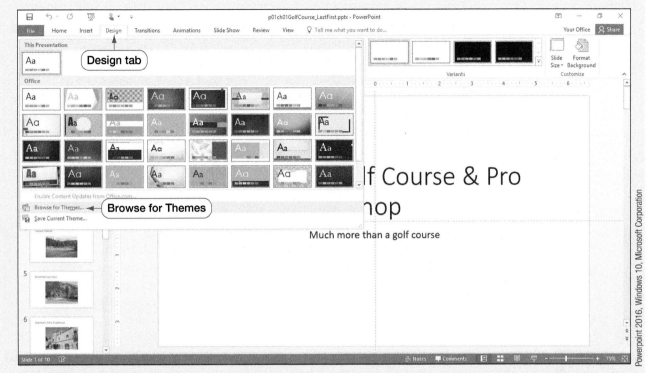

Figure 27 Browse for themes

e. Navigate through the folder structure to the location of your student data files, and then double-click **p01ch01RedBluff**.

The Red Bluff template is now applied to the existing slide show.

f. Click the **File** tab, click **Save As**, and then double-click **This PC**. In the Save As dialog box, navigate to the location where you are saving your project files, and then change the file name to p01ch01GolfCourse_LastFirst using your last and first name. Click **Save**.

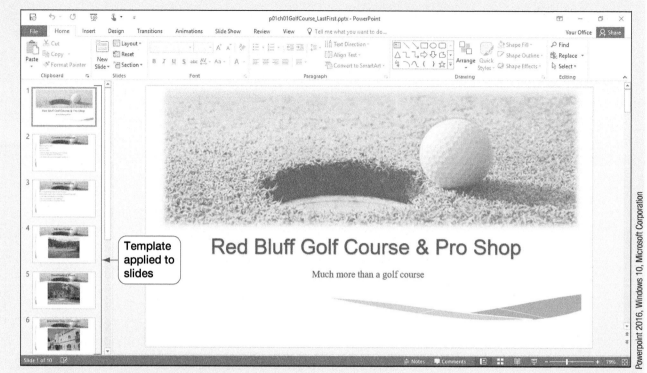

Figure 28　Red Bluff template applied

g. Click each of the **slides** in the left pane, and make note of the changes.

h. **Save** 🖫 , exit PowerPoint, and then submit your files as directed by your instructor.

Concept Check

1. What is the difference between the following presentation purposes: inform, persuade, prepare, and tell a story? p. 765–766

2. What questions might you ask to help you define the purpose and scope of your presentation? p. 766

3. How can storyboards be used to help plan a presentation? p. 770

4. List three presentation views in PowerPoint. p. 772, 775

5. Explain when it is appropriate to use Outline View. p. 780

6. Describe a situation when changing a slide layout improves its readability. p. 786

7. What are some benefits of using applying Design Themes to a presentation? p. 787–788

8. What is white space and what role does it play when deciding how to edit and move content on a slide? p. 794

9. For what reason would you use the Insights Pane? p. 795

10. Explain when you would save a slide show as a PowerPoint Show versus a PDF. p. 798–799

11. List three options for printing a presentation. p. 799–801

12. Describe one benefit of creating a presenation from a template. p. 802

Key Terms

Design theme   787
Left pane   773
Normal view   772
Notes pane   773
Outline View   772
PDF   799
Pecha Kucha   768
PowerPoint Show   798

Reading view   775
Sizing handles   786
Slide footer   791
Slide layout   786
Slide pane   773
Slide placeholder   794
Slide Show view   775
Slide Sorter view   775

Smart Lookup 795
Spelling tool   795
Storyboard   770
Target audience   765
Template   802
Thesaurus tool   795
White space   794

Visual Summary

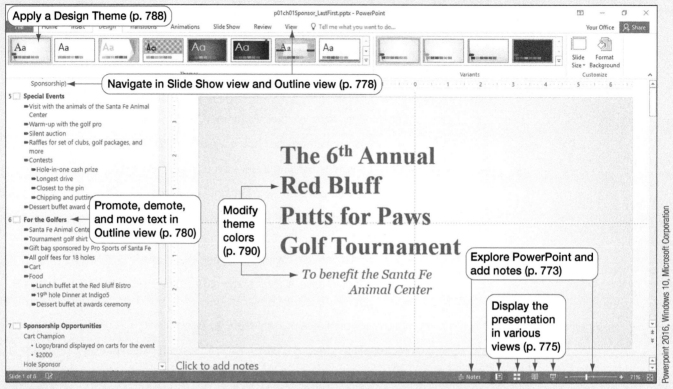

Apply a Design Theme (p. 788)

p01ch01Sponsor_LastFirst.pptx - PowerPoint

Navigate in Slide Show view and Outline view (p. 778)

Promote, demote, and move text in Outline view (p. 780)

Modify theme colors (p. 790)

Explore PowerPoint and add notes (p. 773)

Display the presentation in various views (p. 775)

Powerpoint 2016, Windows 10, Microsoft Corporation

Figure 29

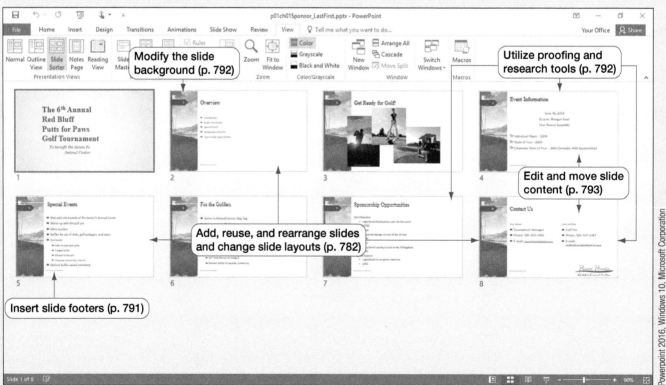

Modify the slide background (p. 792)

Utilize proofing and research tools (p. 792)

Edit and move slide content (p. 793)

Add, reuse, and rearrange slides and change slide layouts (p. 782)

Insert slide footers (p. 791)

Powerpoint 2016, Windows 10, Microsoft Corporation

Figure 30

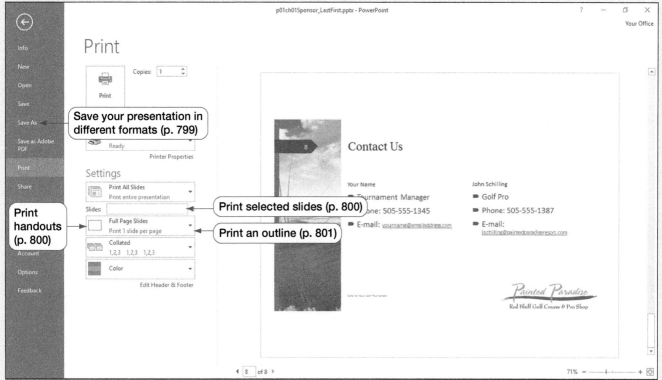

Figure 31

Powerpoint 2016, Windows 10, Microsoft Corporation

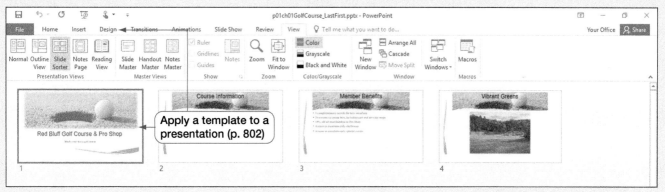

Figure 32

Powerpoint 2016, Windows 10, Microsoft Corporation

Practice 1

Student data files needed:

 p01ch01Products.pptx

p01ch01LogoPT.jpg

You will save your files as:

p01ch01Products_LastFirst.pptx

p01ch01ProductsPDF_LastFirst.pdf

Gift Shop Product Line Presentation

Sales & Marketing

The Painted Treasures gift shop manager requested your assistance in improving a presentation that she will make to the staff to introduce them to some new products for the shop. You will modify and reorganize the slides, apply a theme to the presentation, make minor modifications to the theme, and proofread the slides. You will print handouts of the slides to distribute to the staff for taking notes during the presentation, and you will save the file in PDF format so it can be posted on the resort's training website.

a. Start PowerPoint, click **Open Other Presentations**, and then double-click **This PC**. Navigate to the location of your student files, and then double-click **p01ch01Products**. Click the **File** tab, click **Save As**, double-click **This PC**, and then navigate to where you are saving your files. Change the **File name** to p01ch01Products_LastFirst using your last and first name, and then click **Save**.

b. In the left pane, click **Slide 1**. Click the **Design** tab, and in the Themes group, click the **Ion Boardroom** theme, and then, in the Variants group, click the **orange/brown Variant**—the fourth variant.

c. You decide to change the fonts. Click the **View** tab, and in the Master Views group, click **Slide Master**. In the Background group, click **Fonts**, and then click **Office**.

d. In the Background group, click **Colors**, and then click **Customize Colors**. Click the **Text/Background - Dark 2** arrow, and then select **More Colors**. Click the **Custom** tab, and then type 241 in the Red box, 90 in the Green box, and 41 in the Blue box. Click **OK**.

e. Click the **Accent 5** arrow, and then select **More Colors**. On the Custom tab, type 40 in the Red box, 83 in the Green box, and 160 in the Blue box. Click **OK**, and then click **Save**. Click **Close Master View**.

f. Click **Slide 1**, click the **Insert** tab, and in the Images group, click **Pictures**. Browse to your data files, select **p01ch01LogoPT**, and then click **Insert**.

g. Right-click the **image**, and then click **Size and Position**. In the Format Picture pane, click the **Position** arrow, and type 1.5" in the Vertical position box. Close the Format Picture pane.

h. Click the **Format** tab, and in the Picture Styles group, click **Drop Shadow Rectangle**, the fourth from left.

i. Right-click the image again, and then click **Copy**. Click the **View** tab, and in the Master Views group, click **Slide Master**. Scroll up to the **Ion Boardroom Slide Master slide**, right-click, and then click **Paste, Use Destination Theme**.

j. Right-click the **image** again, and then click **Size and Position**. Click the **Size** arrow, and then type 2 in the Width box. Click the **Position** arrow. Type 0.1" in the Horizontal position box, and then type 0.1" in the Vertical position box.

k. Close the Format Picture pane, and return to **Normal** view. With Slide 1 selected, click the **Design** tab, and in the Customize group, click **Format Background**. Check **Hide background graphics**. Select the **image** on Slide 1, and set it to **Align Center**.

l. Insert the following text in the Slide footer: Copyright 2018, Painted Paradise Resort & Spa for all slides except the Title Slide.

m. Click the **Home** tab, and in the Slides group, click the **New Slide** arrow, and then click **Title and Content**. In the title placeholder of the new slide, type Our Goals. In the body placeholder, type the following.

- Introduce our new product lines
- Increase sales by 18%
- Have fun!

n. Select the **text** you just typed, and change the font size to **24**.

o. On Slide 1, select the **subtitle text**, and then click **Increase Font Size** to **24**.

p. Click **Slide 5**. Select the **second line of body text**, press and hold Ctrl, and then select the **fourth** and **sixth lines**. In the Paragraph group, click **Increase List Level**. Select all of the **body text**, and then set the font size to **20**.

q. Click **Slide 4**, and select the **Content Placeholder**, displaying the text Comfort, Beauty, and Style. Move the **placeholder** down until the there is no background behind the text. It is acceptable if some of the placeholder overlaps the picture.

r. On Slide 4, click the **top sizing handle** of the Content Placeholder beginning with Cashmere Blankets, and drag it down until it aligns with the top of the picture on the left.

s. Click **Slide 6**. Select the **jewelry items**, including the **bulleted items** under each type of jewelry, and then set the font size to **20**. Drag the **top sizing handle** down until the placeholder aligns with the bottom of the title placeholder background.

t. Click **Slide 7**, change the font size of the body text placeholder to 24. Move the picture to the top right corner of the body text placeholder. Use the guides to help with exact placement.

u. Click **Slide 3**, and in the Slides group, click **Layout**, and then select **Two Content**. Select the text beginning with **Ask** and continuing through **Suggest additional items based on purchase**, and then drag the text to the placeholder on the right. In the Font group, click **Increase Font Size** once to change the font to size **20**.

v. Drag the **top sizing handle** of the left placeholder down to visually balance the text and so that the first bullet of the text box on the left aligns with the one on the right. Click **Increase Font Size** once to change the font to size **20**.

w. Drag **Slide 3** on the Slide pane to the end of the slide show. Click **Slide 4** on the Slide pane, and drag it to the Slide 3 position. Delete **Slide 7**, "Contact Us."

x. Click the **Slide Show** button in the status bar, and hold the left and right mouse buttons down at the same time for two seconds to begin at the first slide. Press [Enter] to advance through the slides.

y. Click the **File** tab, click **Save As**, and then double-click **This PC**. In the Save As dialog box, navigate to the location where you are saving your project files, and then change the **file name** to p01ch01ProductsPDF_LastFirst using your last and first name. In the Save as type box, select **PDF**, and then click **Save**.

z. On the File tab, click **Print**, click the **Full Page Slides** arrow, and then click **3 Slides** in the Handouts group. Click the **Color arrow**, and then click **Grayscale**. If your instructor directs you to submit a printed copy, click **Print**.

aa. **Save** the presentation, exit PowerPoint, and then submit your file(s) as directed by your instructor.

Problem Solve 1

MyITLab®
Grader
Homework

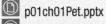
Student data files needed:

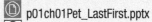
You will save your files as:

p01ch01Pet.pptx

p01ch01PetPic.jpg

p01ch01Pet_LastFirst.pptx

p01ch01PetPDF_LastFirst.pdf

Adopt a Pet Presentation

Sales &
Marketing

Joe works at the local Humane Society, and he has put together a presentation that he will use at community events to raise awareness about pet issues and to encourage people to adopt a shelter pet. You volunteer at the shelter, and your job will be to modify and reorganize the slides, apply a theme to the presentation, and make minor modifications to the theme. You will print handouts of the slides to distribute to people to take home after the presentation, and you will save the file in PDF format so it can be posted on the shelter's website.

a. Open the PowerPoint file, **p01ch01Pet.** Save your file as p0ch01Pet_LastFirst, using your last and first name.

b. Apply the **Facet** theme, and select the **fourth Variant** of the theme.

c. On **Slide 1**, format a background for the slide using the file **p01ch01PetPic.** Apply transparency at **85%.** Repeat this for **Slide 8.**

d. Insert a footer that reads Copyright 2018, County Humane Society. Have it appear on every slide but the title slide.

e. On **Slide 8**, center the title and the body text over the white space on the slide, and remove the bullets from the three lines of body text. For the three lines of body text, increase the font size to **24.** Change the color of the body text to **Black, Background 1.**

f. Move **Slide 3** between Slide 5 and Slide 6.

g. Format the picture on **Slide 3** with Picture Style **Drop Shadow Rectangle.** Repeat this for the three pictures on the other slides.

h. Change the layout of **Slide 3** to **Two Content.** Drag the top sizing handle of the right placeholder down so that it aligns with the top of the picture. Make sure the left edge of the placeholder does not overlap the picture.

i. Change the layout of **Slide 7** to **Two Content.** Select the text beginning with the third bullet point and extending to the end of the placeholder. Drag the selected text to the placeholder on the right. You may need to move the picture temporarily to do this.

j. Drag the bottom-sizing handle of the left placeholder up so it aligns with the top of the picture. Move the picture to **2.19"** horizontal position and **3.92"** vertical position.

k. Move the right placeholder to the right so it no longer overlaps the picture.

l. View the slide show from the beginning, and then save the presentation.

m. Save the presentation, and then save the presentation as p01ch01PetPDF_LastFirst.pdf.

n. Close the presentation and the PDF. Exit PowerPoint, and submit your files as directed by your instructor.

Critical Thinking

What is the main purpose of this presentation? To inform? To persuade?

Who is the target audience of this presentation? Could there be multiple audiences?

What are some ways in which you could improve this presentation to better engage the audience?

Perform 1: Perform in Your Career

Student data files needed:

Blank PowerPoint presentation

p01ch01Pesto.docx

You will save your file as:

p01ch01Pesto_LastFirst.pptx

Cooking Class Presentation

Information Technology

You are the executive chief of a large, upscale restaurant. The Women's Center, a nonprofit community organization, has invited you to run cooking classes during the annual herb sale, which is the Women's Center's primary fundraiser. You need to prepare a presentation to use during your cooking demonstration. Your audience will be educated men and women who love to garden but might have only rudimentary cooking skills. Your presentation needs to include recipes as well as instructions and tips for a successful outcome.

a. Start **PowerPoint**, and create a new presentation using the Organic template. If the Organic template is unavailable, select a template of your choosing from the available options. You may use an Office.com template in place of a built-in template if you prefer. Click the **File** tab, click **Save As**, double-click **This PC**, and then navigate to where you are saving your files. Change the **File name** to p01ch01Pesto_LastFirst using your last and first name, and then click **Save**.

b. Navigate to the location of your student files, and then double-click **p01ch01Pesto** to open the Word document. You will use the contents of this document in the presentation.

c. In the presentation file, type Basil as the presentation title and type Pesto - Green Nectar as the subtitle.

d. Insert a new slide, using the Section Header Layout. Type Pesto in the title placeholder.

e. Insert a new slide, using the Title and Content Layout. Type Pesto Ingredients in the slide title placeholder. Copy the ingredient list for pesto from the Word document, and paste it into the PowerPoint slide in the content placeholder.

f. Insert a new slide, using the Title and Content Layout. Type Pesto Directions in the slide title placeholder. Copy the instructions for pesto from the Word document, and paste it into the PowerPoint slide in the content placeholder.

g. Format each sentence on the Pesto Directions slide as a separate bullet point. Make four of the lines into sub-bullets.

h. Add another section header slide, and title this section Bruschetta.

i. Add two Title and Content slides. Copy and paste the bruschetta ingredients in the first slide, and title it Bruschetta Ingredients. Copy and paste the bruschetta directions to the second slide, and title it Bruschetta Directions. Format each sentence in the directions as a separate bullet point.

j. If directed by your instructor, print your file as handouts with six slides to a page. Print only slides **2** through **7**.

k. Save the presentation, exit PowerPoint and Word, and submit your file as directed by your instructor.

Additional Chapter Cases are available at www.pearsonhighered.com/youroffice

Additional
Cases

Microsoft PowerPoint 2016

| Chapter 2 | TEXT AND GRAPHICS |

OBJECTIVES

Prepare Case

The Red Bluff Caddy School Presentation

The Red Bluff Golf Course & Pro Shop is sponsoring a caddy school. You will create the first-day presentation for training. The audience will be people 18 to 25 years old who are interested in learning about golf and who want to be caddies at the golf club. You will modify a presentation and add appropriate graphics before passing it along to John Schilling, the golf pro, for final approval.

Student data files needed for this chapter:

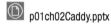 p01ch02Caddy.pptx

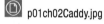 p01ch02Caddy.jpg

p01ch02GolfBall.jpg

p01ch02ProShop.jpg

p01ch02GolfGirl.jpg

p01ch02Green.jpg

p01ch02Pink.jpg

p01ch02Blue.jpg

p01ch02Bullet.png

You will save your file as:

 p01ch02Caddy_LastFirst.pptx

Using Text Effectively

The content of a presentation, especially the text, is a very important element of the slide show. As a presenter, one must ensure the accuracy of their words. People remember and believe more of what they see on the screen than what they hear. In this section, you will carefully review the content provided to you because making retractions or corrections after a presentation is difficult.

Modify Text

As one uses PowerPoint, they will make a lot of decisions. They will decide how to group content items. They will select fonts for the text elements. They will align the text and organize it on the slides. They will edit the content to improve the layout of slides.

After a discussion on font selections, you will begin to modify the Caddy School presentation to improve the readability of the slides. You will also align the text to better organize the information.

Understanding Print-Friendly and Screen-Friendly Fonts

Typography, the art of selecting and arranging text on a page, is an interesting topic for in-depth study. Understanding some basic concepts enables a person to produce slides that are easy to read. People read printed pages and screen pages differently, which affects the choices they makes for the fonts in a slide show.

Printer-friendly fonts have characteristics that make them easy to read on paper, as shown in Figure 1. They are usually printed in black ink on a white page giving them high contrast, which improves the readability of the text. Serif fonts are considered formal, businesslike, and powerful. Often, **serif fonts**, such as Times New Roman, are used for large blocks of text. The serifs, or small lines at the ends of the letters, provide guidelines for the eye to follow as the text is read. These fonts move the eye quickly across the page. Black-and-white printing is also less expensive than printing with color.

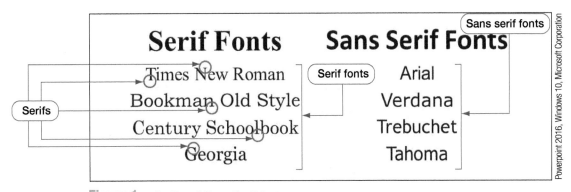

Figure 1   Serif and Sans Serif fonts

Screen-friendly fonts are easy to read on the screen, help to protect the eyes from strain, and reduce stress. Because of the resolution of the text on displayed slides, fonts on slides must maintain their integrity at great size. **Sans serif fonts**, such as Verdana and Trebuchet, were designed specifically for screens. "Sans" means "without" in Latin, and sans serif fonts do not have serifs at the ends of the letters. Sans serif fonts give the text a casual, modern feel. The serif font Georgia is also a good screen-friendly font. Often, in presentations, the title of slides is displayed in a serif font, while the content of the slide is set in a sans serif font. Screen-friendly fonts have an additional benefit: One can use color without additional expense. Be aware that colors must still be selected that have a good amount of contrast to make the text easy to read. One should avoid color combinations that are hard on the eyes, such as a red background with turquoise text. Select two or three colors to use consistently throughout a presentation. Remember that your goal is to have people be able to read the slides.

 CONSIDER THIS | **Selecting Color for Accessibility**

Did you know that about 8% of males and 0.5% of females are color-blind? How can you accommodate these individuals as you select colors and format important concepts and information? Are you limited to black and white?

Making Font Selections

Generally, in designing slides, a sans serif font is used for the majority of the text; a serif font may occasionally be used for emphasis. Text should be a mixture of uppercase and lowercase characters, even for headings. It is more difficult to read text that is written in all capitals. Hyphenated words should be avoided on slides when possible. Tracking between the parts of hyphenated words is difficult when the slide is projected. It is a good idea to use bold for emphasis. Italic text is hard to read, and underlined text may be confused with hyperlinks.

Font size is also important. The goal is for the slides to be read. Text that is too small frustrates the audience. The minimum font size you should use for the body text is 18 point. Of course, larger is better. Slide titles are set in a larger font than the body of the slide.

Providing an Appropriate Amount of Text on a Slide

As you create content for the slides, try to think like a headline writer, striving for the fewest words possible to convey the point. For instance, replace "Our goal is to increase sales by 55% in the coming year" with "Goal — Increase sales 55%." Use bullet points rather than complete sentences. Remove repetitive words, replacing them with a heading. Rather than placing a number-rich table on a slide, summarize the numbers. Focus the audience on the purpose by covering one major point or concept per slide.

A worthwhile best practice is the **rule of six**, also known as the 6 × 6 rule. This rule calls for a maximum of six lines per slide, not including the title, and six words per line. The rule helps to ensure that the slides are readable. You should not worry if you occasionally have more words on a line. This is a guideline. The goal is to put the absolute essence of the message on the slides. As a presenter, you want the audience to interact with you — not to spend all their time reading the screen. Remember that the slide show is a visual aid, meant to support a presentation.

Opening and Saving the File

In this exercise, you will open the file for the first-day training presentation and save it with a new name.

P02.00

To Open and Save the File

a. Start **PowerPoint**, click **Open Other Presentations** in the left pane, and then double-click **This PC**. Navigate through the folder structure to the location of your student data files, and then double-click **p01ch02Caddy**. A rough draft of the first-day caddy training presentation opens.

b. Click the **File** tab, click **Save As**, and then double-click **This PC**. In the **Save As** dialog box, navigate to the location where you are saving your project files, and then change the file name to p01ch02Caddy_LastFirst using your last and first name. Click **Save**.

Modifying Fonts in a Presentation

In this exercise, you will modify the fonts used in the Red Bluff Golf Course & Pro Shop Caddy School presentation to improve readability.

P02.01

To Modify Fonts in a Presentation

a. If necessary, click **Slide 1**, and then select the text **Red Bluff Golf Course & Pro Shop Caddy School**. On the Home tab, in the Font group, click the **Font** arrow, and then select **Calibri**. Notice that the words are in small caps.

SIDE NOTE

Pin the Ribbon
If your ribbon is collapsed, pin your ribbon open. Click the Home tab. In the lower right-hand corner of the ribbon, click Pin the Ribbon ⊞.

b. In the Font group, click the **Font Dialog Box Launcher** ⊡. In the Font dialog box, uncheck **Small Caps**, and then click **OK**.
   The words "Caddy School" appear on the same line as the rest of the title. Because these words are not related to the Red Bluff Golf Course & Pro Shop, it is best to separate them.

c. Click to position the insertion point before the word **Caddy**, and then press Enter.

d. Select the **title placeholder** — or border — so that you see a solid line instead of a dotted line. In the Font group, click the **Font Size** arrow, and then select **40**.

e. Click the **View** tab, and then, in the Show group, if necessary click **Ruler** to display the ruler. Drag the **left sizing handle** of the title placeholder to the 4" mark to the left of 0 on the horizontal ruler. The title text should fit in the placeholder.

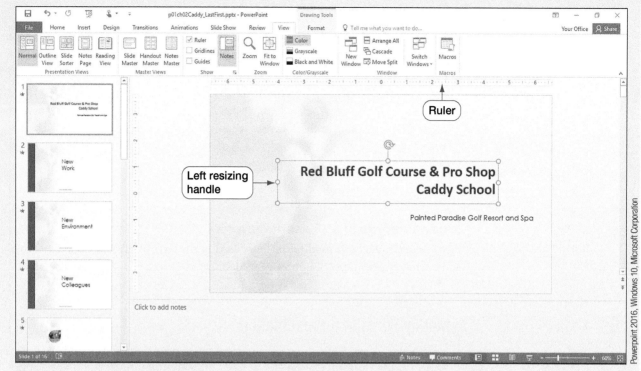

Figure 2 Title slide font modified

    f. **Save** the presentation.

Aligning Text

Proper text alignment provides organization to the text and enables the audience to read the material more easily. On the Home tab, the Paragraph group contains options to Align Left, Center, Align Right, and Justify text. Most of the body text that you type on slides should be left-aligned. In Western cultures, people begin reading at the left side of the page and are comfortable with this alignment. Center alignment is sometimes used in titles. It is difficult to read large amounts of text that is centered, so it is a good idea not to center the slide body text. Right alignment is used for emphasis or for artistic reasons and with limited amounts of text. Often, right alignment is used in placing captions next to photographs that are on the right side of the slide. Justified alignment produces a block with both the left and right margins aligned. Extra spaces are automatically added between the words to achieve the alignment of the margins. This works well for quotations that are longer than one line. In this exercise, you will change alignment in the presentation.

P02.02

To Align Text

  a. Click **Slide 14** from the thumbnails in the left pane.

  b. Click anywhere in the title text of **Case Study**. Click the **Home** tab, in the Paragraph group, click **Align Left** ☰. Alignment is applied to the entire line when you place the insertion point in the line.

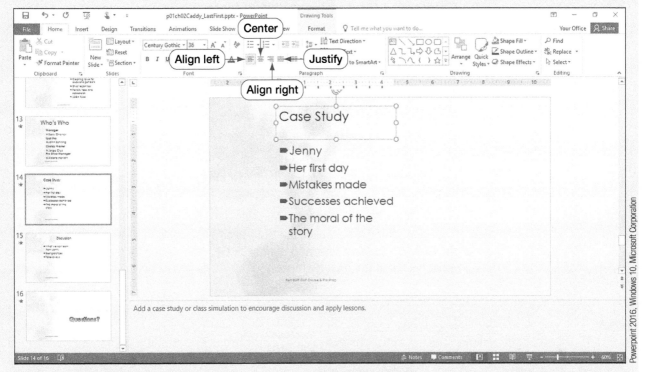

Figure 3 Aligning text

c. Click **Slide 15**. Select the **title placeholder**. On the Home tab, in the Paragraph group, click **Align Left** 🖻. The alignment is applied to the text within the placeholder.

d. **Save** 🖫 the presentation.

Use Text Hierarchy to Convey Organization

As you develop content for a presentation, you will quickly see that there are relationships between the pieces of information. You should group information together and perhaps provide a title so the audience sees the information in an organized way. This helps them to remember the key points of the presentation.

List hierarchy can be shown by using bullets or numbers. Bullets are used to group unordered items into a list. In PowerPoint, you can select different bullet symbols, using the Bullets arrow in the Paragraph group. You can even customize the bullet symbol by changing the color or size. Many people select custom bullet symbols from the Wingdings font because of the graphic nature of the symbols. Numbers are used for **ordered lists** — sequential steps that need to appear in a specific order. The format of numbers can be Roman numerals, Arabic numerals, or letters. The color and size of the numbers can also be adjusted. The starting number for the list can be changed when appropriate.

Applying and Customizing Bulleted Lists

List hierarchy includes indenting subitems on a slide. The first bulleted point may have three or four characteristics, which are indented and have a different bullet character. The Paragraph group contains the commands to increase and decrease the indention of the items. In this exercise, you will change list level and add a picture bullet to the list of employees helping with the caddy school.

To Create and Customize Bulleted Lists

a. Click **Slide 14** on the left hand pane, and select the text of the four bullets below the text "Jenny". On the Home tab, in the Paragraph group, click **Increase List Level** ▣.

b. Click **Slide 13**, and then click in the text **Barry Cheney**. On the Home tab, in the Paragraph group, click the **Bullets** arrow ▦▾.

c. Click **Bullets and Numbering**.

d. In the Bullets and Numbering dialog box, click **Picture**, and next to From a file, click **Browse**. Navigate through the folder structure to the location of your student data files, and then double-click **p01ch02Bullet**. The bullet has now been updated to a custom bullet point.

e. In the Paragraph group, click the **Bullets** arrow, click **Bullets and Numbering**, set the Size to 175 % of text, and then click **OK**. You will apply the new bullet to the other names in the next exercise.

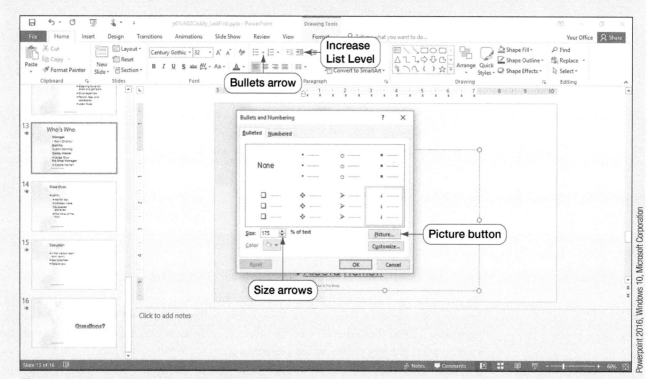

Figure 4   Bullets and Numbering dialog box

f. **Save** ▣ the presentation.

Reuse Formats

The **Format Painter** enables you to select formatting from an existing object or text and apply it to other objects or text within the presentation. This is done quickly by selecting the desired formatted item and then clicking Format Painter to apply the desired selected formatting to additional items — like copy and paste but with a paintbrush. To use Format Painter for multiple instances, such as applying the format to different slides, select the text that contains the desired format to copy, and double-click Format Painter. Once the formatting has been applied to all items, click Format Painter again to toggle it off.

Using the Format Painter

Previously, you created a custom bullet on Slide 13. In this exercise, you will use the Format Painter to apply the new bullet to the other names on the slide.

 P02.04

To Use the Format Painter

a. The second, third, and fourth bullets on Slide 13 need to be the same as the first bullet. If it has not already been selected, select the bullet text **Barry Cheney**.

b. On the Home tab, in the Clipboard group, double-click **Format Painter** . As you move the insertion pointer onto the slide, you will notice a paintbrush icon on the pointer to indicate that the Format Painter is active.

> **Troubleshooting**
>
> If the Format Painter button is clicked once, it will apply formatting to one item and then toggle off by default. When double-clicked, Format Painter will stay toggled after the first use until the button is clicked again to toggle it off, thus allowing multiple uses of the tool. If the feature does not stay toggled on, repeat the text selection for Barry Cheney, and make sure to double-click the button, or try double-clicking faster.

c. Drag the pointer across the text **John Schilling**. The custom bullet was applied. Repeat for **Jorge Cruz** and **Aleeta Herriott**.

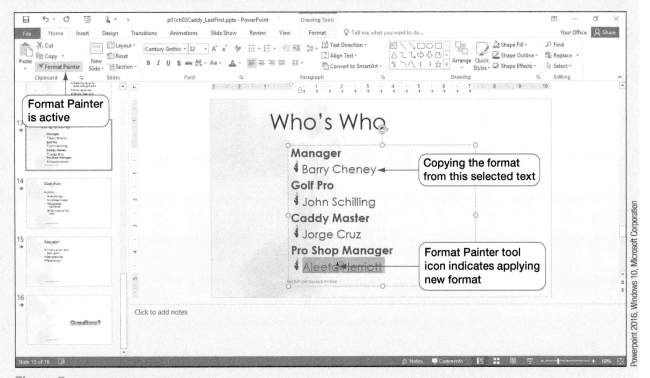

Figure 5 Format Painter

d. In the Clipboard group, click **Format Painter** to return to the normal pointer.

e. **Save** the presentation.

Use Special Symbols

Special **symbols** from various fonts are characters not available on a standard keyboard that can be inserted into text placeholders in PowerPoint. The Symbol button on the Insert tab enables you to add these special symbols to a presentation. A common inserted character is the copyright symbol. Other characters include the trademark symbol, currency signs for different countries, and accents and letters from various languages. For instance, the "e" with acute accent in the word "résumé" can be found in the Symbol dialog box.

Inserting Symbols

The Symbol dialog box displays the special characters available for the selected font. Symbols that have been used recently are displayed at the bottom of the dialog box and can be clicked to reuse the symbols in the current position of the mouse pointer. The character code is the unique number given to the symbol; if known, it can be typed into the box to search for a specific character.

In this exercise, you will update the title slide of the Caddy School presentation to include a new title, your name, and a copyright notification.

To Insert Symbols

a. Click **Slide 1**, and then click to place the insertion point before the text **Painted Paradise**. Press Enter.

b. On the newly inserted line, type Barry Cheney.

c. Position the insertion point before the text **Painted Paradise**. Click the **Insert** tab, and then, in the Symbols group, click **Symbol**.

d. If necessary, click the **Font** box arrow and select (**normal text**). Scroll until you see the © copyright symbol, and then click the © copyright symbol — or alternatively, in the Character code box, type 00A9, click **Insert**, and then click **Close**. The symbol is placed at the insertion point.

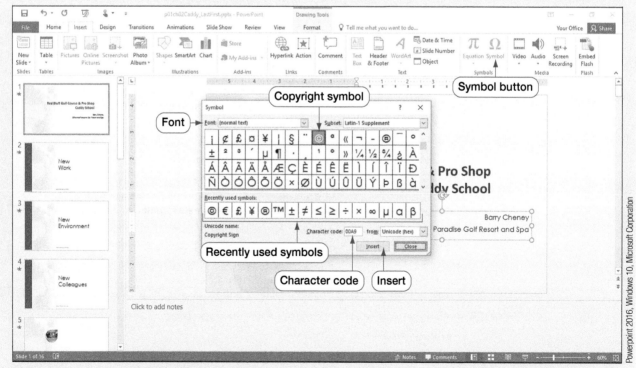

Figure 6   The Symbol dialog box

e. Type the current year, and then press the [Spacebar] to complete the copyright statement.

f. **Save** 🖫 the presentation. If you need to take a break before finishing this chapter, now is a good time.

Selecting and Using Appropriate Graphics

Graphics, in the form of photographs, charts, graphs, and SmartArt, can be valuable assets in presentations. Graphics convey information visually and can evoke a greater understanding of a concept. They also add interest to the presentation.

There are some basic ground rules to consider in selecting graphics. Foremost, the graphics must support the message; otherwise, they will distract and confuse the audience. The graphics should be clear and should be consistent with the design of the presentation and the audience's expectations. For instance, a business audience attending a presentation on policy changes would not appreciate the use of cartoon art, and complex charts and graphs would be incomprehensible to typical audiences.

S S CONSIDER THIS | Selecting Graphics

Graphics add more than just interest to your presentation; they add information, both explicit and implicit. What forms of explicit information can graphics take? What forms of implicit information? Your graphic selections can have unanticipated meanings. Can you recall a time when the presenter's graphic selections were inappropriate or distracting?

Graphics can come from a variety of sources. PowerPoint accesses Office.com to provide high-quality art and photographs. You can even find animated art that provides movement to the graphic. The Internet is a rich resource for graphics, but keep copyright laws in mind. A **copyright** is the right to copy and is often exclusive rights given to the creator of original work. A form of intellectual property, the copyright also gives the holder the right to be credited, to determine who may adapt the work, or in other ways to benefit from it. Of course, photographs that you have taken and other artwork that you have produced can be used in PowerPoint presentations. Keep in mind that large graphics and videos can load very slowly and may make it impossible to e-mail the presentation and otherwise difficult to share it with others.

There are two types of digital graphics: **bit-mapped graphics** and **vector graphics**. Bit-mapped images are stored as pixels, individual dots of color arranged in a grid to represent the image. Photographs are an example of bit-mapped images. Up-scaling bit-mapped images or resizing them larger than their stored size results in a pixilated image — the object edges lose definition and appear rough. Vector graphics are made of formulas that determine the shapes used in an image. They are often smaller in file size than bit-mapped graphics. Because of the formulas, vector graphics are not resolution dependent — not dependent on pixels — and so can be resized without becoming pixelated. For information about graphic file formats, see the quick reference box. In this section, you will insert and manipulate images to balance text and visual representation in your presentation.

Pixelation

Bit-mapped graphic   Vector graphic

Powerpoint 2016, Windows 10, Microsoft Corporation

Figure 7   Vector and Bit-Mapped graphics

QUICK REFERENCE	Graphic File Formats

Common graphic file types are:

- JPEG — **J**oint **P**hotographic **E**xperts **G**roup. Compressed file format for raster — pixmap — data. Commonly used for web-based photographs saved as 24-bit RGB data. The higher the compression, the more data is lost; JPEG is therefore a "lossy" type. Also known as JPG.

- GIF — **G**raphic **I**mage **F**ile format. Uses a color lookup table and supports up to 256 colors per image. For flat, solid colors, GIF is your best option. GIFs are extremely efficient and small in file size when applied to images with few colors, such as a logo. However, images with more than 256 colors will result in color loss' therefore, a JPEG format is the preferred choice when you exceed a 256-color limit.

- TIFF — **T**agged **I**mage **F**ile **F**ormat. Uncompressed, very large files typically used in photo software or page layout software when it is important to maintain resolution without any loss in quality. TIFF has the most flexibility in terms of grayscale and colors for print or web media, including content layers for transparency. Also known as TIF.

- PNG — **P**ortable **N**etwork **G**raphics. Substitute for GIFs and has more features than JPEG. Allows for multibit transparency, a full range of color (16 million colors), and better compression.

Work with Images and Art

In his 1797 book *Remarks on Rural Scenery*, John Thomas Smith explains an idea of Sir Joshua Reynolds about balancing light and dark in paintings. He refers to this revolutionary notion as a "**rule of thirds**," discussing proportions of two-thirds to one-third with particular reference to landscapes. For example, the proportions of a picture could be two-thirds of one element — say, water — to one-third of another — say, land. Further, this picture could be framed in a larger scene so that it occupies one-third, while the sky, for example, occupies the upper two-thirds. Finally, Smith concluded that this general proportion of two and one was "the most picturesque medium in all cases of breaking or otherwise qualifying straight lines and masses and groups."

Today, the rule of thirds is used in photography, graphic design, art, composition, and landscape design. Horizontal and vertical guides are overlaid on a scene, and then the scene is manipulated until it is in balance. Some cameras today place a digital grid overlay in view of the photographer so the scene can be optimized specifically with this rule in mind.

In the grid, two equidistant vertical lines slice the scene into thirds vertically, and two equidistant horizontal lines do the same horizontally. The idea is that the most interesting parts of the scene should fall along these lines or, preferably, at the intersections. The intersections are where the most visual impact or power is derived. In some industries, the intersections are called "**power points**."

Figure 8 Rule of thirds

PowerPoint does not tile this visual grid overlay in thirds automatically, but multiple visual guides can be added manually. This provides the creator of the presentation the ability to ensure that the artwork or the entire slide is in balance.

Adding Guides

The guides will not show in the presentation, but they are an overlay for use while designing a presentation. The idea is to put the most important things at the guide intersections, or the power points. Depending on the use of power points, they may provide more impact than a bulleted list. The **vertical guide** spans the top and bottom of the slide and is used to align objects horizontally, while the **horizontal guide** spans the left and right of the slide and is used to align objects vertically. In this exercise, you will add guides to your slides.

To Add Guides

a. If you took a break, open the **p01ch02Caddy** presentation.

b. On Slide 1, click the **View** tab, and then, in the Show group, click **Guides**. Make sure **Ruler** is also checked.

   The vertical and horizontal guides will be displayed at the zero mark on both the horizontal ruler above the slide and the vertical ruler to the left of the slide in the Slide pane.

c. Drag the **Vertical Guide** to the right until it reaches **2.25** to the right of **0** on the horizontal ruler.

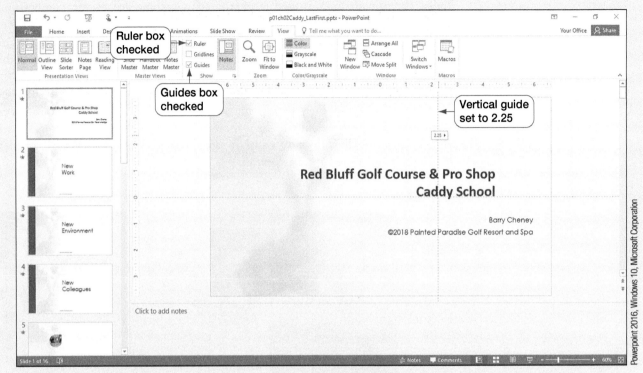

Figure 9 Positioning guides

d. Right-click the **guide** in an area free of text, and click **Add Vertical Guide** on the shortcut menu. Drag this guide to the left until it reaches **2.25** to the left of **0** on the horizontal ruler.

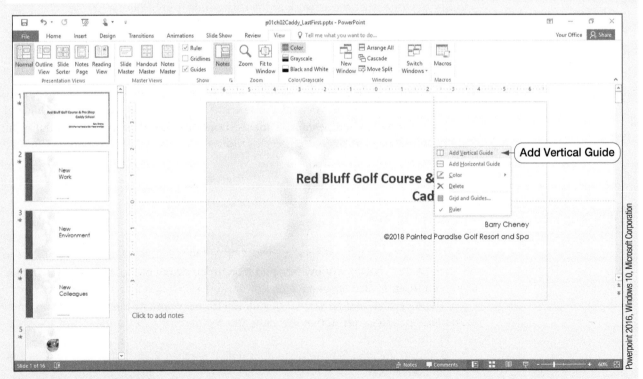

Figure 10 Adding guides

e. Drag the **Horizontal Guide** down until it reaches **1.25** below **0** on the vertical ruler. Because you want to divide the slide into thirds vertically, you need to draw only two equidistant horizontal guides.

f. Right-click the **guide** in an area free of text, and click **Add Horizontal Guide** on the shortcut menu. Drag this guide up until it reaches **1.25** above **0** on the vertical ruler.

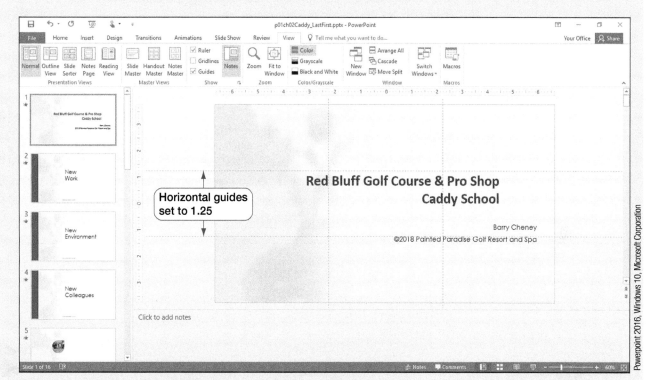

Figure 11   Guides set for Rule of Thirds and power point intersections

> ## Troubleshooting
> If you accidentally add more guides than you want or need, you can right-click a guide and then click **Delete**.

g. Scroll through a couple of slides to see how the guides reveal the balance — or lack thereof — in the layout of these slides.

h. **Save** 🖫 the presentation.

Inserting Graphics

By clicking the graphic icons shown on the **content placeholders** of PowerPoint slides, shortcuts are launched to elements such as pictures, tables, charts, SmartArt graphics, online pictures, or video. Commands on the Insert tab can offer similar options and can also be used to place graphics on the slides. In this exercise, you will insert a few different graphics into the presentation.

To Insert a Graphic

a. Click **Slide 12**. The content placeholder, with multimedia icons, is displayed on the left of the slide.

b. Click **Pictures** in the content placeholder. Navigate through the folder structure to the location of your student data files, and then double-click **p01ch02Caddy**. The photograph appears on the slide, replacing the placeholder. Notice that the image covers two of the guide intersections.

c. Click **Slide 6**. Because there is no content placeholder, to insert an image, click the **Insert** tab, and then, in the Images group, click **Pictures**. Navigate through the folder structure to the location of your student data files, and then double-click **p01ch02GolfGirl**.

    The image is inserted on the slide. You will size and crop it later.

d. Click **Slide 5**. Right-click the **photograph**.

    One of the advantages of using an existing presentation is that if the pictures are already formatted, you can change them and retain the effects. You will change the photograph on Slide 5 using the Change Picture option on the shortcut menu.

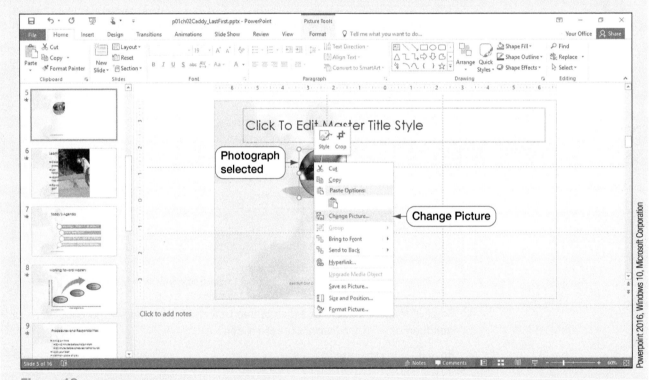

Figure 12   Change picture

e. Click **Change Picture**, then click **Browse**, navigate through the folder structure to the location of your student data files, and then double-click **p01ch02Green**. The photograph automatically adjusts, replacing the previous photograph.

f. Click **Slide 14**, click the **Insert** tab, and then, in the Images group, click **Pictures**. Navigate through the folder structure to the location of your student data files, and then double-click **p01ch02Pink**. The photograph appears on the slide. You will resize it later.

g. **Save** the presentation.

Resizing and Cropping Graphics

Graphics, such as photographs, are easily manipulated by using PowerPoint tools. An object can be resized, making it fit into a placeholder; unwanted portions from photographs can be cropped; and images can be flipped or rotated to improve the design of the slide.

Sizing handles, displayed around a selected graphic, enable it to be resized and moved around the slide. The corner sizing handles increase or decrease the size of the graphic when dragged, while retaining the proportions of the graphic. The side sizing handles increase or decrease the width or height of the graphic. Be careful not to distort the graphic when using the side handles. When you point to a handle to perform a sizing action, the pointer will change to a two-pointed arrow ⟷. Point anywhere else on the object, and a four-pointed arrow pointer ✥ indicates that you can drag the graphic to a new location on the slide.

In this exercise, you will improve the graphics by resizing and cropping them.

To Resize and Crop Graphics

a. Click **Slide 6**, and then click the **photo**.

b. Click the **Picture Tools Format** tab, and in the Size group, click the **Size Dialog Box Launcher** ⤢. If necessary, in the Format Picture pane, click the **Lock aspect ratio** check box to select it. Under Size, click inside the **Height** box, and change the height to 4". The width of the graphic will automatically change in proportion to the height of the object.

Notice that the size of the graphic in inches is displayed in the Size group on the Picture Tools Format tab. You can also use the Size group to resize the graphic.

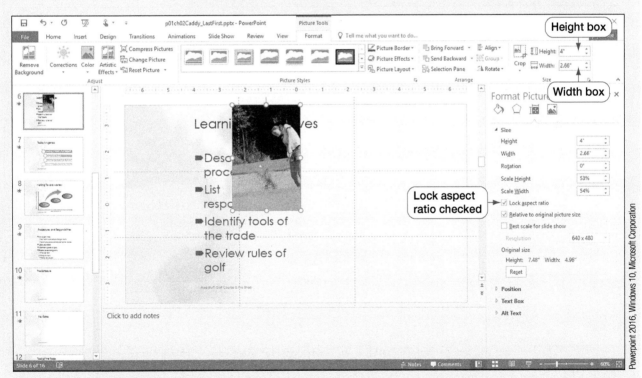

Figure 13   Resizing a graphic

> ## Troubleshooting
> If you make an error in sizing the photograph and want to return to the original size, click Reset in the Format Picture pane.

c. Drag the **image** to the right until the head of the model is near the power point at the intersection of the right vertical guide and the top horizontal guide.

You may notice special alignment guides showing up momentarily on the slide, near the image. The guides are red. In this case, they indicate the position of the image relative to the other elements on the slide.

d. In the Format Picture pane, click the **Position** arrow. Using this area of the Format Picture pane, you can modify the placement of a graphic with more precision.

e. Click inside the **Vertical position** box, and then set it to 2.1". Make sure the From box is set to Top Left Corner. Click **Close** ☒ to close the Format Picture pane. Notice that the image is now over two of the guide intersections.

f. Click **Slide 12**, and then click the **photograph**. You will crop some of the grass in the foreground of the photograph.

g. Click the **Picture Tools Format** tab, and in the Size group, click the **Crop** button. **Cropping handles** appear at the edges of the photograph to enable you to cut away portions of the graphic that you do not need.

The corner cropping handles crop the vertical and horizontal sides of the photograph at one time. The side cropping handles enable you to crop from one direction.

h. Drag the **bottom middle cropping handle** up until the handle is just below the feet of the caddy. The gray area below the cropping handle will be deleted from the image.

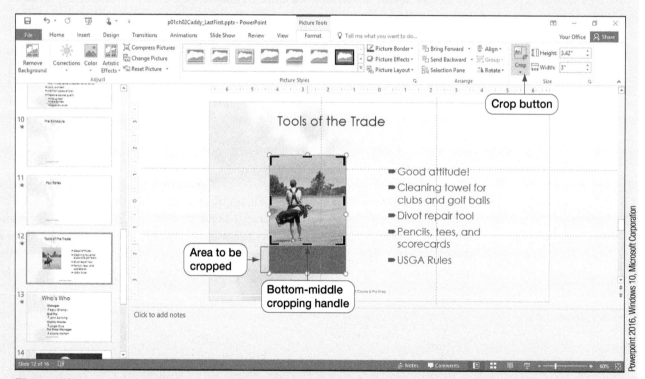

Figure 14 Cropping photos

i. On the Picture Tools Format tab, in the Size group, click the **Size Dialog Box Launcher** ⬚. In the Format Picture pane, click **Picture** 🖼, and then select **Crop**. Click inside the Crop position **Height** box, and, if necessary, change the position to 3.5". Notice that the Format Picture pane allows you to make more precise crops. In the Size group, click the **Crop** button again to confirm the change.

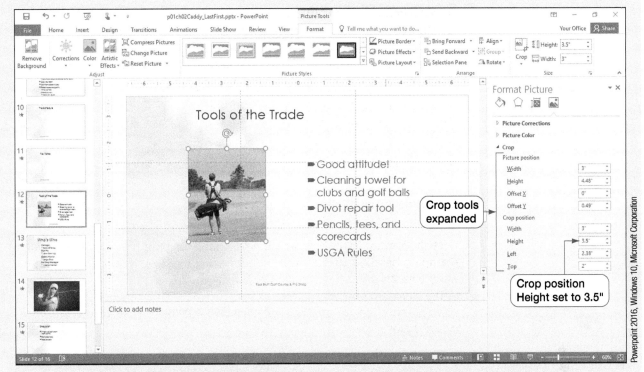

Figure 15 Cropping using the Format Picture pane

j. Click **Size & Properties** 🖼 at the top of the Format Picture pane. In the Size section, click inside the **Scale Width** box, and increase the scale of the picture to 120%, click **Close** ☒ to close the Format Picture pane, and then click anywhere on the slide outside of the photograph. Using the Scale options, you can modify the size of the image by percentages.

k. **Save** 🖫 the presentation.

Rotating and Flipping Graphics

Graphics can be rotated or flipped to improve the design of the slide. For example, photos with faces should face the audience or the center of the slide whenever possible. This reinforces the slide, providing a sense of agreement to the message of the slide. If you find the perfect graphic but the person faces the edge of the slide, the image can be flipped. Beware of words on images that may need to be flipped, such as on a sign in the background, because these will display backwards when flipped. In this exercise, you will rotate and flip a graphic.

REAL WORLD ADVICE	Utilize the New Designer Tool to Create Professional Looking Slides

Those with an Office 365 subscription have access to new features as they are made available. Designer is one of those new features. It allows anyone to create high quality professional slides with only a few clicks. Upload a picture to a slide and Designer will suggest a variety of design options from which to choose. Select the one you like most and you're done. This allows you to spend more time focusing on the content of your presentation and less time about how to design the slides.

To Rotate and Flip Graphics

a. Click **Slide 14**, right-click the **image**, and then click **Size and Position**.

b. In the Format Picture pane, click in the **Width** box, and then type 6" and press Enter.

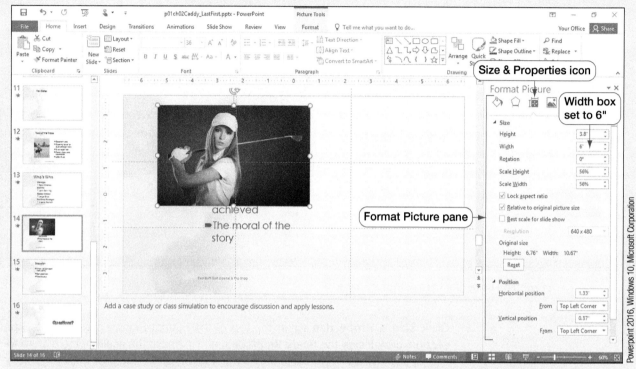

Figure 16 Format Picture pane

c. Click the **body text placeholder** so that its border is a solid line. In the Format Shape pane, if necessary, click **Position** to expand the category.

d. Click in the **Horizontal Position** box, and then type 6.6" and press Enter. This sets the placeholder body text 6.6" from the top left corner of the slide.

e. Select the **photograph**. Click the **Picture Tools Format** tab, and in the Arrange group, click **Rotate**, and then click **Flip Horizontal**. The golfer is now facing the direction of the content, which focuses the attention of the audience to the text.

f. Drag the **rotation handle** to the right to tilt the photograph so that the vertical posture of the model is in line with the left vertical guide. It is okay if the top left corner of the photograph is off the slide. Images arranged in unusual ways can add interest to the slide.

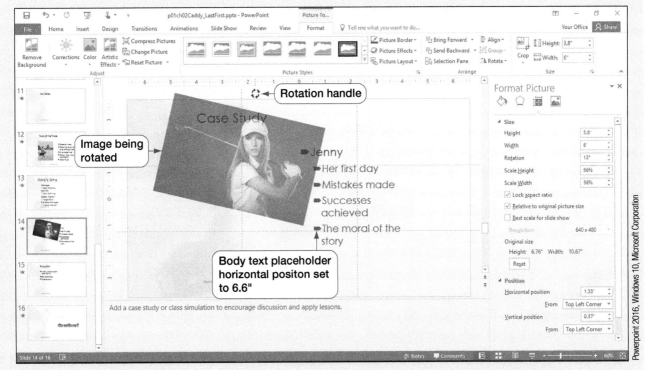

Figure 17 Rotating a graphic

g. In the Format Picture pane, click the **Horizontal position box**, type 0.7", and then press Enter. Click the **Vertical position box**, type 1.3", and then press Enter. The model's face is now behind the top left power point, and the upper right corner of the image covers the first bullet.

h. **Close** × the Format Picture pane.

i. Right-click the **photograph**, point to **Send to Back**, and then click **Send to Back**. This moves the photograph behind the placeholder text on the right, and you can now see the first bullet over the image.

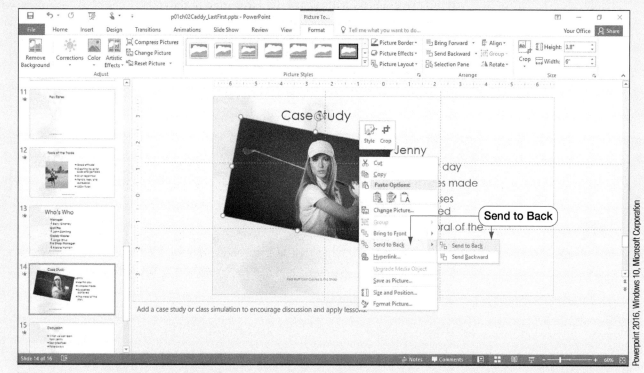

Figure 18 Sending an image to the back

j. Right-click the **photograph**, and then select **Copy**. Right-click **Slide 15** in the left hand pane, and then, under Paste Options, click **Use Destination Theme** 📋.

k. Click the **Picture Tools Format** tab, and in the Arrange group, click **Rotate**, and then click **Flip Horizontal**. With the image selected, press → multiple times to move the picture to the right so the model's face is to the right of the right **Vertical Guide** and you can see all of the text. Click outside of the photograph. Since you used the arrow keys, you maintained the exact same vertical placement as the photo on Slide 14.

l. **Save** 🖫 the presentation.

Changing the Color of Graphics

PowerPoint contains sophisticated tools for modifying images. Using the Corrections tool on the Picture Tools Format tab, you can improve the brightness, contrast, and sharpness of images. The Color tool enables you to change the color of a picture to better match the presentation's color scheme or to improve the quality of the image. Artistic Effects can make the picture look as if it were sketched or painted. You can also **recolor** an image by altering the colors of the image to create a monochromatic effect.

The **Kelvin scale** describes a standard color temperature of light sources. For example, in photographs, the lower numbers on the scale represent the warmer colors of yellow, red, and orange, such as candlelight, while the higher numbers, over 5,000K, represent blue or cooler colors. The color temperature of regular daylight, such as one might see outdoors on a clear day, is 5,500 on the Kelvin scale. The light source in this sense is measured between 1,000K and 25,000K.

In PowerPoint, changing the color tone or temperature of an image seems to work backward. This is because the higher the temperature, the more daylight is added, and therefore the more normal the flesh tones appear. When the temperature drops, the flesh tones appear blue in color, such as at night, even though the temperature represents warmer colors on the Kelvin scale.

In this exercise, you will change the **saturation** of the color of one of the photographs in the presentation — the amount of color in the photograph — and then change the **color tone**, or the temperature, of a photograph, to add more blue to the image. Also, you will use the **Eyedropper tool** to precisely match colors from graphics to create uniformity in the slides. The Eyedropper tool enables you to sample a color and drop it onto an element to make that element's color match the sampled color.

To Change the Color of Graphics

a. Click **Slide 6**, and then click the **photograph**. Click the **Picture Tools Format** tab, and in the Adjust group, click **Color**. Point to the images in the Color Saturation gallery, preview the choices, and then click **Saturation: 200%** to apply more color to the image.

   The color scheme that you select for the template or design theme affects the colors presented in the gallery. In the Recolor gallery, for example, light and dark accent colors from the scheme appear with various black-and-white, sepia, and washout options.

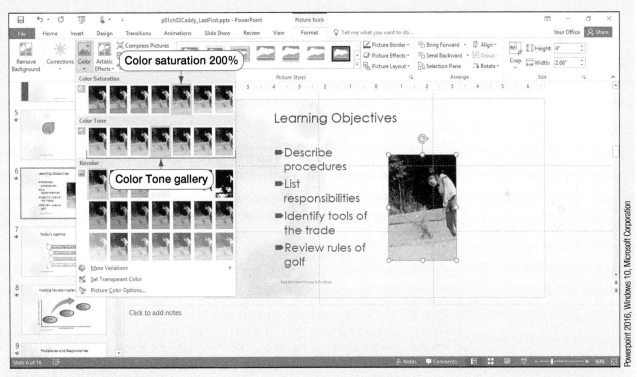

Figure 19 Color galleries

b. In the Adjust group, click **Color**. Point to the images in the **Color Tone** gallery, and then observe that as the temperature in Kelvin goes down, more blue is apparent in the photograph. As the temperature increases, the yellow tones are enhanced as more daylight is added.

c. Click **Temperature: 5300 K**.

   To precisely match color from your photographs to other elements in your presentation, you first need to sample the color. You will use the Eyedropper tool to do this.

d. Right-click the **photograph** on Slide 6, click **Format Picture**, and then, in the Format Picture pane, click **Fill & Line** 🖊.

e. If necessary, click **Fill** to expand the category, and then select **Solid fill**. Click the **Fill Color** arrow, and then click **Eyedropper**.

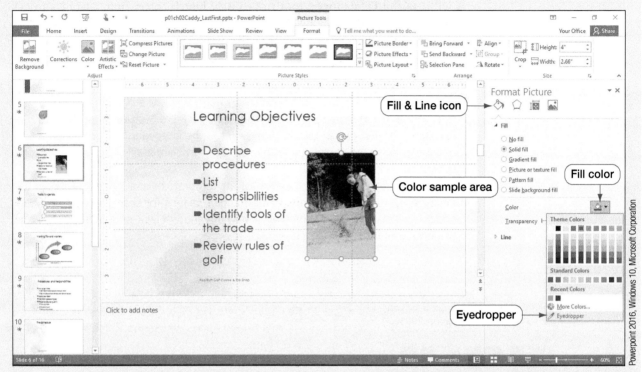

Figure 20   Eyedropper tool

Now you are ready to sample a color from the photograph. Notice that when you point to the photograph, the pointer changes to an Eyedropper.

f. Select and click a **color** from the model's shirt, from somewhere bright blue. The sampled color is now available to use and is shown in the Format Picture pane in the bucket.

g. Click the **placeholder text** to the left of the photograph, and then, if necessary, in the **Format Picture** pane, click **Fill & Line** [icon], and then click **Solid fill**. The sampled color has been applied to the placeholder.

h. Under Fill in the Format Picture pane, click inside the **Transparency** box, and change the transparency to 90%. **Close** ☒ the Format Picture pane.
   Transparency allows some of the slide background to be visible through the placeholder background. The higher the transparency percentage, the more visible is the background.

i. Click the **photograph**. Drag the **top-right sizing handle** of the photograph until the top edge of the picture is even with the top height of the text placeholder box.

j. **Save** ☐ the presentation.

Applying a Picture Style

Picture Styles enable you to add preset effects to your graphics. Options include frames, shadows, and unusual shapes. Having too many styles in the same presentation will detract from the presentation, so be careful to use only a few.

In this exercise, you will use Picture Styles to frame a photograph in the Caddy School presentation, change the border color in another, and add depth to a third.

To Apply a Picture Style

a. Click **Slide 12**, and then click the **photograph**. Click the **Picture Tools Format** tab, and in the Picture Styles group, click **More** ⮟, and then point to the style thumbnails shown in the gallery and observe the Live Preview. The name of the style appears as you point to each thumbnail.

b. Click **Rotated, White** to apply that style to the photograph. This style gives the photograph a 3-D appearance.

c. Click **Slide 6**, and then click the **photograph**. Click the **Picture Tools Format** tab, and in the Picture Styles group, click **Picture Border**, and then click **Brown, Accent 3, Darker 25%**.

d. In the Picture Styles group, click **Picture Border**, point to **Weight**, and then click **3 pt**.

e. With the **photograph** still selected, in the Format Picture pane, click **Shadow**, click the **Presets** button, and then select **Offset Diagonal Bottom Left** — the third thumbnail in the first row of the Outer group.

f. In the Format Picture pane, click the **Size** arrow to increase the size of the shadow to 102%. Click the **Distance** arrow to increase the distance to 10 pt.

Shadows are the result of light. You can adjust where the light source is coming from by adjusting the Angle, how bright the light source is by adjusting the Blur and Transparency, and how far away the foreground objects are from the background by adjusting the Distance.

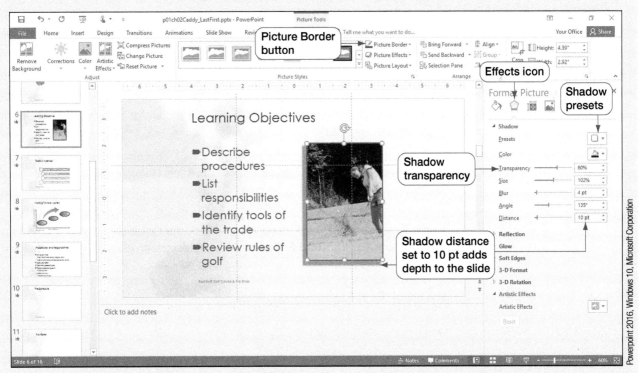

Figure 21   Applying a border

g. In the Format Picture pane, click **Close** ☒ and then **Save** ⊟ the presentation.

Work with Shape and Line Graphics

Lines and shapes can increase understanding of the slides by creating focal points and explaining concepts. Add an arrow to a slide, and the audience will look where it is pointing. Lines and shapes add color and interest. Boxes, which are also considered shapes, enable you to label objects. As you add shapes to slides, keep in mind that the objects should remain consistent with the other graphics and colors in the presentation.

Applying Line Gradients

Gradients can give an illusion of depth to objects. Changing the angle of a gradient fill can indicate a light source. In this exercise, you will work with both.

To Apply Line Gradients

a. Click **Slide 8**, and then click the **left oval**. Press and hold [Shift] while you click once on the other **two ovals**. All three ovals are now selected. Release [Shift].

b. Click the **Drawing Tools Format** tab, and in the Size group, click the **Size Dialog Box Launcher** [▿]. Under Shape Options, click **Fill & Line** [◇].

c. Scroll down the Format Shape pane, click **Line**, and then select **Gradient line**.

d. Click the **Type** arrow, and then select **Radial**. Click the **Direction** arrow, and then select **From Top Right Corner**.

e. Scroll down, and then click inside the **Width** box, and set the width of the line to 4 pt.

f. Under Gradient stops, notice the markers on the gradient line. Click **Stop 1 of 4**, which should be at position 0%. Click the **Color** arrow, and then select **White, Background 1**. This will be the first stop on the radius and will give you the spotlight effect from the top-right corner.

g. Click inside the **Position** box, and set the position to 25%. Notice how the white spotlight effect has moved around the radius.

h. Under Gradient stops, click **Stop 2 of 4**. Click the **Color** arrow, and then select **Light Green, Background 2, Darker 50%**. Click inside the **Position** box, and set the position to 40%.

i. Under Gradient stops, click **Stop 3 of 4**. Click the **Color** arrow, and then select **Light Green, Background 2, Darker 75%**. Click inside the **Position** box, and set the position to 75%. This stop gives the most volume to the shape.

j. Under Gradient stops, click **Stop 4 of 4**. Click the **Color** arrow, and then select **Light Green, Background 2, Darker 25%**. If necessary, click inside the **Position** box and set the position to 100%. Using a lighter color at stop 4 gives the illusion of a secondary light source just off the screen and to the left, rounding out the volume of the shape.

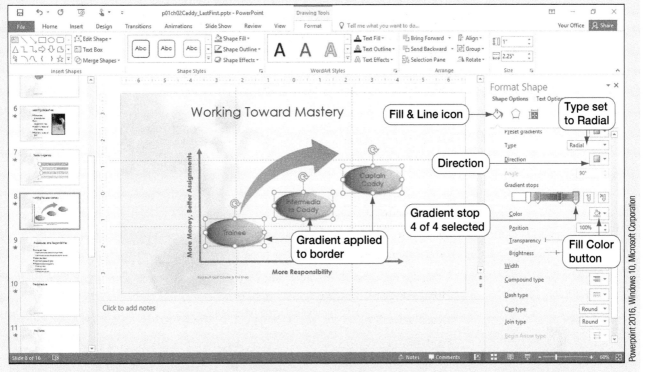

Figure 22   Line gradients

k. **Save** the presentation.

Applying Shape Gradients

Gradients can give an illusion of volume. Changing the angle of a gradient fill can indicate a light source. In the preceding section, you worked with gradient lines. In this exercise, you will apply a gradient fill to a shape to give it volume.

P02.13

To Apply Shape Gradients

a. On Slide 8, make sure that **all three ovals** are still selected. Scroll to the top of the Format Shape pane under Fill.

> ### Troubleshooting
> If all three ovals are not selected, click on one of the ovals to select it. Next, press and hold [Shift], and then click each of the other two ovals once. Last, release [Shift].

b. Under Gradient stops, click **Stop 1 of 4**. Click the **Color** arrow, and then select **White, Background 1**. Click inside the **Position** box, and set the position to 25%. This stop gives the most spotlight to the shape.

c. Under Gradient stops, click **Stop 2 of 4**. Click the **Color** arrow, and then select **Light Green, Background 2, Darker 50%**. Click inside the **Position** box, and set the position to 60%. This stop gives the most volume to the shape.

d. Under Gradient stops, click **Stop 3 of 4**. Click the **Color** arrow, and then select **Light Green, Background 2, Darker 75%**. Click inside the **Position** box, and set the position to 95%. This stop rounds out the left side of the shape.

e. Under Gradient stops, click **Stop 4 of 4**. Click the **Color** arrow, and then select **Light Green, Background 2, Darker 25%**. If necessary, click inside the **Position** box and set the position to 100%. This stop completes the curve of the shape.

f. **Close** × the Format Shape pane. On the Drawing Tools Format tab, in the Size group, click in the **Shape Width** box, and type 2.8". Press Enter.

g. Click the **Home** tab. In the Font group, click **Bold** B.

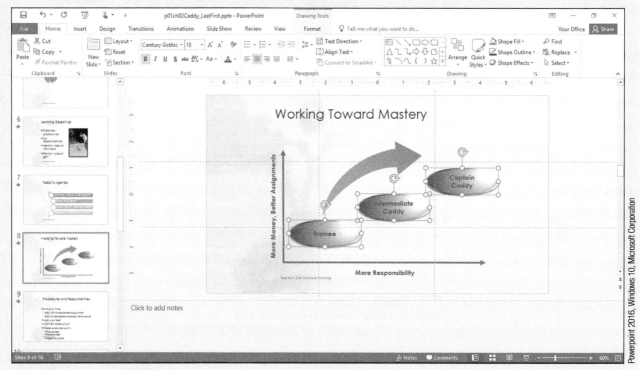

Figure 23 Shape gradients

h. **Save** 🖫 the presentation.

Applying Shape Styles

PowerPoint contains a wide range of shapes in the Illustrations group on the Insert tab. When you select a shape from the gallery, a crosshair pointer enables you to draw the shape on the slide. Sizing handles appear on selected shapes so you can change the shape or rotation of the object you have drawn, similar to sizing handles on images. Shapes can be filled, stacked, aligned, grouped, and merged.

A drop shadow can be added behind a shape element to give the element a light source. This makes it appear as if it is hovering on the slide. However, images with drop shadows that overlap will cast shadows from above onto the objects beneath. To avoid this, design a shape identical to the one you want to overlap, apply a drop shadow to it, insert it exactly behind the image you want to shadow, and then send it to the back of the object. This gives the illusion that the shapes are closely stacked. Also, lines or a border around shapes helps to separate them visually.

In this exercise, you will modify the shapes on a slide in the Caddy School presentation to better suit your message. The objects you create will add visual interest to a few of the plainer slides.

To Apply Shape Styles

a. Click **Slide 2**.

b. Click the **Insert** tab. In the Illustrations group, click **Shapes**, and then, in the Stars and Banners group, select **Wave**. Position the insertion point at approximately 2.5" to the left of the horizontal 0" and 2.5" above the vertical 0". Click and drag to approximately 4" to the right of the horizontal 0" and 2.5" below the vertical 0".

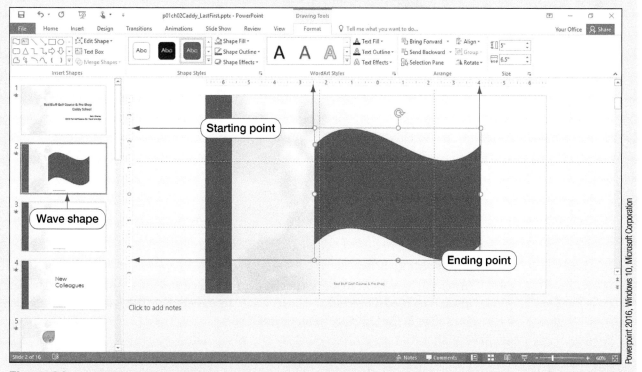

Figure 24 Inserting a wave shape

c. On the Drawing Tools Format tab, in the Shape Styles group, click on the **Shape Effects** arrow. Then point to **Preset**, and under the Presets group, click **Preset 8**. Click anywhere off of the shape to deselect it.

d. Click the **Insert** tab. In the Illustrations group, click on the **Shapes** arrow. Under Lines, click **Line**.

e. Place your insertion point at the **top left corner** of the wave shape. Press and hold Shift while you click and drag to the **bottom** of the slide. Release Shift. Notice that Shift ensures that the line stays straight.

f. With the line still selected, on the Drawing Tools Format tab, in the Shape Styles group, click the **Shape Outline** arrow. Point to **Weight**, and click **6 pt**. Notice that the text looks as though it is on a flag.

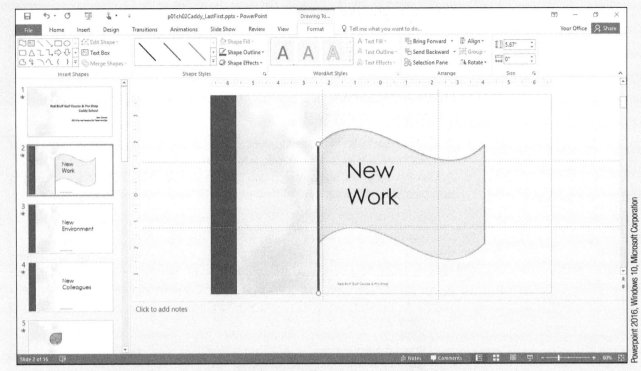

Figure 25 Custom shape

    g. **Save** 🖫 the presentation.

Duplicating Shapes

After you have spent so much time formatting a shape to get it just the way you want it, there is no need to recreate it all over again. In this exercise, you will duplicate the shapes on a slide in the Caddy School presentation.

To Duplicate Shapes

    a. Click the **wave** shape on Slide 2 to select it. Press and hold ⇧Shift. Click the **line** shape. Release ⇧Shift. The line and wave shapes should both be selected.

    b. Right-click one of the shape borders, and select **Copy**. Right-click **Slide 3** in the left pane. Under Paste Options, select **Use Destination Theme** 📋. Repeat this for Slide 4.

    c. **Save** 🖫 the presentation.

Arranging Shapes

PowerPoint has tools that enable you to precisely arrange the shapes you create. You can reorder items that are stacked to bring other shapes forward or send them toward the back. You can group objects so they are treated as one object.

    In this exercise, you will make four boxes for the text on the Procedures and Responsibilities slide. You will begin by moving the text into their respective placeholders to prepare to move the text over the four power points.

To Arrange Shapes

a. Click **Slide 9**. Select the text beginning with **Preserve course quality** and ending with **divots**. On the Home tab, in the Clipboard group, click **Cut** 🔲.

b. In the Slides group, click the **Layout** arrow, and then select **Two Content**. Click inside the top of the right placeholder box, and then, in the Clipboard group, click **Paste** to insert the cut text.

c. Click the **Drawing Tools Format** tab, and in the Size group, set the **Height** of the box to 3".

d. Select the **title** placeholder, and then, on the Drawing Tools Format tab, in the Size group, set the **Height** of the box to 0.8".

e. Select the text **Maintain pace of play**, and then click the **Home** tab. In the Clipboard group, click **Cut** 🔲. On the Drawing Tools Format tab, in the Drawing group, and in the shapes box, select **Text Box**. Click once on any part of the **slide** that does not contain a placeholder to insert the box, and then, in the Clipboard group, click **Paste**. The text was inserted into the new text box. If necessary, click Bksp once to remove the extra space at the end of the pasted content. You will move the text box into place later.

> ### Troubleshooting
> If you accidently dragged the mouse while placing the text box onto the slide, the text box will not expand to accommodate the pasted text. If this happened, simply click Undo in the Quick Access Toolbar and complete the steps again, making sure to click once and not drag the mouse when placing the text box onto the slide.

f. Select the text **Look your best**, and then, on the Home tab, in the Clipboard group, click **Cut** 🔲. On the Drawing Tools Format tab, in the Drawing group, and in the shapes box, select **Text Box**. Click once on any part of the **slide** that does not contain a placeholder to insert the box, and then, in the Clipboard group, click **Paste**. The text was inserted into the new text box. If necessary, click Bksp once to remove the extra space at the end of the pasted content. You will move the text box into place later.

g. Select the text **Arrive on time**, and then, in the Clipboard group, double-click **Format Painter** 🔲. Drag the pointer over the text **Maintain pace of play** and the text **Look your best**. In the Clipboard group, click **Format Painter** 🔲 to toggle it off.

h. **Save** 🔲 the presentation.

Aligning Shapes

PowerPoint has smart tools that enable you to make precision alignments to your shapes and elements in your presentation. You can align two or more shapes in relation to each other, using red **Smart alignment guides** that assist you in aligning elements with other elements on your slide. Some Smart alignment guides assist with equidistance too. The **Equidistant guides** assist you in placing one or more selected objects within equal distance of at least two other slide elements. This is not the same as Distribute Horizontally or Distribute Vertically, which attempt to distribute the space between the middle object or objects of three or more elements in a set between the outer elements.

In this exercise, you will align the text over the four power points.

To Align Shapes

a. On Slide 9, drag the box with the text **Maintain pace of play** until it is positioned under the box beginning with **Preserve course quality**. Smart Alignment guides will appear to assist you in left-aligning this box with the one above it. Drag the **right sizing handle** to the left until the Smart Alignment guide appears, indicating that the widths of the two boxes are the same.

b. Drag the box with the text **Look your best** until it is positioned under the box beginning with **Arrive on time**. Use the Smart Alignment guides to assist you in aligning the **left bullet point** with the one above. Drag the **right sizing handle** to the right until the Smart Alignment guide appears, indicating that the widths of the two boxes are the same. Drag the **top-sizing handle** of this box, using Smart Alignment guides to assist in aligning the top with the top of the bottom box on the right.

c. Edit the text **30 - 40 minutes before shotgun starts** to read 30 - 40 m before shotgun. Edit the text **20 minutes before scheduled normal rounds** to read 20 m before normal rounds. Edit the text **Repair any divots** to read Repair divots.

d. Select the box beginning with **Arrive on time**, and then drag the **bottom sizing handle** up until a red horizontal Smart Alignment guide appears, indicating that it is the same height as the top box on the right.

e. Click any one of the **boxes**, press and hold Shift, and then click **each box** to select all four content boxes. Slowly drag the group of boxes upward until two multiple sets of Smart Alignment guides appear with equidistant guides above and below the group.

   Arrows will appear between the guides indicating that the distances between the objects are the same. If you have trouble getting the equidistant guides to appear, position the boxes as shown below.

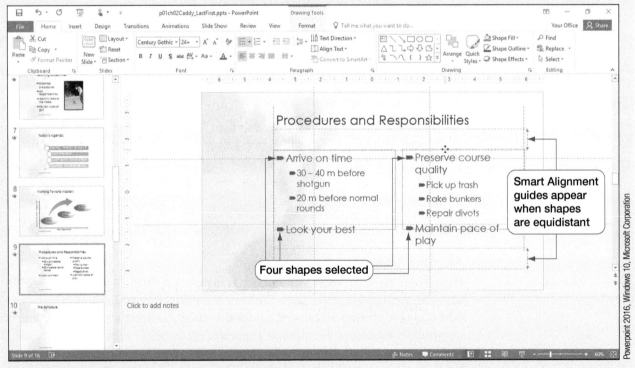

Figure 26 Aligning shapes

f. **Save** 🔲 the presentation.

Merging Shapes

Sometimes to get the perfect shape, you need to customize what is available. Using the Merge Shapes feature in PowerPoint, you can create custom shapes from one or more built-in shapes. Such variations include union, taking the sum of two or more shapes; combine, the sum of two or more shapes, less their overlapping parts; or intersect, the overlap between two or more shapes. Other variations include fragment, breaking shapes into smaller parts along their overlapping lines; and subtract, removing whole parts of a shape using the outline of another shape. In this exercise, you will create a Welcome slide and merge a WordArt shape with an image.

To Merge Shapes

a. Click **Slide 5**. Click the **Insert** tab, and then, in the Images group, click **Pictures**. Navigate through the folder structure to the location of your student data files, and then double-click **p01ch02ProShop**.

b. Click the **Insert** tab, and in the Text group, click **WordArt**. Click **Fill - White, Outline - Accent 1, Shadow** — the fourth option in the first row. Type Welcome in the box. The size of the box expands to accommodate the word.

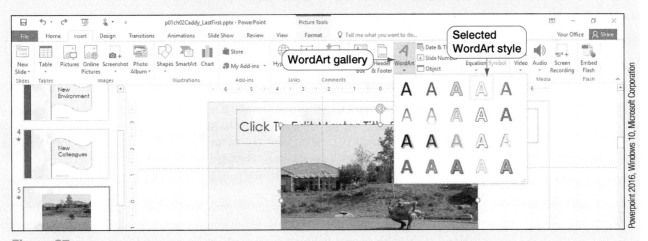

Figure 27 WordArt gallery

Just as shapes can be filled in and modified with effects, text can be enhanced with the use of **WordArt**, which is text that has been enhanced with color, outlines, shadows, and special effects. Used for small amounts of text, WordArt adds color and interest to your presentation.

c. Click the **border** of the WordArt box. Click the **Home** tab, and then, in the Font group, change the Font Size to 80. Use the Format Picture pane to position the WordArt box with a horizontal position of 2.83" and a vertical position of 3.65" from the top left corner.

d. Click the **picture** to select it, press and hold Shift, and then click the **WordArt** box. Both objects should be selected. Click the **Drawing Tools Format** tab, and in the Insert Shapes group, click the **Merge Shapes** arrow, and then click **Intersect**. The shapes will now be merged.

Troubleshooting

If the Merge Shapes feature is not working properly, be sure to select the image first and select the WordArt box second.

Figure 28 Merging shapes

e. Drag the **merged shape** down and to the right until it is centered over the lower right power point. The top and bottom sizing handles should be centered on the bottom vertical alignment guide. **Close** ⊠ the Format Picture pane.

f. **Save** ⊟ the presentation. If you need to take a break before finishing this chapter, now is a good time.

Using Elements to Communicate Information

A presentation will likely include many elements: text elements; graphic elements designed to communicate information, such as tables, charts, and SmartArt graphics; and elements that are designed to communicate or invoke emotion, such as pictures and other media.

Create a Table

Tables, which are grids of data arranged in rows and columns, organize information in a way that is meaningful to audiences. Short phrases, single words, and numbers can be placed in the table. Even graphics, such as photographs, can be placed in the cells. The table can be created as a media object directly from the icon on the content placeholder, or the Insert tab can be used to develop the table. Once the table has been created, various styles, table effects, and layouts can be applied. Table cells can be split or merged. Tables can also be a useful tool for laying out the slide format by using tables with transparent lines and backgrounds to keep everything aligned.

REAL WORLD ADVICE	Using an Excel Worksheet as a Source

Often, the data you need to convey in a presentation is already available in an Excel worksheet. You can copy the information from Excel and paste it onto a PowerPoint slide. Options for pasting include the following.

- Using the styles of the slide
- Keeping the source formatting from the worksheet
- Linking the information so changes in the worksheet will be reflected in the presentation
- Inserting the information as a picture
- Keeping the text only and eliminating the worksheet grid
- Creating a table in PowerPoint and then pasting the information from the worksheet into the table

Inserting a Table

In this exercise, you will insert and modify a table to better illustrate the weekly golf schedule in the Caddy School presentation.

To Insert a Table

a. If you took a break, open the **p01ch02Caddy** presentation.

b. Click **Slide 10**. Click the **Insert** tab, and then, in the Tables group, click **Table**. Click **Insert Table** below the table grid. The Insert Table dialog box is displayed.

c. Increase the Number of columns to **8**, increase the Number of rows to **5**, and then click **OK**.

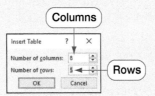

Figure 29 Insert Table dialog box

Powerpoint 2016, Windows 10, Microsoft Corporation

d. Type Caddy in the first cell, press Tab to move to the next cell, and then type the abbreviations for the days of the week — beginning with **Mon** for Monday — in each of the cells on the top row of the table. See the top row in the Table 1 for guidance.

> **SIDE NOTE**
> **Navigating a Table**
> Use arrow keys on the keyboard, or press Tab to move from left to right and press Shift+Tab to move from right to left.

e. Click before the word **Caddy**. Click the **Table Tools Layout** tab, and then, in the Table group, click **Select**, and then click **Select Row**. In the **Alignment** group, click **Center** ☰.

f. In the second row cell of the first column, type Captain. In the third row cell of the first column, type Intermediate, and then, in the fourth row cell of the first column, type Trainee.

Some of the words are broken in the middle so the words fit the cell. Do not worry about that at this time.

g. Continue to fill in the table as shown. The last row will remain blank for now.

Caddy	Mon	Tues	Wed	Thurs	Fri	Sat	Sun
Captain	8 AM	10 AM	8 AM	10 AM	8 AM	7 AM	7 AM
Intermediate	Noon	8 AM	Noon	8 AM	Noon	8 AM	8 AM
Trainee	8 AM	Noon	8 AM	Noon	8 AM	9 AM	9 AM

Table 1

h. **Save** 🖫 the presentation.

Applying Table Styles and Table Effects

Table Styles provide options for color in the table. The Table Style Options on the Table Tools Design tab enable you to specify treatment for the various rows and columns in the table. The Header Row command affects the first row of the table, where the column headers appear, by applying a stronger color to the background of the cells and displaying the words in a bold font. Banded rows or banded columns highlight the rows or columns with different colors. This assists the audience as they read the information in the table. Styles can be applied to the total row, first column, and last column to highlight totaled information in the table. The color of individual cells on the table can also be changed after applying a table style, by using the Shading tool.

Table Effects further enhance a table by providing visual effects such as cell bevels, borders, table shadows, and reflections. Applying simple table effects can improve the readability of the table. However, use caution in using styles and effects, and avoid overuse, as the table can quickly become difficult for the audience to read.

In this exercise, you will update the Caddy School Schedule table with Table Styles and Table Effects.

To Apply Table Styles and Table Effects

a. If necessary, click anywhere on the **table** on Slide 10. Click the **Table Tools Design** tab, and then, in the Table Styles group, click **More**. Point to the **thumbnails** in the gallery to see a live preview of the slide, and then, under Best Match for Document, click **Themed Style 1 - Accent 3** in the top row.

   The brown colors of the table coordinate with the colors of the background graphic.

b. Select the **cells** containing the caddy ranks: **Captain**, **Intermediate**, and **Trainee**. In the Table Styles group, click the **Shading** arrow, and then click **Brown, Accent 3, Lighter 60%**.

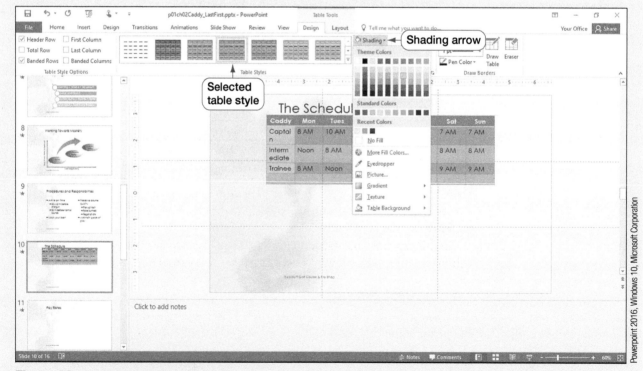

Figure 30 Applying a table style

c. Select the **data in the second through fourth rows** of the table. On the Table Tools Design tab, in the Table Styles group, click the **Borders** ⊞ arrow, and then select **All Borders**. Adding a border to the cells in the table enables your audience to differentiate between the cells of the table.

d. Click a **cell** in the table. In the Table Styles group, click **Effects** ⟲, point to **Shadow**, and then select **Offset Diagonal Bottom Left**. The shadow is applied to the entire table and helps to maintain consistency with the other graphics in the presentation.

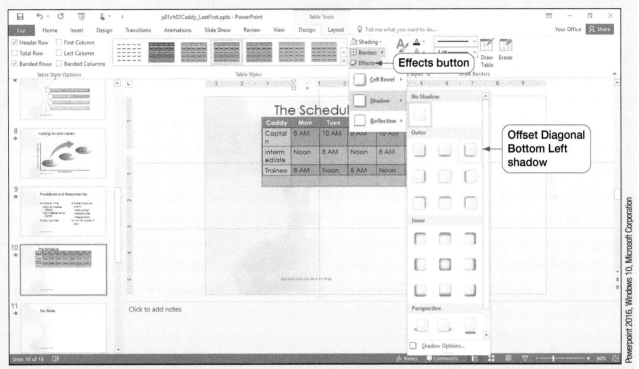

Figure 31 Selecting table effects

e. **Save** ⊟ the presentation.

Changing the Table Layout

The Table Tools Layout tab enables changes to be made, such as adding rows and columns to the table. Unnecessary rows or columns can also be deleted. Cells of the table can be merged into a single cell, and a single cell can be split into multiple cells. The Table Tools Layout tab contains alignment tools that enable content of the cells to be aligned horizontally and vertically in the cells. The direction of the text and width of the cell margins can also be modified.

In this exercise, you will add a row to the table below the column heading row, and you will merge cells in this row. You will also delete the extra row at the bottom of the table.

To Change the Table Layout

a. Click in the **Captain** cell in the table. Click the **Table Tools Layout** tab, and in the Rows & Columns group, click **Insert Above**. A new row is placed between the column headings and the table data.

b. Select the second row **cells** under Mon through Thurs of the table. In the Merge group, click **Merge Cells**, and then type Weekday Times in the merged cell. In the Alignment group, click **Center** ☰. The cells are merged to show that the cells below are all related to the weekday times.

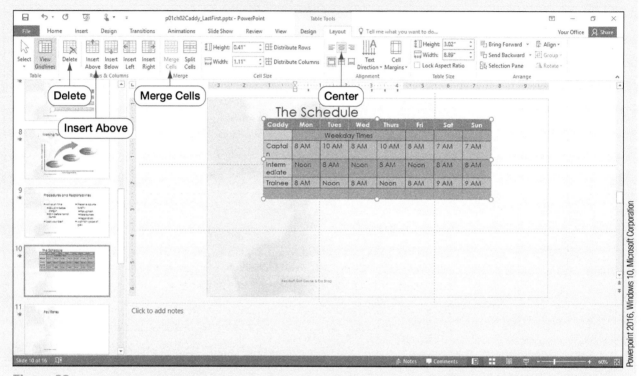

Figure 32 Modifying the table layout

c. Select the second row **cells** under Fri through Sun of the table. In the Merge group, click **Merge Cells**, and then type Weekend Times. In the Alignment group, click **Center** ☰.

d. The extra row of the table is not needed. Click any **cell** in the last row of the table. In the Rows & Columns group, click **Delete**, and then click **Delete Rows**.

e. Click the cell containing the **Intermediate** caddy rank. In the Cell Size group, click the **Table Column Width** arrow to increase the size until the word **Intermediate** fits on a single line. The width should be 1.8".

f. Select the **column headers** for the days of the week. In the Cell Size group, click in the **Table Column Width** box, type 1, and then press Enter.

g. With any cell selected, on the Table Tools Layout tab, in the Arrange group, click **Align**, and then click **Align Center**. Click **Align** again, and then click **Align Middle**. Notice that the table is now centered both horizontally and vertically on the slide.

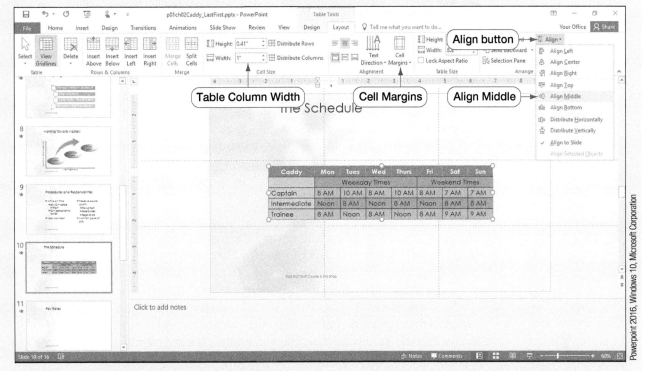

Figure 33 Modifying column and table alignment

h. Select the entire **top row** of the table. In the Alignment group, click **Cell Margins**, and then click **Wide**. The size of the cells containing the headers seems to have increased, but in reality, a wider margin was put around the words.

i. Select the word **Caddy** in the table, and then drag it to the first cell of the second row. This improves the balance of the table. With the word **Caddy** selected, click the **Home** tab, and in the **Font** group, click **Font Color** A ·, and then click **White, Background 1**.

> **Troubleshooting**
> If the cell seems extra tall, you may have included the paragraph mark in the selection of the word. Click after the word "Caddy," and press Delete to remove the paragraph break.

j. **Save** 🖫 the presentation.

Create and Insert Charts

Just as pictures can tell a story in a presentation, **charts** of numeric data assist the audience in grasping the message. Charts can be persuasive tools in presentations, giving the audience the essence of the problem and the solution. Large amounts of numbers are often difficult to read on the screen, but they can be distilled into charts that describe the real meaning of the data. The message of the chart should stand out as a single statement.

PowerPoint has tools that enable you to enter the data into a worksheet window and then create a chart. A wide variety of chart types are available. After the chart has been created, the data can be edited, and the characteristics of the chart, including the design, layout, and format can be modified.

As charts are created for use in presentations, it is important to critically evaluate them to ensure that the information is correct and that they make sense. Often, just switching the data in the rows and columns gives a whole new meaning to the chart. To critically evaluate a chart, ask yourself the following questions.

- What is the one thing you are trying to convey with the chart?
- What is the core information you want to include?
- Does the chart add to the message of the slide? Is it easy to read?
- Does the chart ethically represent the data and not misrepresent it?

Inserting a Chart

Charts are created by first selecting the type of chart to insert onto a slide. The type of chart relates to the type of data being used. For instance, a pie chart is used to show the relationship of each part to the whole, and a line chart shows trends over a period of time. A column or bar chart shows the item relates to another item.

After you select the chart type, a worksheet table window opens and displays default data. You then replace the default data with actual data, and the chart appears on the slide in Live Preview. In this exercise, you will create a stacked column chart to show the pay rate information in the Caddy School presentation.

To Insert a Chart

a. Click **Slide 11**, and then click **Insert Chart** in the content placeholder. In the Insert Chart dialog box, click the **Column** type in the left pane, and then, in the right pane, click **Stacked Column**, and then click **OK**.

The worksheet opens showing the Live Preview of the default data. The categories represent the columns, and the series provide the numeric data.

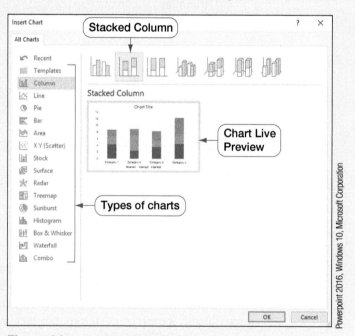

Figure 34   Inserting a chart

b. If necessary, resize the worksheet window, and type the following information over the existing data.

	Base	Average Tips
Trainee	10	8
Intermediate	12.5	13
Captain	15	20

As you type, you should notice that the PowerPoint slide is updated in Live Preview. The final row and last column of the default worksheet are unneeded, so you will delete them.

c. Drag the **bottom-right corner** of the range — the blue square — up and to the left so only the data used — columns A - C and rows 1 - 4 — are selected. Close $\boxed{\times}$ the worksheet window. Review the chart to ensure that the data is correct.

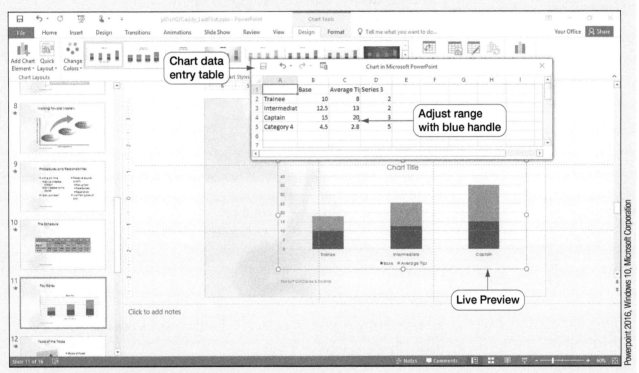

Figure 35 Inserting chart data

d. **Save** 🖫 the presentation.

Changing the Chart Type

Usually, confusion with a chart occurs because the wrong choice was made for a chart type or the horizontal and vertical axes are reversed. PowerPoint makes it easy for you to experiment with the various types of charts to improve your message.

In this exercise, you will change the chart type to a 3-D version that will fit with the other elements of the presentation better.

P02.23

SIDE NOTE
Viewing Chart Type Names
You can hover your mouse pointer over each chart type to see the name of each chart.

To Change the Chart Type

a. On Slide11, click the **chart** if necessary.
   The Chart Tools Design tab enables you to change the type of chart, the layouts, and the styles.

b. In the Type group, click **Change Chart Type**. In the Change Chart Type dialog box, click **3-D Stacked Column**. Click **OK**. The 3-D effect is consistent with other graphics in your presentation.

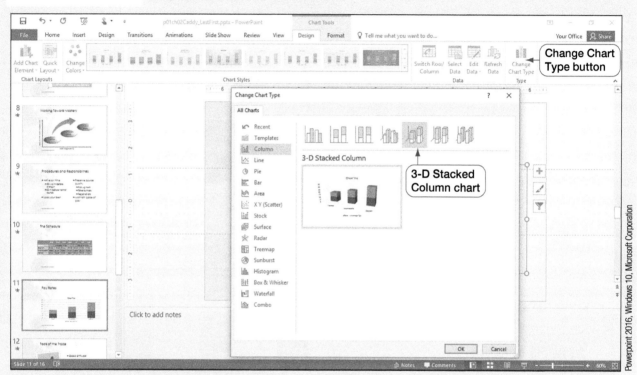

Figure 36 Changing the chart type

c. In the Chart Styles group, click **More** [▾], and then click **Style 6**.

d. **Save** [💾] the presentation.

Changing the Chart Layout

The Chart Tools Design tab contains tools for adding descriptive labels to the chart, which can increase the audience's understanding of the material. The horizontal and vertical axes should be labeled. The legend enables the audience to match the bars with the caddy ranks. Data labels enable you to show the value of each of the bars on the table. This is beneficial if you do not use the gridlines in your chart. You can also display the data that you used to place the numeric data into the chart if necessary.

In this exercise, you will change the layout of the chart, using the Quick Layout templates.

P02.24

SIDE NOTE

Chart Styles

In addition to predefined chart layouts, you can select from various chart styles by clicking the Chart Styles button to the right of the chart.

To Change the Chart Layout

a. Click the **chart** on Slide 11, if necessary, to select it. Under the Chart Tools Design tab, in the Chart Layouts group, click **Quick Layout**, and then click **Layout 1**.

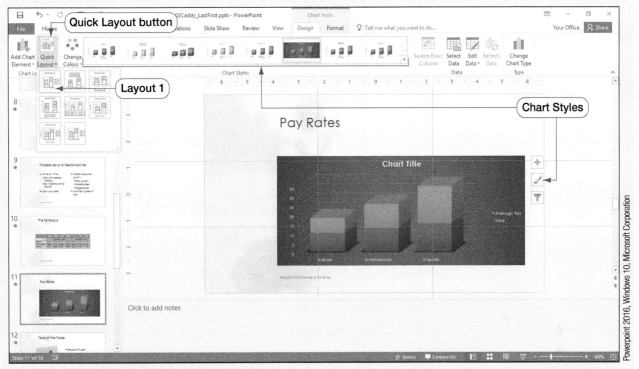

Figure 37   Modifying the chart layout

b. **Save** 🖫 the presentation.

Changing Chart Elements

Individual elements on the chart, such as the title, series bars, axes, legend, and gridlines can be selected and modified by using the Chart Tools Format tab.

In this exercise, you will add a descriptive title to the chart.

 P02.25

To Change Chart Elements

a. Click the **chart** on Slide 11, if necessary, to select it. Click **Chart Title** to select the title placeholder border.

If a solid border is displayed around the chart title, the text within the placeholder will automatically be replaced when you type a new title. If the border is displayed as a dashed line border, it is necessary to click and drag to select the text that you intend to replace.

    b. Type Pay Per Hour, in Dollars. **This will remove the words "Chart Title" and give a proper title.**

    c. **Save** ⊟ the presentation.

Create a SmartArt Graphic

SmartArt graphics add color, shape, and emphasis to the text in presentations. Specialty graphics such as list, hierarchy, process, pyramid, and cycle charts are preformatted by using the color scheme in the slide show. The gallery contains a number of versions for each chart type. A wide range of graphic types are available. For instance, Process graphics show a sequence of steps, while Cycle graphics represent a circular flow of stages or tasks. Hierarchy and Relationship graphics show how items relate, such as you might find on a company's organizational chart.

Using SmartArt

The agenda on Slide 7 gives you an opportunity to effectively use SmartArt. In this exercise, you will change the SmartArt graphic style that already exists on Slide 7, using the SmartArt Styles gallery.

 P02.26

To Use SmartArt

    a. Click **Slide 7**, and then click the SmartArt illustration **border**. Click the **SmartArt Tools Design** tab, and in the SmartArt Styles group, click **More** ⊡, and then, under Best Match for Document, click **Intense Effect**.

       The Intense Effect provides some shadow effects that helps to tie this object into the other elements in the presentation. It is also important that the style chosen does not make it more difficult for the information on the slide to be read. The SmartArt Tool tabs provide many options for modifying the design or format of the graphic.

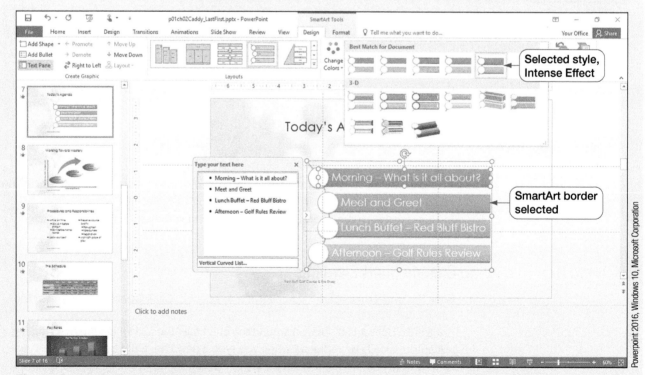

Figure 38 SmartArt Styles gallery

Troubleshooting

You can reset the graphic to the original version at any time. To do so, under the Smart Tools Design tab, in the Reset group, click Reset Graphic.

b. On the Smart Tools Design tab, in the Create Graphic group, make sure **Text Pane** is toggled on to display the "Type your text here" pane. You will use the Text pane to quickly edit the information on the SmartArt graphic.

Similar to Outline view, the SmartArt Text pane enables you to concentrate on content without the visualizations. You can add additional bullet points at the end of the graphic by clicking after the last bullet point and pressing Enter. Use the arrow keys or click the bullet points to move within the Text pane. You can move the bullet text up and down on the graphic, using tools on the SmartArt Tools Design tab, and you can promote or demote text as needed.

c. In the Text pane, replace the text **Morning - What is it all about?** with the text Welcome, Caddy Overview.

d. Press ↓ twice to move to the bullet point **Lunch Buffet** in the Text pane, and then delete the text **Buffet**. In the next bullet point, delete the text **Afternoon - ,** leaving only the words **Golf Rules Review**. Close the Text pane by clicking **Close** ✕ in the Text pane.

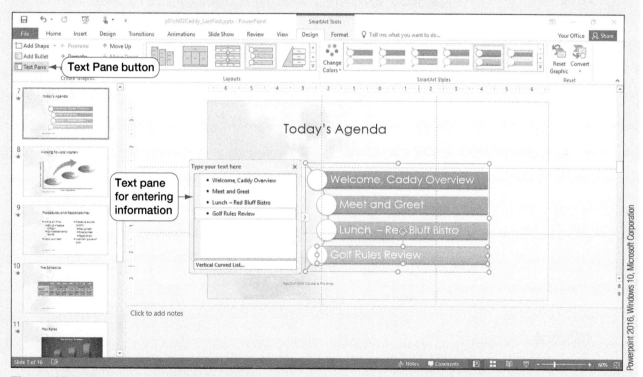

Figure 39 Editing text in a SmartArt graphic

e. **Save** 🖫 the presentation.

Customizing SmartArt

SmartArt can be customized in a variety of ways. One way is by adding images. Also, the colors used in SmartArt graphics are based on the colors in the theme or template used for the presentation. Choices for coloring the graphics include Primary Theme Colors, Colorful combinations, and Accent color options. You can also recolor the individual shapes using the Shape Fill and Shape Outline tools on the Format tab. Shape effects, such as shadows and bevels, can be applied to the individual shapes. In this exercise, you will add a relevant image for each agenda item.

 P02.27

To Customize SmartArt

a. On Slide 7, click the **top circle**, next to the first agenda item, on the SmartArt graphic. Click the **SmartArt Tools Format** tab, and then, in the Shape Styles group, click the **Shape Fill** arrow, and then click **Picture**. Click **Browse**, and then navigate through the folder structure to the location of your student data files, and then double-click **p01ch02GolfBall**.

b. Click the **second circle** to the left of the second agenda item. On the SmartArt Tools Format tab, in the Shape Styles group, click the **Shape Fill** arrow, and then click **Picture**. Click **Browse**, and, if necessary navigate through the folder structure to the location of your student data files, and then double-click **p01ch02Blue**.

c. Click the **third circle** to the left of the third agenda item. On the SmartArt Tools Format tab, in the Shape Styles group, click the **Shape Fill** arrow, and then click **Picture**. Click **Browse** and, if necessary navigate through the folder structure to the location of your student data files, and then double-click **p01ch02ProShop**.

d. Click the **fourth circle** to the left of the fourth agenda item. On the SmartArt Tools Format tab, in the Shape Styles group, click the **Shape Fill** arrow, and then click **Picture**. Click **Browse**, and, if necessary navigate through the folder structure to the location of your student data files, and then double-click **p01ch02Pink**.

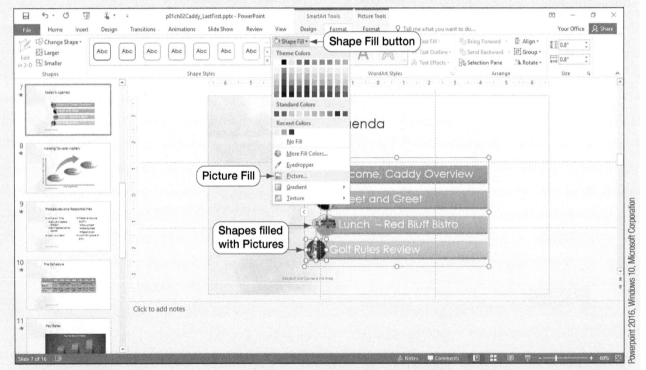

Figure 40   Modifying SmartArt

e. View the presentation in Slide Show view. Exit Slide Show view when finished.

f. **Save** 🖫 the presentation, exit PowerPoint, and then submit your file as directed by your instructor.

Concept Check

1. What are some things you should consider when selecting fonts for a presentation? p. 814

2. When would you use numbered lists instead of bulleted lists? p. 817

3. Describe the usefulness of the Format Painter tool. p. 818

4. Explain what special symbols are. p. 820

5. Explain the rule of thirds. p. 822, 823

6. List two things that gradients do for shapes when applied appropriately. p. 836, 837

7. Tables organize information into columns and rows in a way that is meaningful to the audience. List three things you can do to tables to make them more visually understandable. p. 846, 847

8. Explain when using a chart is beneficial to your presentation. p. 849, 851

9. List three benefits of using SmartArt graphics. p. 854, 855

Key Terms

Bit-mapped graphic   821
Chart   849
Color tone   833
Content placeholder   825
Copyright   821
Cropping handles   828
Equidistant guides   841
Eyedropper tool   833
Format Painter   841
Horizontal guide   823
Kelvin scale   832

List hierarchy   817
Ordered list   817
Picture Styles   834
Power points   823
Printer-friendly fonts   813
Recolor   832
Rule of six   814
Rule of thirds   822
Sans serif font   814
Saturation   833
Screen-friendly fonts   814

Serif font   813
Smart alignment guides   841
SmartArt graphic   854
Symbol   820
Table   844
Transparency   834
Vector graphic   821
Vertical guide   823
WordArt   843

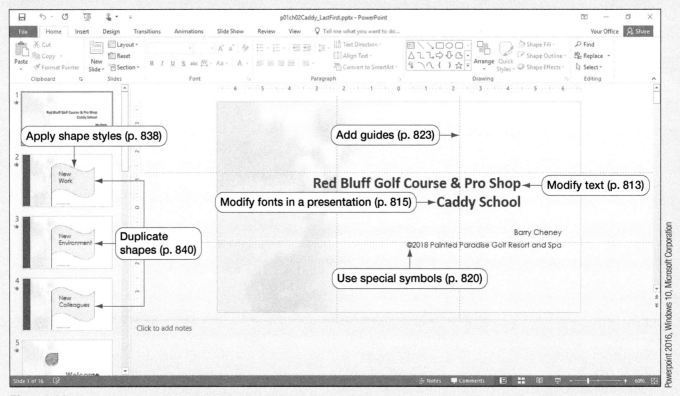

Figure 41

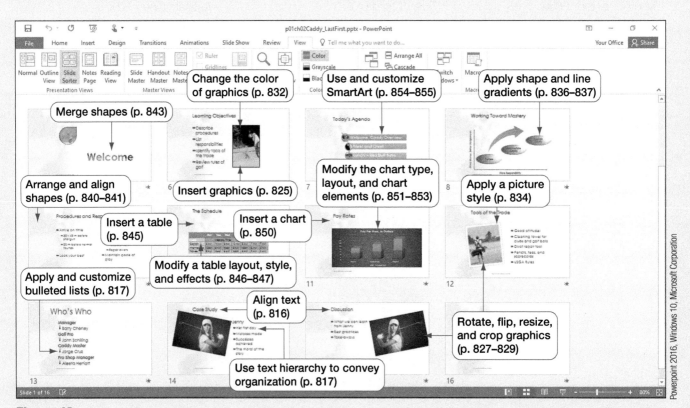

Figure 42

Student data files needed:

Sales &
Marketing

p01ch02Destination.pptx

p01ch02DestAlbum.pptx

p01ch02DestBouquet.jpg

You will save your file as:

p01ch02Destination_LastFirst.pptx

Planning Your Destination Wedding Seminar

Painted Paradise Resort and Spa is the perfect place for a destination wedding. Patti Rochelle, the corporate event planner, has several wedding planners on her staff. She would like to hold quarterly seminars to help brides-to-be plan for their special day. Seminars will be held on a Saturday morning and will feature a continental breakfast. Each seminar will begin with a presentation outlining the benefits of holding a wedding at Painted Paradise Resort and Spa. The audience also will include prospective grooms as well as parents of the couples. After the presentation, everyone attending will tour the resort to look at the various venues available for both the ceremony and the reception.

a. Start **PowerPoint**, click **Open Other Presentations** in the left pane, and then double-click **This PC**. Navigate through the folder structure to the location of your student data files, and then double-click **p01ch02Destination**. Click the **File** tab, click **Save As**, and double-click **This PC**. In the **Save As** dialog box, navigate to the location where you are saving your project files, and then change the file name to p01ch02Destination_LastFirst using your last and first name. Click **Save**.

b. Click **Slide 1**, click the **title placeholder**, and then type Planning Your Destination Wedding. Click in the **subtitle placeholder**, and type Painted Paradise Golf Resort & Spa, select the text just typed, and then change the font size to 28.

c. Click **Slide 3**. Click the **Insert** tab, and then in the Images group, click **Pictures**. Navigate to the location of your student data files, and then double-click **p01ch02DestBouquet**.

d. On the Picture Tools Format tab, in the Size group, click the **Size Dialog Box Launcher**. In the Format Picture pane, If necessary, click **Lock aspect ratio** to select it, and then decrease the Scale Height to 75%. Close the Format Picture pane. In the Pictures Styles group, click **Soft Edge Rectangle**. Drag the **picture** to the bottom right corner of the slide.

e. Click **Slide 4**, and then click **Insert Table** in the content placeholder. Change the number of columns to 3, change the number of rows to 4, and then click **OK**. Type the following data in the table.

Wedding Type	Guests	Room
Small	Up to 50	Pueblo Room
Medium	50 to 250	Eldorado Room
Large	250 to 500	Musica Room

f. On Slide 4, click a **cell** in the table. Click the **Table Tools Design tab**, and in the Table Styles group, click **Themed Style 2 - Accent 4**. In the Table Style Options group, click the **Banded Rows** check box to remove the banded row formatting.

g. Click the **Table Tools Layout** tab, and in the Table Size group, change the Table Size Height to 4". Select all of the **cells** in the table, and then, in the Alignment group, click **Center**. With the text selected, click **Center Vertically** in the Alignment group.

h. Click the **Home** tab, and then, in the Font group, increase the font size to 24. Drag the table down so the top edge is in line with the bottom of the picture in the top-right corner.

i. Click **Slide 5**, and then click the **chart**. Click the **Chart Tools Design** tab, and in the Data group, click **Edit Data**. Add the following data to the worksheet, beginning with the cell immediately below the text Groom's Attire.

Photography	2,000
Miscellaneous	1,300

j. Close the chart worksheet. On the Chart Tools Design tab, in the Chart Layouts group, click **Quick Layout**, and then click **Layout 6**. In the Chart Layouts group, click **Add Chart Element**, point to **Chart Title**, and then click **None**.

k. Click **Slide 6**, and then click the **SmartArt graphic**. Click the **SmartArt Tools Design** tab, and in the Layouts group, click **More**, and then click **Circle Arrow Process**.

l. On the SmartArt Tools Design tab, in the SmartArt Styles group, click **Change Colors**, and then click **Transparent Gradient Range - Accent 4**. In the SmartArt Styles group, click **More**, and then, under 3-D, click **Polished**.

m. Set vertical guides to 2.25 to the right and left of 0 on the horizontal ruler. Set horizontal guides to 1.25 above and below 0 on the vertical ruler. Click the **border** of the first box to the right of the rings so it has a solid border. Press and hold Shift, then click the three remaining **boxes**. Drag the **right sizing handle** of the top box until the red alignment guide is at 2.5" to the right of 0 on the horizontal ruler.

n. Drag the **boxes** until the center sizing handle of the top box is just to the right side of the right vertical alignment guide. Click the **Home** tab, and then, in the Font group, increase the font size to 16.

o. On the Home tab, in the Slides group, click the **New Slide** arrow, and then click **Reuse Slides**. In the Reuse Slides pane, click **Browse**, and then click **Browse File**. Navigate to the location of your student data files, and then double-click **p01ch02DestAlbum**. In the Reuse Slides pane, click **Slide 2** to **Slide 7** in succession. In the left pane, select the slides you just added. Click the **Design** tab, and in the Customize group, click **Format Background**. In the Format Background pane, click **Hide background graphics** to remove the image in the upper right corner.

p. Close the Reuse Slides pane and the Format Background pane. Delete **Slide 13**. Click **Slide 1**, and then click the **photograph**. Click the **Picture Tools Format** tab, and in the Size group, click the **Crop arrow**, and then click **Fill**. Click in a blank area to deselect the photograph.

q. Click the **Slide Show** tab, and then, in the Start Slide Show group, click **From Beginning**. Review the slides.

r. **Save** the presentation, exit PowerPoint, and then submit your file as directed by your instructor.

Problem Solve 1

Homework

Student data files needed: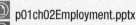

p01ch02Employment.pptx

p01ch02Employ1.jpg

You will save your file as: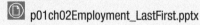

p01ch02Employment_LastFirst.pptx

Employment Opportunities for College Students

Human Resources

The Director of Human Resources at Painted Paradise Golf Resort and Spa has prepared a presentation to be shown to local college students informing them about job opportunities at the resort. The presentation contains the information that the director would like to include, but it has not yet been formatted. You have been asked to review the presentation and make it more visually appealing. You will apply a theme to the presentation, make minor modifications to the theme.

a. Open the PowerPoint file **p01ch02Employment**. Save your file as p01ch02Employment_LastFirst using your last and first name.

b. Set up guides using the Rule of thirds: **vertical guides** at 2.25 to the right and left of 0 on the horizontal ruler and **horizontal guides** to 1.25 above and below 0 on the vertical ruler.

c. Apply the **Organic** theme and the **Second** Organic Variant to the presentation.

d. Select the **text** of the first bullet on **Slide 4**, and then increase the font size to **32**. Remove the bullet from the text. Select the text of the remaining bullets on the slide, and then increase the font size to **24**. In the left placeholder, insert the photograph **p01ch02Employ1**. Drag the image to the right until it is centered on the left vertical guide.

e. Add the following bullets to the end of the text in the placeholder on Slide 5.

Display merchandise attractively
Possess excellent communication skills

f. Click **Slide 3**, and then click the **photograph**. Drag the photograph down until its top edge is aligned with the top edge of the placeholder text with bullets. Crop the image by setting the Crop position height to 2.2" and the Crop position width to 2.0" on the Format Picture pane. Add the Picture Style **Drop Shadow Rectangular** to the image.

g. Repeat the Drop Shadow for the image on **Slide 6**. For the image on **Slide 6**, set the Picture Color Tone Presets to **Temperature: 8800**, and then set the Color Saturation to **Saturation: 200%**. Center the picture on the right vertical guide, and center it vertically with the text box on the left.

h. For the image on **Slide 4**, apply the **Rotated, White** picture style in the Picture Styles group.

i. Click **Slide 2**, and then click the **SmartArt** object border to select the entire object. Set the size by checking **Lock aspect ratio** and then setting the height to 3.8". Set the horizontal position to 3.9" from **Top Left Corner**, and set the vertical position to 2.78" from **Top Left Corner**.

j. On **Slide 2**, select and format the three first-level bullet shapes of the SmartArt object with **Gradient fill**, Preset **Top Spotlight - Accent 2**. Set the Type to **Radial** and the Direction **From Top Right Corner**.

k. Continuing with the gradient fill, click the **Add Gradient Stop** button to add an additional stop, and set the four gradient stops as follows.

Stop 1 of 4, Position: 0%, Color: **White, Background 1**

Stop 2 of 4, Position: 36%, Color: **Red, Accent 2, Lighter 40%**

Stop 3 of 4, Position: 70%, Color: **Red, Accent 2, Darker 25%**

Stop 4 of 4, Position: 100%, Color: **Brown, Accent 1, Darker 50%**

l. Continuing with the three selected shapes, apply a **gradient line**, and accept the defaults.

m. Click **Slide 7**. Size the table to 3.2" high and 8.5" wide. Click **Size & Properties** in the Format Shape pane to set the horizontal position of the table to 2.4" From **Top Left Corner** and the vertical position to 3" from **Top Left Corner**. Apply **Dark Style 2 – Accent 1/Accent 2** from the Table Styles. Add a **Soft Round Cell Bevel** effect to the table header row.

n. **Save** the presentation, exit PowerPoint, and submit your file as directed by your instructor.

Student data file needed:

 p01ch02Result.pptx

You will save your file as:

 p01ch02Result_LastFirst.pptx

Production &
Operations

Girls Inc Fundraiser Results Presentation

You are the chair of the fundraising committee for Girls, Inc. an organization that strives to inspire girls to be strong, smart, and bold by providing them with life-changing experiences and solutions to the unique challenges girls face. You need to prepare a presentation that will report the results of the fundraiser to the board members at the next meeting.

a. Open the PowerPoint file, **p01ch02Result**. Save your file as p01ch02Result_LastFirst using your last and first name.

b. Change the title font color to **Orange Accent 4**.

c. On slide 2, insert a row in the table between the rows for **Globe** and **Lemon**. Type Genovese Basil, 231, 334 in the appropriate cells.

d. Decrease the width of the second and third columns in the table.

e. Center the table headings. Left-align the plant names in the first column. Right-align the numbers.

f. Center the resized table horizontally and vertically on the slide.

g. Create a new slide 3. Use the table data in Slide 2 to create a **Clustered Column** chart.

h. Change the chart layout type to a **3-D Clustered Column** and the chart style to **Style 5**.

i. Edit the Vertical Axis Title to read Sales.

j. Delete the placeholder for the chart title.

k. Add a title to the chart slide with the text Most Varieties Increase Sales.

l. Create a new Slide 4 with the title Steps to Success. Add a SmartArt object using the **Chevron Accent Process** layout. Add the text Plan, Communicate, Work, to the SmartArt boxes.

m. Move the basil drawing from the last slide to the title slide. Enlarge the picture, and position it in the upper left corner.

n. Click the final slide, and type Thank You! as the title text. **Reset** the slide layout to **Title and Content**. Click the body text placeholder, and type the text Girls, Inc.™ can continue to empower girls all over the country because of you. Remove the leading bullet. Include the Trademark symbol after **Inc.**.

o. **Save** the presentation, exit PowerPoint, and submit your file as directed by your instructor.

Additional
Cases

Additional Chapter Cases are available at www.pearsonhighered.com/youroffice

Understanding the Art of Presentation

This business unit had two outcomes:

Learning Outcome 1:

Understand the purpose of PowerPoint and how to utilize the available tools to create effective and engaging presentations that are tailored to your audience.

Learning Outcome 2:

Arrange and format text in a presentation to ensure optimal readability and comprehension by your audience and to leverage graphics and images to enhance your presentations.

In Business Unit 1 Capstone, students will demonstrate competence in these outcomes through a series of business problems at various levels from guided practice to problem solving an existing presentation to performing to create new presentations.

More Practice 1

Student data files needed:

- p01Deals.pptx
- p01DealsCont.pptx
- p01DealsGolf.jpg
- p01DealsMassg.jpg
- p01DealsRes.jpg
- p01DealsTheme.thmx

You will save your files as:

- p01Deals_LastFirst.pptx
- p01DealsPDF_LastFirst.pdf

Painted Paradise Resort & Spa Special Deals

Sales & Marketing

The Painted Paradise Resort & Spa offers special deals to families and couples. The deals include various services such as golf, spa treatments, lodging, and meals. They are designed to persuade people to come to the resort and enjoy a perfect getaway. The deals are described in PowerPoint presentations that are sent via e-mail or shared online.

You will create a graphic-rich presentation to feature the Last Minute Deal, the Two Perfect Days Deal (for couples), and the Girls' Camp (for adults). You will use a theme, modify the colors and font of the theme, and reuse slides. You will make use of WordArt, a table to detail the Girls' Camp options, special symbols, and a custom footer.

You might notice that there is more text than would normally be used in a slide show. This is because you will not be delivering the slide show as a presenter. Instead, your audience will view it online. You will carefully check the spelling and proofread the document before saving the file as a PowerPoint PDF file.

a. Open the PowerPoint file **p01Deals**. Save your file as p01Deals_LastFirst using your last and first name.

b. On **Slide 1**, type your first and last name in the slide title placeholder, and then type today's date after the colon in the content area.

c. Click the **Design** tab, and then, in the Themes group, click **More**, and then click **Browse for Themes**. Navigate through the folder structure to the location of your student data files, and then double-click **p01DealsTheme** to apply the theme to the presentation. In Slide Master view, change the theme fonts to **Corbel** fonts, and then close this view.

d. Insert a **Title Slide Layout** as Slide 2, and then type Special Deals for You from the Painted Paradise Golf Resort & Spa as the presentation title. Change the font size to **44**. Add A passion for helping people relax as the subtitle. Modify the subtitle font to **italic**, and align the text to the **right**.

e. On **Slide 2**, add a **Rectangle** shape, **2"** in height and **5"** in width, to the top right area of the slide. Make the following changes to the shape.

- Type The time to relax is when you don't have time for it in the shape. Press Enter, and then type Sidney J. Harris.
- Select the **quotation text**, apply the WordArt style **Fill - White, Outline - Accent 1, Shadow**, and then increase the size of the font to **32**.
- Insert the Wingdings symbol with a character code of **122** in front of the name **Sidney**. Align the author's name to the right.
- Add an **Offset Diagonal Bottom Left** shadow to the shape.

f. In Slide Master view, create a new theme colors palette by changing the theme color Text/Background - Light 2 setting to **Blue, Text 2, Darker 50%**. Save the Theme Colors as SpecialDealsColors_LastFirst using your last and first name.

g. Reuse all slides from the **p01DealsCont** file, adding them to the end of the current presentation. On the Insert tab, insert **Date and time** footers to all of the slides except the title slide, click **Fixed**, and then replace the default date with Offers good through August 30. Click **Footer**, and then type Reserve now at www.paintedparadiseresort.com.

h. Using **Outline view**, make the following modifications.

- Delete the Resort Special Deals slide (Slide 4).
- Drag **Slide 7** to position **5**.
- Drag **Slide 8** to position **7**.
- On **Slide 9**, select the **Wine and appetizer buffet** line, and drag it below the Lunch line. Add Poppable Pastries and coffee in-room breakfast at the bottom of the feature list on **Slide 9**. Drag the **Poppable Pastries** line into position above the Lunch line.

i. In Normal view, on **Slide 3**, edit the graphic boxes to highlight each of the deals: **Last Minute Deals**, **Two Perfect Days**, and **Girl's Camp**.

j. Add a new **Title and Content** slide after **Slide 4**. Type Savings Highlights in the title placeholder. Insert a **3-D Stacked Column** chart, and then complete the worksheet as follows.

	Normal Pricing	Last Minute Deal 1	Last Minute Deal 2
Room	575	500	500
Spa Treatment	230	200	0
Golf	250	0	215
Meals	120	104	104

k. On the Chart Tools Design tab, in the Data group, click **Select Data**, and then switch the rows and columns in the chart. In the **Chart Layouts** group, click **Add Chart Element**, point to **Legend**, and then click **Top**. Click **Add Chart Element** again, point to **Chart Title**, and then click **None**. Edit the data by adding the following column to the end of the worksheet, and then close the chart data sheet.

Last Minute Deal 3
500
200
215
104

l.   Change the layout of **Slide 4** to **Two Content**. Add the photograph from the student data files named **p01DealsMassg**. Modify the photograph as follows.

   • Resize the photograph to a height of **2.9"**.

   • Adjust the position of the photograph to have a horizontal position of **5.25"** from the top left corner and a vertical position of **4"** from the top left corner.

   • Apply the **Drop Shadow Rectangle** picture style.

m.   On **Slide 4**, to insert the photograph of a woman with a golf club from the student data files, select **p01DealsGolf**. Modify the photograph as follows.

   • Resize the photograph to a height of **2.9"**.

   • Adjust the position of the photograph to have a horizontal position of **5.25"** from the top left corner and a vertical position of **1"** from the top left corner.

   • Apply the **Drop Shadow Rectangle** picture style.

n.   On **Slide 4**, select the **body text** placeholder, and right-click. Select **Format Shape**. In the Format Shape pane, under Text Options and then Text Box, set the Vertical alignment to the middle of the placeholder. If the right column content text placeholder is visible, delete it.

o.   On **Slide 6**, drag the **right sizing** handle of the body text placeholder to the left until it is at the left edge of the photograph.

p.   On **Slide 7**, modify the photograph as follows.

   • Alter the color to **Red, Accent color 1 Light**.

   • Resize the photograph to a height of **2.5"**.

   • Adjust the position of the photograph to have a horizontal position of **0.5"** from the top left corner and a vertical position of **3.03"** from the top left corner.

   • Apply the **Soft Edge Oval** picture style.

   • Drag the **left sizing** handle of the body text placeholder to place the text to the right of the photograph.

q.   On **Slide 8**, modify the photograph of the couple dancing by setting the **Color Tone** to **Temperature: 4700 K**. Apply the **Soft Edge Rectangle** picture style to the **couple dining** photograph. Use the **Format Painter** to apply the style to the other two photographs, and then select **all three photographs** and distribute them horizontally.

r.   On **Slide 9**, select the photograph, and then modify it as follows.

   • Resize the photograph to a height of **3"**.

   • Adjust the position of the photograph to have a horizontal position of **4.67"** from the top left corner and a vertical position of **4"** from the top left corner.

   • Change the Color Saturation to **200%**.

   • Apply the **Drop Shadow Rectangle** picture style.

s.   On **Slide 10**, insert the **Registered Sign** symbol after the word **Poppable**. This symbol is an "R" inside a circle. Modify the symbol's font effect to **Superscript**. Change the text **Poppable® Pastries** to the font color **Red, Accent 1, Darker 25%**, and change the font style to **italic**.

t.   Add a new **Title and Content** slide after Slide 10. Type The Girls' Camp Deal in the title placeholder. Add a table to the slide with **two columns** and **six rows**. Type the following information in the table.

Number of Guests	Cost per Guest
2	$500
3	$450
4	$400
5	$350
6	$300

u. Modify the table on **Slide 11** as follows.
- Resize the table to a height of **4.5"** and a width of **4.5"**.
- Center the text, and then, in the Alignment group, click **Center Vertically**.
- Apply the **Medium Style 3 - Accent 1** style to the table.
- On the Table Tools Layout tab, in the Arrange group, click **Align**, and then click **Align Center**.

v. On **Slide 12**, insert the photograph **p01DealsRes**, and resize it to a height of **3."** Drag the **photograph** to the bottom-center on the slide until the Smart Guides appear at the bottom center of the photograph. Apply the picture style **Simple Frame, White**.

w. Review the slides, carefully proofreading each item and making necessary corrections. Check the spelling, and then save the presentation. Save the file in PDF format, give it the name **p01DealsPDF_LastFirst**, and use the **Minimum size** button above **Publish**.

x. Save the presentation, exit PowerPoint, and then submit your file as directed by your instructor.

Problem Solve 1

MyITLab®
Grader
Homework

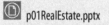
Student data file needed:
p01RealEstate.pptx

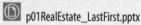
You will save your file as:
p01RealEstate_LastFirst.pptx

Selling New York

Using U.S. Census and New York State Real Property data, you have constructed a presentation to contrast the property values of metropolitan areas with those of the rest of the state. Next you focused on two similar towns in Suffolk County to make a case for living in a suburb north of the Long Island Expressway. The presentation will be shown by realtors to potential landowners. Your job now will be to add a theme, modify the layout of several slides, and manipulate the information elements in the presentation to be more appealing.

Sales & Marketing

a. Open the PowerPoint file **p01RealEstate**. Save your file as p01RealEstate_LastFirst using your last and first name.

b. Add vertical and horizontal guides at **2.25"** and **1.25"**, respectively, to help you adhere to the rule of thirds.

c. On the Title Slide, type A Tale of Two Towns in the subtitle placeholder. Apply the **Wood Type** theme to the presentation.

d. Apply a footer with the text Selling New York on all slides except the Title Slide. Apply Slide numbers.

e. On **Slide 4**, type Real Property Values, 2018 into the Title placeholder. Replace the Chart Title with the text Top 10 Municipalities With Most Land Parcels. Modify the chart to **4.7"** in height, and modify its vertical position to **2.2."**. Apply **Layout 8** to the chart, and change the vertical Axis Title to Dollars. Delete the horizontal Axis Title.

f. On **Slide 2**, move the text box to **1.8"** vertical position and horizontal position.

g. On **Slide 5**, in the Title placeholder, type Municipal Value: Parcels & Sq. Miles, and then apply **Style 6** to the Chart. Adjust the font size of the horizontal and vertical axis values to **18**. Adjust the font size of the data labels to **16**.

h. On **Slide 7**, type A Tale of Two Towns in the Title placeholder. Change the font size of the table to **20**. Adjust the width of the table to **11"**, and then center on the slide horizontally and vertically. Set Cell Margins to **Normal**, and adjust the width of the Full Value and Population columns so the data and headings fit on one line.

i. On **Slide 8**, increase the font size of the horizontal and vertical axis values to **20**.

j. On **Slide 9**, change the Chart Title to Huntington Nearly Twice as Valuable as Babylon, and then change the font size of the horizontal and vertical axis values to **18**.

k. On **Slide 10**, change the font of the vertical axis to **18**.

l. On **Slide 10**, insert WordArt with the text Living Large in Huntington. Apply the style **Gradient Fill – Gray-50%, Accent 1, Reflection** to the WordArt. Center the WordArt between the chart and the footer.

m. Save the presentation, exit PowerPoint, and then submit your file as directed by your instructor.

Problem Solve 2

Student data files needed:

 p01Funding.pptx

 p01Malala.jpg

 p01Photo.jpg

You will save your file as:

 p01Funding_LastFirst.pptx

Malala Fund Presentation

Sales & Marketing

The Malala Fund is an international organization focusing on empowering adolescent girls through secondary education in the most vulnerable communities around the world. You have been asked to improve the presentation provided, using the skills you have developed throughout this business unit.

a. Open the PowerPoint file **p01Funding**. Save your file as p01Funding_LastFirst using your last and first name.

b. Create a custom font group using **Baskerville Old Face** as the Heading font and **Arial** as the Body font. Name the custom font group FundingFonts_LastFirst using your last and first name.

c. On **Slide 1**, type The Malala Fund in the title placeholder. In the subtitle placeholder, type Empowering girls all over the world with access to quality education.

d. Use the options on the Design tab to create a custom background using the **p01malala.jpg** picture included in your student files. Modify the background picture as follows.
   - Set the Transparency to **70%**
   - Set Offset left to **-16%**
   - Set all other Offsets to **0%**
   - Apply to all slides

e. To every slide except the title slide, apply slide numbers and add a footer that contains the text, More info at www.malala.org.

f. On **Slide 2**, modify the SmartArt by applying the **Moderate Effect** SmartArt Style, and change the color to **Transparent Gradient Range - Accent 1**.

g. On **Slide 3**, use the tools in the Format Shape pane to modify the SmartArt in the following manner:
   - Apply a **Gradient fill** with a **Rectangular** type and a direction of **From Bottom Right Corner**.
   - Adjust **Stop 1 of 3** to have a **Blue, Accent 1, Darker 50%** color, a position of **0%**, and a transparency of **0%**.
   - Adjust **Stop 2 of 3** to have a **Blue, Accent 1, Darker 25%** color, a position of **50%**, and a transparency of **40%**.
   - Adjust **Stop 3 of 3** to have a **Blue, Accent 1, Lighter 40%** color, a position of **100%**, and a transparency of **40%**.

h. On **Slide 4**, modify the SmartArt by applying the **Moderate Effect** SmartArt Style and change the color to **Gradient Loop - Accent 1**. Further modify the SmartArt by changing the fill of each of the three shapes containing the bullet point with the same **Gradient fill** described in step g for Slide 3.

i. On **Slide 5**, modify the SmartArt by applying the **Moderate Effect** SmartArt Style, and change the color to **Transparent Gradient Range - Accent 1**.

j. On **Slide 6**, modify the SmartArt by applying the **Moderate Effect** SmartArt Style, and change the color to **Transparent Gradient Range - Accent 1**.

k. On **Slide 7**, use the tools in the Format Shape pane to modify the SmartArt in the same manner as you did on Slide 3.

l. On **Slide 8**, at the end of the sentence in the body placeholder, press Enter, type Donate Now at www.malala.org, and then press the Spacebar to create a hyperlink. Select the text just typed, and remove the italics and center the text inside the content placeholder.

m. Insert the **p01Photo.jpg** picture from your student files into Slide 8.

n. Resize the picture to have a height of **3"** and a width of **4.49"**.

o. Change the Color Saturation to **200%**.

p. Apply the **Center Shadow Rectangle** Picture Style. Align the photo with the left side of the title placeholder, and adjust the vertical position to be **4"** from the Top Left Corner.

q. Save the presentation, exit PowerPoint, and then submit your file as directed by your instructor.

Critical Thinking

Considering that the purpose of this presentation is to inform the audience about the Malala Fund and to persuade people to donate money, what other elements could be included in the presentation to increase its effectiveness? Give at least two examples.

Perform 1: Perform in Your Life

Student data files needed:

- Blank PowerPoint presentation
- p01FamStory.docx
- p01FamilyPic1.jpg
- p01FamilyPic2.jpg
- p01FamilyPic3.jpg

You will save your files as:

- P01Family_LastFirst.pptx
- P01FamilyShow_LastFirst.ppsx

My Family Presentation

Information Technology

In this project, you will create a slide show based on your family using the skills you have learned in this business unit. This would be great to show at a family reunion. You have many options for the organization of this presentation. You could focus on each member of your family on individual slides. You could highlight past generations of your family. Plan to include between seven and ten slides. Use the file p01FamStory to draw some thumbnails and plan the content of your slides.

Select an appropriate template, changing the colors or fonts. Create an outline with the titles and body content for your slides. Change the slide layouts as needed to accommodate the information on the slides. Slide footers should include your name and the slide number. Pay attention to the graphic details of this presentation, selecting appropriate digital photographs you may have and shapes to assist you in telling your family story. Use SmartArt creatively, perhaps to develop a family tree. Use a chart in your presentation as well as a table.

You will print an outline of the presentation, so you will know what is on each slide as you speak to the audience. You will save the presentation in PowerPoint Show format so it is easy to start.

a. Open and print **p01FamStory** to plan the content of your slides. Start **PowerPoint**, select a theme, and save the presentation as p01Family_LastFirst using your last and first name.

b. Modify the colors or fonts of the template appropriately.

c. Create seven to ten slides, with titles and body content.

d. Modify the layouts of the slides appropriately. To every slide except the title slide, add a footer that contains your first and last name and the slide number.

e. On the title slide, include your first and last name and a copyright notice with the copyright symbol.

f. Add photographs and shapes to slides in the presentation. Use vertical and horizontal guides to observe the rule of thirds. If you do not have access to any family photos, you may use the ones included with your data files.

g. Create a SmartArt graphic on a slide for a family tree.

h. Create a table on a slide to describe some aspect of your family.

i. Create a chart on a slide.

j. Check the spelling throughout the presentation. Ignore the spelling of proper names, and correct any other misspelled words. Review each slide in Slide Show view.

k. Save the presentation. Save the presentation again as a PowerPoint Show named p01FamilyShow_LastFirst. Print an outline of your presentation. Exit PowerPoint, and then submit your files as directed by your instructor.

Perform 2: Perform in Your Career

Student data files needed:

Blank PowerPoint presentation

p01HealthStore.docx

p01Dentistry.jpg

p01Nurses.jpg

p01Pharmacist.jpg

p01PhysicalTherapist.jpg

p01Preparation.jpg

p01Radiology.jpg

You will save your files as:

p01Health_LastFirst.pptx

p01HealthShow_LastFirst.ppsx

Career Day

Human Resources

As the administrative manager of the American Health Group, you have been asked to discuss health care careers during the Fall Career Expo at the local high school. Your audience will be mainly ninth and tenth graders who are deciding what careers they wish to pursue. Your presentation will discuss at least five options in the health care field. Consider nurses, doctors, therapists, medical records personnel, phlebotomists, EMT workers, psychologists, optometrists, dentists, chiropractors, and other health care careers as you prepare the presentation. You will deliver the presentation to about 30 people at one time in a classroom situation. You will need to do enough research to adequately present the material.

a. Open and print **p01HealthStore** to plan the content of your slides. Start **PowerPoint**, select a theme, and then save the presentation as p01Health_LastFirst using your last and first name.

b. Modify the colors or fonts of the template appropriately.

c. Create seven to twelve slides, with titles and body content.

d. Modify the layouts of the slides appropriately. To every slide except the title slide, add a footer that contains your first and last name, the slide number, and the current date.

e. On the title slide, include your first and last name and a copyright notice with the copyright symbol.

f. Add photographs and shapes to slides in the presentation. Be sure you have appropriate permissions for any photograph or image you use. You may also use any of the photographs included in your data files. Use vertical and horizontal guides to observe the rule of thirds when placing images on the slides.

g. Create a SmartArt graphic on a slide.

h. Create a table on a slide to either describe each career path or show local training programs for each career.

i. Create a chart on a slide.

j. Type notes in the Notes pane that reflect your research for this project.

k. Check the spelling throughout the presentation. Ignore the spelling of proper names, while correcting any other misspelled words. Review each slide in Slide Show view.

l. Save the presentation. Save the presentation again as a PowerPoint Show named p01HealthShow_LastFirst. Print an outline of your presentation. Exit PowerPoint, and then submit your files as directed by your instructor.

Perform 3: Perform in Your Team

Student data files needed:

Blank PowerPoint presentation

p01Airplane.jpg

p01BeachResort.jpg

p01Mountain.jpg

p01Park.jpg

p01Restaurant.jpg

You will save your file as:

p01Tourism_TeamName.pptx

Research & Development

Dream Travel Presentation

You are a high school senior in a geography course who has been assigned to research and prepare a presentation on a country you dream of traveling to someday. You have been assigned to work with a group of fellow classmates whose task it is to create a travel presentation about a country of your choice that you have studied in class. Arrange to meet with your group to assign specific tasks to each member, who is then responsible for researching and writing an informational slide (or more) to include in the slide show. Once a rough draft has been prepared, format and design the document with slide layouts that are not only readable and informative but also visually appealing to promote travel to and within this country. Incorporate a tourism design theme with varied visual elements and include cultural opportunities in your presentation's content.

a. Divide the informational slides to be researched and written evenly among the group members. Suggested slide topics include the following.
   - Title slide containing the country, group name, and course information
   - Content slide of major airlines that travel to your destination
   - Content slide of hotels or resorts at your destination
   - Content slide of restaurants at your destination
   - Content slide of activities to be enjoyed at your destination
   - Additional content slides of your choice, including, but not limited to:
      - Historical information
      - Sightseeing/Tour Opportunities
      - Shopping
      - Activity Highlights
      - Geographical Map of Country
      - Travel Route
      - Souvenirs
      - Languages Spoken
      - Other information of your choice
      - Slide containing an appropriate chart of potential travel expenses (e.g., a comparison of airline costs or a breakdown of total travel expenses)
      - Closing slide that lists websites with more information about your destination.

b. Research your topic(s) and write a rough draft of the content before continuing on with the PowerPoint portion of the project.

c. Select one group member to set up the document by completing steps d through f.

d. Open your browser, and navigate to www.onedrive.com, www.drive.google.com, or any other instructor-assigned location. Be sure all members of the group have an account.

e. Start **PowerPoint**, and then create a new blank document. Save the document as p01Tourism_TeamName using the name assigned to your group by your instructor.

f. Share the file with the other members of your group, and make sure that each group member has the appropriate permissions to edit the presentation.

g. Each group member will then type the rough draft content slides within the presentation file.

h. As a group, select a design theme for the entire slide show. Adjust theme colors and fonts as desired. You might want to incorporate flag colors of your chosen country. Ensure enough contrast between background and text for readability. Maintain a consistent feel throughout your presentation.

i. Use varied slide layouts for interest.

j. Incorporate visuals (e.g., SmartArt, ClipArt, Pictures, spreadsheet charts, tables, placeholder shading, shapes, and symbols) on your slides. Apply Picture Effects to enhance your images. Be sure you have appropriate permissions for any photograph or image you use. You may also use any of the photographs included in your data files.

k. Correct any spelling or grammatical errors.

l. Review your presentation by running it full-screen. Make any other improvements you think necessary.

m. Save the presentation, exit PowerPoint, and then submit your file as directed by your instructor.

Perform 4: How Others Perform

Student data file needed:

 p01FitnessData.pptx

You will save your file as:

 p01Fitness_LastFirst.pptx

Fitness Presentation

Production & Operations

You are a volunteer at your local fitness facility, River Bluffs Fitness Center. The Wellness Coordinator is responsible for conducting seasonal orientation sessions for new members of the center, which includes a presentation on facility hours, activities offered, membership rates, and camps, as well as general facility and staff information. Your supervisor has already started a presentation file with much of the required information and graphics. You have been asked to complete the slide show for tomorrow evening's summer orientation presentation for new members of the fitness center.

a. Open the PowerPoint file **p01FitnessData**. Save your file as p01Fitness_LastFirst using your last and first name.

b. On Slide 1, decrease the title text **River Bluffs Fitness Center Orientation** to a font size of **48**.

c. On Slide 2, add Membership Forms to the bottom of the bulleted list in the content placeholder. Move the content placeholder up approximately **1/2"** to better position alongside the image.

d. On Slide 3, use the Thesaurus proofing tool to change the word Prospects to **Options**. Adjust line spacing of bulleted list to **2.0**.

e. On Slide 4, apply the **Soft Edge Rectangle** picture style to both images.

f. Rearrange slides so that the slide titled Summer Sports Camps is Slide 5 and the slide titled Give is Slide 6.

g. On Slide 5, adjust the line spacing of the bulleted list to **1.5**. Apply a **Dark Green Accent 2** picture border to the image.

h. On Slide 6, using the Linear Venn layout from the Relationship category, insert a SmartArt graphic. Delete one of the circular shapes before entering the words Mentor, Volunteer, and Donate in the remaining three shapes. Apply the **Inset SmartArt** style and **Colorful Range-Accent Colors 2 to 3** to the graphic. Move the SmartArt graphic to the left about **1"**.

i. On Slide 7, insert an Online Picture by searching for teamwork in the Bing Image Search tool. Insert the image of linked stick people. Position and resize the image along the right side of the bulleted list.

j. Insert a new slide below Slide 2. Be sure the new slide has a Title and Content slide layout. Enter 2018 Membership Rates as the title. Insert a 4 × 4 table, and enter the following information.

Description	Annual	Continuous	Introductory
Youth	$173.00	$15.50	$50.55
Adult	$590.00	$51.00	$175.00
Family	$840.00	$72.00	$240.00

k. Adjust the font size of all text to **24**, and adjust the height of the table to **2.5"**. Center-align the column headings **Annual**, **Continuous**, and **Introductory**. Right-align the dollar amounts in the last three columns.

l. Correct any spelling or grammatical errors.

m. Review your presentation by running it full-screen. Make any other improvements you think necessary.

n. Save the presentation, exit PowerPoint, and then submit your file as directed by your instructor.

PowerPoint Business Unit 2

Collaborating and Invoking Emotion with the Audience

Thousands of business presentations are created each and every day using PowerPoint, and most of them are forgettable. They have become so predictable and commonplace that thousands of mediocre presentations bore audiences to the point of sleep or, to use the phrase coined by Angela Garber, create "Death by PowerPoint." With a little investment of time, you can learn to use the more advanced features of PowerPoint to take your presentations to the next level.

Learning Outcome 1:

Utilize advanced PowerPoint elements to create high-quality presentations using transitions and animations, embedded media files, and photo albums.

Real World Success

"Learning how to use PowerPoint as a way to reinforce my presentations, not be the presentations, has helped me throughout my entire college experience. Many of my classes require one or more presentations, and my classmates are always coming to me for advice."

- Benjamin, current student

Learning Outcome 2:

Customize PowerPoint to create a brand using themes, slide masters, and layouts, and collaborate with others using comments and speaker notes.

Real World Success

"I interned for a small business last summer, and their sales team was continually creating presentations for various events where they would have an opportunity to inform people about their products. I noticed that each presentation had a completely different look and feel to it as each presentation has a different individual authoring it. I took the initiative to create a custom template that incorporated colors and themes from the company logo, and it was a big hit!"

- Blake, recent graduate

Microsoft PowerPoint 2016

Chapter 3 | MULTIMEDIA AND MOTION

Prepare Case

The Turquoise Oasis Spa Presentation for Marketing

The Turquoise Oasis Spa manager, Meda Rodate, has asked you to create a presentation to send to people who make inquiries about the spa. This presentation is to introduce people to the spa by showing photographs of the spa, detailing the treatments, and giving other useful information for first-time spa guests.

The presentation will be distributed via a PDF and as an e-mail attachment. Custom slide shows will be developed from the presentation for specific clients, such as brides who want to enjoy the spa before their wedding.

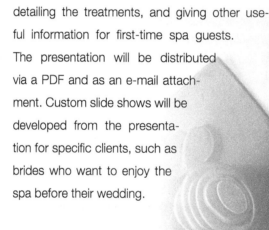

OBJECTIVES

1. Use transitions and animations. p. 877

2. Create hyperlinks within a presentation. p. 885

3. Apply and modify multimedia in presentations. p. 892

4. Create a PowerPoint photo album. p. 898

5. Create a custom slide show. p. 904

6. Save a presentation in multiple formats. p. 907

Valua Vitaly/Shutterstock

Student data files needed for this chapter:

 p02ch03Spa.pptx

 p02ch03Greeting.wav

 p02ch03Music.mp3

 p02ch03Reflexology.mpg

p02ch03Spa1.jpg

p02ch03Spa2.jpg

p02ch03Spa3.jpg

p02ch03Spa4.jpg

p02ch03Spa5.jpg

p02ch03SpaTheme.thmx

p02ch03SpaMeda.jpg

p02ch03PaintBrush.jpg

You will save your files as:

 p02ch03Spa_LastFirst.pptx

 p02ch03SpaAlbum_LastFirst.pptx

 p02ch03SpaCustom_LastFirst.pptx

 p02ch03SpaVideo_LastFirst.mp4

p02ch03SpaHandouts_LastFirst.docx

Using Motion and Multimedia in a Presentation

Motion, such as transitions and animations, along with multimedia elements, such as audio and video, can enhance presentations. Motion and animation can invoke emotion in the audience; multimedia can break up a presentation and is often used to explain concepts in a way that appeals to people who have different learning styles. Multimedia can also add entertainment value to your presentation while maintaining a professional appearance.

Multimedia objects are applied in a variety of ways in PowerPoint. Simple transitions and animations of the slides and content can engage the audience. Hyperlinks enable moving through the presentation in a nonsequential slide order or using the resources of the Internet. Buttons and triggers enable the start of multimedia actions. Sounds and recorded narrations enhance slide shows that are self-playing in kiosks or on DVDs. Movies can be embedded into presentations to engage your audience.

As always, use caution when applying multimedia to your slide shows. Remember that you are the focus of the presentation, and the multimedia should support you and your message. Too much multimedia also tires your audience. Remember the KISS principle: Keep It Short and Simple!

In this section, you will apply a variety of multimedia features to your presentation to support the marketing message of the spa.

Use Transitions and Animations

PowerPoint 2016 has some powerful tools for creating transitions and animations in a presentation. **Transitions** are defined as the visual and audio elements that occur as the slides change. When used effectively, transitions can add a professional quality to your presentations. **Animations** refer to the movement of elements, such as text and graphics, on a slide.

Transitions and animations have many settings, with opportunities to apply multiple actions to a slide. Consider the purpose of the slide, and select the elements that support the message. It is important to maintain consistency with the transitions and animations within the presentation. Suppose you want to build interest in a product. You may decide to list the individual components of the product, one by one, and then make the big reveal at the end of the slide. This animation method works well if you want to focus the audience's attention on one bullet point at a time.

Transitions can also be used to automatically advance the slides after a set amount of time. As you know, most of the time, slides are advanced by an individual clicking the mouse button or a remote slide presenter or by pressing a key on the keyboard. Slides that play on a **kiosk** — which is a computer system that provides information to people in nontraditional places such as museums, grocery stores, or banks — should have automatic transitions. You have the option to make each of the slides advance after a set amount of time, as indicated on the Transitions tab.

Opening the Starting File

The staff at the Turquoise Oasis Spa have put together a basic PowerPoint presentation. In this exercise, you will enhance the presentation by adding effective transitions, animations, and other multimedia objects.

 P03.00

To Get Started

a. Start **PowerPoint**, click **Open Other Presentations** in the left pane, and then double-click **This PC**. Navigate through the folder structure to the location of your student data files, and then double-click **p02ch03Spa**. The spa presentation will open. Look through the presentation to get a feel for what it is about.

b. Click the **File** tab, click **Save As**, and then double-click **This PC**. In the **Save As** dialog box, navigate to the location where you are saving your project files, and then change the file name to p02ch03Spa_LastFirst, using your last and first name. Click **Save**.

Applying Effective Transitions

Slide transitions can take many different forms in a presentation. The Transitions tab contains the options that are applied to the slides, which are divided into three categories of transition types: Subtle, Exciting, and Dynamic Content. Sounds can be applied to the transitions. You can modify the length of time it takes for the transition to occur and can determine the action, such as a mouse click, that causes it to occur. If you want to have a self-playing presentation, such as one that might be displayed in a kiosk, you can use the Transitions tab to set up the changing of the slides.

The presentation meets the minimum requirements that Meda Rodate asked for, but to be an effective marketing tool, it needs to engage the recipient and invoke a desire to come to the spa. In this exercise, you will begin the process of improving the presentation by adding transitions.

 P03.01

To Apply Transitions

a. Click **Slide 2**, and then click on the **Transitions** tab, in the Transitions to This Slide group, click **More** ⊽ to reveal all of the available transitions. Notice the organization of the transitions into the three categories: Subtle, Exciting, and Dynamic Content.

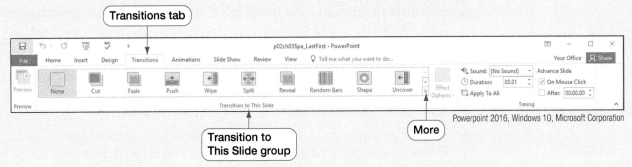

Transitions tab

Transition to This Slide group

More

Powerpoint 2016, Windows 10, Microsoft Corporation

Figure 1 Transitions

SIDE NOTE

Select Multiple Adjacent Slides

You can select multiple slides by clicking the first slide in the range, and then pressing and holding Shift while clicking the last slide in the range.

SIDE NOTE

Select Nonadjacent Slides

You can select multiple slides by pressing and holding Ctrl while clicking on the slides you wish to select.

b. Explore some of the various transitions, and think about what kind of emotion they may invoke.

c. Click the **Reveal** transition. This transition brings with it a feeling of calm relaxation, perfect for a relaxing day at the spa.

d. Select **Slides 3** through **12**, and then in the Transitions to This Slide group, click **Reveal** to apply this transition to all the slides except the title slide.

e. Select **Slides 2** through **7**. In the Transition to This Slide group, click **Effect Options**, and then click **Smoothly From Left**. Slides 8 - 12 now have the default effect option of Smoothly From Right.

f. Click **Slide 12**. In the Transition to This Slide group, click **Effect Options**, and then select **Through Black From Right**. This change in transition effect will help to signal the end of the presentation.

g. Select **Slides 2** through **12**. On the Transitions tab, in the Timing group, click in the **Duration** box, type **2.3** and then press Enter to reduce the duration of the Reveal transition.

h. Press F5 to view the slide show from the beginning. Navigate through the slides, and then exit the presentation when you have reviewed each transition.

i. Click **Save** 🔲.

Editing Transitions

As you work with transitions, you may want to change settings you have made. For instance, in the project you are working on, you may decide that the transitions need to occur more quickly, or you could modify the effects applied to the individual slides.

Keep in mind that you should have some consistency in the way the transitions occur. In your project, you selected a single transition type, but you then applied different effect options to the transitions on different slides. In this exercise, you will modify the speed of the transitions and add a sound to some of the slide transitions.

To Modify Transitions

a. Click **Slide 5**. On the Transitions tab, in the Timing group, click the **Sound** arrow, and then select **Chime** from the list of available sounds.

b. In the Preview group, click **Preview** to preview the gentle chime sound along with the transition. Adding a transition sound to select slides is one way to add emphasis to specific content.

c. Click **Slide 12**, and then in the Timing group, click the **Sound** arrow, and then click **Other Sound.**

d. Navigate to the student data files, click **p02ch03Greeting**, and then click **OK**.

Notice the audio file plays instantly upon adding it to the slide and will play automatically when this slide appears in the presentation. You will change this later so that the audio will play only when the photograph is clicked.

e. Press F5 to view the slide show from the beginning. Navigate through the slides, and then press Esc at the end of the slide show to return to Normal view.

f. Click **Save** 🖫.

Animating Objects for Emphasis

Animations affect the individual objects on the slide. Bullet points, text, and graphics can be timed to appear on the slide. The three major animation groups are Entrance, Emphasis, and Exit. In the **Entrance animation**, the action happens as the object enters the slide, and in the **Exit animation**, the action occurs as the object leaves the slide. The **Emphasis action** is applied to the object after it is displayed on the slide. Another animation option is to set up a motion path to move the object.

Animations can be started in one of three ways. You can start the animation by clicking the mouse. The animation can be set up to play with any previous action on the slide. You can also set up the animation to play after another animation. You can set the **duration**, or length of time an animation effect takes to play, in parts of a second. You can also **delay** the action, causing it to play after a certain number of seconds. When you select a content placeholder, you have the choice to apply the effect to the text as One Object, All at Once, or By Paragraph. The One Object option treats all of the text in the text box as a single animation. The All at Once animation may appear to be the same as the One Object animation, but with different animation types, such as the Fly In, it will be more evident. The By Paragraph animation applies the action to elements of the placeholder object one at a time.

 CONSIDER THIS | **Appropriate Animations and Sounds**

Using animations and sound that enhance your presentation is a skill that is developed over time. Can you describe a presentation in which you saw appropriate, engaging animations and sound used? Can you describe a situation in which animations or sounds distracted from the presentation?

REAL WORLD ADVICE | **Create Movielike Motion with Morph**

Available only to Office 365 subscribers, this new feature makes it easier to do simple animations in your presentation. Morph can animate not only images and text, but also 3-D shapes or be applied at a word or even character level. Duplicate the slides you want morphed together, move the objects based on how you want them to animate, and click the Morph button under Transitions.

Select animations carefully while keeping in mind the important points being made by the slide. Emphasize those points. In this exercise, you will apply animations to the tour slides, making the photographs appear one after the other. This will give the feeling of walking through the spa.

P03.03

To Animate Objects

a. Click **Slide 2**. Click the **Reception Area** photograph, press and hold Shift, and then click the **Reception Area** text box to select both objects. Click the **Animations** tab, and in the Animation group, click **Fade** to apply the Fade animation to both selected objects.

Notice the two small numbered boxes next to the objects. The same number indicates that the animations applied to the objects will occur simultaneously.

> **Troubleshooting**
>
> If the Fade animation is not visible, click **More** ⬇ , and then in the Entrance group, click Fade.

b. Select the **photo** and **text box** again. In the Timing group, click the **Start** arrow. Click **With Previous**, click the **Duration** box, type 1.3 and then press Enter. In the Preview group, click **Preview** to view the animation. Notice that changing the start from On Click to With Previous has changed the animation sequence number from 1 to 0 on the photo and the associated text box.

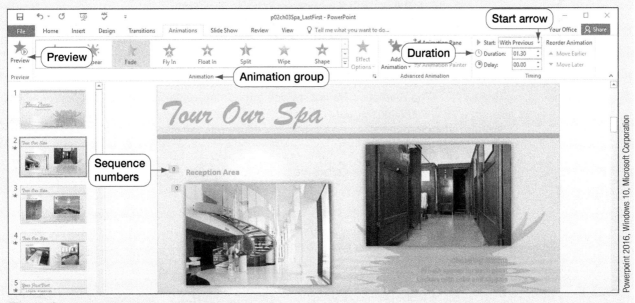

Figure 2   Animations Tab

c. Click the **Changing Rooms** photograph, press and hold Shift, and then click the **Changing Rooms** text box. In the Animation group, click **Fade**.

d. Select the photo and text box again. In the Timing group, click the **Start** arrow, and then click **With Previous**. Click the **Duration** box, type 1.3 and then press Enter. Click the **Delay** box, type 1.3 and then press Enter.

Notice the numbers next to all the objects are zero, indicating that their animations are triggered by the display of the slide. After a 1.3 second delay, the Changing Rooms objects will appear with the same Fade animation.

e. Click the **Reception Area** photograph. In the Advanced Animation group, double-click **Animation Painter** to copy the animation settings so they can be applied to multiple objects.

f. Complete the following to use the Animation Painter to apply the animations to other objects.

- Click **Slide 3**, and then click the **Showers** photograph to apply the animation formatting to the image.

- Click **Slide 4**. Click the **Private Jacuzzi** photograph, and then click the **Private Jacuzzi** text.

- Click the **Animation Painter** to return the mouse pointer to normal.

g. Click **Slide 2**. Click the **Changing Rooms** photograph, and in the Advanced Animation group, double-click **Animation Painter**.

h. Complete the following to use the Animation Painter to apply the animations to other objects.

- Click **Slide 3**, and then apply the animation to the **Sauna** photograph.

- Click **Slide 4**, and then apply the animation to the **Couples Massage** photograph and text. Click the **Animation Painter** to return the mouse pointer to normal.

i. Click **Slide 3**. Select the **text box** with the text **Showers**, **Private**, and **Wheelchair accessible**, and in the Animation group, click **Fade**.

Notice the animation sequence applied to the text is 1, which means the text will appear after both images.

j. In the Advanced Animation group, click **Animation Pane**.

The Animation Pane provides a roadmap of the order and duration in which the animations occur. The numbers indicate the order, and the bars indicate the duration.

k. In the Animation Pane, click the **Up** arrow [▲] to reorder the text animation to occur before the Sauna photograph (Picture 12) but after the Showers photograph (Picture 13).

l. In the Timing group, click the **Start** arrow, and then click **With Previous** so that the Showers text appears with the Showers photograph. In the Timing group, click in the **Duration** box, type 1.3 and then press [Enter].

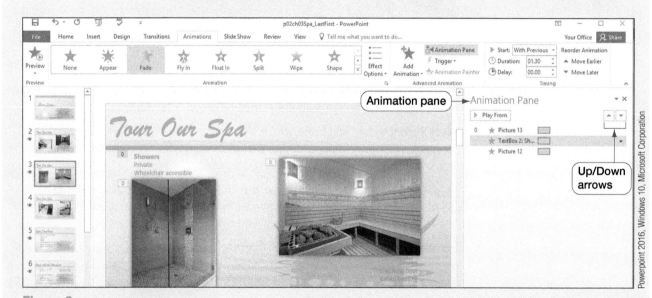

Figure 3 Animation Pane

m. Select the **text box** with the text **Sauna**, **Therapeutic heat**, **Zoned heating**, and **Ocean sounds**. On the Animations tab, in the Animation group, click **Fade**. After the animation preview occurs, reselect the text, click the **Start** arrow, and then click **With Previous** so that the Sauna text appears with the Sauna photograph. Click in the **Duration** box, type 1.3 and then press Enter.

n. Close ☒ the Animation Pane, press F5 to view the slide show from the beginning, and then click through the first five slides to review the animations and transitions. Press Esc to return to Normal view.

o. Click **Save** 🖫.

Adding Motion Paths

Creating a motion path animation is another simple way to engage your audience. PowerPoint 2016 provides several basic motion paths including lines, arcs, turns, loops, and even custom paths that you design. The object simply follows the motion path that you define with the same options for when to start, duration, and delay that other animations have.

In this exercise, you will add an image of a paintbrush to Slide 11, apply a custom motion path to the image, and adjust the settings to create the illusion of the paintbrush painting the pricing table. This simple animation can draw the audience's attention to the content of the slide.

 P03.04

To Add a Motion Path

a. Click **Slide 11**.

b. Click the **Insert** tab, and then in the Images group, click **Pictures**. Browse to your student data files, click **p02ch03PaintBrush**, and then click **Insert**.

c. Click the **Format** tab, and then in the Adjust group, click **Remove Background**. Drag the lower right-corner **sizing handle** toward the lower right corner of the image to include the entire paintbrush handle. In the Refine group, click **Mark Areas to Keep**, and click on the two purple areas of the metal brush handle to keep this part of the brush image. In the Close group, click **Keep Changes** to remove the background color from the image.

d. In the Size group, click the **Shape Width** 🔲 box, type 6.0" and then press Enter.

e. Right-click the **paintbrush** image, and then click **Size and Position**. Click **Position** to expand the section. Click the **Horizontal position** text box, type 7.3", click the **Vertical position** text box, and then type 3.5". Close the **Format Picture** pane.

f. Click the **Animations** tab, and then in the Animation group, click **More** 🔽, scroll down, and then in the Motion Paths group, click **Custom Path**.

g. Drag a **zigzag** pattern, starting from the tip of the paintbrush to the top left-corner of the pricing table, and then zig back and forth as you work your way down the table.

h. Once you have reached the bottom of the table, drag one more line so that the custom path ends just below the table, and then press Enter to create the custom path.

i. Once the custom path has been created, you will see a green arrow indicating the start of the motion path and a red arrow indicating the end of the motion path. Make any adjustments necessary so that the motion path end point does not block any of the information in the pricing table.

> ### Troubleshooting
> Once the motion path is created, you may see that PowerPoint shifts the path to the right of the table. Using the Preview button is the best way to see the custom path in action.

j. In the Preview group, click **Preview** to see the custom path in action. The default duration of the custom path is too fast for the painting effect you are trying to create.

k. Click the **paintbrush** picture, and then in the Timing group, click in the **Duration** box, type 4.25 and then press [Enter].

l. In the Timing group, click the **Start** arrow, and then click **With Previous**. Now that the paintbrush has a custom path animation, you will add an animation to the pricing table, giving it an effect of being painted by the paintbrush.

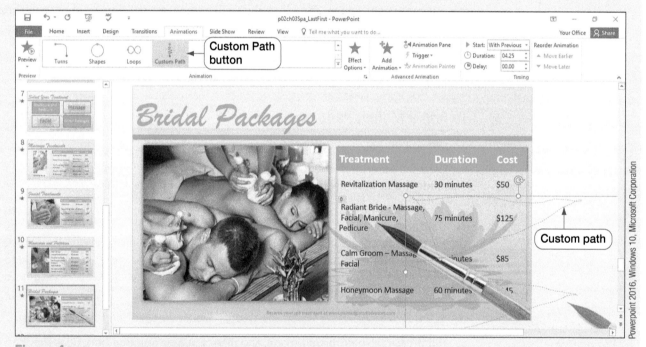

Figure 4   Custom motion path

m. Click the **pricing table**. In the Animation group, click **Wipe** to apply the Wipe animation to the photograph.

n. In the Animation group, click **Effect Options**, and then select **From Top**. In the Timing group, click the **Start** arrow, and then select **With Previous**. Click in the **Duration** box, type 3.5, and then press [Enter]. Click the **Delay** box, type 0.5 and then press [Enter].

  The .50-second delay will allow the paintbrush animation to begin moving before the pricing table animation begins.

Troubleshooting

Depending on how long your zigzag custom path is, you may need to adjust the animation durations and delay for the effect to look good.

o. Click **Slide Show** 🖵 on the status bar to view the slide in presentation mode. Press [Esc] to return to Normal view.

p. Click **Save** 🖫.

Create Hyperlinks Within a Presentation

Hyperlinks are objects, such as text or graphics, which provide a path to additional resources. Hyperlinks serve two purposes in PowerPoint. You can hyperlink to slides that are not in the normal progression of the slides. Hyperlinks can also link to Internet resources, such as e-mail and the web. This gives the audience an opportunity to interact with the presentation.

You will begin by setting links from Slide 7, where the treatments are listed, to the slides later in the presentation that contain the appropriate information. You will also create a hyperlink back to Slide 7 so the audience can select another treatment option. Later, you will hide the slides so the only way to view them is to click the hyperlink.

Linking to Other Slides

Objects of all types can be set as hyperlinks in the slide show. This means that a graphic or text can link to a different slide. As with hyperlinks on the web, a 🖑 is displayed to indicate a hyperlink as the slide show is displayed if the mouse pointer hovers over the link.

It is important to provide a way back to the original slide so the audience is not left at a dead end in the presentation. Again, a graphic or text object can be used to link back to the original slide. In this exercise, you will provide a link to each of the treatment option slides. In a future exercise, you will add the link back to Slide 7, which lists the options.

 P03.05

SIDE NOTE

Insert Hyperlink Dialog Box

If you close the Insert Hyperlink dialog box too soon, you can right-click the box, and then click Edit Hyperlink in the shortcut menu to return to the dialog box.

To Create Hyperlinks to Other Slides

a. Click **Slide 7**. Select the **Manicure and Pedicure SmartArt box**, click the **Insert** tab, and then in the Links group, click **Hyperlink**.

b. In the Insert Hyperlink dialog box, click **Place in This Document** on the left.

c. In the Select a place in this document list, select **10. Manicures and Pedicures**.

d. Click **ScreenTip**, located in the top-right corner of the Insert Hyperlink dialog box. In the ScreenTip text box, type Check out our manicure and pedicure offerings.

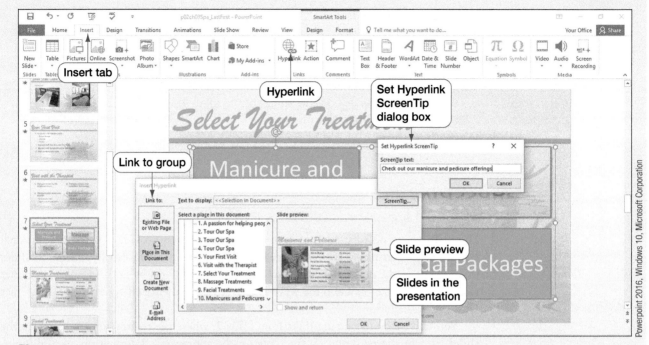

Figure 5   Creating hyperlinks in a presentation

e. Click **OK**, and then click **OK** again.

f. Click **Slide Show** 🖵 on the status bar to view the slide in presentation mode.

Notice that if you hover your pointer over the Manicure and Pedicure box, the ScreenTip text appears. And if you click the box, the slide transitions to Slide 10.

g. Press [Esc] to return to Normal view.

h. Click **Slide 7**, and then complete the following to create a hyperlink to the Massage Treatments slide.

- Select the **Massage box**, and then on the Insert tab, in the Links group, click **Hyperlink**.

- In the Select a place in this document list, select **8. Massage Treatments**.

- Click **ScreenTip**. The Set Hyperlink ScreenTip dialog box opens. In the ScreenTip text box, type Relax with a professional massage, click **OK**, and then click **OK** again.

i. Complete the following to create another hyperlink to the Facial Treatments slide.

- Select the **Facial box**, and then in the Links group, click **Hyperlink**.

- In the Select a place in this document list, select **9. Facial Treatments**.

- Click **ScreenTip**. The Set Hyperlink ScreenTip dialog box opens. In the ScreenTip text box, type Look years younger with our facial treatments, click **OK**, and then click **OK** again.

j. Complete the following to create another hyperlink to the Bridal Packages slide.

- Select the **Bridal Packages box**, and then click **Hyperlink**.

- In the Select a place in this document list, select **11. Bridal Packages**.

- Click **ScreenTip**. The Set Hyperlink ScreenTip Dialog Box opens. In the ScreenTip text box, type Options for the bride and groom, click **OK**, and then click **OK** again.

k. Press F5 to view the slide show from the beginning. As you view the slides, check each hyperlink to verify that it goes to the correct slide. You can right-click the slide and then click **Last Viewed** to return to Slide 7 after checking each hyperlink.

As you continue through the presentation, you will notice that the slides promoting the various services are repeated. In a later exercise, you will hide those slides.

l. Press Esc to return to Normal view.

m. Click **Save** 🖫.

Creating Hyperlinks to Websites

Two types of hyperlinks, to a web page or to an e-mail address, link the audience to these Internet resources. An active Internet connection is required for these links to work. When someone clicks a hyperlink to a web page, the default browser opens and the page is displayed. When the e-mail hyperlink is clicked, the default e-mail application opens.

In this exercise, you will add an e-mail link for Meda Rodate and a website hyperlink to the Painted Paradise Resort & Spa.

 P03.06

SIDE NOTE

Hyperlinks

Hyperlinks should always appear on a single line. If the URL does not need to be viewed, create descriptive text to use instead, or you could use TinyURL.

TinyURL is a URL-shortening service on the web that provides short aliases that can be used for redirection to long URLs.

To Create Hyperlinks to the Internet

a. Click **Slide 12**. Click at the end of the **phone number**, and then press Enter to move to the next line. Type E-mail: and then press the Spacebar once.

b. Click the **Insert** tab, in the Links group, click **Hyperlink**, and then under Link to, click **E-mail Address**.

c. In the **Text to display** text box, type mrodate@paintedparadiseresort.com. In the **E-mail address** text box, type mrodate@paintedparadiseresort.com again. Notice that PowerPoint automatically adds the words mailto: before the e-mail address.

d. In the **Subject** text box, type Important request from presentation. Click **OK**. Providing an automatic subject line gives Meda or her staff a way to recognize that the e-mail came from this link in the presentation.

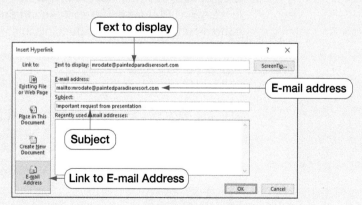

Figure 6 Setting up an e-mail hyperlink

e. If necessary, click at the end of the **e-mail address text**, and then press Enter once. Type Website: and then press the Spacebar once.

f. On the Insert tab, in the Links group, click **Hyperlink**, and then under Link to, click **Existing File or Web Page**.

g. In the **Text to display** text box, type www.paintedparadiseresort.com. In the **Address** text box, again type www.paintedparadiseresort.com. Notice that PowerPoint adds "http://" before the typed URL.

h. Click **ScreenTip**. The Set Hyperlink ScreenTip dialog box opens. Click in the **ScreenTip** text box, and then type Visit our website, click **OK**, and then click **OK** again.

i. Click the **Animations** tab, and then in the Animation group, click **Fade**. In the Timing group, click the **Start** arrow, and then click **With Previous**. Click in the **Duration** box, type 2.0 and then press Enter.

j. Click **Slide Show** 🖵 on the status bar to view the slide in presentation mode. Confirm that clicking the hyperlinks, start the correct Internet resource — the default browser or e-mail application.

k. Close each application after it opens. Press Esc to return to Normal view.

l. Click **Save** 🖫.

Adding Action Buttons

Action buttons are special shapes that are predefined to include actions that help you navigate through slides. The buttons are available on the Insert tab in the Shapes gallery. If the shape you wish to use is not available in the Shapes gallery, you can either modify an existing shape or combine shapes together to make new shapes. The actions include moving to a previous slide or the next slide, skipping to the first or last slide of the presentation, playing a sound or movie, opening a document, or opening a Help feature.

In this exercise, you will add Action buttons to your presentation to return to Slide 7 from each of the treatment slides. You also will modify the shape by changing the colors to better blend with your presentation.

To Add and Modify Action Buttons

a. Click **Slide 8**. Click the **Insert** tab, and then in the Illustrations group, click **Shapes**. In the Action Buttons group, click **Action Button: Back or Previous** ◁. Click the bottom-right corner of the **slide** to place the graphic.

b. In the Action Settings dialog box, click the **Hyperlink to** arrow, select **Slide...**, and then in the Hyperlink to Slide dialog box, click **7: Select Your Treatment**. Click **OK**, and then click **OK** again.

c. With the Back or Previous shape selected, click the **Drawing Tools Format** tab, and then in the Size group, click the **Shape Height** 🔟 box, type 0.6", and press Enter. Click the Shape Width 🔲 box, type 0.8", and then press Enter.

d. In the Arrange group, click **Align**, click **Align Right**, click **Align** again, and then click **Align Bottom**.

The shape is now aligned to the bottom-right corner of the slide.

e. In the Shapes Styles group, click **More** ⏷, and then select **Moderate Effect-Dark Teal, Accent 1**, located in the fifth row of the second column from the left.

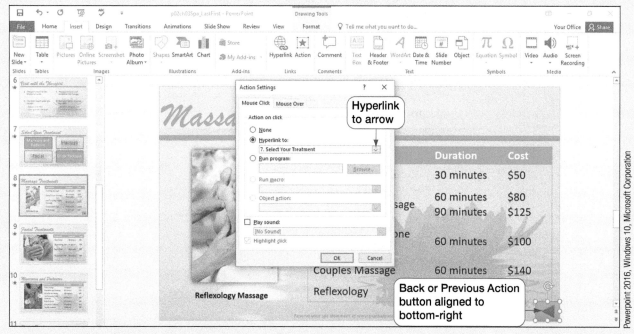

Figure 7 Action buttons

f. Right-click the **Action Button: Back or Previous** shape and then select **Copy**. Click **Slide 9**, right-click the slide, and then under Paste Options, select **Use Destination Theme** 📋. Repeat the pasting of the **Action Button: Back or Previous** shape on **Slide 10** and **Slide 11**.

g. Click **Slide 7**, and then click **Slide Show** 🖵 on the status bar. Click each **link**, and then click the **Action** buttons on the resulting slides to ensure they work correctly. Press [Esc] to return to Normal view.

h. Click **Save** 🖫.

Hiding Slides

There are a number of reasons why you might want to hide slides in a presentation. In this project, you want to hide the treatment detail slides unless the person viewing the presentation clicks on a hyperlink. In other cases, you may want to anticipate questions your audience might have and place some hidden slides within your presentation to reveal if they ask these questions.

In this exercise, you will hide Slides 8 - 11 in the presentation. They will open only if someone clicks a link on Slide 7. With the Back buttons you set up, they can return to Slide 7 to view other treatments

To Hide Selected Slides

a. Click **Slides 8** through **11.**

b. Click the **Slide Show** tab, and then in the Set Up group, click **Hide Slide** to hide slides 8 - 11 from the presentation. Notice the slide images fade and slashes are placed through the slide numbers.

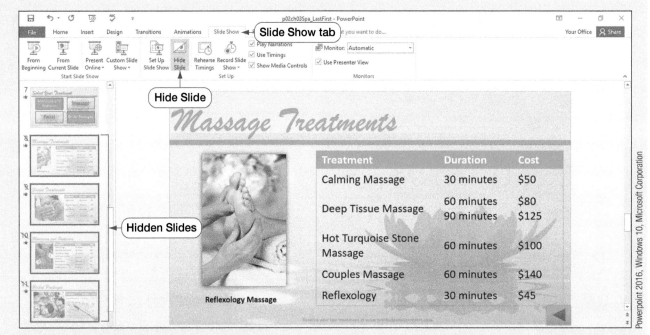

Figure 8 Hiding slides

c. Click **Slide 7**, and then click **Slide Show** 🖵 on the status bar to view the presentation from the current slide. Click each **link**, and then click the **Back or Previous Action** button to return to Slide 7.

d. Press Enter to advance to the next visible slide.

Notice the next visible slide is Slide 12 with Meda Rodate. Hidden slides are accessible via links or by using the See All Slides command when you right-click a slide during a slide show.

e. Press Esc to return to Normal view, and then click **Save** 🖫.

Adding a Trigger

Triggers are set on objects that already contain animation; this enables you to create movement, reveal additional objects, play a sound or movie, or emphasize objects. The trigger object can be a graphic or text, and it must be clicked for the animation to occur.

In your project, Meda begins speaking as soon as Slide 12 is displayed. It can be disconcerting for people to suddenly hear someone speaking when they did not expect it. In this exercise, you will change the transition and apply a trigger to Meda's photograph to play her recorded message when someone clicks the photograph.

REAL WORLD ADVICE | **Making Sound Choices**

When working on a slide show, consider the audience as you add audio to your presentation. Will they view your presentation in a quiet location where sound would not be appreciated, such as in the office or library? Also consider the likelihood they will have speakers or a headset, and that the sound may be turned up. If you are making the presentation in person, make sure the sounds you select add to the value of the presentation.

P03.09

To Add a Trigger

a. Click **Slide 12**. Click the **Transitions** tab, and then in the Timing group, click the **Sound** arrow. Click **[No Sound]** to remove the sound from the transition, if a sound is showing.

b. Click the **Insert** tab, and then in the Illustrations group, click **Shapes**. In the Basic Shapes group, click the **Oval** shape, and then drag an oval over Meda's face. You will animate the oval to play the recording Meda made and later hide the oval behind her photograph.

c. With the **Oval** shape selected, click the **Format** tab, and then in the Size group, click the **Shape Height** box, type 1.9", and press Enter. Click the Shape Width box, type 1.2", and then press Enter.

d. Right-click the **Oval** shape, and then click **Size and Position**. Click **Position** to expand the section. Click the **Horizontal position** box, type 1.6", click the **Vertical position** box, and then type 3.7". Close the **Format Shape** pane.

e. Click the **Animations** tab, and then in the Animation group, click **Appear**.

f. In the Advanced Animation group, click **Animation Pane**. Click the **black** arrow to the right of the oval name, and then click **Effect Options**.

g. In the Appear dialog box, on the Effect tab, click the **Sound** arrow, and then click **p02ch03Greeting**.

h. Click the **Timing** tab, and then click **Triggers**. Click the **Start effect on click of**, and then click **Picture 8**.

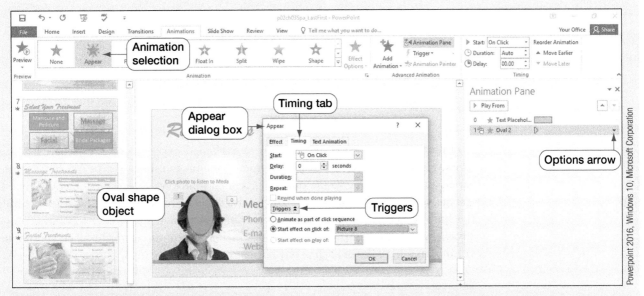

Figure 9   Adding a trigger

i. Click **OK**. The recording begins to play as a preview of the animation.

j. Click the **oval** to select it. Click the **Format** tab, and then in the Arrange group, click the **Send Backward** arrow, and then click **Send to Back**. Notice the oval is no longer visible, as it is behind the photograph of Meda Rodate.

k. Click the **Animations** tab, in the Advanced Animation group, click **Animation Pane** to close the Animation Pane.

l. Click **Slide Show** 🖳 on the status bar. Click **Meda's photograph** to listen to her message, and then press Esc to return to Normal view.

m. Click **Save** 🖫.

Apply and Modify Multimedia in Presentations

As with other elements added to a presentation, sounds and videos are inserted using the Insert tab. Sounds can be found and added from audio files, such as MP3 or WAV files. As the audio is added, a player with a Play button is automatically added to the slide. With the player selected, you can modify the way the sound is played, having it play automatically when the slide is displayed, or when the Play button is clicked. Audio can play across slides so a background song continues to play as the user advances the slides. Audio can be looped so it continues to play until it is stopped. The audio file can be set to fade in at the beginning of the playback and fade out at the end. If the file is too long, it can be trimmed.

PowerPoint 2016 supports a wide variety of multimedia formats and includes more built-in codecs than ever before so you do not have to install them on your computer for certain file formats to work.

QUICK REFERENCE	Supported Audio File Formats
File Format	**Extension**
AIFF audio file	.aiff
AU audio file	.au
MIDI file	.midi or .mid
MP3 audio file	.mp3
Advanced Audio Coding — MPEG-4 audio file	.m4a or .mp4
Windows audio file	.wav
Windows Media audio file	.wma

In some cases, video is the only way to explain a concept to your audience. At other times, video can be used to emphasize something on the slide. Videos can come from a variety of sources. A video file can be embedded from your disk drive, OneDrive online storage, or YouTube. YouTube videos can also be embedded into a presentation by using the Embed code under the Share option for a particular video. One consideration, as always, is making sure that you are not violating someone's copyright when you import video from other sources such as any online resources.

QUICK REFERENCE	Supported Video File Formats
File Format	**Extension**
Windows Media file	.asf
Windows video file	.avi
MP4 video file	.mp4, .m4v, or .mov
Movie file	.mpg or .mpeg
Adobe Flash media	.swf
Windows Media video file	.wmv

PowerPoint can also add bookmarks to both audio and video files. Bookmarks mark sections of the file so the user can jump to a certain point in the file before starting the playback. This is useful if you want the focus to be on a part of the audio file as a sound bite during a presentation but also want to have the entire file available if the user decides to play the complete file for the audience.

Keep in mind that when video is added to a presentation, the file size increases significantly. Also, a slide might be slow to display if a large file is embedded.

Inserting Audio Files

To set the mood for the spa presentation, you will play a short musical file on the first slide. It will start automatically and not require a player. In this exercise, you will trim the file to create a smaller presentation file. You will also adjust the volume so it is a gentle musical interlude.

 P03.10

To Add an Audio File to a Presentation

a. Click **Slide 1.** Click the **Insert** tab, in the Media group, click the **Audio** arrow, and then click **Audio on My PC.**

b. If necessary, navigate to your student files, click **p02ch03Music**, and then click **Insert.** On the player controls, click **Play/Pause** ▶ to listen to the song.

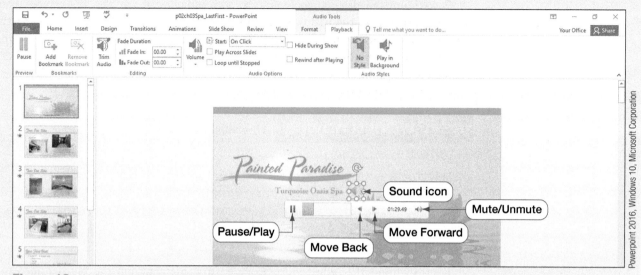

Figure 10 Adding audio and the player controls

c. Click the **Audio Tools Playback** tab, and then in the Editing group, click **Trim Audio**. In the **End Time** box, select the numbers, type 15.5 and then press Enter.

d. On the Audio Tools Playback tab, in the Editing group, click the **Fade In** box, type 5.0 and then press Enter. Click the **Fade Out** box, type 5.0 and then press Enter.

e. In the Audio Options group, click the **Volume** arrow, and then click **Medium**. Click **Play/Pause** ▶ to listen to the edited song.

f. In the Audio Options group, click the **Start** arrow, select **Automatically**, and then click **Hide During Show**.

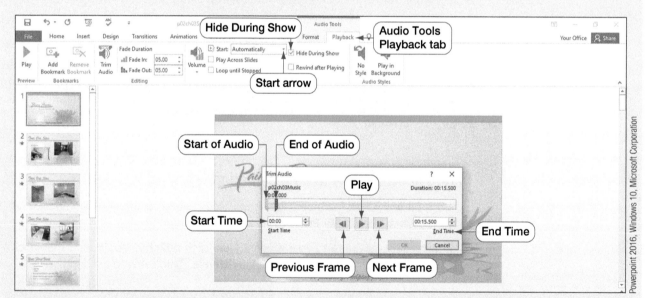

Figure 11 Trimming audio

g. Click **Slide Show** 🖵 on the status bar. You may continue through the slide show or press Esc to return to Normal view. Click **Save** 🖫.

The audio clip is a nice introduction to the spa presentation by setting the mood. However, if someone viewing the presentation does not have the volume turned up, they will not lose any important information by not hearing the clip.

Recording Narration

Slide narration is a useful addition to presentations when you will not be making the presentation in person. You can record the narration as you view the slides using a simple recorder available in PowerPoint, or you can record the narration in a different sound software application, such as Audacity, and add the narration to the slides as a part of the transitions or animations, as you did with the audio files earlier.

CHAPTER 3

REAL WORLD ADVICE	Recording Narration and Slide Advances

The Slide Show tab contains options for setting up the slide show with timed advancement of the slides as well as recorded narration. If you will not be giving the presentation in person, this method works well. The slides are displayed full screen as you record your presentation. You record the narration and advance each slide. When you have reached the end of the slide show, you will be asked whether you want to retain the timings. This method of preparing a presentation works well for distance learning, sales presentations, and kiosks.

Slide 5 contains notes for you to record as narration. The computer you use will need a microphone so you can record the notes. In this exercise, you will modify the sound object so the narration begins when the slide is displayed and the player does not show on the slide. If you do not have a microphone, read the procedure but skip the steps.

 P03.11

To Record Slide Narration

a. Click **Slide 5.** If necessary, click Notes in the status bar to show the slide notes. Drag the **border** between the Slide pane and the Notes pane up until you can see both paragraphs of text in the Notes pane.

b. Click the **Insert** tab, and then in the Media group, click the **Audio** arrow, and then select **Record Audio**.

Read through the text in the Notes pane before you begin to record. This will save you some time and let you experiment with the inflections of your voice.

> **Troubleshooting**
>
> The Record Audio tool will be available only if you have a built-in or plugged-in microphone. Skip the Record Narration steps if you do not have a microphone available.

c. If necessary, drag the **Record Sound** dialog box up so you can see the notes. Click the **Record** button, and then begin reading the notes into the microphone. Click the **Stop** button when you have completed the reading. Click **Play** to review the recording.

> **Troubleshooting**
>
> If you would like to re-record the audio, click Cancel, and then repeat Steps b and c.

d. In the Name box, type Slide 5 Recording.

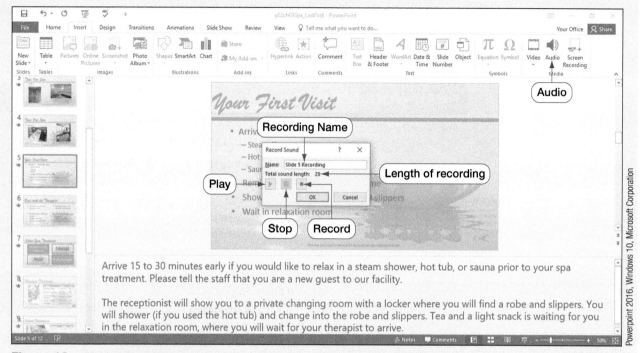

Figure 12   Recording slide narration

e. Click **OK** to save the recording to the slide.

f. Click the **Speaker** 🔊 that appears in the center of the slide, and then click the **Playback** tab.

g. In the Audio Options group, click the **Start** arrow, select **Automatically**, and then click **Hide During Show**.

h. Click **Slide Show** 🖳 on the status bar. Review **Slide 5**, and then press Esc to return to Normal view. Readjust the Notes pane so it takes up less space. Click **Save** 🖫.

Inserting Video Files

Video clips are engaging to the audience. They provide movement on the screen. They can be used to show live action of a procedure, as you might do in training. You can creatively use video to introduce products, provide support to your sales staff, and present customer testimonials.

In this exercise, you will replace the Reflexology Massage photograph on Slide 8 with a short video.

P03.12

To Add Video to a Presentation

a. Click **Slide 8**, click the **reflexology** photograph, and then press Delete.

b. Click the **Insert** tab, and then in the Media group, click the **Video** arrow, and then select **Video on My PC**. Navigate to your student files, click **p02ch03Reflexology**, and then click **Insert**.

c. Click the **Format** tab, in the Size group, click the **Video Width** box, type 4.0" and then press Enter. In the Size group, click **Crop**, and then drag the **middle-right sizing handle** in slightly to remove the green bar on the right side of the video. Click **Crop** again to accept the crop adjustment and to keep the video selected.

d. Drag the **video** to the left beside the table and above the **Reflexology Massage** box.

e. Click the **Playback** tab, and then in the Video Options group, click the **Start arrow**, select **Automatically**, click **Loop until Stopped**, and then click **Hide While Not Playing**.

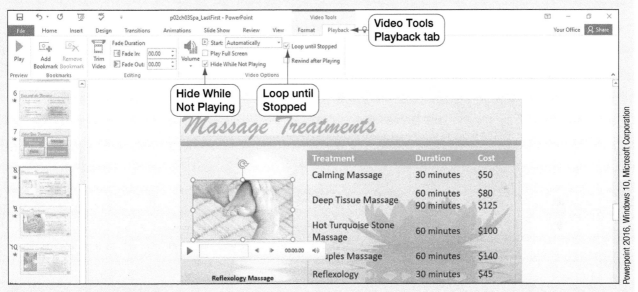

Figure 13 Video embedded

f. Click **Slide Show** on the status bar, and then review the slide. Press Esc twice when you have finished watching the video.

g. Click **Save** and close the presentation. If you need to take a break before finishing this chapter, now is a good time to take a break.

Creating Photo Albums and Custom Shows

Two additional features of PowerPoint that can enhance your presentations are the Photo Album feature and Custom Slide Shows. Both are easily created with just a few tools available in PowerPoint 2016.

The **Photo Album** feature of PowerPoint is an efficient way to insert a large number of photographs into a slide show just by selecting the photographs you want to include in the presentation. You do not have to individually insert, resize, or arrange the pictures on the slides. This saves you time and effort, and produces a professional looking album of photographs.

A **custom slide show** is a subset of slides in a larger presentation. Think of it as a presentation within a presentation. You create a main presentation and then create custom shows within the presentation for your targeted audience.

In this section, you will create and modify a photo album. You will also create two custom slide shows.

Create a PowerPoint Photo Album

Available on the Insert tab, the Photo Album button opens a dialog box that enables you to select the photographs from a storage location, such as a disk drive or a USB drive. Once the photographs are in the album, you can preview them in the dialog box and change the rotation, brightness, and contrast. You can change the order of the photographs. Text can be added to the slide at this stage or added with boxes after the presentation has been created. You can modify the layout of the pictures on the page, specify the shape of the frames around the photographs, and apply a theme.

REAL WORLD ADVICE | **Using a Photo Album in Business**

Most people turn to PowerPoint's Photo Album feature when they have a lot of vacation or family photos to make into a presentation, but photo albums also have uses in the business world. Consider these ideas:

- Product catalog, showing the items and a short description
- Product history album, showing photographs of different stages toward completion of a project, such as a building project
- Owner's manual, showing photographs of important parts of the machinery
- Training manual, showing a group of figures with comments
- Testimonials from satisfied customers with photographs of them enjoying the product
- Meet the staff album, showing photographs of everyone on the staff with their names and other important information

---

It is important to note that when you use the Photo Album feature in PowerPoint, a new file will be generated. The photo album is not added into the current open presentation. Once the album has been created, the slides can be reused in other slide shows.

Continuing with the spa chapter, you will create a photo album that will introduce members of the spa staff. You will later combine these album slides with the slides from the spa presentation.

Selecting Photographs

The most efficient way to select the photographs for the album is to group all of the pictures in a single folder. This makes it easier to select the ones you need. For instance, in the photo album you will create in this chapter, the photographs you will use begin with the same code and name, p02ch03Spa. If necessary, you can update a photo album and add more photographs later, using the Edit Photo Album feature.

CONSIDER THIS | **Using Social Networking Photographs**

Given the popularity of social networking sites such as Facebook, what pictures could be found of you on the Internet? Is it ethical to use a picture from one of these sites without permission? Are there situations in which it would be illegal?

In this exercise, you will create a small photo album with photographs of the members of the staff. It will be added to the spa presentation later.

P03.13

To Create a Photo Album

a. If you took a break, open the **p02ch03Spa_LastFirst** presentation.

b. Click the **File** tab, click **New**, and then click **Blank Presentation**.

Troubleshooting

If you closed PowerPoint and not just the presentation from the previous exercise, Start PowerPoint, and then in the Start screen, click Blank Presentation.

c. Click the **Insert** tab, and then in the Images group, click **Photo Album**, and then click **New Photo Album**.

d. In the Photo Album dialog box, click **File/Disk**, and then navigate to your student files. Select all five of the files beginning with **p02ch03Spa1** through **p02ch03Spa5**, and then click **Insert**.

Troubleshooting

You can select multiple files at once by clicking the first file name, pressing Shift, and then clicking the last file name, or you can select nonadjacent files by pressing Ctrl, while clicking each file name.

e. Click each **file name** in the Pictures in album box to see a preview of each file. Click **Save** 🔚.

The files are not in the correct order. You will arrange them in a later part of the project. One of the photos is displayed sideways. You will correct that in the next part of the project.

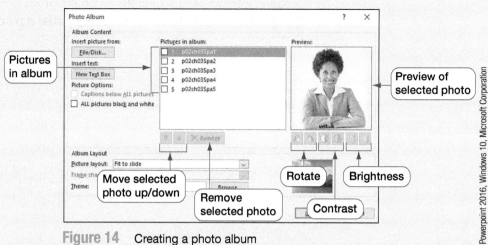

Figure 14   Creating a photo album

Modifying Photographs

Once imported into a photo album, photographs can be modified with some simple tools. They can be rotated in 90-degree increments, either clockwise or counterclockwise. The contrast and brightness of the photographs can be adjusted in the Photo Album dialog box. You can also specify that all pictures be converted to black-and-white in the photo album without changing the original picture color.

When the photo album is created, you will be able to make more sophisticated adjustments, such as altering the color temperature and color tone. In this exercise, you will adjust the brightness and contrast of a photograph and rotate one of the photographs.

P03.14

To Modify the Photographs with the Photo Album Tools

a. In the Pictures in album box, select **p02ch03Spa5** by clicking the check box next to the file name, and then click **Rotate 90 degrees Clockwise** once. Deselect **p02ch03Spa5**.

> **Troubleshooting**
>
> If you clicked the wrong button and the woman is now displayed upside down, continue clicking the button until she is in the correct orientation.

b. Select **p02ch03Spa1** in the Pictures in album box, click **Decrease Brightness** once, and then click **Increase Contrast** twice. Deselect **p02ch03Spa1**.

c. Click **Save** .

Arranging Photographs

There are a number of layouts to select from when creating a photo album in PowerPoint. A picture can fill the slide or be placed in the middle of the slide, or you can have two or four pictures per slide. There is an option to place a title on each of the slide pages, regardless of the number of photographs on the slide. You can also choose from seven frame shapes that will hold the photographs.

Photographs can be moved in the photo album with the arrow buttons at the bottom of the Pictures in album box. If you will be placing two or more photographs on a slide, you can also control which photograph appears on the right or left by the order in which you place the file names.

You have decided to display one photograph per slide with a title. In this exercise, you will specify a center shadow rectangle for the frame shape. You will also move the files into the correct order.

To Alter the Arrangements of Photographs in the Photo Album

a. In the Album Layout group, click the **Picture layout** arrow, and then select **2 pictures with title.**

b. Click the **Frame shape** arrow, and then select **Center Shadow Rectangle**.

c. Select **p02ch03Spa5**, and then click **Up** ⬆ four times to move the photograph into position 1. Deselect **p02ch03Spa5**.

d. Select **p02ch03Spa2**, and then click **Down** ⬇ three times to move this file to the end of the list. Deselect **p02ch03Spa2**.

e. Click **Save** 🖫.

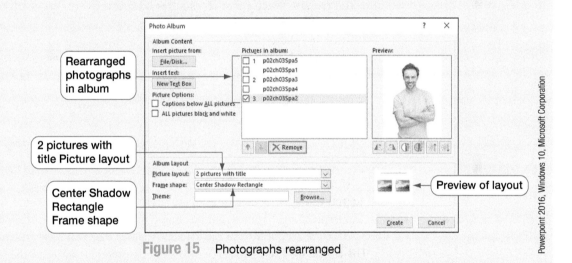

Figure 15 Photographs rearranged

Powerpoint 2016, Windows 10, Microsoft Corporation

Inserting Text

Text can be added to slides in two ways from the Photo Album dialog box. You can add boxes that you will later fill with text or you can add **captions**, which are boxes that describe the photographs. The default captions will be the names of the files, which are not something you want the audience to see, so do not forget to update the captions if you use them. If you later decide you do not want to use the boxes, they can be replaced with other objects or deleted.

In this exercise, you will add text boxes to each of the slides that will introduce a staff member of the spa.

To Add Text to a Photo Album

a. Select **p02ch03Spa5** in the Pictures in album list, and then click **New Text Box** under the Insert text heading. The box appears in the list under the photograph file name that was highlighted. Deselect **p02ws03Spa5**.

b. Complete the following to add a text box to the remaining slides with photographs.

- Select **p02ch03Spa1**, and then click **New Text Box.** Deselect **p02ch03Spa1**.

- Select **p02ch03Spa3**, and then click **New Text Box.** Deselect **p02ch03Spa3**.

- Select **p02ch03Spa4**, and then click **New Text Box.** Deselect **p02ch03Spa4**.

- Select **p02ch03Spa2**, and then click **New Text Box.** Deselect **p02ch03Spa2**.

- Click **Save** 🖫.

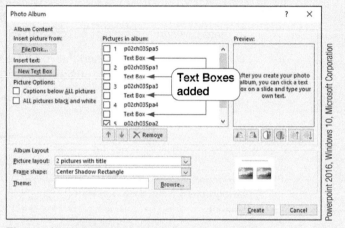

Figure 16   Text boxes added

Selecting a Theme

Just as you can add themes to a presentation, you can add a theme to a photo album. The Microsoft Office themes that are stored on your computer during the installation of Office 2016 are available. You can also use themes that you have created.

The theme for the Introduction to the Spa presentation is available in your student data files. In this exercise, you will apply the theme to your photo album to maintain consistency with the spa presentation because you will be reusing slides from the album in the spa presentation.

 P03.17

To Add a Theme to a Photo Album

a. In the Photo Album dialog box, under Album Layout, click **Browse**. Navigate to your student files, click **p02ch03SpaTheme**, and then click **Select**.

b. Click **Create**, and then press [F5] to view the slide show from the beginning. Review the slides in the Photo Album presentation, and then press [Esc] to return to Normal view.

c. Click the **File** tab, click **Save As**, and then double-click **This PC**. In the **Save As** dialog box, navigate to the location where you are saving your project files. Type p02ch03SpaAlbum_LastFirst, using your last and first name. Click **Save** 🖫.

Editing a Photo Album

As you can see, it is quick work to select photographs and place them on slides using the Photo Album feature of PowerPoint. Depending on selections you make, you may need to edit the slides. Once the photo album has been created, the slides can be modified using the normal PowerPoint tools. You can resize and move the photographs, modify the appearance of the photographs, and add text.

After reviewing the slides, you realize that you did not include Meda Rodate in the staff photo album. In this exercise, you will return to the Photo Album dialog box to add her photograph. You will also add text to the presentation in Normal view.

To Add Text and Edit the Photo Album

a. Click the **Insert** tab, in the Images group, click the **Photo Album** arrow, and then select **Edit Photo Album** to open the Edit Photo Album dialog box.

b. Click **File/Disk**, click **p02ch03SpaMeda**, and then click **Insert**.

c. Select **p02ch03SpaMeda**, click the **Up** arrow ⬆ to move the photograph into position 1.

d. Click **New Text Box** under the Insert text heading. Deselect **p02ws03SpaMeda**. A new text box will be inserted under the **p02ws03SpaMeda** photo.

Figure 17   Editing a photo album

e. Click **Update** to display the revised photo album.

f. Click **Slide 2**, select the title placeholder, and then type Meda Rodate, Spa Manager. Select the words **Text Box**, and then type Meda has over ten years of experience in spa management. If necessary, select the text you have just typed in the text box, click the **Home** tab, and then in the Paragraph group, click **Align Left** ≣.

g. Complete the following to add information to each to the remaining slides.

   • Click **Slide 3**, select the title placeholder, and then type Irene Kai, Salon Manager. Select the words **Text Box**, and then type Irene strives to make clients feel comfortable and pampered when they come to the Turquoise Oasis Spa.

   • Click **Slide 4**, select the title placeholder, and then type Kelly Mathews, Receptionist. Select the words **Text Box**, and then type Kelly is dedicated to making our spa clients feel welcome and relaxed.

- Click **Slide 5**, select the title placeholder, and then type Jason Niese, Massage Therapist. Select the words **Text Box**, and then type Jason views massage as an important part of health and well-being.

- Click **Slide 6**, select the title placeholder, and then type Kendra Mault, Massage Therapist. Select the words **Text Box**, and then type Kendra is passionate about massage and the many benefits it provides.

- Click **Slide 7**, select the title placeholder, and then type Leslie Dixon, Nail Technician. Select the words **Text Box**, and then type Leslie strives to stay on top of new trends and to continue to learn new techniques.

Figure 18 Slide 7 of the photo album

h. Click **Slide 1**, click the **title** placeholder, and select the text **Photo Album**. Type Meet Our Staff. In the subtitle placeholder, ensure that your name was added. If not, type to add your first and last name.

i. Click **Save** 🖫, and then close the presentation.

The photo album was modified to create a staff introduction slide presentation to include with the Introduction to the Spa presentation. Later, you will reuse the slides in the photo album in the Introduction to the Spa slide show and create a customized presentation.

Create a Custom Slide Show

In a custom slide show, you select the slides from the main presentation and group them to create a customized presentation. Perhaps you do not need all of the slides in a presentation because your audience has different characteristics or needs. Using the Custom Slide Show feature, you can select just the slides you want to display. Another advantage of creating custom slide shows is that you can display the slides in a different order than in the original slide show.

Customizing a Slide Show

All of the slides that you will need in a custom slide show must be in the same slide presentation. You cannot select slides from different presentations. Because you want to use slides from both the photo album and the Introduction to the Spa presentation, you will save the spa presentation with a new name, and reuse the slides from the photo album.

Once the slides have been combined into the same presentation, you will build the custom show. Only certain slides will be selected. You will also modify some parts of the new spa presentation so it functions more efficiently.

 P03.19

To Create Custom Slide Shows

a. If necessary, open the **p02ch03Spa_LastFirst** presentation file. Click the **File** tab, click **Save As**, and then double-click **This PC**. In the **Save As** dialog box, navigate to the location where you are saving your project files, and then change the file name to p02ch03SpaCustom_LastFirst, using your last and first name. Click **Save**.

b. Click **Slide 11**. On the Home tab, in the Slides group, click the **New Slide** arrow, and then select **Reuse Slides**. Click **Browse** in the Reuse Slides pane, and then click **Browse File**. Navigate to where you saved **p02ch03SpaAlbum_LastFirst**, and double-click the **file name**.

c. Click **Keep source formatting** at the bottom of the Reuse Slides pane to select this option. Click **Slides 2** through **7** in the Reuse Slides pane to add them to the presentation. Be sure to click each slide only once to avoid inserting multiple slides into the presentation.

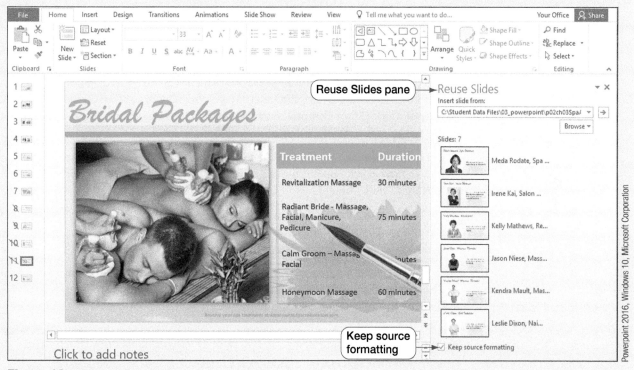

Figure 19 Reuse Slides pane

d. **Close** ⊠ the Reuse Slides pane.

e. Click the Slide Show tab, in the Start Slide Show group, click **Custom Slide Show**, and then select **Custom Shows**. In the Custom Shows dialog box, click **New**. Select the **Custom Show 1** text, and then in the Slide show name box type Facilities-Staff.

f. Under Slides in presentation, select **1. A passion for helping people relax** through **4. Tour Our Spa**.

g. Select **12. Meda Rodate, Spa Manager** through **17. Leslie Dixon, Nail Technician**. Click **Add**.

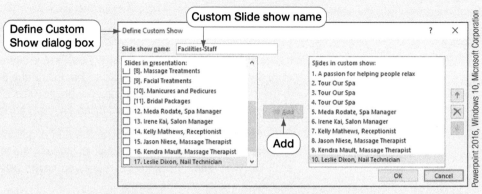

Figure 20   Creating a custom slide show

h. Click **OK**, and then click **Close**. Save 🔲 the presentation. You have created the presentation, and you will now display it as a custom slide show.

i. On the Slide Show tab, click the **Custom Slide Show** arrow, and then select **Facilities-Staff**. Navigate through the presentation making sure that it all works, noting that there are no transitions on the slides that were reused from the photo album.

j. Click **Slide 12**, press and hold ⇧Shift, and then click **Slide 17** to select the six slides. Click the **Transitions** tab, and then in the Transitions to This Slide group, click **Reveal**. Click **Effect Options**, and then select **Smoothly From Right** if needed. In the timing group, click the **Duration** box and type 2.3.

k. Click the **Slide Show** tab, and then in the Start Slide Show group, click **Custom Slide Show**. Click **Facilities-Staff**, and then review each slide. Press [Esc] to return to Normal view.

    You notice that you did not add the Reservations Information slide to the presentation. You will need to go back and edit the presentation to include Slide 18.

l. In the Start Slide Show group, click **Custom Slide Show**, and then click **Custom Shows**. The Facilities-Staff custom show is selected because it is the only show. Click **Edit**.

m. Click **18. Reservations Information** in the Slides in presentation box. Click **Add**. The slide will be added to the presentation at the end, which is exactly where you want it to be. Click **OK**, and then click **Close**.

n. Click the **Slide Show** tab, and then in the Start Slide Show group, click **Custom Slide Show**. Click **Facilities-Staff**, and then review each slide. Press [Esc] to return to Normal view.

    While viewing the custom presentation again, you notice that the slides with the staff members are missing the footer. You will need to fix this so that all of the slides are consistent.

o. Click **Slides 12** through **17**. Click the **Insert** tab, in the Text group, click **Header & Footer**, and then click **Footer** to select it. In the Footer box type Reserve your spa treatment at www.paintedparadiseresort.com. Click the **Don't show on title slide check box** to deselect it, and then click **Apply**.

p. Click **Save** ⊟. On the Slide Show tab, in the Start Slide Show group, click **Custom Slide Show**, click **Facilities-Staff**, and then review each of the slides in the presentation to ensure that the footer is on all of the slides with the exception of slide 18 and the first slide. Press ⎋ to return to Normal view. You will now create another custom slide show to focus on the facilities at the Turquoise Oasis Spa.

q. If necessary, click the **Slide Show** tab, and then in the Start Slide Show group, click **Custom Slide Show**, and select **Custom Shows**. Click **New**, select the **Custom Show 1** text, then type Facilities in the Slide show name box. Click **1. A passion for helping people** through **6. Visit with the Therapist** in the Slides in presentation box. Click **18. Reservations Information**, and then click **Add**, click **OK**, and then click **Close**.

r. In the Start Slide Show group, click **Custom Slide Show**, and then select **Facilities** to view the newly created custom slide show. Press ⎋ to return to Normal view.

s. Click **Save** ⊟, and then **close** the presentation.

Now, with a single presentation, you have two customized presentations to share with different audiences. The presentation can be used with guests who are new to the spa.

If you need to take a break before finishing this chapter, now is a good time to take a break.

Saving and Sharing a Presentation

PowerPoint can save your presentation files in a variety of formats and allows you to easily share your presentation with others. Using the Share tab on the File tab, you can share your presentation files in a variety of ways, depending on whether or not your presentation file is saved locally, on a SharePoint site, or on OneDrive. Using the Invite People option, you can invite people to view or collaborate with you on your presentation, generate a link to share with others, and give them view or edit permissions. You can post your presentation to various social networks like such as Facebook, Twitter, and LinkedIn. Using the E-mail option, you can send a presentation via an e-mail as either a PowerPoint, PDF, or XPS attachment, or as a link. Using the Present Online option, you can set up the presentation to be broadcast to remote viewers by sending them a link so they can view the slides on the web in real time as you display them. Slides can also be published to a slide library or SharePoint site so other people can access and update the presentation.

In this section, you will explore various options to save and share your presentation with others. You will also learn how to export your presentation in various formats.

Save a Presentation in Multiple Formats

Using the Export tab on the File tab, you can save the presentation in different types of file formats. You can create a PDF or XPS document. These file formats retain the fonts, formatting, and images exactly as you created them in PowerPoint, and the content cannot be easily changed. You can export the presentation as a video with automatic timings to advance the slides to be displayed on computer monitors, projectors, mobile devices, or DVDs.

The Export tab also has the option to Create Handouts. Handouts allow you to create Word documents with the slides and notes. This enables you to make modifications in layout and format to the handouts. You can also add additional content to the handouts. When you use this option to create the handouts, changes you make to the slide presentation will automatically update the handout.

Saving and Sending a Presentation via E-Mail

You have a number of options to select from when you use the E-mail option on the Share tab. You can attach the PowerPoint file in its native format (.pptx) to an e-mail message. You can e-mail a link to a shared location on a server so others can view it and make modifications. The file can be saved in PDF format and attached to an e-mail message. You can do the same for an XPS file. The file can also be sent as an Internet fax if you have a fax service provider.

In this exercise, you will share the Spa presentation via e-mail as a PDF attachment to yourself so you can see the result. Keep in mind that the various formats create files of different sizes. Generally, a PDF file is smaller than an XPS file. Both of these types are smaller than the PowerPoint format of .pptx. Consider the content of the presentation as you select the file type. PDF and XPS files do not enable internal hyperlinks to other slides, play audio or video, or display slide transitions or animations. If these things are necessary for your presentation, you need to send the file in PowerPoint format.

 P03.20

To Send the Presentation as a PDF

a. Open PowerPoint, under Recent, double-click **p02ch03Spa_LastFirst**. If the file is not available under Recent, click **Open Other Presentations**, navigate to the location where you store your project files, and then double-click **p02ch03Spa_LastFirst**.

b. Click the **File** tab, and then click **Share**.

c. Click **Email**, and then click **Send as PDF**. PowerPoint will now publish the slides as a PDF and attempt to launch your default desktop e-mail program.

> ### Troubleshooting
> If you do not have a desktop e-mail client configured, you may not be able to complete these steps. Ask your instructor for additional information.

d. Type your e-mail address in the To field. Type your instructor's e-mail address in the Cc field. Select the Subject text, which is the file name, and then type Introduction to the Spa First Last, using your first and last name. Click in the **Message** box, and then type I am sending you this presentation in PDF format. It is a smaller file, but you will not be able to hear the audio or see the animations. Press [Enter], and then type Enjoy! Press [Enter] again, and then type your first and last name.

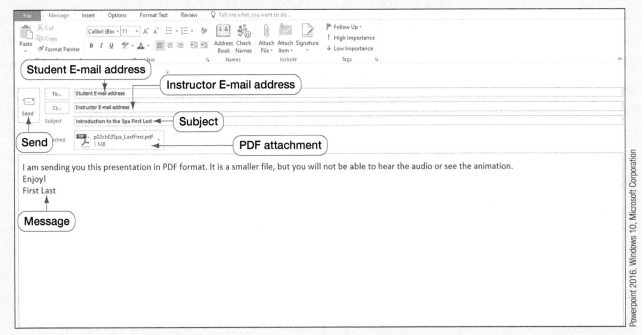

Figure 21 Sending a presentation as a PDF

e. Click **Send**. Navigate to your inbox to which the e-mail was sent. Open the message when it arrives, and then click the **attachment link**. Your default PDF reader opens the file and the presentation is displayed in PDF format.

f. Scroll through the PDF to advance the slides. Notice the speaker icon replaces audio. There are no transitions. On the Select Your Treatment slide, click a **hyperlink**. It will not link to the hidden slides because those slides were not saved as part of the PDF file. Click the **e-mail hyperlink** for Meda and an e-mail message window opens. Close the window without sending a message to Meda.

g. Close the PDF.

Saving a PowerPoint Presentation as a Video

PowerPoint videos display the slides with all of the features that you build into the slide. The animations, transitions, audio, and video work as they do in the normal Slide Show view. Be aware that hidden slides are not part of the video and that hyperlinks do not work. Once you have created the video, it can be distributed via DVD, the Internet, or e-mail.

Saving a presentation as a video provides an opportunity to create the presentation in one of three different overall file sizes. You can create the video for presentation quality which will have the highest quality (1920 × 1080) but also the largest file size. Internet quality has a medium file size and moderate quality (1280 × 720), and Low Quality has the smallest file size but also the lowest quality (852 × 480). The file is saved as an MPEG-4 Video (mp4) and can be played using Windows Media Player, iTunes, or any other desktop video player.

In this exercise, you will create the video in low quality to minimize storage space. Because the slides were not set up to advance automatically, you will use the timings provided on the Create a Video pane to advance the slides.

P03.21

To Export a PowerPoint Presentation as a Video

a. Click the **File** tab, and then on the **Export** tab, click **Create a Video**.

b. Click the **Presentation Quality** arrow, and then select **Low Quality**.

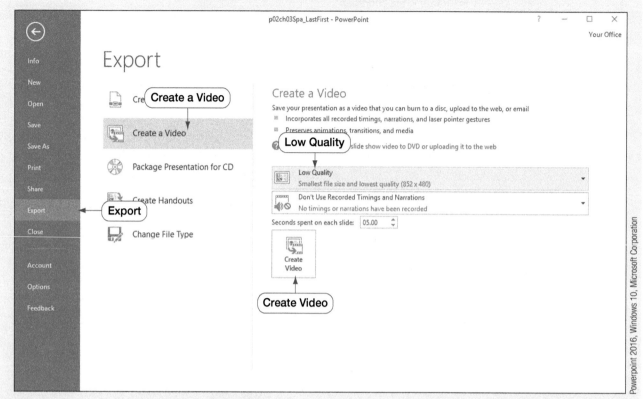

Figure 22 Exporting a presentation as a video

c. Click **Create Video**. The Save As dialog will open. Save your file as p02ch03SpaVideo_LastFirst, using your last and first name and then click **Save**.

The video will be processed and stored in the location where you save your project files. This process can take quite a bit of time. Notice the status bar at the bottom of the window reports that it is creating a video. Wait until it is finished before proceeding to the next step.

d. Navigate to where you are storing your completed files, and then open **p02ch03SpaVideo_LastFirst** to play it.

Notice the slides advance automatically after five seconds of display. If media elements are on the slide, such as the music on the first slide, those elements will play before the five-second counter begins. If you have slides with a lot of text, you may have to increase the time the slides are displayed before creating the video so people can read the whole slide before it advances.

e. Close the media player, and then return to the **p02ch03Spa** presentation.

REAL WORLD ADVICE **Video Considerations**

As you consider the size limitations that some people have on their e-mail inbox, you may turn to YouTube or your OneDrive as alternative storage locations for the video. You could then provide a link to the video in the e-mail message that you send to your intended audience.

CONSIDER THIS | **YouTube Privacy**

If you use YouTube as a storage location for presentation video, privacy can become a concern. In what circumstances would YouTube be an appropriate storage location? What type of presentation video should not be placed on YouTube?

Creating Handouts in Word Format

PowerPoint creates handouts by showing the slides in full-slide format or thumbnail format. There are times when you might want to have the handouts in Word format so you can manipulate them using Word. For instance, you may want to add additional content to the handouts or change the layout. You could also use this document as a beginning point for creating training materials, with details of procedures, for the audience to take with them after viewing a presentation.

You will create a Word document that contains thumbnails of the slides and the notes. You will add your name and today's date to the first page of the document. Do not print the document unless directed by your instructor.

To Create Handouts

a. Click the **File** tab, and then click **Export**. Click **Create Handouts**, and then click **Create Handouts**.

The Send to Microsoft Word dialog box shows five options. You can place notes or blank lines next to the slides or below them. You can also send only the outline to Word. In this dialog box, you have the option to paste the slides into the Word document or to use the Paste Link option, which creates linked slides in the Word document that are updated if the original slides in PowerPoint are altered at a later time.

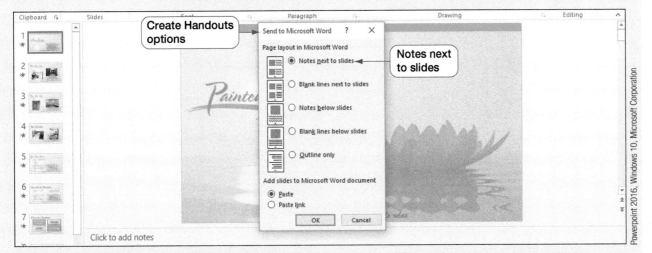

Figure 23 Exporting a presentation to print handouts

b. The first option, with Notes next to slides is already selected, so click **OK**.

A new Word document will open on your desktop. You may have to click the application on the taskbar to view the file. It will take a little time for the document to completely render. The first several slides do not have notes. Notice that the hidden slides are also shown in the Word document.

c. Scroll down the document until you see **Slide 5**. Notes were on that slide as well as Slide 6. Scroll back to the top of the document. Click in front of the text **Slide 1**, and then type your first and last name. Press ⌷Space⌷ and then type today's date press ⌷Enter⌷.

d. In the Word document, click the **File** tab. Click **Save As**, and then double-click **This PC**. In the **Save As** dialog box, navigate to the location where you are saving your project files, and then save the file as p02ch03SpaHandouts_LastFirst, using your last and first name. Click **Save** ⌷🖫⌷, close **Word**, and then click **Close** ⌷×⌷ to close **PowerPoint**. Submit your files as directed by your instructor.

Concept Check

1. Your supervisor, Larry Houck, has asked you to add some pizzazz to a quarterly report presentation that he created. His intended audience for the presentation includes his boss and the upper management of the company. What types of transitions or animations might you use to engage this audience? Discuss your reasons. p. 877

2. Larry, your supervisor, asked you to create a presentation comparing three laptop computers that the department is considering purchasing. You have decided to add hyperlinks to the websites of the three companies on which you have focused your research. What are some key points to keep in mind for using these hyperlinks? What kind of internal hyperlinks — to slides within the presentation — might you use? p. 885

3. As a volunteer at a local animal shelter, you decide you want to add some audio to a presentation you have created. What kinds of sounds would you use? How would this audio improve the delivery of your message? Would this change your distribution plans? If so, how? p. 892

4. Continuing with your work on the animal shelter presentation, you have decided to photograph all of the animals that are up for adoption and create a presentation to persuade people to support the shelter by adopting or making donations. Describe how you would use the Photo Album feature of PowerPoint to create the presentation. How would you distribute the presentation to people who might adopt or make a donation? p. 897

5. PowerPoint allows for the creation of custom slide shows. Discuss some of the uses and benefits of creating custom slide shows from a presentation. p. 904

6. A PowerPoint presentation can be exported into several different formats. Discuss the benefits and limits of a PDF and video export? p. 907

Key Terms

Action button 888
Animation 877
Caption 901
Custom slide show 898
Delay 880

Duration 880
Emphasis action 880
Entrance animation 880
Exit animation 880
Hyperlink 885

Kiosk 877
Photo Album 898
Transition 877
Trigger 890

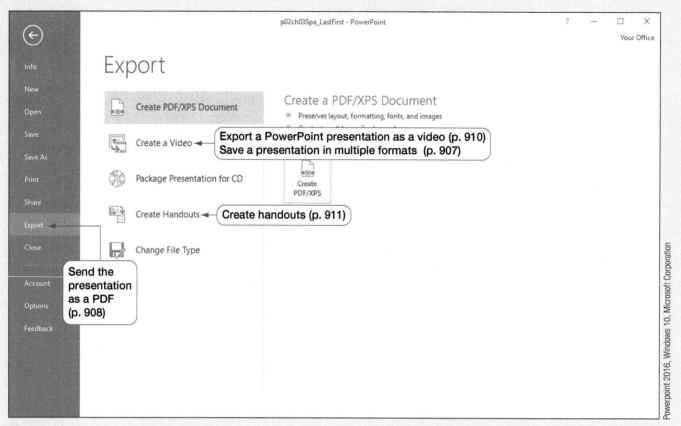

Figure 24

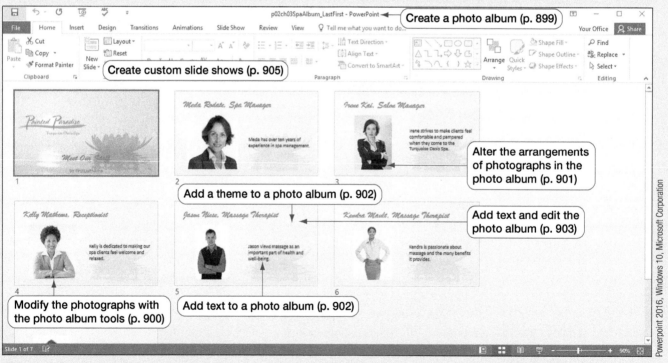

Figure 25

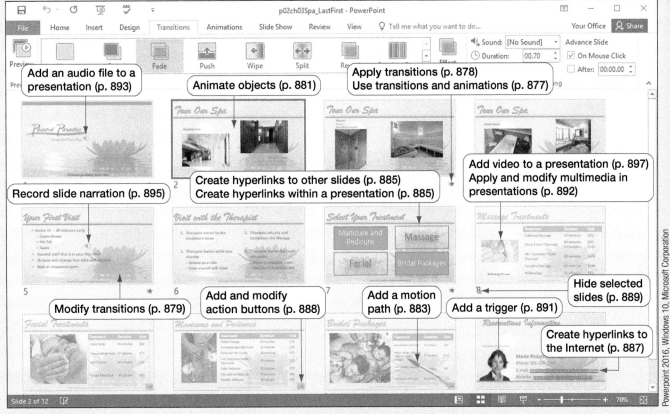

Figure 26

Practice 1

Student data files needed:

 Blank PowerPoint presentation

p02ch03ProductsTheme.thmx

p02ch03SpaProducts1.jpg

p02ch03SpaProducts2.jpg

p02ch03SpaProducts3.jpg

p02ch03SpaProducts4.jpg

p02ch03SpaProducts5.jpg

p02ch03SpaProducts6.jpg

You will save your file as:

p02ch03Products_LastFirst.pptx

Spa Product Album

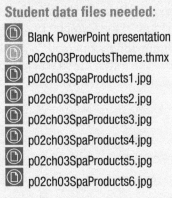

Sales & Marketing

The marketing team at the Spa would like to promote a few of their products that are available for purchase. In this exercise, you will create a PowerPoint Photo Album featuring images of these products.

a. Start **PowerPoint**, and then in the PowerPoint Start screen, double-click **Blank Presentation**.

b. Click the **Insert** tab, in the Images group, click the **Photo Album** arrow, and then select **New Photo Album**.

c. In the Photo Album dialog box, click **File/Disk**. Navigate to where you are storing your student files, select all six files beginning with **p02ch01SpaProducts1** through **p02ch03SpaProducts6**, and then click **Insert**.

d. Make the following changes in the Photo Album dialog box.

- Select **p02ch03SpaProducts2**, and then click **Rotate 90 degrees counter-clockwise** once. Deselect **p02ch03SpaProducts2**.
- Select **p02ch03SpaProducts6**, click **Increase Brightness** twice, and then click **Increase Contrast** twice. Deselect **p02ch03SpaProducts6**.
- Under Album Layout, click the **Picture layout** arrow, and then click **2 pictures with title**.
- Under Album Layout, click the **Frame shape** arrow, and then click **Center Shadow Rectangle**.
- Under Picture Options, click **Captions below ALL pictures**.
- Under Album Layout, to the right of Theme box click **Browse**. Navigate to your student files, click **p02ch03ProductsTheme**, and then click **Select**.
- Click **Create**.

e. On the **File tab**, click **Save As**, and then double-click **This PC**. In the **Save As** dialog box, navigate to the location where you are saving your project files, and then change the file name to p02ch03Products_LastFirst, using your last and first name. Click **Save**.

f. Click **Slide 1**. Select the **Photo Album** text, and then type Salon Products.

g. In the subtitle placeholder, select the **text**, and then type Featured Products for Sale. With the text selected, on the Home tab, in the Paragraph group, click **Center**.

h. Select **Slides 1** through **4**. Click the Transitions tab, and then in the Transition to This Slide group, click **Reveal**. In the **Timing** group, click the **Duration** box, type 2.5 and then press Enter.

i. Click **Slide 2** and make the following changes.
- Click the **Title placeholder**, and then type Nail Care Products.
- Select the file name **p02ch03SpaProducts1**, and then type Dry Your Nails Fast.
- Select the file name **p02ws03SpaProducts2**, and then type Hundreds of Colors.
- Click the **p02ch03SpaProducts1** photo. Click the **Animations** tab, and then in the Animation group, click **Fade**. In the timing group, click the **Start** arrow, and then click **With Previous**. In the Duration box type 1.0.
- Click the **p02ch03SpaProducts2** photo. Click the **Animations** tab, and then in the Animation group, click **Fade**. In the timing group, click the **Start** arrow, and then click **After Previous**. In the Duration box type 1.0, and then in the Delay box type 1.0.

j. Click **Slide 3** and make the following changes.
- Click the **Title placeholder**, and then type Luxury Bath Products.
- Select the file name **p02ch03SpaProducts3**, and then type Homemade Soaps.
- Select the file name **p02ws03SpaProducts4**, and then type Aromatic Bath Oils.
- Click the **p02ch03SpaProducts3** photo. Click the **Animations** tab, and then in the Animation group, click **Fade**. In the timing group, click the **Start** arrow, and then click **With Previous**. In the Duration box type 1.0.
- Click the **p02ch03SpaProducts4** photo. Click the **Animations** tab, and then in the Animation group, click **Fade**. In the timing group, click the **Start** arrow, and then click **After Previous**. In the Duration box type 1.0, and then in the Delay box type 1.0.

k. Click **Slide 4** and make the following changes.
- Click the **Title placeholder**, and then type Home Facial Products.
- Select the file name **p02ch03SpaProducts5**, and then type Cucumber Anti-Aging Cream.
- Select the file name **p02ws03SpaProducts6**, and then type Natural Face Mask.

- Click the **p02ch03SpaProducts5** photo. Click the **Animations** tab, and then in the Animation group, click **Fade**. In the timing group, click the **Start** arrow, and then click **With Previous**. In the Duration text box type 1.0.

- Click the **p02ch03SpaProducts6** photo. Click the **Animations** tab, and then in the Animation group, click **Fade**. In the timing group, click the **Start** arrow, and then click **After Previous**. In the Duration box type 1.0, and then in the Delay box type 1.0.

l. Save your presentation, exit PowerPoint, and then submit your file as directed by your instructor.

Problem Solve 1

Homework

Student data files needed:

 p02ch03Adventures.pptx

p02ch03AdventuresTheme.thmx

p02ch03Adventure.mp3

You will save your file as:

 p02ch03Adventures_LastFirst

Outdoor Adventures Presentation

Sales & Marketing

Outdoor Adventures is a business that specializes in providing people with the equipment and training needed for such activities as mountain climbing, skydiving, and whitewater rafting. The management would like you to help them put together a PowerPoint presentation that can be used to show to companies that might be interested in including Outdoor Adventures in their corporate retreats.

a. Start **PowerPoint**. Navigate to the location of your student files, and then double-click **p02ch03Adventures**. Save the presentation as p02ch03Adventures_LastFirst.

b. Apply the **p02ch03AdventuresTheme** theme located in the student files to the presentation.

c. On **Slide 1**, apply the **Fly Through** transition. In the Timing group, set the **Duration** to 1.5, and then click **Apply To All**.

d. Make the following changes to **Slide 1**.

- Insert the **p02ch03Adventure.mp3** audio file.

- Trim the audio file to end at 00:20:15.

- Apply a 3-second fade in and a 3-second fade out.

- Adjust the appropriate playback setting for the music to start **automatically** and to hide the player during the show.

- Adjust the volume to play at medium level.

e. Make the following changes to **Slide 3**.

- Apply the **Zoom** animation to the photograph. Adjust the timing so that the animation occurs **After Previous** and the **Duration** is set to 0.5.

- Select the placeholder with the bullet list. Apply the **Fade** animation to the list. Adjust the timing so that the animation occurs **After Previous**, the **Duration** is set to 1.0 and the **Delay** is set to 0.5.

f. Using the **Animation Painter**, set the same animation settings to **Slides 4** through **8** for each of the photos and bullet list placeholders. This will make the animation sequence the same for **Slides 3** through **8**.

g. Click **Slide 10**. Add an e-mail hyperlink next to E-mail: with the text to display reiterf@outdooradventures.com. Include a Subject line that reads Question from Adventure Presentation.

h. Click **Slide 2**. Make the following changes.

- Click the **SmartArt box** with the text Mountain biking. Insert a hyperlink to Slide 3. Add a ScreenTip that reads Check out our mountain biking adventures.

- Click the **SmartArt box** with the text Mountain climbing. Insert a hyperlink to Slide 4. Add a ScreenTip that reads We take mountain climbing to a new height.

- Click the **SmartArt box** with the text Hiking. Insert a hyperlink to Slide 5. Add a ScreenTip that reads We have some great hiking adventures.

- Click the **SmartArt box** with the text Whitewater rafting. Insert a hyperlink to Slide 6. Add a ScreenTip that reads Want some excitement in your life, take a rafting trip with us.

- Click the **SmartArt box** with the text Skydiving. Insert a hyperlink to Slide 7. Add a ScreenTip that reads You will love this adventure.

- Click the **SmartArt box** with the text Zip line tours. Insert a hyperlink to Slide 8. Add a ScreenTip that reads A must for the outdoor enthusiast.

i. Click **Slide 3**. Select the text Adventure Options in the lower-right corner of the slide. Insert a hyperlink to **Slide 2**. Add a ScreenTip that reads Click to return to the main menu - Adventure Options.

j. Select the **textbox with the hyperlink Adventure Options**, and then right-click and click **Copy**.

k. Click **Slide 4**. Right-click on an open area of the slide and click **Paste**.

l. Repeat Step k for **Slides 5** through **8**.

m. Hide **Slides 3** through **8**.

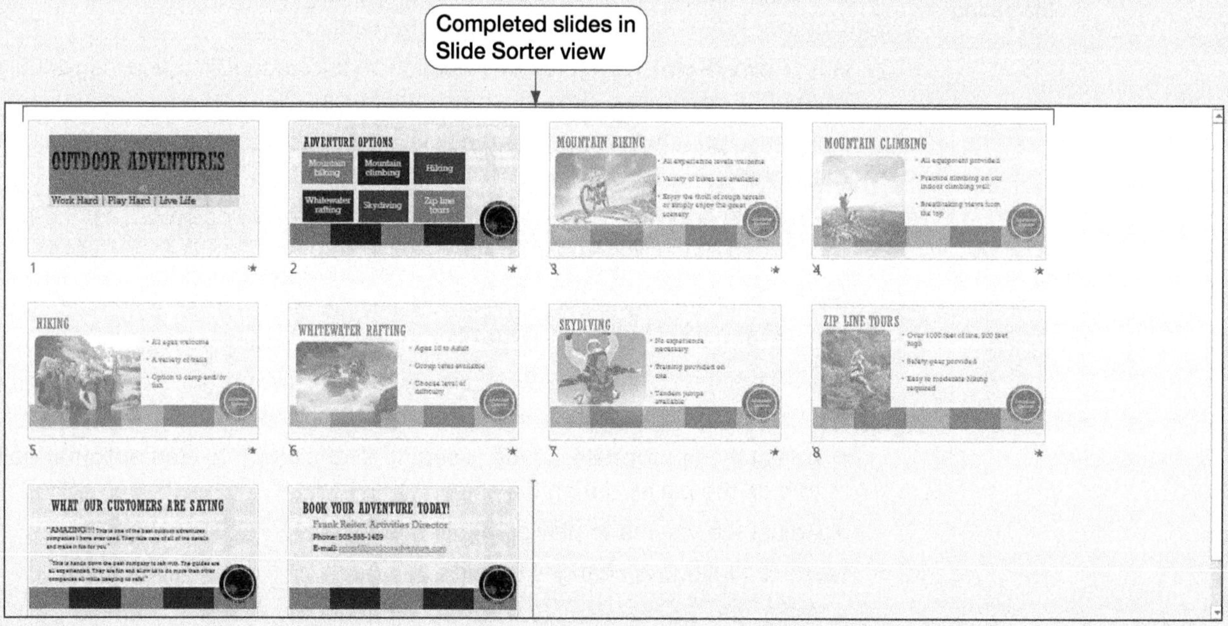

Completed slides in Slide Sorter view

Figure 27

n. Preview the presentation to make sure that all links are working properly.

o. Save the presentation, exit PowerPoint, and then submit your file as directed by your instructor.

Critical Thinking

As you use images, audio, and video in your presentations, it can be very tempting to use the Internet for finding resources. What do you need to know before taking files from the Internet? Can you use these resources in your presentation? If so, under which terms? What are your best options for finding images and multimedia resources?

Student data files needed:

 p02ch03Job.pptx

p02ch03Resume.jpg

p02ch03Education.jpg

P02ch03Awards.jpg

You will save your file as:

p02ch03Job_LastFirst.pptx

Job Qualifications Presentation

Human Resources

You are seeking an internship position at a local business. In addition to a traditional resume and cover letter, you would like to prepare a PowerPoint presentation summarizing your qualifications for the position. In this exercise, you will create a PowerPoint presentation, using the file provided, outlining your qualifications.

a. Start **PowerPoint**. Navigate to the location of your student files, and then double-click **p02ch03Job**. Save the presentation as p02ch03Job_LastFirst, using your last and first name.

b. On **Slide 1**, type your first and last name in the title placeholder, and type Qualifications in the subtitle placeholder. Add the **p02ch03Resume.jpg** image to the slide. Place the image appropriately on the slide, keeping in mind good slide design. Apply a picture style to the image.

c. On **Slide 2**, add a photograph of yourself to the picture placeholder. Crop the image to show only your head and shoulders.

d. Apply a **Fade** animation to the photo.

e. In the textbox to the right of the photo, type Click photo to hear my statement.

f. Add an introduction statement to the Notes pane of **Slide 2**. This statement should include your name and a sentence or two explaining why you are qualified for the position.

g. Insert an audio recording of the notes into **Slide 2**.

   • Use the Animation Pane to adjust the timing of the recording to occur when the photograph is clicked.

   • Ensure that the audio player is hidden during the presentation.

h. On **Slide 3** type a summary of qualifications. Include at least four bullet points.

   • Apply an Entrance animation to each bullet point. Be sure your animation choice is subtle and does not distract from the presentation. Take into consideration the type of presentation.

   • Each bullet animation should automatically follow the preceding one with a 1-second delay.

i. On **Slide 4** type any work experience you have.

   • Apply the same Entrance animation from the previous step (step h) to each bullet point. You want your presentation to flow, so you will use the same subtle animation.

   • Each bullet animation should automatically follow the preceding one with a 1-second delay.

j. On **Slide 5** type your education background, including when you graduated high school and your expected graduation date from college, along with majors(s), minor(s), and relevant course work. Add the **p02ch03Education.jpg** image to the slide. Place the image appropriately on the slide, keeping in mind good slide design. Apply a picture style to the image.

- Apply the same Entrance animation from the previous step (step h) to each bullet point. You want your presentation to flow, so you will use the same subtle animation.
- Each bullet animation should automatically follow the preceding one with a 1-second delay.

k. On **Slide 6** type your awards and accomplishments, such as dean's list, school elections, or competitions. Add the **p02ch03Award.jpg** image to the slide. Place the image appropriately on the slide, keeping in mind good slide design. Apply a picture style to the image.

- Apply the same Entrance animation from the previous step (step h) to each bullet point. You want your presentation to flow so you will use the same subtle animation.
- Each bullet animation should automatically follow the preceding one with a 1-second delay.

l. Apply a transition to the slides. The transition should be the same for all slides. Ensure that the transition is appropriate for the message you are trying to convey.

m. Add a footer to all of the slides except Slide 1. Include your e-mail address and the current date.

n. Save your presentation, exit PowerPoint, and then submit your file as directed by your instructor.

Additional
Cases

Additional Chapter Cases are available at www.pearsonhighered.com/youroffice

Microsoft PowerPoint 2016

Chapter 4 | CUSTOMIZATION AND COLLABORATION

OBJECTIVES

1. Create a custom template using the slide master p. 922

2. Customize the notes master and customize the handouts master p. 933

3. Develop a presentation from a custom template and outline p. 939

4. Use slide sections to organize and prepare a presentation p. 941

5. Create comments, and navigate comments p. 943

6. Create and use speaker notes p. 946

7. Mark presentations as final and apply password protection p. 948

8. Develop skills in delivering presentations p. 949

9. Understand how to use Office Mix p. 958

Prepare Case

Corporate Identity Template

The management of the Painted Paradise Turquoise Oasis Spa understands the importance of developing a corporate identity recognizable by employees and the public. You have been asked to create a professional PowerPoint template that will be used by the Turquoise Oasis Spa as the beginning point for slide shows. The specifications from management include developing a color theme, a font theme, and custom page layouts. The color scheme will help to create branding for the spa. You will use many of the things you already know about developing slides as you create the template. Once the template is finished, you will collaborate with the spa manager, Irene Kai, to create a quarterly report using the template. You will assist her in creating speaker notes and developing a template for handouts. You will also work with Irene to prepare her for the actual presentation to the board of directors, giving her advice on overcoming presentation nervousness, being prepared, and engaging the audience. Irene has also learned of a new tool for creating interactive presentations and wants you to learn more about Office Mix.

Zadorozhnyi Viktor/Shutterstock

Student data files needed for this chapter:

 Blank PowerPoint presentation

 p02ch04Comments.pptx

p02ch04Outline.docx

p02ch04SpaBackground.jpg

p02ch04Irene.jpg

You will save your files as:

 p02ch04Template_LastFirst.potx

 p02ch04Presentation_LastFirst.pptx

 p02ch04Update_LastFirst.pptx

p02ch04Notes_LastFirst.docx

p02ch04Delivery_LastFirst.pptx

Creating a Corporate Identity with a Custom Template

Corporations throughout the world take pride in their **corporate identity**. Visual identities are carefully crafted to make products recognizable. Logos, color schemes, and fonts are used for years to ensure that customers identify with the product. Think about how you recognize one soft drink from another just by looking at the colors on the can. People visiting foreign countries are often surprised to recognize the golden arches of McDonald's.

Corporate identities are normally developed by the marketing group of a company. They conduct market research, costs analysis, and other studies to build the identity. They hire professional designers to produce pieces of the overall identity, such as the logo, with guidance from studies. They develop guidelines for the use of the corporate materials, often specifying the exact placement of the logo on a page, or the exact color numbers for the colors used in advertising. Each branch of the organization is expected to use the identity to create consistency and present a unified public view of the company.

In this section, you will work toward creating a custom template for the Turquoise Oasis Spa, using custom colors, fonts, and layouts.

Create a Custom Template Using the Slide Master

Templates provide predefined layouts, theme colors, fonts, and sample content which enable a company to quickly produce consistent and professional slide shows. This consistency aspect of the template begins with the **slide master**. The slide master is a special template slide that defines the fonts, placement of footers, background colors, and other characteristics for the presentation. The slide master also contains layouts for the template. In the slide master, new layouts can be added, layouts can be deleted, and modifications to the existing layouts can occur. For instance, if you wanted the title of the slides to appear along the bottom of the slides, you would move the title placeholder to the location on the slide master, not on each individual slide.

In the Slide Master view, the larger slide thumbnail represents the slide master, referred to as the Office Theme Slide Master. The smaller thumbnails represent the different layouts available. If global changes need to be made that affect all slides, those changes should be made on the Office Theme Slide Master.

The slide master tools are available on the View tab. While working in the slide master view, all of the other PowerPoint tools are available. When work is completed in the slide master, it is very important that the Slide Master view before beginning to populate a presentation with information. Otherwise, the information added to the slides becomes part of the template.

Opening the Starting File

This chapter focuses on building a template for a presentation. The template can be reused so an identity emerges over time. A template is also somewhat secure because most casual PowerPoint users do not know how to modify a template. In this exercise, you will modify a slide master, the handout master, and the notes master.

 P04.00

To Get Started

a. Start **PowerPoint**, and then on the Start screen, click **Blank Presentation**.

b. Click the **File** tab, click **Save As**, and then double-click **This PC**. In the **Save As** dialog box, click **Save as type**, click **PowerPoint Template**, navigate to the location where you are saving your project files, and then change the file name to p02ch04Template_LastFirst, using your last and first name. Click **Save**.

SIDE NOTE
Pin the Ribbon
If your ribbon is collapsed, pin your ribbon open. Click the Home tab. In the lower right-hand corner of the ribbon, click Pin the Ribbon ⊣.

Troubleshooting
Once you change the Save As file type to PowerPoint template (*.potx), the Save As dialog box will direct you to a Custom Office Template directory. Be sure to change the storage location so the file is saved with your project files.

Modifying the Slide Master Theme

A theme adds color and font consistency to a normal presentation. By setting up the colors and fonts in Slide Master view, you customize the template. You can add background colors, textures, or pictures to all of the slide layouts or to individual slide layouts. It is easier to set up the background for all of the slides using the slide master, but keep in mind that anything you put on the slide master is locked in the slide layouts and cannot be changed without changing the slide master. For instance, if you put a shape on the slide master, it will appear in the same location on every slide layout.

In this exercise, you will begin the project by opening the slide master and adding background colors to the slide master.

P04.01

To Modify the Slide Master Theme

a. Click the **View** tab, and then in the Master Views group, click **Slide Master**.
   The Slide Master tab appears on the ribbon with the slide master and the layout slides. You will begin by adding a background to the slides.

Figure 1 Slide Master tab

Powerpoint 2016, Windows 10, Microsoft Corporation

SIDE NOTE
Using the Theme Slide Master
The default slide layout when Slide Master view opens is the Title Slide Layout. You can apply different formatting to each of the layouts or apply them to the slide master.

b. Scroll up and click the **Office Theme Slide Master**, which is the first thumbnail in the left pane and appears larger than all the others. In the Background group, click the **Colors** arrow, and then click **Blue II**.

   You are basing your color choices on the **Blue II** color scheme, but you will modify some of the background and accent colors. These accents will help to create a brand for the spa.

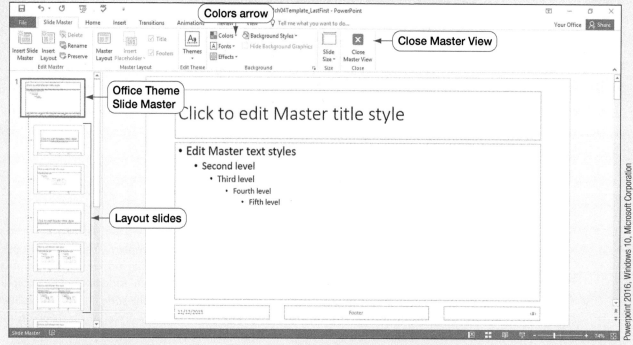

Figure 2 Slide Master view

c. In the **Background** group, click **Colors**, and then select **Customize Colors**. In the Create New Theme Colors dialog box, click the **Text/Background - Dark 2** arrow, and then select **More Colors**. On the Custom tab, type 129 for **Red**, 177 for **Green**, 172 for **Blue**, and then click **OK**.

d. Click the **Text/Background - Light 2** arrow, and then select **More Colors**. Type 180 for **Red**, 163 for **Green**, 130 for **Blue**, and then click **OK**.

e. Click the **Accent 1** arrow, and then select **More Colors**. Type 170 for **Red**, 230 for **Green**, 228 for **Blue**, and then click **OK**.

f. Click the **Accent 2** arrow, and then select **More Colors**. Type 112 for **Red**, 56 for **Green**, 0 for **Blue**, and then click **OK**.

g. Click the **Accent 3** arrow, and then select **More Colors**. Type 208 for **Red**, 234 for **Green**, 124 for **Blue**, and then click **OK**.

h. Click the **Hyperlink** arrow, and then select **More Colors**. Type 226 for **Red**, 242 for **Green**, 176 for **Blue**, and then click **OK**.

i. Click the **Followed Hyperlink** arrow, and then select **More Colors**. Type 84 for **Red**, 42 for **Green**, 0 for **Blue**, and then click **OK**.

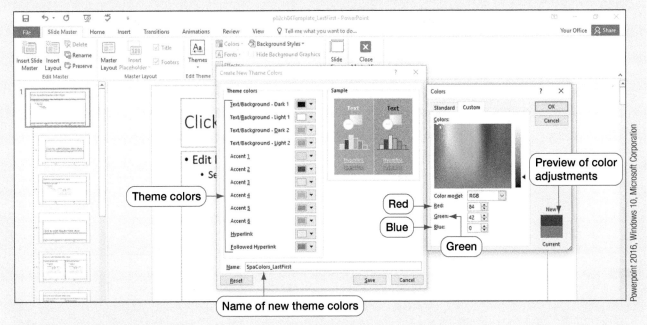

Figure 3 Edit theme colors

j. Type SpaColors_LastFirst, using your last and first name, in the Name box, and then click **Save**.

> With the color scheme modified, you will now focus your attention on the font selection.

k. In the Background group, click the **Fonts** arrow, and then select **Customize Fonts**.

l. In the Create New Theme Fonts dialog box, click the **Heading font** arrow, scroll down, and then click **Trebuchet MS**.

> **Troubleshooting**
>
> If the Trebuchet MS font is not available, use another sans serif font, such as Calibri or Arial.

m. Click the **Body font** arrow, scroll down, and then select **Verdana**.

n. Type SpaFonts_LastFirst, using your last and first name, in the Name box, and then click **Save**.

> With the font selections made, you will turn your attention to the effects. The effects enable you to make selections that determine the format of graphic elements.

o. In the Background group, click the **Effects** arrow, and then select **Smokey Glass**.

> Now you have set the theme properties. Next, you will change the background of the Office Theme Slide Master and add a rectangle shape.

p. In the Background group, click the **Background Styles** arrow, and then select **Style 11**.

q. Click the **Insert** tab, and then in the Illustrations group, click **Shapes**. In the Rectangles group, select the **Rectangle**.

r. Drag a rectangle shape at the bottom of the slide to fit across the entire width of the slide, and then make the following modifications.

- If necessary, click the **Drawing Tools Format** tab, and then in the Shape Styles group, click the **More**, and then select **Subtle Effect – Lime, Accent 3**.

- Right-click the **rectangle shape**, and then select **Format Shape**. In the Format Shape pane, click **Fill & Line**, if necessary.

- In the Format Shape pane, click **Fill**, and then click **Gradient fill**, if necessary.

- Under Gradient stops, click **Stop 1 of 2**, click the **Color** arrow, and then select **Aqua, Accent 1**.

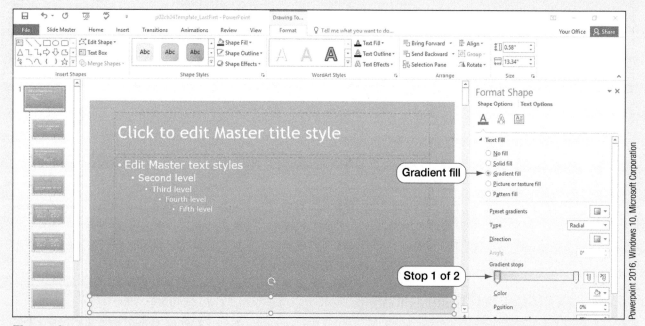

Figure 4   Change gradient fill

- If necessary, click the **Drawing Tools Format** tab. In the Size group, type .58" in the Shape Height box and 13.34" in the Shape Width box.

- In the Arrange group, click **Align**, select **Align Bottom**.

- In the Arrange group, click the **Send Backward** arrow, and then select **Send to Back**.

    This will send the shape backward and the footer placeholders will move to the front and will be visible.

- In the Shape Styles group, click the **Shape Outline** arrow, and then select **No Outline**.

- Click the **Shape Effects** arrow in the Shape Styles group, point to **Shadow**, and then in the Outer group, select **Offset Top**.

s. Select the text **Click to edit Master title style**, click the **Home** tab, and then in the Font group, click **Text Shadow**.

Figure 5 Modified Office Theme Slide Master

    t. **Save** 🖫 the presentation.

Customizing Slide Master Layouts

By default, Master Slide view provides you with 11 different layouts that can be used in a presentation. You can edit or delete existing layouts or create new ones that fit the needs of the organization or presenter.

    In this exercise, you will further customize the template by deleting unnecessary layouts, editing the title layout, customizing the slide footers, and creating a new slide layout.

 P04.02

SIDE NOTE

Deleting Slide Layouts
Alternatively, you can select the slide layout you wish to delete and press Delete.

To Customize Slide Master Layouts

    a. Scroll to the bottom of the slide master layouts in the left pane, click **Vertical Title and Text Layout**, and then click the **Slide Master** tab. In the Edit Master group, click **Delete**.

       The slide layout is removed, and the previous slide (Title and Vertical Text Layout) in the pane is selected. You will delete this layout next.

> **Troubleshooting**
> Point to the slide layout in the left pane to view the names of the layouts.

    b. Press Delete to delete the **Title and Vertical Text Layout**. Continue deleting the following layouts:

      • Picture with Caption Layout

      • Content with Caption Layout

      • Blank Layout

      • Title Only Layout

- Comparison Layout

- Section Header Layout

This leaves four slides in the left pane: the Office Theme Slide Master, Title Slide Layout, Title and Content Layout, and Two Content Layout.

SIDE NOTE

Modifying Slide Footers

When working with footers in Slide Master view, you are setting up the formats, not the actual footer text.

---

c. Click the **Office Theme Slide Master** thumbnail. Click the **slide number footer** placeholder on the right side of the slide, and then press Delete to delete the entire placeholder. Do this for all of the slide layouts.

d. If necessary, click the **Office Theme Slide Master** thumbnail. Click the **center footer**, click the **Drawing Tools Format** tab, and then in the Size group, type 5.5" in the Shape Width box, and then press Enter. In the Arrange group, click **Align**, and then select **Align Right**.

e. Click the **left footer**. In the Size group, type 4.5" in the Shape Width box, and then press Enter. In the Arrange group, click **Align**, and then select **Align Left**.

f. Select the **right footer** placeholder, click the **Home** tab, in the Font group, click the **Font Color** arrow, and then under Theme Colors select **Black, Background 1**.

g. Select the **left footer** placeholder, click the Home tab, in the Font group, click the **Font Color** arrow, and then select **Black, Background 1**.

h. Click the **Title Slide Layout** in the left pane. Click the **Slide Master** tab, in the Background group, click the **Background Styles** arrow, and then select **Format Background**.

i. In the Format Background pane, under Fill click the **Picture or texture fill** option button. Under Insert picture from, click **File**. Navigate to where you are storing your student files, and double-click to insert **p02ch04SpaBackground**.

j. In the Format Background pane, click in the **Transparency** box, type 35%, and press Enter. This will make the text on the Title layout easier to read.

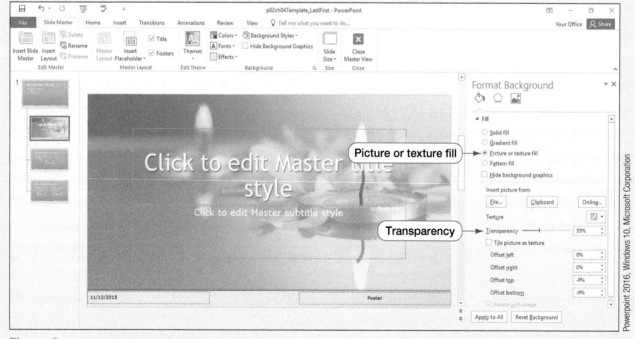

Figure 6   Format Background pane

k. **Close** ☒ the Format Background pane.

l. Click to select the **title placeholder border**, and then click the **Home** tab. In the Font group, click the **Font Color** arrow, and then select **Black, Background 1**.

m. Click to select the **subtitle placeholder border**. On the Home tab, in the Font group, click the **Font Color** arrow, and then select **Black, Background 1**.

n. With the subtitle placeholder still selected, click the **Drawing Tools Format** tab, in the Size group, type 0.6" in the Shape Height ⬍ box, and then press Enter.

o. Right-click the **subtitle placeholder**, and then select **Size and Position**. Click **Position** to expand the section. Click the **Horizontal position** box, and then type 0.1", and press Enter. Click the **Vertical position** box, and then type 6.3", and press Enter.

p. Click the **title placeholder**, and then click the **Horizontal position** box, and then type 0.1", and press Enter. Click the **Vertical position** box, and then type 3.6", and press Enter. Close the Format Shape pane.

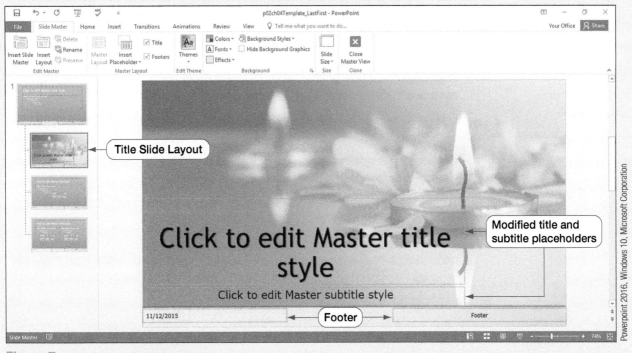

Figure 7 Modified Title Slide Layout

q. **Save** 🖫 the presentation.

Adding a New Slide Layout

Just as slides can be added to regular slide shows, you can insert additional slide layouts into the template. In this exercise, you will add a layout that will contain Irene's contact information, since you know that she always uses this type of slide in her presentations.

To Add Slide Master Layouts

a. Click the **Slide Master** tab, and then in the Edit Master group, click **Insert Layout**.

b. In the Edit Master group, click **Rename**, select the **text** in the Layout name box in the Rename Layout dialog box, and then type Contact Information. Click **Rename**.

  The slide appeared with just a title placeholder. You decide to create a text and picture placeholder to hold the contact information.

c. On the Slide Master tab, in the Master Layout group, click the **Insert Placeholder** arrow, and then select **Picture**.

d. Drag under the title placeholder to create a **picture** placeholder.

e. Click the **Drawing Tools Format** tab, and then in the **Size** group, type 4.5" in the Shape Height box and 3.07" in the Shape Width box. **Press** Enter.

f. Right-click the picture placeholder, and then click **Size and Position**. If necessary, click **Position** to expand the section. Click the **Horizontal position** box, type 0.55", and press Enter. Click the **Vertical position** box, type 2.0", and press Enter.

g. Click the **Slide Master** tab, in the Master Layout group, click the **Insert Placeholder** arrow, and then select **Text**.

h. Drag under the title placeholder and to the right of the picture placeholder to create a **text** placeholder.

i. On the **Drawing Tools Format** tab, in the Size group, type 4.5" in the Shape Height box and 9.4" in the Shape Width box.

j. In the Format Shape pane, click the **Horizontal position** box, and 3.8", and press Enter. Click the **Vertical position** box, type 2.0", and press Enter.

  Now that the two placeholders are in place, you need to adjust the title placeholder so that the items are aligned nicely on the slide.

k. Click the **title placeholder,** click the **Horizontal position** box in the Format Shape pane, type 0.55", and then press Enter. Click the **Vertical position** box. If necessary, type 0.4", and then press Enter. **Close** ✕ the Format Shape pane.

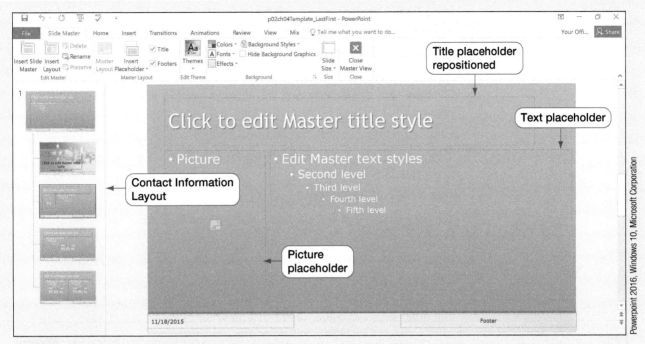

Figure 8 Contact Information layout

I. **Save** 🖫 the presentation.

Your Contact Information layout may appear in a different layout order in the left pane than pictured above in Figure 8. It does not matter where this layout is shown, because you will apply the layouts to slides that are in the correct order.

Placing Text on the Slide

In some cases, the text that will appear on slides will be consistent between presentations. For instance, the template you have been working on will always be used by Irene Kai for presentations related to the spa. To save time, you can place and format text in the template that will always be displayed when the template is opened. It is important to note that this must be done with Slide Master view closed; otherwise, the text that you add will be placeholder text that will not be displayed on the slide.

In this exercise, you will add the name of the spa and the slogan to the title slide. You will also make some minor adjustments to the fonts and add Irene's picture.

To Add Text and a Photo to the Slide Layout

a. Click the **Slide Master** tab, and then in the Close group, click **Close Master View**.

b. Click the title placeholder text on **Slide 1**, and then type Turquoise Oasis Spa. Select the **text** you just typed, and then on the Home tab, in the Font group, click **Increase Font Size** Ａ̇ twice to increase the font size to **72**.

c. Click the subtitle placeholder, and then type A Passion for Relaxation. Select the **text** you just typed, and then in the Font group, click **Italic** 𝐼 .

d. On the Home tab, in the Slides group, click the **New Slide** arrow, and then select **Contact Information**. Click the title placeholder, and then type Contact Information.

e. In the Picture placeholder, click the **picture icon**, navigate to where you are saving your student files, select **p02ch04Irene**, and then click **Insert**.

f. On the **Picture Tools Format** tab, in the Picture Styles group, click **More**, and then select **Center Shadow Rectangle**.

g. Click the **text** placeholder, and then click in front of the text **Click to add text**. Press Bksp to remove the bullet point, and then type Irene Kai, Spa Manager. Press Enter twice. In the Paragraph group, click **Bullets**.

h. Type Appointments, press Enter, and then press Tab. Type Phone: 505.555.7329, and then press Enter.

i. Type E-mail: appointments@paintedparadiseresort.com, and then press Enter.

j. In the Paragraph group, click **Decrease List Level**, type Questions/Concerns, press Enter, and then press Tab.

k. Type Phone: 505. 555.7328, press Enter, type E-mail: ikai@paintedparadiseresort .com, and then press Enter. Press Bksp to remove the bullet.

Figure 9   Contact Information layout with text

l. **Save** the presentation.

When creating PowerPoint templates, you must remember to close Slide Master view before finalizing any changes made to the template and before closing PowerPoint. If you open a .potx template file by double-clicking the file name, PowerPoint will create a new Presentation with the template applied. If you need to make any changes to the template itself, you will need to Save As a .potx file type and replace the previous version. Alternatively, use the Open command within PowerPoint or click the file name in the Recent files list to open the template file as a .potx file.

Customize the Notes Master

Many corporations, businesses, and organizations have guidelines for materials that are printed. They may require content such as a copyright notice or a privacy statement. They may expect the use of a standard format for all documents. The speaker notes can be customized so certain things will appear on the printed document in the **notes master**. The notes master determines the layout of elements, such as the slide thumbnail and notes placeholder, on the speaker notes pages.

By default, the notes printed from PowerPoint contain headers and footers. They include a space for a customized header along with the current date at the top of the page, a space for a customized footer, and the page number at the bottom. The default items can be removed from the notes or modified in placement and text. A graphic of the slide appears above the notes in standard layout, but that can be modified as needed. The size of the text can be increased or decreased, and fonts can be edited on the notes pages.

Modifying Headers and Footers

You modify the headers and footers through the View tab, using Notes Master view. Using Notes Master view, you have access to the other tabs within PowerPoint so you can modify fonts, for example.

In this exercise, you will modify the header and footer on the notes master to customize the areas for the Turquoise Oasis Spa. You will do this on the template so the customization is available in each presentation Irene creates using the template. Later, you will apply the template to the presentation to update it.

To Customize the Notes Master Header and Footer

a. Click the **View** tab, and then in the Master Views group, click **Notes Master**.

b. Click the **Header** box, type Turquoise Oasis Spa, and then press Enter. Type Irene Kai, Spa Manager.

c. Click the **Footer** box, and then type Confidential, All Rights Reserved. Press the Spacebar, type the current year. Select the **footer text**, click the **Home** tab, and then in the Font group, click the **Font Size** arrow, and then increase the font size to **14**.

d. Click in front of the **page number** symbol in the bottom right placeholder, and then type Slide. Press the Spacebar once to leave a blank space in between the word and the page number symbol. Select the **text** in the slide number footer, and then increase the font size to **18**.

This footer will print the number of the slide. The larger font will enable Irene to more easily keep track of where she is in the presentation.

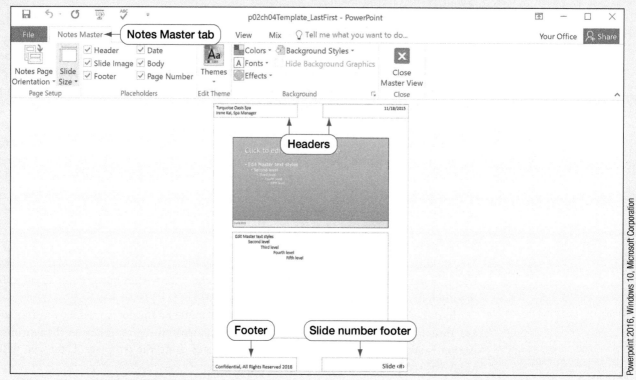

Figure 10   Notes Master

e. **Save** 🔲 the presentation.

Modifying Slide and Notes Placeholders

Many people do not realize that you can change the slide image and the notes placeholder on the notes page. If you make the image smaller, there is more room for notes. You can also change the font size in the notes placeholder so the text is easier to read as a presenter. If you like your pages in landscape orientation, you can change the orientation on the notes master. In this exercise, you will customize the Notes Master layout and the notes placeholders.

To Customize the Notes Master Layout and Notes Placeholders

a. Click the **Notes Master** tab, in the Page Setup group, click **Notes Page Orientation** arrow, and then select **Landscape**.

b. Click the **slide image**. Click the **Drawing Tools Format** tab, and then in the Size group, in the Shape Height box 🔲 type 2.2". Press Enter.

c. In the Arrange group, click **Align**, and then select **Align Left**.

d. Click the **border** of the notes placeholder, and then drag the **center-top sizing handle** up to just below the slide image. In the Arrange group, click **Align**, and then select **Align Left**. Drag the **center-right sizing handle** to the right to expand the notes placeholder to the right edge of the slide.

e. Select **all the text** in the notes placeholder, click the **Home** tab, and then in the Font group, increase the font size to **16** to make reading the notes easier.

f. Click the **Insert** tab, and then in the Illustrations group, click **Shapes**, and in the Lines group, select **Line**. Hold Shift, and then drag a horizontal line to the right of the slide image that ends near the right edge of the notes page.

- Right-click the **line**, and then select **Copy**. Right-click the **line**, and then under Paste Options, select **Use Destination Theme** 📋. Paste the line four times so there are a total of five lines.

- If necessary, drag the **lines** onto the page, and then place them roughly next to the slide image, spaced equally apart from each other.

- Click the first line, hold Shift, and then click each of the lines. Click the **Drawing Tools Format** tab, and then in the Arrange group, click **Align**, and then select **Distribute Vertically**.

- Click **Align** again, and then select **Align Right**.

  These lines will be used for last-minute notes that Irene might want to write on the printouts. She may want to note the name of the contact person for the presentation, or list pertinent information that she would like to work into the presentation. For instance, she may talk to someone in the audience prior to the presentation and might want to include that person's name and a short story about that person.

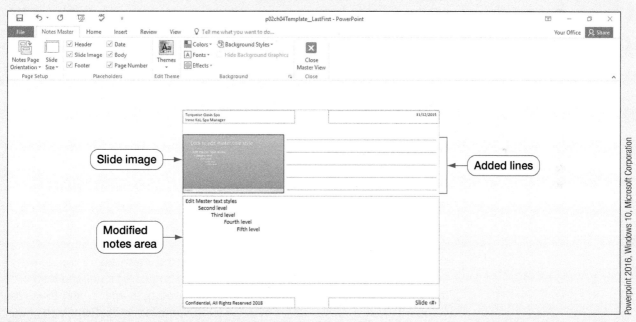

Figure 11 Modifying notes placeholders

g. Click the **Notes Master** tab, and then in the Close group, click **Close Master View**.

h. **Save** 🖫 the presentation.

Customize the Handout Master

Just as the notes master can be customized, changes can be made to the **handout master**, which determines the layout of elements, such as the header and footer, on the handout pages. In this case, the corporate office may be even more vigilant about changing the printouts, as these are handed directly to audience members.

Handouts pages are good places to list contact and company information. A copyright notice may be required on the page. Using Handout Master view, handouts can be specified to be printed in either portrait or landscape orientation. It is interesting to note that slide placeholders cannot be moved or modified in a handout master.

Modifying the Headers and Footers

In this exercise, you will add Irene's contact information to the header and place a standard copyright notice on the handouts. You will also move the page number to the top of the slide and include the word "Page" next to it. You will remove the date placeholder.

To Customize the Handout Master Headers and Footers

a. Click the **View** tab, and then in the Master Views group, click **Handout Master**.

b. Click the **Header** placeholder, type Irene Kai, Turquoise Oasis Spa, and then press Enter. Type ikai@paintedparadiseresort.com. Select the **header text**. Click the **Home** tab, in the Font group, click the **Font** arrow, select **Trebuchet MS**. Click the **Font Size** arrow, and then click **14**.

c. Click the **Handout Master** tab, and then in the Placeholders group, click **Date** to deselect it. Click the **page number footer**, press Shift to constrain movement, and drag the placeholder up to the position that the Date placeholder occupied in the top right corner. Click in front of the **page number symbol**, and then type Page:. Be sure to include a space after the colon.

d. Drag the **left middle sizing handle** of the page number placeholder to the right so the placeholder is just the size that is needed to accommodate the text.

e. Click the **header** placeholder, and then drag the **center bottom sizing handle** down so the text fits within the placeholder.

f. Click inside the **Footer** placeholder. Click the **Insert** tab, and then in the Symbols group, click **Symbol**. In the Symbol dialog box, click the **Subset** arrow and then select **Basic Latin**. Scroll down to the row below the lowercase x, click to select the **Copyright Sign** (character code 00A9 in the normal text font), and then click **Insert**. Click **Close**. Type the current year followed by a space, and then type Turquoise Oasis Spa. Select the **text**. Click the **Home** tab, in the Paragraph group, click **Center** ☰, and then increase the font size to **14**. Drag the **right middle sizing handle** of the placeholder to the right edge of the page.

g. Move the footer placeholder up about .5" from the bottom of the page. Moving the footer up will allow it to fit within the default page margins of the page when printed.

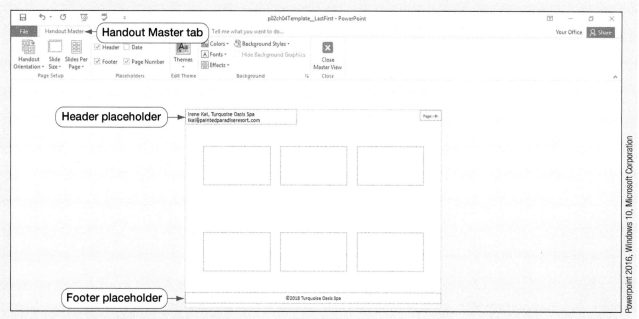

Figure 12   Modifying the handout master

h. **Save** 🖫 the presentation.

Setting up the Page

Some people prefer to see handout pages in a landscape orientation, while others prefer portrait orientation. You can change the orientation of the pages as well as the slide images. Since PowerPoint 2016 has been optimized for widescreen monitors and tablets, slides are typically displayed in a 16:9 ratio, making them wider than they are tall. For this reason, you will generally display the slides in landscape orientation to avoid distorting them. Selecting a portrait or landscape handout orientation makes no difference in the size or shape of the slide images, so it becomes a matter of personal preference.

REAL WORLD ADVICE   **Printing Handouts**

When you using handouts for your presentation, it is important to have a good idea of how they will supplement your message. Of course, you want to print handouts that are valuable tools for the audience, and you probably want to avoid printing handouts that do not contribute information. This helps you to be more environmentally conscious because you are not using printing resources, such as paper and ink, for unnecessary handouts. You should also consider when to distribute the handouts. Do you want the audience members to use the handouts for supplemental notes during your presentation? Are you distracted by people turning the pages or rustling the paper? There are many things you should take into consideration before printing handouts.

In this exercise, you will print a sample handouts and notes page using the two slides that were added to the template.

P04.08

To Print Handouts and Notes

a. Click the **Handout Master** tab, and then in the Close group, click **Close Master View**.

b. Click the **File** tab, click **Print**, and then click **Full Page Slides**. In the Handouts group, select **2 Slides**.

c. Review the preview of the handout page, and then click **Print** if your instructor requests a copy of the printout.

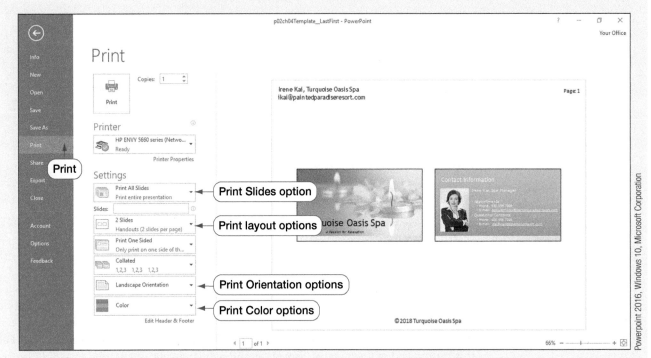

Figure 13   Printing handouts

d. If you printed the handouts in Step c, click the **File** tab if necessary, and then click **Print**.

e. Click **2 Slides**, and then in the Print Layout group, select **Notes Pages**. Click the **Next Page** and **Previous Page** arrows at the bottom of the Preview pane to review the Notes Pages print layout. Click **Print** if your instructor requests a copy of the printout.

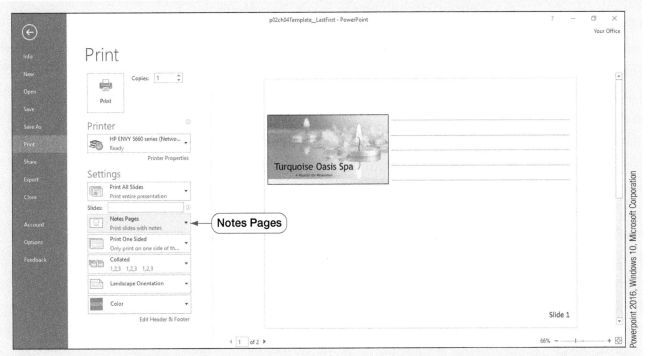

Figure 14 Printing notes

    f. **Save** the presentation and **close** PowerPoint.

Develop a Presentation from a Custom Template and Outline

Custom templates are accessed in the same way that you use other templates. Begin a new PowerPoint presentation, and select the template. As slides are added, the layouts that are a part of the template are available on the Home tab.

    Sometimes it is more convenient to add content to a slide show by importing it from a file created in another application such as Word or Notepad as opposed to starting from scratch. If the outline was created using heading styles, the slides will be created with the hierarchy of data reflected in the outline. If the outline does not have heading styles applied, each item on the outline will appear on a different slide. Content created on the Outline tab of Word flows into the PowerPoint slides very well.

Using a Custom Template

In this exercise, you will create a new presentation using the spa template.

P04.09

To Create a Presentation Based on a Template

    a. Navigate to the location where you are saving your project files, and then open **p02ch04Template_LastFirst**. PowerPoint opens the file as a new presentation using the template.

    b. Click the **File** tab, click **Save As**, and then double-click **This PC**. In the **Save As** dialog box, navigate to where you are saving your project files, and change the file name to p02ch04Presentation_LastFirst, using your last and first name. Click **Save**.

Importing an Outline into a Presentation

Irene created an outline in Word that she would like you to include in the presentation. In this exercise, you will import the outline and set the layout for each slide. You will make modifications to the imported text to improve the consistency with the PowerPoint presentation.

P04.10

SIDE NOTE

Outlines in Different Formats

Outline file formats suitable for importing into PowerPoint include .docx, .txt, rtf, and others.

To Import an Outline into a Presentation

a. On **Slide 1**, on the Home tab, in the Slides group, click the **New Slide** arrow, and then select **Slides from Outline**.

b. Navigate to the location of your student data files, click **p02ch04Outline**, and then click **Insert**.

The slides flow into the presentation but do not have the same corporate branding that the spa is looking to incorporate into the presentations. Since the slides were imported from an external source, layouts and font colors are not applied.

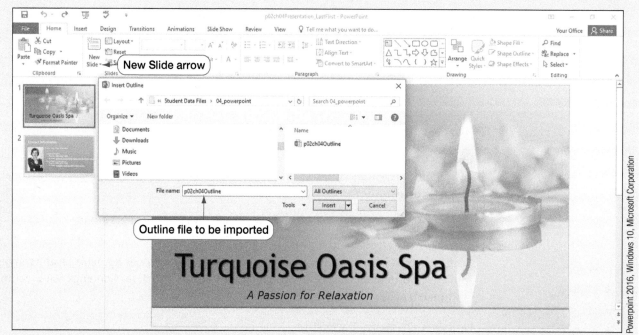

Figure 15   Importing a Word outline

c. Select **Slides 2** through **10**, and then in the **Slides** group, click **Reset**. This restores all the imported fonts, font styles, and font colors on the selected slides to the default settings of the template.

d. Click **Slide 8**, click inside the **text** placeholder, and then on the Home tab, in the Paragraph group, click **Bullets** ▭ ▾ to remove the bullet from the quotation.

e. Click **Slide 9**, click inside the **text** placeholder, and on the Home tab, in the Paragraph group, click **Bullets** ▭ ▾ to remove the bullet from the quotation.

f. **Save** ▭ the presentation.

Use Slide Sections to Organize and Prepare a Presentation

Slide sections are organizational tools for use on the Slides tab. Section titles can be placed between groups of slides and then collapsed or expanded. This means that you can see sections you want to work with, while minimizing sections you do not need to see. This is very beneficial when you have a large slide show, saving you time as you search for a slide.

In this exercise, you will assign sections to the slides and experiment with collapsing or expanding the sections.

 P04.11

To Assign Slides to Sections

a. In the left pane, click the gap between **Slide 2** and **Slide 3**. On the Home tab, in the Slides group, click the **Section** arrow, and then select **Add Section**.

Notice that the section was created and all subsequent slides 3–10 were placed in the section. You will now rename the section.

b. Click **Section**, and then select **Rename Section**. In the Rename Section dialog box, type Solutions as the Section name, and then click **Rename**.

c. Right-click between **Slide 5** and **Slide 6**, and then select **Add Section**. Right-click **Untitled Section**, select **Rename Section**, and then type Inspire Employees. Click **Rename**.

d. Right-click between **Slide 6** and **Slide 7**, and then select **Add Section**. Right-click **Untitled Section**, select **Rename Section**, and then type Financial Success. Click **Rename**.

e. Add a section entitled Feedback between **Slide 7** and **Slide 8**.

f. Add a section entitled Future between **Slide 9** and **Slide 10**.

g. Right-click the first section entitled **Default Section**, and then rename it **Introduction**.

h. On the Home tab, in the Slides group, click the **Section** arrow, and then select **Collapse All**. Click the arrow ▷ next to the Solutions section to expand it.

Notice that when the sections are collapsed, you see the section name along with the number of slides that belong to that section. With the section expanded, you see three slides in the Solutions section.

i. Click the arrow ◢ next to the **Solutions** section to collapse it. Click the arrow ▷ next to the **Feedback** section to expand it.

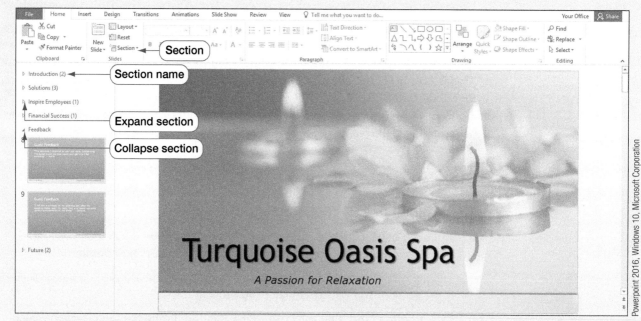

Figure 16 Slide sections

j. In the Slides group, click the **Section** arrow, and then select **Expand All**.

k. **Save** 🖫 the presentation. If you need to take a break before finishing this chapter, now would be a good time to take a break.

Collaborating and Presenting

In business, being able to collaborate effectively with coworkers is a valuable skill. Microsoft provides many methods for collaboration through its Office applications and OneDrive. By using Microsoft's OneDrive and PowerPoint Web App, you can share your presentation and collaborate with anyone on virtually any device even if the other person does not have PowerPoint installed on his or her device. In this section, you will learn how to add comments, view comments, and delete comments in a presentation.

 CONSIDER THIS | **Working in a Team**

Teamwork is common in today's corporate world. You may find yourself collaborating on a presentation as a team member. What challenges would you anticipate in working on a presentation in a team? How could you overcome those challenges?

REAL WORLD ADVICE **Restrict Access**

Sharing your presentation with others in a shared folder can lead to unauthorized changes being made to your presentation. It is a good idea to use the PowerPoint Restrict Access feature. It is located on the File tab, in the Info section, under Protect Presentation. For you to be able to use this feature, your computer will need to be set up for Information Rights Management though Microsoft Office.

Create Comments

The Comments feature provides a way for you to add your input about the presentation, whether to collaborate with others or for your own personal use. This is also an excellent way to keep track of changes that others have suggested. **Comments** are short notes attached to the presentation. They appear in comment boxes that look like speech callouts. When the speech callout icon is clicked, a Comments pane is displayed, showing the names of the commenters along with their messages, when the comment was made, and possibly their photos if they were logged into a Microsoft Account. Comments do not show while in presentation view.

In this exercise, you will add comments to the presentation, asking Irene for additional content.

P04.12

To Add Comments to a Presentation

a. If you took a break, open the **p02ch04Presentation_LastFirst** presentation.

b. Click **Slide 2**. Click the **Review** tab, and then in the Comments group, click **New Comment**, type This slide could use some nice photographs of some of your employees. Press Enter.

> Notice that below your comment is a section for Reply. In PowerPoint, the comments have been redesigned so they mimic a conversation and are not just isolated comments.

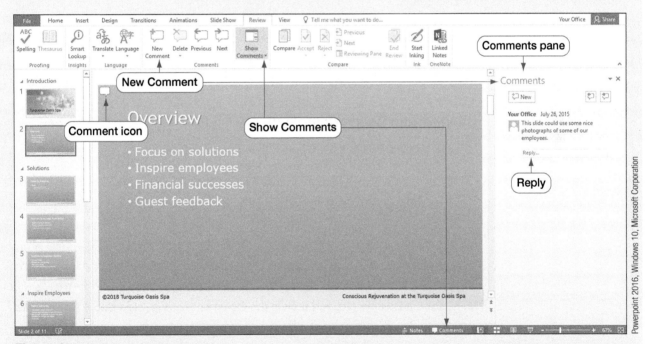

Figure 17 Creating comments

c. Click **Slide 9**, and then in the Comments group, click **New Comment**. Type Irene, can we get a photograph from Jacquie's wedding? **Close** ☒ the Comments pane. You will update the presentation to include the actual footer text before sending the presentation to Irene.

d. Click the **Insert** tab, and then in the Text group, click **Header & Footer**. In the Header and Footer dialog box, on the Slide tab, click the **Date and time** check box to select it, and click **Fixed**. Select the date text in the box to replace the contents of this box. Type the current year and then press [Spacebar]. Type Turquoise Oasis Spa. Click **Footer** to select it, and then click in the Footer box and type Conscious Rejuvenation at the Turquoise Oasis Spa. Click **Don't show on title slide** to select it, and then click **Apply to All**.

You may have noticed that you cannot access the symbols while viewing the Header & Footer dialog box. You will modify the footer, return to the Header & Footer dialog box, and then apply the modifications to all slides.

e. Click in front of the year on the footer. On the Insert tab, in the Symbols group, click **Symbol**, and then click **Copyright Symbol** (character code 00A9 in the normal text font). Click **Insert**, click **Close**, and then in the Text group click **Header & Footer**. Notice the copyright symbol is now in front of the date in the footer dialog box. Click **Apply to All**.

f. **Save** 🖫 and **close** the presentation.

Navigate Comments

When a file is returned to you with comments, the comment icons will appear on the slides. You can click each slide in the presentation and search for the icons, but this takes time. Instead, you can use the Comments group on the Review tab to move to the next comment or the previous comment. You can also edit comments and delete comments in this group.

You sent the file to Irene for her review. She sent it back to you with her comments. In this exercise, you will review the changes Irene made to the file and the comments she added.

P04.13

SIDE NOTE

Showing Comments
Alternatively, you can click Comments in the status bar at the bottom to open the Comments pane.

To View and Delete Comments

a. Start **PowerPoint**, click **Open Other Presentations** in the left pane, and then double-click **This PC**. Navigate through the folder structure to the location of your student data files, and then double-click **p02ch04Comments**.

The presentation that Irene has modified opens. She added some photographs, added new comments, and replied to some comments.

b. Click the **File** tab, click **Save As**, and then click **This PC**. In the **Save As** dialog box, navigate to where you are saving your project files, and change the file name to p02ch04Update_LastFirst, using your last and first name. Click **Save**.

c. Click the **Review** tab, and then in the Comments group, click **Show Comments**.

The Comments pane opens to the right, and Irene's comment on Slide 1 is displayed.

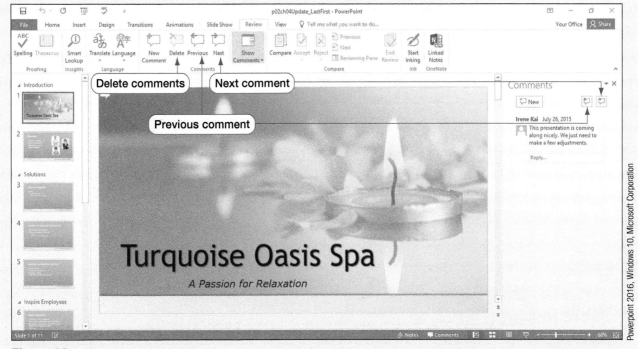

Figure 18 Reviewing comments

d. On the Review tab, in the Comments group, click **Next** to view the next comment. Notice on Slide 2 that Irene has replied to your comment.

e. Continue clicking **Next** to review the other comments.

f. Click **Slide 1**, in the Comments pane, click the **comment**. On the Review tab, in the Comments group, click **Delete** to delete the comment.

g. Click **Slide 2**, click the comment, and then click **Delete** to delete the comment thread since it has been addressed.

h. Click **Slide 3**, click the **Insert** tab, and then in the Illustrations group, click **SmartArt**. Click **Relationship** on the left, click the **Opposing Arrows** SmartArt illustration, and then click **OK**.

- In the **top text** placeholder, type Increase Profitability.

- Select the **text** you just typed, and then reduce the font size to **36**.

- Click the **bottom text** placeholder, and then type Reduce Employee Turnover.

- Select the **text** you just typed, and then reduce the font size to **36**.

- Delete the **bulleted list** behind the SmartArt illustration, and then delete the **text placeholder**.

- Click the **SmartArt illustration** border, and then click the **SmartArt Tools Design** tab. In the SmartArt Styles group, click the **Subtle Effect**. In the SmartArt Styles group, click the **Change Colors** arrow and select **Gradient Range – Accent 3**.

- Right-click the SmartArt illustration border, and then select **Size and Position**. Click **Position** to expand the section. In the Format Shape pane, click the **Horizontal position** box, type 4.45" and then press Enter. Click the **Vertical position**, type 0.52", and then press Enter.

- Click the **slide title** placeholder border. Click the **Horizontal position** box, and then type 0", and press (Enter). Click the **Vertical position** box, and then type 0.17", and press (Enter). **Close** [×] the Format Shape pane.

You have finished the suggested changes made by Irene, so you will now delete all remaining comments.

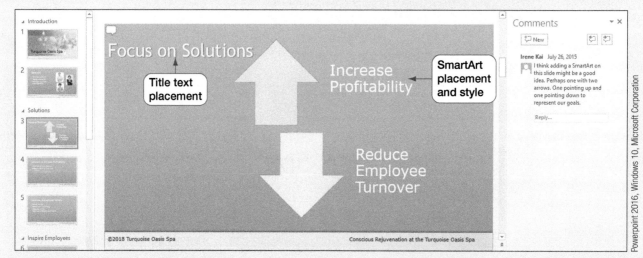

Figure 19 SmartArt illustration

i. In the Comments pane, click the **comment** to select it. Click the **Review** tab, in the Comments group, click **Delete** to delete the comment since it has now been addressed.

j. Click **Slide 8**. In the Comments pane, click the **comment** to select it, and then click **Delete** to delete the comment.

k. Click **Slide 9**. In the Comments pane, click the **comment** to select it, and then click **Delete** to delete the comment thread.

l. **Close** [×] the Comments pane.

m. **Save** [⊟] the presentation.

Create and Use Speaker Notes

Speaker notes, displayed in the Notes pane of the PowerPoint window, enable you to write the words you will say during the presentation and store them with the actual presentation. You can later print the notes for reference during the presentation, or if you are using a dual display screen system or are projecting your presentation, you can show the audience the slides while you view the notes in Presenter view.

There are some tips you should consider while creating speaker notes. Avoid writing complete sentences. This will help keep you from reading word for word from the notes. Organize the notes with numbers or letters in outline format. Use the Export feature on the File tab to create handouts in Microsoft Word, in order to see notes on the side or below the slide pictures. Having a picture of the slide on the notes enables you to stay on track during the presentation. By converting the presentation file to Word, you can then modify the font size of the notes, making it larger and easier to read in a darkened room.

While Irene was reviewing the presentation and adding comments, she also added some speaker notes to a few of the slides. In this exercise, you will create some additional speaker notes in the presentation. You will then create a Word document with the notes.

To Add and Print Speaker Notes

a. Click **Slide 1**. Click **Notes** in the status bar, and then drag the **border** between the Slide pane and the Notes pane upward so you have more room to type notes. The slide becomes smaller but is still clear enough for you to read.

b. Click the **Notes** pane, and then type Introduce yourself. Press Enter. Click the **Home** tab, and then in the Paragraph group, click **Increase List Level** 🔳 Type Name, and then press Enter. Type Spa Manager, and then press Enter. Click **Decrease List Level** 🔳 and then type Quarterly report on the successes of the spa.

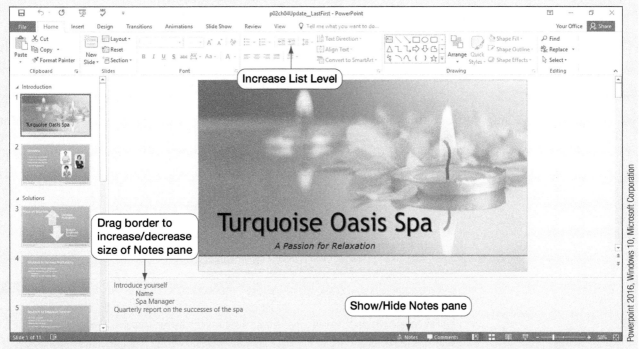

Figure 20   Speaker notes

c. Browse through the presentation, and then examine the notes on **Slides 3, 5, 7,** and **10**.

d. Continue adding speaker notes to the Notes pane of each slide as noted in the table, using Increase List Level and Decrease List Level as needed.

Slide 4	Product display makeover
	Mobile marketing extremely successful
	On low-booked days — increased walk-ins by 25%
Slide 6	Worked to develop the employees
	Recognized
	Encouraged
	Offered hands-on management training
	One-on-one coaching

e. **Save** 🔲 the presentation. Click the **File** tab, click **Export**, click **Create Handouts**, and then click **Create Handouts**.

f. Leave **Notes next to slides** selected, and then click **OK**. Click the **Word application** when it appears on the taskbar.

g. Select the **Notes** column in the Word document by clicking above the Slide 1 Notes third column when the ⬇ is displayed. Click the **Home** tab, in the Font group, click **Decrease Font** A⁻ once.

h. Click **Save** 🖫 in the Word document, navigate to the location where you are saving your project files, and then change the file name to p02ch04Notes_LastFirst, using your last and first name. Click **Save**.

i. **Close** ✕ the Word document.

Mark Presentations as Final and Apply Password Protection

The use of passwords protects presentations from being accessed by unauthorized people. This keeps others from opening and modifying the documents. On a shared server, a SharePoint site, or OneDrive, you may want to use this feature when you have completed the presentation. On the Info tab on the File tab, you can mark the file as final and make it read-only. This makes the presentation viewable but does not allow modifications. You may also encrypt the presentation with a password. People who do not have the password cannot view or modify the presentation. You can also restrict the permission of people so they cannot edit, copy, or print the presentation. An invisible digital signature can be added to the presentation, ensuring the integrity of the document.

REAL WORLD ADVICE | **Before Marking a Presentation as Final**

It is important to consider who will be viewing the presentation and what version of PowerPoint they will be using. Under the File tab, on the Info tab, you will find options under the Check for Issues button. If people may be viewing your presentation with an earlier version of PowerPoint, you will want to check for any compatibility issues. If you will be publishing your presentation to the web, you will also want to check for any accessibility issues for people with visual impairments. The Accessibility Checker will inform you of ways to ensure people with visual impairments can get the most out of your presentation.

In this exercise, you will protect the presentation with a password and then mark the presentation as final.

To Encrypt a Presentation with a Password and Mark as Final

a. In the **p02ch04Update_LastFirst** presentation, click the **File** tab, on the **Info** tab, click **Protect Presentation**, and then select **Encrypt with Password**.

Notice the Caution message in the Encrypt Document dialog box. PowerPoint does not provide a password recovery system, so if you lose your password, you will not be able to access the presentation.

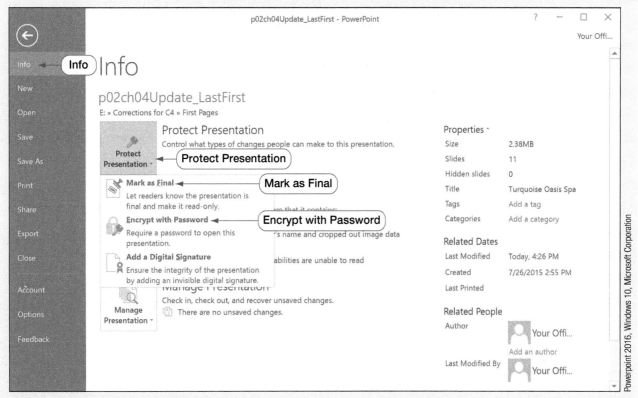

Figure 21 Protecting Presentations

b. Type SpaPresentation for the password, and then click **OK**. Type the same password again to confirm, and then click **OK**.

Click **Save** 🖫 and **Close** the presentation, but leave PowerPoint open.

c. Click the **File** tab, in the Recent list, click the **p02ch04Update_LastFirst** presentation file to open it. Type SpaPresentation as the password, and then click **OK**.

   The presentation opens, and you can make edits to the slides. You will need to share the password with anyone who will be editing, viewing, or presenting the presentation.

d. Click the **File** tab, on the **Info** tab, click **Protect Presentation**, and then select **Mark as Final**.

e. Read the warning message, and then click **OK**.

f. Read the information message that is displayed, and then click **OK**.

   Notice the yellow bar across the top of the window. Notice the Ribbon is not visible above the yellow bar. A Marked as Final icon also appears in the status bar at the bottom. The file has been marked as final, but edits are still possible if someone ignores the warning and clicks Edit Anyway.

g. **Close** the presentation and exit **PowerPoint**. If you need to take a break before finishing the chapter, now is a good time.

Delivering a Presentation

At some time in your career, you will probably be asked to make a presentation. For some people, this causes great anxiety, while for others it seems natural to speak in front of a crowd. There is a wide variety of advice about giving presentations. In the long run, it is a skill you build over time, and the real key is practice. Business schools all over the world recognize the importance of developing presentation and public speaking skills, and they offer many courses that require presentations for assignments and some in lieu of final examinations. In this section, you will explore methods for preparing and delivering a presentation.

Develop Skills in Delivering Presentations

Once you have completed the slides for the presentation, you should practice using them. Project the presentation with the actual equipment you will use, if possible, and practice using the speaker notes, advancing the slides, and looking out into the imaginary audience. You may feel a little funny talking out loud to an empty room, but saying the actual words and hearing them will help to make them flow off your tongue more easily during the real presentation. It is a good idea to enlist a few people to watch a practice session and ask for their honest feedback. They can make you aware of verbal and nonverbal distracters, such as excessively clearing your throat, jingling change in your pocket, or talking too softly. They may also suggest improvements to the content of your presentation. If you do not have people to help you practice, record yourself with a video or audio recorder so you can review the practice session.

Overcoming Presentation Nervousness

Rest assured even the most accomplished presenter occasionally suffers from presentation nervousness. Most people are nervous in the few minutes leading up to being introduced and in the minutes just after the presentation has begun. There are many things you can do to lessen the effects of the anxiety. Remember to breathe. Take deep breaths, filling your lungs and breathing out through your mouth. Even during your presentation, taking a full breath gives you time to straighten out your thoughts, relax, and give the audience a little break. It is like adding white space to your presentation. Smile at your audience. Nod your head. Use hand gestures. These physical movements help to relax your body and reassure your mind that you are in control.

Remind yourself that you are prepared. You have your materials at hand. Your speech has been polished through practice. For the most part, audiences want you to succeed and will support you if you make a genuine effort.

REAL WORLD ADVICE	Memorizing Your Presentation

You may have observed presenters who do not seem to have any notes at all. They may have given the speech so many times it comes to mind naturally, or they may have memorized what they want to say. There is a difference between memorizing the presentation and memorizing the outline. If you are comfortable with the material, memorizing the outline will not only help keep you on track during the presentation but also enable you to choose the actual language you use on the fly. If specific things need to be said during a presentation, then memorizing it is the best way to deliver all of the parts. This takes some time and practice to accomplish, and in some cases, the delivery may seem "canned."

Last-minute changes or accidents add stress to the presentation. As you prepare, think about the possible problems and try to frame emergency actions. You will be ready for the unexpected if you have previously thought it through. If something unexpected does happen, evaluate whether you can do anything about it. If you can, do it. If you cannot, do not overreact to the situation. The audience may not even know that the widget you planned to hold up did not arrive on time or that you are wearing your travel clothes because your luggage went to a different city. Good presenters do not let internal or external forces ruin their presentations.

In this exercise, you will develop slides that focus on fears involved in presentation delivery.

P04.16

To Review Speaker Fears

a. Start **PowerPoint**, and then on the Start screen click **Blank Presentation**. On Slide 1 in the title placeholder, type Presentation Delivery. In the subtitle placeholder, type First Last, using your first and last name.

b. Click the **File** tab, click **Save As**, and then double-click **This PC**. In the **Save As** dialog box, navigate to where you are saving your project files, and change the file name to p02ch04Delivery_LastFirst, using your last and first name. Click **Save**.

c. Insert a **Title and Content slide** as **Slide 2**, in the title placeholder, type Five Fears People Have, and then in the content placeholder list **five fears** that people might have about presenting in front of an audience.

d. Classify each of the fears as Internal or External. Each classification should contain two or more bullet points with at least two subpoints for each listed bullet.

e. Develop one or two methods of minimizing each of the fears.

f. **Save** ⊟ the presentation.

Being Prepared

From bringing extension cords to having multiple versions of your presentation saved on a USB flash drive, computer hard drive, and OneDrive, you can never be too prepared for a presentation. As discussed in the previous section, practice is the best way to arrive prepared for your speech. Arrive 15 minutes to an hour prior to the presentation. If at all possible, you should check the seating arrangements, lighting, audio equipment, handouts, laser pointers, and the projection equipment prior to the presentation. If you bring your own presentation equipment, make sure you have all of the cords to plug the projector into your computer and into the wall. Be sure you have the cord for the computer, even if you have a fully charged battery. You might need a long extension cord. It is a good idea to bring an extra bulb for the projector. A book light might be a handy tool to use for reading your notes if the room will be darkened. Another consideration is what you have on the background of your desktop because the audience may see this displayed on the screen at some point. Be sure that the background is appropriate for a public view.

Walking around the room prior to the presentation gives you a feel for how you might be able to move and engage the audience during the speech. Find out where the light switch is and how to work the microphone if you will be using one. Decide where you will place your computer, the projector, other visual aids, and handouts. If possible, place the projector, focus it on the screen, and test it prior to the audience arrival. Better yet, open your presentation and have it queued to the first slide so the audience will not see you fumble through your directories looking for the PowerPoint file. Having the presentation ready to go gets you off to a running start and adds professionalism to your presentation.

REAL WORLD ADVICE | **Displaying a Presentation**

If at all possible, avoid displaying your presentation from a USB flash drive. These devices slow down animations, crash more easily than a computer will, and introduce other problems. If possible, copy the presentation from the USB flash drive onto the desktop of the computer, and launch the desktop version before your speech. Remember to delete the it from the desktop of the computer after your speech if you are using someone else's computer.

Presenters are a little like airline flight attendants. They need to know where the emergency exits are, the location of the restrooms, and where the refreshments are served. They need to know when the presentation should begin and end. The presenter is viewed as the leader during a speech, so take charge.

Another aspect of being prepared centers on your appearance. You will be more confident if you are comfortable in your clothing. Do not wear a hat during your presentation unless its presence is part of the speech, and then remove the hat as soon as your point has been made. For instance, you might be playing the role of a coach, complete with a ball cap and whistle. As soon as you have blown the whistle, catching the attention of the audience, remove the cap for a more professional appearance. Make a last-minute stop in front of a mirror before your presentation. Check your smile. No spinach between your teeth? Check your hair. Make sure all zippers are secured. Give yourself a thumbs-up, and head out to meet the audience.

In this exercise, you will create a checklist you can use to ensure that you are prepared for your presentation.

To Create a Preparedness Checklist

a. In the Slides group click the **New Slide** arrow and then select **Title and Content**. This will be **Slide 3** in the presentation.

b. In the title placeholder, type Presentation Checklist.

c. In the content placeholder type a list of 10 to 12 items that you should have when you arrive at a presentation. If necessary, apply **Bullets** ⬚ to the list.

d. Insert three additional **Title and Content slides** for Slides 4 through 6. In the title placeholder for Slide 4 through Slide 6 type Scenario Reactions.

e. React to the following scenarios by listing what you would do if they happened during your presentation. On Slide 4, type the first question listed below and then your answer. On Slide 5, type the second question and then your answer. On Slide 6, type the third question and then your answer.

   1. You are about four minutes into delivering your presentation. The bulb on the projector burns out. What would you do?

   2. During the luncheon prior to your speech, you spilled coffee on your clothing. What would you do?

   3. As you were coming to the stage, you heard thunder in the distance. About 10 minutes after you began your speech, the lights went out. What would you do?

f. **Save** ⬚ the presentation.

Engaging Your Audience

From shaking hands and introducing yourself to audience members prior to the presentation until you have completed your speech, you should strive to engage your audience and make a connection. Your enthusiasm for the topic should draw the audience into your presentation. You should speak with confidence.

Make eye contact with audience members. If possible, look directly at the person who introduced you or arranged for you to speak, and mention his or her name in the first few sentences when you speak. Then turn your head to the other side of the audience, make eye contact with someone else, and continue speaking. You should maintain eye contact for one to three seconds per person. Do not focus on just the front row, but also look to the middle and back of the crowd. It is important that you do not face the projection screen and give your presentation with your back to the audience. Avoid standing in front of the screen, where you will be blinded by the projector light and mask the presentation content from the audience. Use a laser pointer or the annotation tools in PowerPoint to focus the attention of the audience on specific parts of the slide.

REAL WORLD ADVICE | **Do Not Be Afraid of Silence**

If one of your slides is filled with a lot of text, do not be afraid of a little silence to give the audience members time to read it. It is extremely difficult to retain what you have read while you are trying to actively listen to the presenter and vice versa.

If at all possible, leave the lights on in the presentation room. This enables you to see the audience, discourages dozing, and increases the interactivity. If the projector is not powerful enough to use with all of the lights on, try to shut off just the lights closest to the projector.

Use natural gestures during your speech. Avoid putting your hands in your pockets or behind your back, crossing your arms, or wringing your hands. If possible, move toward the audience during your presentation. Occasionally take a step to one side or the other, but avoid pacing. Do not look at your feet.

REAL WORLD ADVICE | **Break Up the Presentation**

Depending on the age of your audience and the degree of interest in your topic, the average attention span ranges from 10 to 20 minutes. If you are giving a long presentation, be prepared with a few appropriate distractions, such as a short video, a joke, or an engaging animation if you notice that your audience is losing interest. This can easily grab their attention for a few more slides and make the overall presentation memorable and engaging.

Your voice is a tool during the presentation. Be interested enough in what you are saying that you do not use a monotone voice to deliver the message. If you find yourself falling into a monotone, take a deep breath. Also, many speakers have problems with the speed at which they speak. Presentation nerves make them talk faster. When giving a presentation, slow down. This helps your voice to take on a lower pitch, which projects authority and power. The volume of your speech is something you can check during your presentation preparations, or you can ask your audience whether they can hear you. Practice helps you learn how to project your voice so it is clear. You might want to take a bottle of water with you to the podium to moisten your throat during nonspeaking portions of your presentation.

S S **CONSIDER THIS** | **Using a Microphone**

Most people hesitate to use a microphone, but some people cannot project their voices well enough to be heard. What are some situations in which you should use a microphone if you have that option?

Another aspect of engaging your audience is the question-and-answer portion of the presentation. Many speeches end with "Are there any questions?" It is more advisable to ask "What questions can I answer?" Assume that people in the audience will have questions.

As an audience member asks a question, make eye contact and listen to the full question. Rephrase the question to help clarify it and to give you some time to frame your response. This also helps to make sure the audience heard the question you are about to answer. Be honest and sincere in your reply, and try to involve the whole audience with your response. It helps to think about possible questions your audience might ask prior to the presentation, so you have answers in mind. In this exercise, you will practice making your presentation.

To Practice Your Presentation Skills

a. Use the **Presentation Delivery** slides you developed in the last two exercises and practice presenting the material while looking in a mirror. Do you seem friendly? Sincere? Knowledgeable?

b. If possible, record your voice while you are practicing the presentation, and then review the recording, evaluating whether you have nervous habits that need to be addressed, such as clearing your throat or saying, "um."

c. Practice the speech one more time in front of a mirror, or if possible, use a video camera to record your practice. Evaluate your performance. Were you speaking clearly? Did you need to use the notes to explain or expand on the points made on the slides?

d. After Slide 6, insert a **Title and Content** slide to the presentation, in the Title placeholder, type Evaluation. Write a short evaluation of your practice sessions, and then, if necessary, apply **Bullets** ▤ for each comment.

e. **Save** 🖫 the presentation.

Introducing and Providing a Roadmap for Your Audience

As you begin your presentation, you should let the audience know your purpose and provide an overview of your presentation. You may have a slide or two that lays out the points you will make at the beginning of your presentation. You should prepare the audience for any unusual activities you have planned, such as group work or a game.

Your initial comments should focus on gaining the attention of the audience members. People have many distractions from their own life or job that they bring to your presentation, such as a difficult meeting they had with their boss. You need to draw them into your agenda. Have a clear preview sentence memorized so it is easy to state. For instance, you might say, "I would like to tell you why sales are down this quarter, and propose a plan for improvement."

Your roadmap might be organized in a variety of ways. You may break up the topic into patterns such as past, present, and future. You might present your topic as steps, each of which needs to be completed before the next step occurs. You might use a pro-and-con approach to the topic. It is easier to keep the attention of audience members if they have some idea of where they are in the presentation and where you are going to take them.

Another approach to presentations that can be used in place or alongside the roadmap method is making sure that the audience knows the "destination" before you begin taking them down the road. For example, if you are about to begin a section of your presentation that explains how profits had increased by 25%, then start off with, "Profits are up 25% and here is why!" This will grab the audience members' attention and provide them with a reason to keep listening if they already know where they are going and are excited about it. This method is often implemented by using the title of a slide or the top bullet point to present the "destination." This way it is known from the start why the slides are of significance.

In this exercise, you will create a roadmap for your presentation.

To Create an Introduction

a. After Slide 7, insert a **Title and Content** slide to the presentation, and then in the Title placeholder, type Attention Getters. List four ways in which you could gain the attention of your audience at the beginning of your presentation, and then, if necessary, apply **Bullets** to each new thought.

b. After Slide 8, insert three additional **Title and Content** slides to the presentation.

c. Click **Slide 9**. In the title placeholder type Road Map 1, and then on the slide develop a general roadmap for number 1 listed below. Click **Slide 10**, type Road Map 2 in the title placeholder and develop your roadmap on the slide for number 2 listed below. Click **Slide 11**, type Road Map 3 in the title placeholder and develop the roadmap on the slide for number 3 listed below.

   1. The spa is rolling out a new customer relationship management electronic system. This system records past treatments and products the customer has purchased and provides additional information about the customer, such as phone number, e-mail address, and how often he or she visits the spa.

   2. The spa is reorganizing, hiring new management, and undergoing construction for a new area.

   3. The lead massage therapist is retiring, and you have been asked to speak about the person at the retirement luncheon.

d. **Save** and then **close** the presentation, and then close PowerPoint.

Annotating Slides

As you make your presentation, you may want to emphasize certain points on your slides. You have probably seen presenters use laser pointers for this purpose. If you decide to use a laser pointer, keep in mind that "dancing" the pointer all over the screen is very distracting. Try to point to the area you want to emphasize, and then turn off the pointer rather than moving it back and forth over the area. Generally, your audience will see the location and focus on it very quickly.

PowerPoint goes one step better by enabling you to **annotate**, or make notations or marks on the slides during your presentation. You can use an arrow to point to objects or a pen or highlighter to make long-lasting notations on the slides. You can even select the color of the ink or highlighter. When you close PowerPoint, a warning message will ask whether you want to save the annotations with the file or not. As in so many other things, it is important to practice using the mouse to draw on the slides prior to using the tool in front of an audience.

In this exercise, you will annotate your presentation.

To Use Annotation Tools

SIDE NOTE
Recent Presentations
This presentation file may also be under the Recent heading on the Start screen.

a. Start **PowerPoint**, click **Open Other Presentations** in the left pane, and then double-click **This PC**. Navigate to the location where you are saving your project files, and then double-click **p02ch04Update_LastFirst**.

b. Type SpaPresentation when the Password dialog box appears, click **OK**, and then click **Edit Anyway** in the yellow bar at the top.

Point Options

Pointing to the lower left corner of the slide will also bring up pointer options as an alternative to the right-click method.

c. Press [F5] to start the presentation from the beginning. Right-click **Slide 1**, point to **Pointer Options**, point to **Ink Color**, and then select **Dark Blue**.

d. Drag an underline below the slogan **A Passion for Relaxation**.

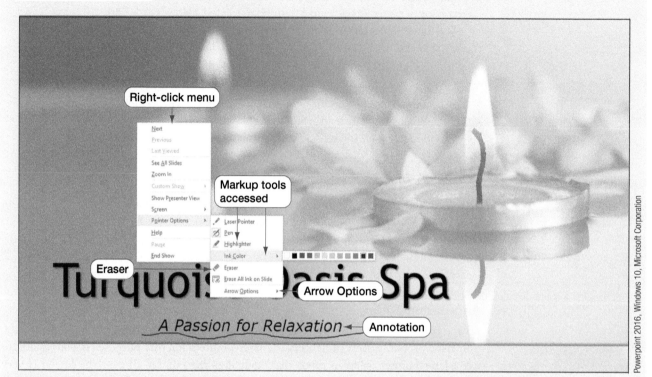

Figure 22 Annotating presentations

> ## Troubleshooting
> When the pen annotation tool is being used, the left mouse button no longer advances the slide. You can press [Enter], the letter "N", or the arrow keys to navigate through slides.

e. Press [Enter] to advance to the next slide. Right-click and point to **Pointer Options**, and then select **Highlighter**. Highlight the word **solutions**.

f. Right-click the **slide**, point to **Screen**, and then select **Show/Hide Ink Markup** to hide the markup on the slide. Repeat this step to display the markup again.

g. Press [Esc] to return to Normal view, and then click **Keep** when you see the warning **Want to keep your ink annotations?** Click **Slide 1** on the Slides tab, and then confirm the ink is still visible.

h. Click the **ink annotation** on Slide 1 to select it, and then press [Delete]. Slide annotations that have been kept can be manipulated in Normal view.

i. **Save** 🖫 and **close** the presentation.

j. Open the file again, type the password SpaPresentation and then click **OK**. Click **Slide 2**, and then confirm the highlighting is still visible on the word **solutions**.

You can save annotations for future use or to distribute them with a slide show you are sending to others.

k. **Close** the presentation and exit **PowerPoint**.

Displaying the Presentation in Presenter View

If your computer can be attached to two monitors, PowerPoint can display the speaker notes on one monitor, usually the laptop, and the presentation slides on the second monitor while in **Presenter view**. As shown in Figure 23, the computer displays Presenter view, and speaker notes are displayed on the right. Information such as which slide you are currently on and how long the presentation has lasted is easily available. Icons on the window enable you to move forward and backward through the presentation. Annotation tools are easily accessed in the window. The next slide in the slide show is displayed so that you are reminded of what is next.

PowerPoint 2016 is automatically configured to display Presenter view if two displays are detected. However, you can check by clicking Use Presenter View on the Slide Show tab in the Monitors group. Here, you can also select which monitor will display Presenter view. If you only have one monitor, you can still use Presenter view. While in Slide Show view, right-click a slide, and then click Show Presenter View.

In PowerPoint 2016, many enhancements have been made to Presenter view. Presenter view now offers zooming onto a specific part of a slide and seeing all slides in a presentation at once, as well as more controls over presentation timing with Pause, Resume, and Restart buttons. Also, you now have easier access to the laser pointer tool.

Figure 23 Presenter view

Powerpoint 2016, Windows 10, Microsoft Corporation

Concluding Your Presentation

The conclusion of the presentation is one of the most important parts because it gives you the opportunity to encourage the audience to fulfill the purpose of your presentation. You should review the roadmap and remind the audience of the content. You can summarize the main points or ask the audience what they have learned. You can tell a story that emphasizes the content. You can emphasize the importance of action and the benefits the audience members will gain.

In most cases, the conclusion of a presentation includes a question-and-answer period. You should set up some time limits so everyone knows when the Q&A will end. Be concise with your answers, and resist the urge to argue with someone who asks a question or challenges you. If you cannot answer the question, admit it, and offer to get back to the person at a later time with the answer.

REAL WORLD ADVICE	When to Accept Questions

Some presenters encourage audience members to participate in the presentation by asking questions or making comments as they think of them. Other presenters prefer to have the audience members hold their questions until the end of the presentation. The size of the audience and the environment of the presentation will help you decide which tactic to use. Keep in mind that questions during your presentation may distract you or the audience and keep you from making all of your points. Regardless of when you accept questions, be sure to repeat the question or paraphrase it so the audience can clearly hear what the question was. This also gives you a chance to frame your response.

When your time is up, thank the audience for their attention. If audience members applaud, acknowledge the response. Some presenters ask the audience to fill out an evaluation form. This can offer you valuable insight into the pluses and minuses of your presentation. After the presentation, be available to speak with members of the audience. Thank the people who arranged for you to speak. Reward yourself for a job well done.

Working with Office Mix

Office Mix is a powerful new tool that turns PowerPoint presentations into interactive lessons. Using Office Mix, you can record presentations, annotate slides, and insert quizzes, polls, videos, screen captures, and screen recordings, which PowerPoint "mixes" into what Microsoft describes as "an interactive, playable presentation" that others can view on the Office Mix website. In addition, content from Kahn Academy, CK-12 Foundation content, PhET Interactive Simulations and other apps, and web pages can be added.

Once the presentation is complete, it can be uploaded to the Office Mix website to publish and share the link. Individuals can watch on any device with a web browser. Office Mix also allows you to check your viewers' progress online, allowing you to see who watched the mix and how well they did on quizzes.

Create an Office Mix

To create an Office Mix, you must install the Office Mix add-in. At the time of writing, Office Mix works with the following versions of PowerPoint: PowerPoint 2016, PowerPoint 2013 SP1, Office 2016, Office 2013 SP1, and Office 365. The Office Mix add-in will not work with previous versions of PowerPoint or Office.

To get started, log onto the Office Mix website at https://mix.office.com, and download Office Mix. A sign-in is required with an organizational account if your organizaton uses Office 365, or you can sign in with a Microsoft, Google, or Facebook account. If you have an Outlook, Hotmail, Xbox, or Skype account, you have a Microsoft ID and are all set.

Once installed, Office Mix will add an additional tab called Mix at the end of the PowerPoint ribbon.

Powerpoint 2016, Windows 10, Microsoft Corporation

Figure 24   Mix tab added

In the Update group of the Mix tab, you will see an Update Office Mix button. Updates are made available often as Microsoft works to incorporate suggestions from users to this add-in. When an update is available, the button is active. When the current update has been applied to PowerPoint, the update button will be dimmed or "grayed out," making it inactive. At the time of the book printing, the current update was applied. You may notice that your Mix tab has some additional elements and a slightly different arrangement than the one shown in Figure 24.

Creating a Slide Recording

The slide recording feature in Office Mix allows you to add a recording of your presentation enhanced with the options to add video, audio, and/or inkings to your slides. If you choose to add video to your slide recording, you will have the option to record in full screen or in a thumbnail in the corner of your slide. The inking feature allows you to add inking annotations to your presentation in several color choices.

If your presentation contains effects such as animations, transitions, and sound effects, keep in mind that your presentation will not record triggered animations, sound effects not recorded in Office Mix, or hyperlinks to inside tables or to custom shows.

Creating a Screen Recording

Imagine that you are a corporate trainer and you need to create a lesson or demonstration on creating formulas using absolute and mixed references in Excel. Typically, you would need a third-party application to record your screen captures. These screen capture applications are usually expensive and have a high learning curve to use.

With Office Mix's built-in Screen Recording feature, you can easily record yourself demonstrating how to create these formulas step by step in Excel. Audio is automatically built in so that you can record your voice as you go through each of the steps.

When the screen recording is complete, it is automatically embedded into the PowerPoint slide. Once you select the recording, a toolbar appears below, with controls including a Play/Pause button.

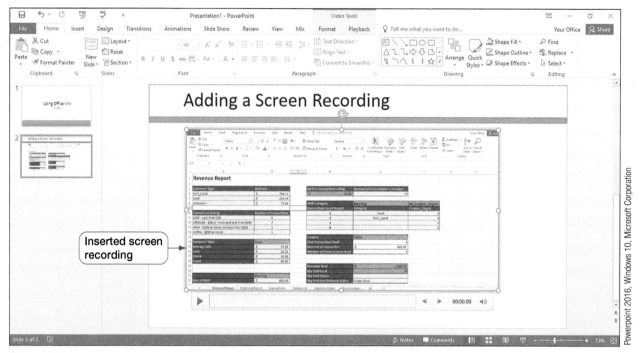

Figure 25 Embedded screen recording

Because the screen capture is embedded as a video into PowerPoint, you are able to use the video tools in PowerPoint to make enhancements to your embedded screen recording.

Inserting Quizzes, Apps, and Web pages

Office Mix is not just limited to screen and slide recordings. Within PowerPoint, you are able to insert quizzes, web pages, and interactive apps such Khan Academy and CK-12 Foundation content to create interactive lessons which can be uploaded to video streaming or social networking websites. Figure 26 shows content available at the time of the printing of the book. More apps are continually being added. Your options may be different than those shown.

Figure 26 Lab apps for Office

Adding quiz formats is easy. You can insert standard quiz formats: true/false, multiple choice, multiple response, free response, and polls. You can set multiple attempts, add hints, set a timer, change the order of multiple choice questions, and provide feedback. Once the quiz is taken, an individual sees immediately whether he or she has chosen the correct answer and any feedback you have added.

Uploading to Mix

Publishing your mix is as easy as uploading to the web and adding permissions for who can view it. Your mix can be viewed in any web browser on any device. Office Mix analytics shows you data about who watched your mix, how much time they spent on each slide, and how they answered your quiz and poll questions. You can even export that data to Microsoft Excel for further analysis.

Concept Check

1. You have been working on a template for your company that will be used by all of the salespeople when they visit customers in the field. The sales people want to create their own customized presentations so they can add the name of the customer and other information to the slide show. What kinds of information would you include on a template for this use? p. 922

2. What purpose do handouts and presentation notes have? What are some things to consider when creating handouts? p. 936

3. When creating a presentation from an outline in Word, what are some things to consider? p. 939

4. What are some benefits of using slide sections to organize a presentation? p. 941

5. Steve Michaels, the vice president of production at your company, requested your input on a presentation he plans to present to the board of directors. He wants feedback on the design of his slides, and he wants you to write some of the text of his presentation. What PowerPoint tools will you use to provide the feedback and text? p. 942

6. What benefits do speaker notes provide? What are some things to consider when creating speaker notes? p. 946

7. Why would you want or need to encrypt a presentation? Why would you want or need to mark a presentation as final? p. 948

8. The board of directors meeting is today, and Steve is in the hospital. You have been asked to make his presentation. You have never made a speech to the board, and you are becoming increasingly nervous. What will you do to control your nerves before the presentation? Once you get into the board room, how will you engage the members of the board and get them to agree to the proposal Steve was making? p. 950

9. You have been asked to create an in-house training on how to create a template in PowerPoint using Office Mix. What tools of Office Mix would be effective to make the presentation engaging and interactive? p. 958

Key Terms

Annotate   955
Comment   943
Corporate identity   922
Handout master   936

Notes master   933
Office Mix   958
Presenter view   957
Slide master   922

Slide section   941
Speaker notes   946
Template   922

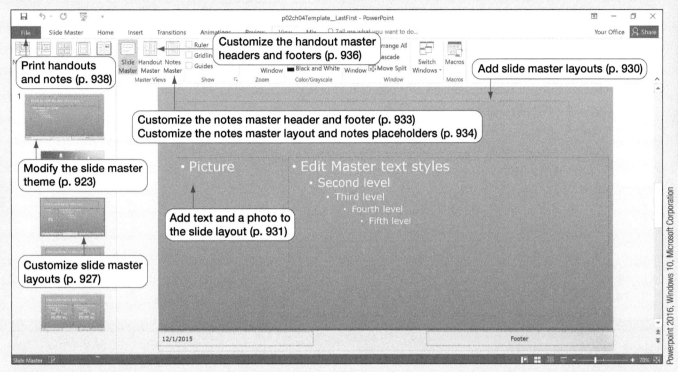

Figure 27

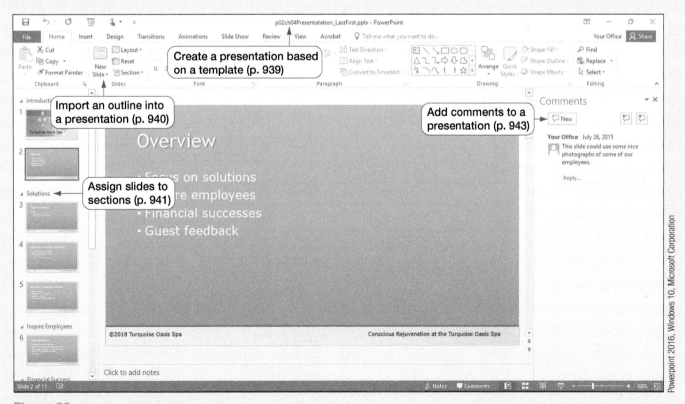

Figure 28

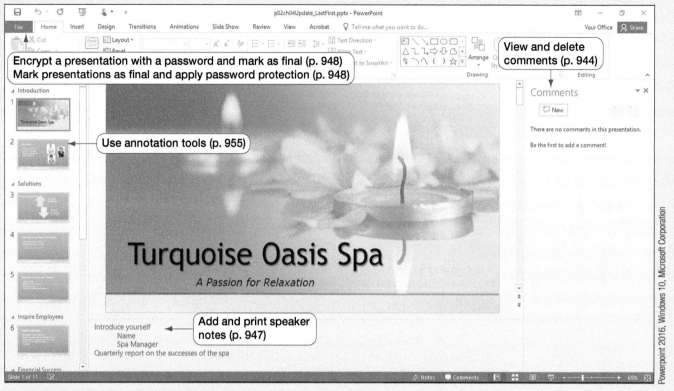

Figure 29

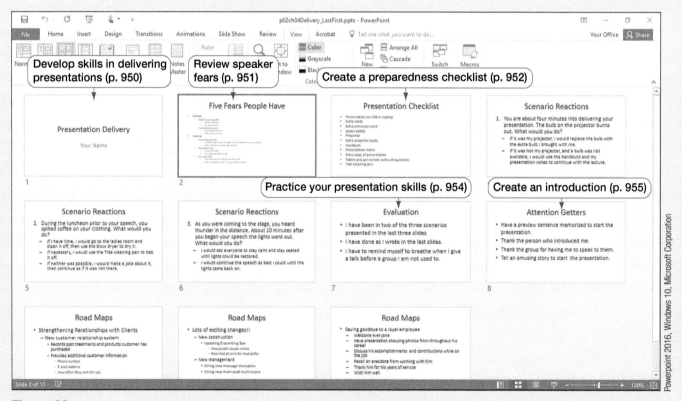

Figure 30

Student data files needed:

 p02ch04Promo.pptx

 p02ch04Fac1.jpg

p02ch04Fac2.jpg

p02ch04Fac3.jpg

You will save your file as:

 p02ch04Promo_LastFirst.potx

Sales & Marketing

Promotional Template

The Turquoise Oasis Spa is working on promoting its remodeled facilities. The manager has asked you to create a template that will be used for various promotional presentations and a few planned events around town. You will create a new layout slide that will be included in all presentations with pictures of the new changes.

a. Start **PowerPoint**. Navigate to the location of your student data files, and then open **p02ch04Promo**.

b. Click the **File** tab, click **Save As**, and then double-click **This PC**. In the **Save As** dialog box, click **Save as type**, and then click **PowerPoint Template**. Navigate to the location where you are saving your project files, and then change the file name to p02ch04Promo_LastFirst, using your last and first name. Click **Save**.

c. Click the **View** tab, and then in the Master Views group, click **Slide Master**. Scroll to the top of the left pane, and then click **Office Theme Slide Master**.

d. In the Background group, click the **Colors** arrow, and then select **Customize Colors.**

• Change the **Accent 2** color to 132 for **Red**, 118 for **Green**, and 88 for **Blue**.

• Change the **Accent 5** color to 38 for **Red**, 108 for **Green**, and 112 for **Blue**.

• Name the custom theme PromoTheme_LastFirst, using your last and first name and then click **Save**.

e. In the Background group, click the **Fonts** arrow, and then select **Customize Fonts**.

• Select **Candara** as the Heading Font.

• Select **Verdana** as the Body Font.

• Name the custom font PromoFont_LastFirst, using your last and first name and then click **Save**.

f. In the Background group, click the **Background Styles** arrow, and then select **Style 3**.

g. Click the **border** of the title placeholder. Click the **Home** tab, in the Font group, change the **Font Color** to **White, Text 1** and then add the **Shadow** effect.

h. Click the **border** of the content placeholder. Change the text color to **White, Text 1**.

i. Click the **Insert** tab, and then in the Text group, click **Header & Footer**. Click **Footer** to select it, and then type Turquoise Oasis Spa. If necessary, click **Don't show on title slide**, and then click **Apply to All**.

j. Delete the following layouts from the template:

• Vertical Title and Text Layout

• Title and Vertical Text Layout

• Picture with Caption Layout

• Content with Caption Layout

• Blank Layout

• Comparison Layout

• Section Header Layout

k. If necessary, click the **Slide Master** tab. In the Edit Master Group, click **Insert Layout**. Rename the layout to New Facilities.

l. On the Slide Master tab, in the Master Layout group, click the **Insert Placeholder** arrow, and then select **Picture**.

m. Drag under the title placeholder to create a **picture** placeholder.

n. Click the **Drawing Tools Format** tab, and then in the **Size** group, type 3.8" in the **Shape Height** box and 3.6" in the **Shape Width** box.

o. Right-click the picture placeholder, and then click **Size and Position**. Click **Position**, click in the **Horizontal position** box, and then type 0.9". Click the **Vertical position** box, and then type 2.5".

p. Select the **picture placeholder**, and then press Ctrl+D to duplicate the picture placeholder. In the Format Shape pane, click the **Horizontal position** box, and then type 4.9". Click the **Vertical position** box, and then type 2.5".

q. With one of the picture placeholders selected, again duplicate the placeholder by pressing Ctrl+D. In the Format Shape pane, click the **Horizontal position** box, and then type 8.9". Click the **Vertical position** box, and then type 2.5".

r. Click **Save**, click the **Slide Master** tab, and then click **Close Master View**.

s. On slide 1, click the title placeholder text, and then type Turquoise Oasis Spa.

t. Click the subtitle placeholder text, and then type Rolling Out the Welcome Mat.

u. On the Home tab, click the **New Slide** arrow, and then select **New Facilities**.

v. Click the title placeholder and type Our New Facilities.

w. Select the first picture placeholder on the left. Click the pictures icon in the content holder. Navigate to where your student data files are located, click **p02ch04Fac1** and then click **Insert**.

x. Select the middle picture placeholder and insert **p02ch04Fac2** from your student data files.

y. Select the picture placeholder on the right and insert **p02ch04Fac3** from your student data files.

z. Select the first picture, press Ctrl, and then select the other two pictures. Click the **Picture Tools Format** tab, under the Picture Styles group, click **Reflected Perspective Right**.

aa. Save the presentation, exit PowerPoint and then submit your file as directed by your instructor.

Problem Solve 1

MyITLab®
Grader
Homework

Student data files needed:

- p02ch04Cafe.pptx
- p02ch04FoodSafetyOutline.docx
- p02ch04Cafe.jpg
- P02ch04Training1.jpg
- P02ch04Training2.jpg
- P02ch04Training3.jpg
- P02ch04Training4.jpg

You will save your file as:

- p02ch04Cafe_LastFirst.pptx

Human
Resources

Food Safety Employee Training

Kayden's Kafe is a unique cafe/deli that serves sandwiches, soups, and salads, plus freshly brewed coffee, espresso, tea, and bakery items made daily from scratch. The managers are hiring staff for the upcoming summer season and would like you to help them customize a presentation on food safety. In this exercise, you will import an outline from a Word document and then customize the slide master and notes master.

a. Start **PowerPoint.** Open the file **p02ch04Cafe**, and then save the presentation as p02ch04Cafe_LastFirst, using your last and first name.

b. In the title placeholder, type Kayden's Kafe. In the subtitle placeholder, type New Staff Training.

c. Import the outline file **p02ch04FoodSafetyOutline**, located in your student data files, into the presentation.

d. Go to the slide master, and then make the following changes to the **Office Theme Slide Master**.

   • Select **Red Orange** as the Theme Colors.

   • Format the Background Style to **Style 5**.

   • Change the Master title style font to **Arial Rounded MT Bold**, set the font size to **60**, and add a Shadow effect.

   • Change the first bullet text to font size **32**.

e. Make the following changes to the **Title Slide Master**.

   • Change the font color for both the title and subtitles to White, Background 1.

   • Insert the **p02ch04Cafe** as a picture background with a transparency of **20%**. Hide the background graphics.

f. Close **Master View** and then **Reset** Slides 2 through 6 so that the changes you have made apply to the imported slides.

g. Click **Slide 2** and select the four bullet points. Right-click the selected text, in the pop-up menu, select **Convert to SmartArt**, and then click the **More SmartArt graphics ...** at the bottom of the dialog box. In the Choose a SmartArt Graphic dialog box, click **Picture** in the left panel, and then select **Title Picture Lineup**.

h. Make the following changes and adjustments to the SmartArt.

   • Apply the **Intense Effect** style.

   • Under Change Colors select **Colorful Range - Accent colors 5 to 6**.

   • Click the **picture icon** for preventing cuts and insert the **p02ch04Training1** file from your student data files.

   • Click the **picture icon** for avoiding falls and insert the **p02ch04Training2** file from your student data files.

   • Click the **picture icon** for fires and burns and insert the **p02ch04Training3** file from your student data files.

   • Click the **picture icon** for poisons and insert the **p02ch04Training4** file from your student data files.

i. Insert a Comment on Slide 2, type I think this looks much better with the SmartArt choice. Should we make other changes to slides 3-6?

j. Insert a Comment on Slide 6, type We need to add a summary slide at the end.

k. In the Notes section of Slide 5, type Suggest that the staff take First Aid training at the local Red Cross.

l. Open the notes master and make the following changes.

   • Change the orientation to Landscape.

   • Increase the size of the notes to 16.

   • Clear the page number and date from the notes.

   • Type Kayden's Kafe Training in the header.

   • Type First Last, using your first and last name in the footer.

m. Close the Notes master.

n. Save the presentation, exit PowerPoint, and then submit your file as directed by your instructor.

Student data files needed:

 Blank PowerPoint presentation

 p02ch04NonverbalOutline.docx

You will save your files as:

 p02ch04InHouseTraining_LastFirst.potx

 p02ch04Nonverbal_LastFirst.pptx

Customer Service Presentation

Human Resources

You work in the Human Resources department of your company as an in-house trainer. You need to ensure that all of your training presentations have a similar "look and feel." You will develop a PowerPoint template, save it, and then use it to create a brief presentation on nonverbal communication that you will use in one of your training sessions.

a. Open a new blank PowerPoint presentation and save as p02ch04InHouseTraining_LastFirst.potx. (Note the file extension denoting the file is a PowerPoint template).

b. Begin by making the following changes to the **Office Theme Slide Master**.

- Create a customized set of Theme Colors, based on one of the color sets available. Change at least one background color and two accent colors. Think about the look and feel you wish your template to represent as you choose each of the colors. The colors of the theme should complement each other. Name the customized theme colors Training_LastFirst, using your last and first name.

- Create an appropriate background for your slides. Use solids, gradients, textures, or background styles. Do not add a photograph.

- Create a customized Theme Font with your choice of heading and body fonts. Choose font sizes and colors for each of the text placeholders as appropriate. Name the customized fonts TrainingFonts_LastFirst.

- Add at least one shape to the template. Remember that placement of the shapes should not hinder the presentation design such that placement of items on the slide becomes difficult. Filled rectangles and lines are always a good choice.

c. Click the **Title Slide Layout** and make changes that you think are needed. Be sure the title is readable with the background you have chosen. Add at least one additional appropriate shape.

d. Create a **new custom layout** that will be used to display your photo and contact information as the in-house trainer. Rename the custom layout PresenterInfo. Close the Master View and add a new PresenterInfo slide. Type Contact Information for the slide title, and add a photo and appropriate contact information in the appropriate placeholders.

e. Save the template and close the file.

f. Navigate to the folder where you are saving your completed files. Double-click the template you just created. Save the file as p02ch04Nonverbal_LastFirst.

g. Click the title slide and type Nonverbal Communication Skills in the Title placeholder. In the Subtitle placeholder, type First Last, using your first and last name.

h. Import the Word outline document **p02ch04NonverbalOutline**.

i. Reset the imported slides if needed.

j. Use a SmartArt illustration on Slide 2 that would best represent the bullet information.

k. Add two or three callout shapes to Slide 3. Format and place the shapes on the slide to add emphasis and design.

l. For slides 4-7, add a comment to each slide noting what changes you might make to the slide to make the slide more appealing to your audience. It is important to remember that slide after slide of bulleted text does not make for an engaging presentation.

m. Save your presentation, exit PowerPoint, and then submit your files as directed by your instructor.

Additional Cases

Additional Chapter Cases are available at www.pearsonhighered.com/youroffice

Collaborating and Evoking Emotion with the Audience

This business unit had two outcomes:

Learning Outcome 1:

Utilize advanced PowerPoint elements to create high-quality presentations using transitions and animations, embedded media files, and photo albums.

Learning Outcome 2:

Customize PowerPoint to create a brand using themes, slide masters, and layouts, and collaborate with others using comments and speaker notes.

In Business Unit 2 Capstone, students will demonstrate competence in these outcomes through a series of business problems at various levels from guided practice to problem solving an existing presentation to performing to create new presentations.

More Practice 1

Student data files needed:

- p02Vacation.pptx
- p02Logo.jpg
- p02V1.jpg
- p02V2.jpg
- p02V3.jpg
- p02V4.jpg
- p02V5.jpg
- p02V6.jpg
- p02V7.jpg
- p02V8.jpg
- p02V9.jpg
- p02V10.jpg
- p02V11.jpg
- p02V12.jpg
- p02V13.jpg
- p02V14.jpg
- p02Resort.jpg
- p02Reservations.jpg

You will save your files as:

- p02VTplate_LastFirst.potx
- p02Vacation_LastFirst.pptx
- p02VAlbum_LastFirst.pptx
- p02VVideo_LastFirst.mp4

Family Vacation Presentation

Sales & Marketing

Production & Operations

Timothy Smith, the marketing manager of the Painted Paradise Resort & Spa, is interested in marketing to families who might want to spend a vacation at the resort. The recreational facilities, including the golf course, spa, pool, and nearby hiking trails, make this an attractive destination for all members of the family. The restaurants at the resort make it convenient and cost-effective to feed the family. Timothy has asked you to create a template and develop a sample presentation to advertise the benefits of a Painted Paradise vacation. You will create a template that appeals to children and parents. You will develop a template for handouts as a part of the main template. You will develop a photo album of photographs from around the resort. Hyperlinks will be added to a slide. You will add transitions and animations to the slides, along with audio. In addition, because Timothy wants to post the presentation on the resort's website, you will create a video of the presentation. He has also requested that you deliver the presentation at his next staff meeting, so you will create some speaker notes and make some planning comments on the slides.

a. Start **PowerPoint**, navigate to the location of your student data files, and open **p02Vacation**. Click the **File** tab, click **Save As**, and then double-click **This PC**. Change the **Save as type** to **PowerPoint Template**, and then navigate to the location where you are saving your project files. Change the file name to p02VTemplate_LastFirst, using your last and first name. Click **Save**.

b. Click the **View** tab, and then in the Master Views group, click **Slide Master**. Click the **Office Theme Slide Master** thumbnail, and then in the Background group, click **Colors**. Click the **Yellow Orange** theme colors. Click **Colors** again, and then click **Customize Colors**. Change the **Accent 3** color to 191 for **Red**, 30 for **Green**, and 46 for **Blue**. In the Name box, type VacationColors_LastFirst, using your last and first name, to create a new color group. Click **Save**.

c. In the Background group, click **Fonts**, and then select the **Trebuchet MS** theme fonts. Click **Background Styles**, and then select **Style 2**.

d. Select the **text** in the title placeholder. Click the **Format** tab, and then in the WordArt Styles group, click **Text Effects**, point to **Shadow**, and then select **Perspective Diagonal Upper Left**. With the text still selected, click the **Home** tab, and then in the Font group increase the font size to **54**.

e. Delete the left footer placeholder, which currently holds the date. Similarly, delete the right footer placeholder, which holds the page number field. Click in the **center footer** place-holder, and change the font color to **Black, Text 1, Lighter 25%**. Click the **Format** tab, and then in the Size group, change the value in the **Shape Width** box to 11.5". In the Arrange group, click **Align**, and then select **Align Center** to center-align the box on the slide.

f. Click the **Title Slide Layout** thumbnail. In the Master Layout group, deselect **Footers**. Click the **Insert** tab, in the Images group, click **Pictures**, and then insert the **p02mpLogo** picture from your student data files. On the Format tab, in the Size group, change the value in the **Shape Width** box to 8.5". Right-click the **logo** image, and then click **Size and Position**. Click **Position** to expand the section. Click the **Horizontal position** box, type 0", click the **Vertical position** box, and then type 2.6". Close the **Format Picture** pane.

g. In the Adjust group, click **Color**, and then select **Set Transparent Color**. With the new pointer, point to the **white background** of the logo, and then click to make the logo image background transparent. With the logo still selected, click the **Animations** tab, and then in the Animation group, apply the **Float In** animation effect. In the Timing group, change the **Duration** to 1.50, and then select **With Previous**.

h. Click the **title** placeholder. In the Animation group, apply the **Wipe** animation, click **Effect Options**, and then select **From Left**. In the Timing group, set the **Duration** to 1.50, click the **Start** arrow, and then select **After Previous**. In the Preview group, click **Preview** to view the result.

i. Click the **Section Header Layout** thumbnail, and then press Delete. Similarly, delete the following layouts.
   - Two Content Layout
   - Blank Layout
   - Picture with Caption Layout
   - Title and Vertical Text Layout
   - Vertical Title and Text Layout

j. Click the **View** tab, and then in the Master Views group, click **Handout Master**. In the Background group, click **Background Styles**, and then select the **Style 9** background style. Select the **TrebuchetMs** theme fonts.

k. Delete the date placeholder. In the **Header** placeholder, type Painted Paradise Resort & Spa. Press Enter, and then type First Last, using your first and last name. Click the **Format** tab, and then in the Arrange group, click **Align,** and then select **Align Center**. Select all the text in the header placeholder, click the **Home** tab, and then in the Paragraph group, click **Center** to center the text within the placeholder.

l. In the **Footer** placeholder, type All Offers Subject to Availability. Place the insertion point in front of the page number symbol, type Page, and then press Spacebar. Click the **Handout Master** tab, and then in the Close group, click **Close Master View**. Save and close the template. Exit PowerPoint.

m. Next, you will create a presentation based on the template. Navigate through the folder structure to the location where you are saving your project files, and then double-click **p02VTemplate_LastFirst**. Save the presentation as p02Vacation_LastFirst, using your last and first name.

n. Click the **title** placeholder, type The Destination for Your Next Vacation!

o. Click the **Insert** tab, and then in the Images group, click the **Photo Album** arrow, and then select **New Photo Album**. Click **File/Disk**, navigate to the location of your student data files, select the following photographs, and then click **Insert**.
   - p02V1
   - p02V2
   - p02V3
   - p02V4
   - p02V5
   - p02V6
   - p02V7
   - p02V8
   - p02V9
   - p02V10
   - p02V11
   - p02V12
   - p02V13
   - p02V14

p. Click the **p02V4** check box to select picture 4. Click the **Up** arrow three times to move picture **4** to position **1**. Click the **p02V4** check box to deselect the picture. Using the same technique, move pictures **p02V5** and **p02V6** into positions **3** and **4**. Move picture **p02V11** into position **6**. Move picture **p02V14** to position **8**. Remove pictures **p02V12** and **p02V13**. Click the **Picture layout** arrow, and then select **2 pictures with title**. Click the **Frame shape** arrow, and then select **Rounded Rectangle**. Click **Create**, and then save the new album where you are saving your project files as p02VAlbum_LastFirst, using your last and first name. Click the **File** tab, and then click **Close**.

q. With the **p02Vacation_LastFirst** file open, click the **Home** tab, and then in the Slides group, click the **New Slide** arrow, and then select **Reuse Slides**. In the Reuse Slides pane, click **Browse**, and then click **Browse File**. Navigate to where you are saving your project files, and then double-click **p02VAlbum_LastFirst**. In the Reuse Slides pane, click **Slide 2** to add it to the presentation. Similarly, click **Slides 3-7**, in that order, to add them to the presentation. Close the Reuse Slides pane.

r. Type the following titles on the following slides.

Slide number	Title
2	Whether You Bike or Hike
3	Golf with Family or Friends
4	Swim or Sun
5	Visit the Spa
6	Catch a Snack or Dine
7	Our Suites or Queens

s. After **Slide 6**, add a **Title and Content** layout slide. Click in the **title** placeholder, type Make Painted Paradise Resort & Spa, and then press Enter. Type Your Vacation Destination. Select all of the **text** within the placeholder, and then center the text within the placeholder. Click the **Pictures** icon in the content placeholder, and then insert the **p02Resort** picture. On the **Format** tab, in Picture Styles group, select **Reflected Rounded Rectangle**.

t. After **Slide 7**, add a new **Comparison** layout slide. Click in the top **title** placeholder, and then type Painted Paradise Deals! In the **left column heading** placeholder, type Family of 4 Deal - 3 Nights, press Enter, and then type $595. Select the **text** in the placeholder, **center** the text and increase the font size to **26**. In the **right column heading** placeholder, type Large Family Deal - 4 Nights, press Enter, and then type $895. Select the **text** in the placeholder, **center** the text and increase the font size to **26**. Select the **left column heading**, press and hold Ctrl, and then select the **right column heading**. Click the **Format** tab, in the Shape Styles group, click the **Shape Fill** arrow, and then click **Light Yellow, Background 2, Darker 50%**.

u. Select the **left body** placeholder, press and hold Ctrl, and then select the **right body** placeholder. On the **Format** tab, in the Shape Styles group, click the **Shape Fill** arrow, and then click **Light Yellow, Background 2, Darker 10%**. With the two body placeholders still selected, click the **Home** tab, in the Paragraph group, click the **Bullets** arrow, and then select **None**. Type the following text in the body placeholders.

Double-Queen Room	Family Suite-Sleeps 8
Round of Golf for 2	Round of Golf for 4
Spa Package for 2	Spa Package for 4
Access to Water Park	Access to Water Park
Family Meal at Indigo5	Family Meal at Indigo5
Daily Breakfast at Red Bluff Bistro	Daily Breakfast at Red Bluff Bistro

v. After **Slide 9**, add a new **Content with Caption** layout slide. Click the **Pictures** icon in the right body content placeholder, and then insert the **p02Reservartions** picture. On the **Format** tab, in the Arrange group, click **Align Objects**, and then select **Align Middle**. In the Picture Styles group, click **More**, and then select **Rounded Diagonal Corner, White**.

w. In the **title** placeholder, type Make Your Reservations Today. **Center** the text within the placeholder, and change the font size to **44**.

x. In the **left content** placeholder, press Enter, type www.paintedparadiseresort.com, and then press Enter twice. Notice that a hyperlink with a red font was automatically inserted. Type 505-555-1792. Press Enter twice, and then type Timothy Smith, Marketing Manager. Select all the **text** within the placeholder, and then **center** the text within the placeholder.

y. With the text still selected, change the font size to **28**. Change the **Shape Width** of the placeholder to 6.0", and then change the **Shape Height** to 4.2". Apply the **Red, Accent 3** font color to the phone number and to the text **Timothy Smith, Marketing Manager**.

z. Select the title placeholder, and change the **Shape Width** of the placeholder to 6.0", and then change the **Shape Height** to 1.5".

aa. Right-click the title placeholder and then click **Size and Position**. Click **Position** to expand the section. Click the **Horizontal position** box, type 0.2", click the **Vertical position** box, and then type 0.4". Click the **body text** placeholder, click the **Horizontal position** box, type 0.1", and then click the **Vertical position** box, and then type 2.0". Close the Format Shape pane.

bb. Select **Slides 2–10**. Click the **Transitions** tab, and then in the Transition to This Slide group, apply the **Cube** transition, click the **Effect Options** arrow, and then select **From Bottom**. In the Timing group, set the duration of the transition to 1.5.

cc. Click **Slide 2**. Apply the **Zoom** animation to the title placeholder. Adjust the timing so that the animation occurs **With Previous** and the **Duration** is set to 1.0. Using the **Animation Painter**, set the same animation settings to **Slides 3-9** for each of the titles.

dd. Click **Slide 10**. Apply the **Split** animation to the title placeholder. Adjust the timing so that the animation occurs **With Previous** and the **Duration** is set to 1.0.

ee. Click the **Insert** tab, in the Text group, click **Header & Footer**. Insert a footer with the text www.paintedparadiseresort.com to all of the slides except the title slide.

ff. Click the **File** tab, click **Export**, and then click **Create a Video**. Click **Presentation Quality**, and then select **Internet Quality**. Click **Create Video**. Save the video where you are saving your project files with the name p02VVideo_LastFirst, using your last and first name.

gg. Click **Slide 1**, click the **Review** tab, and then in the Comments group, click **New Comment**. Type This presentation will be given to the marketing staff under the direction of Timothy Smith. Don't forget the computer, power supply, extension cords, and projector. Close the Comments pane.

hh. In the speaker notes for **Slide 8**, type This slide can be updated as needed.

ii. Prepare to print Handouts with **2 Slides** per page. Review each page of the handout. Notice that page 2 contains the comment that was typed on Slide 1. Print the handout if directed by your instructor. Press Esc to return to the presentation.

jj. Save and close the presentation file, and then exit PowerPoint. Submit your files as directed by your instructor.

Problem Solve 1

Student data files needed:

p02Mobile.pptx

p02MOutline.docx

p02SmartPhone.jpg

p02MMarketing.jpg

p02MVideo.mp4

You will save your file as:

p02Mobile_LastFirst.pptx

Mobile Restaurant Marketing Pitch Presentation

Sales & Marketing

As an avid smartphone user, you are aware of mobile marketing. You can sign up for special offers and deals that are for smartphone users only. You have been thinking about the implications of this type of marketing for the Painted Paradise Resort & Spa, and have been asked to make a presentation at the next meeting of the Board of Directors. You will use the slide master tools to create backgrounds on different slide layouts for consistency in the presentation, but you will not create an actual template. You have created an outline of important points, which you will import into the presentation. You have found an interesting video to embed in the presentation. Transitions and animations will be used in the slide show. You will add speaker notes to use during your persuasive presentation. The handout master will be modified to produce customized handouts of some of the key slides of the presentation.

a. Open **p02Mobile** and save your file as p02Mobile_LastFirst, using your last and first name.

b. Open the **Slide Master** view. Set the theme colors to **Blue Warm**.

c. Change the theme fonts to **Gill Sans MT**.

d. Apply the **Style 5** background style.

e. Click the **Retrospect Slide Master** thumbnail at the top of the left pane. Select all of the text in the body content placeholder, and then click the **Home** tab. In the Font group, click **Increase Font Size** until the font size displayed is **28+**.

f. Select the **title placeholder text** and increase the font size to **54**.

g. With the text still selected, on the **Format** tab, in the WordArt Styles group, click **Fill – Blue-Gray, Accent 1, Shadow**. Apply the **Shadow, Offset Bottom** text effect.

h. Click the **Title and Content** Layout. Insert the **p02SmartPhone** picture. Change the height of the image to 4.5". Change **the Horizontal position** to 0.6" and the **Vertical position** to 2.0".

i. Close the Master View, and then save the presentation.

j. Click the **title** slide. In the title placeholder, type Mobile Marketing. Center the text in the placeholder. In the subtitle placeholder, type Presented by First Last, using your first and last name. Insert the image **p02MMarketing**. Change the height of the image to 4.0". Change **the Horizontal position** to 0.9" and the **Vertical position** to 0.6".

k. Create new slides using the outline named **p02MOutline**. **Reset** slides **2–8**.

l. Apply the **Title and Content** layout to **slides 2–8**.

m. Select **Slide 6**, and then insert a **text box** over the screen of the phone. Change the Text Fill for the text box to **White, Background 1**. Type Indigo5 Specials, and then press **Enter** twice. Type Lunch: Sweet Potato Hash, and then press **Enter** twice. Type Dinner: Prime Rib w/Potato. Include a space after each of the colons. Select **Indigo5 Specials**, center the text and change the font color to **Blue-Gray, Accent 1**. Change the height of the text box to 2.8" and the width to 1.8". Change the **Horizontal position** to 1.24" and the **Vertical position** to 2.76". Close the Format Shape pane.

n. Select **Slide 7**, click the **Design** tab, and then in the Customize group, click **Format Background**. In the Format Background pane, select **Hide background graphics**. Close the Format Background pane.

o. On **Slide 7**, click the **Insert Video** button in the content placeholder, and then click **Browse.** Navigate to the location of your student files and then double-click **p02MVideo**. Add an **Outer Shadow Rectangle** video style. Set the playback video option to **Loop until Stopped** and click in the body placeholder to **Start Automatically**.

p. Select **Slide 8**, press **Enter** and type Mobile Marketing Association. Select the text and add www.mmaglobal.com as a hyperlink. Click to the right of the text, press **Enter**. Type mobiThinking and add www.mobithinking.com as a hyperlink. Click to the right of the text, press **Enter.** Type Mobile Marketing Watch and add mobilemarketingwatch.com as a hyperlink.

q. Select **Slides 2–8**, and then apply the **Push** transition with the effect option of **From Right**.

r. Select **Slide 2**, and then animate each bullet point individually with the **Fade** animation. Set the animation to start when the mouse button is **clicked**, with a duration of 2.00.

s. Add the following speaker notes to the presentation:

Slide	Note
4	Show examples
5	Click to show each bullet
8	Play video and discuss available apps

t. Select **Slide 1**, and then insert the following comment (include the period): Bring cellphone and iPad.

u. Compress the Media to a **Low Quality**. Review the presentation, and then save the presentation. Exit PowerPoint. Submit your file as directed by your instructor.

Critical Thinking

The purpose of this presentation is to persuade the audience of the value of mobile marketing. Including charts would be a great way to support your position on why mobile marketing would be an important strategy for Painted Paradise Resort & Spa. What types of data should you research to include? What types of charts would best represent the data? Would another PowerPoint element be more effective? Give at least two examples.

Problem Solve 2

Student data files needed:

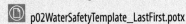

p02WaterSafety.pptx

p02WaterSafetyOutline.docx

p02Buddy.jpg

p02Lifeguard.jpg

p02Float1.jpg

p02Float2.jpg

p02Float3.jpg

P02Float4.jpg

p02NoGlass.jpg

You will save your files as:

p02WaterSafetyTemplate_LastFirst.potx

p02WaterSafety_LastFirst.pptx

Water Safety Presentation

Production & Operations

The resort staff has noticed that several guests are not following the rules and good safety practices in the pool area. Julie Rholfing, the VP of Special Projects for the resort has asked that a PowerPoint presentation be developed to educate and reinforce pool rules and pool safety. She has started the presentation and created an outline for the presentation. She has asked you to finish the presentation.

You will begin the project by creating a template based on the presentation Julie has started. You will import an outline that she has provided. Additionally, you will add photographs, SmartArt, and transitions to the presentation. Some slides will be hidden. Links between slides will allow nonsequential viewing of the slides. You will customize the handout master.

a. Open the PowerPoint file **p02WaterSafety** and then save your file as a PowerPoint template as p02WaterSafetyTemplate_LastFirst.

b. Customize the theme colors and change the **Hyperlink** color to **Blue, Accent 6, Darker 25%**. Change the **Followed Hyperlink** color to **Blue, Accent 6, Darker 50%**. Save the new theme color group with the name WaterSafety_LastFirst, using your last and first name.

c. Create a custom font group using **Lucida Sans** as the Heading font and **Gill Sans MT** as the Body font. Name the custom font group WaterSafety_LastFirst, using your last and first name.

d. Click the **Office Theme Slide Master**. Format the background adding a gradient fill. Under **Preset gradients**, select **Top Spotlight - Accent 2**.

e. Select the **title** placeholder and increase the font size to **48**.

f. Customize the top level bullet with a character code of 00BB with a size of **90%**, using the color **Aqua, Accent 1, Darker 25%**. Customize the second-level bullet with character code 203A with a size of 85%, using the **Aqua, Accent 1, Darker 25%**.

g. Close the Slide Master view, and then open the **Handout Master**. Remove the date placeholder. In the header placeholder, type Painted Paradise Resort & Spa. Type your First Last name on the second line of the header placeholder. Center-align the header placeholder on the page, and then center the text within the placeholder. Close the Master View.

h. Save and close the template. Exit PowerPoint. Create a new presentation based on the template file you just created, and then save the presentation as p02WaterSafety_LastFirst, using your last and first name.

i. Import the outline file **p02WaterSafteyOutline** into the presentation. **Reset** the slides so that the template settings apply to the imported slides.

j. Click **Slide 2**. Convert the bulleted list to a **Basic Block List** SmartArt illustration. Apply the **Intense Effect** SmartArt Style and change the color to **Colorful - Accent Colors**.

k. Click **Slide 3.** Remove the bullet in front of the quote. Increase the font size of the quoted text to **48**. Remember to include the quotes when adjusting the font size. **Center align** the text. Apply **bold** formatting to the text **Drowning** within the quote.

l. Click **Slide 4**. Change the slide layout to **Picture with Caption**. Increase the font size of the Buddy Up text to **48** and the two lines of text underneath to **28**. Insert the **p02Buddy.jpg** picture. Apply the **Beveled Oval, Black** picture style.

m. Click **Slide 5**. Convert the bulleted list to a **Vertical Bullet List** SmartArt illustration. Apply the **Moderate Effect** SmartArt Style.

n. Click **Slide 6**. Insert the **p02Lifeguard.jpg** picture. Change the height of the picture to 3.0". Apply the **Beveled Oval, Black** picture style. Change the horizontal position to 9.3" and the vertical position to 0.5".

o. Click **Slide 7**. Convert the bulleted list to a **Vertical Picture Accent List** SmartArt illustration. Apply the **Intense Effect** SmartArt Style and change the color to **Colorful - Accent Colors**. In the top picture placeholder insert the **p02Float1** picture into the top picture placeholder. Insert the **p02Float2** picture into the middle picture placeholder. Insert the **p02Float3** picture into the bottom picture placeholder.

p. Click **Slide 8**. Convert the bulleted list to a **Lined List** SmartArt illustration. Apply the **Intense Effect** SmartArt Style and change the color to **Dark 1 Outline**.

q. Click **Slide 9**. Insert the **p02NoGlass.jpg** picture. Change the height of the picture to 3.8". Apply the **Beveled Oval, Black** picture style. Change the horizontal position to 7.1" and the vertical position to 2.6".

r. Click **Slide 10**. Change the slide layout to **Title Only**. Center the text in the title placeholder. Insert the **p02Float4.jpg** picture. Change the height of the picture to 3.9". Apply the **Simple Frame, Black** picture style. Change the horizontal position to 4.7" and the vertical position to 2.3".

s. Click **Slide 2.** Click the **SmartArt box** shape border with the text Buddy Up. Insert a hyperlink to Slide 4. Add the ScreenTip Click the link to learn more! Finish linking the remainder of the SmartArt boxes to the appropriate slides. Add the same ScreenTip for each.

t. Click **Slide 4**. Insert a **Custom Action Button** in the bottom right corner of the slide. Set the hyperlink to **Slide 2**. Type Main Menu in the button. Apply the **Intense Effect - Aqua, Accent 1** style. Change the height to 0.6" and the width to 1.5". Change the horizontal position to 11.7" and the vertical position to 6.8".

u. Copy the action button to **Slides 5-9**.

v. In Slide Sorter view, drag **Slide 3** so that it becomes **Slide 2**.

w. Hide slides **4-9**.

x. Add a new slide with the **Title and Content** layout at the end of the presentation. Type For More Information... in the Title placeholder. Remove the bullet in the content placeholder and type Painted Paradise Resort & Spa. On the next line type www.paintedparadiseresort.com. Press **Enter** to activate the hyperlink. Center the text in the content holder, change the font size to **44**, and then change the content holder vertical position to 2.74".

y. Apply the **Ripple** transition to all slides.

z. Save the presentation, exit PowerPoint, and submit your files as directed by your instructor.

Perform 1: Perform in Your Life

Student data file needed:

 Blank PowerPoint presentation

You will save your files as:

 p02Reunion_LastFirst.pptx

 p02RVideo_LastFirst.mp4

High School Reunion Presentation

Sales & Marketing

Human Resources

As a member of the reunion planning committee for your high school class, you will be creating a PowerPoint presentation to show your classmates' current photographs. Make sure you have permission to use the photographs that you are including in your presentation. Do not assume you can just take them from Facebook or other sources without consent of the owner. For this project, you are to create only a small number of slides to use as an example of how a presentation for your entire class would look. You want to share this idea with the committee before you spend a lot of time producing the presentation. You will use PowerPoint's Photo Album feature to quickly create a presentation with photographs and text. You will modify the colors to reflect your school colors. You will create the video in a small format so you can get approval for it before creating the larger video file.

a. Start **PowerPoint**, and then create a blank presentation. Create a photo album based on a group of 10–20 photographs. Add **captions** to the slides. Apply a **design theme**, keeping in mind that you can alter the colors of the theme to reflect your school colors after you have created the photo album. Apply the **Center Shadow Rectangle** frame shape to all of the pictures. Adjust the size and position of the photos, if necessary.

b. After creating the photo album, save it as p02Reunion_LastFirst.

c. On the title slide, insert an appropriate title and subtitle, and then add a graphic or photograph that associates the presentation with your high school. The title slide should contain a copyright notice, with the copyright symbol, the four-digit year, a comma, and your name (©2018, Your Name). The high school website address (URL) should appear somewhere on the title slide as a hyperlink.

d. If your computer has a microphone, record an audio for one slide.

e. Apply transitions to the slides.

f. Add animations to elements on the slides.

g. Modify the theme as needed for colors and fonts.

h. Insert text boxes as needed to provide brief information about the people on the slide. Insert the name of each person in the caption box.

i. Create speaker notes on each slide with the names of the people pictured and a short snippet of information about each person, such as where the person lives now and whether the person is married and has children.

j. Save the presentation after you have made the modifications listed here.

k. Save the presentation as a video as p02RVideo_LastFirst, using your last and first name.

l. Click **Compress Media**, saving it as **Low Quality**. Save and close the presentation file, and then exit PowerPoint. Submit your files as directed by your instructor.

Perform 2: Perform in Your Career

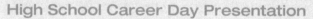

Student data file needed:

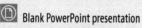 Blank PowerPoint presentation

You will save your file as:

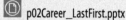 p02Career_LastFirst.pptx

High School Career Day Presentation

Research and Development

Human Resources

You have been working in your chosen career field for more than three years and have been asked by a local high school teacher to make an informal presentation to a group of students on Career Day. The overall topic is your chosen career field. Specific subtopics should include required education level, work environment, job duties, pay, and job outlook. Once you have prepared a rough draft outline in Word, you will import the outline into PowerPoint. You will then format and design an informative and visually appealing presentation to promote student interest in further exploring your career field. Incorporate a design theme related to your career, customize your presentation, and prepare to deliver your presentation.

a. Prepare a rough draft outline of your presentation topics in Microsoft Word. You will not need to submit this outline to your instructor; its purpose is to gather your initial presentation ideas.

b. Start **PowerPoint** and create a new blank file with the name p02Career_LastFirst, using your last and first name. Import your Word outline into your new PowerPoint file.

c. Create a customized set of theme colors for all slides, based on an existing theme of your choosing. Customize any two accent colors. Name the custom theme colors CareerColors_LastFirst, using your last and first name.

d. Create a customized theme font for all slides, with your choice of heading and body fonts. Name the custom theme fonts CareerFonts_LastFirst, using your last and first name.

e. Apply any text effects to the master title style. Be sure the title is readable with the background style you chose.

f. Customize the Title Slide Layout to your liking. When customizing this layout, consider that the title slide's purpose is to introduce your presentation — in this case, your career. Incorporate at least one shape illustration into the Title Slide Layout design.

g. Add additional speaker notes, as you deem necessary.

h. Add slide sections between groupings of slides, if you deem it appropriate. Use your customized Title Slide Layout for these slides.

i. Apply transitions to each of the slides. Add animation if you feel it is needed.

j. Customize the Handout Master Headers and Footers. In the Header placeholder, type your first and last name and your career. Adjust the font to match your theme font(s) and enlarge the text slightly. Delete the date and page number placeholders.

k. Correct any spelling or grammatical errors.

l. Review your presentation by running it in Presenter view. Consider how PowerPoint annotation tools may be used during presentation delivery. Make any other improvements you think necessary.

m. Save and close the presentation file, and exit PowerPoint.

n. Submit your file as directed by your instructor.

Perform 3: Perform in Your Team

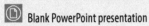
Student data file needed:
 Blank PowerPoint presentation

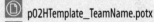
You will save your files as:
 p02HTemplate_TeamName.potx
 p02HHS_TeamName.pptx

HHS Training

Production & Operations

Human Resources

You are one of the trainers for the U.S. Department of Health & Human Services. Your group is responsible for training the staff. You will create a presentation that reviews a topic covered on the www.hhs.gov website. Examples of possible topics are the Health Insurance Portability & Accountability Act of 1996, MedlinePlus, prevention of diseases, and so on. Your audience will be medical workers and staff members such as receptionists, records managers, and insurance processors. You may have new employees as part of the audience, but for the most part, this is refresher training. Most of the time, the presentation will be given to groups of 10 to 12 people during coffee meetings that normally last about 15 minutes.

a. Select one team member to set up the documents by completing steps b–d.

b. Open your browser and navigate to www.onedrive.com, www.drive.google.com, or any other instructor-assigned storage location. Be sure all members of the team have an account on the chosen system, most likely a Microsoft or Google account.

c. Start **PowerPoint**. Create a template. Have your team decide whether to use a standard or widescreen slide size, and then if necessary, make the slide size change in the template from within Slide Master view. Save your file as p02HTemplate_TeamName where TeamName is the name assigned to your team by your instructor.

d. Share the file with the other members of your team and make sure that each team member has the appropriate permissions to edit the document. Divide the work evenly among team members.

e. You should make adjustments to the template background, colors, fonts, and other design elements. Modify the handout master to include a header with your team name, the current date, and the text HHS. Save the template, and then close the template file.

f. Begin a new presentation, using the template, based on your research. Name this file p02HHS_TeamName. Be sure to provide an introduction and roadmap.

g. The title slide should contain a title and a list of the team members.

h. Add appropriate transitions to each of the slides.

i. If you choose to use animation, animate text elements on slides so they appear individually, allowing you to focus the attention of the audience on one major point at a time.

j. Create speaker notes for each slide.

k. Incorporate visuals (e.g., SmartArt, photographs, spreadsheet charts, tables, placeholder shading, shapes, and symbols) on your slides. Apply Picture Effects to enhance your images. Be sure you have appropriate permissions for any photograph or image you use.

l. In an appropriate location, include a hyperlink to the external website http://www.hhs.gov with the display U.S. Dept. of Health & Human Services.

m. Insert an appropriate video related to your presentation. YouTube is a good resource to consider for a video source. Make sure that you abide by copyright. Trim the video if needed so that its running time is under two minutes. Apply a video style. Adjust the start of the video to occur when the video is clicked.

n. The final slide of the presentation should contain a conclusion.

o. Add comments to the title slide describing how you would prepare for this presentation. Provide a checklist of items that you should remember to take with you to the presentation.

p. Add comments to the introduction/roadmap slide describing what you will do during the presentation to engage the audience. Save the presentation.

q. Create a custom slide show that does not contain the video slide. Type No Video in the Slide show name box.

r. Carefully proofread the presentation, and then save the presentation.

s. Review your presentation by running it full-screen. Make any improvements you think necessary.

t. Once the assignment is complete, share the documents with your instructor or turn in as your instructor directs. Make sure that the instructor has permission to edit.

u. Review your presentation by running it full-screen. Make any further improvements you think necessary.

v. Save the presentation, exit PowerPoint, and then submit your files as directed by your instructor.

Perform 4: How Others Perform

Student data files needed:
p02Yoga.pptx
p02YBackground.pptx
p02YMusic.mp3

You will save your file as:
p02Yoga_LastFirst.pptx

The Yoga for You Presentation

Sales & Marketing

A local yoga studio, 2 Yogis, wants to advertise to the community through a PowerPoint presentation to be shown at an upcoming fitness event. Maddie Wollman has asked you to review the presentation that she started and to comment on it. She has little experience in creating presentations, so she wants your input. Her target audience includes people who are interested in being fit and reducing the stress in their lives. She expects the potential students to be in the age range of 15 to 50 years old. She knows they will stop by her booth for only a few moments, and she needs to quickly catch their attention and engage them.

a. Open the PowerPoint file **p02Yoga**. Save your file as p02Yoga_LastFirst, using your last and first name.

b. The presentation was created with the standard slide size. You prefer using the widescreen slide size. Change the slide size to widescreen in the Slide Master.

c. Review the presentation in Slide Show view. You may want to watch it several times to evaluate the content and design. Pay special attention to the color choices, the fonts for readability, and the animations chosen.

d. Insert **p02YBackground** as a background on the title slide. Set the transparency as needed. Make changes to the fonts, WordArt, and color scheme in the slide master. Keep in mind the topic as you design the slide master for improvement. Your color scheme and fonts should go along with the background photograph to make the presentation look cohesive and set the right tone for this type of presentation.

e. Place comments on each of the slides in the presentation on the changes you have made and why you have made the changes. Similar changes can be grouped together in one comment.

f. Insert the audio file **p02YMusic.mp3** on the title slide. Have it start automatically and have it play throughout all of the slides in the presentation. Keep it hidden during the show.

g. Correct any spelling or grammatical errors.

h. Review your presentation by running it full-screen. Make any other improvements you think necessary.

i. Save the presentation, exit PowerPoint, and submit your file as directed by your instructor.

Integrated Projects

Chapter 1

WORD AND EXCEL INTEGRATION

OBJECTIVES

1. Link an object   p. 985
2. Update a linked object   p. 988
3. Embed an object p. 993
4. Modify an embedded object   p. 996

Prepare Case

Sales & Marketing

Updated Menu

The Indigo5 is an upscale restaurant that is always striving to stay one step ahead of its clientele. On the basis of marketing and customer analysis over the past year, Alberto Dimas, restaurant manager, has decided to add new selections to the menu. He is writing a memo in Word to his staff to inform them of these new additions. He would like to include a chart he created in Excel. Alberto will also write a memo to William Mattingly, CEO of the Painted Paradise Resort & Spa, informing him of customer trends for the past year. The memo will include a line chart to add visual impact. Your assignment is to practice linking and embedding the charts from Excel into the Word documents.

Evgeny Litvinov/Shutterstock

Student data files needed for this chapter:

 i01ch01IndigoMenu.docx

 i01ch01IndigoData.xlsx

 i01ch01IndigoMemo.docx

i01ch01IndigoReport.xlsx

You will save your files as:

 i01ch01IndigoMenu_LastFirst.docx

 i01ch01IndigoData_LastFirst.xlsx

 i01ch01IndigoMemo_LastFirst.docx

 i01ch01IndigoReport_LastFirst.xlsx

Object Linking and Embedding

An **object** is any item that can be selected and manipulated independently of surrounding text. Examples include pictures, shapes, charts, tables, sound clips, and videos. Using **OLE (Object Linking and Embedding)** — a feature in Microsoft Office — an object can be inserted into a file as either a linked object or an embedded object.

The program that creates the object is called the **source program**, and the file where the object is created is called the **source file**. The program into which you insert the object is called the **destination program**, and the file into which you insert the object is called the **destination file**.

A **linked object** is inserted into a document as a link that is still connected to the source file where it was originally created. When the object is updated in the source file, it will also be updated in the destination file. This is particularly useful if you have inserted the linked object into several different documents, because they will all be updated automatically whenever changes are made to the source file. This means that you can make a change one time and the same change will be reflected in all objects that are linked to the source.

An **embedded object** is an object that is inserted into a document but is not connected to the file in which it was created. Changes made to the source of an embedded object will not be automatically updated in the embedded copy as they are with a linked object, and changes to the embedded object will not be reflected in the source. However, you can use the tools in the source program to update the embedded object in the destination file. There may be times when this is exactly what you want, since you can make changes in the destination file without changing the source file.

REAL WORLD ADVICE | **To Link or Embed?**

Sometimes it is easier to copy and paste an object, but when you do, you lose the advantages that come with linking and embedding. The choice to link or embed is determined primarily by how you want to update your object. If you want to update the object in its original source program, you would choose to link the object to the destination file. For example, suppose you create a chart in Excel that has data that will change frequently. When you link the chart to a Word document, any changes you make to the chart in Excel will be reflected in Word. On the other hand, if you want the ability to update the chart in the destination file, you would choose to embed the chart. The advantages and disadvantages of linking and embedding are shown in Table 1.

	Copy & Paste	Linking	Embedding
Where copied object is located	Destination file where it is pasted	Source file where it is created	Destination file where it is inserted
How copied object is updated	In the destination file with limited options	In the source file	In the destination file
Advantages	Simple way to create a copy of an object and paste it in another location	A single chart can be displayed in multiple files and updated only in the source file. Destination file size is reduced.	The destination file is a self-contained file that is not dependent on a source file
Disadvantages	Objects have to be updated in both the source and destination files	Must have access to source file to make changes to object	Objects may have to be updated in both the source and destination files. Destination file size is increased.

Table 1 Comparison of different methods of copying objects

Linking Objects

When an object is linked, information can be updated if the source file is modified. A linked object is stored in the source file. The destination file stores only the location of the source file, and it displays a representation of the linked object. Linking keeps the size of the destination document small. Use linked objects if the size of the destination file is a consideration. Linking is also useful when the data source is maintained by someone else and must be shared among users. In this section, you will link an object, modify the object in the source file, and then update the object in the destination file.

Link an Object

Linking an object is advantageous because the data can be updated in the source file and the changes are reflected in the destination file. The data can be any object, including a chart, table, range of cells, or SmartArt graphic. An object can be linked to several documents, which will all be automatically updated when changes are made to the source file.

Linking an Excel Chart to a Word Document

When you link an Excel chart to a Word document, any changes you make to the Excel data will update the chart not only in Excel, but also in the linked Word document. The chart is still part of the source file, which is the Excel document, while the destination file, which is the Word document, contains the link file that is automatically updated. In this exercise, you will link an Excel chart to an existing Word document.

 IP01.00

SIDE NOTE
Pin the Ribbon
If your ribbon is collapsed, pin your ribbon open. Click the Home tab. In the lower right-hand corner of the ribbon, click Pin the Ribbon ⊡.

To Link an Excel Chart to a Word Document

a. Start **Word**, click **Open Other Documents** in the left pane, and then double-click **This PC**. Navigate through the folder structure to the location of your student data files, and then double-click **i01ch01IndigoMenu**. Maximize the Word window if necessary.

b. Click the **File** tab, click **Save As**, and then double-click **This PC**. Navigate to the location where you are saving your project files, and then change the file name to i01ch01IndigoMenu_LastFirst, using your last and first name. Click **Save**.

c. Insert a **left-aligned footer** with the file name, and then click **Save** 🔲. Click **Minimize** ⊟ to minimize the Word window.

d. Start **Excel**, and then open **i01ch01IndigoData**. Maximize the Excel window if necessary.

e. Click the **File** tab, click **Save As**, and then navigate to the location where you are saving your project files. Change the file name to i01ch01IndigoData_LastFirst, using your last and first name. Click **Save**.

f. Insert a **footer** with the file name in the left section of the Menu worksheet, and then click **Save** 🔲.

g. Click the **Menu** worksheet tab if necessary. Click the **chart border** once to select the pie chart. A border will appear around the edge of the object and the Chart Tools contextual tabs are displayed.

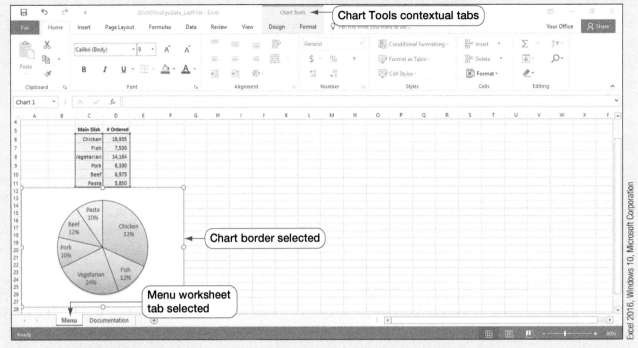

Figure 1 Chart selected in Excel

h. On the Home tab, in the Clipboard group, click **Copy** 📋 to copy the chart to the Clipboard. Click **Minimize** ▭ to minimize the Excel window.

i. Click **Word** 📘 on the taskbar to display the Word document. On the Home tab, in the Paragraph group, click **Show/Hide** ¶ to show paragraph marks, and then click at the end of the second body paragraph after **vegetarian dishes**. Press Enter twice to insert a blank line and start a new paragraph.

j. On the Home tab, in the Clipboard group, click the **Paste** arrow, and then select **Paste Special**.

k. In the Paste Special dialog box, click the **Paste link** option, and then in the As box, select **Microsoft Excel Chart Object**.

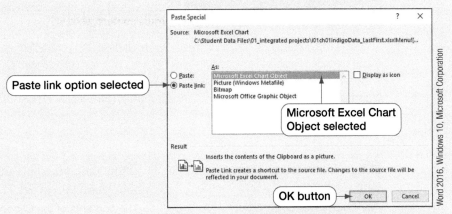

Figure 2 Paste Special dialog box with Paste link option selected

l. Click **OK**. The chart is pasted in the Word document as a linked object.

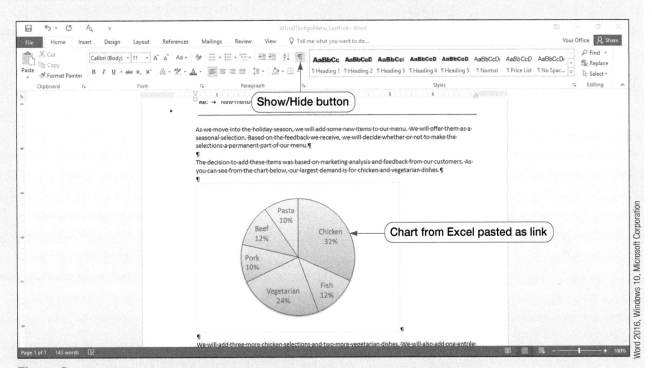

Figure 3 Word document with linked Excel chart

m. Click **Save** 🔲, and then click **Minimize** ⊟ to minimize the Word window.

If the source file is in Excel and you choose Paste link As:	Depending on what has been copied, this will be inserted:
Microsoft Excel Chart Object	The contents of the Clipboard
Bitmap	The contents of the Clipboard as a bitmap picture
Picture (Windows Metafile)	The contents of the Clipboard as a Windows metafile
Picture (GIF)	The contents of the Clipboard as a GIF picture
Picture (PNG)	The contents of the Clipboard as a PNG picture
Picture (JPEG)	The contents of the Clipboard as a JPEG picture
Microsoft Office Graphic Object	The contents of the Clipboard as shapes
Microsoft Excel Worksheet Object	The contents of the Clipboard
Formatted Text (RTF)	The contents of the Clipboard as text with font and table formatting
Unformatted Text	The contents of the Clipboard without any formatting
HTML Format	The contents of the Clipboard in HTML format
Unformatted Unicode Text	The contents of the Clipboard as text without any formatting

Table 2 Comparing Paste link options

SIDE NOTE

A Link Is Not the Same as a Hyperlink

A link between a source file and a destination file is different from a hyperlink. A hyperlink is a navigation tool; a link is not.

Update a Linked Object

When both the source file and the destination file are open and data is changed in the source file of a linked object, the data will be updated in the destination file only if you manually update the link for the object. This gives you control over when and how to update a link in the destination file.

When the destination file is closed and then opened, the linked object is automatically updated unless you turn off automatic updates in the Links options.

Updating a Linked Excel Chart in a Word Document

When data related to a chart is changed in Excel, the chart in Excel is automatically updated. However, the chart may or may not be automatically updated in the destination file depending on whether the destination file is open or closed. In this exercise, you will make changes to a chart in Excel and then manually update the chart in the Word document, which is open.

 IP01.01

To Update a Linked Excel Chart in a Word Document

a. Click Excel ![Excel icon] on the taskbar to display the Excel workbook.

b. Click the **chart** to select it if necessary. Under Chart Tools, on the Design tab, in the Type group, click **Change Chart Type**. Select **3-D Pie**, and then click **OK**.

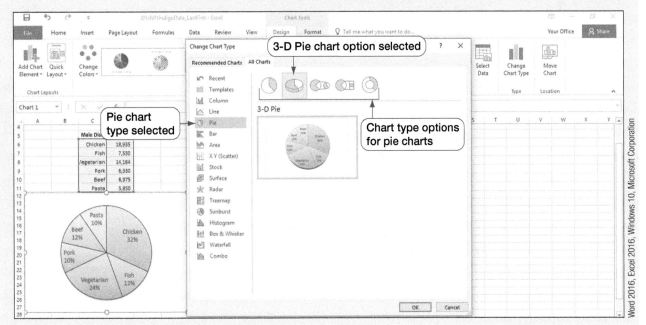

Figure 4   Change Chart Type options for Pie chart

c. In the Chart Layouts group, click the **Add Chart Element** arrow, point to **Chart Title**, and then select **Above Chart**. In the formula bar, type Main Dishes Ordered by Type and then press Enter. Click the **Home** tab, and then in the Font group, click **Bold** B to apply bold to the title.

d. Click cell **D7**, type 9000 to change the number of Fish dishes ordered, and then press Enter. The percentage for Fish in the chart changes from 12% to 15% to reflect this change.

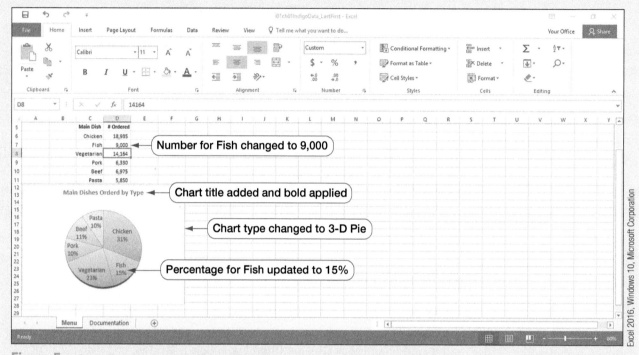

Figure 5 Chart Type and data in Excel changed

e. Click the **Documentation** worksheet tab, and then complete the following:

- Click cell **A8**, then type today's date in mm/dd/yyyy format, and then press Enter.

- Click cell **B8**, then type your name in Firstname Lastname format, and then press Enter.

- Click cell **C8**, type Changed chart type to 3-D Pie, and then press Enter.

- In cell **C9**, type Added chart title, and then press Enter.

- In cell **C10**, type Changed number of Fish dishes in cell D7 to 9000, and then press Enter.

f. Click **Save** 🖫, and then click **Minimize** ▭ to minimize the Excel window.

g. Click **Word** on the taskbar to display the Word document.

h. Click the **chart** to select it, right-click the **chart**, and then on the shortcut menu, select **Update Link**. The chart is updated with the changes you made in Excel.

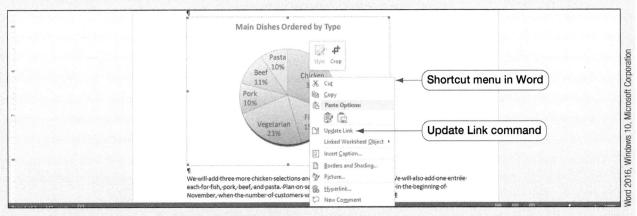

Figure 6   Shortcut menu with Update Link command

Troubleshooting

Did you get an error message? If you changed the name of the source file or moved the source file to a new folder, the update will not work. If Excel cannot find the source file in the same folder as the destination file, it will break the link with the destination file. To have the object linked again, you will have to open the Links dialog box and change the source file to the new location or new file name or move the source file to the same folder as the destination file.
To change the source file, do the following.

1. Right-click the object in the destination file.

2. Point to Linked Worksheet Object, and then click Links.

3. Click Change Source, select the new location or name of the source file, and then click Open. Click OK.

---

i. On the Home tab, in the Paragraph group, click **Center** ≡ to center the chart horizontally in the document. Click **Show/Hide** ¶ to hide paragraph marks.

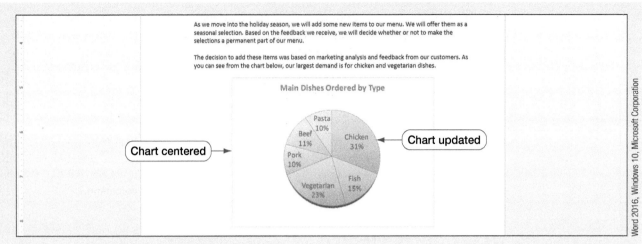

As we move into the holiday season, we will add some new items to our menu. We will offer them as a seasonal selection. Based on the feedback we receive, we will decide whether or not to make the selections a permanent part of our menu.

The decision to add these items was based on marketing analysis and feedback from our customers. As you can see from the chart below, our largest demand is for chicken and vegetarian dishes.

Main Dishes Ordered by Type

Pasta 10%
Beef 11%
Chicken 31%
Pork 10%
Fish 15%
Vegetarian 23%

Chart centered

Chart updated

Word 2016, Windows 10, Microsoft Corporation

Figure 7 Chart updated and centered in Word

j. Click **Save** 🖫, and then click **Close** ☒ to close Word.

k. Click **Excel** 📊 on the taskbar to display the Excel workbook, and then click **Close** ☒ to close Excel.

$\$$ CONSIDER THIS | **To Link or Not to Link?**

Teamwork is an important part of business. When files are sent between team members, linking can easily cause errors because of the source file. Do you think you should not use links when working in a team? Why or why not?

REAL WORLD ADVICE | **Teamwork and Linking Files**

There are a number of options you can choose when setting up links to help preserve those links, especially when files are being shared by several people. Right-click a linked object, point to Linked Worksheet Object, and then select Links to open the Links dialog box, where you will find the options listed in Table 3.

Action	Effect	Advantages	Disadvantages
Manual Update	When the destination file opens, the user will not get a message about a linked object.	If the user of the destination file is unfamiliar with Word, the manual update will not cause any confusion over what to do.	The destination file object will not be automatically updated to reflect changes made in the source file.
Locked	The object will not be updated.	When someone else is given a file, you may want to have control over what data they see, so having an object that cannot be updated may be beneficial.	The link will not be updated even though it has not been broken.
Change Source	Changes the source file where the object is found.	If a source file has been renamed or moved, the source file for the object can be changed to the new name or location.	If the source file has been renamed or moved but you do not know the new name or where it has been moved, this option will not help.
Break Link	The destination file and source file will no longer be linked by the object.	There is no need to worry about moving a source file or changing its name.	Changes made in the source file will no longer be reflected in the destination file.

Table 3 Links options

Embedding Objects

When you embed an object, the object is physically stored in the destination file along with all the information needed to manage the object. After embedded objects have been inserted, they become part of the destination file and are not linked to the source file. A document that contains embedded objects will be larger than one containing the same objects as links. Changes can be made to the object in the destination file. These changes will not be automatically reflected in the source file. If you also want to make changes in the source file, you will have to make those changes manually. In this section, you will embed an object and then modify it in the destination file, using tools from the source program.

Embed an Object

For certain purposes, embedding offers several advantages over links. Users can transfer documents with embedded objects to other computers or other locations on the same computer without breaking a link. Embedding can also be useful when you do not want changes to be reflected in the source file.

Embedding an Excel Chart in a Word Document

An Excel chart embedded in a Word document becomes part of the document, and any changes made to the chart will remain in the document. Changes made to the chart in the Word document will not be reflected in the Excel worksheet. In this exercise, you will embed an Excel chart in a Word document.

To Embed an Excel Chart in a Word Document

a. Start Word, and then open **i01ch01IndigoMemo**. Maximize the Word window if necessary.

b. Click the **File** tab, click **Save As**, and then navigate to the location where you are saving your project files. Change the file name to i01ch01IndigoMemo_LastFirst, using your last and first name. Click **Save**.

c. Insert a **left-aligned footer** with the file name, and then click **Save** 🗗. Click **Minimize** ⊟ to minimize Word.

d. Start **Excel**, and then open **i01ch01IndigoReport**.

e. Click the **File** tab, click **Save As**, and then navigate to the location where you are saving your project files. Change the file name to i01ch01IndigoReport_LastFirst, using your last and first name. Click **Save**.

f. Insert the **file name** in the left section of the footer on the Customers worksheet, and then click **Save** 🗗. Maximize the Excel window if necessary.

g. Click the **Customers** worksheet tab if necessary. Select the line chart by clicking the **chart border** once. A border appears around the edge of the object.

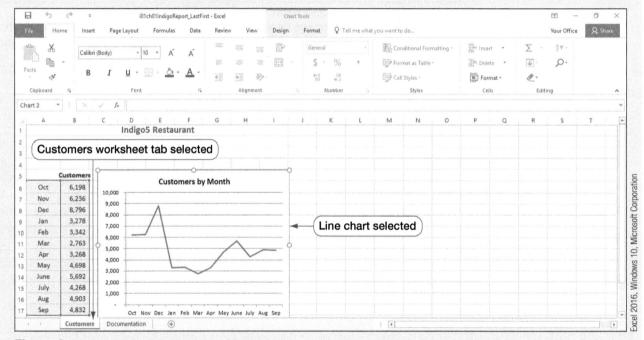

Figure 8 Excel worksheet with chart selected

h. On the Home tab, in the Clipboard group, click **Copy** 📋 to copy the chart to the Clipboard. Click **Minimize** ⊟ to minimize the Excel window.

i. Click **Word** on the taskbar. On the Home tab, in the Paragraph group, click **Show/Hide** ¶ to show paragraph marks. Click at the end of the last sentence of the last paragraph. Press [Enter] twice to insert a blank line and start a new paragraph.

j. On the Home tab, in the Clipboard group, click the **Paste** arrow, and then select **Paste Special**. In the Paste Special dialog box, click the **Paste** option, and then in the As box, select **Microsoft Excel Chart Object**.

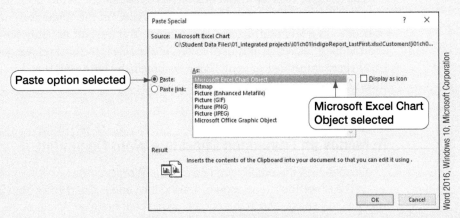

Figure 9 Paste Special Dialog box with Paste option selected

k. Click **OK**. The chart is embedded in the Word document.

l. On the Home tab, in the Paragraph group, click **Show/Hide** ¶ to hide paragraph marks, and then click **Save** 🖫.

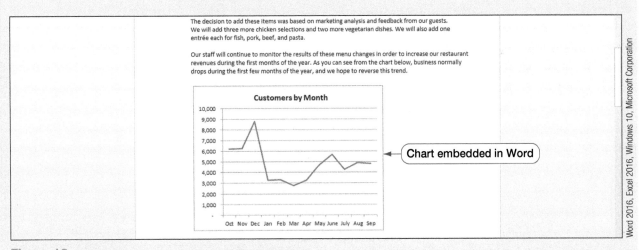

Figure 10 Word document with embedded Excel chart

Modify an Embedded Object

When you edit an embedded object in the destination file, the changes affect only the object in the destination file. This is what makes it different from linking or using a copy and paste command.

Modifying an Embedded Chart in a Word Document

Modifying an embedded chart in a Word document will change the chart in the document, but the chart in the Excel workbook will remain unchanged. Alternatively, changing the chart in Excel will not change the chart in the Word document. However, the embedded chart can be edited by using Excel tools in the Word document because it was embedded as a Microsoft Excel Chart Object. You can edit not only the chart options but also the Excel data that was used to create the chart. In this exercise, you will modify an Excel chart embedded in your Word document by changing the chart type, editing the title, and revising data.

 IP01.03

To Modify an Embedded Chart in a Word Document

a. Double-click the embedded line chart in Word.

The Chart Tools tabs appear, making the various Chart Tools from Excel available. The worksheet tabs in the original worksheet are also visible at the bottom of the object, with an additional tab for Chart1.

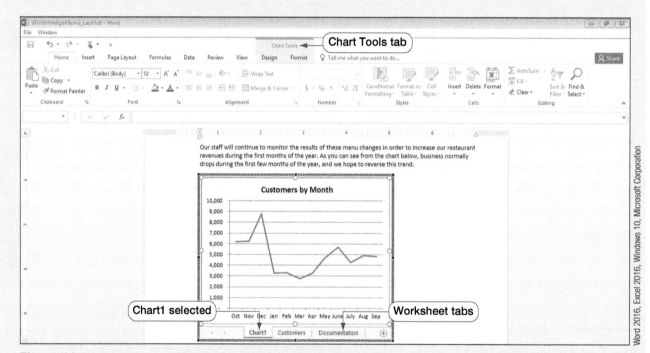

Figure 11 Chart Tools showing editing options available

b. Under Chart Tools, on the Design tab, in the Type group, click **Change Chart Type**. Select **Line with Markers**, the fourth option.

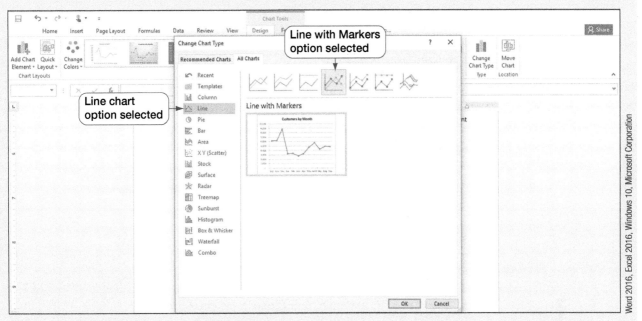

Figure 12   Change Chart Type options for Line chart

c. Click **OK**. The line chart in the Word document changes to add markers.

d. Click the **chart title** to select it, and then click the title again to place the insertion point within the placeholder. Change the title to read Customer Analysis by Month.

e. Click the **Customers** worksheet tab. Click cell **B6**, change the Oct Customers to 8000, and then press Enter. The chart is updated to show this change.

f. Click the **Chart1** worksheet tab to see the change reflected in the chart. Click outside the chart to deselect it.

g. Click the **border** of the chart to select it. On the Home tab, in the Paragraph group, click **Center** to center the chart horizontally in the document. Click outside the chart to deselect it.

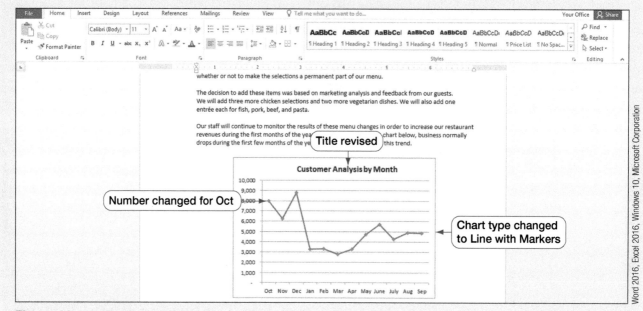

whether or not to make the selections a permanent part of our menu.

The decision to add these items was based on marketing analysis and feedback from our guests. We will add three more chicken selections and two more vegetarian dishes. We will also add one entrée each for fish, pork, beef, and pasta.

Our staff will continue to monitor the results of these menu changes in order to increase our restaurant revenues during the first months of the ye... chart below, business normally drops during the first few months of the ye... this trend.

Title revised

Number changed for Oct

Customer Analysis by Month

Chart type changed to Line with Markers

Word 2016, Excel 2016, Windows 10, Microsoft Corporation

Figure 13   Chart changed in Word

h. Click **Save** 🖫, and then click **Close** ☒ to close Word.

Modifying a Chart in an Excel Workbook

The chart and data in the Excel workbook have not changed. If you want to make sure that both documents reflect the changes made in the Word document, you will need to make the same changes manually in the Excel workbook. In this exercise, you will update the chart and data in the Excel workbook to correspond to the changes that you made to the chart and data in the Word document. Note that there may be times when you will choose not to update the source document.

To Modify a Chart in an Excel Workbook

a. Click Excel 🅧 on the taskbar to display the Excel workbook.

b. Click the **chart border** to select the chart. The Chart Tools contextual tabs appear, making the various Chart Tools available.

c. Under Chart Tools, on the Design tab, in the Type group, click **Change Chart Type**, select **Line with Markers**, the fourth option, and then click **OK**.

d. Click the **chart title** to select it, and then click the placeholder again to place the insertion point within the title placeholder. Change the title to read Customer Analysis by Month, and then click outside the chart.

e. Click cell **B6**, change the Oct Customers to 8000, and then press Enter.

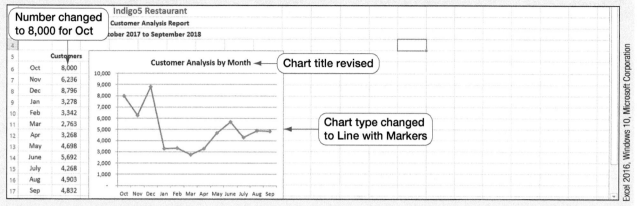

Figure 14 Chart changed in Excel

f. Click the **Documentation** worksheet tab, and then complete the following.

- Click cell **A8**, then type today's date in mm/dd/yyyy format, and then press Enter.

- Click cell **B8**, then type your name in Firstname Lastname format, and then press Enter.

- Click cell **C8**, type Changed chart type to Line with Markers, and then press Enter.

- In cell **C9**, type Revised chart title, and then press Enter.

- In cell **C10**, type Changed Oct Customers in cell B6 to 8000, and then press Enter.

g. Click **Save** 🖫, and then click **Close** ☒ to close Excel. Submit your files as directed by your instructor.

1. Describe what is meant by linking an object. Give an advantage and a disadvantage of linking. p. 985

2. How are linked objects updated? Give an example of when you might want to link an object. p. 988

3. Describe what is meant by embedding an object. When might you want to embed an object instead of linking it? p. 993

4. Explain how an embedded object is modified. Give an example of when you might want to embed an object. p. 996

Key Terms

Destination file   984
Destination program   984
Embedded object   984

Linked object   984
Object   984
OLE (Object Linking and
   Embedding)   984

Source file   984
Source program   984

Visual Summary

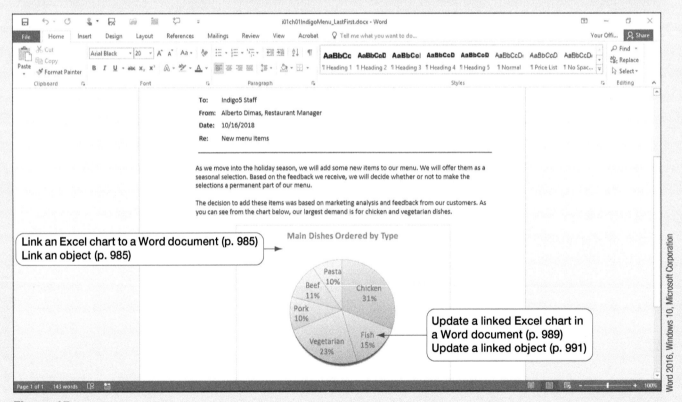

Link an Excel chart to a Word document (p. 985)
Link an object (p. 985)

Update a linked Excel chart in a Word document (p. 989)
Update a linked object (p. 991)

Word 2016, Windows 10, Microsoft Corporation

Figure 15

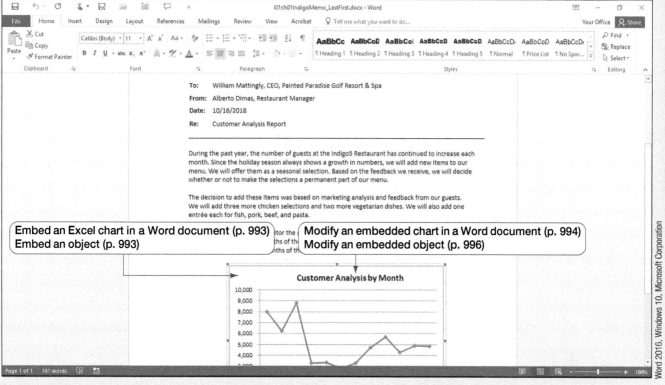

The two callout boxes in Figure 16 contain:

Embed an Excel chart in a Word document (p. 993)
Embed an object (p. 993)

Modify an embedded chart in a Word document (p. 994)
Modify an embedded object (p. 996)

Figure 16

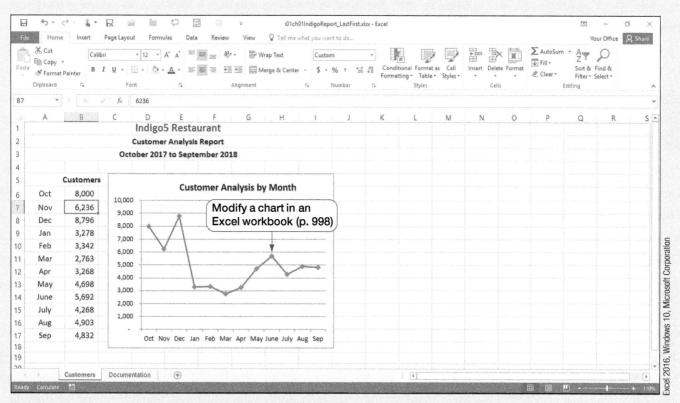

Modify a chart in an Excel workbook (p. 998)

Figure 17

Student data files needed:

 i01ch01WeddingPlan.docx

 i01ch01WeddingCost.xlsx

You will save your files as:

 i01ch01WeddingPlan_LastFirst.docx

 i01ch01WeddingCost_LastFirst.xlsx

Wedding Planning

Sales & Marketing

The staff in the Event Planning department would like to promote full-service weddings at the Painted Paradise Resort & Spa. A full-service wedding includes all aspects of the planning and execution of the event. One staff member wrote a short description in Word promoting the service, and another staff member put together a sample budget and time line in Excel. Your job is to link the budget and embed the timeline in the Word document.

a. Start **Word**, and then open **i01ch01WeddingPlan**.

b. Click the **File** tab, click **Save As**, and then navigate to the location where you are saving your project files. Save the file as i01ch01WeddingPlan_LastFirst, using your last and first name. Click **Save**.

c. Insert a **left-aligned footer** with the file name, and then click **Save**. Click **Minimize** to minimize the Word window.

d. Start **Excel**, and then open **i01ch01WeddingCost**.

e. Click the **File** tab, click **Save As**, and then navigate to the location where you are saving your project files. Save the file as i01ch01WeddingCost_LastFirst, using your last and first name. Click **Save**.

f. Insert the **file name** in the left section of the footer on the Budget worksheet, and then click **Save**. Maximize the Excel window if necessary.

g. Select the range of cells **A4:C17**. On the Home tab, in the Clipboard group, click **Copy** to copy the data to the Clipboard. Click **Minimize** to minimize the Excel window.

h. Click **Word** on the taskbar to display the document. Click the blank line below **Budget Worksheet**, and then press Enter to go to a new line.

i. On the Home tab, in the Clipboard group, click the **Paste** arrow, and then select **Paste Special**. Select the **Paste link** option button, and then select **Microsoft Excel Worksheet Object**. Click **OK**.

j. On the Home tab, in the Paragraph group, click **Center** to center the table horizontally. Click **Save**, and then close Word.

k. Click **Excel** on the taskbar to display the workbook. Change the **Average Cost of the Coordinator** to 750, and change the **Average Cost of the Ceremony** to 1500. Click **Save**, and then click **Minimize** to minimize the Excel window.

l. Start **Word**, and then open **i01ch01WeddingPlan_LastFirst**. Click **Yes** to the warning about updating links. If the data was not updated, right-click the **table**, and then click **Update Link**. Click **Save**, and then click **Minimize** to minimize the Word window.

m. Click **Excel** on the taskbar to display the workbook. Click the **Timeline** worksheet tab, click the **SmartArt graphic** to select it, and then click the **top border** to ensure that the entire SmartArt graphic is selected. A border will appear around the edge of the object. On the Home tab, in the Clipboard group, click **Copy** to copy the SmartArt graphic to the Clipboard. Click **Minimize** to minimize the Excel window.

n. Click **Word** on the taskbar to display the document. Place the insertion point in front of the **Wedding Timeline** heading, and then press Ctrl+Enter to insert a page break and move the heading to the top of page 2.

o. Click the blank line below **Wedding Timeline**. On the Home tab, in the Clipboard group, click the **Paste** arrow, and then select **Paste Special**. Select the **Paste** option, and then select **Microsoft Office Graphic Object**. Click **OK**.

p. Click the embedded **SmartArt graphic**. Under SmartArt Tools, on the Design tab, in the SmartArt Styles group, select **Change Colors**, and then change the color to **Accent 3 - Gradient Range - Accent 3**. Change the heading for **1 Month** to 1-2 Months. Click outside of the SmartArt graphic to deselect it. Click **Save**, and then close Word.

q. Click **Excel** on the taskbar to display the workbook. Click the **Timeline** worksheet tab. Change the heading for **1 Month** to 1-2 Months. Do not change colors.

r. Click the **Documentation** worksheet tab, and then complete the following:
   - Click cell **A8**, then type today's date in mm/dd/yyyy format, and then press Enter.
   - Click cell **B8**, then type your name in Firstname Lastname format, and then press Enter.
   - Click cell **C8**, type Changed the Average Cost of the Coordinator to 750, and then press Enter.
   - In cell **C9**, type Changed the Average Cost of the Ceremony to 1500, and then press Enter.
   - In cell **C10**, type Changed heading from 1 Month to 1-2 Months.

s. Click **Save**, and then close Excel. Submit your files as directed by your instructor.

Practice 2

Student data files needed:

 i01ch01RaceFlyer.docx

 i01ch01RaceBudget.xlsx

You will save your files as:

 i01ch01RaceFlyer_LastFirst.docx

 i01ch01RaceBudget_LastFirst.xlsx

Running Event

Customer Service

The Event Planning department is excited about organizing a new competitive 5K and 10K run/walk at the resort. The event is designed to bring families to the resort for the weekend and will include a cookout, prizes, and opportunities to tour the resort. The flyer for the event was created in Word and has some charts that would be nice to include in the financial report that was created in Excel. Your assignment is to link and embed the data from Word into Excel.

a. Start **Word**, and then open **i01ch01RaceFlyer**.

b. Click the **File** tab, click **Save As**, and then navigate to the location where you are saving your project files. Change the file name to i01ch01RaceFlyer_LastFirst, using your last and first name. Click **Save**.

c. Insert a **left-aligned footer** with the file name, and then click **Save**. Click **Minimize** to minimize the Word window.

d. Start **Excel**, and then open **i01ch01RaceBudget**.

e. Click the **File** tab, click **Save As**, and then navigate to the location where you are saving your project files. Change the file name to i01ch01RaceBudget_LastFirst, using your last and first name. Click **Save**.

f. Insert a **left-aligned footer** with the file name on the Budget worksheet, and then click **Save**. Maximize the Excel window if necessary.

g. Click **Word** on the taskbar to display the document. Select the **table** with the registration fees. On the Home tab, in the Clipboard group, click **Copy** to copy the table to the Clipboard. Click **Minimize** to minimize the Word window.

h. Click **Excel** on the taskbar to display the workbook. On the Budget worksheet, select cell **D3**. On the **Home** tab, in the Clipboard group, click the **Paste** arrow, and then select **Paste Special**. Select the **Paste link** option, and then select **Microsoft Word Document Object**. Click **OK**. Click **Save**, and then close Excel.

i. Click **Word** on the taskbar to display the document. Change the **Day of Race** amounts to $35 for the **5K** and $45 for the **10K**. Click **Save**, and then click **Minimize** to minimize the Word window.

j. Start **Excel**, and then open **i01ch01RaceBudget_LastFirst**. Click **Enable Content** in the Security Warning bar. The Day of Race amounts are updated. Click **Save**, and then click **Minimize** to minimize the Excel window.

k. Click **Word** on the taskbar to display the document. Click the **SmartArt** graphic once to select it, and then click the **top border** to ensure that the entire SmartArt object is selected. A border will appear around the edge of the object. On the Home tab, in the Clipboard group, click **Copy** to copy the SmartArt graphic to the Clipboard. Click **Minimize** to minimize the Word window.

l. Click **Excel** on the taskbar to display the workbook. Select cell **E12**. On the Home tab, in the Clipboard group, click the **Paste** arrow, and then select **Paste Special**. Select the **Paste** option, and then select **Microsoft Office Drawing Object**. Click **OK**.

m. Click the embedded **SmartArt** graphic. Change the order of the text to read **Race Run Walk**. Click outside the SmartArt graphic to deselect it.

n. Click the **Bold** tab, and then in the Page Setup group, click **Orientation**, and then select **Landscape**. In the **Scale to Fit** group, click the **Width** arrow, and then select **1 page** so the table and SmartArt graphic will print on the same page as the budget.

o. Click the **Documentation** worksheet tab, and then complete the following:

- Click cell **A8**, then type today's date in mm/dd/yyyy format, and then press Enter.
- Click cell **B8**, then type your name in Firstname Lastname format, and then press Enter.
- Click cell **C8**, type Inserted linked table in cell D3, and then press Enter.
- In cell **C9**, type Inserted embedded SmartArt graphic in cell E12, and then press Enter.
- In cell **C10**, type Changed order of text in SmartArt graphic, and then press Enter.
- In cell **C11**, type Changed orientation to Landscape and to fit 1 page.

p. Click **Save**, and then close Excel.

q. Click **Word** on the taskbar to display the document. Click the embedded **SmartArt graphic**. Change the order of the text to read **Race Run Walk**. Click outside the SmartArt to deselect it. Click **Save**, and then close Word. Submit your files as directed by your instructor.

Problem Solve 1

Student data files needed:
- i01ch01ShopReport.docx
- i01ch01ShopAnalysis.xlsx

You will save your files as:
- i01ch01ShopReport_LastFirst.docx
- i01ch01ShopAnalysis_LastFirst.xlsx

Gift Shop Update

Finance & Accounting

The resort's gift shop, Painted Treasures, is reporting its revenue and staffing for the first quarter of the year. A short document has been created with a description of the analysis in Word, but the numbers, charts, and graphics are all in Excel. Your assignment is to link the chart created in Excel to the Word document and embed the organization chart created in Excel in the Word document.

a. Start **Word**, open **i01ch01ShopReport**, and then save it as i01ch01ShopReport_LastFirst, using your last and first name.

b. Start **Excel**, open **i01ch01ShopAnalysis**, and then save it as i01ch01ShopAnalysis_LastFirst, using your last and first name.

c. Click the **Revenue** worksheet tab, copy the pie chart, and then paste it in the Word document after the first body paragraph as a linked Microsoft Excel Chart Object.

d. In the source file, add a **chart title** above the pie chart with the title Gift Shop Sales by Segment. In the Word document, update the link to reflect this change.

e. In the source file, on the **Staffing** worksheet tab, copy the **organization chart**, and then paste it in the Word document after the second body paragraph as an embedded Microsoft Office Graphic Object.

f. In the destination file, change the **Manager** name to First Last, using your first and last name.

g. Resize the pie chart and the SmartArt graphic so everything fits on one page, delete any blank pages, and then center the pie chart horizontally on the page. Save the document and close Word.

h. In the source file, change the **Manager** name in the SmartArt graphic to your own name. If requested by your instructor, update the Documentation worksheet appropriately. Save the workbook and close Excel. Submit your files as directed by your instructor.

Problem Solve 2

Student data files needed:

 i01ch01ItemsFlyer.docx

 i01ch01ItemsList.xlsx

You will save your files as:

 i01ch01ItemsFlyer_LastFirst.docx

i01ch01ItemsList_LastFirst.xlsx

Gift Shop Preview

Sales & Marketing

People have been asking for articles with the Painted Paradise logo that can be purchased as souvenirs of their resort visit. Susan Brock, Painted Treasures Gift Shop manager, has decided to add some new, low-cost items to meet this need. She has created a worksheet with the names of new items, wholesale cost, and retail cost. Susan has asked you to create a flyer advertising a preview of the new items with just the item name and the retail cost. After embedding the data from the Excel worksheet in the Word document, you will format it attractively.

a. Start **Word**, open **i01ch01ItemsFlyer**, and then save it as i01ch01ItemsFlyer_LastFirst, using your last and first name. Insert a **left-aligned footer** with the file name, and then save the flyer.

b. Start **Excel**, open **i01ch01ItemsList**, and then save it as i01ch01ItemsList_LastFirst, using your last and first name. Click the **New Items** worksheet tab, and then insert a footer with the file name in the left section. Save the workbook.

c. Select cells **A1:C10**, and then click **Copy**.

d. Click **Word** on the taskbar, and then show paragraph marks and other hidden formatting symbols. Position the insertion point in front of the **second section break**. Paste the **table** as an embedded Microsoft Excel Worksheet Object.

e. Double-click the **embedded table**. Delete the middle column that lists wholesale prices.

f. Select cells **A1:B10**, and then increase the font size to **18**. Increase the width of column **B** so the heading **Retail Price** is on one line, and then middle-align the heading. Click the **View** tab, and then in the Show group, deselect **Gridlines** to remove gridlines from the table.

g. Deselect the table, and then hide the paragraph marks. Save the document, and then close Word and Excel. Submit your files as directed by your instructor.

Critical Thinking

In the preceding exercise, you were instructed to embed the data from Excel on new items for sale into a Word flyer? Why does it make more sense in this instance to embed rather than link?

Perform 1: Perform in Your Career

Student data files needed:

 Blank Word document

 Blank Excel workbook

You will save your files as:

 i01ch01PhotoLetter_LastFirst.docx

 i01ch01PhotoQuote_LastFirst.xlsx

Photography Quotes for Potential Customers

Sales & Marketing

You are an independent photographer who specializes in small events and small groups, including families. You frequently send out quotes to potential clients. Your quote form is kept in Excel, but the letters you send out are in Word. You therefore need to link your workbook data with the letter you send to potential clients. Your quote must include the date of the event, a customer name, a description of the job and its location, the approximate number of hours the job will take, extra travel time required, and any special requests. You need the flexibility to change the data in Excel and have it change in Word at the same time.

a. Start **Word**, and then create a letter to potential clients. Include a return address, date, greeting, and closing, and then save the letter as i01ch01PhotoLetter_LastFirst, using your last and first name. Insert a left-aligned footer.

b. Start **Excel**, and then create a **quote sheet** for your services. Include a heading with your company information and headings for the date of the event, customer name, job location and description, number of hours required, extra travel time involved, any special requests, and the cost of the job. Save the file as i01ch01PhotoQuote_LastFirst, using your last and first name. Insert a footer in the left section of the Excel workbook with the file name.

c. Complete the quote for a fictitious client. Copy the data for the quote, and then paste it into your Word document so it is linked to Excel. Save **i01ch01PhotoLetter_LastFirst** with the linked data.

d. Submit your files as directed by your instructor.

Perform 2: How Others Perform

Student data files needed:

 i01ch01SurveyReview.docx

 i01ch01SurveyData.xlsx

You will save your files as:

 i01ch01SurveyReview_LastFirst.docx

 i01ch01SurveyData_LastFirst.xlsx

Computer Students Survey

Information Technology

Your professor has surveyed 100 students to determine how comfortable they are with the four major Microsoft Office applications. A student assistant has compiled the survey results using Excel and has written a Word document summarizing the outcome. The professor plans to administer the survey again at the end of the semester to assess how comfort levels have changed. She would like to enter new data results in the Excel worksheet and then automatically update both the table and the chart in the Word document. However, what the student assistant has done is not working properly. You have been asked to look at both documents and make any revisions necessary to link the data in the Excel file to the Word file so changes made to the Excel data can be easily updated in the table and chart in the Word document.

a. Open **i01ch01SurveyReview**, and then save it as i01ch01SurveyReview_LastFirst, using your last and first name. Insert a left-aligned footer with the file name, and save the workbook.

b. Determine how the objects were pasted into the document. Do you think the table was linked, embedded, or copied and pasted? What about the chart?

c. Open **i01ch01SurveyData**, and then save it as i01ch01SurveyData_LastFirst, using your last and first name. Insert a left-aligned footer with the file name on the Survey worksheet, and then save the workbook.

d. In the Word document, make corrections to the table and chart so that when changes are made to the data in Excel, those changes will be reflected in the Word document. Save the document.

e. In the Excel workbook, in cell D5, change the **Very Comfortable** value to **8**, and then in cell **D8**, change the **Very Uncomfortable** value to **64**. If requested by your instructor, update the Documentation worksheet appropriately. Save the workbook, and then close Excel.

f. In the Word document, update the table and the chart. Make sure the changes made in Excel are reflected in the Word document. Submit your files as directed by your instructor.

Additional
Cases

Additional Chapter Cases are available at www.pearsonhighered.com/youroffice

Integrated Projects

Sales & Marketing

OBJECTIVES

1. Prepare Excel data for export to Access p. 1010

2. Import Excel data into Access p. 1011

3. Prepare Access data for a mail merge p. 1015

4. Export Access query results into Word p. 1017

Prepare Case

Coupon Mailing

Indigo5 is an upscale restaurant whose managers are always looking for ways to promote good relationships with current customers. Over the past year, the restaurant has used comment cards to collect customer suggestions. Customers are promised a special treat if they indicate their birthday month. This information is maintained in an Excel workbook. Each month, the restaurant sends out coupons for a free dessert for two to customers with birthdays in the following month. Your assignment is to import the Excel data into Access, query Access for all birthdays in April, and then use the Mail Merge feature in Word to create coupons based on the results of the Access query.

Andrey Armyagov / Shutterstock

Student data files needed for this chapter:

 i01ch02PromoNames.xlsx   i01ch02PromoCoupon.docx

You will save your files as:

 i01ch02PromoNames_LastFirst.xlsx   i01ch02PromoMerge_LastFirst.docx

 i01ch02Promo_LastFirst.accdb

Use Excel Data in Access

Both Excel and Access can be used to collect, sort, and store data, but Access generally has more sophisticated tools to accomplish those tasks. However, Excel has capabilities such as formulas, functions, and charts that are lacking in Access. Deciding where to store your data depends on what kind of data you have and what you want to do with it, as summarized in Table 1.

	Excel	Access
How data is stored	In worksheets using rows and columns	In a relational structure of multiple tables
What is stored best	Numbers and formulas	Text, numbers, other objects
Advantages	What-if models and analysis PivotTables Charts and graphs Conditional formatting, color bars, and other visual displays	Generates reports Multiple users Data entry forms Connecting multiple databases Data extraction

Table 1   Storing data in Excel and Access

Data can be exchanged between Access and Excel to take advantage of the strengths of each program. There are multiple ways to exchange data between the two programs, as shown in Table 2.

Data from Access to Excel	Data from Excel to Access
Copy and paste	Copy and paste
Connect to Access database	Import data directly
Export data directly	Link to Excel worksheet

Table 2   Sharing data

Import has two different meanings in referring to Excel and Access. When data is imported into Excel from Access, a permanent connection is created. As the data in Access is updated, the data in Excel is also updated automatically.

When data is imported into Access from Excel, there are two options in the Get External Data dialog box. If you select the Import the source data into a new table in the current database option, changes made to the source data will not be reflected in the database. If you select the Link to the data source by creating a linked table option, Access will create a table that will maintain a link to the source data in Excel. Changes made to the source data in Excel will be reflected in the linked table. In this section, you will import Excel data into Access and export Access data to Word.

REAL WORLD ADVICE   **No Need to Fear Access**

Most people in business either are very comfortable with Excel or have some familiarity with it. Not as many people are familiar with Access, and some even avoid it. Excel is therefore used more for data collection purposes than is necessary or appropriate, since much of the process could be done more easily in Access. Having knowledge of both programs is critical so you can make decisions about which program is best to use for your purpose. You will also be able to move data between the two programs. For example, if your data in Access needs to be subtotaled and charted, you can import the data into Excel, apply subtotals, and then chart the data. On the other hand, if you do a lot of data entry, it would be beneficial to create a form in Access to make entering data more user-friendly.

Prepare Excel Data for Export to Access

Data in Excel can be easily imported into an Access table. Because all data is stored in tables in Access, the data in Excel must be in a list form. An example may be an address book, a list of inventory items, or a list of employees.

Preparing an Excel List for Export

Before data is imported into Access, you need to make sure the data is compatible. The data should have column headings that will become the field names in the Access table. The rows in Excel will become the records in the Access table, so there should be no blank rows in the data you are importing. In this exercise, you will edit a list of data in Excel so it can be imported easily into Access.

IP02.00

To Prepare an Excel Data for Exporting to Access

SIDE NOTE
Pin the Ribbon
If your ribbon is collapsed, pin your ribbon open. Click the Home tab. In the lower right-hand corner of the ribbon, click Pin the Ribbon.

a. Start **Excel**, and then open **i01ch02PromoNames**. Maximize the Excel window if necessary.

b. Click the **File** tab, click **Save As**, and then navigate to the location where you are saving your project files. Change the file name to i01ch02PromoNames_LastFirst, using your last and first name. Click **Save**.

c. Click the **Birthdays** worksheet tab if necessary. Insert a **footer** with the file name in the left section, and then click **Save**.

d. Scroll through the list of names, and notice the blank rows. Select row **257** by clicking on the row number. On the Home tab, in the Cells group, click **Delete**. Repeat these steps to delete rows **75**, **19**, and **9**.

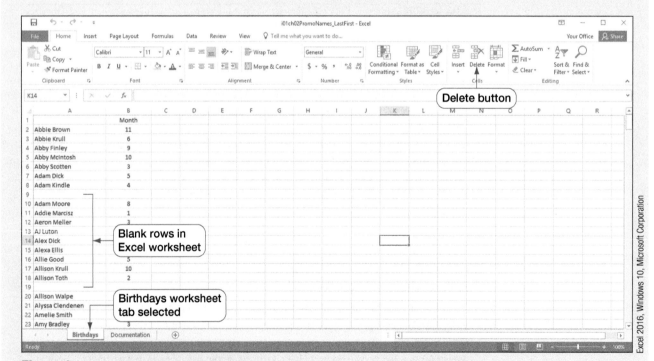

Figure 1 Blank rows in Excel worksheet

e. Press Ctrl + Home to return to cell A1. In cell **A1**, type Name, and then press Enter. In cell **A2**, using all lowercase letters, replace the existing name with your first and last name. Make sure that you do not capitalize your first and last name. You will learn the reason later in this exercise. In cell **B2**, change the Month to 4.

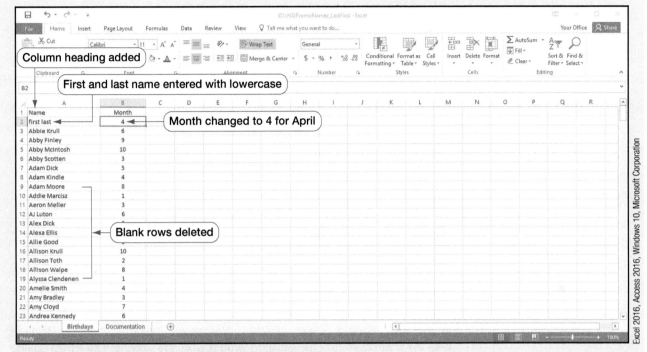

Figure 2   Excel worksheet edited for export to Access

f. Click the **Documentation** worksheet tab. Update the Documentation worksheet as directed by your instructor.

g. Click **Save** 🖫, and then click **Close** ✕ to close Excel.

Import Excel Data into Access

When you import data from Excel into Access, Access stores the data in a new or existing table without making changes to the data in Excel. You can import only one worksheet at a time, so if you have multiple worksheets, you will have to repeat the steps for each sheet. If your data is on a worksheet with other unwanted data, you can create a **named range**, which is a specific name you give to a range of cells other than the cell references for the data in Excel. Then, in Access, you can specify that you want to import only the data in your named range.

REAL WORLD ADVICE   **Data in Two Places**

Once you have imported data from Excel into Access, the data is stored in two different places and may or may not be linked, depending on the option you selected in the Get External Data dialog box. If a change to a record is made in Excel, it will change the record in Access only if you selected the Link to the data source by creating a linked table option. However, data imported from Access into Excel may be updated. Trying to maintain the same records in two different programs is not good business practice. It is better to import or export data for a specific one-time purpose, such as to query the data or create a chart from data.

CONSIDER THIS | **Creating Connections**

As you complete this project, you change the data in two places because a permanent connection does not exist. What recommendations might you make for processing comment cards and birthday data from the customer?

Importing an Excel List into an Access Table

The **Import Spreadsheet Wizard** will walk you through the steps to import your Excel data into an Access table. When you import data, the wizard provides three options: create a new table with the data, append the Excel data to an existing table, or create a linked table. In this exercise, you will import Excel data into a new Access table that will be called tblBirthdays.

IP02.01

To Import an Excel List into an Access Table

a. Start Access 🔲, click **Blank desktop database**, and then in the File Name box type i01ch02Promo_LastFirst, using your last and first name.

b. Click **Browse** 🔲, navigate to the location where you are saving your files, click **OK**, and then click **Create**.

c. Click the **External Data** tab, and then in the Import & Link group, click **Excel**. In the Get External Data - Excel Spreadsheet dialog box, click **Browse**, and then navigate to the location where you are saving your files. Select **i01ch02PromoNames_LastFirst**, and then click **Open**.

d. Make sure **Import the source data into a new table in the current database** is selected.

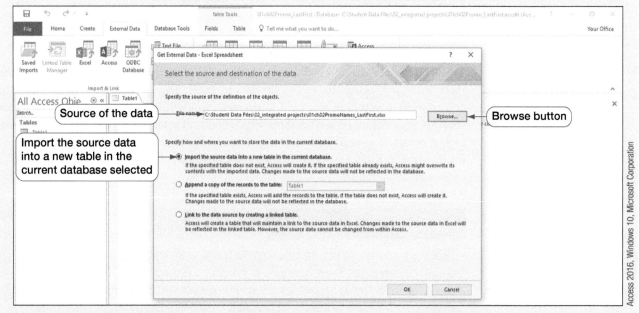

Figure 3 Get External Data: Excel spreadsheet dialog box

e. Click **OK**. The Import Spreadsheet Wizard opens. In the Import Spreadsheet Wizard dialog box, make sure **Show Worksheets** is selected, and then select **Birthdays**. Click **Next**.

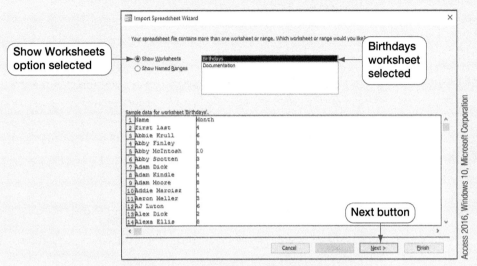

Figure 4   Import Spreadsheet Wizard

f. Select **First Row Contains Column Headings**.

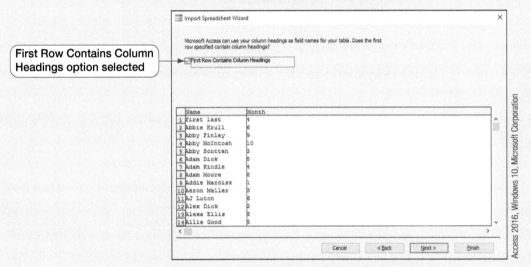

Figure 5   First Row Contains Column Headings

g. Click **Next**, and then click **Next** again. Make sure **Let Access add primary key** is selected, and then click **Next**.

h. In the Import to Table text box, type tblBirthdays for the name of the new table.

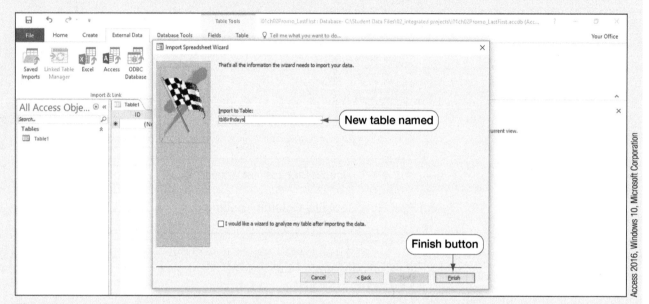

Figure 6 Name new table

i. Click **Finish**, do not select the Save import steps check box, and then click **Close**.

> **Troubleshooting**
> Did you receive an error that says, "An error occurred trying to import file"? If so, then the import failed. If a dialog box opened that prompted you to save the import steps of the operation, then the import worked, but some data may be missing. Start by opening your source file and compare it to the Access table — your destination file. If there are only a few missing pieces of information, you can add that information to the table manually. If there are large pieces or whole columns of data missing, compare column headings and data types, revise your source data, and try to import again.

j. In the Navigation Pane, double-click the **tblBirthdays** table to open it. Scroll down the list of names to make sure they were imported correctly. Click **Close** ✕ to close the tblBirthdays table.

k. Click ✕ to close the Table1 table, which is open by default. Leave the database and Access open.

Use Access Data in Word

Access data, whether it was entered in Access directly or imported from an Excel workbook, can be used in a Word document. One common example of using Access data in a Word document is to create a **mail merge**, which is a process that simplifies the task of preparing documents that contain identical formatting, layout, and text but in which certain portions of each document vary. In this section, you will create an Access query from an existing Access table and then use the results to create a mail merge document in Word.

Prepare Access Data for a Mail Merge

Data for a mail merge in Word can come from either an Access table or a query. If the data is coming from a query, the query must be created first.

Querying Data in an Access Database

To find the customers with birthdays in a particular month, you need to query the birthdays table with the birthday month as the criteria. In this exercise, you will create a query to find all customers with April birthdays.

 IP02.02

To Create a Query in an Access Database

a. Click the **Create** tab, and then in the Queries group, click **Query Design**. In the Show Table dialog box, select **tblBirthdays**, and then click **Add** to add the tblBirthdays table to the query.

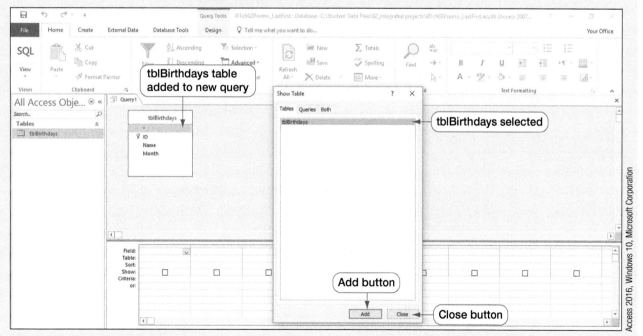

Figure 7   Table added to Query1

b. Click **Close** [×] to close the Show Table dialog box. In the tblBirthdays table box, double-click **Name**, and then double-click **Month** to add the fields to the query design grid.

c. Click the **Show** check box under Month to deselect the check box and hide this field. In the **Criteria** row for the Month field, type 4 to query for all birthdays in April.

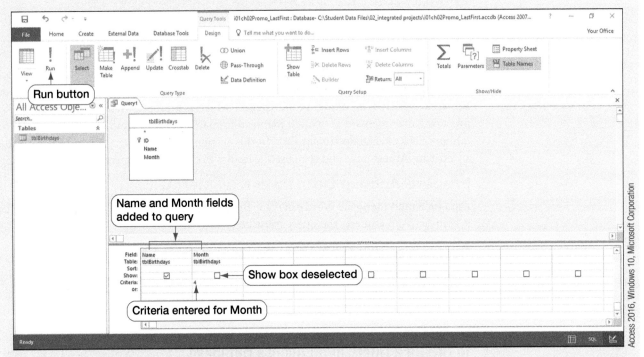

Figure 8   Query design grid for April birthdays

d. Click **Save** [icon]. In the Save As dialog box, type qryAprilBirthdays in the Query Name box, and then click **OK**.

e. On the Design tab, in the Results group, click **Run** to run the query. This retrieves 20 records with the names of people with April birthdays. In the **Name** field, double-click the **right border** to automatically adjust the width of the column so all names are visible.

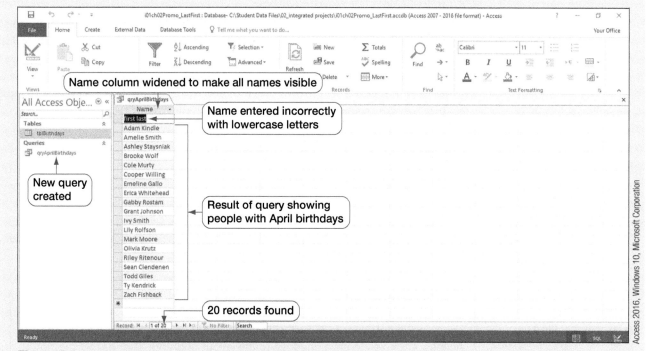

Figure 9 Results of running query

f. Click **Close** ⊠ to close the qryAprilBirthdays query, and then close Access.

Export Access Query Results into Word

Word has no import command to import data from Access; therefore, the data must be exported from Access to be opened in Word. The exception to this is a mail merge, which will be discussed below. When you use the export command in Access to export the data in a form or datasheet, that data is exported as a **Rich Text Format (.RTF)** file, a format that retains the formatting of the original document. It is then stored in a new Word document. From the new Word document, you can copy and paste the object into another existing Word document. Alternatively, you can copy data from an Access table, query, form, or report and paste it into an existing document.

CONSIDER THIS | RTF Files

Exporting data to an RTF file to use in another document takes two steps: creating the RTF file and copying and pasting it into another file. Are there advantages to this method versus a direct copy and paste into a document?

If the data in Access is going to be used in a Word mail merge document, then the Word Mail Merge Wizard can be used to export the data, and an RTF file is not necessary. You can use the results of an Access query or any other data stored in an Access table to merge into a Word document to create customized letters or labels.

Exporting Data for a Mail Merge

To export a list of data from Access to Word, the **Word Mail Merge Wizard** can be used to help create a new mail merge document or to employ an existing mail merge document from which to create form letters. The wizard can be started in either Access or Word. When the wizard is started in Access, it gives you the option either to create a new Word document or to use an existing one. In this exercise, you will link your data to an existing Word document to create customized birthday coupons for the customers listed in the Access query you just created.

SIDE NOTE
Security Warning
When you open a database, you will see a Security Warning bar just below the ribbon. Microsoft disables certain features to maintain security and prevent viruses from entering your computer.

To Merge Access Query Results into Word

a. Start **Access**, and then open **i01ch02Promo_LastFirst**.

b. Click **Enable Content** in the SECURITY WARNING bar. In the Navigation Pane, double-click the **qryAprilBirthdays** query to open it. Click the **External Data** tab, and then in the Export group, click **Word Merge**. The Microsoft Word Mail Merge Wizard opens.

> **Troubleshooting**
> Did you receive an error that says, "The Mail Merge Wizard cannot continue because the database is in exclusive mode"? If so, click OK, and then close Access. Click Yes to save changes to the layout of qryAprilBirthdays if prompted. Start Access, and open i01ch02Promo_LastFirst.

c. If necessary, select **Link your data to an existing Microsoft Word document**, and then click **OK**.

d. Navigate to the location of your student data files, select **i01ch02PromoCoupon**, and then click **Open**.

e. Click **Word** 📰 on the taskbar to display the birthday coupon. Maximize the Word window if necessary. In the Mail Merge pane, under Selected recipients, make sure **Use an existing list** is selected. Note that [qryAprilBirthdays] in "i01ch02Promo_LastFirst" is displayed under Use an existing list.

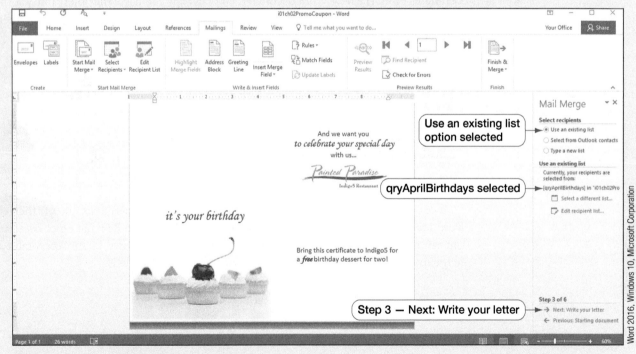

Figure 10   Mail Merge pane open in Word

f. Click **Next: Write your letter** at the bottom of the Mail Merge pane.

g. Click the **Happy Birthday coupon**, and then decrease the zoom size so the entire coupon is displayed. Click before **Bring** on the coupon to place the insertion point.

h. In the Mail Merge pane, under **Write your letter**, click **More items**. In the Insert Merge Field dialog box, if necessary, select **Database Fields**, and then, in the Fields box, make sure **Name** is selected. Click **Insert**, and then click **Close**.

i. Press ⏎ twice so there is a blank line after the field. Right-click **<<Name>>**, select **Edit Field** from the shortcut menu, and then in the Field dialog box, under Format, select **Title case**.

You have just added a **format field switch** that determines the use of uppercase and lowercase letters. By selecting Title case, you specify that the first letter of all names will be capitalized even if the names were entered incorrectly in the Excel worksheet. Remember that you were asked to type your first and last names using lowercase letters earlier in this chapter. Without the format switch, your first and last names would not be capitalized on the birthday coupon. If you choose First capital, only the first name will be capitalized.

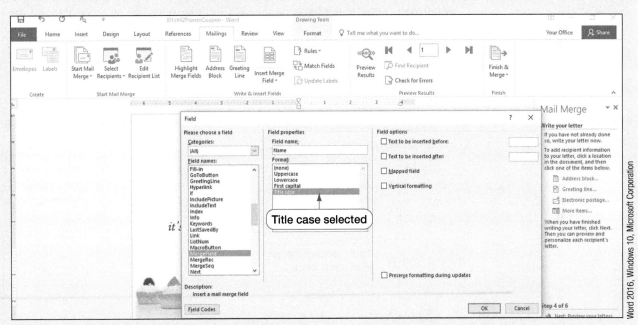

Figure 11 Edit Merge Field to add format switch

j. Click **OK** to close the Field dialog box. Select **<<Name>>**. Click the **Home** tab, in the **Font** group, click **Bold** B .

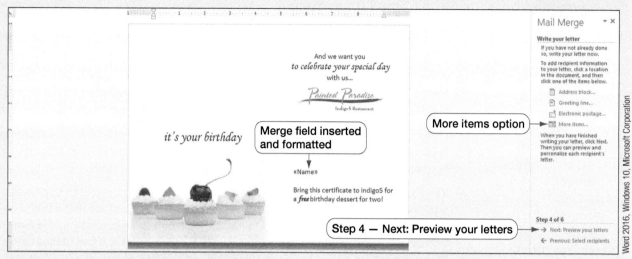

Figure 12 Name field inserted and formatted

k. In the Mail Merge pane, click **Next: Preview your letters**. The first certificate should display your first and last name with initial caps. Under **Preview your letters**, at the top of the Mail Merge pane, click the **arrow** button to scroll through the names of several other recipients with April birthdays.

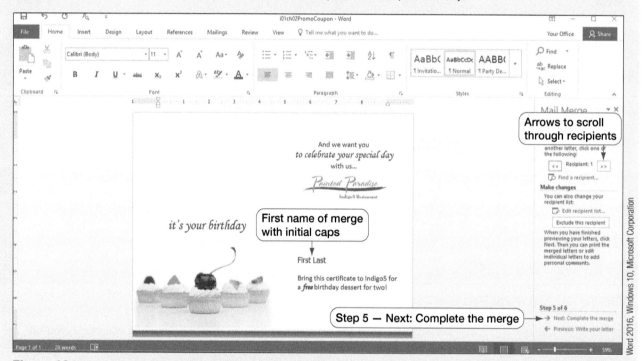

Figure 13 Completed merge with names inserted in coupons

l. Click **Next: Complete the merge**. Under Merge, click **Edit Individual letters** to merge the individual coupons in a new document.

m. In the Merge to New Document dialog box, if necessary, select **All**, and then click **OK**. A new document opens with one page for each coupon. Scroll through the document to examine several of the coupons.

n. Click the **File** tab, click **Save As**, and then navigate to the location where you are saving your project files. Name this document i01ch02PromoMerge_LastFirst, using your last and first name, and then click **Save**.

o. Click **Close** ☒ to close i01ch02PromoMerge_LastFirst. Click **Close** ☒ to close i01ch02PromoCoupon without saving the changes. Click **Close** ☒ to close Access.

Concept Check

1. Why is it important to prepare your Excel data before importing it into Access? What kinds of things should you look for? p. 1010

2. Why would you want to import data into Access from Excel? Why would you want to import data into Excel from Access? p. 1011

3. Why would you create a query in Access to export to Word? Give an example. p. 1015

4. What is one common error you may get when you use the Mail Merge Wizard to export data from Access? How can you prevent this error? p. 1017

Key Terms

Format field switch   1019
Import   1009
Import Spreadsheet Wizard   1012

Mail merge   1015
Named range   1011
Rich Text Format (.RTF)   1017

Word Mail Merge Wizard   1018

Visual Summary

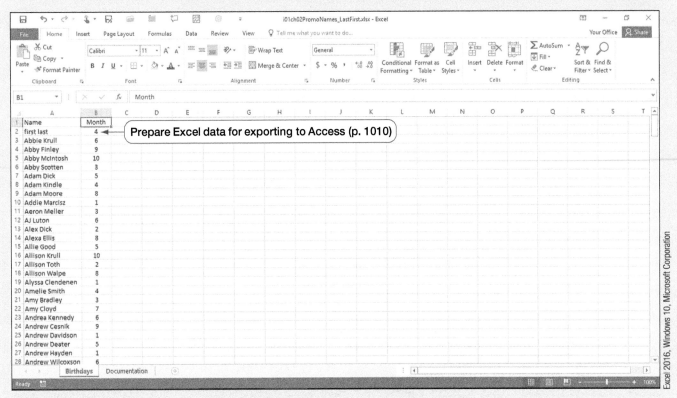

Figure 14

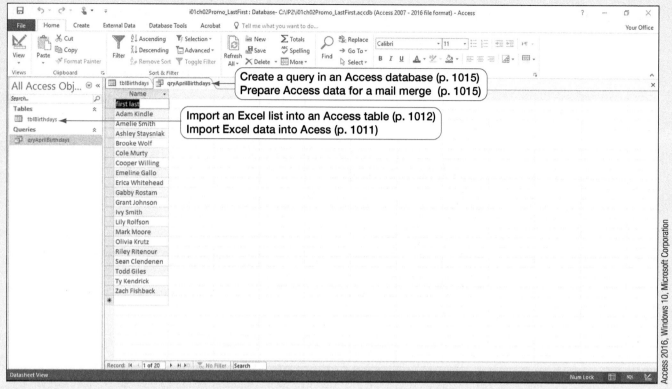

Create a query in an Access database (p. 1015)
Prepare Access data for a mail merge (p. 1015)

Import an Excel list into an Access table (p. 1012)
Import Excel data into Acess (p. 1011)

Figure 15

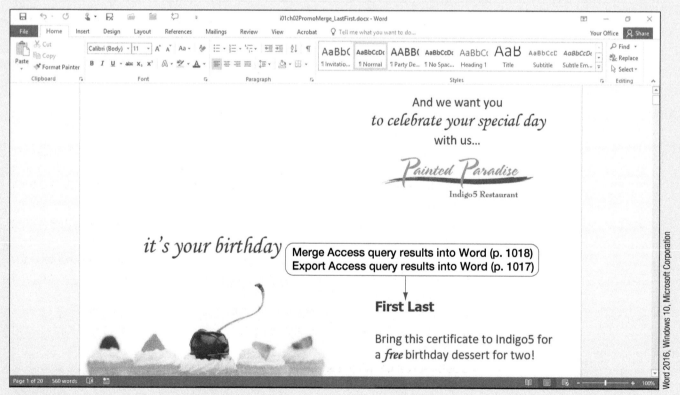

And we want you
to celebrate your special day
with us...

Painted Paradise

Indigo5 Restaurant

it's your birthday

Merge Access query results into Word (p. 1018)
Export Access query results into Word (p. 1017)

First Last

Bring this certificate to Indigo5 for
a *free* birthday dessert for two!

Figure 16

Student data file needed:

 i01ch02LibraryList.xlsx

You will save your files as:

 i01ch02LibraryList_LastFirst.xlsx

 i01ch02Library_LastFirst.accdb

i01ch02LibraryMerge_LastFirst.docx

Library Conference

Customer Service

Painted Paradise Resort Event Planning is getting ready for an onsite library conference. Library directors from all over Florida will be attending. Some directors will be speaking or giving presentations. You have been assigned to create name tags for just the attendees, since presenters will have special badges. Information has been kept in an Excel workbook with the name of the library director, the name of the library, and the status indicating whether the director is an attendee or a presenter. You will have to import the Excel list into Access and then use Word Merge to create name tags for all attendees.

a. Start **Excel**, and then open **i01ch02LibraryList**. Maximize the Excel window if necessary.

b. Click the **File** tab, click **Save As**, and then navigate to the location where you are saving your project files. Change the file name to i01ch02LibraryList_LastFirst, using your last and first name. Click **Save**.

c. If necessary, click the **Conference** worksheet tab, and then select **row 42**. On the Home tab, in the Cells group, click **Delete**. Repeat the same steps for **row 18**.

d. In cell **A2**, replace the existing name with your first name and last name, and then save the workbook. Close Excel.

e. Start **Access**, click **Blank desktop database**, and then in the File Name box, type i01ch02Library_LastFirst, using your last and first name. Click **Browse**, and then navigate to the location where you are saving your project files. Click **OK**, and then click **Create**.

f. Click the **External Data** tab, and then in the Import & Link group, click **Excel**. Click **Browse**, navigate to the location where you are saving your student files, select **i01ch02LibraryList_LastFirst**, and then click **Open**.

g. Make sure **Import the source data into a new table in the current database** is selected, and then click **OK**.

h. In the Import Spreadsheet Wizard dialog box, make sure **Show Worksheets** is selected, select **Conference**, and then click **Next**. Select **First Row Contains Column Headings**, click **Next**, and then click **Next** again. Make sure **Let Access add primary key** is selected, and then click **Next**.

i. Type tblDirectors for the name of the new table, and then click **Finish**. Click **Close** without saving the import steps.

j. In the Navigation Pane, open the new table **tblDirectors**. Double-click the **right border** of the Director field and the Library field to automatically fit the column widths. Click **Save**, and then close both the tblDirectors table and the Table1 table.

k. Click the **Create** tab, and then in the Queries group, click **Query Design**. In the Show Table dialog box, click **Add** to add the **tblDirectors** table to the query, and then click **Close**.

l. Double-click **ID**, **Director**, **Library**, and **Status** to add the fields to the query grid. In the Criteria line for the Status field, type Attendee.

m. On the Design tab, in the Results group, click **Run**. You should see results only for the Attendees of the conference and not for the Presenters. Click **Save**, type qryAttendees for the Query Name, and then click **OK**. Close the query, and then close the database.

n. Open **i01ch02Library_LastFirst**. Click **Enable Content** if necessary. Open the **qryAttendees** query. Click the **External Data** tab, and then in the **Export** group, click **Word Merge**.

o. In the Microsoft Word Mail Merge Wizard dialog box, select **Create a new document and then link the data to it**, and then click **OK**.

p. Click **Word** on the taskbar, and then click **Maximize** if necessary. In the Mail Merge pane, under Select document type, select **Labels**. Click **Next: Starting document**.

q. Under Change document layout, click **Label options**. In the Label Options dialog box, under Label information, in the Label vendors box, select **Avery US Letter**, and then under Product number select **5390 Name Badges Insert Refills**. Click **OK**.

r. In the Mail Merge pane, click **Next: Select recipients**, and then click **Next: Arrange your labels**. Under Arrange your labels, click **More items**. In the Insert Merge Field dialog box, double-click **Director** and **Library**, and then click **Close**.

s. Resize the document so you can see the text on the nametag. Click between <<Director>> and <<Library>>, and then press Enter to place "Library" on a new line. Select both **<<Director>>** and **<<Library>>**. Click the **Home** tab, and then in the Font group, increase the font size to **18**. Select only **<<Director>>**, and then in the Font group, click **Bold**.

t. In the Mail Merge pane, under Replicate labels, click **Update all labels**. Click the **Table Selector** in the top left corner of the table to select all the records. Under Table Tools, on the Layout tab, in the Alignment group, click **Align Center**.

u. With the table still selected, click the **Home** tab, and then in the Paragraph group, click the **Borders** arrow, and then select **All Borders** to place borders around all labels.

v. In the Mail Merge pane, click **Next: Preview your labels**, and then click **Next: Complete the merge**. Under Merge, click **Edit individual labels**. In the Merge to New Document dialog box, under Merge records, select **All** if necessary, and then click **OK**.

w. Click **Save**, locate the folder where you are saving your files, and then name the file i01ch02LibraryMerge_LastFirst. Click **Save**, and then close the document. Close the mail merge document called Document1 without saving it. Close Access. Submit your files as directed by your instructor.

Practice 2

Student data files needed:

 i01ch02EventPoster.docx

 i01ch02EventList.xlsx

You will save your files as:

i01ch02EventPoster_LastFirst.docx

i01ch02EventList_LastFirst.xlsx

i01ch02Event_LastFirst.accdb

Corporate Challenge Event

Sales and Marketing

Painted Paradise Resort Event Planning is coordinating an upcoming corporate challenge event on the grounds of the resort. The events will include a 5K Fun Run, a 100-Meter Sprint, a 400-Meter Relay, a Tug of War, and a Water Balloon Toss. Each event will need a poster with the name of the event and a list of participants. Your assignment is to create the poster for the 5K Fun Run. The participant information is in an Excel list. You will import that list into Access, query for that particular event, and then export the list of participants to a poster in Word. You will also format the poster attractively.

a. Start **Word**, and then open **i01ch02EventPoster**. Maximize the Word window if necessary.

b. Click the **File** tab, click **Save As**, and then navigate to the location where you are saving your files. Change the file name to i01ch02EventPoster_LastFirst, using your last and first name. Click **Save**.

c. Start **Excel**, and then open **i01ch02EventList**. Maximize the Excel window if necessary.

d. Click the **File** tab, click **Save As**, and then navigate to the location where you are saving your project files. Change the file name to i01ch02EventList_LastFirst, using your last and first name. Click **Save**.

e. Select **row 103**. On the Home tab, in the Cells group, click **Delete**. Repeat these steps for **rows 59**, **36**, and **12**.

f. In cell **B1**, type **Event** for the column heading. In cell **A2**, replace the existing name with your first name and last name. Click **Save**, and then close Excel.

g. Start **Access**, click **Blank desktop database**, and then in the File Name box, type i01ch02Event_LastFirst, using your last and first name. Click **Browse**, and then navigate to the location where you are saving your files. Click **OK**, and then click **Create**.

h. Click the **External Data** tab, and then in the Import & Link group, click **Excel**. Make sure **Import the source data into a new table in the current database** is selected, and then click **Browse**. Navigate to the location where you are saving your project files, select **i01ch02EventList_LastFirst**, and then click **Open**. Click **OK**.

i. In the Import Spreadsheet Wizard dialog box, make sure **Show Worksheets** is selected, and then if necessary, select **Participants**. Click **Next**. Select **First Row Contains Column Headings**, click **Next**, and then click **Next** again.

j. Make sure **Let Access add primary key** is selected, and then click **Next**. In the Import to Table box, type tblEvents, and then click **Finish**. Click **Close** without saving the import steps.

k. In the Navigation Pane, open the **tblEvents** table. Double-click the **right border** of the Name field and the Event field to automatically fit the column widths.

l. Click the **Create** tab, and then in the Queries group, click **Query Design**. In the Show Table dialog box, make sure **tblEvents** is selected, click **Add**, and then click **Close** to close the dialog box. Double-click the **Name** and **Event** fields to add them to the query grid.

m. Click **Show** under the Event field to deselect the check box and hide this field. Click the **Criteria** line for the Event field, and type 5K Fun Run. Click **Save**, name the query qry5KFunRun, and then click **OK**.

n. On the Design tab, in the Results group, click **Run**. Double-click the **right border** of the Name field to automatically widen the column. Click **Save**.

o. Click the **Select All** button in the upper left corner of qry5KFunRun to select all the records. Click the **Home** tab, and then in the Clipboard group, click **Copy**.

p. Click **Word** on the taskbar. In the Word document **i01ch02EventPoster_LastFirst**, on the Home tab, in the Paragraph group, click **Show/Hide** to show paragraph marks. Click the first paragraph mark under the heading Event Participants, and then in the **Clipboard** group, click **Paste**.

q. Click the **table selector** to select the entire table, and then in the Paragraph group, click **Center**. Select the **first two rows**, and then delete them, leaving only the names. Click the **table selector** to select the table, and then in the Font group, increase the font size to **14**. Place the insertion point in front of your name, and drag to select the names — not the table names, and then in the Paragraph group, click **Center**. In the Paragraph group, click the **Borders** arrow, and then select **No Border**. Click **Show/Hide** to turn off the paragraph marks. Click **Save**, and then close Word.

r. Close Access, and then select **Yes** to save all changes when asked. Submit your files as directed by your instructor.

Merchandise Labels

Production &
Operations

Painted Treasures Gift Shop staff would like to put merchandise labels on the different items they carry to help them quickly manage inventory and ring up sales based on the category of merchandise. The item list is in an Excel spreadsheet, and the labels are in Word. Your assignment is to import the Excel list into Access, then find the records for all items except those categorized as "Other." You will use Word Mail Merge to create labels for the queried data.

a. Start **Excel**, open **i01ch02ItemsList**, and then save it to your project files as i01ch02ItemsList_LastFirst. Insert the **file name** in the left section of the footer.

b. Prepare the Excel list for importing into Access by deleting any blank rows, and then save the workbook. If requested by your instructor, update the **Documentation** worksheet to reflect the changes that have been made.

c. Import the data into a new Access database called i01ch02Items_LastFirst. Do not save the import steps. Save the new table, and name it tblInventory.

d. Query the **tblInventory** table for records in all categories except Other. Show fields **Items** and **Category**. Save the new query as qryCategories.

e. Use Word Mail Merge to create labels in a new Word document using the records in the **qryCategories** query. For Label options, select **Avery US Letter** as the Label vendor, and select Product number **18160 Address Labels**.

f. Add the **Items** field on the first line of the label and the **Category** field on the second line of the label. Increase the font size to **14**, and then center the text so the information fits well on the label.

g. Complete the merge, and then save the new document as i01ch02ItemsMerge_LastFirst. Close the document, and then close all documents in Word without saving.

h. Close Access, and then close Excel. Submit your files as directed by your instructor.

Art Sale Newsletter

Sales and
Marketing

Susan Brock, manager of Painted Treasures Gift Shop, has just received a shipment of amazing African art. She would like to send out a newsletter to customers who live in the local area telling them of these new acquisitions. Susan has been keeping data about past customers in an Excel worksheet that lists names and addresses. She has created a newsletter in Word, and she would like you to take over the task of merging the names of customers who will receive the newsletter. Your assignment is to import the Excel list into Access and then find the names for all customers who live in New Mexico. You will use Word Mail Merge to create personalized newsletters addressed to each individual.

a. Start **Excel**, and then open **i01ch02ArtList**. Save it to your project files as i01ch02ArtList_LastFirst, using your last and first name. Insert the **file name** in the left section of the footer, and then save the document. Prepare the list for exporting to Access by deleting any blank rows. Save the workbook.

b. Import the data into a new Access database called i01ch02Art_LastFirst. Do not save the import steps. Save the new table, and name it tblAddresses.

c. Change the first name in the table to your own name. Query the **tblAddresses** table for records of all people who live in **NM**. Show fields **First Name** and **State**. Save the new query as qryNewMexico.

d. Use Word Merge to create newsletters that address each recipient by first name using **i01ch02ArtNews**. Add the **First Name** field after the word **Dear** and before the colon at the top of the newsletter, using the correct spacing. Complete the merge, save the new document as i01ch02ArtMerge_LastFirst, using your last and first name and then close the document.

e. Close all documents in Word without saving. Close Access, and then close Excel. Submit your files as directed by your instructor.

Perform 1: Perform in Your Career

Student data files needed:

 Blank Word document

 Blank Excel workbook

Blank Access database

You will save your files as:

 i01ch02Book_LastFirst.accdb

 i01ch02BookAward_LastFirst.docx

 i01ch02BookList_LastFirst.xlsx

i01ch02BookMerge_LastFirst.docx

Book Award Certificates

Customer Service

You are a teacher and would like to reward your students for completing a reading program that lasted the entire school year. The students would choose a book to read each week. On Fridays, they would sit at a special table, have pizza for lunch, and discuss the book. Some children read just a few books, but others read almost one a week. You would like to print certificates for students who read 25 books or more. You have been tracking your students in Excel with the students' names and number of books read. You will need to import the data into Access, query the data for names of students who deserve the award, and then use the query results in a Word document that shows each student's name and the number of books read.

a. Start **Word**, and then create an award certificate for your students. You may use a template and modify it as necessary. Save the file as i01ch02BookAward_LastFirst, using your last and first name, and then close Word.

b. Open **Excel**, and create a list of names and number of books read for at least 25 students. The highest possible number of books read is 32. The first record should have your name as the student and 28 books read. Save the file as i01ch02BookList_LastFirst, using your last and first name.

c. Import the **Excel** list into an Access database called i01ch02Book_LastFirst. Name the new table tblBooksRead. Query the table for students who read 25 books or more. Save the query as qryStudents.

d. Use Word Mail Merge to create award certificates with the results of your query. Include the student's name and the number of books read. Save the merged document as i01ch02BookMerge_LastFirst, using your last and first name. Close all documents without saving. Submit your files as directed by your instructor.

Student data files needed:

 i01ch02SalesNews.docx

i01ch02SalesData.xlsx

i01ch02SalesReps.accdb

You will save your files as:

 i01ch02SalesNews_LastFirst.docx

i01ch02SalesReps_LastFirst.accdb

i01ch02SalesMerge_LastFirst.docx

Sales and
Marketing

Quarterly Newspaper

Barbie Keilman makes one-of-a kind jewelry. Since this consumes a great deal of her time, she has hired five of her friends to help sell her jewelry. Each of the friends hosts several parties during the month where she exhibits Barbie's latest creations and takes orders. To avoid conflicts, each friend covers a certain neighborhood in the city. You have been asked to create a newsletter to keep Barbie and her friends informed of sales during each quarterly period. Barbie hopes this will motivate her friends to increase sales. You have been asked to include a chart to illustrate sales visually and a table that ranks the sales staff for the quarter. Then you will need to personalize each newsletter with each person's name and area.

a. Start **Word**, open **i01ch02SalesNews**, and then save it as i01ch02SalesNews_LastFirst, using your last and first name. Insert a left-aligned footer with the file name.

b. Start **Excel**, and then open **i01ch02SalesData**. Copy the data for first quarter sales, and then paste it at the bottom of the newsletter under the text Year to Date Sales. Copy the column chart, and then paste it under the sales data. Adjust size as necessary, and format attractively. Save the Word document.

c. Start Access, and then open **i01ch02SalesReps**. Change the name of the North area's sales rep to your own name. Save the file as i01ch02SalesReps_LastFirst, using your last and first name.

d. Complete a mail merge to add each sales rep's name and area to the newsletter. Save the merged document as i01ch02SalesMerge_LastFirst, using your last and first name. Close all documents without saving. Submit your files as directed by your instructor.

Additional
Cases

Additional Chapter Cases are available at www.pearsonhighered.com/youroffice

Integrated Projects

Chapter 3 | WORD, EXCEL, ACCESS, AND POWERPOINT INTEGRATION

OBJECTIVES

1. Work in Outline view p. 1030
2. Create a PowerPoint presentation from a Word outline p. 1034
3. Insert Access data into a PowerPoint presentation p. 1036
4. Import Access data into Excel p. 1040

Prepare Case

Indigo5 Restaurant Training

Determined to remain a top-rated restaurant, Indigo5 requires that all staff members undergo extensive training in customer service every quarter. Alberto Dimas, restaurant manager, has written an outline in Word for the training seminar, listing topics he wants to cover. Survey results ranking customers' satisfaction with food and service for the past year have been kept in an Access database. Your assignment is to complete a PowerPoint presentation using the Word outline. You will include a data table with satisfaction rankings from the previous quarter; you will then import the Access data into Excel to create a chart that summarizes the survey results.

Natalia Mylova/Shutterstock

Student data files needed for this chapter:

 i01ch03ServeOutline.docx

 i01ch03ServeChart.xlsx

i01ch03ServeShow.pptx

i01ch03ServeSurvey.accdb

You will save your files as:

 i01ch03ServeOutline_LastFirst.docx

 i01ch03ServeChart_LastFirst.xlsx

 i01ch03ServeShow_LastFirst.pptx

Integrating Word and PowerPoint

Text can easily be copied from Word to PowerPoint, but sometimes a copy and paste is not efficient or effective. Copying and pasting large amounts of text can be time consuming, and deciding how to split up text for different PowerPoint slides can often be overwhelming.

To use Word text efficiently in a PowerPoint presentation, a Word outline can be used as a starting point. An **outline** is a hierarchical representation of paragraphs, which are recognized in Word by nonprinting, end-of-paragraph marks. A paragraph can be a blank line, one or two words, or multiple sentences. When you type a paragraph into a document in **Outline view**, Word automatically assigns heading styles to each paragraph to create different levels. At the top of the hierarchy are **Level 1** paragraphs. Paragraphs at the next level are **Level 2**. These outlining levels correspond to the Heading styles available for formatting located on the Home tab, in the Styles group. Paragraphs already formatted with heading styles will appear at different levels in Outline view. Paragraphs that have not been formatted with heading styles will appear as **body text** in Outline view. In this section, you will create a PowerPoint presentation from a Word outline.

Work in Outline View

When Outline view is opened, a new Outlining tab is displayed on the ribbon with tools available for formatting paragraphs. The Promote button and Demote button are used to move paragraphs to different levels. When you **promote** a paragraph, you move it to a higher level in the outline. When you **demote** a paragraph, you move it to a lower level in the outline.

As your outline develops, it is often helpful to see only one level at a time. If a paragraph has levels below it, a plus sign appears at the beginning of the line. If these levels are displayed, double-clicking the plus sign temporarily hides all the lower levels below that paragraph. To redisplay all subheadings under a heading, double-click the plus sign again. You can also select text and use the **Expand** [+] and **Collapse** [−] buttons in the Outline Tools group to expand and collapse paragraphs.

If you select a heading that includes collapsed subordinate text, the collapsed text is also selected, even though it is not visible. Any changes you make to the heading, such as moving, copying, or deleting, also affect the collapsed text.

A minus sign at the beginning of the line is assigned to paragraphs with no lower levels below them. Paragraphs that have a simple bullet point — that is, no plus or minus sign — are body text and cannot be collapsed or expanded. You can click Show Level to choose which levels to view at one time. When you click Show Level and select Level 2, only Level 1 and Level 2 paragraphs will be visible. Table 1 lists the outline tools and their functions.

Tool	Name	Function
←	Promote	Moves selected heading and subtext by promoting them—moving them up one level and to the left
→	Demote	Moves selected heading and subtext by demoting them—moving them down one level and to the right
⇐	Promote to Heading 1	Changes the selected paragraph(s) to Heading 1
⇒	Demote to Body Text	Changes the selected paragraph(s) to Body Text
▲	Move Up	Moves selected heading and subtext up
▼	Move Down	Moves selected heading and subtext down
+	Expand	Expands selected headings and subtext groups
−	Collapse	Collapses selected headings and subtext groups
Body Text	Outline Level	Shows the level where the insertion point is located

Table 1   Outline tools and their functions

Working with Levels in Outline View

You can view a Word document in Outline view at any time. When you switch to Outline view, your paragraphs are displayed by levels. You can make changes to the levels of the paragraphs either in Print Layout view or directly in Outline view. In this exercise, you will open a Word document, view it in Outline view, and make changes to the paragraph levels in Outline view.

SIDE NOTE
Pin the Ribbon
If your ribbon is collapsed, pin your ribbon open. Click the Home tab. In the lower right-hand corner of the ribbon, click Pin the Ribbon 📌.

To Work with a Document in Outline View

a. Start Word, and then open **i01ch03ServeOutline**. Maximize the Word window if necessary.

b. Click the **File** tab, click **Save As**, and then double-click **This PC**. In the **Save As** dialog box, navigate to the location where you are saving your project files, and then change the file name to i01ch03ServeOutline_LastFirst, using your last and first name. Click **Save**.

c. Insert a **left-aligned footer** with the file name, and then click **Save** 💾. Double-click in the document, and then press Ctrl+Home to move the insertion point to the beginning of the document.

Figure 1 Word outline in Print Layout view

d. Click the **View** tab, and then in the Views group, click **Outline**. Notice in the Outline Tools group, in the Outline Level box, that all paragraphs are considered Body Text.

Figure 2   Word outline in Outline view

e. Press Ctrl+A to select all the lines of text. On the Outlining tab, in the Outline Tools group, click **Promote** ←.

All lines of text are promoted to Level 1. The font type and font size change, and a minus sign is displayed at the beginning of each line to visually show that the paragraphs are Level 1 and not body text. Click a blank area of the document to deselect the text.

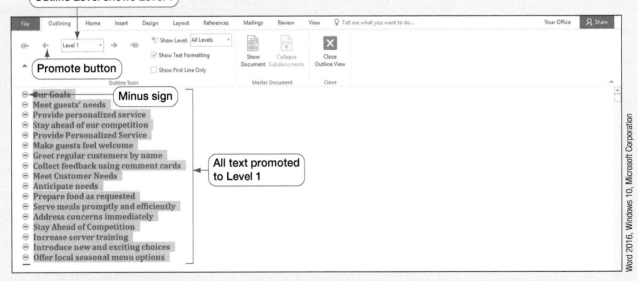

Figure 3   Text promoted to Level 1

f. Place the insertion point at the beginning of the second line, which says **Meet guests' needs**, and then in the **Outline Tools** group, click **Demote** →.

This moves the paragraph to Level 2 and decreases the font size. Note the button in front of the first paragraph has changed from a minus sign to a plus sign because there is now a paragraph at a level below.

g. Select the next two lines, **Provide personalized service** and **Stay ahead of our competition**, and then in the **Outline Tools** group, click **Demote** →.

h. Select lines **6** through **8**, and then click **Demote** →. Select lines **10** through **13**, and then click **Demote** →. Select lines **15** through **17**, and then click **Demote** →.

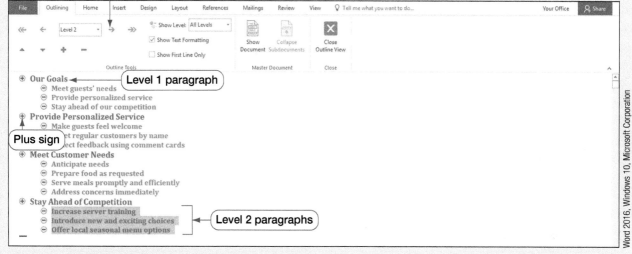

Figure 4   Outline with Level 1 and Level 2 paragraphs

i. Click **Save** 🖫.

REAL WORLD ADVICE   **Optional Outlining Method**

You may want to use the Styles options on the Home tab to create your outline instead of using Outline view. Select a paragraph and then, on the Home tab, in the Styles group, select a style — Heading 1, Heading 2, and so on — to create different levels of paragraphs. By using the Style method, you will see the different formatting of the text, but you will not see the plus and minus signs as you do in Outline view.

Rearranging a Word Outline

After you have created an outline, you can move paragraphs from one part of the outline to another without changing their levels. The Outlining tab has Move Up and Move Down buttons that will move selected lines up or down one or more lines at a time. This does not change the levels, only the position of the paragraphs within the outline. In this exercise, you will rearrange your paragraphs in Outline view.

IP03.01

To Rearrange the Outline

a. Press `Ctrl`+`Home` to move the insertion point to the beginning of the document.

b. Click the **plus sign** in front of **Meet Customer Needs** to select that paragraph and the four paragraphs below. On the Outlining tab, in the Outline Tools group, click **Move Up** ▲ four times so all five lines are above **Provide Personalized Service**.

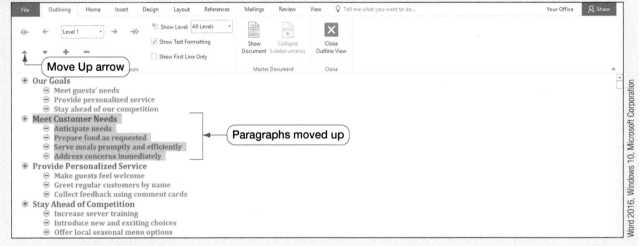

Figure 5   Paragraphs moved up

c. In the Close group, click **Close Outline View** to return to Print Layout view.

d. Click **Save** 🖫, and then click **Close** ✕ to close Word.

Create a PowerPoint Presentation from a Word Outline

It is easy to create slides for a PowerPoint presentation from a Word outline. PowerPoint automatically uses the highest level of paragraphs in the outline as slide titles on new slides and the lower-level text as bulleted text. Each level after the first-level slide text displays one level lower, using a bullet or number outline. Once the slides have been created, you can modify them as necessary in PowerPoint by changing the formatting or the levels of text.

Creating PowerPoint Slides from a Word Outline

PowerPoint offers a command that allows you to import an outline. In this exercise, you will open the PowerPoint presentation that Alberto Dimas has already created. Then you will use the Word outline to create new PowerPoint slides.

 IP03.02

To Create PowerPoint Slides from a Word Outline

a. Start PowerPoint, and then open **i01ch03ServeShow**.

b. Click the **File** tab, click **Save As**, and then double-click **This PC**. In the **Save As** dialog box, navigate to the location where you are saving your project files, and then change the file name of the presentation to i01ch03ServeShow_LastFirst, using your last and first name. Click **Save**.

c. On the Home tab, in the Slides group, click the **New Slide** arrow, and then select **Slides from Outline**.

d. In the Insert Outline dialog box, navigate to the location where you are saving your project files, select **i01ch03ServeOutline_LastFirst**, and then click **Insert**. Four new slides are inserted from the outline.

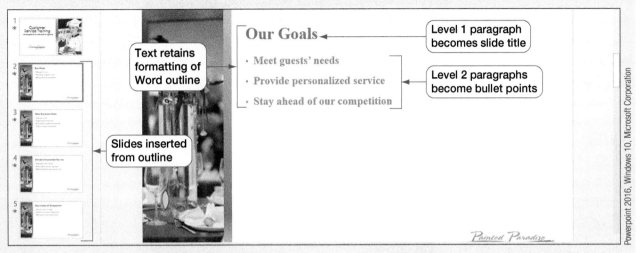

Figure 6 PowerPoint slides inserted from Word outline

Troubleshooting

PowerPoint cannot make slides from an open Word document. If you get an error message when you try to select a file, make sure the file is closed, and then try selecting the Slides from Outline command again.

Resetting Formatting of Slides Inserted from an Outline

When you insert slides into a PowerPoint presentation from an outline, the new slides retain some of the formatting from the Word document. Notice that the font on the new slides does not really match the font on the title slide. This would be even more noticeable if your presentation already contained several other slides before you inserted new ones. The title slide uses the Century Gothic font, and the slides inserted from the outline use the Times New Roman font. The text on the new slides is formatted in shades of blue used for Heading 1 and Heading 2 styles. You would like the new slides to match the title slide. To accomplish this, you can use the **reset** function, which returns the position, size, and formatting of slide placeholders to the default settings determined by the slide master. In this exercise, you will reset the four inserted slides to match the title slide.

To Reset Formatting of Slides Inserted from an Outline

SIDE NOTE

Another Way to Reset
You can also right-click a slide or group of slides and then select Reset Slide from the shortcut menu.

a. In the left pane, with Slide 2 already selected, hold down Shift, and then click **Slide 5**. The four slides you inserted are selected. On the Home tab, in the Slides group, click **Reset**. The four slides now reflect the format determined by the slide master and match the title slide.

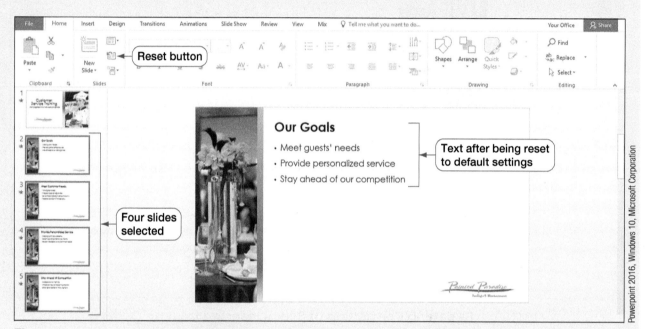

Figure 7 Slides reset to default settings

b. Click the **Insert** tab, and then in the Text group, click **Header & Footer**. In the Header and Footer dialog box, click the **Notes and Handouts** tab. Click **Footer** to select it, and then type i01ch03ServeShow_LastFirst, using your last and first name. Click **Apply to All**.

c. Click **Save**. Click **Minimize** to minimize the PowerPoint window to the taskbar.

Integrating Access and PowerPoint

Data can be shared between PowerPoint and Access. Access tables and queries can be copied and pasted directly into a PowerPoint presentation. The data is therefore shared but not linked, so any changes made to the data in Access will not be reflected in data that is copied and pasted in PowerPoint. In this section, you will practice copying data from Access and then pasting it to a PowerPoint slide.

Insert Access Data into a PowerPoint Presentation

Unlike exporting data in Access to Word or Excel, there is no import or export command for moving Access data to a PowerPoint presentation. Instead, simple Copy and Paste commands are used.

Copying and Pasting Access Data

Because data must be copied and pasted from Access to PowerPoint, any data from a table or query can easily be selected, copied, and pasted using the commands on the Clipboard. In this exercise, you will copy the results of a query in Access and paste it onto a slide in PowerPoint.

To Copy and Paste Access Query Results to a PowerPoint Slide

a. Start Access, and then open **i01ch03ServeSurvey**.

b. If necessary, click **Enable Content** in the SECURITY WARNING bar. In the Navigation Pane, double-click the query **qrySummary** to open it in Datasheet view.

c. Click **Select All** ⬜ in the top left corner of the query datasheet. This selects all the records in the query datasheet.

SIDE NOTE
Security Warning
Microsoft disables some features to prevent malicious software from entering your computer through a database file. If you trust the contents, click Enable Content.

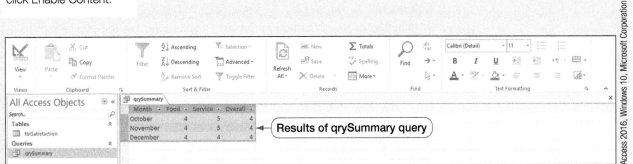

Figure 8   Query showing summary of customer satisfaction

SIDE NOTE
Queries and Tables
You opened and copied query results in steps b through d. You can open and copy a table the same way.

d. On the Home tab, in the Clipboard group, click **Copy** 📋, and then close Access.

e. Click **PowerPoint** 🅿️ on the taskbar to display the PowerPoint window. With the **i01ch03ServeShow_LastFirst** presentation open, click **Slide 3** to select it.

f. Click the **Home** tab, and then in the Clipboard group, click **Paste**. Point to the top of the table, and when your mouse pointer turns into a four-sided arrow ⬌, drag the **table** below the text.

The query results are now pasted as a table into PowerPoint.

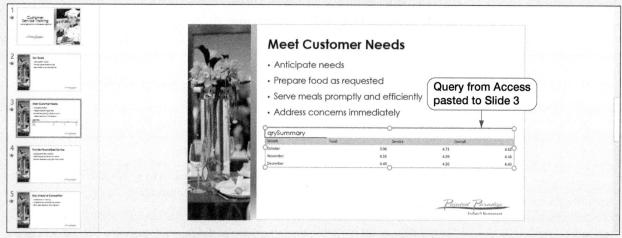

Figure 9   Query pasted from Access

Access 2016, Powerpoint 2016, Windows 10, Microsoft Corporation

g. With the table selected, on the Home tab, in the Font group, click the **Font Size** arrow, and then select **18**. The font size for all text in the table is increased.

h. Select the title **qrySummary**, and then type Satisfaction Survey Results as the new title. Select the Satisfaction Survey Results title. On the Home tab, in the paragraph group, click **Center**.

i. Click the **top border** of the table to make sure the entire table is selected. Under Table Tools, on the **Design** tab, in the Table Style Options group, click **Header Row**. In the Table Styles group, select the **Dark Style 1 - Accent 1** style to apply the style to the table.

j. Select all of the cells in the second row of the table. In the Table Styles group, click the Shading 🖿 arrow, and then select **Lavender, Accent 1, Darker 25%**. Select the cells in the second row again. On the Home tab, in the Font group, click **Bold** B.

k. With the table still selected, under Table Tools, on the **Layout** tab, in the Table Size group, change the **Height** 🔲 to 2.5" and change the **Width** 🔲 to 7.5".

l. Select the text in the **second through fourth** columns of the table. In the **Alignment** group, click **Center** ☰ and **Center Vertically** 🔲 to center the text horizontally and vertically within the cells.

> ### Troubleshooting
>
> In the Access database, the query was formatted so no decimal places were displayed in the number. When the data is copied to the Clipboard, the actual data is copied, not the displayed data. Therefore, when you paste the table into PowerPoint, there will be two decimal places showing. If necessary, you can type over the numbers that are copied and replace them with a rounded number.

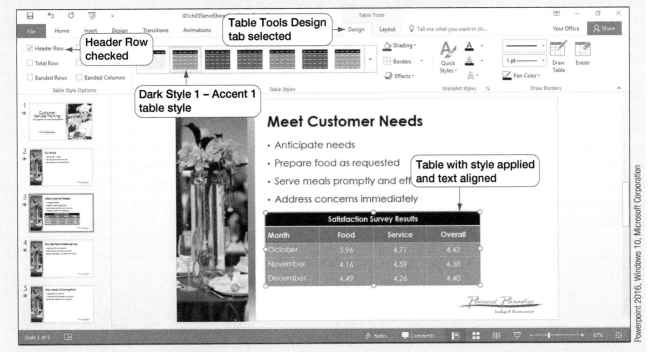

Figure 10 Table after formatting

m. Click **Save** , and then click **Minimize** ☐ to minimize PowerPoint on the taskbar.

S₅ CONSIDER THIS | **Paste Options**

You are performing a simple copy and paste with the data from Access. There are other options under Paste Special that you could have used. What are they? When would you want to use Paste Special rather than Paste?

Integrating Access, Excel, and PowerPoint

You can bring data into Excel from Access by using the Copy and Paste commands, by importing Access data into Excel, or by exporting Access data into the worksheet. The method you choose to use will determine whether the data is linked and can be automatically updated from one program to another. An import will create a permanent connection between Excel and Access, while a simple copy and paste will not. Table 2 shows the results of various methods of sharing data between Access and Excel. In this section, you will import data from Access into Excel, create a chart from the imported data, and then link the chart to a slide in PowerPoint.

Sharing Data Between Access and Excel	Type of Connection	Results
To bring data into Excel from Access:		
Copy and paste	None	No connection between Excel and Access after the copy and paste
Import Access data into Excel (in Excel)	Permanent	Can refresh the data in Excel when changes are made in Access
Export Access data into an Excel worksheet (in Access)	None	No connection between Excel and Access, but export steps can be saved for future use
To bring data into Access from Excel:		
Copy and paste	None	No connection between Access and Excel after the copy and paste
Import an Excel worksheet into an Access datasheet (in Access)	None	No connection between Access and Excel
Link to an Excel worksheet from an Access table (in Access)	Permanent	Can refresh the data in Access when changes are made in Excel

Table 2   Sharing data between Access and Excel

Import Access Data into Excel

When you import data from an Access database into an Excel worksheet, a permanent connection is created, and when data is changed in the database, the data can be refreshed in the worksheet. If you use the Copy and Paste commands or export the Access data, you create a copy of the data that cannot be updated.

Creating a Chart with Imported Access Data

There may be times when you have data in Access and realize that the data could be shown better as a chart. Access does not have charting capabilities. If the chart is a one-time project and will not need to be updated, then a copy and paste of the data will be sufficient. However, if the data will be frequently updated in Access and will therefore require the chart to be updated also, a link would be a better option. In this exercise, you will import data from Access into Excel so when the data is changed in Access, the change is reflected in Excel.

 IP03.05

To Import Access Data into Excel

a. Start Excel, and then open **i01ch03ServeChart**. Maximize the Excel window if necessary.

b. Click the **File** tab, click **Save As**, and then double-click **This PC**. In the **Save As** dialog box, navigate to the location where you are saving your project files, and then change the file name to i01ch03ServeChart_LastFirst, using your last and first name. Click **Save**.

c. Make sure the **Satisfaction** worksheet tab is selected. Insert the **file name** in the left section of the footer, and then click **Save** 🖫.

d. Click cell **A3**. Click the **Data** tab, and then in the Get External Data group, click **From Access**.

e. Navigate to the folder where your student data files are located, select **i01ch03ServeSurvey**, and then click **Open**.

f. In the Select Table dialog box, select **qrySummary** if necessary, and then click **OK**. This selects the Access query that has the data you want to import to create the desired chart.

Figure 11   Select Table dialog box

g. In the Import Data dialog box, verify that **Table** is selected and that the Existing worksheet text box contains **=$A$3**. This tells Excel where to put the data table in the worksheet.

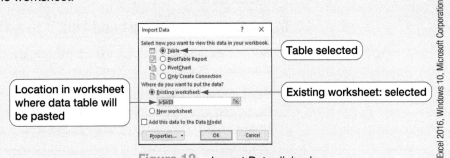

Figure 12   Import Data dialog box

h. Click **OK**. Select cells **B4:D6**. Click the **Home** tab, and then in the Number group, click **Decrease Decimal** until the numbers are formatted with only two decimal places. Click **Save**.

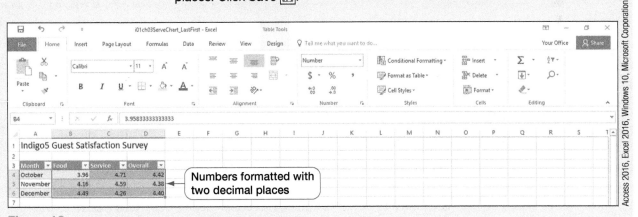

Figure 13   Data table from Access formatted in Excel

Linking an Excel Chart to a PowerPoint Presentation

After you have created a chart in Excel with Access data, you can use that chart in another program such as PowerPoint. If you link the chart to the presentation, then when the data is updated in Access, it can be refreshed in Excel and PowerPoint at the same time. In this exercise, you will link the Excel chart you create from the Access data to a slide in your PowerPoint presentation.

To Create an Excel Chart and Link it to a PowerPoint Slide

a. Select cells **A3:D6**. Click the **Insert** tab, and then in the Charts group, click **Insert Column or Bar Chart** , and then select 3-D Clustered Column.

b. Point to the **top left edge** of the chart. When your mouse pointer changes to a four-sided arrow , drag the **chart** so the **top left** corner is in cell **A8** and the **bottom right** corner is in or close to cell **G22**.

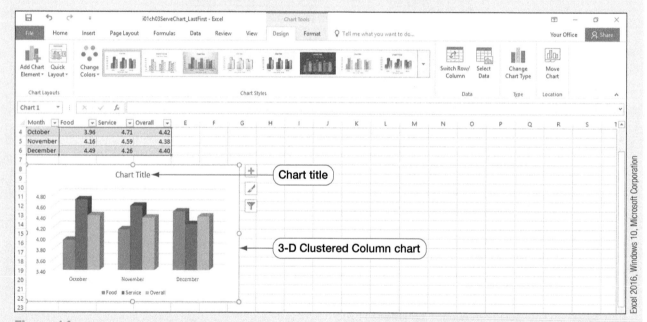

Figure 14 Column chart inserted

c. Click **Save** . With the chart still selected, click on the **Home** tab, and then in the Clipboard group, click **Copy** to copy the chart to the Clipboard.

d. Click **Minimize** to minimize the Excel window to the taskbar.

e. Click **PowerPoint** on the taskbar to restore the PowerPoint window. Click **Slide 4** to select it. On the Home tab, in the Clipboard group, click the **Paste** arrow, and then select **Paste Special**. Select **Paste link**, choose **Microsoft Excel Chart Object**, and then click **OK**.

Troubleshooting

If you close Excel before you paste the chart into PowerPoint, then Paste Special will give you only the option to Paste but not Paste link. If you closed Excel before you pasted the chart in this exercise, open Excel, copy the chart again, and keep Excel open while you paste the chart into PowerPoint.

f. Click **Excel** ⊞ on the taskbar to restore the Excel window. Select the **Chart Title** text, type Summary of Customer Surveys and press [Enter].

g. Click the **top border** of the chart to select it. Under Chart Tools, on the Design tab, in the Chart Styles group, click **Change Colors**, and then under Colorful, select **Color 4**.

h. Click the **Documentation** worksheet tab. Update the Documentation worksheet as directed by your instructor.

i. Click **Save** 🖫, and then click **Close** ✕ to close Excel.

j. Click **PowerPoint** 🖭 on the taskbar to restore the PowerPoint window. Click **Slide 4** if necessary. Note that the chart in the presentation now shows the chart title you added in Excel as well as the color change. Move the **chart** below the text. With the chart selected, under Drawing Tools, on the Format tab, in the Arrange group, click **Align Objects** 🖫, and then click **Align Center**.

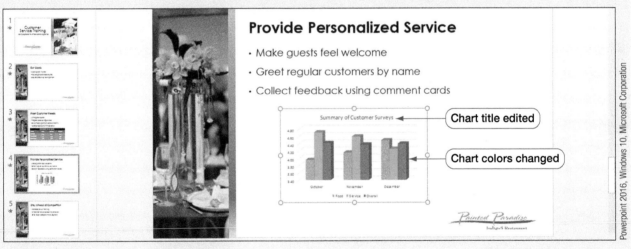

Figure 15   Chart updated in PowerPoint

k. Click **Save** 🖫, and then click **Close** ✕.

REAL WORLD ADVICE   Link, Embed, or Copy and Paste?

As you recall, the source file is the file from which the original data comes, and the destination file is the file to which the data is copied. When a chart is linked to an Excel worksheet, any changes in the worksheet are made to the linked chart as well. This is helpful if you are planning to change the data on a regular basis, such as for a monthly or quarterly report. If you do not plan on changing the original data but would like the option to make changes to the chart in the destination file, then you can embed the chart. This allows you to change layout, design, and formatting options of the chart in either the destination or the source file but not both. If you do not need that kind of flexibility, then copying and pasting is the simplest method for copying the chart from one file to another.

1. How is working in Outline view in Word different from working in Print Layout view? What is the advantage to being able to expand and collapse the different-level paragraphs in an outline? p. 1030

2. How do you prepare a Word outline so it can be imported into PowerPoint as slides? p. 1034

3. Why would you want to export Access data to Excel before using it in another application, such as PowerPoint? p. 1036

4. What is the difference between copying and pasting data from Access to Excel and exporting data from Access to Excel? Why would you copy and paste? When would you use an export? p. 1040

Key Terms

Body text 1030	Level 1 1030	Promote 1030
Collapse 1030	Level 2 1030	Reset 1030
Demote 1030	Outline 1030	
Expand 1030	Outline view 1030	

Visual Summary

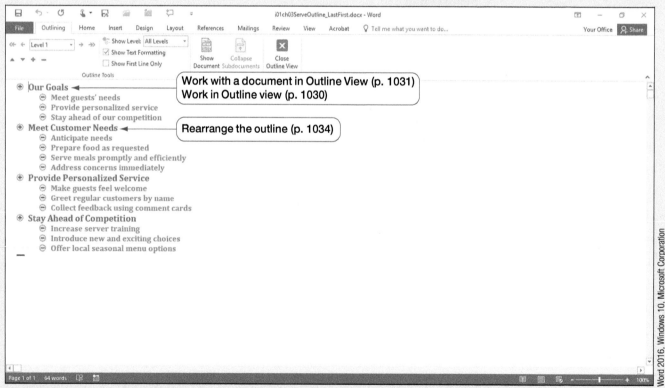

Work with a document in Outline View (p. 1031)
Work in Outline view (p. 1030)

Rearrange the outline (p. 1034)

Word 2016, Windows 10, Microsoft Corporation

Figure 16

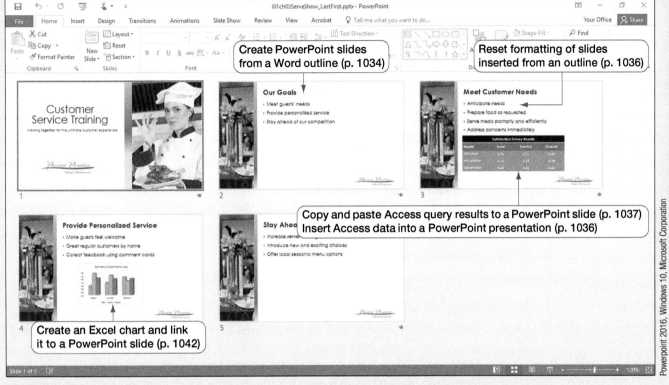

Figure 17

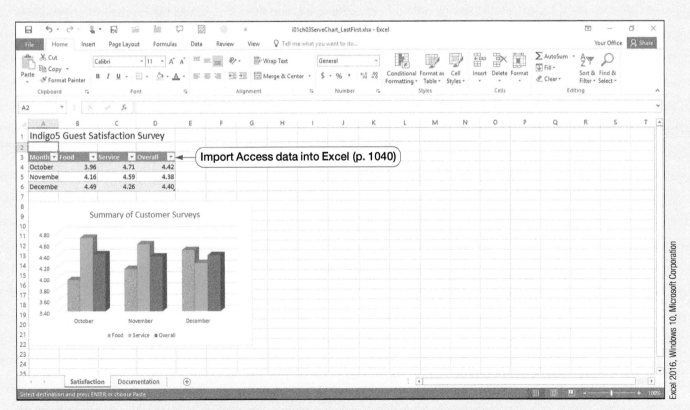

Figure 18

Student data files needed:

📄 i01ch03FundOutline.docx

📄 i01ch03FundShow.pptx

📄 i01ch03FundChart.xlsx

📄 i01ch03FundResult.accdb

You will save your files as:

📄 i01ch03FundOutline_LastFirst.docx

📄 i01ch03FundShow_LastFirst.pptx

📄 i01ch03FundChart_LastFirst.xlsx

Auction Fundraiser

Finance &
Accounting

Patti Rochelle, corporate event planner, has been asked to put together a presentation to summarize the recent auction fundraiser her group has coordinated. She has put together an outline in Word and an Access database with donor information. Your assignment is to use the Word outline to create PowerPoint slides and then to import Access data into Excel to create charts to include in the presentation.

a. Start Word, and then open **i01ch03FundOutline**. Maximize the Word window if necessary.

b. Click the **File** tab, click **Save As**, and then double-click **This PC**. In the **Save As** dialog box, navigate to the location where you are saving your project files, and then change the file name to i01ch03FundOutline_LastFirst, using your last and first name. Click **Save**. Insert a **left-aligned footer** with the file name.

c. Click the **View** tab, and then in the Views group, click **Outline**. Select **all the lines of text**, and then click **Promote** so all lines are promoted to Level 1. Demote all lines except **Gold Level Donations**, **Silver Level Donations**, **Major Donors**, and **Donor Summary**. In the Close group, click **Close Outline View** to return to Print Layout view. Save the document, and then close Word.

d. Start PowerPoint, and then open i01ch03FundShow.

e. Click the **File** tab, click **Save As**, and then navigate to the location where you are saving your project files. Change the file name to i01ch03FundShow_LastFirst, using your last and first name, and then click **Save**.

f. On the Home tab, in the Slides group, click the **New Slide** arrow, and then select **Slides from Outline**. Locate the folder where you are saving your project files, select **i01ch03FundOutline_LastFirst**, and then click **Insert**.

g. Click **Slide 2**, hold down [Shift], and then click **Slide 5** to select the four slides. On the Home tab, in the Slides group, click **Reset**.

h. Insert the **file name** in a footer on **Notes and Handouts**, click **Apply to All**, and then click **Save**. Click **Minimize** to minimize the PowerPoint window to the taskbar.

i. Start **Excel**, and then open **i01ch03FundChart**. Maximize the Excel window if necessary.

j. Click the **File** tab, click **Save As**, and then navigate to the location where you are saving your project files. Change the file name to i01ch03FundChart_LastFirst, using your last and first name. Click **Save**. Insert the **file name** in the left section of the footer.

k. Click cell **A4**. Click the **Data** tab, and then in the Get External Data group, click **From Access**. Navigate to the location of your student data files, select **i01ch03FundResult**, and then click **Open**.

l. In the Select Table dialog box, select **qrySummary**, and then click **OK**. In the Import Data dialog box, verify that **Table** is selected and that the Existing worksheet text box contains =$A$4. Click **OK**.

m. Select cells **B5:E7**. Click the **Home** tab, and then in the Number group, click **Accounting Number Format** to format the numbers with a dollar sign and two decimal places.

n. Select cells **A4:B7**. Click the **Insert** tab, and in the Charts group, click **Insert Pie or Doughnut Chart**, and then under the 3-D Pie category, select **3-D Pie**. Move the chart so the **top left** corner is in cell **A9** and the **bottom right** corner is in or close to cell **E23**.

o. Select the **chart**, and then change the chart title to Summary of Donor Values. Under Chart Tools, on the Design tab, in the Chart Styles group, click **Change Colors**, and then select **Color 2**. In the Chart Layouts group, click the **Add Chart Element** arrow, point to **Data Labels**, and then select **Best Fit**. Click **Save**.

p. If requested by your instructor, update the **Documentation** worksheet to reflect the changes that have been made, and then save the workbook.

q. Click the **Summary** worksheet tab if necessary. Select the **chart**. Click the **Home** tab, and then in the Clipboard group, click **Copy**.

r. Click **PowerPoint** on the taskbar to restore the PowerPoint window. Click **Slide 5** to select it. On the Home tab, in the Slides group, click the **Layout** arrow, and then select **Title Only**. In the Clipboard group, click the **Paste** arrow, and then select **Paste Special**. Click **Paste link**, select **Microsoft Excel Chart Object**, and then click **OK**.

s. With the chart selected, under Drawing Tools, on the Format tab, in the Size group, increase the **Shape Height** to 4". Save the presentation, and then close PowerPoint, saving changes if prompted. Close Excel. Submit your files as directed by your instructor.

Practice 2

Student data files needed:

🔲 i01ch03GuestOutline.docx

🔲 i01ch03GuestShow.pptx

🔲 i01ch03GuestList.accdb

You will save your files as:

🔲 i01ch03GuestOutline_LastFirst.docx

🔲 i01ch03GuestShow_LastFirst.pptx

Marriage Presentation

Customer Service

The staff in Event Planning has been asked to create a short PowerPoint presentation to celebrate an upcoming marriage. The bride and groom have given Patti Rochelle, corporate event planner, a Word outline listing topics they want in the presentation. The presentation will run continuously in an alcove during the reception. The guest list has been maintained in an Access database. Your assignment is to create a PowerPoint presentation from the Word outline and insert a query table into the presentation to show how many guests, by state, will be at the ceremony.

a. Start Word, and then open **i01ch03GuestOutline**. Maximize the Word window if necessary.

b. Click the **File** tab, click **Save As**, and then navigate to the location where you are saving your project files. Change the file name to i01ch03GuestOutline_LastFirst, using your last and first name. Click **Save**. Insert a **left-aligned footer** with the file name.

c. Click the **View** tab, and then in the Views group, click **Outline**. Select **all the lines of text**, and then click **Promote** so all the lines are promoted to Level 1. Demote all lines except **The Bride**, **The Groom**, **The Bridal Party**, and **Our Guests**. Click **Close Outline View** to return to Print Layout view. Click **Save**, and then close Word.

d. Start **PowerPoint**, and then open **i01ch03GuestShow**.

e. Click the **File** tab, click **Save As**, and then navigate to the location where you are saving your project files. Change the file name to i01ch03GuestShow_LastFirst, using your last and first name. Click **Save**.

f. On the Home tab, in the Slides group, click the **New Slide** arrow, and then select **Slides from Outline**. Navigate to the location where you are saving your files, select **i01ch03GuestOutline_LastFirst**, and then click **Insert**.

g. Click **Slide 2**, hold down Shift, and then click **Slide 5** to select the four slides. On the Home tab, in the Slides group, click **Reset**. With the slides still selected, click **Layout**, and then select **Title and Content**. Click Save, and then click Minimize to minimize the PowerPoint window to the taskbar.

h. Start **Access**, and then open **i01ch03GuestList**. If necessary, click **Enable Content** in the SECURITY WARNING bar.

i. In the Navigation Pane, double-click the query **qryStates** to open it in Datasheet view. Click **Select All** at the top left corner of the query datasheet to select all the records in the query datasheet. On the Home tab, in the Clipboard group, click **Copy**. Close Access.

j. Click **PowerPoint** on the taskbar to restore the PowerPoint window. Click **Slide 5** to select it. On the Home tab, in the Slides group, click the **Layout** arrow, and then select **Two Content**. Click the **right** placeholder, and then in the Clipboard group, click **Paste**.

k. With the table selected, on the Home tab, in the Font group, click the **Font Size** arrow, and then select **14**. Replace the title **qryStates** with **Home States of Guests**, and then increase the font size of the title to **16**. Resize the columns, starting with the column on the left. Center the title and column headings. Center the number of guests under the column **Guests**. Align the table so it is centered in the right area of the slide.

l. Select the **table**. Under Table Tools, on the Design tab, in the Table Styles group, select the **Light Style 1 - Accent 3** style to apply the style to the table.

m. In the left placeholder, click in front of **Jill**. On the Home tab, in the Paragraph group, click **Bullets** to remove the bullet, and then in the Paragraph group, click **Align Right** to move the names to the right side of the placeholder. Select the text **Jill and John**, and then in the Font group, click **Italic**. Save the presentation, and then close PowerPoint. Submit your files as directed by your instructor.

Problem Solve 1

Student data files needed:

 i01ch03BoardOutline.docx

i01ch03BoardShow.pptx

i01ch03BoardList.accdb

You will save your files as:

i01ch03BoardOutline_LastFirst.docx

i01ch03BoardShow_LastFirst.pptx

i01ch03BoardChart_LastFirst.xlsx

Sales Presentation

Finance & Accounting

The manager of Painted Treasures Gift Shop needs to give a sales presentation to the resort's board of directors each month. There is an existing Access database with information on items sold as well as a Word outline with the basic information for the presentation. Your assignment is to create a PowerPoint presentation from the Word outline, copy Access query results into the presentation, and finally, import the Access data into Excel to create a chart to include on one of the slides.

a. Start Word, and then open **i01ch03BoardOutline**. Save the file to your project folder with the file name i01ch03BoardOutline_LastFirst, using your last and first name.

b. In Outline view, promote and demote the paragraphs so **January Trends**, **January Sales by Category**, and **February Strategy** are all Level 1 paragraphs. The other paragraphs should all be Level 2. Close Outline view, save the file, and then close Word.

c. Start **PowerPoint**, and then open **i01ch03BoardShow**. Save the presentation as i01ch03BoardShow_LastFirst, using your last and first name. Insert new slides using the file **i01ch03BoardOutline_LastFirst**. Reset the new slides that you inserted. Insert the **file name** in a footer on **Notes and Handouts**, click **Apply to All**, and then click **Save**.

d. Start **Excel**, open a new blank workbook, and then save it to your student folder as i01ch03BoardChart_LastFirst, using your last and first name. Save the workbook.

e. Get external data from the query **qryJanuarySales** in the Access database **i01ch03BoardList**. Insert the table in cell **A1**, and then format cells **B2:B9** with the **Accounting** format. Create a **3-D Clustered Column** chart from the data table. Delete the chart title, which will not be needed because the title of the slide explains what the data represents. Change the color of the chart to **Color 3** and apply the **Style 12** chart style. Move the chart below the data table. Save the workbook.

f. Copy the **column chart** to the Clipboard. In the PowerPoint presentation, select **Slide 3**, and change the layout of the slide to Title Only. Paste the **Excel chart** as a link to the slide. Increase the size of the chart so it fits well on the slide and would be visible to the audience in the back of the room. Align the chart so it fits well on the slide and all text is visible. Save the presentation, and then minimize PowerPoint.

g. Start **Access**, open **i0ch03BoardList**, and then click **Enable Content**. Copy the **qryJanuarySales** query results to the Clipboard, and then close Access.

h. In the PowerPoint presentation, change the layout of **Slide 2** to **Two Content**. Paste the **table** on the right side of the slide. Increase the font size, replace the title, and then resize the columns. Apply a style to the table, and then make any additional formatting changes to improve the appearance of the table. Align the table so it fits well on the slide and all the text is visible. Save the presentation, and then close PowerPoint. Submit your files as directed by your instructor.

Problem Solve 2

Student data files needed:

📄 i01ch03TrendOutline.docx

📄 i01ch03TrendShow.pptx

📄 i01ch03TrendData.accdb

You will save your files as:

📄 i01ch03TrendOutline_LastFirst.docx

📄 i01ch03TrendShow_LastFirst.pptx

📄 i01ch03TrendCharts_LastFirst.xlsx

New Gift Items

Sales & Marketing

The manager and staff of the Painted Treasures Gift Shop have been brainstorming to find ways to expand inventory and increase sales. They have been researching trends in the gift shop industry and have developed several different possibilities. They want to create a presentation for Painted Paradise management detailing their ideas. Data has been kept in an Access database with information about potential new items, wholesale cost, and suggested sale price. There is also an outline in Word showing the topics they would like to cover. Your assignment is to create a PowerPoint presentation from the Word outline, import the Access data into Excel, and then create charts for the presentation.

a. Start Word, and then open **i01ch03TrendOutline**. Save the file to your project folder with the file name i01ch03TrendOutline_LastFirst, using your last and first name.

b. Using **Outline** view, promote and demote the paragraphs so **Luxuries and indulgences**, **Green Products**, and **Soft Goods** are all Level 1 paragraphs. The other paragraphs should all be Level 2. Close Outline view, save the file, and then close Word.

c. Start **PowerPoint**, and then open **i01ch03TrendShow**. Save the presentation as i01ch03TrendShow_LastFirst, using your last and first name. Note that the manager has already created two slides. Click **Slide 2** to select it, and then insert new slides from **i01ch03TrendOutline_LastFirst**. Reset the new slides that you inserted. Click **Save** and then minimize PowerPoint.

d. Start **Excel**, open a new blank workbook, and then save it as i01ch03TrendCharts_LastFirst, using your last and first name.

e. Import data from the Access database **i01ch03TrendData** by importing the datasheets from the three queries: **qryLuxuries**, **qryGreenProducts**, and **qrySoftGoods**. Use a separate worksheet for each datasheet, and name the worksheet tabs appropriately.

f. Format numbers on all worksheets as **Currency**. Insert a line chart using the **Line with Markers** style on each worksheet showing the cost and retail price for each item in that category. Move the chart under the data. Change the chart titles to match the name of the categories, and then save the workbook.

g. If requested by your instructor, add the **Documentation** worksheet, and then complete it to reflect the changes that have been made. Save the workbook.

h. Copy each chart and paste it on the corresponding slide in the PowerPoint presentation. Move each chart so it fits well on the slide and all text is visible. Increase the font size on the charts if necessary. Save the presentation and then close PowerPoint. Close Excel. Submit your files as directed by your instructor.

Perform 1: Perform in Your Career

Student data files needed:

- Blank Word document
- Blank Excel workbook
- Blank Access database
- Blank PowerPoint presentation

You will save your files as:

- i01ch03GrantOutline_LastFirst.docx
- i01ch03GrantShow_LastFirst.pptx
- i01ch03GrantRatio_LastFirst.accdb
- i01ch03GrantChart_LastFirst.xlsx

Grant Presentation

Information
Technology

You are the principal of a new and innovative high school, and you are looking for ways to increase the technology available to your students. You have learned of a grant that would pay for tablets for each student to use during the school year. You would like your school to become a leader in technology, and you have Access data that shows how most schools are lacking in this area. Along with writing the grant proposal, you need to create a presentation for the school board with the grant proposal information. The project name is Technology Grant Proposal. The grant presentation must include the following information:

- An introduction to your school with background information and a mission statement
- A problem statement that identifies the problems the project will address
- A comparison of student-to-computer ratios of area schools
- A project summary of what your school will need
- A list of key benefits the project will provide your school
- A budget for the project

a. Start Word, and then create a Word outline that will eventually become your PowerPoint slides. You must include the bulleted information above in your presentation. There should be Level 1 and Level 2 paragraphs for each slide. Save the document with the file name i01ch03GrantOutline_LastFirst, using your last and first name. Save the document and then close Word.

b. Start **PowerPoint**, and then create slides from the Word outline you created in step a. Add a title and subtitle to the presentation on Slide 1. Apply a theme to the presentation. Save the presentation with the file name i01ch03GrantShow_LastFirst, using your last and first name.

c. Start **Access**, and then create a new database called i01ch03GrantRatio_LastFirst, using your last and first name. Add the following fields after the ID field: School Name, School Enrollment, and Computer Ratio. Add at least 12 records to fill in this table. The first record should have your first and last name as the School Name, followed by HS. The records should show that the maximum Computer Ratio is 4:1. That is, all records should be 4:1, 5:1, or higher. Save the database.

d. Copy all the records in the Access table, and then paste the data sheet into an appropriate slide in your PowerPoint presentation. You will need to Resize the columns, apply a style to the table, and then save the presentation.

e. Start **Excel**, and then create a budget for the project. Assume that there are 426 students. Include the cost of the tablet, the cost of any additional hardware or software, and the estimated cost of maintenance per student and for the total project. Create a chart for the data. Save the workbook with the file name i01ch03GrantChart_LastFirst, using your last and first name. Insert the file name in the left section of the footer.

f. If requested by your instructor, add the Documentation worksheet, and then complete it to reflect the changes made.

g. Link the Excel data and the chart to a slide in your PowerPoint presentation. Save the workbook, and then close Excel.

h. Save the PowerPoint presentation. Close all applications. Submit your files as directed by your instructor.

Perform 2: How Others Perform

Student data files needed:

 i01ch03ClassShow.pptx

 i01ch03ClassOutline.docx

i01ch03ClassList.accdb

You will save your files as:

 i01ch03ClassOutline_LastFirst.docx

 i01ch03ClassShow_LastFirst.pptx

 i01ch03ClassCharts_LastFirst.xlsx

Productions & Operations

Presentation Gone Wrong

The local university offers special classes for people who are 50 years old or more. Some of the classes last only one day; others span several weeks. Various excursions are also offered that could be day trips or might extend over a weekend. Your friend works in the Continuing Education office and has put together a presentation to show how many students have signed up for these classes. He created an outline in Word and tried to create PowerPoint slides using the Slides from Outline feature, but he ended up with a slide for each class instead of a slide for each type of class. The types of classes are One Day Classes, Multi-Week Courses, and Excursions. When students register, their data is entered in an Access database. Queries have been created to track the number of students in each class and in each type of class. Your friend would like to import this data into Excel to create charts, but he cannot do that until he corrects the presentation. He has asked for your help.

a. Start PowerPoint, and then open **i01ch03ClassShow**. Examine the way the slides were created from the Word outline. Close PowerPoint.

b. Start **Word**, and then open **i01ch03ClassOutline**. Save the file as i01ch03ClassOutline_LastFirst, using your last and first name.

c. Edit the outline so the three types of classes will be the titles on three different slides and the class names will be the details on each slide. Save the document, and then close Word.

d. Start **PowerPoint**, open a new presentation, and then save it as i01ch03ClassShow_LastFirst, using your last and first name. Insert slides from the outline **i01ch03ClassOutline_LastFirst**. There should be a title slide and three slides from the Word outline. Add an appropriate title and subtitle to Slide 1. Save the presentation, and then minimize PowerPoint.

e. Start **Excel**, open a new workbook, and then save it as i01ch03ClassCharts_LastFirst, using your last and first name. Change the orientation to **Landscape** and change the width to **1 page**. Save the workbook.

f. Import data from the Access database **i01ch03ClassList** by importing the datasheets from the three queries: qryOneDay, qryMultiWeek, and qryExcursions. Use a separate worksheet for each datasheet and name the worksheet tabs appropriately. Create a column chart on each worksheet showing the number of students enrolled for each type of class. Change the chart titles to match the names of the worksheets, and then save the workbook.

g. If requested by your instructor, add the Documentation worksheet, and then complete to reflect the changes that have been made. Save the workbook.

h. Click **PowerPoint** on the taskbar to restore the PowerPoint window. Link each chart to the appropriate slide in the PowerPoint presentation. Move and size each chart, if necessary, so it fits attractively on the slide. Apply a Design theme that coordinates with the colors of the charts. Save the presentation, and then close PowerPoint. Close Excel. Submit your files as directed by your instructor.

Additional
Cases

Additional Chapter Cases are available at www.pearsonhighered.com/youroffice

Online materials can be found in the Student Resources located at www.pearsonhighered.com/youroffice.

Microsoft Office Specialist Word 2016 (Core)			
Chapter	MOS Obj #	Objective	Your Office Heading
1	**Create and Manage Documents**		
	1.1	**Create a Document**	
Ch1	1.1.1	Create a Blank Document	Create a New Document
Online	1.1.2	Create a Blank Document Using a Template	
Online	1.1.3	Open a PDF in Word for Editing	
Ch3	1.1.4	Insert Text from a File or External Source	Insert Text from Another Document
	1.2	**Navigate Through a Document**	
Ch2	1.2.1	Search for Text	Proofread a Document
Online	1.2.2	Insert Hyperlinks	
Online	1.2.3	Create Bookmarks	
Online	1.2.4	Move to a Specific Location or Object in a Document	
	1.3	**Format a Document**	
Ch4	1.3.1	Modify Page Setup	Change Page Setup
Ch3	1.3.2	Apply Document Themes	Use Themes
Online	1.3.3	Apply Document Style Sets	
Ch4	1.3.4	Insert Headers and Footers	Insert a Header and Footer
Ch2	1.3.5	Insert Page Numbers	
Online	1.3.6	Format Page Background Elements	
	1.4	**Customize Options and Views for Documents**	
Ch2	1.4.1	Change Document Views	Explore the Word Interface
Ch4	1.4.2	Customize Views by Using Zoom Settings	Insert and Delete Text
Online	1.4.3	Customize the Quick Access Toolbar	
Ch1	1.4.4	Split the Window	Split the Window
Ch1	1.4.5	Add Document Properties	Insert and Delete Text
Ch1	1.4.6	Show or Hide Formatting Marks	Explore the Word Interface
	1.5	**Print and Save Documents**	
Ch1	1.5.1	Modify Print Settings	Print a Document
Ch1	1.5.2	Save Documents in Alternative File Formats	Save and Close a Document
Ch1	1.5.3	Print All or Part of a Document	Print a Document
Online	1.5.4	Inspect a Document for Hidden Properties or Personal Information	
Online	1.5.5	Inspect a Document for Accessibility Issues	
Online	1.5.6	Inspect a Document for Compatibility Issues	

Microsoft Office Specialist Word 2016 (Core)			
Chapter	**MOS Obj #**	**Objective**	**Your Office Heading**
2	**Format Text, Paragraphs, and Sections**		
	2.1	**Insert Text and Paragraphs**	
Ch2	2.1.1	Find and Replace Text	Proofread a Document
Ch1	2.1.2	Cut, Copy and Paste Text	Create a New Document
Ch2	2.1.3	Replace Text by Using AutoCorrect	Proofread a Document
Ch1	2.1.4	Insert Special Characters	Add Bullets, Numbers, and Symbols
	2.2	**Format Text and Paragraphs**	
Ch1	2.2.1	Apply Font Formatting	Format Characters
Online	2.2.2	Apply Formatting by Using Format Painter	
Ch4	2.2.3	Set Line and Paragraph Spacing and Indentation	Working with Paragraph Spacing
Online	2.2.4	Clear Formatting	
Online	2.2.5	Apply a Text Highlight Color to Text Selections	
Ch1	2.2.6	Apply Built-in Styles to Text	Understand Word Styles
Ch3	2.2.7	Change Text to WordArt	Use WordArt
	2.3	**Order and Group Text and Paragraphs**	
Ch4	2.3.1	Format Text in Multiple Columns	Work with Columns
Ch4	2.3.2	Insert Page, Section, or Column Breaks	Work with Columns
Online	2.3.3	Change Page Setup Options for a Section	
3	**Create Tables and Lists**		
	3.1	**Create a Table**	
Ch3	3.1.1	Convert Text to Tables	Create a Table
Online	3.1.2	Convert Tables to Text	
Ch3	3.1.3	Create a Table by Specifying Rows and Columns	Create a Table
Ch3	3.1.4	Apply Table Styles	Create a Table
	3.2	**Modify a Table**	
Ch3	3.2.1	Sort Table Data	Create a Table
Online	3.2.2	Configure Cell Margins and Spacing	
Ch3	3.2.3	Merge and Split Cells	Create a Table
Ch3	3.2.4	Resize Tables, Rows, and Columns	Create a Table
Online	3.2.5	Split Tables	
Online	3.2.6	Configure a Repeating Row Header	
	3.3	**Create and Modify a List**	
Online	3.3.1	Create a Numbered or Bulleted List	
Online	3.3.2	Change Bullet Characters or Number Formats for a List Level	
Online	3.3.3	Define a Custom Bullet Character or Number Format	
Ch2	3.3.4	Increase or Decrease List Levels	
Online	3.3.5	Restart or Continue List Numbering	
Online	3.3.6	Set Starting Number Value	

Microsoft Office Specialist Word 2016 (Core)			
Chapter	MOS Obj #	Objective	Your Office Heading
4	**Create and Manage References**		
	4.1	**Create and Manage Reference Markers**	
Ch2	4.1.1	Insert Footnotes and Endnotes	Format a Research Report
Online	4.1.2	Modify Footnote and Endnote Properties	
Ch2	4.1.3	Create Bibliography Citation Sources	Develop a Bibliography or Works Cited Page
Online	4.1.4	Modify Bibliography Citation Sources	
Ch2	4.1.5	Insert Citations for Bibliographies	
Online	4.1.6	Insert Figure and Table Captions	
Online	4.1.7	Modify Caption Properties	
	4.2	**Create and Manage Simple References**	
Online	4.2.1	Insert a Standard Table of Contents	
Online	4.2.2	Update a Table of Contents	
Online	4.2.3	Insert a Cover Page	
5	**Insert and Format Graphic Elements**		
	5.1	**Insert Graphic Elements**	
Online	5.1.1	Insert Shapes	Insert Simple Shapes
Ch2	5.1.2	Insert Pictures	Insert Graphics
Ch1	5.1.3	Insert a Screen Shot or Screen Clipping	
Ch3	5.1.4	Insert Text Boxes	Insert a Text Box
	5.2	**Format Graphic Elements**	
Ch3	5.2.1	Apply Artistic Effects	Insert Graphics
Ch3	5.2.2	Apply Picture Effects	Insert Graphics
			Apply Picture Effects
Online	5.2.3	Remove Picture Backgrounds	
Ch3	5.2.4	Format Objects	
Ch3	5.2.5	Apply a Picture Style	Add Quick Styles to Images
Ch3	5.2.6	Wrap Text Around Objects	Insert Graphics
Ch3	5.2.7	Position Objects	Work with Columns
Online	5.2.8	Add Alternative Text to Objects for Accessibility	
	5.3	**Insert and Format SmartArt Graphics**	
Ch4	5.3.1	Create a SmartArt Graphic	Create SmartArt
Ch4	5.3.2	Format a SmartArt Graphic	Create SmartArt
Ch4	5.3.3	Modify SmartArt Graphic Content	Create SmartArt

Microsoft Office Specialist Excel 2016 (Core)			
Chapter	MOS Obj #	Objective	Your Office Heading
1		**Create and Manage Worksheets and Workbooks**	
	1.1	**Create Worksheets and Workbooks**	
Ch1	1.1.1	Create a Workbook	Creating a New Workbook
Online	1.1.2	Import Data from a Delimited Text File	Import Files
Ch1	1.1.3	Add a Worksheet to an Existing Workbook	Deleting, Inserting, Renaming, and Coloring Worksheet Tabs
Ch1	1.1.4	Copy and Move a Worksheet	Moving or Copying a Worksheet
	1.2	**Navigate in Worksheets and Workbooks**	
Online	1.2.1	Search for Data within a Workbook	Find and Replace Data
Ch1	1.2.2	Navigate to a Named Cell, Range, or Workbook Element	Navigating Between Worksheets
Online	1.2.3	Insert and Remove Hyperlinks	Insert Hyperlinks
	1.3	**Format Worksheets and Workbooks**	
Ch1	1.3.1	Change Worksheet Tab Color	Deleting, Inserting, Renaming, and Coloring Worksheet Tabs
Ch1	1.3.2	Rename a Worksheet	Deleting, Inserting, Renaming, and Coloring Worksheet Tabs
Ch1	1.3.3	Change Worksheet Order	Moving or Copying a Worksheet
Ch1	1.3.4	Modify Page Setup	Changing Page Orientation and Print Range
Ch1	1.3.5	Insert and Delete Columns or Rows	Inserting and Deleting Columns or Rows
Ch2	1.3.6	Change Workbook Themes	Changing Themes
Ch1	1.3.7	Adjust Row Height and Column Width	Adjusting Column Width and Row Height
Ch1	1.3.8	Insert Headers and Footers	Adding Headers and Footers
	1.4	**Customize Options and Views for Worksheets and Workbooks**	
Online	1.4.1	Hide or Unhide Worksheets	
Ch2	1.4.2	Hide or Unhide Columns and Rows	Hiding Worksheet Rows
Online	1.4.3	Customize the Quick Access Toolbar	
Ch1	1.4.4	Change Workbook Views	Using Worksheet Views
Online	1.4.5	Change Window Views	
Online	1.4.6	Modify Document Properties	
Ch2	1.4.7	Change Magnification by Using Zoom Tools	Showing Functions and Formulas
Ch2	1.4.8	Display Formulas	Showing Functions and Formulas
	1.5	**Configure Worksheets and Workbooks for Distribution**	
Ch1	1.5.1	Set a Print Area	Changing Page Orientation and Print Range
Ch1	1.5.2	Save Workbooks in Alternative File Formats	Exporting a Workbook to PDF
Ch1	1.5.3	Print All or Part of a Workbook	Using Print Preview and Printer Selection
Ch1	1.5.4	Set Print Scaling	Changing Page Margins and Scaling
Ch1	1.5.5	Display Repeating Row and Column Titles on Multipage Worksheets	Using Print Titles
Online	1.5.6	Inspect a Workbook for Hidden Properties or Personal Information	
Online	1.5.7	Inspect a Workbook for Accessibility Issues	
Online	1.5.8	Inspect a Workbook for Compatibility Issues	

Microsoft Office Specialist Excel 2016 (Core)			
Chapter	**MOS Obj #**	**Objective**	**Your Office Heading**
2	**Manage Data Cells and Ranges**		
	2.1	**Insert Data in Cells and Ranges**	
Ch1	2.1.1	Replace Data	Dragging and Dropping
			Modifying Cell Information
Ch1	2.1.2	Cut, Copy, or Paste Data	Cutting, Copying, and Pasting
Ch2	2.1.3	Paste Data by Using Special Paste Options	Using Paste Options/Paste Special
Ch1	2.1.4	Fill Cells by Using AutoFill	Using Series (AutoFill)
Ch1	2.1.5	Insert and Delete Cells	Inserting and Deleting Cells, Clearing Cells, and Cell Ranges
	2.2	**Format Cells and Ranges**	
Ch1	2.2.1	Merge Cells	Merging and Centering Versus Centering Across
Ch2	2.2.2	Modify Cell Alignment and Indentation	Aligning Cell Content
Ch2	2.2.3	Format Cells by Using Format Painter	Copying Formats
Ch1	2.2.4	Wrap Text within Cells	Wrapping Text and Line Breaks
Ch2	2.2.5	Apply Number Formats	Number Formatting
Ch2	2.2.6	Apply Cell Formats	Number Formatting
Ch2	2.2.7	Apply Cell Styles	Using Built-In Cell Styles
	2.3	**Summarize and Organize Data**	
Ch4	2.3.1	Insert Sparklines	Exploring Sparklines
Online	2.3.2	Outline Data	Create Outlines
			Collapse Groups of Data in Outlines
Ch2	2.3.3	Insert Subtotals	Using Tables and the Total Row
Ch2	2.3.4	Apply Conditional Formatting	Highlighting Values in a Range with Conditional Formatting
3	**Create Tables**		
	3.1	**Create and Manage Tables**	
Ch2	3.1.1	Create an Excel Table from a Cell Range	Applying Table Styles
Ch2	3.1.2	Convert a Table to a Cell Range	Applying Table Styles
Online	3.1.3	Add or Remove Table Rows and Columns	
	3.2	**Manage Table Styles and Options**	
Ch2	3.2.1	Apply Styles to Tables	Applying Table Styles
Ch2	3.2.2	Configure Table Style Options	Applying Table Styles
Ch2	3.2.3	Insert Total Rows	Using Tables and the Total Row
	3.3	**Filter and Sort a Table**	
Ch2	3.3.1	Filter Records	Using Tables and the Total Row
Online	3.3.2	Sort Data by Multiple Columns	Sort Data on Multiple Columns
Online	3.3.3	Change Sort Order	Applying Table Styles
Online	3.3.4	Remove Duplicate Records	Remove Duplicates
4	**Perform Operations with Formulas and Functions**		
	4.1	**Summarize Data by Using Functions**	
Ch3	4.1.1	Insert References	Using Relative Cell Referencing
			Using Absolute Cell Referencing
			Using Mixed Cell Referencing

Microsoft Office Specialist Excel 2016 (Core)			
Chapter	MOS Obj #	Objective	Your Office Heading
Ch2	4.1.2	Perform Calculations by Using the SUM Function	Using the SUM Function by Selecting Destination Cells
Ch2	4.1.3	Perform Calculations by Using MIN and MAX Functions	Using MIN and MAX
Ch2	4.1.4	Perform Calculations by Using the COUNT Function	Using COUNT and AVERAGE
Ch2	4.1.5	Perform Calculations by Using the AVERAGE Function	Using COUNT and AVERAGE
	4.2	**Perform Conditional Operations by Using Functions**	
Ch3	4.2.1	Perform Logical Operations by Using the IF Function	Using Logical Functions
Online	4.2.2	Perform Logical Operations by Using the SUMIF Function	The SUMIF Function
Online	4.2.3	Perform Logical Operations by Using the AVERAGEIF Function	The AVERAGEIF Function
Online	4.2.4	Perform Statistical Operations by Using the COUNTIF Function	The COUNTIF Function
	4.3	**Format and Modify Text by Using Functions**	
Ch3	4.3.1	Format Text by Using RIGHT, LEFT, and MID Functions	Using Text Functions
Ch3	4.3.2	Format Text by Using UPPER, LOWER, and PROPER Functions	Using Text Functions
Ch3	4.3.3	Format Text by Using the CONCATENATE Function	Using Text Functions
5	**Create Charts and Objects**		
	5.1	**Create Charts**	
Ch4	5.1.1	Create a New Chart	Creating Charts in an Existing Worksheet
Online	5.1.2	Add Additional Data Series	Add a Data Series to a Chart
Ch4	5.1.3	Switch between Rows and Columns in Source Data	Correcting a Confusing Chart
Ch4	5.1.4	Analyze Data by Using Quick Analysis	Creating Pie Charts
	5.2	**Format Charts**	
Ch4	5.2.1	Resize Charts	Modifying a Chart's Position Properties
Ch4	5.2.2	Add and Modify Chart Elements	Modifying an Existing Chart
Ch4	5.2.3	Apply Chart Layouts and Styles	Creating Charts in an Existing Worksheet
			Changing the Data and Appearance of a Chart
Ch4	5.2.4	Move Charts to a Chart Sheet	Placing Charts on a Chart Sheet
	5.3	**Insert and Format Objects**	
Ch4	5.3.1	Insert Text Boxes and Shapes	Inserting Objects
Ch2	5.3.2	Insert Images	Inserting a Picture
Online	5.3.3	Modify Object Properties	Add Styles and Effects to Objects
			Adding Color to Chart Objects
Online	5.3.4	Add Alternative Text to Objects for Accessibility	

Microsoft Office Specialist Access 2016			
Chapter	**MOS Obj #**	**Objective**	**Your Office Heading**
1		**Create and Manage a Database**	
	1.1	**Create and Modify Databases**	
Ch1	1.1.1	Create a Blank Desktop Database	
Ch3	1.1.2	Create a Database from a Template	Using Quick Start Templates
Online	1.1.3	Create a Database by Using Import Objects or Data from Other Sources	Merge Databases
			Created Linked Tables from External Data Sources
Online	1.1.4	Delete Database Objects	Delete Tables, Queries, Forms, and Reports
	1.2	**Manage Relationships and Keys**	
Ch2	1.2.1	Create and Modify Relationships	Create a One-to-Many Relationship
			Create a Many-to-Many Relationship
Ch2	1.2.2	Set the Primary Key	Understand and Designate Keys
Ch2	1.2.3	Enforce Referential Integrity	Understand Referential Integrity
Ch2	1.2.4	Set Foreign Keys	Understand and Designate Keys
Ch2	1.2.5	View Relationships	Understand Relationships between Tables
	1.3	**Navigate Through a Database**	
Ch3	1.3.1	Navigate Specific Records	Understand the Purpose of Tables
Ch3	1.3.2	Create and Modify a Navigation Form	Use Navigation Forms
Ch3	1.3.3	Set a Form as the Startup Option	Set a Form as the Startup Option
Online	1.3.4	Display Objects in the Navigation Pane	Maneuver in the Navigation Pane
Ch1	1.3.5	Change Views of Objects	Maneuver in the Navigation Pane
	1.4	**Protect and Maintain Databases**	
Online	1.4.1	Compact a Database	Compact and Repair a Database
Online	1.4.2	Repair a Database	Compact and Repair a Database
Ch3	1.4.3	Back Up a Database	Back Up a Database
Online	1.4.4	Split a Database	Split a Database
Online	1.4.5	Encrypt a Database with a Password	Encrypt a Database with a Password
Online	1.4.6	Recover Data From Backup	
	1.5	**Print and Export Data**	
Ch4	1.5.1	Print Reports	Create a Report Using the Report Wizard
Online	1.5.2	Print Records	
Online	1.5.3	Save a Databases as a Template	Save Databases as Templates
Ch4	1.5.4	Export Objects to Alternative Formats	
2		**Build Tables**	
	2.1	**Create Tables**	
Ch2	2.1.1	Create a Table	Create a Table in Design View
Ch2	2.1.2	Import Data into Tables	Import Data from Other Sources
Ch2	2.1.3	Create Linked Tables from External Sources	
Ch3	2.1.4	Import Tables from other Databases	Understand the Purpose of Tables
Online	2.1.5	Create a Table from a Template with Application Parts	
	2.2	**Manage Tables**	
Ch1	2.2.1	Hide Fields in Tables	Hide Fields in Tables
Online	2.2.2	Add Total Rows	

Microsoft Office Specialist Access 2016			
Chapter	**MOS Obj #**	**Objective**	**Your Office Heading**
Online	2.2.3	Add Table Descriptions	
Online	2.2.4	Rename Tables	
	2.3	**Manage Records in Tables**	
Ch4	2.3.1	Update Records	Navigate and Edit Records in Datasheets
Ch1	2.3.2	Add Records	Understand the Purpose of Tables
Ch2	2.3.3	Delete Records	Enter Data Manually
Ch2	2.3.4	Append Records from External Data	Import Data from Other Sources
Ch3	2.3.5	Find and Replace Data	Find and Replace Records in the Datasheet
Ch3	2.3.6	Sort Records	Sort Table and Query Results
Ch3	2.3.7	Filter Records	Find and Replace Records in the Datasheet
	2.4	**Create and Modify Fields**	
Ch2	2.4.1	Add Fields to Tables	Understand Masks and Formatting
Ch3	2.4.2	Add Validation Rules to Fields	Add a Validation Rule to Fields
Online	2.4.3	Change Field Captions	Change Field Captions
Ch2	2.4.4	Change Field Sizes	Create a Table in Design View
Ch2	2.4.5	Change Field Data Types	Create a Table in Design View
Online	2.4.6	Configure Fields to Auto-Increment	Configure Fields to Auto-Increment
Online	2.4.7	Set Default Values	Set Default Values
Ch3	2.4.8	Using Input Masks	Understand Masks and Formatting
Online	2.4.9	Delete Fields	Enter Data Manually
3	**Create Queries**		
	3.1	**Create a Query**	
Ch1	3.1.1	Run a Query	Understand the Purpose of Queries
Online	3.1.2	Create a Crosstab Query	Create Crosstab Queries
Online	3.1.3	Create a Parameter Query	Create Parameter Queries
Online	3.1.4	Create an Action Query	Create Action Queries
Ch3	3.1.5	Create a Multi-Table Query	Create Queries in Design View
Ch3	3.1.6	Save a Query	Create Queries in Design View
	3.2	**Modify a Query**	
Online	3.2.1	Rename a Query	
Ch3	3.2.2	Add Fields	Create Queries in Design View
Online	3.2.3	Remove Fields	
Ch3	3.2.4	Hide Fields	Define Selection Criteria for Queries
Ch1	3.2.5	Sort Data Within Queries	Understand the Purpose of Queries
Ch3	3.2.6	Format Fields Within Queries	Create Aggregate Functions
	3.3	**Create Calculated Fields and Grouping within Queries**	
Ch3	3.3.1	Add Calculated Fields	Create Calculated Fields
Online	3.3.2	Set Filtering Criteria	Understand the Purpose of Queries
Ch3	3.3.3	Group and Summarize Data	Create Aggregate Functions
Ch3	3.3.4	Group Data by Using Comparison Operators	Define Selection Criteria for Queries
Ch3	3.3.5	Group Data by Using Arithmetic and Logical Operators	Define Selection Criteria for Queries
4	**Create Forms**		
	4.1	**Create a Form**	
Ch3	4.1.1	Create a Form	Understand the Purpose of Forms

Chapter	MOS Obj #	Objective	Your Office Heading
Online	4.1.2	Create a Form from a Template with Application Parts	Understanding Application Parts
Ch3	4.1.3	Save a Form	Understand the Purpose of Forms
	4.2	**Configure Form Controls**	
Ch3	4.2.1	Move Form Controls	
Online	4.2.2	Add Form Controls	
Online	4.2.3	Modify Data Sources	
Ch3	4.2.4	Remove Form Controls	
Ch3	4.2.5	Set Form Control Properties	
Ch3	4.2.6	Manage Labels	
Ch4	4.2.7	Add Sub-Forms	Create a Form Using the Form Wizard
	4.3	**Format a Form**	
Online	4.3.1	Modify Tab Order	Modify Tab Order in Forms
			Auto Order Forms
Online	4.3.2	Configure Print Settings	Modify a Form's Design
Online	4.3.3	Sort Records By Form Field	Sort Records
Online	4.3.4	Apply a Theme	Modify a Form's Design
Online	4.3.5	Control Form Positioning	
Online	4.3.6	Insert Backgrounds	Insert Backgrounds
Online	4.3.7	Insert Headers and Footers	Modify a Form's Design
Ch3	4.3.8	Insert Images	Modify a Form's Design
5	**Create Reports**		
	5.1	**Create a Report**	
Ch4	5.1.1	Create a Report Based on The Query or Table	Understand Referential Integrity
Online	5.1.2	Create a Report in Design View	
Ch4	5.1.3	Create a Report by Using a Wizard	Understand the Purpose of Reports
	5.2	**Configure Report Controls**	
Ch4	5.2.1	Group and Sort Fields	Customize a Report
Ch4	5.2.2	Modify Data Sources	Modify Data Sources
Ch4 Online	5.2.3	Add Report Controls	Create a Report Using the Report Wizard
			Add Report Controls
Ch4	5.2.4	Add and Modify Labels	Create a Report Using the Report Wizard
	5.3	**Format a Report**	
Ch4	5.3.1	Format a Report into Multiple Columns	Format Reports into Multiple Columns
Online	5.3.2	Add Calculated Fields	Create a Report Using the Report Wizard
Ch4	5.3.3	Control Report Positioning	
Ch4	5.3.4	Format Report Elements	Customize a Report
Ch4	5.3.5	Change Report Orientation	Create a Report Using the Report Wizard
Ch4	5.3.6	Insert Header and Footer Information	Create a Report Using the Report Wizard
Ch4	5.3.7	Insert Images	Insert Images
Ch4	5.3.8	Apply a Theme	

Microsoft Office Specialist PowerPoint 2016			
Chapter	MOS Obj #	Objective	Your Office Heading
1	**Create and Manage Presentations**		
	1.1	**Create a Presentation**	
Ch2	1.1.1	Create a New Presentation	Create a Custom Template Using the Slide Master
Ch2	1.1.2	Create a Presentation Based on a Template	Using a Template to Create a New Presentation
Ch2	1.1.3	Import Word Document Outlines	Develop a Presentation from a Custom Template and Outline
	1.2	**Insert and Format Slides**	
Ch1	1.2.1	Insert Specific Slide Layouts	Add, Reuse, and Rearrange Slides and Change Slide Layouts
Online	1.2.2	Duplicate Existing Slides	
Online	1.2.3	Hide and Unhide Slides	
Ch1	1.2.4	Delete Slides	Navigate in Slide Show View and Outline View
Ch1	1.2.5	Apply a Different Slide Layout	Add, Reuse, and Rearrange Slides and Change Slide Layouts
Ch2	1.2.6	Modify Individual Slide Backgrounds	Understand the Purpose and Benefits of Using Themes
Ch1	1.2.7	Insert Slide Headers, Footers, and Page Numbers	Understand the Purpose and Benefits of Using Themes
	1.3	**Modify Slides, Handouts, and Notes**	
Online	1.3.1	Change the Slide Master Theme or Background	
Online	1.3.2	Modify Slide Master Content	
Online	1.3.3	Create a Slide Layout	
Online	1.3.4	Modify a Slide Layout	
Online	1.3.5	Modify the Handout Master	
Online	1.3.6	Modify the Notes Master	
	1.4	**Order and Group Slides**	
Ch4	1.4.1	Create Sections	Use Slide Sections to Organize and Prepare a Presentation
Ch1	1.4.2	Modify Slide Order	
Ch4	1.4.3	Rename Sections	Use Slide Sections to Organize and Prepare a Presentation
	1.5	**Change Presentation Options and Views**	
Ch1	1.5.1	Change Slide Size	
Ch1	1.5.2	Change Views of a Presentation	Navigate in Slide Show View and Outline View
Online	1.5.3	Set File Properties	
	1.6	**Configure a Presentation for Print**	
Ch1	1.6.1	Print All or Part of a Presentation	Preview and Print a Presentation
Online	1.6.2	Print Notes Pages	
Ch1	1.6.3	Print Handouts	Preview and Print a Presentation
Ch1	1.6.4	Print in Color, Grayscale, or Black and White	Preview and Print a Presentation

Microsoft Office Specialist PowerPoint 2016

Chapter	MOS Obj #	Objective	Your Office Heading
	1.7	**Configure and Present a Slide Show**	
Online	1.7.1	Create Custom Slide Shows	
Online	1.7.2	Configure Slide Show Options	
Online	1.7.3	Rehearse Slide Show Timing	
Ch1	1.7.4	Present a Slide Show by Using Presenter View	Develop Skills in Delivering Presentations
2		**Insert and Format Text, Shapes, and Images**	
	2.1	**Insert and Format Text**	
Ch1	2.1.1	Insert Text on a Slide	Add, Reuse, and Rearrange Slides and Change Slide Layouts
Ch2	2.1.2	Apply Formatting and Styles to Text	Modify Text
Ch2	2.1.3	Apply WordArt Styles to Text	Work with Shape and Line Graphics
Online	2.1.4	Format Text in Multiple Columns	
Ch2	2.1.5	Create Bulleted and Numbered Lists	Use Text Hierarchy to Convey Organization
Online	2.1.6	Insert Hyperlinks	
	2.2	**Insert and Format Shapes and Text Boxes**	
Ch3	2.2.1	Insert or Replace Shapes	Work with Shape and Line Graphics
Ch3	2.2.2	Insert Text Boxes	Work with Shape and Line Graphics
Online	2.2.3	Resize Shapes and Text Boxes	
Ch3	2.2.4	Format Shapes and Text Boxes	Work with Shape and Line Graphics
Online	2.2.5	Apply Styles to Shapes and Text Boxes	
	2.3	**Insert and Format Images**	
Ch1	2.3.1	Insert Images	Work with Images and Art
Ch3	2.3.2	Resize and Crop Images	Work with Images and Art
Ch3	2.3.3	Apply Styles and Effects	Work with Images and Art
	2.4	**Order and Group Objects**	
Ch3	2.4.1	Order Objects	Work with Shape and Line Graphics
Ch3	2.4.2	Align Objects	Work with Shape and Line Graphics
Online	2.4.3	Group Objects	
Online	2.4.4	Display Alignment Tools	
3		**Insert Tables, Charts, SmartArt, and Media**	
	3.1	**Insert and Format Tables**	
Ch4	3.1.1	Create A Table	Create a Table
Ch4	3.1.2	Insert and Delete Table Rows and Columns	Create a Table
Ch4	3.1.3	Apply Table Styles	Create a Table
Online	3.1.4	Import a Table	Import Tables from External Sources
	3.2	**Insert and Format Charts**	
Ch4	3.2.1	Create a Chart	Create and Insert Charts
Online	3.2.2	Import a Chart	Import Charts from External Sources
Online	3.2.3	Change the Chart Type	
Ch4	3.2.4	Add a Legend to a Chart	Create and Insert Charts
Online	3.2.5	Change the Chart Style of a Chart	

Microsoft Office Specialist PowerPoint 2016			
Chapter	MOS Obj #	Objective	Your Office Heading
	3.3	**Insert and Format SmartArt Graphics**	
Online	3.3.1	Create SmartArt Graphics	
Ch3	3.3.2	Convert Lists to SmartArt Graphics	
Ch3	3.3.3	Add Shapes to SmartArt Graphics	
Online	3.3.4	Reorder Shapes in SmartArt Graphics	
Online	3.3.5	Change the Color of SmartArt Graphics	
	3.4	**Insert and Manage Media**	
Ch3	3.4.1	Insert Audio and Video Clips	Apply and Modify Multimedia in Presentations
Ch3	3.4.2	Configure Media Playback Options	Apply and Modify Multimedia in Presentations
Ch3	3.4.3	Adjust Media Window Size	Apply and Modify Multimedia in Presentations
Online	3.4.4	Set the Video Start and Stop Time	
Online	3.4.5	Set Media Timing Options	
4	**Apply Transitions and Animations**		
	4.1	**Apply Slide Transitions**	
Ch1	4.1.1	Insert Slide Transitions	Use Transitions and Animations
Ch1	4.1.2	Set Transition Effect Options	Use Transitions and Animations
	4.2	**Animate Slide Content**	
Ch4	4.2.1	Apply Animations to Objects	Use Transitions and Animations
Ch4	4.2.2	Apply Animations to Text	Use Transitions and Animations
Ch4	4.2.3	Set Animation Effect Options	Use Transitions and Animations
Online	4.2.4	Set Animation Paths	
	4.3	**Set Timing for Transitions and Animations**	
Ch1	4.3.1	Set Transition Effect Duration	Use Transitions and Animations
Online	4.3.2	Configure Transition Start and Finish Options	
Ch4	4.3.3	Reorder Animations on a Slide	
5	**Manage Multiple Presentations**		
	5.1	**Merge Content from Multiple Presentations**	
Ch3	5.1.1	Insert Slides from Another Presentation	
Online	5.1.2	Compare Two Presentations	
Online	5.1.3	Insert Comments	Create Comments
Online	5.1.4	Review Comments	Create Comments
	5.2	**Finalize Presentations**	
Online	5.2.1	Protect a Presentation	
Online	5.2.2	Inspect a Presentation	
Ch1	5.2.3	Proof a Presentation	
Online	5.2.4	Preserve Presentation Content	
Online	5.2.5	Export Presentations to Other Formats	

Glossary

A

ABS function a function that returns the absolute value of a number, that is, the number without its negative sign.

Absolute cell reference the exact address of a cell when both the column and the row need to remain constant regardless of the position of the cell when the formula is copied to other cells.

Action buttons a special shape that is predefined to include actions that navigate through slides.

Action Center the place where notifications appear and where a user can quickly get to most Windows 10 settings.

Active cell the cell that is the recipient of an action, such as a click, calculation, typing, or paste; identified by the thick green border. Only the active cell can have data entered into it.

Active window the window in which you can move the mouse pointer, type text, or perform other tasks.

Active worksheet the worksheet that is visible in the Excel application window. The active worksheet tab has a white background with bold letters and a thick bottom border.

Address bar in File Explorer a toolbar immediately below the ribbon that displays the current file path and allows users to perform searches for files.

Add-ins for Office enhancements for the features in Office that can be installed from the Microsoft Store.

Adobe PDF file a file format that is easy to send through e-mail and preserves the original document look and feel so it opens the same way every time for the recipient.

Aggregate function perform arithmetic operations, such as averages and totals, on records displayed in a table or query.

Alignment guides green lines that automatically appear, in moving an object, to help align the object with the text. The guides disappear when the object is released or when the guides are no longer needed.

All Markup a view in which tracked changes and comments are visible.

Anchor indicates the paragraph with which an object is associated.

AND function a logical function that returns TRUE if all logical tests supplied are true; otherwise, it returns FALSE.

Animation the movement of elements on a slide.

Annotate make notations or marks on slides as you give a presentation.

Annotated bibliography a special type of bibliography that compiles references along with a short paragraph summarizing or reviewing the value of the source to the research paper.

APA a writing style guide preferred by the social sciences.

App application software that must be installed from the Windows Store.

Append row the first blank row at the end of the table in Access.

Application software programs that help the user perform specific tasks, such as word processing.

Application Start screen the first screen that is seen when a program is opened but an existing program file is not open. In this screen, you can select a blank document, workbook, presentation, database, or one of many application-specific templates.

Apps for Office apps that enhance Office and run in the side pane to provide extra features such as web search, dictionary, and maps.

Area chart a chart that emphasizes the magnitude of change over time and depicts trends.

Argument variables or values a function requires in order to calculate a solution. A value passed to a function, either as a constant or a variable.

Attribute information about an entity.

AutoCorrect a feature that corrects common typographical errors and misspellings as they are typed.

AutoFill a feature that copies information from one cell or a series in adjacent cells into adjacent cells in the direction in which the fill handle is dragged.

AutoFit a method to change the column width of the data to match the widest data entered in that field.

AutoRecovery a feature that will attempt to recover any changes made to a document since your last save if something goes wrong.

AVERAGE function a function that returns an average or mean from a specified range of cells.

B

Backstage view provides access to the file-level features, such as saving a file, creating a new file, opening an existing file, printing a file, and closing a file, as well as program options.

Backup database an extra copy of a database created in case the database is lost. Access appends the current date to the file name.

Banding alternating the background color of rows and/or columns to assist in tracking information.

Bar chart a chart that displays data horizontally and is used for comparison among individual items.

Bar tab positions a vertical bar under the tab stop.

Bibliography a list of references used in the development of a research paper.

Bit-mapped graphic an image created with pixels or bits in a grid; the most common example is photographs, which are typically saved in JPEG file format.

Block a common business letter style in which all text is left-aligned and single-spaced except for double spacing between paragraphs.

Body text in an outline, text that has not been formatted with heading styles.

Bootcamp mac software that allows the user to decide which operating system Mac operating system or Windows to run.

Bound control   a control on a report or form whose data source is a field in the table.

Browser   a program that allows the user to view web pages.

Built-in cell   style predefined and named combination of cell and content formatting properties.

Built-in function   a function included in Excel that can be categorized as financial, statistical, mathematical, date and time, text, or so on.

Bullet   a symbol that appears before each item to create a list of items, or identifies a summary point.

Business communication   communication between members of an organization for the purpose of carrying out business activities.

C

Calculated control   a control on a report or form whose data source is a calculated expression.

Caption   box linked to photographs within a photo album.

Cardinality   the number of instances of one entity that relate to one instance of another entity. Cardinality is expressed as one-to-many, many-to-many, or one-to-one.

Cell   the intersection of a row and a column in a table or worksheet.

Cell alignment   allows cell content to be left-aligned, centered, and right-aligned on the horizontal axis, as well as top-aligned, middle-aligned, and bottom-aligned on the vertical axis.

Cell range   the cells in the worksheet that have been selected.

Cell reference   a reference to a particular cell or cell range within a formula or function instead of a value.

Center tab   aligns the middle of the text under the tab stop.

Centered   text aligned horizontally between margins at the center of the page.

Character style   sets the formatting of font, font size, color, and emphasis to individual characters or selections.

Chart   a graphical representation of numeric data.

Chart sheet   a special worksheet that is dedicated to displaying chart objects.

Chicago   a writing style guide that is primarily concerned with the preparation and editing of papers and books for publication.

Citation   a reference to a published or unpublished source used in the development of a paper.

Cleansing text   removing unwatned chartacters, rearranging data in a cell or correcting erroneous data.

Click   a single press of the left mouse button.

Clipboard   a temporary storage location where information that was cut or copied is stored until you paste, move, or clear the information.

Clipboard pane   a pane that shows the most recent cut or copied items that you can paste.

Close   the command to close an Office file without exiting the associated program.

Cloud computing   computing resources either hardware or software being used by another computer over a network. Files that are stored in a remote location can be stored, accessed, and edited.

Cloud storage   a type of storage that allows the user to keep files on the Internet rather than on the client computer.

Collapse   to hide lower levels in an outline.

Color tone   the temperature of a photo image.

Column   a vertical set of cells that encompasses all the rows in a worksheet.

Column chart   a chart that is used to compare data across categories and show change, sometimes over time.

Combination chart   a chart that displays two different types of data by using multiple chart types in a single chart object.

Comment   a text box, similar to a sticky note, that is attached to a cell in a worksheet in which you can enter notes or give instructions

Compacting   an Access feature that rearranges objects in your database to use disk space more efficiently.

Comparison operator   an operator used in a query to compare the value in a database to the criteria value entered in the query.

Composite key   a primary key composed of two fields.

Compressed file   a file that contains many files grouped together and reduces the file size; the most common file extension is .zip and files are referred to as zipped.

Conditional formatting   allows the specification of rules that apply formatting to cells or specific controls, as determined by the rule outcome.

Constant   a number that does not change.

Content placeholder   an element that appears on the slide with shortcut icons for inserting tables, charts, SmartArt graphics, pictures, online pictures, or videos.

Contextual tabs   a ribbon tab that contains commands related to selected objects so you can manipulate, edit, and format the objects. This ribbon tab does not appear unless the object is selected.

Contiguous cell range   a range consisting of multiple selected cells, all of which are directly adjacent to at least one other cell in the selected range.

Control   a part of a form or report that is used to enter, edit, or display data.

Copy   duplicate a selection to the Clipboard while leaving the original in the same location.

Copyright   the right to copy and is often exclusive rights given to the creator of original work. A form of intellectual property, the copyright also gives the holder the right to be credited, to determine who may adapt the work, or in other ways to benefit from it.

Corporate identity   the visual elements, such as a logo, that make a company and its products recognizable.

Cortana   a clever personal assistant that can search your PC and the web and can set reminders, among other things.

Cortana's Notebook   software that keeps track of what the user likes and wants Cortana to do.

COUNT function   a function that returns the number of cells in a range of cells that contain numeric data.

COUNTA function   a function that returns the number of cells within a range that contain any type of data.

Cropping handles   lines around selected graphic objects that enable the user to cut away unneeded portions.

Crosstab query   a special type of query used when you want to describe one field in terms of two or more other fields in the table.

CSE   a writing style guide preferred by the sciences.

Custom slide show   a subset of a PowerPoint presentation containing only part of the slides in the presentation.

Cut   removes a selection from its original location to the Clipboard.

D

Data facts about people, events, things, or ideas

Data bar graphical display of data that is overlaid on the data in the cells of the worksheet.

Data point an individual piece of data being charted.

Data series A group of related data values to be charted.

Data source a file that contains variable information that is used in a mail merge process.

Data type the characteristic that defines the kind of data that can be entered into a field, such as numbers, text, or dates. The data type tells Access how to store and display the field.

Data visualization the graphical presentation of data with a focus on qualitative understanding.

Database a collection of data.

Database management system (DBMS) database management software that can be used to organize, store, manipulate, and report on your data.

Datasheet view a view of an Access object that shows the data.

Date and time functions functions that are used for entering the current day and time into a worksheet as well as for calculating the intervals between dates.

Date data data recognized by Excel as a date; takes the form of a serial number, with the number 1 representing January 1, 1900.

DATEDIF function a function that enables you to calculate the time between two dates.

Decimal tab tab stop at which text aligns so that the decimal points line up.

Default a setting that is automatically in place unless you specify otherwise.

Delay the length of time in seconds before an animation or transition plays.

Delimiter a character used in a text file to separate the fields; it can be a paragraph mark, a tab, a comma, or another character.

Demote to move a paragraph to a lower level in the outline.

Design theme a set of elements, such as a color palette, font group, and slide backgrounds that enable you to create consistent slides.

Design view a view of an Access object that shows the detailed structure of a table, query, form, or report.

Desktop background the picture or pattern that is displayed on the desktop.

Destination cell the cell that received the result of an operations such as Paste or an AutoSum function.

Destination file the file into which a linked or embedded object is inserted.

Destination program the program into which a linked or embedded object is inserted.

Device driver software that tells the computer how to communicate with a piece of hardware such as a printer.

Dialog box a user window that provides more options or settings beyond those provided on the ribbon.

Dialog Box launcher an icon in a group that opens a corresponding dialog box or task pane.

Document a letter, memo, report, brochure, resume, or flyer.

Draft view a document view that provides the most space possible for typing, without displaying margins.

Drop cap a design element in which the first letter of a paragraph is shown as a large graphic representation of the letter.

Duration the length of time in seconds that it takes an animation or transition to play.

E

Edge the Windows 10 default browser and PDF reader.

Edge Hub the place where a user can manage favorites, a reading list, downloads, and browsing history.

Edit mode a mode that allows you to edit or change the contents of a field or change the name of a file or folder.

Embedded chart an object located on the same worksheet with the data.

Embedded object an object that is inserted into a document that is not connected to the source file where it was created. Any updates must be made in the new document.

Emphasis action the effect that occurs after an object is displayed on a slide.

Endnote a reference that appears in a numerical list at the end of a paper, providing information on the source.

Entity person, place, item, or event about which you want to keep data.

Entrance animation the effect that occurs as objects enter the slide.

Equidistant guides red guidelines that appear briefly to assist the user in placing one or more selected objects an equal distance from at least two other slide elements.

Exit animation the effect that occurs as objects leave the slide.

Expand to show lower levels in an outline.

Expression Builder a tool that helps you build calculated fields correctly by providing a list of expressive elements, operators, and built-in functions.

Eyedropper tool a tool that enables the user to sample a color of one element and then drop that color onto another element.

F

Field a specific piece of information that is stored in every record and, when formatted, appears as a column in a database table. An item of information in a worksheet column that is associated with something of interest.

Field size the maximum length of a data field or a range of values.

File stored information associated with a particular file type or program.

File Explorer formerly known as Windows Explorer, a program that is used to create and manage folders and files.

File Explorer address bar the toolbar immediately below the ribbon that allows users to browse folders as he or she would in a web browser.

File extension three or four characters after the file name that is preceded by a period and that is used by the Windows operating system to determine which programs should be used to open a file.

File list in File Explorer the right pane of the File Explorer window, which opens initially to recent folders and files.

File path the physical location of the file starting with a letter that represents the drive and separating folders with a "\".

Fill color the background color of a cell.

Filter a condition applied temporarily to a table or query to show a subset of the records.

Filter by selection selecting a value in a record and filtering the records that contain only the values that match what has been selected.

Financial functions functions that are used for common financial calculations such as interest rates, payments, and analyzing loans.

Find and Replace the process of finding a specified item, formatting, or punctuation and replacing it with another.

Find command a command used to find records in a database with a specific value.

Find Duplicates Query Wizard finds duplicate records in a table or a query.

FIND function a function that searches for a specified string of text in a larger string of text and returns the position number where the specified text begins

Find Unmatched Query Wizard finds records in one table that do not have related records in another table.

Firewall software that controls incoming and outgoing network traffic.

First-line indent an indent style in which the first line of a paragraph is indented a specified distance from the left margin by default, at 1/2 inch.

Flash Fill recognizes patterns in data as you type and automatically fills in values for text and numeric data.

Folder a container used to store related documents or files.

Font a style of displaying characters, numbers, punctuation, and special characters. Also the way letters in words look, including the size, weight, and style.

Font group font combinations, for the headings and body content, that become part of a theme.

Footer text or graphics that are printed in the bottom margin of a document.

Footnote a reference to a source that is placed numerically at the bottom of the page in which the reference is made.

Foreign key a field in a table that stores the value of the primary key of a related table for the purpose of creating a relationship.

Form an object that allows you to enter or view your table data.

Form view data view of a form.

Format specifies how data is displayed.

Format field switch a method that determines the format of contents of fields, such as the use of uppercase and lowercase letters.

Format Painter a tool that allows you to copy a format and apply it to other selections.

Formatting mark a special character that is displayed in a document to indicate where nonprinting characters, such as Enter, Tab, or Spacebar, are located.

Formula performs a mathematical calculation (or calculations) using information in the active worksheet and other worksheets to calculate new values; it can contain cell references, constants, functions, and mathematical operators.

Function a built-in formula that performs operations against data based on a set of inputs, such as SUM or AVERAGE function. Some functions, called null functions, do not require arguments.

Function Arguments a dialog box that provides additional information and previews the results of a function being constructed.

G

Gallery a set of menu options that appear when you click the arrow next to a button.

Gesture recognition a feature for devices with touch capability that allows the user to control the computer with finger gestures instead of mouse clicks.

Grand total controls added to a report to perform calculations on all records.

Graphical format the presentation of information in charts, graphs, and pictures.

Graphical user interface (GUI) an interface that uses visual icons.

Gridlines lines that go across charts to help gauge the size of the bars, columns, or data lines.

Group a collection of records along with some introductory and summary information about the records. A logical groupings of commands on the ribbon.

Group footer the area of a report where summary information about a group is included.

Group header the area of a report where introductory information about a group is included.

H

Handout master the layout of elements, such as the header and footer, on the handout pages.

Hanging indent an indent style in which the first line begins at the left margin and all other lines in the paragraph are indented.

Hard return inserted into a document when you press Enter.

Header text or graphics that are printed in the top margin of a document.

Help a window opened via the Help button or the F1 key.

Horizontal guide a guideline set at 0 on the vertical ruler by default to assist in the placement of elements on a slide. A user can add many horizontal guides.

Hyperlink an object, such as text or a graphic, that provides a path to nonlinear slides or to Internet resources, such as e-mail or websites

I

IF function a logical function that returns one of two values depending upon whether the supplied logical test being evaluated is true or false.

Import Spreadsheet Wizard a tool that provides step-by-step instructions in Access to help successfully import data from Excel.

Importing the process of copying data from another file, such as a Word file or Excel workbook, into a separate file, such as an Access database.

Indexed folders locations that the Windows search tool has already searched and for which it has produced a keyword list.

Information data that has been manipulated and processed to make it meaningful.

Input mask controls how data is entered by creating a consistent template. An input mask can also control the way that data is stored.

Insertion point The blinking black bar that indicates the position where the next character you type will be placed.

INT function rounds down any decimal values to the nearest whole integer.

J

Join a connection between two tables based on a common field, used to create a relationship.

Join lines the lines connecting tables in the Relationship tab.

Junction table a table that breaks down a many-to-many relationship into two one-to-many relationships.

Justified text that is aligned so that it is spread evenly between the left and right margins.

K

Kelvin scale   a photographic control feature found on many cameras but also used in postprocessing. Allows a user to match white balance with available light. The scale ranges from 2,000 to 10,000; a cold blue tint can be applied to photographs at the low end, and an extremely red-orange tone can be applied at the highest end.

Keyboard shortcut   keyboard equivalents for software commands that allow you to keep your hands on the keyboard instead of reaching for the mouse to perform actions.

KeyTips   a form of keyboard shortcut. Pressing the Alt button will display KeyTips (or keyboard shortcuts) for items on the Ribbon and the Quick Access Toolbar.

Kiosk   a stand-alone computer system that provides information to people in nontraditional places, such as museums, grocery stores, banks, sporting events, and more.

L

Label control   an unbound control. It may be the name of a field or other text you manually enter.

Landscape orientation   for page layout and printing purposes, landscape indicates that the page is wider than it is tall.

Layout Selector   a tool that allows you to move a whole table at one time.

Layout view   shows data and allows limited changes to a form or report design.

Leader   a row of dots or dashes that are displayed before a tab stop.

LEFT function   returns the characters in a text string based on the number of characters you specify, starting with the far left character in the string.

Left indent   fndenting an entire paragraph from the left margin.

Left pane   a pane in PowerPoint on the left of the screen that allows you to select a slide.

Left tab   aligns the left edge of the text under the tab stop.

Left-aligned   text that is aligned flush with the left margin, with a ragged right edge.

Legend   an index withing a chart that provides information about the data.

Level 1   the highest level in a Word outline.

Level 2   the second highest level in a Word outline.

Line chart   a chart that is used to convey change in data over a period of time; good for showing trends.

Line spacing   space between lines in a paragraph.

Linked object   an object that is inserted into a document as a link that is still connected to the source file where it was originally created. Updates are made in the source file.

List hierarchy   the relationship of text elements on the slide, usually depicted with groups and subgroups.

Live Layout   a feature that reflows the text around an object in real time as it is dragged to a new position.

Live Preview   a feature that shows the results that would occur in your file if you were to click that particular option.

Live Tile   a tile that provides a constant stream of information.

Lock Screen   the screen that displays when you start the computer or leave it for a period of time.

Logical functions   functions that return a result, or output, based upon evaluating whether a logical test is true or false.

Logical operator   an operator used in a query used to combine two or more criteria.

Login Screen   the screen where a user can enter login credentials.

Lookup and reference functions   functions that look up matching values in a table of data.

M

Mail merge   a process that simplifies the task of preparing documents that contain identical formatting, layout, and text but in which certain portions of each document vary.

Main document   a document that consists primarily of text that will not change during a mail merge process.

Main form   the primary or first table selected in creating a form.

Many-to-many relationship   a relationship between tables in which one record in one table has many matching records in a second table and one record in the second table has many matching records in the first table.

Margin   the empty space at the top, bottom, left, and right edges of a document.

Mathematical operator   parentheses ( ), exponentiation ^, division /, multiplication *, addition +, or subtraction –.

MAX function   a function that examines all numeric values in a specified range and returns the maximum value.

Maximize   the button located in the top right corner of the title bar that enlarges a window to its maximum size, which offers the largest workspace.

MEDIAN function   a function used to measure the central tendency or the location of the middle of a set of data.

Merge & Center   a feature that combines selected cells into a single cell and then centers the text within that single cell.

Merge field   reference to a field in the data source of a mail merge process.

Microsoft Word 2016   the word-processing software that is included in the Microsoft Office 2016 suite.

MIN function   a function that examines all numeric values in a specified range and returns the minimum value.

Mini toolbar   a toolbar that appears after text has been selected and that contains buttons for the most commonly used formatting commands, such as font, font size, font color, center alignment, indents, bold, italic, and underline.

Minimize   the button that reduces a window to a taskbar button.

Mixed cell reference   using a combination of absolute cell referencing and relative cell referencing for a cell address within a formula by preceding either the column letter or the row value with a dollar sign to "lock" as absolute while leaving the other portion of the cell address as a relative reference.

MLA   a writing style guide preferred by the humanities.

MODE function   a function that returns the most frequently occurring value in a range of data.

MODE.MULT function   a function that returns the most frequently occurring values in a range of data.

MODE.SNGL function   a function that returns the most frequently occurring value in a range of data.

Modified block   a business letter style in which the body is left-aligned and single-spaced except for double spacing between paragraphs and the date and closing are left-aligned slightly to the right of center.

Monospaced font   a font in which all the characters use the same amount of horizontal space.

Most Recently Used list   a list maintained by Office of your most recently modified files: documents, spreadsheets, databases, and presentations.

Mouse pointer   an arrow that shows the position of the mouse.

Multiple virtual desktops   a feature that allows the user to configure different desktops and experiences for different purposes and to switch easily between them.

Multiplier effect   when Access joins two tables without a common field, each record in the first table is matched with each record in the second table.

N

Name Manager   used to create, edit, delete, or troubleshoot named ranges in a workbook.

Named range   a cell or group of cells that have been given a name, other than the default column and row cell address reference, that can then be used within a formula or function.

Natural primary key   A primary key that has a logical relationship or meaning in the data.

Navigation bar   provides a way to move through records in table, query, report, and form objects.

Navigation mode   a mode that allows you to move from record to record or from field to field using keystrokes and the Navigation bar.

Navigation pane   the pane that in File Explorer displays locations where users can find files, such as Quick Access, OneDrive, This PC, Network, and possibly more, depending on the computer. Also a pane that enables you to move around within your document, search for content, and manipulate the organization of headings; provides a set of related features for navigating and searching for content.

Navigation Pane (Access)   the window in Access that shows all the objects in the database.

Network in File Explorer   allows users to browse files found on network drives rather than on local drives.

Newsletter   a printed or electronic news report for a group.

Noncontiguous cell range   a range consisting of multiple selected cells, at least one of which is not directly adjacent to at least one other cell in the selected range.

Nonprinting character   a character that is included in a document but does not print, such as Enter, Tab, and Spacebar.

Normal view   the default view of PowerPoint that displays the Left hand pane (thumbnails) and the Slide pane work area.

Normalization   the process of minimizing the duplication of information in a relational database through effective table design.

Notes master   the layout of elements, such as the slide thumbnail and notes placeholder, on the speaker notes pages.

Notes pane   a pane in PowerPoint that allows you to add speaker notes that the audience will not see.

NOW function   a function used to display the current date and time in a cell.

Numeric data   data that contains only the digits 0[en]9 and possibly a period (.) for a decimal place and/or a hyphen to indicate negativity.

Number data type   a data type that can store only numeric data. The data field will be used in calculations.

Numeric key   a primary key with a number data type. AutoNumber is often used for numeric keys.

O

Object   a table, form, query, or report. An item that can be selected and manipulated independently of surrounding text.

Office Background   an artistic design displayed in the upper right in the title bar of Office.

Office Backstage   a feature that provides access to the file-level commands, such as saving a file, creating a new file, opening an existing file, printing a file, and closing a file, as well as program options and account settings.

Office Clipboard   a clipboard within Office that can hold up to 24 selections of text or graphics that can be pasted into Office documents.

Office Mix   an add-in to PowerPoint that turns PowerPoint presentations into interactive lessons.

Office Online   a web-based suite of Microsoft Office applications with core functionality, including Word Online, Excel Online, PowerPoint Online, and OneNote Online.

Office Theme   a color scheme used by Office.

OLE (Object Linking and Embedding)   a feature in Microsoft Office that allows you to insert an object into a file as either a linked object or an embedded object.

One-to-many relationship   a relationship between two tables in which one record in the first table corresponds to many records in the second table; the most common type of relationship in Access.

One-to-one relationship   a relationship between tables in which a record in one table has only one matching record in the second table.

OneDrive   an online cloud computing technology provided by Microsoft and integrated with Office 2016 that offers a certain amount of free collaborative storage space.

Operating system   system software that controls and coordinates computer hardware operations so that other programs can run efficiently.

OR function   a logical function that returns TRUE if any one logical test supplied is true; otherwise, it returns FALSE.

Order of operations   the order in which Excel processes calculations in a formula that contains more than one operator.

Ordered list   sequential numbered steps that need to appear in a specific order.

Orphan   the first line of a paragraph when the line is alone at the bottom of a page.

Orphan (Access)   a foreign key in one table that does not relate to a primary key in another table.

Outline   a hierarchical representation of paragraphs, which are recognized by a nonprinting end-of-paragraph mark.

Outline view   a document view that shows levels of detail and organization, as identified by headings and subheadings.

Outline View (PowerPoint)   a pane in Normal view used to place content on the slide in a hierarchy relationship.

P

Page break   the break where one page ends and another one begins.

Page Break Preview   a view that does not show page margins, headers, or footers, but allows you to manually adjust the location of page breaks.

Page Layout view   a view that shows page margins, print headers and footers, and page breaks.

Pane   a smaller window that often appears to the side of the program window and offers options or helps you to navigate through completing a task or feature.

Paragraph spacing   space between paragraphs.

Paragraph style   sets the alignment, spacing, and indentation formatting to a paragraph of text.

Paste   placing a cut or copied selection in a new location.

Paste Preview   a feature that shows the effect of a paste operation before the paste occurs.

PDF (Portable Document Format) a file type that preserves most formatting attributes of a source document regardless of the software in which the document was created.

Pecha Kucha a unique format for presentations, which automatically displays 20 slides for 20 seconds each, during which the presenter speaks. The idea is that practicing presenting in this way will help you become more concise and clear.

Photo Album an efficient way to place a large number of photographs into a presentation.

Picture a visual representation of an image that can be drawn, painted, or photographed.

Picture Styles preset effects applied to graphics to create borders, shapes, or effects such as shadowing or bevelling.

Pie chart a chart that displays a comparison of each value to a total.

Placeholder a container for text or graphics, used on the layout to position the objects on the slide.

Plagiarism the act of falsely claiming ideas or phrasing as one's own when in fact another person originated them.

PMT function a function used to calculate a payment amount based on constant payments and a constant interest rate.

Portable Document Format (PDF) a file type that preserves most formatting attributes of a source document regardless of the software in which the document was created.

Portrait orientation for page layout and printing purposes, portrait indicates the page is taller than it is wide.

Power points the intersections of equidistant horizontal and vertical guides, which serve to break a scene into thirds.

PowerPoint Show a slide show that opens full screen without the need for the PowerPoint application first.

Presentation an oral performance aid that uses slides or stand-alone silent presentation, such as that at a kiosk.

Presenter view the view that is configured to display automatically if a projector or two monitors are connected to the computer. Allows you to control various aspects of the presentation and view speaker notes on one monitor while the audience sees the presentation on the other monitor or the screen. Can also be manually displayed by right-clicking a slide during the slide show and clicking Show Presenter View.

Primary key the field that uniquely identifies a record in a table.

Primary sort field the first field chosen in a multiple field sort.

Print Layout a document view that shows top, bottom, left, and right margins.

Print Preview backstage view of how a document, workbook, presentation, table, or other object will appear when printed.

Printer-friendly fonts fonts that are easy to read on a printed page.

Program application software that the user will install directly from a download installer, or from the company that wrote the program.

Promote to move a paragraph to a higher level in the outline.

Property sheet a list of properties for fields in which you can make precise changes to each property associated with the field.

Proportional font a font in which the characters use varying amounts of horizontal space, depending on how much they need.

Protected View a view of the file in which the contents can be seen and read but cannot be edited, saved, or printed the contents until editing is enabled. By default, Office will open files from e-mail or a web browser in this view.

Q

Query an object that retrieves specific data from one or more database objects either tables or other queries and then, in a single datasheet, displays only the data you specify.

Query by example a type of query in which a sample of the data is set up as criteria.

Query design grid selected fields in a query. Shown at the bottom of a query's Design view.

Query workspace displays the source for data in the query. Shown at the top of a query's Design view.

Quick Access allows users to browse through locations they have previously marked as important.

Quick Access Toolbar located at the top left of the Office window, it can be customized to display commonly used buttons.

Quick Analysis a contextual tool that appears when you select data in a worksheet and offers single-click access to formatting, charts, PivotTables, and Sparklines.

R

Read Mode an interactive view of the document that minimizes distractions and menus to leave more room for the pages themselves; optimized for touch screens.

Reading view a PowerPoint view where the slides are displayed full screen, with buttons on the status bar to move to the next or previous slide, or to a menu of slides.

Recolor altering the colors of a photograph or other graphic to create a monochromatic effect.

Recommended Charts a feature that quickly analyzes a selection in a worksheet and recommends chart types that best fit your data.

Record all of the categories of data that pertain to one person, place, thing, event, or idea and that are formatted as a row in a worksheet or database table.

Record selector the small box at the left of a record in Datasheet view and Form view that is used to select an entire record.

Recycle Bin a temporary storage place for deleted files from your computer until they are restored or permanently deleted.

Redundancy data that is repeated in more than one place in the database, an indicator of poor design.

Relational database three-dimensional database software that can connect data in separate tables to form a relationship when common fields exist and can offer reassembled information from multiple tables.

Relational database three-dimensional database software that it is able to connect data in separate tables to form a relationship when common fields exist, offering reassembled information from multiple tables.

Relationship an association between two tables based on a common field.

Relative cell reference default cell reference in a formula to a cell address position that will automatically adjust when the formula is copied or extended to other cells; the cell being referenced changes relative to the placement of the formula.

Replace command a command used to automatically replace values in a table or query.

Report an object that summarizes the fields and records from a table or query in an easy-to-read format suitable for printing.

Report view a view that allows you to see what the printed report will look like in a continuous page layout.

Reset to return position, size, and formatting of slide placeholders to the default settings determined by the slide master.

Restore Down a button that, when a window is at its maximum size, will restore the window to a previous, smaller size. When a window is in the Restore Down mode, this button expands the window to its full size.

RGB a color system in which red, green, and blue are combined in various proportions to produce other colors.

Ribbon the row of tabs with buttons across the top of the application where you will find most of the commands for the application. The ribbon differs from program to program, but each program has two tabs in common: the File tab and the Home tab.

Ribbon Display Options three options for ribbon display: Auto-Hide Ribbon, Display Tabs, and Display Tabs and Command.

Ribbon group a collection of related commands on a ribbon tab.

Rich Text Format (.RTF) a file format that retains the formatting of the original document when you import it into another program.

Right indent indenting an entire paragraph from the right margin.

Right tab aligns the right edge of the text under the tab stop.

Right-aligned text that is aligned flush with the right margin, with a ragged left edge.

Roaming settings a group of settings that offer synced user-specific data that affects the Office experience

ROUND function a function that is used to round a number to a specific number of digits.

Row a horizontal set of cells that encompasses all the columns in a worksheet.

Rule of six a rule that advises the use of no more than six words per line and no more than six lines per slide.

Rule of thirds a method of dividing a scene so as to leave two-thirds canvas and one-third subject, thereby framing the subject. A scene is manipulated beneath a grid of intersecting horizontal and vertical lines until it is in balance.

Ruler a horizontal and vertical bar at the top and side of a document showing measurements.

S

Sans serif font a font that does not have end strokes (serifs) on the letters.

Saturation the amount of color intensity.

Scatter chart a chart that shows the relationship between numeric variables.

Screen-friendly fonts fonts that can be read easily from a distance when projected on a screen.

ScreenTip a small box that provides a name or other information about the object to which you are pointing.

Secondary sort field the second and subsequent fields chosen in a multiple field sort.

Section a document area that can be formatted differently from other sections.

Semi-block a business letter style in which the body is left-aligned and single-spaced, the date and closing are centered, and each paragraph is indented 1/2 inch.

Serif font a font that includes small lines or strokes (serifs) at the end of letter characters, which provide a visual guideline connection between letters and words.

Shake shaking the title bar of a window to minimize all other windows.

Short Text data type a data type that can store either text or numeric characters.

Shortcut menu a list of context-sensitive commands related to a selection that appears when you right-click.

Simple Markup a view in which tracked changes and comments are hidden by default.

Sizing handle small boxes or circles in the center and corners of the border surrounding an object that can be used to resize the object.

Slide footer information that is displayed at the bottom of the slide that can include the slide number, date, and other information.

Slide layout the placement of objects, such as the title and body content, on the slide.

Slide master a special slide used to create a template; details fonts, placement of footers, background colors, and other characteristics of the presentation.

Slide pane the large work area, in Normal view, that displays one slide at a time allowing the user to add, edit, and format content.

Slide placeholder a container for text and graphic elements that can be moved and resized to improve the use of the white space on the slides.

Slide section an organizational tool in PowerPoint that can expand and collapse a group of slide thumbnails in the left pane.

Slide Show view the full-screen display of a slide presentation, as it would be shown to an audience.

Slide Sorter view a PowerPoint view where the slides are displayed as thumbnails, enabling you to rearrange slides and review transitions.

Smart alignment guides red alignment guides that appear briefly to assist the user in placing one or more selected objects on a slide relative to other objects on the same slide. Equidistant guides are an example of smart alignment guides.

Smart Lookup a research tool that provides access to a variety of reference books, dictionaries, research websites, and business and financial sites.

SmartArt graphics a graphic object that presents information visually.

Snap a quick way to arrange open windows by dragging them to the edges of your screen.

Snip a picture of your current screen taken with the Snipping Tool.

Soft return the automatic wrapping of text from one line to the next when a line reaches the right margin.

Sort field a field used to determine the order of the records in a table.

Sorting the process of rearranging records into a specific order.

Source cell(s) the cell(s) that contain the data supplied to a function.

Source file the file in which a linked or embedded object is stored.

Source program the program used to create a linked or embedded object.

Sparkline small charts embedded into cells on a spreadsheet, providing a way to graphically summarize a row or column of data in a single cell with a miniature chart.

Speaker notes notes that are stored with the presentation in the Notes pane.

Special operator an operator used to compare text values in a query.

Spelling & Grammar a tool that locates misspellings and errors in grammar and word usage.

Spelling tool   used to check the spelling of the presentation, offer suggestions for misspelled words, provide audible pronunciations of words, and suggest synonyms.

Split form   a form created from one table with a Form view and a Datasheet view in the same window.

Spreadsheet   a two-dimensional grid that can be used to model quantitative data and perform accurate and rapid calculations with results ranging from simple budgets to financial and statistical analyses.

Status bar   is located at the bottom of a window.

Storyboard   conceptual drawings of a story that enables you to plan and visualize how everything comes together in a scene or sequence of shots.

Style   a set of formatting characteristics that you can apply to selected text.

Style guide   a set of standards for creating a document.

Subform   the form created for the secondary table records in creating a form from two or more tables.

Subreport   the report section created for the secondary table records in creating a report from two or more tables.

SUBTOTAL Function   a function that will only run calculations on the data that is in the subset when a filter is applied. Also, a function that can return any of 11 different values including all of the AutoSum functions, the product, standard deviation, and variance.

Subtotals   controls added to a report to perform calculations on a group of records.

SUM Function   a function that adds of all numeric information in a specified range, list of numbers, list of cells, or any combination.

Symbol   a character not available on a standard keyboard, such as the copyright symbol or foreign language accent marks.

Syncing   a process that ensures that the same versions of your files are both on the local computer and in the cloud.

Syntax   the structure and order of the function and the arguments needed for Excel to run a function.

System software   software that controls and coordinates computer hardware operations so that other programs can run efficiently.

T

Tab selector   a button that changes the type of tab stop that is inserted into the ruler in Word.

Tab stop   a location where the insertion point will stop when the tab key is pressed.

Table   an organized grid of information, arranged in rows and columns.

Table (Access)   the database object that stores data organized in an arrangement of columns and rows and is the foundation of an Access database.

Table selector   the icon at the top left corner of a table that enables the selection of the entire table.

Table style   a predefined set of formatting properties that determine the appearance of a table.

Tablet mode   a mode in which every interaction is expected to be done via touch. The directions in this book are written assuming that a mouse is used.

Tabular format   the presentation of information such as text and numbers in tables.

Target audience   the general characteristics of the group of people to whom you are planning to present.

Taskbar notification area   displays information about the status of programs running in the background, a clock, the option to safely remove devices such as USB flash drives, and other options that can be customized.

Taskbar   the bar at the bottom of the desktop containing the Start button, a Cortana search box, a series of buttons representing pinned apps and all open programs, and the taskbar notification area.

Tell me what you want to do   a help tool in the title bar of Office applications that can launch commands in addition to accessing traditional help.

Template   a file with predefined layouts, theme colors and fonts, and sample content that enables you to quickly produce a professional, consistent slide show.

Template (Access)   a database shell that provides tables, forms, queries, and reports.

Text box   a bound control that represents the actual value of a field or a drawing object that can contain text.

Text box control   a bound control. Represents the actual value of a field.

Text data   can contain any combination of printable characters, including letters, numbers, and special characters available on any standard keyboard.

Text filter   filters that allow you to create a custom filter to match all or part of the text in a field that you specify.

Text function   a function that manages, manipulates, and formats text data.

Text wrap   the way in which text wraps around an object.

Theme   a set of design elements such as fonts, styles, colors, and effects associated with a theme name that enables you to create professional, color-coordinated documents quickly.

Thesaurus   a research tool that enables you to select synonyms for words in the presentation.

This PC   allows the user to view the contents of the computer's storage devices, including the hard drive, CD/DVD drive, and attached USB flash drives.

Tile   a picture representation of a program or application.

Time data   data recognized by Excel as representing time; represented as a decimal value, where .1 is 144 minutes, .01 is 14.4 minutes, and so on.

Title bar   the bar at the top of a window that displays a file or folder name and contains buttons for minimizing, maximizing or restoring down, and closing a window.

TODAY function   a function that is used to return the current date into a cell.

Toggle   a button that reverses its action when it is clicked or enacted a second time.

Toggle button   a type of button that turns the feature on with one click and turns the feature off with a second click.

Total row   a temporary row that can be added to the end of a datasheet that allows for statistical calculations of field values.

Touch mode   applies to touch screen devices; the ribbon and shortcut menus are enlarged to make selecting commands with your fingertip easier.

Track Changes   a tool in Word that enables you to keep track of all additions, deletions, and formatting changes in a document.

Transition   the visual and audio elements that occur as the slides change.

Transparency   a measure of the opacity of an object; used to reduce the opacity of foreground objects so background objects can be seen. Opacity and transparency are inversely related.

Trendline   a line that uses current data to show a trend or general direction of the data.

Trigger   text or graphic that enables animation to occur.

U

Unbound control   a control on a form or report that does not have a source of data.

URL (Uniform Resource Locator)   a website address.

USB drive   a small and portable storage device, popular for moving files back and forth between a lab, office, and/or home computer.

USB flash drive   a small storage device that plugs into your computer's USB port and may hold small or large amounts of information.

V

Vector graphic   object-oriented graphics based on geometric formulas, most often used for line art graphics found in logos or 3-D programs.

Vertical guide   a guideline set at 0 on the horizontal ruler by default to assist in the placement of elements on a slide. A user can add many vertical guides.

View   one of several perspectives of an object.

Virtualization   software that mimics Windows in order to run Office on a Mac.

Virus   malicious code intended to harm your computer, use your computer's resources, or collect sensitive information about the user.

VLOOKUP function   a function that matches a provided value in a table of data and returns a value from a subsequent column; also helps to retrieve values located in another location and is used when your comparison values are located in a column (vertically) to the left of the data you want to find.

W

Watermark   text or picture that appears behind document text.

Web Layout   a document view that displays pages as they would appear in a web browser.

What-if analysis   changing values in spreadsheet cells to investigate the effects on calculated values of interest; allows you to examine the outcome of the changes to values in a worksheet.

White space   space in a document or worksheet that does not contain data of any kind, allowing the user's eyes to rest.

Widow   the last line of a paragraph when the line is alone at the top of a page.

Wildcard   a special character that represents zero or more characters, depending on the wildcard.

Wildcard character   characters, such as an asterisk (*) or question mark (?), that substitute for other characters when used in a selection.

Window   is what displays when you open a program or app; windows have standard features across all programs and apps and give Windows its name.

Windows Defender   built-in virus protection for Windows 10.

Windows Hello   a feature new to Windows 10 that allows the operating system to use the camera to recognize your face rather than requiring you to type a password.

Wizard   a step-by-step guide for performing complex tasks.

Word Mail Merge Wizard   a feature that can help to create a new mail merge document or employ an existing mail merge document to create form letters.

Word processing   software that enables you to create, edit, and print documents.

Word Start screen   the screen that is displayed when Word is launched.

Word wrap   the feature whereby Word automatically wraps text from one line to the next.

WordArt   a feature that allows the user to modify text to include shadows, outlines, colors, gradients, and 3-D effects.

Workbook   an Excel file that contains one or more worksheets.

Works cited   a list of sources actually referenced in a research paper.

Worksheet   each instance of a spreadsheet; a grid of columns and rows in which data is entered.

Index